Berlitz®

Ocean Cruising
& Cruise Ships 2003

by Douglas Ward
President
The Maritime Evaluations Group

Editorial

Written by
Douglas Ward

Editorial Director
Brian Bell

Editorial address
Berlitz Publishing
PO Box 7910, London SE1 1WE
United Kingdom
Fax: (44) 20-7403 0290
berlitz@apaguide.co.uk

Distribution

United States
Langenscheidt Publishers, Inc.
46-35 54th Road, Maspeth, NY 11378
Fax: (1) 718 784 0640

Canada
Thomas Allen & Son Ltd
390 Steelcase Road East
Markham, Ontario L3R 1G2
Fax: (1) 905 475 6747

UK & Ireland
GeoCenter International Ltd
The Viables Centre, Harrow Way
Basingstoke, Hants RG22 4BJ
Fax: (44) 1256 817988

Worldwide
Apa Publications GmbH & Co.
Verlag KG (Singapore branch)
38 Joo Koon Road, Singapore 628990
Tel: (65) 6865 1600. Fax: (65) 6861 6438

Printing

Insight Print Services (Pte) Ltd
38 Joo Koon Road, Singapore 628990
Tel: (65) 6865-1600. Fax: (65) 6861-6438

©2003 Apa Publications GmbH & Co.
Verlag KG (Singapore branch)
All Rights Reserved

*Berlitz Trademark Reg. U.S. Patent Office
and other countries. Marca Registrada.
Used under licence from the Berlitz
Investment Corporation*

First Edition 1985
Thirteenth Edition 2003
Reprinted 2003

CONTACTING THE AUTHOR
Although every effort is made to
provide accurate information, we live
in a fast-changing world and would
appreciate it if readers would call our
attention to any outdated information by
writing to Douglas Ward at:

The Maritime Evaluations Group
Canada House, 1 Carrick Way
New Milton, Hants BH25 6UD
United Kingdom
shipratings@hotmail.com

www.berlitzpublishing.com

FROM THE AUTHOR

Ever since my very first trans-atlantic crossing, in July 1965, aboard Cunard Line's 83,673-ton ocean liner RMS *Queen Elizabeth* (then the largest passenger ship in the world), I have been captivated by passenger ships and the sea. To date, I have completed just over 5,000 days at sea, participating in more than 880 cruises, 150 transatlantic crossings, and countless Panama Canal transits, shipyard visits, ship christenings, maiden voyages, I am still fascinated by and absorbed in every aspect of cruising and cruise ships.

Speak to anyone who has been on a cruise – they'll almost certainly be enthusiastic in their praise. So will you – that is, *if you choose the right ship, for the right reasons*. This book is designed to help you do just that. It is a comprehensive source of information about cruising and the ships that offer to take you away from the pressures, stresses, and confines of daily life ashore.

When you first look into taking a cruise, you will be confronted by an enormous and bewildering choice. Reading this book will simplify that choice and you will leave for your cruise as well informed as most specialists in the industry. In fact, professional cruise sales agents already use this book as a valuable reference source.

From time to time, the media reports on criminal aspects of the cruise industry, such as rape and environmental pollution. The international cruise industry, which consists of more than 80 ocean-going cruise operators carrying more than 10 million passengers a year, provides an extremely safe and hassle-free way to take a vacation. Indeed, with fewer than 100 cases of alleged rape among more than 10 million passengers, life ashore seems perilous by comparison.

Of course, the terrorist attacks on the US on September 11, 2001, had an impact. Some cruise lines went out of business, some tightened their belts and cut standards, and some tried hard to carry on as normal in an increasingly competitive environment. As in many industries, however, the financially strong will survive.

Standards have suffered from cost-cutting exercises as the major cruise lines tried to recover from the discounting that has plagued the marketplace, led by lines based in North America. Nevertheless, the industry still

HOW TO USE THIS BOOK

This book is divided into two main parts, followed by a short section of practical information and useful addresses. The first part (Questions and Answers, The Cruising Experience, Different Kinds of Cruises, Choosing the Right Cruise) helps you define what you are looking for in a cruise vacation and what kind of accommodation to select, and supplies valuable advice on what to know before you go. It provides a wealth of information, including a look at life aboard

ship and how to get the best from it; the cuisine, dining and "alternative" dining rooms; nautical terminology; how the ship's hierarchy works; and advice about going ashore. Alternative cruises, such as expedition cruises, sail-cruise ships, coastal and river cruises, and freighters, are discussed, too, culminating with that ultimate travel experience: the around-the-world cruise.

The main section of the book contains profiles of 254 ocean-going cruise vessels. From large

provides vacation experiences seldom matched in product delivery, cleanliness and hygiene by land-based resorts. And the value for money is better today than it has been for the past 20 years.

Unfortunately, many things that used to be included in the price of a cruise now cost extra. This "onboard revenue" compensates the industry for the fact that basic prices are as low now as in 1980. Discounted pricing has done one thing, however, and that is to open up cruising to a much wider socio-economic base than ever before.

The ratings of cruise ships have, therefore, undergone some changes, too, since September 11, 2001. I am pleased to report, however, that some ships have even *improved* their product and standing in the international cruise industry; these changes are reflected in this book.

I love my work, and I strive to provide you with the kind of information that will help you decide which ship will give you the best possible vacation. This book is a tribute to everyone who has made my seafaring experiences possible, and I would like

Another sailing, another show: many ships lay on lavish entertainment.

to thank all cruise lines for their excellent cooperation and assistance during the complicated scheduling, sailing, inspection, evaluation and rating processes. Without the complete cooperation of the cruise lines, this book would not be possible. Note that the three ships of Peter Deilmann Reederei (*Berlin, Deutschland, Lili Marleen*) are not included in this book at the specific request of Mr Peter Deilmann.

— *Douglas Ward*

to small, from unabashed luxury to ships for the budget-minded, new and old, they are all here. The ratings and evaluations are a painstaking documentation of the author's personal work. He travels constantly throughout the world, and is at sea for approximately nine months each year.

The attraction of cruising lies in the variety of ships, cruise lines, products and choices available. This book is intended to help you make informed decisions, given the enormous differ-

ences between ships, service standards, and cruise lines today.

All evaluations of cruise ships have been made objectively, without bias, partiality, or prejudice. In almost all instances, the ships have all been visited recently by the author or one of his team members in order to update or adjust earlier ratings or to assess current status. Passenger comments and feedback are also taken into account in the final evaluations (*see form, page 640*).

Most of the statistical infor-

mation contained in the 254 detailed profiles was supplied and checked by the cruise lines and ship owners. Any errors or updated information should be sent to the author at the address shown on the facing page.

Please note that the author's constant cruise and ship inspection schedule means that he is seldom on land, and regrets that he is no longer able to answer all letters. But all comments will be studied and will help maintain the authority of the next edition.

Introduction

The Cruising Experience

Different Kinds of Cruises

Choosing the Right Cruise

The Ships and their Ratings

Practical Information

Maps

Tables and Charts

WHY TAKE A CRUISE?

*We answer the questions about ocean cruising most frequently asked
both by those new to this type of vacation and by regulars*

Compared to most land vacations, cruises offer so much more. For a start, your initial fare includes your accommodation, all meals and in-between snacks, entertainment, lectures, social functions, participation events, movies, and use of the ship's facilities, including the fitness center, casino (no entry charge, and you don't have to be a member), and perhaps air tickets to get to and from your cruise ship. The hassles of an ordinary land-based vacation are completely eliminated in one very neat package.

With the outstanding choice of cruises, ships and itineraries available for every budget, a cruise represents almost unlimited potential. More than 250 ocean-going cruise ships visit almost 2,000 destinations throughout the world, and new ships are being constantly introduced. Cruising is a year-round vacation for singles, couples, families with children, and those of senior years. You are transported from place to place in a highly civilized manner. You can be as active, or as relaxed and pampered as you like. Most cruise ships have a well equipped medical center.

Early booking means greater savings, and a better choice of accommodation. Many lines allow you to extend your vacation and have special pre- and post-cruise hotel/resort or safari game-park extra stay packages available at appealing rates.

Why are cruises so popular?

Over 10 million people throughout the world took a cruise last year. Cruising is popular today because it takes you away from the pressures and strains of contemporary life by offering an escape from reality. Cruise ships are really self-contained resorts, without the crime, which can take you to several destinations in the space of just a few days.

The sea has always been a source of adventure, excitement, romance, and wonder. It is beneficial and therapeutic, and, because you pay in advance, you know what you will spend on your vacation without any hidden surprises. There is no traffic (except when you go ashore in ports of call), and no pollution. The hassles of ordinary travel are almost eliminated in one pleasant little package. And, you can save a substantial amount of money over a regular land-based vacation.

PRECEDING PAGES: P&O's *Oriana* arrives in Sydney.
LEFT: Cunard's *Queen Elizabeth 2* crosses the Atlantic.

Then there are the sights. Some of the world's most beautiful places are seen best from the decks of cruise ships. Indeed, there's simply no other way to see the dramatic, awe-inspiring beauty of Antarctica, Alaska's Inside Passage and its glaciers, the Galápagos Islands, the Panama Canal, or Vietnam's haunting Halong Bay. Up-close and personal is just one of the reasons that cruising is such a valuable experience. It's no wonder that 85 percent of passengers want to go again. And again. And again. Cruising is addictive.

Has terrorism had an effect?

Yes. In the weeks after the September 11, 2001, attacks on the United States, several cruise lines went out of business or filed for bankruptcy protection. Seven ocean-going and one river cruise lines, and 22 ocean-going ships were affected (plus three river cruise vessels). Among them were: American Hawaii Cruises (1 ship), Delta Queen Coastal Cruises (1 ship), Dreamline Cruises (1 ship), Renaissance Cruises (10 ships), United States Lines (1 ship), Valtur Tourism (1 ship).

In addition, the Delta Queen Steamboat Company suspended sailings aboard two of its three Mississippi riverboats: *American Queen, Delta Queen* and *Mississippi Queen* (although all are now back in operation). In 2001, before September 11, several small cruise lines also ceased operations: Great Lakes Cruises (1 ship), Hyundai Cruises (3 ships), Marine Expeditions (3 ships).

Many cruise lines had to redeploy their ships, while others suffered a dramatic drop in passenger numbers. With fixed operating costs, several had cash flow problems, and new bookings dried up. Thus, the unfortunate effect of the "fallout" after the attacks translated to a lack of confidence (particularly in North Americans) in traveling by air. With the deep discounting to attract passengers, their return to cruising was swift.

Has quality declined as a result?

Yes, unfortunately it has. In the mass market, a cruise aboard the ships of the "Big Eight" cruise lines (Carnival Cruise Lines, Celebrity Cruises, Costa Cruises, Holland America Line, Norwegian Cruise Line, P&O Princess Cruises, Royal Caribbean International, and Star Cruises) has become a "not so inclusive" product, and passengers are asked to pay extra for all sorts of things that were formerly included. The cruise lines have also raised their prices for many items, including drinks and spa treatments, among others. While it's still an excellent value for the money vacation, the quality is going down, particularly among the large ships. For better quality, you will need to pay more money. Indeed, there is more distance now between the cruise ships belonging to the "Big Eight" cruise lines and the (generally smaller) more upscale ships, particularly in terms of crew, food, service and training.

Other effects of cost cutting include the withdrawal of hospitality services such as stewards and stewardesses who show you to your cabin when you first embark. Examples of large lines that have dispensed with this service include P&O Princess Cruises and Royal Caribbean International, whose meager staff on duty at the ship side of the gangway, now merely point you in the direction of your deck, or to the ship's elevators. However, despite the cost cutting, cruise fares remain at pre-1980 levels, an indication of the incredible value of a cruise when compared to a land-based vacation.

What exactly *is* a cruise?

A cruise is a vacation. It is an antidote to (and escape from) the stress and strain of life ashore. It offers you a chance to relax and unwind in comfortable surroundings, with attentive service, good food, and a ship that changes the scenery for you. It is virtually a hassle-free, and, more importantly, a crime-free vacation. You never have to make blind choices. Everything's close to hand, and there are always polite people to help you. A cruise vacation provides great value for money, variety (in ship size, destinations, facilities, cuisine, entertainment, activities and shore excursion opportunities), a chance to explore new places, meet new people, make friends, and, above all, provides the ingredients for you to have a wonderful vacation.

How long does one last?

It can be as short or as long as you want. Cruise lines offer cruises from as little as three nights to more than six months (there are even passengers who stay aboard some ships all year round, and disembark only when the ship has to go into dry dock for refits and refurbishments).

Aren't all ships and cruises similar?

Far from it. Look through this book and you will see that ships range from under 200 feet (60 meters) to over 1,000 feet (300 meters) in length. They carry from under 100 to almost 4,000 passengers; facilities, food, and service vary according to the size of the ship. Ambience ranges from

ultra-casual to very formal (starchy and reserved). Entertainment ranges from amateur dramatics to full-fledged high-tech production shows, from the corner cabaret to a world-famous headliner, and everything in between.

Isn't cruising just for old people?

Nothing could be further from the truth. Indeed, the average age of passengers gets younger each year. Although those of silver years have found cruising to be a very safe way to travel the world, the average age of first-time passengers is now well under 40. Remember also that even wrinkly old people can have fun, too, and many of them have more get-up-and-go than many people under the age of 40.

On a typical cruise you'll meet singles, couples, families with children of all ages (including single parents and grandparents), honeymooners, second- or third-time honeymooners, groups of friends, and college buddies are all passengers. In fact, today's passengers are likely to be your next-door neighbors.

Won't I get bored?

Usually, it's the men who ask this question, but get them aboard and it is almost guaranteed that there won't be enough time in the day to do all the things they want to do – as long as you choose the right ship, for the right reasons. There are more things to do aboard today's ships than there is on almost any Caribbean island. So, whether you want to lie back and be pampered, or go nonstop, you can do it on a cruise vacation, and you will only have to pack and unpack once. Finally, just being at sea provides a sense of freedom that few other places can offer.

Where can I go on a cruise?

There are over 30,000 different cruises to choose from each year, and almost 2,000 cruise destinations in the world. A cruise can also take you to places inaccessible by almost any other means, such as Antarctica, the North Cape, the South Sea islands, and so on. In fact, if you close your eyes and think of almost anywhere in the world where there's water, there's probably a cruise ship or river vessel to take you there.

Isn't cruising expensive?

Compare what it would cost on land to have all your meals and entertainment provided, as well as transportation, fitness and sports facilities, social activities, educational talks, parties, and other functions, and you will soon realize the incredible value of a cruise. Further, a ship is a destination in itself, which moves to other destinations. No land-based resort could ever do that.

At your service: the crew of the *Queen Elizabeth 2*.

Simply give yourself a vacation budget, and go to your professional travel supplier with it. The rest, as they say, will be taken care of.

A seven-day cruise is advertised for $400 a person. Is this too good to be true?

As a rule, yes. Consider that a decent hotel room in New York costs at least $200 per night (plus taxes) *without meals* or *entertainment*; it stands to reason that something is not quite as it seems. Before booking, read the fine print. Look at all the additional costs such as tips to cabin and dining room stewards, shore excursions, drinks (plus a 15 percent gratuity), plus getting to and from the ship. That $400 per person could well be for a four-berth cabin adjacent to the ship's laundry or above the disco, but in any event, not in a desirable location (just like a $50 hotel room in New York).

Why does it cost more to cruise in Europe and the Far East than in the Caribbean?

There are two reasons:
● Almost all aspects of operations, including fuel costs, port charges, air transportation, supplying food to the ships, are much higher in Europe.
● Companies can make more money (called yield) than in the cut-price Caribbean, where sun, sea, and sand are the principal attractions, whereas sightseeing, architecture, culture, and other things are part of a more enriching cruise experience.

Additionally, the price of shore excursions in Europe is also high. Indeed, in April 2002, Greece raised the price of admission to all ancient sites and museums. For example, the price of admission to the Acropolis was more than doubled, from 5.87 euros (about $8.30/£3.60) to 12 euros (about $10.50/£7.35).

How inclusive is "all-inclusive"?

That's rather like asking how much sand is on the beach! For cruise passengers, it typically means that transportation, accommodation, food, and entertainment are wrapped up in one neat package. Today on land, however, "super clubs" offer everything "all-in" including drinks. While that concept works better aboard small ships (those carrying less than 500 passengers), the large cruise ships (those carrying more than 1,000 passengers) provide more facilities and more reasons for you to spend money on board, so "all-exclusive" might be a better term.

Is cruising for singles?

Yes, indeed. A cruise vacation is ideal for those traveling alone (over 25 percent of all passengers are solo travelers), because it is easy to meet other people in a noncompetitive environment. Many ships also have dedicated cabins for singles as well as special add-on rates for single occupancy of double cabins. Some cruise lines will even find a cabin mate for you to share with, if you so desire. However, be aware that in cabins

Family cruising is the industry's biggest growth sector.

that have three or four berths, personal privacy will be non-existent.

Why is it so expensive for singles to travel alone?

Almost all cruise lines base their rates on double occupancy. Thus, when you travel alone, the cruise (cabin) portion of your fare reflects an additional supplement. While almost all new ships are built with cabins for double occupancy, some older ships do have single occupancy cabins.

Do cruises suit honeymooners?

Absolutely. A cruise is the ideal setting for romance, for shipboard weddings (these can be arranged in some ports, depending on local regulations), receptions, and honeymoons. Most decisions are already made for you, so all you have to do is show up. Most ships have double-, queen- or king-sized beds, too. And for those on a second honeymoon, many ships now perform a "renewal of vows" ceremony (some charge for this).

And what about children?

Also yes. In fact, a cruise provides families with more quality time than any other type of vacation (family cruising is the largest growth segment in the cruise industry). Activities are tailored to various age groups (Disney has cruise ships dedicated to families and children). In addition, a cruise is educational, allows children to interact in a safe, crime-free environment, and takes them to destinations in comfortable and familiar sur-

A cruise is ideal in many ways for honeymooners.

roundings. In fact, children have such a good time aboard ship and ashore, you may have difficulty getting them home after the cruise (if you choose the right ship). And you as parents (or single parent) will get time to enjoy life, too.

Can I find a quiet, serene cruise, away from children and noise?

Yes. If you don't like crowds, noise, long lines, there are some beautiful small ships ready to cater to your every whim. Perhaps a sail-cruise vessel or a river or barge cruise could also provide the right antidote. There are so many choices. Companies with ships that are totally child-free: P&O Cruises (*Arcadia*), Saga Cruises (*Saga Rose*), Swan Hellenic Discovery Cruises (*Minerva/Minerva II*).

How pregnant can I be when I take a cruise?

You can be *very* pregnant. Typically though, most cruise lines will *not* allow a mother-to-be to cruise past their 28th week of pregnancy. You may be required to produce a doctor's certificate.

Is there a cruise with no ports of call?

Yes, but it isn't really a cruise. It's a transatlantic *crossing*, from New York to Southampton, England, aboard Cunard Line's *Queen Elizabeth 2*. While I have been advising cruise lines for years that a ship doing occasional three-, four-, or seven-

day cruises to nowhere would be welcomed by many repeat passengers, no cruise line has yet taken the initiative. Many passengers are so "allergic" to places that are really tourist rip-off destinations that they really want nothing more than to be aboard a ship at sea, with all the creature comforts of home.

Will I need a passport?

Yes, you will, particularly in these days of heightened security checks, when some form of photo ID is obligatory almost everywhere. You can usually apply for a passport at your local post office. In capital cities, and, possibly, other major cities, there will be a passport office where you can apply in person, or at short notice.

What size of ship is best?

Ships really come in three discernable sizes: Small, Mid-Size, and Large.
● Choose a Large Ship (these carry over 1,000 passengers up to almost 4,000) if you like lots of people, big-city facilities and entertainment.
● Choose a Mid-Sized ship (500–1,000 passengers) for a small-town atmosphere, with some entertainment and a small choice of facilities.
● Choose a Small Ship (these carry 50 to 500 passengers) if you are seeking a quiet, serene vacation, probably without children, and you don't need much entertainment – just really good food and relaxation.

See "Selecting the Right Ship" *(page 114).*

Should I book early?

The further you book ahead, the greater will be any discount applied by the cruise line. You'll also get the cabin you want, in the location you want, and you may also be upgraded. When you book late (close to the sailing date), you may get a low price, but you typically won't get the cabin or location you might like, or (worse still), in ships with two seatings for dinner, you won't be able to choose early or late seating.

Can I dine when I want to?

Yes, you can – well, almost. Most major cruise lines have introduced "flexible dining" which

It's even possible to play mini-golf at sea.

allows you to choose (with some limitations) when you want to eat, and with whom you dine. Just like going out to restaurants ashore, reservations may be required (you may also have to wait), and occupants of the most expensive suites get priority. Aboard large cruise ships (1,000-plus passengers) the big evening entertainment shows typically are staged twice, so you end up with the equivalent of two-seating dining anyway.

What is "alternative" dining?

Some ships now have alternative dining spots other than the main restaurant. These usually cost extra – typically between $15 and $25 a person, but the food quality is decidedly better, as is pre-

sentation, service, and ambiance. Most alternative dining spots are also typically more intimate, and much quieter than the main dining rooms.

Do ships have different classes?

Not really. Gone are the class distinctions and the pretensions of formality of the past. Differences are now found mainly in the type of accommodation chosen; in the price you pay for a larger cabin (or suite), the location of your cabin (or suite), and whether or not you have butler service.

What does category guarantee mean?

It means you have purchased a specific grade of accommodation (just as in a hotel), although the *actual* cabin may not have been assigned to your booking yet. Your cabin may be assigned before you go, or when you arrive for embarkation.

What's the difference between an "outside" and an "interior" cabin?

An "outside" (or "exterior") cabin doesn't mean it's outside the ship; it simply means that it has a window (or porthole) with a view of the outside, or there is a private balcony for you to physically be (or look) outside. An "interior" cabin means that it does not have a view of the outside, but it will have artwork or curtains on one wall instead of a window or patio-like (balcony) door.

Isn't it hard to find one's way around large ships?

Well, it can take at least a few hours, or a day or so. However, in general, remember that decks are horizontal, while stairs are vertical. The rest comes naturally, with practice.

I like large ships, but find it hard to escape from constant noise. What's the answer?

I understand your problem. Simply contact the hotel manager and let him (or her) know that volume levels are unacceptable and to please do something about it. If enough people do this, things will have to change for the better. Or you could take earplugs!

Can I send and receive e-mails on board?

Sometimes, depending on your service provider. Aboard most ships, e-mail facilities have now been added to some degree or other. Several ships now sport an Internet café, or Internet Centers. For many companies, e-mail has now become an important revenue generator. One cruise ship, *Europa* (Hapag-Lloyd Cruises) even has a *full* personal computer in *every* cabin with 24 hour internet/e-mail connectivity (e-mails are free), while some other ships have installed computers in their most expensive suites.

Can I learn about computers while on a cruise?

Yes. Crystal Cruises, Cunard Line and Seabourn Cruise Line are just three examples of cruise lines that provide computers and learning classes. Indeed, the Computer Learning Centers aboard *Crystal Harmony, Crystal Symphony* and *QE2*, each have almost two-dozen computer workstations or laptops for class use.

Can I go shopping in ports of call?

Yes, you can. Many passengers with a black belt in shopping engage in "retail therapy" when visiting ports of call such as Dubai, Hong Kong, Singapore, St. Martin, and St. Thomas, among so many others. Just remember you will have to carry all your purchases home at the end of your cruise.

Do I have to leave the ship in each port of call?

Absolutely not. In fact, many repeat passengers enjoy being aboard "their" ships when there are virtually no other passengers aboard.

Can I fly in the night before or stay an extra day after the cruise?

Cruise lines often do offer pre- and post-cruise stay packages that can be purchased at an additional cost. The advantage is that you don't have to do anything else. All will be taken care of, as they say. If you book a hotel on your own, however, you may have to pay an "air deviation" fee (payable if you do not take the cruise line's air arrangements, or you want to change them).

Can I pre-book seats on flights?

With packaged vacations such as cruises, it is normally not possible to reserve airline seats prior to check-in, and, although the cruise line will typically forward your requests for preferred seating, these may not be guaranteed.

Where did all the money go?

Apart from the cruise fare itself, there could be other incidentals such as government taxes, port charges, air ticket tax. Once on board, extra costs

will typically include drinks, mini-bar items, cappuccino and espresso coffees, shore excursions, surfing the Internet, sending or receiving e-mails, health spa treatments, casino gaming, photographs, laundry and dry-cleaning, babysitting services, wine tasting, bottled water placed in your cabin, and the services of the medical department.

A cruise aboard a ship belonging to one of the major cruise lines (Carnival Cruise Lines, Celebrity Cruises, Costa Cruises, Holland America Line, Norwegian Cruise Line, Princess Cruises, Royal Caribbean International, Star Cruises) could be compared to buying a car, whereby automobile manufacturers offer a basic model at a set price,

"Rock climbing" on the *Voyager of the Seas'* funnel.

with optional extras to be added. These cruise lines will tell you that income generated on board helps to keep the basic cost of a cruise reasonable.

What if I don't like my cruise?

Given today's standards, it's almost certain that you *will* enjoy your cruise vacation. One company – Carnival Cruise Lines – has a Vacation Guarantee that states that if you do not like the cruise, the ship, or other aspect of the vacation, you can disembark in the first port of call, and the line will return all your money. Now, that's an excellent guarantee that less than one-tenth of 1 percent of its passengers take up. Other lines would do well to follow this example. ❑

CRUISING'S IRRESISTIBLE GROWTH

Outpaced by jet aircraft, passenger liners seemed destined for the scrapyard.

Then they began transforming themselves into floating resorts

In 1835, a curious advertisement appeared in the first issue of the *Shetland Journal*. Headed "To Tourists" it proposed an imaginary cruise from Stromness in Scotland, round Iceland and the Faroe Islands, and hinted at the pleasures of cruising under the Spanish sun in winter. Thus, it is said, the journal's founder, Arthur Anderson, invented the concept of cruising. Just two years later, Anderson, along with his partner Brodie Wilcox, founded the great Peninsular Steam Navigation Company (later to become P&O).

Soon after, Samuel Cunard started his transatlantic sailings, from Liverpool to Halifax, across the most dangerous ocean in the world, the North Atlantic, with a steam-powered sailing vessel, *Britannia*, on July 4, 1840. Every year since then, a Cunard ship has operated scheduled transatlantic liner service between the old and new worlds.

Sailing for leisure soon caught on. Even writers

such as William Makepeace Thackeray and Charles Dickens boarded ships for the excitement of the voyage, not just to reach a destination. The Victorians, having discovered tourism, promoted the idea widely. Indeed, Thackeray's account of his legendary voyage in 1844, from Cornhill to Grand Cairo by means of the P&O ships of the day, makes fascinating reading, as does the account by Dickens of his transatlantic crossing aboard a Cunard ship in 1842. Ruger's American Line's *Quaker City*, which journeyed from London to the Black Sea in 1867, was the subject of Mark Twain's *The Innocents Abroad*, published in 1869.

In the 1920s, cruising became the thing to do for the world's well-to-do. Being pampered in such grand style was fashionable – and is still the underlying concept of cruising. The ship took you and your belongings anywhere, and fed you, accommodated you, relaxed you, and entertained you. At the same time, it even catered for your servants – who, of course, accompanied you.

The First Booze Cruises

Cruising for Americans was helped greatly by Prohibition in the 1930s. After all, just a few miles out at sea, you were free to consume as much liquor as you wanted. And cheap three- and four-day weekend "booze cruises" out of New York were preferable to "bathtub gin." Then came short cruises, with destinations as well as alcohol. In time, the short cruise was to become one of the principal sources of profit for the steamship companies of the day.

In the 1930s a battle raged between the giant cruising companies of the world, as Britain, France, Germany, and the United States built liners of unprecedented luxury, elegance, glamour, and comfort. Each country was competing to produce the biggest and best afloat. For a time, quality was somehow related to smokestacks: the more a ship had the better. Although speed had always been a factor, particularly on the transatlantic run, it now became a matter of national ambition.

The first ship designed specifically for cruising from the US after World War II was *Ocean Monarch* (Furness Withy & Company Ltd), which was awarded a gold medal by the US Academy of Designing for "outstanding beauty and unusual design features of a cruise ship." Its maiden voyage was from New York to Bermuda

in 1951. I worked aboard the ship for a short time.

One of the most renowned cruise liners of all time was Cunard's *Caronia* (34,183 tons), conceived in 1948. It was designed and built to offer a transatlantic service in the peak summer months only and then spend the rest of the year doing long, expensive cruises. One outstanding feature was a single giant mast and one smokestack, the largest of its time. The hull was painted four shades of green, supposedly for the purposes of heat resistance and easy identification. Known as the "Green Goddess," it was one of the first ships to provide a private adjoining bathroom for every cabin – a true luxury.

The Birth of Modern Cruising

In June 1958, the first commercial jet aircraft flew across the Atlantic and forever altered the economics of transatlantic travel. It was the last year in which more passengers crossed the North Atlantic by sea than by air. In the early 1960s, passenger-shipping directories listed over 100 passenger lines. Until the mid-1960s, it was cheaper to cross the Atlantic by ship than by plane, but the appearance of the jet aircraft changed that rapidly, particularly with the introduction of the Boeing 747 in the early 1970s. In 1962, more than 1 million people crossed the North Atlantic by ship; in 1970, that number was down to 250,000.

The success of the jumbo jets created a fleet of unprofitable and out-of-work passenger liners that appeared doomed for the scrap heap. Even the famous big "Queens," noted for their regular weekly transatlantic service, were at risk. Cunard White Star Line's *Queen Mary* (80,774 tons) was withdrawn in September 1967. Cunard Line's sister ship *Queen Elizabeth*, at 83,673 tons the largest passenger liner ever built (until 1996), made its final crossing in October 1968.

Ships were sold for a fraction of their value. Many lines went out of business and ships were scrapped. Those that survived attempted to mix transatlantic crossings with voyages south to the sun. The Caribbean (including the Bahamas) became appealing, cruising became an alternative, and an entire new industry was born, with new lines being formed exclusively for cruising.

Then came smaller, more specialized ships, capable of getting into the tiny ports of developing Caribbean islands (there were no commercial airlines taking vacationers to the Caribbean then, and few hotels). Instead of cruising long distances south from more northerly ports such as New York, companies established their headquarters in Florida. This not only avoided the cold weather, choppy seas, and expense of the northern ports but also saved fuel costs with shorter runs to the Caribbean. Cruising was reborn. California became the base for cruises to the Mexican Riviera, and Vancouver on Canada's west coast became the focus for summer cruises to Alaska.

Flying passengers to embarkation ports was the next logical step, and soon a working relationship emerged between the cruise lines and the airlines. Air/sea and "sail and stay" packages thrived – joint cruise and hotel vacations with inclusive pricing. Some of the old liners came out of mothballs, purchased by emerging cruise lines and refurbished for warm-weather cruising operations, often with their interiors redesigned and refitted. During the late 1970s, the modern cruise industry grew at a rapid rate.

Cruising Today

Today's cruise concept hasn't changed much from that of earlier days, although it has been improved, refined, expanded, and packaged for ease of consumption. No longer the domain of affluent, retired people, the cruise industry today, is vibrant and alive with passengers of *every* age and socio-economic background. Cruising is no longer the shipping business, but the hospitality industry (although some cruise ship staff appear to be in the hostility industry).

New ships are generally larger than their counterparts of yesteryear, yet cabin size has become "standardized" to provide more space for entertainment and other public facilities. Today's ships boast air conditioning to keep out heat and humidity; stabilizers to keep the ship on an even keel; a high level of maintenance, safety, and hygiene; and more emphasis on health and fitness facilities.

Cruise ship design has moved from the traditional, classic, rounded profiles of the past (example: *Queen Elizabeth 2*) to the extremely boxy shapes with squared-off sterns and towering superstructures today (examples: *Infinity, Millennium, Summit*). Although ship lovers lament these design changes, they have resulted from the need to squeeze as much as possible in the space provided (you can squeeze more in a square box than you can in a round one, although it may be less aesthetically appealing). Form follows function, and ships have changed from ocean transportation to floating vacation resorts.

Although ships have long been devoted to eating and relaxation in comfort (promulgating the maxim "Traveling slowly unwinds you faster"), ships today offer more activities, and more learning and life-enriching experiences than

---

DID YOU KNOW?

● that the first vessel built exclusively for cruising was Hamburg-Amerika Line's two-funnel yacht, the 4,409-ton *Princessin Victoria Luise*? This luxury ship even included a private suite for the German kaiser.

● that the first ship to be fitted with real stabilizers (not an autogyro device) was the Peninsular & Oriental Steam Navigation Company's 1949-built 24,215-ton *Chusan*?

● that the first consecrated oceangoing Roman Catholic chapel aboard a passenger ship was in Compagnie Generale Transatlantique's *Ile de France* of 1928?

● that the latest life rafts called Hydrostatic Release Units (HRU), designed in Britain and approved by the Royal Navy, are now compulsory on all British-registered ships? Briefly, an HRU is capable of automatically releasing a life raft from its mountings when a ship sinks (even after it sinks) but can also be operated manually at the installation point, saving precious time in an emergency.

---

before. And there are many more places you can visit on a cruise: from Antarctica to Acapulco, Bermuda to Bergen, Dakar to Dominica, Shanghai to St. Thomas, or if you prefer, perhaps nowhere at all.

The cruise industry is a $15 billion business worldwide and still growing. It provides employment to a growing number, both directly (there are over 100,000 shipboard officers, staff and crew, as well as about 15,000 employees in cruise company offices), and indirectly (suppliers of foodstuffs and mechanical and electrical parts, port agents, transport companies, destinations, airlines, railways, hotels, car rental companies). In 2001, over 10 million people worldwide took a cruise, packaged and sold by cruise lines through tour operators and travel agents.

Building a Modern Cruise Ship

More than any other type of vessel, a cruise ship has to fulfill fantasies and satisfy exotic imaginations. It is the job of the shipyard to take those fantasies and turn them into a steel ship without unduly straining the laws of naval architecture and safety regulations, not to mention budgets.

Although no perfect cruise ship exists, turning owners' dreams and concepts into ships that embody those ideals is the job of specialized marine architects and shipyards, as well as consultants, interior designers, and a mass of specialist suppliers. Computers have simplified this complex process, although shipboard management and operations personnel often become frustrated with designers who are more idealistic than they are practical. Ships represent a compromise between ideals and restrictions of space and finance, the solution being to design ships for specific areas and conditions of service.

Ships used to be constructed in huge building docks, from the keel (backbone) up. Today, ships are built in huge sections, then joined together in an assembly area (typically as many as 60 or more sections for a large ship). The sections may not even be constructed in the shipyard, although they will be assembled there.

Formerly, passenger spaces were slotted in wherever there was space within a given hull. Today, computers provide highly targeted ship design, enabling a new ship to be built within two years instead of within the four or five years it took in the 1950s.

The maximum noise and vibration levels allowable in the accommodation spaces and recreational areas are stipulated in any owner's contract with the shipyard. Vibration tests are carried out once a ship is built and launched, using a finite method element of evaluation; this embraces analyses of prime sources of noise and excitation,

namely the ship's propellers and main engines.

Prefabricated cabin modules, including *in situ* bathrooms complete with toilets and all plumbing, are used today. When the steel structure of the relevant deck is ready, with main lines and insulation installed, cabin modules are then affixed to the deck, and power lines and sanitary plumbing are swiftly connected. All waste and power connections, together with hot/cold water mixing valves, are arranged in the service area of the bathroom and can be reached from the passageway outside the cabin for maintenance.

Cruising Tomorrow

Current thinking in ship design follows two distinct paths: large ships or smaller ships.

● Large ships, where "economy of scale" helps the operator to keep the cost per passengers down. Three companies (Carnival Cruise Lines, Princess Cruises, and Royal Caribbean International) have ships measuring over 100,000 tons, accommodating over 3,000 passengers, with the "bigger is better" principle being pursued for all it's worth. These ships are, however, limited to the Caribbean, being too wide to transit the Panama Canal (non-Panamax).

● Small ships, where the "small is exclusive" concept has gained a strong foothold, particularly in the luxury category. Cruise lines offer high-quality ships of low capacity, which can provide

Previous pages and above: classic cruising posters

a highly personalized range of quality services.

Other cruise lines have expanded by "stretching" their ships. This is accomplished literally by cutting a ship in half, and inserting a newly constructed midsection, thus instantly increasing capacity, adding more accommodation and public rooms, while maintaining the same draft. "Stretched" ships include: *Black Watch* (ex-*Royal Viking Star*), *Carousel* (ex-*Nordic Prince*), *Norwegian Dream* (ex-*Dreamward*), *Norwegian Majesty* (ex-*Royal Majesty*), *Norwegian Star I* (ex-*Royal Viking Sea*), *Norwegian Wind* (ex-*Windward*), *Sundream* (ex-*Song of Norway*), and *Westerdam* (ex-*Homeric*).

Whatever direction the design of cruise vessels takes in the future, ships are becoming increasingly environmentally friendly. With growing concern, particularly in eco-sensitive areas such as Alaska and the South Pacific, better safeguards against environmental pollution and damage are being built into the vessels.

The cruise industry is fast approaching "zero discharge," which means that nothing is discharged into the world's oceans at any time. This is an easier objective for the latest batch of ships to attain, since older ships usually have a more difficult time achieving this ambitious target because of their outdated equipment. ❏

At the helm of the *Queen Mary*, withdrawn in 1967.

A Chronology of Modern Cruising

1960 Passenger shipping directories listed more than 30 companies operating transatlantic voyages. Many ships were laid up from 1960 to 1970, and most were sold for a fraction of their value. *Britannic,* the last passenger ship to wear the White Star Line colors, went out of service.

1962 Compagnie Générale Transatlantique's liner *France*, at 1,035 ft the longest passenger ship ever built, entered service from Le Havre to New York.

1963 Cunard Line's RMS *Queen Elizabeth* made an experimental cruise from New York to the West Indies. As a result, full air conditioning was fitted in 1965–66 to facilitate more extensive cruising.

1965 The Orient Steam Navigation Company was absorbed into the P&O Group. The new company became known as the Peninsular & Oriental Steam Navigation Company. Stanley B. McDonald founded Princess Cruises.

1966 Soviet transatlantic service was reopened with the Black Sea Shipping Company's *Aleksandr Pushkin* inaugurating service between Montreal and Leningrad (now St. Petersburg) for the first time since 1949. The Norwegian company Klosters Reederei joined Miami businessman Ted Arison in marketing Caribbean cruises from Miami. Sanford Chobol founded Commodore Cruise Line.

1967 Cunard withdrew the transatlantic liner *Queen Mary* from service.

1968 Cunard's *Queen Elizabeth* withdrawn. Cunard refused delivery of *Queen Elizabeth 2* from its builder, John Brown, in December, because of unacceptable turbine vibration levels. Repairs led to a five-month delay to its maiden transatlantic crossing. Boise Cascade purchased Princess Cruises from its founder, Stanley B. McDonald, who bought back the line two years later.

1969 Lars-Eric Lindblad's *Lindblad Explorer*, designed for close-in expedition cruising, was launched. Royal Caribbean Cruise Line was founded by a consortium of Norwegian shipping companies. The loss-making liner *United States* was laid up.

1970 Royal Viking Line was founded by a consortium of three partners (Bergen Line, A.F. Klaveness, and Nordenfjeldske) who each contributed one ship (*Royal Viking Sea, Royal Viking Sky,* and *Royal Viking Star*). Germany's Norddeutscher Lloyd and Hapag (Hamburg American Line) merged as Hapag-Lloyd.

1971 Cunard Line was sold to Trafalgar House Investments.

1972 Ted Arison founded Carnival Cruise Lines. It began with just one ship, *Mardi Gras* (ex-*Empress of Canada*). It ran aground on its first voyage.

1973 Sitmar Cruises began operations from Syd

ney with a single ship, *Fairstar* (a converted troop carrier formerly operated by Bibby Line).

1974 P&O bought Princess Cruises. Compagnie Générale Transatlantique laid up the loss-making *France*. The Port Authority of New York and New Jersey opened its Passenger Ship Terminal. Royal Cruise Lines' first ship, *Golden Odyssey*, built to accommodate the equivalent load of a Boeing 747 aircraft (425 passengers), was introduced.

1975 *Island Princess* and *Pacific Princess* (Princess Cruises) become the "stars" in the American television show *The Love Boat*.

1976 The Italian Line and Lloyd Triestino ceased transatlantic passenger operations.

1977 World Explorer Cruises was founded with a single ship, *Universe*. Holland America Line absorbed Monarch Cruise Lines.

1978 Richard Hadley founded United States Cruises.

1979 American Hawaii Cruises was formed. In June, SS *France* was purchased by Lauritz Kloster, rebuilt for Caribbean cruises, renamed *Norway* and transferred to Norwegian Caribbean Lines.

1980 Sea Goddess Cruises was founded by Helge Naarstad. Denmark's United Steamship Company (DFDS) founded Scandinavian World Cruises to operate one-day cruises from Miami (the company subsequently became SeaEscape).

1981 Transatlantic service provided by Soviet-registered ships was discontinued because of a US embargo. Astor Cruises was formed in the UK.

1982 The British government chartered Cunard's *Queen Elizabeth 2* and P&O Cruises' *Canberra* for use as troop carriers during the Falklands War between Argentina and Britain. B&I Line's *Uganda* was used as a hospital ship.

1983 P&O appointed Jeffrey Sterling as chairman

in order to fend off an unwanted takeover bid by Cunard Line's owners, Trafalgar House, which purchased Norwegian America Cruises (NAC), together with *Sagafjord* and *Vistafjord*. Premier Cruise Lines was founded. Salen-Lindblad Cruising's *Lindblad Explorer* became the first passenger ship to successfully navigate the Northwest Passage, sailing 4,790 miles (7,700 km) from Saint John's, Newfoundland, to Point Barrow, Alaska.

1984 Sundance Cruises was founded by Stanley B. McDonald with a single ship, *Sundancer*. Also founded were Dolphin Cruise Line and Premier Cruise Lines. Windstar Sail Cruises re-launched the age of commercial sail.

1985 The Chandris Group of Companies acquired Fantasy Cruises from GoGo Tours, renaming it Chandris Fantasy Cruises in the US and Chandris Cruises in the UK.

1986 Signet Cruise Line was founded in Norway. Owing to a lawsuit brought by an American who claimed the right to the name Signet, the company changed its name to Seabourn Cruise Line. Eastern Cruise Lines, Western Cruise Lines, and Sundance Cruises merged to become Admiral Cruises. Cunard acquired Sea Goddess Cruises, together with *Sea Goddess I* and *Sea Goddess II*.

1987 Carnival Cruise Lines made its first public stock offering. Cunard's *Queen Elizabeth 2* was converted at a German shipyard from steam turbine to diesel-electric power, the largest conversion in maritime history. Bahama Cruise Line became Bermuda Star Line. Ocean Cruise Lines merged with Pearl Cruises. Princess Cruises replaced almost 500 unionized British

---

The *Canberra* is escorted back into Southampton after having been a troop carrier in the 1982 Falklands War.

hotel and catering staff aboard its five ships.
1988 Commodore Cruise Lines sold its *Bohème* to the Church of Scientology; it was renamed *Freewinds*. Crystal Cruises was formed as a wholly-owned division of Japan's Nippon Yusen Kaisha (NYK). Royal Caribbean Cruise Line merged with Admiral Cruises to form Royal Admiral Cruises (later Royal Caribbean Cruises). Carnival Cruise Lines acquired Holland America Line, including its land-based hotel/transport operations and Windstar Cruises. Seabourn Cruise Line's first ship, *Seabourn Pride*, entered service.
1989 American Cruise Lines, which operated small vessels for intracoastal cruising, went into bankruptcy. The Chandris Group of Companies announced the creation of Celebrity Cruises, which ordered two new cruise ships, to be named *Horizon* and *Zenith*. Ocean Quest International was formed to provide seven-day cruises for scuba diving enthusiastst; the venture failed after a diver died in a hyperbaric decompression chamber. Renaissance Cruises was formed by Fearnley & Eger (a 120-year-old Oslo-based shipping concern) to build and market eight small premium cruise vessels. The Panama Canal celebrated its 75th birthday. Lars-Eric Lindblad's Lindblad Travel company went into bankruptcy.
1990 Starlite Cruises (part of the Piraeus-based Lelakis Group) was formed to provide ships for

WHO GOES CRUISING

The Maritime Evaluations Group has analyzed by nationality the breakdown of passengers choosing to take an oceangoing cruise vacation:

United States	6,900,000
UK *	800,000
Asia (not including Japan)	800,000
Germany	392,000
Canada	300,000
Italy	250,000
Australasia	200,000
Japan	200,000
France	225,000
Rest of Europe	250,000
Cyprus **	75,000
Freighter Passengers	3,000
Total	10,395,000

* This figure includes 120,000 British passengers who took a two- to seven-day cruise from Cyprus in conjunction with a resort/hotel stay.
** Local Cyprus market only.
Note: The above numbers do not include the approximately 1 million passengers who took a river/inland waterway cruise, nor the 300,000 passengers who took a coastal cruise aboard the ships of Norwegian Coastal Voyages. All figures for 2001.

one-day and seven-day cruises. Ocean Cruise Lines was purchased by Croisières Paquet, itself owned by the French giant Accor leisure company. Japan Cruise Line entered the cruise market in Japan with its new 606-passenger *Orient Venus* for charters and incentive cruises for Japanese companies. At the start of the Gulf War, the US government chartered *Cunard Princess* for six months for use as a rest and relaxation center for US service personnel in the Persian Gulf.
1991 Carnival Cruise Lines acquired a 25 percent stake in Seabourn Cruise Line. Renaissance Cruises was sold to an international group of investors. Effjohn International purchased Crown Cruise Line. Seawind Cruise Line commenced cruise operations. Nippon Yusen Kaisha (NYK) purchased Salen Lindblad Cruising.
1992 Costa Cruise Lines introduced its new Euro-Luxe cruise concept with the debut of *CostaClassica*. Admiral Cruises ceased operations. Carnival Cruise Lines deployed *Mardi Gras* to accommodate 600 staff members made homeless by the Hurricane Andrew. The Chandris Group of Companies and Overseas Shipholding Group (OSG) signed an agreement to form a joint venture company called Celebrity Cruise Lines, Inc. Chargeurs and Accor, the French property and leisure industries group that own Paquet Cruises and Ocean Cruise Lines, purchased a 23 percent stake in Costa Crociere, the parent company of Costa Cruises.
1993 Carnival Cruise Lines formed Fiesta Marina Cruises for the Spanish-speaking Latin American market; it was phenomenally unsuccessful. Cunard and Effjohn announced a joint venture, good for 10 years, and formed Cunard Crown Cruises. George Poulides founded Festival Cruises. SeaQuest Cruises ceased operations. *Frontier Spirit* was returned to its Japanese owners and was chartered as *Bremen* to Germany's Hanseatic Tours.
1994 Delta Queen Steamboat Company changed its corporate name to American Classic Voyages Company; it owns American Hawaii Cruises and the Delta Queen Steamboat Company. Trafalgar House, Cunard's parent company, signed an agreement to purchase the rights to the name Royal Viking Line, together with *Royal Viking Sun*. *Royal Viking Queen* went to Royal Cruise Line, becoming *Queen Odyssey* and later *Seabourn Legend*. Radisson Diamond Cruises and Seven Seas Cruise Line merged to become Radisson Seven Seas Cruises. Star Cruises was founded.
1995 British company Airtours purchased *Southward* from Norwegian Cruise Line and *Nordic Prince* from Royal Caribbean Cruises.
1996 Kloster Cruise (the parent company of Norwegian Cruise Line and Royal Cruise Line) announced the closure of its Royal Cruise Line division. *Crown Odyssey* and *Royal Odyssey* went to

Norwegian Cruise Line as *Norwegian Crown* and *Norwegian Star*, respectively. *Queen Odyssey* went to Seabourn Cruise Line and renamed *Seabourn Legend*. *Star Odyssey* was sold to Fred Olsen Cruise Lines and renamed *Black Watch*. Baltic Line and Sunshine Cruise Lines ceased cruise operations. Cunard (together with parent company Trafalgar House) was purchased by Kvaerner.

1997 Hapag-Lloyd acquired Hanseatic Tours, together with its expedition ship, *Hanseatic*. Carnival Corporation, jointly with Airtours, purchased the shares of Costa Cruises. Celebrity Cruises was bought by Royal Caribbean International for $1.3 billion. P&O Cruises' *Canberra* was withdrawn from service and sent to Pakistan for scrap.

1998 Australia repealed its cabotage laws, allowing international cruise ships to dock and operate from Australian ports without restrictions. Kvaerner sold Cunard for $500 million to a consortium that included Carnival Corporation. Orient Lines, together with its single ship *Marco Polo,* was purchased by Norwegian Cruise Line.

1999 Crown Cruise Line was reintroduced as an upscale division of Commodore Cruise Line. The company chartered *Crown Dynasty* and later purchased the ship for $86.2 million.

2000 Star Cruises took full control of Norwegian Cruise Line (including Orient Lines) after purchasing the outstanding shares held by the Carnival Corporation. The P&O Group separated its cruising activities from the rest of the group, placing more emphasis on what it sees as its core business; it has four cruise divisions – Aida Cruises,

The Queen Mary 2, Cunard's huge new transatlantic ocean liner, is due to make its debut in January 2004.

P&O Cruises, P&O Cruises (Australia), and Princess Cruises. Costa Cruises became 100% owned by the Carnival Corporation.

2001 Spain's Pullmantur bought *Oceanic* (formerly Premier Cruise Lines' *Big Red Boat I*) and *Seawind Crown* (formerly operated by Premier Cruise Lines) for the Spanish-speaking market. The Carnival Corporation sold its 25.1% shareholding in Airtours. Carnival Corporation sold the company's *Seabourn Goddess I* and *Seabourn Goddess II* to Norwegian shipowner Atle Brynestad and partner Larry Pimentel. Renaissance Cruises ceased operations after the September 11 terrorist attacks on the US. American Hawaii Cruises, United States Lines and Delta Queen Coastal Cruises all ceased operations. P&O Princess and Royal Caribbean Cruises Limited announced a merger, bringing together nine different brands: A'ROSA Cruises, Aida Cruises, Celebrity Cruises, P&O Cruises, P&O Cruises (Australia), Princess Cruises, Royal Caribbean International, Seatours, and Swan Hellenic.

2002 Valtur Tourism ceased its cruise operations; the Italian company had one ship (*Valtur Prima*). SeaDream Yacht Club began operations with two ships, *SeaDream I* and *SeaDream II*. Start-up cruise line Imperium Cruises chartered two of the former Renaissance Cruises ships: *R7* and *R8*. Golden Sun Cruises became Golden Star Cruises and started operating *Aegean I*. ❏

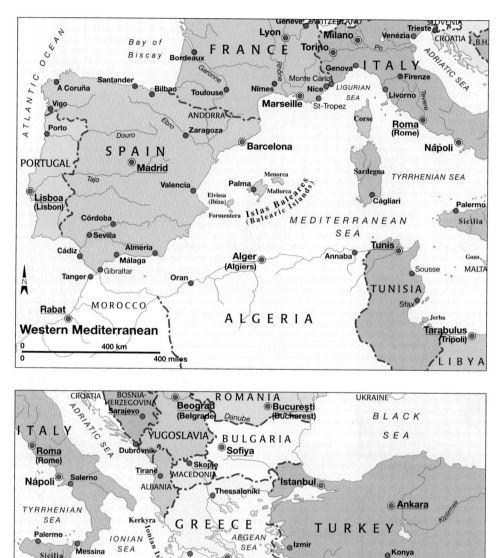

Western Mediterranean

ATLANTIC OCEAN

Bay of Biscay

FRANCE

SWITZERLAND

SLOVENIA

Genève
Lyon
Milano
Venézia
Trieste
CROATIA
B.H.

Bordeaux
Garonne
Torino
Po
ADRIATIC SEA

Santander
Bilbao
Toulouse
Nîmes
Monte Carlo
Genova
ITALY
Firenze

A Coruña
Rhône
Nice
LIGURIAN SEA
Livorno

Vigo
St-Tropez
Tevere

Porto
Douro
Ebro
ANDORRA
Marseille
Corse
Roma
(Rome)

SPAIN
Zaragoza
Barcelona
Nápoli

PORTUGAL
Madrid
Tajo

Menorca
Sardegna
TYRRHENIAN SEA

Valencia
Palma
Mallorca
Eivissa
(Ibiza)
Islas Baleares
(Balearic Islands)
Cágliari
Palermo

Lisboa
(Lisbon)
Córdoba
Formentera
MEDITERRANEAN SEA
Sicilia

Sevilla
Almería
Málaga
Alger
(Algiers)
Annaba
Tunis
Gozo
MALTA

Cádiz
Gibraltar
Sousse

Tanger
Oran
TUNISIA

Rabat
MOROCCO
Sfax

ALGERIA
Jerba

Tarabulus
(Tripoli)

LIBYA

0   400 km
0   400 miles

Eastern Mediterranean

ITALY

CROATIA
BOSNIA-HERZEGOVINA
Sarajevo
ROMANIA
Beograd
(Belgrade)
Danube
Bucureşti
(Bucharest)
UKRAINE

ADRIATIC SEA
YUGOSLAVIA
BLACK SEA

Roma
(Rome)
Dubrovnik
Skopje
BULGARIA
Sofiya

Nápoli
Salerno
Tiranë
MACEDONIA
Istanbul

TYRRHENIAN SEA
ALBANIA
Thessaloniki
Ankara

Palermo
Kerkyra
GREECE
TURKEY
Kızılırmak

Sicilia
Messina
IONIAN SEA
Ionian Islands
AEGEAN SEA
Izmir

Catania
Patra
Athina
(Athens)
Konya
Adana

Gozo
Valletta
MALTA
Antalya

Ródhos
Nicosia
SYRIA

Kríti
CYPRUS
Lemesos
LEBANON
Beirut

MEDITERRANEAN SEA
Dimashq
(Damascus)
Amman

Tel Aviv-Yafo
Yerushalayim
(Jerusalem)
JORDAN

Eastern Mediterranean
LIBYA
El Iskandarîya
(Alexandria)
Bur Sa'id
(Port Said)
ISRAEL
Dead Sea

EGYPT
El Qâhira
(Cairo)

0   400 km
0   400 miles

The Baltic and Northern Europe

0   200 km

0   200 miles

N

NORWEGIAN SEA

BARENTS SEA

Nordkapp

Vardø

Murmansk

Tromsø

Inarijärvi

Monchegorsk

Lofoten

Vesterålen

Narvik

Vestfjorden

Lokan tekojärvi

Bodø

Kovdozero

Arctic Circle

Mo i Rana

Luleälven

Kemi   FINLAND   RUSSIA

Perämeri   Oulu

Bottenviken

Oulujärvi

Kokkola   Kajaani

Pielinen

SWEDEN   Umeå

Trondheim   *Storsjön*   Vaasa   Kuopio   Joensuu

Ljungan   Jyväskylä   Mikkeli

Sundsvall

NORWAY   *Lågen*   Tampere   Kouvola

Pori   Hämeenlinna   Kotka   Vyborg

Bergen   Gävle   Turku   Helsinki   Sankt-Peterburg

Oslo   *Dalälven*   Åland   (St Petersburg)

Uppsala

Stavanger   Västerås   Gulf of Finland   Tallinn

Örebro   *Vänern*   Hiiumaa   ESTONIA   RUSSIA

Kristiansand   *Skagerrak*   Norrköping   Saaremaa   Tartu   Pskovskoye oz.

NORTH SEA   Göteborg   Linköping

Vättern   *Gulf of Bothnia*

Ålborg   Borås   Jönköping   Gotland   Gulf of Riga   Riga   LATVIA

Kattegat   Öland   Liepāja   *Daugava*   Daugavpils

DENMARK   Århus   Helsingborg

København   Klaipeda   LITHUANIA

(Copenhagen)

Esbjerg   Odense   Malmö   BALTIC SEA   Kaunas   BELARUS

Bornholm   Kaliningrad   *Neman*

Bremen,   Kiel   Gdynia   Vilnius   Minsk

Bremerhaven,   RUSSIA

Hamburg   GERMANY   Rostock   POLAND

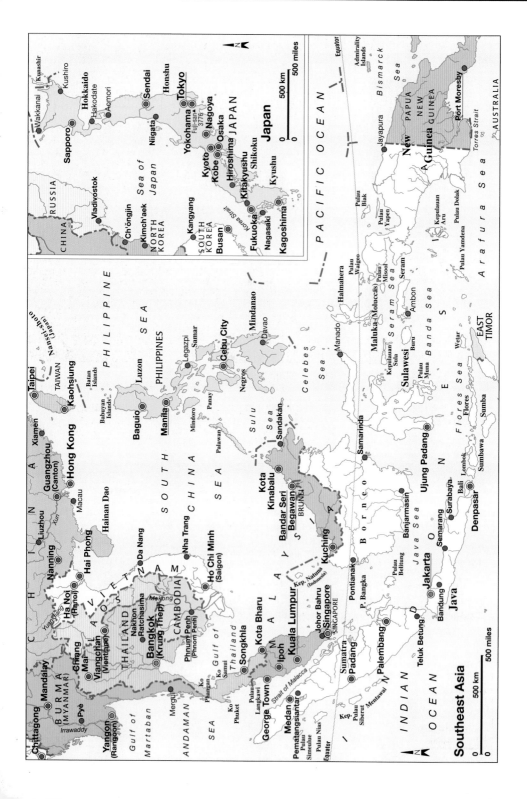

While the *Crystal Symphony* contains a cinema, Sydney provides an opera house.

Australasia

0   500 km

0   500 miles

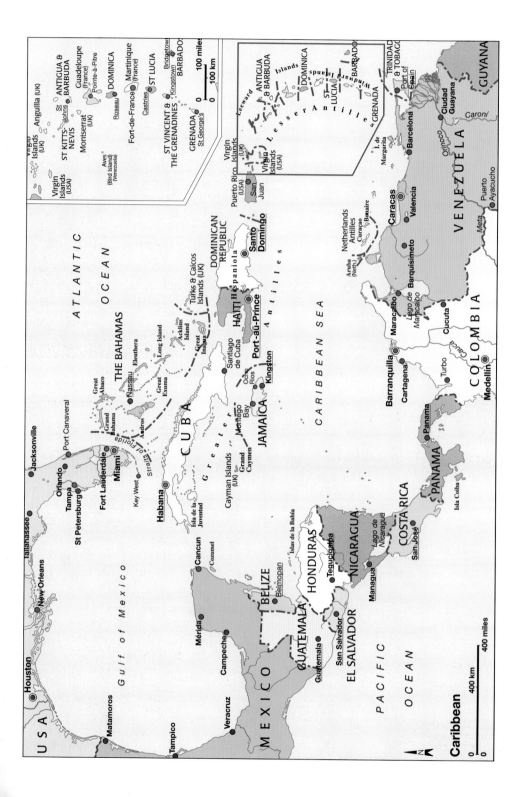

Caribbean

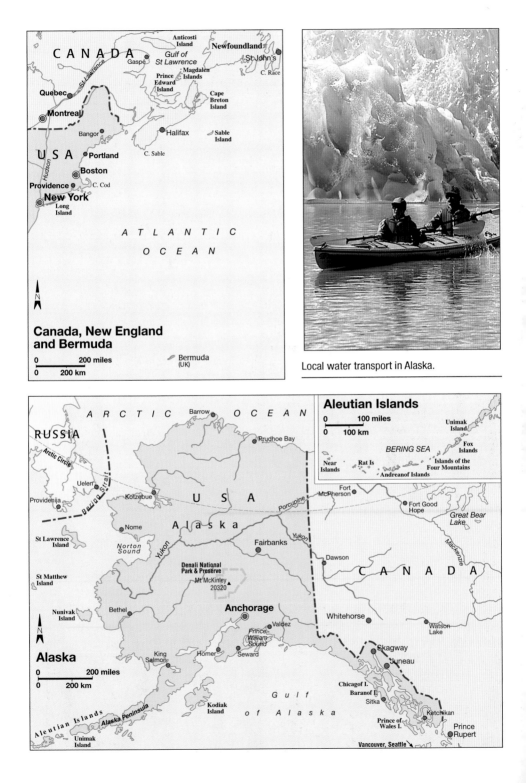

Canada, New England and Bermuda

CANADA

Anticosti Island
Newfoundland
St John's
Gaspé
Gulf of St Lawrence
C. Race
Prince Edward Island
Magdalen Islands
Quebec
Cape Breton Island
Montreal
St Lawrence

USA

Bangor
Halifax
Sable Island
Portland
C. Sable
Hudson
Boston
Providence
C. Cod
New York
Long Island

ATLANTIC OCEAN

N

0   200 miles
0   200 km

Bermuda (UK)

Local water transport in Alaska.

Alaska

ARCTIC   Barrow   *OCEAN*

RUSSIA

Arctic Circle

Prudhoe Bay

Uelen

Bering Strait

Providenija

Kotzebue

U S A

Porcupine

Fort McPherson

Fort Good Hope

Great Bear Lake

St Lawrence Island

Nome

Alaska

Yukon

Fairbanks

Yukon

Dawson

Mackenzie

St Matthew Island

Norton Sound

Denali National Park & Preserve
Mt McKinley
20320

C A N A D A

Nunivak Island

Bethel

Anchorage

Whitehorse

Watson Lake

N

Prince William Sound

Valdez

King Salmon

Homer

Seward

Skagway

Juneau

Alaska

0   200 miles
0   200 km

Aleutian Islands   Alaska Peninsula

Chicagof I.
Baranof I.
Sitka

Kodiak Island

Gulf of Alaska

Prince of Wales I.

Ketchikan

Prince Rupert

Unimak Island

Vancouver, Seattle

Aleutian Islands

0   100 miles
0   100 km

Unimak Island

BERING SEA

Fox Islands

Near Islands

Rat Is

Islands of the Four Mountains

Andreanof Islands

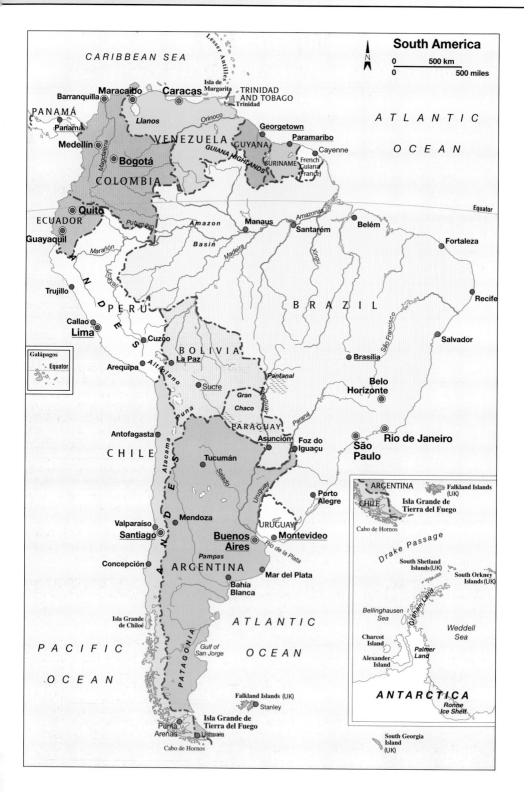

WHERE TO?

Cruise lines currently visit just under 2,000 destinations, so there's

almost certainly a ship to take you where you want to go

Because itineraries vary widely, depending on each ship and cruise, it is wise to make as many comparisons as you can by reading the cruise brochures for descriptions of the ports of call. Several ships may offer the same or similar itineraries simply because these have been tried and tested. Narrow the choice further by noting the time spent at each port, and whether the ship actually docks in port or lies at anchor. Then, compare the size of each vessel and its facilities.

Caribbean Cruises

There are over 7,000 islands in the Caribbean Sea, although many are small or uninhabited. Caribbean cruises are usually destination-intensive cruises in a warm, sunny climate that cram between four and eight ports into one week, depending on whether you sail from a Florida port or from a port already in the Caribbean, such as Barbados or San Juan. This means you could be visiting at least one port a day, with little time at sea for relaxation (the *original* "port-a-cabin"). This kind of island-hopping leaves little time to explore a destination. Although you see a lot of places in a week, by the end of the cruise you may need another week to unwind. *Note*: June to November is hurricane season in the Caribbean (including the Bahamas and Florida).

● **Eastern Caribbean** cruises include ports such as Barbados, Dominica, Martinique, Puerto Rico, St. Croix, St. Kitts, St. Martin, and St. Thomas.
● **Western Caribbean** cruises typically include ports such as Calica, Cozumel, Grand Cayman, and Playa del Carmen.
● **Southern Caribbean** cruises typically include ports such as Antigua, Aruba, Barbados, La Guaira (Venezuela), and Grenada.

Private Islands

Several cruise lines with Bahamas/Caribbean itineraries feature a "private island" (also called an "out-island"). This is a small island close to Nassau in the Bahamas outfitted with all the ingredients to make an all-day beach party a "nice day out." Also available are water sports, scuba, snorkeling, crystal-clear waters, warm sands, even a hammock or two, and, possibly, massage in a beach cabana. There are no reservations to make, no tickets to buy, and no hassles with taxis. But be aware that you may be sharing your private island with more than 2,000 others.

Norwegian Cruise Line was the first to feature a private island, in 1977. Today, Disney Cruise Line, whose first ship debuted in 1998, has the most extensive facilities of all on its private island (which is owned, not leased, like all others).

Some islands change names depending on the day of the week, and what ship is in. Beaches idyllic for 200 people can be noisy and crowded with 2,000 or more passengers from a large ship anchored for a "beach barbecue." Cruise lines have their own names for these islands *(see table below)*.

One bonus is that a "private island" will not be cluttered with hawkers and hustlers, as are so many Caribbean beaches. And, because they *are* private, there is security, and no fear of passengers being mugged, as occurs in some islands.

Private island beach days are not all-inclusive, however, and attract high prices for snorkel gear (and mandatory swim vest), pleasure craft, and

Private Islands			
Cruise Line	**Name of Island**	**Location**	**First Used**
Celebrity Cruises	Catalina Island	Dominican Republic	1995
Costa Cruises	Serena Cay	Dominican Republic	1996
Disney Cruise Line	Castaway Cay	Bahamas	1998
Holland America Line	Half Moon Cay	Bahamas	1997
Norwegian Cruise Line	Great Stirrup Cay	Bahamas	1977
Princess Cruises	Princess Bay	Mayreau, Genadines	1986
Princess Cruises	Princess Cays	Eleuthera, Bahamas	1992
Royal Caribbean International	Coco Cay	Bahamas	1990
Royal Caribbean International	Labadee	Haiti	1986

"banana" boat fun rides; it has become yet another way for cruise lines to increase revenue. However, it costs a lot of money to develop a private island. Examples: Disney Cruise Line spent $25 million developing and outfitting Castaway Cay (formerly known as Gorda Cay), while Holland America Line spent $16 million developing Half Moon Cay.

Europe/Mediterranean Cruises

Traveling within Europe (including the Baltic, Black Sea, Mediterranean, and Norwegian fjord areas) makes economic sense. European and Mediterranean cruises are popular because:
● So many of Europe's major cosmopolitan cities – Amsterdam, Barcelona, Copenhagen, Genoa, Helsinki, Lisbon, London, Monte Carlo, Nice, Oslo, St. Petersburg, Stockholm, and Venice – are on the water. It is far less expensive to take a cruise than to fly and stay in decent hotels (and have to pay for food and transport).
● You will not have to try to speak or understand different languages when you are aboard ship as you would ashore (if you choose the right ship).
● Aboard ship you use a single currency (typically US dollars or euros).
● A wide variety of shore excursions are offered.
● Lecture programs provide you with insights before you step ashore. Small ships are arguably better than large ships, as they can obtain berthing space (large ships may have to anchor in more of the smaller ports, so it can take time to get to and from shore – a frustrating inconvenience). Many Greek islands are accessible only by shore tender. Some companies give you more time ashore than others, so compare itineraries in the brochures.

Alaska Cruises

These are especially popular because:
● They offer the best way to see the state's magnificent shoreline and glaciers.
● Alaska is a vast, relatively unexplored region.
● There is a wide range of shore excursions, including many floatplane and helicopter tours.
● There are many excursions. These include "dome car" rail journeys to Denali National Park to see North America's highest peak, Mt. McKinley.
● Pre- and post-cruise journeys to Banff and Jasper National Parks can be made from Vancouver.
There are two popular cruise routes:
The Inside Passage Route, which usually includes visits to tidewater glaciers, such as those found in Glacier Bay's Hubbard Glacier or Tracy Arm (just two of the 15 active glaciers along the 62-mile/100-km Glacier Bay coastline). Typical ports of call might include Juneau, Ketchikan, Skagway, and Haines.
The Glacier Route, which usually includes the

Gulf of Alaska during a one-way cruise between Vancouver and Anchorage. Typical ports of call might include Seward, Sitka, and Valdez.

Two major cruise lines, Holland America Line and Princess Cruises, have such comprehensive facilities ashore (hotels, tour buses, even trains) that they are committed to Alaska for many years. Holland America Line-Westours and Princess Tours (a division of Princess Cruises) have, between them, invested more than $300 million in Alaska; Holland America Line-Westours is the state's largest private employer. Other lines depend on what's left of the local transportation for their land tours. In 2001, for example, Holland America Line took 115,000 passengers to Alaska, while Princess Cruises took 180,000.

In ports where docking space is limited, some ships anchor rather than dock. Many cruise brochures unfortunately do not indicate which ports are known to be anchor (tender) ports.

With more than 660,000 cruise passengers visited Alaska in 2001 and several large ships likely to be in port on any given day, there's so much congestion in many of the small Alaska ports that avoiding crowded streets is an unpleasant part of the cruise experience. Even nature is retreating; with more humans around, wildlife is becoming harder to spot. And some of the same shops can now be found in Alaska as well as in the Caribbean.

The more adventurous might consider one of the more unusual Alaska cruises to the far north, around the Pribilof Islands (superb for bird watching) and into the Bering Sea.

Transcanal Cruises

These take you through the Panama Canal, constructed by the United States after the failure of a French effort started by Ferdinand de Lesseps (although first conceived by Charles I of Spain). The French labored for 20 years, beginning in 1882 with a labor force of over 10,000, but disease and financial problems defeated them (over

---

DID YOU KNOW?

● that Alaska has two time zones? Most of Alaska is one hour behind Pacific Standard Time, whereas the Aleutian Islands are two hours behind Pacific Standard Time.
● that the Pacific Ocean has a tide of 22 feet (6.7 meters) and the Atlantic Ocean has a tide of only 8 inches (20.3 centimeters)?
● that the Wallace Line is not a new cruise company, but the scientific demarcation separating Asia and Oceania?
● that the average time for a ship to pass through the Panama Canal is eight hours? The fastest transit time was set by the USS Manley at 4 hours and 38 minutes.

The *Regal Princess* in Gaillard Cut, the Panama Canal.

22,000 people died of disease and pestilence). The US took over the building effort in 1904 and the waterway opened on August 15, 1914, shaving over 7,900 nautical miles off the distance between New York and San Francisco. The cost was an astonishing $387 million (in 1914 terms). The Panama Canal runs from *northwest* to *southeast* (not west to east), covering 51 miles (82 km) of locks and gates and dams, and the best way to experience this engineering wonder is from the deck of a cruise ship. Control of the canal passed from the US to Panama in 2000. A proposed $4 billion widening of the canal and new locks, to be built by 2010, will enable those "post-Panamax" ships (such as *Adventure of the Seas, Carnival Destiny, Carnival Triumph, Carnival Victory, Diamond Princess, Explorer of the Seas, Golden Princess, Grand Princess, Star Princess,* and *Voyager of the Seas*) to use it.

Between the Caribbean and the Pacific, a ship is lifted 85 ft (26 meters) in a continuous flight of three steps at Gatun Locks to Gatun Lake through which it will travel to Gaillard Cut where the Canal slices through the Continental Divide. It will be lowered at Pedro Miguel Locks 31 ft (9.4 meters) in one step to Miraflores Lake, then the remaining two steps to sea level at Miraflores Locks before passing into the Pacific. Ships move through the locks under their own power, guided by towing locomotives. The 50-mile (80-km) trip across the Isthmus of Panama takes 8–9 hours.

Panama Canal cruises typically depart from Fort Lauderdale or San Juan, calling at one or two Caribbean islands before entering the canal and ending in Acapulco, Los Angeles, or San Francisco.

Australasia and Orient Cruises

If you like the idea of cruising in Australasia, Southeast Asia, or the Orient and you live in Europe or North America, be aware that the flying time to get to your port of embarkation and ship will be long. It's advisable to arrive at least two days before the cruise, as time changes and jet lag can be severe. The area has so much to offer that it's worth taking a cruise of at least 14 days.

Choose an itinerary, then read about the proposed destinations. Your cruise or travel agent will provide essential background, as will the wide range of Berlitz Pocket Guides. Australia, New Zealand, the islands of the South Pacific, Hong Kong, China, Japan, Indonesia, Malaysia, Singapore, and Thailand are superb destinations.

Where To?

Today's cruise ships roam all over the world. For simplicity, some areas are grouped together on the following pages, together with the companies and, in most cases, the cruise lines that serve them.

Cruise lines with several ships tend to switch ships to operate certain itineraries from year to year, so we have not provided the names of ships. When it was compiled, the list was as accurate as possible, given the fact that many companies had not released their latest full itineraries. ❑

The cruise lines: Who goes where

KEY
✔ = Frequent and infrequent calls
● = Year-round calls
See notes on page 28

	Alaska	Antarctica	Amazon	Arabian Gulf (Red Sea)	Around Britain	Around Africa	Around South America	Around the World	Atlantic Isles (Canaries/Madeira)	Australia/New Zealand/S. Pacific	Bahamas	Bermuda (summer season contract)	Canada/New England
Abercrombie & Kent	✔	✔								✔			
Aida Cruises													
Airtours Sun Cruises/My Travel			✔							✔			
American Canadian Caribbean Line													✔
American Cruise Lines													
Canodros													
Carnival Cruise Lines	✔										●		✔
Celebrity Cruises	✔						✔				●	✔	
Classic International Cruises													
Classical Cruises													
Clipper Cruise Line	✔	✔	✔		✔			✔					✔
Club Med Cruises										✔			
Costa Cruises										✔			
Cruise West	✔												
Crystal Cruises	✔		✔			✔	✔	✔	✔	✔			✔
Cunard Line			✔		✔		✔	✔	✔	✔			✔
Delphin Seereisen			✔					✔	✔				✔
Disney Cruise Line											●		
Festival Cruises/First European Cruises									✔				
Fred Olsen Cruise Lines			✔		✔				✔				✔
Galapagos Cruises													
Glacier Bay Cruises	✔												
Golden Star Cruises													
Hapag-Lloyd Cruises	✔	✔	✔	✔	✔	✔	✔	✔		✔			✔
Hebridean Island Cruises					✔								
Holland America Line	✔						✔	✔	✔	✔	●		✔
Imperial Majesty Cruise Line											●		
Island Cruises													
Islas Galapagos y Turismos													

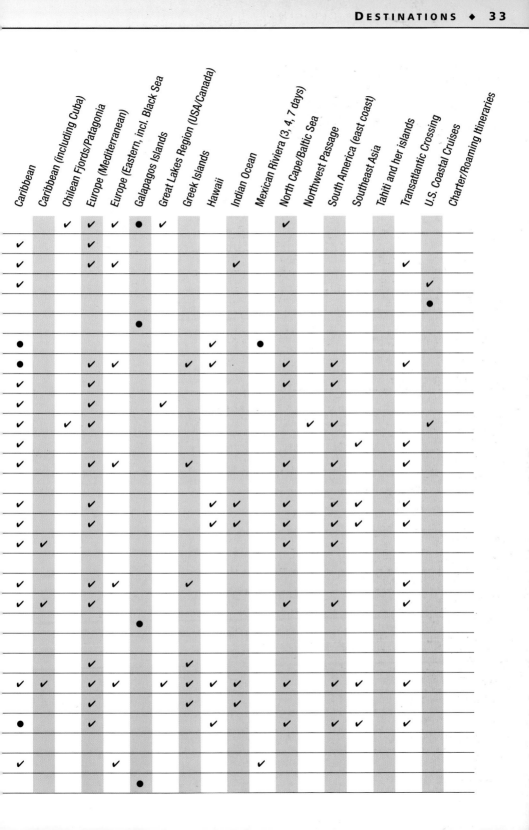

Caribbean	Caribbean (including Cuba)	Chilean Fjords/Patagonia	Europe (Mediterranean)	Europe (Eastern, incl. Black Sea)	Galapagos Islands	Great Lakes Region (USA/Canada)	Greek Islands	Hawaii	Indian Ocean	Mexican Riviera (3, 4, 7 days)	North Cape/Baltic Sea	Northwest Passage	South America (east coast)	Southeast Asia	Tahiti and her islands	Transatlantic Crossing	U.S. Coastal Cruises	Charter/Roaming Itineraries
		✔	✔	✔	●	✔					✔							
✔			✔															
✔			✔	✔					✔							✔		
✔																		✔
																		●
					●													
●								✔		●								
●			✔	✔			✔	✔			✔		✔			✔		
✔			✔								✔		✔					
✔			✔			✔												
✔		✔	✔									✔	✔					✔
✔															✔		✔	
✔			✔	✔			✔				✔		✔			✔		
✔			✔					✔	✔		✔		✔	✔		✔		
✔			✔					✔	✔		✔		✔	✔		✔		
✔	✔										✔		✔					
✔			✔	✔			✔									✔		
✔	✔		✔								✔		✔			✔		
					●													
			✔				✔											
✔	✔		✔	✔		✔	✔	✔	✔		✔		✔	✔		✔		
			✔				✔		✔									
●			✔								✔		✔	✔		✔		
✔				✔						✔								
					●													

	Alaska	Antarctica	Amazon	Arabian Gulf (Red Sea)	Around Britain	Around Africa	Around South America	Around the World	Atlantic Isles (Canaries/Madeira)	Australia/New Zealand/S. Pacific	Bahamas	Bermuda (summer season contract)	Canada/New England
Klien Tours													
Kristina Cruises													
Lindblad Expeditions	✓												
Louis Cruise Lines													
Majestic International Cruises													
Mano Maritime													
Mediterranean Shipping Cruises						✓							
Metropolitan Touring													
Mitsui OSK Passenger Line								✓					
New Paradise Cruises													
Noble Caledonia		✓		✓	✓								
Norwegian Cruise Line	✓										●	✓	✓
Nouvelle Frontieres													
NYK Cruise Line								✓		✓			
Orient Lines		✓						✓		✓			
P&O Cruises			✓						✓	✓			✓
P&O Cruises (Australia)										●			
Phoenix Seereisen	✓		✓	✓		✓	✓	✓	✓	✓			✓
Plantours & Partner			✓		✓	✓		✓	✓				
Ponant Cruises			✓										
Princess Cruises	✓	✓			✓			✓	✓	✓	●	✓	✓
Pullmantur Cruises													
Quark Expeditions		✓											
Radisson Seven Seas Cruises		✓	✓	✓			✓		✓	●			✓
Regal Cruises							✓						✓
Royal Caribbean International	✓				✓				✓		●	✓	✓
Royal Olympic Cruises			✓	✓			✓						
Saga Cruises								✓					
St. Helena Shipping					✓								

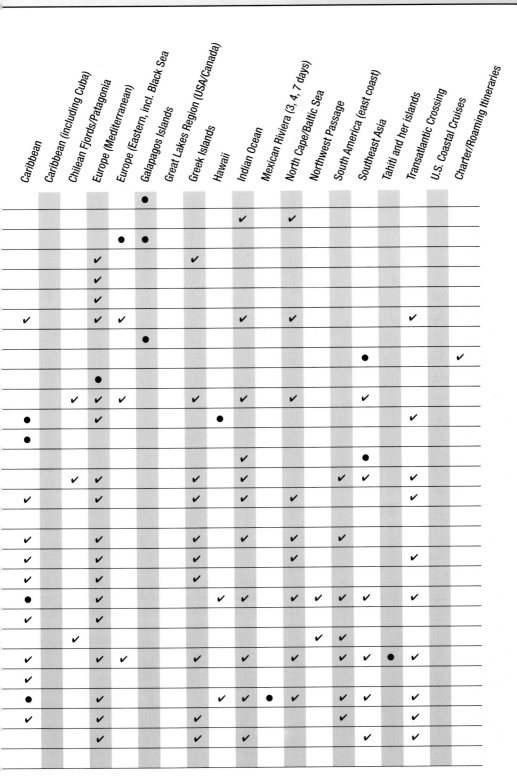

Caribbean	Caribbean (including Cuba)	Chilean Fjords/Patagonia	Europe (Mediterranean)	Europe (Eastern, incl. Black Sea)	Galapagos Islands	Great Lakes Region (USA/Canada)	Greek Islands	Hawaii	Indian Ocean	Mexican Riviera (3, 4, 7 days)	North Cape/Baltic Sea	Northwest Passage	South America (east coast)	Southeast Asia	Tahiti and her islands	Transatlantic Crossing	U.S. Coastal Cruises	Charter/Roaming Itineraries
					●													
									✓		✓							
				●	●													
			✓				✓											
			✓															
			✓															
✓			✓	✓					✓		✓					✓		
					●													
														●				✓
			●															
	✓		✓	✓			✓		✓		✓			✓				
●			✓					●							✓			
●																		
									✓					●				
	✓		✓				✓		✓			✓	✓			✓		
✓			✓				✓		✓		✓					✓		
✓			✓				✓		✓		✓		✓					
✓			✓				✓				✓					✓		
✓			✓				✓											
●			✓					✓	✓		✓	✓	✓	✓		✓		
✓			✓															
	✓											✓	✓					
✓		✓	✓				✓		✓		✓		✓	✓	●	✓		
✓																		
●			✓					✓	✓	●	✓		✓	✓		✓		
✓			✓				✓						✓			✓		
			✓				✓		✓						✓	✓		

	Alaska	Antarctica	Amazon	Arabian Gulf (Red Sea)	Around Britain	Around Africa	Around South America	Around the World	Atlantic Isles (Canaries/Madeira)	Australia/New Zealand/S. Pacific	Bahamas	Bermuda (summer season contract)	Canada/New England
Sea Cloud Cruises													
Seabourn Cruise Line	✔		✔		✔		✔	✔	✔				✔
SeaDream Yacht Club													
Seetours			✔				✔	✔	✔				✔
Silversea Cruises			✔				✔	✔	✔	✔			✔
Society Expeditions	✔	✔			✔			✔					
Spanish Cruise Line													
Star Clippers										✔			
Star Cruises				✔						✔			
Star Line Cruises													
Swan Hellenic Cruises					✔	✔							
Thomson Cruises					✔				✔				
Transocean Tours	✔		✔		✔		✔	✔	✔	✔			✔
Venus Cruise (Japan Cruise Line)	✔									✔			
Windjammer Barefoot Cruises													
Windstar Cruises										✔			
World Explorer Cruises	✔												

Notes

Bahamas: Only those ships that feature year-round cruises to the Bahamas are included.

Bermuda (summer): Only the five cruise lines (featuring five ships) that have long-term Bermuda government contracts for weekly summer season cruises to Bermuda are listed here, although several other companies operate cruises that include Bermuda infrequently throughout the year.

New England/Canada: These cruises are typically seven-day northbound voyages between New York and Montreal or southbound voyages from Montreal to New York. Of course, these can be combined to make a 14-day round-trip voyage.

Caribbean: Note that there are several more companies than those listed here whose ships visit the Caribbean infrequently, but their schedules are seldom known far enough in advance to be included.

Alaska: These cruises are operated between May and September only.

Mexican Riviera Year-Round (three/four/seven days): Ships based on the US West Coast.

Hawaii: One ship, Norwegian Cruise Line's Norwegian Star, sails year-round in Hawaii. A number of other cruise lines have ships that call at Hawaii, and some now cruise from there on a regular basis, although the archaic US Cabotage laws still linger. The Passenger Services Act (known commonly as the Jones Act) states

Caribbean	Caribbean (including Cuba)	Chilean Fjords/Patagonia	Europe (Mediterranean)	Europe (Eastern, incl. Black Sea)	Galapagos Islands	Great Lakes Region (USA/Canada)	Greek Islands	Hawaii	Indian Ocean	Mexican Riviera (3, 4, 7 days)	North Cape/Baltic Sea	Northwest Passage	South America (east coast)	Southeast Asia	Tahiti and her islands	Transatlantic Crossing	U.S. Coastal Cruises	Charter/Roaming Itineraries
✔			✔												✔			
✔			✔				✔	✔	✔		✔		✔	✔	✔			
✔			✔															
✔			✔								✔		✔	✔		✔		✔
✔		✔	✔				✔		✔		✔		✔	✔		✔		
	✔																	
✔			✔															
✔			✔											✔		✔		
														●				
			✔						✔									
							✔		✔		✔		✔					
✔			✔						✔							✔		
✔	✔		✔				✔		✔		✔		✔	✔		✔		
														●				
●																		
✔			✔											✔		✔		

that only US flag ships (there are no major oceangoing US-flagged ships at present) can embark and disembark passengers in US ports without first going to a foreign port (a US flag ship is one that is registered in the United States). Norwegian Cruise Line's Norwegian Star also goes to a foreign island – Fanning Island.

Antarctica: The Antarctic Peninsula is definitely not a destination for cruise ships carrying more than 200 passengers (evacuation in the event of an emergency would prove virtually impossible). To operate in this region, where ice can easily crush a ship within the hour when weather deteriorate (as it often does), a ship must have an "ice-strengthened" or "ice-hardened" hull capable of breaking through pack-ice in the for-mative stage. All shore excursions are included; rubber-inflatable Zodiac landing craft are used for venturing ashore (there are no docks on the Antarctic continent or islands in the Antarctic Peninsula), and landings can be very wet. The austral summer (December through February) is the only time ships can travel to the Antarctic Peninsula, where many nations have their research stations, because the ice is so dense during the winter months that the continent (which, at its smallest, is the size of North America) swells to twice its summer size.

Roaming Ships: Cruise lines with "roaming" ships constantly roam around the world, mostly on non-repeating itineraries of varying cruise lengths.

LIFE ABOARD

This A to Z survey covers the astonishing range of facilities that modern

cruise ships offer and tells you how to make the most of them

Air-Conditioning

Cabin temperature can be regulated by an individually controlled thermostat, so you can adjust it to suit yourself. Public room temperatures are controlled automatically. Air temperatures are often kept cooler than you may be used to.

Art Auctions

Aboard many large and mid-size ships, art auctions form part of the entertainment. They are fun participation events, but don't expect to purchase an heirloom, as most of the art pieces are pure drivel. It's funny how so many identical pieces can be found aboard so many ships! Also, the charges for getting art pieces framed and sent home can be daunting (in other words, a rip-off).

Baby-Sitting

In some ships, stewards, stewardesses, and other staff may be available as babysitters for an hourly charge. Make arrangements at the reception desk/purser's office. Note that aboard some ships, evening baby-sitting services may not start until late in the evening (it is wise to check times and availability *before* you book your cruise).

Beauty Salon/Barber Shop

Make appointments as soon after boarding as possible (particularly on short cruises). Appointment times fill up rapidly, especially before social events such as a captain's cocktail party. Charges are comparable to those ashore. Typical services: haircut for men and women, styling, permanent waving, coloring, manicure, pedicure, leg waxing.

Bridge Visits

Check the *Daily Program* for navigation bridge visits. In most large ships, bridge visits are not allowed for insurance and security reasons. In others, although personal visits are forbidden, a *Behind the Scenes* video on how the ship is run may be shown on the cabin television system.

Cashless Cruising

It is now the norm to cruise cash-free, and to settle your account with one payment (by cash or credit card) prior to disembarking on the last

LEFT: Keeping track of time – an elaborate astrological clock in the atrium lobby of the *Amsterdam*.

day. Often this is arranged by making an imprint of a credit card prior at embarkation, permitting you to sign for everything. Before the end of the cruise, a detailed statement is delivered to your cabin. Some cruise lines may discontinue their "cashless" system for the last day of the cruise, which can be most irritating.

Note that ships visiting a "private island" on a Bahamas/Caribbean itinerary will probably ask you to pay cash for beverages, water sports and scuba diving gear, and other items that you purchase ashore.

Casino Gaming

While most passengers do not choose a cruise in order to gamble, many cruise ships have casinos, where a range of table games is played (typically blackjack or 21, Caribbean stud poker, roulette, craps, and baccarat). Playing chips and cash change are available from the cashier or from banknote acceptance machines. Children under 18 are not allowed in the casino. The casino will be closed in port due to international customs regulations, and taking photographs in the casino is usually forbidden. German- and Japanese-registered ships are not permitted to operate casinos that give cash prizes.

Most cruise lines show videos that give information on how to play the various table games, as well as free lessons to entice players. Remember that casinos provide entertainment rather than a hard-core gambling environment, and there is no charge to enter any shipboard casino (all you need is luck).

Comment Cards

On the last day of the cruise you will be asked to fill out a company "comment card." Some cruise lines offer "incentives" such as a bottle of champagne. Be truthful when completing this form, as it serves as a means of communication between you and the cruise line. Pressure from staff to write "excellent" for everything is rampant aboard cruise ships. But if there *have* been problems with the service or any other aspect of your cruise, do say so.

Communications

Most ships now have a direct-dial satellite telephone system. In addition, all ships are given an

Low stakes on the high seas: many ships have casinos.

internationally recognized call sign, made up of a combination of several letters and digits. When the ship is at sea, you can call from your cabin (or the ship's radio room) to anywhere in the world:
● via radiotelephone (a slight/moderate background noise might be noticed).
● via satellite (which will be as clear as your own home phone).

Direct dial satellite calls (this service started in 1986) are more expensive, but are completed instantly. Some ships also have credit card telephones located in public areas; these also connect instantly, via satellite. Satellite calls can also be made when the ship is in port (radiotelephone calls cannot). Satellite telephone calls cost between US$5 and $15 per minute, depending on the type of communications equipment the ship carries (the latest systems are digital). Calls are charged to your onboard account.

Your relatives and friends can reach you by calling the High Seas Operator in most countries (in the United States, dial 1-800-SEA-CALL). The operator will need the name of the ship, together with the ocean code (Atlantic is 871; Pacific is 872; and the Indian Ocean is 873).

Cruisespeak

The following terminology is used aboard today's cruise ships. The correct nautical terminology is given, while the words that follow are what many cruise lines now use:

Cabin: Penthouse Suite, Junior Suite, Stateroom, or Room
Cabin Service: Room Service
Passenger: Guest
Purser's Office: Guest Relations Desk or Front Office

Customs Regulations

All countries vary in the duty-free allowances granted by their own customs service, but you will be informed aboard your cruise ship of the allowable amounts for your nationality and residency.

Daily Program

The *Daily Program* contains a list of the day's activities, entertainment, and social events. It is normally delivered to your cabin the evening before the day that it covers. Read it carefully, so that you know what, when, and where things are happening.

Death at Sea

What happens if someone dies at sea? Typically, it happens more on long cruises, where passengers are generally older. Bodies are put in a special refrigeration unit for removal at the port of disembarkation, or the body can be flown home from a wayward port of call (more complicated, owing to the paperwork). Note that flying a body home usually involves a large expense. A burial at sea can also be arranged aboard ship (some people have a body cremated at home, return to their favorite cruise ship, and have the ashes scattered at sea).

Departure Tax

If you are disembarking in a foreign port and flying home, be advised that there could be a departure tax to pay (in local currency) at the airport.

Disembarkation

During the final part of your cruise, the cruise director will give an informal talk on customs, immigration, and disembarkation (sometimes called "debarkation") procedures. The night before your ship reaches its final destination, you will be given a customs form to fill out. Any duty-free items bought from the shop on board must be included in your allowance (save the receipts in case a customs officer wishes to see them).

The night before arrival, place your main baggage outside your cabin on retiring (or before 4am). It will be collected and off-loaded on arrival. Leave out fragile items, liquor, and the clothes you intend to wear for disembarkation and onward travel (it is amazing just how many people pack everything, only to find they are in an embarrassing position on disembarkation day). Anything left in your cabin will be considered hand luggage to be hand-carried off when you leave.

On disembarkation day, breakfast will typically be early. It might be better to miss breakfast and sleep later, providing announcements on the ship's public address system do not wake you (it may be possible to turn off such announcements). Even worse than early breakfast, is the fact that you will be commanded (requested, if you are lucky) to leave your cabin early, only to wait in crowded public rooms – sometimes for hours. To add insult to injury, your cabin steward (after he has received his tip, of course) will knock on the door to take the sheets off the bed so the cabin can be made up for the incoming passengers. Cruise aboard the smaller "upscale" ships and this will not happen.

Before leaving the ship, remember to claim any items you have placed in the ship's safety deposit boxes and leave your cabin key in your cabin. Passengers cannot go ashore until all baggage has been off-loaded, and customs and/or immigration inspections or pre-inspections have been carried out. In most ports, this takes two to three hours after arrival. It is wise to leave at least three hours from the time of arrival to catch a connecting flight or other transportation. Once off the ship, you will identify your baggage on the pier before going through customs inspection (delays are usually minimal). Porters may be there to assist you.

Engine Room

In almost all passenger ships, the engine room is off-limits to passengers, and visits are not allowed, for insurance and security reasons. In some ships, a technical information leaflet may be available. Aboard others, a Behind the Scenes video may be shown on the cabin television system. For more specific or detailed information, contact a member of the ship's engineering staff via the purser's office.

Gift Shops

The gift shop/boutique/drugstore will offer a selection of souvenirs, gifts, toiletries, and duty-free items, as well as a basic stock of essential items. You will find duty-free items, such as perfumes, watches, and so on, very competitively priced, and buying onboard ship may save you the hassle of shopping ashore. Opening hours are posted at the store and in the Daily Program.

Health/Fitness/Spa Facilities

The latest ships have elaborate spas where (for an extra fee) whole days of treatments are on offer. Stress reducing and relaxation treatments are practiced combined with the use of seawater, which contains minerals, micronutrients, and vitamins. Massages might include Swedish remedial massage, shiatsu, and aromatherapy treatments. You can even get a massage on your private balcony aboard some ships.

Most ships provide plenty of opportunity for exercise.

Launch (Tender) Services

Enclosed or open motor launches (called "tenders") are employed on those occasions when your cruise ship is unable to berth at a port or island. In such cases, a regular launch service is operated between ship and shore for the duration of the port call. Details of the launch service will be provided in the Daily Program. When stepping on or off a tender, remember to extend "forearm to forearm" to the person assisting you. Do not grip their hands because this simply has the effect of immobilizing the helper.

Launderette

Some ships are fitted with self-service launderettes, equipped with washers, dryers, and ironing facilities. There is sometimes a charge for washing powder and for use of the machines.

Laundry and Dry Cleaning

Most ships offer a full laundry and pressing service. Some ships may also offer dry-cleaning facilities. A detailed list of services (and prices) can be found in your cabin. Your steward will collect and deliver your laundry or dry cleaning.

Library

Most cruise ships have a library offering a good selection of books, reference material, and periodicals. A small deposit (refundable on return of the book) is sometimes required when you borrow a book. Note that aboard the small luxury ships, the library is open 24 hours a day, and no deposit is required. Aboard large ships, you will probably find that the library is open only a couple of hours each morning and afternoon. *Aurora*, *Oriana* and *QE2* are examples of ships with full-time, qualified librarians (aboard most other ships a member of the cruise staff or entertainment staff – with no knowledge of books or authors – staffs the library). The library is typically where you will find board games such as Scrabble, backgammon, and chess.

Lifeboat Drill

There have been few recent incidents requiring the evacuation of passengers although two cruise ships have been totally lost following collisions (*Jupiter*, 1988, and *Royal Pacific*, 1992). Travel by ship, however, remains one of the safest means of transportation. Even so, it cannot be stressed enough that attendance at lifeboat drill is not only required but makes sense, and participation is mandatory. You must, at the very least, know your boat station and how to get to it in the event of an emergency.

If other passengers are lighthearted about the drill, do not let that affect your seriousness of purpose. Be sure to note your exit and escape pathways and learn how to put on your lifejacket correctly. The drill takes no more than 15 minutes of your time and is a good investment in playing safe (the *Royal Pacific* sank in just 16 minutes following a collision).

A Passenger Lifeboat Drill must be conducted on board within 24 hours of leaving the embarka-

The *Oriana*'s library contains a table made by Britain's Lord Linley, son of the late Princess Margaret.

Those who've seen *Titanic* don't mind lifeboat drills.

tion port (within 6 hours would be more desirable). You will hear an announcement from the bridge, which goes something like this: "Ladies and Gentlemen, may I have your attention, please. This is the captain speaking to you from the bridge. In 15 minutes time, the ship's alarm bells will signal emergency lifeboat drill for all passengers. This is a mandatory drill, conducted in accordance with the requirements of the Safety of Life at Sea Convention. There are no exceptions."

Here is an example of an announcement from the navigation bridge: "The emergency signal is a succession of seven or more short blasts followed by one long blast of the ship's whistle, supplemented by the ringing of the electric gongs throughout the ship. On hearing this signal, you should make your way quickly but quietly to your cabin, put on warm clothing and your lifejacket, then follow the signs to your emergency boat station, where you will be kept fully informed over the loudspeakers through which I am speaking to you now."

Lost Property

Contact the reception desk/purser's office immediately if you lose or find something on the ship. Notices regarding lost and found property may be posted on the bulletin boards.

Mail

You can buy stamps and mail letters aboard most ships. Some ships use the postal privileges and stamps of their flag of registration, while others buy local stamps at ports of call. Mail is usually taken ashore by the ship's port agent just before the ship sails. A list of port agents and mailing addresses will be sent with your tickets and documents before you leave for your cruise, so you can advise friends and family how they can send mail to you.

Massage

Make appointments for a massage as soon after embarkation as possible, in order to obtain the time and day of your choice. Larger ships have more staff and offer more flexibility in appointment times. The cost averages about $2 a minute. In some ships, a massage service is available in your cabin (or on your private balcony), if it is large enough to accommodate a portable massage table.

Medical Services

Except for ships registered in England or Norway, there are no mandatory international maritime requirements for cruise lines to carry a licensed physician or to have hospital facilities aboard. However, in general, all ships carrying over 50 passengers do have hospital facilities and do carry at least one licensed doctor aboard ship (ships registered in England and Norway have both, without exception). Usually, there is a reasonably equipped hospital in miniature, although the standard of medical practice and of the physicians themselves may vary from line to line. Most shipboard doctors are generalists; there are no cardiologists or neurosurgeons. Doctors are often employed as outside contractors and therefore will

There are plenty of organized diversions.

charge for use of their services, including sea-sickness shots (except for Russian and Ukrainian registered vessels, where medical services are free). UK passengers should note that ships fall outside the UK National Health Service scheme.

Regrettably, many cruise lines place a low priority on providing medical services (there are, however, some exceptions). Most shipboard physicians are not certified in trauma treatment or medical evacuation procedures, for example. Most ships that cater to North American passengers tend to carry doctors licensed in the United States, Canada, or Britain, but aboard many other ships, doctors come from a variety of countries and disciplines. Some medical organizations, such as the American College of Emergency Physicians, have created a special division for cruise medicine.

Cunard Line's *QE2*, which carries a total of 2,921 passengers and crew, has a fully equipped hospital with one surgeon, one doctor, a staff of six nurses, and two medical orderlies; contrast this with Carnival's *Sensation*, which carries up to 3,514 passengers and crew, with just one doctor and two nurses.

There is wide variation between standards and equipment. Obviously, any ship that features long-distance cruises, with several days at sea, should have better medical facilities and a better qualified staff than one that is engaged in a standard seven-day Caribbean cruise, with a port of call to make almost every day.

There is, at present, no agreed industry-wide standard relating to the standard of medical certification that is required by cruise ships. Most ship doctors are necessarily of the general practice type, but often, short-term contracts can mean poor continuity and differing standards.

Ideally, a ship's medical staff should be certified in Advanced Cardiac Life Support. The minimal standard medical equipment should include an examination room, isolation ward/bed, X-ray machine (to verify the existence of broken or fractured bones), cardiac monitor (EKG) and defibrillator, oxygen-saturation monitor (to determine a patient's blood-oxygen level), external pacemaker, oxygen, suction and ventilators, hematology analyzer, culture incubator, and a mobile trolley intensive care unit.

Note that any *existing* health problems that require treatment on board must be reported at the time of booking.

Movies

In most cruise ships a dedicated movie theater is an essential part of the ship's public-room facilities. The movies are recent, often selected by the cruise line from a special licensed film- or video-leasing service. Many of the latest ships have replaced or supplemented the ship's movie theater with television sets and video players in each cabin.

News and Sports Bulletins

The world's news and sports results are reported in the ship's newspaper or placed on the bulletin board that is normally located near the purser's office or in the library. For sports results not listed, ask at the purser's office; it may be possible for the results to be obtained for you.

Passenger Lists

All ships of yesteryear provided passenger lists with each passenger's name and hometown or region. Today, only a handful of companies carry on the tradition (perhaps some passengers are traveling with someone they should not!).

Photographs

Professional photographers take pictures of passengers throughout the cruise, including their arrival on board. They cover all main events and social functions, such as the captain's cocktail party. The photographs can be viewed without any obligation to purchase (the price is likely to be in excess of $6 for a postcard-sized color photograph).

Postcards and Writing Paper

These are available from the writing room, library, purser's office, or your room steward. Aboard many ships, they are available for a modest sum.

Purser's Office

This is also known as the Reception Office, guest relations, or information desk. Centrally located, this is the nerve center of the ship for general passenger information and problems. Opening hours are posted outside the office and given in the *Daily Program*. In some ships, the purser's office is open 24 hours a day.

Religious Services

Interdenominational services are conducted on board, usually by the captain or staff captain. A few older ships (and Costa Cruises' ships) have a small private chapel. Denominational services may be offered by specially invited or fellow-passenger members of the clergy.

Room Service

Beverages and snacks are available at most times. Liquor is normally limited to the opening hours of the ship's bars. Your room steward will advise you of the services. There's no charge for room service.

Safety First

In an increasingly regulated world, the importance of safety cannot be overplayed. The training of

TOP 30 PET PEEVES – MINE AND OTHER PASSENGERS'

● Passengers who do not possess a credit card (particularly older Asian passengers) are made to feel inferior at the check-in/embarkation desks, particularly in the United States. Some cruise lines have the temerity to ask for a $500 deposit in cash, just for the "privilege" of securing an onboard charge card. No hotel on land does this. Simply refuse, and say that if you cannot trust me, then refund my cruise fare.

● Aboard the large, high-tech ships, getting Cabin Services, or the "Guest Relations Desk," or the Operator to answer the telephone can be an exercise in frustration, patience, and gross irritation.

● Aboard many ships, 15 percent is automatically added to wine bills. Thus, a wine waiter makes much more money on a more expensive bottle of wine, whether he knows anything about that wine (or how to decant and serve it, for example) or not. For doing just the same job for a wine costing $125 as for a wine costing $15 he makes a lot more. Therefore, insist on adding your own gratuity, and politely refuse to be told how much you have to tip.

● Cruise brochures that use models, and provide the anticipation of an onboard product that a ship cannot deliver; the result is disappointment for passengers.

● Cruise brochures that state that their ship has a "small ship feel, big ship choice" when it really caters to more than 1,000 passengers (often more than 2,000).

● Constant, irritating, and repetitive announcements for bingo, horse racing, art auctions, and the latest gizmos for sale in the shops.

● "Elevator" music playing continuously in passageways and on open decks (even worse: rock music).

● Any announcement that is repeated. Any announcement that is repeated.

● Flowers in one's cabin that, are not watered or refreshed by the steward.

● Bathrobes provided but never changed for the duration of the cruise.

● Skimpy towels.

● Mini-bar/refrigerators that do not provide limes and lemons for drink mixes.

● Remote control units that need an instruction manual to understand their operation for turning on the television and getting a video player to work.

● In-cabin announcements at any time, except for emergencies (they are completely unnecessary for programmed events and shore excursions).

● Garnishes, when "parsley with everything" seems to be the rule of the seagoing entree experience.

● Baked Alaska parades.

● Paper, plastic, or polystyrene plastic cups for drinks of any kind.

● Paper napkins for meals or informal buffets (they should be linen or cotton).

● Plastic plates (often too small) for buffets.

● Buffets where only cold plates are available, even for hot food items.

● Repetitious breakfast and luncheon buffets and uncreative displays.

● Artwork placed aboard ships, but with the cruise line not caring or knowing enough about it to place the name of the artist and the year of creation alongside, whether it be a painting or a sculpture.

● Shopping lecturers, shopping videos, art auctions, and carpet auctions.

● Shore-side porters who take your bags when you get off the bus, or out of your car, then stand there until you tip them before they move your bags or drop them (worst ports: Ft. Lauderdale and Miami).

● Cabin stewards/stewardesses who place small folded pieces of paper in cabin door frames to show when their passengers have left their cabins.

● Audiovisual technicians who think that the volume level of the show should equal that for a rock concert for 250,000 people.

● Bands scheduled to play in a lounge that do not start playing until passengers walk in and sit down.

● Private island days, when the tender ride to get to the island is longer than the flight to get to the ship.

● Ships that ask you to settle your shipboard account before the morning of disembarkation.

● Long lines and waiting periods for disembarkation.

crew in relation to safety and security has become extremely important – so much so that new international regulations will soon require all crew to undergo basic safety training *before* they are allowed to join and work aboard any cruise ship. No longer will crew be recruited with the intention of providing on-the-job training.

Safeguards for passengers include lifeboats and life rafts. Since the introduction of the 1983 amendments to Chapter III of the *Safety of Life at Sea* (SOLAS) *Convention 1974* (which came into effect in 1980), much attention has been given to safety. The SOLAS conventions are subscribed to by all member countries of the United Nations, under the auspices of the International Maritime Organization (IMO).

All cruise ships built since July 1, 1986, must have either totally enclosed or partially enclosed lifeboats (only ships built before this date can have open lifeboats). These have diesel engines that will still operate when the lifeboat is inverted.

The 1990 SOLAS standards on stability and fire protection (mandating the enclosing of all stairways and the installation of sprinkler and smoke detection systems and "low-location" lighting) for all new ship construction took effect on October 1, 1997. Existing ships have been given another five years to comply (the retrofitting of sprinkler systems in particular is an expensive measure that may not be considered viable by owners of older ships).

October 1, 1997, was the deadline whereby all cruise ships must:
● Use smoke detectors and smoke alarms in all passenger cabins, corridors, stairway enclosures, and other public spaces.
● Have and use low-level lighting showing routes of escape (such as in corridors and stairways).
● Make all fire doors throughout the ship controllable from the ship's navigation bridge, and their status displayed thereon.
● Make all fire doors that are held open by hinges capable of release from a remote location.
● Use a general emergency alarm that is audible in all cabins.

In 2010, the use of combustible materials in cruise ship construction (allowed under the previous SOLAS 60 regulations) will be forbidden.

The crew attends frequent emergency drills, the lifeboat equipment is regularly tested, and the fire-detecting devices, and alarm and fire-fighting systems are checked throughout the ship. If you spot fire or smoke, use the nearest fire alarm box, alert a member of staff, or contact the bridge.

As from July 1, 2002, all ocean-going cruise ships on international voyages are required to carry voyage data recorders (VDRs – similar to black boxes carries by aircraft).

Sailing Time

In each port of call, the ship's sailing and all-aboard times are posted at the gangway. The all-aboard time is usually half an hour before sailing (ships cannot wait for individual passengers who are delayed).

Seasickness

The French term *mal de mer* may sound quaint, but the malady has been nauseating to seafarers since the Phoenicians. Fortunately, seasickness is rare these days, even in rough weather (less than 3 percent of all passengers become seasick). Ships have stabilizers – large underwater "fins" on each side of the hull – to counteract any rolling motion. Nevertheless, it is possible to develop some symptoms – anything from slight nausea to vomiting.

Seasickness occurs when the brain receives confusing messages from the body's sensory organs, causing an imbalance of receptors in the inner ear. The mind and brain are accustomed to our walking or riding on a nonmoving surface. If the surface itself moves in another direction, a signal is sent to the brain that something's wrong. Continuous mixed signals result in headaches, clammy skin, dizziness, paleness, and yawning, soon followed by nausea and vomiting. There is still no explanation for the great difference in individual susceptibility to seasickness.

Both old-time sailors and modern physicians have their own remedies, and you can take your choice or try them all (but not at the same time):
● When you notice the first movement of a ship, go out on deck and walk back and forth. You will find that your knees, which are our own form of stabilizer, will start getting their feel of balance and counteraction. This is the sign that you are "getting your sea legs."
● Get the fresh sea breeze into your face (arguably the best antidote of all), and if nauseated, suck an orange or a lemon.
● When on deck, focus on a steady point, such as the horizon.
● Eat lightly. Do not make the mistake of thinking a heavy meal will keep your stomach well anchored. It will not.
● Dramamine (dimenhydrinate, an anti-histamine and sedative, which was introduced just after World War II) will be available in tablet (chewable) form on board the ship.
● Scopoderm (also known as Transderm Scop), known as "The Patch" (manufactured by Ciba-Geigy), has an ingredient known as scopolamine, which has proven effective. It was reintroduced in 1997 after being taken off the market for several years. Possible side effects are dry mouth, blurred vision, drowsiness and problems with urinating.
● If you are really distressed, the ship's doctor

Senior officers have become more security-conscious.

can give you an injection to alleviate discomfort. It may make you drowsy, but the last thing on your mind will be staying awake at the movie.

● Try Travel Oil, an aromatherapy oil made by Borealis Healthcare in the UK. It is a natural alternative to drug-based medications. Applied to the temples and across the forehead, there are no side effects.

● Another natural preventive is ginger in powder form. Mix half a teaspoon in a glass of warm water or milk, and drink it before sailing. This is said to settle any stomach for a period of up to eight hours.

● "Sea Bands" (or "Aquastraps") are a drug-free method of controlling motion sickness. These are slim bands (in varying colors) that are wrapped around the wrist, with a circular "button" that presses against the acupressure point Pericardium 6 (*nei kuan*) on the lower arm. Attach them a few minutes before you step aboard and wear on both wrists throughout the cruise.

● Another drug-free remedy can be found in ReliefBand, a watch-like device worn on the wrist. It is said to 'emit gentle electrical signals that interfere with nerves that cause nausea.'

All this being said, bear in mind that in addition to stabilizers in the hull, most cruises are in warm, calm waters and most cruise ships spend much time along the coast or pull into port regularly. The odds are very much against being seasick.

Security

A recognized standard of passenger ship protection exists, following the hijacking of *Achille Lauro* in 1985, and the terrorist attacks and atroc-

ities that occurred in New York and Washington in September 2001. Cruise lines reached this recognized standard as a result of several factors: a moral obligation which, like safety, is inherent in the industry; passenger expectation; and the firmer, more formal pressures being applied across the world by governments and coast guards. You will be required to go through metal detection devices at the gangway, and your baggage will be subject to more stringent inspection.

All cabins can be locked, and it is recommended that you keep your cabin locked at all times when you are not there. Old-style keys are made of metal and operate a mechanical lock; most will be plastic key cards that operate electronically coded locks. Cruise lines do not accept responsibility for any money or valuables left in cabins and suggest that you store them in a safety deposit box at the purser's office, or, if one is supplied, in your in-cabin personal safe.

You will be issued a personal boarding pass when you embark (the latest high-tech passes may include your photo, lifeboat station, restaurant seating, and other pertinent information). This serves as identification and must be shown at the gangway each time you board (you may also be asked for a separate photo ID, such as a driver's license). The system of boarding passes is one of many ways in which cruise lines ensure passenger safety.

Shipboard Etiquette

Cruise lines want you to have a good vacation, but there are some rules to be observed.

● In public rooms, smoking and nonsmoking sections are available. In the dining room, however, cigar and pipe smoking are not permitted at all.
● If you take a video camera with you, be aware that you are not allowed to tape any of the professional entertainment shows and cabarets because of regulations designed to prevent international copyright infringement.

It is all right to be casual when on vacation, but not to enter a ship's dining room in just a bathing suit. Bare feet, likewise, are not permitted. If you are uncomfortable eating with the typical 10-piece dining room cutlery setting, you don't have to fret; some cruise lines have introduced etiquette classes to help you.

Shipboard Injury

Slipping, tripping, and falling are the major sources of shipboard injury. This does not mean that ships are unsafe, but there are some things you can do to minimize the chance of injury. If you *do* suffer from injury aboard ship, feel it is the cruise line's fault, and want to take some kind of legal action against the company, you should be aware of the following:

In the United States, Appendix 46, Section 183(b) of the US Civil Code requires that "the injured passenger notify the cruise line in writing within six months from the date of the injury to file a claim and suit must be filed within one year from the date of injury." So, if you file a claim after the one-year period, the cruise line will probably seek a summary judgment for dismissal.

It is imperative that you first *read your ticket*. The passenger ticket is a *legal contract* between passenger and cruise line. It will invariably state that you must file suit in the state (or country) designated in the ticket. Thus, if a resident of California buys a cruise, and the cruise line is based in Florida, then the lawsuit must be filed in Florida. If you reside in the US and you purchase a cruise in the Mediterranean and the cruise line is based in Italy, then you would have to file suit in Italy. This is known as the Forum Clause. (Part of a typical contract is reproduced on page 573.)

One area in which passengers may not be able to sue a cruise line is in the event of injury or accident when they are on a shore excursion advertised and sold aboard ship. This is because the tour operators are independent contractors. So, when you buy your shore excursion, ask if the ship's insurance fully covers you under the terms of the passenger ticket contract.
In your cabin: Note that aboard many ships, particularly older vessels, there are raised lips separating the bathroom from the sleeping area.

Do not hang anything from the fire sprinkler heads located on most cabin ceilings.

On older ships, it is wise to note how the door lock works. Some require a key on the inside in order to unlock the door. Leave the key in the lock, so that in the event of a real emergency, you do not have to hunt for the key.
On deck: Aboard older ships, watch for raised lips in doorways leading to open deck areas. Be alert and do not trip over them.

Wear sensible shoes with rubber soles (not crepe) when walking on deck or going to pool and lido areas. Do not wear high heels.

Walk with caution when the outer decks are wet after being washed, or if they are wet after rain. This warning applies especially to metal decks. There is nothing more painful than falling onto a solid steel deck.

Do not throw a lighted cigarette or cigar butt, or knock out your pipe, over the ship's side. The sea might seem like a safe place to throw such items, but they can easily be sucked into an opening in the ship's side or onto an aft open deck area, only to cause a fire.

Shore Excursions

In the past, shore excursions were limited to city tours and venues that offered folkloric dances by local troupes, the shore excursions offered today are almost limitless, and include flight-seeing, float-plane rides, cross-country four-wheel drive trips, mountain biking, and even overland safaris. Indeed, be careful or you could end up spending far more on shore excursions than the price of your cruise.

Cruise lines plan and oversee shore excursions assuming that you have not seen a place and aim to show you its highlights in a comfortable manner and at a reasonable price. Buses, rather than taxis or private cars, are often used. This cuts costs and allows the tour operator to narrow the selection of guides to only those most competent, knowledgeable, and fluent in whatever language the majority of passengers speak, while providing some degree of security and control.

Brochure descriptions of shore excursions include artistic license, often written by personnel who haven't visited the port of call. All cruise lines should adopt the following definitions in their descriptive literature and for their lectures and presentations: The term "visit" should mean actually entering the place or building concerned. The term "see" should mean viewing from the outside (as from a bus, for example).

Shore excursions are timed to be most convenient for the greatest number of participants, taking into account the timing of meals on board (these may be altered according to excursion times). Departure times are listed in the descriptive literature and in the *Daily Program*, and may or may not be announced over the ship's public

Shopping ashore at Charlotte Amalie, US Virgin Islands.

address system. There are no refunds if you miss the excursion. If you are hearing impaired, therfore, make arrangements with the shore excursion manager to assist you in departing for your excursions at the correct times.

The ship's representative supervising the shore excursion program is the eyes and ears of the cruise line, and can recommend to the head office that any excursion be suspended if it is not up to standard. Shore excursion staff will be dockside dispatching the excursions in each port.

Most excursions give little in-depth history, and the general knowledge of guides is often limited. City excursions are basically superficial. To get to know a city intimately, go alone or with a small group. Take a taxi or bus, or walk directly to the places that are of most interest to you.

Many ships operate dive-in excursions at a reasonable price that includes all equipment. Instruction is offered on board, and underwater cameras can often be rented, too.

When you buy a shore excursion from the cruise line, you are fully covered by the ship's insurance; arrange it on your own and you are not covered when you step off the ship.

Shore excursion booking forms should be forwarded with your cruise tickets and documents. In some ships, they can be booked via the interactive television system in your cabin.

Book early, particularly those listed as "limited participation." This means that places are restricted, sold on a first-come, first-served basis. Where shore excursions can be booked

before the sailing date, they are often sold out.

For cancellations, most ships require a minimum of 24 hours' notice before the advertised shore excursion departure time. Refunds are at the discretion of the cruise line.

Take along only what is necessary; leave any valuables aboard ship, together with any money and credit cards you do not plan to use. Groups of people are often targets for pickpockets in popular sightseeing destinations and major cities. Also, beware of excursion guides who give you a colored disk to wear for "identification." He may be marking you as a "rich" tourist for local shopkeepers.

Going solo? If you hire a taxi for sightseeing, negotiate the price in advance, and don't pay until you get back to the ship or to your final destination. If you are with friends, hiring a taxi for a full- or half-day sightseeing trip can often work out far cheaper than renting a car, and you also avoid the hazards of driving. Naturally, prices vary according to destination, but if you can select a driver who speaks your language, and the taxi is comfortable, even air-conditioned, you are ahead.

Shopping

Many cruise lines that operate in Alaska, the Bahamas, the Caribbean, and the Mexican Riviera openly engage a company that provides the services of a "shopping lecturer." The shopping lecturer promotes selected shops, goods, and services heavily, fully authorized by the cruise line (which receives a commission from the same). This relieves the cruise director of any responsibilities, together with any questions concerning his involvement, credibility, and financial remuneration.

Shopping maps, with "selected" stores highlighted, are placed in your cabin. Often, they come with a "guarantee" such as: "Shop with confidence at each of the recommended stores. Each merchant listed on this map has been carefully selected on the basis of quality, fair dealing, and value. These merchants have given Cruise Line X a guarantee of satisfaction valid for thirty (30) days after purchase, excluding passenger negligence and buyers' regret, and have paid a promotional fee for inclusion as a guaranteed store."

Know in advance just what you are looking for, especially if your time is limited. But if time is no problem, browsing can be fun.

When shopping time is included in shore excursions, be wary of stores recommended by tour guides; the guides are likely to be receiving commissions from the merchants.

Shop around before you buy. Good shopping hints and recommendations are often given in the port lecture at the start of your cruise.

When shopping for local handicrafts, make sure they have indeed been made locally.

Be wary of "bargain-priced" name brands, as they may well be counterfeit and of dubious quality. For watches, check the guarantee. Some shopping information may be available in information literature about the port and this should be available at the ship's shore excursion office.

Remember that the ship's shops are also duty free and, for the most part, competitive in price. The shops on board are closed while in port, however, due to international customs regulations.

Sports Facilities

The variety of sports facilities on board depends on the size of the ship. Facilities typically include: badminton, basketball practice area, golf driving cage, horseshoes, jogging track, miniature putting green, paddle tennis, quoits, ring toss, shuffleboard, skeet shooting, squash (rarely), table tennis, and volleyball.

Sun

Cruising to the sun? Note that the closer you get to the equator the more potent and penetrating are the rays. They are most harmful when the sun is directly overhead. Use a protective sun lotion (15–30 factor), and reapply it every time you go for a swim or soak in the pool or ocean. Start with just 15 minutes' exposure and gradually work your way up to an hour or so. It is better to go home with a suntan than sunburn.

Surviving a Shipboard Fire

Shipboard fires generate heat, smoke, and often panic. In the unlikely event that you are in one, try to remain calm and think logically and clearly.

When you board the ship and get to your cabin, check the way from there to the nearest emergency exits fore and aft. Count the number of cabin doorways and other distinguishing features to the exits in case you have to escape without the benefit of lighting, or in case the passageway is filled with smoke and you cannot see clearly. New ships will use the "low location" lighting systems more and more, which are either the electroluminescent or photoluminescent type.

Exit signs are located just above floor level, but aboard older vessels the signs may be above your head, which is virtually useless, as smoke and flames always rise. Note the nearest fire alarm location and know how to use it in case of dense smoke and/or no lighting. In future, it is likely that directional sound evacuation beacons will be mandated; these will direct passengers to exits, escape-ways and other safe areas and appear to be better than the present visual aids, which can be all but useless if the compartment you are in is completely surrounded by smoke.

If you are in your cabin and there is fire in the passageway outside, first put on your lifejacket and feel for the cabin door. If the door handle is hot, soak a towel in water and use it to turn the handle of the door. If there is a raging fire in the passageway, cover yourself in wet towels and go through the flames. It may be your only means of escape, unless you have a balcony cabin.

Check the passageway. If there are no flames, or if everything looks clear, walk to the nearest emergency exit or stairway. If there is smoke in the passageway, crawl to the nearest exit. If the exit is blocked, then go to an alternate one.

It may take considerable effort to open a fire door to the exit, as they are heavy. Don't use the elevators, as they may stop at a deck that is on fire or full of smoke.

In the event of fire in your cabin, report it immediately by telephone. Then get out of your cabin if you can and close the door behind you to prevent any smoke or flames from entering the passageway. Finally, sound the alarm and alert your neighbors.

Swimming Pools

Most ships have outdoor or indoor swimming pools, or both. They may be closed in port owing to local health regulations and/or cleaning. Opening hours will be listed in the *Daily Program*. Diving is not allowed, since pools are shallow. Parents should note that most pools are unsuper-

A nursery pool to keep kids cool

vised. Be aware that some ships use excessive chlorine or bleaching agents for cleaning; these could cause bathing suit colors to run.

Television

Television programming is obtained from a mixture of satellite feeds and onboard videos. Some ships can lock-on to live international news programs (such as CNN or BBC World News), or to text-only news services, for which cruise lines pay a subscription fee. Satellite television reception is sometimes poor, however, due to the fact that ships constantly move out of the narrow beam being downloaded from the satellite and they therefore cannot "track" the signal as accurately as a land-based facility.

Tipping (Gratuities)

Many travelers feel that the ship should host its passengers, and that the passengers should not host the crew by means of tips, so the question of tipping is awkward and embarrassing. In some ships, there are subtle suggestions made regarding tips; in others, cruise directors get carried away and are simply dictatorial regarding tipping.

Some ships offer hints on tipping via the in-cabin video system. Some cruise brochures state "tipping is not required." They may not be required, but will definitely be expected by the ship's staff. Here are the accepted cruise industry standard for gratuities:

Dining room waiter: $3–$4 per person per day;
Busboy: $1.50–$2 per day;
Cabin steward/stewardess: $3–$3.50 per person per day;
Butler: $5–$6 per person per day.

Aboard many ships, a gratuity of 10 or 15 percent is automatically added to your bar check, whether you get good service or not.

Tips are normally given on the last evening of a cruise of up to 14 days' duration. For longer cruises, you would extend half of the tip halfway through and the rest on your last evening. *Note*: Aboard some Greek-flagged ships, gratuities are pooled and given to the chief steward, who gives them out at the end of each cruise ($8–$10 per person per day is the norm).

Gratuities are included in the cruise fare aboard a small number of ships (principally those in the luxury end of the market), where no extra tipping is permitted (in theory). Gratuities (at a rate of about $10 per person, per day) are increasingly being added automatically to onboard accounts by most of the major cruise lines.

Origin of the word "tip": Before the introduction of postage stamps in 1840, coachmen who transported passengers were often asked to carry a letter or other package. A small recompense was given for this service, called a "tip" – which stands for "to insure personal service." Hence, when in the future some special

When show business goes to sea: the Las Vegas-like grand atrium of Carnival Cruise Lines' *Fascination*.

service was provided, particularly in the hospitality industry, tips became an accepted way of saying thank-you for services rendered.

Valuables

Many ships now have a small personal safe installed in each cabin. However, items of special value should be kept in a safety deposit box in the purser's office. You will then have simple and convenient access to your valuables during the cruise.

Visitors

Passes to enable friends and relations to see you on board prior to sailing must always be arranged in advance, preferably at the time you make your booking. Clear announcements will be made when it is time for all visitors to go ashore. Unfortunately, bon voyage parties, such as those you may have seen in the movies, are virtually a thing of the past. They are no longer possible (with the exception of ships operating around-the-world cruises) owing to increased security concerns and insurance regulations.

Water Sports

Some small ships have a water sports platform that is lowered from the ship's stern or side. These ships carry windsurfers, waterski boats, jet skis, water skis, and scuba and snorkel equipment, usu-

ally at no extra charge. Some may also feature an enclosed swimming "cage" for areas of the world where unpleasant fish might be lurking.

Although such facilities look good in the cruise brochures, in many cases ships seem reluctant to use them. This is because many itineraries have too few useful anchor ports. Also, the sea must be in an almost flat calm condition, which is seldom the case. Another more prosaic reason is simply because of strict insurance regulations.

Wine and Liquor

The cost of drinks on board is generally lower than on land, since ships have access to duty-free liquor. Drinks may be ordered in the dining room, at any of the ship's bars or from room service. Some lines charge "corkage," a fee to deter passengers from bringing their own wines into the dining room.

In the dining room, you can order wine with your meals from an extensive and reasonably priced wine list. For wine with your dinner, it's worth making an effort to place your order at lunchtime, as wine waiters are always at their busiest at the evening meal.

In some ships, a duty-free sales point allows you to purchase wine and liquor to drink in your cabin. You will not normally be permitted to bring these purchases into the dining room or other public rooms, nor indeed any duty-free wine or liquor purchased in port. These regulations are made to protect bar sales, which are a substantial source of onboard revenue for the cruise line. ❏

WHAT TO DO IF...

Twenty practical tips for a good cruise experience

❶ Your luggage does not arrive at the ship.
If you are part of the cruise line's air/sea package, the airline is wholly responsible for locating your luggage and delivering it to the next port. If you arranged your own air transportation it is wholly *your* problem. Always have easy-to-read name and address tags both *inside* as well as *outside* your luggage. Keep track of claim documents and give the airline a detailed itinerary and list of port agents (usually included with your documents).

❷ *You* miss the ship.
If you miss the ship's departure (due to late or non-performing flight connections, etc), and you are traveling on an air/sea package, the airline will arrange to get you to the ship. If you are traveling "cruise-only," however, and have arranged your own air transportation, then *you* are responsible for onward flights, hotel stays, and transfers. Many cruise lines now have "deviation" desks, where (for a fee) you can adjust airline flights and dates to suit personal preferences. If you arrive at the port just as your ship is pulling away, see the ship's port agent immediately.

❸ Your cabin is too small.
Almost all cruise ship cabins are too small (I am convinced that some are designed for packages rather than people). When you book a cruise, you pay for a certain category and type of cabin but have little or no control over which one you actually get. See the hotel manager as soon as possible and explain what is wrong with the cabin (noisy, too hot, etc). If the ship is full (most are nowadays), it will be difficult to change. However, the hotel manager will probably try to move you from known problem cabins, although they are not required to do so.

❹ Your cabin has no air-conditioning, it is noisy, or there are plumbing problems.
If there is anything wrong in your cabin, or if there is something wrong with the plumbing in your bathroom, bring it to the attention of your cabin steward immediately. If nothing gets better, complain to the hotel manager. Some cabins, for example, are located above the ship's laundry, generator, or galley (hot); others may be above the disco (noisy). If the ship is full, it may be difficult to change.

❺ You have noisy cabin neighbors.
First, politely tell your neighbors that you can hear them brushing their hair as the cabin walls are so thin, and would they please not bang the drawers shut at 2am! If that does not work, complain to the purser or hotel manager, and ask them to attend to the problem.

❻ You have small children and the brochure implied that the ship has special programs for them, but when on board you find out it is not an all-year-round program.
In this instance, either the brochure was misleading, or your travel agent did not know enough about the ship or did not bother to ask the right questions. If you have genuine cause for complaint, then see your travel agent when you get home. Most ships generally will try to accommodate your young ones (large ships – those carrying more than 1,000 passengers – have more facilities), but may not be covered by their insurance for "looking after" them throughout the day, as the brochure seemed to promise. Again, check thoroughly with your travel agent *before* you book.

❼ You do not like your dining room seating.
Most "standard" market ships operate two seatings for dinner (sometimes this applies to all meals). When you book your cruise, you are asked whether you want the first or second seating. The line will make every attempt to please you. But if you want second seating and are given first seating (perhaps a large group has taken over the entire second seating, or the ship is full), there may be little the restaurant manager can do.

❽ You want a table for two and are put at a table for eight.
Again, see the restaurant manager and explain why you are not satisfied. A little gratuity should prove helpful.

❾ You cannot communicate with your dining room waiter.
Dining room waiters are probably of a nationality and tongue completely foreign to yours, and all they can do is smile. This could prove frustrating for a whole cruise, especially if you need something out of the ordinary. See the restaurant manager, and tell him you want a waiter with whom

you can communicate. If he does not solve the problem, see the hotel manager.

❿ The food is definitely not "gourmet" cuisine as advertised in the brochure.
If the food is not as described (for example, whole lobster in the brochure, but only cold lobster salad once during the cruise, or the "fresh squeezed" orange juice on the breakfast menu is anything but), inform the maître d' of the problem.

⓫ A large group has taken over the ship.
Sometimes, large groups have blocked (pre-booked) several public rooms for meetings (seemingly every hour on the hour in the rooms you want to use). This means the individual passenger (that is you) becomes a second-class citizen. Make your displeasure known to the hotel manager immediately, tell your travel agent, and write a follow-up letter to the line when you return home.

⓬ A port of call is deleted from the itinerary.
If you only took the cruise because the ship goes to the place you have wanted to go for years, then read the fine print in the brochure *before* you book. A cruise line is under *no* obligation to perform the stated itinerary. For whatever reason (political unrest, weather, mechanical problems, no berth space, safety, etc.), the ship's captain has the ultimate say.

⓭ You are unwell aboard ship.
Do not worry. There will be a qualified doctor (who generally operates as a concession, and therefore charges) and medical facilities, including a small pharmacy. You will be well taken care of. Although there are charges for medical services rendered, almost all cruise lines offer insurance packages that include medical coverage for most eventualities. It is wise to take out this insurance when you book.

⓮ You have a problem with a crew member.
Go to the hotel manager or chief purser and explain the problem (for single women this could be a persistent cabin steward with a master door key). No one will do anything unless you complain. Cruise ships try to hire decent staff, but, with so many crew, there are bound to be a few bad apples. Insist on a full written report of the incident, which must be entered into the ship's daily log by the staff captain (deputy captain).

⓯ You leave some personal belongings on a tour bus.
If you find you have left something on a tour bus, and you are back on board your ship, the first thing to do is advise the shore excursion manager or the purser's office. The shore excursion manager will contact the tour operator ashore to ascertain whether any items have been handed in to their office.

⓰ The cruise line's air arrangements have you flying from Los Angeles via Timbuktu to get to your cruise ship.
Fine if your cruise ship is in Timbuktu (difficult, as it is inland). Most cruise lines that have low rates also use the cheapest air routing to get you to your ship. That could mean flights from a central hub. Be warned: you get what you pay for. Ask questions *before* you book.

⓱ You fly internationally to take a cruise.
If your cruise is a long distance away from your home, then it usually makes good sense to fly to your cruise embarkation point and stay for at least a day or two before the cruise. Why? Because you will be better rested and you will have time to adjust to any time changes. You will step aboard your ship already relaxed and ready for a real vacation.

⓲ The ship's laundry ruins your clothes.
If any of your clothing is ruined or discolored by the ship's laundry, first tell your cabin steward(ess), and then follow up by going to the purser's office and getting it registered as a proper complaint. Take a copy of the complaint with you, so you can follow up when you get home. Unfortunately, you will probably find a disclaimer on the laundry list saying something to the effect that liability is limited to about $1 per item, which is not a lot. So, although the laundry and dry cleaning facilities generally work well, things can occasionally go wrong just like ashore.

⓳ You have extra charges on your bill.
Check your itemized bill carefully. Then talk to the purser's office and ask them to show you the charge slips. Finally, make sure you are given a copy of your bill, *after* any modifications have been made.

⓴ You're unhappy with your cruise experience.
You (or your travel agent) ultimately choose the ship and cruise. But if your ship does not meet your specific lifestyle and interests, or the ship performs less well than the brochure promises, then let your travel agent and the cruise line know as soon as possible. If your grievance is valid, many cruise lines will offer a credit, good towards a future cruise. But do be sure to read the fine print on the ticket. ❏

CUISINE

Anyone wanting to eat 24 hours a day could do so aboard many ships,
and the variety of food would keep boredom at bay

Dining is the single most talked- and written-about aspect of the cruise experience. There is a thrill of anticipation that comes with dining out in a fine restaurant. The same is true aboard ship, where dining in elegant, friendly, and comfortable surroundings stimulates an appetite sharpened by the bracing sea air.

Attention to presentation, quality, and choice of menu in the honored tradition of the transatlantic luxury liners has made cruise ships justly famous. Cruise lines know that you will spend more time eating on board than doing anything else, so their intention is to cater well to your palate, within the confines of a predetermined budget.

The "intelligent standardization" of the food operation and menus translates, of course, to cost-effectiveness in the process of food budgeting for any cruise line. Being able to rationalize expenditure *and* provide maximum passenger satisfaction is, therefore, almost a science today. Quite simply, *you get what you pay for*. Aboard low-priced cruises, you will get portion-controlled frozen food that has been reheated. To get fresh food (particularly fresh fish and the best cuts of meats), cruise lines must pay significantly more, adding to the cruise price.

Cruise lines put maximum effort into telling passengers how good their food is, often to the point of being unable to deliver what is shown in the brochures. But not all meals aboard all ships are gourmet affairs by any stretch of the imagination. In general, cruise cuisine compares favorably with the kind of "banquet" food served in a standard hotel or family restaurant – in other words, almost tasteless.

Most ships cannot offer a real "gourmet" experience because the galley (ship's kitchen) may be striving to turn out hundreds of meals at the same time. What you *will* find is a good selection of palatable, pleasing, and complete meals served in comfortable surroundings, in the company of good friends – and *you* do not have to do the cooking. Maybe you will even dine by candlelight, a pleasant way to spend any evening.

Food from hell

Experienced passengers who "collect" cruises have seen it, smelled it, and tasted it all before aboard ship: real rubber duck-foul (fowl) food, fit only to be stuffed, painted, and used as children's toys in their bathtubs. Talk about rock-hard lobster, fish with the elasticity of a baseball bat, inedible year-old shrimp, veterinarian-rejected chicken, and grenade-quality meats. Not to mention teary-eyed or hammer-proof cheese, soggy salty crackers, unripe fruits, and coffee that looks (and tastes) like army surplus paint. Or yellow-green leaves that could be either garnish or an excuse for salad. Sadly, it is all there, in the cruise industry's global cafeteria.

Most ships feature self-serve buffets for breakfast and luncheon, one of the effects of discounted fares (and less staff are required). Strangely, passengers do not seem to mind lining up for self-service food (this somehow reminds me of school lunches). But while buffets look fine when they are fresh, after a few minutes of passengers serving themselves, they do not. And, one learns soon enough that the otherwise sweet little old ladies can become ruthlessly competitive at buffet opening time. Passengers should not have to play guessing games when it comes to

Asian stir-fry aboard the *Crystal Symphony*.

food, but many cruise lines forget to put labels on food items; this slows down any buffet line. Labels on salad dressings, sauces, and cheeses would be particularly useful.

Passengers have different preferences and tastes. Some like their food plain, while some like it spicy; some like *nouvelle cuisine*, some like meat and potatoes (and lots of it). Some try new things, some stick with the same old stuff. It is all a matter of personal taste. Cruise lines tend to cater to general tastes. The best ships offer food cooked more or less individually to your liking. Some people are accustomed to drinking coffee out of polystyrene plastic cups and eating food off paper plates at home. Others wouldn't dream of doing that and expect fine dining, with food correctly served on fine china, just as they do at home.

If you are *left-handed*, tell your waiter at your first meal exactly how you want your cutlery placed and to make sure that tea or coffee cup handles are turned in the correct direction (this is impossible with a fish knife, of course). It would be better if right- or left-hand preferences were established when you book, and the cruise lines informed the ship.

Menus are displayed outside the dining room each day so that you can preview each meal. Suite occupants have menus delivered. When looking at the menu, one thing you will never have to do is to consider the price: it is all included.

Healthy Eating

With today's emphasis on low-cholesterol and low-salt diets, most ships have "spa" menus, with calorie-filled sauces replaced by spa cuisine. Some include basic nutritional information, such as the calorie count and fat, protein, and carbohydrate content, on their "spa" menus, or for selected "light" items on regular menus (mostly for dinner, seldom for breakfast or luncheon).

If you are vegetarian, vegan, macrobiotic, counting calories, want a salt-free, sugar-restricted, low-fat, low-cholesterol, or any other diet, advise your travel agent at the time of booking, and get the cruise line to confirm that the ship can actually handle your dietary requirements. Note that cruise ship food does tend to be liberally sprinkled with salt, and that vegetables are often cooked with sauces containing dairy products, salt, and sugar.

The Dining Room

Aboard many ships, the running and staffing of dining rooms is contracted to a specialist maritime catering organization. Ships that cruise in waters away from their home country find that professional catering companies do an excellent job. The quality is generally to a good standard. However, ships that control their own catering staff and food are often those that go to great lengths to ensure that their passengers are satisfied.

The Big 8 Cruise Lines: How They Score on Cuisine and Service

Food	Carnival Cruise Lines	Celebrity Cruises	Costa Cruises	Holland America Lines	Norwegian Cruise Line	Princess Cruises	Royal Caribbean Int.	Star Cruises
Dining Room/Cuisine	6.3	8.6	6.4	7.2	6.2	7.2	7.1	7.0
Buffets/Informal Dining	6.0	8.1	5.7	6.1	5.7	6.5	6.4	6.7
Quality of Ingredients	6.0	8.7	6.2	7.1	6.3	6.9	6.9	8.0
Afternoon Tea/Snacks	4.2	7.1	5.1	5.6	4.8	5.9	5.4	5.6
Wine List	7.8	8.2	5.6	6.0	6.1	6.6	6.1	6.4
Overall Food Score	6.06	8.14	5.8	6.4	5.82	6.62	6.38	6.74
Service								
Dining Rooms	5.8	8.3	6.1	7.0	6.7	7.3	7.2	7.1
Bars	6.8	8.0	6.4	7.1	6.8	7.5	7.3	6.8
Cabins	6.6	8.1	6.8	7.4	6.4	7.5	7.3	7.2
Open Decks	6.0	7.6	5.8	6.6	6.2	6.8	6.4	6.0
Wines	5.7	8.0	5.3	6.1	6.4	6.2	6.1	7.1
Overall Service Score	6.18	8.00	6.08	6.84	6.50	7.06	6.80	6.84
Combined food/service score	6.12	8.07	5.94	6.62	6.16	6.84	6.59	6.79

Self-service buffets are a popular option.

Which Seating?

Open Seating: It's also called Freestyle Dining (Norwegian Cruise Lines), or Personal Choice Dining (Princess Cruises), this simply means that you can sit at *any* available table, with whomever *you* wish, at *whatever time* you choose (within dining room opening hours). So, just turn up, and you'll be seated, just like going out to a restaurant ashore. However, this is a little bit of an anomaly aboard the large cruise ships, as the principal entertainment program is typically set at two shows each night, which, in effect, limits your choice of dining times.

Single Seating: you can choose *when* you wish to eat (within dining room hours) but have an assigned table for the cruise.

Two Seatings: you are assigned (or choose) one of two seatings, early or late. Typical meal times for two-seating ships are:

      Breakfast: 6.30am–8.30am
      Lunch: 12 noon–1.30pm
      Dinner: 6.30pm–8.30pm

Some ships operate two seatings only for dinner, while others operate on a two-seating arrangement for all meals.

Four Seatings: you choose the time (only Carnival Cruise Lines currently operates four seatings). Dinner is at 5.30pm, 6.45pm, 7.30pm or 8.45pm. Hoever, two seatings apply aboard *Carnival Legend, Carnival Pride* and *Carnival Spirit*.

Note: Some ships that operate in Europe (the Mediterranean) or South America will probably have later meal times. Dinner hours may also vary

when the ship is in port to allow for the timing of shore excursions.

Smoking/Nonsmoking

Many ships have totally nonsmoking dining rooms, while some provide smoking (cigarettes only, not cigars or pipes) and nonsmoking sections. Nonsmokers who wish to sit in a no-smoking area should tell the restaurant manager when reserving a table. Note that at open seating breakfasts and luncheons in the dining room (or informal buffet dining area), smokers and nonsmokers may be seated close together.

The Captain's Table

The captain usually occupies a large table in or near the center of the dining room on "formal" nights. The table seats eight or more people picked from the passenger or "commend" list by the hotel manager. If you are invited to the captain's table, it is gracious to accept, and you will have the chance to ask all the questions you like about shipboard life.

Dining Room Staff

The restaurant manager (also known as the Maître d' Hotel – not to be confused with the ship's Hotel Manager) is an experienced host, with shrewd perceptions about compatibility. It is his responsibility to seat you with compatible fellow passengers. If a table reservation has been arranged prior to boarding, you will find a table assignment/seating card in your cabin when you embark. If not, make your reservation with the restaurant manager or one of his assistants immediately after you embark.

Unless you are with your own family or group of friends, you will be seated next to strangers. Tables for two are a rarity; most tables seat four, six, or eight. It is a good idea to ask to be seated at a larger table, because if you are a couple seated at a table for four and you do not get along with your table partners, there is no one else to talk to. And remember, if the ship is full, it may be difficult to change tables once the cruise has started.

If you are unhappy with any aspect of the dining room operation, the sooner you tell someone the better. Don't wait until the cruise is over to send a scathing letter to the cruise line – it's too late then to do anything positive.

The best waiters are those trained in European hotels or hotel/catering schools. They excel in fine service and will learn your likes and dislikes quickly. They normally work aboard the best ships, where dignified professionalism is expected and living conditions are good.

A Typical Day

From morning till night (and beyond), food is offered to the point of overkill, even aboard the most modest cruise ship.

6am: hot coffee and tea on deck for early risers. Full breakfast: typically with as many as 60 different items, in the main dining room. For a more casual meal, you can serve yourself buffet-style at an indoor/outdoor deck café (the choice may be more restricted than in the main dining room, yet adequate).

Lunchtime: with service in the dining room, buffet-style at an informal café, or at a separate grill for hot dogs and hamburgers, and a pizzeria, where everything is cooked right in front of you but usually presented with less style than at a fast food restaurant.

4pm: Afternoon tea, in the British tradition, complete with finger sandwiches and cakes. This may be served in one of the main lounges to the accompaniment of live music (it may even be a "tea-dance") or recorded classical music.

Dinner: the main event of the evening, and apart from the casualness of the first and last nights, it is formal in style.

Midnight Buffet: This is without a doubt the most famous of all shipboard meals. They are grand spreads, often based around a different theme each night, (seafood, Oriental, tropical fruit fantasy, chocoholic, etc.). There may be a Gala Midnight Buffet (usually on the penultimate evening), for which the chefs pull out all the stops.

Plate Service vs. Silver Service

Plate Service: When the food is presented as a complete dish, it is as the chef wants it to look; color combinations, the size of the component parts, and their positioning on the plate. All are important. In most cruise ships, "plate service" is now the norm. It works well and means that most people seated at a table will be served at the same time and can eat together, rather than let their food become cold, as can be the case with silver service.

Silver Service: When the component parts are brought to the table separately, so that the diner, not the chef, can choose what goes on the plate and in what proportion. Silver service is best when there is plenty of time (few cruise ships provide silver service today). What some cruise lines class as silver service is actually silver service of vegetables only, with the main item, be it fish, fowl, or meat, already positioned on the plate.

National Differences

The different nationalities among passengers present their own special needs and requirements. Here are some examples:

Inspirational dining experience aboard the *Inspiration*.

Asian, British, German, and other European passengers like boiled eggs served in real china eggcups for breakfast. North Americans rarely eat boiled eggs, and most often put the eggs into a bowl and eat them with a fork.

German passengers tend to prefer breads (especially dark breads) and a wide variety of cheeses for breakfast and lunch. They tend to like yellow (not white) potatoes. They also have an obvious liking for German draught or bottled beers rather than American canned beers.

The French like soft – not flaky – croissants, and may request brioches and confitures.

Japanese passengers like "bento box" breakfasts of salmon and eel, and vegetable pickles, as well as Japanese rice, which is very different from Chinese rice.

Southern Italians like to have red sauce with just about everything, while northern Italians like less of the red sauces and more white sauces and flavorings, such as garlic, with their pasta.

Australian passengers like to have "vegemite" to spread on bread and toast.

North Americans like weak coffee with everything – often before, during, and after a meal. This is why, even on the most upscale ships, sugar is placed on tables (also for iced tea). North Americans tend to eat and run, whereas Europeans, for example, like to dine in a more leisurely fashion, treating mealtimes as a social occasion.

Most passengers agree that cruise coffee is appalling, but often it is simply the chlorinated water that gives it a different taste. Europeans prefer strong coffee, usually made from the coffee beans of African countries such as Kenya. North Americans usually drink the coffee from Colombia or Jamaica.

European tea drinkers like to drink tea out of teacups, not coffee or sports mugs (very few cruise ships know how to make a decent cup of tea, so British passengers in particular should be aware of this).

Alternative Dining

A number of ships now have "alternative" dining rooms, for which reservations must be made. These typically incur an extra charge ($20–$25), for which you get much better food, presentation and service than in the ship's main dining room(s), which tend to be large and noisy. Note, however, that the costs can quickly add up, just like they can when you dine out ashore. Let's take, as an example, David's Supper Club aboard *Carnival Pride*. The food is excellent (but the portions are large), and the ambiance is quiet and refined, but if you are a couple and you have just two glasses of wine each (Grgich Hills Chardonnay, for example, at $12.50 a glass), and pay the cover charge, that's $100 for dinner (if you want caviar, it's an extra $29 for a 1-ounce serving).

The Executive Chef

The executive chef plans the menus, orders the food, organizes his staff, and arranges all the meals on the menus. He makes sure that menus are not repeated, even on long cruises. On some cruises, he works with guest chefs from restaurants ashore to offer tastes of regional cuisine. He may also purchase fish, seafood, fruit, and various other local produce in "wayside" ports and incorporate them into the menu with a "special of the day" announcement.

The Galley

The galley ("kitchen") is the heart of all food preparation on board. At any time of the day or night, there is plenty of activity, whether it is baking fresh bread at 2am, making meals and snacks for passengers and crew around the clock, or decorating a special birthday cake. The staff, from executive chef to pot-washer, all work together as a team, each designated a specific role, with little room for error.

The galley and preparation areas consist of the following sections (the names in parentheses are the French names given to the person who is the specialist in the area of expertise):

Fish Preparation Area (Poissonnier): This area contains freezers and a fully equipped preparation room, where fish is cleaned and cut to size before it is sent to the galley.

Meat Preparation Area (Butcher/Rotisseur): This area contains separate freezers for meat and poultry. Their temperatures are kept at around 10°F (–17°C). There are also defrosting areas kept at 35°–40°F (2°–4°C). Meat and poultry are sliced and portioned before being sent to the galley.

Vegetable Preparation Area (Entremetier): Vegetables are cleaned and prepared in this area.

What's on the Menu

HEALTHY CHOICE MENU

Our Healthy Choice Menu reflects today's awareness of lighter, more balanced diets. In response to these nutritional needs, Princess Cruises offers dishes that are low in cholesterol, fat, and sodium but high in flavor.

USA: Fresh Fruit Cup California Style
China: Won Ton and Vegetable Soup
New Zealand: John Dory Fillet Maori Style
Austria: Kranz Cake, Warm Vanilla Custard Sauce

VEGETARIAN MENU

USA: Fresh Fruit Cup California Style
Greece: Greek Salad, Mediterranean Dressing
Italy: Risotto with Asparagus
France: Puff Pastry Vegetable Roll with Tomato Sauce
Switzerland: Vacherin Suisse
Assorted International Cheese and Crackers

ALWAYS AVAILABLE

Classic Caesar Salad
Broiled North Sea Silver Salmon Fillet
Grilled Skinless Chicken Breast
Grilled Black Angus Sirloin Steak
Baked Potato and French Fries can be requested in addition to the daily vegetable selection.

APPETIZERS

Italy: Cocktail di Granseola Costa Esmeralda
Crabmeat Served in Half Cantaloupe Melon with Aurora Sauce
France: Smoked Breast of Strasbourg Duckling

England: Cured York Rolls on a Bed of Fresh Baby Leaves
USA: Fresh Fruit Cup California Style

Soups

China: Won Ton and Vegetable Soup
Scotland: Mutton and Barley Soup
Polynesia: Chilled Tropical Fresh Fruit Cream Soup

Salad

Greece: Greek Salad, Mediterranean Dressing

Princess Favorite

Italy: Risotto con Pollo e Asparagi
A Combination of Italian Carnaroli Rice with Green Asparagus Tips and Strips of Chicken Finished with Freshly Grated Parmesan Cheese and Herbs

ENTRÉES

New Zealand: John Dory Fillet Maori Style
Norway: Rainbow Trout Seven Sisters Fjord Fashion
Poached and Served with a Delicate Dill Sauce. Potatoes au Gratin
Holland: Glazed Milk-Fed Veal Leg Ancienne
Sliced and Served with a Mushroom Morel Cream Sauce, Hollandaise Potatoes
Australia: Oven-Baked Spring Leg of Lamb Aussie Style
Coated with Mustard and Aromatic Herbs Flavored with Mint
USA: Surf and Turf
Filet Mignon and Jumbo Shrimp from the Grill with Browned Red New Potatoes and Bâtonnet Vegetables

Sauce Preparation Area (Saucier): This is where the sauces are prepared.

Soup Preparation Area (Potagier): Soups are made in huge tureens.

Cold Kitchen (Garde Manger): This is the area where all cold dishes and salads are prepared, from the simplest sandwich (for room service, for example) to the works of art that grace the buffets. The area is well equipped with mixing machines, slicing machines, and refrigeration cabinets where prepared dishes are stored until required.

Bakery and Pastry Shop (Baker): This area provides the raw ingredients for preparing food, and contains dough mixers, refrigerators, proving ovens, ovens, and containers in all shapes and sizes. Dessert items, pastries, sweets, and other confectionery are prepared and made here.

Pantry: This is where cheese and fruits are prepared, and where sandwiches are made.

Dishwashing Area: This area contains huge conveyor-belt dishwashing machines. Wash and rinse temperatures are carefully controlled to comply with public health regulations. This is where all cooking utensils are scrubbed and cleaned, and where the silverware is scrupulously polished.

Hygiene Standards

Galley equipment is in almost constant use, and regular inspections and maintenance help detect potential problems. There is continual cleaning of equipment, utensils, bulkheads, floors, and hands.

Cruise ships sailing from or visiting US ports

The informal Lido Café aboard the Europa.

are subject to in-port sanitation inspections. These are voluntary, not mandatory inspections, based on 42 inspection items, undertaken by the United States Public Health (USPH) Department of Health and Human Services, under the auspices of the Centers for Disease Control. The cruise line pays for each ship inspection. A similar process takes place in Britain under the Port Health Authority, which has even more stringent guidelines.

A tour of the galley proves to be a highlight for some passengers, when a ship's insurance company permits. A video of *Behind the Scenes*, for use on in-cabin television, may be provided instead.

In accordance with internationally accepted standards, all potable water brought on board, or produced by distillation aboard cruise ships, should contain a free chlorine or bromine residual equal to or greater than 0.2 ppm (parts per million). This is why drinking water served in the dining room often tastes of chlorine.

Waste Disposal

Cruise ships must be capable of efficient handling of garbage and waste materials, as trash generated by passengers and crew must be managed, stored, and disposed of efficiently and economically. The larger the ship, the more waste is created, and the greater the need for reliable disposal systems.

Trash includes bottles, cans, corrugated cartons, fabrics, foodstuffs, paper products, plastic containers, as well as medical waste, sludge oil, wet waste, and so on. The sheer magnitude of waste materials can be highly problematic, especially on long cruises. If solid waste is not burnable, or cannot be disposed of overboard (this must be biodegradable), it must be stored for later off-loading and disposal on land.

Although the latest breed of cruise ships is equipped with "zero-discharge" facilities, many older cruise ships still have a way to go when it comes to garbage handling. One method of dealing with food waste is to send it to a waste-pulping machine that has been partially filled with water. Cutting mechanisms reduce the waste and allow it to pass through a special sizing ring to be pumped directly overboard or into a holding tank or an incinerator when the ship is within three-mile limits.

Whichever method of waste disposal is chosen, it, as well as the ship, must meet the extremely stringent demands of Annex V of MARPOL 73/78 international regulations.

Caviar

Although it might seem like it from menu descriptions, most ships do not serve Beluga caviar, but the less expensive and more widely available Sevruga and Sevruga Malossol (low-salt) caviar. Even more widely served aboard the standard cruise ships is Norwegian lumpfish "caviar." If you are partial to the best caviar, you might want to know that Cunard's QE2 is reputed to be the world's largest single buyer of caviar (spending about $500,000 a year), after the Russian and the Ukrainian governments.

Those who have not tasted good caviar may find it very salty. That's because the eggs are taken fresh from a sleeping female sturgeon (it takes about 20 years for a female beluga sturgeon to mature, and caviar is taken from onlh three of 29 varieties of female sturgeon). The eggs are then passed through a screen to separate them from other fibrous matter, then mixed with salt, which acts as a preservative and also promotes the taste. The more salt added, the better the caviar is preserved; the less salt added the finer the taste.

The process is done by highly skilled labor, which adds to its cost. The two countries that produce most of the world's caviar are Iran and Russia (both countries produce farmed sturgeon stock, which is released into the Caspian Sea continually to replenish dwindling stocks). In general, Russian caviar is more highly salted than caviar from Iran. And just as each vineyard produces different wines, so each fishery will produce different-tasting caviar. Additionally, there are about 400 species of sturgeon, so grades can differ.

The Caspian Sea is the spawning ground for 90 percent of the world's caviar-producing sturgeon. There are three types that are fished for caviar.

● The giant beluga is hardest to find and the most expensive. It can weigh 1,500 pounds (680 kg) or more. One fish can yield up to 20 pounds (9 kg) of caviar, and its smoky-gray eggs are the largest (they are also the most delicate).

● The ossetra this takes about 13 years to mature, and weighs up to 40 pounds (18 kg). These are the most durable eggs (they are also smaller) and range in color from a darkish brass to olive green.

● The sevruga weighs about six pounds. It also has small eggs, ranging in color from soft gray to dark gray.

There is also a fourth type of sturgeon, known as a sterlet, which produces a translucent golden egg, although it is hard to find (before 1917 all the golden caviar was sent to the Tsar in Russia).

There was a time when sturgeon was found in abundance. So much so that caviar was often placed on the bars of London and New York as a snack to promote the sale of beer and ale. Caviar is a natural accompaniment for good champagne, but good champagne (like anything else of high quality) doesn't come cheap. What most ships use as champagne, for the Captain's Welcome Aboard Cocktail Party, for example, just about passes as champagne. Some ships feature a caviar and champagne bar on board, offering several varieties of caviar at extra cost.

Champagne

Champagne making is a real art (in France itself the production of Champagne is restricted to a very small geographic area). Unlike wine, it is bottled in many sizes, ranging from the minute to the ridiculously huge, and with a variety of names to match:

Quarter bottle . . . . . . 18.7 centiliters
Half bottle (split) . . . 37.5 centiliters
Bottle . . . . 75 centiliters

What Wine Costs		
CELLAR MASTER SUGGESTIONS		
	Glass	Bottle
Fumé Blanc Robert Mondavi, Napa Valley	$5.50	$21.00
Chardonnay Cuvaison, Napa Valley		$34.00
Cabernet Sauvignon Wente Estate, Livermore Valley	$5.50	$22.00
Cabernet Sauvignon Guenoc Estate, Lake County		$24.00

Magnum.	2 bottles
Jeroboam	4 bottles
Rehoboam	6 bottles
Methuselah	8 bottles
Salmanazar	12 bottles
Balthazar	16 bottles
Nebuchadnezzar . . .	20 bottles

The three main grape-growing districts in Champagne are: the Montagne de Reims, to the south and east of Reims; the Vallée de la Marne, surrounding the river; and the Côtes des Blancs, south of Epernay. The first two mainly grow the dark pinot-noir and pinot-meunier grapes; the latter grows the white chardonnay variety (all are used in making champagne). Removing the husks before full fermentation prevents the dark grapes from coloring the wine red. If pink champagne is required, the skins are left in the grape mix for a longer time to add color.

Although the Champagne area has been producing wines of renown for a long time, its vintners were unable to keep their bubbles from fizzling out until a monk in the Abbey of Haut-villiers, whose name was Dom Perignon, came up with the solution. The bubbles – escaping carbonic acid gas – had always escaped, until Dom Perignon devised a bottle capable of containing the champagne without it exploding from the bottle, a common occurrence in local cellars.

The legacy of this clever monk is that the champagne bottle is the strongest bottle made today. Its thickness is concentrated around the bottle's base and shoulders. Dom Perignon's bottle was aided by the coincidental development of the cork.

Even after his work, champagne was not the perfect elixir enjoyed today. It was rather cloudy due to residual sediment (dead yeast cells). Its bubbles, therefore, could not be truly relished visually until la Veuve Cliquot (the Widow Cliquot) devised the system of *remuage* in the nineteenth century. Rather than laying the bottles down horizontally for their period of aging, she put them in a special rack, called a pupitre, which held them at a 45-degree angle, with the neck of the bottle facing down. Each day, the bottles are given a short, sharp, quarter turn so as to shake the sediment, which gradually settles in the neck of the bottle.

Once this is complete, a process called *dégorgement* freezes the neck of the bottle. It is then uncorked and internal pressure ejects the ice containing the sediment. Obviously, this means that the bottle is a little less than totally full, so the champagne is topped up with what is called the *dosage*, which is a sweet champagne liqueur.

The degree of sweetness of this addition depends on the tastes of the market to which the champagne is ultimately destined. After the *dosage* is added, the permanent cork is forced in and wired up. The bottles then remain in the cellar of the winery until they are ordered. Each bottle is then washed and labeled prior to being shipped for sale. ❑

ENTERTAINMENT ABOARD

*After food, the most subjective part of any mainstream cruise is the
entertainment, which has to be diversified and innovative but never controversial*

Ask 1,000 people what they'd like to see as part of any evening entertainment program, and you'll get 1,000 different answers. It's all a matter of personal taste and choice. Whatever one expects, the days are gone when you would have been entertained by waiters doubling as singers, although a few bar waiters are still known to perform tray-spinning effects to boost their tips.

Many passengers, despite having paid so little for their cruise, expect to see top-notch entertainment, "headline" marquee-name cabaret artists, the world's most "popular" singers, and the most dazzling shows with slick special effects, just as one would find in the best venues in Las Vegas, London, or Paris. There are many reasons why it is not exactly so. International star acts invariably have an entourage that accompanies them to any venue: their personal manager, their musical director (often a pianist or conductor), a rhythm section (with bass player and drummer), even their hairdresser. On land, one-night shows are possible, but with a ship, an artist cannot always disembark after just one night, especially when it involves moving equipment, costumes,

Some of the larger ships mount spectacular shows.

and baggage. This makes the whole matter logistically and financially unattractive for all but the very largest ships on fixed itineraries, where a marquee-name act might be a marketing plus.

When you are at home you can bring the world's top talent into your home via television. Cruise ships are a different matter. Most entertainers don't like to be away from their "home base" for long periods, as they rely on telephone contact. Most don't like the long contracts that the majority of ships must offer in order to amortize the cost.

So many acts working aboard cruise ships are interchangeable with so many other acts also working aboard cruise ships. Ever wonder why? Entertainers aboard ship must also *live* with their audiences for several days (sometimes weeks) – something unheard-of on land – as well as work on stages aboard older ships that weren't designed for live performances. However, there is no question that cruise ships are the new location for vaudeville acts, where a guaranteed audience is a bonus for many former club-date acts, as well as fresh acts trying to break in to the big time on land.

Many older (pre-1970) ships have extremely limited entertainment spaces, and very few ships provide proper dressing rooms and backstage

facilities for the storage of costumes, props, or effects, not to mention the extensive sound and lighting equipment most live "name" artists demand or need. Only the latest ships provide the extensive facilities needed for presenting the kind of high-tech shows one would find in Las Vegas, London, or New York, for example. These feature elaborate electronic backdrops, revolving stages, orchestra pits, multi-slide projection, huge stage-side video screens, pyrotechnic capabilities, and the latest light-mover and laser technology. Even the latest ships often lack enough dressing room and hanging space for the 150 costumes required in a single typical ship production show.

However, more emphasis has been placed on entertainment since the mid-1970s. Entertainment on today's large mainstream ships is market-driven. In other words, it is directed toward that segment of the industry that the cruise line's marketing department is specifically targeting (discounting notwithstanding). This is predom-inantly a family audience, so the fare must appeal to as broad an age range as possible – a tall order for any cruise line's director of entertainment.

A cruise line with several ships in its fleet will normally employ an entertainment department comprising an entertainment director and several assistants, and most cruise lines have contracts with one or more entertainment agencies that specialize in entertainment for cruise ships.

It is no use, for example, in a company booking a juggler who needs a floor-to-ceiling height of 12 feet but finds that the ship has a show lounge with

a height of just 7 feet (although I did overhear one cruise director ask if the act "couldn't he juggle sideways"); or an acrobatic knife-throwing act (in a moving ship?); or a concert pianist when the ship only has an upright honky-tonk piano; or a singer who sings only in English when the passengers are German-speaking.

Indeed, the hardest audience to cater to is one of mixed nationalities (each of whom will expect entertainers to cater exclusively to their particular linguistic group). Given that cruise lines are now marketing to more international audiences in order to fill ships, the problem of finding the right entertainment is far more acute.

The more upscale cruise lines (typically those operating small ships) offer more classical music, even some light opera, more guest lecturers and top authors than the seven-day package cruises heading for warm-weather destinations.

Part of the entertainment experience aboard large cruise ships is the glamorous "production show," the kind of show you would expect to see in any good Las Vegas show palace, with male and female lead singers and Marilyn Monroe look-alike dancers, a production manager, lavish backdrops, extravagant sets, grand lighting, special effects, and stunning custom-designed costumes. Unfortunately, many cruise line executives, who know little or nothing about entertainment, still regard plumes and huge feather boas paraded by showgirls who *step*, but don't *dance*, as being desirable. Some cruise ships have coarse shows that are not becoming to either

DID YOU KNOW?

● that Roy, of the famous Siegfried & Roy (Siegfried Fischbacher and Roy Uwe Ludwig Horn) illusion act, used to be a steward aboard the German liner *Bremen*? Siegfried was a bartender aboard the same ship. That's how they met.

● that musical instruments of some of the stars of rock and pop can be found aboard Holland America Line's *Zaandam*? They were acquired from the "Pop and Guitars" auction at Christie's in London, and a Fender Squire Telecaster guitar signed by Mick Jagger, Keith Richards, Charlie Watts, Ronnie Wood and Bill Wyman of The Rolling Stones; A Conn Saxophone signed on the mouthpiece by former US President Bill Clinton; an Ariana acoustic guitar signed by David Bowie and Iggy Pop; a Fender Stratocaster guitar signed in silver ink by the members of the rock band Queen; a Bently "Les Paul" style guitar signed by various artists, including Carlos Santana, Eric Clapton, BB King, Robert Cray, Keith Richards and Les Paul.

● that the Cunard White Star Line's *Queen Mary* was the first ship to have a system of colored lights that varied according to music (chromosonics)?

● that Verdi wrote an opera to commemorate the opening of the Suez Canal? Its name is *Aïda*.

● that the 212-passenger *Seabourn Legend* was the star of the film *Speed 2: Cruise Control*, released in 1997 in the US? The film was shot on location in Marigot, the capital of the French side of the tiny two-nation Caribbean island of St. Martin/St. Maarten. The filming called for the building of almost a complete "town" at Marigot, into which the ship crashes.

● that *Titanic*, the stage musical, cost $10 million to mount in New York in 1997? That's $2.5 million more than it cost to build the original ship that debuted in 1912. The play debuted at the Lunt-Fontanne Theater in April 1997 (the ship sank on April 14, 1912).

● that the Hollywood film that cost the most money – but also made the most – was based aboard a passenger liner? The film, *Titanic*, was released in 1997.

● that the cruise ship used in the 1974 movie *Juggernaut*, in which seven bombs in oil drums were placed aboard, was *Maxim Gorkiy*? The film starred Richard Harris, Omar Sharif, David Hemmings, and Anthony Hopkins.

dancer or passenger. Such things went out of vogue about 20 years ago. Shows that offer more creative costuming and real dancing win more votes today.

Book back-to-back seven-day cruises (on alternating eastern and western Caribbean itineraries, for example), and you should note that entertainment is generally geared to seven-day cruises. Thus, you will probably find the same two or three production shows and the same acts on the second week of your cruise. The way to avoid seeing everything twice is to pace yourself. Go to some shows during the first week and save the rest for the second week.

Regular passengers will notice that they seem to see the same acts time after time on various ships. For the reasons given above (and more), the criteria narrow the field even though there are many fine land-based acts. In addition, ship entertainers need to enjoy socializing. Successful shipboard acts tend to be good mixers, are presentable when in public, do not do drugs or take excess alcohol, are not late for rehearsals, and must cooperate with the cruise director and his or her staff as well as with the band.

Sadly, with cruise lines forever looking for ways to cut costs, entertainment has of late been a major target for some companies (particularly the smaller operators). Cutting costs translates to

Music aboard cruise ships caters for many tastes.

bringing on, for example, lower-cost singers (who often turn out to be non-reading, vocally-challenged persons) and bands that cannot read charts (musician-speak for musical arrangements) brought on board by cabaret acts.

Show Biz at Sea

In today's high-tech world, staging a lavish 45 to 50-minute production show involves the concerted efforts of a range of experienced people, and a cost of $500,000 to $1 million a show isn't unheard-of. Weekly running costs (performers' salaries, costume cleaning and repair, royalties, replacement audio and videotapes, and so on) all add up to an expensive package for what can be a largely unappreciative and critical audience.

Who's Who

Although production companies differ in their approach, the following gives some idea of the various people involved behind the scenes.

Executive Producer
Transfers the show's concept from design to reality. First, the brief from the cruise line's director of entertainment might be for a new production show (the average being two major shows per seven-day cruise). After deciding on an initial concept, they then call in the choreographer, vocal coach, and musical arranger.

Choreographer
Responsible for auditioning the dancers and for creating, selecting, and teaching the routines.

Musical Director
Coordinates all musical scores and arrangements; trains the singers in voice and microphone techniques, projection, accenting, phrasing, memory, and general presentation; and oversees session singers and musicians for the recording sessions.

Musical Arranger
After the music has been selected, the musical arrangements must be made. Just one song can cost as much as $2,000 for a single arrangement for a 12-piece orchestra.

Costume Designer
Provides creative original designs for a minimum of seven costume changes in one show lasting 45 minutes. The costumes must also be practical, as they will be used repeatedly.

Costume Maker
Buys all materials, and must be able to produce all required costumes in the time frame allotted.

Graphic Designer
Provides all the set designs, whether they are physical one- two- or three-dimensional sets for the stage, or photographic images created on slide film, video, laser disk, or other electronic media.

Lighting Designer
Creates the lighting patterns and effects for a

It's not only the ship that's moving…

production show. Sequences and action on stage must be carefully lit to the best advantage. The completed lighting plot is computerized.

Bands/Musicians

Before the big production shows and artists can be booked, bands and musicians must be hired, often for long contracts. Naturally, live musicians are favored for a ship's show band, as they are excellent music readers (necessary for all visiting cabaret artists and for big production shows). Big bands are often placed in some of the larger ships for special sailings, or for world cruises, on which ballroom dancing plays a large part. Most musicians work to contracts of about six months.

Other Entertainment

Most cruise ships organize acts that, while perhaps not nationally recognized "names," can provide two or three different shows during a seven-day cruise. These will be male/female singers, illusionists, puppeteers, hypnotists, and even circus acts, with wide age-range appeal.

There are comedians and comedy duos who perform "clean" material and who may find employment year-round on what is now known as the "cruise ship circuit." These popular comics enjoy good accommodation, are stars while on board, and often go from ship to ship on a standard rotation every few days. There are

raunchy, late-night "adults only" comedy acts in some of the ships with younger, "hip" audiences, but few have enough material for several shows.

The larger a ship, the larger the entertainment program will be. In some ships, the cruise director may "double" as an act, but most companies prefer him/her to be strictly an administrative and social director, allowing more time to be with passengers. Most passengers find that being entertained "live" is an experience far superior to that of sitting at home in front of a television set, watching its clinical presentation.

Playing the game

Television game shows should be the next audience participation event aboard the large ships with the huge showlounges. Disney Cruise Line has "Who Wants to be a Mouseketeer?" These professionally produced game shows, which are licensed from television companies, involve all passengers seated in a ship's show lounge because interactive buttons are wired into every seat. The game shows are great fun, and provide good entertainment. While they are quite expensive to mount, they provide something different from the costumed production show extravaganzas that cost the cruise lines millions to produce. ❑

CRUISING FOR ROMANTICS

With more and more people taking solo trips, the possibility of

a shipboard romance has a special attraction for many

Back in 1932, Warner Bros. released the film *One Way Passage*, a bittersweet story starring Kay Francis and William Powell. Remember the shipboard romance between Bette Davis and Paul Henreid in the film *Now, Voyager*? Or Irene Dunne and Charles Boyer in *An Affair to Remember*? All involved oceangoing passenger ships and romance. Then there was *Gentlemen Prefer Blondes*, in which Marilyn Monroe and Jane Russell starred. In the early 1950s, Howard Hughes presented Jane Russell in an RKO movie called *The French Line*, which depicted life on board one of the great ocean liners of the time – the SS *Liberté* – as being exciting, frivolous, promiscuous, and romantic. The movie was, in fact, made on board the great ship.

Today that same romantic attraction is still very much in vogue. In 1997, in the Hollywood blockbuster *Titanic*, Kate Winslet and Leonardo Di Caprio showed young love and its great adventure aboard the stricken ocean liner on its maiden voyage across the North Atlantic.

While you may not believe in mermaids, romance does happen. More than 2 million cruise passengers (more than 25 percent of all cruise passengers) traveled as singles in 2001. About 25 percent of all calls to travel agents are made by singles and single parents. Cruise lines are just waking up to this fact and are trying to help by providing special programs for single passengers. Some cruise lines or tour operators advertise special cruises for singles, but remember that the age range could be anything from 7 to 70.

Make no mistake about it: the world of cruising is made for couples. Singles are an expensive afterthought. Indeed, many singles are prejudiced against cruising because most cruise lines charge a single occupancy supplement for anyone traveling alone. The reason is that the most precious commodity aboard any cruise ship is space. Every square foot must be used for essential facilities or revenue-earning areas. Since a single cabin is often as large as a double and uses the same electrical wiring, plumbing, and fixtures – and thus is just as expensive to build – cruise lines naturally feel justified in charging supplements or premiums for those who are occupying single cabins.

Single cabins are often among the most expensive, when compared with the per-person rates for double occupancy cabins. From the point of view of the crew, it takes as much time to clean a single cabin as it does a double. And, of course, there is only one tip instead of two.

Single Supplements

If you want to travel alone and not share a cabin, you can pay either a flat rate for the cabin or a single "supplement" if you occupy a double cabin. Some lines charge a fixed amount – $250, for instance – as a supplement, no matter what the cabin category, ship, itinerary, or length of cruise. Single supplements, or solo occupancy rates, vary between lines, and sometimes between ships. Check with your travel agent for the latest rates.

Guaranteed Single Rates

Although some singles travel with friends or family, many others like to travel alone. For this reason, cruise lines have established several programs to accommodate them. One is the "Guar-

LEFT: fountain in the atrium of the *Statendam*.
RIGHT: fun activities bring singles together.

Getting together in the hot tub aboard the *Imagination*.

anteed Single" rate, which provides a set price without having to be concerned about which cabin to choose. Some cruise lines have guaranteed singles' rates, but the line and *not* the passenger picks the cabin. If the line does not find a roommate, the single passenger may get the cabin to himself/herself at no extra charge.

Guaranteed Share Programs

A "Guaranteed Share" program allows you to pay the normal double-occupancy rate, but the cruise line will find another passenger of the same sex to share the double cabin with you. Some cruise lines do not advertise a guaranteed-share program in their brochures but will often try to accommodate such bookings, particularly when demand for space is light. You could book a guaranteed share basis cabin only to find that you end up with a cabin to yourself. As cruise lines are apt to change such things at short notice, it is best to check with your travel agent for the latest rates, and read the fine print.

Cruising for Single Women

Any single woman can take a cruise vacation knowing that she is going to be as safe – if not safer – than she would be in any major vacation destination, but that does not mean that a cruise ship is a totally safe, completely hassle-free environment. Common sense should be the rule. Undoubtedly though, cruising is a great way to relax, and if you are seeking that special someone, cruising somehow brings people closer together.

There is always someone to talk to, be they couples or other singles, and cruising is not a "meat market" where you are always under observation. The easiest way to meet other singles, however, is to participate in scheduled activities. Be a little assertive, and get the cruise director or cruise staff to introduce you to other singles.

In the dining room, ask the restaurant manager to seat you with other singles, or a mix of singles and couples. Single black women should note that there is often a dearth of single black men for dancing or socializing with (they simply have not discovered cruising yet).

If you *are* looking for romance, however, beware of the lure of the uniform, of an easy affair or fling with a ship's officer (or member of the crew). They get to see new faces every week (or every cruise), and thus the possible risk of sexually transmitted diseases should be borne in mind.

Gentlemen Cruise Hosts

The female-to-male passenger ratio is high (as much as eight-to-one on world cruises and other long voyages), especially for passengers of middle to senior years, so some cruise lines provide male social hosts, specially recruited as dance and bridge partners, and company during social functions. First used to good effect aboard Cunard Line's *QE2* in the late 1970s, gentlemen hosts are now employed by a number of cruise lines (particularly those carrying a large number of elderly passengers).

They generally host a table in the dining room, appear as dance partners at all cocktail parties and dance classes, and accompany women on shore excursions. These gentlemen, usually over 55 years of age and/or retired, are outgoing, mingle well, are well groomed, and enjoy cruise ships and traveling around the world almost free of charge.

If you think you would like such a job, do remember that you'll have to dance for several hours most nights, and dance just about every kind of dance well! Crystal Cruises, Cunard, Holland America Line, and Silversea Cruises, among others, provide gentlemen hosts, especially on the longer voyages and world cruises.

The *Love Boat* Connection

Two famous television shows, *The Love Boat* (US) and *Traumschiff* (Germany), have given a tremendous boost to the concept of cruising as the ultimate romantic vacation, although what is shown on the screen does not quite correspond to reality. Indeed, the real captain of one ship, when he was asked the difference between his job and that of the captain of *The Love Boat*, remarked: "On TV they can do a retake if things are not right the first time around, whereas I have to get it right the first time!"

Ships are indeed romantic places (a fact that underpinned the 1997 blockbuster Hollywood movie *Titanic*). There's nothing quite like standing on the aft deck of a cruise ship with your loved one – your hair blowing in the breeze – as you sail over the moonlit waters to yet another discovery. Of course, a full moon only occurs once a month, so check the calendar to make sure the timing of *your* moonlit cruise is perfect.

There is no doubt that cruises provide excellent opportunities for meeting people of similar interests. So if you are looking for romance, and if you choose the right ship, the odds are reasonably in your favor.

Getting Married Aboard Ship

As in all those old black-and-white movies, a ship's captain can indeed marry you when at sea (unless the ship's country of registry prohibits, or does not recognize, such marriages). In practice, however, this service is rarely offered by cruise lines today. You would need to inquire in your country of domicile (or residence) whether such a marriage is legal, and ascertain what paperwork and blood tests are required.

The onus to provide the *validity* of such a marriage is yours. The captain could be sued and perhaps held criminally liable if he marries a couple that are not legally entitled to be married (for example, an underage male or female who do not

have the consent of a parent or guardian, or if one or both parties are not legally divorced).

It is a simple matter to arrange to get married aboard almost any cruise ship when the ship is alongside in port, provided you take along your own registered minister. Carnival Cruise Lines, Holland America Line, and Princess Cruises, among others offer special wedding packages. These include the services of a minister to marry you, wedding cake, champagne, bridal bouquet and matching boutonniere for the bridal party, a band to perform at the ceremony, and an album of wedding photos.

Carnival Cruise Lines' program includes a marriage ceremony on a beach in Grand Cayman or St. Thomas. Princess Cruises offers weddings on a beach in St. Thomas (prices range from $525 to $1175 per package). Or you could arrange a romantic wedding Disney-style on its private island, *Castaway Cay*.

Princess Cruises features weddings aboard *Golden Princess, Grand Princess* (which had the first oceangoing wedding chapel aboard a contemporary cruise vessel), and *Star Princess*, performed by the ship's captain (the wedding is legal because of the ship's registry, Bermuda). There are three packages, Pearl, Emerald, and Diamond; the costs are $1,400, $1,800, and $2,400, respectively. A Wedding Coordinator at the line handles all the details. What better way than to be married aboard ship *and* have your honeymoon aboard, too?

Even if you can't get married aboard ship, you could have your wedding reception aboard one. Many cruise lines offer outstanding facilities and provide complete services to help you plan your reception. Contact the Director of Hotel Services at the cruise line of your choice. The cruise line should go out of its way to help, especially if you follow the reception with a honeymoon cruise.

UK-based passengers should know that P&O Cruises hosts a series of cruises called the "Red-Letter Anniversary Collection" for those celebrating 10, 15, 20, 25, 30, 35, 40, 45, 50, 55, or 60 years of marriage. Gifts you will receive with the compliments of P&O Cruises include a brass carriage clock, leather photograph album, free car parking at Southampton, or free first-class rail travel from anywhere in the UK (check with your travel agent for the latest details).

A cruise also makes a fine, no-worry honeymoon vacation, and a delightful belated honeymoon getaway if you had no time to spare when you were married. You will feel as if you are in the middle of a movie set as you sail away to fairytale places, though actually, the ship is a destination in itself.

Renewal of Vows

There has recently been an upsurge in cruise lines performing "renewal of vows" ceremonies. A cruise is a wonderful setting for reaffirming to one's partner the strength of commitment. A handful of ships have a small chapel where this ceremony can take place; otherwise it can be anywhere aboard ship (a most romantic time is at sunrise or sunset on the open deck). The renewal of vows ceremony is conducted by the ship's captain and a nondenominational text reaffirms the love and trust between "partners, lifetime friends, and companions."

Although some companies, such as Carnival Cruise Lines, Celebrity Cruises, Holland America Line, and Princess Cruises, have complete packages for purchase, which include music, champagne, hors d'oeuvres, certificate, corsages for the women, and so on, most other companies do not charge (yet). The ship's photographer usually records the event (it is, after all, a revenue-generating photo opportunity) and will have special photo albums embossed with the cruise line's logo.

Cruising for Honeymooners

Cruising is popular as a honeymoon vacation. The advantages are obvious: you pack and unpack only once; it is a hassle-free and crime-free environment; and you get special attention, if you want it. It is also easy to budget in advance, as one price often includes airfare, cruise, food, entertainment, several destinations, shore excursions, and pre- and post-cruise hotel stays.

Once you are married, some cruise lines make a point of offering discounts to entice you to book a future (anniversary) cruise. Just think, no cooking meals, everything will be done for you. You can think of the crew as your very own service and kitchen staff.

Although no ship as yet provides bridal suites (hint, hint), many ships do provide cabins with queen-sized or double beds. Some, but by no means all, also provide tables for two in the dining room should you wish to dine together without having to make friends with others.

Some cruise ships feature Sunday departures, so couples can plan a Saturday wedding and reception before traveling to their ship. Pre- and post-cruise hotel accommodation can also be arranged.

Most large ships accommodate honeymoon couples well; however, if you want to plan a more private, intimate honeymoon, it would be a good idea to try one of the smaller, yacht-like cruise vessels such as those of Radisson Seven Seas Cruises, Seabourn Cruise Line, Silversea Cruises, or Windstar Cruises.

And what could be more romantic for honeymooners than to stroll, by themselves on deck, to the forward part of the ship, above the ship's bridge. This is the quietest (except perhaps for some wind noise) and most dimly lit part of the ship, and an ideal spot for stargazing and romancing.

Cruise lines offer a variety of honeymoon packages, just as hotels and resorts on land do. Although not all cruise lines provide all services, typically they might include:

❤ Private captain's cocktail party for honeymooners.

❤ Tables for two in the dining room.

❤ Set of crystal champagne or wine glasses.

❤ Honeymoon photograph with the captain, and photo album.

❤ Complimentary champagne (imported or domestic) or wine.

❤ Honeymoon cruise certificate.

❤ Champagne and caviar for breakfast.

❤ Flowers in your suite or cabin.

❤ Complimentary cake.

❤ Special T-shirts.

Finally, remember to take a copy of your marriage license or certificate, for immigration (or marriage) purposes, as your passports will not yet have been amended.

Also, remember to allow extra in your budget for things like shipboard gratuities (tips), shore excursions, and spending money ashore.

If your romance includes the desire to sleep in a large bed next to your loved one, check with your travel agent and cruise line to make sure the cabin you have booked has such a bed. Better still, book a suite. But check and double-check to avoid disappointment.

If you need to take your wedding gown aboard for a planned wedding somewhere along the way – in Hawaii or Bermuda, for example – there is usually space to hang it in the dressing room next to the stage in the main showlounge, especially aboard large ships. ❑

DID YOU KNOW?

● that motion pictures' most famous on-screen odd couple, Jack Lemmon and Walter Matthau, played gentlemen dance hosts intent on defrauding rich widows aboard a Caribbean cruise ship? Called *Out to Sea*, the 1997 Martha Coolidge film also starred Gloria DeHaven, Dyan Cannon, Hal Linden, Elaine Stritch, and Brent Spiner. The "cruise ship" interior was filmed at Raleigh Studios in Hollywood.

● that Epirotiki Line's *Jupiter* was used to carry the 61 finalists of the Miss Universe contest in 1976 (Epirotiki Line is now part of Royal Olympic Cruises)?

● that on Valentine's Day, 1998, some 5,000 couples renewed their vows aboard the ships of Princess Cruises?

CRUISING FOR FAMILIES

When parents decide to take their children with them on a cruise,

it's important to choose a ship with the right facilities

Yes, you *can* take your children on a cruise. In fact, once you get them aboard, you will hardly see them at all, if you choose the right ship and cruise. Family cruises can give parents a welcome break; no one has to cook, or do the dishes, make the beds, drive, or find a place to park. Families can do different things on a cruise, and parents don't have to be concerned about the whereabouts of their children. Where else can you go out for a night on the town without having to drive, and be home in a moment should the baby-sitter need you? Dad can sleep in. Mom can go swimming and join an aerobics class.

The children can join in the organized activities that go on all day long. Whether you share a cabin with them or whether they have their own separate but adjoining cabin, there will be plenty to keep them occupied. Aboard several ships that cruise in the Caribbean, you will even find favorite life-sized cartoon characters.

Some cruise lines have token family programs, with limited activities and only a couple of general staff allocated to look after children, even though their brochures might claim otherwise. But cruise lines that are really serious about family cruise programs dedicate complete teams of kids', "tweens and teens" counselors, who run special programs that are off-limits to adults. They also have facilities such as high chairs in the dining room, cots, and real playrooms. Most entertainment for children is designed to run simultaneously with adult programs. For those cruising with very young children, baby-sitting services may also be available. For example, *QE2* has real children's nurses and even trained English National Nursing Examination Board-qualified nannies. *Aurora, Oceana* and *Oriana* have a "night nursery" for children of two to five years of age.

Parents, of course, have long realized that children cost more as they age. For example, children under two years travel free on most cruise lines (and airlines). If older, they cost money.

There's no better vacation for families than a ship cruise, especially at holiday time, whether it is at Christmas and New Year, Easter, or during the long summer school vacation. Active parents can have the best of all worlds, family togetherness, social contact, and privacy. Cruise ships provide a very safe, crime-free, encapsulated environment, and give junior passengers a lot of free-

dom without parents having to be concerned about where their children are at all times. A cruise also allows youngsters a chance to meet and play with others in their own age group. And, because the days aboard are long, youngsters will be able to spend time with their parents or grandparents, as well as with their peers. They can also tour the ship's bridge, meet senior officers and learn about the navigation, radar, and communications equipment, as well as being able to see how the ship operates. They will be exposed to different environments, experience many types of food, travel to and explore new places, and participate in any number of exciting activities.

Cruise ships can be full of children, or they can provide quiet moments. But aboard the busiest ships, adults will rarely get to use the swimming pools alone as they will be overcome with children having a truly good time.

Many cruise lines, recognizing the needs of families, have added a whole variety of children's programs to their daily activities. Some ships have separate swimming pools and play areas for chil-

Cruising increasingly provides activities for children.

The water slide aboard *Disney Magic*.

dren, as well as junior discos, video rooms, and teen centers.

In some ships, stewards, stewardesses, and other staff may be available as private babysitters for an hourly charge (otherwise, *group* babysitting may be available). Make arrangements at the reception desk/purser's office. Aboard some ships, evening baby-sitting services may not start until late in the evening (check details *before* booking your cruise).

Cruise lines serious about children divide them into five distinct age groups, with various names to match, according to cruise line and program: Toddlers (ages 2–4); Juniors (ages 5–7); Intermediate (ages 8–10); Tweens (ages 11–13); and Teens (ages 14–17). It often seems to be children under 12 who get the most from a cruise.

DID YOU KNOW?

● that the French liner *Ile de France* was the first, and only, ship to have a real carousel in the children's playroom? This was also the ship used in the 1960 movie *The Last Voyage*, with Robert Stack and Dorothy Malone.

● that a 15-foot-high Goofy hangs upside down over the stern of *Disney Magic*? What is he doing? Why, painting the ship, of course!

● that Carnival Cruise Lines and Mattel teamed up to produce a nautical-themed Barbie Doll? She can be found in the gift shops aboard all the company's ships.

● that Carnival Cruise Lines carried more than 300,000 children aboard its ships in 2001?

Disney Goes Cruising

In 1998, Disney Cruise Line entered the family cruise market with a big splash. The giant entertainment and theme park company introduced the first of two large ships (each has two funnels) to cater specifically to families with children. The two ships, *Disney Magic* and *Disney Wonder,* are family cruise ships that cater to 1,750 adults and up to 1,000 children, with the whole of the Disney organization to support the shipboard entertainment program. For more comments, see *Disney Magic* and *Disney Wonder* in the listings section.

General Information

Parents with babies can rest assured that they will find selected baby foods on board ships that cater to children (along with cribs and high chairs, but do ask your travel agent to check first). If you need something out of the ordinary, or that special brand of baby food, or a high chair in the restaurant, a crib, baby bathtub, baby stroller (few ships have them available for rent), or monitoring service, let your travel agent know *well in advance*, and get them and the cruise line to *confirm in writing* that the facilities and items you need will be available on board. Most cruise lines are accommodating and will do their best to obtain what is needed, provided enough notice is given.

Parents using organic baby foods, such as those obtained from health food stores, should be aware that cruise lines buy their supplies from major general food suppliers and not the smaller specialized food houses.

Although many ships have full programs for

children during days at sea, these may be limited when the ship is in port. Ships expect you to take your children with you on organized excursions, and sometimes (though not always) there are special prices for children. If the ship has a playroom, it might be wise to find out if it is open and supervised on all days of the cruise.

When going ashore, remember that if you want to take your children swimming or to the beach, it is wise to phone ahead to a local hotel with a beach or pool. Most hotels will be perfectly happy to show off their property to you, hoping for your future business.

Some cruise ships in the Caribbean area have the use of a "private" island for a day. A lifeguard will be on duty, and there will be water sports and snorkeling equipment you can rent. Remember, however, that the beaches on some "private" islands are fine for 200 passengers, but with 2,000 they become crowded, and standing in line for beach barbecues and changing and toilet facilities becomes a necessary part of the experience.

Although the sun and sea might attract juniors to the warm waters of the Caribbean, children aged seven and over will find a Baltic, Black Sea, or Mediterranean cruise a delight. They will also have a fine introduction to history, languages, and different cultures.

Children's Rates

Most cruise lines offer special rates for children sharing their parents' cabin. The cost is often lower than third and fourth person share rates. To get the best possible rates, however, it is wise to book early. And do not overlook booking an interior (no-view) cabin; you will rarely be in it anyway.

You should note that, although many adult cruise rates include airfare, most children's rates do not. Also, although some lines say children sail "free," they must in fact pay port taxes as well as airfare. The cruise line will get the airfare at the best rate, so there is no need to shop around.

If you have very young children and can get to your ship without having to fly, you'll save yourself the hassles of struggling though airports (with heightened security and longer lines) with pushchairs, strollers, and other paraphernalia.

Single Parents

Only a handful of cruise lines so far have introduced their versions of the "Single Parent Plan." This offers an economical way for single parents to take their children on a cruise, with parent and child sharing a two-berth cabin, or parent and children sharing a three-berth cabin. Single parents will pay approximately one-third the normal single-person rate for their children, and there will be plenty of activities for both parent and child(ren) to enjoy.

Family Reunions

A cruise can provide the ideal place for a family reunion (either with or without children). Here are some tips to take into account when planning one.

Let your travel agent do the planning and make all the arrangements (ask for a group discount if the total in your group adds up to more than 15). Make sure that together you choose the right cruise line, for the right reasons.

Book 12 months in advance if possible so that you can arrange cabins adjacent or close to each other (arrange for everyone to be at the same dinner seating, if the ship operates two seatings).

If anyone in the group has a birthday or anniversary, tell your travel agent to arrange a special cake (most cruise lines do not charge extra for this). Special private parties can also be arranged, although there will be an additional cost. If the group is not too large, you may be able to request to dine at the captain's table.

Arrange shore excursions as a group (in some ports, private arrangements may prove unbeatable). Finally, get everything in writing (particularly cabin assignments and locations). ❏

THE BEST CHOICE FOR CHILDREN

These cruise lines and ships have been selected by the author for their excellent children programs and care (not all ships of a particular cruise line have been chosen):

Aida Cruises (*AIDAcara, AIDAaura, AIDAvita*)
Carnival Cruise Lines (*Carnival Conquest, Carnival Destiny, Carnival Glory, Carnival Legend, Carnival Pride, Carnival Spirit, Carnival Triumph, Carnival Victory, Ecstasy, Elation, Fantasy, Fascination, Imagination, Inspiration, Paradise, Sensation*)
Celebrity Cruises (*Century, Constellation, Galaxy, Infinity, Mercury, Millennium, Summit*)
Cunard (*Queen Elizabeth 2*)
Disney Cruise Line (*Disney Magic, Disney Wonder*)
Norwegian Cruise Line (*Norway, Norwegian Dawn, Norwegian Sky, Norwegian Star, Norwegian Sun*)
P&O Cruises (*Aurora, Oceana, Oriana*)
Princess Cruises (*Diamond Princess, Golden Princess, Grand Princess, Star Princess*)
Royal Caribbean International (*Adventure of the Seas, Brilliance of the Seas, Explorer of the Seas, Radiance of the Seas, Serenade of the Seas, Voyager of the Seas*)
Star Cruises (*Star Pisces, SuperStar Leo, SuperStar Virgo*)
Thomson Cruises (*The Emerald, The Topaz*)

Note that *Aurora, Disney Magic, Disney Wonder, Oceana, Oriana* and *QE2* cater to children (and babies) of all ages particularly well, while most other ships in the above list do not typically provide good facilities (or individual babysitting services for children under 3 years old).

CRUISING FOR THE PHYSICALLY CHALLENGED

*A relaxed environment, lots of social contact and organized entertainment
are the attractions. But it's important to choose the right ship*

The advantages of a cruise for the physically challenged are many, apart from the obvious ones of no packing and unpacking:
● Good place for relaxation and self-renewal.
● Pure air at sea (no smog, pollen or pollution).
● Spacious public rooms.
● Excellent medical facilities close by.
● Specialized dietary requirements can be met.
● The staff will generally be very helpful.
● Varied entertainment.
● Gambling (but, as yet, no wheelchair-accessible gaming tables or slot machines).
● Security (no crime on board).
● Different ports of call.

But there are also significant disadvantages:
● There is *no* barrier-free cruise ship in existence. Although some of the newest and largest ships have been well designed, they are not barrier-free, so be prepared to accept the possibility of frustration when trying to access some areas (self-serve buffets are a particular handicap for many).
● Very few ships have access-help lifts installed at swimming pools (exception: P&O Cruises) or thalassotherapy pools or shore tenders (exception: Holland America Line).
● Unless cabins are specifically designed for the physically challenged, problem areas include the entrance, furniture configuration, closet hanging rails, and beds.
● Cabin bathrooms: doors that open inward are useless; the grab bars, wheel-in shower stall, toiletries cabinet should be at an accessible height.
● Elevator doorways: the width of the door is important for wheelchair passengers; controls are often not at a height suitable for operation from a wheelchair (except in the newer ships).
● Sometimes having to wait behind hordes of able-bodied passengers who really do not need to use the elevators.
● Access to outside decks is not often provided through electric-eye doors that open and close automatically. Rather it is provided through doorways that have to be opened manually.
● Cruise lines, port authorities, airlines, and various allied services are slowly improving their facilities for the physically challenged. Not all are in wheelchairs, of course, but all have needs that the cruise industry is (slowly) working to accommodate. Few cruise lines show photographs of passengers in wheelchairs (Princess Cruises is an exception).

The design of ships has traditionally worked against the mobility-limited. To keep water out or to prevent water escaping from a flooded cabin or public area, raised edges (known as "coamings" or "lips") are often placed in doorways and across exit pathways. Also, cabin doorways are often not wide enough to accommodate even a standard wheelchair. A "standard" cabin door is about 24 inches (60 cm) wide.

Cabins designed for the mobility-limited typically have doors that are about 30 inches (76 cm) wide. "Standard" bathroom doors are normally only about 22 inches (56 cm) wide, whereas those designed for wheelchairs are about 28–30 inches (71–76 cm) wide. Ask your travel agent to confirm the width of cabin and bathroom doors. Remember to allow for the fact that your knuckles on either side of a wheelchair can add to the width of your wheelchair. Beds in cabins for the physically challenged aboard most ships are not equipped with a "panic" button, adjacent to a bedside light switch (*Carnival Destiny, Carnival Triumph* and *Carnival Victory* are examples of ships that have them installed).

Bathroom doors are a particular problem, and the door itself, whether it opens outward into the cabin or inward into the bathroom, only compounds the problems of maneuvering a wheelchair within a cramped space. Four cabins for the physically challenged in the *QE2,* however, have electrically operated sliding doors into the bathroom, a completely level entrance into both cabin and bathroom, and remote-controlled lights, curtains, and doors, as well as a door intercom and alarm.

Bathrooms in many older ships are small and full of plumbing fixtures, often at odd angles, awkward when moving about from the confines of a wheelchair. The bathrooms aboard new ships are more accessible, but the plumbing is often located beneath the complete prefabricated module, making the floor higher than that in the cabin, which means a ramp must be fitted in order to wheel in.

Some cruise lines will, if given advance notice, remove a bathroom door and hang a fabric curtain in its place. Many lines will provide ramps for the bathroom doorway, where a sill or "lip" is encountered.

It was once the policy of almost all cruise lines to discourage the mobility-limited from taking a cruise or traveling anywhere by ship for reasons of safety, insurance, and legal liability. But a cruise is the ideal holiday for the physically challenged, as it provides a relaxed environment with plenty of social contact, organized entertainment, and activities. Despite most brochures declaring that they accept wheelchairs, few ships are well fitted to accommodate them. Some cruise lines openly state that all public restrooms and cabin bathrooms are inaccessible to wheelchair-bound passengers.

What about safety? Curiously, only three cruise ships currently provide direct access ramps to the lifeboats; they are *Crystal Harmony, Crystal Symphony* and *Europa.*

The list overleaf pertains to all the ships reviewed in this book and provides a guide as to their accessibility (the author, or one of his staff, personally wheels around each ship to check).

Once you've decided on your ship and cruise, the next step is to select your accommodation. There are many grades of cabin, depending on size, facilities, and location. Choose a cruise line that permits you to choose a specific cabin, rather than one that merely allows you to select a price category, then assigns you a cabin just before your departure date or, worse, at embarkation.

What Cabins Should Include:

● No "lip" or threshold at the cabin door, which should be a minimum of 35 inches wide (89 cm).
● Bedside "panic" button linked to the navigation bridge (which is staffed 24 hours a day).

Author Douglas Ward checks out a ship's facilities.

● Enough space to maneuver a wheelchair between entrance, bed, closet, and bathroom.
● Closet with "pull down" clothes rail.
● Telephone mounted at wheelchair height (not high up on wall).
● Mirrors that can be used when seated in a wheelchair (full-length).
● Safe or lockable drawer that is reachable at wheelchair height.
● Convenient electrical outlet for battery charger (for electronic wheelchair users)

What Bathrooms Should Include:

● Outward opening door.
● No "lip" at bathroom door.
● No "lip" into shower stall.
● Shower stall (with detachable showerhead located at head height when seated in a wheelchair).
● Shower chair that folds up when not in use, and grab rails.
● Grab rails for toilet.
● Toilet with electric automatic seat pad cleaner.
● Sink at low enough height for wheelchair to move up close.
● Emergency (panic) button in or adjacent to shower (for falls).

The following tips will help you choose wisely:
● If the ship does not have any specially equipped cabins for the physically challenged, book the best outside cabin in your price range or choose another ship. However, be careful as you may find that even cruise brochures that state that a ship has "wheelchair accessible" cabins fail to say whether the wheelchair will fit through the *bathroom* door, or whether there is a "lip" at the door. Find out whether the wheelchair can fit into the shower area. Get your travel agent to check, and recheck the details. Do not take "I think so" as an answer. Get specific measurements.
● Choose a cabin close to an elevator. Not all elevators go to all decks, so check the deck plan carefully. Smaller and older vessels may not even have elevators, making access to many areas, including the dining room, difficult if not impossible.
● Avoid, at all costs, a cabin down a little alleyway shared by several other cabins, even if the price is attractive. The space along these alleyways is very limited and entering one of these cabins in a wheelchair is likely to be difficult.
● Cabins located amidships are less affected by vessel motion, so choose something in the middle of the ship if you are concerned about rough seas, no matter how infrequently they might occur.
● The larger (and therefore the more expensive) the cabin, the more room you will have to maneuver in. Nowhere does this assume more importance than in the bathroom.
● If your budget allows, pick a cabin with a bath

rather than just a shower, because there will be considerably more room, especially if you are unable to stand comfortably enough.

● Meals in some ships may be served in your cabin, on special request. This is a decided advantage should you wish to avoid dressing for every meal. There are, however, few ships that have enough actual space in the cabin for dining tables.

● If you want to join other passengers in the dining room and your ship offers two fixed-time seatings for meals, choose the second. Then you can linger over your dinner, secure in the knowledge that the waiter will not try to rush you.

● Space at dining room tables is limited in many ships. When making table reservations, therefore, tell the restaurant manager that you would like a

table that leaves plenty of room for your wheelchair, so that it leaves plenty of room for waiters – and other passengers – to get past.

● Find a travel agent who knows your needs and understands your requirements, but follow up on all aspects of the booking yourself so that there will be no last-minute slip-ups.

● Make sure that the cabin you booked is so stated on the final passenger ticket contract. Also make sure that the contract specifically states that if, for any reason, the cabin is not available, that you will get a full refund *and* transportation back home as well as any hotel bills incurred.

● Take your own wheelchair with you, as ships carry only a limited number of wheelchairs; these are provided for emergency hospital use only. An

Which Ships Best Cater for the Physically Challenged

Ship	Grade	Ship	Grade	Ship	Grade	Ship	Grade
Adonia	A	Caronia	C	Explorer of the Seas	A	Mercury	B
Adventure of the Seas	A	Carousel	D	Fantasy	C	Millennium	A
A'ROSA Blu	B	Celebration	D	Fascination	C	Minerva	C
Aegean I	D	Century	B	Flamenco	D	Minerva II	B
AIDAcara	B	Clelia II	D	Flying Cloud	D	Mistral	B
AIDAvita	B	Clipper Adventurer	D	Fuji Maru	D	Mona Lisa	C
Akademik Sergey		Clipper Odyssey	C	Funchal	D	Monarch of the Seas	C
Vavilov	D	Club Med 2	D	Galapagos Explorer II	D	Monterey	D
Albatros	D	C. Columbus	C	Galaxy	B	Nantucket Clipper	D
Ambasador I	D	Constellation	A	Golden Princess	A	Navigator of the Seas	A
American Eagle	D	Coral Princess	B	Grand Princess	A	Niagara Prince	D
American Glory	D	Costa Allegra	D	Grande Caribe	D	Nippon Maru	C
Amsterdam	B	Costa Atlantica	B	Grande Mariner	D	Noordam	C
Arcadia	B	Costa Classica	B	Grandeur of the Seas	B	Nordic Empress	C
Arion	D	Costa Europa	C	Hanseatic	D	Norway	B
Astor	C	Costa Marina	D	Hebridean Princess	D	Norwegian Dawn	A
Astoria	C	Costa Mediterranea	B	Hebridean Spirit	D	Norwegian Dream	C
Asuka	C	Costa Romantica	B	Holiday	D	Norwegian Majesty	D
Atalante	D	Costa Tropicale	D	Horizon	B	Norwegian Sea	D
Aurora	A	Costa Victoria	B	Imagination	C	Norwegian Sky	B
Ausonia	D	Crown Odyssey	B	Infinity	A	Norwegian Star	A
Azur	D	Crystal Harmony	A	Inspiration	C	Norwegian Sun	B
Black Prince	D	Crystal Serenity	A	Island Escape	D	Norwegian Wind	C
Black Watch	C	Crystal Symphony	A	Jubilee	D	OceanBreeze	D
Bolero	D	Dawn Princess	A	Kapitan Dranitsyn	D	Ocean Majesty	D
Braemar	C	Delphin	D	Kapitan Khlebnikov	D	Oceana	A
Bremen	D	Diamond Princess	B	Kristina Regina	D	Oceanic	C
Brilliance of the Seas	B	Disney Magic	B	Le Levant	D	Odysseus	D
Calypso	D	Disney Wonder	B	Le Ponant	D	Olympic Countess	D
Caribe	D	Ecstasy	C	Legacy	D	Olympic Explorer	C
Carnival Conquest	B	Elation	C	Legend of the Seas	B	Olympic Voyager	C
Carnival Destiny	B	Enchantment of		Lirica	NYR	Oosterdam	B
Carnival Glory	B	the Seas	B	Maasdam	B	Oriana	B
Carnival Legend	B	Endeavour	D	Majesty of the Seas	C	Orient Venus	D
Carnival Pride	B	Europa	B	Mandalay	D	Pacific Sky	C
Carnival Spirit	B	European Stars	B	Marco Polo	C	Pacific Venus	C
Carnival Triumph	B	European Vision	B	Maxim Gorkiy	D	Paloma I	D
Carnival Victory	B	Explorer	D	Melody	C	Paradise	C

alternative is to rent an electric wheelchair, which can be delivered to the ship on your sailing date.

● If you live near the port of embarkation, arrange to visit the ship yourself to check its suitability for your accessibility requirements (most cruise lines will be helpful in this regard).

● Hanging rails in the closets on most ships are positioned too high for someone who is wheelchair-bound to reach (even the latest ships seem to repeat this basic error). Many cruise ships, however, have cabins specially fitted out to suit the mobility-limited. They are typically fitted with roll-in closets and have a pull-down facility to bring your clothes down to any height you want.

● Elevators are a constant source of difficulty for wheelchair passengers. Often the control buttons are located far too high to reach, especially those for upper decks.

● Doors on upper decks that open onto a Promenade or Lido Deck are very strong, are difficult to handle, and have high sills. Unless you can get out of your wheelchair, these doors can be a source of annoyance, even if there is help at hand, as they open inward or outward (they should ideally be electrically operated sliding doors).

● Advise any airline you might be traveling with of any special needs well ahead of time so that arrangements can be made to accommodate you without last-minute problems.

● Advise the cruise line repeatedly of the need for proper transfer facilities, in particular buses or vans with wheelchair ramps.

Ship		Ship		Ship		Ship	
Paul Gauguin	C	Sensation	C	Star Princess	A	Van Gogh	D
Polaris	D	Serenade	D	Statendam	C	Veendam	C
Polynesia	D	Seven Seas Mariner	A	Stella Solaris	D	Vision of the Seas	B
Princesa Cypria	D	Seven Seas Navigator	B	Summit	A	Vistamar	D
Princesa Marissa	D	Silver Cloud	C	Sunbird	C	Volendam	B
Princesa Victoria	D	Silver Shadow	A	Sundream	D	Voyager of the Seas	A
Princess Danae	D	Silver Star	D	Sun Bay	D	Wilderness Adventurer	D
Prinsendam	A	Silver Whisper	A	Sun Bay II	D	Wilderness Discoverer	D
Professor Molchanov	D	Silver Wind	C	Sun Princess	A	Wind Song	D
Professor Multanovskiy	D	Song of Flower	D	SuperStar Aries	B	Wind Spirit	D
Queen Elizabeth 2	B	Sovereign of the Seas	C	SuperStar Capricorn	C	Wind Star	D
Queen Mary 2	NYR	Spirit of '98	D	SuperStar Gemini	C	Wind Surf	C
R-5 Blue Dream	B	Spirit of Alaska	D	SuperStar Leo	B	World Discoverer	D
Radiance of the Seas	B	Spirit of Columbus	D	SuperStar Virgo	B	World Renaissance	D
Radisson Diamond	C	Spirit of Discovery	D	The Emerald	D	Yamal	D
Regal Empress	D	Spirit of Endeavour	D	The Iris	D	Yankee Clipper	D
Regal Princess	B	Spirit of Glacier Bay	D	The Jasmine	D	Yorktown Clipper	D
Rhapsody	D	Spirit of Oceanus	D	The Topaz	D	Zaandam	B
Rhapsody of the Seas	B	Splendour of the Seas	B	The World	A	Zenith	B
Rotterdam	A	Star Clipper	D	Thomson Spirit	C	Zuiderdam	B
Royal Clipper	D	Star Flyer	D	Triton	D		
Royal Princess	B	Star Pisces	D	Universe Explorer	D		
Royal Star	D						
Ryndam	C						
Saga Rose	C						
St. Helena	D						
Sapphire	D						
Seabourn Legend	D						
Seabourn Pride	D						
Seabourn Spirit	D						
SeaDream I	D						
SeaDream II	D						
Sea Bird	D						
Sea Cloud	D						
Sea Cloud II	D						
Sea Lion	D						
Sea Princess	A						
Seawing	D						

KEY   A) Recommended as most suitable for wheelchair passengers
B) Reasonably accessible for wheelchair passengers
C) Moderately accessible for wheelchair passengers
D) Not suitable for wheelchair passengers

● The following ships of Carnival Cruise Lines have double-width entertainment deck promenades that are good for wheelchair passengers, but the public restrooms are not accessible. In addition, although the cabin bathrooms are equipped with shower stalls and grab rails, the bathrooms have a steel "lip" and are therefore neither suitable nor accessible when stepping out of a wheelchair: Celebration, Ecstasy, Elation, Fantasy, Fascination, Holiday, Imagination, Inspiration, Jubilee, Paradise, Sensation.

● Crystal Harmony and Crystal Symphony (Crystal Cruises) are the only ships presently in operation that provide special access ramps from an accommodation deck directly to the ship's lifeboats (Crystal Serenity joins the fleet in July 2003).

● Regal Princess (Princess Cruises) has large outside cabins for the physically challenged, although they have lifeboat-obstructed views.

Embarkation

Even if you've alerted the airline and arranged your travel according to your needs, there is still one problem to surmount when you arrive at the cruise embarkation port to join your ship: the actual boarding. If you embark at ground level, the gangway to the ship may be level or inclined. It will depend on the embarkation deck of the ship and/or the tide in the port.

Alternatively, you may be required to embark from an upper level of a terminal, in which case the gangway could well be of the floating loading-bridge type, like those used at major airports. Some have flat floors; others may have raised lips spaced every three feet (awkward to negotiate in a wheelchair, especially if the gangway is made steeper by a rising tide).

Tendering Ashore

Cruise lines should (but don't always) provide an anchor emblem in brochures for those ports of call where a ship will be at anchor instead of alongside. If the ship is at anchor, be prepared for an interesting but safe experience. The crew will lower you and your wheelchair into a waiting tender (ship-to-shore launch) and then, after a short boat-ride, lift you out again onto a rigged gangway or integral platform. If the sea is calm, this maneuver proceeds uneventfully; if the sea is choppy, your embarkation could vary from exciting to harrowing.

Fortunately (or not) this type of embarkation is rare unless you are leaving a busy port with several ships all sailing the same day. Holland America Line is currently the only company that has made its shore tenders accessible to wheelchair passengers, with a special boarding ramp and scissor lift so that wheelchair passengers can see out of the shore tender's windows.

Wheelchairs

Wheelchair passengers with limited mobility should use a collapsible wheelchair. By limited mobility, I mean a person able to get out of the wheelchair and step over a sill or walk with a cane, crutches, or other walking device.

The chart on the preceding pages indicates the best cruise ships for wheelchair accessibility. Remember to ask questions before you make a reservation. Examples:

● Does the cruise line's travel insurance (with a cancellation/trip interruption) cover you for any injuries while you are aboard ship?

● Are any public rooms or public decks aboard the ship inaccessible to wheelchairs (for instance, it is sometimes difficult to obtain access to the outdoor swimming pool deck)?

● Will you be guaranteed a good viewing place in the main showroom from where you can see the shows if seated in a wheelchair?

● Will special transportation be provided to transfer you from airport to ship?

● If you need a collapsible wheelchair, can this be provided by the cruise line?

● Do passengers have to sign a medical release?

● Do passengers need a doctor's note to qualify for a cabin for the physically challenged?

● Will crew be on hand to help, or must the passengers rely on their own traveling companions for help?

● Are the ship's tenders accessible to wheelchairs?

● How do you get from your cabin to the lifeboats (which may be up or down several decks) in an emergency if the elevators are out of action and cannot be used?

Waivers

Passengers who do not require wheelchairs but are challenged in other ways, such as those who have impaired sight, hearing, or speech, present their own particular requirements. Many of these can be avoided if the person is accompanied by an able-bodied companion experienced in attending to their special needs. In any event, some cruise lines require physically challenged passengers to sign a waiver.

Hearing Impaired

Many people suffer from hearing loss; in fact the loss of hearing makes up the largest group of disabilities in almost any country (it affects some 28 million Americans, for example). Those affected should be aware of problems aboard ship:

● Hearing the announcements on the public address system.

● Use of the telephone.

● Poor acoustics in key areas (for example, boarding shore tenders).

Take a spare battery for your hearing aid. More new ships have cabins specially fitted with colored signs to help those who are hearing impaired. Crystal Cruises' *Crystal Harmony, Crystal Serenity* and *Crystal Symphony*, and Celebrity Cruises' *Century, Galaxy,* and *Mercury* have movie theaters that are fitted with special headsets for the hearing impaired.

Unfortunately, many ships make life difficult for the hearing impaired, with constant, irritating, and repetitive announcements. It is often difficult for the hearing impaired to distinguish important or useful announcements from those that are of little or no importance.

Finally, when going ashore, particularly on organized excursions, be aware that most destinations are simply not equipped to handle the hearing impaired. ❑

ALTERNATIVE CRUISES

The choice includes river cruises, nature expeditions, sail-cruise ships,
freighter travel, ocean crossings, and round-the-world trips

Coastal Cruises

Europe

There is year-round coastal cruising along the shores of Norway to the Land of the Midnight Sun aboard the ships of Norwegian Coastal Voyages (known locally as the Hurtig-Ruten, or "Highway 1"). The fleet consists of small, comfortable, working express coastal packet steamers and contemporary cruise vessels that deliver mail, small packaged goods, and foodstuffs, and take passengers, to the communities spread on the shoreline.

This is a 2,500-mile (4,000-km) journey from Bergen in Norway to Kirkenes, close to the Russian border (half of which is north of the Arctic Circle) and takes 12 days. You can join it at any of the 34 ports of call and stay as long as you wish (the ships sail every day of the year). In 2000, the company carried almost 300,000 passengers.

The service started in 1893 and is run by a combination of three companies. The ships can accommodate between 144 and 674 passengers. The newest ships in the fleet have an elevator that can accommodate a wheelchair passenger.

Archipelago hopping can be done along Sweden's eastern coast, too, by sailing in the daytime and staying overnight in one of the many small hotels. One vessel sails from Norrtalje, north of Stockholm, to Oskarshamn, near the Baltic island of Öland, right through the spectacular Swedish archipelago. You can also cruise from the Finnish city of Lappeenranta to the Estonian city of Viborg without a visa, thanks to perestroika. Point-to-point coastal transportation between neighboring countries, major cities, and commercial centers is big business in Northern Europe.

Scotland

The fishing town of Oban, two hours west of Glasgow by road, perhaps seems an unlikely point to start a cruise, but it is the base for one of the world's finest cruise experiences. *Hebridean Princess* is an absolute gem, with Laura Ashley-style interiors. This ship carries passengers around some of Scotland's most magnificent coastline and islands. Take lots of warm clothing, however (layers are ideal), as the weather can be somewhat unkind. As an alternative, there's *Lord of the*

Exploring Norway's fjords at close quarters.

Glens, another treat for small ship lovers, cruising in style through the lakes and canals of Scotland.

United States

In the US, coastal vessels flying the American flag offer a change of style from big oceangoing cruise ships. On these cruises, informality is the order of the day. Accommodating up to 226 passengers, the ships are more like private parties – there's no pretentiousness. Unlike large cruise ships, these small vessels are rarely out of sight of land. Their operators seek out lesser-known areas, offering in-depth visits to destinations inaccessible to larger ships, both along the eastern coast and in Alaska.

During the past few years, there has been little growth in this segment of the cruise market, although this is now changing. If you are the sort of person who prefers a small country inn to a larger resort, this type of cruise might appeal to you. The ships, each of which measures under 2,500 tons and is classified as a "D-class" vessel, are subject neither to the bureaucratic regulations nor to the union rules that sounded the death knell for large US-registered ships.

These vessels are restricted to cruising no more than 20 miles (32 km) off shore, at a comfortable 12 knots. Public room facilities are limited, and because the vessels are of American registry, there is no casino. For entertainment, passengers are usually left to their own devices. Most vessels are in port during the evening, so you can go ashore for the local nightlife. Getting ashore is extremely easy; passengers can be off in a matter of minutes, with no waiting at the gangway.

Accommodation is in outside-view cabins (some open directly onto the deck, not convenient when it rains), each with a picture window and small bathroom. The cabins are small but cozy, and closet space is very limited, so take only what you absolutely need. There's no room service, and you turn your own bed down at night. Cabins are closer to the engines and generators so noise can be considerable at night. The quietest cabins are at the bow, and most cruising is done during the day so passengers can sleep better at night. Tall passengers should note that the overall length of beds rarely exceeds 6 feet (1.82 meters) maximum.

The principal evening event is dinner in the dining room, which accommodates all passengers at once. This can be a family-style affair, with passengers at long tables, and the food passed around. The cuisine is decidedly American, with fresh local specialties featured.

These vessels usually have three or four decks, and no elevators. Stairs can be on the steep side and are not recommended for people with walking difficulties. This kind of cruise is good for those who do enjoy a family-type cruise experience in pleasant surroundings. The maxim "You just relax, we'll move the scenery" is very appropriate in this case.

A small selection of coastal and inland cruise vessels is featured in the profiles in Part Two, since they are small and specialized and have limited facilities.

River and Barge Cruises

Whether you want to cruise down the Nile, along the mighty Amazon or the lesser Orinoco, the stately Volga or the primal Sepik, the magnificent Rhine or the "blue" Danube, along the mystical Ayeyarwady (formerly the Irrawaddy) or the "yellow" Yangtze – to say nothing of the Don and the Dnieper, the Elbe, or Australia's Murray – there's a river vessel and cruise to suit you.

What sort of person enjoys cruising aboard river vessels? Well, anyone who survives well without dressing up, bingo, casinos, discos, or entertainment, and those who want a totally unstructured lifestyle. In 2002, over *1 million* people took a river/inland waterway cruise.

European River Cruising

Cruising down one of Europe's great waterways is a soothing experience – it's quite different from sailing on an open sea, where motion has to be taken into consideration (rivers are calm). These cruises provide a constant change of scenery, often passing through several countries, each with its own history and architecture, in a weeklong journey. River vessels are always close to land and provide a chance to visit cities and areas inaccessible to large ships. Indeed, watching stunning scenery slip past your floating hotel is one of the most relaxing and refreshing ways to absorb the beauty that has inspired poets and artists through the centuries. A cruise along the Danube, for example, will take you through four countries and from the Black Forest to the Black Sea.

Norwegian Coastal Express Ships

Ship	Tonnage	Built	Berths
Finnmarken	12,000	2002	675
Kong Harald	11,200	1993	490
Midnatsol	6,100	1982	322
Narvik	4,073	1982	314
Nordkapp	11,386	1996	490
Nordlys	11,200	1994	490
Nordnorge	11,386	1997	490
Polarlys	12,000	1996	490
Richard With	11,205	1993	490
Trollfjord	12,000	2002	674
Vesteralen	6,261	1983	314

Coastal Cruise Vessels (more than 10 cabins)

Ship	Cruise Line	Cabins	Region	Built
Ambassador I	Marco Polo Cruises	45	Galapagos Islands	1959
American Eagle	American Cruise Lines	27	USA Coastal Cruises	2000
American Glory	American Cruise Lines	27	USA Coastal Cruises	2002
Aranui*	Campagnie Polynesienne de Transport Maritime	25	Tahiti/Marquesas	1984
Callisto	Classical Cruises	17	Greek Isles	
Coral Princess	Coral Princess Cruises	27	Australia (Great Barrier Reef)	1988
Coral Princess II	Coral Princess Cruises	25	Australia (Great Barrier Reef)	1987
Corinthian	Ecoventura/Galapagos Network	45	Galapagos Islands	1967
Executive Explorer	Glacier Bay Cruises	25	Alaska	1986
Grande Caribe	American Canadian Caribbean Line	48	USA Coastal Cruises	1997
Grande Mariner	American Canadian Caribbean Line	50	USA Coastal Cruises	1999
Halcyon	Various operators	24	Greek Islands, Mediterranean	1990
Haumana	Bora Bora Cruises	19	Tahiti and Islands	1997
Isabela II	Metropolitan Touring	20	Galapagos Islands	1989
Lycianda	Blue Lagoon Cruises	21	Yasawa Islands (Fiji)	1984
Mare Australis	Cruceros Australis	66	Patagonia	2002
Mystique Princess	Blue Lagoon Cruises	36	Yasawa Islands (Fiji)	1996
Nantucket Clipper	Clipper Cruise Line	51	USA Coastal Cruises	1984
Nanuya Princess	Blue Lagoon Cruises	25	Yasawa Islands (Fiji)	1987
Niagara Prince	American Canadian Caribbean Line	42	USA Coastal Cruises	1994
Pegasus	Classical Cruises	23	Greek Islands, Mediterranean	1992
Reef Endeavour	Captain Cook Cruises	75	Australia (Great Barrier Reef)	1995
ReefEscape	Captain Cook Cruises	59	Australia	1987
Santa Cruz	Metropolitan Touring	43	Galapagos Islands	1979
Sea Bird	Lindblad Expeditions	35	Alaska, Baja	1981
Sea Lion	Lindblad Expeditions	35	Alaska, Baja	1982
Sea Voyager	Lindblad Expeditions	33	Central America	1982
Shearwater	Various operators	40	Worldwide	1962
Spirit of '98	Cruise West	48	Alaska	1984
Spirit of Alaska	Cruise West	39	Alaska	1980
Spirit of Columbia	Cruise West	39	Alaska	1979
Spirit of Discovery	Cruise West	25	Alaska	1982
Spirit of Endeavor	Cruise West	51	Alaska	1983
Spirit of Glacier Bay	Cruise West	43	Alaska	1971
Spirit of Oceanus	Cruise West	50	Alaska/South Pacific	1991
Sydney 2000	Captain Cook Cruises	60	Australia	1979
Temptress Explorer	Temptress Adventure Cruises	50	Central America	1970
Tropic Sun	Aquanaut Cruise Lines	18	Galapagos Islands	1967
Wilderness Adventurer	Glacier Bay Cruises	38	Alaska	1983
Wilderness Discoverer	Glacier Bay Cruises	43	Alaska	1992
Wilderness Explorer	Glacier Bay Cruises	18	Alaska	1969
Yasawa Princess	Blue Lagoon Cruises	33	Yasawa Islands (Fiji)	1984
Yorktown Clipper	Clipper Cruise Line	69	USA Coastal Cruises	1988

KEY   * = Coastal Freighter

In 1840–41, the Marquess of Londonderry, a member of the British aristocracy, traveled across Europe along the Rhine and Danube Rivers. She then wrote about these experiences, which were published in London in 1842, in a book entitled *A Steam Voyage to Constantinople*. And who could forget the romance implied by Johann Strauss's famous waltz "The Blue Danube"? The new Rhine-Main-Danube waterway, at 2,175 miles (3,500 km), is the longest waterway in Europe. It connects 14 countries, from Rotterdam on the North Sea to Sulina and Izmail on the Black Sea, and offers river travelers some of the most fascinating sights anywhere.

River vessels are long and low in the water, and their masts fold down in order to negotiate low bridges. Although small when compared to oceangoing cruise ships, they have a unique and friendly international atmosphere. The most modern of them are air-conditioned and offer the discreet luxury of a small floating hotel, with several public rooms including a dining room, observation lounge, bar, heated swimming "dip" pool (some even have a heated indoor pool), sauna, solarium, whirlpool, gymnasium, massage, hairdresser, and shop kiosk.

Although the cabins may be small, with limited closet space (take casual clothing, as informality is the order of the day), they are functional. Most have an outside view (facing the river), with a private bathroom, and will prove very comfortable for a one-week journey. Romantics should note that twin beds are the norm (they can seldom be pushed together). Many cabins in the latest vessels feature a personal safe, a mini-bar, a television, and an alarm clock/radio. The ceilings are rather low, and the beds are short.

River cruising in Europe has reached a very sophisticated level, and you can be assured of good service and meals of a consistently high European standard. Dining is a pleasant although not always a gourmet experience (the best food is that catered by Austrian and Swiss companies). While lunch is generally a buffet affair, dinners feature a set menu consisting of three or four courses.

Typical rates for river cruises are from $800 to over $3000 per person for a one-week cruise, including meals, cabin with private facilities, side trips, and airport/railway transfers. If you are already in Europe, many cruises can be purchased "cruise-only" for greater flexibility.

Tip: It is best to go for an outside-view cabin on a deck that does not have a promenade deck walkway outside it. Normally, cabins on the lowest deck have a four-berth configuration. It does not matter which side of the vessel you are on, as you will see a riverbank and scenery on both sides.

River Cruising: Russia

Perhaps the best way to get to know Russia is on a river/inland waterway cruise. Often referred to as the "Waterways of the Tsars," the country benefits from a well-developed network of rivers, lakes, and canals. Geographically, river routes for tourists are divided into three main areas: Central European Russia, Northwestern European Russia, and Asian Russia.

In the days before privatization, Rechtflot was the Russian government's management overlord, with 21 shipping companies and a combined fleet of more than 5,000 vessels, which together carried more than 20 million passengers and about 500 million tons of cargo each year. Today, there are about 80 river cruise vessels that carry international tourists.

In the Central Basin, Moscow is the hub of river tourism, and the newly opened waterways between Moscow and St. Petersburg allow a seven-day cruise link between the present and former capitals.

The best-known Russian rivers are the Don, Moskva, Neva, and Volga, but the lesser known Belaya, Dvina (and North Dvina) Irtysh, Kama, Ob (longest river in Siberia), Oka, Svir, Tura, and Vyatka connect the great system of rivers and lakes in the vast Russian hinterland.

Many Russian vessels are chartered to foreign (non-Russian) cruise wholesalers and tour packagers. The vessels do vary quite a lot in quality and facilities. Some are air-conditioned and most are clean.

One unusual Russian river vessel worth mentioning, *Rossiya*, is used for state visits and is extremely elegant and fitted throughout with exceptionally fine materials. Cruises include the services of a cruise manager and lecturers. Some companies also specialize in pre- or post-cruise "home stays" as part of a cultural package.

River Cruising: The Nile

A journey along the Nile, the world's longest (and historically the greatest) river, is a journey back in time, to over 4,000 years before the birth of Christ, when the Pharaohs thought they were immortal. Even though time proved them mistaken, the people who lived along the riverbanks formed one of the greatest civilizations the world has known. The scenery has changed little in over 2,000 years. The best way to see it, of course, is by riverboat.

In all, there are over 7,000 departures every year aboard approximately 300 Nile cruise vessels, many offering standards of comfort, food, and service that vary between very good and extremely poor. Most have a swimming pool, lounge, piano bar, and disco. A specialist lecturer in ancient Egyptian history accompanies almost

Tourist boats dominate the Nile, but there are better alternatives for cruising this historic river.

all sailings, which cruise the 140 miles between Aswân and Luxor in four or five days. Extended cruises, typically of seven or eight days, cover about 295 miles (475 km) and visit Dendera and Abydos. The longest cruises, of 10 to 12 days, cover 590 miles (950 km) and include visits to Sohâg, El Amarna, Tuna El Gabal, and Ashmuneim, ending in Cairo.

Most Nile cruises include sight-seeing excursions, which are accompanied by experienced, trained guides who may reside on board, or who may meet the boat at each call. Multilingual guides also accompany each cruise.

River Cruising: China

There are now several new river vessels featuring cruises along the Yangtze, the world's third-longest river, particularly through the area known as the Three Yangtze River Gorges, a 100-mile (160-km) stretch between Nanjin Pass in the east and White King City in the west. The Yangtze stretches 3,900 miles (6,300 km) from Shanghai through the very heartland of China. The Three Gorges include the 47-mile-long (76-km) Xiling Gorge, the 25-mile-long (40-km) Wu Gorge, and the 28-mile-long (45-km) Qutang Gorge (known locally as "Wind Box Gorge"). The Lesser Three Gorges (or Three Small Gorges) are also an impressive sight, often part of the main cruise but also reached by small vessels from Wushan. If

possible, take a cabin with a balcony. It is worth the extra money, and the view is better.

Note that standards of hygiene are generally far lower than you may be used to at home. In China, rats and rivers often go together, and rat poison may well be found under your bed.

Among the best operators are Regal China Cruises (*Elaine*, *Jeannie*, and *Sheena*, 258 passengers) and Victoria Cruises (*Victoria*, *Victoria Pearl*, and *Victoria III*, 154 passengers). All have Chinese- and western-style restaurants, a beauty salon, a small health club with sauna, and private mah-jong and karaoke rooms. Fine Asian hospitality and service prevail, and cabins are kept supplied with fresh towels and hot tea. There are several other operators, but do check on the facilities, meet-and-greet service, and the newness of the vessels before booking. The best time of the year to go is May–June, and late August–October (July and early August are extremely hot and humid).

Note that the new $60 billion hydroelectric Sanxia (Three Gorges) Dam, the world's largest (first envisioned by Sun Yat-sen in 1919), is presently under construction, essentially blocking off this major tourist attraction and creating a reservoir that will be 375 miles long (600 km), and 575 feet deep (175 meters), with an average width of 3,600 feet (1,100 meters). It is scheduled for full completion in 2009, and will submerge 13 cities, 140 towns, 1,352 villages, 657 factories and 66 million acres of cultivated land (more than 1½ million people will be relocated). Once completed, it will raise the Yangtze River 150 feet (45 meters), and cruise vessels of up to 10,000 tons will be able to sail up the Yangtze from the Pacific Ocean.

Ayeyarwady (Irrawaddy) River (Myanmar)

How about the *Road to Mandalay*? Orient Express Hotels operates a fine river cruise vessel in Myanmar (formerly known as Burma). The river vessel *Road to Mandalay* operates weekly between Mandalay and Pagan, along the Ayeyarwady (formerly Irrawaddy) River. Or there are two smaller vessels: *Pandaw*, a stern-wheeler built in Scotland in 1947, and *Pandaw II*, a slightly larger replica, introduced in 2001.

River Murray (Australia)

The fifth-largest river in the world, the Murray, was the lifeblood of the pioneers who lived on the driest continent on earth. Today, the river flows for more than 1,250 miles (2,760 km) across a third of Australia, its banks forming protected lagoons for an astonishing variety of bird and animal life. Paddlewheel boats such as *Murray Princess* offer most of the amenities found aboard America's *Mississippi Queen*. There are even six cabins for the physically disabled.

Barge Cruising: Europe

Smaller and more intimate than river vessels, and more accurately called boats, "cruise barges" ply the inland waterways and canals of Europe from spring to fall, when the weather is best. Barge

A cruise barge is a convenient way to see Europe.

cruises (usually of 3 to 13 days' duration) offer a completely informal atmosphere, and a slow pace of life, for up to a dozen passengers. They chug along slowly in the daytime, and moor early each evening, giving you time to pay a visit to a local village and get a restful night's sleep. The inland waterways of Europe all adhere to the CEVNI regulations (Code Européan des Voies de la Navigation Intérieur), a United Nations instrument with international authority and relevance.

Cruise barges tend to be beautifully fitted out with rich wood paneling, full carpeting, custom-built furniture and tastefully chosen fabrics. Each barge has a dining room/lounge-bar and is equipped with passenger comfort in mind. Each barge captain takes pride in his vessel, often acquiring some rare memorabilia to be incorporated into the decor.

Locally grown fresh foods are usually purchased and prepared each day, allowing you to live well and feel like a houseguest. Most cruise barges can also be chartered exclusively so you can just take your family and friends, for example.

The waterways of France especially offer beauty, tranquility, and a diversity of interests, and barge cruising is an excellent way of exploring an area not previously visited. Most cruises include a visit to a famous vineyard and wine cellar, as well as side trips to places of historic, architectural, or scenic interests. Shopping opportunities are limited, and evening entertainment is always impromptu. You will be accompanied by a crew member familiar with the surrounding country-side. You can even go hot-air ballooning over the local countryside and land to a welcome glass of champagne and your flight certificate. Although

The *American Queen* steamboat on the Mississippi.

ballooning is an expensive extra, the experience of floating over such pastoral landscapes is something to treasure.

How you dine on board a barge will depend on the barge and area; dining ranges from home-style cooking to outstanding nouvelle cuisine, with all the trimmings. Often, the barge's owner, or spouse, turns out to be the cook, and you can be assured that the ingredients are all very fresh.

Barging on the canals often means going through a constant succession of locks. Nowhere is this more enjoyable and entertaining than in the Burgundy region of France where, between Dijon and Mâcon, for example, a barge can negotiate as many as 54 locks during a six-day cruise. Interestingly, all lockkeepers in France are women.

Rates typically range from $600 to more than $3,000 per person for a six-day cruise. I do not recommend taking children. Rates include a cabin with private facilities, all meals, good wine with lunch and dinner, other beverages, use of bicycles, side trips, and airport/railway transfers. Some operators also provide a hotel the night before or after the cruise. Clothing, by the way, is totally casual at all times – but, at the beginning and end of the season, take sweaters and rain gear.

Steamboating: United States

The most famous of all river cruises in the United States are those aboard the steamboats of the mighty Mississippi River. Mark Twain, an outspoken fan of Mississippi cruising, at one time said: "When man can go 700 miles an hour, he'll want to go seven again."

The grand traditions of the steamboat era are maintained by the *American Queen*, and by the older, smaller *Delta Queen* and *Mississippi Queen* (Delta Queen Steamboat Company), all of which are powered by steam engines that drive huge wooden paddlewheels at the stern.

The smallest and oldest of the three boats, the 174-passenger *Delta Queen*, was built on Scotland's Clydeside in 1926, and was placed on the US National Register of Historic Places in 1989. She gained attention when President Carter spent a week aboard her in 1979.

Half a century younger, the $27-million, 400-passenger *Mississippi Queen* was constructed in Jefferson, Indiana, where nearly 5,000 steamboats were built during the 19th century. *Mississippi Queen* was designed by James Gardner of London (creator of Cunard's *QE2*).

Traveling aboard one of the steamboats makes you feel you've stepped into the past. There's a certain charm and old-world graciousness as well as delightful woods, brass, and flowing staircases. And once a year, boats challenge one another in the Great Steamboat Race, a 10-day extravaganza.

Steamboat cruises last from 2 to 12 days, and during the year there are several theme cruises, with big bands and lively entertainment. The steamboats cruise up and down the Mississippi and Ohio rivers. The food is "Americana" fare, which means steak, and shrimp, Creole sauces, fried foods, and few fresh vegetables. ❑

● For more detailed information and examples of river vessels, see the companion volume to this book, the *Berlitz Guide to River Cruising* (published spring 2003).

Expedition/Nature Cruises

With so many opportunities to cruise in Alaska and in the Baltic, Caribbean, Mediterranean, and Mexican Riviera areas, you may be surprised to discover that a small but growing group of enthusiasts is heading out for strange and remote waters. But there are countless virtually untouched areas to be visited by the more adventurous, whose motto might be "see it before it is spoiled." Such passengers tend to be more self-reliant and more interested in doing or learning than in being entertained.

Passengers become "participants" and take an active role in almost every aspect of the voyage, which is destination-, exploration-, and nature-intensive. Naturalists, historians, and lecturers (rather than entertainers) are aboard each ship to provide background information and observations about wildlife. Each participant receives a personal logbook, illustrated and written by the wildlife artists and writers who accompany each cruise. The logbook documents the entire voyage and serves as a great source of information as well as a complete mémoire of your cruise. Adventure cruise companies provide expedition parka and waterproof boots, but you will need to take waterproof trousers (for Antarctica and the Arctic).

You can walk on pack ice in the Arctic Circle, explore a gigantic penguin rookery on an island in the Antarctic Peninsula, the Falkland Islands or South Georgia, or search for "lost" peoples in Melanesia. Or you can cruise close to the source of the Amazon, gaze at species of flora and fauna in the Galapagos Islands (Darwin's laboratory), or watch a genuine dragon on the island of Komodo (from a comfortable distance, of course).

Briefings and lectures bring cultural and intel-

An expedition cruise party comes ashore in Antarctica.

lectual elements to expedition cruise vessels. There is no formal entertainment as such; passengers enjoy this type of cruise more for the camaraderie and learning experience, and being close to nature in the extreme. The ships are designed and equipped to sail in ice-laden waters, and yet they have a shallow enough draft to glide over coral reefs.

Expedition cruise vessels can, nevertheless, provide comfortable and even elegant surroundings for up to 200 passengers, and offer first-class food and service. Without traditional cruise ports at which to stop, a ship must be self-sufficient, capable of long-range cruising, and totally environmentally friendly.

Expedition cruising came about as a result of people wanting to find out more about this remarkable planet of ours, its incredible animal, bird, and marine life. Lars-Eric Lindblad pioneered the activity in the late 1960s. A Swedish American, he was determined to turn travel into adventure by opening up parts of the world tourists had not visited.

After chartering several vessels for cruises to Antarctica (which he started in 1966), he organized the design and construction of a ship that was capable of going almost anywhere in comfort and safety.

In 1969, *Lindblad Explorer* was launched. The ship earned an enviable reputation in adventure travel. Lindblad sold it to Salen-Lindblad Cruising in 1982. They subsequently resold it to Society

Passenger Ships through the Northwest Passage

1984 *Lindblad Explorer* (Capt. Hasse Nilsson)

1985 *World Discoverer* (Capt. Heinz Aye)

1988 *Society Explorer* (Capt. Heinz Aye)

1991 *Frontier Spirit* Ship returned at Flaxman Island – trip cancelled (Capt. Heinz Aye)

1992 *Frontier Spirit* (Capt. Hainz Aye)

1994 *Kapitan Khlebnikov*

1995 *Hanseatic* (Capt. Hartwig von Harling)

1995 *Kapitan Khlebnikov* (Capt. Hartwig von Harling

1996 *Hanseatic* Grounded Simpson Street for 10 days – passengers taken aboard *Kapitan Dranitsyn* (Capt. Hartwig von Harling)

1997 *Hanseatic* (Capt. Heinz Aye)

1998 *Kapitan Khlebnikov*

1998 *Hanseatic* (Capt. Heinz Aye)

Expeditions, which renamed it *Society Explorer* (the ship is presently operated by Abercrombie & Kent as *Explorer*).

Specialist adventure and expedition cruise companies provide in-depth expertise and specially constructed vessels, usually with ice-hardened hulls that are capable of going into the vast reaches of the Arctic and Antarctica.

Expedition/Nature Cruise Areas

Buddha was once asked to express verbally what life meant to him. He waited a moment – then, without speaking, held up a single rose. Several "destinations" on our planet cannot be adequately described by words. They have instead to be experienced, just as a single rose.

The principal adventure cruise areas of the world are Alaska and the Aleutians, the Amazon and the Orinoco, Antarctica, Australasia and the Great Barrier Reef, the Chilean fjords, the Galapagos Archipelago, Indonesia, Melanesia, the Northwest Passage, Polynesia, and the South Pacific. Baja California and the Sea of Cortez, Greenland, the Red Sea, East Africa, the Réunion Islands and the Seychelles, West Africa and the Ivory Coast, and the South China Seas and China Coast are other adventure cruise destinations growing in popularity.

To put together cruise expeditions, companies turn to knowledgeable sources and advisors. Scientific institutions are consulted; experienced world explorers and naturalists provide up-to-date reports on wildlife sightings, migrations, and other natural phenomena. Although some days are scheduled for relaxation or preparing for the days ahead, participants are kept physically and mentally active. Speaking of physical activity, it is unwise to consider such an adventure cruise if you are not completely ambulatory.

Antarctica

It's the ultimate place to chill-out, and perhaps the most intriguing destination on earth. It was first sighted only in 1820 by the American sealer Nathaniel Palmer, British naval officer Edward Bransfield, and Russian captain Fabian Bellingshausen. For most, it is just a wind-swept frozen wasteland (it has been calculated that the ice mass contains almost 90 percent of the snow and ice in the world). For others, however, it represents the last pristine place on earth, empty of people, commerce, and pollution, yet offering awesome icescape scenery and a truly wonderful abundance of marine and bird life. There are no germs and not a single tree.

More than 12,000 people visited the continent – the only smoke-free continent on earth – in 2001, yet the first human to come here did so within a generation of man landing on the moon. There is not a single permanent inhabitant of the continent, whose ice is as much as 2 miles thick. Its total land mass equals more than all the rivers and lakes on earth and exceeds that of China and India combined. Icebergs can easily be the size of Belgium. The continent has a raw beauty and an ever-changing landscape, but do take sunscreen, as there is no pollution and it is easy to get sunburned when the weather is good.

Once part of the ancient land mass known as Gondwanaland (which also included Africa, South

---

DID YOU KNOW?

● that passengers once asked the operations director of a well-known expedition cruise ship where the best shops were in Antarctica? His reply: "On board, madam!"

● that Quark Expeditions had the good fortune of making maritime history in July/August 1991, when its chartered Russian icebreaker, *Sovetskiy Soyuz*, made a spectacular 21-day voyage to negotiate a passage from Murmansk, Russia, to Nome, Alaska, across the North Pole? The ship followed the trail that had been set in 1909 by Admiral Peary, who crossed the North Pole with 56 Eskimos, leaving by sled from Ellesmere Island. Although the polar ice cap had been navigated by the US nuclear submarines *Skate* and *Nautilus*, as well as by dirigible and airplane, this was the first passenger ship to make the hazardous crossing (planning for it took over two years).

● that in 1984, Salen Lindblad Cruising made maritime history by successfully negotiating a westbound voyage through the Northwest Passage, a 41-day epic that started from St. John's, Newfoundland, in Canada, and ended at Yokohama, Japan? The expedition cruise had taken two years of planning and was sold out just days after it was announced. The search for a Northwest Passage to the Orient attracted brave explorers for more than four centuries. Despite numerous attempts and loss of life, including Henry Hudson in 1610, a "white passage" to the East remained an elusive dream. Amundsen's 47-ton ship *Gjoa* eventually navigated the route in 1906, taking three years to do so. It was not until 1943 that a Canadian ship, *St. Roch*, became the first vessel in history to make the passage in a single season. *Lindblad Explorer* became the 34th vessel, and the first cruise vessel, to complete the Northwest Passage.

● that the most expensive expedition cruise excursion was a cruise/dive to visit the resting place of RMS *Titanic* aboard the two deep-ocean submersibles *Mir I* and *Mir II* used in James Cameron's Hollywood blockbuster. Just 60 participants went as up-close-and-personal observers in 1998, and another 60 were taken in 1999.

The *Bremen* in Lamaire Channel, Antarctic Peninsula.

America, India, Australasia, and Madagascar), it is, perhaps, the closest thing on earth to another planet, and it has an incredibly fragile ecosystem that needs international protection.

Although visited by "soft" expedition cruise ships and even "normal"-sized cruise ships with ice-hardened hulls, the more remote "far side" – the Oates and Scott Coasts, McMurdo Sound, and the famous Ross Ice Shelf – can be visited only by real icebreakers such as *Kapitan Dranitsyn*, *Kapitan Khlebnikov*, and *Yamal* (they carry 100 passengers or fewer), as the winds can easily reach more than 100 mph (160 km/h).

There are no docks in Antarctica, so venturing "ashore" is done by Zodiacs – rubber inflatable craft, an integral part of the Antarctica experience. Be aware that you *can* get stuck even aboard these specialized expedition ships, as did *Clipper Adventurer* in February 2000, in an ice field – it had to be rescued by an Argentine Navy icebreaker.

Note to photographers: take plastic bags to cover your camera, so that condensation forms inside the bag and not on your camera when changing from the cold of the outside Antarctic air to the warmth of your expedition cruise vessel. Make sure you know how to operate your camera with gloves on (taking them off even for a short time could induce frostbite in poor weather conditions).

The Arctic

Want some Northern Exposure? Try the Arctic. The Arctic is an ocean surrounded by continents, whereas Antarctica is an ice-covered continent surrounded by ocean. The Arctic Circle is located at 66 degrees, 33 minutes, and 3 seconds north, although this really designates where 24-hour days and nights begin. The Arctic is best defined as that region north of which no trees grow, and where water is the primary feature of the landscape. It is technically a desert (receiving less than 10 inches of rainfall a year) but actually teems with wildlife. It has short, cool summers; long, cold winters; and frequent high winds. Canada's Northwest Territories, which cover 1.3 million square miles, is part of the Arctic region. Photographers should note the practical advice given for Antarctica.

Galápagos

A word of advice about the Galápagos Islands: do not even think about taking a cruise with a "non-Ecuadorian flag" ship; the Ecuadorians jealously guard their islands and prohibit the movement of almost all non-Ecuadorian-registered cruise vessels within its boundaries. The best way to see this place that Darwin loved is to fly to Quito and cruise aboard an Ecuadorian-registered vessel.

The government of Ecuador set aside most of the islands as a wildlife sanctuary in 1934, while uninhabited areas were declared national parks in 1959. The national park includes approximately 97 per cent of the islands' landmass, together with 20,000 sq. miles (50,000 sq. km) of ocean. The Charles Darwin Research Station was established in 1964, and the government created the Galápagos Marine Resources Reserve in 1986.

Note that the Galápagos National Park tax is presently about $100 per person. Smoking is prohibited on the islands of the Galápagos, and visitors are limited to 50,000 a year.

Greenland

The world's largest island, Greenland, in the Northern Hemisphere's Arctic Circle, is technically a desert 82 percent covered with ice (actually compressed snow) up to 11,000 feet thick. Greenland's rocks are among the world's oldest (the 3.8 billion-year-old Isukasia formations), and its ecosystem is one of the newest.

Forget Alaska, the glacier at Jacobshavn (also known as Ilulissat) is the fastest moving in the world and creates a new iceberg every five minutes. Greenland is said to have more dogs than people, and these provide the principal means of transport for the Greenlanders.

The Environment

Since the increase in environmental awareness, adventurers have banded together to protect the environment from further damage. In the future, only those ships that are capable of meeting new "zero discharge" standards, such as those introduced in the Arctic by the Canadian Coast Guard, will be allowed to proceed through environmentally sensitive areas.

Expedition cruise companies are very concerned about the environment (none more than Hapag-Lloyd Cruises and Quark Expeditions), and they spend much time and money in educating both crews and passengers about safe environmental procedures.

An "Antarctic Traveler's Code" has been created, the rules of which are enforced by all expedition cruise companies, based on the Antarctic Conservation Act of 1978 to protect and preserve the ecosystem, flora, and fauna of the Antarctic continent, as well as Recommendation XVIII-1, adopted at the Antarctic Treaty Meeting, Kyoto, 1994. Briefly, the Act makes it unlawful, unless authorized by regulation or permit issued under the Act, to take native animals or birds, to collect any special native plant or introduce species, to enter certain special areas (SPAs), or to discharge or dispose of any pollutants. To "take" means to remove, harass, molest, harm, pursue, hunt, shoot, kill, trap, capture, restrain, or tag any native mammal or bird, or to attempt to do so.

Under the Act, violators are subject to civil penalties, including a fine of up to $10,000 and one year imprisonment for each violation. The Act is found in the library of each adventure/expedition ship that visits the continent.

Will large cruise ships ever cruise in Antarctica? Not in the foreseeable future. Ships are limited to a maximum of 400 passengers, so the likelihood of a mega-ship zooming in on the penguins with 2,000-plus passengers is unlikely (nor would it be possible to rescue passengers and crew in the event of an emergency).

The Companies

Abercrombie & Kent
This well-known company operates the older, basic, but still highly suitable *Explorer* (the former *Society Explorer*).

Clipper Cruise Lines
This company operates *Clipper Adventurer*, a small ship with a hull that is ice-hardened.

Hapag-Lloyd Cruises
This company operates *Bremen* and *Hanseatic*, small, high-tech expedition cruise vessels. Both ships have fine, rather luxurious appointments (*Bremen* is less luxurious than *Hanseatic*) and are marketed to both English- and German-speaking passengers.

Lindblad Expeditions
This company operates *Polaris*, a small expedition vessel operating in the Galápagos Islands, which features comfortable appointments and creature comforts (see listings section for details). In addition, two small vessels, *Sea Bird* and *Sea Lion* (former Exploration Cruise Lines vessels) operate "soft" coastal cruises in protected coastal areas in the United States, including Alaska.

Quark Expeditions
Quark Expeditions charters Russian-owned nuclear- or diesel-powered icebreakers fitted with some outstanding amenities and decent creature comforts for up to 100 passengers. The operator, a pioneer in this specialized segment of the cruise industry, concentrates on itineraries to the Antarctic, the Arctic, and North Polar regions. Among the vessels chartered are the superb *Kapitan Dranitsyn, Kapitan Khlebnikov, Professor Molchanov, Professor Multanovskiy,* and *Yamal.*

Society Expeditions
After losing one ship (*World Discoverer*) in the Solomon Islands in 1999, Society Expeditions, which has had a checkered history, has re-emerged with another ship of the same name, *World Discoverer*, to operate expedition-style cruises.

Sail-powered Cruise "Yachts"

Thinking of a cruise but really want to sail, to be free as the wind? Have you been cruising on a conventional large cruise ship that is more like an endurance test? Whatever happened to the *romance* of sailing? Think no more, for the answer, to quote a movie title, is "back to the future."

Think about cruising under sail, with towering masts, the creak of taut ropes and washing-powder-white sails to power you along? There is simply nothing that beats the thrill of being aboard a

The *Wind Spirit*, one of three identical vessels.

multi-mast tall ship, sailing under thousands of square feet of canvas through waters that mariners have sailed for centuries.

This is cruising in the traditional manner, aboard authentic sailing ships, contemporary copies of clipper ships, or aboard the latest high-tech cruise-sail ships. Even the most jaded passengers will, I am convinced, enjoy the exhilaration of being under sail.

There are no rigid schedules, and life aboard equates to an unstructured lifestyle, apart from meal times. Weather conditions may often dictate whether a scheduled port visit will be made or not, but passengers sailing on these vessels are usually unconcerned with being ashore anywhere. They would rather savor the thrill of being one with nature, albeit in a comfortable, civilized setting, and without having to do the work themselves.

Real Tall Ships

While we have all been dreaming of adventure, a pocketful of designers and yachtsmen committed pen to paper, hand in pocket and rigging to mast, and came up with a potpourri of stunning vessels to delight the eye and refresh the spirit.

Look in the listings section for these true, working tall ships: *Royal Clipper*, *Sea Cloud*, *Sea Cloud II*, *Star Clipper*, and *Star Flyer*. Of these, *Sea Cloud* has a history that spans over 70 years – a true veteran working sailing ship that still is at the height of luxury under sail.

In the Caribbean, Windjammer Barefoot Cruises also operates a fleet of five tall ships offering very basic fun-and-sun cruises: *Flying Cloud*, *Legacy*, *Mandalay*, *Polynesia*, and *Yankee Clipper*. Only shorts and T-shirts are needed. Although cabin towels are provided, you'll need to take your own beach towels. Only one vessel is certified by the US Coast Guard, the others are not, although they do comply with most international safety regulations.

Contemporary Sail-Cruise Ships

To combine sailing with push-button automation, try *Club Med 2* (Club Méditerranée) or *Wind Surf* (Windstar Cruises) – with five tall aluminum masts, they are the world's largest sail-cruise ships – and *Wind Song*, *Wind Spirit*, and *Wind Star* (Windstar Cruises), with four masts. Not a hand touches the sails; they are computer controlled from the navigation bridge. These ships are contemporary oceangoing robots. There's little sense of sailing as the computer controls keep the ship on a steady, even keel.

From a yachtsman's viewpoint, the sail-to-power ratio is poor. That's why these cruise ships with sails have engine power to get them into and out of port. (The Star Clipper ships, by contrast, do it by sail alone, except when there is no wind, which is infrequent.). You should be aware that on some itineraries, when there is little wind, you could well be under motor power for most of the cruise, with only a few hours spent under sail. The four Windstar Cruises' vessels and one Club Med ship are typically under sail for about 40 percent of the time.

It was a Norwegian living in New York, Karl Andren, who first turned the concept of a cruise vessel with sails into reality. "Boyhood dream stuff," he said. The shipyard (Société Nouvelle des Ateliers et Chantiers du Havre – or ACH, as it is known locally), enjoyed the challenge of building these most unusual vessels.

The shipyard had much experience in the design and construction of cable-laying ships using the hydraulic power of servomechanisms. This was a concept that was adopted for the Windstar's automatic computer-controlled sail rig. Gilbert Fournier, the shipyard president and an expert computer programmer, became fascinated with the project. Three ships (a fourth was planned but never built) were delivered to Windstar Cruises. These ships carry mainly North American passengers, whereas the Club Med vessel caters primarily to French-speaking passengers.

Another slightly smaller but very chic vessel is the sleek *Le Ponant*. This three-mast ship caters to just 64 French-speaking passengers in elegant, yet casual, high-tech surroundings, developing the original Windstar concept to an advanced state of contemporary technology.

Freighter Travel

More than 3,000 passengers presently travel by freighter each year, and the number is growing as passengers become further disenchanted with the large resort ships that form a major part of the cruise industry today. Traveling by freighter is also the ultimate way to travel for those seeking a totally unstructured voyage without entertainment or other diversions.

There are about 250 cargo ships (freighters and container vessels) offering berths, with German operators now accounting for about more than half of the ships. True freighters – the general break-bulk carrier ships and feeder container vessels, carry up to 12 passengers. Freighter schedules change constantly, depending on the whim of the owner and the cargo to be carried, whereas container ships travel on regular schedules. For the sake of simplicity, they are all termed freighters.

Today's freighters have changed dramatically over the past few years, as cost management and efficiency have become the most relevant factors for successful ship operators. Container ships today are operated as the passenger' liners used to be – running line voyages on set schedules, or name-day voyages, as they are presently termed.

Passengers opting for this type of travel typically include independent types (anyone allergic to traveling in groups), retirees, relocating executives, people with family connections in other countries, graduates returning home from an overseas educational establishment, or professors on sabbatical. Because there are no medical facilities, maximum age limits are imposed by most freighter companies and anyone over the age of 65 must produce a medical certificate of good health.

What do you get when you book a freighter voyage? You get a cabin with double or twin beds, a small writing table, and a private bathroom. You also get good company, cocktails with conversation, hearty food (you'll eat in one seating with the ship's officers), an interesting voyage, a lot of water, and the allure of days at sea. What don't you get? Entertainment, bingo, horse racing, and other mindless parlor games (unless you take them with you). You will certainly have time to relax and unwind completely, read books (some freighters have a small library), or play card games, or board games with the few other passengers that will be on board.

The accommodation aboard today's freighters will typically consist of a spacious and well-equipped outside-view cabin high above the water line, with a large window rather than a porthole, comfortable lounge/sitting area, and private facilities – generally far larger than most standard cruise ship cabins.

While freighter travel can be less expensive than regular cruise ship travel on a per day basis ($75–$150), remember that freighter voyages are of much longer duration. A typical voyage lasts about 30 days or more, so the cost of a voyage can actually add up to a considerable amount. Most voyages are sold out far in advance (often more than a year ahead), so do plan ahead, and remember to purchase trip cancellation insurance.

What to take with you? Casual clothing (do check with the freighter line concerned, as some require you to dress properly for dinner – that means jacket and tie), all medication, cosmetics, and personal toiletry items, hair dryer, multi-voltage converter plug, washing powder, and other sundry items. There may be a small "shop" on board (for the crew) but only the bare essentials like toothpaste will be available. Remember to take some extra photos of yourself in case the ship makes unannounced port stops and visas are required. The only gratuities you will need to give are for the waiter and cabin steward, at about $1–$2 per day, per person.

FREIGHTERS THAT TAKE PASSENGERS

The following lines offer regular passenger voyages year-round:
American President Lines, Australia New Zealand Direct Lines, Bank Line, Blue Star Line, Canada Maritime, Chilean Lines, Cho Yang Shipping, Columbus Line, Egon Oldendorff, Great Lakes Shipping, Hamburg-Sud, Hanseatic Shipping Company, Hapag-Lloyd, Ivaran Lines, Lykes Brothers Steamship Company, Mediterranean Shipping Company, Nauru Pacific Line, Safmarine Cruises, and United Baltic Corporation.

FREIGHTER BOOKINGS, INFORMATION

Traveltips Cruise & Freighter Association
P.O. Box 580188, Flushing, NY 11358, USA
Freighter World Cruises
180 South Lake Avenue, Suite 335, Pasadena,
CA 91101, USA
The Cruise People
88 York Street, London W1H 1DP, England
Strand Voyages
Charing Cross Shopping Concourse, Strand, London
WC2N 4HZ, England
Sydney International Travel Centre
75 King Street, Level 8, Sydney 2000, Australia

Note that freighters can, and do, sometimes cancel port calls due to various reasons. So, if it's the itinerary, or a certain port that attracts you, be aware that it doesn't always go according to plan. In other words, if you can't accept last minute changes or disappointment, don't consider freighter cruising.

Crossings

By "crossings," I mean crossings 3,000 miles (4,800 km) or so that constitute the North Atlantic, although crossings might also include any other major stretch of water, such as the Pacific or the Indian Ocean.

The North Atlantic

Crossing the North Atlantic by ship is an adventure, when time seems to be totally suspended. It really is the most delicious way of enjoying life aboard ship. It actually takes little more than a long weekend. After the embarkation procedures have been completed, you will be shown to the gangway. Cross the gangway from pier to ship and you are in another world. It is a world that provides a complete antidote to the pressures of contemporary life ashore, and it allows you to practice the fine art of doing nothing, if you so wish. After the exhilaration of a North Atlantic crossing, the anticipation of landfall among passengers throughout any ship is nothing short of electric.

Hemmed in by the polar ice caps, the Atlantic Ocean divides Europe and Africa from the Americas. It is three times the size of North America and contains the world's longest mountain range, which extends (undersea) over 7,000 miles (11,000 km) and rises over 6,000 feet (1,800 meters) above the ocean floor. The only points of this ridge that rise to the surface are at St. Helena (Ascension), St. Paul's Rocks (the Azores), and Tristan da Cunha. The ocean's average width is 2,500 miles (4,000 km).

Although half the size of the Pacific Ocean, the Atlantic Ocean receives more than half of the water drainage of the world (four times that of the Pacific Ocean). Its average depth is 18,900 feet (5,800 meters) and its greatest depth, which is known as the Milwaukee Depth, goes down beyond 30,240 feet (9,217 meters).

Crossing the North Atlantic by passenger vessel should really be considered an art form. I have done it myself 149 times and always enjoy it immensely. I consider crossings as rests in musical parlance, for both are described as "passages." Indeed, musicians do often "hear" rests in between notes. So if ports of call are the musical notes of a voyage, then the rests are the days at sea – a temporary interlude, when the indulgence of the person and psyche are of paramount importance.

Experienced mariners will tell you that a ship only behaves like a ship when it is doing a crossing, for that's what a real ship is built for. Yet the days when ships were built specifically for crossings are almost gone. The only ship offering a regularly scheduled transatlantic service (a "crossing") is Cunard's *Queen Elizabeth 2*, a 70,327-grt ship, built with an incredibly thick hull, designed to hold well against the worst weather the North Atlantic has to offer. Indeed, captains work harder on an Atlantic crossing than on regular cruising schedules.

The most unpredictable weather in the world, together with fog off the Grand Banks of Newfoundland, can mean that the captain will spend torturous hours on the bridge, with little time for socializing. When it is foggy, the crew of *QE2* are often pestered by passengers wanting to know if the ship has yet approached latitude 41°46' north, longitude 50°14' west – where White Star Line's *Titanic* (43,326-tons) struck an Arctic iceberg on that fateful April night in 1912.

There is something magical in "doing a crossing." It takes you back to the days when hordes of passengers turned up at the piers of the ports of New York, Southampton, Cherbourg, or Hamburg, accompanied by chauffeurs and steamer trunks, jewels and finery, ablaze in a show of what they thought was best in life. Movie stars of the 1920s, '30s, and '40s often traveled abroad on the largest liners of the day, to arrive refreshed and ready to dazzle European fans.

Excitement and anticipation precede a crossing. First there is the hubbub and bustle of check-in, then the crossing of the threshold on the gangway before being welcomed into the calmness aboard, and finally escorted to one's accommodation for the next several days. Once the umbilical cord of the gangway is severed, bow and stern mooring lines are cast off, and with three long blasts on the ship's deep whistle, the *QE2* is pried gently from its berth. The ship sails silently down the waterway, away from the world, as serene as a Rolls-Royce, as sure as the Bank of England. Passengers on deck often observe numerous motorboats trying to keep up with the giant liner as it edges down the Hudson River, past Battery Park City, the Statue of Liberty, the restored Ellis Island, then out toward the Verrazano-Narrows Bridge, and out to the open sea.

Coming westbound, arriving in New York by ship is one of the world's thrilling travel experiences. Following a six-day crossing aboard the *QE2*, where five of the days are 25 hours long (but only 23 hours long on an eastbound crossing), everything else is an anticlimax.

QE2 can also accommodate up to 12 cars a crossing, just in case you really do not want to be parted from your wheels. It also provides kennels, so you can even take your pet, although when crossing eastbound to Southampton, they may have to be quarantined for up to six months. The *QE2* is a distillation of more than 150 years of transatlantic traditions and an oasis of creature comforts offered by no other ship.

QE2 is still special – greater part liner, smaller part cruise ship – a legend in its own lifetime, and the only ship featuring regularly scheduled crossings throughout the year. Vast amounts of money have been spent on refurbishment over time.

During the ship's initial planning stages, naval architect Dan Wallace and director of engineering Tom Kameen were responsible for its design – for a high-speed, twin-screw ship capable of carrying out safely a six-day transatlantic crossing. Cunard's chairman, Sir Basil Smallpiece, invited James Gardner and Dennis Lennon, well-known industrial designers, as general design coordinators. Gardner concentrated on exterior aesthetics, while Lennon, in addition to designing the restaurant interiors – the basic shape of which had already been determined by structural and operational requirements – was also concerned with the introduction of a design signature that would be immediately apparent throughout the ship; for example, in the staircases and corridors. The aim was that the interior design of the *QE2* would emphasize the "classless" ship concept.

January 2004 sees the introduction of a larger running mate to *QE2* when *Queen Mary 2*

Queen Elizabeth 2 sails along the Mersey into Liverpool.

(dubbed *QM2*) takes to the North Atlantic. This new ship, at 150,000 tons the world's largest passenger ship, is destined to knock your socks off. *Queen Mary 2* will also feature regularly scheduled transatlantic crossings throughout the year.

Apart from the *QE2*'s regular crossings, a number of cruise ships feature transatlantic crossings. Although they are little more than repositioning cruises – a way of moving ships that cruise the Mediterranean in summer to the Caribbean in winter, and vice versa – they offer more chances to experience the romance and adventure of a crossing, usually in the spring and in the fall. These are particularly good for those wanting uninterrupted days at sea and plenty of leisure time.

Most cruise ships operating repositioning crossings actually cross the Atlantic using the "sunny southern route" – typically departing from southern ports such as Ft. Lauderdale, San Juan, or Barbados, and ending the journey in Lisbon, Genoa, or Copenhagen via the Azores or the Canary Islands off the coast of northern Africa. In this way, they avoid the more difficult weather often encountered in the North Atlantic. The crossings take longer, however: between eight and 12 days.

World Cruises and Segments

The ultimate classic voyage for any experienced traveler is a round-the-world cruise. This is defined as the *complete* circumnavigation of the earth in a continuous one-way voyage. The ports of call are carefully planned for their interest and

diversity, and the entire voyage can last as long as six months.

Ships that sail from cold to warm climates – typically during January, February, and March, when the weather in the southern hemisphere is at its best – give you the experience of crisp, clear days, sparkling nights, delicious food, tasteful entertainment, superb accommodation, delightful company, and unforgettable memories. It is for some the cultural, social, and travel experience of a lifetime, and for the few who can afford it, an annual event. Note that most passengers who regularly sail on the around-the-world voyages take them in a westbound direction, thus gaining time instead of losing it (one hour for each degree that the ship crosses).

The concept of the world sea cruise first became popular in the 1920s, although it has existed since the 1880s (although the first actual around-the-world voyage was made by Ferdinand Magellan in 1519). A world cruise aboard a modern ship means experiencing stabilized, air-conditioned comfort in luxury cabins, and extraordinary sight-seeing and excursions on shore and overland. In some ships, every passenger will get to dine with the captain at least once.

A world cruise gives you the opportunity to indulge yourself, while being hermetically sealed against outside unpleasantness (except when you go ashore). Although at first the idea may sound totally extravagant, it need not be, and fares can be as low as $100 a day to more than $3,000 a day. Alternately, you can book just a segment of the cruise if that fits your pocket and interest. There is a difference in what you get for your money, however. For example, aboard ships rated at four stars

Early-morning exercise on *Universe Explorer*.

Cruise ships in Biscayne Bay, Miami.

or more, shuttle buses from your ship to the center of town (or attraction) will probably be included; this is not so aboard ships rated three stars or less.

Traditionally, ships operating around-the-world cruises do so in a *westbound* direction, gaining one hour each time the ship passes through a time zone. However, some ships occasionally make their around-the-world cruises in an *eastbound* direction, so those days get progressively shorter by one hour each time you go through a time zone (at some point you'll get back the one whole day you lost). Needless to say, most passengers prefer the *westbound* direction.

Special Features

Some of the special events planned for a world cruise will typically include:
- Celebrity entertainers
- World-renowned lecturers
- Themed formal balls and parties
- Equator crossing ceremony
- International dateline crossing ceremony
- Overnight and multi-day overland excursions
- Personalized stationery

Planning and Preparation

Few enterprises can match the complexity of planning and preparing for a world cruise. For example, more than 675,000 main meals will be prepared in the galleys during a typical *QE2* world cruise. Several hundred professional entertainers, lecturers, bands, and musicians must all be booked about a year in advance of the voyage. In addition, crew changeovers during the cruise must be organized. A ship the size of the *QE2* requires two major crew changes during the three-month-long voyage.

Because a modern world cruise ship has to be totally self-contained, a warehouse-full of spare parts (electrical, plumbing, and engineering supplies, for example) must be planned for, ordered,

DID YOU KNOW?

- that the first regular steamship service across the North Atlantic was inaugurated on March 28, 1838, when the 703-ton steamer *Sirius* left London for New York via Cork, Ireland?
- that the winter of 1970–71 was the first time since 1838 that there was no regular passenger service on the North Atlantic?
- that the first scheduled transatlantic advertisement appeared in the *New York Evening Post* on October 27, 1817, for the 424-ton sailing packet *James Monroe* to sail from New York to Liverpool on January 5, 1818, and for *Couvier* to sail from Liverpool to New York on January 1?
- that the following are just some of the personalities that have crossed in the *QE2*? Carl Sagan, Joan Fontaine, Larry Hagman, Ben Lyon, Joan Rivers, Elaine Stritch, and Arthur Schlesinger, Jr., Rod Stewart?
- that the *QE2* is still the fastest passenger ship in service?
- that since the ship's maiden voyage in 1969, the *QE2* has traveled more than 4 million nautical miles, and carried almost 2 million passengers?
- that Cunard Line held the record from 1940 to 1996 for the largest passenger ship ever built (RMS *Queen Elizabeth*)?

loaded, and stored somewhere aboard ship prior to sailing. For just about every shipboard department, the same basic consideration will apply: once at sea, it will be impossible to pick up a replacement projector bulb, air-conditioning belt, table tennis ball, saxophone reed, or anything else that the ship might run out of.

The cruise director will have his/her hands full planning entertainment and social events for a long voyage. It is not like the "old days" when an occasional game of bingo, horse racing, or the daily tote would satisfy passengers.

A cruise line must give advance notice of the date and time that pilots will be needed, together with requirements for tugs, docking services, customs and immigration authorities, or meetings with local dignitaries and the press. Then there is the organization of dockside labor and stevedoring services at each port of call, plus planning and contracting of bus or transportation services for shore excursions. Other preparations include reserving fuel at various ports on the itinerary.

World Cruise Segments

Cruises to exotic destinations – China, the Orient, the South Pacific, around Africa, the Indian Ocean, and around South America – offer all the delights associated with a world cruise. The cruise can be shorter and hence less expensive, yet offer the same elegance and comfort, splendid food, delightful ambience, and interesting, well-traveled fellow passengers.

An exotic voyage can be a totally self-contained cruise to a specific destination, lasting anywhere from 30 days to more than 200 days (*Europa*'s 2003 world cruise lasts for an astonishing 239 days). Or you can book a segment of a world cruise to begin at one of its ports of call, getting off at another port. "Segmenting" is ideal for those who wish to be a part of a world cruise but have neither the time nor the money for the prolonged extravagance of a three- to six-month vacation.

Segment cruising involves flying either to or from your cruise (or both). You can travel to join your exotic cruise at one of the principal ports such as Genoa, Rio de Janeiro, Acapulco, Honolulu, Sydney, Hong Kong, Singapore, Bangkok, Colombo, Mumbai (Bombay), Mombasa, or Athens, depending on the ship and the itinerary.

Ships that roam worldwide during the year offer the most experienced world cruises or segments. Most of these world cruise ships operate at about 75 percent capacity, thus providing considerably more space for passengers than they would normally have.

Going P.O.S.H.

This colloquialism for "grand" or "first-rate" has its origin in the days of ocean steamship travel between England and India. Wealthy passengers would, at considerable cost, book round-trip passage as "Port Outward, Starboard Home." They would thus secure a cabin on the cooler side of the ship while crossing the unbearably hot Indian Ocean under the sun. Abbreviated as P.O.S.H., the expression soon came to be applied to first-class passengers who could afford that luxury. (*Brewers*

Around the World Cruises 2003–4

Ship	Company	Days	Date	From (Start)
Albatros	Phoenix Seereisen	130	December 21, 2002	Genoa
Amsterdam	Holland America Line	108	January 4, 2003	Ft. Lauderdale
Astor	Transocean Tours	153	December 22, 2002	Nice
Asuka	NYK Cruises	103	March 11, 2003	Yokohama
Aurora	P&O Cruises	91	January 6, 2003	Southampton
Crystal Symphony	Crystal Cruises	104	January 19, 2003	Ft. Lauderdale
Delphin	Delphin Seereisen	136	December 12, 2002	Genoa
Deutschland	Peter Deilmann Cruises	136	December 18, 2002	Las Palmas
Europa	Hapag-Lloyd Cruises	239	November 25, 2002	Malta
Maxim Gorkiy	Phoenix Seereisen	139	December 21, 2002	Bremerhaven
Nippon Maru	Mitsui OSK Passenger Line	103	April 4, 2003	Tokyo
Oriana	P&O Cruises	92	January 8, 2003	Southampton
Pacific Venus	Venus Cruise	100	March 21, 2003	Yokohama
Queen Elizabeth 2	Cunard Line	107	January 5, 2003	Southampton
Saga Rose	Saga Cruises	104	January 5, 2003	Southampton
Seven Seas Mariner	Radisson Seven Seas Cruises	108	January 21, 2003	Los Angeles

* Not including ports of embarkation and disembarkation

WORLD CRUISES ◆ 99

Dining in style on *Seabourn Pride*.

Dictionary of Phrase and Fable, Cassell Ltd).

However, the reality is that the monsoon winds that blow in and out of the Asian area shift between winter and summer, so that the sheltered side of a ship would change according to the season. Further, in looking at deck plans of ships of the period, most cabins were located *centrally*, with indoor promenades or corridors along each side, so the actual definition of the origin of P.O.S.H. could be said to be taken as artistic license.

Around the World Cruises 2003–4

This table below includes ships that are presently scheduled to operate an around-the-world cruise in 2003–4. The number of ships operating around-the-world cruises is down slightly from the previous year – one of the predictable after-effects of the ship redeployment that took place after the terrorist attacks on New York and Washingtdon D.C. on September 11, 2001.

Note that the number of ports visited varies from a low of 26 (NYK Cruises' *Asuka*) to a high of 125 (Hapag-Lloyd Cruises' *Europa*). ❑

Date (Finish)	To	Direction	Number of Ports *
April 30, 2003	Genoa	Westbound	62
April 22, 2003	Ft. Lauderdale	Westbound	42
23 May, 2003	Bremerhaven	Eastbound	76
June 22, 2003	Kobe	Westbound	26
April 8, 2003	Southampton	Westbound	28
May 3, 2003	Los Angeles	Westbound	37
26 May, 2003	Nice	Westbound	56
May 4, 2003	Venice	Westbound	59
July 21, 2003	Hamburg	Westbound	125
May 9, 2003	Bremerhaven	Westbound	70
July 15, 2003	Kobe	Westbound	27
April 9, 2003	Southampton	Eastbound	28
June 29, 2003	Kobe	Westbound	32
April 17, 2003	New York	Westbound	33
April 19, 2003	Southampton	Westbound	30
May 9, 2003	Ft. Lauderdale	Eastbound	44

DID YOU KNOW?

● that the Dollar Steamship Line featured a round-the-world cruise that started October 15, 1910, from New York, aboard the ss *Cleveland*? The cruise was advertised as "one-class, no overcrowding" voyage. The cost was "$650 and up," according to an advertisement placed by the Frank Clark Travel Agency, of the Times Building in New York.

● that a round-the-world cruise was made in 1922–23 by Cunard's *Laconia* (19,680 grt), a three-class ship that sailed from New York? The itinerary included many of the ports of call that are still popular with world cruise travelers today. The vessel accommodated 350 persons in each of its first two classes, and 1,500 in third class, giving a total capacity of 2,200 passengers, more than many ships of today.

Choosing the Right Cruise

WHAT'S NEW FOR 2003

Look out for more internet cafés, health spas,

entertaining architecture – and self-correcting pool tables

The cruise industry is still buoyant, and the introduction of new ships continues at a steady pace. More than 30 new ships are scheduled for delivery between January 2003 and December 2005, at a cost of about $12 billion, fueled by the continuing increase in demand for high-value cruise vacations.

New ships incorporate the latest in sophisticated high-tech electronic navigation and safety equipment, recent advances in propulsion technology and the best in advanced ship design and construction, offering passengers an unprecedented number of options, choice of facilities, and dining and entertainment experiences.

The world's largest ever cruise ship is scheduled to debut in early 2004: *Queen Mary 2*, measuring a whopping 150,000 tons. The largest ships at present are the Royal Caribbean International's *Adventure of the Seas*, *Explorer of the Seas* and *Voyager of the Seas*, introduced in 2001, 2000, and 1999, respectively – all measuring approximately 137,300 tons); these ships are floating leisure playgrounds aimed at the standard cruise marketplace. Is bigger better? That's up to the individual, but it can be rather like being in a large shopping mall environment as opposed to a smaller boutique environment, or "all-exclusive" versus "all-inclusive" cruising.

Propulsion

The latest ships are now powered by gas turbines, or by diesel-electric or diesel-mechanical propulsion systems that propel them at speeds of up to 28 knots (only Cunard Line's *QE2*, with a top speed of more than 30 knots, is faster).

A new technology is now incorporated into propulsion design, the "pod" system. Briefly, pods, which resemble huge outboard motors, replace internal electric propulsion motors, shaft lines, rudders and their machinery, and are compact, self-contained units that typically weigh about 170 tons each. Pod units *pull*, rather than *push*, a ship through the water. When going ahead, pod units face with the propeller forward (ships can go astern either by rotating the pods 180 degrees or by reversing the thrust). A vessel's turning circle diameter is reduced considerably, and vibration at the ship's stern is virtually eliminated.

LEFT: planning the next cruise.

New ships will incorporate everything that is seen to be environmentally friendly, such as "enviro-engines" that provide power without visible smoke, "enviro-laundries," – maybe even "enviro-entertainment"! How about recruiting some "enviro-passengers?"

Exteriors

The indented, cascading after-decks of ships such as *Aurora*, *Oriana*, *Norwegian Star*, *SuperStar Leo* and *SuperStar Virgo* are both stunning and practical – overlooking aft pool areas. Other cruise ships take the "block" approach and fill in stern areas with cabins that have an aft-facing view (*Carnival Destiny*, *Carnival Triumph*, *Carnival Victory*, for example), or multilevel dining rooms with huge expanses of glass windows (*Century*, *Constellation*, *Galaxy*, *Infinity*, *Mercury*, *Millennium*, and *Summit*, for example), or other public rooms and facilities.

The most instantly recognizable exteriors are those of *AIDAcara* and *AIDAvita*, with huge bold red lips and brown eyes adorning their prows. Yet other ships now have huge slogans painted on their white sides (Royal Caribbean international's slogan "Like No Vacation On Earth" for example).

Some ships are downright ugly, no matter how you look at them (examples: *Infinity*, *Millennium*, *Summit*), and display designers gone mad with trying to create a "yacht-like" exterior – to a ship of 90,000 tons.

Interiors

Both "retro" and "contemporary" are "in," as interior designers try to create luxurious, welcoming interiors reminiscent of Europe's grand hotels.

Large ships have interiors that include such things as multi-deck-high atriums, large theaters complete with revolving stages, hydraulic orchestra pits, huge scenery stowage spaces, internet cafes, computer learning centers, and in-cabin interactive television – not to mention billiard (pool) tables that self-correct aboard a moving ship. Some ships have two atrium lobbies instead of one (*Carnival Destiny*, *Carnival Triumph*, *Carnival Victory*, *Galaxy*, and *Mercury*), while the industry's largest trio: *Adventure of the Seas*, *Explorer of the Seas* and *Voyager of the Seas* feature a large *horizontal*, rather than a *vertical* atrium, rather reminiscent of a city shopping walkway, and extremely popular (particularly among North Americans).

As for contemporary, among the most stunning, bold, and graphic interiors are those that are found in the ships of Carnival Cruise Lines. Somehow, lilac neon, fiber optics, mosaics, and multicolored carpeting go together here although they never would in *any* setting other than a Las Vegas hotel. It is all a feast for the eyes and mind (entertainment architecture, as the interior designer calls it), but for many (especially for European passengers) it could be sensory overload (but a good advertisement for the fiber optic and lighting industries).

Ships have become instant floating art museums (some are better than others), with collections of artwork costing several million dollars per ship. For example: $12 million (*Voyager of the Seas*); $6 million (*Vision of the Seas)*; $4 million (*Enchantment of the Seas*); $3.8 million (*Century)*; $3 million (*Galaxy*); $2.5 million (*Sun Princess*); $2 million (*Veendam*); $1 million (*AIDAcara, Inspiration*). However, it is not the money spent that's important; it is the fact that artwork now forms a more important integral part of the physical interior decor than ever before, and particularly so with large ships, with ever larger wall spaces to cover.

Computer-Driven Cruising

Can you send and/or receive emails when aboard your cruise ship? Yes, you can, at least aboard some ships – but at a price. As an example, Crystal Cruises imposes a set-up charge of $5, plus $3 for each page of email messages. Many ships have now introduced internet cafés, where you can "do" coffee and email – typically at a cost of $0.75 to $1 per minute.

Most cruise lines have web sites on the internet *(see listing at the end of the book)*. Computers link almost all departments and functions aboard the latest ships, and (somewhat inflexible) interactive television systems let you order wine, arrange shore excursions, play casino games, go shopping, and order pay-per-view movies, all from the comfort of your cabin.

Computers cannot yet pour you a drink, although you can order one, accompanied by a light snack. But, order a croissant with your breakfast and the "point and select" system won't bother to ask whether you'd like it warm or cold. Oh, well, that's technology for you; as long as you are a "standard" photofit passenger, it'll work for you. Otherwise, call room service (sort of defeats the purpose, doesn't it?).

Spas: The Ultimate Pampership

Health and fitness spas are among the hottest passenger (revenue) facilities in the latest cruise ships, with more space than ever devoted to them. The basic sauna, steam room, and massage facility has evolved into huge, specially designed spas that include the latest in high-tech muscle exercising, aerobic and weight-training machines, and relaxation treatments, such as: hydrotherapy and thalassotherapy baths, jet blitz, rasul (graduated steam and all-over body mud cleansing), seaweed wraps, and hot and cold stone massage.

Ships with large spas locate them on the uppermost decks of the latest ships, and feature large floor-to-ceiling ocean-view windows. Treatment rooms (some will have integral showers) are flexible and can be adapted to incorporate the latest trends, gimmicks, and themes.

Traditional Japanese and Indonesian design elements have been included, with rock gardens, running water, shoji screens and hot tea help to create a serene environment in the spas aboard several ships. Among the ships with such designs and features: *Century, Constellation, Galaxy, Mercury, Millennium, Star Princess,* and *Summit*. There are large coed saunas (holding as many as 30-persons), with large glass walls and exterior views (*AIDAcara, AIDAvita*).

For Smokers

Cigar smoking is quite in vogue, and special cigar bars and lounges have been created aboard several ships, including: *Adventure of the Seas, Century, Constellation, Crystal Harmony, Crystal Serenity, Crystal Symphony, Europa, Explorer of the Seas, Galaxy, Horizon, Infinity, Mercury, Millennium, Mistral, Norwegian Dawn, Norwegian Sky, Norwegian Star, Norwegian Sun, Seven Seas Mariner, SuperStar Virgo, Summit, Voyager of the Seas,* and *Zenith.* The nicest are aboard *Europa, Infinity, Millennium* and *Summit*.

For Nonsmokers

Carnival Cruise Lines' *Paradise* is the first and only cruise ship to be totally nonsmoking (even the shipyard workers who built the ship were not allowed to smoke – officially). Think you can smoke anyway? Forget it – there's a fine if you do (crew and other passengers can detect cigarette smoke within five miles). You will be fined $250 *and* asked to leave at the next port (at *your* expense). Meanwhile, nonsmokers will be pleased to know that many ships now feature totally nonsmoking dining rooms and show lounges.

Dining and Service

What's really in vogue are what are termed "*alternative*" restaurants – particularly aboard the new large ships. These are typically à la carte restaurants where you *must* make a reservation, and pay for the

The *Royal Clipper* under full sail.

privilege of dining in small, intimate places with the best in food and service.

Some ships, such as *Norwegian Dawn, Norwegian Star, SuperStar Leo* and *SuperStar Virgo* feature as many as 10 different restaurants and eateries, some of which incur an extra charge – just like going out ashore.

Several ships now pay homage to past transatlantic liners of the past in the décor of their dining rooms or alternative restaurants; examples include the Normandie Restaurant aboard *Carnival Pride*, the Ocean Liners Restaurant aboard *Constellation*, the Olympic Restaurant aboard *Millennium*, the United States Restaurant aboard *Infinity*, and the Normandie Restaurant aboard *Summit*. Many ships now charge extra for better dining experiences.

Many new ships now feature flexible dining and 24-hour casual eateries, so you can eat (or snack) when you want. Although the concept is good, the delivery often is not (it is typically self-service eating, and not the *dining* experience most passengers envisage).

Also hot (in culinary-speak) is the fact that several cruise lines have aligned themselves with well-known chefs and brand names ashore in order to provide an "authenticity" to their product, and to produce even more of a "wow" effect, at least in terms of marketing.

Examples include Crystal Cruises (Wolfgang Puck); Cunard Line (Daniel Boulud); Radisson Seven Seas Cruises (Le Cordon Bleu); Seabourn Cruise Lines (Charlie Palmer); Silversea Cruises (Relais & Châteaux).

Two-deck-high dining rooms are back in vogue: *Amsterdam, Century, Carnival Legend, Carnival Pride, Carnival Spirit, Costa Atlantica, Dawn Princess, Galaxy, Legend of the Seas, Infinity, Maasdam, Mercury, Millennium, Nordic Empress, Rotterdam, Ryndam, Splendour of the Seas, Statendam, Summit, Sun Princess, Veendam* and *Volendam* have them. Not to be outdone, *Adventurer of the Seas, Explorer of the* Seas and *Voyager of the Seas* (and two others on order) have dining halls that are three decks high.

What's Not So Hot in 2003

● The large floating resorts that travel by night and are in port during the day provide little connection to nature and the sea, the ship being the destination (small town takes to water). Almost everything is designed to keep you *inside* the ship – to spend money, thus increasing onboard revenue and shareholder dividends.

● Entertainment – either production shows or

cabaret acts – it's all so much the same no matter what ship you are aboard. It's time for more creative thinking.

● Aggressive, young, so-called "cruise directors" who insist on interposing themselves into every part of your cruise, day and night. Public address systems are *consistently* overused by these bouncy youngsters, and are too loud, and too intrusive, which hardly makes for a restful cruise. Some of these cruise directors may make excellent cheerleaders, but seem unable to communicate with anyone over the age of 25.

● Homogenous accommodation. As identically sized standard cabins are the same shape and layout (good for incentive planners, but not for individual passengers), they also tend to be the same colors: eggshell white, off-white, or computer-colored beige. Although such colors are welcome after days in the sun, they quickly become tedious on voyages over long stretches of water. Only bold bedspreads or the occasional color prints that adorn a spare wall bring relief. Plain ceilings are also boring. Close to useless are wall-mounted hairdryers (which have poor directed pressure) in modular bathrooms; they should, instead, be located in the vanity desk or dressing area.

● Calling passengers "guests" is becoming widespread. It is confusing, however, and nautically incorrect (a guest in one's house doesn't pay). Further, the word "guest" cannot be translated into some languages. Passengers *pay* to be aboard ship. Ships are different from hotels, and should remain so. They provide a nautical experience and move through water; passengers have cabins and suites, and decks, not floors. However, several cruise lines prefer to think they think they are in the hotel business – but that's because hoteliers, ex-airline people, and accountants run them, not shipping people.

● The use of "hotel-speak" is further invading the industry. Royal Caribbean International, for example, now calls its in-cabin refrigerators "Automatic Refreshment Centers."

● Two things that have almost disappeared: streamers and free champagne, formerly provided at bon voyage parties on deck on sailing day (exception: world cruises and Japanese-registered cruise ships). Instead, waiters hustle you to buy a "bon voyage" cocktail, or some "Bahamaramamaslammer" in a plastic or polystyrene sports cup. The little goodies, such as travel bags, and extensive personal amenity kits, have been taken away by the bean counters of many of the world's cruise lines, believing that passengers won't notice. Believe me, they *do*.

● As for food, you should note that ships that feature 7-day cruises repeat menu cycles each week. If, for example, you take two, back-to-back 7-day

Eastern and Western Caribbean cruises, the menu will probably be repeated for the second week (so will the whole entertainment program and the cruise director's spiel, jokes, and activities).

Cruise ship food and service standards have suffered more lately due to deep discounting. Ships carrying over 1,000 passengers cannot seem to deliver what is portrayed in the cruise brochures consistently. Also, because of the acute shortage of waiters who speak good English (the majority of passengers being North American), many cruise lines have had to train personnel from Caribbean basin, Central American countries and eastern Europe; their command of the English language is often less than adequate.

One thing that *should* go pier-side is the amateurish, intrusive "Baked Alaska Parade." Popular with first-time passengers, it is old hat for many. It's time the cruise lines were more creative. The industry should also find a better way to sing "Happy Birthday" than the present waiter-induced chant that usually sounds like a funeral dirge.

● In the seven-day cruise market (particularly from US ports) disembarkation is still an untidy and hostile process. Passengers are unceremoniously dumped ashore, with little help after the trying procedures of locating their luggage and going through customs inspection. Poor representation once they get to their respective airports for check-in may be an added ordeal. Of particular concern is the fact that the same procedure applies to all passengers, whether they are in the finest penthouse suite or the smallest interior (no-view) cabin. The final impression of these seven-day cruises, therefore, is poor. The worst disembarkation ports: Ft. Lauderdale, Los Angeles, Miami, and San Juan.

Environmental Concerns

Cruise ships refine oil, treat human waste, and incinerate garbage, but that's not enough today, as pressure continues to mount for clean oceans. Engine emissions are now subject to the provisions of Marpol Annexe VI.

Cruise ships and their operating companies also have a unique position among all shipping interests. They are not likely to damage the ocean environment as compared with oil tankers, although spillage of any kind is regrettable.

Other environmental concerns involve the condition of the air aboard ships. Of particular note is the fact that a ship's air-conditioning system can provide an ideal site for mold growth such as that found in the aerospora group (including *Cladosporium sp.*). Thus it is vital that cruise lines not skimp on maintenance, and the replacement of filters and other items in air-conditioning systems is very important. ❏

MAKING THE RIGHT CHOICES

There are ships and cruises to suit every taste, but the variety can be bewildering.

We help you find your way through the hyperbole of the brochures

Despite constant cruise company claims that theirs has been named the "Best Cruise Line" or "Best Cruise Ship," *there really is no such thing* – only what's good, and right, for you. Most ship owners want to be a "luxury" cruise operator, and most passengers want to sail aboard one of the top-rated "luxury" ships. But *few* operators can really deliver a five-star ship, product, and crew.

What a Cruise Is

A cruise is a vacation. It offers you a chance to relax and unwind in comfortable surroundings, with attentive service, good food, and a ship that changes the scenery for you. It is a virtually hassle-free and crime-free vacation. You never have to make blind choices. Everything's close at hand, and there are always polite people to help you.

What a Cruise Is Not

Some cruises simply aren't relaxing despite cruise brochures proclaiming that "you can do as much or as little as you want to." For example, large ships that carry 3,000 or more passengers tend to cram lots of passengers into small cabins and provide nonstop activities that do little but insult the intelligence and assault the wallet.

Price is, of course, the key factor for most people. The cost of a cruise provides a useful guideline to a ship's ambience, type of passengers, and degree of luxury, food, and service.

The amount you are prepared to spend will determine the size, location, and style of shipboard accommodation you get. Be wary of cruise lines that offer huge discounts – it either means that the product was unrealistically priced at source or that there'll be a reduction in quality somewhere. Ships are as individual as fingerprints: each can change its "personality" from cruise to cruise, depending on the character of passengers (and crew).

Passengers encompass all types of personalities and lifestyles, from affluent, reserved, and mature to active, athletic, fun-loving, and youthful, or family-oriented, or conservation-minded, or adventurous, or wild fun seekers. They may be well traveled, or honeymooners on their first cruise, or veteran passengers who cruise several times a year.

How Long?

The standard of luxury, comfort, and service is generally in direct proportion to the length of the cruise. To operate long, low-density voyages, cruise lines must charge high rates to cover the extensive preparations, high food and transportation costs, port operations, fuel, and other expenditures. The length of cruise you choose will depend on the time and money at your disposal and the degree of comfort you are seeking.

The popular standard length of a cruise is seven days, although cruises can vary from two-day party cruises to a slow exotic voyage around the world of up to 180 days. If you are new to cruising and want to "get your feet wet," try a short cruise first.

Which Ship?

There's something to suit virtually all tastes, so it is important to take into account your own personality and vacation requirements when selecting a ship.

Ships are measured (not weighed) in gross tons (gt) and come in three principal size categories:
Small Ships: for up to 500 passengers (typically measure 2,000–25,000 tons)
Mid-Size Ships: for 500–1,000 passengers (typically measure 25,000–50,000 tons)
Large Ships: for over 1,000 passengers (typically measure 50,000–150,000 tons)

Whatever the physical dimensions, all cruise ships provide the same basic ingredients: accommodation, activities, entertainment, plenty of food, good service, and ports of call, although some do it much better than others (and charge more).

Space

To get an idea of the amount of the space around you, look at the Passenger Space Ratio given for each ship in the listings section (tonnage divided by number of passengers).
Passenger Space Ratio:
50 and above – the ultimate
30 to 50 – very spacious
20 to 30 – reasonably spacious
10 to 20 – moderate to high density
10 or below – extremely cramped

Small Ships (up to 500 Passengers)

Choose a small ship for an intimate cruise experience and a small number of passengers. Some of the most exclusive cruise ships in the world belong in this group (but so do most of the coastal vessels with basic, unpretentious amenities, sail-cruise ships, and the expedition-style cruise vessels that take passengers to see nature).

Choose this size ship if you do not need much entertainment, large ship facilities, gambling casinos, several restaurants, and if you don't like to wait in lines for anything. If you want to swim in the late evening, or have champagne in the Jacuzzi at midnight, it is easier aboard small ships than aboard larger ships, where more rigid programs lead to inflexible, passenger-unfriendly thinking.

Small Ships: Advantages
● More like small inns than mega-resorts.
● Easy to find your way around, and signage is usually clear and concise.
● At their best in warm weather areas.
● Capable of true culinary excellence, with fresh foods cooked individually to order.
● Most provide an "open seating" in the dining room; this means that you can sit with whomever you wish, whenever you wish, for all meals.
● Provide a totally unstructured lifestyle, offering a level of service not found aboard most of the larger ships, and no or almost no announcements.
● Provide an "open bridge" policy, allowing passengers to go to the navigational bridge at almost any time (except during difficult maneuvers and in cases of difficult weather conditions).
● Some small ships have a hydraulic marina water sports platform located at the stern and carry equipment such as jet skis, windsurfers, a water ski powerboat, and scuba and snorkeling gear.
● Go to the more off-beat ports of call that larger ships can't get into.
● When the ship is at anchor, going ashore is easy and speedy, with a continuous tender service.

Small Ships: Disadvantages
● Do not have the bulk, length, or beam to sail well in open seas in inclement weather conditions.
● Do not have the range of public rooms or open spaces that large ships can provide. Options for entertainment, therefore, are limited.

Mid-Size Ships (500–1,000 Passengers)
Choose a mid-size ship if you want to be among up to 1,000 passengers. They are well suited to the smaller ports of the Aegean and Mediterranean, and are more maneuverable than larger ships. Several of these ships operate around-the-world cruises and other long-distance cruising itineraries to exotic destinations not really feasible aboard many of the ships in the small or large ship categories.

There is a big difference in the amount of space available. Accommodation varies from large "penthouse suites" complete with butler service to tiny interior (no-view) cabins.

These ships will generally be more stable at sea than "small ships", due to their increased size and draft. They provide more facilities, more enter-tainment, and more dining options. There is some entertainment, and more structured activities than aboard small ships, but less than aboard large ships.

Mid-Size Ships: Advantages
● They are neither too large, nor too small; their size and facilities often strike a happy balance.
● It is an easy matter to find one's way around.
● They generally sail well in areas of inclement weather, being neither high-sided like the large ships, nor of too shallow draft like some of the small ships.
● Lines seldom form (except for ships that are approaching 1,000 passengers), but if they do, they are likely to be short.
● They appear more like traditional ships than most of the larger vessels, which tend to be more "boxy" in shape and profile.

Mid-Size Ships: Disadvantages
● They do not offer as wide a range of public rooms and facilities as do large ships.
● Few have large show lounges for large-scale production shows; hence entertainment tends to be more of the cabaret variety.

Large Ships (1,000–4,000 Passengers)
Choose a large ship if you enjoy being with lots of other people, in a big-city environment, you enjoy being sociable, and like to experience plenty of entertainment and dining (no, make that *eating*) options. Large ships provide a well packaged standard or premium cruise vacation experience, usually in a seven-day cruise. Aboard large cruise ships, it is the interaction between passengers and crew that determines the quality of the experience.

Large ships have extensive facilities and programs for families with children of all ages. But if you meet someone on the first day and want to meet them again, make sure you appoint a place and time, or you may not see them again (apart from the size of the ship, they may be at a different meal seating). These ships have a highly structured array of activities and passenger participation events each day, together with large entertainment venues, and the most lavish production shows at sea.

It is in the standard of service, entertainment, lecture programs, level of communication, and finesse in dining services that really can move these ships into high rating categories, but they must be exceptional to do so. Choose higher-priced suite accommodation and the service improves.

Large ships are run on a highly programmed basis. It is difficult, for example, to go swimming in the late evening, or after dinner (decks are cleaned and pools are often netted over by 6pm – too early). Having champagne delivered to outdoor hot tubs late at night is virtually impossible. Large ships

Ships like *Voyager of the Seas* have a big-city feel.

have lost the flexibility for which cruise ships were once known, and have become victims of company "policy" legislation and insurance regulations. There can be a feeling of "conveyor-belt" cruising.

Large Ships: Advantages
● Have the widest range of public rooms and facilities, often a wraparound promenade deck outdoors, and more space (but more passengers).
● Generally better flexibility in dining options.
● The newest ships have state-of-the-art electronic interactive entertainment facilities (good if you like computers and high-tech gadgetry).
● Generally sail well in open seas in inclement weather conditions.
● There are more facilities and activities for people of all ages, particularly for families with children.

Large Ships: Disadvantages
● Trying to find your way around the ship can prove frustrating.
● Lines to wait in: for embarkation, the purser's office (information desk), elevators, informal buffet meals, fast food grills, shore tenders, shore excursions, immigration, and disembarkation.
● They resemble floating hotels (but with constant announcements), and so many items cost extra. They are like retail parks surrounded by cabins.
● Signage is often confusing; there will be a lack of elevators at peak times.
● The larger the ship, the more impersonal the service (unless you have "butler" service in a penthouse suite).

● You will probably have to use a sign-up sheet to use gymnasium equipment such as treadmills or exercise bicycles.
● There are too many announcements (they could be in several languages).
● Dining room staff is so programmed to provide speedy service, it is almost impossible to sit and dine in leisurely fashion.
● Food may well be rather bland (cooking for 2,000 is not quite the same as cooking for a little dinner party of 20).
● Telephoning room service can be frustrating, particularly in those ships with automatic telephone answering systems that state "your call will be answered by room service personnel in the order it was received."
● Room service breakfast is not generally available on the day of disembarkation.
● In early evening, some take the deck chairs away, or strap them up so they can't be used.
● The in-cabin music aboard the latest ships is supplied through the television set, and it may be impossible to turn off the picture (so much for quiet, romantic late-night music, and darkened cabins).
● When the ship is at anchor (few ports can accept large ships alongside their docking facilities), you will need to stand in line, or wait in a lounge, for a "tender ticket" – then wait until your ticket number is called – to go ashore by ship-to-shore craft. This can take an hour or more. Getting back on board could take some time, too, and you could be standing out in the hot sun for a long time.
● Some large ships have only two main passenger staircases. In an emergency, the evacuation of more than 2,000 passengers could prove difficult. ❏

THE BIG 8 CRUISE LINES

Is big necessarily beautiful? We compare what the world's

top cruise companies have to offer when it comes to cuisine and service

All eight offer one thing: a well-packaged cruise (generally of seven days) that includes interesting itineraries, plenty of food, reasonable service, and a good selection of entertainment and large-scale production shows, most of which lean heavily on the use of technical effects and great lighting. The ships also provide large casinos, shopping malls, and extensive spa and fitness facilities. Most ask you to pay port taxes, insurance, gratuities to staff over and above the cruise fare, and for many additional items.

The lines differ in the facilities, space, food, and service featured, together with subtle differences in the delivery of the cruise product. Here are some of the positive and negative differences among the Big Eight cruise lines. Note that changes, upgrading and downgrading of products and services, may have occurred since this book was completed.

Carnival Cruise Lines

This is the world's largest and most successful single cruise line. It specializes in cruises for the young at heart, with constant upbeat music, and passenger participation games typically found in a jolly, adult summer camp atmosphere. While some might appear almost degrading, they are nevertheless well liked by passengers who associate such activities with "fun" – the line's theme. All the ships have incredibly imaginative multicolored, upbeat décor (each ship has its own décor theme).

Carnival *does not* try to sell itself as a "luxury" or "upscale" cruise line and consistently delivers *exactly* what its brochures say, for which there is a huge, growing first-time cruise audience. However, the company provides a well-packaged cruise vacation, with smart new ships that have the latest high-tech entertainment facilities and features, and extra-cost alternative dining spots. Shore excursions are booked via in-cabin ("Fun Vision") television systems.

With almost identical large ships, the company does a fine job of providing almost nonstop activities. If you don't mind drinks in plastic glasses (on deck and in casual Lido dining spots) and basic hamburger/hot dog and fast foods in abundance, this line provides them almost round-the-clock (pizzas *are* available 24 hours a day). The company provides excellent "dazzle and sizzle" production shows and a lot of nighttime entertainment options for party people, as well as some excellent children's programming (ideal for young families).

Carnival features "Total Choice" dining aboard most of its ships – where you choose one of four seating times for dinner: 5.45pm. 6.30pm; 8pm or 8.45pm (exceptions: *Carnival Legend, Carnival Pride, Carnival Spirit*, which feature two seatings). Although the menu choice looks good, the cuisine delivered is quite unmemorable. But, if you like pizzas, the largest ships in the fleet serve an average of 800 pizzas per day. All ships also have a serve-yourself casual Lido Buffet – for breakfast, lunch *and* dinner – so you don't need to dress to go to the formal dining room(s).

The cabins throughout the fleet are a decent size. Carnival will help you have fun all the way, but do not expect the finesse or small details you might find with some of the lesser-known lines. Major sources of passenger complaints include hospitality at embarkation and disembarkation (particularly the shore-side staff), and the large number of security staff aboard ship (these comments are also true of Royal Caribbean International).

This is lively, action-filled cruising, with constant music everywhere – in all bars and lounges, throughout all public spaces, accommodation hallways, open decks (including pool decks), and even elevators. In fact, there's no escape from noise pollution (volume equals ambiance is the equation the company has successfully worked to for years).

Carnival has grown dramatically over the past few years and has improved its product substantially. In 1996, it introduced a "Vacation Guarantee" program (the first of its kind in the industry) to great success – particularly for first-time passengers who don't know whether they will enjoy cruising (few passengers ever consider leaving the cruise); the program has been extended.

Celebrity Cruises

In the 1990s (its formative years), Celebrity Cruises established an outstanding reputation for its cuisine, particularly in the dining rooms, with its formal presentation and service. All meals *are* made from scratch, and no pre-packaged, boxed, or pre-prepared items are used at all – which is an admirable achievement, and different from all others in the Big Eight group. The sauces accompanying the main dishes, in particular, are excellent. Thus, there is a good degree of *taste* that is often lacking aboard the larger ships of today. The waiters (many from Eastern European countries) are well trained and it is generally easy to communi-

Carnival Victory cruises out of its Miami base.

cate with them. There are several tables for two in the dining room, although dining room chairs would be more comfortable if they had armrests.

Another reason this line provides a high-quality cruise experience is the fact that each ship simply has much more staff than other ships of comparable size and capacity. This is noticeable in the housekeeping and food and beverage departments, which provide a superior product. The artwork in the latest ships in the fleet is also stunning, and comprises what is probably the most remarkable collection of contemporary art in the cruise industry today.

Two ships in its present eight-ship fleet (*Horizon* and *Zenith*) have complete wraparound teak promenade decks (*Century, Constellation, Galaxy, Infinity, Mercury, Millennium* and *Summit* do not). The ships are always spotlessly clean, being vacuumed and polished around the clock. There are more cleaners and service personnel aboard Celebrity Cruises' ships (per passenger) than in any of the other Big Eight cruise lines. In fact, there are more crew members per passenger than aboard any of the others in the Big Eight cruise lines. It is the line's commitment to providing a superior product that fully justifies the additional expenditure on all the details and staff necessary.

At present, the high standards established by Celebrity Cruises are to be continued under new owner Royal Caribbean International. At present, the standard of food and its delivery remain the best of any of the Big Eight cruise lines, although standards, sadly, do appear to be dropping.

Costa Cruises

This company specializes in cruises for Europeans (or passengers with European tastes), and particularly Italians (during the summer European season). The ships have a definite European "feel" to them, in their decor and manner of product delivery, which is very laid-back.

The food is really standard hotel banquet fare, disappointing and unmemorable, as is the service, which displays little or no finesse (it is hard to find an Italian waiter anywhere – something the company was once known for). The company does, however, present good Italian pasta dishes, which are always popular, and, on formal nights, dining by candlelight. But there are no wine waiters. The self-serve buffets are particularly poor – arguably the worst of all the Big Eight.

The cabins tend to be on the mean side in size, but the décor is fresh and upbeat, and the bathrooms are very practical units (some ships have sliding doors), an excellent alternative to those that open inward, taking space from the bathroom).

This is lively, action-filled, noisy cruising, with music everywhere – in almost all bars and lounges, all public spaces, accommodation hallways, and the open decks (including the pool deck).

What is good is the variety of public rooms, lounges, and bars, many of which provide fairly intimate spaces, and the more European atmosphere.

The entertainment and shows are geared toward the international clientele. Costa Cruises is the only company to have a chapel aboard each of its ships, with Roman Catholic Mass featured daily.

Carnival Corporation, parent company of Costa Cruises, purchased part of the company in 1997 and the rest in 2000.

Holland America Line

This line, whose new ships get larger and larger, features teakwood outdoors promenade decks fleet-wide, whereas most rivals have artificial grass or some other form of indoor-outdoor carpeting. The ships are very clean and well maintained.

The food is adequate, though not memorable, the result of food quality, presentation, and service having become very standardized in recent years. The ingredients are mostly from pre-packaged goods, and, although the menu variety looks reasonable, the taste, on the whole, is dull. Dining room service is too fast but provided by friendly, smiling Indonesian and Filipino waiters whose communication skills leave much to be desired. The company does, however, offer free cappuccino and espresso coffees, and free ice cream during certain hours of the day, as well as hot hors d'oeuvres in all bars – something other major lines seem to have dropped, or charge extra for.

When it comes to buffets, the line uses more canned fruits (liked by older passengers because they are soft) than do, say, Celebrity Cruises or Princess Cruises, but about the same amount as can be found aboard the ships of Costa Cruises or Norwegian Cruise Line.

The company's claim to "five-star" ships in its brochures is erroneous and misleading. The ships are extremely pleasant and have an elegant "feel" to them, with some fine, somewhat eclectic artwork from the Dutch East and West Indies. What is excellent is the fact that social dancing is always on the menu. This is something that older passengers, in particular, enjoy. However, communication with many of the smiling staff *can* prove frustrating, and passenger care (for which Holland America Line used to be well known) has become mediocre. Training and service finesse have suffered considerably with the introduction of several new ships, and the dilution of qualified staff.

The suites and cabins are of good proportions, and come nicely equipped. They are quite comfortable, and Holland America Line also provides a good array of personal toiletry amenities. An additional bonus item is a canvas tote bag provided for all passengers, which is a nice extra and useful for shopping or for going to the beach. When you first walk aboard a Holland America Lines ship, you will be escorted to your cabin by a steward – something that most other major lines have ceased to do.

Carnival Corporation, the parent company of Carnival Cruise Lines, wholly owns Holland America Line, which it bought in 1988.

Norwegian Cruise Line

The senior officers are the only thing that's Norwegian. This cruise line provides a good product for a youthful, active, sports-minded audience, but most of the staff is from the Caribbean basin, and, in general, do not have the finesse of those ships with more European staff. The cabins are reasonably attractive and functional, although closet and drawer space is very limited in the newest ships.

NCL features Freestyle Dining – which means you turn up and a table will be found for you – so you can change tables every night and dine with whom you want (this feature may not be available in all dining spots aboard all ships). While this works best aboard the newer ships, aboard ships such as *Norwegian Dream* and *Norwegian Wind* it simply creates food outlets instead of restaurants, and doesn't work well. It also works better for individuals rather than for large groups. Although menu descriptions sound appetizing, in essence most food seems overcooked and unmemorable; lighter fare is available in a "bistro" setting aboard all ships in the fleet for those that want to "eat and run." Sports fans will find sports bars and memorabilia aboard these ships.

There is lively music everywhere – in almost all bars and lounges, throughout all public spaces, accommodation hallways, and open decks.

As for entertainment, the production shows are of the colorful, well-choreographed, slightly belittling, noisy, high-energy type. Note that *all* passengers are automatically charged $10 per person, per day for gratuities. Norwegian Cruise Line was purchased in 2000 by Star Cruises, and, as a result, is replacing its older ships with brand new vessels.

Princess Cruises

Despite promoting itself alluringly as "The Love Boat," Princess Cruises provides only a few tables for two in the dining rooms of *Dawn Princess, Grand Princess* and *Sun Princess*, while other ships only have larger tables.

The line was once known for its good food but today it is very much standardized, run-of-the-mill fare (Alaska cruises do, however, feature fresh Alaska salmon). Sadly, there are no longer any wine waiters in the dining rooms. However, the casual dining options have improved, particularly in the Horizon Court, although plastic plates, rather than trays, are used (passengers tend to take less if there are not trays).

Princess Cruises has also introduced freestyle dining – you turn up and a table will be found for you (not available in all restaurants in all ships) – so you can change tables every night, and dine with whom you want, when you want.

The cabins are generally of generous proportions (exceptions: *Dawn Princess, Sea Princess,* and *Sun Princess*) and reasonably well designed. They are well- equipped and comfortable, with warm décor and practical bathrooms. All ships have Filipino and other cabin staff and some European staff in front-line service areas.

The company's Shore Excursion Program is arguably the best run of any of the Big Eight companies. Entertainment tends to be very traditional, with a mix of elegant production shows and the usual cabaret acts, but volume levels often increase beyond the bearable. The company charges for so many extra items that the product has, like that of other large lines, turned into almost all-exclusive cruising. The UK-based P&O Group, which also owns Aida Cruises, P&O Cruises and P&O Cruises (Australia), wholly owns Princess Cruises.

Royal Caribbean International

Brilliance of the Seas, Enchantment of the Seas, Grandeur of the Seas, Legend of the Seas, Radiance of the Seas, Rhapsody of the Seas, Splendour of the Seas, and *Vision of the Seas* have slightly larger cabins than in the earlier ships *Majesty of the Seas, Monarch of the Seas*, and *Sovereign of the Seas*.

The company places more emphasis than most on passenger participation activities, such as Art Auctions, Passenger Talent Show, Masquerade Parade, Country & Western Jamboree, and so on. It is all very predictable, and the same programming is featured aboard all its ships, because it is tried, tested, and proven, if perhaps a little "old hat."

Although Royal Caribbean International's food is of approximately the same standard as that aboard Carnival Cruise Line ships, Carnival's ships have larger cabins, as do the ships of Celebrity Cruises, Holland America Line, and Princess Cruises. French, Italian, Oriental, Caribbean, and American are the main themes for the menus for different nights. Wine lovers should note that there are no vintages on the wine lists (because they are all so young).

The ships are shapely, with well-rounded sterns, and interesting design profiles that make them instantly recognizable. Most feature a trademark Viking Crown Lounge, set around the funnel stack, either in front of it or part way up it. Large, brightly lit casinos are provided, as are shopping galleries that passengers have to walk through to get almost anywhere else. It is all cleverly designed to extract maximum revenue – in a nice way, of course.

There is lively music everywhere – in almost all bars and lounges, throughout all public spaces, accommodation hallways, open decks, and even elevators. In fact, there's no escape from music and other noise pollution.

Royal Caribbean International also owns Celebrity Cruises, although the two brands are thankfully kept separate as far as the onboard product (particularly the food and service) is concerned.

Star Cruises

The company, established in 1994, has a diverse fleet of ships and caters to many nationalities and types of passengers, but markets principally to Australians, Europeans (particularly British and German passengers), Indians, and Southeast Asians. It operates in the Pan-Asia region.

Since its inception as an operator of ships primarily for casino gaming, the company has partly made the transition into a "normal" cruise line (although casino gaming remains an important part of the ships' entertainment facilities). The original intention was to have 12 ships, one for each sign of the zodiac. Passengers book in one of two classes: "Balcony Class" and "Non-Balcony Class."

Star Pisces operates short cruises for serious casino players, while *MegaStar Aries,* and *MegaStar Capricorn* are two small and finely outfitted luxury ships for VIP club members, private charters, and for testing new routes (and are thus not suitable for inclusion in this book).

The purpose-built new, large ships *SuperStar Leo* and *SuperStar Virgo* (which have many restaurants and dining spots and more entertainment for the company's activity-oriented Asian vacationers) are all fine cruise ships.

Star Cruises is the *only* cruise line to have its own simulator center, an outstanding training facility for its Scandinavian navigation officers. Star Cruises' parent company, Genting Berhad, owns a string of land-based resorts and hotels, huge tracts of land for development, and other interests including entertainment, aviation, power stations, oil and gas units, and rubber and palm oil plantations.

There is lively music everywhere – in almost all bars and lounges, throughout all public spaces, accommodation hallways, open decks, and even elevators. In fact, there's no escape from music and other noise pollution.

This cruise line is young, but is now the third largest cruise company in the world (Star Cruises wholly owns Norwegian Cruise Line and Orient Lines). Although service levels and finesse are inconsistent, and the company often moves its ships to different base ports and itineraries at short notice, the hospitality aboard the ships is very good, as is the choice of food available for many different ethnic nationalities. ❑

● *For how the Big 8 cruise lines scored on cuisine and service, see the chart on page 56.*

The big eight cruise lines

KEY

(1) = Selected suites only
(2) = On request only
(3) = In the shower unit only: CostaVictoria
(4) = On back-to-back cruises only (turnaround day)

A look at this chart shows just what cruise lines do (or do not) provide in your cabin and bathroom

CRUISE LINE	Carnival Cruise Lines		Celebrity Cruises		Costa Cruises	
	Standard Cabins	Suites	Standard Cabins	Suites	Cabins	Suites
CABIN						
Bed Linen: Duvets (not sheets/blankets)	No	No	No	Yes	No	No
Bed Linen: 100% Cotton	No	No	No	No	Yes	Yes
Bed Linen: 50% Cotton/50% Polyester	Yes	Yes	Yes	Yes	No	No
Pillowcases: 100% Cotton	No	No	No	No	No	No
Towels: 100% Cotton	No	No	Yes	Yes	Yes	Yes
Towels: 86% Cotton/14% Polyester	Yes	Yes	No	No	No	No
Non-Allergenic Pillows	No	No	No	No	Yes (2)	Yes (2)
Fresh Fruit Bowl	No	No	No	Yes	Yes (2)	Yes (2)
Fresh Flowers	No	No	No	Yes	Yes (2)	Yes (2)
Telephone	Yes	Yes	Yes	Yes	Yes	Yes
Personal Safe	Yes	Yes	Yes	Yes	Yes	Yes
Personalized Stationery	No	No	No	Yes	No	No
Television	Yes	Yes	Yes	Yes	Yes	Yes
VCR Player	No	Yes	No	Yes	No	No
CD Player	No	No	No	Yes (7)	No	No
MP3 Player	No	No	No	No	No	No
Shoe Shine	No	No	No	Yes	Yes	Yes
Continental Breakfast	Yes	Yes	Yes	Yes	Yes	Yes
Full In-Cabin Breakfast/Lunch/Dinner Service	No	No	Yes	Yes	No	Yes
Complimentary Espresso/Cappuccino Coffees	Yes	Yes	No	Yes	No	No
Free Local Newspaper in Port (when available)	No	No	No	Yes	No	No
Complimentary Pressing Service (First 24 Hours)	No	No	No	Yes	No	Yes
CABIN BATHROOM						
Real Glasses in Bathroom	Yes	Yes	Yes	Yes	Yes	Yes
Soap/Shampoo Dispenser Unit	No	No	No	No	Yes (3)	Yes (3)
Soap	Yes	Yes	Yes	Yes	Yes	Yes
Shampoo	No	No	No	No	Yes	Yes
Conditioner	No	No	No	No	Yes	Yes
Combined Shampoo/Conditioner	Yes	Yes	Yes	Yes	No	No
Foaming Bath Oil	No	No	No	Yes	No	No
Hand Lotion	No	Yes	Yes	Yes	Yes	Yes
Mouthwash	No	No	No	Yes	No	No
Shower Cap	No	No	No	Yes	Yes	Yes
Loofah Sponge	No	No	No	Yes	No	No
Hairdryer	Yes (11)	Yes (11)	Yes	Yes	Yes	Yes
Weight Scale	No	No	No	Yes	No	No
Bathrobes	Yes (9)	Yes	No	Yes	No	Yes
Shaving/Make-Up Mirror	No	Yes (11)	No	Yes	No	No

(5) = Deluxe cabins only
(6) = Royal Suite only
(7) = Penthouse Suite only
(8) = All outside-view suites and cabins (all ships)

(9) = SuperStar Leo and SuperStar Virgo only
(10) = Brilliance of the Seas and Radiance of the Seas only
(11) = Not all ships

Holland America Line		Norwegian Cruise Line		Princess Cruises		Royal Caribbean International		Star Cruises (9)	
Standard Cabins	Suites	Standard Cabins	Suites	Standard Cabins	Suites	Standard Cabins	Suites	Standard Cabins	Suites (Balcony Class)
No	No	No	No	No	No	No	No	Yes	No
No	No	On request	On request	No	No	Yes (10)	No	Yes	Yes
Yes	Yes	Yes	Yes	Yes	Yes	Yes	Yes	No	No
No	No	No	No	No	No	Yes (10)	No	Yes	Yes
No	No	Yes	Yes	Yes	Yes	Yes	Yes	Yes	Yes
Yes	Yes	No	No	No	No	No	No	No	No
No	No	No	No	Yes	Yes	Yes	Yes	No	No
Yes	Yes	Yes (2)	Yes	Yes	Yes	No	No	No	Yes
Yes	Yes	No	Yes	No	Yes	No	No	No	Yes
Yes	Yes	Yes	Yes	Yes	Yes	Yes	Yes	Yes	Yes
No	Yes	No	No	No	No	No	No	No	No
Yes	Yes	Yes	Yes	Yes	Yes	Yes	Yes	Yes	Yes
No	Yes	No	Yes (1)	No	No	No	Yes (6)	No	Yes
No	No	No	Yes (1)	No	No	No	Yes (6)	No	Yes
No	No	No	No	No	No	No	No	No	No
No	No	No	No	No	Yes	No	No	No	No
Yes	Yes	Yes	Yes	Yes	Yes	Yes	Yes	No	Yes
Yes	Yes	Yes	Yes	Yes	Yes	Yes	Yes	No	No
No	No	No	No	No	No	No	No	No	Yes
No	No	No	No	Yes (4)	Yes (4)	No	No	No	Yes (2)
No	Yes	No	No	No	No	No	No		
Yes	Yes	Yes	Yes	Yes	Yes	Yes	Yes	Yes	Yes
No	No	No	No	No	No	No	No	No	No
Yes	Yes	Yes	Yes	Yes	Yes	Yes	Yes	Yes	Yes
No	No	No	No	Yes	Yes	Yes	Yes	No	Yes
No	No	No	No	Yes	Yes	No	Yes (5)	No	Yes
Yes	No	Yes	Yes	No	No	No	No	Yes	No
No	Yes	No	Yes (1)	No	No	No	No	No	Yes
Yes	Yes	Yes	Yes	Yes	Yes	No	Yes (5)	No	Yes
No	No	No	No	No	No	No	No	No	Yes
Yes	Yes	Yes	Yes	Yes (2)	Yes (2)	Yes	Yes	Yes	Yes
No	No	No	No	No	No	No	No	No	No
No	Yes	Yes	Yes	Yes	Yes	No	No	Yes	Yes
No	No	No	Yes (1)	No	No	No	No	No	Yes
No	Yes	No	Yes	Yes	Yes	No	Yes	No	Yes
No	No	No	No	No	No	No	No	No	Yes

SELECTING THE RIGHT SHIP

Are new ships better than old? Should you consider a maiden voyage?

Is corporate cruising good value? Are theme cruises fun?

A ship built before 1980 is considered to be an old ship. However, this really depends on the level of maintenance it has received, and whether it has operated on short or longer cruises (short cruises get more passenger through-put, and, therefore, more wear and tear). Yet many passengers do like older ships, as they tend to have fewer synthetic materials in their interior décor.

Although it is inevitable that some older tonnage cannot match the latest in high-tech ships, it should be noted that ships today are not constructed to the same high standards, or with the same loving care, as in the past.

New Ships: Advantages

● Incorporate the latest in high-tech electronic equipment and the best in advanced ship design and construction.
● Meet the latest safety and operating standards as laid down by international maritime conventions.
● Feature more public room space, with public rooms and lounges built out to the sides of the hull (enclosed promenade decks are no longer regarded as essential).
● Offer more standardized cabin layouts and fewer categories.
● Are more fuel-efficient.
● Have a shallower draft, which makes it easier for them to enter and leave ports.
● Have bow and stern thrusters, so they seldom require tug assistance in many ports, thus reducing operating costs.
● Have plumbing and air-conditioning systems that are new and work.
● Have diesel engines mounted on rubber to minimize vibration.
● Usually have the latest submersible lifeboats.

New Ships: Disadvantages

● Do not "take the weather" as well as older ships (the experience of sailing across the North Atlantic in November on one of the new large ships can be unforgettable). Because of their shallow draft, these ships roll, even when there is the slightest puff of wind.
● Tend to have smaller standard cabins, which can mean narrow, short beds.
● Have thin hulls and therefore do not withstand the bangs and dents as well as older, more heavily plated vessels.
● Have décor made mostly from synthetic mate-rials (due to stringent regulations) and therefore could cause problems for those passengers who are sensitive to such materials.
● Have toilets of the powerful vacuum suction "barking dog" type.
● Are powered mainly by diesel (or diesel-electric) engines, which inevitably cause some vibration; although on the latest vessels, the engines are mounted on pliable, floating rubber cushions and are, therefore, virtually vibration-free.
● Have cabin windows that are completely sealed instead of portholes that can be opened.

Pre-1970 Ships: Advantages

● Have strong, plated hulls (often riveted) that can withstand tremendously hard wear and tear; they "take the weather" well.
● Have large cabins with long, wide beds/berths, because passengers needed more space in the days when voyages were much longer.
● Have a wide range of cabin sizes, shapes, and grades that are more suited to those families traveling with children.
● Have toilets that are of the "gentle flush" variety instead of the powerful "barking dog" vacuum toilets found aboard newer ships.
● Are powered by steam turbines, which are virtually free of vibration or noise and are considerably quieter and smoother than modern vessels.
● Have portholes that sometimes actually open.
● Have interiors that are built from more traditional materials such as wood and brass, with less use of synthetic fibers (less likely to affect anyone who is allergic to synthetics).
● Have deep drafts that help them to achieve a smooth ride in the open seas.

Pre-1970 Ships: Disadvantages

● They are not so fuel-efficient and, therefore, are more expensive to operate than the new ships.
● Need a larger crew, because of the more awkward, labor-intensive layouts of the ships.
● Have a deep draft (necessary for a smooth ride) but need tugs to negotiate ports and tight berths.
● Have increasing difficulty in complying with the current international fire, safety, and environmental regulations.
● Are usually fitted with older-type open lifeboats.
● If 10 years or older, they are more likely to have plumbing and air-conditioning problems in cabins and public areas.

The captain sets the tone for service and hospitality.

The Crew

You can estimate the standard of service by looking at the crew-to-passenger ratio (provided in the ship profiles in this book). The best service levels are aboard ships that have a ratio of one crew member to every two passengers, or higher. The best ships in the world, from the point of view of crew living and working conditions, also tend to be the most expensive ones (the adage "you get what you pay for" tends to be true).

Most ships now have multinational crews, with one or two exceptions. The crew mixture gives the impression of a ship being like a miniature United Nations. If the crew is happy, the ship will be happy, too, and passengers will sense it.

Corporate Cruising

Corporate, incentive organizations and seagoing conferences provide a growing market for cruise companies, who are typically eager to provide their ships for whole-ship charters. Cruise ships of all sizes, types and styles can provide an exciting venue for between 100 and 3,000 participants. Corporate organizers realize the benefits when they don't have to deal with such things as accommodation, food or entertainment for their delegates or participants, as these items are already in place.

Cruise companies have specialized departments and personnel to deal with all the details. Corporate organizers don't even have to think about car rentals either. Many of the larger ships have almost identical cabin sizes and configurations, a bonus for incentive houses. Corporate cruising clients can also make for a welcome change for the shipboard crew, who are used to dealing with participants out for a good time. Corporate passengers also get to see what cruising is all about, and could well turn into long-term cruise devotees.

Maiden/Inaugural Voyages

There is an element of excitement in taking the maiden voyage of a new cruise ship, or in joining the inaugural voyage of a recently refurbished, reconstructed, or stretched vessel.

If you have a degree of tolerance and you are not bothered by some inconvenience, slow or nonexistent service in the dining room, fine; otherwise, wait until the ship has been in service for at least three months. Then again, if you book a cruise on the third or fourth voyage, and there is a delay in the ship's introduction, you could find yourself on the maiden voyage.

One thing is certain — any maiden voyage is a collector's item, but Murphy's Law prevails: "If anything can go wrong, it will." For example:

● A strike, a fire, or a shipyard bankruptcy, are some of the possible causes of delay to a new ship.

● Service aboard new or recently refurbished ships (or a new cruise line) is likely to be uncertain at best and could be a complete disaster. An existing cruise line may use experienced crew from its other vessels to help "bring out" a new ship, but they may be unfamiliar with the ship's layout and may have problems training other staff.

● Plumbing and electrical items tend to cause the most problems, particularly aboard reconstructed and refurbished vessels. Examples: toilets that do not flush or do not stop flushing; faucets incorrectly marked, where "hot" really means "cold"; room thermostats mistakenly fitted with reverse wiring; televisions, audio channels, lights, and electronic card key locks that do not work; electrical outlets incorrectly indicated; and "automatic" telephones that refuse to function.

● The galley (kitchen) of a new ship causes perhaps the most consternation. Even if everything works and the executive chef has ordered the right supplies, they could be anywhere other than where they should be. Imagine if they forgot to load the seasoning, or if the eggs arrived shell-shocked.

● Items such as menus, postcards, writing paper, or TV remote control units, door keys, towels, pillowcases, glassware, and perhaps even toilet paper may be missing, lost in the bowels of the ship, or simply not ordered.

● In the entertainment department, items such as spare spotlight bulbs may not be in stock. Or there may be no hooks in the dressing rooms to hang costumes on (many older ships do not even have dressing rooms). Or what if the pianos arrived damaged, or "flip" charts for the lecturers didn't show up? Manuals for high-tech sound and lighting equipment may be in a foreign language.

Theme Cruises

If there's a theme, there's probably a cruise to suit. Each year, an ever richer variety of theme cruises is available, with many cultural, ecological, and educational subjects.

Typical topics include: Adventure, Antiques, Archaeological, Art Lovers, Astronomy, Backgammon, Ballroom and Latin Dancing, Big Band, Blues Festival, Bridge, Chess Tournament, Classical Music, Computer Science, Country and Western, Diet and Nutrition, Educational, Exploration, Fashion, Film Festival, Food and Wine, Gardening, Holistic Health, Gay/Lesbian, Jazz Festival, Movie Buffs, Murder Mystery, Naturalist/Nude, Octoberfest, Ornithology, Photography, Scottish Dancing, Sequence Dancing, Singles, Steamboat Race, Superbowl, Theatrical, and Wine Tasting.

Signs You've Chosen the Wrong Ship

● When, just after you've embarked, a waiter hands you a drink in a tall plastic glass from a whole tray of drinks of identical color and froth, then gives you a bill to sign without having the courtesy to say "Welcome Aboard."

● When your "luxury" cabin has walls so thin you can hear your neighbors combing their hair.

● When the brochure's "full bathtub" turns out to be "a large sink" located at floor level.

● When you wanted a quiet, restful cruise, but your travel agent booked you aboard a ship with 300 baseball fans and provided them all with signed baseball bats and boom boxes for their use on deck (solution: read this book thoroughly first).

● When you packed your tuxedo, but other passengers take "formal" attire to mean clean cut-off jeans and a less stained T-shirt.

● When the "medical facility" is located in the purser's office and consists of a box of adhesive bandages with instructions in a foreign language.

● When the gymnasium equipment is kept in the restaurant manager's office.

● When you have a cabin with an "obstructed view" (this will usually mean there is a lifeboat hanging outside it), and it is next to or below the disco. Or the laundry. Or the garbage disposal facility. Or the anchor.

● When "fresh selected greens" means a sprig of parsley on the entrée plate, at every lunch and dinner seating (boring even on a three-day cruise).

● When the cruise director tries to sell passengers a watch, or a piece of art, over the ship's public address system.

● When front-row seats at a rock concert would be quieter than a poolside deck chair at midday.

● When you hear *Achy-Breaky Heart*, *Hot! Hot! Hot!*, the *Macarena*, or *Yellow Bird* 10 times during the first day.

● When you have to buy shin pads to prevent injury from the 600 children that try to run you down in the passageways.

● When the cruise brochure shows your cabin with flowers and champagne, but you get neither.

● When the bottled water on your dining room table comes with a bill ever so quickly if you dare to open the bottle.

● When the brochure says "Butler Service," but you have to clean your own shoes, get your own ice, and still tip twice the amount you would for an "ordinary" cabin steward.

● When the Beer Drinking or Hog Calling Contest, Knobby Knees Contest, and Pajama Bingo are listed as "enrichment lectures."

● When the "fresh-squeezed orange juice" you just ordered means fresh-squeezed, but last week, or the week before that, on land, and then poured into industrial-size containers, before transfer to your polystyrene plastic cup on deck.

● When the brochure says tipping is not required, but your waiter and cabin steward tell you otherwise and threaten they will break your kneecaps if you do not hand them something that approaches what to you is a large sum of money.

● When the cruise director thoughtfully telephones you at 2.30am to tell you that the bingo jackpot is up to $1,000.

● When, on the final day, the words "early breakfast" means 5am, and "vacate your cabin by 7.30am" means you must spend about three hours sitting in the show lounge waiting for disembarkation, with 500 available seats, your hand luggage, and 2,000 other passengers, probably playing bingo.

● When on deck, you notice a large hole in the bottom of one or more of the ship's lifeboats.

● When the cabin steward tries to sell you a timeshare in his uncle's coal mine in wherever he is from, at a greatly reduced price, or says you must go without soap and towels for a week.

● When the proclaimed "five-course gourmet meal" in the dining room turns out to be four courses of salty chicken soup and a potato.

● When the "Deck Buffet" means that there are no tables and chairs, only the deck, to eat off.

● When the brochure shows photos of smiling young couples, but you and your spouse/partner are the only ones under 80.

● When the library is located in the engine room.

● When the captain tells you he is really a concert pianist and his diploma is really for the piano, not navigation. ❑

CHOOSING THE RIGHT CABIN

Does cabin size count? Are suites sweeter than cabins?

Is a balcony desirable? What about location?

Ideally, you should feel at home when at sea, so it is important to choose the right accommodation for your needs. Like houses ashore, all cabins have good and not-so-good points. Choose wisely, for if you find your cabin (incorrectly called a "stateroom" by some companies) is too small when you get to the ship, it may be impossible to change it or to upgrade, as the ship could very well be completely full.

Cruise lines designate cabins only when deposits have been received (they may, however, guarantee the grade and rate requested). If this is not done automatically, or if you come across a disclaimer such as one spotted recently – "All cabin assignments are confirmed upon embarkation of the vessel" – get a guarantee in writing that your cabin will not be changed on embarkation.

There are three main types of accommodation, but many variations on each theme:

● **Suites:** (the largest living spaces, typically with a private balcony); and "junior" suites (with or without private balcony).

● **Outside-view cabins:** a large picture window or one or more portholes (with or without private balcony).

● **Interior (no-view) cabins:** so called because there is no window or porthole.

Private Balconies

Balconies are in. A private balcony (or "veranda," or "terrace") is just that. It is a balcony (or mini-terrace) adjoining your cabin where you can sit, enjoy the view, dine, or even have a massage. There's something very civilized (if slightly anti-social) about sitting on one's balcony sipping champagne, or having breakfast "à la deck" in some exotic place. It is also pleasant to get fresh air and to escape cold (air-conditioned) cabins. The value of a private balcony, for which you pay a premium, comes into its own in warm weather areas. One thing is almost certain: once you have a private balcony, you'll be hooked. Balconies are like cruises: they're addictive. Indeed, some ships have enough private balconies for more than 800 budding Juliets to be wooed by their Romeos.

Some private balconies are not so private, however. Balconies not separated by full floor-to-ceiling partitions (examples: *Carnival Destiny, Carnival Triumph, Carnival Victory, Maasdam, Norway, Oriana, Ryndam, Seven Seas Mariner, Statendam,* and *Veendam*) don't quite cut it. You

Zodiac Suite bedroom aboard *SuperStar Leo*.

could get noise or smoke from your neighbor, but when all things are in your favor, a balcony is a wonderful extra. Some ships have balconies with full floor-to-ceiling privacy partitions *and* an outside light (examples: *Century, Galaxy, Mercury,* and *Radisson Diamond*). Note that some partitions in *Century, Galaxy,* and *Mercury* are of the full type, while some are of the partial type, depending on deck and location. Another downside of private balconies is that you cannot escape the loud music being played on the open swimming pool deck atop the ship – particularly annoying when "island night" goes on until the early morning hours and you just want to sit quietly on the balcony.

Some suites with forward-facing private balconies may not be so good, as the wind speed can make them all but unusable. And when the ship drops anchor in ports of call, the noise pollution can be deafening.

All private balconies (except French balconies – *see below*) have railings to lean on, but the balconies in some ships have solid steel plates between railing and deck, so you cannot look out to sea when you are seated (examples: *Costa*

Typical Cabin Layouts

The following rates are typical of those you can expect to pay for ❶ a seven-day and ❷ a 10-day Caribbean cruise aboard a modern cruise ship. The rates are per person and include free roundtrip airfare or low-cost air add-ons from principal North American gateways

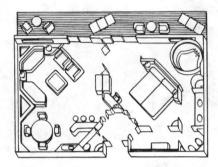

Luxury outside suite with private verandahh, separate lounge area, vanity area, extra-large double or queen-sized bed, bathroom with tub, shower, and extensive closet and storage space.

❶ $2,250 ❷ $4,000

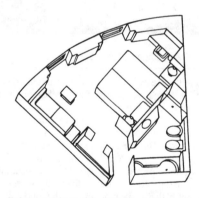

Deluxe outside cabin with lounge area, double or twin beds, bathroom with tub, shower, and ample closet and storage space.

❶ $2,250 ❷ $2,850

■ Note that in some ships, third- and fourth-person berths are available for families or friends wishing to share. The upper Pullman berths, not shown on these cabin layouts, are recessed into the wall above the lower beds.

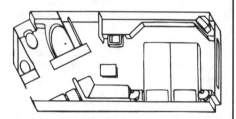

Large outside double with bed and convertible daytime sofabed, bathroom with shower, and good closet space.

❶ $1,750 ❷ $2,450

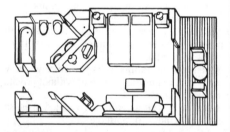

Standard outside double with twin beds (plus a possible upper third/fourth berth), small sitting area, bathroom with shower, and reasonable closet space.

❶ $1,450 ❷ $1,975

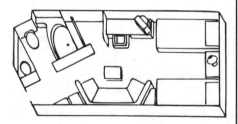

Inside double with two lower beds that may convert into daytime sofabeds (plus a possible upper third/fourth berth), bathroom with shower, and fair closet space.

❶ $1,250 ❷ 1,750

Classica, *Costa Romantica*, *Dawn Princess*, and *Sun Princess*). Better are those ships with balconies that have clear glass (examples: *Aurora, Brilliance of the Seas, Century, Galaxy, Mercury, Nordic Empress,* and *Radiance of the Seas*) or horizontal bars.

Don't be fooled by brochure-speak. A French balcony is one where the doors open to fresh air, but there's no balcony for you to step onto.

How Much?

The amount you pay for accommodation is directly related to the size of the cabin, its location, and the facilities and services provided.

● There are no set standards; each line implements its own system according to ship size, age, construction, and profit potential.

● Many cruise lines still *do not* give cabin sizes in their brochures, but you will find the size range in the ship profiles in the listings section.

● If this is your first cruise, choose the most expensive cabin you can afford. If it is too small (and most cabins *are* small), the cruise might fall short of your expectations.

● It may be better to book a low-grade cabin on a good ship than a high-grade cabin on a poor ship.

● If you are in a party of three or more and do not mind sharing a cabin, you will achieve a substantial saving per person, so you may be able to book a higher-grade cabin without paying extra.

Cabin Sizes

Cabins are like miniature hotel rooms and provide more or less the same facilities, except space. Ships necessarily have space limitations and utilize space efficiently. Viewed by most owners and designers as little more than a convenient place for passengers to sleep, shower, and change, cabin space is often compromised in favor of large public rooms and open areas. In some of the smaller interior (no-view) and outside cabins, changing clothes is a challenge; and to take a shower, you need to be an acrobat.

The latest ships come with more standardized cabin sizes, because they are made in modular form (I, and others, consider 170 sq. ft/15.7sq. meters to be the *minimum* acceptable size for a "standard" cruise ship cabin today). They all have integrated bathrooms (mostly made from non-combustible phenolic-glass-reinforced plastics) fitted into the ship during construction.

Older (pre-1970) ships had more spacious cabins (there were more days at sea, fewer ports of call, and fewer entertainment rooms). This encouraged many to spend a great deal of time in their cabins, often entertaining other passengers. Ask your travel agent for the dimensions of the cabin you have selected.

Cabin Location

● An "outside-view" cabin is recommended for first-time passengers: an "interior (no-view)" cabin has no portholes or windows, making it more difficult to orient you or to gauge the weather or time.

● Cabins located in the center of a ship are more stable and tend to be noise and vibration-free. Ships powered by diesel engines (this applies to most new and modern vessels) create and transmit some vibration, especially at the stern.

● Take into account personal habits when choosing the location of your cabin. For example, if you like to go to bed early, avoid a cabin close to the disco. If you have trouble walking, choose a cabin close to the elevator.

● Generally, the higher the deck, the higher the cabin price, and the better the service. This is an inheritance from transoceanic times, when upper-deck cabins and suites were sunnier and warmer.

● Cabins at the bow (front) of a ship are slightly crescent-shaped, given that the outer wall follows the curvature of the ship's hull. But they can be exposed to early morning noises, such as the anchor being dropped at ports where the ship cannot dock.

● Cabins with interconnecting doors are fine for families or close friends, but the wall between them is usually thin, so you can plainly hear anything that's being said next door.

● Many brochures now indicate cabins that have "obstructed-views." Cabins on lower decks are closer to engine noise and heat, especially at the aft of the vessel and around the engine casing. Be aware that in many older ships, elevators will probably not operate to the lowermost decks.

Facilities

Cabins provide some, or all, of the following:
● Private bathroom (generally small and compact) fitted with shower, washbasin, and toilet. Higher-grade cabins and suites may have full-size bathtubs. Some even have a whirlpool bath and/or bidet, a hairdryer, and more space.
● Electrical outlets for personal appliances, usually 110 and/or 220 volts.
● Multi-channel radio, TV (regular satellite channels or closed circuit), and VCR or DVD player.
● Two beds or a lower and upper berth (possibly, another one or two upper berths) or a double-, queen-, or king-size bed. In some ships, twin beds can be pushed together to form a double.
● Telephone, for inter-cabin or ship-to-shore communication.
● Depending on cabin size, a chair, or chair and table, or sofa and table, or even a separate lounge/sitting area (higher accommodation grades).
● Refrigerator and bar (higher grades).
● Vanity/desk unit with chair or stool.
● Personal safe.
● Closet space, some drawer space, plus storage room under beds for suitcases.
● Bedside night stand/table unit.
● Towels, soap, shampoo, and conditioner. (Many ships, particularly the "upscale" ones, provide a greater selection of items.)

Many first-time passengers are surprised to find their cabin has twin beds. Double beds are a comparative rarity except in the higher-priced suites. Aboard some ships you will find upper and lower berths. A "berth" is a nautical term for a bed held in a wooden or metal frame. A "Pullman berth" tucks away out of sight during the day, usually into the bulkhead or ceiling. You climb up a short ladder at night to get into an upper berth.

The Suite Life

Suites are the most luxurious and spacious of all shipboard accommodation, and typically come with butler service. A suite (literally a "suite of rooms") is a place where you could get lost in. It should measure a *minimum* 400 sq.ft. (37 sq. meters), and comprise a lounge or sitting room separated from a bedroom by a solid door (not just a curtain); a bedroom with a large bed; one or more bathrooms, and an abundance of closet, drawer, and other storage space. Many lines inaccurately describe some accommodation as suites, when they are nothing more than a large cabin with a curtain that divides sitting and sleeping areas.

Some ships devote whole decks or sections of decks to suites. Cruise lines know some passengers will pay handsomely for the best and quietest accommodation. They'll also expect the best service and preferential treatment throughout the ship.

Suites are best on long voyages with several days at sea. Be aware that in large ships (those carrying more than 1,000 passengers), there may be a whole deck or two devoted to penthouses and suites, but you will have to share the rest of the ship with those in lower-priced accommodation. That means there is no preferential seating in the showroom, the dining rooms, or on sunbathing decks. You may, however, get separate check-in facilities and preferential treatment upon disembarkation, but your luggage will be lumped together with everyone else's. ❑

Opposite Page: *Costa Victoria* in Venice, Italy.

The 10 Largest Suites Afloat

Ship	Cruise Line	Total (sq. ft)	Total (sq. m)
The World	Residensea	3,423.2	301.3
Norwegian Star	Norwegian Cruise Line	3,030.1	281.5
Constellation	Celebrity Cruises	2,530.0	235.0
Infinity	Celebrity Cruises	2,530.0	235.0
Millennium	Celebrity Cruises	2,530.0	235.0
Summit	Celebrity Cruises	2,530.0	235.0
Seven Seas Mariner	Radisson Seven Seas Cruises	1,580.0	146.7
Century	Celebrity Cruises	1,535.0	142.5
Galaxy	Celebrity Cruises	1,535.0	142.5
Mercury	Celebrity Cruises	1,535.0	142.5

Note: The spaces shown include balconies

THIS YEAR'S WORLD BEATERS

Having reviewed 254 cruise ships, Berlitz names the best performers for 2003

and explains why they deserve their maritime Oscars

BERLITZ FIVE-STARS-PLUS (***** +) CLUB

For this 2003 edition, only one ship has achieved the score required for it to be awarded membership in this most exclusive club.

Europa   (Hapag Lloyd Cruises)   1857 points   ***** +

Why? Because there is outstanding cuisine and attentive, friendly, very attentive, yet unobtrusive personal service from a staff dedicated to working aboard the world's finest cruise ship. But it's not just the ship itself and its facilities and appointments that contribute to the ship's high rating – it's also in the extensive array of details and personal attention from a fine, dedicated crew. It all adds up to the very best and most luxurious cruise ship and cruise experience available today – unless you have your own private motor yacht. Additionally, thanks to the pod propulsion system, there is absolutely no vibration anywhere.

BERLITZ FIVE-STARS (* * * * *) CLUB

For this 2003 edition, only 22 ships have achieved the score required for them to be awarded membership in the prestigious 5-star club.

	points
SeaDream I	1790
SeaDream II	1790
Seabourn Legend	1785
Seabourn Pride	1785
Seabourn Spirit	1785
Queen Elizabeth 2 (Grill Class)	1763
Crystal Symphony	1758
Silver Shadow	1757
Silver Whisper	1757
Hanseatic	1740
Silver Cloud	1729
Silver Wind	1729
Crystal Harmony	1725
Sea Cloud II	1709
Hebridean Spirit	1707
Sea Cloud	1704
Seven Seas Mariner	1703
Constellation	1701
Hebridean Princess	1701
Infinity	1701
Millennium	1701
Summit	1701

This year's runners-up: *SeaDream I* (above) and *SeaDream II*.

Almost all the ships feature one seating or open-seating dining, extremely comfortable accommodation, the very best in terms of seagoing cuisine, and highly personal service. There may be ships that have larger penthouse suites, balconies, show lounges, health spas and other appointments, but aboard the ships in the *Berlitz Five-Stars Club*, what counts is the cuisine and service, and the attention to detail. At a time when many cruise lines are making economies, these criteria are more important than ever.

LEFT: 2003's winning ship, *Europa*, operated by Hapag Lloyd Cruises, explores the Caribbean.

HOW WE EVALUATE THE SHIPS

The facilities count, of course, but just as important are the

standards of food, service, staff and hospitality

I have been evaluating and rating cruise ships and the onboard product professionally since 1980. In addition, I am provided with regular reports from a small team of trained professional passengers. The ratings are conducted with *total objectivity*, from a set of predetermined criteria and a modus operandi designed to work *globally*, not just regionally, across the entire spectrum of ocean-going cruise ships today, in all segments of the marketplace.

As I have stressed earlier in this book, there really is no "best cruise line in the world" or "best cruise ship" – only the ship and cruise that is *right for you*. Therefore, different criteria are applied to ships of different sizes, styles, and market segments throughout the world. Since so many new ships are of similar dimensions, but with different decor, more emphasis is placed on the standard of the dining experience, and the service and hospitality aspects of the cruise.

This section includes 254 oceangoing cruise ships in service (or due to enter service) and chosen by the author for inclusion when this book was completed. Almost all except the newest ships have been carefully evaluated, taking into account more than 400 separate inspection points based on personal cruises, visits and revisits to ships, as well as observations and comments from my reporting team. These are channeled into 20 major areas, each with a possible 100 points. The maximum possible score for any ship is therefore 2,000 points.

For the sake of clarity and at-a-glance user-friendliness, these are provided in the five main sections (Ship, Accommodation, Food, Service, Cruise Operation).

Cruise lines, ship owners, and operators should note that ratings, like stocks and shares, can go *down* as well as *up* each year, due to increased competition, the introduction of newer ships with more custom-designed facilities, and other market- or passenger-driven factors.

The ratings more reflect the *standards* of the cruise product delivered to passengers (the software), and less the physical plant (the hardware). Thus, although a ship may be the latest, most stunning vessel in the world in terms of design and decor, if the food, service, staff, and hospitality are not so good, the scores and ratings will reflect these aspects more clearly.

The stars beside the name of the ship at the top of each page relate directly to the Overall Rating. The highest number of stars awarded is **five stars** (✶✶✶✶✶), and the lowest is one star. This system is universally recognized throughout the hospitality industry. A plus (**+**) indicates that a ship deserves just that little bit more than the number of stars attained. However, I must emphasize that it is the number of points achieved rather than the number of stars attained that perhaps is more meaningful to anyone comparing ships.

What The Ratings Mean

1,851–2,000 points   ✶✶✶✶✶ **+**

You can expect to have an outstanding luxury cruise experience – in fact, it doesn't get any better than this. It should be truly memorable, and with the highest attention to detail, finesse, and highly personal service (how important you are made to feel is critically important). The decor must be elegant and tasteful, measured by restraint and not flashiness, with fresh flowers and other decorative touches in abundance, and the layout of the public rooms might well be in accordance with the principles of *feng shui*.

Any ship with this rating must be just about unsurpassable in the cruise industry, and it has to be very, very special, with service and hospitality levels to match. There must be the very highest quality surroundings, comfort and service levels, the finest and freshest quality foods, including all breads and rolls baked on board. Highly creative menus, regional cuisine, and dining alternatives should provide maximum choice and variety, and special orders will be part of the dining ritual.

Dining room meals (particularly dinners) are expected to be grand, memorable affairs, correctly served on the finest china, with a choice of wines of suitable character and vintage available, and served in the correct-sized sommelier glasses of the highest quality (Reidel or Schott).

The service staff will take pleasure in providing you with the ultimate personal, yet unobtrusive, attention with the utmost of finesse, and the word "no" should definitely not be in their vocabulary. This really is the very best of the best in terms of refined, unstructured living at sea, but it may cause serious damage to your bank statement.

1,701–1,850 points   *****
You can expect to have a truly excellent cruise experience that should be very memorable, and with the finesse and attention to detail commensurate with the amount of money paid. The service and hospitality levels will be extremely high from all levels of officers and staff, with strong emphasis on fine hospitality training (all service personnel members *must* make you feel important).

The food will be commensurate with the high level expected from what is virtually the best that is possible, while the service should be very attentive yet unobtrusive. The cuisine should be quite memorable, with ample taste. Special orders should never present a problem, with a creative cuisine that will be of a very high standard. There must be a varied selection of wines, which should be properly served in glasses of the correct size (not simply a standard size glass for white and one for red wines).

Entertainment is expected to be of prime quality and variety. Again, the word "no" should not be in the vocabulary of any member of staff aboard a ship with this rating. A cruise aboard a ship with this high rating may well cause damage to your bank statement, particularly if you choose the most spacious grades of accommodation. Few things will cost extra once you are on board, and brochures should in fact be more "truthful" than those for ships with a lower rating.

1,551–1,700 points   **** +
You should expect to have a high-quality cruise experience that will be quite memorable, and just a little short of being excellent in all aspects. Perhaps the personal service and attention to detail could be slightly better, but, nonetheless, this should prove to be a fine all-round cruise experience, in a setting that is extremely clean and comfortable, with few lines anywhere, a caring attitude from service personnel, and a good standard of entertainment that appeals to a mainstream market. The cuisine and service will be well rounded, with mostly fresh ingredients and varied menus that should appeal to almost anyone, served on high quality china.

All in all, this should prove to be an extremely well rounded cruise experience, probably in a ship that is new or almost new. There will probably be less "extra cost" items than ships with a slightly lower rating, but you get what you pay for these days.

1,401–1,550 points   ****
You should expect to have a very good quality all-round cruise experience, most probably aboard a modern, highly comfortable ship that will provide a good range of facilities and services. The food and service will be quite decent overall, although decidedly not as "gourmet" and fanciful as the brochures with the always-smiling faces might have you believe.

The service on board will be well organized, although it will perhaps be a little robotic and impersonal at times, and only as good as the cruise line's training program allows. You will probably notice a lot of things cost extra once you are on board, although the brochure typically is vague and tells you that the things are "available" or are an "option." However, you should have a good time, and only a moderate amount of damage will be done to your bank statement.

1,251–1,400 points   *** +
You should expect to have a decent quality cruise experience, from a ship where the service levels should be good, but perhaps without the finesse that could be expected from a more upscale environment. The crew aboard any ship achieving this score should reflect a positive attitude with regard to hospitality, and a willingness to accommodate your needs, up to a point. Staff training will probably be in need of more attention to detail and flexibility.

Food and service levels in the dining room(s) should be reasonably good, although special orders or anything out of the ordinary might prove more difficult. There will probably be a number of extra-cost items you thought were included in the price of your cruise – although the brochure typically is vague and tells you that the things are "available" or are an "option."

1,101–1,250 points   ***
You can expect to have a reasonably decent, middle-of-the-road cruise experience, with a moderate amount of space and quality in furnishings, fixtures, and fittings. The cabins are likely to be a little on the small side (dimensionally challenged). The food and service levels will be quite acceptable, although not at all memorable, and somewhat inflexible with regard to special orders, as almost everything is standardized.

Crew attitude could certainly be improved, the level of hospitality and cleanliness will be moderate but little more, and entertainment will probably be weak. A good option, however, for those looking for the reasonable comforts of home without pretentious attitudes, and little damage to their bank statement.

951–1,100 points   ** +
You should expect to have a cruise experience that will be below the average in terms of accommodation (typically with cabins that are dimensionally challenged), quality of the ship's facilities,

food, wine list, service, and hospitality levels, in surroundings that are completely unpretentious. In particular, the food and its service will probably prove to be most disappointing and rather typical of roadside café standards.

There will be little flexibility in the levels of service, hospitality and staff training, which will be no better than poor. Thus, the overall experience will be commensurate with the small amount of money you paid for the cruise.

801–950 points   **

You should expect to have a cruise experience of modest quality aboard a ship that is probably in need of more attention to maintenance and service levels, not to mention hospitality. The food is likely to be quite tasteless and homogenized, and of low quality, and service will leave much to be desired in terms of attitude, which will tend to be mediocre at best.

Staff training is likely to be minimal, and turnover will probably be high. The "end-of-pier" entertainment could well leave you wanting to read a good book.

651–800 points   * +

You can expect to have only the most basic cruise experience, with little or no attention to detail, from a poorly trained staff that is probably paid low wages and to whom you are just another body. The ship will, in many cases, probably be in need of much maintenance and upgrading, and will probably have few facilities.

Cleanliness and hygiene may well be questionable, and there will be absolutely no finesse in personal service levels, with poor attitude from the crew, and dismal entertainment as significant factors in the low score and rating. On the other hand, the price of a cruise is probably alluringly low.

601–650 points   *

You can expect to have a cruise experience that is the absolute bottom of the barrel, with almost nothing in terms of hospitality or finesse. You can forget about attention to detail – there won't be any. This will be the kind of experience that would equal a stay in the most basic motel, with few facilities, a poorly trained, uncaring staff, most of whom will have undergone a hospitality bypass, and a ship that is in need of better maintenance and upgrading.

The low cost of a cruise aboard any cruise ship with this rating should provide a clue to the complete lack of any quality. This will be particularly true in the areas of food, service, and entertainment. In other words, this could well be a totally forgettable cruise experience.

Distribution of points

These are the percentage of the total points available which are allocated to each of the main areas evaluated:

- ● **The Ship**   25%
- ● **Accommodation**   15%
- ● **Cuisine**   15%
- ● **Service**   20%
- ● **Entertainment**   7.5%
- ● **The Cruise Experience** 17.5%

The Ship

Hardware/Maintenance/Safety

This score reflects the general profile and condition of the ship as hardware, its age and maintenance, hull condition, exterior paint, decking and caulking, swimming pool and surrounds, deck furniture, shore tenders, lifeboats, life rafts, and other safety items. It also reflects interior cleanliness (public restrooms, elevators, floor coverings, wall coverings, stairways, passageways, and doorways), food preparation areas, refrigerators, garbage handling, compacting, and incineration, and waste disposal facilities.

Outdoor Facilities/Space

This score reflects the overall space per passenger on open decks, crowding, swimming pools/whirlpools and their surrounds, lido deck areas, number and type of deck lounge chairs (with or without cushioned pads) and other deck furniture, outdoor sports facilities, shower enclosures and changing facilities, towels, and quiet areas (those without music).

Interior Facilities/Space/Flow

This score reflects the use of common interior public spaces, including enclosed promenades; passenger flow and points of congestion; ceiling height; lobby areas, stairways, and all passenger hallways; elevators; public restrooms and facilities; signage, lighting, air-conditioning and ventilation; and degree of comfort and density.

Decor/Furnishings/Artwork

This score reflects the overall interior decor and color scheme; hard and soft furnishings, wood (real, imitation, or veneer) paneling, carpeting (tuft density, color, and practicality), fit and finish (seams and edging), chairs (comfort, height, and support), ceilings and decor treatments, reflective surfaces, artwork (paintings, sculptures, and atrium centerpieces), and lighting.

Spa/Fitness Facilities

This score reflects any health spa, wellness center, and fitness facilities; location and accessibility; lighting and flooring materials; fitness and muscle-training machines and other equipment; fitness programs; sports and games facilities; indoor swimming pools; whirlpools; grand baths; aqua-spa pools; saunas and steam rooms; rasul, the various types of massage (Swedish Remedial, Shiatsu, Ayurvedic, Reflexology), and other treatment rooms; changing facilities; jogging and walking tracks; and promenades.

Accommodation

Cabins: Suites and Deluxe Grades

This score reflects the design and layout of all grades of suites and deluxe grade cabins, private balconies (whether full floor-to-ceiling partition or part partitions, balcony lighting, balcony furniture). Also beds/berths, furniture (its placement and practicality), and other fittings; closets and other hanging space, drawer space, and bedside tables; vanity unit, bathroom facilities, washbasin, cabinets, and toiletries storage; lighting, air-conditioning, and ventilation; audiovisual facilities; quality and degree of luxury; artwork; bulkhead insulation, noise, and vibration levels. Suites should not be so designated unless the sleeping room is completely separate from the living area.

Note that some large cruise ships now have whole decks devoted to superior grade accommodation, with a significant difference between this accommodation and that of "standard" cabins.

Also the soft furnishings and details such as the information manual (list of services); paper and postcards (including personalized stationery); telephone directory; laundry lists; tea- and coffee-making equipment; flowers (if any); fruit (if any); bathroom personal amenities kits, bathrobes, slippers, and the size, thickness, quality, and material content of towels.

Cabins: Standard Sizes

This score reflects the design and layout (whether outside or inside), beds/berths, furniture (its placement and practicality), and other fittings. Also taken into account: closets and other hanging space, drawer space, bedside tables, and vanity unit; bathroom facilities, washbasin, cabinets, and toiletries storage; lighting, air-conditioning and ventilation; audiovisual facilities; quality and degree of fittings and furnishings; artwork; bulkhead insulation, noise, and vibration levels.

In addition, we have taken into account the usefulness of the information manual (directory of services); paper and postcards (including stationery); telephone directory; laundry lists; tea- and coffee-making equipment; flowers (if any); fruit (if any); and bathroom amenities kits, bathrobes, slippers, and the size, thickness, quality, and material content of towels.

Cuisine

This section forms 15 percent of the whole rating system and is very important, as food is often the main feature of today's cruises. Cruise lines put maximum emphasis on promising passengers how good their food will be, often to the point of being unable to deliver what is promised. Generally, the standard of food is good. The rule of thumb is: if you were to eat out in a good restaurant, what would you expect? Does the ship meet your expectations? Would you come back again for the food?

There are perhaps as many different tastes as there are passengers. The "standard" market cruise lines cater to a wide range of tastes, while the more exclusive cruise lines can offer better quality food, cooked individually to your taste. As in any good restaurant, you get what you pay for.

Dining Room/Cuisine

This score reflects the physical structure of dining rooms; window treatments; seating (alcoves and individual chairs, with or without armrests); lighting and ambience; table set-ups; the quality and condition of linen, china, and cutlery; and table centerpieces (flowers). It also reflects menus, food quality, presentation, food combinations, culinary creativity, variety, design concepts, appeal, taste, texture, palatability, freshness, color, balance, garnishes, and decorations; appetizers, soups, pastas, flambeaus, tableside cooking; fresh fruit and cakes; the wine list (and connoisseur wine list), price range, and wine service. Alternative dining venues are also checked for menu variety, food and service quality, décor and noise levels.

Informal Dining/Buffets

This score reflects the hardware (including the provision of hot and cold display units, sneeze guards, tongs, ice containers and ladles, and serving utensils); buffet displays (which have become quite disappointing and institutionalized); presentation; trays and set-ups; correct food temperatures; food labeling; breakfast, luncheon, deck buffets, midnight buffets, and late-night snacks; decorative elements such as ice carvings; and staff attitude, service, and communication skills.

Quality of Ingredients

This score reflects the overall quality of ingredients used, including consistency and portion size; grades of meat, fish, and fowl; and the price paid by the cruise line for its food product per passenger per day. It is the quality of ingredients that most dictates the eventual presentation and quality of the finished product as well as its taste. Also included is the quality of tea and coffee (better quality ships are expected to provide more palatable tea and coffee).

Tea/Coffee/Bar Snacks

This score reflects the quality and variety of teas and coffees available (including afternoon teas/coffees and their presentation); whether mugs or cups and saucers are presented or available;

whether milk is served in the correct open containers or in sealed packets; whether self-service or graciously served. The quality of such items as cakes, scones, and pastries, as well as bar/lounge snacks, hot and cold canapés, and hors d'oeuvres also forms part of this section.

Service

Dining Room

This score reflects the professionalism of the restaurant staff: the maître d'hotel, dining room managers, head section waiters, waiters and assistant waiters (busboys), and sommeliers and wine waiters. It includes place settings and correct service (serving, taking from the correct side), communication skills, attitude, flair, dress sense (uniform), and finesse. Waiters should note whether passengers are right- or left-handed and, aboard ships with assigned table places, make sure that the cutlery and glasses are placed on the side of preference. Cutlery and wine glasses are also included.

Bars

This score reflects the lighting and ambience; overall service in bars and lounges; noise levels; communication skills (between bartenders and bar staff and passengers); staff attitude, personality, flair and finesse; correct use of glasses (and correct size of glasses); billing and attitude when presenting the bill (aboard those ships where a charge is made).

Cabins

This score reflects the cleaning and housekeeping staff, butlers (for penthouse and suite passengers), cabin stewards/stewardesses and their supervisory staff, attention to detail and cleanliness, in-cabin food service, linen and bathrobe changes, and language and communication skills.

Open Decks

This score reflects steward/stewardess service for beverages and food items around the open decks; service for placement and replacement of towels on deck lounge chairs, self-help towels, and emptying of used towel bins; general tidiness of all associated deck equipment; and the availability of service at nonstandard times (in the evening or early morning, for example).

Gratuities

In the Other Comments section at the end of each rating, all gratuities are usually at extra cost unless specifically included in the price. Likewise, insurance and port taxes are also at extra cost unless they are specifically stated as included.

Entertainment

On specialist ships, such as those featuring expedition cruises, or tall ships, where entertainment is not a feature, it is the lecture program that forms this portion of the evaluations.

The score reflects the overall entertainment program and content as designed and targeted to specific passenger demographics. Cruise ship entertainment has to appeal to passengers of widely varying ages and types. Included is the physical plant (stage/bandstand) of the main showlounge; technical support, lighting, follow spotlight operation and set/backdrop design; sound and light systems (including laser shows); recorded click-tracks and all special effects; variety and quality of large-scale production shows (including story, plot, content, cohesion, creativeness of costumes, relevancy, quality, choreography, and vocal content); cabaret; variety shows; game shows; singers; visual acts; bands and solo musicians.

The Cruise Experience

Activities Program

This score reflects the variety, quality, and quantity of daytime activities and events. The rating includes the cruise director and cruise staff (including their visibility, availability, ability, and professionalism), sports programs, participation games, special interest programs, port and shopping lecturers, and mind-enrichment lecturers.

This score also reflects any water sports equipment carried (including banana boat, jet skis, scuba tanks, snorkeling equipment, waterski boat and windsurfers), instruction programs, overall staff supervision, the marina (usually located aft) or side-retractable water sports platforms, and any enclosed swimming area (if applicable).

Movies/Television Programming

This score reflects movies screened in onboard theaters, including screen, picture and sound quality; videos screened on the in-cabin television system; other televised programming, including a ship's own television station programming; content; and entertainment value. Cabin television audio channels are also included in this section.

Hospitality Standard

This score reflects the level of hospitality of the crew and their attention to detail and personal satisfaction. It includes the professionalism of senior officers, middle management, supervisors, cruise staff, and general crew; social contact, appearance, and dress codes or uniforms; atmosphere and ambience; motivation; communication skills (most important); the general ambience and the attention to detail.

Overall Product Delivery

This score reflects the quality of the overall cruise as a vacation experience – what the brochure states and promises (real or implied), which reflects on the level of expectation versus the onboard product delivery and level of hospitality and services received.

Notes on the Rating Results

Cruise ship evaluations and ratings have of necessity become tougher and much more complex. Although a ship may be the newest, with all the latest high-tech facilities possible, passengers reiterate that it is the onboard food and service that often disappoints.

Cruise companies defend themselves by stating that their passengers are willing to accept lesser quality with regard to food in return for lower prices. However, this attitude only results in a downward spiral that affects food quality, freshness, variety, creativity, and presentation, as well as service, quality of personnel, crew training, safety, maintenance, and other related items.

Cuts in food quality, crew wages and detail items are typically made by cruise companies in the hope that passengers will not notice them. However, in the final analysis, it is the little things that add to points lost on the great scorecard.

The ratings are intended to help the cruise companies to take note of their product, listen to their income-generating passengers, and return some of the items and the finesse currently missing in the overall cruise vacation experience, while adjusting fares to better reflect long-term growth of this good value-for-money vacation. ❏

WHAT THE DESCRIPTIONS MEAN

Ship Size
● Small Ship (up to 500 passengers)
● Mid-Size Ship (500–1,000 passengers)
● Large Ship (over 1,000 passengers)

Lifestyle
Designated as Standard, Premium, or Luxury, according to a general classification into which segment of the market the ship falls. It should thus further allow you to choose the right size ship and cruise experience to fit your lifestyle.
● Those designated as Standard are the least expensive.
● Those designated as Premium are more expensive (than Standard), have generally better food, service, and facilities.
● Those designated as Luxury are the most expensive and provide the best in facilities, food, and service, and the finest cruise experience possible.

Cruise Line
The cruise line and the operator may be different if the company that owns the vessel does not market and operate it.

First Entered Service
Where two dates are given, the first is the ship's maiden passenger voyage when new, and the second is the date it began service for the current operator.

Propulsion
The type of propulsion is given (i.e. gas turbine, diesel, diesel-electric, or steam turbine), together with the output (at 100 percent), expressed as MW (megawatts) or kW (kilowatts) generated.

Propellers
Number of propellers or azimuthing pods (in which a propeller is mounted externally, replacing conventional propeller and shaft).

Passenger Capacity
The number of passengers is based on:
● Two lower beds/berths per cabin, plus all cabins for single occupancy.
● All available beds/berths filled (Note: This figure may not always be accurate, as cruise lines often make changes by adding or taking away third/fourth berths according to demand).

Passenger Space Ratio (Tons Per Passenger)
Achieved by dividing the gross registered tonnage by the number of passengers.

Crew to Passenger Ratio
Achieved by dividing the number of passengers by the number of crew (lower beds/all possible beds and berths filled).

Cabin Size Range
From the smallest cabin to the largest suite (including "private" balconies/verandahs), these are provided in square feet and square meters, rounded up to the nearest number.

Wheelchair-accessible Cabins
Cabins designed to accommodate passengers with mobility problems.

Dedicated Cinema/seats
A "yes" means that there is a separate cinema dedicatedly solely to showing large-screen movies throughout the day and during the evening. This is distinct from a show lounge that may be used to screen movies during the day (afternoon) and live shows in the evening. The number of seats is provided where known.

Removed 2006

A'Rosa Blu
NOT YET RATED

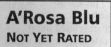

Large Ship: ....70,285 tons	Passengers	Cabin Current: ....110 and 220 volts
Lifestyle: ....Standard	(lower beds/all berths): 1,596/1,910	Elevators: 9
Cruise Line: ...A' Rosa Cruises (Seetours)	Pass. Space Ratio	Casino (gaming tables): ....Yes
Former Names: ....Crown Princess	(lower beds/all berths): 44.0/36.7	Slot Machines: ....Yes
Builder: ....Fincantieri Navali (Italy)	Crew/Passenger Ratio	Swimming Pools (outdoors): 2
Original Cost: ....$276.8 million	(lower beds/all berths): 2.3/2.7	Swimming Pools (indoors): 0
Entered Service: ...July 1990/June 2002	Navigation Officers: ....European	Whirlpools: 4
Registry: ....Great Britain	Cabins (total): 798	Fitness Center: ....Yes
Length (ft/m): 804.0/245.08	Size Range (sq ft/m): 188.3–538.2/	Sauna/Steam Room: ....Yes/Yes
Beam (ft/m): 105.8/32.25	17.5–50.0	Massage: ....Yes
Draft (ft/m): 26.9/8.21	Cabins (outside view): 620	Self-Service Launderette: ....Yes
Propulsion/Propellers: .....diesel-electric	Cabins (interior/no view): 171	Dedicated Cinema/Seats: Yes/169
(24,000kW)/2	Cabins (for one person): 0	Library: ....Yes
Passenger Decks: 11	Cabins (with private balcony): 184	Classification Society: ....RINA
Total Crew: 677	Cabins (wheelchair accessible): 10	

OVERALL SCORE: NYR (OUT OF A POSSIBLE 2,000 POINTS)

ACCOMMODATION: There are 10 different accommodation price categories to choose from, and these include suites and junior suites (both with private balconies), outside view cabins and interior (no view) cabins, and special cabins for the handicapped. Generally speaking, accommodation on the higher decks will cost more (location is everything). Occupants of accommodation designated as suites (there are 14 of them) and junior suites (there are 36) also have a private lounge to play in.

In general, the cabins are well designed and have large bathrooms as well as good soundproofing. Walk-in closets, refrigerator, personal safe, and an interactive video system are provided in all cabins, as are chocolates on your pillow each night. Twin beds convert to queen-size beds in standard cabins. Bathrobes and personal toiletry amenities are provided, and all cabins feature a small refrigerator and color television. You should note that the outside-view handicapped cabins have views that are obstructed by lifeboats, as do some other cabins on the same deck (Deck 8). Some cabins can accommodate a third and fourth person.

SUITES/JUNIOR SUITES: The 14 most expensive suites – each has a large private balcony – are quite well laid out in a practical design that positions most things in just about the right place. The bedroom is separated from the living room by a heavy wooden door, and there are televisions in both rooms. The closet and drawer space is actually very generous, and there is enough of it even for two back-to-back cruises.

BERLITZ'S RATINGS

	Possible	Achieved
Ship	500	NYR
Accommodation	200	NYR
Food	400	NYR
Service	400	NYR
Entertainment	100	NYR
Cruise	400	NYR

DINING: There are many choices for eating, from self-serve restaurants to full-service dining spots and casual eateries, so you'll need to plan your eating habits around the many spots aboard this ship.

Seetours has cleverly divided what was formerly the ship's principal restaurant into two separate dining spots; Markt (Market) Restaurant, and the Bella Donna Restaurant. The Markt Restaurant is a self-serve buffet-style eatery, similar in style to the one found aboard *AIDAcara* and *AIDAvita*. There are few tables for two (most are for four, six or eight), and the most desirable tables (for six persons) are those that overlook the stern. The Bella Donna Restaurant is also a full-service dining spot, with à la carte items cooked to order (some at extra cost). Both restaurants have smoking and non-smoking sections, which provides the ship's German-speaking passengers a choice.

The wine list is average, with a heavy emphasis on Austrian and German wines. Note that 15 percent is added to all beverage bills, including wines (whether you order a €15 bottle or a €100 bottle, although it involves the same amount of service).

Fine food lovers will probably head for Rossini, the elegant Italian restaurant, which features candlelit dining with excellent food (including regional specialties) and personal service.

Other alternative dining spots include the Buena Vista Restaurant (featuring Mexican and South American cuisine), a self-serve lido buffet called the California Grill (open 24 hours a day). There's also an Asia Bistro (with wok preparation, and themed evening buffet such as Indonesian, Thai, and Vietnamese cuisines), as well as the Dolce Vita Eiscafé. A Japanese sushi bar (all items are at extra cost) is part of the middle level of the three-deck high lobby, located quite conveniently adjacent to the shops.

For sweet snacks during the day, a Confiserie (patisserie) is located in the ship's spacious lobby area, between the reception desk and internet center. As might be expected, many of the alternative eateries feature items that are at extra cost.

OTHER COMMENTS: For many years this ship was operated by Princess Cruises as *Crown Princess* – in fact, it was the first ship in the 70,000-ton range to be built for that company. It was originally ordered by Sitmar Cruises and debuted in 1990 (Princess Cruises purchased Sitmar Cruises in 1988). The ship was moved to the A'Rosa brand marketed by Germany's Seetours and began operations in June 2002 under the ship's new name, the catchy (well, sort of) but not quite so easy to pronounce *A'Rosa Blu*, operating cruises specifically for the German-speaking family market.

In case you are confused about the brand name, A'Rosa Cruises (like Aida Cruises) is part of Seetours, which is itself a part of P&O Princess Cruises. Actually, if you take a river cruise in Europe, you may see them again – the company has two river vessels, *A'Rosa Bella* and *A'Rosa Donna* (some have called the pair BellaDonna).

The first thing you'll notice is the ship's catchy exterior markings on its bows – a pair of bright red lips holding – you guessed it – a huge, red rose. Perhaps the ship's more ideal name would have been *A'Rosa Red* instead of *A'Rosa Blu* (*blue* roses are, after all, extremely hard to find)?. Of course, training the animation staff to hold a red rose in their mouths (as in the line's jazzy, but virtually unreadable brochure) might prove a little tricky.

The ship has an interesting, jumbo-airplane look to it when viewed from the front, with a dolphin-like upper structure made of lightweight aluminum alloy (designed by the renowned Italian architect Renzo Piano), and a large swept back funnel (also made from aluminum alloy) placed aft. The new funnel design covers the original one, which looked more like a stark-upright garbage can.

The ship's interiors received a complete makeover after delivery to Seetours in 2002. Perhaps the area that received most attention, however, was concentrated in what was formerly the observation dome/casino; this was set high atop the ship in the "dolphin head" (the

casino has now been scaled down in size and relocated to a lower deck). The whole space has been very nicely turned into Spa Rosa – an extensive, two-deck wellness center, measuring some 1,300 sq. meters (almost 14,000 sq. ft), with a staircase that connects the two levels. Treatments include various types of massage (including hot stone massage, shiatsu and other Asiatic touch treatments), as well as a Turkish steam bath (Hammam).

The refit/refurbishment program was aimed at providing the kinds of facilities that are in line with the tastes of young, active German-speaking families and single passengers. The interior layout is rather disjointed, however, and will take a little getting used to. Some innovative and elegant styling of the period is mixed with traditional features and a reasonably spacious interior layout. An understated decor of soft pastel shades is highlighted by some very colorful artwork and splashes of color.

The atrium lobby is three decks high and is quite elegant. It features a grand staircase with fountain sculpture (a good setting for stand-up cocktail parties). Facilities include a library, internet café, business center, bike station (mountain bikes are available for rent), and seven bars.

Cruises are designated not in 7-day Caribbean or Mediterranean terms, but by colorful descriptions such as BLU Cotton, BLU Coconut, BLU Mambo, BLU Salsa, BLU Viking, and so on (well, at least it's original, but a little confusing). This ship should provide you with a pleasant cruise experience in surroundings that are at once elegant and comfortable, and the young, vibrant staff will make you feel welcome. Watch out for those rich red lips, and let me know if you see the man with the red rose in his teeth anywhere on board.

WEAK POINTS: Standing in line for anything such as embarkation, disembarkation, shore tenders and for self-serve buffet meals is an inevitable aspect of cruising aboard all ships that carry more than 1,000 passengers. Sadly, there is no decent forward observation viewpoint outdoors. There is also no wrap-around promenade deck outdoors (the only walking space being along the port and starboard sides of the ship). In fact, there is very little contact with the outdoors at all. The sunbathing space is also *extremely* limited when the ship is full (which should be most of the time). There are many support pillars in the public rooms that obstruct the sight lines and impede passenger flow. There is no indoor swimming pool – something that many of the more traditional German-speaking passengers will probably miss.

Adonia
NOT YET RATED

Large Ship:	...............77,499 tons	Passengers		Cabin Current:	........110 and 220 volts
Lifestyle:	...................Standard	(lower beds/all berths):	.....2,016/2,272	Elevators:	11
Cruise Line:	............P & O Cruises	Passenger Space Ratio		Casino (gaming tables):	............Yes
Former Names:	..........*Sea Princess*	(lower beds/all berths):	.......38.4/34.1	Slot Machines:	....................Yes
Builder:	.............Fincantieri (Italy)	Crew/Passenger Ratio		Swimming Pools (outdoors):	3
Original Cost:	...........$300 million	(lower beds/all berths):	.........2.3/2.5		(+2 for children)
Entered Service:	.... Dec 1998/May 2003	Navigation Officers:	............British	Swimming Pools (indoors):	0
Registry:	.................Great Britain	Cabins (total):	975	Whirlpools:	5
Length (ft/m):	.............857.2/261.3	Size Range (sq ft/m):	......158.2–610.3/	Fitness Center:	....................Yes
Beam (ft/m):	...............105.6/32.2		14.7–56.7	Sauna/Steam Room:	..........Yes/Yes
Draft (ft/m):	..................26.5/8.1	Cabins (outside view):	652	Massage:	...........................Yes
Propulsion/Propellers:	.....diesel-electric	Cabins (interior/no view):	372	Self-Service Launderette:	...........Yes
	(46,080kW)/2	Cabins (for one person):	0	Dedicated Cinema/Seats:	..........No
Passenger Decks:	10	Cabins (with private balcony):	410	Library:	.........................Yes
Total Crew:	850	Cabins (wheelchair accessible):	18	Classification Society:	....Lloyds Register

---

OVERALL SCORE: NYR (OUT OF A POSSIBLE 2,000 POINTS)

ACCOMMODATION: There are 19 different cabin grades, designated as: suites (with private balcony), mini-suites (with private balcony), outside-view twin-bedded cabin with balcony, outside-view twin-bedded cabin, and interior (no view) twin-bedded cabins. Although the standard outside-view and interior (no view) cabins are a little small, they are well designed and functional in layout, and have earth tone colors accentuated by splashes of color from the bedspreads. Proportionately, there are quite a lot of interior (no view) cabins.

Many of the outside-view cabins have private balconies, and all seem to be quite well soundproofed, although the balcony partition is not floor to ceiling type, so you can hear your neighbors clearly (or smell their smoke). Note: the balconies are very narrow, and only just large enough for two small chairs, and there is no dedicated outdoor balcony lighting. Many cabins have third- and fourth-person upper bunk beds – these are good for families with children.

There is a reasonable amount of closet and abundant drawer and other storage space in all cabins; although this is adequate for a 7-night cruise, it would be tight for longer. Also provided are a color television, and refrigerator. Each night a chocolate will appear on your pillow. The cabin bathrooms are practical units, and come complete with all the details one needs, although again, they really are tight spaces, best described as one person at-a-time units. Fortunately, they have a shower enclosure of a decent size, a small amount of shelving for your personal toiletries, real glasses, a hairdryer and a bathrobe.

BERLITZ'S RATINGS

	Possible	Achieved
Ship	500	NYR
Accommodation	200	NYR
Food	400	NYR
Service	400	NYR
Entertainment	100	NYR
Cruise	400	NYR

SUITES: The largest accommodation can be found in six suites (Orcades, Orion, Orissa, Oronsay, Orsova, Orontes), two on each of three decks located at the stern of the ship, each with its own large private balcony. These suites are well laid out, and have large bathrooms with two sinks, a Jacuzzi bathtub, and a separate shower enclosure. The bedroom features generous amounts of wood accenting and detailing, indented ceilings, and television sets in both bedroom and lounge areas. The suites also have a dining room table and four chairs.

MINI-SUITES: These typically have two lower beds that convert into a queen-sized bed. There is a separate bedroom/sleeping area with vanity desk, and a lounge with sofa and coffee table, indented ceilings with generous amounts of wood accenting and detailing, walk-in closet, and larger bathroom with Jacuzzi bathtub and separate shower enclosure.

STANDARD OUTSIDE-VIEW/INTERIOR (NO VIEW) CABINS: A reasonable amount of closet and abundant drawer and other storage space is provided in all cabins – adequate for a 7-night cruise (but a little tight for longer cruises), as are a television and refrigerator. A chocolate is placed on your pillow each night. The cabin bathrooms are practical, and come with all the details one needs, although they really are tight spaces, best as one-person at-a-time units. They do, however, have a decent shower enclosure, a small amount of shelving for personal toiletries, real glasses, hairdryer and a bathrobe.

Note that P&O Cruises features the BBC World channel on the in-cabin color television system (when available, depending on cruise area), as well as movies (there is no dedicated theater aboard this ship).

DINING: There are two main dining rooms, Maggiore and Trasimeno. Both dining rooms are non-smoking, as are the dining rooms aboard all ships of P & O Cruises, and which one you are assigned to will depend on the location of your accommodation. Each has its own galley and each is split into multi-tier sections, which help create a feeling of intimacy, although there is a lot of noise from the waiter stations, which are adjacent to many tables. Breakfast and lunch are provided in an open seating arrangement; dinner is in two seatings.

The cuisine will be decidedly British – a little adventurous at times, but always, always there will be plenty of curry dishes and other standard British items – but with good presentation. However, you should not expect exquisite dining – this is British hotel catering that does not pretend to offer caviar and other gourmet foods – but what the company does present is attractive and tasty, with some excellent gravies and sauces to accompany meals. In keeping with the Britishness of P&O Cruises, the desserts are always enjoyable. A statement in the onboard cruise folder states that P&O Cruises does not knowingly purchase genetically modified foods. The service is provided by a team of friendly stewards – most of who are from the island of Goa – with which P&O has had a long relationship.

On most cruises, a typical menu cycle will include a Sailaway Dinner, Captain's Welcome Dinner, Chef's Dinner, Italian Dinner, French Dinner, Captain's Gala Dinner, and Landfall Dinner. The wine list is reasonable, but the company has, sadly, seen fit to eliminate all wine waiters. Note that 15 percent is added to all beverage bills, including wines (whether you order a £10 bottle or a £100 bottle of wine, even though it takes the same amount of service to open and pour the wine).

The Pavilion self-serve buffet, open 24 hours a day, is located above the navigation bridge, and has some commanding views. At night, this large room (there are two food lines – one each on both port and starboard sides), which resembles a food court, can be transformed into an informal dinner setting with sit-down waiter service.

Outdoors on deck, with a sheltered view over the Riviera Pool, the Riviera Grill features fast-food items for those who don't want to change for their sunbathing attire. For informal eats, there is also *Café Corniche*, for pizzas and light snacks; it is located on the uppermost level of the four deck high atrium lobby.

In addition, there's also a patisserie (for cappuccino/espresso coffees and pastries), a wine/caviar bar (Premier Cru). The cabin service menu is very limited, and presentation of the food items featured is poor.

OTHER COMMENTS: Although large (and the identical twin to *Oceana*), this all-white ship has a profile that is well balanced by a large, stylish, swept-back buff-colored funnel, which contains a deck tennis/basketball/volleyball court in its sheltered aft base. Originally built for Princess Cruises as *Sea Princess*, the ship is now marketed to British passengers as part of the P&O Cruises fleet. There is a wide, teak wrap-around promenade deck outdoors, some real teak steamer-style deck chairs (with royal blue cushioned pads), and 93,000 sq. ft (8,640 sq. meters) of outdoors space. A great amount of glass area on the upper decks provides plenty of light and connection with the outside world.

The ship actually absorbs passengers quite well, and some areas have an almost intimate feel to them, which is what the interior designers intended. The interiors are very attractive, with warm colors and welcoming decor that includes countless wall murals and other artwork. The signs around the ship could be better, however.

There is a wide range of public rooms to choose from, with several intimate rooms and spaces so that you aren't overwhelmed by large spaces. The decor is tasteful, with attractive color combinations that are warm and don't clash (nothing is brash). The interior focal point is a large four-deck-high atrium lobby with winding, double stairways, complete with two panoramic glass-walled elevators.

The main public entertainment rooms are located under three cabin decks. There is plenty of space, the traffic flow is good, and the ship absorbs people well. There are two show lounges (Limelight, and Spotlight), one at each end of the ship; one is a superb 550-seat, theater-style show lounge (movies are also shown here) and the other is a 480-seat cabaret-style lounge with bar.

A glass-walled health spa complex is located high atop ship with gymnasium and high-tech machines. One swimming pool is "suspended" aft between two decks (there are two other pools (and two pools for children), although they are not large for the size of the ship).

The library is a very warm room and has several large buttery leather chairs for listening to compact audio discs, with ocean-view windows. There is a conference center for up to 300, as well as a business center, with computers, copy and fax machines. The collection of artwork is good, particularly on the stairways, and helps make the ship feel smaller than it is, although in places it doesn't always seem coordinated. The Monte Carlo Club Casino, while large, is not really in the main passenger flow and so it does not generate the "walk-through" factor found aboard so many ships.

The most traditional room aboard is the Wheelhouse Lounge/Bar, which is decorated in the style of a late 19th-century gentleman's club, complete with wood paneling and comfortable seating. The focal point is a large ship model from the P&O collection archives: *Arandora Star*.

Ballroom dance aficionados will be pleased to note that there are several good-sized wooden dance floors aboard this ship. The ship always carries a professional dance couple as hosts and teachers, and there is plenty of dancing time included in the entertainment programming.

Children have their own Treasure Chest (for ages 2–5), The Hideout (for 6–9 years olds), and for older children (aged 10–13) there is The Buzz Zone.

At the end of the day – as is the case aboard most large ships – you will be well attended if you live in the top-grade accommodation; if you do not, you will merely be one of a very large number of passengers. One nice feature is the captain's cocktail party – it is typically held in the four-deck-high main atrium – so you can come and go as you please – and there's no standing in line to have your photograph taken with the captain if you don't want to.

However, note that in the quest for increased onboard revenue (and shareholder value), even birthday cakes are an extra-cost item, as are espressos and cappuccinos (fake ones, made from instant coffee, are available in the dining rooms). Also at extra cost are ice cream, and bottled water (these can add up to a considerable amount on an around-the-world cruise, for example). You can expect to be subjected to a stream of flyers advertising daily art auctions, "designer" watches, "inch of gold/silver" and other promotions. For gratuities (which are optional), you should typically allow £3.50 ($5.25) per person, per day.

Adonia is being transferred from the Princess Cruises fleet (its previous name was *Sea Princess*) to the UK-based parent company P&O Cruises, to begin cruising in May 2003. *Adonia* will replace *Arcadia*, which will be placed into a new cruise line, named Ocean Village, and targeted to a younger audience. *Adonia* will cater to an adults-only clientele, with a more relaxed (come as you wish, dress up if you wish) dress code. Many of the public rooms will have undergone name changes to better reflect the tastes of P&O's mainly British passengers.

Note that this book was published before *Sun Princess* left the Princess Cruises fleet to P&O Cruises to become *Adonia*. Although not yet rated as *Adonia*, the evaluations and ratings in effect when the ship was operated as *Sun Princess* (1,539 points, 4 Stars) are expected to be reasonably similar when the ship is re-evaluated.

WEAK POINTS: There are a number of dead ends in the interior layout, so it's not as user-friendly as it should be. Standing in line for embarkation (an "express check-in" option is available by completing certain documentation 40 days in advance of your cruise), disembarkation, shore tenders and for self-serve buffet meals is an inevitable aspect of cruising aboard all large ships. Shuttle buses, which used to be provided in the various ports, are no longer complimentary when provided (except on the around-the-world cruise).

There is no escape from repetitious announcements (for activities that bring revenue, such as art auctions, bingo, horse racing) that intrude on your cruise vacation (depending on itinerary).

The digital voice announcing elevator deck stops is irritating to passengers (many of whom tell me they would like to rip out the speaker system). There are a number of dead ends in the interior layout, so it's not as user-friendly as it should be. The cabin numbering system is extremely illogical, with numbers going through several hundred series on the same deck.

The swimming pools are quite small considering the number of passengers carried, and the pool deck is cluttered with white, plastic deck lounge chairs, without cushioned pads. Waiting for tenders in anchor ports can prove irritating, but again, it is now typical of large ship operations. Shuttle buses, which used to be provided free in some ports, are no longer complimentary.

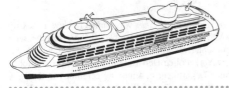

Adventure of the Seas
★★★★

Large Ship:	137,276 tons	Total Crew:	1,185
Lifestyle:	Standard	Passengers	
Cruise Line:	Royal Caribbean International	(lower beds/all berths):	3,114/3,838
		Passenger Space Ratio	
Former Names:	none	(lower beds/all berths):	44.0/35.7
Builder:	Kvaerner Masa-Yards (Finland)	Crew/Passenger Ratio	
Original Cost:	$500 million	(lower beds/all berths):	2.6/3.2
Entered Service:	Nov 2001	Navigation Officers:	Scandinavian
Registry:	The Bahamas	Cabins (total):	1,557
Length (ft/m):	1,020.6/311.1	Size Range (sq ft/m):	151.0–1,358.0/
Beam (ft/m):	155.5/47.4		14.0–126.1
Draft (ft/m):	28.8/8.8	Cabins (outside view):	939
Propulsion/Propellers:	diesel-electric	Cabins (interior/no view):	618
	(75,600kW)/3 azimuthing pods	Cabins (for one person):	0
Passenger Decks:	14	Cabins (with private balcony):	765

Cabins (wheelchair accessible):	26
Cabin Current:	110 volts
Elevators:	14 (6 glass-enclosed)
Casino (gaming tables):	Yes
Slot Machines:	Yes
Swimming Pools (outdoors):	3
Swimming Pools (indoors):	0
Whirlpools:	6
Fitness Center:	Yes
Sauna/Steam Room:	Yes/Yes
Massage:	Yes
Self-Service Launderette:	No
Dedicated Cinema/Seats:	No
Library:	Yes
Classification Society:	Det Norske Veritas

OVERALL SCORE: 1,537 (OUT OF A POSSIBLE 2,000 POINTS)

ACCOMMODATION: There is an extensive range of 22 cabin categories in four major groupings: Premium ocean-view suites and cabins, Promenade-view (interior-view) cabins, Ocean-view cabins, and Interior (no view) cabins. Many cabins are of a similar size – good for incentives and large groups, and 300 have interconnecting doors – good for families.

A total of 138 interior (no view) cabins have bay windows that look *into* a horizontal atrium – first used to good effect aboard the Baltic passenger ferries *Silja Serenade* (1990) and *Silja Symphony* (1991) with interior (no view) cabins that look into a central shopping plaza. Regardless of what cabin grade you choose, however, all except for the Royal Suite and Owner's Suite feature twin beds that convert to a queen-sized unit, television, radio and telephone, personal safe, vanity unit, mini-bar (called an Automatic Refreshment Center) hairdryer and private bathroom.

The largest accommodation includes luxuriously appointed penthouse suites (whose occupants, sadly, must share the rest of the ship with everyone else, except for their own exclusive, and private, concierge club). The grandest is the Royal Suite, which is positioned on the port side of the ship, and measures 106.5 sq. meters/1,146 sq. ft). It features a king-sized bed in a separate, large bedroom, a living room with an additional queen-sized sofa bed, baby grand piano (no pianist is included, however), refrigerator/wet bar, dining table, entertainment center, and large bathroom.

Slightly smaller, but still highly desirable are the Owner's Suites (there are 10, all located in the center

BERLITZ'S RATINGS		
	Possible	Achieved
Ship	500	431
Accommodation	200	160
Food	400	252
Service	400	294
Entertainment	100	83
Cruise	400	317

of the ship, on both port and starboard sides, each measuring 43 sq. meters/468 sq. ft) and four Royal Family suites (each 53 sq. meters/574 sq. ft), all of which feature similar items. However, the four Royal Family suites, which have two bedrooms (including one with third/fourth upper Pullman berths) are at the stern of the ship and have magnificent views over the ship's wake (and seagulls).

No matter what grade of accommodation you choose, all cabins feature twin beds that convert to a queen-sized bed, a private bathroom with shower enclosure (towels are 100 percent cotton), as well as interactive, closed circuit and satellite television, and pay-per-view movies. Cabins with "private balconies" are not so private, as the partitions are only partial, leaving you exposed to your neighbor's smoke or conversation. The balcony decking is made of Bolidt – a sort of rubberized sand – and not wood, while the balcony rail is of wood.

DINING: The main dining room (total capacity 1,919) is undoubtedly large and is set on three levels, all of which are named after composers (Mozart, Strauss, Vivaldi). A dramatic staircase connects all three levels. However, all three feature exactly the same menus and food. There are also two small private wings for private groups: La Cetra, and La Notte, each seating 58 persons. The dining room is totally non-smoking, there are two seatings, and tables are for four, six, eight 10 or 12. The place settings, china and cutlery are of good quality.

The cuisine is typical of mass banquet catering that offers standard fare comparable to that found in American family-style restaurants ashore. The food costs are well below that for sister company Celebrity Cruises, and so you should not expect the same food quality. While the menu descriptions sound tempting, the actual food may be somewhat disappointing and unmemorable. The menu descriptions make the food sound better than it is (which is consistently below average), mostly disappointing and without much taste. However, a decent selection of light meals is provided, and there's a vegetarian menu. The selection of breads, rolls, fruit and cheese is quite poor. Caviar (once a standard menu item) incurs a hefty extra charge. There is no good caviar, and special orders, tableside carving and flambeau items are not offered. Dinner menus typically include a Welcome-Aboard Dinner, French Dinner, Italian Dinner, International Dinner, Captain's Gala Dinner.

While USDA prime beef is very good, other meats may not be (they are often disguised with gravies or heavy sauces). Most of the fish (apart from salmon) and seafood is overcooked and lacking in taste. Green vegetables are scarce, although salad items are plentiful. Rice is often used to replace potatoes and other sources of carbohydrates. Breads and pastry items are generally good (although some items, such as croissants, for example, may not be made on board). Dessert items are very standardized, and the selection of cheeses is poor (almost all come from the USA, known mostly for its processed, sliced, colored cheeses), as is the choice of accompanying crackers.

ALTERNATIVE DINING OPTIONS: These are for casual and informal meals at all hours and include:
● *Cafe Promenade*: for continental breakfast, all-day pizzas, pastries, desserts and specialty coffees (sadly provided in paper cups).
● *Windjammer Café*: for casual buffet-style breakfast, lunch and light dinner (except the last night of the cruise).
● *Island Grill*: (this is actually a section inside the Windjammer Café), for casual dinner (no reservations necessary) featuring a grill and open kitchen.
● *Portofino*: an "upscale" (non-smoking) Euro-Italian restaurant (98 seats) for dinner (reservations required).
● *Johnny Rockets*, a retro 1950s all-day, all-night eatery that features hamburgers, malt shakes (at extra cost), and jukebox hits, with both indoor and outdoor seating.
● *Sprinkles*: for round-the-clock ice cream and yoghurt.

OTHER COMMENTS: *Adventurer of the Seas* is a stunning, large, floating leisure resort, sister to *Explorer of the Seas* and *Voyager of the Seas*, which debuted in 2000 and 1999, respectively, and two others still to come. The exterior design is not unlike an enlarged version of the company's *Vision*-class ships. The ships are, at present, the largest cruise vessels in the world in terms of tonnage measurement (but, to keep things in perspective, the ships are not quite as long as Norwegian Cruise Line's *Norway*, and will be eclipsed in January 2004 when Cunard Line's *Queen Mary 2* debuts).

Adventure of the Seas was named in New York City by Mayor Giuliani on November 10, 2001, together with representatives from the Fire Department of New York, New York Police Department, and the Port Authority Police Department in a moving ceremony at the New York Passenger Terminal at Pier 88. At that time, Royal Caribbean International made a $50,000 contribution to the Twin Towers Relief Fund, in the aftermath of the terrorist atrocities inflicted on the city.

The ship's propulsion is derived from three pod units, powered by electric motors (two azimuthing, and one fixed at the centerline) instead of conventional rudders and propellers, in the latest configuration of high-tech propulsion systems.

With large proportions, the ship provides more facilities and options, and caters to more passengers than any other Royal Caribbean International ship has in the past, and yet the ship manages to have a healthy passenger space ratio (the amount of space per passenger). Being a "non-Panamax" ship, it is simply too large to go through the Panama Canal, thus limiting its itineraries almost exclusively to the Caribbean (where only a few islands can accept it), or for use as a floating island resort. Spend the first few hours exploring all the many facilities and public spaces aboard this vessel and it will be time well spent.

Although the ship is large, the accommodation hallways are warm and attractive, with artwork cabinets and wavy lines to break up the monotony. In fact, there are plenty of decorative touches to help you avoid what would otherwise be a very clinical environment.

Embarkation and disembarkation take place through two stations/access points, designed to minimize the inevitable lines (that's over 1,500 people for each access point). Once inside the ship, you'll need good walking shoes, particularly when you need to go from one end to the other – it really is quite a long way.

The four-decks-high Royal Promenade, which is 393.7 ft (120 meters) long, is the main interior focal point (it's a good place to hang out, to meet someone, or to arrange to meet someone). The length of two football fields, it has two internal lobbies (atria) that rise to as many as 11 decks high. Restaurants, shops and entertainment locations front this winding street and interior "with-view" cabins look into it from above. It is designed loosely in the image of London's fashionable Burlington Arcade – although there's not a real brick in sight, and I wonder if the designers have ever visited the real thing. It is, however, an imaginative piece of design work, and most passengers (particularly those who enjoy shopping malls) enjoy it immensely.

The super-atrium houses a "traditional" pub, with draft beer and plenty of "street-front" seating (North American passengers always seem to sit down, while British passengers prefer to stand at the bar). There is also a Champagne Bar, a Sidewalk Café (for continental breakfast, all-day pizzas, specialty coffees and desserts), Sprinkles (for round-the-clock ice cream and yoghurt), and a sports bar. There are also several shops – jewelry shop, gift shop, liquor shop and the logo souvenir shop. Altogether, the Royal promenade is a nice place to see and be seen, and it sees action throughout the day and night. Comedy art has its place here, too, for example in the *trompe l'oeil* painter climbing up the walls). The Guest Reception and Shore Excursion counters are located at the aft end of the promenade, as is an ATM machine. Things to watch for: look up to see the large moving, asteroid-like sculpture (constantly growing and contracting), parades and street entertainers.

Arched across the promenade is a captain's balcony. Meanwhile, in the center of the promenade is a stairway that connects you to the deck below, where you'll find Schooner Bar (a piano lounge) and the colorful Casino Royale. This is naturally large and full of flashing lights and noises. Casino gaming includes blackjack, Caribbean stud poker, roulette, and craps.

Aft to the casino is the Aquarium Bar, while close by are some neat displays of oceanographic interest. Royal Caribbean International has teamed up with the University of Miami's Rosenstiel School of Marine and Atmospheric Science to study the ocean and the atmosphere. A small onboard laboratory is part of project.

Action man and action woman can enjoy more sporting pursuits, such as a rock-climbing wall that's 32.8 ft high (10 meters). It is located outdoors at the aft end of the funnel. You'll get a great "buzz" being 200 ft (70 meters) above the ocean while the ship is moving – particularly when it rolls.

There's also a rollerblading track, a dive-and-snorkel shop, a full-size basketball court and 9-hole golf driving range. A ShipShape health spa measures 15,000 sq. ft (1,400 sq. meters), includes a large aerobics room, fitness center (with the usual stairmasters, treadmills, stationary bikes, weight machines and free weights), treatment rooms, men's and women's sauna/steam rooms, while another 10,000 sq. ft (930 sq. meters) is devoted to a Solarium (with magrodome sliding glass roof) for relaxation after you've exercised too much.

There's also a regulation-size ice-skating rink (Studio B), featuring *real*, not fake, ice, with "bleacher" seating for up to 900, and the latest in broadcast facilities. Ice Follies shows are presented here. Slim pillars obstruct clear-view arena stage sight lines, however.

If ice-skating in the Caribbean doesn't appeal, you may enjoy the stunning two-deck library (open 24 hours a day). A grand $12 million has been spent on permanent artwork. Drinking places include a neat Aquarium Bar, complete with 50 tons of glass and water in four large aquariums (whose combined value is over $1 million).

Other drinking places include the small and intimate Champagne Bar, Crown & Anchor Pub, and a Connoisseur Club – for cigars and cognacs. Lovers of jazz might appreciate High Notes, an intimate room for cool music, or the Schooner Bar piano lounge. Golfers might enjoy the 19th Hole – a golf bar.

Show lovers will find that the Palace Showlounge is quite a dramatic room that seats 1,350 and spans the height of five decks; it features a hydraulic orchestra pit and huge stage areas.

There is a television studio, located adjacent to rooms that could be used, for example, for trade show exhibit space. Lovers can tie the knot in the wedding chapel in the sky, called the Skylight Chapel (on the upper level of the Observation Lounge, and even has wheelchair access via an electric stairway lift). Outdoors, the pool and open deck areas provide a resort-like environment.

Children's facilities are extensive. "Aquanauts" is for 3–5 year olds; "Explorers" is for 6–8 year olds; "Voyagers" is for 9–12 year olds. Optix is a dedicated area for teenagers, including a daytime club (with several computers), soda bar, and dance floor. "Challenger's Arcade" features an array of the latest video games. Paint and Clay is an arts and crafts center for younger children. Adjacent is Adventure Beach, an area for all the family; it includes swimming pools, a water slide and game areas outdoors.

In terms of sheer size, this ship dwarfs all other ships in the cruise industry, but in terms of personal service, the reverse tends to be the case, unless you happen to reside in one of the top suites. Royal Caribbean International does, however, try hard to provide a good standard of programmed service from its hotel service staff. Remember to take lots of extra pennies – you'll need them to pay for all the additional-cost items.

The ship is large, so remember that if you meet someone somewhere, and want to meet them again you'll need to make an appointment (arrange to meet along the Royal Promenade) – for this really is a large, Las Vegas-style American floating resort-city for the lively of heart and fleet of foot.

WEAK POINTS: Standing in line for embarkation, disembarkation, shore tenders and for self-serve buffet meals is an inevitable aspect of cruising aboard all large ships. Lines for check-in, embarkation and disembarkation (it's better if you are a non-US resident and stay at an RCI-booked hotel, as all formalities can be completed there and then you'll simply walk on board to your cabin). Suites and cabins with private balcony have Bolidt floors (a substance that looks like rubberized sand) instead of wood.

If you have a cabin with a door that interconnecting door to another cabin, be aware that you'll probably be able to hear *everything* your next-door neighbors say and do. Bathroom toilets are explosively noisy – like a barking dog.

You'll need to plan what you want to take part in wisely as almost everything requires you to sign-up in advance (many activities take place only on sea days). The cabin bath towels are small and skimpy. There are very few quiet places to sit and read – almost everywhere there is intrusive acoustic wallpaper (background music). Although the menus and food variety offered have been upgraded since the introduction, remember that you get what you pay for.

Aegean I
★★

Mid-Size Ship: . . . . .11,563 tons	Total Crew: 200	Cabins (wheelchair accessible): 0
Lifestyle: . . . . .Standard	Passengers	Cabin Current: . . . . .220 volts
Cruise Line: . . . . .Golden Star Cruises	(lower beds/all berths): 560/682	Elevators: 2
Former Names: . . . .*Aegean Dolphin,*	Passenger Space Ratio	Casino (gaming tables): . . . . .Yes
Dolphin, Aegean Dolphin, Alkyon, Narcis	(lower beds/all berths): 20.6/16.8	Slot Machines: . . . . .Yes
Builder: . . . .Santierul N. Galatz (Romania)	Crew/Passenger Ratio	Swimming Pools (outdoors): 1
Original Cost: .n/a	(lower beds/all berths): 2.8/3.4	Swimming Pools (indoors): 0
Entered Service: 1974/May 2002	Navigation Officers: . . . . .Greek	Whirlpools: 0
Registry: .Greece	Cabins (total): 280	Fitness Center: . . . . .Yes
Length (ft/m): 460.9/140.5	Size Range (sq ft/m): 134.5–290.6/	Sauna/Steam Room: . . . . .Yes/No
Beam (ft/m): 67.2/20.5	12.5–27.0	Massage: . . . . .Yes
Draft (ft/m): 20.3/6.2	Cabins (outside view): 198	Self-Service Launderette: . . . . .No
Propulsion/Propellers: . . . . .diesel	Cabins (interior/no view): 82	Dedicated Cinema/Seats: Yes/172
(10,296kW)/2	Cabins (for one person): 0	Library: . . . . .Yes
Passenger Decks: 8	Cabins (with private balcony): 8	Classification Society: . . .Lloyd's Register

---

OVERALL SCORE: 897 (OUT OF A POSSIBLE 2,000 POINTS)

ACCOMMODATION: This ship has nine different cabin price grades. Most of the cabins have an outside-view, and most are of the same size and configuration, although the largest cabins can be found on Sun Deck. All cabins feature a small refrigerator and telephone. They are reasonably spacious considering the size of the ship, and they are quite pleasantly decorated, although closet, drawer and luggage storage space for two is limited (it certainly is not enough for a long cruise), but adequate for one; the walls and ceilings are very plain (perhaps more artwork would help). Note that the cabin soundproofing is extremely poor, and you can hear almost everything that's happening in the adjacent cabin(s).

The bathrooms are partly tiled, although they are small and basic, and only just adequate, but there really is little space for personal toiletry items. Bathrobes are typically only provided for occupants of accommodation designated as suites (although this also depends on anyone who may charter and operate the vessel). All toilets are of the non-vacuum type and are quiet, although the toilet seats are extremely high, at 20 inches (52 cm).

There are two suites on Sun Deck – the largest accommodation aboard this ship. Although the lounge area is not even curtained off from the sleeping area, it is quite large. The bathroom features a full size bathtub, although the "lip" (step) into the bathroom is unnecessarily high (11 inches/28 cm).

DINING: The dining room, located on one of the lowest passenger decks, features restful colors, and has mostly large tables (there are no tables for two). It is a no-smoking room, there are two seatings, and the ceilings are plain. There is a decent amount of space around each table, allowing waiters the room to provide a decent service, although this tends to be quite hurried at times.

A mixture of Continental and Greek cuisine is featured, with only a limited selection of breads, cheeses and fruits, which tend to be very standard items.

For casual meals, small (limited choice) self-serve breakfast and lunch buffets are available on the Lido Deck aft, where a popular outdoor gyro and salad bar is available, although the standards of food handling and hygiene leave much to be desired.

OTHER COMMENTS: Golden Star Cruises had a slight name change in 2002, from Golden Sun Cruises (the company then had three ships, namely, *Aegean I, Aegean Spirit* and *Arcadia,* each put into the company by three separate owners). The profile of this ship looks reasonably smart – in some ways almost contemporary – although the stern is very square and angular, the result of an extensive $26 million conversion, which involved a "chop and stretch" operation between 1986 and 1988.

The open deck space can be said to be moderately good, but it is certainly not enough when the ship is full, and that means it could be difficult to find good sunbathing space. Also, the number of deck lounge chairs is very limited.

Inside, the public rooms are quite tastefully decorated in soft, mostly pastel colors, although there is much use

BERLITZ'S RATINGS		
	Possible	Achieved
Ship	500	224
Accommodation	200	97
Food	400	175
Service	400	205
Entertainment	100	37
Cruise	400	159

of mirrored surfaces. There is a reasonable showlounge, laid out in a single-level amphitheater-style, although 10 pillars obstruct the sight lines from many seats. The Belvedere Lounge, which is set high atop the ship and forward, features a smart piano bar and good ocean views through large windows.

A dialysis station is a useful addition to medical facilities, although the beauty salon and "spa" facilities are cramped and poor.

In general, the service, from a mainly Greek hotel staff could be said to be selectively friendly (when they want to be), although there is certainly little finesse. Many members of the ship's crew, including officers, can be seen smoking in public areas (this would be totally against the regulations of almost all non-Greek cruise companies, or any company that is serious about the hospitality industry).

This ship really caters best primarily to European passengers who don't expect much in the way of food and service and just want to take a 3- or 4-day cruise to get around some of the islands in the Aegean Sea, the ship performing more as a water-taxi with full board included. The ship is often placed under charter to various operators, and cruises are sold by a number of different organizations in many countries. Thus, *Aegean I*

will provide you with a basic cruise experience in moderately comfortable but very densely populated surroundings, but at a reasonable price – therefore you should not expect the spit and polish that other ships might provide in the same price range. The onboard currency is the euro.

WEAK POINTS:
Although at first glance the ship appears to have a good range of nicely decorated public rooms, on closer inspection some of the materials used in their construction are held together by the "patch and fix" method of shipbuilding and refurbishment, which is definitely below internationally accepted standards. There are too many unnecessary announcements (often made in several languages, depending on the passenger mix and cruise).

The teakwood decking around the swimming pool is not in good condition. The gangway is narrow and steep in some ports. There are no cushioned pads for the deck lounge chairs (lying on a towel on plastic ribbing is no fun for more than a few minutes). The poor attitude and hospitality from most officers and crew is unacceptable, and officers should learn to turn their two-way radios down.

AIDAcara
★★★★

Large Ship: ....38,600 tons	Total Crew: 370	Cabins (wheelchair accessible): 4
Lifestyle: ....Standard	Passengers	Cabin Current: ....110 and 220 volts
Cruise Line: ......Aida Cruises (Seetours)	(lower beds/all berths): 1,186/1,230	Elevators: 5
Former Names: ....*Aida*	Passenger Space Ratio	Casino (gaming tables): ....No
Builder: ....Kvaerner Masa-Yards	(lower beds/all berths): 32.5/31.3	Slot Machines: ....No
(Finland)	Crew/Passenger Ratio	Swimming Pools (outdoors): 1
Original Cost: ....DM300 million	(lower beds/all berths): 3.2/3.3	Swimming Pools (indoors): 0
Entered Service: ....June 1996	Navigation Officers: ....German	Whirlpools: 3
Registry: ....Great Britain	Cabins (total): 593	Fitness Center: ....Yes
Length (ft/m): 634.1/193.3	Size Range (sq ft/m): 145.3–376.7/	Sauna/Steam Room: ....Yes/Yes
Beam (ft/m): 90.5/27.6	13.5–35.0	Massage: ....Yes
Draft (ft/m): 20.3/6.2	Cabins (outside view): 391	Self-Service Launderette: ....Yes
Propulsion/Propellers: ....diesel	Cabins (interior/no view): 202	Dedicated Cinema/Seats: ....No
(21,720kw)/2	Cabins (for one person): 0	Library: ....Yes
Passenger Decks: 9	Cabins (with private balcony): 4	Classification Society: Germanischer Lloyd

OVERALL SCORE: 1,529 (OUT OF A POSSIBLE 2,000 POINTS)

ACCOMMODATION: There are five grades: A-outside (182.9 sq. ft/17 sq. meters); B-outside (145.3 sq. ft/13.5 sq. meters); C-Interior (156 sq. ft/14.5 sq. meters); Junior Suite (269.1 sq. ft/25 sq. meters); Suite (376.7 sq. ft/ 35 sq. meters). The decor is bright, splashy, youthful, and contemporary. All cabins are accented with multi-patterned fabrics, wood-trimmed cabinetry (with nicely rounded edges) and rattan furniture. The twin beds have duvets, and a fabric canopy from headboard to ceiling. Windows feature full pull-down blackout blinds.

Grades A, B, and C have just a small amount of drawer space, but, as you will not need many clothes, this is not really a drawback. Some cabins in grades A, B and C have one bed and a convertible daytime sofa bed. All cabin bathrooms are compact, but well designed, feature showers, and wall-mounted soap/shampoo dispensers, so there is no wastage of throwaway plastic bottles (environmentally friendly). But you should bring your own conditioner, hand lotion, or any other personal toiletry items. Cotton bathrobes are provided. Although bathrooms do not have a hairdryer, one is located in the vanity unit in the cabin. There is no cabinet for personal toiletry items.

Four Suites have a forward-facing private balcony (all four share the same, ship-wide balcony, as there are no partitions for privacy) and more luxurious furnishings and fittings. Seating in the cabin lounge area is in contemporary rattan chairs. There is a wall unit that houses a television that can be turned for viewing from either lounge or bedroom, and a refrigerator.

BERLITZ'S RATINGS

	Possible	Achieved
Ship	500	415
Accommodation	200	148
Food	400	296
Service	400	289
Entertainment	100	71
Cruise	400	310

Suites and Junior Suites have a generous amount of closet, drawer and other storage space, a stocked mini-bar, and a VCR. Bathrooms have a full-size bathtub and hairdryer.

The cabins are cleaned and beds are made each morning, but not in the evening. For anyone allergic to natural fibers, down-filled duvets and pillows can be replaced with those made of synthetic materials.

DINING: There are two large self-service buffet restaurants: "Caribbean" and "Market" (open almost 24 hours a day) and Maritime Restaurant, an à la carte restaurant, with waiter and sommelier service.

The standard of food offered at the serve yourself buffet islands is good to very good, with creative presentation and good table-clearing service. There is no standing in long lines, as is common aboard most other cruise ships. There is always a fine selection of breads, cheeses, cold cuts, fruits and make-your-own teas (with a choice of more than 30 types of loose-leaf regular and herbal teas, as well as coffee).

At peak times, the buffet restaurants may remind you of motorway cafés (albeit elegant ones), with all their attendant noise, but a good selection of foods is provided (more than 1,200 items). You can sit where you want, when you want, and with whom you want, so dining really becomes a socially interactive occasion. Because of the two large self-serve buffet rooms and dining concept, the crew to passenger ratio looks poor; but this is because there really are no waiters as such (except in the à la carte Maritime Restaurant), only staff for clearing tables.

The Maritime Restaurant, which has 74 mostly high-back seats, has an intimate dining atmosphere. It is open for dinner only, and features a set five- or six-course menu that is changed every few days. There is no extra charge, except for additional à la carte menu items (such as sevruga caviar, smoked salmon, châteaubriand, rib-eye steak), and for wines. Reservations are made each morning of the day you want to eat in the Maritime Restaurant, at the reception desk.

OTHER COMMENTS: The ship (originally the *Aida*, the name was changed in 2001) has a contemporary profile, is well proportioned, and has a swept-back funnel and wedge-shaped stern. There is no mistaking the red lips painted on the bows, as well as the blue eyes of Aïda (from Verdi's opera, written to commemorate the opening of the Suez Canal in 1871).

AIDAcara is known as a "Club Ship," offering a sea-going version of Germany's popular Robinson Clubs. In case you are confused about the brand name, Aida Cruises (like A'Rosa Cruises) is part of Seetours, which is itself a part of P&O Princess Cruises. Actually, if you take a river cruise in Europe, A'Rosa Cruises operates two river vessels, *A'Rosa Bella* and *A'Rosa Donna* (some have called the pair BellaDonna).

This fun ship includes a whole army of "animateurs" (like the GOs of Club Med, but better) who enjoy leading a variety of activities by day (they also act as escorts for shore excursions), and as entertainers by night, acting in the colorful, often funny, shows alongside the professional entertainers. They (along with other staff) also interact with passengers throughout the ship, and can drink with them at the bars – something not permitted aboard most cruise ships.

There is a wrap-around promenade deck outdoors, good for strolling, or for sitting in a deck lounge chair and just taking in the sea air. Outside on deck, the swimming pool and surrounding area has several cascading levels at the forward end for deck chairs and sun lounging, plus a basketball court, although the pool itself is small.

Inside, there is no wasted space, and the public rooms are open and flow into each other instead of being contained spaces. The "you are here" (deck plan) signs are excellent, and finding your way round is a simple matter. The decor is upbeat and trendy, and will appeal to younger passengers, particularly those who may not have cruised before. A large observation lounge is set high atop the ship overlooking the bow. There is a wide array of intimate public rooms and spaces from which to choose.

The fitness, wellness and sports programming is among the most extensive in the cruise industry. The "Wellness Center" is aft on Deck 10. It measures 11,840 sq. ft (1,100 sq. meters), and contains two saunas (one seats more than 20 persons and has glass ocean-view walls), massage and other treatment rooms, and large lounging area. Forward and outside the wellness center, is an FKK (FreiKoerperKultur) nude sunbathing deck.

One popular feature are the more than two dozen "Hit Bikes" (mountain bikes with tough front and rear suspension units) for conducted biking excursions in each port of call – the concept and concession of Austrian Downhill Champion Skier Erwin Resch. In addition, there is a 400-meter (1,312-ft) jogging track.

Central to all social interactions is the Aida Lounge, which features novel "lollipop stick" decorations on the bar counter. The bar itself, at 162.4 ft (49.5 meters) long, is the longest bar aboard any cruise ship. The feel is youthful, colorful, unpretentious, casual, relaxed, and sporting.

This is a family-friendly ship, with plenty of activities for younger family members (children are split into two age groups: Seepferdchen, from 4 to 7 years; Sharks, from 8 to 13 years). There is a diverse selection of children's and youth programs – good for families. Children can make their own menus for the week (together with the chef), and get to go into the galley to make cookies and other items – a novel idea that more ships could adopt.

The ship caters best to first-time passengers and youthful German-speaking couples seeking good value for money in a fun environment. The dress code is simple: "casual" (no dinner jackets or ties) at all times.

There are two alternating itineraries in the Mediterranean during the summer, and in the winter, there are two alternating itineraries in the Caribbean. Alternating 7-night itineraries can be combined for a 14-day cruise. In addition, packages created by tour operators such as Jahn Reisen and Seetours can add land stays for an even longer cruise and resort holiday experience. This presents a good amount of flexibility.

About 20 nationalities are represented among the crew, who are upbeat and cheerful, and really want passengers to have a good time in an unstuffy atmosphere. And they do, for this is a young, vibrant, and fun ship, with plenty of passenger participation in all kinds of events. The brochure accurately describes the casual, young, fun and active lifestyle (whenever I sail aboard the ship, few passengers appear to be over the age of 40).

Aida Cruises/Seetours also has a whole range of hotels you can book to extend your vacation either before or after your cruise. All port taxes and gratuities are included, and, with very reasonable cruise fares, it is almost cheaper than staying home, and better value than almost any land-based vacation. The euro is the currency used on board.

WEAK POINTS: Standing in line for embarkation, disembarkation, shore tenders and for self-serve buffet meals is an inevitable aspect of cruising aboard all large ships. There is a charge for use of the washing machines and the dryers in the self-service launderette. The swimming pool is too small for the number of passengers carried – particularly during the hot winter (Caribbean) season.

Sadly, the shows have become increasingly amateurish – not as good as they were when the ship debuted.

AIDAvita
NOT YET RATED

Large Ship: ....42,200 tons	Passengers	Cabin Current: ....220 volts
Lifestyle: ....Standard	(lower beds/all berths): 1,266/1,582	Elevators: 6
Cruise Line: ....Aida Cruises	Passenger Space Ratio	Casino (gaming tables): ....No
(Seetours)	(lower beds/all berths): 33.3/26.6	Slot Machines: ....No
Former Names: ....none	Crew/Passenger Ratio	Swimming Pools (outdoors): 2
Builder: ....Aker MTW (Germany)	(lower beds/all berths): 3.0/3.7	Swimming Pools (indoors): 0
Original Cost: ....$350 million	Navigation Officers: ....German	Whirlpools: 5
Entered Service: ....Apr 2002	Cabins (total): 633	Fitness Center: ....Yes
Registry: ....Great Britain	Size Range (sq ft/m): 145.3–344.4/	Sauna/Steam Room: ....Yes/Yes
Length (ft/m): 666.6/203.2	13.5–32.0	Massage: ....Yes
Beam (ft/m): 92.2/28.1	Cabins (outside view): 422	Self-Service Launderette: ....Yes
Draft (ft/m): 20.7/6.3	Cabins (interior/no view): 211	Dedicated Cinema/Seats: ....No
Propulsion/Propellers: ...diesel-electric/2	Cabins (for one person): 0	Library: ....Yes
Passenger Decks: 10	Cabins (with private balcony): 60	Classification Society: .....Germanischer
Total Crew: 418	Cabins (wheelchair accessible): 4	Lloyd

OVERALL SCORE: NYR (OUT OF A POSSIBLE 2,000 POINTS)

ACCOMMODATION: There are seven grades of accommodation: Suite (344.4 sq. ft/32 sq. meters), including balcony; A-outside-view (188.3 sq. ft/17.5 sq. meters) with balcony; A-outside-view (182.9 sq. ft/17 sq. meters) without balcony: B-outside-view (145.3 sq. ft/13.5 sq. meters); C-interior (no view: 156.0 sq. ft/14.5 sq. meters). All suites and cabins are designed for two persons; however, a total of 94 cabins also have two extra beds/berths for children, and some cabins have interconnecting doors (useful for families with children).

The decor is bright, splashy, youthful, and contemporary. All cabins are accented with multi-patterned fabrics, wood-trimmed cabinetry (with nicely rounded edges) and rattan furniture. The twin beds have duvets, and a fabric canopy from headboard to ceiling. Windows feature full pull-down blackout blinds. Some cabins in the center of the ship have views obstructed by lifeboats. All cabin bathrooms are compact, but well designed, feature showers, and wall-mounted soap/shampoo dispensers, so there is no wastage of throwaway plastic bottles (environmentally friendly), but you should bring your own conditioner, hand lotion, or any other personal toiletry items. Cotton bathrobes are provided. Although the bathrooms do not have a hairdryer, one is located in the vanity unit in the cabin.

There are two large suites, located at the front of the ship, each with its own private balcony. These offer much more space, including more drawer and storage space, and better quality furniture and furnishings, as one would expect.

BERLITZ'S RATINGS

	Possible	Achieved
Ship	500	NYR
Accommodation	200	NYR
Food	400	NYR
Service	400	NYR
Entertainment	100	NYR
Cruise	400	NYR

DINING: There are two large self-serve buffet restaurants: "Calypso" and "Market", with a wide range of food (more than 1,200 items) available almost 24 hours a day. In addition, there is an à la carte restaurant, the "Maritim Restaurant", with waiter and sommelier service.

The standard of food offered at the self-serve buffet islands is good to very good, with creative presentation and good table-clearing service. The islands cut down on the waiting time for food, as is common aboard most other cruise ships of a similar size and passenger carry. There is always a fine selection of breads, cheeses, cold cuts, fruits and make-your-own teas (with a choice of more than 30 types of loose-leaf regular and herbal teas, as well as coffee).

At peak times, the buffet restaurants may remind you of motorway cafes (albeit elegant ones), with all their attendant noise, but a good selection of foods is provided (more than 1,200 items). You can sit where you want, when you want, and with whom you want, so dining really becomes a socially interactive occasion. Because of the large buffet rooms and self-serve dining concept, the actual crew to passenger ratio looks poor; but this is because there really are no waiters as such (except in the à la carte restaurant), only staff for clearing tables.

The "Maritim Restaurant", which features mostly high-back seats, has an intimate dining atmosphere. It is open for dinner only, and features a set five- or six-course menu, changed every two or three days. There is no extra charge, except for special à la carte menu items (such as sevruga caviar, smoked salmon, châteaubriand, rib-eye steak), and for wines. Reservations are made each morning of the day you want to eat in the Maritim Restaurant, at the reception desk.

Aft of the funnel, the Calypso Terraces provide a casual dining alternative, complete with a large bar – and seating outdoors (as well as seating under a sail-cloth canopied cover).

OTHER COMMENTS: *AIDAvita* is a "Club Ship" (and a slightly larger sister to *AIDAcara*) and offers a sea-going version of Germany's popular Robinson Clubs. The ship has a contemporary profile, is well proportioned, and has a swept-back funnel and wedge-shaped stern. Its bows feature the red lips, as well as the blue eyes, of Aïda (from Verdi's opera of the same name, written to commemorate the opening of the Suez Canal in 1871). In case you are confused about the brand name, Aida Cruises (like A'Rosa Cruises) is part of Seetours, which is itself a part of P&O Princess Cruises. Actually, if you take a river cruise in Europe, A'Rosa Cruises operates two river vessels, *A'Rosa Bella* and *A'Rosa Donna* (some have called the pair BellaDonna).

There is a good amount of open deck and sunbathing space, including some rather nice, quiet space above the navigation bridge. There is one egg-shaped swimming pool, set in a "beach-like" environment with splash and play areas (these facilities are larger and better than aboard *AIDAcara*.

This fun ship includes a whole army of "animateurs" (like the GOs of Club Med, but better) who enjoy leading a variety of activities by day (they also act as escorts for shore excursions), and as entertainers by night, acting in the colorful, often funny, shows alongside the professional entertainers. They (along with other staff) also interact with passengers throughout the ship, and can drink with them at the bars – something not permitted aboard most cruise ships.

Inside, there is no wasted space, and the public rooms are open and flow into each other instead of being contained spaces. The "you are here" (deck plan) signs are excellent, and finding your way round is a simple matter. The decor is upbeat and trendy, and will appeal to younger passengers, particularly those who may not have cruised before. A large observation lounge is set high atop the ship overlooking the bow. There is a wide array of intimate public rooms and spaces from which to choose.

The fitness, wellness and sports programming is among the most extensive in the cruise industry. An excellent wellness center – called Body and Soul – is located forward on Deck 12. It measures approximately 11,840 sq. ft (1,100 sq. meters), and contains two saunas (one seats more than 20 persons and has glass ocean-

view walls), massage and other treatment rooms, and large lounging area. Forward and outside the wellness center, is an FKK (FreiKoerperKultur) nude sunbathing deck. The "Hit Bikes" (mountain bikes with tough front and rear suspension units) for conducted biking excursions in each port of call are the concept and concession of Austrian Downhill Champion Skier Erwin Resch.

This certainly is going to be a family-friendly ship, with plenty of activities for younger family members (children are split into two age groups: Seepferdchen, from 4 to 7 years; Sharks, from 8 to 13 years). There is a diverse selection of children's and youth programs – good for families. Children can make their own menus for the week (together with the chef), and get to go into the galley to make cookies and other items – a novel idea that more ships could adopt.

The ship caters best to first-time passengers and youthful German-speaking couples seeking good value for money in a fun environment. The dress code is simple: "casual" (no dinner jackets or ties) at all times.

During the summer, *AIDAvita* sails itineraries in the Mediterranean, and in the winter, the ship sails in the Caribbean. Alternating 7-night itineraries can be combined for a 14-day cruise. In addition, packages created by tour operators such as Jahn Reisen, Seetours and TUI can add land stays for an even longer cruise and resort holiday experience. This presents a good amount of flexibility.

About 20 nationalities are represented among the crew, who are upbeat and cheerful, and really want passengers to have a good time in an unstuffy atmosphere. And they do, for this is definitely a young, vibrant, and fun ship, with plenty of passenger participation in all kinds of events. The brochure quite accurately describes the casual, young, fun and active lifestyle (whenever I sail aboard the ship, few passengers appear to be over the age of 40).

Aida Cruises/Seetours also has a whole range of hotels you can book to extend your vacation either before or after your cruise. All port taxes and gratuities are included, and, with rates that are extremely attractive, it is almost cheaper than staying home, and better value than almost any land-based vacation. If you've cruised aboard the (slightly) smaller sister ship *AIDAcara* before, I am certain you'll also like this newer, slightly larger ship, whose final score is expected to be similar, if not a few points more than *AIDAcara*. The euro is the currency used on board.

WEAK POINTS: Standing in line for embarkation, disembarkation, shore tenders and for self-serve buffet meals is an inevitable aspect of cruising aboard all large ships.

Akademik Sergey Vavilov ★★

Small Ship: ....6,231 tons	Passengers
Lifestyle: ....Standard	(lower beds/all berths): 80/80
Cruise Line: ....Poseidon Arctic	Passenger Space Ratio
Expeditions	(lower beds/all berths): 77.8/77.8
Former Names: ....none	Crew/Passenger Ratio
Builder: ....Hollming (Finland)	(lower beds/all berths): 1.7/1.7
Original Cost: ....n/a	Navigation Officers: ....Russian
Entered Service: 1988	Cabins (total): 40
Registry: ....Russia	Size Range (sq ft/m): ....n/a
Length (ft/m): 386.4/117.8	Cabins (outside view): 38
Beam (ft/m): 59.7/18.1	Cabins (interior/no view): 0
Draft (ft/m): 19.3/5.9	Cabins (for one person): 0
Propulsion/Propellers: diesel/2	Cabins (with private balcony): 0
Passenger Decks: 4	Cabins (wheelchair accessible): 0
Total Crew: 45	Cabin Current: ....110/220 Volts

Elevators: 0
Casino (gaming tables): ....No
Slot Machines: ....No
Swimming Pools (outdoors): 1
Swimming Pools (indoors): 0
Whirlpools: 0
Fitness Center: ....Yes
Sauna/Steam Room: ....Yes/No
Massage: ....No
Self-Service Launderette: ....No
Dedicated Cinema/Seats: ....No
Library: ....Yes
Classification Society: ....Russian
Shipping Register

OVERALL SCORE: 942 (OUT OF A POSSIBLE 2,000 POINTS)

ACCOMMODATION: The accommodation is arranged over three decks. With the exception of a single "suite," which is quite large for the size of the ship, almost all other cabins are extremely small (dimensionally challenged is a better description), very utilitarian, and clinical, although all have a small desk and a reasonable amount of closet space. There are two-berth cabins with shower and toilet, or there are two-bed cabins on the lowest deck, whose occupants must share an adjacent bathroom and toilet.

DINING: There are two dining rooms (the galley is located between them), and all passengers are accommodated in a single seating. The meals are hearty international fare, with no frills. When under charter to various specialist operators, western chefs oversee the food operation, which is basic and uninspiring.

OTHER COMMENTS: This vessel was originally specially constructed for the former Soviet Union's polar and oceanographic research program and should not be taken as a cruise ship, although it was converted in the early 1990s to carry passengers, and then refurbished in 1996 and fitted out specifically for expedition cruising. This is the sister ship to *Akademik Ioffe*. Although the ship was, for years, chartered by such distinguished operators

BERLITZ'S RATINGS

	Possible	Achieved
Ship	500	218
Accommodation	200	83
Food	400	194
Service	400	191
Entertainment	N/A	N/A
Cruise	500	256

as Quark Expeditions, it is now operated by Russia's own Poseidon Arctic Expeditions, in conjunction with the owners of the vessel, the P.P. Shirsov Institute of Oceanology. Has an ice-hardened steel hull, which makes the vessel ideally suited to cruising in both the Arctic and Antarctic regions. There is an open bridge policy, so all passengers have access to the navigation bridge. There are several Zodiac landing craft for close-in shore excursions and nature observation trips. The ship has a seawater swimming pool outdoors, but it is really small.

Inside, the limited public rooms consist simply of a library and lounge/bar. The dining rooms also serve as a lecture room. This ship does have good medical facilities.

This is expedition style cruising, in a very small ship with limited facilities and the most basic product delivery. However, it provides a somewhat primitive, but genuine adventure experience, taking you to places others can only dream about. The bigger ships cannot get this close to Antarctica, but this little vessel will sail you close to the face of the ice continent.

WEAK POINTS: Although there is a swimming pool, it is very, very small, and is best described as nothing more than a "dip" pool. The food is extremely basic, as is the service, and the ship's interior decor.

Albatros
★★★

Mid-Size Ship: ....24,803 tons	Total Crew: 340	Cabins (wheelchair accessible): 0	
Lifestyle: ....Standard	Passengers	Cabin Current: ....110 volts	
Cruise Line: ....Phoenix Seereisen	(lower beds/all berths): 827/1,571	Elevators: 3	
Former Names: ....*Dawn Princess,*	Passenger Space Ratio	Casino (gaming tables): ....Yes	
Sitmar Fairwind, FairWind, Sylvania	(lower beds/all berths): 29.9/15.7	Slot Machines: ....Yes	
Builder: ....John Brown & Co. (UK)	Crew/Passenger Ratio	Swimming Pools (outdoors): 3	
Original Cost: ....n/a	(lower beds/all berths): 2.4/4.6	Swimming Pools (indoors): 0	
Entered Service: ....June 1957/Aug 1993	Navigation Officers: ....European	Whirlpools: 0	
Registry: ....The Bahamas	Cabins (total): 457	Fitness Center: ....Yes	
Length (ft/m): 608.2/185.40	Size Range (sq ft/m): 89.3–240.0/	Sauna/Steam Room: ....Yes/No	
Beam (ft/m): 80.3/24.49	8.3–22.3	Massage:.........................Yes	
Draft (ft/m): 29.3/8.94	Cabins (outside view): 232	Self-Service Launderette: ....Yes	
Propulsion/Propellers: .....steam turbine	Cabins (interior/no view): 215	Dedicated Cinema/Seats: Yes/300	
(18,300kW)/2	Cabins (for one person): 0	Library: ....No	
Passenger Decks:.................11	Cabins (with private balcony): 0	Classification Society: ...Lloyd's Register	

OVERALL SCORE: 1,144 (OUT OF A POSSIBLE 2,000 POINTS)

ACCOMMODATION: There is a wide range of cabin sizes and configurations (in 28 price categories), a throwback to the days when it was a ship operating transatlantic crossings, all of which feature really heavy-duty furniture, fittings, strong doors, and eclectic décor with colors that don't really match. All cabins have a decent amount of storage space (some of the larger cabins have wood-paneled walls), although closet and storage space could become limited for long voyages, particularly in the smaller, lower-grade cabins. Most cabins have painted metal perforated ceiling tiles, although, thankfully, there's almost no plastic anywhere. Duvets are standard, rather than sheets and blankets.

The bathrooms are quite large, with cabinets and shelf space for toiletries in most, and toilets that are of the quiet (non-vacuum) type, although the plumbing is exposed. All passengers are provided with 100 percent cotton towels and bathrobes and some personal toiletry amenities (soap, shampoo, body lotion, and shower gel).

Accommodation designated as suites have more space, and a sleeping area that can be curtained off. Anyone booking a suite or one of the top five grades receives Phoenix VIP service, which includes flowers, a separate check-in desk and priority disembarkation. All suites are located on Jupiter Deck, and have names: 105 (Dresden), 106 (Nurnberg), 107 (Bonn), 108 (Baden Baden), 114 (Potsdam), 115 (Weisbaden), 116 (Heidelberg), 117 (Lubeck), 120 (Bach), 121 (Beethoven), 122 (Haydn), 124 (Weimar), 126 (Bremen), 127 (Mozart), 128 (Aarchen), 131 (Bamberg), 133 (Augsberg), 135

BERLITZ'S RATINGS

	Possible	Achieved
Ship	500	263
Accommodation	200	115
Food	400	221
Service	400	254
Entertainment	100	44
Cruise	400	232

(Freiburg), 136 (Magdeburg), 138 (Kiel), 140 (Düsseldorf), 142 (Hannover), 143 (Erfurt), 145 (Baunschweig), 146 (Köln), 147 (Frankfurt), 149 (Regensburg), 150 (München), 155 (Berlin), 157 (Hamburg).

DINING: There are two dining rooms, both moderately charming and comfortable (with moderately high ceilings, and portholes), but tables are quite close together. This means the rooms are also quite noisy (although some would call this "ambience"). There are two seatings. The menu is reasonably creative, the choice is rather limited, and the food is best described as "down home basic." In other words, do not expect the finest of meats, or fish, or cheeses, but what is provided is adequate for passengers seeking low-priced cruises.

The service is quite friendly and attentive, in true European style (the mainly Filipino waiters do speak a limited amount of German), although there is little finesse in their style of service. Still, it is unpretentious. Because there are two seatings for meals, one cannot dine leisurely.

Table wines are included for lunch and dinner, although the quality is less than good. There is also an additional wine list with some (slightly) better quality wines featured, at very reasonable prices. However, the wine glasses are very small (too small for red wine).

OTHER COMMENTS: *Albatros* is a vintage all-white classic ship with a forthright profile and a single, large, centrally placed funnel painted in the turquoise/aquamarine blue of Phoenix Seereisen. The ship is sturdily constructed, and has a riveted hull that is virtually impossible to find today, as well as a deep draft that makes it very stable at sea, having been built as a two-class liner specifically for Cunard Line's transatlantic crossings in the late 1950s. Since August 1993 the ship has been under long-term charter to Phoenix Seereisen from V-Ships, the owners and operators.

Albatros is an unpretentious ship that has an interesting old-world ambience and charm that somehow helps to make up for the lack of finesse associated with more upscale, newer cruise products.

There is plenty of open deck and sunbathing space, although this quickly becomes cramped and crowded when the ship is full, particularly around the three aft swimming pools (one of which is for the use of children, as Phoenix Seereisen appeals particularly well to families with children). Particularly popular are two long sheltered promenade decks, which are ideal for strolling or just sitting on one of the many decks lounge chairs.

Inside the ship, a great deal of dark wood paneling and trim that was used in its original interiors has been retained (although there is also much use of laminated paneling). There are also many solid brass accents throughout the interiors and public rooms. There is a small library, with a selection of both hardback and paperback books (most of which are old), as well as limited amount of reference material.

There are, however, relatively few public rooms from which to choose (fortunately, most are located on one fore-to-aft promenade deck). Public rooms are typically crowded (particularly at night), and it is extremely difficult to get away from the smell of stale cigarette smoke. There are also many "thresholds" or high sills to step over at doorways, particularly to the outside decks and pool area, and so the ship cannot be recommended to anyone confined to a wheelchair under any circumstances. In fact, anyone with walking difficulties would be wise to consider a newer ship to cruise aboard.

The show lounge is not a show lounge, but a room for "cabaret" acts. The sight lines to the stage are obstructed from many seats by 10 thick pillars. Entertainment is really of the low-cost "end-of-pier" type –

the sort that you would have typically seen in the 1960s.

Phoenix Seereisen features extensive, interesting destination-intensive itineraries, and young, friendly Phoenix Seereisen staff members are aboard every cruise to help with shore excursions. There is a very informal atmosphere and a very relaxed, casual dress code prevails throughout.

Although the ship has been generally well maintained, remember that this *is* an old ship, having been designed for transatlantic service. Thus, the layout is somewhat disjointed, accommodation passageways are narrow, and they have many twists and turns. Because this is a steam ship, you should be aware of the possibility of black soot falling on the aft decks occasionally; in other words, do not wear white.

This ship should prove to be good for a first cruise experience with fellow German-speaking passengers and crew, providing that your expectations are not at all high. All in all, however, the onboard product delivered is rather sloppy when compared to other similarly priced cruises.

There are two styles of cruising, according to the brochure: Classic and Modern. Cruises designated "classic" are generally longer cruises (including around-the-world cruises) where the dress code is more formal. Cruises designated "modern" are shorter cruises (typically of 10 days or less) where the dress code is very relaxed and casual.

Far from being a new ship, *Albatros* performs and behaves extremely well in most sea condition, and the resulting product is both entertaining and reasonably priced for the popular market seeking an ocean-going holiday in totally relaxed, unstuffy and unpretentious surroundings. It represents a decent value for money cruise holiday. The currency on board is the euro.

WEAK POINTS: The itineraries are busy, and short cruises mean that the ship has to work hard to keep up. The Lido Café breakfast and lunch buffets are extremely poor, particularly in the way food is displayed, and there are not enough seats. The entertainment is consistently second-rate. The ship could be much cleaner than it is. Stale cigarette smoke is everywhere.

Removed 2006

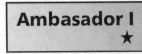

Ambasador I
★

Small Ship:	.............2,573 tons	Total Crew:	68	Cabin Current:	..........220 volts (DC)

Small Ship: ....2,573 tons
Lifestyle: ....Standard
Cruise Line: ....Islas Galapagos Turismos
y Vapores
Former Names: .....Jedinstvo/Aquanaut
Ambassador/Atlas Ambassador
Builder: .....Brodogradiliste (Yugoslavia)
Original Cost: ....n/a
Entered Service: 1959/1993
Registry: ....Ecuador
Length (ft/m): 296.2/90.30
Beam (ft/m): 42.7/13.03
Draft (ft/m): 14.0/4.45
Propulsion/Propellers: ....diesel
(7,060kw)/2
Passenger Decks: 5

Total Crew: 68
Passengers
(lower beds/all berths): 114/160
Passenger Space Ratio
(lower beds/all berths): 22.5/16.0
Crew/Passenger Ratio
(lower beds/all berths): 1.9/2.3
Navigation Officers: ....International
Cabins (total): 62
Size Range (sq ft/m): 95.0–190.0/
8.8–17.6
Cabins (outside view): 43
Cabins (interior/no view): 19
Cabins (for one person): 10
Cabins (with private balcony): 0
Cabins (wheelchair accessible): 0

Cabin Current: ....220 volts (DC)
Elevators: 0
Casino (gaming tables): ....No
Slot Machines: ....No
Swimming Pools (outdoors): 1
Swimming Pools (indoors): 0
Whirlpools: 0
Fitness Center: ....No
Sauna/Steam Room: ....No/No
Massage: ....No
Self-Service Launderette: ....No
Dedicated Cinema/Seats: ....No
Library: ....Yes
Classification Society: ....Jugoslavenski
Registrar Brodova

OVERALL SCORE: 620 (OUT OF A POSSIBLE 2,000 POINTS)

ACCOMMODATION: Depending on which tour operator is marketing the ship, there are, in general, five cabin grades (the higher the deck, the higher the price), with accommodation spread over three decks. Almost all cabins really are very small, with only the most minimal amount of furniture, fittings and furnishings. The bathrooms are tiny, and the plumbing leaves much to be desired. The cabins are, thus, barely adequate and not very comfortable. Some cabins have upper/lower berths, and some also accommodate three or four persons.

DINING: The dining room is reasonably pleasant, and accommodates all passengers in a single seating, but there are no tables for two. The service is quite forgettable, as is the food.

OTHER COMMENTS: This is a real vintage style of ship – now well over 40 years old – and was formerly owned and operated by a Yugoslavian shipping company. The ship has a single, squat, blue funnel placed squarely amidships. This is not a handsome vessel, by any stretch of the imagination, and maintenance is of the "patch here, patch there" type. There is only a small amount of outdoor deck space for sunbathing, as the decks are quite cluttered.

Inside the ship there is only one main public room, the main lounge, which is used for just about every public activity, including lectures and recaps.

BERLITZ'S RATINGS

	Possible	Achieved
Ship	500	115
Accommodation	200	67
Food	400	131
Service	400	149
Entertainment	100	20
Cruise	400	138

This small cruise ship operates cruises of the Galapagos Islands, although the price is not really very modest. It's adequate only so long as you do not expect much. Although the ship can carry more passengers, there is a limit of 86 passengers for these cruises, set by the Galapagos National Park regulations.

Think of the ship simply as the most basic transportation to get you between the islands, but don't consider this ship if you like contemporary décor and styling, or good food and service.

If you *are* going on a Galapagos cruise, it is important that you remember to take with you: passport, short and long-sleeve cotton shirts, good walking shoes, windbreaker, mosquito repellent (mosquitos are at their worst between December and July, particularly in Bartolome), sunglasses with retaining strap, any personal medication. You will need to take a flight from Quito to San Cristobal (via Guayaquil) to join your cruise. The Galapagos National Park tax is an additional $100 per person (approximate), payable *in cash* when you land at your incoming airport.

WEAK POINTS: The cruise prices are extremely high for what you get, and for such an old vessel with limited facilities. It's simply basic, basic, basic, all the way. The public passageways are quite dark, and the carpeting is well worn. The swimming pool is really tiny – it is merely a "dip" pool.

American Eagle
★★

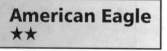

Small Ship:	...............1,480 tons	Passengers		Cabin Current:	...............110 volts
Lifestyle:	..................Standard	(lower beds/all berths):	..........49/49	Elevators:	1
Cruise Line:	.....American Cruise Lines	Passenger Space Ratio		Casino (gaming tables):	.............No
Former Names:	.................none	(lower beds/all berths):	.......30.2/30.2	Slot Machines:	.....................No
Builder:	.......Chesapeake Shipbuilding	Crew/Passenger Ratio		Swimming Pools (outdoors):	0
	(USA)	(lower beds/all berths):	.........2.2/2.2	Swimming Pools (indoors):	0
Original Cost:	.....................n/a	Navigation Officers:	.........American	Whirlpools:	0
Entered Service:	............Apr 2000	Cabins (total):	27	Fitness Center:	.....................No
Registry:	........................USA	Size Range (sq ft/m):	......176.0–382.0/	Sauna/Steam Room:	............No/No
Length (ft/m):	.............174.0/53.00		16.3–35.4	Massage:	........................No
Beam (ft/m):	..............40.5/12.30	Cabins (outside view):	27	Self-Service Launderette:	...........No
Draft (ft/m):	.................6.5/1.98	Cabins (interior/no view):	0	Dedicated Cinema/Seats:	...........No
Propulsion/Propellers:	.........diesel/2	Cabins (for one person):	5	Library:	...........................No
Passenger Decks:	4	Cabins (with private balcony):	6	Classification Society:	. .American Bureau
Total Crew:	22	Cabins (wheelchair accessible):	2		of Shipping

---

OVERALL SCORE: 827 (OUT OF A POSSIBLE 2,000 POINTS)

ACCOMMODATION: There are cabins for couples and singles, six suites, as well as two wheelchair-accessible cabins. All of the cabins feature twin beds, a small desk with chair, and clothes hanging space. The six suites also have a color television, VCR and compact disc (audio) player. All cabins have a private bathroom with separate shower enclosure, washbasin and toilet (none of the cabins has a bathtub), as well as windows that open.

DINING: The dining salon, located in the latter third of the vessel, has large, panoramic picture windows on three of its sides. It has open seating (there are no assigned tables), so you can sit where you like, and with whom you wish, although dining times are set. There are no tables for two, and the chairs do not have armrests The food is very much American fare – good and wholesome, featuring regional cuisines, and presented and served in a basic, unfussy manner. Note that there is little or no choice of entrées, and only one appetizer, one soup, etc. There is no wine list, although basic white and red low-quality American table wines are included. On the last morning of each cruise, only continental breakfast is available.

OTHER COMMENTS: American Cruise Lines is the resurrection of a company with the same name that existed between 1974 and 1989. It now features intra-coastal waterway cruising, as well as sailings in New England and the Hudson River Valley. *American Eagle* is a new

BERLITZ'S RATINGS

	Possible	Achieved
Ship	500	249
Accommodation	200	110
Food	400	196
Service	400	170
Entertainment	100	10
Cruise	400	92

ship that was built specifically for coastal cruising and cannot venture far into open seas away from the coastline (a sister vessel is planned, with more balcony cabins). The ship's uppermost deck is open (good for scenery observation), and there are tables and chairs, a few deck lounge chairs, and a small putting green.

There are just two public lounges. The main one – the observation lounge – is located forward and has windows on three sides (an open bar is set up each afternoon). This becomes the principal meeting place for passengers. A second, smaller lounge is sandwiched between cabins on the same deck.

The whole point of a cruise aboard this ship is to get close to the inland areas, cities and town of America's intra-coastal waterways and coastline. There's no waiting in line – you can board whenever you want. The ship docks in the center, or within walking distance of most towns on the itineraries. The dress code is "no ties casual."

WEAK POINTS: It really is *extremely* expensive for what you get, compared even to those ships of a similar size and purpose (although this is a new ship and the cabins are of a better size and are slightly better equipped). Although there is an elevator, it does not go to the uppermost deck (Sun Deck). The limited choice of food is very disappointing – particularly in view of the high cost of the cruises. There are no health spa facilities – not even a sauna or steam room, or massage – and there are no medical facilities.

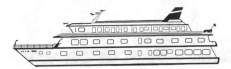

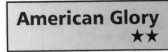

American Glory
★★

Small Ship:	...............1,480 tons	Passengers	Cabin Current:	...............110 volts
Lifestyle:	...................Standard	(lower beds/all berths):	.........49/49	Elevators:	1
Cruise Line:	......American Cruise Lines	Passenger Space Ratio		Casino (gaming tables):	.............No
Former Names:	.................none	(lower beds/all berths):	.......30.2/30.2	Slot Machines:	.....................No
Builder:	.......Chesapeake Shipbuilding	Crew/Passenger Ratio		Swimming Pools (outdoors):	0
	(USA)	(lower beds/all berths):	.........2.2/2.2	Swimming Pools (indoors):	0
Original Cost:	....................n/a	Navigation Officers:	.........American	Whirlpools:	0
Entered Service:	.............July 2002	Cabins (total):	27	Fitness Center:	....................No
Registry:	........................USA	Size Range (sq ft/m):	......176.0–382.0/	Sauna/Steam Room:	............No/No
Length (ft/m):	.............174.0/53.00		16.3–35.4	Massage:	...........................No
Beam (ft/m):	...............40.5/12.30	Cabins (outside view):	27	Self-Service Launderette:	...........No
Draft (ft/m):	..................6.5/1.98	Cabins (interior/no view):	0	Dedicated Cinema/Seats:	...........No
Propulsion/Propellers:	..........diesel/2	Cabins (for one person):	5	Library:	..............................No
Passenger Decks:	4	Cabins (with private balcony):	14	Classification Society:	. .American Bureau
Total Crew:	22	Cabins (wheelchair accessible):	3		of Shipping

---

OVERALL SCORE: 835 (OUT OF A POSSIBLE 2,000 POINTS)

ACCOMMODATION: There are cabins for couples and singles, seven suites, as well as five wheelchair-accessible cabins. All of the cabins feature twin beds, a small desk with chair, and clothes hanging space. The seven most expensive cabins also have a color television, VCR and compact disc (audio) player. All cabins have a private bathroom with separate shower enclosure, washbasin and toilet (none of the cabins has a bathtub), as well as windows that open. Accommodation designated as suites also have a private balcony, although this is very narrow.

DINING: The dining salon, located in the latter third of the vessel, has large, panoramic picture windows on three of its sides. Open seating is featured (there are no assigned tables), so you can sit where you like, and with whom you wish, although dining times are set. There are no tables for two, and the chairs do not have armrests The food is very much American fare – good and wholesome, featuring regional cuisines, and presented and served in a basic, unfussy manner. There is little or no choice of entrées, and only one appetizer, one soup, etc. There is no wine list, although basic white and red low-quality American table wines are included. On the last morning of each cruise, only continental breakfast is available.

OTHER COMMENTS: American Cruise Lines is the resurrection of a company with the same name that existed between 1974 and 1989. It now features intra-coastal waterway cruising, as well as sailings in New England and the Hudson River Valley. *American Glory*, together

BERLITZ'S RATINGS

	Possible	Achieved
Ship	500	257
Accommodation	200	110
Food	400	196
Service	400	170
Entertainment	100	10
Cruise	400	92

with sister ship *American Eagle* are new ships that were built specifically for coastal cruising and cannot venture far into open seas away from the coastline. The ship's uppermost deck is open (good for scenery observation), and there are tables and chairs, a few deck lounge chairs, and a small putting green.

There are just two public lounges. The main one – the observation lounge – is located forward and has windows on three sides (an open bar is set up each afternoon). This becomes the principal meeting place for passengers. A second, smaller lounge is sandwiched between cabins on the same deck.

The point of a cruise aboard this ship is to get close to the inland areas, cities and town of America's intra-coastal waterways and coastline. There's no waiting in line – you can board whenever you want. The ship docks in the center, or within walking distance of most towns on the itineraries. The dress code is "no ties casual." The score is expected to be marginally better than for sister ship *American Eagle*, due to some improvements in construction and the addition of more balcony cabins.

WEAK POINTS: It really is *extremely* expensive for what you get, compared even to ships of a similar size and purpose (although this is a new ship and the cabins are of a better size and are slightly better equipped). Although there is an elevator, it does not go to the uppermost deck (Sun Deck). The limited choice of food is very disappointing – particularly in view of the high cost. There are no health spa facilities – not even a sauna or steam room, or massage – and there are no medical facilities.

Amsterdam
★★★★

Large Ship:	.61,000 tons
Lifestyle:	Premium
Cruise Line:	Holland America Line
Former Names:	none
Builder:	Fincantieri (Italy)
Original Cost:	$400 million
Entered Service:	Oct 2000
Registry:	The Netherlands
Length (ft/m):	780.8/238.00
Beam (ft/m):	105.8/32.25
Draft (ft/m):	25.5/7.80
Propulsion/Propellers:	diesel-electric (37,500 kW)/2 azimuthing pods (15.5 MW each)
Passenger Decks:	12
Total Crew:	600
Passengers (lower beds/all berths):	1,380/1,653
Passenger Space Ratio (lower beds/all berths):	44.2/36.9
Crew/Passenger Ratio (lower beds/all berths):	2.3/2.7
Navigation Officers:	Dutch
Cabins (total):	690
Size Range (sq ft/m):	184.0–1,124.8/ 17.1–104.5
Cabins (outside view):	557
Cabins (interior/no view):	133
Cabins (for one person):	0
Cabins (with private balcony):	172
Cabins (wheelchair accessible):	20
Cabin Current:	110 and 220 volts
Elevators:	12
Casino (gaming tables):	Yes
Slot Machines:	Yes
Swimming Pools (outdoors):	1
Swimming Pools (indoors):	1 (magrodome cover)
Whirlpools:	2
Fitness Center:	Yes
Sauna/Steam Room:	Yes/Yes
Massage:	Yes
Self-Service Launderette:	Yes
Dedicated Cinema/Seats:	Yes/235
Library:	Yes
Classification Society:	Lloyd's Register

OVERALL SCORE: 1,543 (OUT OF A POSSIBLE 2,000 POINTS)

ACCOMMODATION: This is spread over five decks (some cabins have full or partially obstructed views), and is in 16 grades: 11 with outside views, 5 interior grades (no view). There are four penthouse suites, and 50 suites (14 more than aboard sister ship *Rotterdam*). No cabin is more than 130 feet (40 meters) from a stairway, which makes it very easy to find your way from cabins to public rooms. Although 81 percent of cabins have outside views, only 25 percent of those have balconies.

All of the "standard" interior and outside cabins are tastefully furnished, and have twin beds that convert to a queen-sized bed (the space is a little tight for walking between beds and the vanity unit, however). There is a decent amount of closet and drawer space, although this will prove tight for the longer voyages featured. The fully tiled bathrooms are disappointingly small (particularly on long cruises), the shower tubs are very small, and the cupboards for one's personal toiletries are quite basic. There is little detailing to distinguish the bathrooms from those aboard the *Statendam*-class ships. All cabin televisions feature CNN and TNT, as well as movies, and ship information and shopping channels.

There are 50 Verandah Suites and four Penthouse Suites on Navigation Deck (more than sister ship *Rotterdam*, due to the fact that the deck has been extended aft, and a swimming pool moved one deck higher). The suites all share a private Concierge Lounge with a concierge to handle such things as special dining arrangements, shore excursions and special requests, although

BERLITZ'S RATINGS

	Possible	Achieved
Ship	500	430
Accommodation	200	165
Food	400	282
Service	400	272
Entertainment	100	78
Cruise	400	316

strangely there are no butlers for these suites, as aboard ships with similar facilities. The lounge, with its wood detailing and private library is accessible only by private key-card.

The four Penthouse Suites are the ultimate in civilized living spaces aboard *Amsterdam*. Each has a separate steward's entrance, as well as a separate bedroom with king-size bed, vanity desk, large walk-in closet with excellent drawer and hanging space, living room, dining room seating up to eight), wet bar, and pantry. The bathroom is large, and has a big oval Jacuzzi bathtub, separate shower enclosure, two washbasins, separate toilet and bidet. There is also a guest bathroom with toilet and washbasin. There is a good-sized private balcony.

Suite occupants get extra special things such as personal stationary, complimentary laundry and ironing, cocktail-hour hors d'oeuvres and other goodies, as well as priority embarkation and disembarkation.

DINING: The main dining room, La Fontaine, spans two levels, and has a huge stained-glass ceiling measuring almost 1,500 sq. ft (140 sq. meters), with a floral motif. There are tables for two, four, six or eight (there are few tables for two). There is open seating for breakfast and lunch, with two seatings for dinner (with both smoking and no-smoking sections). Rosenthal china and fine cutlery are featured (although there are no fish knives).

Unfortunately, Holland America Line food isn't as nice as the china it's placed on. It may be adequate for most passengers who are not used to better food, but it doesn't match the standard found aboard other ships in the premium segment of the industry. While USDA beef is of a good quality, fowl tends to be battery-tough, and most fish is overcooked and has the consistency of a baseball bat. What are also definitely *not* luxurious are the endless packets of sugar, and packets (instead of glass jars) of breakfast jam, marmalade and honey, and poor quality teas. While these may be suitable for a family diner, they do not belong aboard a ship that claims to have "award-winning cuisine." Dessert and pastry items are of good quality (specifically for American tastes), although there is perhaps too much use of canned fruits and jellies. Forget the selection of "international" cheeses, however, as most of it didn't come from anywhere other than the USA – a country known for its processed, highly colored processed "cheese" slices, and not for fine cheese making. Note that Holland America Line can provide Kosher meals, but these are prepared ashore, frozen, and brought to your table sealed in their original containers (there is no Kosher kitchen on board).

ALTERNATIVE (RESERVATIONS REQUIRED) DINING SPOT: There is also an alternative 88-seat *Odyssey Restaurant*, available to all passengers on a reservation-only basis (priority reservations are given to passengers occupying suite grade accommodation). There is no extra charge for dining in the *Odyssey Restaurant*, which features better food and presentation than in the main dining room. The whimsically surreal artwork features scenic landscapes. The cuisine is decidedly California-Italian in style, with small portions and few vegetables.

As another alternative, the Lido Buffet is open for casual dinners on all except the last night of each cruise, in an open-seating arrangement. Tables are set with crisp linens, flatware and stemware. A set menu is featured, and this includes a choice of four entrées.

For casual breakfasts and lunches, the Lido Buffet provides old-style, stand-in-line serve-yourself canteen food – adequate for those used to TV dinner-tray food, but most definitely not lavish, as the brochures claim. Salad items appear adequate, but are quite tasteless, like the iceberg lettuce that doesn't seem to go away.

OTHER COMMENTS: *Amsterdam* is a close sister ship to *Rotterdam*, and has a nicely raked bow, as well as the familiar interior flow and design style. The ship has twin funnels that may be well recognized by Holland America Line's former passengers. *Amsterdam* was the first ship in the Holland America Line fleet to feature an azimuthing pod propulsion system. Each pod has a forward-facing propeller that can be turned through 360 degrees, and houses an electric motor and propeller, replacing the traditional long shaft, propeller and rudder system of the past. The pods are powered by a diesel-electric system.

The interior public spaces also carry on the same layout and flow as found aboard *Rotterdam*. The interior café is best described as restrained and formal, with much

use of medium and dark wood accenting. As a whole, the café of this ship is extremely refined, with much of the traditional ocean liner detailing so loved by frequent Holland America Line passengers. Much of the artwork features items from Holland America Line's glorious past, as well as items depicting the history of the city of Amsterdam from the 17th through the 20th centuries.

The interior focal point is a three-deck high atrium, in an oval, instead of circular, shape. A whimsical "Astrolobe" is the featured centrepiece in this atrium. Also clustered in the atrium lobby are the reception desk, shore excursion desk, photo shop and photo gallery.

The ship has three principal passenger stairways, which is so much better than two from the viewpoint of safety, flow and accessibility. There is a magrodome-covered pool on the Lido Deck between the mast and the ship's twin funnels, watched over by a sculpture of a brown bear catching salmon.

There are children's and teens' play areas, although these really are token gestures by a company that traditionally does not cater well to children. Popcorn is available at the Wajang Theatre for moviegoers, while adjacent is the popular Java Café. The casino, located in the middle of a major passenger flow on one of the entertainment decks, has blackjack, roulette, poker and dice tables alongside the requisite rows of slot machines.

Amsterdam is an extremely comfortable ship in which to cruise, with some fine, elegant and luxurious decorative features. However, these are marred by the poor quality of dining room food and service and the lack of understanding of what it takes to make a "luxury" cruise experience, despite what is touted in the company's brochures.

Holland America Line also provides cappuccino and espresso coffees and free ice cream during certain hours of the day aboard its ships, as well as hot hors d'oeuvres in all bars – something other major lines seem to have dropped, or charge extra for.

Gratuities are extra, and they are added to your shipboard account at $10–$13 per day, according to the accommodation grade chosen. Refreshingly, the company does not add an automatic 15% gratuity for beverage purchases. Perhaps the ship's best asset is its friendly and personable Filipino and Indonesian crew, although communication can prove frustrating at times.

WEAK POINTS: Standing in line for embarkation, disembarkation, shore tenders and for self-serve buffet meals is an inevitable aspect of cruising aboard all large ships. With one whole deck of suites (and a dedicated, private concierge lounge, with preferential passenger treatment), the company has in effect created a two-class ship. The charge to use the washing machines and dryers in the self-service launderette is petty and irritating, particularly for the occupants of high-priced accommodation. Communication (in English) with many of the staff, particularly in the dining room and informal buffet areas, can prove frustrating. The room service menu is limited, and room service is very basic. Non-smokers should note that typically, there will be many smokers to avoid.

Arcadia
★★★ +

New one in 2006

Large Ship: ....63,524 tons	Total Crew: 650	Cabins (wheelchair accessible): 8
Lifestyle: ....Standard	Passengers	Cabin Current: ....110 and 220 volts
Cruise Line: ...P&O Cruises/Ocean Village	(lower beds/all berths): 1,461/1,549	Elevators: 9
Former Names: *Star Princess, FairMajesty*	Passenger Space Ratio	Casino (gaming tables): ....Yes
Builder: ....Chantiers de L'Atlantique	(lower beds/all berths): 43.4/38.5	Slot Machines: ....Yes
(France)	Crew/Passenger Ratio	Swimming Pools (outdoors): 3
Original Cost: ....$200 million	(lower beds/all berths): 2.2/2.3	Swimming Pools (indoors): 0
Entered Service: .... Mar 1989/Dec 1997	Navigation Officers: ....British	Whirlpools: 4
Registry: ....Great Britain	Cabins (total): 748	Fitness Center: ....Yes
Length (ft/m): 810.3/247.00	Size Range (sq ft/m): 179.7–529.6/	Sauna/Steam Room: ....Yes/No
Beam (ft/m): 105.6/32.20	16.7–49.2	Massage: ....Yes
Draft (ft/m): 26.9/8.20	Cabins (outside view): 583	Self-Service Launderette: ....Yes
Propulsion/Propellers: .....diesel-electric	Cabins (interior/no view): 165	Dedicated Cinema/Seats: Yes/205
(39,000kW)/2	Cabins (for one person): 64	Library: ....Yes
Passenger Decks: 12	Cabins (with private balcony): 50	Classification Society: ...Lloyd's Register

OVERALL SCORE: 1,374 (OUT OF A POSSIBLE 2,000 POINTS)

ACCOMMODATION: There are 12 different cabin grades: eight outside and four interior (no view) categories. Almost all of the interior (no view) and outside-view standard-grade cabins for two are of an excellent size and layout, and are quite well equipped, with good wooden drawer and other storage space, plus some under-bed space for luggage), and walk-in (open) closets. But, the sound insulation between cabins is poor (televisions late at night can be irritating, as can loud children). A number of cabins also feature third and fourth person berths (in which case the drawer and storage space becomes tight, and there is only one personal safe). Some cabins can also be designated for single occupancy.

The decently sized modular bathrooms have good shower enclosures, and retractable clothes line. Only suites and mini-suites have bathtubs, as the ship was built for American passengers (who prefer showers). Personal toiletry amenity kits typically include a shower cap, nail files, sewing kit, cotton buds and lint remover. Soap is provided, and a soap/shampoo dispenser is fitted into the shower enclosure.

There are 14 suites and 36 mini-suites (each named after P&O ships of the past), and more living space, with a separate bedroom and lounge. Each has a private balcony (although the partitions are not of the full floor-to-ceiling type, so you may hear your neighbors).

All suites and standard cabins have large walk-in closets, personal safe, refrigerator, television, VCR, telephone, trouser press, retractable clothesline and hairdryer. Suite bathrooms have a bathtub and separate

BERLITZ'S RATINGS		
	Possible	Achieved
Ship	500	367
Accommodation	200	146
Food	400	238
Service	400	274
Entertainment	100	75
Cruise	400	274

shower enclosure, while mini-suite bathrooms have a wooden floor, bathtubs with an integral shower. Both suite and mini-suite occupants get bathrobes and slippers.

Room service for breakfast, afternoon tea and snacks for suite occupants is very basic, and should be upgraded. Apart from a limited continental breakfast menu, no other room service items are available in the standard (non-suite) cabins. Music is available only through the TV set; there is no way to obtain any of the music channels without having a television picture on.

DINING: The Pacific Restaurant has two levels (there are two steps up to the center, raised section), but it can be fairly noisy. There are tables for two, four, six, eight or 10, mostly in small sections that give an almost cozy feel to the room. There are two seatings, both non-smoking.

The food is typical of P&O, unpretentious and not at all memorable. Although the menu choice is reasonably varied, the quality of meat and fish is very ordinary (don't expect Scottish Black Angus beef, for example). If you like "meat and two veg" fare and enjoy a curry a day, you'll be fine here, but if you like anything more adventurous, forget it. Vegetarian dishes are incorporated into the menu each day, although the selection is limited. The service is warm and friendly. As on all P&O ships, the "Great British Breakfast" is always popular.

The indoor-outdoor "Conservatory" buffet restaurant (it is open for breakfast and lunch, and for the occasional alternative special theme self-serve buffet dinner, such as "Gateway to India ") is small and crowded, particularly when the ship is full. There is also the Al fresco Pizzeria (one standard pizza plus two different special pizzas are featured each day on a 7-day rotation, although the pizza slices are bread-based, and not made from pizza dough), an ice cream bar (Sundaes), a patisserie, and a caviar bar. All informal dining spots are non-smoking.

OTHER COMMENTS: The ship was originally designed and built for Sitmar Cruises, which was absorbed into Princess Cruises in 1988 prior to the ship's completion. The ship was extensively refurbished in late 1997 at the Harland & Wolff shipyard in Belfast, and reconfigured specifically for British cruise passengers. It is well proportioned, and has a good amount of open deck space for sunbathing around twin swimming pools (one has a sit-in bar – a first for P&O Cruises), as well as on the open decks aft of the funnel. Eight bells are sounded each day at noon, and relayed throughout the ship's public areas, in true nautical tradition.

The interiors feature restrained styling mixed with traditional shipboard decor, including some pleasing art deco touches (stainless steel balustrades), so nothing jars the senses, is garish, or out of place. A large selection of artwork provides some warmth to what would otherwise be a rather clinical, staid interior.

There is a lack of public rooms (although most have high ceilings) for the number of passengers carried; there are few little nooks and crannies, and almost nowhere that could be called a quiet room.

The focal point of a three-deck-high foyer is highlighted by a stainless steel kinetic sculpture (it resembles a Swiss Army knife) that brings one's attention to the multi-deck horseshoe-shaped staircase. Afternoon tea dances are held here.

The largest public room is the two-deck-high Palladium show lounge; it is horseshoe-shaped, with main and balcony levels, and there are adequate sight lines from most of the banquette-style seating, which was improved in the ship's latest refit in January 2000.

There is a domed observation lounge atop the ship (the Horizon Lounge). Although it is a little out of the traffic flow, it is a restful spot for cocktails, although it turns into a night-spot/discotheque, with accompanying thumping music. Several shops (one always carries chocolates and other sweeties for the British, who like to snack) and a dedicated cinema complete the picture.

Out on the open deck (Deck 12), there are two swimming pools; the forward pool is for adults (new, sloping steps were installed in the latest refit), while the aft pool is reserved for families and children. Four Jacuzzis are set on a raised platform, and two shower cubicles stand adjacent to the Splash Bar.

Little vignettes of the former P&O liner Canberra are displayed in the small Canberra Room, while the necessary cricket memorabilia are displayed resplendently in the wood paneled "The Oval" pub, which also has a central (wooden) dance floor.

The Monte Carlo casino offers three blackjack tables and two roulette tables, plusf 79 slot machines. Although the library has a good selection of books, it is too small, has poor lighting, few comfortable chairs, and is located out of the main passenger flow. There is a beauty salon, gymnasium, and sauna/steam room complex low down in the ship, although not particularly inviting.

Arcadia provides a traditional large ship ambience for the many British repeat passengers who enjoy such facilities and a degree of anonymity, all in unpretentious surroundings. Thankfully, there are few announcements.

There is always a good mix of entertainment aboard the ships of P&O Cruises, and this includes the Stadium Theatre Company, which provides the production shows. In addition, standard British cabaret acts provide entertainment suited to British tastes.

P&O Cruises has a fine program of special theme cruises, including antiques, The Archers (a long-running British radio program), art appreciation, classical music, comedy, cricket, gardening, jazz, motoring, popular fiction, Scottish dance, sequence dancing are among the themes. Check with your travel agent to see what is available at the time you want to cruise. Most of Canberra's crew was transferred to Arcadia and the ship features an interesting assortment of cruise itineraries.

A coach service for passengers embarking and disembarking in Southampton covers much of the UK (it is operated by Eavesway Travel); car parking is also available (one rate for undercover, one rate for open compound), and is operated by Andrews Garage.

In spring 2003, Arcadia will be moved from P&O Cruises to a subsidiary company, Ocean Village. It will be renamed Ocean Village, and will be targeted at an even younger, dress-down clientele who want to take a cruise in unstuffy, unpretentious surroundings – in other words, no-frills cruising (see page 401). The onboard currency is the British pound.

WEAK POINTS: Standing in line for embarkation, disembarkation, shore tenders and for self-serve buffet meals is an inevitable aspect of cruising aboard all large ships. There is a permanent odour of stale cigarettes in many areas of the ship. There is no full wrap-around promenade deck outdoors (open port and starboard walking areas stretch only partly along the sides). As "acoustic wallpaper" is everywhere, there is no "music-less" bar for a drink and quiet conversation. The female (digitally recorded) voice and her constant "mind the doors" reminders every time the elevator doors close are extremely irritating. Shuttle buses, which used to be provided free in some ports, are no longer complimentary. The stairways and passageways are dull; the library is too small. Although the company caters to (young) couples and families, the size of the cabins with third and fourth (upper) berths is far too small. The sauna/steam room area is in need of a complete revamp.

Arion
★★

Venice 8/10/05

Small Ship: ....6,000 tons	Total Crew: 120	Cabin Current: ....220 volts
Lifestyle: ....Standard	Passengers	Elevators: 1
Cruise Line: ....Classic International	(lower beds/all berths): 334/340	Casino (gaming tables): ....Yes
Cruises	Passenger Space Ratio	Slot Machines: ....Yes
Former Names: ....Astra I, Istra	(lower beds/all berths): 17.7/17.6	Swimming Pools (outdoors): 1
Builder: ......Brodgradiliste (Yugoslavia)	Crew/Passenger Ratio	Swimming Pools (indoors): 0
Original Cost: ....n/a	(lower beds/all berths): 2.7/2.8	Whirlpools: 0
Entered Service: 1965/1999	Navigation Officers: ....Portuguese	Fitness Center: ....No
Registry: ....Panama	Cabins (total): 169	Sauna/Steam Room: ....No/No
Length (ft/m): 381.5/116.3	Size Range (sq ft/m): ....n/a	Massage: ....No
Beam (ft/m): 54.1/16.5	Cabins (outside view): 142	Self-Service Launderette: ....No
Draft (ft/m): 18.3/5.6	Cabins (interior/no view): 27	Dedicated Cinema/Seats: ....No
Propulsion/Propellers: ....diesel	Cabins (for one person): 4	Library: ....Yes
(11,030kW)/2	Cabins (with private balcony): 0	Classification Society: ...Bureau Veritas
Passenger Decks: 5	Cabins (wheelchair accessible): 0	& Rinave

OVERALL SCORE: 859 (OUT OF A POSSIBLE 2,000 POINTS)

ACCOMMODATION: There are 12 cabin price grades – rather a lot for such a small ship (however, this may depend on tour operators that charter the vessel). Except for the top two grades, the cabins are modest in size and features, and one would not want to spend much time in them. Cabins 1–8, which have windows, have lifeboat-obstructed views. Higher deck cabins have windows, while others have portholes. Some cabins have a twin bed arrangement (side by side), while others are "L"-shaped. Each cabin has a small TV set. There is little closet and storage space (so take the minimal amount of clothing). The bathrooms are tiny and basic, yet adequate.

DINING: Although the dining room is warm and mildly attractive, with decent place settings, there are few tables for two, and the tables are very close together (leaving little room for waiters to serve properly). The chairs do not have armrests. There is only one seating. The food is limited in variety The Portuguese waiters are quite friendly, attentive, and may occasionally smile. The wine list is quite basic, and the wine glasses are small. Casual breakfasts and luncheons can be taken in the Lindo Lounge, just forward of the swimming pool and open deck aft.

OTHER COMMENTS: *Arion* (the name comes from a poet who, according to legend, was saved from drowning by dolphins) is a small ship, built for close-in cruises of the Dalmatian coast, and has a typical low-built early 1960s profile. The ship was extensively (and lovingly) recon-

BERLITZ'S RATINGS

	Possible	Achieved
Ship	500	186
Accommodation	200	82
Food	400	177
Service	400	218
Entertainment	100	37
Cruise	400	159

structed by its new owners, Classic International Cruises (even the navigation bridge has been relocated forward) after the company purchased the ship at auction in Haifa in 1999.

The ship is being operated under charter to various tour operators, and thus attracts an international mix of passengers who enjoy cruising aboard the smaller ships that have some character. There is not a lot of open deck space, although the ship does have a small, enclosed teakwood promenade deck. The small swimming pool is really only a "dip" pool, but it is adequate considering the size of the ship.

There are few public rooms, but the owner has done a pleasing job of making the interiors much more attractive than before the reconstruction, although the lighting in some places could be better. There is a show lounge, although it is only one deck in height, and the sight lines are quite restricted from many seats.

The ship has some interesting itineraries, at the very lowest prices. It is particularly suited to "nooks and crannies" ports of call, such as those found in the Mediterranean. The dress code is extremely casual and there is a relaxed ambience.

WEAK POINTS: Because this is a small ship, there are few public rooms and facilities, and very little open deck space. The interior passageways are narrow and not very well lit. The public rooms are always crowded and it is hard to get away from cigarette smokers. There are no cushioned pads for the deck lounge chairs. The ship is not suitable for wheelchair or other disabled passengers.

St. Petersburg 6/6/05

Astor
★★★★

Mid-Size Ship: . . . . .20,606 tons	Total Crew: 300	Cabin Current: . . . . .220 volts
Lifestyle: . . . . .Premium	Passengers	Elevators: 3
Cruise Line: . . . . .Transocean Tours	(lower beds/all berths): 590/650	Casino (gaming tables): . . . . .No
Former Names: . . . . .*Fedor Dostoyevskiy,*	Passenger Space Ratio	Slot Machines: .No
Astor (II)	(lower beds/all berths): 34.9/31.7	Swimming Pools (outdoors): 1
Builder: . . . . . . .Howaldtswerke Deutsche	Crew/Passenger Ratio	Swimming Pools (indoors): 1
Werft (Germany)	(lower beds/all berths): 1.9/2.1	Whirlpools: 0
Original Cost: . . . .$65 million	Navigation Officers: . . .Russian/Ukrainian	Fitness Center: . . . . .Yes
Entered Service: . . . . . Feb 1987/Apr 1997	Cabins (total): 295	Sauna/Steam Room: . . . . .Yes/No
Registry: . . . . .The Bahamas	Size Range (sq ft/m): 140.0–280.0/	Massage: . . . . .Yes
Length (ft/m): 579.0/176.50	13.0–26.0	Self-Service Launderette: . . . . .No
Beam (ft/m): 74.1/22.61	Cabins (outside view): 199	(ironing room)
Draft (ft/m): 20.0/6.10	Cabins (interior/no view): 96	Dedicated Cinema/Seats: . . . . .No
Propulsion/Propellers: . . . . .diesel	Cabins (for one person): 0	Library: . . . . .Yes
(15,400kW)/2	Cabins (with private balcony): 0	Classification Society: . . . . .Germanischer
Passenger Decks: 7	Cabins (wheelchair accessible): 0	Lloyd

OVERALL SCORE: 1,486 (OUT OF A POSSIBLE 2,000 POINTS)

ACCOMMODATION: The accommodation, spanning 18 price categories, is spread over three decks, and comprises 32 suites and 263 outside-view and interior (no view) cabins. No matter what grade of accommodation is chosen, rosewood cabinetry and plain beige walls is the norm – a restful environment. All suites and cabins with outside-view windows have blackout blinds (good for cruises to the land of the midnight sun).

SUITES: The suites (279.8 sq.ft/26 sq. meters) are tastefully decorated in pastel colors, and have rosewood cabinetry and accents. Each has a separate bedroom (with brass clock), lounge/living room (another brass clock), with mini-bar/refrigerator. The bathroom has a decent size cabinet for personal toiletry items, as well as a sit-in bathtub/shower combination, toilet, and a white enamel washbasin. A wide array of bathroom amenities is provided, including built-in hairdryer, soap, shampoo, shower cap, comb, sewing kit, shoe polish, shoehorn, clothes lint collector, nail file, matches, and a basket of fruit, replenished daily.

OUTSIDE-VIEW AND INTERIOR (NO VIEW) CABINS: These cabins (139.9 sq. ft/13 sq. meters) are well appointed and tastefully decorated in fresh pastel colors, and have dark wood accents and cabinetry, making them very restful. There is plenty of closet and drawer space, as well as some under-bed storage space for luggage. The bathrooms are very practical, and each has a decent size

BERLITZ'S RATINGS

	Possible	Achieved
Ship	500	388
Accommodation	200	151
Food	400	294
Service	400	295
Entertainment	100	63
Cruise	400	295

cabinet for personal toiletry items, as well as all the necessary fittings, including a white enamel washbasin.

OUTSIDE-VIEW FAMILY (4-BERTH) CABINS: These large cabins (258.3 sq.ft/24 sq. meters) have two lower beds, one upper berth and one sofa bed – good for families with children. The tiled bathroom has a shower enclosure, white enamel washbasin and toilet.

No matter what grade of accommodation you choose, all passengers get European duvets, 100 percent cotton towels, cotton bathrobe, soap, shampoo, shower cap, sewing kit and a basket of fruit. The cabin service menu is very limited and could be better, although German-speaking passengers in general seldom use room service for food items. There is an extra charge for sandwiches, and little else is available. However, there is plenty of food elsewhere around the ship. Note that there is an extra charge for freshly-squeezed orange juice, as aboard all ships in the German-speaking market.

DINING: The Waldorf Dining Room is reasonably elegant, well laid-out, and operates two seatings. It also has two small wings (good for private parties or groups of up to 30). The service throughout is friendly and unpretentious, and the food quality and presentation has received some attention from the food caterer. The menus are reasonably attractive, and both quality and presentation are acceptable standard fare, but nothing special. In addition to the regular entrees (typically three entrees for dinner), there may also be a pasta dish, and a vegetarian specialty dish. The wine list contains a decent selection of wines from many regions, and all at inexpensive to moderate price levels.

The casual breakfast and lunch buffets (both in the restaurant and another lounge) are reasonably well presented, and constantly refreshed, although they tend to be somewhat repetitive; the choice of foods is limited and there is room for improvement.

OTHER COMMENTS: *Astor* was the original name for this ship, the larger of two ships bearing this same name in the 1980s (the other being the present Transocean Tours ship *Arkona*), originally built for the now-defunct Astor Cruises. Its previous owners, the now defunct AquaMarin Cruises, again brought back the ship's name to *Astor* from its previous name *Fedor Dostoyevskiy*.

This is an attractive modern ship with a raked bow, a large square funnel and a nicely balanced contemporary profile. The ship was constructed in the best German tradition (slightly larger than the first *Astor* (presently renamed *Astoria*), and has been well maintained and refurbished throughout the years. Introduced by Transocean Tours in 1996, this ship was placed under a long-term charter agreement until 2007 from its present owners, Russia's Sovcomflot. *Astor* and its (slightly smaller) sister ship *Astoria* now operate in tandem – two ships of a similar size and with very similar facilities (even built in the same shipyard, with the same bathroom fittings and washbasins), the same conservative decor and ambiance – operating as one product.

This ship represents an excellent mix of traditional and contemporary styling. Built to a high standard in a German shipyard, fine teakwood decking and polished wooden rails are seen outside almost everywhere.

There is an excellent amount of open deck and sunbathing space, as well as cushioned pads for the deck lounge chairs. There is a basketball court for active passengers, as well as a large deck chess game on an aft deck, and the usual shuffleboard courts.

The interior fittings are of extremely fine quality. There is a supremely comfortable and varied array of public rooms and conference facilities, most of which have high ceilings. Public rooms include a show lounge

(unfortunately with 14 pillars to obstruct the sight lines), a Captain's Club lounge, a library and card room, and two large boutiques. A wood-paneled Hansa Tavern (with good German lager on draught) is a fine retreat, and extremely popular as a late night drinking club.

On one of the lower decks, there is an indoor swimming pool of a decent size, as well as a sauna, relaxation room, gymnasium, and beauty salon.

Transocean Tours features interesting and well-designed destination-intensive worldwide itineraries, and cruises are provided at a very attractive price. The Russian/Ukrainian hotel staff is friendly without being obtrusive, although you may find the occasional one or two crew that appears to have had a hospitality bypass.

This ship, which caters exclusively to German-speaking passengers, provides a certain degree of style, comfort and elegance, and a fine leisurely cruise experience in a relaxed, spacious setting (there is no crowding anywhere) that is less formal than a ship such as *Europa*. In typical German style, a Fruhschoppen with the appropriate music, Bavarian sausages and free beer is presented on the open lido deck once each cruise.

The ship can be booked at any DERPART, Transmarin or UDR travel agency, and represents a good choice for those seeking a well-packaged cruise in fine contemporary surroundings. Transocean Tours staff can be found aboard every cruise, some of which are designated as special-theme cruises.

The currency aboard *Astor* is the euro. Port taxes, insurance and gratuities to staff *are all included* in the cruise fare. Drinks prices are inexpensive, particularly when compared to land-based prices.

A service provided by ABX Logistics will collect your luggage from your house, and transport it to the ship for you (this saves having to carry it); when you return, the service will collect it from the ship and bring it to your house – all for a nominal fee (this service is only available to/from certain ports).

WEAK POINTS: The show lounge has pillars obstructing the sight lines, and the stage is also the dance floor, and cannot be raised for shows; entertainment, therefore, is mostly cabaret-style. The bathroom towels are small and should be larger.

Astoria
★★★★

Mid-Size Ship: . . . . .18,591 tons	Total Crew: 243	Cabins (wheelchair accessible): 0
Lifestyle: . . . . .Premium	Passengers	Cabin Current: . . . . .220 volts
Cruise Line: . . . . .Transocean Tours	(lower beds/all berths): 500/618	Elevators: 3
Former Names: . . . . .Arkona, Astor	Passenger Space Ratio	Casino (gaming tables): . . . . .No
Builder: . . . . . . .Howaldtswerke Deutsche	(lower beds/all berths): 36.0/30.0	Slot Machines: .No
Werft (Germany)	Crew/Passenger Ratio	Swimming Pools (outdoors): 1
Original Cost: . . . .$55 million	(lower beds/all berths): 2.1/2.5	Swimming Pools (indoors): 1
Entered Service: . . . . .Dec 1981/Feb 2002	Navigation Officers: . . . . .European	Whirlpools: 0
Registry: . . . . .The Bahamas	Cabins (total): 259	Fitness Center: . . . . .Yes
Length (ft/m): 539.2/164.35	Size Range (sq ft/m): 150.0–725.0/	Sauna/Steam Room: . . . . .Yes/No
Beam (ft/m): 74.1/22.60	13.4–65.3	Massage: . . . . .Yes
Draft (ft/m): 20.0/6.11	Cabins (outside view): 183	Self-Service Launderette: . . . . .No
Propulsion/Propellers: . . . . .diesel	Cabins (interior/no view): 76	Dedicated Cinema/Seats: . . . . .No
(13,200kW)/2	Cabins (for one person): 0	Library: . . . . .Yes
Passenger Decks: 8	Cabins (with private balcony): 0	Classification Society: Germanischer Lloyd

OVERALL SCORE: 1,476 (OUT OF A POSSIBLE 2,000 POINTS)

ACCOMMODATION: The accommodation, of which there are 18 price categories, is spread over three decks, and comprises one Senator Suite, 34 suites and 263 outside-view and interior (no view) cabins.

SENATOR SUITE: This Boat Deck suite (725 sq. ft/65.3 sq. meters) is simply lovely, and has just about everything needed for refined, private living aboard this ship. There is a separate bedroom with double bed, living room with sofa, dining table and chairs. The tiled bathroom features a large bathtub, separate shower enclosure, and plenty of storage space for personal toiletry items.

SUITES: Suites (269.1 sq. ft/25 sq. meters) have a separate bedroom with double bed, living room with sofa, dining table and chairs. The tiled bathroom has a large bathtub, separate shower enclosure, and plenty of storage space for personal toiletry items.

OUTSIDE-VIEW CABINS/INTERIOR (NO VIEW) CABINS: The standard cabins (139.9 sq. ft/13 sq. meters) are quite well appointed and decorated, and all feature crisp, clean colors (some might find them plain, as are the ceilings). The bathrooms are quite compact units, although there is a decent-sized shower enclosure. They are fully tiled, however, and have a decent cabinet for storing personal toiletry items.

No matter what grade of accommodation you choose, all passengers get 100 percent cotton towels, and bathrobe. The cabin service menu is very limited and

BERLITZ'S RATINGS		
	Possible	Achieved
Ship	500	378
Accommodation	200	151
Food	400	295
Service	400	295
Entertainment	100	62
Cruise	400	295

could be better, although German-speaking passengers in general seldom use room service for food items. There is an extra charge for sandwiches, and little else is available; however, there is plenty of food elsewhere around the ship. Note that there is an extra charge for fresh-squeezed orange juice, as aboard all ships in the German-speaking market.

DINING: The Astoria Restaurant, located high in the ship, has big, ocean-view picture windows and is reasonably attractive, with dark wood paneling and restful décor; two seatings are featured. The food is adequate to very good, though choice is somewhat limited, but the service, by some charming waitresses, does help. The occasional formal candlelight dinners provide a romantic ambiance. The wine list contains a decent selection of wines from many regions, and all at inexpensive to moderate price levels.

The self-serve buffets (for breakfast and luncheon) are varied, although the presentation could be improved. The cabin service food menu is very limited.

OTHER COMMENTS: *Astoria* is a traditional style of cruise ship (slightly smaller than her sister ship *Astor*), originally constructed for the now defunct Astor Cruises. The ship cruised under the Seetours banner from October 1985 and continued until February 2002, when it was transferred to its new operators, Transocean Tours. The ship underwent a very slight name change, to *Astoria*. Some minor modifications took place so that *Astor* and *Astoria* now operate in tandem – two ships of a similar size and with very similar facilities (even built in the same shipyard, with the same bathroom fittings and washbasins), the same conservative decor and ambiance – operating as one product.

Astoria is a well-constructed modern vessel with a well-balanced profile. There is a very good amount of open deck and sunbathing space for its size, with some excellent teakwood decking and polished railings. There is a good amount of open deck and sunbathing space, as well as cushioned pads for the deck lounge chairs. For the sports-minded, there is a large volleyball court.

Astoria, like its sister ship *Astor*, has beautifully appointed interior fittings and decor, with a great deal of rosewood paneling and wood accents throughout. The ship has been maintained extremely well. Subdued lighting and a soothing ambience is highlighted by good artwork throughout the ship. There are good meetings facilities, a fine library, and, perhaps more important, an excellent pub with draught German beer.

Subdued lighting and soothing ambience, highlighted by fine artwork throughout make for a pleasant, relaxing cruise experience. There are good meetings facilities, and a fine, well-stocked library. There is an excellent pub (naturally with draught German lager) looking aft over the sun deck, which is definitely the late-night meeting place.

There is also an excellent indoor spa and fitness center, with a good range of facilities that include a swimming pool, fitness center, and three sun-bed rooms for tanning sessions. In addition, sophisticated hospital facilities include oxygen multi-step therapy. Passengers who use dialysis machines will find that Transocean Tours operates several special cruises, complete with specially trained medical personnel (dialysis equipment I installed aboard *Astoria*).

There are many cigarette and cigar smokers. The ship features good traditional European-style hotel service, and a mostly Ukrainian service staff. The reception desk is open 24 hours daily.

Astoria features good value for money cruising in contemporary comfort, and is best recommended for passengers who appreciate quality, fine surroundings, good food, and excellent destination-intensive itineraries, all packaged neatly in a relaxed, informal ambience. Many cruises have special themes. Transocean Tours staff is available aboard every cruise; they will go out of their way to make sure that you will have an excellent cruise experience in very comfortable surroundings. The ship has many repeat passengers, who enjoy the extremely friendly, mostly German crew (who provide a fun crew show). The currency aboard *Astoria* is the euro. Port taxes, insurance and gratuities to staff *are all included* in the cruise fare.

A service by ABX Logistics will collect your luggage from your house, and transport it to the ship for you (this saves having to carry it); when you return, the service will collect it from the ship and bring it to your house – all for a nominal fee.

WEAK POINTS: There is no wrap-around promenade deck outdoors. The show lounge has 14 pillars obstructing the sight lines, and the stage is also the dance floor and cannot be raised for shows; entertainment, therefore, is mostly cabaret-style. Finally, non-smokers should note that there are many cigarette and cigar smokers, and it is often hard to get away from them.

Removed 2006

Asuka
★★★★ +

Mid-Size Ship: ....28,856 tons	Total Crew: 262	Cabins (wheelchair accessible): 2
Lifestyle: ....Premium	Passengers	Cabin Current: ....110 volts
Cruise Line: ....NYK Cruises	(lower beds/all berths): 600/618	Elevators: 5
Former Names: ....none	Passenger Space Ratio	Casino (gaming tables): ....Yes
Builder: .....Mitsubishi Heavy Industries	(lower beds/all berths): 48.0/46.6	Slot Machines: ....Yes
(Japan)	Crew/Passenger Ratio	Swimming Pools (outdoors): 1
Original Cost: ....$150 million	(lower beds/all berths): 2.2/2.3	Swimming Pools (indoors): 0
Entered Service: ....Dec 1991	Navigation Officers: ....Japanese	Whirlpools: 3
Registry: ....Japan	Cabins (total): 300	Fitness Center: ....Yes
Length (ft/m): 632.5/192.81	Size Range (sq ft/m): 182.9–649.0/	Sauna/Steam Room: ....Yes/Yes
Beam (ft/m): 81.0/24.70	17.0–60.3	Massage: ....Yes
Draft (ft/m): 21.6/6.6	Cabins (outside view): 300	Self-Service Launderette: ....Yes
Propulsion/Propellers: ....diesel	Cabins (interior/no view): 0	Dedicated Cinema/Seats: Yes/97
(17,300kW)/2	Cabins (for one person): 0	Library: ....Yes
Passenger Decks: 8	Cabins (with private balcony): 108	Classification Society: Nippon Kaiji Kyokai

OVERALL SCORE: 1,660 (OUT OF A POSSIBLE 2,000 POINTS)

ACCOMMODATION: There are seven accommodation categories (Suite, and grades A, B, C, D, F and J), although in reality there are just five types of suites and cabins. Three decks (8, 9 and 10) have suites and cabins with a private balcony (note that the floor is laid with green simulated turf, and there is no outside light). No matter what grade of accommodation you choose, all suites and cabins have ocean views, although some are slightly obstructed by the ship's gangway, when it is in the raised (stowed) position; there are no interior (no view) cabins.

In all grades, the cabinetry featured is thick, cherry wood, with nicely rounded edges. The cabin insulation is excellent. There is a good amount of closet and drawer space, including some lockable drawers and a personal safe. Facilities include a hot water (tea-making) unit (with a selection of both western and Japanese teas), refrigerator (stocked with beer and cold coffee – the kind you find in street corner vending machines in Japan), 100 percent cotton bathrobe, yukata (cotton house robe), slippers, and down duvets (instead of sheets/blankets).

All grades feature bathrooms with full, deep bathtubs (while the "club" suite bathrooms are of generous proportions, the standard bathrooms are rather small), and all have a tiled floor and bath/shower area. The range of personal toiletry items includes soap, shampoo, rinse, toothbrush/toothpaste, comb, shower cap, razor set, and vanity pack for ladies.

Two suites provide the largest accommodation (one is decorated in blue, the other in salmon); these are larger versions of the "A" grade cabins. Each has a separate bed-

BERLITZ'S RATINGS

	Possible	Achieved
Ship	500	418
Accommodation	200	169
Food	400	340
Service	400	334
Entertainment	100	80
Cruise	400	319

room, with walk-in closet that includes a luggage deck, and twin beds that convert to a queen-sized bed), sofa, two chairs and coffee table, large vanity desk, plenty of drawer space, and large color television; The marble-clad bathroom is large and has a whirlpool bathtub set alongside large ocean-view windows overlooking the private balcony, and twin washbasins set in a marble surround; a living room, and separate guest bathroom. The private balcony is quite large and has a tall tropical plant set in a glass display enclosure.

"A" grade cabins are excellent living spaces, and feature twice the size and space of the standard cabins in categories "D," "F" and "J." They are very nicely decorated and outfitted, and have twin beds (convertible to a queen-sized bed), sofa, two chairs and coffee table, large vanity desk, plenty of drawer space, and large color television. However, when in its twin bed configuration, the room's *feng shui* is not good, as one of the beds is facing a large mirror at the writing/vanity desk -- which is not permissible. Many have a private balcony (with full floor-to-ceiling partition and a green synthetic turf floor, although there is no outside light), with floor-to-ceiling sliding door (the door handles are quite awkward, however). In addition to all the standard cabin amenities, an illuminated walk-in closet (with long hanging rail and plenty of drawer space) is provided. The bathrooms are partly tiled and of generous proportions, and include a glass-fronted (plastic) toiletries cabinet, and two washbasins set in a thick marble surround. Four new suites were added to Panorama Deck 10 during a 1999 drydock in what was previously an unused space.

The room service menu is small (it is, in effect, rarely used by Japanese passengers), but it does include such things as continental breakfast, and light snacks throughout the day and evening. Sashimi and sushi items are available during the hours when the sushi bar is open (typically 6pm–11pm), at extra cost.

DINING: The Four Seasons dining room is totally a no-smoking area, and cellular phones are thankfully not permitted (many people take mobile phones with them, particularly on the short cruises that are so popular in Japan). It is laid out in two sections, with ocean-view windows along one side only (in the aft section), and along two sides (forward section only), has a good amount of space around the tables, although there are only a few tables for two. There are two seatings, and both Japanese and Western cuisine is featured daily – traditional Japanese breakfast and luncheon in the restaurant (western cuisine in the Lido Café), and Japanese dinners, with the occasional western dinner. There is a limited, but very reasonable, selection of second-tier wines.

"Umihiko" is a small alternative dining spot. It is an à la carte sushi bar (with both counter and table seating) that features superb fresh seafood, beautifully prepared and presented (at extra cost), together with a good selection of Japanese sake. It is open also for lunch as well as dinner on some short cruises, and for dinner (and occasionally lunch) on longer cruises.

For casual breakfasts and lunches, an informal, now improved, upgraded and expanded self-serve Lido Café is provided, with indoor-outdoor seating, and a bar. This popular eatery now provides better indoor seating, and an improved layout that is much more user-friendly.

A traditional *washitsu* room (in which room the floor is covered in tatami mats, and no shoes are allowed) is provided for special afternoon tea ceremonies, haiku readings and other traditional Japanese ceremonies. The entrance has a small black stone and wood entrance.

OTHER COMMENTS: When introduced in 1991, *Asuka* was the first all-new large ship specially designed for the still slow growing Japanese cruise market, and the largest cruise ship constructed in Japan for the local market. But it is quickly becoming outdated, although a refurbishment in 2001 refreshed some of the interiors.

The ship has pleasing exterior styling and profile, with a large, rounded, but squat funnel. There is a good amount of open deck space (although Japanese passengers do not use it much, as most are not keen on sunbathing). There is a wide wrap-around teakwood promenade deck outdoors, good for strolling.

The "cake-layer" stacking of the public rooms hampers passenger flow and makes it somewhat disjointed, although the ship's Japanese passengers do like the separation of public rooms. There are many intimate public rooms and plenty of space so that there is never a feeling of crowding. There is an excellent, spacious true Japanese grand bath with large ocean-view windows,

two baths, one hot tub, sauna, a proper steam room with wood floor and wood ceiling, several washing stations, showers, and vanity desk with grooming aids. The massage room, however, is located away from the grand bath area and would be better if integrated.

The interior decor is elegant but understated, with pleasing color combinations, quality fabrics and fine soft furnishings. Fascinating Japanese artwork is featured, including a four-deck-high mural located on the wall of the main foyer staircase by Noriko Tamara, called "Song of the Seasons." The Mariner's Club, decorated in the style of an English gentleman's club with wood paneled walls and deep leather chairs, and a bar is a popular evening spot.

Cellular pay phones are located in one of the deck foyers, good for use when the ship features short cruises around Japan. The entertainment is typically an interesting mix of western acts (including colorful production shows), and traditional Japanese acts (including storytellers). There are good facilities for meetings and groups.

As for the dress code, there is a mix of formal and informal nights, while during the day the dress code is very casual. In case you want to do your own laundry, there is a self-service launderette, which has 12 washing machines. One nice touch is the fact that streamers are still thrown when the ship is cruising around Japan – a maritime tradition that so many other cruise ships have ceased. Gratuities are neither expected, nor allowed. Note that children under 10 are not generally accepted, except during special summer festival and holiday cruises.

Asuka has, over the years, gathered a loyal following, perhaps because the ship provides an extremely comfortable and serene environment in which to cruise, particularly for its annual around-the-world cruise and the longer cruises in Southeast Asia and South Pacific. Regular passengers enjoy these because many more activities, lecturers and entertainers are planned than on the short cruises typical throughout much of the summer. Now that the ship is more than 10 years old, however, the refurbished areas (new carpeting throughout, expanded Lido Café) tend to show up some of the other areas that need attention.

A specialist courier company provides an excellent luggage service and will collect your luggage from your home before the cruise, and deliver it back to your home after the cruise (this service is available only in Japan). In the spring of 2002, *Asuka* went into a shipyard for some upgrading of public rooms and accommodation areas. The onboard currency is the Japanese yen.

WEAK POINTS: There is no butler service in the Asuka Club suites. The ship is in need of further refurbishment and upgrading in some areas in order to compete effectively in the international marketplace. The green turf on the upper, outermost deck is a patchwork quilt and makes it look sloppy when compared with other areas. The white caulking of teakwood decking looks dirty and would be better if replaced by black caulking.

Removed 2006

Atalante
★

Small Ship: ....13,562 tons	Total Crew: 170	Cabins (wheelchair accessible): 0
Lifestyle: ....Standard	Passengers	Cabin Current: ....220 volts DC
Cruise Line: ....New Paradise Cruises	(lower beds/all berths): 518/705	Elevators: 0
Former Names: ....*Tahitien*	Passenger Space Ratio	Casino (gaming tables): ....Yes
Builder: .....Direction des Construction	(lower beds/all berths): 26.1/19.2	Slot Machines: ....Yes
et Armes Navales (France)	Crew/Passenger Ratio	Swimming Pools (outdoors): 2
Original Cost: ....n/a	(lower beds/all berths): 3.0/4.1	Swimming Pools (indoors): 0
Entered Service: ....May 1953/Dec 1992	Navigation Officers: ......Cypriot/Greek	Whirlpools: 0
Registry: ....Cyprus	Cabins (total): 260	Fitness Center: ....No
Length (ft/m): 548.5/167.20	Size Range (sq ft/m): 129.1–247.5/	Sauna/Steam Room: ....No/No
Beam (ft/m): 67.9/20.70	12.0–23.0	Massage: ....No
Draft (ft/m): 20.7/6.30	Cabins (outside view): 171	Self-Service Launderette: ....No
Propulsion/Propellers: ....diesel	Cabins (interior/no view): 89	Dedicated Cinema/Seats: ....No
(7,700kW)/2	Cabins (for one person): 2	Library: ....No
Passenger Decks: 7	Cabins (with private balcony): 0	Classification Society: ....Bureau Veritas

OVERALL SCORE: 645 (OUT OF A POSSIBLE 2,000 POINTS)

ACCOMMODATION: The cabins, in 10 different price grades, are all rather small and spartan, although most are decorated in pastel shades. While many cabins have two lower beds, there are many that also have third- and fourth-person upper Pullman berths (good for families with children or friends who don't mind sharing in order to keep the per person price low). There is a limited amount of closet space, but you really do not need much clothing for this casual cruise. Additional cabins installed in a 1993 refit are noisy and harder squeaky, which makes them quite difficult to sleep in. The top grade cabins also have a refrigerator, and a little more space; otherwise there is little to distinguish them.

DINING: The Venus Dining Room is located low down in the ship and always seems to have a musty odor and aroma of stale food. Self-serve buffets are featured for most meals, and the food really is quite basic – with few choices and poor presentation. Service is provided mainly by Greek waiters, who are friendly but are completely without finesse, and very little training. There is also a small cafeteria for casual snacks.

OTHER COMMENTS: Now well over 40 years of age, *Atalante*, a former passenger-car liner, is well worn. The ship has a small, squat funnel amidships and a really long foredeck (something not generally found aboard new ships). This is quite a stable ship at sea, however,

BERLITZ'S RATINGS

	Possible	Achieved
Ship	500	135
Accommodation	200	67
Food	400	135
Service	400	158
Entertainment	100	30
Cruise	400	120

with a deep draft, and rides well. There is a generous amount of open deck and sunbathing space, but the outdoor decking is well worn, as are the deck lounge chairs.

The number of public rooms is very limited, and the layout is quite awkward and very disjointed. The main public room is the show lounge, an uncomfortable room that is immersed in high volume, low quality shows and cabaret. Recent decor changes are for the better, although much of the interior decor is dated, yet adequate and comfortable for those who do not want the glitz of newer ships. Much emphasis is placed on duty-free shopping.

This ship is perhaps acceptable for younger, budget-minded passengers wanting to party and travel with just the basics and without the need for much service. The ship operates two- and three-night short, casual cruises from Cyprus to Egypt and Israel. The onboard currency is the Cyprus pound. There will be a wide variety of nationalities on board, so international language skills may be useful.

WEAK POINTS: The ceilings in the public rooms are low. The nightlife is disco-loud, as is the music. There is no finesse anywhere, although the staff is reasonably enthusiastic. Many passengers smoke, so it is difficult to get away from the smell of stale smoke everywhere. This ship has passed its "sell-by" date and really should be retired or replaced by newer tonnage.

Aurora
★★★★

Large Ship:	76,152 tons	
Lifestyle:	Standard	
Cruise Line:	P&O Cruises	
Former Names:	none	
Builder:	Meyer Werft (Germany)	
Original Cost:	$375 million	
Entered Service:	May 2000	
Registry:	Great Britain	
Length (ft/m):	885.8/270.0	
Beam (ft/m):	105.6/32.2	
Draft (ft/m):	25.9/7.9	
Propulsion/Propellers:	diesel-electric (40,000kW)/2	
Passenger Decks:	10	
Total Crew:	816	
Passengers		
(lower beds/all berths):	1,868/1,975	
Passenger Space Ratio		
(lower beds/all berths):	40.7/38.5	
Crew/Passenger Ratio		
(lower beds/all berths):	2.2/2.4	
Navigation Officers:	British	
Cabins (total):	934	
Size Range (sq ft/m):	150.6–953.0/ 14.0–88.5	
Cabins (outside view):	655	
Cabins (interior/no view):	279	
Cabins (for one person):	0	
Cabins (with private balcony):	406	
Cabins (wheelchair accessible):	22 (8 with private balcony)	
Cabin Current:	110 and 220 volts	
Elevators:	10	
Casino (gaming tables):	Yes	
Slot Machines:	Yes	
Swimming Pools (outdoors):	3 (1 with magrodome)	
Swimming Pools (indoors):	0	
Whirlpools:	5	
Fitness Center:	Yes	
Sauna/Steam Room:	Yes/Yes	
Massage:	Yes	
Self-Service Launderette:	Yes	
Dedicated Cinema/Seats:	Yes/200	
Library:	Yes	
Classification Society:	Lloyd's Register	

OVERALL SCORE: 1,548 (OUT OF A POSSIBLE 2,000 POINTS)

ACCOMMODATION: There are five principal grades of accommodation, in 26 price categories. Included are 2 two-level penthouses, 10 suites with balconies, 18 mini-suites with balconies, 368 cabins with balconies, 225 standard outside-view cabins, 16 interconnecting cabins for families, and 279 interior (no view) cabins. All grades, from the largest to the smallest, provide the following common features: polished cherry wood laminate cabinetry, full-length mirror, tea and coffee-making facilities, as well as a personal safe, refrigerator, television, individually-controlled air-conditioning; twin beds that convert to a queen-size double bed, sofa and coffee table. There are four whole decks of cabins with private balconies (this is about 40 percent of all cabins), and these feature easy-to-open sliding glass floor-to-ceiling doors; the partitions are of the almost full floor-to-ceiling type – so they really are quite private – and cannot be overlooked from above.

Cabin insulation could be much better (particularly poor is the noise created by the magnetic catches in drawers and on the closet doors). Also, the TV sets provide only monaural sound. Although most doorways are 26 inches (66 cm) wide, the measurement of actual access is 2 inches (5 cm) less because of the doorframe; however, some doorways are only 21.5 inches (55 cm) wide.

A good range of Molton Brown personal amenities (shampoo, body lotion, shower gel) is provided for all accommodation designated as penthouse suites, suites or mini-suites. For all other accommodation, only soap is provided, together with a "sport wash" combination soap

BERLITZ'S RATINGS

	Possible	Achieved
Ship	500	429
Accommodation	200	161
Food	400	271
Service	400	307
Entertainment	100	82
Cruise	400	298

and shampoo in a dispenser in the shower (so take your favorite shampoo and conditioner), and a small pouch of assorted personal care items. All grades get a Molton Brown "hair and body sport wash" dispenser mounted in all bathrooms, as well as thick, 100 percent cotton bathrobes, and 100 percent cotton towels.

PENTHOUSE SUITES: The largest accommodation consists of two penthouse suites (named Library Suite and Piano Suite), each 953 sq. ft (88.5 sq. meters). They have forward-facing views, being located forward directly underneath the navigation bridge (the blinds must be drawn at night so as not to affect navigation). Each is spread over two decks in height, and connected by a beautiful wood curved staircase. One suite features a baby grand piano (playable manually, or it can be set to play electronically), while the other features a private library. The living area is on the lower deck (Deck 10), and incorporates a dining suite (a first in a P&O ship) and a small private balcony. In the bedroom, upstairs, there is a walk-in closet, while the bathroom features porcelain and polished granite, with twin basins, bathtub and separate shower enclosure. There is also a small private balcony. Butler service is provided.

SUITES: Accommodation designated as suites (there are 10 of them) measure about 445 sq. ft (41.3 sq. meters). They have a separate bedroom with two lower beds that convert to a queen-sized bed. There is a walk-in dressing area and closet, with plenty of drawer space, trouser press and ironing board. The lounge features a sofa, armchairs, dining table and chairs, writing desk, television, radio and stereo system. The marble-clad bathroom has a whirlpool bath, shower and toilet. The private balcony has space for two deck lounge chairs, plus two chairs and two tables. Butler service is provided.

MINI-SUITES: These measure 325 sq. ft (30.1 sq. meters), and have a separate bedroom area with two lower beds that convert to a queen-sized bed. There are one double and two single closets, a good amount of drawer space, binoculars, a trouser press and ironing board. Each private balcony has a blue plastic deck covering, one deck lounge chair, one chair and table, and exterior light.

STANDARD OUTSIDE-VIEW/INTERIOR (NO VIEW) CABINS: Accommodation designated as double cabins with private balcony measure about 175 sq. ft (16.2 sq. meters). They have two lower beds that convert to a queen-sized bed. The sitting area has a sofa and table. There's also a vanity table/writing desk, and a private balcony with blue plastic deck covering, two chairs (with only a small recline) and small table. Note that a 110-volt (American) socket is located *underneath* the vanity desk drawer – in a difficult to access position.

Outside-view or interior (with no view) cabins have two lower beds that convert to a queen-sized bed, closet (but very few drawers), and measure 150 sq. ft (14 sq. meters). The bathroom has a mini-bath/shower and toilet, or shower and toilet.

All bathrooms in all grades (except those designated as suites) are compact, modular units, and have mirror-fronted cabinets, although the lighting is quite soft (not strong enough for the application of make-up), and, in cabins with bathtubs, the retractable clothesline is located too high for most people to reach (you may need to stand on the side of the bathtub to use it – this could prove unsafe).

There are 22 wheelchair-accessible cabins, well outfitted for the physically challenged passenger, and almost all are located within very easy access to elevators. However, one cabin (D165 on Deck 8) is located between forward and mid-ships stairways, and it is difficult to access the public rooms on Deck 8 without first going to the deck below, due to several steps and tight corners. All other wheelchair-accessible cabins are well positioned, and eight of them have a private balcony.

DINING: The two main dining rooms, Alexandria and Medina (each seats 525) feature tables for 2, 4, 6, 8 and 10, and there are two seatings. Medina, the midships restaurant, features a slight Moorish theme décor, while Alexandria, with windows on three sides, features Egyptian décor. Both restaurants are non-smoking, and both have more tables for two aboard this ship than in the equivalent restaurants aboard close sister ship *Oriana*. The china is Wedgwood, the silverware is by Elkington.

The cuisine is very British – a little adventurous at times, but always with plenty of curry dishes and other standard British items – but with good presentation (better than other ships in the P&O Cruises fleet). You should not expect exquisite dining, though – this is British hotel catering that doesn't pretend to offer caviar and other gourmet foods. But what it does present is attractive and tasty, with some excellent gravies and sauces to accompany meals. In keeping with the Britishness of P&O Cruises, the desserts are always good. A statement in the onboard folder states that P&O Cruises does not knowingly purchase genetically modified foods. The service is provided by a team of friendly stewards from the island of Goa, with which P&O has had a long relationship.

In addition to the two formal dining rooms, there are several other dining options. You can, for example, also have dinner in the 24-hour, 120-seat French bistro-style restaurant, Café Bordeaux, for which there is a cover charge (for dinner only). Breakfasts and lunches are also featured here, as are several types of coffees: espresso, cappuccino, latte, ristretto, as well as flavored coffees.

Casual, self-serve breakfasts and lunches can be taken in a dazzlingly colorful eatery named "The Orangery." Other casual dining spots include the Sidewalk Café (for fast food items poolside), a French patisserie (for pastries and coffee), champagne bar and, in a first for a P&O cruise ship, Raffles coffee and chocolate bar (but without the ceiling fans). All informal dining spots are non-smoking.

OTHER COMMENTS: *Aurora* (named after the goddess of the Dawn in mythologies such as Greek, Melanesian and Slavonic mythologies named after the goddess of dawn, or perhaps the carnation Dianthus Aurora, or it could be the famous Northern and Southern Lights – aurora borealis and aurora australis) was built specifically for the growing British traditional cruise market. The ship, the flagship of P&O Cruises, is based at Southampton, England. *Aurora* is a close sister ship and running mate to the company's popular *Oriana*, although *Aurora* has more space per passenger.

As ships evolve, slight differences in layout occur, as is the case with *Aurora*. One big difference can be found in the addition of a large, magrodome-covered indoor/outdoor swimming pool (good for use in all weathers). The stern superstructure is nicely rounded and has several tiers that overlook the aft decks, pool and children's outdoor facilities. There is a good amount of open deck and sunbathing space, an important plus for the outdoors-loving mainly British passengers. There is an extra-wide wrap-around promenade deck outdoors, with plenty of (white plastic) deck lounge chairs.

The ship's interiors are gentle, welcoming and restrained, with good colors and combinations that don't clash. The public rooms and areas have been designed in such a way that each room is individual, and yet there appears to be an open, yet cohesive flow throughout all of the public areas – something difficult to achieve when a number of designers are involved.

There is good horizontal passenger flow, and wide passageways help to avoid congestion. Very noticeable are the fine, detailed ceiling treatments.

Being a ship for all types of people, specific areas have been designed to attract different age groups and lifestyles. The focal point is a four-decks-high atrium lobby and a dramatic, calming, 35-ft (10.6-meter) high, Lalique-style sculpture (it's actually made of fiberglass) of two mythical figures behind a veil of water. At the top of the atrium is the ship's library (larger and in a different location than *Oriana*).

The carpeting throughout the ship is of an excellent quality, much of it custom designed and made of long-lasting 100 percent wool. There are original artworks by all-British artists that include several tapestries and sculptures. For a weird experience, try standing on the midships staircase and look at the oil on canvas paintings by Nicholas Hely Hutchinson – they are curved – and this has a dramatic effect on one's ability not to be seasick while cruising through the Bay of Biscay.

Other features include a virtual reality games room, 12 lounges/bars (among the nicest are Andersons – similar to Anderson's aboard *Oriana*, with a fireplace and mahogany paneling, and the Crows Nest – complete with a lovely one-sided model of one of P&O's former liners: *Strathnaver* of 1931 (scrapped in Hong Kong in 1962). There is also a golf simulator (extra charge), and a cinema that doubles as a concert and lecture hall.

There are special facilities and rooms for children and teenagers – even a night nursery, and a whole deck outdoors to play on (swimming pools and whirlpools included just for the youngsters). In addition, 16 cabins have interconnecting doors – good for families with children (or maid). At peak holiday times (summer, Christmas, Easter) there could be 400 or more children on board. However, the ship absorbs them well, and the children's programming helps keep them occupied.

The Oasis Spa is located midships and almost atop the ship. It is moderately large, and provides all the standard alternative treatment therapies (note that the sauna and steam room are co-ed – so you'll need a bathing suit). A gymnasium has the latest high-tech muscle toning equipment. There's a beauty salon with a spiral staircase, and a relaxation area overlooking the forward swimming pool.

The library also houses several writing desks, as well as large leather audio listening chairs (in which you can relax – or fall asleep – with a good compact disc), and three computer stations with internet access. The library has a good range of hardback books (and a librarian), and skillfully crafted inlaid wood tables. On the second day of almost any cruise, however, the library will have been almost stripped of books by word-hungry passengers. The library also sells some nautical books.

Ballroom dance fans will make use of the four good-sized wooden dance floors. The ship always carries a professional dance couple as hosts and teachers, and plenty of dancing time is included in the programming.

Children and teens have "Club Aurora" programs with their own rooms ("Toybox," "Jumping Jacks" and "Decibels"), and their own outdoor pool. Children can be entertained until 10pm, which gives parents time to have dinner and go dancing. All cabins also have a baby-listening device. A night nursery for small children (ages 2 to 5) is available at no extra charge (6pm–2am). Teenagers have their own hangout, Decibels.

There is a wide variety of mainly British entertainment, from production shows to top British "names" and lesser artists. There is also a program of theme cruises (antiques, The Archers, art appreciation, classical music, comedy, cricket, gardening, jazz, motoring, popular fiction, Scottish dance, sequence dancing are examples).

In this ship, P&O Cruises has improved on the facilities of older sister ship *Oriana*, with larger cabins and suites and with more dining options and choice of public areas. *Aurora* provides a decent, standardized cruise experience – good value for the money – for its mainly British passengers (of all dialects) and is ideal for those who don't want to fly to join a cruise, as the ship sails from Southampton. Each year, it has an around-the-world cruise; this is excellent value for money.

However, in the quest for increased onboard revenue (and shareholder value), even birthday cakes now cost extra, as do espressos and cappuccinos (fake ones, made from instant coffee, are available in the dining rooms). Also at extra cost are ice cream, and bottled water (these can add up to a considerable amount on an around-the-world cruise). The onboard currency is the British pound. For gratuities, you should typically allow £3.50 ($5.25) per person, per day.

A fine British brass band send-off accompanies all sailings. Other touches include church bells that sound throughout the ship for the interdenominational Sunday church service. A coach service for passengers embarking or disembarking in Southampton covers much of the UK. Car parking is available (one rate for under-cover parking, one rate for an open compound).

WEAK POINTS: The layout is a little disjointed in places, with several dead-ends and some poor signage in places. The hours of opening of the Reception Desk (7am–7pm when I last sailed) are too short. Except for the suites, no cabins have illuminated closets. The cabin ceilings are disappointingly plain. Shuttle buses, once provided in the various ports, are no longer complimentary when provided (except on the around-the-world cruise). Standing in line for embarkation, disembarkation, shore tenders and for self-serve buffet meals is an inevitable aspect of cruising aboard all large ships. During the school holidays, there will be many children aboard; this can irritate some older passengers. The cost of sending emails (from the four computers in the library) is high, at £3 ($4.50) for 10 minutes. "Cashless Cruising" doesn't include tips (for an around-the-world cruise, this means carrying more than $750 in cash), or stamps, or condoms (available in machines in the public toilets).

Removed 2005

Ausonia
★★ +

Mid-Size Ship: ....12,609 tons	Total Crew: 280	Cabin Current: ....220 volts
Lifestyle: ....Standard	Passengers	Elevators: 1
Cruise Line: ....Louis Cruise Lines/	(lower beds/all berths): 508/701	Casino (gaming tables): ....Yes
First Choice	Passenger Space Ratio	Slot Machines: ....Yes
Former Names: ....none	(lower beds/all berths): 24.8/17.9	Swimming Pools (outdoors): 1
Builder: ....Cantieri Riuniti dell' Adriatico	Crew/Passenger Ratio	Swimming Pools (indoor): 0
(Italy)	(lower beds/all berths): 1.8/2.5	Whirlpools: 1
Original Cost: ....n/a	Navigation Officers: ......Greek/Cypriot	Fitness Center: ....Yes
Entered Service: ....Sept 1957/May 1998	Cabins (total): 254	Sauna/Steam Room: ....Yes/No
Registry: ....Cyprus	Size Range (sq ft/m): 69.9–269.1/	Massage: ....Yes
Length (ft/m): 522.5/159.26	6.5–25.0	Self-Service Launderette: ....No
Beam (ft/m): 69.8/21.29	Cabins (outside view): 152	Dedicated Cinema/Seats: Yes/125
Draft (ft/m): 21.4/6.54	Cabins (interior/no view): 102	Library: ....Yes
Propulsion/Propellers: .....steam turbine	Cabins (for one person): 1	Classification Society: ...Registro Navale
(12,799kW)/2	Cabins (with private balcony): 0	Italiano (RINA)
Passenger Decks: 8	Cabins (wheelchair accessible): 0	

OVERALL SCORE: 996 (OUT OF A POSSIBLE 2,000 POINTS)

ACCOMMODATION: From suites to standard interior and outside cabins, all are small and compact, yet reasonably comfortable, in six cabin grades. They have all the basics, including a private bathroom and adequate closet space for frugal packers (drawer space is limited, however).

The uppermost cabin grades have a full-sized bathtub (two suites have whirlpool baths), while all others have showers. There are several family cabins. Some interior and outside standard cabins have upper and lower berths.

DINING: The no-smoking dining room, located high up in the vessel, has good ocean views from large picture windows, and features fine china and pleasant table settings. Tables are for four, six or eight, in two seatings. Friendly, efficient service with well programmed flair and attention is provided. The international cuisine provides a good mix of Continental fare, with some regional Mediterranean specialties and British favorites. The selection of fruits and cheeses is limited. The basic wine list provides an inexpensive range and a decent choice.

OTHER COMMENTS: *Ausonia* is an all-white ship that has a classic steamship profile, with a large, single funnel placed amidships. There is a decent amount of open deck and sunning space although the swimming pool is tiny (a "dip" pool). The ship was bought by Louis Cruise Lines in 1997, and underwent extensive refurbishing and upgrading in 1998. Under its previous owners it had

BERLITZ'S RATINGS		
	Possible	Achieved
Ship	500	146
Accommodation	200	93
Food	400	260
Service	400	241
Entertainment	100	48
Cruise	400	208

not been well maintained, and still needs a lot of attention to detail. It has also undergone much mechanical and galley upgrading.

Most of the public rooms are located on one deck (Corfu Deck), so it's easy to find one's way around. Most of the public areas have had upgraded décor and color changes, and are now lighter and more cheerful, with new soft furnishings.

The number of public lounges and rooms is, however, limited. The Majorca Lounge (main showlounge) is pleasantly decorated, although the sight lines to the stage area are quite poor, due to the fact that a large number of pillars obstruct the view; the seats on the raised sections on the port and starboard sides are slightly better. There is also a small nightclub, casino, duty-free shop, an enclosed "winter garden" lounge/reading area on the starboard side, and a cinema.

This ship is presently under a charter arrangement to the UK's First Choice Holidays, and will provide a decent, no-frills first cruise experience for those who choose to cruise on a limited budget (as long as your expectations are not too grand), with all the basics in place. Hopefully, the ship and cruise will exceed your expectations. The onboard currency is the British pound.

WEAK POINTS: There are few public rooms. Many passengers are heavy smokers and it is difficult to avoid them. Has a narrow gangway (this can be steep in some ports). You can book the deck you want your cabin to be on, but cabins are assigned by First Choice Cruises.

Azur
★★ +

Removed 2006

Mid-Size Ship	.............14,717 tons	Passengers		Cabin Current:	...............220 volts
Lifestyle:	..................Standard	(lower beds/all berths):	.........720/850	Elevators:	3
Cruise Line:	............Festival Cruises	Passenger Space Ratio		Casino (gaming tables):	.............Yes
Former Names:	.....*The Azur, Azur, Eagle*	(lower beds/all berths):	........20.4/17.3	Slot Machines:	......................Yes
Builder:	...Dubigeon-Normandie (France)	Crew/Passenger Ratio		Swimming Pools (outdoors):	2
Original Cost:	......................n/a	(lower beds/all berths):	..........2.0/2.4	Swimming Pools (indoors):	0
Entered Service:	.... May 1971/Apr 1994	Navigation Officers:	.............Greek	Whirlpools:	0
Registry:	....................Panama	Cabins (total):	361	Fitness Center:	....................Yes
Length (ft/m):	...........465.8/142.00	Size Range (sq ft/m):	.......94.7–212.0/	Sauna/Steam Room:	............Yes/No
Beam (ft/m):	...............71.8/21.90		8.8–19.7	Massage:	.........................No
Draft (ft/m):	.................18.7/5.73	Cabins (outside view):	148	Self-Service Launderette:	...........No
Propulsion/Propellers:	...........diesel	Cabins (interior/no view):	213	Dedicated Cinema/Seats:	.......Yes/175
	(16,300kW)/2	Cabins (for one person):	2	Library:	.........................Yes
Passenger Decks:	7	Cabins (with private balcony):	0	Classification Society:	....Bureau Veritas
Total Crew:	350	Cabins (wheelchair accessible):	2		

OVERALL SCORE: 1,008 (OUT OF A POSSIBLE 2,000 POINTS)

ACCOMMODATION: Most of the cabins are of a decent size, but many also have upper berths, thus accommodating three or four persons. There are many interior (no view) cabins (there are more interiors than outsides). These are, naturally, the least expensive, but they have a limited amount of storage space (the under-bed storage space is good, however). Although the cabins are plain, they are furnished and decorated in soft earth tones accented by brightly colored soft furnishings. All have a private bathroom, nicely refurbished with tiled floor, shower, retractable clothes drying line, and good storage space for personal toiletries.

A number of deluxe cabins have a full bathtub/shower combination, hairdryer, illuminated closets, minibar/refrigerator, and plenty of closet, drawer and under-bed storage space.

There are two outside cabins for the physically challenged, but the ship really cannot be recommended for anyone in a wheelchair, as access to most of it is difficult at best, and, to some areas, access in a wheelchair is absolutely impossible.

The cabin insulation is poor throughout the ship. Housekeeping is provided by a friendly group of cabin staff who hail from Goa.

DINING: The dining room has a low ceiling. It is a non-smoking room, is reasonably charming and has large ocean-view windows on three sides, but the chairs are not really comfortable, and the tables are incredibly cramped. Two seatings are featured (the first seating is

BERLITZ'S RATINGS		
	Possible	Achieved
Ship	500	200
Accommodation	200	95
Food	400	217
Service	400	251
Entertainment	100	48
Cruise	400	197

extremely rushed). The food is reasonably good, and its presentation is attractive, as are the menus. There is a rather limited selection of breads, fruits and cheeses. Multilingual waiters provide the service. Meal hours can vary, depending on the itinerary (and shore excursions). The wine list is decent (the wines are young, however), and prices are modest.

Informal breakfast and lunch buffets are adequate but never seem to look very attractive, the result of a food concession that is used to the repetition and routine of doing things the same way all the time. There is, however, plenty of food, much like you'd get at a cheap banquet. Unfortunately, there are just not enough seats available for the number of persons that use the buffet each day, and the result is total congestion.

OTHER COMMENTS: This fairly smart, though somewhat stubby-looking ship (the first ship that this relatively new cruise line placed into service) has a very short bow and twin tall funnels and was constructed as a cruise-ferry. There is a modest amount of open deck space for sunbathing, and this becomes really tight when the ship is full (which is most of the time).

There are no cushioned pads for the plastic deck lounge chairs. The two swimming pools (located on different decks, one atop the ship, the other aft) are very small (more like "dip" pools).

Inside, the layout is a little awkward to get used to at first, with many stairways in the aft section of the ship that have short, steep steps (this is typical of its original cruise-ferry construction). There is a reasonable selection of public rooms and several bars, with light, upbeat decor and the use of many mirrored surfaces (if you wear glasses, reflections could prove a problem). The show lounge has extremely poor sight lines, and a low ceiling, although it is good for group meetings and lectures. A cinema (it is unusual for a ship of this size to have one) is used for movies and lectures. There is almost always lively action in the casino (which has its own bar), although the room is somewhat out of the main passenger flow. A two-deck-high indoor volleyball court is a bonus for sports fans, although it is located adjacent to the children's playroom.

The ship looks really neat and tidy in most areas, but in some others it looks unkempt and sloppy, the result of uneven refurbishments.

Festival Cruises has done a good job of creating a totally European product in a short space of time, and garnered a good name for honest, value-for-money cruising. Festival Cruises (known in the US as First European Cruises) provides destination-intensive cruises principally aimed at Europeans. The ship is a popular vessel for those seeking a friendly environment, and should appeal to the young, active set looking for a good first cruise experience to a host of destinations, at a very attractive price. Add the ingredients of friendly service, totally unpretentious but reasonably tasty food, and a mix of international passengers speaking many different languages. So what you get is decent enough value for the money, despite the fact that the ship is really tired and well worn in places. Choose this ship, therefore, not for the ship itself but for the itineraries and destinations.

The ship provides all announcements, daily programs, news, entertainment, and shore excursions in five languages. The onboard currency is the euro.

WEAK POINTS: It is difficult to find quiet spaces, as music is playing constantly in all public rooms and open spaces (for ambience? or annoyance?). Although there are three elevators, they are so small and cramped that they hold no more than three persons (or one large person). The cabins really are small and cramped (particularly those with third and fourth upper berths). Smokers are everywhere, and are difficult to avoid (in typical European fashion, ashtrays are simply moved – if used at all – to wherever smokers happen to be sitting).

The constant announcements in several languages are incredibly irritating. The constant push for onboard revenue is also irritating (you have to pay extra even for a visit to the ship's navigation bridge). The poolside towels are small and thin. The show lounge is really inadequate – no more than a poor cabaret room. The seats in the cinema seats are not staggered, and so sight lines can be awkward. The ship is tired, like Blackpool, and has perhaps passed its sell-by date.

Black Prince   MO
★★ +

Small Ship: ....11,209 tons	Passengers	Cabin Current: ....230 volts
Lifestyle: ....Standard	(lower beds/all berths): 442/472	Elevators: 2
Cruise Line: .....Fred Olsen Cruise Lines	Passenger Space Ratio	Casino (gaming tables): ....Yes
Former Names: ....none	(lower beds/all berths): 25.3/23.7	Slot Machines: ....No
Builder: ....Fender Werft (Germany)	Crew/Passenger Ratio	Swimming Pools (outdoors): 1
Original Cost: ....$20 million	(lower beds/all berths): 2.2/2.3	Swimming Pools (indoors): 1
Entered Service: 1966	Navigation Officers: ....European	Whirlpools: 2
Registry: ....Norway	Cabins (total): 234	Fitness Center: ....Yes
Length (ft/m): 470.4/143.40	Size Range (sq ft/m): 80.7–226.0/	Sauna/Steam Room: ....Yes/No
Beam (ft/m): 66.6/20.30	7.5–21.0	Massage: ....Yes
Draft (ft/m): 20.0/6.10	Cabins (outside view): 167	Self-Service Launderette: ....No
Propulsion/Propellers: ....diesel	Cabins (interior/no view): 67	Dedicated Cinema/Seats: ....No
(12,310kW)/2	Cabins (for one person): 29	Library: ....Yes
Passenger Decks: 7	Cabins (with private balcony): 0	Classification Society: ....Det Norske
Total Crew: 200	Cabins (wheelchair accessible): 2	Veritas

OVERALL SCORE: 1,093 (OUT OF A POSSIBLE 2,000 POINTS)

ACCOMMODATION: There is a wide range of cabin sizes and configurations (the brochure lists 14) to choose from (from dimensionally challenged to quite adequate), and a good percentage of cabins are particularly reserved for single passengers. Do note, however, that many cabins have poor air-conditioning, and hard beds, and some cabins have second-person beds that fold down at night and are used as seating by day. No matter what grade of accommodation you choose, duvets are provided, the bathroom towels are of 100 percent cotton and are quite large, and a hairdryer is also supplied. A package of Gilchrist & Soames personal toiletry items (bath gel, shampoo/conditioner, sewing kit, shower cap) is provided for all passengers.

The outside-view suites are reasonably decent (particularly comfortable are the Gran Canaria and Lanzarote suites, with their wood-paneled walls) and nicely appointed. Other cabins are small, but reasonably well equipped (except for the lowest grades, which are very small and rather utilitarian), and tastefully decorated, for a smaller ship. There is a charge for room service. The upper grade cabins also have a refrigerator.

DINING: The dining room actually has three sections, named Fleur de Lys, Royal Garter, and The Gallery (a narrow section that joins – or separates – them both). All sections are non-smoking, and have big picture windows. There are two seatings (sometimes, first- and second-seating diners exchange seatings, a pleasant arrangement).

Alternatively, the Balblom Restaurant, located atop

BERLITZ'S RATINGS		
	Possible	Achieved
Ship	500	271
Accommodation	200	109
Food	400	209
Service	400	236
Entertainment	100	51
Cruise	400	217

the ship, provides another choice for dining (reservations required).

Fred Olsen Cruise Lines features above average cuisine that is attractively presented, with a good range of fish, seafood, meat and chicken dishes, as well as vegetarian options. The food is generally of good quality, with a decent selection of main course items to suit most British tastes. Breakfast buffets tend to be quite repetitious, although they appear to satisfy most.

Communication with the Filipino waiters can prove a little frustrating at times (although it is better now than it has been in the past, and smiles can compensate). There is a reasonably decent range of wines, at moderate prices, but few of the wine stewards have much knowledge of wines.

OTHER COMMENTS: *Black Prince* is a traditional style of ship (the name is 14th-century, originally referring to the son of Edward III). Solidly built (in the first instance for winter cruising and summer North Sea crossings), the ship has been well maintained, but does have a rather ungainly profile, and does tend to pitch heavily in unkind seas.

There are few public rooms, the principal one being the Neptune Lounge, the ship's show lounge, which has two levels (although sight lines to the stage are quite restricted from many seats). Another lounge, the Aquitaine Lounge, sits in the front part of the ship, and tends to be the quiet room – good for reading an absorbing book. The ship's small casino located on the starboard side of this lounge.

The one facility that is extremely good is the indoor fitness/leisure center (added in 1996), complete with an indoor swimming pool (an unusual facility for such a small ship), and health spa area with its own juice bar.

The décor has a very homely, restrained, feel and ambience, with soft lighting and no glitz anywhere. Many of the soft furnishings are hand-tailored on board by the Filipino crew. The ship has good wooden stairways throughout, although the steps are a little steep. An ironing room is provided – another useful addition for the ship's mainly British passengers.

Although the names sound similar, *Black Prince* is not at all like the larger *Black Watch*, which has many more facilities and is altogether a better ship at sea. *Black Prince* does have a friendly feel and an unstuffy ambience, an almost totally Filipino staff, and is well suited to the informal, older, British passenger. However, note that the standards of cleanliness, food and service have been slipping lately. While there are many repeat passengers who would not dream of trying another ship, some newcomers will feel that this is an old, tired ship that should be heading for retirement – soon, particularly in light of the increased competition from other, newer, and better ships.

So, what are the good points about cruising aboard *Black Prince*? Well, the ship, which was originally constructed for long-distance cruising, has settled in well under the Fred Olsen Cruise Lines brand, and should provide you with a good, well-rounded cruise experience, with well organized cruises, interesting itineraries, complimentary shuttle buses in many ports of call, a reasonably comfortable (but quite basic) ship, a decent standard of food, and with service from a generally friendly, mostly Filipino staff.

Black Prince is geared specifically towards older British passengers who appear intent on seeking out the world's duty-free shops, with British entertainment, acts and production shows. It all translates to good value for money cruises for a fair price. Port taxes are included for UK passengers sailing from Dover or Southampton. For the ship's mainly British passengers, the National Express coach network works in conjunction with Fred Olsen Cruise Lines to provide a dedicated Cruiselink service via London's Victoria Coach Station to the UK departure ports of Dover or Southampton.

The Filipino crew is generally friendly by nature, although the feeling that many passengers have is that the ship now operates more for the crew than for its passengers. Standards of product delivery and professionalism have fallen over the past few years (a stronger onboard middle management with properly recognized training is needed), and hence the score for this ship now reflects this lower quality. The onboard currency is the British pound.

Weak Points: It is often difficult to get away from smokers, and the service has become overly casual and sloppy of late. The company lists recommended gratuities of £4 ($6) per passenger per day, which, to some, seems a lot. The air-conditioning is inconsistent; in particular in many cabins it is not good (the ship was built when forced air circulation was the norm).

Black Watch
★★★★

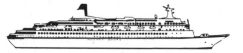

Mid-Size Ship: . . . . .28,492 tons	Total Crew: 310
Lifestyle: . . . . .Standard	Passengers
Cruise Line: . . . . .Fred Olsen Cruise Lines	(lower beds/all berths): 761/843
Former Names: . . . .*Star Odyssey,*	Passenger Space Ratio
Westward, Royal Viking Star	(lower beds/all berths): 37.4/33.7
Builder: . . . . .Wartsila (Finland)	Crew/Passenger Ratio
Original Cost: . . . .$22.5 million	(lower beds/all berths): 2.4/2.7
Entered Service: . . .June 1972/Nov 1996	Navigation Officers: . . . . .European
Registry: . . . . .The Bahamas	Cabins (total): 400
Length (ft/m): 674.1/205.47	Size Range (sq ft/m): 135.6–819.1/
Beam (ft/m): 82.6/25.20	12.6–76.1
Draft (ft/m): 24.7/7.55	Cabins (outside view): 352
Propulsion/Propellers: . . . . .diesel	Cabins (interior/no view): 48
(13,400kW)/2	Cabins (for one person): 38
Passenger Decks: 8	Cabins (with private balcony): 9

Cabins (wheelchair accessible): 4
Cabin Current: . . . . .110 and 220 volts
Elevators: 4
Casino (gaming tables): . . . . .Yes
Slot Machines: . . . . .Yes
Swimming Pools (outdoors): 2
Swimming Pools (indoors): 0
Whirlpools: 3
Fitness Center: . . . . .Yes
Sauna/Steam Room: . . . . .Yes/Yes
Massage: . . . . .Yes
Self-Service Launderette: . . . . .Yes
Dedicated Cinema/Seats: Yes/156
Library: . . . . .Yes
Classification Society: Det Norske Veritas

OVERALL SCORE: 1,429 (OUT OF A POSSIBLE 2,000 POINTS)

ACCOMMODATION: There are 18 price categories of accommodation (plus one for the owner's suite, whose price is not listed in the brochure), including four grades of cabins for those traveling solo (these are spread across most of the accommodation decks, and not just the lower decks, as some lines do). The wide range of accommodation provides something for everyone, from spacious suites with separate bedrooms, to small (interior – no view) cabins. While most cabins are for two persons, some can accommodate a third, fourth, or even a fifth person.

In all grades of accommodation, duvets are provided, the bathroom towels are of 100 percent cotton and are quite large, and a hairdryer is provided. A package of Gilchrist & Soames personal toiletry items (bath gel, shampoo/conditioner, sewing kit, shower cap) is supplied to all passengers. Occupants of suite grade accommodation also get a cotton bathrobe and cold canapés each evening (as well as priority seating in the dining rooms). The room service menu is quite limited and could be improved (although there is an abundance of food available at most times of the day). The suites and cabins on Decks 7, 8, and 9 are quiet units, a number of cabins located in the aft section of Decks 3, 4 and 5 can prove to be uncomfortable, with noise from throbbing engines and generator units a major source (particularly from cabins adjacent to the engine casing).

OUTSIDE-VIEW/INSIDE (NO VIEW) CABINS: Spread across Decks 3, 4, 5, 7 and 8, all cabins (approximately 135–200 sq. ft/12.6–18.5 sq. meters) are quite well equipped, and

BERLITZ'S RATINGS

	Possible	Achieved
Ship	500	371
Accommodation	200	158
Food	400	268
Service	400	281
Entertainment	100	73
Cruise	400	278

there is plenty of good (illuminated) closet, drawer and storage space (the drawers are metal and tinny, however, and in some closets they consist of wire baskets – like you might find in inexpensive hotels in Europe). No-smoking cabins are available. Some cabin bathrooms have awkward access, and insulation between some of the lower grade cabins could be better. The bathrooms are of a decent size. All have had a facelift, with new toiletries cabinets, washbasin facings, and re-tiled floors. Some cabins have a small bathtub, although many have only a shower enclosure.

DELUXE/BRIDGE/JUNIOR SUITES: These suites 240–260 sq. ft/22.2–24.1 sq. meters), on Decks 7 and 8, have a large sleeping area and lounge area with larger ocean view picture windows and refrigerator, more hooks for hanging bathrobes, outerwear and luggage; and a bathroom with bathtub and shower (cabin 8019 is the exception, with a shower instead of a bathtub).

MARQUEE SUITES: These suites (approximately 440 sq. ft/40.8 sq. meters) have a large sleeping area and lounge area with larger ocean view picture windows and refrigerator, more hooks for hanging bathrobes, outerwear and luggage; and a bathroom with bathtub and shower.

PREMIER SUITES: Anyone wanting the largest accommodation on board (apart from one owner's suite), should consider one of nine suites, each of which is named after a place: Amalfi (9006), Lindos (9002), Nice (9004), each measuring 547.7 sq. ft/50.8 sq. meters;

Seville (9001), Singapore (9003), Carmel (9005), Bergen (9007), Waterford (9009), each measuring 341.7 sq ft/31.7 m2; and Windsor (9008), measuring 574.8 sq. ft/53.4 sq. meters. These suites feature a separate bedroom with ample closet and other storage space, lounge with large windows (with large television and VCR, refrigerator and mini-bar), and bathroom with full-size bathtub and shower, and separate toilet.

OWNER'S SUITE: This measures 819.1 sq. ft/76.1 sq. meters (including the balcony), or 625.4 sq. ft/58.1 sq. meters (excluding the balcony). It consists of a foyer leading into a lounge, with sofa, table and chairs, and audio center (television, CD player, video player), refrigerator and mini-bar. A separate bedroom has a double bed, and ample closet and drawer space. A second bedroom has two bunk beds (good for families with children). The bathroom is large and has a full-size bathtub, separate shower enclosure, toilet, and two washbasins. There is a large (almost) private balcony with space enough for a table and six chairs, plus more space for a couple of deck lounge chairs. It is located just aft of the navigation bridge on the starboard side of the ship.

DINING: The Glentanar Dining Room has a high ceiling, a white sail-like focal point at its center, and ample space at each table. It is a totally non-smoking dining room, and the chairs are comfortable and have armrests. There is also a smaller offshoot of the dining room called the Orchid Room, which can be reserved for a more intimate (and quieter) dining experience (suite occupants get first choice for seats in this room). While breakfast is typically in an open seating arrangement, there are two seatings for lunch and dinner. Two cold food display counters are provided for passengers to help themselves to breakfast and lunch items.

The Garden Café (also a non-smoking room) is a small, more casual dining spot with a light, breezy décor that will remind you of a garden conservatory. It sometimes features special themed dinners, such as French, Indian, or Thai. There is a self-help salad bar and hot food display so you can eat with the minimum of fuss from waiters, although they are available for service when you need them. The room is also the location for late-night snacks.

Fred Olsen Cruise Lines features above-average cuisine that is attractively presented, with a good range of fish, seafood, meat and chicken dishes, as well as vegetarian options. The food is generally of good quality, with a decent selection of main course items to suit most British tastes. Breakfast buffets tend to be quite repetitious, although they appear to satisfy most.

Communication with the Filipino waiters can prove a little frustrating at times (although it is better now than it has been in the past, and smiles can compensate to some extent). There is a reasonably decent range of wines, at moderate prices, but few of the wine stewards have much knowledge of wines.

OTHER COMMENTS: Acquired by Fred Olsen Cruise Lines in late 1996, this handsome ship, originally built for long-distance cruising for the now-defunct Royal Viking Line (actually built for one of the three original shipping partners in the line – Bergenske Dampskibsselskab), has a sharply raked bow and a sleek appearance that was "stretched" in 1981 with the addition of a mid section. The ship's name is taken from the famous Scottish Black Watch regiment, although the ship itself is an all-white color.

There is an excellent amount of open deck and sunbathing space, and a good health-fitness area high atop the ship, as well as a wide wrap-around teakwood promenade deck (with wind-breaker on the aft part of the deck). Sports facilities include a large paddle tennis court, golf practice nets, shuffleboard and ring toss.

The interior décor is quiet and restful, with wide stairways and foyers, soft lighting and no glitz anywhere aboard this ship although many passengers find the artwork a little drab (it is, in reality, rather more Scandinavian eclectic than anything). In general, good materials, fabrics (including the use of the Black Watch tartan) and soft furnishings add to a pleasant ambience and comfortable feeling experienced throughout the public rooms, most of which are quite spacious and have high, indented ceilings.

There is a wide selection of public rooms, most of which (including the main dining room) are located on one deck in a horizontal layout that makes access easy. An observation lounge (called The Observatory) high atop the ship, is decorated in nautical memorabilia, has commanding views and is a popular spot – particularly when the ship leaves ports of call in the evenings (Boddington's and Stella Artois beers are available on draught here, and in all bars throughout the ship). There is a good cinema (few ships today have a dedicated cinema) with a steeply tiered floor, and a pleasant library (with an adjacent computer/internet access room containing two computer terminals), and a card room.

One of the most popular rooms is the Braemar Room, a large lounge close to the restaurant. It has a self-help beverage corner for coffees and teas (open 24 hours a day), comfortable chairs, and large ocean-view windows along one side. Afternoon tea is served here. On one wall is an old iron figurehead from a ship called *Braemar Castle* (it's one of several iron figureheads found aboard this ship, from a collection owned by the Olsen family).

Smokers will appreciate a special cigar and pipe smoking room (The Cove), as well as a bar (Pipers Bar) for general smoking (these are the only two locations inside the ship where smoking is permitted).

The casino consists of two blackjack tables and a roulette table, located in a passageway opposite the Starlite Nightclub; a separate room houses a clutch of rarely used slot machines. A self-serve launderette (very useful on the longer cruises operated by this ship) has four washing machines, five dryers, and a couple of irons in a large user-friendly room.

So, what are the good points about cruising aboard *Black Watch*? Well, the ship, which was originally constructed for long-distance cruising, has settled in well under the Fred Olsen Cruise Lines brand, and should provide you with a good, well-rounded cruise experience. The cruises are well organized, with interesting itineraries, complimentary shuttle buses in many ports of call. *Black Watch* is a very comfortable (not luxurious) ship, with a good standard of food and service. The ship is geared specifically towards the older British passenger who appears intent on seeking out the world's duty-free shops, with British entertainment, acts and production shows, and a friendly, mostly Filipino staff and decent (though not faultless) service.

All in all, Fred Olsen Cruise Lines has come a long way from humble beginnings, and now offers extremely good value for money cruises in a relaxed environment that provides passengers with many of the comforts of home. Port taxes are included for UK passengers sailing from Dover or Southampton.

For the ship's mainly British passengers, the National Express coach network works in conjunction with Fred Olsen Cruise Lines to provide a dedicated Cruiselink service via London's Victoria Coach Station to the UK departure ports of Dover or Southampton. The onboard currency is the British pound.

WEAK POINTS: Although being kept in good condition, do remember that this ship is more than 30 years old, which means that little problems such as gurgling plumbing, creaking joints, and other idiosyncrasies can occur occasionally, and air conditioning may not be all that it should be (this is particularly true in some cabins). The company lists recommended gratuities of £4 ($6) per passenger per day, which, to some, seems a lot. Only a few suites have private balconies.

WIND SPEEDS

A navigational announcement to passengers is normally made once or twice a day, giving the ship's position, temperature, and weather information.

Various winds affect the world's weather patterns. Such well-known winds as the Bora, Mistral, Northwind, and Sirocco, among others, play an important part in the makeup of weather at and above sea level. Wind velocity is measured on the Beaufort scale, a method that was devised in 1805 by Commodore Francis Beaufort, later Admiral and Knight Commander of the Bath, for measuring the force of wind at sea. Originally, it measured the effect of the wind on a fully rigged man-of-war (which was usually laden with cannons and heavy ammunition). It became the official way of recording wind velocity in 1874, when the International Meteorological Committee adopted it.

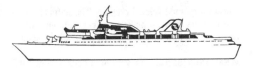

Removed 2006

Mid-Size Ship: . . . . .15,781 tons	Passengers	Cabin Current: . . . . .110 and 220 volts
Lifestyle: . . . . .Standard	(lower beds/all berths): 802/984	Elevators: 4
Cruise Line: . . . . . . .Spanish Cruise Line	Passenger Space Ratio	Casino (gaming tables): . . . . .Yes
Former Names: . . . .*Starward*	(lower beds/all berths): 19.6/16.0	Slot Machines: . . . . .Yes
Builder: . . . . .A.G. Weser (Germany)	Crew/Passenger Ratio	Swimming Pools (outdoors): 2
Original Cost: .n/a	(lower beds/all berths): 2.4/2.9	Swimming Pools (indoors): 0
Entered Service: . . . .Dec 1968/May 2001	Navigation Officers: . . . . .Greek	Whirlpools: 0
Registry: . . . . .Panama	Cabins (total): 401	Fitness Center: . . . . .Yes
Length (ft/m): 525.9/160.30	Size Range (sq ft/m): 111.9–324.0/	Sauna/Steam Room: . . . . .Yes/No
Beam (ft/m): 74.9/22.84	10.4–30.1	Massage: . . . . .Yes
Draft (ft/m): 22.5/6.86	Cabins (outside view): 237	Self-Service Launderette: . . . . .No
Propulsion/Propellers: . . . . .diesel	Cabins (interior/no view): 164	Dedicated Cinema/Seats: Yes/210
(12,950kW)/2	Cabins (for one person): 0	Library: . . . . .Yes
Passenger Decks: 7	Cabins (with private balcony): 0	Classification Society: . . . . . . .Det Norske
Total Crew: .330	Cabins (wheelchair accessible): 2	Veritas

---

OVERALL SCORE: 1,034 (OUT OF A POSSIBLE 2,000 POINTS)

ACCOMMODATION: Except for five decent sized suites, the cabins are very compact units that are moderately comfortable, and are decorated in soft colors, accented by colorful soft furnishings. They are, however, adequate for a one-week cruise, particularly as this company specializes in destination-intensive cruises. While the closet space is limited, there are plenty of drawers, although they are metal and tinny. The bathrooms are small and tight, and the towels are not large, although they are made of 100 percent cotton; the toilets are of the "gentle flush" and not the "barking dog suction" variety as found aboard newer ships. The insulation between cabins could be better (each cabin has a notice asking passengers to keep the audio system to a minimum to avoid "cabin rage" complaints from neighbors).

The five suites (all, strangely, with Jamaican names) are of a good size, with a "privacy" curtain between the hallway/closet and the sleeping/lounging area. There is plenty of space to walk in these suites, which feature separate vanity desk, curtained-off closet, plenty of drawer and storage space for luggage, a lounge with a sofa that converts into an additional bed, drinks table and two chairs. The bathroom has a small but deep bathtub with shower.

DINING: This ship has a dining room (non-smoking) that is cheerful and charming, with some prime tables overlooking the stern (most are for four, six or eight). There are two seatings (Spanish dining hours are much later than those of most other nationalities). The reasonable

BERLITZ'S RATINGS

	Possible	Achieved
Ship	500	231
Accommodation	200	101
Food	400	215
Service	400	237
Entertainment	100	50
Cruise	400	200

food selection is totally geared to Spanish tastes. The service is cheerful, friendly, and comes with a smile (remember, this *is* an inexpensive, informal cruise experience, so you should not expect haute cuisine). The wine list is acceptable, but the wines, for the most part, are very young.

In addition, breakfast and lunch buffets are provided indoors at Signals Café, with seating provided outdoors at tables set around the aft swimming pool (but space is tight and there simply isn't enough of it). There is a good selection of bread and bread rolls, cold cuts of meat, fresh fruits and cheeses at the buffets, which are presented reasonably well, given the space limitations.

OTHER COMMENTS: This ship has a fairly contemporary upper profile with dual swept-back funnels, and is an ideal size for cruising in the Mediterranean region. *Bolero* was formerly a Caribbean-based ship owned and operated for many years by Norwegian Cruise Line. Festival Cruises acquired the ship in 1995. In May 2001 *Bolero* commenced operations for Spanish Cruise Line (Festival Cruises is a one-third owner of the new cruise line, together with Spanish tour operator Iberojet, and Spanish ferry operator Transmed, parent company of Spanish Cruise Line).

The open deck and sunbathing space is very limited (some of the decks are of plain steel, painted blue), and cluttered with plenty of white, plastic deck lounge chairs and blue/yellow sun umbrellas for shade at the aft outdoor decks. Just forward of the twin blue funnels is an enclosed basketball/volleyball court), while aft of the mast is a large solarium-style shielded housing, with multi-level lounge/bar/disco that is adjacent to one of the ship's two swimming pools.

Inside the ship, there is a good choice of public rooms for this size of vessel, and they feature clean, contemporary furnishings and upbeat, cheerful fabric colors and décor. There is a good, steeply tiered dedicated cinema, with good sight lines.

Bolero is a comfortable vessel, ideal for Mediterranean cruises, with a warm, friendly, and lively ambience. A reasonably attractive ship, it should prove a good choice for first-time passengers seeking a destination-intensive cruise at very attractive prices.

Spanish Cruise Line provides a totally Spanish shipboard life and cruise experience in rather crowded, though moderately comfortable (certainly not elegant or glitzy) surroundings, at a very modest price that translates to very good value for money. The staff is friendly and they try hard to make you feel welcome, like a member of a family. The onboard currency is the euro.

WEAK POINTS: This is a very high-density vessel that really does feel crowded when full (some might call it "ambience"). Has a less than handsome "duck-tailed" sponson stern (this acts rather like a stabilizer). Smokers are everywhere, and are difficult to avoid (in typical European fashion, ashtrays are simply moved – if used at all – to wherever smokers happen to be sitting). There are no cushioned pads for the deck lounge chairs. The diesel engines are noisy and tend to "throb" in some parts of the vessel (particularly when the ship is going full speed), including in many cabins on the lower decks. Cabins do not have TV sets. There are simply too many loud, repetitive announcements (all in Spanish).

MO ——

Braemar
★★★ +

Mid-Size Ship: . . . . .19,089 tons	Total Crew: .320	Cabin Current: . . . . . . .110 and 220 volts
Lifestyle: . . . . .Standard	Passengers	Elevators: 5
Cruise Line: . . . . .Fred Olsen Cruise Lines	(lower beds/all berths): 729/821	Casino (gaming tables): . . . . .Yes
Former Names: . . . .*Crown Dynasty,*	Passenger Space Ratio	Slot Machines: . . . . .Yes
Norwegian Dynasty, Crown Majesty,	(lower beds/all berths): 26.1/23.8	Swimming Pools (outdoors): 1
Cunard Dynasty, Crown Dynasty	Crew/Passenger Ratio	Swimming Pools (indoors): 0
Builder: . .Union Navale de Levante (Spain)	(lower beds/all berths): 1.8/2.0	Whirlpools: 2
Original Cost: . . . .$100 million	Navigation Officers: . . . . . .Scandinavian	Fitness Center: . . . . .Yes
Entered Service: . . . .July 1993/Aug 2001	Cabins (total): 377	Sauna/Steam Room: . . . . .Yes/Yes
Registry: . . . . .Panama	Size Range (sq ft/m): 139.9–349.8/	Massage: . . . . .Yes
Length (ft/m): 537.4/163.81	13.0–32.5	Self-Service Launderette: . . . . .No
Beam (ft/m): 73.8/22.50	Cabins (outside view): 251	Dedicated Cinema/Seats: . . . . .No
Draft (ft/m): 17.7/5.40	Cabins (interior/no view): 126	Library: . . . . .No
Propulsion/Propellers: . . . . .diesel	Cabins (for one person): 21	Classification Society: . . . . . . .Det Norske
(13,200kW)/2	Cabins (with private balcony): 16	Veritas
Passenger Decks: 7	Cabins (wheelchair accessible): 4	

OVERALL SCORE: 1,325 (OUT OF A POSSIBLE 2,000 POINTS)

ACCOMMODATION: There are 16 accommodation price categories, and, no matter whether you choose a suite or standard outside-view or interior (no view) cabin, the higher the deck, the higher the price (in real estate terminology, this translates to location, location, location). No matter what grade of accommodation you choose, a small television, and hairdryer are provided (some are awkward to retract from their wall-mount holders), as are European duvets. The bathroom towels are of 100 percent cotton and are quite large (bathrobes are available upon request in suite-grade accommodation). A package of Gilchrist & Soames personal toiletry items (soap, bath gel, sewing kit, shampoo/conditioner, shower cap) is provided for all passengers. Note that there is no separate audio system in the cabins, so the only music you can obtain is from one of the television channels, but you'll have to leave the picture on (suites, however, do have a CD music system).

STANDARD (OUTSIDE-VIEW)/INSIDE (NO VIEW) CABIN GRADES: The standard outside-view and interior (no view) cabins, almost all of which are the same size, are really quite small, although they are nicely furnished, and trimmed with blond wood cabinetry. Most of them have broad picture windows (some deluxe cabins on Deck 6 and Deck 7 have lifeboat-obstructed views). They are practical and comfortable, with wood-trimmed accents and multi-colored soft furnishings, but there very little drawer space, and the closet (hanging) space

BERLITZ'S RATINGS

	Possible	Achieved
Ship	500	364
Accommodation	200	135
Food	400	237
Service	400	255
Entertainment	100	61
Cruise	400	273

is extremely limited (the ship having been purpose-built originally only for 7-day cruises). So, as there is little room for luggage, take only the clothing that you think necessary. Each of the outside-view cabins on Deck 4 has a large picture window, while those on the lower Decks 2 and 3 have a porthole. They are quite well equipped, with a small vanity desk unit, a minimal amount of drawer space, curtained windows, and personal safe (hard to reach as it is positioned close to the floor in many cabins – so you'll need to kneel down for access).

Each cabin has a private bathroom (of the "me first, you next" variety) with a tiled floor, small shower enclosure (with curtain you'll probably need to dance with, particularly if you are of above-average size), toiletries cupboard, washbasin, and low-height toilet (of the barking dog vacuum variety), and some under-sink storage space (there's also an electrical socket for shavers).

When the ship was bought by Fred Olsen Cruise Lines a number of cabins were changed from double-occupancy units to cabins for the single traveler, as aboard other ships operated by the company – a nice touch for the many singles not wishing to share.

Some cabins do unfortunately suffer from inadequate soundproofing; passengers in cabins on Deck 4 in particular are disturbed by anyone running or jogging on the promenade deck above. A copy machine is almost constantly in use opposite Cabin 4110, and you will be subject to noise from the constant opening and closing of the door opposite this cabin. Cabins on the lowest deck

(Deck 2) in the center of the ship (between cabins 2061-2079) are subject to some noise from the adjacent engine and generator room.

SUITES: On Deck 7, accommodation that is designated as suites all feature a name as well as a number, as follows: 7001 (Owner's Suite); 7002 (Buenos Aires); 7003 (Cartagena); 7004 (Lima); 7005 (Cartagena); 7006 (New York); 7007 (Washington, D.C.); 7008 (Honolulu); 7009 (La Habana); 7010 (Hamilton); 7011 (Rio de Janeiro); 7012 (Balboa); 7014 (Willemstad); 7016 (Toronto); 7018 (Santiago); 7031 (San Francisco); 7032 (Mexico City); 7033 (Montevideo); 7034 (Bridgetown).

While they are not large, the suites do feature a sleeping area that can be curtained off from the living area. All of the suites are decorated in individual styles befitting their name, and each has its own small CD player/music system.

DINING: The Thistle Restaurant is a pleasing and attractive totally non-smoking restaurant, with large oceanview windows on three sides; its focal point is a large oil painting on a wall behind buffet food display counter. However, it is rather tight on space, and the tables are extremely close together, making proper service quite difficult for the waiters. There are tables for two, four, six or eight; the Porsgrund china features the familiar Venus pattern. The ambience, however, is quite warm, and service is friendly and quite attentive. There are two seatings for dinner, and open seating for breakfast and lunch. A varied menu is provided. The salad items are quite poor and very basic, with little variety, although there is a decent choice of dessert items. For breakfast and lunch there are two food display counters so that you can help yourself, but at peak times these create much congestion (the layout is less than ideal).

Casual breakfasts and luncheons can be taken in the self-service buffet that is located in the Palms Café, although these tend to be repetitive. Both indoor and outdoor seating is available. Although it is the casual dining spot, tablecloths are provided.

As this book was being completed, a barbeque grill was being planned for the pool deck; this will be a welcome addition, particularly when the ship operates in the Caribbean.

OTHER COMMENTS: This ship was purchased by Fred Olsen Cruise Lines in spring 2001 and renamed *Braemar* following the demise of Crown Cruise Line, the ship's previous operator. Following an extensive refurbishment, *Braemar* started operating cruises targeted mostly at British and Scandinavian passengers.

This is quite a handsome-looking mid-sized ship for informal cruising, with attractive exterior styling, and a lot of glass space that provides contact with the outside. It will provide a refreshing change for those who do not want to cruise aboard the larger (some say warehouse-size) ships. Surprisingly, however, the ship does roll somewhat, quite probably due to its shallow draft design (meant for warm weather cruise areas).

There is quite a good amount of open deck and sunbathing space for a ship of this size, and this incorporates two outdoors bars (one aft and one midships adjacent to the swimming pool) that feature Boddington's and Stella Artois beers on draught. Four open decks, located aft of the funnel, provide good, quiet, places to sit and read, and teak chairs add a touch of elegance to these decks.

The promenade deck is laid with teakwood decking, and the promenade deck is a complete wrap-around deck. Passengers can also go right to the bow of the ship (this provides a photo opportunity for camera users inspired by the vision of Kate Winslet and Leonardo di Caprio spreading their arms on the bow of *Titanic*). Blue plastic mat-style floor covering is used on the deck where the swimming pool is located; it may look a bit tacky, but it works well in the heat of the Caribbean, where the ship was meant to spend most of its time.

Inside, there is a pleasant five-deck-high, glass-walled atrium, offset to the starboard side. Off-center stairways appear to add a sense of spaciousness to a clever interior design that surrounds passengers with light. The interior decor in public spaces is warm and inviting, with contemporary, but not brash, art-deco color combinations. The artwork is quite colorful and pleasant, in the Nordic manner.

The Neptune Showlounge sits longitudinally along one side of the ship, with amphitheater-style seating in several tiers, but its layout is less than ideal. There are both smoking and non-smoking sections (the majority being non-smoking).

In what was formerly a casino, the Braemar Room is now an open-plan style of lounge, with its own bar, split by a walkway that leads to the showlounge (forward) and the shops (midships). Despite being open, it has cozy seating areas and is very comfortable, with a tartan carpet; one section is for smokers, the other, for non-smokers. A model of the first Fred Olsen ship named *Braemar* (4,775 tons) is displayed in the center of the room, as is a large carved wood plaque bearing the name Braemar Castle in Scotland. There is a baby grand piano (typically played during cocktail hours), otherwise this lounge is good for reading as there is no piped music to disturb the gentle, homely feeling.

The (mostly) Filipino staff is friendly and attentive, and the hospitality factor is reasonably good, although the standard of service itself and attention to detail is quite poor when compared with ships that have European staff. This is particularly noticeable in the restaurant and other food service areas. Training to a better standard of food service and product delivery is needed, and this, I am pleased to say, is slowly being achieved. All in all, Fred Olsen Cruise Lines has come a long way from its humble beginnings, and now offers extremely good value for money cruises in a relaxed environment that provides passengers with many of the comforts of home. The onboard currency is the British pound.

WEAK POINTS: The ship has had a number of lives under different operators, and, although Fred Olsen Cruise Lines has spent huge sums of money in interior refinishing, there remain many areas in passenger hallways where you'll find scuffed paneling and other wall coverings.

Do expect some crowding for the self-serve buffets, tenders, and the few elevators aboard this ship. British passengers should note that no suites or cabins have bathtubs. There is often congestion between first- and second-seating passengers at the entrance to the show lounge. The show lounge itself has congestion problems, is poorly designed for passenger movement, several pillars (15) obstruct the sight lines to the stage, and the seating arrangement is poor.

Non-smokers should be aware that the typical passenger mix may include many passengers who smoke, and it may be difficult to avoid them, given the space constraints of the ship. The health spa facilities are quite limited. There is no self-service launderette (although there is one ironing room). The company charges for shuttle buses in many ports of call.

RULES OF THE ROAD

Ships, the largest moving objects made by man, are subject to stringent international regulations. They must keep to the right in shipping lanes, and pass on the right (with certain exceptions). When circumstances raise some doubt, or shipping lanes are crowded, ships use their whistles in the same way an automobile driver uses directional signals to show which way he will turn. When one ship passes another and gives a single blast on its whistle, this means it is turning to starboard (right). Two blasts mean a turn to port (left).

The other ship acknowledges by repeating the same signal. Ships switch on navigational running lights at night — green for starboard, red for port, plus two white lights on the masts, the forward one lower than the aft one.

Flags and pennants form another part of a ship's communication facilities and are displayed for identification purposes. Each time a country is visited, its national flag is shown. While entering and leaving a port, the ship flies a blue-and-white vertically striped flag to request a pilot, while a half red, half white flag (divided vertically) indicates that a pilot is on board. Cruise lines also display their own "house" flag from the mast.

A ship's funnel (smokestack) is one other means of identification, each line having its own design and color scheme. The size, height, and number of funnels were points worth advertising at the turn of the century.

Most ocean liners of the time had four funnels and were called "four-stackers."

There are numerous customs at sea, many of them older than any maritime law. Superstition has always been an important element, as in the following example quoted from the British Admiralty Manual of Seamanship: "The custom of breaking a bottle of wine over the stem of a ship when it is being launched originates from the old practice of toasting prosperity to a ship with a silver goblet of wine, which was then cast into the sea in order to prevent a toast of ill intent being drunk from the same cup. This was a practice that proved too expensive, and it was replaced in 1690 by the breaking of a bottle of wine over the stem."

Bremen
★★★★

Small Ship:	.6,752 tons
Lifestyle:	Premium
Cruise Line:	Hapag-Lloyd Cruises
Former Names:	*Frontier Spirit*
Builder:	Mitsubishi Heavy Industries (Japan)
Original Cost:	$42 million
Entered Service:	Nov 1990/Nov 1993
Registry:	The Bahamas
Length (ft/m):	365.8/111.51
Beam (ft/m):	55.7/17.00
Draft (ft/m):	15.7/4.80
Propulsion/Propellers:	diesel (4,855kW)/2
Passenger Decks:	6
Total Crew:	94
Passengers	
(lower beds/all berths):	164/184
Passenger Space Ratio	
(lower beds/all berths):	41.1/36.6
Crew/Passenger Ratio	
(lower beds/all berths):	1.7/1.9
Navigation Officers:	European
Cabins (total):	82
Size Range (sq ft/m):	174.3–322.9/ 16.2–30.0
Cabins (outside view):	82
Cabins (interior/no view):	0
Cabins (for one person):	0
Cabins (with private balcony):	18
Cabins (wheelchair accessible):	2
Cabin Current:	110 and 220 volts
Elevators:	2
Casino (gaming tables):	No
Slot Machines:	No
Swimming Pools (outdoors):	1
Swimming Pools (indoors):	0
Whirlpools:	0
Fitness Center:	Yes
Sauna/Steam Room:	Yes/No
Massage:	No
Self-Service Launderette:	No
Lecture/Film Room:	Yes (seats 164)
Library:	Yes (open 24 hours)
Zodiacs:	12
Helicopter Pad:	Yes
Classification Society: Germanischer Lloyd	

OVERALL SCORE: 1,461 (OUT OF A POSSIBLE 2,000 POINTS)

ACCOMMODATION: This comes in only four different configurations. All cabins have an outside view (the cabins on the lowest deck have portholes; all others have good-sized picture windows).

All of the cabins are well equipped for the size of the vessel. Each cabin features wood accenting, a color television (small), telephone, refrigerator (soft drinks are provided and replenished daily, at no charge), vanity desk (with 110v American-style and 220v European-style electrical sockets) and sitting area with small drinks table. Cabins have either twin beds (convertible to a queen-sized bed, but with individual European duvets) or double bed, according to location. There is also a small indented area for outerwear and rubber boots, while a small drawer above the refrigerator unit provides warmth when needed for such things as wet socks and gloves.

Each cabin has a private bathroom (of the "me first, you next" variety) with a tiled floor, shower enclosure (with curtain), toiletries cupboard, washbasin (located quite low, as the ship was built in Japan) and low-height toilet (vacuum type, with delay), and a decent amount of under-sink storage space (there's also an electrical socket for shavers). Large towels and 100 percent cotton bathrobes are provided for all passengers, as is a range of personal toiletry items (shampoo, body lotion, shower gel, soap, and shower cap).

Each cabin has a moderate amount of (illuminated) closet space (large enough for two weeks for two persons, but very tight for more than that cruise length)

BERLITZ'S RATINGS		
	Possible	Achieved
Ship	500	349
Accommodation	200	150
Food	400	298
Service	400	311
Entertainment	N/A	N/A
Cruise	500	353

although the drawer space is limited (suitcases can be stored under the beds). The beds feature European cotton duvets. Some Sun Deck and Bridge Deck cabins also have a small balcony (the first expedition cruise vessel to have them) with blue plastic (easily cleanable) decking and wooden handrail, but no exterior light. The balconies, which have two teak chairs and drinks table, are, however, quite small and narrow, with part partitions and doors that open outwards onto the balcony.

Two Sun Deck suites have a separate lounge area with sofa and coffee table, bedroom (with large wall clock), large walk-in closet, and bathroom with a bathtub and two washbasins.

DINING: The dining room features open seating when operating for mixed German and International passenger cruises, and open seating for breakfast and lunch and one seating for dinner (with assigned seats) when operated only as German-speaking cruises. It is fairly attractive, with pleasing décor and colors; it also has big picture windows. The food is extremely good, and made with high-quality ingredients. Although the portions are small, the presentation is appealing to the eye. There is always an excellent choice of freshly made breads and pastries, and a good selection of cheeses and fruits. Dinner typically includes a choice of two appetizers, two soups, an entremets (in-between course), two entrees (main courses) and two or three desserts, plus a cheese board. There is always a vegetarian specialty, as well as a healthy (light) eating option. The service is also good, with smartly dressed bi-lingual (German- and English-speaking) waiters and waitresses.

As an alternative to the dining room, breakfast and luncheon buffets are available in "The Club," or outside on the Lido Deck (weather permitting), where "The Starboard Bar/Grill" is also operated for hamburgers and other grilled food items.

OTHER COMMENTS: This purpose-built expedition cruise vessel (formerly *Frontier Spirit*, for the now defunct US-based Frontier Cruises) has a handsome, wide, though squat, contemporary profile and decent equipment. Its wide beam provides decent stability and the vessel's long cruising range and ice-hardened hull provides the ship with access to remote destinations. The ship carries the highest ice classification for passenger vessels. In 1993 Hapag-Lloyd spent $2 million in refurbishment costs to reconfigure the restaurant and make other changes to the ship, and, in another refurbishment in 2000, the hull color was changed from blue to white. This is one of the few ships that will allow you to take a tour of the engine room. It is the sixth ship to bear the name *Bremen* for Hapag-Lloyd; the others being introduced in 1858 (*Bremen I*), 1897 (*Bremen II*), 1923 (*Bremen III*), 1929 (*Bremen IV*), and 1959 (*Bremen V*).

Zero-discharge of waste matter is fiercely practiced; this means that absolutely nothing is discharged into the ocean that does not meet with the international conventions on ocean pollution (MARPOL). All the equipment for in-depth marine and shore excursions is provided, including a boot-washing station with three water hoses and boot cleaning brushes.

An open bridge policy applies. There is almost a wrap-around walking deck (you must go up and down the steps at the front of the deck to complete the "wrap"). A large open deck aft of the mast provides a good viewing platform (also useful for sunbathing on warm-weather cruises). There is a small fitness room, and a decent sized sauna.

The ship has a good number of public rooms for its size, including a forward-facing observation lounge/lecture room (with portside bar), and a main lounge (called the Club) with a high ceiling, bandstand, dance floor and large bar, and an adjacent library with 12 bookcases (most books are in German).

Bremen features superb, well-planned destination-intensive itineraries, with good documentation, port information, and maps. The ship provides a good degree of comfort (although it is not as luxurious as the slightly larger sister ship *Hanseatic*). There is also a reception desk (open 24 hours a day), a fine array of expert lecturers, a friendly crew, and no annoying "elevator" music played in the hallways or on the open decks all add to the enjoyable cruise experience you should have aboard this ship.

Bremen is a very comfortable, practical, and unpretentious expedition cruise vessel (perhaps arguably a better expedition vessel than sister ship *Hanseatic*, and, although not as luxurious in its interiors and appointments, the ship has a very loyal following).

Cruises aboard this ship will provide you with a fine learning and expedition experience, and operates particularly well when featuring Antarctic cruises (all shore landings and tours are included, as is seasickness medication). The onboard ambience is completely casual, comfortable, unstuffy (no tux needed), friendly, and very accommodating. Passengers also appreciate the fact that there are no mindless parlour games, no television (on expedition cruises, although there are videos daily) no bingo, no horseracing, no casino, and no music in hallways or on open decks.

ARCTIC/ANTARCTIC CRUISES: When the ship goes to cold weather/ice areas such as the Arctic or Antarctic, red parkas (waterproof outdoor jackets) are supplied, as are waterproof rubber (Wellington) boots. You should, however, take some waterproof trousers and several pairs of thick socks, plus "thermal" underwear. Each of the fleet of 12 Zodiacs (rubber-inflatable landing craft) is named after a place: Amazon, Antarctic, Asmat, Bora Bora, Cape Horn, Deception, Jan Mayen, Luzon, Pitcairn, San Blas, Spitzbergen, and Ushuaia. On Arctic and Antarctic cruises, it is particularly pleasing to go to the bridge wings late at night to stargaze under pollution-free skies (the watch officers will be pleased to show you the night skies).

Note that special sailings may be under the auspices of various tour operators, although the ship is operated by Hapag-Lloyd Cruises. Thus, your fellow passengers (I prefer to refer to them as expedition cruise participants) may well be from many different countries. Insurance, port taxes and all staff gratuities are typically included in the cruise fare, and an expedition cruise logbook is also typically provided at the end of each expedition cruise for all participants – a superb reminder of what's been seen and done during the course of your adventure experience. The onboard currency is the euro.

WEAK POINTS: The ship does not have a "bulbous bow" and so is liable to deep pitching in some sea conditions (it does, however, have stabilizers). The dining room has 12 pillars placed in inconvenient positions (the result of old shipbuilding techniques). The swimming pool is very small, as is the open deck space around it, although there are both shaded and open areas. In-cabin announcements cannot be turned off (on cruises in the Arctic and Antarctic, announcements are often made at or before 7am on days when shore landings are permitted). Sadly, the ship was not built with good cabin insulation, the result being that you can hear your neighbors brushing their hair.

Bathrooms are subject to gurgling plumbing noises (between the washbasin and shower enclosure) due to their design and construction. There is only one boot washing station (two would be better, and more in keeping with the requirements of an expedition cruise vessel).

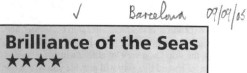

✓ Barcelona 09/09/05

Brilliance of the Seas
★★★★

Large Ship:	90,090 tons
Lifestyle:	Standard
Cruise Line: Royal Caribbean International
Former Names:	none
Builder:	Meyer Werft (Germany)
Original Cost:	$350 million
Entered Service:	July 2002
Registry:	The Bahamas
Length (ft/m):	961.9/293.2
Beam (ft/m):	105.6/32.2
Draft (ft/m):	27.8/8.5
Propulsion/Propellers:	Gas turbine/ 2 pods (19.5 MW each)
Passenger Decks:	13
Total Crew:	869
Passengers (lower beds/all berths):	2,188/2,500
Passenger Space Ratio (lower beds/all berths):	41.1/36.0
Crew/Passenger Ratio (lower beds/all berths):	2.5/2.8
Navigation Officers:	Norwegian
Cabins (total):	1,094
Size Range (sq ft/m):	165.8–1,216.3/ 15.4–113.0
Cabins (outside view):	813
Cabins (interior/no view):	237
Cabins (for one person):	0
Cabins (with private balcony):	577
Cabins (wheelchair accessible):	24
Cabin Current:	110 volts
Elevators:	9
Casino (gaming tables):	Yes
Slot Machines:	Yes
Swimming Pools (outdoors):	2
Swimming Pools (indoors):	0
Whirlpools:	3
Fitness Center:	Yes
Sauna/Steam Room:	Yes/Yes
Massage:	Yes
Self-Service Launderette:	No
Dedicated Cinema/Seats:	Yes/40
Library:	Yes
Classification Society:	Det Norske Veritas

OVERALL SCORE: 1,546 (OUT OF A POSSIBLE 2,000 POINTS)

ACCOMMODATION: There is a wide range of suites and standard outside-view and interior (no view) cabins to suit different tastes, requirements, and depth of wallet, in 10 different categories and 19 different price groups.

Apart from the largest suites (the 6 owner's suites), which feature king-sized beds, almost all other cabins have twin beds that convert to a queen-sized bed (all sheets are of 100 percent Egyptian cotton, although the blankets are of nylon). All cabins feature rich (but faux) wood cabinetry, including a vanity desk (with hairdryer), faux wood drawers that close silently (hooray), television, personal safe, and three-sided mirrors. Some cabins have ceiling recessed, pull-down berths for third and fourth persons, although closet and drawer space would be extremely tight for four persons (even if two of them are children), and some have interconnecting doors (so families with children can cruise together, in separate, but adjacent cabins. Note that audio channels are available through the television; however, if you want to go to sleep with soft music playing in the background you'll need to put a towel over the television screen, as it is impossible to turn the picture off.

Most bathrooms feature tiled accenting and a terrazzo-style tiled floor, and a shower enclosure in a half-moon shape (it *is* rather small, however, considering the size of many typical North American passengers), 100 percent Egyptian cotton towels, a small cabinet for personal toiletries and a small shelf. In reality, there is little space to stow personal toiletries for two (or more).

The largest accommodation consists of a family suite with two bedrooms. One bedroom has twin beds (con-

BERLITZ'S RATINGS

	Possible	Achieved
Ship	500	433
Accommodation	200	163
Food	400	259
Service	400	298
Entertainment	100	81
Cruise	400	312

vertible to queen-sized bed), while a second has two lower beds and two upper Pullman berths, a combination that can sleep up to eight persons (this would be suitable for large families).

Occupants of accommodation designated as suites also get the use of a private Concierge Lounge (where priority dining room reservations, shore excursion bookings and beauty salon/spa appointments can be made).

DINING: Minstrel is the name of the main dining room, which spans two decks (the upper deck level has floor-to-ceiling windows, while the lower deck level has windows). It seats 1,104, and has Middle Ages music themed decor. There are tables for two, four, six, eight or 10 in two seatings for dinner. Two small private dining rooms (Zephyr, with 94 seats and Lute, with 30 seats) are located off the main dining room. No smoking is permitted in the dining venues.

The cuisine in the main dining room is typical of mass banquet catering that offers standard fare comparable to that found in American family-style restaurants ashore. While menu descriptions are tempting, the actual food may be somewhat disappointing and unmemorable. The menu descriptions make the food sound better than it is (which is consistently below average), mostly disappointing and without much taste. However, a decent selection of light meals is provided, and a vegetarian menu is available. The selection of breads, rolls, fruit and cheese is quite poor, however, and could do more improvement. Caviar (once a standard menu item) incurs a hefty extra charge. There is no good caviar; special orders, tableside carving and flambeau items are not offered. Menus typically include a "Welcome Aboard" Dinner, French Dinner, Italian Dinner, International Dinner, Captain's Gala Dinner.

For a change form the main dining room, there are two alternative dining spots: "Portofino," with 112 seats, featuring Italian cuisine, and "Chops Grille Steakhouse," with 95 seats and an open (show) kitchen, featuring premium chops and steaks. Both alternative dining spots have food that is of a much higher quality than in the main dining room. There is an additional charge of $20 per person (this includes gratuities to staff), and reservations *are* required for both dining spots, which are typically open between 6pm and 11pm. Be prepared to eat a *lot* of food (perhaps this justifies the cover charge). The dress code is smart casual.

Also, casual meals can be taken (for breakfast, lunch and dinner) in the self-serve, buffet-style Windjammer Café, which can be accessed directly from the pool deck. It has islands dedicated to specific foods, and indoors and outdoors seating.

Additionally, there is the Seaview Café, open for lunch and dinner. Choose from the self-serve buffet, or from the menu for casual, fast food seafood items including fish sandwiches, popcorn shrimp, fish 'n' chips, as well as non-seafood items such as hamburgers and hot dogs. The décor, naturally, is marine- and ocean related.

OTHER COMMENTS: This is the second Royal Caribbean International ship to use gas turbine power instead of the more conventional diesel or diesel-electric combination. Pod propulsion power is also provided, instead of the previously conventional rudder and propeller shafts.

Brilliance of the Seas is a streamlined, looking contemporary ship, and features a two-deck-high wraparound structure in the forward section of the funnel. Along the ship's port side, a central glass wall protrudes, giving great views (cabins with balconies occupy the space directly opposite on the starboard side). The gently rounded stern has nicely tiered decks, which gives the ship an extremely well-balanced look.

The décor is contemporary, yet elegant, bright and cheerful, designed for active, young and trendy types. The artwork is abundant and truly eclectic. A nine-deck high atrium lobby has glass-walled elevators (on the port side) that travel through 12 decks, face the sea and provide a link with nature and the ocean.

The Centrum (as the atrium is called), has several public rooms connected to it: the guest relations (the erstwhile purser's office) and shore excursions desks, a Lobby Bar, Champagne Bar, the Library, Royal Caribbean Online, the Concierge Club, and a Crown & Anchor Lounge. A great view can be had of the atrium by looking down through the flat glass dome high above it.

Other facilities include a three decks high show lounge (Pacifica Theatre), with 874 seats (including 24 stations for wheelchairs); a second entertainment lounge for cabaret shows; and conference rooms. There's also a

Champagne Bar, and a large Schooner Bar that houses maritime art in an integral art gallery, not to mention the necessary Casino Royale. There's also a small, deeply tiered, dedicated screening room for movies (with space for two wheelchairs), as well as a 194-seat conference center, and a business center.

The Viking Crown Lounge, set around the ship's funnel, functions as an observation lounge during the daytime. In the evening, the space features Starquest, a futuristic, high-energy dance club, and Hollywood Odyssey, a more intimate and relaxed entertainment venue for softer mood music and "black-box" theater.

For the internet-connect set, Royal Caribbean Online is a dedicated computer business center that features 12 IBM computers with high-speed internet access for sending and receiving emails.

As aboard *Adventure of the Seas, Explorer of the Seas, Radiance of the Seas* and *Voyager of the Seas* (the largest ships in the RCI fleet), there is a 30-ft high (9-meter) rock-climbing wall with five separate climbing tracks (to take part, you'll need to sign up). Other sports facilities include a golf course, jogging track, basketball court, 9-hole miniature golf course (with novel decorative ornaments), and an indoor/outdoor country club with golf simulator.

Health and fitness facilities have themed décor, and include a 10,176 sq.-ft (945 sq.-meter) solarium with whirlpool and counter current swimming under a retractable magrodome roof, gymnasium (with 44 cardiovascular machines), 50-person aerobics room, sauna and steam rooms, and therapy treatment rooms. There is also an exterior jogging track.

Youth facilities include Adventure Ocean, an "edutainment" area with four separate age-appropriate sections for junior passengers: Aquanaut Center (for ages 3–5); Explorer Center (for ages 6–8); Voyager Center (for ages 9–12); and the Optix Teen Center (for ages 13–17). There is also Adventure Beach, which includes a splash pool complete with waterslide; Surfside, with computer lab stations with entertaining software; and Ocean Arcade, a video games hangout.

It is clear that this second of a new generation of RCI ships (more are to follow) has been constructed specifically for longer itineraries, with more space and comfortable public areas, larger cabins and more dining options – for the young, active, hip and trendy set. The onboard currency is the US dollar.

WEAK POINTS: Many of the "private" balcony cabins are not very private, as they can be overlooked by anyone standing in the port and starboard wings of the Solarium, and from other locations. Standing in lines for embarkation, the reception desk, disembarkation, for port visits, shore tenders and for the self-serve buffet stations in the Windjammer Café is an inevitable aspect of cruising aboard this large ship. There are no cushioned pads for the deck lounge chairs. Spa treatments are extravagantly expensive.

Calypso
★★ +

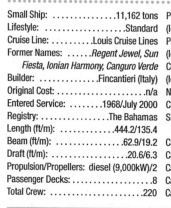

Small Ship: ....11,162 tons	Passengers		Cabin Current: ....110 volts
Lifestyle: ....Standard	(lower beds/all berths): 486/596		Dining Rooms: 1
Cruise Line: ....Louis Cruise Lines	Passenger Space Ratio		Elevators: 2
Former Names: ......*Regent Jewel, Sun*	(lower beds/all berths): 22.9/18.8		Casino (gaming tables): ....Yes
Fiesta, Ionian Harmony, Canguro Verde	Crew/Passenger Ratio		Slot Machines: ....Yes
Builder: ....Fincantieri (Italy)	(lower beds/all berths): 2.2/2.7		Swimming Pools (outdoors): 1
Original Cost: ....n/a	Navigation Officers: ....European		Swimming Pools (indoors): 0
Entered Service: 1968/July 2000	Cabins (total): 243		Whirlpools: 0
Registry: ....The Bahamas	Size Range (sq ft/m): 135–244/		Fitness Center: ....Yes
Length (ft/m): 444.2/135.4	12.5–22.6		Sauna/Steam Room: ....Yes/No
Beam (ft/m): 62.9/19.2	Cabins (outside view): 158		Massage: ....Yes
Draft (ft/m): 20.6/6.3	Cabins (interior/no view): 85		Self-Service Launderette: ....No
Propulsion/Propellers: diesel (9,000kW)/2	Cabins (for one person): 0		Dedicated Cinema/Seats: ....No
Passenger Decks: 8	Cabins (with private balcony): 0		Library: ....Yes
Total Crew: 220	Cabins (wheelchair accessible): 2		Classification Society: ...Lloyd's Register

OVERALL SCORE: 1,062 (OUT OF A POSSIBLE 2,000 POINTS)

ACCOMMODATION: The ship features mostly cabins with an outside view, which are quite attractive, with warm, pastel colors, although the fabrics and soft furnishings could be of better quality. The cabin bathrooms all have showers, but none have bathtubs.

The cabins are really quite small and barely adequate, so take as little clothing as possible. Some cabins have double beds, while most others have twin beds, and many feature third and fourth berths (good for families). Has a limited cabin service menu.

DINING: The dining room is located aft. It is reasonably attractive and well decorated, although its layout is somewhat awkward, as it is positioned on two slightly different levels. There are two seatings, with tables for four, six, and eight persons. Good general cuisine and service standards are provided, and attractive buffets feature plenty of cheeses and cold cuts of meat, which are essential to German-speaking passengers.

OTHER COMMENTS: This former Strintzis Line ferry (which operated Mediterranean ferry services) was extensively reconstructed in Greece (although its resulting exterior profile is certainly less than attractive) and then operated by the now-defunct Regency Cruises before being placed under a five-year bare-boat charter

BERLITZ'S RATINGS		
	Possible	Achieved
Ship	500	212
Accommodation	200	97
Food	400	224
Service	400	249
Entertainment	100	55
Cruise	400	225

to Transocean Tours. Following this, the ship was laid-up in Greece for two years prior to being purchased by Louis Cruise Lines, the ship's present owners and operators.

The ship carries a predominantly German-speaking clientele who seek to travel to interesting and somewhat offbeat destinations in modest surroundings, at a very modest price.

One really practical feature is the ship's enclosed wooden promenade deck, good for strolling. There are plenty of public rooms, bars and lounges to use considering the size of the ship. The fit and finish of the vessel is disappointingly poor, as is the quality of some of the interior decoration.

A cozy, relaxed, and unpretentious ambience is what many passengers want, and get, aboard this ship. The dress code is very relaxed, and formal attire is definitely not required. So, those seeking a casual cruise experience in unstuffy surroundings should be comfortable aboard this ship, which caters well to first-time passengers. The onboard currency is the euro.

WEAK POINTS: This really is a high-density ship, which means that it is very crowded when full, so expect some lines to form for shore excursions and buffets. Expect a large number of smokers. There are very steep, narrow stairways on the outer decks.

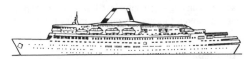

Removed 2006

Caribe
★★ +

Small Ship: ....15,000 tons	Total Crew: 280	Cabin Current: ....110 and 220 volts
Lifestyle: ....Standard	Passengers	Elevators: 2
Cruise Line: ....Festival Cruises	(lower beds/all berths): 500/560	Casino (gaming tables): ....Yes
Former Names: *Valtur Prima, Italia Prima,*	Passenger Space Ratio	Slot Machines: ....Yes
Italia I, Positano, Surriento, Fridtjof Nansen,	(lower beds/all berths): 30.0/26.7	Swimming Pools (outdoors): 1
Volker, Volkerfreundschaft, Stockholm	Crew/Passenger Ratio	Swimming Pools (indoors): 0
Builder: ....Varco Chiapella (Italy)	(lower beds/all berths): 1.7/2.0	Whirlpools: 1
Original Cost: $150 million (reconstruction)	Navigation Officers: ....European	Gymnasium: ....Yes
Entered Service: ....Feb 1948/May 1994	Cabins (total): 250	Sauna/Steam Room: ....Yes/Yes
Registry: ....Italy	Size Range (sq ft/m): 129.2–376.7/	(Turkish Bath)
Length (ft/m): 525.2/160.10	12.0–35.0	Massage: ....Yes
Beam (ft/m): 68.8/21.04	Cabins (outside view): 218	Self-Service Launderette: ....No
Draft (ft/m): 24.6/7.5	Cabins (interior/no view): 32	Dedicated Cinema/Seats: ....No
Propulsion/Propellers: ....diesel	Cabins (for one person): 0	Library: ....Yes
(14,500kW)/2	Cabins (with private balcony): 8	Classification Society: ...Registro Navale
Passenger Decks: 7	Cabins (wheelchair accessible): 0	Italiano

---

OVERALL SCORE: 1,005 (OUT OF A POSSIBLE 2,000 POINTS)

ACCOMMODATION: There are several grades of accommodation from which to choose. No matter which grade of accommodation or price level you choose, all cabins feature a mini-bar, television, and personal safe. Each cabin has a large Italian fresco above the bed, although the ceilings are quite plain. All cabin bathrooms have a combination bathtub/shower, as well as a good amount of indented space for one's personal toiletries.

Eight suites each feature a small private balcony, although the sight lines are quite limited. Each suite has a separate lounge/living area, with table and chairs; the bedroom features twin beds that convert to a queen-sized bed. The bathrooms in the suites and junior suites feature Jacuzzi bathtubs with showers.

The cabins on Sole Deck forward have lifeboat-obstructed views, and those suites located on Portofino Deck may, late at night, be subject to noise from the public rooms located on the deck above.

DINING: The single, large Grand' Italia Restaurant is set on a lower deck in the center of the vessel. It is quite attractive, and has tables for two, four, six and eight. There is one seating for dinner. As you might expect, Italian cuisine is featured, with decent pasta dishes, together with some regional specialties. Standard house wines are typically included for lunch and dinner. There is a limited selection of breads, fruits and cheeses, far too much use of canned fruits, and a poor cabin service menu.

For casual meals, there is also a self-serve buffet

BERLITZ'S RATINGS		
	Possible	Achieved
Ship	500	258
Accommodation	200	111
Food	400	195
Service	400	217
Entertainment	100	40
Cruise	400	184

for breakfast and lunch in Il Giardino, although the selection is really quite basic.

OTHER COMMENTS: This ship has certainly had a busy past life, and is presently one of the oldest ships in service in the cruise industry. The former ocean liner made history when, as *Stockholm* (its original name) it rammed and sank the *Andrea Doria* in July 1956. The ship was reconstructed as a cruise ship in 1994 using its old, riveted hull, but with a completely new superstructure, and a somewhat ungainly profile, took on a new lease of life as *Italia Prima*. More recently, the ship was renamed *Valtur Prima* in 1999, and, when Valtur Tourism (the ship's charter operators) failed in 2001, the ship was chartered by Festival Cruises, renamed *Caribe* in April 2002, and began cruising again.

Because the ship's maneuverability at slow speeds is quite poor, stability is questionable, despite the addition of a large sponson stern apron, so tugs are required in most ports of call.

Outdoors facilities include a wrap-around teakwood promenade deck. Heavy duty, real wood "steamer" deck chairs are provided, although there are no cushioned pads for them. The sunbathing space outdoors is, however, very limited, and definitely not sufficient when the ship is full.

The ship's interiors are decorated in contemporary Italian style. There is a good selection of public rooms to choose from, including a 400-seat auditorium for meetings, and a number of smart boutiques. The décor is reasonably contemporary and splashes of color keep it upbeat; it is complemented by a good selection of colorful artwork. The Afrodite Spa also sports a Turkish bath, which is quite an unusual feature aboard cruise vessels today. There is also a small chapel.

Although the ship's interiors are quite attractive, your cruise experience will depend on what is spent on the food and the service staff, whose attitude and communication skills lacks any kind of finesse. The ship sails from Havana, Cuba on 7-night cruises within the Caribbean (a Cuban visa is necessary). Golfers can choose from several golf packages, including play at one course in Havana, Cuba.

The currency used aboard ship is US dollar. Passengers can opt for an optional "drinks included" package, although this applies only to drinks taken in the dining room.

WEAK POINTS: *Caribe* really is a high-density ship, particularly when it is full, and there is little space for passengers to move around in. The "you are here" deck plans are not easy to read, and could be improved. The small swimming pool is really only a "dip" or "plunge" pool. There is no observation lounge with forward-facing views over the ship's bows. The hallways on the accommodation decks are quite narrow. Sight lines in the single-level show lounge are extremely poor. In the cinema, the seats are not staggered and so the sight lines are poor.

Carnival Conquest
NOT YET RATED

Large Ship: ....110,000 tons	Passengers	Cabin Current: ....110 volts
Lifestyle: ....Standard	(lower beds/all berths): 2,974/3,700	Elevators: 18
Cruise Line: ......Carnival Cruise Lines	Passenger Space Ratio	Casino (gaming tables): ....Yes
Former Names: ....none	(lower beds/all berths): 36.9/29.7	Slot Machines: ....Yes
Builder: ....Fincantieri (Italy)	Crew/Passenger Ratio	Swimming Pools (outdoors): 3
Original Cost: ....$500 million	(lower beds/all berths): 2.5/3.1	(+1 with magrodome)
Entered Service: ....Dec 2002	Navigation Officers: ....Italian	Swimming Pools (indoors): 0
Registry: ....Panama	Cabins (total): 1,487	Whirlpools: 7
Length (ft/m): 951.4/290.0	Size Range (sq ft/m): 179.7–482.2/	Fitness Center: ....Yes
Beam (ft/m): 116.4/35.5	16.7–44.8	Sauna/Steam Room: ....Yes/Yes
Draft (ft/m): 27.0/8.2	Cabins (outside view): 917	Massage: ....Yes
Propulsion/Propellers: .....diesel-electric	Cabins (interior/no view): 570	Self-Service Launderette: ....Yes
(63,400kW)/2	Cabins (for one person): 0	Dedicated Cinema/Seats: ....No
Passenger Decks: 13	Cabins (with private balcony): 574	Library: ....Yes
Total Crew: 1,160	Cabins (wheelchair accessible): 25	Classification Society: ...Lloyd's Register

OVERALL SCORE: NYR (OUT OF A POSSIBLE 2,000 POINTS)

ACCOMMODATION: There are 20 accommodation price grades, in 7 different grades: suites with private balcony; deluxe outside-view cabins with private balcony; outside-view cabins with private balcony; outside-view cabins with window; cabins with a porthole instead of a window; interior (no-view) cabins; interior (no-view cabins) with upper and lower berths. There are five decks of cabins with private balcony – more than any other Carnival ship to date – over 150 more than *Carnival Destiny, Carnival Triumph* or *Carnival Victory*, for example.

There are even "fitness" cabins aboard this ship – in a block of 18 cabins located directly around and behind the Nautica Spa; so, fitness devotees can get out of bed and go straight to the treadmill without having to go through any of the public rooms first.

The standard cabins are of good size and come equipped with all the basics, although the furniture is rather square and angular, with no rounded edges. Three decks of cabins (eight on each deck, each with private balcony) overlook the stern. Most cabins with twin beds can be converted to a queen-size bed format.

A gift basket is provided in all grades of accommodation; it includes aloe soap, shampoo, conditioner, deodorant, breath mints, candy, and pain relief tablets (albeit all in sample sizes).

Note: If you book accommodation in one of the suites (Category 11 or 12 in the Carnival Cruise Lines brochure) you automatically qualify for "Skipper's Club" priority check-in at any US homeland port – useful for getting ahead of the crowd.

BERLITZ'S RATINGS

	Possible	Achieved
Ship	500	NYR
Accommodation	200	NYR
Food	400	NYR
Service	400	NYR
Entertainment	100	NYR
Cruise	400	NYR

DINING: There are two principal dining rooms on *Carnival Conquest*: the Renoir Restaurant, with 744 seats, and the larger Monet Restaurant, with 1,044 seats. Both are two decks high, and both have a balcony level for diners (the balcony level in the Monet Restaurant is larger). Two additional wings in the Renoir Restaurant, named Cassat and Pissaro, provide room to accommodate large groups in a private dining arrangement.

Dining is in *four* seatings, for greater flexibility: 6pm, 6.45pm, 8pm and 8.45pm (these times are approximate). Although the menu choice looks good, the actual cuisine delivered is typically adequate, but quite unmemorable.

Casual eaters will find a serve-yourself Lido Buffet – for breakfast and lunch, while for dinner this turns into the Seaview Bistro for use as a casual alternative eatery – for those that do not want to dress to go to the formal dining rooms (typically between 6pm and 9pm. These include specialty stations where you can order omelets, eggs, fajitas, Chicken Caesar salad, and pasta and stir-fry items. And, if you are still hungry, there's always a midnight buffet around the corner.

Although Carnival meals stress quantity, not quality, the company constantly works hard to improve its cuisine. However, food and its taste are still not the company's strongest points (you get what you pay for, remember). While menu items sound good, their presentation and taste leave much to be desired. While meats are of a high quality, fish and seafood is not. Presentation is simple, and few garnishes are used. Many meat and fowl dishes are disguised with gravies and sauces. The selection of fresh green vegetables, breads, rolls, cheeses and fruits is limited, and there is too much use of canned fruit and jellied desserts.

However, do remember that this is banquet catering, with all its attendant standardization and production cooking (it is, therefore, difficult to ask for anything remotely unusual or off-menu). The selection of breads, rolls, cheeses and fruits is limited (there is too much use of canned fruit).

Although there is a decent wine list, there are no wine waiters (the waiters are expected to serve both food and wine, which does not work well), or decent sized wine glasses. However, the waiters do sing and dance (be prepared for *Simply the Best, Hot, Hot, Hot,* and other popular hits), and there are constant waiter parades; the dining room is show business – all done in the name of gratuities at the end of your cruise. If you like pizzas, this ship typically serves an average of more than 800 pizzas *every* day.

The Cezanne Restaurant is the ship's casual self-serve international food court-style lido deck eatery, which has a capacity of over 1,200. Its décor reflects the style of a 19th-century French café. It has two main serving lines; it is adjacent to the aft pool and can be covered by a magrodome glass cover in inclement weather. Included in this eating mall are Paul's deli, PC's Wok (Chinese cuisine, with wok preparation), a 24-hour pizzeria, and a patisserie (there's an extra charge for yummy pastries, however), as well as a grill for fast foods such as hamburgers and hot dogs. Each night, the Cezanne Restaurant is turned into the "Seaview Bistro," and provides a casual (dress down) alternative to eating in the main dining rooms, serving pasta, steaks, salads and desserts (typically between 6pm and 9pm).

ALTERNATIVE (RESERVATIONS-ONLY, EXTRA COST) DINING:

The Point is the name of the reservations-only, extra cost, alternative dining spot. The décor includes wall murals in the style of Seurat's famous *Le Cirque* (The Circus). Fine table settings, china and silverware are featured, as well as leather-bound menus. This eatery features prime American steaks, such as a filet mignon (9 ounces), porterhouse steak (24 ounces) and New York strip loin steak (be prepared for huge cuts of meat – which are shown to you at your table before you order), and broiled lobster tail, as well as stone crab claws (five of them) – they come flash-frozen courtesy of the famed Joe's Stone Crabs of South Miami Beach.

The décor features the colorful, playful works of Goerges-Pierre Seurat. Reservations are required and there is a cover charge of $25 per person (for service and gratuity). A connoisseur's wine list is also available (typically including such delightful wines as Opus One and Château Lafite-Rothschild). The food is very good, and the ambiance is quiet and refined, but if you are a couple and you have just two glasses of wine each (Grgich Hills Chardonnay or Merlot, for example, at $12.50 a glass), and pay the cover charge, that's $100 for dinner (if you want caviar, it's an extra $29 for a 1-ounce serving). But you may think it's worth it.

OTHER COMMENTS: *Carnival Conquest* is the 19th new-build for this very successful cruise line. It is presently the largest ship in the Carnival Cruise Lines fleet, and has the same well-balanced profile as the earlier ships of a similar, but slightly smaller type: *Carnival Destiny, Carnival Triumph* and *Carnival Victory.* The ship, whose bows are extremely short, has the distinctive, large, swept-back wing-tipped funnel that is the trademark of Carnival Cruise Lines, in the company colors of red, white and blue. However, due to its size, the ship is unable to transit the Panama Canal, and is thus dedicated to itineraries in the Caribbean.

This is quite a stunning ship, built to impress at every turn. Although the ship's bows are extremely short, the profile is well balanced, and features Carnival's trademark large wing-tipped funnel in the company colors of red, white and blue. Amidships on the open deck is a long water slide (200 ft/60 meters in length), as well as tiered sunbathing decks positioned between two swimming pools and several hot tubs. As aboard all Carnival ships, there is a "topless" sunbathing area set around the funnel base (can't be seen from the pool deck below).

The layout is logical, so finding your way around is not difficult. Joe Farcus, the interior designer who designs all the interiors for all Carnival ships, has done a fine job. The décor is all about the world's great Impressionist painters, such as Degas, Monet and Van Gogh. You'll also find large Murano glass flowers on antiqued brass stems in several public areas. It is very imaginative, and a fantasy land for the artist in you (it is not as glitzy as the "*Fantasy*"-class ships).

As for public areas, there are three decks full of lounges, 10 bars and lots of rooms to play in. There are two atriums: the largest, the Atelier Atrium (in the forward third of the ship) goes through nine decks, while the aft atrium goes through three decks. The ship features a doublewide indoor promenade, nine-deck-high, glass-domed rotunda atrium lobby, and a large (15,000-sq-ft/1,400-sq.-meter) Nautica Spa.

The Toulouse-Lautrec Showlounge is a multi-deck showroom seating 1,400, and serves as the venue for Carnival's ritzy-glitzy Las-Vegas-style razzle-dazzle production shows each cruise. It features a revolving stage, hydraulic orchestra pit, superb sound, and seating on three levels (the upper levels being tiered through two decks). There is a proscenium over the stage that acts as a scenery loft (there are two large-scaled Vegas-like razzle-dazzle production shows each cruise). The smaller Degas Lounge features cabaret-style entertainment and adult comedy shows.

For those who like to gamble, the Tahiti casino is certainly large and action-packed; there are also more than 320 slot machines. There are also several other nightspots for just about every musical taste (except for opera, ballet and classical music lovers).

Children are provided with good facilities, including their own two-level Children's Club (including an outdoor pool), and are well cared for with "Camp Carnival," the line's extensive children's program.

This ship is one of the great floating playgrounds for young, active adults who enjoy constant stimulation, close contact with lots and lots of others, as well as the three Gs – glitz, glamour and gambling that together amount to Splash Vegas. It is a live board game with every move executed in typically grand, colorful, fun-filled Carnival Cruise Lines style. This is also a fine vessel for large incentive groups.

Potential passengers of other nationalities should note that this is definitely an all-American experience and product, with all its attendant glitz and jazzy/rock sounds – a real "life on the ocean rave." Forget fashion – having fun is the *sine qua non* of a Carnival cruise.

Gratuities are automatically added to your onboard account at $9.75 per person, per day (the amount charged when this book was completed); you can have this amount adjusted, although you'll have to visit the information desk to do so.

However, this is a large ship, with lots of people everywhere, and that means some waiting in lines, particularly for shore excursions, buffets, embarkation and disembarkation (although the port of Miami has greatly improved terminal facilities specifically for this ship, with some 90 check-in desks). It also means a very impersonal cruise experience. For such a large ship, there really is not much open deck space per passenger; so on any sea days you can expect some crowding. The onboard currency is the US dollar.

WEAK POINTS: It is difficult to escape from noise and loud music (it's even played in accommodation hallways and elevators), not to mention smokers, and masses of people walking around in unsuitable clothing, clutching plastic sport drinks bottles, at any time of the day or night. Many of the private balconies are not so private, and can be overlooked from various public locations. You have to carry a credit card to operate the personal safes, which is inconvenient.

You'll be subjected to a stream of flyers advertising daily art auctions, "designer" watches, "inch of gold/silver" and other promotions, while "artworks" for auction are strewn throughout the ship.

There are too many pillars obstructing passenger flow and sight lines throughout the ship; they are everywhere. Indeed, the many pillars in the dining room make it extremely difficult for the waiters and the proper service of food. Standing in line for embarkation, disembarkation, shore tenders and for self-serve buffet meals is inevitable aboard all large ships. Stage smoke appears to be in constant use during the production shows, and volumes are of the ear-splitting type. The public toilets are spartan and could do with some cheering up.

Carnival Destiny
★★★★

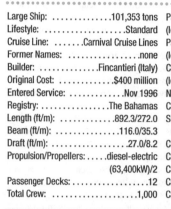

Large Ship: ....101,353 tons	Passengers	Cabin Current: ....110 volts
Lifestyle: ....Standard	(lower beds/all berths): 2,642/3,400	Elevators: 18
Cruise Line: ....Carnival Cruise Lines	Passenger Space Ratio	Casino (gaming tables): ....Yes
Former Names: ....none	(lower beds/all berths): 38.3/29.8	Slot Machines: ....Yes
Builder: ....Fincantieri (Italy)	Crew/Passenger Ratio	Swimming Pools (outdoors): 3
Original Cost: ....$400 million	(lower beds/all berths): 2.6/3.4	(+1 with magrodome)
Entered Service: ....Nov 1996	Navigation Officers: ....Italian	Swimming Pools (indoors): 0
Registry: ....The Bahamas	Cabins (total): 1,321	Whirlpools: 7
Length (ft/m): 892.3/272.0	Size Range (sq ft/m): 179.7–482.2/	Fitness Center: ....Yes
Beam (ft/m): 116.0/35.3	16.7–44.8	Sauna/Steam Room: ....Yes/Yes
Draft (ft/m): 27.0/8.2	Cabins (outside view): 806	Massage:.........................Yes
Propulsion/Propellers: .....diesel-electric	Cabins (interior/no view): 515	Self-Service Launderette:..........Yes
(63,400kW)/2	Cabins (for one person): 0	Dedicated Cinema/Seats: ....No
Passenger Decks:.................12	Cabins (with private balcony): 418	Library: ....Yes
Total Crew: 1,000	Cabins (wheelchair accessible): 25	Classification Society: ...Lloyd's Register

OVERALL SCORE: 1,455 (OUT OF A POSSIBLE 2,000 POINTS)

ACCOMMODATION: Over half of all cabins have an ocean-view, and at 225 sq. ft./21 sq. meters they are the largest in the standard market. They are spread over four decks and have private balconies (with glass rather than steel balustrades, for better, unobstructed ocean views), extending over the ship's side. The balconies have bright fluorescent lighting.

The standard cabins are of good size and come equipped with all the basics, although the furniture is rather square and angular, with no rounded edges. Three decks of cabins (eight on each deck, each with private balcony) overlook the stern (with three days at sea on each of two alternating itineraries, vibration is kept to a minimum).

There are eight penthouse suites, and each has a large private balcony. Although they are quite lavish in their appointments, at only 483 sq. ft (44.8 sq. meters), they are really quite modest when compared to the best suites even in many smaller ships. There are also 40 other suites, each of which features a decent sized bathroom, and a good amount of lounge space, although they are nothing special.

In those cabins with balconies (more cabins have balconies aboard this ship than those that do not), the partition between each balcony is open at top and bottom, so you can hear noise from neighbors (or smell their cigarettes). It is disappointing to see three categories of cabins (both outside and interior) with upper and lower bunk beds (lower beds are far more preferable, but this is how the ship accommodates an extra 600 over and above the lower bed capacity).

BERLITZ'S RATINGS

	Possible	Achieved
Ship	500	430
Accommodation	200	165
Food	400	219
Service	400	269
Entertainment	100	85
Cruise	400	287

The cabins feature soft color schemes and more soft furnishings in more attractive fabrics than some other ships in the fleet. Interactive "Fun Vision" technology lets you choose movies on demand (for a fee). The bathrooms, which have good-sized showers, feature good storage space in the toiletries cabinet. A gift basket is provided in all grades of accommodation; it includes aloe soap, shampoo, conditioner, deodorant, breath mints, candy, and pain relief tablets (albeit all in sample sizes).

Note: If you book accommodation in one of the suites (Category 11 or 12 in the Carnival Cruise Lines brochure) you automatically qualify for "Skipper's Club" priority check-in at any US homeland port – useful for getting ahead of the crowd.

DINING: The ship's two dining rooms (the Galaxy, forward, with windows on two sides, has 706 seats; the Universe, aft, with windows on three sides, has 1,090 seats); both are non-smoking. Each spans two decks (a first for any Carnival ship), and incorporate a dozen pyramid-shaped domes and chandeliers, and a soft, mellow peachy color scheme.

The Universe dining room features a two-deck-high wall of glass overlooking the stern. There are tables for four, six and eight (and even a few tables for two that the line tries to keep for honeymooners). Dining is now in *four* seatings, for greater flexibility: 6pm, 6.45pm, 8pm and 8.45pm (these times are approximate). Although the menu choice looks good, the actual cuisine delivered is adequate, but quite unmemorable.

Casual eaters will find a serve-yourself Lido Buffet – open for breakfast and lunch, while for dinner this turns into the Seaview Bistro for use as a casual alternative eatery – for those that do not want to dress to go to the formal dining rooms (typically between 6pm and 9pm. These include specialty stations where you can order omelets, eggs, fajitas, Chicken Caesar salad, and pasta and stir-fry items. And, if you are still hungry, there's always a midnight buffet around the corner!

Carnival meals stress quantity, not quality, although the company constantly works hard to improve the cuisine. While passengers seem to accept it, few find it stays in their mind after the cruise. Food and its taste are not the company's strongest points (you get what you pay for, remember).

While menu items sound good, their presentation and taste leave much to be desired. While meats are of a high quality, fish and seafood is not. Presentation is simple, and few garnishes are used. Many meat and fowl dishes are disguised with gravies and sauces. The selection of fresh green vegetables, breads, rolls, cheeses and fruits is limited, and there is too much use of canned fruit and jellied desserts. However, do remember that this is banquet catering, with all its attendant standardization and production cooking (it is, therefore, difficult to ask for anything remotely unusual or off-menu). The selection of breads, rolls, cheeses and fruits is limited (there is too much use of canned fruit).

Although there is a decent wine list, there are no wine waiters (the waiters are expected to serve both food and wine, which does not work well), or decent sized wine glasses. However, the waiters do sing and dance (be prepared for *Simply the Best, Hot, Hot, Hot, Hot,* and other popular hits), and there are constant waiter parades; the dining room is show business – all done in the name of gratuities at the end of your cruise. If you like pizzas, this ship typically serves an average of more than 800 pizzas *every* day.

The dining room entrances have comfortable drinking areas for pre-dinner cocktails. There are also many options for casual dining, particularly during the daytime. The Sun and Sea Restaurant is two decks high; it is the ship's informal international food court-style eatery, which is adjacent to the aft pool and can be covered by a magrodome glass cover in inclement weather. Included in this eating mall are a Trattoria (for Italian cuisine, with made-to-order pasta dishes), Happy Valley (Chinese cuisine, with wok preparation), a 24-hour pizzeria, and a patisserie (extra charge for pastries), as well as a grill (for fast foods such as hamburgers and hot dogs).

At night, the area becomes the "Seaview Bistro" (it typically operates between 6pm and 9pm), providing a casual (dress down) alternative to eating in the main dining rooms. It serves pasta, steaks, salads and desserts. The good thing is that, if you really want to eat 24 hours a day, you can do it aboard this ship, which has something for (almost) everyone.

OTHER COMMENTS: *Carnival Destiny* is Carnival's 11th new ship for this very successful cruise line. However, because of its size, the ship is unable to transit the Panama Canal, and is thus dedicated to itineraries in the Caribbean. The ship, whose bows are extremely short, has the distinctive, large, swept-back wing-tipped funnel that is the trademark of Carnival Cruise Lines, in the company colors of red, white and blue.

It is quite a stunning ship, built to impress at every turn, with the most balanced profile of all the ships in the Carnival fleet, although the ship's bows are extremely short. Amidships on the open deck is a very long water slide (200 ft/60 meters in length), as well as tiered sunbathing decks positioned between two swimming pools and several hot tubs. As aboard all Carnival ships, there is a "topless" sunbathing area set around the funnel base (can't be seen from the pool deck below).

Inside, Joe Farcus, the interior designer who designs all the interiors for the ships of Carnival Cruise Lines, has done a fine job. The decor is a fantasyland for the senses (though nowhere near as glitzy as the "*Fantasy*"-class ships).

The layout is logical, so finding your way around is easy. As for public areas, there are three decks full of lounges, 10 bars and lots of rooms to play in. The ship features a doublewide indoor promenade, nine-deck-high, glass-domed rotunda atrium lobby, and a large (15,000 sq. ft/1,393.5 sq. meter) Nautica Spa. The three-level (non-smoking) Palladium showlounge is stunning, and features a revolving stage, hydraulic orchestra pit, superb sound, and seating on three levels (the upper levels being tiered through two decks). There is a proscenium over the stage that acts as a scenery loft (there are two large-scaled Vegas-like razzle-dazzle production shows each cruise).

For those who like to gamble, the Millionaire's Club Casino is certainly large and action-packed; there are also more than 320 slot machines.

An additional feature that this ship has which the *Fantasy*-class ships do not have is the Flagship Bar, located in the Rotunda (atrium), which faces forward to glass-walled elevators. Another feature is the All Star Bar – a sports bar with tables that featuring sporting memorabilia.

Children are provided with good facilities, including their own two-level Children's Club (including an outdoor pool), and are well cared for with "Camp Carnival," the line's extensive children's program.

From the viewpoint of safety, passengers can embark directly into the lifeboats from their secured position without having to wait for them to be lowered, thus saving time in the event of a real emergency.

However, this is a large ship, with lots of people everywhere, and that means some waiting in lines, particularly for shore excursions, buffets, embarkation and disembarkation (although the port of Miami has greatly improved terminal facilities specifically for this ship, with some 90 check-in desks). It also means a very impersonal cruise experience. For such a large ship, there really is not much open deck space per passenger; so on any sea days you can expect some crowding.

This ship is one of the great floating playgrounds for young, active adults who enjoy constant stimulation, close contact with lots and lots of others, as well as the three Gs – glitz, glamour and gambling that together amount to Splash Vegas. It is a live board game with every move executed in typically grand, colorful, fun-filled Carnival Cruise Lines style. This is also a fine vessel for large incentive groups. Potential passengers of other nationalities should note that this is definitely an all-American experience and product, with all its attendant glitz and jazzy/rock sounds – a real "life on the ocean rave." Forget fashion – having fun is the *sine qua non* of a Carnival cruise. Gratuities are automatically added to your onboard account at $9.75 per person, per day (the amount charged when this book was com-

pleted); you can have this amount adjusted, although you'll have to visit the information desk to do so. The onboard currency is the US dollar.

WEAK POINTS: The terraced pool deck is really cluttered, and there are no cushioned pads for the deck chairs. Getting away from people and noise is difficult. The Photo Gallery, adjacent to the atrium/purser's office, becomes extremely congested when photos are on display. Standing in line for embarkation, disembarkation, shore tenders and for self-serve buffet meals is an inevitable aspect of cruising aboard all large ships.

There is absolutely no escape from unnecessary and repetitious announcements (particularly for activities that bring revenue, such as art auctions, bingo, horse racing) that intrude constantly into your cruise, and a great deal of hustling for drinks, although it is sometimes done with a knowing smile.

PLIMSOLL MARK

The safety of ships at sea and all those aboard owes much to the 19th-century social reformer Samuel Plimsoll, a member of the British Parliament concerned about the frequent loss of ships due to overloading. In those days, some shipowners would load their vessels down to the gunwales to squeeze every ounce of revenue out of them. They gambled on good weather, good fortune, and good seamanship to bring them safely into port. Consequently, many ships went to the bottom of the

sea – the result of their buoyancy being seriously impaired by overloading.

Plimsoll helped to enact legislation that came to be known as the Merchant Shipping Act of 1875. This required shipowners to mark their vessels with a circular disc 12 inches (30 cm) long bisected by a line 18 inches (46 cm) long, as a measure of their maximum draft; that is, the depth to which a ship's hull could be safely immersed at sea.

The Merchant Shipping Act of 1890 went even further, and

required the Plimsoll mark (or line) to be positioned on the sides of vessels in accordance with tables drawn up by competent authorities.

The Plimsoll mark is now found on the ships of every nation. The Plimsoll mark indicates three different depths: the depth to which a vessel can be loaded in fresh water, which is less buoyant than salt water; the depth in summer, when seas are generally calmer; and the depth in winter, when seas are much rougher.

Carnival Glory
NOT YET RATED

Large Ship:	110,000 tons	Passengers	
Lifestyle:	Standard	(lower beds/all berths):	2,974/3,700
Cruise Line:	Carnival Cruise Lines	Passenger Space Ratio	
Former Names:	none	(lower beds/all berths):	36.9/29.7
Builder:	Fincantieri (Italy)	Crew/Passenger Ratio	
Original Cost:	$500 million	(lower beds/all berths):	2.5/3.1
Entered Service:	Summer 2003	Navigation Officers:	Italian
Registry:	Panama	Cabins (total):	1,487
Length (ft/m):	951.4/290.0	Size Range (sq ft/m):	179.7–482.2/
Beam (ft/m):	116.4/35.5		16.7–44.8
Draft (ft/m):	27.0/8.2	Cabins (outside view):	917
Propulsion/Propellers:	diesel-electric	Cabins (interior/no view):	570
	(63,400kW)/2	Cabins (for one person):	0
Passenger Decks:	13	Cabins (with private balcony):	574
Total Crew:	1,160	Cabins (wheelchair accessible):	25

Cabin Current:	110 volts
Elevators:	18
Casino (gaming tables):	Yes
Slot Machines:	Yes
Swimming Pools (outdoors):	3
(+1 with magrodome)	
Swimming Pools (indoors):	0
Whirlpools:	7
Fitness Center:	Yes
Sauna/Steam Room:	Yes/Yes
Massage:	Yes
Self-Service Launderette:	Yes
Dedicated Cinema/Seats:	No
Library:	Yes
Classification Society:	Lloyd's Register

OVERALL SCORE: NYR (OUT OF A POSSIBLE 2,000 POINTS)

ACCOMMODATION: There are 20 accommodation price grades, in 7 different grades: suites with private balcony; deluxe outside-view cabins with private balcony; outside-view cabins with private balcony; outside-view cabins with window; cabins with a porthole instead of a window; interior (no-view) cabins; interior (no-view cabins) with upper and lower berths. There are five decks of cabins with private balcony – like sister ship *Carnival Conquest*. Most cabins with twin beds can be converted to a queen-size bed format. Note that if you book accommodation in one of the suites (Category 11 or 12 in the Carnival Cruise Lines brochure) you automatically qualify for "Skipper's Club" priority check-in at any US homeland port – useful for getting ahead of the crowd.

There are even "fitness" cabins aboard this ship – a block of 18 cabins located directly around and behind the Nautica Spa; so fitness devotees can get out of bed and go straight to the treadmill without having to go through any of the public rooms first.

DINING: There are two principal dining rooms. Both are two decks high, and both have a balcony level for diners (the balcony level in one is larger than the other). Two additional wings provide room to accommodate large groups in a private dining arrangement.

Dining is in *four* seatings, for greater flexibility: 6pm, 6.45pm, 8pm and 8.45pm (these times are approximate). Although the menu choice looks good, the actual cuisine delivered is typically adequate, but quite unmemorable.

The wine list is both varied and good, although note

BERLITZ'S RATINGS

	Possible	Achieved
Ship	500	NYR
Accommodation	200	NYR
Food	400	NYR
Service	400	NYR
Entertainment	100	NYR
Cruise	400	NYR

that there are no wine waiters (the waiters are expected to serve both food and wine, which does not work well), or decent sized wine glasses. However, the waiters do sing and dance (be prepared for *Simply the Best, Hot Hot Hot,* and other popular hits), and there are constant waiter parades; the dining room is show business – all done in the name of gratuities at the end of your cruise. If you like pizzas, this ship typically serves an average of more than 800 pizzas *every* day.

There is also a casual self-serve international food court-style lido deck eatery. It has two main serving lines; it is adjacent to the aft pool and can be covered by a magrodome glass cover in inclement weather. Included in this eating mall are Paul's deli, PC's Wok (Chinese cuisine, with wok preparation), a 24-hour pizzeria, and a patisserie (there's an extra charge for yummy pastries, however), as well as a grill for fast foods such as hamburgers and hot dogs. Each night, the Cezanne Restaurant is turned into the "Seaview Bistro," and provides a casual (dress down) alternative to eating in the main dining rooms, serving pasta, steaks, salads and desserts (typically between 6pm and 9pm).

ALTERNATIVE (RESERVATIONS-ONLY, EXTRA COST) DINING: There is one reservations-only, extra cost, alternative dining spot. Fine table settings, china and silverware are featured, as well as leather-bound menus. This eatery features prime American steaks, such as a filet mignon (9 ounces), porterhouse steak (24 ounces) and New York strip loin steak (be prepared for huge cuts of meat – which are shown to you at your table before you order), and broiled lobster tail, as well as stone crab claws (five of them) – they come flash-frozen courtesy of the famed Joe's Stone Crabs of South Miami Beach. The décor features the colorful, playful works of Goerges-Pierre Seurat. Reservations are required and there is a cover charge of $25 per person (for service and gratuity). A connoisseur's wine list is also available (typically including such delightful wines as Opus One and Chateau Lafite-Rothschild). The food is very good, and the ambiance is quiet and refined, but if you are a couple and you have just two glasses of wine each (Grgich Hills Chardonnay or Merlot, for example, at $12:50 a glass), and pay the cover charge, that's $100 for dinner (if you want caviar, it's an extra $29 for a 1-ounce serving). But you may think it's worth it.

OTHER COMMENTS: *Carnival Glory* is the 20th new ship for this very successful cruise line. It is, together with sister ship *Carnival Conquest*, the largest ship in the Carnival Cruise Lines fleet, and has the same generally well-balanced profile as the earlier ships of a similar type: *Carnival Conquest, Carnival Destiny, Carnival Triumph* and *Carnival Victory*. The ship is unable to transit the Panama Canal, due to its size. The ship, whose bows are extremely short, has the distinctive, large, swept-back wing-tipped funnel that is the trademark of Carnival Cruise Lines, in the company colors of red, white and blue.

The ship's interior décor is all about the world's great Impressionist painters. Joe Farcus, the interior designer who has designed all of the ship interiors for Carnival Cruise Lines, has done a great job, and tastefully so. The decor is well done, and a fantasyland for the artist in you (and not as glitzy as the "*Fantasy*"-class ships). The layout is logical, so finding your way around is easy.

There are two atriums: the largest (in the forward third of the ship) goes through nine decks, while the aft atrium goes through three decks. There are nightspots for just about every musical taste (except for opera, ballet and classical music lovers).

The show lounge is a multi-deck showroom, and serves as the venue for Carnival's ritzy-glitzy Las-Vegas-style production shows. A smaller lounge features cabaret-style entertainment and adult comedy shows.

Note that this ship is not yet rated, although the score is expected to be similar to those of close sister ships *Carnival Destiny, Carnival Triumph* and *Carnival Victory*. The onboard currency is the US dollar.

WEAK POINTS: It is difficult to escape from noise and loud music (it's even played in accommodation hallways and elevators), not to mention smokers, and masses of people walking around in unsuitable clothing, clutching plastic sport drinks bottles, at any time of the day or night. Many of the private balconies are not so private, and can be overlooked from various public locations. You have to carry a credit card to operate the personal safes, which is inconvenient. You'll be subjected to a stream of flyers advertising daily art auctions, "designer" watches, "inch of gold/silver" and other promotions, while "artworks" for auction are strewn throughout the ship.

There are too many pillars obstructing passenger flow and sight lines throughout the ship; they are everywhere. Indeed, the many pillars in the dining room make it extremely difficult for the waiters and the proper service of food. Standing in line for embarkation, disembarkation, shore tenders and for self-serve buffet meals is an inevitable aspect of cruising aboard all large ships. Stage smoke appears to be in constant use during the production shows, and volumes are of the ear-splitting type. The public toilets are spartan and could do with some cheering up.

Carnival Legend
★★★★

Large Ship:	85,920 tons	Passengers	
Lifestyle:	Standard	(lower beds/all berths):	2,124/2,680
Cruise Line:	Carnival Cruise Lines	Passenger Space Ratio	
Former Names:	none	(lower beds/all berths):	40.4/32.0
Builder:	Kvaerner Masa-Yards	Crew/Passenger Ratio	
Original Cost:	$375 million	(lower beds/all berths):	2.2/2.6
Entered Service:	Aug 2002	Navigation Officers:	Italian
Registry:	Panama	Cabins (total):	1,062
Length (ft/m):	959.6/292.5	Size Range (sq ft/m):	185.0–490.0/
Beam (ft/m):	105.6/32.2		17.1–45.5
Draft (ft/m):	25.5/7.8	Cabins (outside view):	849
Propulsion/Propellers:	diesel-electric	Cabins (interior/no view):	213
	(62,370 kW)/2 azimuthing pods	Cabins (for one person):	0
	(17.6 MW each)	Cabins (with private balcony):	750
Passenger Decks:	12	Cabins (wheelchair accessible):	16
Total Crew:	1,030	Cabin Current:	110 volts

Elevators:	12
Casino (gaming tables):	Yes
Slot Machines:	Yes
Swimming Pools (outdoors):	2+1 children's pool
Swimming Pools (indoors):	1 (indoor/outdoor)
Whirlpools:	5
Fitness Center:	Yes
Sauna/Steam Room:	Yes/Yes
Massage:	Yes
Self-Service Launderette:	Yes
Dedicated Cinema/Seats:	No
Library:	Yes
Classification Society:	Registro Navale Italiano (RINA)

OVERALL SCORE: 1,474 (OUT OF A POSSIBLE 2,000 POINTS)

ACCOMMODATION: There are 20 accommodation price categories to choose from. The range of accommodation includes suites (with private balcony), outside-view cabins with private balcony, 68 ocean view cabins with French doors (pseudo balconies that have doors which open, but no balcony to step out onto), and a healthy proportion of standard outside-view to interior (no view) cabins.

Regardless of the grade of accommodation chosen, all cabins feature spy-hole doors, and have twin beds that can be converted into a queen-sized bed, individually controlled air-conditioning, television, and telephone. A number of cabins on the lowest accommodation deck have views that are obstructed by lifeboats. Note that some cabins that can accommodate a third and fourth person have *very little* closet space, and there's only one personal safe. There is no separate radio in each cabin – instead, audio channels are provided on the in-cabin television system (however, you can't turn the picture off – not very romantic for late at night sounds with your loved one). A gift basket of (sample sized) personal amenities is now provided in all grades of accommodation; it includes aloe soap, shampoo, conditioner, deodorant, breath mints, candy, and pain relief tablets. Note that if you book one of the suites (Category 11 or 12 in the Carnival Cruise Lines brochure), you automatically qualify for "Skipper's Club" priority check-in at any US homeland port – useful for getting ahead of the crowd.

Among the most desirable suites and cabins are those

BERLITZ'S RATINGS

	Possible	Achieved
Ship	500	435
Accommodation	200	154
Food	400	234
Service	400	270
Entertainment	100	86
Cruise	400	295

on five of the aft-facing decks; these feature private balconies with views overlooking the stern and ship's wash. You might think that these units would suffer from vibration, but they don't, a bonus provided by the pod propulsion system.

For the ultimate in extra space, it would be worth your while trying one of the large deluxe balcony suites on Deck 6, with its own private teakwood balcony. These tend to be quiet suites, with a large lounge and sleeping areas, a good size bathroom with twin (his 'n' hers) washbasins, toilet and bidet, and whirlpool bathtub. These feature twin beds that convert to a queen-sized bed, three (illuminated) closets, and a huge amount of drawer space. The balcony has an outside light, and a wide teakwood deck with smoked glass and wood railing (you could easily seat 10 people with comfort and still have space left over).

In order to keep things in perspective, you should note that even the largest suites are actually quite small when compared with suites aboard other ships of a similar size – for example, Celebrity Cruises' *Constellation, Infinity, Millennium,* and *Summit,* where penthouse suites measure up to 2,530 sq. ft (235 sq. meters). Carnival Cruise Lines has fallen behind in the move to larger living spaces, and, with this ship, lost an opportunity to provide more space for those seeking it. However, Carnival's philosophy has always been to get its passengers out into public areas to socialize, and spend money (this is, after all, a vacation).

DINING: This ship features a single, large, two-decks-high, 1,300-seat main dining room called Truffles Restaurant, with seating on both upper and main levels. Its huge ceiling features large murals of a china pattern made famous by Royal Copenhagen, and wall-mounted glass display cases feature fine china – plates, soup tureens and platters. The galley is located underneath the restaurant, with waiter access by escalators. There are tables are for two, four, six or eight, and small rooms on both upper and lower levels can be closed off for groups of up to 60. Dining is in two seatings (main and late) for lunch and dinner, while breakfast is in an open seating arrangement.

Carnival meals stress quantity, not quality, although the company constantly works hard to improve the cuisine. While passengers seem to accept it, few find it worth remembering. Food and its taste are still not the company's strongest points (you get what you pay for).

Although there is a decent wine list, there are no wine waiters (the waiters are expected to serve both food and wine, which does not work well, as their knowledge is limited). The service is highly programmed, but entertaining and friendly. Unlike in most restaurants ashore, the waiters sing and dance (be prepared for *Simply the Best, Hot, Hot* and other popular hits), and there are constant waiter parades. But to Carnival, the dining room is pure show business – all done in the name of gratuities at the end of your cruise.

For casual eaters, while there is no lido café, the Unicorn Café is an extensive eatery that forms the aft third of Deck 9 (part of also wraps around the upper section of the huge atrium). Mural of unicorns abound everywhere. It includes a central area with small buffet counters (deli sandwich corner, Asian corner, rotisserie, and International counter); there are salad counters, a dessert counter, and a 24-hour Pizzeria counter, all of which form a large eatery with both indoor and outdoor seating. Note that movement around the buffet area is *very slow*, and requires you to stand in line for everything. Each night, the Unicorn Cafe changes its name to Seaview Bistro, for casual, serve-yourself dinners in a dress-down setting (typically open between 6pm and 9.30pm).

The good thing is that, if you want to eat 24 hours a day, you can do it aboard this ship, which has something for (almost) everyone.

ALTERNATIVE (RESERVATIONS-ONLY, EXTRA COST) DINING: The Golden Fleece Supper Club is a more upscale dining spot atop the ship, with just 156 seats. It features a show kitchen where chefs can be seen preparing their masterpieces. It is located on two of the uppermost decks of the ship, above the Unicorn Grille, in the lower, forward section of the funnel housing, with great views over the multi-deck atrium. The décor is set around the Greek legend of Jason and the Argonauts. The bar is the setting for a large sculpture of the Golden Fleece. Fine table settings, china and silverware are featured, as well as leather-bound menus. This eatery fea-tures prime American steaks, such as a filet mignon (9 ounces), porterhouse steak (24 ounces), New York strip loin steak (be prepared for huge cuts of meat – which are shown to you at your table before you order), and broiled lobster tail, as well as stone crab claws (five of them) – they come flash-frozen courtesy of the famed Joe's Stone Crabs of South Miami Beach. Reservations are required and there is a cover charge of $25 per person (for service and gratuity). A connoisseur's wine list is also available (typically including such delightful wines as Opus One and Chateau Lafite-Rothschild). The food is very good, and the ambiance is generally quiet and refined, but if you are a couple and you have just two glasses of wine each (Grgich Hills Chardonnay or Merlot, for example, at $12.50 per glass), and pay the cover charge, that's $100 for dinner (and if you want caviar, it's an extra $29 for a 1-ounce serving). But you may think it's worth it.

OTHER COMMENTS: *Carnival Legend* (sister ship to *Carnival Pride* and *Carnival Spirit*) is the 18th new ship for this very successful cruise line. Its launch made headlines in 2002 when actress Judi Dench, the celebrity chosen to break the traditional bottle of champagne on its hull, had difficulty doing so; a final hefty heave smashed the bottle, drenching Dame Judi with champagne.

The ship, whose bows are extremely short, has the distinctive, large, swept-back wing-tipped funnel that is the trademark of Carnival Cruise Lines, in the company colors of red, white and blue.

The first thing that regular passengers will notice is the length of this ship – longer than the company's larger trio (*Carnival Destiny, Carnival Triumph, Carnival Victory*), and only a hair's breath shorter than Cunard Line's *Queen Elizabeth 2* (which the Carnival Corporation, Carnival Cruise Lines' parent company, owns). The new design makes the ship look much sleeker than any other in the Carnival Cruise Lines fleet (except for sisters *Carnival Pride* and *Carnival Spirit*) – a process of continuing ship design and evolvement.

When you first walk into the ship, you'll be greeted by the immense size of a dramatic lobby space that spans eight decks. The atrium lobby presents a stunning wall decoration that is best seen from any of the multiple viewing balconies on each deck above the main lobby floor level. Take a drink from the lobby bar and look upwards – the surroundings are simply stunning, with a mural of the Colossus of Rhodes (one of the seven wonders of the world).

The interior décor is dedicated to the world's great legends, from wonders of the ancient world and heroes of antiquity to 20th-century jazz masters and great athletes – an eclectic mix that somehow works well, thanks to the imagination of interior designer Joe Farcus, who calls his design "entertainment architecture."

There are two whole entertainment/public room decks, the upper of which also features an exterior promenade deck - something new for this fun cruise line.

Although it doesn't go around the whole ship, it's long enough to do some serious walking on. Additionally, there is also a jogging track outdoors, located around the ship's mast and the forward third of the ship.

Without doubt, the most dramatic room aboard this ship is the Follies Showlounge. It spans three decks in the forward section of the ship, and recalls the movie palaces of the 1920s. Spiral stairways at the back of the lounge connect all three levels. Stage shows are best seen from the upper three levels, from where the sight lines are reasonably good. Directly underneath the show lounge is the Firebird Lounge, has a bar in its starboard aft section.

A small wedding chapel is located forward of the uppermost level of the two main entertainment decks, adjacent to the library and internet center. Other facilities include a winding shopping street with several boutique stores (including all the usual Carnival logo items), photo gallery, video games room, an observation balcony in the center of the vessel (at the top of the multideck atrium), and a large Club Merlin Casino, with its castle-like atmosphere (damsels, knights and wizards are painted on the walls).

A large health spa, called the Body Beautiful Spa, spans two decks, is located directly above the navigation bridge in the forward part of the ship and features 13,700 sq. ft (1,272 sq. meters) of space. Facilities on the lower level include a solarium, eight treatment rooms, lecture rooms, sauna and steam rooms for men and women, a beauty parlor; the upper level consists of a large gymnasium with floor-to-ceiling windows on three sides, including forward-facing ocean views, and an aerobics room with instructor-led classes (some at extra cost).

There are two centrally located swimming pools outdoors, and one of the pools can be used in inclement weather due to its retractable magrodome (glass dome) cover. There are two whirlpool tubs, located adjacent to the swimming pools. A winding water slide that spans two decks in height is located at an aft, upper deck. Another smaller pool is available for children. There is also an additional whirlpool tub outdoors.

In the medical department, Tele-Radiology is installed in this ship. This system enables shipboard physicians to digitally transmit X-rays and other patient information to shore-side facilities – useful for peace of mind for passengers and crew.

Carnival Legend is a fine, large floating playground for the young and young-at-heart, active adults who enjoy constant stimulation, participation events, close contact with lots and lots of others, as well as the three Gs – glitz, glamour and gambling. It's cruising Splash Vegas-style, and akin to a live board game with every move executed in typically grand, colorful, fun-filled Carnival Cruise Lines style. It could also prove to be an interesting vessel for large incentive groups.

Potential passengers of other nationalities should note that this is definitely an all-American experience and product, with all its attendant glitz and jazzy/rock sounds – a real "life on the ocean rave." However, this is a large ship, with lots of people everywhere, and that means some waiting in line, particularly for shore excursions, buffets, embarkation and disembarkation. It also means a very impersonal cruise experience.

Expect intrusive announcements (particularly for activities that bring revenue, such as art auctions, bingo, horse racing) that intrude constantly into your cruise, and a great deal of hustling for drinks, although it is sometimes done with a knowing smile. Forget fashion – having fun is the *sine qua non* of a Carnival cruise.

Soft-drinks packages can be purchased for adults and children. Gratuities are automatically added to your onboard account at $9.75 per person, per day (the amount charged when this book was completed). You can have this amount adjusted, although you'll have to visit the information desk to do so. The onboard currency is the US dollar.

WEAK POINTS: The information desk in the lobby is really quite small, and can become quite congested, particularly on embarkation day and days at sea. It is difficult to escape from noise and loud music (it's even played in accommodation hallways and elevators), not to mention smokers, and masses of people walking around in unsuitable clothing, clutching plastic sport drinks bottles, at any time of the day or night. Many of the private balconies are not so private, and can be overlooked from various public locations. You have to carry a credit card to operate the personal safes, which is inconvenient. You'll be subjected to a stream of flyers advertising daily art auctions, "designer" watches, "inch of gold/silver" and other promotions, while "artworks" for auction are strewn throughout the ship.

There are too many pillars obstructing passenger flow and sight lines throughout the ship; they are everywhere. Indeed, the many pillars in the dining room make it extremely difficult for the waiters and the proper service of food. Standing in line for embarkation, disembarkation, shore tenders and for self-serve buffet meals is an inevitable aspect of cruising aboard all large ships.

Stage smoke appears to be in constant use during the production shows, and volumes are of the ear-splitting type. Books and computers are cohabitants in the ship's library/internet center, but anyone wanting a book has to lean over others who may be using a computer – a very awkward arrangement. Public toilets are spartan and could do with some cheering up.

Carnival Pride
★★★★

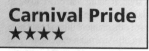

Large Ship: ....85,920 tons	Passengers	Elevators: 12
Lifestyle: ....Standard	(lower beds/all berths): 2,124/2,680	Casino (gaming tables): ....Yes
Cruise Line: ....Carnival Cruise Lines	Passenger Space Ratio	Slot Machines: ....Yes
Former Names: ....none	(lower beds/all berths): 40.4/32.0	Swimming Pools (outdoors): ....2+1
Builder: ....Kvaerner Masa-Yards	Crew/Passenger Ratio	children's pool
Original Cost: ....$375 million	(lower beds/all berths): 2.2/2.6	Swimming Pools (indoors): 1
Entered Service: ....Jan 2002	Navigation Officers: ....Italian	(indoor/outdoor)
Registry: ....Panama	Cabins (total): 1,062	Whirlpools: 5
Length (ft/m): 959.6/292.5	Size Range (sq ft/m): 185.0–490.0/	Fitness Center: ....Yes
Beam (ft/m): 105.6/32.2	17.1–45.5	Sauna/Steam Room: ....Yes/Yes
Draft (ft/m): 25.5/7.8	Cabins (outside view): 849	Massage: ....Yes
Propulsion/Propellers: .....diesel-electric	Cabins (interior/no view): 213	Self-Service Launderette: ....Yes
(62,370 kW)/2 azimuthing pods	Cabins (for one person): 0	Dedicated Cinema/Seats: ....No
(17.6 MW each)	Cabins (with private balcony): 750	Library: ....Yes
Passenger Decks: 12	Cabins (wheelchair accessible): 16	Classification Society: ...Registro Navale
Total Crew: 1,029	Cabin Current: ....110 volts	Italiano (RINA)

OVERALL SCORE: 1,474 (OUT OF A POSSIBLE 2,000 POINTS)

ACCOMMODATION: There are 20 accommodation price categories to choose from, in 6 different grades. The range of accommodation includes suites (with private balcony), outside-view cabins with private balcony, 68 ocean view cabins with French doors (pseudo-balconies that have doors which open, but no balcony to step out onto – although you do get fresh air), and a healthy proportion of standard outside-view to interior (no view) cabins. While the smallest cabin measures a very decent 185 sq. ft (17.1 sq. meters), the largest suite measures a dimensionally challenged 490 sq. ft (45.5 sq. meters) – small when compared with many other ships of a similar size today, although still a healthy chunk of living space.

While the bathrooms are quite compact, they do include a shower enclosure, several shelves, a shaving mirror, and 100 percent cotton towels. A gift basket of (sample sized) personal amenities is now provided in all grades of accommodation; it includes aloe soap, shampoo and conditioner sachets, deodorant, breath mints, candy, and pain relief tablets.

Regardless of the grade of accommodation chosen, all cabins feature spy-hole doors, and have twin beds that can be converted into a queen-sized bed, individually controlled air-conditioning, television, telephone, hairdryer (located in the vanity desk), and neat, yellow glass bedside lights that might just remind you of Tin Man in the film *The Wizard of Oz*. A number of cabins on the lowest accommodation deck (Main Deck) have views that are obstructed by lifeboats. Note that some

BERLITZ'S RATINGS

	Possible	Achieved
Ship	500	435
Accommodation	200	154
Food	400	234
Service	400	270
Entertainment	100	86
Cruise	400	295

cabins that can accommodate a third and fourth person have *very little* closet space, and there's only one personal safe. There is no separate radio in each cabin – instead, audio channels are provided on the in-cabin television system (however, you can't turn the picture off – not very romantic for listening to late-night sounds with your loved one).

Among the most desirable suites and cabins are those on five of the aft-facing decks; these feature private balconies with views overlooking the stern and ship's wash. You might think that these units would suffer from vibration, but they don't, a bonus provided by the two-pod propulsion system.

For the ultimate in extra space, try one of the large deluxe balcony suites on Deck 6 with large private teak-wood balcony. These tend to be quiet suites, with a large lounge and sleeping areas, large bathroom with twin (his 'n' hers) washbasins, toilet and bidet, and whirlpool bathtub. These feature twin beds that convert to a queen-sized bed, three (illuminated) closets, and a huge amount of drawer space. The balcony has an outside light, and wide teak deck with smoked glass and wood railing (you could easily seat 10 people with comfort and still have space left over).

In order to keep things in perspective, you should note that even the largest suites are small when compared with suites aboard other ships of a similar size – for example, Celebrity Cruises' *Constellation, Infinity, Millennium,* and *Summit,* where penthouse suites measure up to 2,530 sq. ft (235 sq. meters). Carnival Cruise Lines has fallen behind in the move to larger living spaces, and, with this ship, lost an opportunity to provide more space for those seeking it. However, Carnival's philosophy has always been to get its passengers out into public areas to socialize, and spend money (this is, after all, a vacation).

Note that if you book accommodation in one of the suites (Category 11 or 12 in the Carnival Cruise Lines brochure) you automatically qualify for "Skipper's Club" priority check-in at any US homeland port – useful for getting ahead of the crowd.

DINING: This ship features a single, large, two-decks-high, 1,300-seat main dining room called the Normandie Restaurant, with seating on both upper and main levels. The décor is designed to give the impression that you are dining in the grand style of the famous French liner *Normandie*, although ship buffs would probably be critical of the results). The galley is located underneath the restaurant, with waiter access by escalators. There are tables for two, four, six or eight, and small rooms on both upper and lower levels can be closed off for groups of up to 60. Dining is in two seatings, main and late, for lunch and dinner, while breakfast is in an open seating arrangement.

Carnival meals tend to stress quantity, not quality, although the company does work hard to improve the cuisine and its presentation. While passengers seem to accept it, few find the meals memorable. Food and its taste are still not the company's strongest points (you get what you pay for, remember), and if you enjoy really good food in a quiet environment, there is an alternative (see under David's Supper Club, below).

While the menu items sound good, presentation and taste leave much to be desired. While meats are generally of a decent quality, fish and seafood is not. The presentation is simple, and few garnishes are used. Many meat and fowl dishes are disguised with gravies and sauces. The selection of fresh green vegetables, breads, rolls, cheeses and fruits is limited, and there is much use of canned fruit and jellied desserts. However, do remember that this is typical of big-ship banquet catering, with all its attendant standardization and production cooking (it is, therefore, difficult to ask for anything remotely unusual or off-menu).

Although there is a decent wine list, there are no wine waiters (the waiters are expected to serve both food and wine, which does not work well, as their knowledge is limited). The service is highly programmed, but entertaining and friendly. Unlike in most restaurants ashore, the waiters sing and dance (be prepared for *Simply the Best, Hot, Hot,* and other such popular hits), and there are constant waiter parades. But to Carnival, the dining room is pure show business – all done in the name of gratuities at the end of your cruise.

For casual eaters, there is the extensive Mermaid's Grille is the equivalent of a lido cafe, which is an eatery that forms the aft third of Deck 9 (part of it also wraps around the upper section of the huge atrium). It includes a central area with small buffet counters (deli sandwich corner, Asian corner, rotisserie, and International counter) in an eclectic mix; there are salad counters, a dessert counter, and a 24-hour Pizzeria counter, all of which form a large eatery with both indoor and outdoor seating. There is plenty of variety, although it's not really inspiring. Note that movement around the buffet area is *very slow*, and requires you to stand in line for everything. Each night, Mermaid's Grille changes its name to Seaview Bistro, for casual, serve-yourself dinners in a dress-down setting (typically open between 6pm and 9.30pm).

In addition, the Piazza Café features specialty coffees, espressos and cappuccinos, special cakes. The good thing is that, if you want to eat 24 hours a day, you can do it aboard this ship, which has something for (almost) everyone.

ALTERNATIVE (RESERVATIONS-ONLY, EXTRA COST) DINING: David's Supper Club is a more upscale dining spot located on two of the uppermost decks of the ship under a huge glass dome, with seating for approximately 150. It features a show kitchen where chefs can be seen preparing their masterpieces. It is located directly above Mermaid's Grille (the self-serve buffet area), in the lower, forward section of the funnel housing, with some superb views over the multi-deck atrium, as well as to the sea. The décor includes a 12-feet high replica of Michaelangelo's famed statue of David. Fine table settings, china and silverware are featured, as are well as leather-bound menus. This eatery features prime American steaks, such as a filet mignon (9 ounces), porterhouse steak (24 ounces), New York strip loin steak (be prepared for huge cuts of meat – which are shown to you at your table before you order), and broiled lobster tail, as well as stone crab claws (five of them) – they come flash-frozen courtesy of the famed Joe's Stone Crabs of South Miami Beach. Reservations are required and there is a cover charge of $25 per person (for service and gratuity). A fine, connoisseur's wine list is also available (typically including such delightful wines as Opus One and Château Lafite-Rothschild). The food and its presentation are very good, and the ambiance is quiet and refined, but if you are a couple and you have two glasses of wine each (Grgich Hills Chardonnay or Merlot, for example, at $12.50 per glass), and pay the cover charge, that's $100 for dinner (and if you want caviar, it's an extra $29 for a 1-ounce serving). But you may think it's worth it.

OTHER COMMENTS: *Carnival Pride* (sister ship to *Carnival Legend* and *Carnival Spirit*) is the 17th new ship for this very successful cruise line. The ship, whose bows are extremely short, has the distinctive, large, swept-back wing-tipped funnel that is the trademark of Carnival Cruise Lines, in the company colors of red, white and blue.

The first thing that regular passengers will notice is the extreme length of this ship – longer than the company's larger trio (*Carnival Destiny, Carnival Triumph, Carnival Victory,* all of which measure over 100,000 tons), and only a hair's breath shorter than Cunard Line's

Queen Elizabeth 2 (which the Carnival Corporation, Carnival Cruise Lines' parent company, owns). Sister ships in the same class are *Carnival Legend* and *Carnival Spirit*, and all three can transit the Panama Canal.

When you first walk into the ship, you'll be greeted by the immense size of a dramatic lobby space that spans eight decks, and décor that includes lots of larger than life nude ladies' breasts, bums, and nude men – all reproductions from the Renaissance period. The atrium lobby presents a stunning 37-ft high (11-meter) reproduction of Raphael's *Nymph Galatea* that is best seen from any of the multiple viewing balconies on each deck above the main lobby floor level. There's no question about it – the surroundings are simply stunning.

The décor is extremely artistic, with art being the theme throughout the ship – even elevator doors and interiors contain reproductions (blown-up, photographic copies that are too grainy for comfort) of some of the great masters of the Renaissance period.

There are two whole entertainment/public room decks, the upper of which also features an exterior promenade deck – something new for this cruise line. Although it doesn't go around the whole ship, it's long enough to do some serious walking on. Additionally, there is also a jogging track outdoors, located around the ship's mast and the forward one-third of the ship.

Without doubt, the most dramatic room aboard is the 1,170-seat Taj Mahal Showlounge, which spans three decks in the forward section of the ship. Spiral stairways at the back of the lounge connect all three levels. Stage shows are best seen from the upper three levels, from where the sight lines are reasonably good. Directly underneath the showlounge is Butterflies, a large lounge, complete with its own bar.

A small wedding chapel is located forward of the uppermost level of the two main entertainment decks, adjacent to the library and internet center. Other facilities include a winding shopping street with several boutique sections for brands such as Fendi, Fossil, Tommy Hilfiger, and a whole array of Carnival logo items. There's also a photo gallery, video games room, an observation balcony in the center of the vessel (at the top of the multi-deck atrium), and a large casino, with gaming tables, slot machines, bar and entertainment.

A large health spa, called the Body Beautiful Spa, spans two decks, is located directly above the navigation bridge in the forward part of the ship and features 13,700 sq. ft (1,272 sq. meters) of space. Facilities on the lower level include a solarium, eight treatment rooms, lecture rooms, sauna and steam rooms for men and women, a beauty parlor; the upper level consists of a large gymnasium with floor-to-ceiling windows on three sides, including forward-facing ocean views, and an aerobics room with instructor-led classes (some at extra cost).

There are two centrally located swimming pools outdoors, and one of the pools can be used in inclement weather due to its retractable magrodome (glass dome) cover. There are two whirlpool tubs, located adjacent to the swimming pools. A winding water slide that spans two decks in height is located at an aft, upper deck. Another smaller pool is available for children. There is also an additional whirlpool tub outdoors.

Tele-Radiology is installed in the medical department aboard this ship. The system enables shipboard physicians to digitally transmit X-rays and other patient information to shore-side facilities.

Carnival Pride is a fine, large floating playground for young and young-at-heart, active adults who enjoy constant stimulation, participation events, close contact with lots and lots of others, as well as the three Gs – glitz, glamour and gambling. It's cruising Splash Vegas-style, and akin to a live board game with every move executed in typically grand, colorful, fun-filled Carnival Cruise Lines style. It could also prove to be an interesting vessel for large incentive groups.

Potential passengers of other nationalities should note that this is definitely an all-American experience and product, with all its attendant glitz and jazzy/rock sounds.

Expect intrusive announcements (particularly for activities that bring revenue, such as art auctions, bingo, horse racing) that intrude constantly into your cruise, and a great deal of hustling for drinks, although it is sometimes done with a knowing smile. Forget fashion– having fun is the *sine qua non* of a Carnival cruise.

Gratuities are added to your onboard account at $9.75 per person, per day (the amount charged when this book was completed); you can have this amount adjusted, although you'll have to visit the information desk to do so. The onboard currency is the US dollar.

WEAK POINTS: The information desk in the lobby is really quite small, and can become quite congested, particularly on embarkation day and days at sea. It is difficult to escape from smokers, crowds and loud music (it's even played in accommodation hallways and elevators). Many private balconies are not so private, and can be overlooked from various public locations. You have to carry a credit card to operate the personal safes, an inconvenience. You'll be subjected to a stream of flyers advertising daily art auctions, 'designer' watches, 'inch of gold/silver' and other promotions, while 'artworks' for auction are strewn throughout the ship.

There are too many pillars obstructing passenger flow and sight lines throughout the ship; they are everywhere. Indeed, the many pillars in the dining room make it extremely difficult for the waiters and the proper service of food. Standing in line for embarkation, disembarkation, shore tenders and for self-serve buffet meals is inevitabl aboard all large ships.

Stage smoke appears to be in constant use during the production shows, and volumes are of the ear-splitting type. Books and computers are cohabitants in the ship's library/internet center, but anyone wanting a book has to lean over others who may be using a computer – a very awkward arrangement. Public toilets are spartan and could do with some cheering up.

Carnival Spirit
★★★★

Large Ship:	.85,920 tons
Lifestyle:	Standard
Cruise Line:	Carnival Cruise Lines
Former Names:	none
Builder:	Kvaerner Masa-Yards
Original Cost:	$375 million
Entered Service:	Apr 2001
Registry:	Panama
Length (ft/m):	959.6/292.5
Beam (ft/m):	105.6/32.2
Draft (ft/m):	25.5/7.8
Propulsion/Propellers:	diesel-electric
	(62,370 kW)/2 azimuthing pods
	(17.6 MW each)
Passenger Decks:	12
Total Crew:	930
Passengers	
(lower beds/all berths):	2,124/2,680
Passenger Space Ratio	
(lower beds/all berths):	40.4/32.0
Crew/Passenger Ratio	
(lower beds/all berths):	2.2/2.6
Navigation Officers:	Italian
Cabins (total):	1,062
Size Range (sq ft/m):	185.0–490.0/
	17.1–45.5
Cabins (outside view):	849
Cabins (interior/no view):	213
Cabins (for one person):	0
Cabins (with private balcony):	750
Cabins (wheelchair accessible):	16
Cabin Current:	110 volts
Elevators:	12
Casino (gaming tables):	Yes
Slot Machines:	Yes
Swimming Pools (outdoors):	2+1
	children's pool
Swimming Pools (indoors):	1
	(indoor/outdoor)
Whirlpools:	5
Fitness Center:	Yes
Sauna/Steam Room:	Yes/Yes
Massage:	Yes
Self-Service Launderette:	Yes
Dedicated Cinema/Seats:	No
Library:	Yes
Classification Society:	Registro Navale
	Italiano (RINA)

OVERALL SCORE: 1,474 (OUT OF A POSSIBLE 2,000 POINTS)

ACCOMMODATION: There are 20 accommodation price categories to choose from. The range of accommodation includes suites (with private balcony), outside-view cabins with private balcony, 68 ocean view cabins with French doors (pseudo balconies that have doors which open, but no balcony to step out onto), and a healthy proportion of standard outside-view to interior (no view) cabins. While the smallest cabin measures a very decent 185 sq. ft (17.1 sq. meters), the largest suite measures a dimensionally challenged 490 sq. ft (45.5 sq. meters), which is small when compared with many other ships of a similar size today.

The bathrooms are quite compact, but include a circular shower enclosure, several shelves, a shaving mirror, and 100 percent cotton towels. A gift basket of (sample sized) personal amenities is now provided in all grades of accommodation; it includes aloe soap, shampoo, conditioner, deodorant, breath mints, candy, and pain relief tablets.

Regardless of the grade of accommodation chosen, all cabins feature spy-hole doors, and have twin beds that can be converted into a queen-sized bed, individually controlled air-conditioning, television, and telephone. A number of cabins on the lowest accommodation deck have views that are obstructed by lifeboats. Note that some cabins that can accommodate a third and fourth person have *very little* closet space, and there's only one personal safe. There is no separate radio in each cabin – instead, audio channels are provided on the in-cabin

BERLITZ'S RATINGS

	Possible	Achieved
Ship	500	435
Accommodation	200	154
Food	400	234
Service	400	270
Entertainment	100	86
Cruise	400	295

television system (however, you can't turn the picture off). Note that if you book one of the suites (Category 11 or 12 in the Carnival Cruise Lines brochure), you automatically qualify for "Skipper's Club" priority check-in at any US homeland port – useful for getting ahead of the crowd.

Among the most desirable suites and cabins are those on five of the aft-facing decks; these feature private balconies with views overlooking the stern and ship's wash. You might think that these units would suffer from vibration, but they don't, a bonus provided by the pod propulsion system.

For the ultimate in extra space, try one of the large deluxe balcony suites on Deck 6 with large private teak balcony. These tend to be quiet suites, with a large lounge and sleeping areas, large bathroom with twin (his 'n' hers) washbasins, toilet and bidet, and whirlpool bathtub. These have twin beds that convert to a queen-sized bed, three (illuminated) closets, and a huge amount of drawer space. The balcony has an outside light, and wide teak deck with smoked glass and wood railing (you could easily seat 10 people with comfort and still have space left over).

In order to keep things in perspective, you should note that even the largest suites are small when compared with suites aboard other ships of a similar size – for example, Celebrity Cruises' *Constellation*, *Infinity*, *Millennium*, and *Summit*, where penthouse suites measure up to 2,530 sq. ft (235 sq. meters). Carnival Cruise Lines has fallen behind in the move to larger living spaces, and, with this ship, lost an opportunity to provide more space for those seeking it. However, Carnival's philosophy has always been to get its passengers out into public areas to socialize, and spend money (this is, after all, a vacation).

DINING: This ship has a single, large, two-decks-high, 1,300-seat main dining room called the Empire Restaurant, with seating on both upper and main levels. The décor is heavily "Napoleonic" (early 19th-century French) style. The galley is located underneath the restaurant, with waiter access by escalators. There are tables are for two, four, six or eight, and small rooms on both upper and lower levels can be closed off for groups of up to 60. Dining is in two seatings, main and late, for lunch and dinner, while breakfast is in an open seating arrangement.

Carnival meals do tend to stress quantity, not quality, although the company constantly works hard to improve its cuisine. However, food and its taste are still not the company's strongest points (you get what you pay for, remember).

Although there is a decent wine list, there are no wine waiters (the waiters are expected to serve both food and wine, which does not work well, as their knowledge is limited). The service is highly programmed, but entertaining and friendly. Unlike in most restaurants ashore, the waiters sing and dance (be prepared for *Simply the Best, Hot, Hot, Hot* and other such poplar hits), and there are constant waiter parades. But to Carnival, the dining room is pure show business – all done in the name of gratuities at the end of your cruise.

For casual eaters, while there is no lido café, there is the extensive La Playa Grille, an eatery that forms the aft third of Deck 9 (part of it also wraps around the upper section of the huge atrium). It includes a central area with small buffet counters (deli sandwich corner, Asian corner, rotisserie, and International counter); there are salad counters, a dessert counter, and a 24-hour Pizzeria counter, all of which form a large eatery with both indoor and outdoor seating. Note that movement around the buffet area is *very slow*, and requires you to stand in line for everything. Each night, La Playa Grille changes its name to Seaview Bistro, for casual, serve-yourself dinners in a dress-down setting (typically open 6pm–9.30pm).

Additionally, there is an outdoor self-serve buffet (adjacent to the fantail pool), which serves fast food items such as hamburgers and hot dogs, chicken and fries, as well as two smaller buffets adjacent to the midships pool area. The good thing is that, if you want to eat 24 hours a day, you can do it aboard this ship, which has something for (almost) everyone.

ALTERNATIVE (RESERVATIONS-ONLY, EXTRA COST) DINING: The Nouveau Supper Club is a more upscale dining spot located on two of the uppermost decks of the ship under a huge glass dome, with seating for approximately 150. It has a show kitchen where chefs can be seen preparing their masterpieces. It is located directly above La Playa Grille Mermaid's Grille, in the lower, forward section of the funnel housing, with some superb views over the multi-deck atrium, as well as to the sea. Fine table settings, china and silverware are used, as well as leather-bound menus. This eatery has prime American steaks, such as a filet mignon (9 ounces), porterhouse steak (24 ounces) and New York strip loin steak (be prepared for huge cuts of meat – which are shown to you at your table before you order), and broiled lobster tail, as well as stone crab claws (five of them) – they come flash-frozen courtesy of the famed Joe's Stone Crabs of South Miami Beach.

The décor features a floral pattern as well as a stained-glass balcony on the upper level, and, in addition, has a stage and dance floor. Reservations are required and there is a cover charge of $25 per person (for service and gratuity). A connoisseur's wine list is also available (typically including such delightful wines as Opus One and Château Lafite-Rothschild). The food is very good, and the ambiance is quiet and refined, but if you are a couple and you have just two glasses of wine each (Grgich Hills Chardonnay or Merlot, for example, at $12.50 per glass), and pay the cover charge, that's $100 for dinner (and if you want caviar, it's an extra $29 for a 1-ounce serving). But you may think it's worth it.

OTHER COMMENTS: *Carnival Spirit* is the 16th new ship for this very successful cruise line. This ship also has Carnival's trademark large wing-tipped funnel in the Miami-based company's red, white and blue colors. It is just a hair's breath shorter than Cunard Line's *Queen Elizabeth 2* (which Carnival Corporation, the parent company of Carnival Cruise Lines, owns). The design makes the ship look much sleeker than any other in the Carnival Cruise Lines fleet (except for its sister ships), a process of continuing ship design and evolvement. What's new for this ship is the pod propulsion system, which gives the ship more maneuverability, while reducing required machinery space and vibration at the stern.

There are two centrally located swimming pools outdoors, and one of the pools can be used in inclement weather due to its retractable magrodome (glass dome) cover. Two whirlpool tubs, located adjacent to the swimming pools, are abridged by a bar. Another smaller pool is available for children; it incorporates a winding water slide that spans two decks in height. There is also an additional whirlpool tub outdoors.

When you first walk into the ship, you'll be greeted by the immense size of the dramatic lobby space that spans eight decks. The atrium lobby, with its two grand stairways, presents a stunning wall decoration that is best seen from any of the multiple viewing balconies on each deck above the main lobby floor level. Take a drink from the lobby bar and look upwards – the surroundings are simply stunning.

There are two whole entertainment/public room decks, the upper of which also has an exterior promenade deck – something new for this fun cruise line. Although it doesn't go around the whole ship, it's long enough to do some serious walking on. Additionally, there is also a jogging track outdoors, located around the ship's mast and the forward third of the ship.

Without doubt, the most dramatic room aboard this ship is the 1,170-seat Pharaoh's Palace Showlounge, which spans three decks in the forward section of the ship. Spiral stairways at the back of the lounge connect all levels. Stage shows are best seen from the upper three levels, from where the sight lines are reasonably good. Directly underneath the showlounge is Versailles Lounge, a large lounge complete with its own bar.

Other facilities include a winding shopping street with several boutique stores and logo shops. A small wedding chapel is located forward of the uppermost level of the two main entertainment decks, adjacent to the combined library and internet center. Other facilities include a winding shopping street with several boutique stores (including all the usual Carnival logo items), photo gallery, video games room, an observation balcony in the center of the vessel (at the top of the multi-deck atrium), a large casino, and a piano lounge/bar.

The casino is large (one has to walk through it to get from the restaurant to the show lounge on one of the entertainments decks), and is equipped with all the gaming paraphernalia and array of slot machines you can think of.

A large health spa, the Body Beautiful Spa, spans two decks, is located directly above the navigation bridge in the forward part of the ship and has 13,700 sq. ft (1,272 sq. meters) of space. Facilities on the lower level include a solarium, eight treatment rooms, lecture rooms, sauna and steam rooms for men and women, a beauty parlor; the upper level consists of a large gymnasium with floor-to-ceiling windows on three sides, including forward-facing ocean views, and an aerobics room with instructor-led classes (some at extra cost).

There are two centrally located swimming pools outdoors, and one of the pools can be used in inclement weather due to its retractable magrodome (glass dome) cover. There are two whirlpool tubs, located adjacent to the swimming pools. A winding water slide that spans two decks in height is located at an aft, upper (outdoors) deck. Another smaller pool is available for children. There is also an additional whirlpool tub outdoors.

There is a "tele-radiology" system that enables shipboard physicians to digitally transmit X-rays and other patient information to shore-side facilities – useful for peace of mind for passengers and crew.

Carnival Spirit is a fine, large floating playground

for the young and young-at-heart, active adults who enjoy constant stimulation, participation events, close contact with lots and lots of others, as well as the three Gs – glitz, glamour and gambling. It's cruising Splash Vegas-style, and akin to a live board game with every move executed in typically grand, colorful, fun-filled Carnival Cruise Lines style. It could also prove to be an interesting vessel for large incentive groups.

Potential passengers of other nationalities should note that this is definitely an all-American experience and product, with all its attendant glitz and jazzy/rock sounds – a real "life on the ocean rave." However, this is a large ship, with lots of people everywhere, and that means some waiting in line, particularly for shore excursions, buffets, embarkation and disembarkation. It also means a very impersonal cruise experience.

Expect intrusive announcements (particularly for activities that bring revenue, such as art auctions, bingo, horse racing) that intrude constantly into your cruise, and a great deal of hustling for drinks, although it is sometimes done with a knowing smile.

Gratuities are added to your onboard account at $9.75 per person, per day (the amount charged when this book was completed); you can have this amount adjusted, although you'll have to visit the information desk to do so. The onboard currency is the US dollar.

WEAK POINTS: The information desk in the lobby is quite small, and can become quite congested, particularly on embarkation day and days at sea. It is difficult to escape from smokers, noise and loud music (it's even played in accommodation hallways and elevators). Many of the private balconies are not so private, and can be overlooked from various public locations. You'll need to carry a credit card to operate the personal safe in your suite or cabin, which is an inconvenience. You'll be subjected to a stream of flyers advertising various products.

There are too many pillars obstructing passenger flow and sight lines throughout the ship; they are everywhere. Indeed, the many pillars in the dining room make it extremely difficult for the waiters and the proper service of food. Standing in line for embarkation, disembarkation, shore tenders and for self-serve buffet meals is an inevitable aspect of cruising aboard all large ships.

Stage smoke appears to be in constant use during the production shows, and volumes are of the ear-splitting type. Books and computers are cohabitants in the ship's library/internet center, but anyone wanting a book has to lean over others who may be using a computer – a very awkward arrangement. Public toilets are spartan and could do with some cheering up.

Carnival Triumph
★★★★

Large Ship:	.101,509 tons	Passengers		Elevators:	.18
Lifestyle:	Standard	(lower beds/all berths):	.2,758/3,473	Casino (gaming tables):	Yes
Cruise Line:	Carnival Cruise Lines	Passenger Space Ratio		Slot Machines:	Yes
Former Names:	none	(lower beds/all berths):	.36.8/29.2	Swimming Pools (outdoors):	.3
Builder:	Fincantieri (Italy)	Crew/Passenger Ratio			(+1 with magrodome)
Original Cost:	.$420 million	(lower beds/all berths):	.2.3/3.0	Swimming Pools (indoors):	.0
Entered Service:	.Oct 1999	Navigation Officers:	Italian	Whirlpools:	.7
Registry:	The Bahamas	Cabins (total):	.1,379	Fitness Center:	Yes
Length (ft/m):	.893.0/272.2	Size Range (sq ft/m):	.179.7–482.2/	Sauna/Steam Room:	Yes/Yes
Beam (ft/m):	.116.0/35.3		16.7–44.8	Massage:	Yes
Draft (ft/m):	.27.0/8.2	Cabins (outside view):	.853	Self-Service Launderette:	Yes
Propulsion/Propellers:	.diesel-electric	Cabins (interior/no view):	.526	Dedicated Cinema/Seats:	.No
	(34,000 kW)/2 azimuthing pods	Cabins (for one person):	.0	Library:	Yes
	(17.6 MW each)	Cabins (with private balcony):	.508	Classification Society:	.Lloyd's Register
Passenger Decks:	.13	Cabins (wheelchair accessible):	.25		
Total Crew:	.1,100	Cabin Current:	.110 volts		

OVERALL SCORE: 1,455 (OUT OF A POSSIBLE 2,000 POINTS)

ACCOMMODATION: Over half of all cabins are outside (and at 225 sq. ft./21 sq. meters they are the largest in the mainstream cruise market). They are spread over four decks and have private balconies (with glass rather than steel balustrades, for better, unobstructed ocean views), with balconies extending from the ship's side. The balconies also feature bright fluorescent lighting.

BERLITZ'S RATINGS

	Possible	Achieved
Ship	500	430
Accommodation	200	165
Food	400	219
Service	400	269
Entertainment	100	85
Cruise	400	287

The standard cabins are of good size and come equipped with all the basics, although the furniture is rather square and angular, with no rounded edges. Three decks of cabins (eight cabins on each deck, each with private balcony) overlook the stern.

There are eight penthouse suites, and each has a large private balcony. Although they are quite lavish in their appointments, at only 483 sq. ft (44.8 sq. meters), they are really quite small when compared to the best suites even in many smaller ships. There are also 40 other suites, each of which features a decent sized bathroom, and a good amount of lounge space, although they are nothing special.

In the cabins with balconies (more cabins have balconies aboard this ship than those that do not), the partition between each balcony is open at top and bottom, so you may well hear noise from neighbors (or smell their cigarettes. It is disappointing to see three categories of cabins (both outside and interior) with upper and lower bunk beds (lower beds are far more preferable, but this is how the ship accommodates an extra 600 people over and above the lower bed capacity).

The cabins feature soft color schemes and more soft furnishings in more attractive fabrics than any other ship in the fleet. Interactive "Fun Vision" technology lets you choose movies on demand (and for a fee). The bathrooms, which have good-sized showers, feature good storage space in the toiletries cabinet. A gift basket is provided in all grades of accommodation; it includes aloe soap, shampoo, conditioner, deodorant, breath mints, candy, and pain relief tablets (albeit all in sample sizes).

If you book accommodation in one of the suites (Category 11 or 12 in the Carnival Cruise Lines brochure) you automatically qualify for "Skipper's Club" priority check-in at any US homeland port – useful for getting ahead of the crowd.

DINING: The ship's two dining rooms (the London, forward, with windows on two sides, has 706 seats; the Paris, aft, with windows on three sides, has 1,090 seats), and both are non-smoking. Each dining room spans two decks, and incorporates a dozen domes and chandeliers. The Universe dining room features a two-deck-high wall of glass overlooking the stern. There are tables for four, six and eight (and even a few tables for two that the line tries to keep for honeymooners).

Dining is now in *four* seatings, for greater flexibility: 6pm, 6.45pm, 8pm and 8.45pm (times are approximate). Although the menu choice looks good, the actual cuisine delivered is adequate, but quite unmemorable.

All ships also feature a serve-yourself casual Lido

Buffet – for breakfast and lunch, while for dinner this turns into the Sea View Bistro for use as a casual alternative eatery – for those that do not want to dress to go to the formal dining rooms. These include specialty stations where you can order omelets, eggs, fajitas, Chicken Caesar salad, and pasta and stir-fry items. And, if you're still hungry, there's a midnight buffet around the corner.

Carnival meals stress quantity, not quality, although the company constantly works hard to improve the cuisine. However, food and its taste are still not the company's strongest points (you get what you pay for, remember).

While the menu items sound good, their presentation and taste leave much to be desired. While meats are of a high quality, fish and seafood is not. Presentation is simple, and few garnishes are used. Many meat and fowl dishes are disguised with gravies and sauces. The selection of fresh green vegetables, breads, rolls, cheeses and fruits is limited, and there is too much use of canned fruit and jellied desserts.

However, do remember that this is banquet catering, with all its attendant standardization and production cooking (it is, therefore, difficult to ask for anything remotely unusual or off-menu). The selection of breads, rolls, cheeses and fruits is limited (there is too much use of canned fruit).

Although there is a decent wine list, there are no wine waiters (the waiters are expected to serve both food and wine, which does not work well), or decent sized wine glasses. The service is highly programmed, although the waiters are willing and reasonably friendly. However, the waiters do sing and dance (be prepared for *Simply the Best, Hot, Hot, Hot* and other popular hits), and there are constant waiter parades; the dining room is show business – all done in the name of gratuities at the end of your cruise.

The dining room entrances have comfortable drinking areas for pre-dinner cocktails. There are also many options for casual dining, particularly during the day.

The South Beach Club (a lido café) is the ship's informal international self-serve buffet-style eatery, with seating on two levels. Included in this eatery are the New York Deli (typically open 11am–11pm), and the Hong Kong Noodle Company (for Chinese cuisine, with wok preparation), and a 24-hour pizzeria (this ship typically serves an average of more than 800 pizzas *every* day).

There is also a grill for fast foods (such as grilled chicken, hamburgers and hot dogs), and salad bar – all part of the poolside-South Beach Club. In addition, there is a self-serve ice cream and frozen yogurt station (no extra charge).

At night, the South Beach Club is turned into the "Seaview Bistro" (it typically is in operation between 6pm and 9pm) and provides a casual (dress down) alternative to eating in the main dining rooms, serving pasta, steaks, salads and desserts. The good thing is that, if you want to eat 24 hours a day, you can do it aboard this ship, which has something for (almost) everyone.

OTHER COMMENTS: *Carnival Triumph* is Carnival Cruise Lines' 14th new ship for this very successful cruise line. It is unable to transit the Panama Canal due to its size. The ship, whose bows are extremely short, has the distinctive, large, swept-back wing-tipped funnel that is the trademark of Carnival Cruise Lines, in the company colors of red, white and blue.

This is quite a stunning ship, built to impress at every turn, has the most balanced profile of all the ships in the Carnival Cruise Lines fleet, although the bow itself is extremely short. Amidships on the open deck is the longest water slide at sea (200 ft/60 meters in length), as well as tiered sunbathing decks positioned between two swimming pools and several hot tubs. As aboard all Carnival ships, there is a "topless" sunbathing area set around the funnel base (can't be seen from the pool deck below). The Lido Deck space is more expansive than aboard sister ship *Carnival Destiny* (the swim-up bar has been eliminated), and the pool is larger.

Inside the ship, Joe Farcus, the interior designer who has designed all of the ship interiors for Carnival Cruise Lines, has outdone himself, but tastefully so. The ship is simply superb, and a fantasyland for the senses (though nowhere near as glitzy as the "*Fantasy*"-class ships). The layout is logical, so finding your way around is a fairly simple matter.

There are three decks full of lounges, 10 bars and lots of rooms to play in. Like her smaller (though still large) predecessors, this ship features a doublewide indoor promenade, nine-deck-high, glass-domed rotunda atrium lobby, and a huge (15,000 sq. ft /1,400 sq. meter) Nautica Spa. The three-level (non-smoking) Rome show lounge is stunning, and has a revolving stage, hydraulic orchestra pit, superb sound, and seating on three levels (the upper levels being tiered through two decks). There is a proscenium over the stage that acts as a scenery loft (there are two large-scaled Vegas-like razzle-dazzle production shows each cruise).

For those that like to gamble, the Club Monaco is certainly a large (and noisy) casino. There are also more than 320 slot machines.

An additional feature that this ship has which the *Fantasy*-class ships do not have is the Flagship bar, located in the Rotunda (atrium), which faces forward to the glass-walled elevators. A sports bar (Olympic Bar) has tables that feature sports memorabilia.

Children are provided with good facilities, including their own two-level Children's Club (including an outdoor pool), and are well cared for with "Camp Carnival," the line's extensive children's program.

From the viewpoint of safety, passengers can embark directly into the lifeboats from their secured position without having to wait for them to be lowered, thus saving time in the event of a real emergency. Well done.

However, this certainly is a big ship, with lots of people everywhere, and that means some waiting in line, particularly for shore excursions, buffets, embarkation and disembarkation (although the port of Miami has greatly improved terminal facilities specifically for this ship, with some 90 check-in desks). It also means a very impersonal cruise experience. For such a large ship, there really is not much open deck space per passenger; so on any sea days you can expect crowding.

This ship is one of the great floating playgrounds for young, active adults who enjoy constant stimulation, close contact with lots and lots of others, as well as the three Gs – glitz, glamour and gambling that together amount to Splash Vegas. It is a live board game with every move executed in typically grand, colorful, fun-filled Carnival Cruise Lines style. It is a fine vessel for large incentive groups.

Potential passengers of other nationalities should note that this is definitely an all-American experience and product, with all its attendant glitz and jazzy/rock sounds – a real "life on the ocean rave." Forget fashion – having fun is the *sine qua non* of a Carnival cruise.

Sister ships include *Carnival Destiny* and *Carnival Victory*, with *Carnival Conquest* also set to join the fleet in late 2002. Gratuities are automatically added to your onboard account at \$9.75 per person, per day (the amount charged when this book was completed); you can have this amount adjusted, although you'll have to visit the information desk to do so. The onboard currency is the US dollar.

WEAK POINTS: The terraced pool deck is really cluttered, and there are no cushioned pads for the deck chairs. Although the outdoor deck space has been improved, there is still much crowding when the ship is full and at sea. Getting away from people and noise is difficult. The Photo Gallery becomes extremely congested when photos are on display. Standing in line for embarkation, disembarkation, shore tenders and for self-serve buffet meals is an inevitable aspect of cruising aboard all large ships. There is absolutely no escape from unnecessary and repetitive announcements (particularly for activities that bring revenue, such as art auctions, bingo, horse racing) that intrude constantly into your cruise, and a great deal of hustling for drinks, although it is sometimes done with a knowing smile.

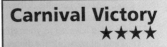

Carnival Victory
★★★★

Large Ship: ....101,509 tons
Lifestyle: ....Standard
Cruise Line: ....Carnival Cruise Lines
Former Names: ....none
Builder: ....Fincantieri (Italy)
Original Cost: ....$410 million
Entered Service: ....Aug 2000
Registry: ....Panama
Length (ft/m): 893.0/272.2
Beam (ft/m): 116.0/35.3
Draft (ft/m): 27.0/8.2
Propulsion/Propellers: .....diesel-electric
(34,000 kW)/2 azimuthing pods
(17.6 MW each)
Passenger Decks: 13
Total Crew: 1,100

Passengers
(lower beds/all berths): 2,758/3,473
Passenger Space Ratio
(lower beds/all berths): 36.8/29.2
Crew/Passenger Ratio
(lower beds/all berths): 2.3/3.0
Navigation Officers: ....Italian
Cabins (total): 1,379
Size Range (sq ft/m): 179.7–482.2/
16.7–44.8
Cabins (outside view): 853
Cabins (interior/no view): 526
Cabins (for one person): 0
Cabins (with private balcony): 508
Cabins (wheelchair accessible): 25
Cabin Current: ....110 volts

Elevators: 18
Casino (gaming tables): ....Yes
Slot Machines: ....Yes
Swimming Pools (outdoors): 3
(+1 with magrodome)
Swimming Pools (indoors): 0
Whirlpools: 7
Fitness Center: ....Yes
Sauna/Steam Room: ....Yes/Yes
Massage: ....Yes
Self-Service Launderette: ....Yes
Dedicated Cinema/Seats: ....No
Library: ....Yes
Classification Society: ...Lloyd's Register

OVERALL SCORE: 1,455 (OUT OF A POSSIBLE 2,000 POINTS)

ACCOMMODATION: Over half of all cabins are outside (and at 225 sq. ft./21 sq. meters they are the largest in the standard market). They are spread over four decks and have private balconies (with glass rather than steel balustrades, for better, unobstructed ocean views), with balconies extending from the ship's side. The balconies have bright fluorescent lighting.

The standard cabins are of good size and have all the basics, although the furniture is square and angular, with no rounded edges. Three decks of cabins (eight on each deck, each with private balcony) overlook the stern (with three days at sea on each of two alternating itineraries, vibration is kept to a minimum).

There are eight penthouse suites, and each has a large private balcony. Although they are quite lavish in their appointments, at only 483 sq. ft (44.8 sq. meters), they are really quite small when compared to the best suites even in many smaller ships. There are also 40 other suites, each of which features a decent sized bathroom, and a good amount of lounge space, although they are nothing special.

In cabins with balconies (more cabins have balconies aboard this ship than those that do not), the partition between each balcony is open at top and bottom, so you may well hear noise from neighbors (or smell their cigarettes. It is disappointing to see three categories of cabins (both outside and interior) with upper and lower bunk beds (lower beds are far more preferable, but this is how the ship accommodates an extra 600 over and above the lower bed capacity).

BERLITZ'S RATINGS

	Possible	Achieved
Ship	500	430
Accommodation	200	165
Food	400	219
Service	400	269
Entertainment	100	85
Cruise	400	287

The cabins have soft color schemes and more soft furnishings in more attractive fabrics than any other ship in the fleet. Interactive "Fun Vision" technology lets you choose movies on demand (and for a fee). The bathrooms, which have good-sized showers, feature good storage space in the toiletries cabinet. A gift basket is provided in all grades of accommodation; it includes aloe soap, shampoo, conditioner, deodorant, breath mints, candy, and pain relief tablets (albeit all in sample sizes).

Note that if you book accommodation in one of the suites (Category 11 or 12 in the Carnival Cruise Lines brochure) you automatically qualify for "Skipper's Club" priority check-in at any US homeland port – useful for getting ahead of the crowd.

DINING: The ship's two dining rooms (the Atlantic, forward, with windows on two sides, has 706 seats; the Pacific, aft, with windows on three sides, has 1,090 seats), and both are non-smoking. Each dining room spans two decks, and incorporate a dozen domes and chandeliers. The Pacific dining room features a two-deck-high wall of glass overlooking the stern. There are tables for four, six and eight (and even a few tables for two that the line tries to keep for honeymooners). Dining is now in *four* seatings, for greater flexibility: 6pm, 6.45pm, 8pm and 8.45pm (these times are approximate). Note that this gives you *very* little time to "dine" – although it should give you some idea of what to expect from your dining experience. Although the menu choice looks good, the actual cuisine delivered is adequate, but quite unmemorable.

All ships also have serve-yourself casual buffets for breakfast and lunch, while for dinner this turns into the Seaview Bistro for use as a casual alternative eatery – for those that do not want to dress to go to the formal dining rooms (it typically is in operation between 6pm and 9pm). These include specialty stations where you can order omelets, eggs, fajitas, Chicken Caesar salad, and pasta and stir-fry items. And, if you are still hungry, there's always a midnight buffet around the corner.

Carnival meals stress quantity, not quality, although the company constantly works hard to improve the cuisine. However, food and its taste are still not the company's strongest points (you get what you pay for).

While the menu items sound good, their presentation and taste leave much to be desired. While meats are of a high quality, fish and seafood is not. Presentation is simple, and few garnishes are used. Many meat and fowl dishes are disguised with gravies and sauces. The selection of fresh green vegetables, breads, rolls, cheeses and fruits is limited, and there is too much use of canned fruit and jellied desserts. However, do remember that this is banquet catering, with all its attendant standardization and production cooking (it is, therefore, difficult to ask for anything remotely unusual or off-menu). The selection of breads, rolls, cheeses and fruits is limited (there is too much use of canned fruit).

Although there is a decent enough wine list, there are no wine waiters (the waiters are expected to serve both food and wine, which does not work well), or decent sized wine glasses. The service is highly programmed, although the waiters are willing and reasonably friendly. However, the waiters do sing and dance (be prepared for *Simply the Best, Hot, Hot, Hot, Hot,* and other popular hits) and there are constant waiter parades. The dining room is show business – all done in the name of gratuities at the end of your cruise.

The dining room entrances have comfortable drinking areas for pre-dinner cocktails. There are also many options for casual dining, particularly during the day.

The Mediterranean Restaurant is the ship's informal international self-serve buffet-style eatery, with seating on two levels. Included in this eatery are the East River Deli (a New York-style deli, open 11am–11pm), the Yangtse Wok (for Chinese cuisine, with wok preparation), and a 24-hour pizzeria (this ship typically serves an average of more than 800 pizzas *every* day).

There is also the Mississippi Barbeque for fast grilled foods (such as grilled chicken, hamburgers and hot dogs), and a salad bar. In addition, there is a self-serve ice cream and frozen yogurt station (no extra charge).

At night, the Mediterranean Restaurant is turned into the "Seaview Bistro" and provides a casual (dress down) alternative to eating in the main dining rooms, serving pasta, steaks, salads and desserts. The good thing is that, if you want to eat 24 hours a day, you can do it aboard this ship, which has something for (almost) everyone.

OTHER COMMENTS: *Carnival Victory* is 15th new ship for this very successful cruise line. It is unable to transit the Panama Canal due to its size. The ship, whose bows are extremely short, has the distinctive, large, swept-back wing-tipped funnel that is the trademark of Carnival Cruise Lines, in the company colors of red, white and blue.

This is quite a stunning ship, built to impress at every turn, has the most balanced profile of all the ships in the Carnival Cruise Lines fleet, although the bow itself is extremely short. Amidships on the open deck is the longest water slide at sea (200 ft /60 meters in length), as well as tiered sunbathing decks positioned between two swimming pools and several hot tubs. As aboard all Carnival ships, there is a "topless" sunbathing area set around the funnel base (it cannot be seen from the pool deck below). The Lido Deck space is more expansive than aboard sister ship *Carnival Destiny* (the swim-up bar has been eliminated), and the pool is larger.

Inside the ship, Joe Farcus, the interior designer who has designed all of the ship interiors for Carnival Cruise Lines, has outdone himself, but tastefully so. The ship's decor is a tribute to the oceans of the world (and nowhere near as glitzy as the "*Fantasy*"-class ships). Seahorses (no, you can't race them), corals and shells are laid throughout the design. The layout is logical, so finding your way around is a fairly simple matter.

There are three decks full of lounges, 10 bars and lots of rooms to play in. Like its smaller (though still large) predecessors, this ship features a doublewide indoor promenade, nine-deck-high, glass-domed rotunda atrium lobby, and a huge (15,000 sq. ft /1400 sq. meter) Nautica Spa. The three-level (non-smoking) Caribbean show lounge is stunning, and features a revolving stage, hydraulic orchestra pit, superb sound, and seating on three levels (the upper levels being tiered through two decks). There is a proscenium over the stage that acts as a scenery loft (there are two large-scaled Vegas-like razzle-dazzle production shows each cruise).

For those who like to gamble, the South China Sea Club is certainly a large (and noisy) casino. There are also more than 320 slot machines.

An additional feature that this ship has which the *Fantasy*-class ships do not have is the Capitol bar, located in the Rotunda (atrium), which faces forward to the glass-walled elevators and sits under the 10-deck-high atrium dome. A sports bar (Aegean Bar) has tables that feature sports memorabilia.

Children are provided with good facilities, including their own two-level Children's Club (including an outdoor pool), and are well cared for with "Camp Carnival," the line's extensive children's program.

From the viewpoint of safety, passengers can embark directly into the lifeboats from their secured position without having to wait for them to be lowered, thus saving time in the event of a real emergency. Well done.

However, this certainly is a big ship, with lots of people everywhere, and that means some waiting in line, particularly for shore excursions, buffets, embarkation and disembarkation (although the port of Miami has greatly improved terminal facilities specifically for this ship, with some 90 check-in desks). It also means a very impersonal cruise experience. For such a large ship, there really is not much open deck space per passenger; so on any sea days you can expect crowding.

This ship is one of the great floating playgrounds for young, active adults who enjoy constant stimulation, close contact with lots and lots of others, as well as the three Gs – glitz, glamour and gambling. It is a live board game with every move executed in typically grand, colorful, fun-filled Carnival Cruise Lines style. It is a fine vessel for large incentive groups.

Potential passengers of other nationalities should note that this is definitely an all-American experience and product, with all its attendant glitz and jazzy/rock sounds – a real "life on the ocean rave." Forget fashion – having fun is the *sine qua non* of a Carnival cruise.

Sister ships include *Carnival Triumph* and *Carnival Triumph*, with *Carnival Conquest* also set to join the fleet in late 2002. Gratuities are automatically added to your onboard account at $9.75 per person, per day (the amount charged when this book was completed); you can have this amount adjusted, although you'll have to visit the information desk to do so. The onboard currency is the US dollar.

WEAK POINTS: The terraced pool deck is really cluttered, and there are no cushioned pads for the deck chairs. Although the outdoor deck space has been improved, there is still much crowding when the ship is full and at sea. Getting away from people and noise is extremely difficult. The Photo Gallery becomes extremely congested when photos are on display. Standing in line for embarkation, disembarkation, shore tenders and for self-serve buffet meals is an inevitable aspect of cruising aboard all large ships.

There is absolutely no escape from unnecessary and repetitious announcements (particularly for activities that bring revenue, such as art auctions, bingo, horse racing) that intrude constantly into your cruise, and a great deal of hustling for drinks, although it is sometimes done with a knowing smile.

Now Saga Ruby.

Caronia
★★★★

MO ✓

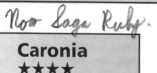

Mid-Size Ship: ....24,492 tons	Passengers	Cabin Current: ....110 volts
Lifestyle: ....Premium	(lower beds/all berths): 679/732	Elevators: 6
Cruise Line: ....Cunard Line	Passenger Space Ratio	Casino (gaming tables): ....Yes
Former Names: ....Vistafjord	(lower beds/all berths): 36.0/33.4	Slot Machines: ....Yes
Builder: ....Swan, Hunter (UK)	Crew/Passenger Ratio	Swimming Pools (outdoors): 1
Original Cost: ....$35 million	(lower beds/all berths): 1.6/1.8	Swimming Pools (indoors): 1
Entered Service: ....May 1973/May 1984	Navigation Officers: ....British	Whirlpools: 2
Registry: ....Great Britain	Cabins (total): 376	Fitness Center: ....Yes
Length (ft/m): 626.9/191.09	Size Range (sq ft/m): 66.7–871.9/	Sauna/Steam Room: ....Yes/No
Beam (ft/m): 82.1/25.05	6.2–81.0	Massage:..........................Yes
Draft (ft/m): 27.0/8.23		Self-Service Launderette: ....Yes
Propulsion/Propellers: ....diesel	Cabins (outside view): 324	Dedicated Cinema/Seats: Yes/190
(17,900kW)/2	Cabins (interior/no view): 52	Library: ....Yes
Passenger Decks: 9	Cabins (for one person): 73	Classification Society: ...Lloyd's Register
Total Crew: 400	Cabins (with private balcony): 25	
	Cabins (wheelchair accessible): 4	

OVERALL SCORE: 1,494 (OUT OF A POSSIBLE 2,000 POINTS)

ACCOMMODATION: According to the brochure, there are 16 cabin categories (four of which are for single travelers wanting a cabin for themselves), from duplex penthouse suites with huge private balconies, to small interior (no view) cabins, in a wide range of different configurations.

The grandest accommodation can be found in two duplex apartments (Caronia Suite and Saxonia Suite). They are really excellent living spaces and occupy two levels. The lower level features a large bedroom and marble-clad bathroom with Jacuzzi bathtub. The upper level features an expansive living room with floor-to-ceiling windows with expansive, unobstructed front and side views, Bang & Olufsen sound system, treadmill, private bar, and a large bathroom (with Jacuzzi bathtub) and separate private sauna. There is a huge, very private balcony outdoors on deck, complete with a two-person hot tub, a teak deck, and great views. A private internal stairway connects the upper and lower levels.

Most other accommodation designated as suites (on Bridge Deck lower level, and Sun Deck) have private balconies are nicely equipped, and have ample closet and drawer space (some also have a large walk-in closet), vanity desk, large beds, and a couple of bookshelves filled with suitable destination books. The marble-clad bathrooms are large and feature a full-sized Jacuzzi bathtub, two washbasins, toilet and bidet.

All other cabins are very well appointed and tastefully redecorated, (all had new bathrooms installed in a 1994 refit), and all feature a refrigerator, mini-bar, personal safe, European duvets (in two thicknesses), and

BERLITZ'S RATINGS		
	Possible	Achieved
Ship	500	370
Accommodation	200	159
Food	400	300
Service	400	310
Entertainment	100	71
Cruise	400	284

thick 100 percent cotton bathrobes. All the wooden furniture has nicely rounded edges. All feature a good amount of closet and drawer space (the closets are illuminated), VCR. The bathrooms feature a whisper-quiet (non-vacuum) toilet.

This ship also has an excellent range of cabins for single travelers (unlike most new ships). Some Sun Deck and Promenade Deck suites have obstructed views. But the smallest cabins really are quite small, with little room to move around.

DINING: The Franconia Dining Room is elegant (although it doesn't have quite the grandeur, high ceiling or grand stairway of sister ship *Saga Rose*), and has been expanded for single-seating dining at assigned tables. There are tables for two, four, six or eight (there are more tables for two than aboard most other cruise ships, the company having recognized that many passengers are single).

Senior officers often host a table for dinner. Single-waiter service is provided in the best European tradition. The tables are a little close together, making it hard for waiters to serve properly in some areas.

An international range of menu items is provided, with a reasonably high standard of quality and variety of ingredients (there is a decent variety of breads at every meal, although the selection is not as good as it used to be). A cold table is set for such things as breads and cheeses at lunchtime, and passengers can help themselves or be served. Salad items, many salad dressings, juices, and cheeses (a selection of more than 40 international cheeses) are always available.

Plate service (where vegetables and entrées are set artistically on the main course plate) is provided. Extra vegetables can always be obtained on request. This is European-style service in the classic seagoing tradition. Waiters are well trained through a good onboard management structure. Although tableside flambeaus cannot be performed at individual tables, they are done in a central location, and waiters collect the finished product to take to their respective tables.

Although the chef has his favorites, menus are not repeated, even on long voyages. Also, one good point about this and other ships in its class (four stars) is that, while the menus are creative, you can order "off-menu" occasionally. Little touches in presentation, such as paper doilies under teacups, soup bowls, and towel-wrapped water jugs put this ahead of some of the more standard cruise products available today.

Apart from the regular menu (typically several appetizers, two or three soups, sorbet, five entrées, two salads, several desserts, and a small selection of international cheeses at every dinner), there is a "light eating" option menu, a vegetarian menu, as well as daily diabetic desserts. Once per cruise a White Star Line menu is recreated in a salute to the past history of the Cunard-White Star Line.

There is a decent wine list with a good selection, and prices typically range from $13 to almost $400. Cappuccino and espresso coffees are available at any time in the dining room, at no charge.

ALTERNATIVE (RESERVATIONS REQUIRED) RESTAURANT: Tivoli is the name of a delightful 40-seat Italian à la carte restaurant (an alternative non-smoking dining spot that is located in what was formerly the upper level of the nightclub) that is elegant and very intimate, and the cuisine (featuring Northern Italian items) is excellent, from a varied menu that features many special dishes daily. It has the feel of a small, exclusive bistro. A tea/coffee station is available 24 hours a day (a machine provides espresso and cappuccino coffees).

CASUAL EATERY: The Lido Deck Cafe is a popular informal dining area with a wide range of self-service buffets that have a different theme daily, as well as for breakfast and lunch. However, lines do develop because both hot and cold items are typically displayed together. Note that when the Lido Deck buffet is in operation, passengers take food into the main lounge, as there are simply not enough tables available. Depending on the type of food provided, the smell often lingers.

OTHER COMMENTS: This ship has classic liner styling and profile, and really does *look* like a ship. This is a finely proportioned vessel, with delightful, rounded, flowing lines, a sleek profile with a good line of sheer, and a large funnel amidships. Following an extensive refit in 1999, the ship changed its name from *Vistafjord* to *Caronia* (the third Cunard ship to bear the name, the

first two being in 1905 and 1947). The royal blue hull shows off the strong, balanced lines, while the profile is further balanced by the orange-red funnel. The ship was built with excellent quality materials, has been well maintained, is smooth and quiet in operation, and a very stable ship at sea (due to its deep draft). Each day, the ship's bell is sounded at noon in fine maritime tradition.

The open decks and sunbathing space are expansive. There is a good teak wrap-around promenade deck outdoors, and the deck lounge chairs have cushioned pads (it's a good place to rest, relax, and read a good book).

Inside, the spacious and elegant public rooms – most of which are located on one deck (Veranda Deck) – have high ceilings and tasteful decor. It's easy to find one's way around, and the ship has an instant homely feel to it. The wide interior stairwells are subtly illuminated. The Garden Lounge is at the front of this deck; behind it the Movie Theater, then the Ballroom (show lounge) and the Lido Café. There's also a library and business center, with several computers and a credit-card operated fax machine, and a small casino.

The ballroom doubles as the ship's show lounge, and it has a fine, large, wooden dance floor, as well as a big band for ballroom dancing (however, at lunchtime, passengers do tend to spill over into it while eating food taken from the Lido Café, which rather ruins the ambience). The ship features conservative, sophisticated, classically oriented entertainment. Few international ships of this size can compete with this ship for the relaxing ambience and service from a well-organized and happy crew. There are refreshingly few announcements and interruptions.

This ship caters best to discerning passengers in a refined, yet friendly manner and with very comfortable surroundings for adults (there any no facilities for children). The ship features good service from a mix or European and Filipino staff. Dance hosts are provided for the many single ladies among the passengers.

Although not shiny and new, the ship has been well cared for, and provides a pleasant, almost gracious and civilized travel experience. The deep discounting that followed the slump in travel after September 2001's terrorist attacks has meant cutbacks and a reduction of the former high standards (the score reflects the cutbacks). The onboard currency is the British pound.

WEAK POINTS: When the ship is full, as is often the case under Cunard Line's new owners (Carnival Corporation), some crowding is evident (the staff is less stressed when there is an occupancy level of 80–90 percent). The Lido Cafe is simply too small, with less than enough seating, so the main lounge becomes an extension of it. Unfortunately, as a result of the recent cost-cutting measures, the standard of product delivery has suffered, and some menu and food items (such as the cheese selection, and a reduction in the number of appetizers and soups featured) have unfortunately been reduced. Passengers do notice such things.

Carousel
★★★

Removed 2006

Large Ship: ....23,149 tons	Passengers	Cabin Current: ....110 volts
Lifestyle: ....Standard	(lower beds/all berths): 1,050/1,158	Elevators: 4
Cruise Line: ......Sun Cruises/My Travel	Passenger Space Ratio	Casino (gaming tables): ....Yes
Former Names: ...._Nordic Prince_	(lower beds/all berths): 22.0/19.9	Slot Machines: ....Yes
Builder: ....Wartsila (Finland)	Crew/Passenger Ratio	Swimming Pools (outdoors): 1
Original Cost: ....$13.5 million	(lower beds/all berths): 2.6/2.8	Swimming Pools (indoors): 0
Entered Service: ....July 1971/May 1995	Navigation Officers: ....International	Whirlpools: 0
Registry: ....The Bahamas	Cabins (total): 525	Fitness Center: ....Yes
Length (ft/m): 637.5/194.32	Size Range (sq ft/m): 119.4–482.2/	Sauna/Steam Room: ....Yes/No
Beam (ft/m): 78.8/24.03	11.1–44.8	Massage: ....Yes
Draft (ft/m): 21.9/6.70	Cabins (outside view): 340	Self-Service Launderette: ....No
Propulsion/Propellers: ....diesel	Cabins (interior/no view): 185	Dedicated Cinema/Seats: ....No
(13,400kW)/2	Cabins (for one person): 0	Library: ....Yes
Passenger Decks: 7	Cabins (with private balcony): 0	Classification Society: ....Det Norske
Total Crew: 400	Cabins (wheelchair accessible): 0	Veritas

OVERALL SCORE: 1,226 (OUT OF A POSSIBLE 2,000 POINTS)

ACCOMMODATION: The cabins are split into just four price grades (Standard, Superior, Promenade and Deluxe) and six types, making it an easy matter to select the type of accommodation you want.

Most cabins are of a similar size (dimensionally challenged comes to mind for most of them) and the insulation between them is quite poor, but do remember that this ship is now over 20 years old. The cabins also have mediocre closets and very little storage space, yet somehow everyone seems to manage (the ship was built originally for Caribbean cruising). They really are adequate for a one-week cruise, as you will need only casual clothes, and, with these destination-intensive cruises, you really will not need many clothes anyway (shoes can always go under the bed).

The bathrooms are very small (they are best described as functional rather than attractive), and the showers have a curtain you will probably need to dance with (larger than average persons may well become frustrated quickly).

The best advice I can give you, therefore, is to take only casual clothing and restrict your packing to the things you really need. Do note that cabin voltage is 110 volts (American two flat-pin sockets are provided), so you may need to take adapters for electrical appliances such as a hairdryer. Note also that, in the past, cabins were not assigned until you arrived at the ship; however, now you *can* book the cabin you want; an extra charge of £50 *per cabin* will be applied for this privilege, which also grants you the right to choose

whether you want to dine at the early or late seating for dinner.

Only the owner's suite contains a refrigerator.

DINING: The dining room, which operates in two seatings, is large, but noisy, and the tables (for four, six or eight) are close together. The catering operation is quite good, however, although all the food seems to taste alike. There is a limited selection of breads, cheeses and fruits. Attentive, friendly but rather frenzied service is normal (particularly for those in the first seating).

So, what's the food like? In a nutshell – it's basic, no-frills cuisine – acceptable for those who don't expect much in the way of presentation or quality, but certainly not memorable. There is plenty of it, however; indeed, it is quantity, not quality, that prevails – but do remember that it is all provided at a low cost – as is a cruise aboard this ship, compared to more expensive cruise products. Presentation is a weak point, and there are no fish knives. So, it's best to remember that, like anything in life, you get what you pay for. If you enjoy going out to eat, and enjoy being adventurous with your food and eating habits, you could be disappointed. There is an adequate, but limited, wine list, and the wines are almost all very young – typical of those you might find in your local supermarket. Wine prices are quite modest, as are the prices for most alcoholic beverages. The same glasses are used for both red and white wines, and they are small.

OTHER COMMENTS: This ship, originally built for and operated by Royal Caribbean International, has a fairly handsome, contemporary look with good lines, a nicely raked bow, and large red funnel. The side of the all-white ship has the company's new corporate logo (My Travel) painted on the side. It was acquired by Sun Cruises/My Travel (one of the UK's "Big Three" tour companies) in 1995. The company provides an activity-filled cruise product in comfortable, but fairly busy surroundings. The ship underwent a $7 million refit in late 1997. While most of the work was below decks, with the fitting of new, better, more powerful generators, some cosmetic work was completed in its interiors.

There is a good, polished wrap-around promenade deck outdoors (it can be slippery when wet) and wooden railings. The open deck space for sunbathing is very crowded and noisy when the ship is full (which is most of the time), but makes for a good party ambience.

The interior layout and passenger flow is sound, with clean, bright decor and some good wooden paneling and trim. The dress code is very casual, good for unstuffy, unpretentious cruising. This is a very affordable cruise, particularly for families with children, and Airtours also has a wide selection of pre- and post-cruise hotel programs. Note, however, that Sun Cruises does not actively market or specialize in cruises for families with children, and the children's/youth facilities are limited (and there is no evening babysitting service for youngsters).

Airtours is known for packaging its products really well, and this ship represents an excellent buy for families who want to cruise, but on a limited budget. Also, if you want a little more than the basics, Sun Cruises/My Travel offers special packages – good for celebrating something special. There are four options: bronze, silver, gold and platinum, with each adding a little extra cost. Want to meet the captain? Go for gold or platinum and you get breakfast in bed with champagne, flowers, fruit basket, and dinner at the captain's table.

Airtours has its own fleet of aircraft, and this is one reason that the company is able to offer complete cruise-air-stay packages at such low rates. Sun Cruises/My Travel does a fine job in getting you and your luggage from airplane to ship without your having to go through immigration in foreign countries whenever possible (this does depend on the itinerary and operational region) – so your cruise vacation is as seamless as it can be.

Sun Cruises/My Travel brochures tell it like it is – so you know before you go exactly what you will get for your money, with the exception of its claim to "first-class food," which is a gross exaggeration. If you want just the basics, you pay the least amount. If you want all the goodies – a wider "premium" seat with extra leg room on your Airtours aircraft, the right to choose your own cabin and dinner seating, breakfast in bed, and dinner with the captain – then you'll pay for all those "privileges." Note that, however you choose to cruise, all gratuities are included. Insurance is also included (but you will be charged for it) unless you decline it on the booking form. The onboard currency is the British pound.

The company will fly you to and from the ship in one of its own modern jet aircraft, and all transfers to/from the ship, are included for good measure. The company really does go out of its way to provide a fine "no-nonsense" good value-for-money vacation, as long as your expectations are not too high. This is *not* the ship if you are looking for a quiet and relaxing vacation. If you have been on a land-based Airtours vacation, you'll know what to expect.

WEAK POINTS: Standing in line for embarkation, disembarkation, shore tenders and for self-serve buffet meals is an inevitable aspect of cruising aboard all large ships. There are many announcements. The accommodation deck hallways are very narrow. Many seats in the show lounge have poor sight lines, obstructed by several pillars. Like the other ships in the fleet, the space per passenger (particularly on the open decks) is very tight when the ship is full (which is most of the time). The cabin televisions are extremely small (except for those in the suites). Note that couples traveling without children may well be surrounded by large number of children during the summer months – and, thus, increased noise levels. The food is of a low quality when compared to many other ships, and the presentation could be improved. There is little choice of tea and coffee. There are no cushioned pads for the deck lounge chairs.

Celebration
★★★ +

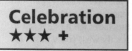

Large Ship:	47,262 tons	Passengers	
Lifestyle:	Standard	(lower beds/all berths):	1,486/1,896
Cruise Line:	Carnival Cruise Lines	Passenger Space Ratio	
Former Names:	none	(lower beds/all berths):	31.8/24.9
Builder:	Kockums (Sweden)	Crew/Passenger Ratio	
Original Cost:	$130 million	(lower beds/all berths):	2.2/2.8
Entered Service:	Mar 1987	Navigation Officers:	Italian
Registry:	Panama	Cabins (total):	743
Length (ft/m):	732.6/223.30	Size Range (sq ft/m):	184.0/17.1
Beam (ft/m):	92.5/28.20	Cabins (outside view):	453
Draft (ft/m):	25.5/7.80	Cabins (interior/no view):	290
Propulsion/Propellers:	diesel	Cabins (for one person):	0
	(23,520kW)/2	Cabins (with private balcony):	10
Passenger Decks:	10	Cabins (wheelchair accessible):	14
Total Crew:	670	Cabin Current:	110 volts

Elevators:	8
Casino (gaming tables):	Yes
Slot Machines:	Yes
Swimming Pools (outdoors):	3
Swimming Pools (indoors):	0
Whirlpools:	2
Fitness Center:	Yes
Sauna/Steam Room:	Yes/No
Massage:	Yes
Self-Service Launderette:	Yes
Dedicated Cinema/Seats:	No
Library:	Yes
Classification Society:	Lloyd's Register

OVERALL SCORE: 1,318 (OUT OF A POSSIBLE 2,000 POINTS)

ACCOMMODATION: This ship has a range of suites, outside-view and interior (no view) cabins. The cabins are quite standard and mostly identical in terms of layout and decor (which means they are good for large groups who generally like to have identical cabins for their participants), are of fairly generous proportions, except for the interior (no view) cabins, which are quite small. They are reasonably comfortable and well equipped, but are nothing special. A gift basket is provided in all grades of accommodation; it includes aloe soap, shampoo, conditioner, deodorant, breath mints, candy, and pain relief tablets (albeit all in sample sizes).

The best accommodation is in the 10 suites, each of which has more space, its own private balcony, a larger bathroom and more closet, drawer and storage space.

Note that if you book accommodation in one of the suites (Category 11 or 12 in the Carnival Cruise Lines brochure) you automatically qualify for "Skipper's Club" priority check-in at any US homeland port – useful for getting ahead of the crowd.

DINING: There are two dining rooms (Horizon and Vista). They are quite cramped when full, and extremely noisy (both are non-smoking), and they have low ceilings in the raised sections of their centers. There are tables are for four, six or eight (there are no tables for two). The décor is bright and extremely colorful, to say the least. Dining is now in four seatings, for greater flexibility: 6pm, 6.45pm, 8pm and 8.45pm (times are approximate).

BERLITZ'S RATINGS

	Possible	Achieved
Ship	500	355
Accommodation	200	143
Food	400	221
Service	400	275
Entertainment	100	74
Cruise	400	250

Carnival meals stress quantity, not quality, although the company constantly works hard to improve its cuisine. While passengers seem to accept it, few find it especially memorable. However, food and its taste are still not the company's strongest points (you get what you pay for, remember).

While the menu items sound good, their presentation and taste leave much to be desired. While meats are of a high quality, fish and seafood is not. Presentation is simple, and few garnishes are used. Many meat and fowl dishes are disguised with gravies and sauces. The selection of fresh green vegetables, breads, rolls, cheeses and fruits is limited, and there is too much use of canned fruit and jellied desserts. However, do remember that this is banquet catering, with all its attendant standardization and production cooking (it is, therefore, difficult to ask for anything remotely unusual or off-menu). The selection of breads, rolls, cheeses and fruits is limited (there is too much use of canned fruit).

Although there is a decent wine list, there are no wine waiters and so the regular waiters are expected to serve both food and wine. The service is highly programmed, although the waiters are willing and reasonably friendly. However, the waiters do sing and dance (be prepared for *Simply the Best, Hot, Hot, Hot, Hot,* and other popular hits), and there are constant waiter parades; the dining room is show business – all done in the name of gratuities at the end of your cruise.

Casual meals can be taken as self-serve buffets in the

Wheelhouse Bar & Grill, although the foods provided are very basic, and quite disappointing, with much repetition (particularly for breakfast) and little variety. At night, the "Seaview Bistro," as the Lido Café is known, provides a casual (dress down) alternative to eating in the main dining rooms, serving pasta, steaks, salads and desserts (it typically is in operation from 6pm to 9pm).

OTHER COMMENTS: *Celebration* is the fourth new ship for this very successful cruise line. The ship's exterior is rather angular, but typical of the space-conscious designs that were introduced in the early 1980s, particularly by Carnival Cruise Lines, in an effort to maximize interior (revenue generating) space. The ship, whose bows are extremely short, has the distinctive, large, swept-back wing-tipped funnel that is Carnival's trademark, in the company colors of red, white and blue. The swimming pools are smaller than one would expect, but the open deck space is good, provided the ship is not full – when, as with most ships, the deck always seems crowded.

Inside, this ship has double-width indoor promenades and a very good selection of public rooms in which to play. The flamboyant interior décor in public rooms is stimulating instead of relaxing, as is the colorful artwork. The interior décor theme is that of New Orleans throughout the public rooms, except for some nautical themes in the Wheelhouse Bar/Grill. There is a large, very active, and noisy casino.

The party atmosphere is good for anyone looking for a stimulating cruise experience. As is the case aboard all Carnival ships, there is a very wide range of entertainment and passenger participation activities from which to choose.

This ship is a floating playground for young, active adults who enjoy constant stimulation, close contact with lots and lots of others, as well as the three Gs – glitz, glamour and gambling. It is a live board game with every move executed in typically grand, colorful, fun-filled Carnival Cruise Lines style. This ship should prove a good choice for families with children (there are so many places for them to explore). There are entertaining dazzle and sizzle shows on stage, which are good for the whole family.

This ship is good if you are taking your first cruise, providing that you like lots of people, noise and lively action. Forget fashion – having fun is the *sine qua non* of a Carnival cruise. *Celebration* operates 4- and 5-day Western Caribbean cruises from Galveston.

Gratuities are automatically added to your onboard account at $9.75 per person, per day (the amount charged when this book was completed); you can have this amount adjusted, although you'll have to visit the information desk to do so. The onboard currency is the US dollar.

WEAK POINTS: There is absolutely no escape from unnecessary and repetitive announcements (particularly for activities that bring revenue, such as art auctions, bingo, horse racing. These intrude constantly into your cruise. There's a great deal of hustling for drinks, although it is sometimes done with a knowing smile. There really is nowhere to go for privacy, peace and quiet, but then you should choose another ship for that. Standing in line for embarkation, disembarkation, shore tenders and for self-serve buffet meals is an inevitable aspect of cruising aboard all large ships.

Century
★★★★ +

√ 08/09/05 Majorca

Large Ship:	70,606 tons	Passengers		Cabin Current:	110 and 220 volts
Lifestyle:	Premium	(lower beds/all berths):	1,750/2,150	Elevators:	9
Cruise Line:	Celebrity Cruises	Passenger Space Ratio		Casino (gaming tables):	Yes
Former Names:	none	(lower beds/all berths):	40.3/32.8	Slot Machines:	Yes
Builder:	Meyer Werft (Germany)	Crew/Passenger Ratio		Swimming Pools (outdoors):	2
Original Cost:	$320 million	(lower beds/all berths):	2.0/2.5	Swimming Pools (indoors):	1 hydropool
Entered Service:	Dec 1995	Navigation Officers:	Greek	Whirlpools:	4
Registry:	The Bahamas	Cabins (total):	875	Fitness Center:	Yes
Length (ft/m):	807.1/246.0	Size Range (sq ft/m):	168.9–1,514.5/	Sauna/Steam Room:	Yes/Yes
Beam (ft/m):	105.6/32.2		15.7–140.7	Massage:	Yes
Draft (ft/m):	24.6/7.5	Cabins (outside view):	569	Self-Service Launderette:	No
Propulsion/Propellers:	diesel	Cabins (interior/no view):	306	Dedicated Cinema/Seats:	Yes/190
	(29,250kW)/2	Cabins (for one person):	0	Library:	Yes
Passenger Decks:	10	Cabins (with private balcony):	61	Classification Society:	Lloyd's Register
Total Crew:	858	Cabins (wheelchair accessible):	8		

OVERALL SCORE: 1,663 (OUT OF A POSSIBLE 2,000 POINTS)

ACCOMMODATION: The wide variety of cabin types includes 18 family cabins, each with two lower beds, two foldaway beds and one upper berth. All cabins have wood cabinetry and accenting, hairdryers in the bathrooms, 100 percent cotton towels, and interactive television and entertainment systems (you can shop, book shore excursions or play casino games interactively in English, German, French, Italian or Spanish). However, the standard 24-hour cabin menu is disappointing, and very limited. There are no cabins for single occupancy.

All cabins feature a personal safe, mini-bar/refrigerator (there is a charge if you use anything, of course) and are nicely equipped and decorated, with warm wood-finish furniture, and none of the boxy feel of cabins in many ships, due to the angled placement of vanity and audio-video consoles at an angle. In addition, all suites on Deck 10 (and the Sky Deck suites on Deck 12) feature butler service and in-cabin dining facilities. Suites that have private balconies also have floor-to-ceiling windows and sliding doors to balconies (a few have outward opening doors).

For the ultimate in accommodation, choose one of two beautifully decorated Presidential Suites, each 1,173 sq. ft (109 sq. meters). These are located amidships in the most desirable position (each can be combined with the adjacent mini-suite via an inter-connecting door, to provide a living space of 1,515 sq. ft (140.7 sq. meters). Each has a marble-floored foyer, a living room with mahogany wood floor and hand-woven rug. Other features include a separate dining area with six-seat dining table; butler's

BERLITZ'S RATINGS

	Possible	Achieved
Ship	500	444
Accommodation	200	177
Food	400	315
Service	400	319
Entertainment	100	78
Cruise	400	330

pantry with wet bar; a wine bar with private label stock, refrigerator and microwave. There is a large private balcony with dining table for two, chaise lounge chairs with cushioned pads, hot tub and dimmer-controlled lighting; master bedroom with king-sized bed, dressed with fine fabrics and draperies, Egyptian cotton bed linen, and walk-in closet with abundant storage space. The all-marble bathroom has a jet-spray shower and whirlpool bath.

All accommodation designated as suites feature European duvets instead of sheets/blankets, fresh flowers, VCR, use of the AquaSpa without charge, and butler service. Electrically operated blinds and other goodies are also standard in some suites.

DINING: A grand staircase connects the upper and lower levels of the splendid two-level Grand Dining Room. Huge windows overlook the stern (electrically operated blinds feature several different backdrops). Each of the two levels has a separate finishing galley. There are two seatings for dinner (open seating for breakfast and lunch), at tables for two, four, six, eight or 10. The dining room is a no-smoking area. The design of the two galleys is excellent, and is such that food that should be hot *does* arrive hot at the table. Three different decorative panels, changed according to theme nights, adorn the huge aft windows. The dining room chairs, which are heavy, should, but do not, have armrests.

All meals, including full dinners, can be served, course-by-course, in all suites and cabins, no matter what accommodation grade you choose. For those who can't live without them, freshly baked pizzas (boxed) can be delivered, in an insulated pouch, to cabins.

Celebrity Cruises has established an enviable reputation for fine dining aboard its ships, and this tradition is being continued. Michel Roux designs the line's menus and exerts tight personal control over their correct cooking and delivery to assure consistency of product. All meals are made from scratch, with nothing pre-cooked or pre-packaged ashore. However, the food served as room-service items is decidedly below the standard of food featured in the dining room.

There is also a large indoor/outdoor Lido café ("Islands") with four separate self-service buffet lines, as well as two-grill serving stations located adjacent to the swimming pools outdoors.

COVA CAFÉ DI MILANO: The Cova Café di Milano is a signature item aboard all the ships of Celebrity Cruises, and a seagoing version of the real Café di Milano originally located next to La Scala Opera House in Milan (it opened in 1817). It is placed in a prominent position, on the second level of the atrium lobby, and several display cases show off the extensive range of Cova coffee, chocolates and alcoholic digestives; this is *the* place to see and be seen. It is a delightful setting (and meeting place) for those who appreciate fine Italian coffees (for espresso, espresso macchiato, cappuccino, latte), pastries and superb cakes in an elegant, refined setting.

OTHER COMMENTS: This ship, which looks externally like a larger version of the company's popular *Horizon/Zenith*, is quite well balanced despite its squared-off stern. It has the distinctive Celebrity Cruises' "X" funnel ("X" being the Greek letter "C" which stands for Chandris, the former owning company). With a high passenger space ratio for such a large ship, there is no real sense of crowding, and the passenger flow is very good. A high crew/passenger ratio of 1:1.9 provides a sound basis for good passenger service.

The interior decor is elegant and understated. Technical and engineering excellence prevails, and there is overindulgence in fire and safety equipment. This is a contemporary ship, with fine public rooms, and an array of Sony television and video screens in many of them. The medical facilities are also excellent.

There is a three-quarter, two-level teak wood promenade deck, and a wrap-around jogging track atop the ship. A stunning, two-level, 1,000-seat show lounge/theater with side balconies features a huge stage, a split orchestra pit (hydraulic), and the latest in high-tech lighting and sound equipment.

One wall of the three-deck-high main foyer (atrium) has nine large television screens providing constantly changing scenery. The atrium is not glitzy, but its décor somehow doesn't closely match the rest of the ship.

There are 4.5 acres (1.8 hectares) of open deck space, together with a fine array of other public rooms and enhanced passenger facilities. An outstanding AquaSpa that measures (9,340 sq ft /870 sq. meters), located forward and high, has some of the more unusual wellness treatments (including a steamy Rasul room), with large panoramic windows and the latest high-tech equipment, all set in a calming environment, complete with shoji screens and Japanese-inspired rock garden.

Wide passageways provide plenty of indoor space for strolling, so there's no feeling of being crowded, and passenger flow is excellent. In fact, the ship absorbs passengers really well. A small, dedicated cinema also doubles as a conference and meeting center with all the latest audio-visual technology.

Cigar smokers will love Michael's Club – a cigar and cognac room of superb taste; a lovely triangular-shaped room, it has become a favorite watering place for those who smoke, with large comfortable chairs and the feel of a real gentlemen's club. Features include a cigar humidor, and a choice of almost 20 different cigars. Those who like gambling will find that the ship's large casino is tightly packed with slot machines and gaming tables, and even has a satellite-linked ATM machine.

Outstanding are the 500 pieces of art that adorn the ship – a $3.8 million art collection that includes many Warhol favorites and some fascinating contemporary sculptures (look for the colored violins on Deck Seven). The "Century Collection" includes a comprehensive survey of the most important artists and the major developments in art since the 1960s, and embraces Abstract Expressionism, Pop, Conceptualism, Minimalism and Neo-Expressionism.

Overall, *Century* is a fine vessel for a big-ship cruise vacation, although some wear and tear and sloppy maintenance show in some areas, although general cleanliness is excellent. There are few announcements. A 15 percent gratuity is automatically added to all bar and wine accounts. The onboard currency is the US dollar.

During the past two years (after Celebrity Cruises was bought by Royal Caribbean International), standards aboard all the ships in the fleet dropped as cuts were made by its new parent. However, as this book was being completed, new management was brought in to bring Celebrity Cruises back to the premium product that was envisioned when the company first started.

WEAK POINTS: Although this is a beautiful ship, the shore excursion operation, embarkation and disembarkation remain weak links in the Celebrity Cruises operation, and the cruise staff is unpolished and has little finesse. Standing in line for embarkation, disembarkation, shore tenders and for self-serve buffet meals is an inevitable aspect of cruising aboard all large ships. The room service menu is poor, and room service food items are below the standard of food featured in the dining room. The inter-active TV system is frustrating to use, and the larger suites have three remotes for TV/audio equipment (one would be better). The officers have become more aloof lately, with far less contact with passengers than in the company's early days.

Clelia II
★★★★

Removed 2006

Small Ship:	...............4,077 tons	
Lifestyle:	...................Premium	
Cruise Line:	.........Golden Sea Cruises	
Former Names:	.......*Renaissance Four*	
Builder:	.....Cantieri Navale Ferrari (Italy)	
Original Cost:	..............$20 million	
Entered Service:	.....Jan 1991/Mar 1998	
Registry:	................The Bahamas	
Length (ft/m):	..............289.0/88.1	
Beam (ft/m):	.................50.1/15.3	
Draft (ft/m):	....................13.4/4.1	
Propulsion/Propellers:	...........diesel	
	(3,514kW)/2	
Passenger Decks:	5	
Total Crew:	55	

Passengers
(lower beds/all berths): 84/84
Passenger Space Ratio
(lower beds/all berths): 48.5/48.5
Crew/Passenger Ratio
(lower beds/all berths): 1.5/1.5
Navigation Officers: ....Greek
Cabins (total): 42
Size Range (sq ft/m): 210.0–538.2/
19.5–50.0
Cabins (outside view): 42
Cabins (interior/no view): 0
Cabins (for one person): 0
Cabins (with private balcony): 4
Cabins (wheelchair accessible): 0

Cabin Current: ....110 volts
Elevators: 1
Casino (gaming tables): ....No
Slot Machines: ....No
Swimming Pools (outdoors): 1
Swimming Pools (indoors): 0
Whirlpools: 1
Fitness Center: ....Yes
Sauna/Steam Room: ....No/Yes
Massage: ....No
Self-Service Launderette: ....No
Dedicated Cinema/Seats: ....No
Library: ....Yes
Classification Society: . . .Lloyd's Register

OVERALL SCORE: 1,546 (OUT OF A POSSIBLE 2,000 POINTS)

ACCOMMODATION: Fine all-outside-view cabins (called "suites" in the brochure) combine highly polished imitation rosewood paneling with lots of mirrors, and fine, hand crafted Italian furniture. All suites have twin beds that can convert to a queen-sized bed, a sitting area with three-person sofa, one individual chair, coffee table, mini-bar/refrigerator (all drinks are at extra cost), color television and VCR, and direct-dial satellite telephone. Note that while closet space is good, space for stowing luggage is tight, and there is little drawer space (each cabin has three drawers, two of which are lockable, plus several open shelves in a separate closet).

Also note that there are no music channels in the cabins, and there is no switch which will turn off announcements off in your cabin.

The number of cabins was reduced from 50 to 42 when the present owners acquired the vessel in 1997, thus providing more space per passenger. Outside each cabin are two brass porthole-shaped lights, which provide a stately, nautical feel to the dark wood-paneled hallways.

The marble bathrooms are compact units that have showers (no bathrooms have a bathtub) with fold-down (plastic) seat, real teakwood floor, marble vanity, large mirror, recessed towel rail (good for storing personal toiletries), and built-in hairdryer. Note: there is a high "lip" into the bathroom.

There are also four VIP "apartments," each consisting of two consecutive adjoining "suites," thus providing a bedroom, large lounge (with red-leather topped office desk), and two bathrooms (his 'n' hers).

BERLITZ'S RATINGS	Possible	Achieved
Ship	500	396
Accommodation	200	168
Food	400	309
Service	400	327
Entertainment	100	57
Cruise	400	289

There is one Presidential Apartment (owner's suite) with an en-suite office, two full separate bedrooms and living room (each with three windows), two bathrooms, and private, though narrow, balcony.

DINING: The Golden Star Restaurant, which has an open seating policy (it can seat up to 100), is bright, elegant and welcoming (non-smoking). It is on the lowest deck and has portholes rather than windows, due to maritime regulations. There are tables for two, four, six, or eight, and you can sit where you like, with whom you like, when you like, in this open seating arrangement. Dinners are normally sit-down affairs — although, depending on the itinerary and length of cruise, there could be an occasional buffet. Breakfast and lunch are usually buffets and can be taken at the poolside (weather permitting), in your suite, or in the restaurant.

The cuisine consists of continental dishes complemented by local (regional) delicacies. The food quality, choice and presentation are all good. While the food is very well presented, the choice of entrées is limited to three for dinner.

OTHER COMMENTS: *Clelia II*, with its royal blue hull and white superstructure, has the look and feel of a contemporary mega-yacht, with handsome styling throughout, although the exterior profile is not particularly handsome. There are two teakwood wrap-around promenade decks outdoors. There is a watersports platform at the stern, and a "Baby Clelia" water jet-propelled shore tender hangs over the stern. The ship also carries jet skis, water-ski boat and sailfish for use when cruising in warm weather areas.

The accommodation is located forward, with public rooms aft. Features pleasing colors and refined and attractive interior décor, with some accents based on Greek design. There is a small library, which also houses the video library, a lounge that can accommodate all passengers (good for use as a lecture room), and a piano bar/lounge.

Originally one of a fleet of eight similar-sized ships operated by Renaissance Cruises, this ship was very nicely refurbished for service in early 1998. Greek artists are featured in many pieces of art around the ship, courtesy of the new owners. With its name change (the new name is also the name of the ship's owner), this charming little ship operates Greek Island cruises during most of the year. It is very comfortable and inviting, and is close

to – but not quite the equal of – some of the other small premium ships (but the price reflects this fact). It will provide you with a destination-intensive, refined, quiet and relaxed cruise, and suits those who don't like crowds, dressing up, scheduled activities, or entertainment.

The ship is often placed under charter to companies such as Abercrombie & Kent, Classical Cruises and other tour packagers for much of the year. No smoking is allowed anywhere inside the ship, only on open decks.

WEAK POINTS: The tiny "dip" pool is not a swimming pool. The open deck and sunbathing space is very limited. The décor consists of plastic woods instead of real woods (it looks almost too perfect in places). There are many slim pillars in the public rooms in odd places. The constant music ("acoustic wallpaper") played throughout the public spaces (including accommodation hallways) is irritating and unnecessary.

SYSTEM CONTROL

The sophisticated state-of-the-art machinery and navigation systems used in the latest generation of cruise ships are such technical marvels that sailors of yesteryear could not even conceive of their invention.

The latest navigation system, known as the "Electronic Chart Precise Integrated Navigation System" (ECPINS) combines the electronics of the latest satellite positioning methods (Global Positioning System) with automatic course plotting, video map displays of the oceans, gyrocompass, echo sounders, sonar Doppler log, wind speed, and various sensors to provide a comprehensive, at-a-glance display of the ship in relation to the rest of the world.

The Compass

This is the instrument by which a ship may be steered on a pre-elected course, and by which bearings of visible objects can be taken in order to fix a ship's position on a navigation chart. There are two kinds:

The magnetic compass uses the inherent magnetic forces within and around the Earth;

The gyrocompass, a relatively recent invention, uses the properties of gyroscopic inertia and precession, ideally to align itself to a true north-south position.

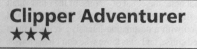

Clipper Adventurer
★★★

Small Ship:	.5,750 tons	Passengers		Cabin Current:	.220 volts	
Lifestyle:	Standard	(lower beds/all berths):	122/122	Elevators:	.0	
Cruise Line:	Clipper Cruise line	Passenger Space Ratio		Casino (gaming tables):	.No	
Former Names:	*Alla Tarasova*	(lower beds/all berths):	47.1/47.1	Slot Machines:	.No	
Builder:	Brodgradiliste Uljanik	Crew/Passenger Ratio		Swimming Pools (outdoors):	.No	
	(Yugoslavia)	(lower beds/all berths):	1.4/1.4	Swimming Pools (indoors):	.No	
Original Cost:	n/a	Navigation Officers:	European	Whirlpools:	.No	
Entered Service:	1976/Apr 1998	Cabins (total):	.61	Fitness Center:	.No	
Registry:	The Bahamas	Size Range (sq ft/m):	119.0–211.0/	Sauna/Steam Room:	Yes/No	
Length (ft/m):	.328.1/100.01		11.0–19.6	Massage:	.No	
Beam (ft/m):	.53.2/16.24	Cabins (outside view):	.61	Self-Service Launderette:	.No	
Draft (ft/m):	.15.2/4.65	Cabins (interior/no view):	.0	Dedicated Cinema/Seats:	.No	
Propulsion/Propellers: diesel (3,884kW)/2		Cabins (for one person):	.0	Library:	Yes	
Passenger Decks:	.5	Cabins (with private balcony):	.0	Classification Society:	Russian Shipping	
Total Crew:	.84	Cabins (wheelchair accessible):	.0		Register	

OVERALL SCORE: 1,175 (OUT OF A POSSIBLE 2,000 POINTS)

ACCOMMODATION: All cabins (there are seven grades, including a dedicated price for single cabin occupancy) have outside views and twin lower beds, with private bathroom with shower, and toilet. The bathrooms are really tiny, although they are tiled, and have all the basics. Several double-occupancy cabins can be booked by those traveling alone (but special rates apply). All cabins have a lockable drawer for valuables, telephone, and individual temperature control. Some have picture windows, while others have portholes. Two larger cabins (called suites in the brochure, which they really are not) are quite well equipped for the size of the vessel.

DINING: Pleasant, though with somewhat dark decor, the dining room, with deep ocean-view windows, seats all passengers at a single seating. The food is a combination of American and Continental cuisine, prepared freshly by chefs trained at some of America's finest culinary institutions. There are limited menu choices, but the food is wholesome, and simply and attractively presented, but certainly not gourmet. Young American waitresses serve the dining room service; their bubbly enthusiasm making up for their lack of finesse.

Casual, self-service breakfast and luncheon buffets are typically taken in the main lounge, as are cocktail-hour hors d'oeuvres and other snacks.

OTHER COMMENTS: *Clipper Adventurer* is a small ship – originally one of eight built for the Murmansk Shipping Company. It has an ice-strengthened (A-1 ice clas-

BERLITZ'S RATINGS		
	Possible	Achieved
Ship	500	292
Accommodation	200	120
Food	400	247
Service	400	242
Entertainment	100	40
Cruise	400	234

sification), and a royal blue hull and white funnel, bow-thruster and stabilizers. But, even with an ice classification, it got stuck in an ice field in the Bellingshausen Sea in 2000. Fortunately, the Argentine Navy icebreaker *Almirante Irizar* freed it.

The ship isn't new, but it had a $15 million refit/conversion in 1997–98, and meets international safety codes and requirements. It specializes in operating close-in expedition-style cruising. There are 10 Zodiac rubber inflatable landing craft for in-depth excursions, and a covered promenade deck.

This is a cozy ship and caters to travelers rather than mere passengers. The dress code is totally casual during the day, although at night many passengers wear jacket and tie. For trekking ashore, take long-sleeved garments.

The public spaces are a little limited, with just one main lounge and bar. There is a small library, with high wingback chairs, and a decent selection of books.

There is no observation lounge with forward-facing views, although there is an outdoor observation area directly below the bridge. Clipper Cruise Line provides its own cruise staff, and experienced historians and naturalist lecturers accompany all cruise expeditions.

Smoking *is* permitted only on the outside decks. Travel insurance is included in the cruise fare. The onboard currency is the US dollar.

WEAK POINTS: The passageways are narrow (it is difficult to pass housekeeping carts), and the stairs are steep on the outer decks. There is no observation lounge with forward-facing views.

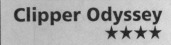

Clipper Odyssey
★★★★

Small Ship: . . . . .5,218 tons	Passengers	Cabin Current: . . . . .115 volts
Lifestyle: . . . . .Premium	(lower beds/all berths): 128/128	Elevators: 1
Cruise Line: . . . . .Clipper Cruise Line	Passenger Space Ratio	Casino (gaming tables): . . . . .No
Former Names: . . . . . . .Oceanic Odyssey,	(lower beds/all berths): 43.4/43.4	Slot Machines: .No
Oceanic Grace	Crew/Passenger Ratio	Swimming Pools (outdoors): 1
Builder: . . . . . . .NKK Tsu Shipyard (Japan)	(lower beds/all berths): 2.4/2.4	Swimming Pools (indoors): 0
Original Cost: . . . .$40 million	Navigation Officers: . . . . .European	Whirlpools: 1
Entered Service: . . . . . Apr 1989/Nov 1999	Cabins (total): .64	Fitness Center: . . . . .Yes
Registry: . . . . .The Bahamas	Size Range (sq ft/m): 182.9–258.3/	Sauna/Steam Room: . . . . .Yes/Yes
Length (ft/m): 337.5/102.9	17.0–24.0	Massage: . . . . .No
Beam (ft/m): 50.5/15.4	Cabins (outside view): 64	Self-Service Launderette: . . . . .No
Draft (ft/m): 14.1/4.3	Cabins (interior/no view): 0	Dedicated Cinema/Seats: . . . . .No
Propulsion/Propellers: diesel (5,192kW)/2	Cabins (for one person): 0	Library: . . . . .Yes
Passenger Decks: 5	Cabins (with private balcony): 8	Classification Society: . . . . . . .Nippon Kaiji
Total Crew: 52	Cabins (wheelchair accessible): 1	Kyokai

OVERALL SCORE: 1,451 (OUT OF A POSSIBLE 2,000 POINTS)

ACCOMMODATION: There are six categories of accommodation. This ship has all-outside cabins that are quite tastefully furnished and feature blond wood cabinetry, twin- or queen-sized beds, living area with sofa, personal safe, mini-bar/refrigerator, television and VCR, and three-sided mirror. All bathrooms feature a deep, half-sized bathtub. Cabins that have private balconies; however note that these are *very small*, almost token gesture balconies, and they have awkward door handles. You should note that the bathroom toilet seats are extremely high.

DINING: The dining room has large ocean view picture windows. It is quite warm and inviting, and all passengers eat in a single seating. The cuisine features fresh foods from local ports, in a mix of regional and some western cuisine, with open seating. A young, friendly American staff provides the service.

OTHER COMMENTS: *Clipper Odyssey* features impressive, though square, contemporary looks and sports twin outboard funnels. The ship was designed in Holland and built in Japan, originally as an attempt to copy the Sea Goddess concept for the Japanese market. There are expansive areas outdoors, considering the size of the

BERLITZ'S RATINGS

	Possible	Achieved
Ship	500	418
Accommodation	200	162
Food	400	271
Service	400	244
Entertainment	100	71
Cruise	400	285

ship – excellent for sunbathing or for spotting wildlife.

There is a decompression chamber for scuba divers, and water sports equipment is carried, as is a fleet of Zodiacs (inflatable landing craft for "soft" expedition use). There is an aft platform, scuba, snorkel, water-ski boat. There is plenty of open deck and sunbathing space. The small swimming pool is just a "dip" pool, however. Has a wide teakwood outdoor jogging track.

Inside, nothing jars the senses, as the interior design concept successfully balances East–West color combinations with some Indonesian accents. The ambience is decidedly warm and intimate, and is for those who seek a small ship where entertainment and loud music isn't a priority. *Clipper Odyssey* will provide a pleasing antidote to cruising aboard the large ships.

Under its new owners, Clipper Cruise Line, the ship operates 3- and 4-day cruises from November through April and 10-day and longer cruises from April to November (islands of the North Pacific region, New Zealand, and Australia's Great Barrier Reef). The onboard currency is the US dollar.

WEAK POINTS: There are lots of pillars in almost all public areas, which do tend to spoil the décor and views.

Club Med 2
★★★★

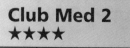

Small Ship:	...............14,983 tons	Main Propulsion:	......a) engines/b) sails	Cabins (for one person): 0

Small Ship: ....14,983 tons
Lifestyle: ....Premium
Cruise Line: ....Club Med Cruises
Former Names: ....none
Builder: ....Ateliers et Chantiers du Havre
(France)
Original Cost: ....$125 million
Entered Service: ....Dec 1992
Registry: ....Wallis & Fortuna
Length (ft/m): 613.8/187.10
Beam (ft/m): 65.6/20.00
Draft (ft/m): 16.4/5.00
Type of Vessel: .....high-tech sail-cruiser
No. of Masts: ....5 (164 ft high)/
7 computer-controlled sails
Sail Area (sq ft/m2): 26,910/2,500

Main Propulsion: ......a) engines/b) sails
Propulsion/Propellers: diesel (9,120kW)/2
Passenger Decks: 8
Total Crew: 200
Passengers
(lower beds/all berths): 394/409
Passenger Space Ratio
(lower beds/all berths): 38.0/36.6
Crew/Passenger Ratio
(lower beds/all berths): 1.9/2.0
Navigation Officers: ....French
Cabins (total): 197
Size Range (sq ft/m): 193.8–322.0/
18.0–30.0
Cabins (outside view): 197
Cabins (interior/no view): 0

Cabins (for one person): 0
Cabins (with private balcony): 0
Cabins (wheelchair accessible): 0
Cabin Current: ....110 and 220 volts
Elevators: 2
Casino (gaming tables): ....No
Slot Machines: ....No
Swimming Pools (outdoors): 2
Whirlpools: 0
Fitness Center: ....Yes
Sauna/Steam Room: ....Yes/No
Massage: ....Yes
Self-Service Launderette: ....No
Library: ....Yes
Classification Society: ....Bureau Veritas

OVERALL SCORE: 1,532 (OUT OF A POSSIBLE 2,000 POINTS)

ACCOMMODATION: There are five suites, and 192 standard cabins (all the same size). All cabins are very nicely equipped and very comfortable, and have an inviting décor that includes much blond wood cabinetry. They all feature a mini-bar/refrigerator, 24-hour room service (but you pay for food), a personal safe, color television, plenty of storage space, bathrobes, and a hairdryer. There are six, four-person cabins, and some 35 doubles are fitted with an extra Pullman berth – good for young families, although this makes them a little more cramped when occupied.

BERLITZ'S RATINGS		
	Possible	Achieved
Ship	500	402
Accommodation	200	164
Food	400	293
Service	400	292
Entertainment	100	76
Cruise	400	305

DINING: There are two main dining rooms, each with tables for one, two or more. Open seating is featured, so you sit with whom you wish. The Odyssey Restaurant has a delightful open terrace for informal meals. Complimentary wines and beers are available with lunch and dinner (there is also an à la carte wine list, with better wines, although these do, of course, cost extra).

Afternoon tea is a delight. The cuisine provides French, continental and Japanese specialties, and the presentation is good.

OTHER COMMENTS: *Club Med 2* is one of a pair of the world's largest high-tech sail-cruisers (her sister ship is

Windstar Cruises' *Wind Surf*), part-cruise ship, part-yacht, like a larger version of the three earlier, smaller Windstar Cruises vessels (*Wind Song, Wind Spirit, Wind Star*).

There are extensive water sports facilities (their use, with the exception of scuba gear, is included in your cruise fare) and an aft marina platform. The water sports equipment includes 12 windsurfers, 3 sailboats, 2 water ski boats, several kayaks, 20 single scuba tanks, snorkels, and 4 motorized water sport boats. The ship's two small swimming pools are saltwater (not freshwater) pools.

Inside, other facilities include a meeting room and a golf simulator (extra charge) as well as a fitness and beauty center, piano bar and lounge.

The onboard activities come under the direction of a large team of young, energetic GOs (*gentiles ordinaires*), who, like their equals on land, have the run of the ship. Although enthusiastic, the entertainment is quite amateurish, although everyone seems to have fun.

This vessel is excellent for more upscale active singles and couples who might like casual elegance rather than the wilder vacation experience of some Club Med resorts, and for those who enjoy water sports. No gratuities are expected or accepted. The onboard currency is the euro or US dollar.

C. Columbus
★★★ +

Small Ship: . . . . .14,903 tons
Lifestyle: . . . . .Standard
Cruise Line: . . . . . . .Hapag-Lloyd Cruises
Former Names: . . . . .none
Builder: . . . .MTW Schiffswerft (Germany)
Original Cost: . . . .$69 million
Entered Service: . . . . .July 1997
Registry: . . . . .The Bahamas
Length (ft/m): 472.8/144.13
Beam (ft/m): 70.5/21.50
Draft (ft/m): 16.8/5.15
Propulsion/Propellers: . . . . .diesel
(10,560kW)/2
Passenger Decks: 6
Total Crew: 170

Passengers
(lower beds/all berths): 410/423
Passenger Space Ratio
(lower beds/all berths): 36.3/35.2
Crew/Passenger Ratio
(lower beds/all berths): 2.4/2.4
Navigation Officers: . . . . .German
Cabins (total): 205
Size Range (sq ft/m): 129.1–322.9/
12.0–30.0
Cabins (outside view): 158
Cabins (interior/no view): 47
Cabins (for one person): 0
Cabins (with private balcony): 2
Cabins (wheelchair accessible): 0

Cabin Current: . . . . .110 volts
Elevators: 3
Casino (gaming tables): . . . . .No
Slot Machines: . . . . .No
Swimming Pools (outdoors): 1
Swimming Pools (indoors): 0
Whirlpools: 0
Fitness Center: . . . . .Yes
Sauna/Steam Room: . . . . .Yes/No
Massage: . . . . .Yes
Self-Service Launderette: . . . . .No
Dedicated Cinema/Seats: . . . . .No
Library: . . . . .Yes
Classification Society: . . . .Germanischer
Lloyd

BERLITZ'S OVERALL SCORE: 1,383 (OUT OF A POSSIBLE 2,000 POINTS)

ACCOMMODATION: The standard cabins are really small, and many of them are interior. All but 10 cabins feature lower berths, but the 16 categories established really are a lot for this size of ship. Except for two forward-facing suites, there are no balcony cabins.

The cabin decor is bright and upbeat, and a good amount of closet and shelf space is provided. The bathrooms are fully tiled and have large shower stalls (none have bathtubs). All cabins feature a mini-bar/refrigerator (all items are at extra cost, as in hotels ashore), personal safe, and hairdryer (bathrobes are available on request, plus a small surcharge).

There are eight suites (each is at least double the size of a standard cabin), and each has a curtained partition between its lounging and sleeping areas, with a wall unit that houses a television that can be turned 360 degrees for viewing from either the lounge or bedroom. Two of the suites located at the bow each have a narrow private veranda (with two teak lounge chairs and coffee table), bedroom (with large wall clock) and lounge area separated by a curtain, two televisions, and an excellent amount of closet, drawer and shelf space. The cabinetry, with its walnut-finish and birds-eye pattern, makes these suites feel warm and luxurious. All the suites have a small room service menu. The bathrooms have a large shower (it is big enough for two), hairdryer, and under-sink storage space. There is 24-hour room service. Only a limited room service menu is available for all cabins.

DINING: There is one large main dining room located at

BERLITZ'S RATINGS

	Possible	Achieved
Ship	500	347
Accommodation	200	146
Food	400	269
Service	400	292
Entertainment	100	61
Cruise	400	268

the stern, with large ocean-view windows on three sides, and seats all passengers in a single seating, with assigned tables. There are just two tables for two), but other tables can accommodate up to 16 – good for family reunions. The cuisine, which has unstuffy presentation, is fairly good, although the menu selection is quite limited (choice of two or three entrées for dinner). There is an excellent selection of fresh-baked breads and rolls every day.

Breakfast and lunch can be taken in the bright, but casual, setting of the Palm Garden, which is also the ship's very comfortable observation lounge. Light dinners also can be taken in the Palm Garden, where a small dance floor adds another dimension.

OTHER COMMENTS: *C. Columbus* has a smart contemporary profile, with a single, large funnel (painted in Hapag-Lloyd's orange/blue colors). Hapag-Lloyd Cruises chartered the ship from the German company Conti Reederei, the owner, until 2002.

The ship also features an ice-hardened hull, which is useful for cold-weather cruise areas. In addition, the bridge "wings" can be folded inwards (as do the overhang lights) flush with the ship's side so that the vessel can enter the locks in the US/Canada Great Lakes region, including the St. Lawrence Seaway and Welland Canal, for which the ship was specifically built.

The ship has a good passenger space ratio. Each deck has a distinctly different color scheme and carpeting, making it easy to find one's way around. There is a reasonable range of public rooms to choose from, most of which are located in a "cake-layer" vertical stacking aft of the accommodation. Although the ceilings in the public rooms are plain and unimaginative (except for the Palm Garden), the décor is really bright and upbeat, and very different to all other ships in the Hapag-Lloyd fleet. The most popular room is arguably the delightful multi-function Palm Garden, which is also the ship's forward-facing observation lounge.

The fit and finish of the ship is a little utilitarian (the mottled gray walls are somewhat cold, but a contrast to the splashes of color found in carpeting and other decorative touches). The artwork chosen is, for the most part, minimal and uncoordinated, yet it all works together to provide cheerful surroundings. Ship buffs will be pleased to find some superb original photographs from the Hapag-Lloyd archives adorning the stairways.

This is a good ship for the standard market German-speaking traveler, and, as such, offers excellent value for the money in very comfortable, unpretentious surroundings. However, you should know that the level of "luxury" is well below that of Hapag-Lloyd's *Europa*, and the experience is completely different (so, of course, is the cruise price). The onboard currency is the euro.

First-time cruise passengers in particular will find this a fresh, comfortable, casual and unpretentious ship for a cruise vacation. You don't need to buy a new wardrobe, and you can leave your tuxedo at home; for this ship you need only informal and casual clothes.

Well-planned itineraries and destination-intensive cruises are featured. Of particular note are the Great Lakes cruises, which are only possible because of the pencil-slim design of *C. Columbus* (the last ocean-going cruise vessel to operate Great Lakes cruises was *World Discoverer* in 1974).

WEAK POINTS: The swimming pool is small (more like a "dip" pool), as is the open deck space. The standard cabins are also very small. There is no wrap-around promenade deck outdoors. The layout and sight lines (including several pillars) in the show lounge are poor.

Constellation
★★★★★

Large Ship: ....91,000 tons	Passengers	Cabin Current: ....110 and 220 volts
Lifestyle: ....Premium	(lower beds/all berths): 1,950/2,450	Elevators: 10
Cruise Line: ....Celebrity Cruises	Passenger Space Ratio	Casino (gaming tables): ....Yes
Former Names: ....none	(lower beds/all berths): 46.6/37.1	Slot Machines: ....Yes
Builder: ....Chantiers de l'Atlantique	Crew/Passenger Ratio	Swimming Pools (outdoors): 2
(France)	(lower beds/all berths): 1.9/2.4	Swimming Pools (indoors): 1
Original Cost: ....$350 million	Navigation Officers: ....Greek	(with magrodome)
Entered Service: ....May 2002	Cabins (total): 975	Whirlpools: 4
Registry: ....The Bahamas	Size Range (sq ft/m): 165.1–2,530.0/	Fitness Center: ....Yes
Length (ft/m): 964.5/294.0	15.34–235.0	Sauna/Steam Room: ....Yes/Yes
Beam (ft/m): 105.6/32.2	Cabins (outside view): 780	Massage: ....Yes
Draft (ft/m): 26.2/8.0	Cabins (interior/no view): 195	Self-Service Launderette: ....No
Propulsion/Propellers: .....gas turbine/2	Cabins (for one person): 0	Dedicated Cinema/Seats: Yes/368
azimuthing pods (39,000kW)	Cabins (with private balcony): 590	Library: ....Yes
Passenger Decks: 11	Cabins (wheelchair accessible): 26	Classification Society: ...Lloyd's Register
Total Crew: 999	(17 with private balcony)	

BERLITZ'S OVERALL SCORE: 1,701 (OUT OF A POSSIBLE 2,000 POINTS)

ACCOMMODATION: There are 20 different grades of accommodation from which to choose, depending on your preference for the size and location of your living space. Almost half of the ship's accommodation features a "private" balcony; approximately 80 percent are outside-view suites and cabins, and 20 percent are interior (no view) cabins. The accommodation is extremely comfortable throughout this ship, regardless of which cabin grade you choose. Suites, naturally, have more space, butler service (whether you want it or not), more and better amenities and more personal service than if you choose any of the standard cabin grades. There are several categories of suites, but those at the stern of the ship are in a prime location and have huge balconies that are really private and not overlooked from above.

Regardless of which grade of accommodation you choose, all suites and cabins have wood cabinetry and accenting, interactive television and entertainment systems (you can go shopping, book shore excursions, play casino games, interactively, and even watch soft porn movies). The bathrooms have hairdryers and 100 percent cotton towels.

PENTHOUSE SUITES: Two Penthouse Suites (on Penthouse Deck) are the largest accommodation aboard. Each occupies one half of the beam (width) of the ship, overlooking the ship's stern. Each measures a huge 2,530 sq. ft (235 sq. meters), consisting of 1,431.6 sq. ft (133 sq. meters) of living space, plus a huge wrap-

BERLITZ'S RATINGS

	Possible	Achieved
Ship	500	454
Accommodation	200	181
Food	400	328
Service	400	330
Entertainment	100	78
Cruise	400	330

around terrace measuring 1,098 sq. ft (102 sq. meters) with 180-degree views. This terrace overlooks the ship's stern, and includes a wet bar, hot tub and whirlpool tub – but much of it can be overlooked by passengers on other decks above.

Features include a marble foyer, a separate living room (complete with ebony baby grand piano – bring your own pianist if you don't play yourself – and a formal dining room. The master bedroom has a large walk-in closet, personal exercise equipment, dressing room with vanity desk, exercise equipment, marble-clad master bathroom with twin washbasins, deep whirlpool bathtub, separate shower, toilet and bidet areas, flat-screen televisions (one in the bedroom and one in the lounge), and electronically controlled drapes. Butler service is standard, and a butler's pantry, with separate entry door, has a full-size refrigerator, temperature-controlled wine cabinet, microwave oven and good-sized food preparation and storage areas. For even more space, an interconnecting door can be opened into the adjacent suite (ideal for multi-generation families).

ROYAL SUITES: Eight Royal Suites, each measuring 733 sq ft (68 sq. meters), are located towards the aft of the ship (four each on the port and starboard sides). Each features a separate living room with dining and lounge areas (with refrigerator, mini-bar and Bang & Olufson CD sound system), and a separate bedroom. There are two entertainment centers with DVD players, and two flat-screen televisions (one in the living area, one in the bedroom), and a large walk-in closet with vanity desk. The marble-clad bathroom has a whirlpool bathtub with integral shower, and there is also a separate shower enclosure, two washbasins and toilet. The teakwood decked balcony is extensive (large enough for on-deck massage) and also features a whirlpool hot tub.

CELEBRITY SUITES: Eight Celebrity Suites, each 467 sq. ft (44 sq. meters), have floor-to-ceiling windows, a separate living room with dining and lounge areas, two entertainment centers with flat-screen televisions (one in the living room, one in the bedroom), and a walk-in closet with vanity desk. The marble-clad bathroom has a whirlpool bathtub with integral shower (a window with movable blind lets you look out of the bathroom through the lounge to the large ocean-view windows). Interconnecting doors allow two suites to be used as a family unit (as there is no balcony, these suites are ideal for families with small children). These suites overhang the starboard side of the ship (they are located opposite a group of glass-walled elevators), and provide stunning ocean views from the glass-walled sitting/dining area, which extends out from the ship's side. A personal computer with wood-surround screen allows direct internet connectivity. Butler service is standard.

SKY SUITES: There are 30 Sky Suites, each 308 sq. ft (28.6 sq. meters), including the private balcony (note that some balconies may be larger than others, depending on the location). Although these are designated as suites, they are really just larger cabins that feature a marble-clad bathroom with bathtub/shower combination. The suites also have a VCR player in addition to a TV set, and have a larger lounge area (than standard cabins) and sleeping area. Butler service is standard.

BUTLER SERVICE: Butler service (in all accommodation designated as suites) includes full breakfast, in-suite lunch and dinner service (as required), afternoon tea service, evening hors d'oeuvres, complimentary espresso and cappuccino, daily news delivery, shoeshine service, and other personal touches.

Suite occupants in Penthouse, Royal, Celebrity and Sky suites also get welcome champagne; a full personal computer in each suite, including a printer and internet access (on request in the Sky Suites); choice of films from a video library; personalized stationery; tote bag; priority dining room seating preferences; private portrait sitting, and bathrobe; and in-suite massage service.

STANDARD OUTSIDE-VIEW/INTERIOR (NO VIEW) CABINS: All other outside-view and interior (no view) cabins feature a lounge area with sofa or convertible sofa bed, sleeping area with twin beds that can convert to a double bed, a good amount of closet and drawer space, personal safe, mini-bar/refrigerator (extra cost), interactive television, and private bathroom. The cabins are nicely decorated with warm wood-finish furni-

ture, and there is none of the boxy feel of cabins in so many ships, due to the angled placement of vanity and audio-video consoles. Even the smallest cabin has a good-sized bathroom and shower enclosure.

WHEELCHAIR-ACCESSIBLE SUITES/CABINS: Wheelchair-accessible accommodation is available in six Sky Suites, three premium outside-view, eight deluxe oceanview, four standard ocean-view and five interior (no view) cabins measuring 347–362 sq. ft (32.2–33.6 sq. meters). They are located in the most practical parts of the ship and close to elevators for good accessibility – all have doorways and bathroom doorways and showers are wheelchair-accessible. Some cabins have extra berths for third or third and fourth occupants (note, however, that there is only one safe for personal belongings, which must be shared).

DINING: The 1,198-seat San Marco Restaurant is the ship's formal dining room. It is two decks high, has a grand staircase connecting the two levels (on the upper level of which is a musicians' gallery), and a huge glass wall overlooking the sea at the stern of the ship (electrically operated blinds provide several different backdrops). There are two seatings for dinner (with open seating for breakfast and lunch), at tables for two, four, six, eight or 10. The dining room is totally no-smoking, and, you should note, that, like all large dining halls, it will prove to be extremely noisy. The menu variety is good, the food has taste, and it is very attractively presented and served in fine European tradition.

In addition to the principal dining room, there are other dining options, particularly for those seeking more casual dining spots. Full service in-cabin dining is also available for all meals (including dinner).

For casual eating, the Seaside Café & Grill is a self-serve buffet area, with six principal serving lines, and around 750 seats; there is also a grill and pizza bar. Each evening, casual alternative dining takes place here (reservations are needed, although there's no additional charge).

ALTERNATIVE (RESERVATIONS-ONLY, EXTRA COST) DINING: The Ocean Liners Restaurant is the ship's alternative dining salon; it is adjacent to the conference center. The décor includes some lacquered paneling from the famed 1920s French ocean liner *Ile de France*. Fine tableside preparation is the feature of this alternative dining room, whose classic French cuisine and service is outstanding (it is masterminded by Michel Roux, owner of a three-star Michelin restaurant near Windsor in England). Menu items have been culled from galleys of the ocean liners of yesteryear. This is haute cuisine at the height of professionalism, for this is, indeed, a room for a full dégustation, and not merely for dinner, featuring the French culinary arts of découpage and flambé. However, with just 115 seats, not all passengers are able to experience it even once during a one-week cruise (reservations are necessary, and a cover charge of $25 per person applies). There's a dine-in wine cellar (with more than 200 labels from around the world), a demonstration galley, and tableside preparation.

COVA CAFÉ DI MILANO: The Cova Café di Milano is a signature item aboard all the ships of Celebrity Cruises, and a seagoing version of the real Café di Milano is located next to La Scala Opera House in Milan (the original opened in 1756). It is located in a prominent position, on the third level of the atrium lobby. It is a delightful meeting place, and *the* place to see and be seen, for those who appreciate fine Italian coffees (for espresso, espresso macchiato, cappuccino, latte), pastries and superb cakes in an elegant, refined setting.

OTHER COMMENTS: *Constellation* is a sister ship to *Infinity, Millennium,* and *Summit* (the *Millennium*-class ships). Jon Bannenberg, the famous mega-yacht designer, dreamed up the exterior featuring a royal blue and white hull, and racy lines in red, blue and gold – although it has turned out to look extremely ungainly (some say downright ugly). This is fourth Celebrity Cruises ship to be fitted with the "pod" propulsion system (and controllable pitch propellers) coupled with a quiet, smokeless, energy-efficient *gas* turbine powerplant (two GE gas turbines provide engine power while a single GE steam turbine drives the electricity generators).

Inside, the ship has the same high-class décor and materials, and public rooms that have made the existing ships in the fleet so user-friendly. Although the main part of the atrium lobby is three decks high, the glass-walled elevators on the port side travel through 11 decks.

Facilities include a combination Cinema/Conference Center, an expansive shopping arcade with 14,447 sq. ft (1,300 sq. meters) of retail store space (with trendy labels such as Fendi, Fossil, Hugo Boss, and Versace), a lavish four-decks-high show lounge with the latest in staging and lighting equipment, a two-level library (one level for English-language books; a second for books in other languages and reference material), card room, music listening room, and an observation lounge/discotheque with outstanding views. Michael's Club, on Promenade Deck, is a haven for those quiet moments for anyone seeking fine cognacs and cigars (about 20 varieties are available). An internet café has almost 20 computers with wood-surround flat screens and internet access.

The artwork throughout the ship (particularly the sculptures) is eclectic, provocative, thoughtful, and intelligent, and at almost every turn another piece appears to break the monotony associated with large spaces.

One delightful feature is a large conservatory located in a glasshouse environment and spreading across a whole foyer. It includes a botanical environment with flowers, plants, tress, mini-gardens and fountains, all designed by the award-winning floral designer Emilio Robba of Paris. It is directly in front of the main funnel and a section of it has glass walls overlooking the ship's side.

Outdoor facilities include two outdoor pools, one indoor/outdoor pool, and six whirlpools. A huge bronze sculpture is on one side of the Sky Deck. It is actually a gorilla holding a fish under its arm, and was created by Angus Fairhurst, is titled "A couple of differences between thinking and feeling."

Wellness facilities include a large AquaSpa (with large thalassotherapy pool under a huge solarium dome), complete with health bar for light breakfast and lunch items, and fresh squeezed fruit and vegetable juices. Spa facilities measuring 25,000 sq. ft (2,300 sq. meters) include 16 treatment rooms, plus eight treatment rooms with showers and one treatment room specifically designed for wheelchair passengers, aerobics room, gymnasium (complete with over 40 machines to help provide you with high-tech muscle training), large male and female saunas (with large ocean-view porthole window), a co-ed thermal suite (containing several steam and shower mist rooms with different fragrances such as chamomile, eucalyptus and mint, and a glacial ice fountain), and beauty salon. Among the different types of massage available is a delightful hot and cold stone massage therapy that lasts almost 1½ hours (about $175).

Sports facilities include a full-size basketball court, compact football, paddle tennis and volleyball, golf simulator, shuffleboard (on two different decks) and a jogging track. Gaming sports include the ship's large Fortunes Casino, with blackjack, roulette, and slot machines.

Families will appreciate the Fun Factory (for children) and The Tower (for teenagers). Children's counselors and youth activities staff are on hand.

Constellation delivers a well-defined North American cruise experience at a very modest price. The "zero announcement policy" means little intrusion. My advice is to book a suite-category cabin for all the extra benefits it brings – it really is worth it. A 15 percent gratuity is automatically added to all bar and wine accounts.

The strong points of a Celebrity cruise include the use of many European staff and service, a fine spa with a good range of facilities, treatments, taste-filled food that is attractively presented and served in the European fine dining tradition, and the provision of many intimate spaces and a superb collection of artwork. During the past two years, standards aboard all Celebrity ships fell as cuts were made by parent company Royal Caribbean International. However, new management has been brought in to put things right.

Aa cruise aboard a large ship such as this provides a wide range of choices and possibilities. It depends how much you are willing to pay. One thing is certain: cruising in a hassle-free, crime-free environment such as this is hard to beat. The onboard currency is the US dollar.

WEAK POINTS: There is, sadly, no wrap-around wooden promenade deck outdoors. Standing in line for embarkation, disembarkation, shore tenders and for self-serve buffet meals is an inevitable aspect of cruising aboard all large ships (however, more flexible embarkation hours do help to spread the flow).

Coral Princess
NOT YET RATED

Large Ship: ....88,000 tons	Passengers	Cabin Current: ....110 volts
Lifestyle: ....Standard	(lower beds/all berths): 1,974/2,590	Elevators: 14
Cruise Line: ....Princess Cruises	Passenger Space Ratio	Casino (gaming tables): ....Yes
Former Names: ....none	(lower beds/all berths): 44.5/33.9	Slot Machines: ....Yes
Builder: Chantiers de l'Atlantique (France)	Crew/Passenger Ratio	Swimming Pools (outdoors): 2
Original Cost: ....$360 million	(lower beds/all berths): 2.1/2.8	(+ 1 splash pool)
Entered Service: ....Dec 2002	Navigation Officers: ....British	Swimming Pools (indoors): 0
Registry: ....Bermuda	Cabins (total): 987	Whirlpools: 5
Length (ft/m): 964.5/294.0	Size Range (sq ft/m): 156–470.0/	Fitness Center: ....Yes
Beam (ft/m): 105.6/32.2	14.4–43.6	Sauna/Steam Room: ....Yes/Yes
Draft (ft/m): 26/7.9	Cabins (outside view): 879	Massage: ....Yes
Propulsion/Propellers: .....gas turbine/2	Cabins (interior/no view): 108	Self-Service Launderette: ....Yes
azimuthing pods	Cabins (for one person): 0	Dedicated Cinema/Seats: ....No
Passenger Decks: 11	Cabins (with private balcony): 727	Library: ....Yes
Total Crew: 900	Cabins (wheelchair accessible): 20	Classification Society: ...Lloyd's Register

OVERALL SCORE: NYR (OUT OF A POSSIBLE 2,000 POINTS)

ACCOMMODATION: There are 33 price categories, in six grades; 16 Suites with balcony (470 sq. ft/43.6 sq. meters); 184 Mini-Suites with balcony (285–302 sq. ft/26.4–28.0 sq. meters); 8 Mini-Suites without balcony (300 sq. ft/27.8 sq. meters; 527 Outside-View Cabins with balcony (217–232 sq. ft/20.1–21.5 sq. meters); 144 Standard Outside-view Cabins (162 sq. ft/15 sq. meters); Interior (no view) Cabins (156 sq. ft/144.5 sq. meters). There are also 20 wheelchair-accessible cabins (217–374 sq. ft/20.1–34.7 sq. meters). All measurements are approximate. Almost all of the out-side-view cabins have private balconies. Some cabins can accommodate a third, or third and fourth person (good for families with children). Some cabins on Emerald Deck (Deck 8) have a view obstructed by lifeboats.

SUITES: There are just 16 suites and, although none are really large, each has a private balcony. All are named after islands (mostly coral-based islands in the Indian Ocean and Pacific Ocean). All suites are located on either Deck 9 or Deck 10. In alphabetical order, they are: Bali, Bora Bora, Catalina, Fiji, Galápagos, Hawaii, Java, Kawai, Lanai, Maldives, Marquesas, Moorea, Seychelles, Sumatra, Tahiti, and Tasmania. In a departure from many ships, *Coral Princess* does not have any suites or cabins with a view of the ship's stern. There are also four Premium Suites, located sensibly in the center of the ship, adjacent to a bank of six elevators. Six other suites (called Verandah Suites) are located further aft.

ALL ACCOMMODATION: All suites and cabins are

BERLITZ'S RATINGS

	Possible	Achieved
Ship	500	NYR
Accommodation	200	NYR
Food	400	NYR
Service	400	NYR
Entertainment	100	NYR
Cruise	400	NYR

equipped with a refrigerator, personal safe, television (with audio channels), hairdryer, satellite-dial telephone, and twin beds that convert to a queen-sized bed (there are a few exceptions). All accommodation has a bathroom with shower enclosure and toilet; note that accommodation designated as suites and mini-suites (there are seven price categories) feature a bathtub.

All passengers receive turndown service and chocolates on pillows each night, plus bath-robes and toiletry amenity kits (larger, naturally, for suite/mini-suite occupants) that typically include soap, shampoo, conditioner, and hand/body lotion. Most out-side cabins on Emerald Deck have views obstructed by the lifeboats. There are no cabins for singles. Princess Cruises typically includes CNN, CNBC, ESPN and TNT on the in-cabin color television system (when available).

DINING: Bordeaux and Provence are the two main din-ing rooms; they are located in the forward section of the ship on the two lowest passenger decks, with the galley all the way forward so it doesn't intersect public spaces. Both are almost identical in design and layout, and have plenty of intimate alcoves and cozy dining spots, with tables for two, four, six, or eight. There are two seat-ings for dinner, while breakfast and lunch are on an open seating basis; you may have to stand in line at peak times, just as in almost any large restaurant ashore. Both dining rooms are non-smoking.

On a seven-day cruise, a menu cycle will typically include a Sailaway Dinner, Captain's Welcome Dinner, Chef's Dinner, Italian Dinner, French Dinner, Captain's

Gala Dinner, and Landfall Dinner. The wine list is reasonable, but not good, and the company has seen fit to eliminate wine waiters. Note that 15 percent is added to all beverage bills, including wines (whether you order a $15 bottle or a $120 bottle, even though it takes the same amount of service to open and pour the wine).

Horizon Court is the ship's casual eatery, located in the forward section of Lido Deck, with superb ocean views. Several self-serve counters provide an array of food for breakfast and lunch buffets, while each evening, bistro-style casual dinners can be taken by those not wishing to go to the ship's more formal dining rooms.

ALTERNATIVE (EXTRA CHARGE) EATERIES: There are two "alternative" dining rooms, both enclosed (i.e. not open areas which passengers can walk through, as in some Princess Cruises ships). Both dining spots incur an extra charge and you must make a reservation: *Sabatini's* is the ship's Italian eatery, with colorful Mediterranean-style decor. *Bayou Café* features Creole food. The room sports a small stage, with baby grand piano, so live music will be part of the dining scenario. *La Pâtisserie*, in the ship's reception lobby coffee, cakes and pastries spot; a good place for informal meetings. *Churchill's* is the cigar and cognac lounge, cleverly sited near a neat little hideaway bar called the Rat Pack Bar.

OTHER COMMENTS: This ship has an instantly recognizable funnel due to two jet engine-like pods that sit high up on its structure (perhaps the designer will add wings one day so that the ship can take off). The propulsion is derived from a "pod" system. The pods, which resemble huge outboard motors, replace internal electric propulsion motors, shaft lines, rudders and their machinery, and are compact, self-contained units that typically weigh about 170 tons each. Pod units *pull*, rather than *push*, a ship through the water. Pods replace the conventional rudder and propeller shafts. Four diesel engines provide the generating power. Electrical power is provided by a combination of four diesel and one gas turbine (CODAG) unit; the diesel engines are located in the engine room, while the gas turbine unit is located in the ship's funnel housing. There are also three bow thrusters and three stern thrusters.

This is the first French-built new ship for Princess Cruises, although the former *Sky Princess* (ordered for Sitmar Cruises, which Princess Cruises bought in 1984) was also built at a (different) French shipyard. The ship's layout is similar to that of the *Grand Princess*-class ships, and sensibly features three major stair towers for passengers (good from the safety and evacuation viewpoint), with plenty of elevators for easy access. For a large ship, the layout is quite user-friendly, and less disjointed than many ships of a similar size.

What is quite pleasing is the fact that sunbathers who use the "quiet" deck forward of the mast have their own splash pool, so they won't have to go down two decks to get to the two main pools in order to cool down – a user-friendly feature long overdue. Strollers will like the ship's full wrap-around exterior promenade deck. Two whole decks provide entertainment rooms, bars and lounges in which to play.

The Princess Theater is two decks high, and, unusually, there is much more seating in the upper level than on the main floor below. A second entertainment lounge (Universe Lounge), more for cabaret-style features, also has two levels (a first for a Princess Cruises ship), and three separate stages – so nonstop entertainment can be featured without constant set-ups.

Surfers can find an AOL Internet Café conveniently located on the top level of the four-deck-high lobby.

It's good to see that the dreaded "fine arts" get their own room, so that paintings to be sold during the art auctions are not spread all over the ship. Adjacent is the Wedding Chapel (a live web-cam can relay ceremonies via the internet). The ship's captain can legally marry (American) couples, due to the ship's registry and a special dispensation (this should, however, be verified when in the planning stage, and may depend on where you live). Princess Cruises offers three wedding packages - Pearl, Emerald, Diamond; the fee includes registration and official marriage certificate. However, to get married *and* take your close family members and entourage with you on your honeymoon is going to cost a lot. The Wedding Chapel can also host "renewal of vows" ceremonies.

The product (particularly the food and entertainment) is totally geared to the North American market; British and other European nationalities (and the occasional Japanese) should feel at home, as long as they realize that the North American product is really about highly organized, packaged cruising. Cruising aboard large ships such as this one has become increasingly an onboard revenue-based product. You can expect to be subjected to a stream of flyers advertising daily art auctions, "designer" watches and the like.

Gratuities to staff are automatically added to your account, at $10 per person, per day (note that gratuities for children are charged at the same rate). If you want to pay less, you'll need to go to the reception desk to have these charges adjusted (that could mean lining up with many other passengers wanting to do the same). The onboard currency is the US dollar.

WEAK POINTS: Standing in line for embarkation (an "express check-in" option is available by completing certain documentation 40 days in advance of your cruise), disembarkation, shore tenders, the purser's desk and for self-serve buffet meals in the Horizon Court is an inevitable aspect of cruising aboard all large ships. There are no butlers – even for the top-grade suites. Cabin attendants have too many cabins to look after (typically 20), which does not translate to fine personal service.

You'll have to live with the many extra charge items (such as for ice cream) and activities (such as yoga and kick boxing classes, typically at $10 per session, and $4 per hour for group babysitting services.

✓ *Lisbon* 5/9/05

Costa Allegra
★★★

Mid-Size Ship: . . . . .28,430 tons
Lifestyle: . . . . .Standard
Cruise Line: Costa Crociere (Costa Cruises)
Former Names: . . . .*Annie Johnson*
Builder: . . . . .Mariotti Shipyards (Italy)
Original Cost: . . . .$175 million
Entered Service: . . . . .Dec 1992
Registry: . . . . .Italy
Length (ft/m): 616.1/187.8
Beam (ft/m): 83.9/25.6
Draft (ft/m): 23.9/7.3
Propulsion/Propellers: . . . . .diesel
(19,200kW)/2
Passenger Decks: 8
Total Crew: 400
Passengers

(lower beds/all berths): 820/1,072
Passenger Space Ratio
(lower beds/all berths): 34.7/26.5
Crew/Passenger Ratio
(lower beds/all berths): 2.0/2.6
Navigation Officers: . . . . .Italian
Cabins (total): 410
Size Range (sq ft/m): 105.4–575.8/
9.8–53.5
Cabins (outside view): 218
Cabins (interior/no view): 192
Cabins (for one person): 0
Cabins (with private balcony): 10
Cabins (wheelchair accessible): 8 (interior)
Cabin Current: . . . . . . .110 and 220 volts
Elevators: 4

Casino (gaming tables): . . . . .Yes
Slot Machines: . . . . .Yes
Swimming Pools (outdoors): 1
Swimming Pools (indoors): 0
Whirlpools: 2
Fitness Center: . . . . .Yes
Sauna/Steam Room: . . . . .Yes/Yes
Massage: . . . . .Yes
Self-Service Launderette: . . . . .No
Dedicated Cinema/Seats: . . . . .No
Library: . . . . .Yes
Classification Society: . . .Registro Navale
Italiano (RINA)

OVERALL SCORE: 1,206 (OUT OF A POSSIBLE 2,000 POINTS)

ACCOMMODATION: The standard cabins are quite light and airy, with splashes of fabric colors, and wood accenting, and are laid out in a practical manner. However, they are small, and there is little closet and drawer space, so take only casual clothing. There are many small interior (no view) cabins, and all cabins suffer from poor soundproofing. Many cabins also have Pullman berths for a third or fourth occupant. The bathrooms are compact, although they do feature good shower enclosures, with sliding circular door instead of the usual limp curtain. The cabin service menu is extremely limited.

On Rousseau Deck there are three forward-facing suites (the largest accommodation on board), each of which features a living room, dinette and wet bar. A further 10 slightly smaller mini-suites feature a small, very narrow balcony, but it is really not private, as it can be seen from the walking track on the deck above.

DINING: The Montmartre Restaurant has 370 seats, and operates in two seatings. It is fairly spacious and has expansive glass windows that look out over the stern, while the port side and starboard side feature large portholes. It is a very noisy room, with tables for four, six, eight or 10 (there are no tables for two). Note that the time for dinner is later when the ship operates in Europe. Romantic candlelight dining is typically part of a formal night. The cuisine is mostly continental, with many Italian dishes included.

Reasonable continental cuisine is featured, but the

BERLITZ'S RATINGS		
	Possible	Achieved
Ship	500	307
Accommodation	200	130
Food	400	218
Service	400	249
Entertainment	100	62
Cruise	400	240

presentation and food quality is not memorable, and is still the subject of many negative comments from passengers. The pasta dishes and cream sauces, however, are very good. So, although there is plenty of food, its quality and presentation often prove disappointing to those who expect better. While the quality of meats is adequate, it could be better, and is often disguised with gravies and rich sauces. Fish and seafood tend to be lacking in taste and are typically overcooked, and green vegetables are hard to come by. However, good pasta dishes are served each day (the pasta is made fresh on board daily), although quantity, not quality, is what appears from the galley. Breads and rolls are typically good, but desserts tend towards their sell-by date.

The service is basically sound, although you will probably note that there are few Italians serving in the dining room, as one might expect aboard the ship of an Italian company. There is a wine list, although there are no wine waiters (the table waiters are expected to serve both food and wine, which does not work well), and almost all wines are young – very young.

The Yacht Club is the informal dining spot, with two small centrally located buffet lines. As for breakfast and lunch buffets are concerned, Costa Cruises comes way down the list; buffets are rather plain, repetitive and unimaginative, and fresh (ripe) fruit and cheese selections are poor. For ice-cream lovers, a gelati cart provides welcome relief at least once each day.

Note that excellent cappuccino and espresso coffees

are always available in various bars around the ship, served in the right sized (proper) china cups.

OTHER COMMENTS: *Costa Allegra* was originally a container ship built for Swedish Johnson Line) that has undergone a skilful transformation into contemporary cruise vessel; this resulted in a jazzy, rather angular-looking ship with a low-slung appearance. There are three bolt-upright yellow funnels that have become a signature for almost all Costa Cruises' ships (exception: *Costa Riviera*). Slightly longer and larger than its sister ship *Costa Marina* (after the addition of a 13.44-meter section), this vessel has a much better standard of interior fit and finish, and more outdoors space than its sister ship. It has an interesting glass-enclosed stern.

There is a high glass-to-steel ratio, with numerous glass domes and walls admitting light, as well as Murano glass light fixtures in some places. There is a good amount of outdoor deck and sunbathing space, although there is no observation lounge with forward-facing views over the ship's bows. Cushioned pads are provided for the deck lounge chairs outdoors.

The decks are named after famous painters. This ship features surprisingly nice interior décor, with cool, restful colors and soft furnishings, as well as domed ceilings and a big use of glass. In the Follies Bergeres show lounge, some 14 pillars obstruct the sight lines to the semi-circular stage from many seats.

Costa Allegro will provide a decent first cruise experience for young adults who enjoy European-style service and a real upbeat, almost elegant atmosphere with an Italian accent and lots of noise. However, few of the officers and crew are actually Italian, as one might expect. The onboard currency is the euro.

WEAK POINTS: There are few public restrooms. The children's room is too small, and the ship is simply not equipped to handle large numbers of children, which are aboard in the summer and at peak holiday periods. The many loud and extended announcements (in several languages) quickly become tiresome – there are no quiet spots to be found anywhere. The opening hours for the small library are really minimal. Tipping envelopes state the amount you are expected to give.

✓ alexandria 11/03

Costa Atlantica
★★★★

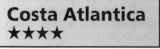

Large Ship: ....85,700 tons	Total Crew: 920	Cabin Current: ....110 volts
Lifestyle: ....Standard	Passengers	Elevators: 12
Cruise Line: ....Costa Crociere	(lower beds/all berths): 2,112/2,680	Casino (gaming tables): ....Yes
(Costa Cruises)	Passenger Space Ratio	Slot Machines: ....Yes
Former Names: ....none	(lower beds/all berths): 40.5/31.9	Swimming Pools (outdoors): 2
Builder: ....Kverner Masa-Yards (Finland)	Crew/Passenger Ratio	(+1 indoor/outdoor)
Original Cost: ....$335 million	(lower beds/all berths): 2.3/2.9	Swimming Pools (indoors): ....No
Entered Service: ....July 2000	Navigation Officers: ....Italian	Whirlpools: ....Yes
Registry:.......................Italy	Cabins (total): 1,056	Fitness Center: ....Yes
Length (ft/m): 959.6/292.5	Size Range (sq ft/m): 161.4–387.5/	Sauna/Steam Room: ....Yes/Yes
Beam (ft/m): 105.6/32.2	15.0–36.0	Massage:........................Yes
Draft (ft/m): 25.5/7.8	Cabins (outside view): 843	Self-Service Launderette: ....No
Propulsion/Propellers: .....diesel-electric	Cabins (interior/no view): 213	Dedicated Cinema/Seats: ....No
(34,000 kW)/2 azimuthing pods	Cabins (for one person): 0	Library: 0
(17.6 MW each)	Cabins (with private balcony): 742	Classification Society: ...Registro Navale
Passenger Decks:.................12	Cabins (wheelchair accessible): 8	Italiano (RINA)

OVERALL SCORE: 1,438 (OUT OF A POSSIBLE 2,000 POINTS)

ACCOMMODATION: There is a healthy (78 percent) proportion of outside-view to interior (no view) cabins. All cabins have twin beds that convert into a queen-sized bed, individually controlled air-conditioning, television, and telephone. Many cabins have their views obstructed by lifeboats on Deck 4 (Roma Deck), the lowest of the accommodation decks, as well as some cabins on Deck 5. Some cabins have pull-down Pullman berths that are fully hidden in the ceiling when not in use.

Some of the most desirable suites and cabins are those with private balconies on the five aft-facing decks (Decks 4, 5, 6, 7, and 8) with views overlooking the stern and ship's wash. The other cabins with private balconies will find the balconies not so private – the partition between one balcony and the next is not a full partition – so you will be able to hear your neighbors (or smell their smoke). However, these balcony occupants all have good views through glass and wood-topped railings, and the deck is made of teak. The cabins are well laid out, typically with twin beds that convert to a queen-sized bed, vanity desk (with built-in hairdryer), large TV set, personal safe, and one closet that features moveable shelves – providing more space for luggage storage. However, the lighting is fluorescent, and much too harsh (the bedside control is for a master switch only – other individual lights cannot be controlled). The bathroom is a simple, modular unit that features shower enclosures with soap dispenser; there is a good amount of stowage space for personal toiletry items.

BERLITZ'S RATINGS

	Possible	Achieved
Ship	500	427
Accommodation	200	152
Food	400	240
Service	400	273
Entertainment	100	64
Cruise	400	282

The largest suites are those designated as Penthouse Suites, although they are really quite small when compared with suites aboard other ships of a similar size (for example, those of Celebrity Cruises' *Century, Galaxy, Mercury, Millennium*). However, they do at least offer more space to move around in, and a slightly larger, better bathroom.

DINING: The Tiziano (main) Dining Room is large in size, and located at the aft section of the ship on two levels, with a spiral stairway between them (the galley itself is located under the dining room, and accessed by escalators). There are two seatings, with tables for two, four, six or eight. Note that dinner on European cruises is typically scheduled at 7pm and 9pm to accommodate the later eating habits of Europeans. Themed evenings are a part of the Costa Cruises tradition, and three different window blinds help create a different feel. However, the artwork is placed at table height, so the room seems more closed-in than it should.

Reasonable continental cuisine is featured, but the presentation and food quality is not memorable, and is still the subject of many negative comments from passengers. The pasta dishes and cream sauces, however, are very good. So, although there is plenty of food, its quality and presentation often prove disappointing. While the quality of meats is adequate, it could be better, and is often disguised with gravies and rich sauces. Fish and seafood tend to be lacking in taste and are typically overcooked, and green vegetables are hard to come by. But good pasta dishes are served each day (the pasta is made fresh on board daily), although quantity, not quality, is what appears. Breads and rolls are typically good, but desserts approach their sell-by date.

The service is basically sound, although there are few Italians serving in the dining room, as one might expect aboard the ship of an Italian company. There is a wine list, although, the table waiters are expected to serve both food and wine, which does not work well), and almost all wines are young – very young.

A reservations-only alternative for dinner, Ristorante Magnifico by Zeffirino, is available six nights a week, with a service charge of $18.75 per person (passengers occupying suites will get a free pass for one evening).

Undoubtedly the place that most people will want to see and be seen is at the Caffe Florian – a replica of the famous indoor/outdoor café that opened in 1720 in St. Mark's Square, Venice. There are four separate salons (Sala delle Stagioni, Sala del Senato, Sala Liberty, and Sala degli Uomini Illustri), and the same fascinating mosaic, marble and wood floors, opulent ceiling art, and special lampshades. Even the espresso/cappuccino machine is a duplicate of that found in the real thing. The only problem is that the chairs are much too small.

Casual breakfast and luncheon self-serve buffet-style meals can be taken in the Botticelli Buffet Restaurant, adjacent to the swimming pools, with seating both indoors and outdoors. A grill (for hamburgers and hot dogs) and a pasta bar are conveniently adjacent to the second pool, while indoors is the Napoli Pizzeria.

Note that excellent cappuccino and espresso coffees are always available in various bars around the ship, served in the right sized (proper) china cups.

OTHER COMMENTS: Longer than the company's largest ship to date (*Costa Victoria*), and only a tad shorter than Cunard Line's *Queen Elizabeth 2*, the new design makes the ship look much sleeker than any other Costa Cruises ship. It is the largest in the fleet, and has basically the same exterior design and internal layout as that of the second ship in the new "8,000" series, *Carnival Spirit*.

There are two centrally located swimming pools outdoors, one of which can be used in inclement weather due to its retractable magrodome cover. A bar abridges two adjacent whirlpool tubs. Another smaller pool is available for children; there is also a winding water slide that spans two decks in height (it starts on a platform bridge located between the two aft funnels). There is an additional whirlpool tub outdoors.

Inside, the layout is somewhat of an extension of that found in previous newbuilds for Costa Cruises – particularly that of *Costa Victoria*. All the deck names are Italian (Roma Deck, Le Notte di Cabiria, La Voce della Luna, La Strada, La Luci del Varieta, for example), with one curious exception, a deck named Ginger and Fred. The interior design is, however, bold and brash – a mix of classical Italy and contemporary features. Good points include the fact that the interior design allows good passenger flow from one public space to another, and there are several floor spaces for dancing, and a range of bars and lounges for socializing.

When you first walk into the ship, you'll be greeted by the immense size of the dramatic lobby space that spans eight decks. The atrium lobby, with its two grand stairways, presents a stunning wall decoration that is best seen from any of the multiple viewing balconies on each deck above the main lobby floor level. Take a drink from the lobby bar and look upwards – the surroundings are quite stunning.

There is a three-deck-high show lounge (the Caruso Theater), with a main floor and two balcony levels around the perimeter. A small chapel is located forward of the uppermost level.

Other facilities include a winding shopping street with several boutique stores (Fendi, Gianni Versace, Paul & Shark Yachting – as well as a shop dedicated to selling Caffe Florian products), photo gallery, video games room, an observation balcony (at the top of the multi-deck atrium), a casino and library (with internet access).

Health spa facilities include a solarium, eight treatment rooms, sauna and steam rooms for men and women, beauty parlor and gymnasium with floor-to-ceiling windows on three sides. There is also a jogging track outdoors.

Costa Cruises has been busy updating its image, and retraining its staff. With the debut of *Costa Atlantica* came many new, better, uniforms for many departments, as well as more choice in a ship that is designed to wow the hip and trendy as well as pay homage to many of Italy's great art and past masters. Food and service levels have been raised to a better standard than that found aboard all other Costa Cruises ships to date. The onboard currency is the US dollar or euro, depending on the region of operation.

WEAK POINTS: There are too many lines; however, standing in line for embarkation, disembarkation, shore tenders and for self-serve buffet meals is an inevitable aspect of cruising aboard all large ships. There is too much use of fluorescent lighting in the suites and cabins, and the soundproofing could be much better; some bathroom fixtures – bath and shower taps in particular – are frustrating to use until you get the hang of them. Some tables in the Tiziano Dining Room have a less than comfortable view of the harsh lighting of the escalators between the galley and the two decks of the dining room.

There are far too many pillars obstructing passenger flow and sight lines throughout the ship; the pillars are everywhere (there is even one in the middle of a winding "shopping street"). The many pillars in the dining room make it extremely difficult for the waiters and the proper service of food. The fit and finish of some of the interior decoration is quite poor. The hospitality levels and service are inconsistent and very spotty, and below the standard of several other "major" cruise lines.

Costa Classica
★★★ +

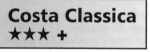

Large Ship: ....52,926 tons	Passengers	Cabin Current: ....110 and 220 volts
Lifestyle: ....Standard	(lower beds/all berths): 1,308/1,766	Elevators: 8
Cruise Line: ....Costa Crociere	Passenger Space Ratio	Casino (gaming tables): ....Yes
(Costa Cruises)	(lower beds/all berths): 40.4/30.0	Slot Machines: ....Yes
Former Names: ....none	Crew/Passenger Ratio	Swimming Pools (outdoors): 2
Builder: ....Fincantieri (Italy)	(lower beds/all berths): 2.1/2.9	Swimming Pools (indoors): 0
Original Cost: ....$287 million	Navigation Officers: ....Italian	Whirlpools: 4
Entered Service: ....Jan 1992	Cabins (total): 654	Fitness Center: ....Yes
Registry:........................Italy	Size Range (sq ft/m): 185.1–430.5/	Sauna/Steam Room: ....Yes/Yes
Length (ft/m): 718.5/220.61	17.2–40.0	Massage:........................Yes
Beam (ft/m): 98.4/30.80	Cabins (outside view): 438	Self-Service Launderette: ....No
Draft (ft/m): 25.0/7.60	Cabins (interior/no view): 216	Dedicated Cinema/Seats: ....No
Propulsion/Propellers: ....diesel	Cabins (for one person): 0	Library: ....Yes
(22,800kW)/2	Cabins (with private balcony): 10	Classification Society: ...Registro Navale
Passenger Decks: 10	Cabins (wheelchair accessible): 6	Italiano (RINA)
Total Crew: 610	(interior)	

OVERALL SCORE: 1,368 (OUT OF A POSSIBLE 2,000 POINTS)

ACCOMMODATION: There are 11 price categories for the accommodation. These include 10 suites, while other cabins are fairly standard in size, shape, and facilities, a higher price being asked for cabins on the highest decks. No matter what grade of accommodation you choose, all suites and cabins feature twin lower beds, color television, telephone, and

BERLITZ'S RATINGS		
	Possible	Achieved
Ship	500	388
Accommodation	200	154
Food	400	218
Service	400	282
Entertainment	100	64
Cruise	400	262

SUITES: The 10 suites, located in the center of Portofino Deck, each have a private rounded balcony, marble-clad bathrooms with Jacuzzi bathtub, and separate shower enclosure. There is plenty of space in the living and sleeping areas, and for the storage of luggage, as these really are very spacious suites.

STANDARD OUTSIDE-VIEW/INTERIOR (NO VIEW) CABINS: In general, the cabins are of a fairly generous size, and are laid out in a practical manner. They have cherry wood veneered cabinetry and accenting, and include a vanity desk unit with a large mirror. There are useful (unusual, for a cruise ship) sliding doors to the bathroom and closets, and the good cabin soundproofing is much appreciated. The soft furnishings are of good quality, but the room service menu is disappointing. The suites feature more space (although they are not large by any means), and hand-woven bedspreads.

Do note that a number of cabins have one or two extra Pullman berths (good for families with small children).

DINING: The Tivoli Dining Room has a lovely indented clean white ceiling, although it is extremely noisy (there are two seatings, with dinner typically at 7pm and 9pm to accommodate the later eating habits of Europeans), and there are a good number of tables for two, as well as tables for four, six or eight. Changeable wall panels help create a European Renaissance atmosphere, albeit at the expense of blocking off windows (but during dinner, it's dark outside anyway – unless you are in the far North). Note that the dinner meal times for European cruises are later than when the ship operates in the Caribbean. Romantic candlelight dining is typically provided on formal nights.

Reasonable continental cuisine is featured, but the presentation and food quality is not memorable, and is still the subject of many negative comments from passengers. The pasta dishes and cream sauces, however, are very good. So, although there is plenty of food, its quality and presentation often prove disappointing to those who expect better. While the quality of meats is adequate, it could be better, and is often disguised with gravies and rich sauces. Fish and seafood tend to be lacking in taste and are typically overcooked, and green vegetables are hard to come by. However, good pasta dishes are served each day (the pasta is made fresh on board daily), although quantity, not quality, is what appears from the galley. Breads and rolls are typically good, but desserts tend towards their sell-by date.

The service is basically sound, although you will probably note that there are few Italians serving in the dining room, as one might expect aboard the ship of an

Italian company. There is a wine list, although there are no wine waiters (the table waiters are expected to serve both food and wine, which does not work well), and almost all wines are young – very young.

For casual eating, the Alfresco Café, located outdoors, is moderately good, depending on what you expect. With its teak deck and traditional canvas sailcloth awning, eating outdoors is a popular pastime. Unfortunately, breakfast and luncheon buffets are really repetitious, quite poor and uncreative; there is little variety, and long lines are typical. The selection of bread rolls, fruits and cheeses is disappointing.

Note that excellent cappuccino and espresso coffees are always available in various bars around the ship, served in the right sized (proper) china cups.

OTHER COMMENTS: *Costa Classica* is an all-white ship (now over 10 years old) with a straight slab-sided profile, which is topped by Costa Cruises' unmistakable trademark trio of tall yellow funnels. This ship has brought Costa into the mainstream of cruising, Italian-style and was part of a multi-million plan to modernize the Costa Cruises (Costa Crociere) fleet.

Inside, the ship features contemporary, innovative Italian design and styling that is best described as befitting European tastes. The design incorporates much use of circles (large portholes instead of windows can be found in cabins on lower decks, and in the dining room, self-serve buffet area, coffee bar, and discotheque, for example).

There is an excellent range of public rooms, lounges and bars from which to choose. A number of specially designed good business and meeting facilities can be found; the rooms provide multi-flexible configurations.

There is some fascinating artwork, including six hermaphrodite statues in one lounge. There is a fine, if unconventional multi-tiered amphitheater-style show lounge, but the seats are bolt upright and downright uncomfortable for more than a few minutes (they remind me of charter aircraft seats). The multi-level atrium is stark and angular, and cold.

The marble-covered staircases look pleasant, but are uncarpeted and are not very practical aboard a modern cruise ship. They are also quite institutional (not to mention just a little dangerous if water or drinks are spilled on them when the ship is moving).

Perhaps the interior is best described as an innovative design project that almost works. A forward observation lounge/nightclub sits atop ship like a lump of cheese, and, unfortunately, fails to work well as a nightclub. Internet access is available from one of several computer terminals in the Internet Cafe.

The staff is reasonably friendly, and, although "spit and polish" of fine service is definitely missing, they will help you to have an enjoyable cruise (especially when pushing for gratuities). Sadly, the dress code has become very casual throughout, even on formal nights. Most passengers will be Italian, with a generous sprinkling of other European nationalities. One night (towards the end of each cruise) is typically reserved for a "Roman Bacchanal," which means that passengers dress up toga-style for dinner and beyond.

In November 2002 the ship is scheduled to enter dry-dock for a $10 million "chop-and-stretch" operation that will increase its tonnage to 78,000, its length to 870.7 feet (265.4 meters), and its passenger capacity to 2,516. The stretch would accommodate a new section of 146.9 ft (44.8 meters) to be added forward of the parallel mid-body. Included in the stretch/refit would be a further 356 passenger cabins (some of which are proposed for single occupancy). On the technical side, the engines will be upgraded for better fuel efficiency, and more generators will be added to cope with the increased demand for electricity and air-conditioning, etc. At the time this book was completed, it was not known if this planned refit would go ahead, although it certainly looks doubtful. The onboard currency is the euro.

WEAK POINTS: Standing in line for embarkation, disembarkation, shore tenders and for self-serve buffet meals is an inevitable aspect of cruising aboard all large ships. There is no wrap-around promenade deck outdoors. The ship's rather slow service speed (19.5 knots) means that itineraries have to be carefully chosen, as the ship cannot compete with the newer ships with faster service speeds (such as Festival Cruises' *European Stars/European Vision*).

The air-conditioning system in the Tivoli Dining Room is noisy. There are too many loud, repetitious and irritating announcements. Shore excursions are very expensive. Tipping envelopes provided in your cabin state the amount you are expected to give.

√ Copenhagen 3/6/05

Costa Europa
★★★ +

Large Ship:	53,872 tons	Passengers		Cabin Current:		110/220 volts
Lifestyle:	Premium	(lower beds/all berths):	1,494/1,744	Elevators:		7
Cruise Line:	Costa Crociere	Passenger Space Ratio		Casino (gaming tables):		Yes
	(Costa Cruises)	(lower beds/all berths):	36.0/30.8	Slot Machines:		Yes
Former Names:	....*Westerdam, Homeric*	Crew/Passenger Ratio		Swimming Pools (outdoors):		2
Builder:	Meyer Werft (Germany)	(lower beds/all berths):	2.4/2.6		(1 with magrodome)
Original Cost:	$150 million	Navigation Officers:	Italian	Swimming Pools (indoors):		0
Entered Service:	May 1986/Apr 2002	Cabins (total):	747	Whirlpools:		2
Registry:	Italy	Size Range (sq ft/m):	129.1–425.1/	Fitness Center:		Yes
Length (ft/m):	797.9/243.23		12.0–39.5	Sauna/Steam Room:		Yes/No
Beam (ft/m):	95.1/29.00	Cabins (outside view):	495	Massage:		Yes
Draft (ft/m):	23.6/7.20	Cabins (interior/no view):	252	Self-Service Launderette:		Yes (5)
Propulsion/Propellers:	diesel (23,830kW)/2	Cabins (for one person):	18	Dedicated Cinema/Seats:		Yes/237
Passenger Decks:	9	Cabins (with private balcony):	0	Library:		Yes
Total Crew:	650	Cabins (wheelchair accessible):	4	Classification Society:	...Lloyd's Register

---

OVERALL SCORE: 1,394 (OUT OF A POSSIBLE 2,000 POINTS)

ACCOMMODATION: There are 13 cabin price categories; these include suites, mini-suites, outside-view cabins, and inside (no view) cabins.

Except for the suite category cabins (there are five suites, each with king size beds, separate lounge area and bathroom with full size bathtub), almost all other cabins are of a similar size. In general, they are generously proportioned units that are well appointed and equipped with almost everything you need. Features include ample closet, drawer and storage space, hairdryer, and good-sized bathrooms (the towels are quite small, however). Unfortunately, there are far too many interior (no view) cabins (over 50 percent of all cabins), and the cabin insulation is rather poor – so you really *can* hear your neighbors brushing their hair. All cabin televisions feature European news channels.

Note that most cabins have twin beds, although there are a number that have the old-style upper and lower berths, so do make sure you request (and get) the kind of cabin with the sleeping arrangements you want when you book. Some of the larger cabins also have a sofa that turns into a bed – good for families with small children. There are four cabins for the handicapped, suitably located, on higher decks, close to elevators.

DINING: The Orion Restaurant is a traditional dining room that has a raised central, cupola-style dome, and port and starboard side portholes are highlighted at night by pleasing lighting. There are two seatings for all meals; note that on European cruises, dinner is typically at 7pm and 9pm to accommodate the later eating habits

BERLITZ'S RATINGS	Possible	Achieved
Ship	500	350
Accommodation	200	142
Food	400	271
Service	400	285
Entertainment	100	71
Cruise	400	275

of Europeans. Also, do take note that dining room tables are extremely close together, and, except for the center section, the ceiling is quite low (being only one deck high), and so the noise level is *extremely* high. The service is reasonable, but communication can prove frustrating sometimes, and smiles from the waiters and assistants can only do so much.

Reasonable continental cuisine is featured, but the presentation and food quality is not memorable, and is still the subject of many negative comments from passengers. The pasta dishes and cream sauces, however, are very good. So, although there is plenty of food, its quality and presentation often prove disappointing to those who expect better. While the quality of meats is adequate, it could be better, and is often disguised with gravies and rich sauces. Fish and seafood tend to be lacking in taste and are typically overcooked, and green vegetables are hard to come by.

However, good pasta dishes are served each day (the pasta is made fresh on board daily), although quantity, not quality, is what appears from the galley. Breads and rolls are typically good, but desserts tend towards their sell-by date.

The Andromeda Restaurant and Sirens Restaurant (both are located in the aft section of the ship) feature breakfast and lunch in self-serve buffet style, but lines and a crowded environment are noisy and not really enjoyable.

Note that excellent cappuccino and espresso coffees are always available in various bars around the ship, served in the right sized (proper) china cups.

OTHER COMMENTS: This was originally a Home Lines cruise ship that underwent an $84 million "chop and stretch" operation in 1990 after being purchased by Holland America Line. You don't even have to look closely to tell where the mid-section was inserted, due to the fact that the windows are larger than the fore and aft sections. The ship was moved to Costa Cruises (a cruise line wholly owned by Carnival Corporation) in 2002. When Costa Cruises took over the ship, no structural changes were made, although some of the soft furnishings were changed and the décor was made to feel brighter and more European in style, although, after a €5 million refit, surprisingly few changes are really noticeable. The funnel, however, looks surprisingly good in Costa Cruises colors.

The ship has good teak outside decks and a wraparound promenade deck with real wooden deck lounge chairs. There is also a good amount of open deck space for sunbathing. There is a magrodome-covered swimming pool deck, but unfortunately it is simply too small for the number of passengers carried.

The ship has elegant, functional, and restful interior decor. The public rooms are decorated in pastel tones, although some décor looks dated. The ship absorbs passengers well, and has good passenger flow, but the layout is a little awkward to learn at first. Good quality furnishings and fabrics are used throughout.

The health and fitness facilities (located on an upper deck) include a fitness center, saunas and massage rooms, although there is no steam room.

Most of the public entertainment rooms are located on one deck, which makes access a simple matter. Entertainment facilities include the Atlante Theater, the ship's two decks high show lounge, with main floor and balcony seating; however, note that several pillars obstruct sight lines from a number of seats. An addition, when Costa Cruises took over the ship, can be found in the Medusa Ballroom, with stage and proper wooden dance floor. Also added were more children's facilities, for the increase in families with children that will inhabit the ship. There are several bars and lounges to choose from, some small and intimate, others larger and noisier. However, there are, fortunately, lots of nooks and crannies to play in – much nicer than the warehouse-style public rooms of the latest, much larger, ships.

Costa Europa is a well-run, modern ship (it is comfortable, but certainly not luxurious) that provides a satisfactory cruise experience, particularly for families with children. There are few Italians among the crew, however (except in key positions), as many are from the Philippines.

The Costa Cruises onboard staff is reasonably friendly, and, although "spit and polish" of fine service is missing, they will help you to have an enjoyable cruise (especially when pushing for gratuities). Sadly, the dress code has become very casual throughout, even on formal nights. Most passengers will be Italian, with a generous sprinkling of other European nationalities, which tends to make for a somewhat noisy, gesture-filled atmosphere on board. One night (towards the end of each cruise) is typically reserved for a "Roman Bacchanal," which means that passengers dress up toga-style for dinner and beyond. Costa Cruises adds an automatic 15 percent for beverage purchases. The onboard currency is the euro.

WEAK POINTS: Standing in line for embarkation, disembarkation, shore tenders and for self-serve buffet meals is an inevitable aspect of cruising aboard all large ships. Communication with staff is not easy; room service is particularly poor. There are no cabins with private balconies. There are too many loud, repetitive and irritating announcements. Shore excursions are very expensive. There is some noticeable vibration in some areas. Tipping envelopes provided in your cabin state the amount you are expected to give.

Costa Marina
★★★

Mid-Size Ship: . . . . .25,441 tons	Passengers	Cabin Current: . . . . .110 and 220 volts
Lifestyle: . . . . .Standard	(lower beds/all berths): 772/1,005	Elevators: 8
Cruise Line: . . . . .Costa Crociere	Passenger Space Ratio	Casino (gaming tables): . . . . .Yes
(Costa Cruises)	(lower beds/all berths): 32.9/25.3	Slot Machines: . . . . .Yes
Former Names: . . . . .Axel Johnson	Crew/Passenger Ratio	Swimming Pools (outdoors): 1
Builder: . . . . .Mariotti Shipyards (Italy)	(lower beds/all berths): 1.9/2.5	Swimming Pools (indoors): 0
Original Cost: . . . .$130 million	Navigation Officers: . . . . .Italian	Whirlpools: 3
Entered Service: . . . . .July 1990	Cabins (total): 386	Fitness Center: . . . . .Yes
Registry: . . . . .Italy	Size Range (sq ft/m): 104.4–264.8/	Sauna/Steam Room: . . . . .Yes/Yes
Length (ft/m): 571.8/174.25	9.7–24.6	Massage: . . . . .Yes
Beam (ft/m): 84.6/25.75	Cabins (outside view): 183	Self-Service Launderette: . . . . .No
Draft (ft/m): 26.1/8.20	Cabins (interior/no view): 205	Dedicated Cinema/Seats: . . . . .No
Propulsion/Propellers: diesel (19,152kW)/2	Cabins (for one person): 0	Library: . . . . .Yes
Passenger Decks: 8	Cabins (with private balcony): 8	Classification Society: . . .Registro Navale
Total Crew: 400	Cabins (wheelchair accessible): 0	Italiano (RINA)

OVERALL SCORE: 1,224 (OUT OF A POSSIBLE 2,000 POINTS)

ACCOMMODATION: Both the outside and interior (no view) cabins are quite comfortable, but have very plain, almost clinical, décor and no warmth. Bathrooms are functional, but there is little space for personal toiletry items. The illuminated cabin numbers outside each cabin are novel. The room service menu is poor.

DINING: The 452-seat Cristal Restaurant is fairly spacious and has expansive glass windows that look out over the stern, while port and starboard sides feature large portholes. There are two seatings and, sadly, there are few tables for two, most of the tables being for four, six or eight. Romantic candlelight dining is typically featured on a formal night.

Reasonable continental cuisine is provided, but the presentation and food quality is not memorable, and is still the subject of many negative comments from passengers. The pasta dishes and cream sauces, however, are very good. So, although there is plenty of food, its quality and presentation often prove disappointing to those who expect better. The quality of meats is good (particularly the dark meats that German-speaking passengers enjoy), although it is often disguised with gravies and rich sauces. Fish and seafood tend to be lacking in taste and are typically overcooked, and green vegetables are hard to come by. However, good pasta dishes are served each day (the pasta is made fresh on board daily), although quantity, not quality, is what appears from the galley. Breads and rolls are typically good, but desserts tend towards their sell-by date.

The service is basically sound, although you will

BERLITZ'S RATINGS		
	Possible	Achieved
Ship	500	312
Accommodation	200	130
Food	400	218
Service	400	249
Entertainment	100	62
Cruise	400	253

probably note that there are few Italians serving in the dining room, as one might expect aboard the ship of an Italian company. There is a wine list, although there are no wine waiters (the table waiters are expected to serve both food and wine, which does not work well), and almost all wines are young – very young.

Note that excellent cappuccino and espresso coffees are always available in various bars around the ship, served in the right sized (proper) china cups.

OTHER COMMENTS: *Costa Marina* is an interesting, though very angular-looking, mid-sized ship, the first of two such ships converted from container carriers to passenger cruise ships (its almost identically designed, though slightly longer sister ship is named *Costa Allegra*). There is a high glass-to-steel ratio, with numerous glass domes and walls. The vessel has a contemporary, cutaway stern that is virtually replaced by a glass wall (which are, in fact, the dining room windows), and a stark upright cluster of three yellow funnels.

Most public rooms are located above the accommodation decks and feature several bars and lounges. This is very much an Italian ship will provide a good first cruise experience for young European passengers.

There is generally good passenger flow throughout its public room spaces, although congestion occurs when first seating passengers move from the dining room to the show lounge and other public rooms, and when second seating passengers move from the public rooms to the dining room.

In the spring of 2002, *Costa Marina* became a ship dedicated to the German-speaking market. The ship underwent a considerable amount of interior redecoration and emerged as an Italian ship for German-speaking passengers ("La Deutsche Vita"). The onboard currency is the euro.

WEAK POINTS: The fit and finish of this vessel are below standard. There is a very limited amount of open deck and sunbathing space. Note that there is no observation lounge with forward-facing views. The swimming pool is really tiny. There are simply too many interior (no view) cabins. There are poor sight lines in the showlounge, with too many pillars (14). The library is really poor. Tipping envelopes provided in your cabin state the amount you are expected to give.

SHIP TALK

Abeam: off the side of the ship, at a right angle to its length.

Aft: near, toward, or in the rear of the ship.

Ahead: something that is ahead of the ship's bow.

Alleyway: a passageway or corridor.

Alongside: said of a ship when it is beside a pier or another vessel.

Amidships: in or toward the middle of the ship; the longitudinal center portion of the ship.

Anchor Ball: black ball hoisted above the bow to show that the vessel is anchored.

Astern: is the opposite of Ahead (i.e., meaning something behind the ship).

Backwash: motion in the water caused by the propeller(s) moving in a reverse (astern) direction.

Bar: sandbar, usually caused by tidal or current conditions near the shore.

Beam: width of the ship between its two sides at the widest point.

Bearing: compass direction, expressed in degrees, from the ship to a particular objective or destination.

Below: anything beneath the main deck.

Berth: dock, pier, or quay. Also means bed on board ship.

Bilge: lowermost spaces of the infrastructure of a ship.

Boat Stations: allotted space for each person during lifeboat drill or any other emergency when lifeboats are lowered.

Bow: the forward most part of the vessel.

Bridge: navigational and command control center.

Bulkhead: upright partition (wall) dividing the ship into compartments.

Bunkers: the space where fuel is stored; "bunkering" means taking on fuel.

Cable Length: a measured length equaling 100 fathoms or 600 feet.

Chart: a nautical map used for navigating.

Colors: refers to the national flag or emblem flown by the ship.

Companionway: interior stairway.

Course: direction in which the ship is headed, in degrees.

Davit: a device for raising and lowering lifeboats.

Deadlight: a ventilated porthole cover to prevent light from entering.

Disembark (also debark): to leave a ship.

Dock: berth, pier, or quay.

Draft (or draught): measurement in feet from the ship's waterline to the lowest point of its keel.

Embark: to join a ship.

Fantail: the rear or overhang of the ship.

Fathom: distance equal to 6 ft.

Flagstaff: a pole at the stern of a ship where the flag of its country of registry is flown.

Free Port: port or place that is free of customs duty and regulations.

Funnel: chimney from which the ship's combustion gases are propelled into the atmosphere.

Galley: the ship's kitchen.

Gangway: the stairway or ramp that provides the link between ship and shore.

Costa Mediterranea
NOT YET RATED

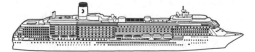

Large Ship: ....85,700 tons	Total Crew: 902	Cabin Current: ....110 volts
Lifestyle: ....Standard	Passengers	Elevators: 12
Cruise Line: ....Costa Crociere	(lower beds/all berths): 2,112/2,680	Casino (gaming tables): ....Yes
(Costa Cruises)	Passenger Space Ratio	Slot Machines: ....Yes
Former Names: ....none	(lower beds/all berths): 40.5/31.9	Swimming Pools (outdoors): 2
Builder: ...Kvaerner Masa-Yards (Finland)	Crew/Passenger Ratio	(+1 indoor/outdoor)
Original Cost: ....$335 million	(lower beds/all berths): 2.3/2.9	Swimming Pools (indoors): ....No
Entered Service: ....May 2003	Navigation Officers: ....Italian	Whirlpools: ....Yes
Registry: ....Italy	Cabins (total): 1,056	Fitness Center: ....Yes
Length (ft/m): 959.6/292.5	Size Range (sq ft/m): 161.4–387.5/	Sauna/Steam Room: ....Yes/Yes
Beam (ft/m): 105.6/32.2	15.0–36.0	Massage: ....Yes
Draft (ft/m): 25.5/7.8	Cabins (outside view): 843	Self-Service Launderette: ....No
Propulsion/Propellers: .....diesel-electric	Cabins (interior/no view): 213	Dedicated Cinema/Seats: ....No
(34,000 kW)/2 azimuthing pods	Cabins (for one person): 0	Library: ....Yes
(17.6 MW each)	Cabins (with private balcony): 742	Classification Society: ...Registro Navale
Passenger Decks: 12	Cabins (wheelchair accessible): 8	Italiano (RINA)

OVERALL SCORE: NYR (OUT OF A POSSIBLE 2,000 POINTS)

ACCOMMODATION: There is a healthy (78 percent) proportion of outside-view to interior (no view) cabins. All of the cabins feature twin beds that can be converted into a queen-sized bed, individually controlled air-conditioning, television, and telephone. Note that some many cabins have their views obstructed by lifeboats - on Deck 4 (Roma Deck), the lowest of the accommodation decks, as well as some cabins on Deck 5. Some cabins feature pull-down Pullman berths that are fully hidden in the ceiling when not in use.

Some of the most desirable suites and cabins are those with private balconies on the five aft-facing decks (Decks 4, 5, 6, 7, and 8) with views overlooking the stern and ship's wash. The other cabins with private balconies will find the balconies not so private – the partition between one balcony and the next is not a full partition, so you will be able to hear your neighbors (or smell their smoke). However, these balcony occupants all have good views through glass and wood-topped railings, and the deck is made of teak. The cabins are well laid out, typically with twin beds that convert to a queen-sized bed, vanity desk (with built-in hairdryer), large television, personal safe, and one closet that features moveable shelves – thus providing more space for luggage storage. However, note that the lighting is fluorescent, and much too harsh (the bedside control is for a master switch only – other individual lights cannot be controlled). The bathroom is a simple, modular unit that features shower enclosures with soap dispenser; there

BERLITZ'S RATINGS		
	Possible	Achieved
Ship	500	NYR
Accommodation	200	NYR
Food	400	NYR
Service	400	NYR
Entertainment	100	NYR
Cruise	400	NYR

is a good amount of stowage space for personal toiletry items.

The largest suites are those designated as Penthouse Suites, although they are really quite small when compared with suites aboard other ships of a similar size (for example, those of Celebrity Cruises' *Century, Galaxy, Mercury,* or *Millennium*). However, they do at least offer more space to move around in, and a slightly larger, better bathroom.

DINING: The main dining room is extremely large and is located at the aft section of the ship on two levels with a spiral stairway between them; the galley itself is located under the dining room, and waiter access is by escalators. There are two seatings, with tables for two, four, six or eight. Note that dinner on European cruises is typically scheduled at 7pm and 9pm to accommodate the later eating habits of Europeans. Themed evenings are a part of the Costa Cruises tradition, and three different window blinds help create a different feel.

There is a wine list, although there are no wine waiters (the table waiters are expected to serve both food and wine, which does not work well), and almost all wines are young – very young.

ALTERNATIVE (RESERVATIONS-ONLY, EXTRA COST) DINING: Ristorante Magnifico by Zeffirino is a more upscale dining spot located on two of the uppermost decks of the ship under a huge glass dome, with seating for approximately 150. It features a show kitchen where chefs can be seen preparing their masterpieces. It is located directly above the self-serve buffet area, in the lower, forward section of the funnel housing, with some superb views over the multi-deck atrium, as well as to the sea. Fine table settings, china and silverware are featured, as are leather-bound menus. Reservations are required and there is a cover charge of $18.75 per person (for service and gratuity). But you may think it's worth it in order to have dinner in a setting that is quieter and more refined than the main dining room.

OTHER VENUES: Undoubtedly the place that most people will want to see and be seen is at the casual Caffe. There are four separate salons. This Caffe is ideal for drinks, music, and people-watching.

Casual breakfast and luncheon self-serve buffet-style meals can be taken in the expansive Buffet Restaurant, which is located adjacent to the swimming pools, with seating both indoors and outdoors. A grill (for hamburgers and hot dogs) and a pasta bar are conveniently located outside adjacent to the second pool, while indoors is a Pizzeria.

Note that excellent cappuccino and espresso coffees are always available in various bars around the ship, served in the right sized (proper) china cups.

OTHER COMMENTS: The first thing that regular passengers will notice is the extremely long length of this ship, which, together with sister ship *Costa Atlantica* makes the ship look much sleeker than any other ship in the Costa Cruises fleet.

Costa Mediterranea sports the now familiar, instantly recognizable yellow upright funnels, with one large funnel and two small exhaust funnels set behind it. The propulsion is provided by two azimuthing "pods" which are hung under the ship's stern (rather like giant outboard motors). These replace the conventional shaft and rudder system (the pods have forward-facing propellers that can be turned through 360 degrees).

There are two centrally located swimming pools outdoors, one of which can be used in inclement weather due to its retractable glass dome (magrodome) cover. A bar abridges two adjacent whirlpool tubs. Another smaller pool is available for children; there is also a winding water slide that spans two decks in height (it starts on a platform bridge located between the two aft funnels). There is also an additional whirlpool tub outdoors.

Inside, the layout is just the same as in sister ship *Costa Atlantica*. The interior design is, however, bold and brash – a mix of classical Italy and contemporary features. Good points include the fact that the interior design allows good passenger flow from one public space to another, and there are several floor spaces for dancing, and a range of bars and lounges for socializing.

When you first walk into the ship, you'll be greeted by the immense size of the dramatic lobby space that spans eight decks. The atrium lobby, with its two grand stairways, presents a stunning wall decoration that is best seen from any of the multiple viewing balconies on each deck above the main lobby floor level. Take a drink from the lobby bar and look upwards – the surroundings are quite stunning.

There is a three-deck-high show lounge, with a main floor and two balcony levels around the perimeter (spiral stairways at the back of the lounge connect all three levels). A small chapel (there is one aboard all the ships of Costa Cruises) is located forward of the uppermost level.

Other facilities include a winding shopping street with several boutique stores (typically Fendi, Gianni Versace, Paul & Shark Yachting are featured), a photo gallery, video games room, observation balcony in the center of the vessel (at the top of the multi-deck atrium), a large casino and a library (with internet access via one of several computer terminals.

Health spa facilities include a solarium, eight treatment rooms, sauna and steam rooms for men and women, beauty parlor and gymnasium with floor-to-ceiling windows on three sides. There is also a jogging track outdoors, located around the ship's mast and the forward third of the ship.

Costa Cruises has, during the recent past, been busy updating its ships and image in the marketplace, and retraining its staff, in order to provide more hospitality and better personal service for its passengers. With the debut of sister ship *Costa Atlantica* came many new, better, uniforms for many departments, as well as more choice in a ship that is designed to wow the hip and trendy. Food and service levels have been raised to a better standard than that found aboard all other Costa Cruises ships to date.

However, do expect irritating announcements (particularly for activities that bring revenue, such as art auctions, bingo, horse racing) that intrude constantly into your cruise, and a great deal of hustling for drinks. The onboard currency is the euro or US dollar, depending on the region of operation.

WEAK POINTS: There are too many lines; however, standing in line for embarkation, disembarkation, shore tenders and for self-serve buffet meals is an inevitable aspect of cruising aboard all large ships. There is too much use of fluorescent lighting in the suites and cabins, and the soundproofing could be much better than it is. Some bathroom fixtures – bath and shower taps in particular – are quite frustrating to use until you get the hang of them. Some tables in the dining room have a less than comfortable view of the harsh lighting of the escalators between the galley and the two decks of the dining room.

Many pillars obstruct passenger flow and sight lines throughout the ship; there is even one right in the middle – actually positioned slightly off-center – of a winding shopping street. Indeed, the many pillars in the dining room make it extremely difficult for the waiters and the proper service of food.

Costa Romantica
★★★ +

Large Ship:	.53,049 tons	Passengers		Cabin Current:	.110 volts
Lifestyle:	Standard	(lower beds/all berths):	.1,356/1,779	Elevators:	.8
Cruise Line:	Costa Crociere	Passenger Space Ratio		Casino (gaming tables):	Yes
	(Costa Cruises)	(lower beds/all berths):	.39.1/29.8	Slot Machines:	Yes
Former Names:	none	Crew/Passenger Ratio		Swimming Pools (outdoors):	.2
Builder:	Fincantieri (Italy)	(lower beds/all berths):	.2.2/2.9	Swimming Pools (indoors):	.0
Original Cost:	$325 million	Navigation Officers:	Italian	Whirlpools:	.4
Entered Service:	Nov 1993	Cabins (total):	.678	Fitness Center:	Yes
Registry:	Italy	Size Range (sq ft/m):	.185.1–430.5/	Sauna/Steam Room:	Yes/No
Length (ft/m):	.718.5/220.61		17.2–40.0	Massage:	Yes
Beam (ft/m):	.98.4/30.89	Cabins (outside view):	.462	Self-Service Launderette:	No
Draft (ft/m):	.25.0/7.60	Cabins (interior/no view):	.216	Dedicated Cinema/Seats:	No
Propulsion/Propellers: diesel (22,800kW)/2		Cabins (for one person):	.0	Library:	Yes
Passenger Decks:	.10	Cabins (with private balcony):	.10	Classification Society:	Registro Navale
Total Crew:	.600	Cabins (wheelchair accessible): 6 (interior)			Italiano (RINA)

OVERALL SCORE: 1,369 (OUT OF A POSSIBLE 2,000 POINTS)

ACCOMMODATION: There are 11 price categories for the accommodation. These include 16 suites, 10 of which have a private semi-circular balcony, while six suites are located in the front of the ship, with commanding views over the ships' bows. The other cabins are fairly standard in size, shape, and facilities, a higher price being asked for cabins located on the highest decks.

SUITES/MINI-SUITES: The 16 suites (with floor-to-ceiling windows) and 18 mini-suites are really quite pleasant (except for the rounded balconies of the 10 suites on Madrid Deck, where a solid steel half-wall blocks the view, whereas a glass half-wall and polished wood rail wood be better). A sliding door separates the bedroom from the living room, and bathrooms are of a decent size. Cherry wood walls and cabinetry help make these suites warm and very attractive.

The six suites at the forward section of Monte Carlo Deck are the largest, and have huge glass windows with commanding forward views, although they do not have balconies.

STANDARD OUTSIDE-VIEW/INTERIOR (NO VIEW) CABINS: All other cabins are of a standard, moderately generous size, and all have nicely finished cherry wood cabinetry and walls (the ceilings are plain). However, the cabin bathrooms and shower enclosures are small. There are a good number of triple and quad cabins that are ideal for families with children. The company's in-cabin food service menu is extremely basic.

BERLITZ'S RATINGS

	Possible	Achieved
Ship	500	389
Accommodation	200	154
Food	400	218
Service	400	282
Entertainment	100	64
Cruise	400	262

DINING: The 728-seat Botticelli Restaurant is better designed and a little less noisy than in the sister ship of the same size (*Costa Classica*, before the ship was due to be "stretched"), and there are several tables for two, four, six or eight. There are two seatings (dinner on European cruises is typically at 7pm and 9pm to accommodate the later eating habits of Europeans), and there are both smoking and non-smoking sections. Romantic candlelight dining is typically featured on a formal night.

Reasonable continental cuisine is provided, but the presentation and food quality is not memorable, and is still the subject of many negative comments from passengers. The pasta dishes and cream sauces, however, are very good. So, although there is plenty of food, its quality and presentation often prove disappointing to those who expect better. While the quality of meats is adequate, it could be better, and is often disguised with gravies and rich sauces. Fish and seafood tend to be lacking in taste and are typically overcooked, and green vegetables are hard to come by.

However, good pasta dishes are served each day (the pasta is made fresh on board daily), although quantity, not quality, is what appears from the galley. Breads and rolls are typically good, but desserts tend towards their sell-by date.

The service is basically sound, although you will probably note that there are few Italians serving in the dining room, as one might expect aboard the ship of an Italian company. There is a wine list, although there are no wine waiters (the table waiters are expected to serve both food and wine, which does not work well), and almost all wines are young – very young.

For informal dining, there is a much improved and more practical buffet layout than in its sister ship, but it is far too small, and buffets are very much standard fare, really unimaginative and quite under-creative, with the exception of some good commercial pasta dishes. One would expect Italian waiters, but, sadly, this is not the case now, with most of the waiters coming from countries other than Italy (many are from the Philippines).

Note that excellent cappuccino and espresso coffees are always available in various bars around the ship, served in the right sized (proper) china cups.

OTHER COMMENTS: *Costa Romantica* is a bold, contemporary ship with an upright yellow funnel cluster of three typical of Italian styling today. Costa is well established in Europe, and Italian-style cruising is something it does well. Sadly, there is no wrap-around promenade deck outdoors, and so contact with the sea is minimal, although there is some good open space on several of the upper levels.

This ship has a much nicer interior design than its sister ship, *Costa Classica*, and the décor is decidedly warmer. Being Italian, it is also chic and very tasteful, and should appeal to both Europeans and sophisticated North Americans. The layout and flow are somewhat disjointed, however. The ship features a good number of business and conference facilities, with several flexible meeting rooms for groups of different sizes.

The multi-level atrium is open and spacious, and has a revolving mobile sculpture. The amphitheater-style, two-deck high, multi-tiered show lounge is quite decent, and has interesting artwork, but the stark upright seating is really uncomfortable (note that 10 very large pillars obstruct the sight lines to the stage from many seats).

There is also a small chapel (in a different location to that in its sister ship), and several intimate public rooms, lounges and bars. Internet access is also available from one of several computer terminals in the Internet Cafe.

Costa Cruises does a good job of providing first-time cruise passengers with a well packaged vacation that is a mix of sophistication and basic fare, albeit accompanied by rather loud music and an international staff that seem to have lost direction. The onboard currency is the euro.

WEAK POINTS: Standing in line for embarkation, disembarkation, shore tenders and for self-serve buffet meals is an inevitable aspect of cruising aboard all large ships. Announcements are many and loud. The ship's rather slow service speed (19.5 knots) means that itineraries have to be carefully chosen, as the ship cannot compete with the newer ships with faster service speeds (such as Festival Cruises' *European Stars/European Vision*).The reception desk staff is quite impersonal, as in a bad hotel, and cigarette smoke is everywhere. Tipping envelopes provided in your cabin state the amount you are expected to give.

Costa Tropicale
★★★

Removed 2006

Large Ship: . . . . .35,190 tons	
Lifestyle: . . . . .Standard	
Cruise Line: . . . . .Costa Crociere	
	(Costa Cruises)
Former Names: . . . .*Tropicale*	
Builder: . . . . . . .Aalborg Vaerft (Denmark)	
Original Cost: . . . .$100 million	
Entered Service: . . . .Jan 1982/June 2001	
Registry: . . . . .Italy	
Length (ft/m): 671.7/204.76	
Beam (ft/m): 86.7/26.45	
Draft (ft/m): 23.3/7.11	
Propulsion/Propellers: diesel (19,566kW)/2	
Passenger Decks: 10	
Total Crew: 550	

Passengers	
(lower beds/all berths): 1,022/1,412	
Passenger Space Ratio	
(lower beds/all berths): 34.4/24.9	
Crew/Passenger Ratio	
(lower beds/all berths): 1.8/2.5	
Navigation Officers: . . . . .Italian	
Cabins (total): 511	
Size Range (sq ft/m): 180.0–398.2/	
	16.7–37.0
Cabins (outside view): 324	
Cabins (interior/no view): 187	
Cabins (for one person): 0	
Cabins (with private balcony): 12	
Cabins (wheelchair accessible): 11	

Cabin Current: . . . . .110 volts	
Elevators: 8	
Casino (gaming tables): . . . . .Yes	
Slot Machines: . . . . .Yes	
Swimming Pools (outdoors): 3	
Swimming Pools (indoors): 0	
Whirlpools: 0	
Fitness Center: . . . . .Yes	
Sauna/Steam Room: . . . . .Yes/No	
Massage: . . . . .Yes	
Self-Service Launderette: . . . . .Yes	
Dedicated Cinema/Seats: . . . . .No	
Library: . . . . .Yes	
Classification Society: . . .Registro Navale	
	Italiano (RINA)

OVERALL SCORE: 1,237 (OUT OF A POSSIBLE 2,000 POINTS)

ACCOMMODATION: There are 12 accommodation categories to choose from. Most of the "standard" interior (no view) and outside-view cabins are all of the standard cookie-cutter variety (although they are of quite a decent size), with an imaginative European-style decor, and just enough closet and drawer space for passengers to manage for a week. The bathrooms are quite plain, but adequate. A number of cabins have third and fourth person upper berths added – these are good for families with children.

The best accommodation can be found in 12 "suites" – each with a small (narrow) semi-private balcony. Naturally, there is more space, with the living and sleeping areas divided. The bathroom is marginally larger, too. However, all of these suites have their views substantially blocked by the positioning of the lifeboats.

DINING: The Riviera Restaurant is located on the ship's lowest deck. It is colorful, very cheerful, brightly lit, but noisy and extremely cramped, which makes correct service quite difficult. There are tables for four, six or eight (there are no tables for two), and dining is in two seatings (dinner on European cruises is typically at 7pm and 9pm to accommodate the later eating habits of Europeans).

Reasonable continental cuisine is featured, but the presentation and food quality is not memorable, and is still the subject of many negative comments from passengers. The pasta dishes and cream sauces, however, are very good. So, although there is plenty of food, its quality and presentation often prove disappointing to

BERLITZ'S RATINGS

	Possible	Achieved
Ship	500	312
Accommodation	200	121
Food	400	217
Service	400	268
Entertainment	100	72
Cruise	400	247

those who expect better. While the quality of meats is adequate, it could be better, and is often disguised with gravies and rich sauces. Fish and seafood tend to be lacking in taste and are typically overcooked, and green vegetables are hard to come by. However, good pasta dishes are served each day (the pasta is made fresh on board daily), although quantity, not quality, is what appears from the galley. Breads and rolls are typically good, but desserts tend towards their sell-by date.

The service is basically sound, although you will probably note that there are few Italians serving in the dining room, as one might expect aboard the ship of an Italian company. There is a wine list, although there are no wine waiters (the table waiters are expected to serve both food and wine, which does not work well), and almost all wines are young – very young.

The Lido Café features self-service buffets, which are very basic, as is the selection of breads, rolls, fruit and cheeses. At night, it becomes a bistro and provides a casual (dress down) alternative to eating in the main dining room.

Note that excellent cappuccino and espresso coffees are always available in various bars around the ship, served in the right sized (proper) china cups.

OTHER COMMENTS: *Costa Tropicale* (whose former name was *Tropicale*) was the first new ship ever ordered by the former owner, Carnival Cruise Lines, and its exterior design led the way for that company's clutch of new buildings during the following years. The ship was acquired by Costa Cruises in January 2001 and given a $24 million dollar refit and refurbishment, including a new yellow funnel, after which it has settled down well into the European itineraries and programs of Costa Cruises. The ship has a fairly distinctive, though somewhat squared-off look.

The interior design is reasonably well laid out, and the ship generally has a good passenger flow. The public rooms are decorated in European colors, which are designed to make everyone feel alive and lively. The show lounge is only one deck high, and the sight lines to the stage are not good from many seats, due to several pillars being positioned in the way. Internet access is also available from one of several computer terminals in the Internet Cafe.

Costa Tropicale is a good ship for families with children, as Costa Cruises goes out of its way to entertain young cruisers as well as their parents, particularly during summer and other busy school holiday periods.

Costa Tropicale now looks spiffy and more contemporary under the Costa Cruises banner, although it is one of the smallest ships in the fleet. This is *not* a luxury cruise product, nor does it pretend to be. But you and your family will probably have fun, and there are plenty of opportunities for gaming and partying. The onboard currency is the euro.

WEAK POINTS: Standing in line for embarkation, disembarkation, shore tenders and for self-serve buffet meals is an inevitable aspect of cruising aboard all large ships. There are so few balcony cabins. Sadly, there is no wrap-around open promenade deck – or any walking space outdoors. The ship has low-quality fittings and cabinetry in many areas. There is noise and loud music everywhere. The health spa is small and has only the most minimal of facilities.

MORE SHIP TALK

Gross Tons (gt): not the weight of a ship but the total navigation of all permanently enclosed spaces above and below decks, with certain exceptions, such as the bridge, radio room, galleys, washing facilities, and other specified areas. It is the basis for harbor dues. International regulations introduced in 1982 required shipowners to remeasure the grt of their vessels (1 grt = 100 cubic ft of enclosed space/2.8 cubic meters). This unit of measure was invented in England centuries ago for taxation purposes, when wine shipped from France was stored in standard-size casks, called tonneaux. Thus a ship carrying twenty casks measured 20 tons, and taxes were applied accordingly.

Helm: the apparatus for steering a ship.

House Flag: the flag denoting the company to which a ship belongs.

Hull: the frame and body of the ship exclusive of masts or superstructure.

Leeward: the side of a ship that is sheltered from the wind.

Luff: the side of a ship facing the wind

Manifest: a list of the ship's passengers, crew, and cargo.

Nautical Mile: one-sixtieth of a degree of the circumference of the Earth.

Pilot: a person licensed to navigate ships into or out of a harbor or through difficult waters, and to advise the captain on handling the ship during these procedures.

Pitch: the rise and fall of a ship's bow that may occur when the ship is under way.

Port: the left side of a ship when facing forward.

Quay: berth, dock, or pier.

Rudder: a finlike device astern and below the waterline, for steering the vessel.

Screw: a ship's propeller.

Stabilizer: a gyroscopically operated retractable "fin" extending from either or both sides of the ship below the waterline to provide a more stable ride.

Starboard: the right side of the ship when facing forward.

Stern: the aftmost part of the ship that is opposite the bow.

Tender: a smaller vessel, often a lifeboat, that is used to transport passengers between the ship and shore when the vessel is at anchor.

Wake: the track of agitated water left behind a ship when in motion.

Waterline: the line along the side of a ship's hull corresponding to the water surface.

Windward: the side of a ship facing the direction in which the wind blows.

Yaw: the erratic deviation from the ship's set course, usually caused by a heavy sea.

Costa Victoria
★★★★

Large Ship:	75,200 tons	Passengers		Cabin Current:	110 and 220 volts
Lifestyle:	Standard	(lower beds/all berths):	1,928/2,464	Elevators:	12
Cruise Line:	Costa Crociere	Passenger Space Ratio		Casino (gaming tables):	Yes
	(Costa Cruises)	(lower beds/all berths):	39.0/30.5	Slot Machines:	Yes
Former Names:	none	Crew/Passenger Ratio		Swimming Pools (outdoors):	2
Builder:	Bremer Vulkan (Germany)	(lower beds/all berths):	2.4/3.0	Swimming Pools (indoors):	1
Original Cost:	$388 million	Navigation Officers:	Italian	Whirlpools:	4
Entered Service:	July 1996	Cabins (total):	964	Fitness Center:	Yes
Registry:	Italy	Size Range (sq ft/m):	120.0–430.5/	Sauna/Steam Room:	Yes/Yes
Length (ft/m):	823.0/251.00		11.1–40.0	Massage:	Yes
Beam (ft/m):	105.5/32.25	Cabins (outside view):	573	Self-Service Launderette:	Yes
Draft (ft/m):	25.6/7.8	Cabins (interior/no view):	391	Dedicated Cinema/Seats:	No
Propulsion/Propellers: diesel (30,000kW)/2		Cabins (for one person):	0	Library:	Yes
Passenger Decks:	10	Cabins (with private balcony):	0	Classification Society:	Registro Navale
Total Crew:	800	Cabins (wheelchair accessible):	0		Italiano (RINA)

OVERALL SCORE: 1,406 (OUT OF A POSSIBLE 2,000 POINTS)

ACCOMMODATION: There are six large Panorama suites (each has third/fourth Pullman berths in a separate, tiny, train-like compartment) and 14 mini-suites (the six suites feature Laura Ashley-style fabrics), all with butler service; 65 percent of all other cabins have outside views, but they are small (for two). While the suites are not large, all other cabins are of rather mean dimensions. Some (only 16) of the interior (no view) cabins accommodate four, while all other cabins are for two or three persons.

All cabins feature wood cabinetry, with a fair amount of closet and drawer space for two for a one-week cruise, excellent air-conditioning, mini-bar/refrigerator, and electric blackout window blind (there are no curtains). The ocean-view cabins have large picture windows. The cabin bathrooms are small but well appointed, and (sensibly) have a sliding door.

There are six cabins for the physically handicapped (each has two bathrooms); all are well located, and adjacent to elevators in the center of the ship.

Note that the personal safe is difficult to reach, and cabin stewards simply have too many cabins to clean, and no help, which means that the service is less than desirable.

DINING: There are two main dining rooms: the 594-seat Minuetto Restaurant, and the 506-seat Fantasia Restaurant, both of which are separated by the main galley. There are two seatings (dinner on European cruises is typically at 7pm and 9pm to accommodate the later eating habits of Europeans), and smoking and no-smoking

BERLITZ'S RATINGS		
	Possible	Achieved
Ship	500	418
Accommodation	200	158
Food	400	220
Service	400	273
Entertainment	100	73
Cruise	400	264

sections in both restaurants. They are expansive (there are a few tables for two, most being for four, six or eight) and feature marble and pine walls. Romantic candlelight dining is typically featured on a formal night. The cuisine is good basic fare, and the presentation is adequate, but nothing special. Somewhat lacking is the use of garnishes to dress the plates. As you would expect, there is always plenty of pasta (the pasta is made fresh on board daily).

Reasonable continental cuisine is featured, but the presentation and food quality is not memorable, and is still the subject of many negative comments from passengers. The pasta dishes and cream sauces, however, are very good. So, although there is plenty of food, its quality and presentation often prove disappointing to those who expect better. While the quality of meats is adequate, it could be better, and is often disguised with gravies and rich sauces. Fish and seafood tend to be lacking in taste and are typically overcooked, and green vegetables are hard to come by. However, good pasta dishes are served each day (the pasta is made fresh on board daily), although quantity, not quality, is what appears from the galley. Breads and rolls are typically good, but desserts tend towards their sell-by date.

The service is basically sound, although you will probably note that there are few Italians serving in the dining room, as one might expect aboard the ship of an Italian company. There is a wine list, although there are no wine waiters (the table waiters are expected to serve both food and wine, which does not work well), and almost all wines are young – very young.

A reservations-only alternative for dinner, *Ristorante Magnifico by Zeffirino*, is available six nights each week, with a service charge of $18.75 per person (passengers occupying suites will get a complimentary pass for one evening).

The ship also features casual breakfast and lunch buffets with indoor/outdoor seating (under a canvas sailcloth canopy for the outdoor section), although the buffet displays are very disappointing. There is also a pizzeria, (it is open in the afternoon and evening) good for casual fast-food devotees who may be used to frozen/re-heated commercial pizzas.

Note that excellent cappuccino and espresso coffees are always available in various bars around the ship, served in the right sized (proper) china cups.

OTHER COMMENTS: *Costa Victoria*'s exterior profile is similar to that of an enlarged version of the popular and very successful *Costa Classica* and *Costa Romantica*, with huge upright yellow funnels that are instantly recognizable. A sister ship, *Costa Olympia* was scheduled for delivery in 1998, but was not completed due to the bankruptcy of the shipyard. Having replaced almost all its older tonnage in the past few years, Costa Cruises now has a good contemporary fleet, operating in the Caribbean, Mediterranean and in South America.

This ship has a fully enclosed bridge. There is an outdoor wrap-around promenade deck (but it is full of deck lounge chairs) as well as a wrap-around jogging track.

Inside the ship is a lovely four-deck-high forward-facing observation lounge (Concorde Plaza) with a "beam-me-up" glass elevator; in the center is a cone-shaped waterfall (huge video screens flank the walls), while "pod" balconies overlook the room's center. It is a stunning space, and has its own bar. Sadly, thick floor-to-ceiling pillars obstruct sight lines from most seats.

The seven-deck-high "planetarium" atrium (a novel, but somewhat impractical design) has four glass elevators that travel up to a clear crystal dome (you can see the weather outside through it). The uppermost level of the atrium is the deck where two outside swimming pools are located, together with four blocks of showers, and an ice cream bar and grill. There is a large forward shopping area, adjacent to the atrium. Ship lovers should look in the Tavernetta Lounge (aft) for 10 paintings of past and present Costa Cruises ships. There is also a small chapel.

Unusual for a new ship (and welcomed by European passengers) is a pleasant (but small) indoor swimming pool, sauna (it is tiny, and there are no adjacent changing or locker facilities, which makes it very user-unfriendly). Also adjacent is a steam room, and gymnasium (limited assortment of equipment), as well as a covered walking/jogging track. There is also a tennis court. Sunbathers on the forward-most section of the outdoor deck close to the mast have their own showers (excellent) and no music (good).

Where this ship differs from most large ships is in its distinct European interior décor, with decidedly Italian styling. The ship is decidedly contemporary without being glitzy – and bold without being brash. Internet access is also available from one of several computer terminals in the Teens Center. The onboard currency is the euro or US dollar, depending on the region of operation.

WEAK POINTS: Standing in line for embarkation, disembarkation, shore tenders and for self-serve buffet meals is an inevitable aspect of cruising aboard all large ships. When inside, there is absolutely no feeling that this is a ship. There are not enough seats in the show lounge. There are no fresh flowers in evidence anywhere. The service is decidedly loud and casual (make that sloppy and inconsistent) and there is little real hospitality. The telephone numbering system is incredibly complicated (try remembering 05313 for the information desk or 06718 to book a massage).

The live music everywhere is loud, very loud, and there are too many repetitive announcements. Tipping envelopes provided in your cabin state the amount you are expected to give. The indigo blue interior walls look pleasant enough, but in the event of a power failure they would make the vessel appear pitch black.

Crown Odyssey
★★★★

Removal 2006

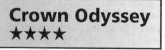

Large Ship:	34,242 tons	Total Crew:	470
Lifestyle:	Premium	Passengers	
Cruise Line:	Orient Lines	(lower beds/all berths):	1,052/1,221
Former Names:	Norwegian Crown,	Passenger Space Ratio	
	Crown Odyssey	(lower beds/all berths):	32.5/28.0
Builder:	Meyer Werft (Germany)	Crew/Passenger Ratio	
Original Cost:	$178 million	(lower beds/all berths):	2.2/2.5
Entered Service:	June 1988/May 2000	Navigation Officers:	European/Norwegian
Registry:	The Bahamas	Cabins (total):	526
Length (ft/m):	615.9/187.75	Size Range (sq ft/m):	153.9–613.5/
Beam (ft/m):	92.5/28.20		14.3–57.0
Draft (ft/m):	23.8/7.26	Cabins (outside view):	410
Propulsion/Propellers:	diesel	Cabins (interior/no view):	116
	(21,330kW)/2	Cabins (for one person):	0
Passenger Decks:	10	Cabins (with private balcony):	16

Cabins (wheelchair accessible):	4
Cabin Current:	110 volts
Elevators:	4
Casino (gaming tables):	Yes
Slot Machines:	Yes
Swimming Pools (outdoors):	1
Swimming Pools (indoors):	1
Whirlpools:	4
Fitness Center:	Yes
Sauna/Steam Room:	Yes/No
Massage:	Yes
Self-Service Launderette:	No
Dedicated Cinema/Seats:	Yes/215
Library:	Yes
Classification Society:	Bureau Veritas

OVERALL SCORE: 1,445 (OUT OF A POSSIBLE 2,000 POINTS)

ACCOMMODATION: There are 18 categories of accommodation to choose from; typically the higher the deck, the more expensive will be your accommodation.

Most cabins (the line calls them staterooms, which they are not) are of the same size and layout, have blond wood cabinetry, an abundance of mirrors, and closet and drawer space, and are very well equipped. Although almost all cabins show some signs of wear and tear, an ongoing refurbishment program keeps them looking good. All cabins feature a color television, hairdryer, thin 100 percent cotton bathrobe, music console (and a button that can be used to turn announcements on or off), personal safe, and private bathroom with shower (many upper grade cabins have a good-sized bathtub). All towels are of 100 percent cotton, although they could be larger; soap, shampoo, body lotion, shower cap and sewing kit are the amenities provided. The cabin soundproofing is generally good, and non-smoking cabins are available.

Some cabins have interconnecting doors, so that they connect to make a two-room suite. You should note that almost all cabins on Deck 8 have lifeboat-obstructed views. Ice machines can be found in all passageways along the accommodation.

The largest accommodation can be found in the 16 suites on Penthouse Deck 10. Each is decorated in a different style, in accordance with the name of the suite (from fore to aft they are: Edinburgh, Inverness, Balmoral, Sandringham, Shalimar, Taj Mahal, Mykonos, Portofino, Bel Air, Hollywood, Bali, Tahiti, Imperial,

BERLITZ'S RATINGS

	Possible	Achieved
Ship	500	401
Accommodation	200	156
Food	400	264
Service	400	274
Entertainment	100	66
Cruise	400	284

Shangri-La, Dynasty, Mandarin). They are very spacious, and provide a sleeping area and separate living room (including some nicely finished wood cabinetry and a huge amount of drawer space), together with a large, white marble-clad bathroom (features a full-sized bathtub with integral shower), and a semi-private balcony (the balcony can be overlooked from the open deck above). Passengers occupying these suites have the use of a concierge, who will arrange private parties, obtain theater tickets, and provide assistance for private shore excursions.

The next most spacious accommodation can be found in cabins with bay windows. These include a separate sleeping area with twin beds, a huge amount of drawer space in a large vanity/writing desk, and a lounge typically with two sofas, tub chairs and heavy glass table, refrigerator and television. Electrically operated window blinds, together with the curtains that front them provide good blackouts for the bay windows. The white marble-clad bathroom is also large and features a full-sized bathtub with integral shower.

There are four wheelchair-accessible cabins; these provide plenty of space to maneuver, and all four include a bathroom with roll-in shower. However, please note that wheelchair accessibility in some of the ports on the many different itineraries operated by this ship (particularly in Europe) may prove to be quite frustrating and wheelchair-accessible transportation will be very limited.

DINING: The Seven Continents Dining Room, which has large picture windows on both port and starboard sides, is large. It is also, unfortunately, extremely noisy (particularly for tables positioned adjacent to the open waiter stations). It has a stained-glass ceiling, and comfortable seating at tables for two, four, six or eight (although the chairs do not have armrests), and two seatings. The dining room is totally non-smoking.

The cuisine, while it is not gourmet either in quality or presentation, is quite adequate for the expectations of Orient Lines' passengers. It is unfussy, yet there is plenty of taste. What is very noticeable is the extensive use of fresh vegetables (whenever they can be obtained). However, you should note that the food quality and presentation is best described as inconsistent.

As for service, the Filipino waiters are generally good, and provide friendly service that is reasonably attentive, although there is a distinct lack of polish, and it is inconsistent. There is a decent, well-priced wine list, although the wines are almost all extremely young, and the Filipino wine waiters have little knowledge of wines, or how to pour them (note that a 15 percent gratuity is automatically added to all wine and drinks bills).

Informal, self-serve buffet-style breakfasts and luncheons (tablecloths are provided) can be taken in the Yacht Club, which also features as an alternative venue for informal dinners (reservations only, and a cover charge of $15 per person).

In addition, casual luncheons can be taken in the Café Italia, located on an open deck aft, adjacent to a sunbathing and whirlpool area, and an open-air bar. This is also used for dining outdoors on selected nights – complete with tablecloths, table umbrellas and fine silverware (this is quite lovely when in ports such as Mykonos or Santorini in Greece).

OTHER COMMENTS: *Crown Odyssey* is a well-designed and built ship, originally constructed for the now defunct Royal Cruise Line, after which Norwegian Cruise Line operated it for several years, before the ship was transferred to Orient Lines in 2000. *Crown Odyssey* has been operated by Orient Lines (a subsidiary of the Star Cruises/Norwegian Cruise Line group) since spring 2000. The ship has quite a handsome exterior profile, and now looks even better, and more balanced, with its royal blue hull and white superstructure.

One nice feature is a full, wrap-around teak promenade deck outdoors, although it does become quite narrow at the fore part of the vessel; a jogging track is also to be found on the uppermost deck outdoors. There is one swimming pool outdoors on an aft lido deck.

Inside, there is generally a good passenger flow,

ample space and fine-quality interiors. Generous amounts of warm woods and marble have been used in the décor, although there are many mirrored surfaces. However, these interiors (particularly the passageways) are now showing signs of wear in many places.

The ship has a spacious layout and a good array of public rooms, including a lobby that is two decks high; a large, gold sculpture of the world (by Pomodoro) is located on the lower level, adjacent to the semi-circular staircase that connects the two levels. On the upper level, boutiques, a piano lounge with bar, and a casino.

There is a theater-style show lounge, where production shows and cabaret are featured, with sight lines that are generally good, but could be better (four pillars obstruct the views from some seats). Off to the port, aft area of the show lounge is a bar.

At the top of the ship is a fine observation lounge (called Top of the Crown) with panoramic views, which, in the evenings, becomes a nightclub. Other facilities include a library, an Internet Center (with four computer terminals), a cinema, and a palm court area.

There is a good Roman-style indoor spa, pool, gymnasium and several beauty treatment rooms, with services provided by Mandara Spa of Bali (a 15 percent gratuity is added to all beauty treatments). Massage can also be provided in the privacy of your suite or cabin.

Crown Odyssey should prove to be an excellent choice for passengers wanting destination-intensive cruising in a ship that has some semblance of European quality, style, and charm, for what is really a very moderate cruise price. Orient Lines specializes in destination-intensive itineraries, and ties in with an extensive pre- and post-cruise program.

All in all, *Crown Odyssey* features extremely good value for money cruises in very comfortable, quite elegant yet unpretentious surroundings, while a friendly and accommodating Filipino crew help make a cruise aboard it a very pleasant, no-hassle experience.

WEAK POINTS: Much of the paneling in the passageways is quite marked and badly scuffed (due, in part, to its very light color), and lets down an otherwise very pleasant ship. Shore excursion and port information could be better. While staff hospitality is generally good, there is little polish or finesse to service. Congestion occurs between first and second seating passengers on days when the captain's cocktail parties are held in the show lounge, and a line forms outside. The production shows, while colorful, are very amateurish, with much material copied from other ships and producers.

Crystal Harmony
★★★★★

Removed 2006

Mid-Size Ship: . . . . .49,400 tons	Passengers	Cabin Current: . . . . . . .115 and 220 volts
Lifestyle: .Luxury	(lower beds/all berths): 960/1,010	Elevators: 8
Cruise Line: . . . . .Crystal Cruises	Passenger Space Ratio	Casino (gaming tables): . . . . .Yes
Former Names: . . . . .none	(lower beds/all berths): 51.4/48.9	Slot Machines: . . . . .Yes
Builder: . . . . .Mitsubishi Heavy Industries	Crew/Passenger Ratio	Swimming Pools (outdoors): 2
(Japan)	(lower beds/all berths): 1.7/1.8	(1 with magrodome)
Original Cost: . . . .$240 million	Navigation Officers: . . . . . . .Scandinavian/	Swimming Pools (indoors): 0
Entered Service: . . . . .July 1990	Japanese	Whirlpools: 2
Registry: . . . . .The Bahamas	Cabins (total): 480	Fitness Center: . . . . .Yes
Length (ft/m): 790.5/240.96	Size Range (sq ft/m): 182.9–947.2/	Sauna/Steam Room: . . . . .Yes/Yes
Beam (ft/m): 97.1/29.60	17.0–88.0	Massage: . . . . .Yes
Draft (ft/m): 24.6/7.50	Cabins (outside view): 461	Self-Service Launderette: . . . . .Yes
Propulsion/Propellers: . . . . .diesel-electric	Cabins (interior/no view): 19	Dedicated Cinema/Seats: Yes/270
(32,800kW)/2	Cabins (for one person): 0	Library: . . . . .Yes
Passenger Decks: 8	Cabins (with private balcony): 260	Classification Society: . . .Lloyd's Register/
Total Crew: .545	Cabins (wheelchair accessible): 4	Nippon Kaiji Kyokai

---

OVERALL SCORE: 1,725 (OUT OF A POSSIBLE 2,000 POINTS)

ACCOMMODATION: There are 10 categories of suites and cabins to choose from: four Crystal Penthouses with private balcony; 26 Penthouse Suites with balcony; 32 Penthouses with balcony; 198 Cabins with balcony; 241 Cabins without balcony.

Regardless of the accommodation category you select, duvets and down pillows are provided, as are lots of other niceties, together with a data socket for connecting a personal laptop computer. All accommodation includes a refrigerator and mini-bar, television, satellite-linked telephone, and hairdryer. A full range of Nutrogena personal toiletry amenities is provided, as is a plush cotton bathrobe. The in-cabin television programming is excellent, and close-captioned videos are provided for the hearing-impaired.

Butlers provide the best in personal service in all the top category suites on Deck 10, where all room service food arrives on silver trays. Afternoon tea trolley service and evening hors d'oeuvres are standard fare in the "butler service" suites.

DECK 10 PENTHOUSES: The four delightful Crystal penthouses measure 948–982 sq. ft (88–91.2 sq. meters) and have a huge private balcony and lounge with audio-visual entertainment center, separate master bedroom with king-sized bed and electric curtains, large walk-in closets, and stunning ocean-view bathrooms that come with jet bathtub, bidet, two washbasins, and plenty of storage space for one's personal toiletry items. These really are among the best in fine, private, pampered liv-

BERLITZ'S RATINGS

	Possible	Achieved
Ship	500	433
Accommodation	200	163
Food	400	345
Service	400	346
Entertainment	100	86
Cruise	400	352

ing spaces at sea, and come with all the best priority perks, including butler service, free laundry service, a wide variety of alcoholic beverages and other goodies – in fact, almost anything you require.

OTHER DECK 10 SUITES: All of the other suites on this deck are worth the asking price, have plenty of space (all feature a private balcony, with outside light), including a separate lounge with large sofa, coffee table and chairs, large television/VCR, and a separate sleeping area that can be curtained off (thick drapes mean you can sleep totally in the dark if you wish). The bathrooms are quite large, and extremely well appointed. In fact, any of the suites on this deck are equipped with everything necessary for refined, private living at sea.

Butlers provide the best in personal service in all the top category suites on this deck (with a total of 132 beds), where all room service food arrives correctly on large silver trays. Afternoon tea trolley service and evening hors d'oeuvres are standard fare in the "butler service" suites.

DECK 9/8/7/5 CABINS: Many of the cabins feature a private balcony (in fact, 50 percent of all cabins have private balconies, with outside lights), and are extremely comfortable, although a little tight for space. They are very compact units, with one-way traffic past the bed, but there is a reasonable amount of drawer and storage space (the drawers *are* small, however) although the closet hanging space is somewhat limited for long voyages. Some cabins in grades G and I have lifeboat-obstructed views. All cabins have a color television, VCR, mini-refrigerator, personal safe, small sofa and coffee table, and excellent soundproofing. The bathrooms, although well appointed, are of the "you first, me next" variety (and size), but they do come with generously sized personal toiletry items and amenities.

DINING: There are several dining choices aboard this pleasant ship. The dining room (totally non-smoking) is moderately elegant, with plenty of space around each table, well-placed waiter service stations and a good number of tables for two, as well as tables for four, six or eight. It is noisy at times (particularly in the raised, center section), making it difficult to carry on a conversation at the larger tables in the center (raised) section.

The food is attractively presented and well served in a friendly but correct manner. It is of a high standard, with high quality ingredients used throughout. The cuisine features a mixture of European specialties and North American favorites. The menus are extremely varied, and special orders are available (including caviar and other treats). All in all, the food is most acceptable and, with the choice of the two alternative dining spots, provides consistently high marks from passengers.

Overall, the food is really good for the size of ship, and, with the choice of the two alternative dining spots, receives high praise. Sadly, dinner in the main dining room is in two seatings, the company having used the space that could have provided a second main dining room, for public areas. While the early seating is simply too rushed for many), with two alternative restaurants, off-menu choices, a hand picked European staff and excellent service, dining is often memorable. Fresh pasta and dessert flambeau specialties are made tableside each day by accommodating headwaiters.

For those who enjoy caviar, it is available, although it is sevruga (malossol) and not beluga (this is hard to find today, and incredibly expensive). The wine list is superb, with an outstanding collection of across-the-board wines, including a mouthwatering connoisseur selection.

Afternoon tea (and coffee) in the Palm Court is good. The choice of sandwiches, cakes and pastries is also good. Needless to say, service is generally excellent.

The two alternative dining spots are Prego (features fine pasta dishes), and Kyoto, featuring pseudo-Japanese and other southeast Asian specialties (there is no extra charge, other than a recommended $6 waiter gratuity per meal that should be included in the cruise fare). The two non-smoking restaurants are intimate, have great views and feature fine food. There should be separate entrance (at present a single entrance serves both).

Additionally, The Bistro (located on the upper level of the two-deck-high lobby) is a casual spot for coffees and pastries, served in the style and atmosphere of a European street café. The Bistro features unusual, Crystal Cruises-logo china that can be purchased in one of the ship's boutiques.

For casual meals, The Lido Café features an extensive self-serve buffet area, located high up in the ship, and with great views from its large picture windows. For casual poolside lunches, there is also the Trident Grill, as well as a, ice cream/frozen yoghurt counter (all at no extra charge).

OTHER COMMENTS: *Crystal Harmony* is a handsome, contemporary ship with raked clipper bow and well-balanced, sleek flowing lines. It has excellent open deck and sunbathing space, and sports facilities that include a paddle tennis court. One of two outdoor swimming pools has a magrodome cover.

There is almost no sense of crowding anywhere, a superb example of comfort by design. There is a wrap-around teakwood deck for walking, and an abundance of open deck and sunbathing space.

Inside, the layout is similar to that of *Crystal Serenity* and *Crystal Symphony,* with a design that shows that form follows function superbly well, combining the best of large ship facilities with the intimacy of rooms found aboard most small ships. There is a wide assortment of public entertainment lounges and small intimate rooms (except for a nightclub/lounge that is simply too large for the number of late-night passengers frequenting it), and passenger flow is excellent. Outstanding are the Vista (observation) Lounge and the supremely tranquil, elegant Palm Court, one of the nicest rooms afloat.

A Business Center has laptop computers, printers, satellite faxes, and phones, and there is a very good book and video library. The theater has high-definition video projection and headsets for the hearing-impaired. There is a self-service launderette on each deck, particularly useful for long voyages.

Fine-quality fabrics and soft furnishings, china, flatware and silver are used throughout. Smokers will enjoy the fine range of cigars available in the Connoisseurs Club (cigar lounge), adjacent to the Avenue Saloon. It incorporates the best in premium brands of liquor and cigars for those who can appreciate (and pay for) such things.

This ship has a very friendly, well-trained, highly professional staff and excellent teamwork (with one of the lowest turnovers of staff in the industry) that is under the direction of a solid, all-European middle management. It is the superb extra attention to detail that makes a cruise aboard this ship so worthwhile, such as almost no announcements, and no background music anywhere. The company pays attention to its fine base of repeat passengers (particularly those in Deck 10 accommodation), and makes subtle changes in operations in order to constantly fine-tune its product.

This ship has just about everything for the discerning, seasoned traveler who wants and is prepared to pay for fine style, space, and the comfort and the facilities of a large vessel capable of longer voyages. *Crystal Harmony* is a fine example of the latest style in contemporary grand hotels afloat and provides abundant choices and flexibility, and an excellent guest lecture program. The passenger mix is approximately 85 percent North American (typically half of these will be from California) and 15 percent other nationalities.

Following a refit in 1997, some of the public rooms were expanded (most notably the casino) and refurbished. Although now over 10 years old (and showing signs of wear in both accommodation and public areas) the ship is being well maintained, and should give pleasure to passengers for many years to come. In 2000 an expanded range of Spa facilities and treatments was introduced, under the aegis of Steiner Platinum Service. A Computer Learning Center was also added, complete with more than 20 desktop and laptop computers. Private lessons are available (although they are expensive, starting at $75 per hour).

The final words: this is announcement-free cruising in a well-tuned, very professionally run, service oriented, ship, the approximate equivalent of a Four Seasons hotel. However, note that the score has gone downwards a little recently, the result of the age of the ship and its facilities, in comparison to other ships available in the discounted marketplace, and the fact that this is still a two-seating ship, which makes it more highly structured in terms of timing than it really should be. The onboard currency is the US dollar.

WEAK POINTS: Your evenings will be necessarily rather structured due to the fact that there are two seatings for dinner (unless you eat in one of the alternative dining spots), and two shows (the show lounge cannot seat all passengers at once). This detracts from the otherwise luxurious setting of the ship and the fine professionalism of its staff. Many passengers feel that gratuities should really be included on a ship that is rated this highly (they can, however, be pre-paid).

THE BRIDGE

A ship's navigation bridge is manned at all times, both at sea and in port. Besides the captain, who is master of the vessel, other senior officers take "watch" turns for four- or eight-hour periods. In addition, junior officers are continually honing their skills as experienced navigators, waiting for the day when they will be promoted to master.

The captain is always in command at times of high risk, such as when the ship is entering or leaving a port, when the density of traffic is particularly high, or when visibility is severely restricted by poor weather.

Navigation has come a long way since the days of the ancient mariners, who used only the sun and the stars to calculate their course across the oceans. The space-age development of sophisticated navigation devices (using satellites) has enabled us to eliminate the guesswork of early navigation (the first global mobile satellite system came into being in 1979).

A ship's navigator today uses a variety of sophisticated instruments to pinpoint the ship's position at any time and establish its course.

Large Ship:	.68,000 tons	Passengers	
Lifestyle:	.Luxury	(lower beds/all berths):	.1,100/1,100
Cruise Line:	.Crystal Cruises	Passenger Space Ratio	
Former Names:	.none	(lower beds/all berths):	.61.8/61.8
Builder: Chantiers de l'Atlantique (France)		Crew/Passenger Ratio	
Original Cost:	.$350 million	(lower beds/all berths):	.1.7/1.7
Entered Service:	.June 2003	Navigation Officers:	.Scandinavian
Registry:	.The Bahamas	Cabins (total):	.550
Length (ft/m):	.820.2/250.0	Size Range (sq ft/m):	.226–1,345.5/
Beam (ft/m):	.111.5/34.0		21–125
Draft (ft/m):	.24.9/7.6	Cabins (outside view):	.550
Propulsion/Propellers:	.2 pods/	Cabins (interior/no view):	.0
	diesel power	Cabins (for one person):	.0
Passenger Decks:	.9	Cabins (with private balcony):	.466
Total Crew:	.635	Cabins (wheelchair accessible):	.8

Cabin Current:	.110/220 volts
Elevators:	.8
Casino (gaming tables):	.Yes
Slot Machines:	.Yes
Swimming Pools (outdoors):	.1
Swimming Pools (indoors):	.1
	(indoor/outdoor)
Whirlpools:	.2
Fitness Center:	.Yes
Sauna/Steam Room:	.Yes/Yes
Massage:	.Yes
Self-Service Launderette:	.Yes
Dedicated Cinema/Seats:	.Yes/202
Library:	.Yes
Classification Society:	.Lloyd's Register

OVERALL SCORE: NYR (OUT OF A POSSIBLE 2,000 POINTS)

ACCOMMODATION: This consists of: four Crystal Penthouses with balcony; 32 Penthouse Suites with Balcony; 66 Penthouses with balcony; 78 superior outside-view cabins with balcony; 286 outside-view cabins with balcony; 84 outside-view cabins without balcony but with large picture windows. There are two whole decks of accommodation designated as suites (Deck 11, and Deck 10), while all other accommodation, while larger than aboard smaller sister ships *Crystal Harmony* and *Crystal Symphony*, is located on Deck 9, 8 and 7.

Regardless of the accommodation category you select, duvets and down pillows are provided, as are lots of other niceties, together with a data socket for connecting a personal laptop computer. All accommodation has a refrigerator and mini-bar, television, satellite-linked telephone, and hairdryer. A full range of Nutrogena personal toiletry amenities is provided, as is a plush cotton bathrobe. The in-cabin television programming is excellent, and close-captioned videos are provided for the hearing-impaired.

Butlers provide the best in personal service in all the top category suites on Deck 10, where all room service food arrives on silver trays. Afternoon tea trolley service and evening hors d'oeuvres are standard fare in the "butler service" suites.

CRYSTAL PENTHOUSES (WITH BALCONY): There are four Crystal Penthouses with private balcony (1,345 sq. ft/125 sq. meters). These are ideally located in the center of the ship on Penthouse Deck 11, each with out-

BERLITZ'S RATINGS

	Possible	Achieved
Ship	500	NYR
Accommodation	200	NYR
Food	400	NYR
Service	400	NYR
Entertainment	100	NYR
Cruise	400	NYR

standing views and large private balconies with outside lighting (they are a slightly different shape to those of the other ships in the fleet). There is a lounge with audio-visual entertainment center, separate master bedroom with king-sized bed and electric curtains, large walk-in closets, large vanity desk.

The marble bathrooms have ocean views; they are stunning and come with a whirlpool bathtub with integral shower, two washbasins, separate large shower enclosure, bidet and toilet, and plenty of storage space for one's personal toiletry items. These really are among the best in fine, private, pampered living spaces at sea, and come with all the best priority perks, including free laundry service.

PENTHOUSE SUITES (WITH BALCONY): There are 32 Penthouse Suites with private balcony (538 sq. ft/50 sq. meters), all located on Penthouse Deck 11. Each has a separate bedroom, walk-in closet and en-suite bathroom with full-size bathtub with integral shower, two washbasins, separate shower enclosure, bidet, toilet, and ample space for one's personal toiletries. The lounge features a large sofa, coffee table and several armchairs, and there is a dining table and four chairs.

PENTHOUSE CABIN (WITH BALCONY): These are 66 of these Penthouse Cabins, and they are located on Penthouse Decks 10 and 11. They measure 403.6 sq. ft/37.5 sq. meters. All come with a private balcony, although eight that are located at the aft of Deck 11 have larger balconies. These units are really large cabins that have a sleeping area that can be curtained off from the lounge area, with its large, long vanity desk. The bathroom is large, and has a full-size bathtub (with integral shower), separate shower enclosure, and a bidet and toilet.

SUPERIOR DELUXE OUTSIDE-VIEW CABINS (WITH BALCONY): The term "deluxe" should not be applied to this accommodation, which really is a standard outside-view cabin that is larger than any standard cabin aboard most other ships, and measures 269 sq. ft (25 sq. meters). The 78 cabins are longer than cabins that don't have a private balcony. It has a sleeping area with clothes closets, small sofa and drinks table, vanity desk with hairdryer. The bathroom has a bathtub with integral shower, two washbasins, and toilet. Large patio doors open to a private balcony.

DELUXE OUTSIDE-VIEW CABINS (WITH BALCONY): The term "deluxe" should not be applied to this accommodation, which really is a standard outside-view cabin that is larger than any standard cabin aboard most other ships, and measures 269 sq. ft (25 sq. meters). The 286 cabins, which are about the same size and shape as the "Deluxe" version mentioned above but located on a "superior" deck (Penthouse Deck 10), are longer than cabins that don't have a private balcony. They have a sleeping area with clothes closets, small sofa and drinks table, vanity desk with hairdryer. The bathroom has a bathtub with integral shower, two washbasins, and toilet. Large patio doors open to a private balcony.

DELUXE OUTSIDE-VIEW CABINS (NO BALCONY): The term "deluxe" should not be applied to this accommodation, which really is a standard outside-view cabin (located on Deck 7, with the wrap-around promenade deck outside each cabin) that is larger than any standard cabin aboard most other ships. The 84 cabins measure 226 sq. ft (21 sq. meters), and have a large window, sleeping area with clothes closets, small sofa and drinks table, vanity desk with hairdryer. The bathroom has a bathtub with integral shower, two washbasins, and toilet.

WHEELCHAIR ACCESSIBLE ACCOMMODATION: Wheelchair-accessible accommodation includes two penthouse grades, two cabins with balconies, and four cabins with large picture windows.

DINING: As in close sister ships *Crystal Harmony* and *Crystal Symphony* there is one main dining room (called the Crystal Dining Room), two alternative dining rooms (reservations are required), and a sushi bar. The Crystal Dining Room is located just aft of the main lobby (and integral lounge/bar Crystal Cove), and has a raised central section. It is totally non-smoking and quite elegant, with a crisp, clean "California Modern" design style that includes plenty of space around each table, well-placed waiter service stations. It is well laid-out, and has a raised, circular central section, although it is somewhat

noisy at times, and not conducive to a fine dining experience. There are tables for two (many positioned adjacent to large windows), four, six or eight.

Sadly, dinner in the main dining room is in two seatings. Clearly the early seating is simply too rushed for many, although with other alternative restaurants, off-menu choices, a hand-picked European staff and excellent service, dining can still be a memorable affair.

ALTERNATIVE DINING SPOTS (RESERVATIONS REQUIRED, NO EXTRA CHARGE): Following the layout and facilities aboard sister ships *Harmony* and *Symphony*, there are two alternative restaurants (one Italian, the other Asian). Both are located aft on Deck 7, and both have excellent views from large picture windows. *Prego* is for Italian food, Italian wines, and service with a flair. *Silk Road* has Asian-California "fusion" food.

There is also a separate sushi bar, with menu items selected by superb Los-Angeles-based Japanese superchef Nobu Matsuhisa, and skillfully prepared on board by a Nobu-trained chef. The alternative dining spots are expected to provide an excellent standard of culinary fare – with food cooked to order at no extra charge (although many Crystal regulars feel the recommended $6 waiter gratuity per meal should be included in the cruise fare rather than be charged to their accounts).

THE BISTRO: Additionally, The Bistro (located on the upper level of the two-deck-high lobby) is a casual spot for coffees and pastries, served in the style and atmosphere of a European street café. The Bistro has unusual, Crystal Cruises-logo china that can also be bought in one of the ship's boutiques.

CASUAL EATERIES: For casual meals, The Lido Café has an extensive self-serve buffet area, located high up in the ship, and with great views from its large picture windows. For casual poolside lunches, there is also the Trident Grill, as well as an ice cream/frozen yoghurt counter (all at no extra charge).

OTHER COMMENTS: The latest (slightly larger) sister ship to the elegant, and successful *Crystal Harmony* and *Crystal Symphony*, this new ship carries forward the same look and profile. *Crystal Serenity* is a contemporary ship with a nicely raked clipper bow and well-balanced lines. While some might not like the "apartment block" look of the ship's exterior, it is the contemporary, "in" look, balconies having become standard aboard almost all new cruise ships.

Podded propulsion is provided. Briefly, two pods, which resemble huge outboard motors, replace internal electric propulsion motors, shaft lines, rudders and their machinery, and are compact, self-contained units that typically weigh about 170 tons each. Although they are at the stern, pod units *pull*, rather than *push*, a ship through the water. Electrical power is provided by the latest generation of environmentally friendly diesel engines.

This ship will have an excellent amount of open deck, sunbathing space, and sports facilities. The aft of two outdoor swimming pools can be covered by a magrodome in inclement weather. There is no sense of crowding anywhere, a superb example of comfort by design, high-quality construction and engineering. There is also a wide wrap-around teakwood deck for walking, pleasingly uncluttered by lounge chairs.

Inside, the layout is similar to that of *Crystal Harmony* and *Crystal Symphony*, with a design that shows that form follows function superbly well, combining the best of large ship facilities with the intimacy of rooms found aboard many small ships. The main lobby houses the reception desk (staffed 24 hours a day), concierge and shore excursion desks, and a lounge/bar (Crystal Cove) with baby grand piano.

However, unlike *CH* and *CS*, forward of the lobby there are no passenger cabins (they have become officers and staff accommodation, which makes sense since this area really is considered to be "back of house").

The Caesar's Palace At Sea casino has been centrally located, with no outside views to distract passengers who are intent on gaming. Instead, the location is adjacent to lifeboats on both sides (in this arrangement, the lifeboats do not obstruct either cabins or public rooms).

This ship has just about everything for the discerning, seasoned traveler who wants and is prepared to pay good money for fine style, abundant space and the comfort and the facilities of a large vessel capable of extended voyages, including an excellent program of guest lecturers. The one thing that lets the product down is the fact that the dining room operation is in two seatings (however, having said that, there are many older passengers who want to eat early, while the line's younger passengers want to dine later, so there is some semblance of balance).

Crystal Cruises takes care of its ships, and its staff, and it is the staff that makes the cruise experience really special. They are a well-trained group that stress hospitality at all times. The ship achieves a high rating because of its fine facilities, service and crew. It is the extra attention to detail that makes a cruise with this ship so special. The passenger mix is approximately 85 percent North American (typically half of these will be from California) and 15 percent other nationalities.

The final word: this new ship should provide you with announcement-free cruising in a well-tuned, very professionally run, service oriented ship, the approximate equivalent of a Four Seasons or Ritz Carlton hotel. The onboard currency is the US dollar.

WEAK POINTS: Your evenings will be necessarily rather structured due to the fact that there are two seatings for dinner (unless you eat in one of the alternative dining spots), and two shows (the show lounge cannot seat all passengers at once). This detracts from the otherwise luxurious setting of the ship and the fine professionalism of its staff. Many passengers feel that gratuities should really be included on a ship that is rated this highly (they can, however, be pre-paid).

Crystal Symphony
★★★★★

Mid-Size Ship: . . . . .51,044 tons	Passengers	Cabin Current: . . . . .110 and 220 volts
Lifestyle: .Luxury	(lower beds/all berths): 960/1,010	Elevators: 8
Cruise Line: . . . . .Crystal Cruises	Passenger Space Ratio	Casino (gaming tables): . . . . .Yes
Former Names: . . . . .none	(lower beds/all berths): 53.1/50.5	Slot Machines: . . . . .Yes
Builder: . . . . .Masa-Yards (Finland)	Crew/Passenger Ratio	Swimming Pools (outdoors): 2
Original Cost: . . . .$300 million	(lower beds/all berths): 1.7/1.8	(1 with magrodome)
Entered Service: . . . . .Mar 1995	Navigation Officers: . . . . . .Scandinavian	Swimming Pools (indoors): 0
Registry: . . . . .The Bahamas	Cabins (total): 480	Whirlpools: 2
Length (ft/m): 777.8/237.10	Size Range (sq ft/m): 201.2–981.7/	Fitness Center: . . . . .Yes
Beam (ft/m): 98.0/30.20	18.7–91.2	Sauna/Steam Room: . . . . .Yes/Yes
Draft (ft/m): 24.9/7.60	Cabins (outside view): 480	Self-Service Launderette: . . . . .Yes
Propulsion/Propellers: . . . . .diesel-electric	Cabins (interior/no view): 0	Massage: . . . . .Yes
(33,880kW)/2	Cabins (for one person): 0	Dedicated Cinema/Seats: Yes/143
Passenger Decks: 8	Cabins (with private balcony): 276	Library: . . . . .Yes
Total Crew: .545	Cabins (wheelchair accessible): 7	Classification Society: . . .Lloyd's Register

OVERALL SCORE: 1,758 (OUT OF A POSSIBLE 2,000 POINTS)

ACCOMMODATION: There are eight categories of accommodation, with the most expensive suites located on the highest accommodation deck (Deck 10). There are two Crystal Penthouses with private balcony; 18 Penthouse Suites with private balcony; 44 Penthouse Cabins with balcony; 214 Cabins with balcony; 202 Cabins without balcony. Some cabins (grades G and I), have obstructed views. Except for the suites on Deck 10, most other cabin bathrooms are very compact units.

Regardless of the accommodation category you select, duvets and down pillows are provided, as are lots of other niceties, together with a data socket for connecting a personal laptop computer. All accommodation features a refrigerator and mini-bar, television, satellite-linked telephone, and hairdryer. A full range of Nutrogena personal toiletry amenities is provided, as is a plush cotton bathrobe. The in-cabin television programming is excellent, and close-captioned videos are provided for the hearing-impaired.

Butlers provide the best in personal service in all the top category suites on Deck 10, where all room service food arrives on silver trays. Afternoon tea trolley service and evening hors d'oeuvres are standard fare in the "butler service" suites.

DECK 10 PENTHOUSES: Two delightful Crystal Penthouses measure 982 sq. ft (91 sq. meters) and have a huge private balcony (with outside light) and lounge with audio-visual entertainment center, separate master bedroom with king-sized bed and electric curtains, large

BERLITZ'S RATINGS

	Possible	Achieved
Ship	500	451
Accommodation	200	175
Food	400	345
Service	400	345
Entertainment	100	88
Cruise	400	354

walk-in closets, and stunning ocean-view marble bathrooms with a whirlpool bathtub, bidet, two washbasins, and plenty of storage space for one's personal toiletry items. These really are among the best in fine, private, pampered living spaces at sea, and come with all the best priority perks, including laundry service.

OTHER DECK 10 SUITES: All of the other suites on this deck have plenty of space (all feature a private balcony, with outside light), including a lounge with large sofa, coffee table and chairs, a sleeping area and walk-in closet. Rich wood cabinetry provides much of the warmth of the décor. The bathrooms are quite large, and are extremely well appointed, with full-sized bathtub and separate shower enclosure, two washbasins, bidet and toilet. In fact, any of the suites on this deck are equipped with everything necessary for refined, private living at sea.

Five butlers provide the best in personal service in all the top category suites on Deck 10 (with a total of 132 beds), where all room service food arrives on silver trays. Afternoon tea trolley service and evening hors d'oeuvres are standard fare in the "butler service" suites.

DECKS 5/6/7/8/9: More than 50 percent of all cabins have private balconies. All are well equipped, and extremely comfortable, with excellent sound insulation. The balcony partitions, however, do not go from floor to ceiling, so you *can* hear your neighbors. Even in the lowest category of standard cabins, there is plenty of drawer space, but the closet hanging space may prove somewhat limited for long voyages. There are generously sized personal bathroom amenities, duvets and down pillows. European stewardesses provide excellent service and attention.

DINING: The main dining room (totally non-smoking) is quite elegant, with crisp design and plenty of space around each table, well-placed waiter service stations. It is well laid out, and features a raised, circular central section, although it is somewhat noisy at times, and not conducive to a fine dining experience. There are tables for two (many of them positioned adjacent to large windows), four, six or eight.

The food is attractively presented and well served (using both plate service as well as silver service). It is of a high standard, with fine quality ingredients used. European dishes are predominant. Menus are extremely varied, and feature a good selection of meat, fish and vegetarian dishes. Special (off-menu) orders *are* available, as are caviar and other culinary niceties.

Overall, the food is really good for the size of ship, and, with the choice of the two alternative dining spots, receives high praise. Sadly, dinner in the main dining room is in two seatings, the company having used the space that could have provided a second main dining room, for public areas. While the early seating is simply too rushed for many), with two alternative restaurants, off-menu choices, a hand-picked European staff and excellent service, dining is often memorable. Fresh pasta and dessert flambeau specialties are made at the table each day by accommodating headwaiters.

The wine list is excellent (though pricey), with an outstanding collection of across-the-board wines, including a mouthwatering connoisseur selection.

Afternoon tea in the Palm Court is a civilized daily event. The Lido provides breakfast and luncheon buffets that are fairly standard fare.

ALTERNATIVE DINING SPOTS (RESERVATIONS REQUIRED, NO EXTRA CHARGE): Two alternative dining spots are the 75-seat *Prego* (featuring fine Italian cuisine, and specializing in good Italian wines), and the revamped 100-seat *Jade Garden* (featuring five contemporary Chinese/French fusion dishes in association with Wolfgang Puck's *Chinois on Main* restaurant in Santa Monica). These rooms are appreciably larger than those aboard *Crystal Harmony*, and set on a lower deck (Deck 6); each restaurant has a separate entrance and themed décor. Both provide an excellent standard of culinary fare, with food cooked to order at no extra charge (although many feel that the recommended $6 waiter gratuity per meal should be included in the cruise fare).

Additionally, The Bistro (located on the upper level of the two-deck-high lobby) is a casual spot for coffees and pastries, served in the style and atmosphere of a European street café. The Bistro has unusual, Crystal Cruises-logo china that can also be purchased in one of the ship's boutiques.

For casual meals, The Lido Café has an extensive self-serve buffet area, located high up in the ship, and with great views from its large picture windows. For casual poolside lunches, there is also the Trident Grill, as well as an ice cream/frozen yoghurt counter (all at no extra charge). Several special themed buffets, with appropriate décor and good service staff dressed accordingly, are provided at the Trident indoor/outdoor pool area. These include the popular Asian Buffet and Follow the Sun buffet.

OTHER COMMENTS: *Crystal Symphony* is a contemporary ship with a nicely raked clipper bow and well-balanced lines. While some might not like the "apartment block" look of its exterior, it is the contemporary, "in" look, balconies having become standard aboard almost all new cruise ships. This ship has an excellent amount of open deck, sunbathing space, and sports facilities. The aft of two outdoor swimming pools can be covered by a magrodome in inclement weather. There is no sense of crowding anywhere, a superb example of comfort by design, high-quality construction and engineering. There is a wide wrap-around teakwood deck for walking, uncluttered by lounge chairs.

Inside, the layout is similar to that of *Crystal Harmony* and *Crystal Serenity,* with a design that shows that form follows function superbly well, combining the best of large ship facilities with the intimacy of rooms found aboard most small ships. The interior décor is restful, with color combinations that don't jar the senses. It has a good mixture of public entertainment lounges and small intimate rooms. Outstanding is the Palm Court, an observation lounge with forward-facing views over the ship's bows– it is tranquil, and one of the nicest rooms afloat (it is larger than aboard the sister ship).

There is an excellent book, video and CD-ROM library (combined with a Business Center). The theater (smaller than aboard sister ship *Crystal Harmony*) features high-definition video projection and headsets for the hearing-impaired. Useful self-service launderettes are provided on each deck. Fine-quality fabrics and soft furnishings, china, flatware and silver are used. Excellent in-cabin television programming (including CNN) is transmitted, as well as close-captioned videos for the hearing-impaired.

In 1999, the ship added a "Connoisseurs Club," located adjacent to the Avenue Saloon. Features in this intimate room include some fine premium brands of liquor and cigars for those who can appreciate (and pay for) such things. Also new is a Computer Learning Center, complete with more than 20 computers. Private lessons are available (although they are expensive, starting at $75 per hour).

In 2000 an expanded range of Spa facilities and treatments was introduced, under the aegis of Steiner Platinum Service.

This ship has just about everything for the discerning,

seasoned traveler who wants and is prepared to pay good money for fine style, abundant space and the comfort and the facilities of a large vessel capable of extended voyages, including an excellent program of guest lecturers.

The one thing that lets the product down is the fact that the dining room operation is in two seatings (however, having said that, there are many older passengers who want to eat early, while the line's younger passengers want to dine later, so there is some semblance of balance).

Crystal Cruises takes care of its ships, and its staff, and it is the staff that makes the cruise experience really special. They are a well-trained group that stress hospitality at all times. The ship achieves a high rating because of her fine facilities, service and crew. It is the extra attention to detail that makes a cruise with this ship so special. The passenger mix is approximately 85 percent North American (typically half of these will be from California) and 15 percent other nationalities.

The final word: this is announcement-free cruising

in a well-tuned, very professionally run, service oriented, ship, the approximate equivalent of a Four Seasons hotel. However, note that the score has gone downwards a little recently, the result of the fact that, in comparison to other ships available in the discounted marketplace, this is still a two-seating ship, which makes it more highly structured in terms of timing than it really should be. The onboard currency is the US dollar.

WEAK POINTS: Your evenings will be necessarily rather structured due to the fact that there are two seatings for dinner (unless you eat in one of the alternative dining spots), and two shows (the show lounge cannot seat all passengers at once). This detracts from the otherwise luxurious setting of the ship and the fine professionalism of its staff. Many passengers feel that gratuities should really be included on a ship that is rated this highly (they can, however, be pre-paid).

Plastic patio furniture on suite and cabin balconies would be better replaced with the more elegant teak variety, to go with the teak decking.

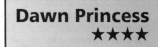

Dawn Princess
★★★★

Large Ship: ....77,499 tons	Passengers		Cabin Current: ....110 and 220 volts
Lifestyle: ....Standard	(lower beds/all berths): 2,100/2,250		Elevators: 11
Cruise Line: ....Princess Cruises	Passenger Space Ratio		Casino (gaming tables): ....Yes
Former Names: ....none	(lower beds/all berths): 36.9/34.4		Slot Machines: ....Yes
Builder: ....Fincantieri (Italy)	Crew/Passenger Ratio		Swimming Pools (outdoors): 4
Original Cost: ....$300 million	(lower beds/all berths): 2.1/2.5		Swimming Pools (indoors): 0
Entered Service: ....May 1997	Navigation Officers: ......British/Italian		Whirlpools: 5
Registry: ....Great Britain	Cabins (total): 975		Fitness Center: ....Yes
Length (ft/m): 857.2/261.3	Size Range (sq ft/m): 158.2–610.3/		Sauna/Steam Room: ....Yes/Yes
Beam (ft/m): 105.6/32.2		14.7–56.7	Massage: ....Yes
Draft (ft/m): 26.5/8.1	Cabins (outside view): 603		Self-Service Launderette: ....Yes
Propulsion/Propellers: .....diesel-electric	Cabins (interior/no view): 372		Dedicated Cinema/Seats: ....No
	(46,080kW)/2	Cabins (for one person): 0	Library: ....Yes
Passenger Decks: 10	Cabins (with private balcony): 446		Classification Society: ...Registro Navale
Total Crew: 900	Cabins (wheelchair accessible): 19		Italiano (RINA)

OVERALL SCORE: 1,539 (OUT OF A POSSIBLE 2,000 POINTS)

ACCOMMODATION: The brochure shows that there are 28 different cabin grades: 20 outside-view and 8 interior (no view) cabins. Although the standard outside-view and interior (no view) cabins are a little small, they are well designed and functional in layout, and have earth tone colors accentuated by splashes of color from the bedspreads. Proportionately, there are quite a lot of interior (no view) cabins. Many of the outside-view cabins have private balconies, and all seem to be quite well soundproofed, although the balcony partition is not the floor-to-ceiling type, so you can hear your neighbors clearly (or smell their smoke). Note: the balconies are very narrow, only just large enough for two small chairs, and there is no dedicated lighting.

A reasonable amount of closet and abundant drawer and other storage space is provided in all cabins – adequate for a 7-night cruise, as are a television and refrigerator. Each night a chocolate will appear on your pillow. The cabin bathrooms are practical, and come complete with most of the things needed, although they really are tight spaces, and are best described as one person at-a-time units. They do, however, have a decent shower enclosure, a small amount of shelving for your personal toiletries, real glasses, a hairdryer and a bathrobe.

The largest accommodation can be found in six suites, two on each of three decks located at the stern of the ship, with large private balcony. These are well laid out, and have large bathrooms with two sinks, a Jacuzzi bathtub, and a separate shower enclosure. The bedroom features generous amounts of wood accenting and detailing,

BERLITZ'S RATINGS

	Possible	Achieved
Ship	500	428
Accommodation	200	162
Food	400	266
Service	400	291
Entertainment	100	86
Cruise	400	306

indented ceilings, and television sets in both bedroom and lounge areas. The suites also have a dining room table and four chairs.

The mini-suites typically have two lower beds that convert into a queen-sized bed. There is a separate bedroom/sleeping area with vanity desk, and a lounge with sofa and coffee table, indented ceilings with generous amounts of wood accenting and detailing, walk-in closet, and larger bathroom with Jacuzzi bathtub and separate shower enclosure.

Note that Princess Cruises features CNN, CNBC, ESPN and TNT on the in-cabin color television system (when available, depending on cruise area).

DINING: There are two main dining rooms, Florentine and Venetian (both are non-smoking, as are all dining rooms aboard the ships of Princess Cruises); each of which has its own galley and each is split into multi-tier sections, which help create a feeling of intimacy, although there is a lot of noise from the waiter stations, which are adjacent to many tables. Breakfast and lunch are provided in an open seating arrangement, while dinner is in two seatings.

Despite the fact that the portions are generous, the food and its presentation are somewhat disappointing, and bland of taste. The quality of fish is poor (often disguised by crumb or batter coatings), the selection of fresh green vegetables is limited, and few garnishes are used. However, do remember that this *is* big-ship banquet catering, with all its attendant standardization and production cooking. Meats are of a decent quality,

although often disguised by gravy-based sauces, and pasta dishes are acceptable (though voluminous), and are typically served by section headwaiters that may also make "something special just for you" – in search of gratuities and good comments. If you like desserts, order a sundae at dinner, as most other desserts are just so-so. Remember that ice cream ordered in the dining room is included, but if you order one anywhere else, you'll have to pay for it.

On any given seven-day cruise, a typical menu cycle will include a Sailaway Dinner, Captain's Welcome Dinner, Chef's Dinner, Italian Dinner, French Dinner, Captain's Gala Dinner, and Landfall Dinner. The wine list is reasonable, but not good, and the company has, sadly, seen fit to eliminate all wine waiters. Note that 15 percent is added to all beverage bills, including wines (whether you order a $15 bottle or a $120 bottle, even though it takes the same amount of service to open and pour the wine).

For some really good meat, however, consider the *Sterling Steakhouse*; it's for those that want to taste four different cuts of Angus beef from the popular "Sterling Silver" brand of USDA prime meats – Filet Mignon, New York Strip, Porterhouse, and Rib-Eye – all presented on a silver tray. There is also a barbecue chicken option, plus the usual baked potato or French fries as accompaniments. This is available as an alternative to the dining rooms, between 6.30pm and 9.30pm only, at an additional charge of $8 per person. However, it is not, as you might expect, a separate, intimate dining room, but is located in a section of the Horizon Buffet, with its own portable bar and some decorative touches to set it apart (from the regular Horizon Buffet).

The Horizon Buffet is open 24 hours a day, and, at night, features an informal dinner setting with sit-down waiter service; a small bistro menu is also available. The buffet displays are, for the most part, quite repetitious, but better than they have been in the last few years (there is no real finesse in presentation, however, as plastic plates are provided, instead of trays). The cabin service menu is very limited, and presentation of the food items featured is poor.

There is also a pâtisserie (for cappuccino/espresso coffees and pastries), a wine/caviar bar, and a pizzeria (complete with cobblestone floors and wrought iron decorative features), and excellent pizzas (there are six to choose from).

OTHER COMMENTS: Although large, this all-white ship has a decent profile, and is well balanced by a large funnel, which contains a deck tennis/basketball/volleyball court in its sheltered aft base. There is a wide, teakwood wrap-around promenade deck outdoors, some real teak steamer-style deck chairs (complete with royal blue cushioned pads), and 93,000 sq. ft (8,640 sq. meters) of space outdoors. A great amount of glass area on the upper decks provides plenty of light and connection with the outside world.

The ship, while large, absorbs passengers well, and has an almost intimate feel to it, which is what the interior designers intended. The interiors are very pretty and warm, with attractive colors and welcoming décor that includes some very attractive wall murals and other artwork. The signage throughout the ship could be better, however.

There is a wide range of public rooms to choose from, with several intimate rooms and spaces so that you don't get the feel of being overwhelmed by large spaces. Features tasteful décor, with attractive color combinations that are warm and don't clash (nothing is brash). The interior focal point is a huge four-deck-high atrium lobby with winding, double stairways, complete with two panoramic glass-walled elevators.

The main public entertainment rooms are located under three decks of accommodation. There is plenty of space, the traffic flow is good, and the ship absorbs people well. There are two show lounges, one at each end of the ship; one is a superb 550-seat, theater-style show lounge (movies are also shown here) and the other is a 480-seat cabaret-style lounge, complete with bar.

A glass-walled health spa complex is located high atop ship and includes a gymnasium with high-tech machines. One swimming pool is "suspended" aft between two decks (there are two other pools, although they are not large for the size of the ship).

The library is a very warm room and has six large buttery leather chairs for listening to compact audio discs, with ocean-view windows. There is a conference center for up to 300, as well as a business center, with computers, copy and fax machines. The collection of artwork is good, particularly on the stairways, and helps make the ship feel smaller than it is, although in places it doesn't always seem coordinated. The casino, while large, is not really in the main passenger flow and so it does not generate the "walk-through" factor found aboard so many ships.

The most traditional room aboard is the Wheelhouse Lounge/Bar, which is decorated in the style of a late 19th-century gentleman's club, complete with wood paneling and comfortable seating. The focal point is a large ship model from the P&O collection archives: aboard *Dawn Princess* it is *Kenya*.

At the end of the day, as is the case aboard most large ships today, if you live in the top suites, you will be well attended; if you do not, you will merely be one of a large number of passengers. One nice feature is the captain's cocktail party – it is typically held in the four-deck-high main atrium – so you can come and go as you please, and there's no standing in line to have your photograph taken with the captain if you don't want to. However, note that cruising aboard large ships such as this one has become increasingly an onboard revenue-based product. You can expect to be subjected to a stream of flyers advertising daily art auctions, "designer" watches, "inch of gold/silver" and other promotions, while "artworks" for auction are strewn throughout the ship.

Note that gratuities to staff are *automatically* added to your account, at $10 per person, per day (gratuities for children are charged at the same rate). If you want to pay less, you'll need to go to the reception desk to have these charges adjusted (that could mean lining up with many other passengers wanting to do the same). The onboard currency is the US dollar.

WEAK POINTS: Standing in line for embarkation (an "express check-in" option is available by completing certain documentation 40 days in advance of your cruise), disembarkation, shore tenders and for self-serve buffet meals is an inevitable aspect of cruising aboard all large ships. There is no escape from unnecessary and repetitive announcements (particularly for activities that bring revenue, such as art auctions, bingo, horse racing) that intrude constantly into your cruise. The in-your-face art auctions are simply overbearing, and the paintings, lithographs and faux, framed pictures that are strewn throughout the ship (and clash irritatingly with the ship's interior décor) are an annoying intrusion into what should be a vacation, not a cruise inside a floating "art" emporium. There are no cushioned pads for the deck lounge chairs on the open lido decks.

The digital voice announcing elevator deck stops is irritating to passengers (many of whom tell me they would like to rip out the speaker system). There are a number of dead ends in the interior layout, so it's not as user-friendly as a ship this size should be. The walls of the passenger accommodation decks are very plain (some artwork would be an improvement). The cabin numbering system is extremely illogical, with numbers going through several hundred series on the same deck.

The swimming pools are quite small for so many passengers, and the pool deck is cluttered with white, plastic deck lounge chairs, which do not have cushioned pads. Waiting for tenders in anchor ports can prove irritating, but typical of large ship operations. Charging for use of the machines and washing powder in the self-service launderette is trifling.

KNOTS AND LOGS

A knot is a unit of speed measuring one nautical mile. (A nautical mile is equal to one-60th of a degree of the earth's circumference and measures exactly 6,080.2 ft (1,852 km). It is about 800 ft (243 meters) longer than a land mile. Thus, when a ship is traveling at a speed of 20 knots (note: this is never referred to as 20 knots per hour), it is traveling at 20 nautical miles per hour.

This unit of measurement has its origin in the days prior to the advent of modern aids, when sailors used a log and a length of rope to measure the distance that their boat had covered, as well as the speed at which it was advancing. In 1574, a tract by William Bourne, entitled A Regiment for the Sea, records the method by which this was done. The log was weighted down at one end while the other end was affixed to a rope. The weighted end, when thrown over the stern, had the effect of making the log stand upright, thus being visible. Sailors believed that the log remained stationary at the spot where it had been cast into the water, while the rope unraveled. By measuring the length of rope used, they could ascertain how far the ship had traveled, and were thus able to calculate its speed.

Sailors first tied knots at regular intervals, eventually fixed at 47 ft 3 inches (14.4 meters) along a rope, then counted how many knots had passed through their hands in a specified time (later established as 28 seconds), and measured by the amount of sand that had run out of an hourglass. They then used simple multiplication to calculate the number of knots their ship was traveling at over the period of an hour.

The data gathered in this way were put into a record, called a logbook. Today, a logbook is used to record the day-to-day details of the life of a ship and its crew as well as other pertinent information.

Delphin
★★★ +

Removed 2006

Small Ship: ....16,214 tons	Passengers	Cabin Current: ....220 volts
Lifestyle: ....Standard	(lower beds/all berths): 466/556	Elevators: 2
Cruise Line: ....Delphin Seereisen	Passenger Space Ratio	Casino (gaming tables): ....No
Former Names: *Kazakhstan II/Belorussiya*	(lower beds/all berths): 35.6/29.8	Slot Machines: ....No
Builder: ....Wartsila (Finland)	Crew/Passenger Ratio	Swimming Pools (outdoors): 1
Original Cost: ....$25 million	(lower beds/all berths): 1.9/2.3	Swimming Pools (indoors): 0
Entered Service: .....Jan 1975/Dec 1993	Navigation Officers: ....Ukrainian	Whirlpools: 0
Registry: ....Malta	Cabins (total): 233	Fitness Center: ....Yes
Length (ft/m): 512.5/156.24	Size Range (sq ft/m): 150.0–492.0/	Sauna/Steam Room: ....Yes/Yes
Beam (ft/m): 71.8/21.90	14.0–45.7	Massage: ....Yes
Draft (ft/m): 20.3/6.20	Cabins (outside view): 128	Self-Service Launderette: ....Yes
Propulsion/Propellers: ....diesel	Cabins (interior/no view): 105	Dedicated Cinema/Seats: ....No
(13,250kW)/2	Cabins (for one person): 0	Library: ....Yes
Passenger Decks: 8	Cabins (with private balcony): 0	Classification Society: .....Germanischer
Total Crew: 234	Cabins (wheelchair accessible): 0	Lloyd

---

OVERALL SCORE: 1,297 (OUT OF A POSSIBLE 2,000 POINTS)

ACCOMMODATION: There are 10 grades of accommodation to choose from. Typically, the higher the deck, the more expensive will be the accommodation.

The Boat Deck suites (located forward) are very large and well equipped, with an abundance of drawers and good closet space, and all feature blond wood furniture, and a refrigerator. The bathrooms are very spacious, and come with full-sized bathtubs and large toiletries cabinet; bathrobes are also provided.

All the other outside-view and interior (no view) cabins are very compact units, yet adequate (but not for an around-the-world cruise), although there is little drawer space, and storage space is tight on the long cruises which this ship often undertakes. All of the beds have European duvets, and all cabins receive fresh flowers each cruise. The bathrooms are small, but there is good space for toiletry items.

DINING: There is one large main dining room – the Pacific Restaurant, which has 554 seats. It has a high ceiling, large ocean-view picture windows, pleasing décor, and seats all passengers in one seating – so there is no need to hurry over meals.

In general, the food is attractively presented (better now that the catering is actively managed in-house), and the variety of foods featured is quite sound. The choice is good (with a heavy reliance on meat and game dishes), although selections for vegetarians are also available. While standard white and red table wines are included for lunch and dinner, there is also an additional wine list

BERLITZ'S RATINGS

	Possible	Achieved
Ship	500	319
Accommodation	200	126
Food	400	257
Service	400	278
Entertainment	100	61
Cruise	400	256

with a reasonably good selection at moderate prices. The gala buffet is very good. Service comes with a smile from attractive Ukrainian waitresses, although communicating with them can prove awkward at times.

For casual meals, breakfast and lunch buffets can be taken in The Lido. The food featured is decent enough, with reasonable choice, although there is some degree of repetition, particularly of breakfast items.

OTHER COMMENTS: *Delphin* is a reasonably smart-looking cruise ship (originally built as one of a series of five vessels in the same class), topped by a square funnel. It was well refitted and refurbished throughout following a shipyard rollover incident (when it was named *Belorussiya*). Its original car decks have long been converted into useful public rooms and additional cabins and the former car loading ramps on the vessel's stern have been fully sealed.

When the ship last underwent a major refurbishment, several new facilities were added. These improved almost all the public areas and added better health/fitness and spa facilities and an improved lido deck (the circular "swimming" pool is small, however, and is really only useful as a "dip" pool).

The promenade decks outdoors are quite reasonable, although there are "lips" which you have to step over in the forward section.

Sports participants will find volleyball, basketball, and table tennis. There is also a fitness center (which features a sauna, solarium, and massage treatments), as well as a dialysis station for up to 26 persons (for cruises when specialist technicians are provided).

The interior decor is quite tasteful and warm, with colors that do not jar the senses. Flower bouquets and colorful artwork enhance the otherwise plain décor throughout.

Delphin will provide a very comfortable cruise experience for those German-speaking passengers who seek destination-intensive cruises, in comfortable, though not luxurious surroundings, at an extremely attractive price. It is *not* a luxury product, nor does it pretend to be. Delphin Seereisen claims it to be a four-star ship/product in its brochure, but the Berlitz score does not quite add up to that in light of the competition in the marketplace (particularly with newer ships with better facilities and layouts), although it is a good product, and the ship's interiors are always in excellent, spotless shape.

Delphin attracts many repeat passengers because of the destination-intensive itineraries and decent level of service. The company continues to spend money on little refinements throughout the ship, which are appreciated by the many loyal repeat passengers. Delphin Seereisen's own onboard cruise director and staff are very good.

Note that all port taxes and insurance are included. The currency on board is the euro.

WEAK POINTS: There are many pillars throughout the public rooms, and these inhibit sight lines. The ceiling height is quite low in most public rooms, and the stairways are quite steep, with steps that are short and difficult to replace without major structural changes (a leftover from its life as a passenger ferry). The gangway is quite narrow. There is no wrap-around promenade deck outdoors and no observation lounge/bar with forward-facing views over the ship's bows.

STEERING

Two different methods can be used to steer a ship:
Electrohydraulic steering uses automatic (telemotor-type) transmission from the wheel itself to the steering gear aft. This is generally used when traffic is heavy, during maneuvers into and out of ports, or when there is poor visibility.
Automatic steering (gyropilot) is used only in the open sea. This system does not require anyone at the wheel because it is controlled by computer. However, aboard all ships, a quartermaster is always at the wheel, for extra safety, and just in case a need should arise to switch from one steering system to another.
Satellite Navigator
Using this latest high-tech piece of equipment, ship's officers can read, on a small television

screen, the ship's position in the open ocean anywhere in the world, any time, and in any weather with pinpoint accuracy.

Satellite navigation systems use the information transmitted by a constellation of orbiting satellites. Each is in a normal circular polar orbit at an altitude of 450 to 700 nautical miles, and orbits the Earth in about 108 minutes.

Data from each gives the current orbital position every two minutes. Apart from telling the ship where it is, it continuously provides the distance from any given point, calculates the drift caused by currents and so on, and tells the ship when the next satellite will pass.

The basis of the satellite navigation is the US Navy Satellite System (NNSS). This first became operational in January

1964 as the precision guidance system for the Polaris submarine fleet and was made available for commercial use in 1967.

The latest (and more accurate) system is the GPS (Global Positioning System), which is now fitted to an increasing number of ships. This uses 24 satellites (18 of which are on-line at any given time) that provide accuracy in estimating a ship's position to plus or minus 6 ft. Another variation is the NACOS (Navigational Command System), which collects information from a variety of sources: satellites, radar, gyroscopic compass, speed log, and surface navigational systems as well as engines, thrusters, rudders, and human input. It then displays relevant computations and information on one screen, controlled by a single keyboard.

Diamond Princess
NOT YET RATED

Large Ship:	.............113,000 tons	Passengers		Cabin Current:	...............110 volts

Large Ship: ....113,000 tons
Lifestyle: ....Premium
Cruise Line: ....Princess Cruises
Former Names: ....none
Builder: .....Mitsubishi Heavy Industries (Japan)
Original Cost: ....$400 million
Entered Service: ....July 2003
Registry: ....Bermuda
Length (ft/m): 951.4/290.00
Beam (ft/m): 123.0/37.50
Draft (ft/m): 26.4/8.05
Propulsion/Propellers: ....gas turbine (25 MW)/2 azimuthing pods (21,000 kW each)
Passenger Decks: 13
Total Crew: 1,238

Passengers
(lower beds/all berths): 2,674/3,100
Passenger Space Ratio
(lower beds/all berths): 42.2/43.4
Crew/Passenger Ratio
(lower beds/all berths): 2.1/2.5
Navigation Officers: ......British/Italian
Cabins (total): 1,337
Size Range (sq ft/m): 168–1,329.3/
15.6–123.5
Cabins (outside view): 1,000
Cabins (interior/no view): 337
Cabins (for one person): 0
Cabins (with private balcony): 750
Cabins (wheelchair accessible): 28
(18 outside/10 interior)

Cabin Current: ....110 volts
Elevators: 14
Casino (gaming tables): ....Yes
Slot Machines: ....Yes
Swimming Pools (outdoors): 4
Swimming Pools (indoors): 0
Whirlpools: 9
Fitness Center: ....Yes
Sauna/Steam Room: ....Yes/Yes
Massage:.........................Yes
Self-Service Launderette:..........Yes
Dedicated Cinema/Seats: ....No
Library: ....Yes
Classification Society: ....Lloyds Register

OVERALL SCORE: NYR (OUT OF A POSSIBLE 2,000 POINTS)

ACCOMMODATION: All passengers receive turndown service and chocolates on pillows each night, as well as bathrobes (on request) and toiletry amenity kits (larger, naturally, for suite/mini-suite occupants) that typically include soap, shampoo, conditioner, and hand/body lotion. A hairdryer is provided in all cabins, sensibly located at the vanity desk unit in the living area. All bathrooms are tiled and have a decent amount of open shelf storage space for personal toiletries. Note that Princess Cruises features BBC World, CNN, CNBC, ESPN and TNT on the in-cabin color television system (when available, depending on cruise area).

You should note that the majority of the outside cabins on Emerald Deck have views obstructed by the lifeboats. Sadly, there are no cabins for singles. Your name is typically placed outside your suite or cabin – making it simple for delivery service personnel but also making it intrusive with regard to your privacy. There is 24-hour room service (note that some items on the room service menu are not, however, available during early morning hours).

Note that most of the balcony suites and cabins can be overlooked from the navigation bridge wing. Cabins with balconies on Baja, Caribe, and Dolphin decks are also overlooked by passengers on balconies on the deck above; they are, therefore, not at all private.

DINING: There are a number of "personal choice" dining options. For formal meals there are four principal dining

BERLITZ'S RATINGS		
	Possible	Achieved
Ship	500	NYR
Accommodation	200	NYR
Food	400	NYR
Service	400	NYR
Entertainment	100	NYR
Cruise	400	NYR

rooms (one more than the similarly sized *Golden, Grand* and *Star Princess*). These offer a mix of two seatings (with seating assigned according to the location of your cabin) or "anytime dining" (where you choose when and with whom you want to eat). All four dining rooms are non-smoking and are split into multi-tier sections in a non-symmetrical design that breaks what are quite large spaces into many smaller sections, for better ambience and less noise pollution.

Specially designed dinnerware and good quality linens and silverware are featured: Dudson of England (dinnerware), Frette Egyptian cotton table linens, and silverware by Hepp of Germany. Note that 15 percent is added to all beverage bills, including wines (whether you order a $15 bottle or a $120 bottle, although it's the same amount of service to open and pour the wine).

Two alternative informal dining areas are provided. Both are open for lunch and dinner (on sea days only); both incur an extra charge, and reservations are needed:

Fabio's is an Italian eatery, with colorful Mediterranean-style décor in the style of a Trattoria. It features Italian-style pizzas and pastas, with a variety of sauces, as well as Italian-style entrees (including tiger prawns and lobster tail – all provided with flair and entertainment by the waiters (by reservation only; expect a cover charge of about $15 per person). Southwestern American food is featured in the other alternative dining spot, and is open for lunch or dinner on sea days only (by reservation only; expect a cover charge of about $8 per person). The cuisine in both of these spots is decidedly better than in the three main dining rooms, with better quality ingredients and significantly more attention to presentation and taste.

A poolside hamburger grill and pizza bar (no additional charge) are additional dining spots for casual bites, while extra charges will apply if you order items to eat at either the coffee bar/patisserie, or the caviar/champagne bar.

Other casual meals can be taken in the Horizon Court, which is open 24 hours a day, with large oceanview on port and starboard sides and direct access to the two principal swimming pools and lido deck (there is no real finesse in presentation, however, as plastic plates are provided).

OTHER COMMENTS: This is the first ship to be constructed by a Japanese shipyard for Princess Cruises (a sister ship, *Sapphire Princess* will debut in 2004). The ship is similar in size and internal layout as *Golden Princess, Grand Princess* and *Star Princess* (although slightly wider). Unlike its half-sister ships *Golden Princess, Grand Princess* and *Star Princess*, however, all of which had a "spoiler" located aft of the funnel, this has been removed from both *Diamond Princess* and *Sapphire Princess*, replaced by an aft-facing nightclub/discotheque structure set around the base of the adjoining the funnel structure, and accessed by an escalator spanning two decks. The view from the nightclub overlooks several aft-facing cascading decks.

The actual hull form in *Diamond Princess* (and sister *Sapphire Princess*, set to debut in 2004) is slightly different to that of other "Grand Class" ships, and is slightly wider. *Diamond Princess* is the first "Grand Class" ship to have a "pod" propulsion system. Briefly, pods, which resemble huge outboard motors, replace internal electric propulsion motors, shaft lines, rudders and their machinery, and are compact, self-contained units that typically weigh about 170 tons each. Although they are located at the stern, pod units *pull*, rather than *push*, a ship through the water. Pods replace the conventional rudder and propeller shafts. Electrical power is provided by a combination of four diesel and one gas turbine (CODAG) unit; the diesel engines are located in the engine room, while the gas turbine unit is located in the ship's funnel housing, on each side of which is a cosmetic pod. For maneuverability, there are also three bow thrusters and three stern thrusters.

The interiors of the ship were overseen and outfitted by the Okura Group, whose Okura Hotel is one of the best in Tokyo. The quality of fit and finish is expected to surpass that of the Italian-built *Golden Princess, Grand Princess* and *Star Princess*.

Unlike the outside decks, there is plenty of space inside the ship (but there are also plenty of passengers), and a wide array of public rooms to choose from, with many "intimate" (this being a relative word) spaces and places to play. The passenger flow has been well thought out, and works with little congestion. The décor is very attractive, with lots of earth tones (well suited to both American and European tastes). In fact, this ship is perhaps the culmination of the best of all that Princess Cruises has to offer from its many years of operating what is now a well-tuned, good quality product.

Four areas center on swimming pools, one of which is two decks high and is covered by a magrodome, itself an extension of the funnel housing. High atop the stern of the ship is a ship-wide glass-walled disco pod (I have nicknamed it the ETR – energy transfer room). It looks like an aerodynamic "spoiler" and is positioned high above the water, with spectacular views from the extreme port and starboard side windows.

The Lotus Spa complex, which has Japanese-style décor, surrounds one of the swimming pools (you can have a massage or other spa treatment in an ocean-view treatment room). Lotus Spa treatments include Chakra hot stone massage, Asian Lotus ritual (featuring massage with reflexology, reiki and shiatsu massage), deep tissue sports therapy massage, lime and ginger salt glow, wild strawberry back cleanse, and seaweed mud wraps, among others devised to make you feel good (and part with your money).

An extensive collection of art works has been chosen, and this complements the interior design and colors well. If you see something you like, you will be able to purchase it on board – it's almost all for sale.

Like sister ships *Golden Princess, Grand Princess* and *Star Princess,* this vessel also features a Wedding Chapel (a live web-cam can relay ceremonies via the internet). The ship's captain can legally marry (American) couples, due to the ship's Bermuda registry and a special dispensation (which should be verified when in the planning stage, according to where you reside). Princess Cruises offers three wedding packages – Pearl, Emerald, Diamond; the fee includes registration and official marriage certificate. However, to get married *and* take your close family members and entourage with you on your honeymoon is going to cost a lot. The "Hearts & Minds" chapel is also useful for "renewal of vows" ceremonies.

For children there is a two-deck-high playroom, teen room, and a host of specially trained counselors. Children have their own pools, hot tubs, and open deck area at the stern of the ship (away from adult areas).

For entertainment, Princess Cruises prides itself on its glamorous all-American production shows, and the shows aboard this ship (typically two per 7-day cruise) will not disappoint. Neither will the comfortable show lounges (the largest of which features $3 million in sound and light equipment, as well as a 9-piece orchestra, and a scenery loading bay that connects directly from stage to a hull door for direct transfer to the dockside). Two other entertainment lounges help spread things around.

Gaming lovers should enjoy what is presently one of the largest casinos at sea (Grand Casino), with more than 260 slot machines; there are blackjack, craps and roulette tables, plus newer games such as Let It Ride Bonus, Spanish 21 and Caribbean Draw Progressive. But the highlight could well be the specially linked slot machines that provide a combined payout.

Other features include a decent library/CD-Rom computer room, and a separate card room. Ship lovers should enjoy the wood-paneled Wheelhouse Bar, finely decorated with memorabilia and ship models tracing part of parent company P&O's history. A high-tech hospital is provided, with live SeaMed tele-medicine link-ups with specialists at the Cedars-Sinai Medical Center in Los Angeles available for emergency help.

Whether this really can be considered a relaxing vacation is a moot point, but with *so many choices* and "small" rooms to enjoy, the ship has been extremely well designed, and the odds are that you'll have a fine cruise vacation, as long as you plan your movements carefully.

Diamond Princess will provide you with a stunning, grand playground in which to roam when you are not ashore. Princess Cruises delivers a fine, well-packaged vacation product, with some sense of style, at an attractive, highly competitive price, and this ship will appeal to those that really enjoy a big city to play in, with all the trimmings and lots of fellow passengers. The ship is full of revenue centers, however, which are designed to help you part with even more money than what is paid for in the price of your cruise ticket. As cruising aboard large ships such as this one has become increasingly an onboard revenue-based product, you can expect to be subjected to a stream of flyers advertising daily art auctions, "designer" watches and the like, while "artworks" for auction are strewn throughout the ship.

The dress code has been simplified – reduced to formal or smart casual (which typically seems to be translated by many as jeans and trainers). Note that gratuities to staff are *automatically* added to your account, at $10 per person, per day (gratuities for children are charged at the same rate). If you want to pay less, you'll need to go to the reception desk to have these charges adjusted (that could mean lining up with many other passengers wanting to do the same). The onboard currency is the US dollar.

WEAK POINTS: If you are not used to large ships, it will take you some time to find your way around this one, despite the company's claim that this vessel offers passengers a "small ship feel, big ship choice." The cabin bath towels are small, and drawer space is limited. There are no butlers – even for the top grade suites (which are not really large in comparison to similar suites aboard some other ships). Cabin attendants have too many cabins to look after (typically 20), which does not translate to fine personal service.

Lines will tend to form for many things aboard large ships, but particularly for the purser's (information) office, and for open seating breakfast and lunch in the four main dining rooms. Long lines for shore excursions and shore tenders are also a fact of life aboard large ships such as this, as is waiting for elevators at peak times, embarkation (an "express check-in" option is available by completing certain documentation 40 days in advance of your cruise) and disembarkation, and booking spa appointments on the day of embarkation.

You'll have to live with the many extra charge items (such as for ice cream, and freshly squeezed orange juice) and activities (such as yoga, group exercise bicycling and kick boxing classes at $10 per session, not to mention $4 per hour for *group* babysitting services – at the time this book was completed). There's also a charge for using the washers and dryers in the self-service launderettes.

Disney Magic
★★★★ +

Large Ship: . . . . .83,338 tons	Passengers	Cabins (wheelchair accessible): 12
Lifestyle: . . . . .Standard	(lower beds/all berths): 1,750/3,325	Cabin Current: . . . . .110 volts
Cruise Line: . . . . .Disney Cruise Line	Passenger Space Ratio	Elevators: 12
Former Names: . . . . .none	(lower beds/all berths): 47.6/25.0	Casino (gaming tables): . . . . .No
Builder: . . . . .Fincantieri (Italy)	Crew/Passenger Ratio	Slot Machines: .No
Original Cost: . . . .$350 million	(lower beds/all berths): 1.8/3.5	Swimming Pools (outdoors): 3
Entered Service: . . . . .July 1998	Navigation Officers: . . . . .European/	Swimming Pools (indoors): 0
Registry: . . . . .The Bahamas	Scandinavian	Whirlpools: 6
Length (ft/m): 964.5/294.00	Cabins (total): .875	Fitness Center: . . . . .Yes
Beam (ft/m): 105.7/32.22	Size Range (sq ft/m): 180.8–968.7/	Sauna/Steam Room: . . . . .Yes/Yes
Draft (ft/m): 26.2/8.0	16.8–90.0	Massage: . . . . .Yes
Propulsion/Propellers: . . . . .diesel-electric	Cabins (outside view): 720	Self-Service Launderette: . . . . .Yes (3)
(38,000kW)/2	Cabins (interior/no view): 155	Dedicated Cinema/Seats: Yes/270
Passenger Decks: 11	Family Cabins: 80	Library: . . . . .No
Total Crew: .945	Cabins (with private balcony): 388	Classification Society: . . .Lloyd's Register

OVERALL SCORE: 1,553 (OUT OF A POSSIBLE 2,000 POINTS)

ACCOMMODATION: Spread over six decks, there are several types of suites and cabins from which to choose; all have been designed for practicality and have space-efficient layouts. Most cabins have common features such as a neat vertical steamer trunk for clothes storage, illuminated closets, a hairdryer located at a vanity desk (or in the bathroom), and bathrobes for all passengers. Many cabins have third- and fourth pull-down berths that rise and are totally hidden in the ceiling when not in use, but the standard interior and outside cabins, while acceptable for two, are extremely tight with three or four. The decor is practical, creative, and colorful, with lots of neat styling touches. Cabins with refrigerators can have them stocked with one of several packages (at extra cost).

The bathrooms, although compact (due to the fact that the toilet is separate from the rest of the bathroom), are really functional units, designed with split-use facilities so that more than one person can use them at the same time (good for families). Many have bathtubs (really shower tubs).

Accommodation designated as suites offer much more space, and extra goodies such as VCRs, CD players, large screen televisions, and extra beds that are useful for larger families. Some of the suites are, however, beneath the pool deck, teen lounge, or informal café, so there could be lots of noise as the ceiling insulation is poor (but the cabin to cabin insulation is good).

Wheelchair-bound passengers have a variety of cabin sizes and configurations to choose from, including suites with a private balcony (unfortunately you cannot get a

BERLITZ'S RATINGS

	Possible	Achieved
Ship	500	444
Accommodation	200	172
Food	400	214
Service	400	303
Entertainment	100	93
Cruise	400	327

wheelchair through the balcony's sliding door) and extra-large bathrooms with excellent roll-in showers, and good closet and drawer space (almost all the vessel is accessible). Note that for the sight-impaired, cabin numbers and elevator buttons are Braille-encoded.

A 24-hour room service is available (suite occupants also get concierge service); however, the room service menu is very limited, as is the cabin breakfast menu. There is a 15 percent service charge for all beverage deliveries (including tea and coffee).

DINING: There are three main dining rooms (all non-smoking), each with over 400 seats, two seatings, and unique themes. Lumiere's has *Beauty and the Beast*; Parrot Cay has a tacky, pseudo-Caribbean theme; Animator's Palate (the most visual of the three) features food and electronic art that makes the evening décor change from black and white to full-color. You will eat in all three dining rooms in rotation (twice per 7-day cruise), and move with your assigned waiter and assistant waiter to each dining room in turn, thus providing a different dining experience (each has a different décor, different menus). As you will have the same waiter in each of the three restaurants, any gratuities go only to "your" waiter. Parrot Cay and Lumiere's have open seating for breakfast and lunch (the lunch menu is pitiful). The noise level in all three dining rooms is extremely high. Note that if the formal nights happen to fall on the evening you are due to eat in Parrot Cay, formal wear and the décor of Parrot Cay Restaurant do not go together, in any shape or form.

In addition, Palo is an elegant 140-seat reservations-only alternative restaurant (with a $5 cover/gratuity charge) featuring Italian cuisine. It has a 270-degree view, and is for adults only (no "Munchkins" allowed); the à la carte cuisine is cooked to order, and the wine list is good (although prices are high). Make your reservations as soon as you board or miss out on the only decent food aboard this ship. Afternoon High Tea is also presented here, on days at sea.

For casual eating, Topsider's is an indoor/outdoor cafe featuring low-quality self-serve breakfast and lunch buffets with very poor choice and presentation, and a buffet dinner for children (consisting mostly of fried foods). There is also an ice cream and frozen yogurt bar (Scoops) that opens infrequently; other fast food outlets include Pluto's (for hamburgers, hot dogs), Pinocchio's, which is open throughout the day but not in the evening (for basic pizza and sandwiches). On one night of the cruise, there is also an outdoor self-serve "Tropical-ifragilisticexpialidocious" buffet.

Overall, the food has improved since the ship was first introduced (it needed to, it was of a very low quality), and is now more attractively presented, although there are still so few green vegetables. Vegetarians and those seeking healthy spa alternatives will be totally underwhelmed, as will those who want spa (light) cuisine. Guest chefs from Walt Disney World Resort prepare signature dishes each cruise, and also host cooking demonstrations.

OTHER COMMENTS: Zip-a-Dee-Do-Dah, Zip-a-Dee-Day! *Disney Magic*'s profile has managed to combine stream-lining with tradition and nostalgia, and has two large red and black funnels designed to remind you of the ocean liners of the past. *Disney Magic* is the first cruise ship built with two funnels since the 1950s. However, one of the funnels is a dummy, and contains a variety of public spaces, including a neat ESPN sports bar and a broadcast center. The ship was actually constructed in two halves, which were then joined together in the shipyard in Venice, Italy. The ship's whistle even plays "When You Wish Upon a Star" (or a sort of sickly version of it). The bow features handsome gold scrollwork that more typically seen adorning the tall ships of yesteryear. There is a wrap-around promenade deck outdoors for strolling.

Disney Cruise Line has not added ostentatious decoration to the ship's exterior. However, Mickey's ears are painted on the funnels; there is also a special 85-ft (26-meter) long paint stripe that cleverly incorporates Disney characters into the whimsical yellow paintwork along each side of the hull at the bow. Cute. The ship's exterior colors are also those of Mickey Mouse himself (call it a well-planned coincidence). Also of note is a 15-ft (4.5-meter) Goofy hanging upside down in a bosun's chair, painting the stern of the vessel.

On deck, a sports deck features a paddle tennis court, table tennis, basketball court, shuffleboard, and golf driving range. An ESPN Skybox Bar features 12 televisions of differing sizes for live (by satellite) sports events and noisy conversation (cigar smokers welcome). There are three outdoor pools: one pool for adults only (in theory), one for children, and one for families (guess which one has Mickey's ears painted into the bottom?). However, there's music everywhere (four different types), and it's impossible to find a quiet spot (in fact, you can sit in many places a get two types of music blaring at you at the same time). The children's pool features a long yellow water slide (available at specified times), held up by the giant hand of Mickey Mouse, although the pool itself really is too small considering the number of small children typically carried.

Inside, the ship is quite stunning, although poorly finished in several places. The Art Deco theme of the old ocean liners has been tastefully carried out (check out the stainless steel/pewter Disney detailing on the handrails and balustrades in the three-deck-high lobby). Most public rooms have high ceilings. The decor is reminiscent of New York's Radio City Music Hall. The interior detailing is stunning, much of it whimsical – pure Disney. The lobby provides a real photo opportunity, with a 6-ft (1.8-meter) high bronze statue of Mickey in the role of a ship's helmsman (there is probably some pixie dust around somewhere, too). Mickey is also visible in many other areas, albeit subtly (for Disney). If you can't sleep, try counting the number of times Mickey's logo appears – it's an impossible task.

There are two large shops and an abundance of Disney-theme clothing, soft toys, collectibles and specialty items. Features a superb, 1,040-seat Walt Disney Theatre (spread over four decks but without a balcony), piano bar, adults-only nightclub/disco, family lounge, and a dedicated cinema (where classic Disney films are shown, as well as first-run movies).

For fitness devotees, a fitness room, part of the spa (measuring 8,500 sq. ft/790 sq. meters) has ocean-view windows that overlook the navigation bridge below. There are several treatment rooms, and a "rain forest" with scented steam rooms, although the pounding from the basketball court located directly above makes relaxing spa treatments impossible, and thus a waste of money.

The children's entertainment areas measure 13,000 sq. ft (1,200 sq. meters); more than 30 children's counselors run the extensive programs. There is also a separate teen club and video game arcade. A child drop-off service is available in the evenings, and private baby-sitting services are available ($11 per hour), as are character "tuck-ins" for children, and character breakfasts and lunches. Strollers are available, at no charge, and parents can be provided with beepers, so that they can also enjoy their time alone, away from their offspring for much of the day.

The entertainment and activities programming for families and children are extremely good. The stage shows (in the 977-seat show lounge) feature Disney themes; "Hercules – A Muse-ical Comedy," "Disney Dreams" (a bedtime story with Peter Pan, Aladdin, the Little Mermaid and others), and "C'est Magique" (featuring a host of fine illusions revolving around Prospero, a 19th-century magician, with some of the background "click" track provided by the Royal Philharmonic Orchestra); sadly, all are performed without a hint of a live orchestra, although lighting and staging are excellent. A show called "Island Magic," which features only Disney characters, is the only show with a "live" orchestra.

Other notable Disney exclusives include the game show "Who Wants to be a Mouseketeer?" The prizes include free cruises and onboard credits of up to $1,000 and Tea with Wendy Darling (from Disney's "Peter Pan").

Adults can play in "Beat Street" This is an adult entertainment area that includes a wacky Hollywood-style street, complete with flashing traffic lights, and three entertainment rooms. "Sessions" is a jazz piano lounge, complete with private headphones for listening to music of all types when no live music is scheduled; "Rockin' Bar D" (for high-energy rock 'n' roll, country music and cabaret acts); and "Off-Beat" (for improvisational comedy involving the audience). During the day, creative enrichment programs have also been added.

Ports of call include St. Maarten, St. Thomas, although the highlight for most is Disney's private island, Castaway Cay. It is an outstanding private island (perhaps the benchmark for *all* private islands for families with children), with its own pier so that the ship can dock alongside – a cruise industry first. There is a post office with its own special Bahamas/Disney stamp, and a whole host of dedicated, well thought-out attractions and amenities for all ages (including a large adults-only beach, complete with massage cabanas).

Disney characters are aboard for all cruises and lots of photo opportunities; they come out to play mainly when children's activities are scheduled. All the artwork throughout the ship's public areas comes from Disney films or animation features, with many original drawings dating from the early 1930s.

This ship should appeal to couples, single parents and multi-generational families (there are few activities for couples during the daytime, but plenty of entertainment at night). Whether cruising with 1,000 (or more) kids aboard will make for a relaxing vacation for those without kids depends on how much noise one can absorb.

Disney Magic has year-round 7-day cruises to the Eastern Caribbean (and Castaway Cay in The Bahamas) – more relaxing than the 3- or 4-day version featured by sister ship *Disney Wonder* – and passengers will find more activities, more lecturers and additional shows that make it all worthwhile. It's all tied up in one encapsulated, well-controlled, seamless, and crime-free environment that promises escape and adventure. American Express cardholders get special treatment and extra goodies.

At Port Canaveral, a special terminal has been con-structed; it's a copy of the original Ocean Terminal used by the transatlantic liners *Queen Elizabeth* and *Queen Mary* in Southampton, England. Transfers between Walt Disney World resorts in Orlando and the ship are included. Special buses feature vintage 1930s/1940s style interior décor (30 sets of Mickey's face and ears can be found in the blue fabric of each seat). Five of the 45 custom-made buses are outfitted to carry wheelchair passengers. Embarkation and disembarkation is an entertainment event rather than the hassle-laden affair that it has become for many cruise lines with large ships (if all the buses do not arrive together).

Disney Magic is the cruise industry's principal floating theme park – a sea-going never-never land. You should be aware, however, that this is a highly programmed, strictly timed and regimented onboard experience, with tickets, lines and reservations necessary for almost everything. Since its introduction, the product has improved almost to the point that Disney now understands that cruise ships *are* different to operate than its theme parks. Parents can relax knowing that security is very good, and all registered children must wear an id bracelet (showing name, cabin number and muster station number), and parents are given pagers for emergencies.

Take mainly *casual* clothing (casual with a capital "C"), although there are two formal nights on the 7-day cruise, and wish upon a star – that's really all you'll need to do to enjoy yourself aboard this stunning ship. The onboard currency is the US dollar. Members of Disney's Vacation Club can exchange points for cruises.

WEAK POINTS: There is no observation lounge with forward-facing views over the ship's bows. There is no dance floor with live orchestra for adults (other than "Rockin Bar D" in Beat Street for throbbing disco/country-style "music"). The elevators are very small, and so is the gymnasium (for such a large ship). It is expensive (but then so is a week at any Disney resort), gratuities are extra, and 15 percent is added to all bar/beverage/wine and spa accounts. Don't even think about it if you are not a Disney fan, or if you don't like kids, lining up and registering for things, and service with only a moderate sprinkling of hospitality.

Standing in line for embarkation, disembarkation, shore tenders and for self-serve buffet meals is an inevitable aspect of cruising aboard all large ships. Lines at various outlets can prove irritating (some creative Disney Imagineering is needed, including a large sprinkling of pixie dust), as can trying to get through to Guest Services by telephone. The food product and delivery has improved, but falls short of less expensive cruise products. There is no proper library – something that many regular cruise passengers miss.

Disney Wonder
★★★★ +

Large Ship: . . . . .85,000 tons	Passengers	Cabin Current: . . . . .110 volts
Lifestyle: . . . . .Standard	(lower beds/all berths): 1,750/3,325	Elevators: 12
Cruise Line: . . . . .Disney Cruise Line	Passenger Space Ratio	Casino (gaming tables): . . . . .No
Former Names: . . . . .none	(lower beds/all berths): 48.5/25.5	Slot Machines: .0
Builder: . . . . .Fincantieri (Italy)	Crew/Passenger Ratio	Swimming Pools (outdoors): 3
Original Cost: . . . .$350 million	(lower beds/all berths): 1.8/3.5	Swimming Pools (indoors): 0
Entered Service: . . . . .Aug 1999	Navigation Officers: European/Norwegian	Whirlpools: 6
Registry: . . . . .The Bahamas	Cabins (total): 875	Fitness Center: . . . . .Yes
Length (ft/m): 964.5/294.00	Size Range (sq ft/m): 180.8–968.7/	Sauna/Steam Room: . . . . .Yes/Yes
Beam (ft/m): 105.7/32.22	16.8–90.0	Massage: . . . . .Yes
Draft (ft/m): 26.2/8.0	Cabins (outside view): 720	Self-Service Launderette: . . . . .Yes (3)
Propulsion/Propellers: . . . . .diesel-electric	Cabins (interior/no view): 155	Dedicated Cinema/Seats: Yes/270
(38,000kW)/2	Family Cabins: 80	Library: . . . . .Yes
Passenger Decks: 11	Cabins (with private balcony): 388	Classification Society: . . .Lloyd's Register
Total Crew: .945	Cabins (wheelchair accessible): 12	

OVERALL SCORE: 1,553 (OUT OF A POSSIBLE 2,000 POINTS)

ACCOMMODATION: Spread over six decks, there are several types of suites and cabins; all have been designed for practicality and have space-efficient layouts that are well thought-out. Most cabins have common features such as a neat vertical steamer trunk used for clothes storage, a hairdryer located at a vanity desk (or in the bathroom), and bathrobes for all passengers. Many cabins have third- and fourth pull-down berths that rise and are totally hidden in the ceiling when not in use, but the standard interior and outside cabins, while acceptable for two, are extremely tight when occupied by three or four persons. The décor is practical, creative, and very colorful, with lots of neat styling touches. Cabins with refrigerators can have them stocked with one of three packages (at extra cost, of course).

The bathrooms, although compact (due to the fact that the toilet is separate from the rest of the bathroom), are really functional units, designed with split-use facilities so that more than one person can use them at the same time (good for families); many have bathtubs (really shower tubs).

The suites, quite naturally, offer much more space and goodies such as VCRs, CD players, large screen televisions, and extra beds that are useful for larger families. Some of the suites are, however, beneath the pool deck, teen lounge, or informal café, so there could be lots of noise as the ceiling insulation is poor (but cabin to cabin insulation is good).

Wheelchair-bound passengers have a variety of cabin sizes and configurations to choose from, including suites

BERLITZ'S RATINGS

	Possible	Achieved
Ship	500	444
Accommodation	200	172
Food	400	214
Service	400	303
Entertainment	100	93
Cruise	400	327

with a private balcony and extra-large bathrooms with excellent roll-in showers, and good closet and drawer space (almost all the vessel is accessible). Wheelchair-bound passengers have a variety of cabin sizes and configurations to choose from, including suites with a private balcony (unfortunately you cannot, get a wheelchair through the balcony's sliding door) and extra-large bathrooms with excellent roll-in showers, and good closet and drawer space (most of the vessel is quite accessible). Note that for the sight-impaired, cabin numbers and elevator buttons are Braille-encoded.

A 24-hour room service is available (suite occupants also get concierge service); the room service menu is limited, however, as is the cabin breakfast menu. There is a 15 percent service charge for beverage deliveries.

DINING: There are three main dining rooms (all non-smoking), each with over 400 seats, two seatings, and unique theme decor. Triton's, Parrot Cay, and Animator's Palate (the most visual of the three) features food and electronic art that make the evening décor change from black and white to full color. You will get to eat in all three dining rooms in rotation, and move with your assigned waiter and assistant waiter to each dining room in turn, thus providing a different dining experience (each has a different décor, different menus). As you will have the same waiter in each of the three restaurants, any gratuities go only to "your" waiter.

Parrot Cay and Triton's have open seating for breakfast and lunch (the lunch menu is poor). The noise level in all three dining rooms is extremely high.

In addition, Palo is an elegant 140-seat reservations-only alternative restaurant (with a $5 cover/gratuity charge) featuring Italian cuisine. It has a 270-degree view, and is for adults only (no "Munchkins" allowed); the à la carte cuisine cooked to order, and the wine list is good (prices are high). Make your reservations as soon as you board or miss out on the only decent food aboard this ship.

For casual eating, Topsider's is an indoor/outdoor café featuring low-quality self-serve breakfast and lunch buffets with very poor choice and presentation, and a buffet dinner for children (consisting mostly of fried foods). There is also an ice cream and frozen yogurt bar (Scoops) that opens infrequently. Other fast food outlets include Pluto's (for hamburgers, hot dogs), and Pinocchio's, which is open throughout the day but not in the evening (for basic, inedible pizza and sandwiches).

Overall, the food has improved since the ship was first introduced, and is now more attractively presented, although there are still so few green vegetables. Vegetarians and those seeking healthy spa alternatives will be underwhelmed – as will those who want spa (light) cuisine. Guest chefs from Walt Disney World Resort prepare signature dishes each cruise, and host occasional cooking demonstrations.

OTHER COMMENTS: *Disney Wonder*'s profile has managed to combine streamlining with tradition and nostalgia, and has two large red-and-black funnels designed to remind you of the ocean liners of the past. *Disney Wonder* is the first cruise ship built with two funnels since the 1950s. However, one of the funnels is a dummy, and contains a variety of public spaces, including a neat ESPN sports bar and a broadcast center. The ship was actually constructed in two halves, which were then joined together in the shipyard in Venice, Italy. The ship's whistle even plays "When You Wish upon a Star" (or a sort of sickly version of it). The bow features handsome gold scrollwork that more typically seen adorning the tall ships of yesteryear. There is a wrap-around promenade deck outdoors for strolling.

Disney Cruise Line has not added ostentatious decoration to the ship's exterior. However, Mickey's ears are painted on the funnels; there is also a special 85-ft (26-meter) long paint stripe that cleverly incorporates Disney characters into the whimsical yellow paintwork along each side of the hull at the bow. Cute. The ship's exterior colors are also those of Mickey Mouse himself (call it a well-planned coincidence). Also of note is a whimsical, 15-ft (4.5-meter) tall Donald Duck and Huey hanging upside down in a bosun's chair, painting the stern.

On deck, a sports deck features a paddle tennis court, table tennis, basketball court, shuffleboard, and golf driving range. An ESPN Skybox Bar has 12 TV sets of differing sizes for live (by satellite) sports events and noisy conversation (cigar smokers welcome). There are three outdoor pools: one pool for adults only (in theory), one for children, and one for families (guess which one has

Mickey's ears painted into the bottom?). However, there's music everywhere (four different types), and it's impossible to find a quiet spot (in fact, you can sit in many places a get two types of music blaring at you at the same time). The children's pool features a long yellow water slide (available at specified times), held up by the giant hand of Mickey Mouse, although the pool itself really is too small considering the number of small children typically carried.

Inside, the ship is visually stunning. The Art Deco theme of the old ocean liners has been tastefully carried out (check out the stainless steel/pewter Disney detailing on the handrails and balustrades in the three-deck-high lobby). Most public rooms have high ceilings. The decor and detailing are stunning, much of it whimsical – pure Disney. Mickey is visible in many areas, albeit subtly (for Disney). If you can't sleep, try counting the number of times Mickey's logo appears – it's an impossible task. The lobby provides a photo opportunity that should not be missed: a 6-ft (1.8-meter) bronze statue of "The Little Mermaid."

There are two large shops and an abundance of Disney-theme clothing, soft toys, collectibles and other specialty items. Features a superb, 1,040-seat Walt Disney Theatre (spread over four decks but designed cinema-style, without a balcony), piano bar, adults-only nightclub/disco, family lounge, and a dedicated cinema (where classic Disney films are shown, as well as first-run movies).

For fitness devotees, a fitness room, part of the spa (measuring 8,500 sq. ft /790 sq. meters) has ocean-view windows that overlook the navigation bridge below. There are several treatment rooms, and a "rain forest" with scented steam rooms.

The children's entertainment areas measure 13,000 sq. ft (1,200 sq. meters), and more than 30 counselors are aboard for any given cruise. There is also a separate teen club and video game arcade. A child drop-off service works in the evenings, private babysitting services are available ($11 per hour), as are character "tuck-ins" for children, and character breakfasts and lunches. Strollers are available, at no charge, and parents can be provided with beepers, so that they can also enjoy their time alone, away from the kids for much of the day.

Entertainment and the activities programming for families and children are outstanding. Stage shows feature Disney themes; "Hercules – A Muse-ical Comedy," "Voyage of the Ghost Ship" (a lighthearted look at cruising), "Disney Dreams" (a bedtime story with Peter Pan, Aladdin, the Little Mermaid and others). Sadly, all are performed without a hint of a live orchestra, although lighting and staging are excellent. A show called "Island Magic," which features only Disney characters, is performed the day before reaching Castaway Cay, and is the only show featuring a "live" orchestra. On the four-day cruise, an additional local Bahamian show takes place outdoors at the middle swimming pool.

For adults, there is "Route 66" – an adult entertainment area that includes a wacky Hollywood-style street, complete with three entertainment rooms. "Cadillac" is a jazz piano lounge, complete with private headphones for listening to music of all types when no live music is scheduled; "Wavebands" (for ear-splitting rock 'n' roll and country music); and "Barrel of Laughs" (for improvisational comedy involving the audience). During the day, creative enrichment programs have been added.

Although Nassau is decidedly unappealing and not tourist-friendly, the highlight of the itinerary is Disney's private island, Castaway Cay. It is an outstanding private island (perhaps the benchmark for *all* private islands), with its own pier so that the ship can dock alongside – a cruise industry first. There is a post office with its own special Bahamas/Disney stamp, and a whole host of dedicated, well thought out attractions and amenities for all ages (including a large adults-only beach, complete with massage cabanas). Watersports equipment (floats, paddleboats, kayaks, hobie cats, aqua fins, aqua trikes, and snorkels) can be rented.

Disney characters are aboard for all cruises and lots of photo opportunities; they come out to play mainly when children's activities are scheduled. All the artwork throughout the ship's public areas comes from Disney films or animation features, with many original drawings dating from the early 1930s.

This ship should appeal to couples, single parents and families alike (there are few activities for couples during the daytime, but plenty of entertainment at night). Whether cruising with 1,000 (or more) kids aboard will make for a relaxing vacation for those without kids depends on how much noise one can absorb (there will probably be even more juniors aboard at peak vacation periods). Disney always points out that 25 percent of Walt Disney World's visitors are adults (these are the *real* kids).

If you bring children, they will have so much fun that they will not want to leave at the end of the cruise. In fact, taking kids is child's play, as Disney makes it all so easy. Parents can relax knowing that security is very good, and all registered children must wear an ID bracelet (showing name, cabin number and muster station number), and parents are given pagers for emergencies.

Disney Wonder has year-round 3- and 4-day cruises to The Bahamas – part of a 7-night vacation package that includes a 3- or 4-day stay at a Walt Disney World resort hotel in Orlando; the cruise then forms the second half of the vacation. It's all tied up in one encapsulated, well-controlled, seamless, and crime-free environment that promises escape and adventure. You can also book just the cruise without the resort stay. American Express cardholders get special treatment and extra goodies. Members of Disney's Vacation Club can exchange points for cruises.

At Port Canaveral, a special terminal has been constructed; it's a copy of the original Ocean Terminal used by the transatlantic liners *Queen Elizabeth* and *Queen Mary* in Southampton, England. Transfers between Walt Disney World resorts in Orlando and the ship are included. Special buses feature vintage 1930s/1940s style interior décor (30 sets of Mickey's face and ears can be found in the blue fabric of each seat). Five of the 45 custom-made buses are outfitted to carry wheelchair passengers. Embarkation and disembarkation is an entertainment event rather than the hassle-laden affair that it has become for many cruise lines with large ships (if all the buses do not arrive together).

Disney Wonder (and sister ship *Disney Magic*) are the cruise industry's floating theme parks – sea-going never-never lands that are rated on their own, in common with all other ships in this book. This rating does not include any additional 3- or 4-day stay at a Disney World resort, which forms part of the total Disney Cruise Line vacation (although it is now possible to book just the cruise).

You should be aware that this is a highly programmed, strictly timed and regimented onboard experience, with tickets, lines and reservations necessary for almost everything. Since its introduction, the product has improved; almost to the point that Disney understands that cruise ships are different to operate than theme parks. Take only *casual* clothing (casual with a capital "C") and wish upon a star – that's really all you'll need to do to enjoy yourself aboard this stunning ship.

The onboard currency is the US dollar.

WEAK POINTS: There is no observation lounge with forward-facing views over the ship's bows. There is no dance floor with live orchestra for adults (other than "Rockin Bar D" in Beat Street for throbbing disco/country-style "music"). The elevators are very small, and so is the gymnasium (for such a large ship). It is expensive (but then so is a week at any Disney resort), gratuities are extra, and 15 percent is added to all bar/beverage/wine and spa accounts. Don't even think about it if you are not a Disney fan, or if you don't like kids, lining up and registering for things, moderate food and service with low-grade hospitality attitude.

Standing in line for embarkation, disembarkation, shore tenders and for self-serve buffet meals is an inevitable aspect of cruising aboard all large ships. Lines at various outlets can prove irritating (some creative Disney Imagineering is needed, including a large sprinkling of pixie dust), as can trying to get through to Guest Services by telephone. The food product and delivery has improved, but falls short of less expensive cruise products. There is no proper library – something that many regular cruise passengers miss.

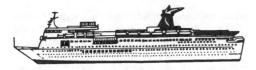

Ecstasy
★★★ +

Large Ship:	.70,367 tons	Passengers	Cabin Current:	.110 volts

Large Ship: ....70,367 tons
Lifestyle: ....Standard
Cruise Line: ....Carnival Cruise Lines
Former Names: ....none
Builder: ...Kvaerner Masa-Yards (Finland)
Original Cost: ....$275 million
Entered Service: ....June 1991
Registry: ....Panama
Length (ft/m): 855.8/260.6
Beam (ft/m): 103.0/31.4
Draft (ft/m): 25.9/7.9
Propulsion/Propellers: .....diesel-electric
(42,240kW)/2
Passenger Decks: 10
Total Crew: 920

Passengers
(lower beds/all berths): 2,052/2,594
Passenger Space Ratio
(lower beds/all berths): 34.2/27.1
Crew/Passenger Ratio
(lower beds/all berths): 2.2/2.8
Navigation Officers: ....Italian
Cabins (total): 1,026
Size Range (sq ft/m): 173.2–409.7/
16.0–38.0
Cabins (outside view): 618
Cabins (interior/no view): 408
Cabins (for one person): 0
Cabins (with private balcony): 54
Cabins (wheelchair accessible): 22

Cabin Current: ....110 volts
Elevators: 14
Casino (gaming tables): ....Yes
Slot Machines: ....Yes
Swimming Pools (outdoors): 3
Swimming Pools (indoors): 0
Whirlpools: 6
Fitness Center: ....Yes
Sauna/Steam Room: ....Yes/Yes
Massage: ....Yes
Self-Service Launderette: ....Yes
Dedicated Cinema/Seats: ....No
Library: ....Yes
Classification Society: ...Lloyd's Register

OVERALL SCORE: 1,385 (OUT OF A POSSIBLE 2,000 POINTS)

ACCOMMODATION: As in sister ships *Elation, Fantasy, Fascination, Imagination, Inspiration, Paradise* and *Sensation*), the standard outside-view and interior (no view) cabins have plain décor. They are marginally comfortable, yet spacious enough and practical (most are of the same size and appointments), with good storage space and well-designed bathrooms.

Those booking one of the outside suites will find more space, whirlpool bathtubs, and some fascinating, rather eclectic decor and furniture. These are mildly attractive, but nothing special, and they are much smaller than those aboard the ships of a similar size of several competing companies.

A gift basket is provided in all grades of accommodation; it includes aloe soap, shampoo, conditioner, deodorant, breath mints, candy, and pain relief tablets (albeit all in sample sizes).

Note that if you book accommodation in one of the suites (Category 11 or 12 in the Carnival Cruise Lines brochure) you automatically qualify for "Skipper's Club" priority check-in at any US homeland port – useful for getting ahead of the crowd.

DINING: The two dining rooms have attractive decor and colors, but are large, crowded and very noisy. The food is adequate, but no more, although Carnival Cruise Lines has made several improvements. Dining in each restaurant is now in four seatings, for greater flexibility: 6pm, 6.45pm, 8pm and 8.45pm (times are approximate).

Carnival meals stress quantity, not quality, although the company constantly works hard to improve the cui-

BERLITZ'S RATINGS

	Possible	Achieved
Ship	500	395
Accommodation	200	151
Food	400	221
Service	400	270
Entertainment	100	81
Cruise	400	267

sine. While passengers seem to accept it, few find it worth remembering. However, food and its taste are still not the company's strongest points (you get what you pay for, remember).

While the menu items sound good, their presentation and taste leave much to be desired. While meats are of a high quality, fish and seafood is not. Presentation is simple, and few garnishes are used. Many meat and fowl dishes are disguised with gravies and sauces. The selection of fresh green vegetables, breads, rolls, cheeses and fruits is limited, and there is too much use of canned fruit and jellied desserts. However, do remember that this is banquet catering, with all its attendant standardization and production cooking (it is, therefore, difficult to ask for anything remotely unusual or off-menu). The selection of breads, rolls, cheeses and fruits is limited (there is too much use of canned fruit).

Although there is a decent wine list, there are no wine waiters (the waiters are expected to serve both food and wine, which does not work well). The service is highly programmed, although the waiters are willing and reasonably friendly. However, the waiters do sing and dance (be prepared for *Simply the Best, Hot, Hot, Hot,* and other popular hits), and there are constant waiter parades; the dining room is show business – all done in the name of gratuities at the end of your cruise.

The Lido café provides the usual casual serve-your-self buffet foods, although it's completely unmemorable. At night, the "Seaview Bistro," as the Lido Café becomes known, provides a casual (dress down) alternative to eating in the main dining rooms, serving pasta, steaks, salads and desserts (it typically is in operation between 6pm and 9pm).

OTHER COMMENTS: *Ecstasy* is the second in the *Fantasy*-class of eight almost identical ships for Carnival Cruise Lines, and the sixth new ship for this very successful cruise line. The ship, whose bows are extremely short, has the distinctive, large, swept-back wing-tipped funnel that is the trademark of Carnival Cruise Lines, in the company colors of red, white and blue.

The general passenger flow is good, and the interior design is clever, functional, and extremely colorful. The neon lighting in the interior decor takes a little getting used to at first, as the color combinations are vivid, to say the least. There is a vintage Rolls-Royce motorcar located on the principal, double-width indoor promenade. The health spa and fitness facilities are decent. A stunning, 10-ton sculpture graces the marble and glass atrium, which spans seven decks. The library has delightful décor, but there are few books. The Chinatown Lounge comes complete with Oriental décor, and features hanging lanterns and smoking dragon. The balconied show lounge is large, but some 20 pillars obstruct the views from several seats.

This ship is one of the great floating playgrounds for young, active adults who enjoy constant stimulation, close contact with lots and lots of others, as well as the three Gs – glitz, glamour and gambling. It is a live board game with every move executed in typically grand, colorful, fun-filled Carnival Cruise Lines style. This ship will provide a great introduction to cruising for the novice passenger seeking an action-packed short cruise experience in contemporary surroundings, with a real swinging party atmosphere, and minimum fuss and finesse. You will have a fine time if you like nightlife and lots of silly participation games. Like life in the fast lane, this is cruising in theme-park fantasyland, and the dress code is extremely casual. The staff will help you have organized fun, and that is what Carnival does best. Want to party? Then this should prove to be a great ship for you. Forget fashion – having fun is the *sine qua non* of a Carnival cruise. The line operates 3- and 4-day Baja Mexico cruises from Los Angeles. Gratuities are automatically added to your onboard account at $9.75 per person, per day (the amount charged when this book was completed); you can have this amount adjusted, although you'll have to visit the information desk to do so. The onboard currency is the US dollar.

WEAK POINTS: Standing in line for embarkation, disembarkation, shore tenders and for self-serve buffet meals is an inevitable aspect of cruising aboard all large ships. This ship is not for those who want a quiet, relaxing cruise experience. There is absolutely no escape from unnecessary and repetitive announcements (particularly for activities that bring revenue, such as art auctions, bingo, horse racing) that intrude constantly into your cruise, and there's a great deal of hustling for drinks orders.

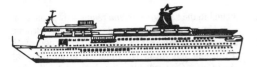

Elation
★★★ +

Large Ship: ....70,367 tons	Total Crew: 920	Cabins (wheelchair accessible): 22
Lifestyle: ....Standard	Passengers	Cabin Current: ....110 volts
Cruise Line: ......Carnival Cruise Lines	(lower beds/all berths): 2,052/2,594	Elevators: 14
Former Names: ....none	Passenger Space Ratio	Casino (gaming tables): ....Yes
Builder: ...Kvaerner Masa-Yards (Finland)	(lower beds/all berths): 34.2/27.1	Slot Machines: ....Yes
Original Cost: ....$300 million	Crew/Passenger Ratio	Swimming Pools (outdoors): 3
Entered Service: ....Mar 1998	(lower beds/all berths): 2.2/2.8	Swimming Pools (indoors): 0
Registry: ....Panama	Navigation Officers: ....Italian	Whirlpools: 6
Length (ft/m): 855.0/260.6	Cabins (total): 1,026	Fitness Center: ....Yes
Beam (ft/m): 103.3/31.5	Size Range (sq ft/m): 173.2–409.7/	Sauna/Steam Room: ....Yes/Yes
Draft (ft/m): 25.9/7.9	16.0–38.0	Massage: ....Yes
Propulsion/Propellers: ....diesel-electric	Cabins (outside view): 618	Self-Service Launderette: ....Yes
42,842 kW)/2 azimuthing pods	Cabins (interior/no view): 408	Dedicated Cinema/Seats: ....No
(14 MW each)	Cabins (for one person): 0	Library: ....Yes
Passenger Decks:.................10	Cabins (with private balcony): 54	Classification Society: ...Lloyd's Register

OVERALL SCORE: 1,387 (OUT OF A POSSIBLE 2,000 POINTS)

ACCOMMODATION: As in sister ships *Ecstasy, Fantasy, Fascination, Imagination, Inspiration, Paradise* and *Sensation*), the standard outside-view and interior (no view) cabins have plain décor. They are marginally comfortable, yet spacious enough and practical (most are of the same size and appointments), with good storage space and well-designed bathrooms.

Those booking one of the outside suites will find more space, whirlpool bathtubs, and some fascinating, rather eclectic decor and furniture. These are mildly attractive, but nothing special, and they are much smaller than those aboard the ships of a similar size of several competing companies.

A gift basket is now provided in all grades of accommodation; it includes aloe soap, shampoo, conditioner, deodorant, breath mints, candy, and pain relief tablets (albeit all in sample sizes).

Note that if you book accommodation in one of the suites (Category 11 or 12 in the Carnival Cruise Lines brochure) you automatically qualify for "Skipper's Club" priority check-in at any US homeland port – useful for getting ahead of the crowd.

DINING: There are two large, lively dining rooms (Imagination and Inspiration). Both are non-smoking. Dining in each restaurant is now in four seatings, for greater flexibility: 6pm, 6.45pm, 8pm and 8.45pm (these times are approximate).

Carnival meals stress quantity, not quality, although the company constantly works hard to improve the cuisine. While passengers seem to accept it, few find it

BERLITZ'S RATINGS		
	Possible	Achieved
Ship	500	395
Accommodation	200	151
Food	400	223
Service	400	270
Entertainment	100	81
Cruise	400	267

worth remembering. However, food and its taste are still not the company's strongest points (you get what you pay for, remember).

While the menu items sound good, their presentation and taste leave much to be desired. While meats are of a high quality, fish and seafood is not. Presentation is simple, and few garnishes are used. Many meat and fowl dishes are disguised with gravies and sauces. The selection of fresh green vegetables, breads, rolls, cheeses and fruits is limited, and there is too much use of canned fruit and jellied desserts. However, do remember that this is banquet catering, with all its attendant standardization and production cooking (it is, therefore, difficult to ask for anything remotely unusual or off-menu). The selection of breads, rolls, cheeses and fruits is limited (there is too much use of canned fruit).

Although there is a decent wine list, there are no wine waiters (the waiters are expected to serve both food and wine, which does not work well). The service is highly programmed, although the waiters are willing and reasonably friendly. However, the waiters do sing and dance (be prepared for *Simply the Best, Hot, Hot, Hot,* and other popular hits), and there are constant waiter parades; the dining room is show business – all done in the name of gratuities at the end of your cruise.

For casual meals, there's The Lido, which, aboard this ship, has some improvements and additions worthy of note, such as: orange juice machine, where you put in oranges and out comes fresh juice (better than the concentrate stuff supplied in the dining room). There's also a sushi bar. Things are looking up, which means more choices. At night, the "Seaview Bistro," as the Lido Café becomes known provides a casual (dress down) alternative to eating in the main dining rooms, serving pasta, steaks, salads and desserts (it typically is in operation between 6pm and 9pm).

OTHER COMMENTS: Although externally angular and not particularly handsome, *Elation* is the seventh in a series of eight ships of the same series and identical internal configuration, but actually the 12th new ship for Carnival Cruise Lines. It is a successful design for this company that targets the mainstream market, and particularly the first-time passenger.

The ship has a bold, forthright, angular appearance that is typical of today's space-creative designs. It is powered by a "pod" propulsion system (this replaces the traditional propeller shaft and rudder combination of most ships), which gives the ship more manoeuvrability, while reducing required machinery space and vibration at the stern. The ship, whose bows are extremely short, has the distinctive, large, swept-back wing-tipped funnel that is the trademark of Carnival Cruise Lines, in the company colors of red, white and blue.

Splashy, showy, public rooms and interior colors – pure Las Vegas, and ideal for those who love it. The theme of the interior décor is composers and their compositions (most of the public rooms have musical names), and the colors, while bright, are less so than aboard previous ships in this series. As in its sister ships, there is a dramatic six-deck-high atrium, appropriately dressed to impress, topped by a large glass dome, and featuring a fascinating, entertaining artistic centerpiece. There are expansive open deck areas and a large, three-deck-high glass-enclosed health spa that is always busy; it includes a gymnasium full of the latest high-tech muscle-pumping machinery, and there is also a banked jogging track outdoors.

There are public entertainment lounges, bars and clubs galore, with something for everyone, including a children's playroom, larger than aboard the previous ships in this series. Some busy colors and design themes

abound in the handsome public rooms – these are connected by wide indoor boulevards and beg your attention and indulgence. There is also a good art collection, much of it bright and vocal. The library is a fine room, as aboard most Carnival ships (but there are few books). One neat feature (not found aboard previous ships in this series) is an atrium bar, complete with live classical music – something new for this company.

The ship has a lavish, yet almost elegant multi-tiered 1,010-seat show lounge and the line's fine, loud, high-energy razzle-dazzle shows. *Ecstasy* operates 7-night Mexican Riviera cruises year-round from the port of Los Angeles, but the ship is arguably better than the ports of call.

This ship is one of the great floating playgrounds for young, active adults who enjoy constant stimulation, close contact with lots and lots of others, as well as the three Gs – glitz, glamour and gambling. It is a live board game with every move executed in typically grand, colorful, fun-filled Carnival Cruise Lines style. Good for those who like big city life ashore and want it on their vacation. Forget fashion – having fun is the *sine qua non* of a Carnival cruise.

Gratuities are automatically added to your onboard account at $9.75 per person, per day (the amount charged when this book was completed); you can have this amount adjusted, although you'll have to visit the information desk to do so. The onboard currency is the US dollar.

WEAK POINTS: Standing in line for embarkation, disembarkation, shore tenders and for self-serve buffet meals is an inevitable aspect of cruising aboard all large ships. This is another ship that provides a rather impersonal cruise experience, as the ship is large and there are so many other passengers. There is absolutely no escape from unnecessary and repetitious announcements (particularly for activities that bring revenue, such as art auctions, bingo, horse racing) that intrude constantly into your cruise, and a great deal of hustling for drinks, although it is sometimes done with a knowing smile.

Enchantment of the Seas ★★★★

Large Ship:	.74,137 tons	Passengers	
Lifestyle:	Standard	(lower beds/all berths):	.1,950/2,446
Cruise Line:	Royal Caribbean International	Passenger Space Ratio	
		(lower beds/all berths):	.38.0/30.3
Former Names:	none	Crew/Passenger Ratio	
Builder:	Kvaerner Masa-Yards (Finland)	(lower beds/all berths):	.2.4/3.2
Original Cost:	$300 million	Navigation Officers:	Norwegian/ International
Entered Service:	July 1997		
Registry:	The Bahamas	Cabins (total):	.975
Length (ft/m):	915.6/279.1	Size Range (sq ft/m):	.158.2–1,267.0/ 14.7–117.7
Beam (ft/m):	105.6/32.2		
Draft (ft/m):	.25.5/7.6	Cabins (outside view):	.576
Propulsion/Propellers:	diesel-electric (50,400kW)/2	Cabins (interior/no view):	.399
		Cabins (for one person):	.0
Passenger Decks:	.11	Cabins (with private balcony):	.212
Total Crew:	.760	Cabins (wheelchair accessible):	.14

Cabin Current:	.110 and 220 volts
Elevators:	.9
Casino (gaming tables):	Yes
Slot Machines:	Yes
Swimming Pools (outdoors):	.1
Swimming Pools (indoors):	.1
(indoor/outdoor w/sliding glass roof)	
Whirlpools:	.6
Fitness Center:	Yes
Sauna/Steam Room:	Yes/Yes
Massage:	Yes
Self-Service Launderette:	No
Dedicated Cinema/Seats:	No
Library:	Yes
Classification Society:	Det Norske Veritas

OVERALL SCORE: 1,521 (OUT OF A POSSIBLE 2,000 POINTS)

ACCOMMODATION: All standard outside-view and interior (no view) cabins feature twin beds that convert to a queen-size bed. There is a reasonably good amount of closet space for a one-week cruise, and an adequate amount of drawer space, although under-bed storage space for luggage is limited. The bathrooms are practical, but the decor is plain. The category A and B cabins also have a VCR.

BERLITZ'S RATINGS

	Possible	Achieved
Ship	500	430
Accommodation	200	166
Food	400	248
Service	400	302
Entertainment	100	81
Cruise	400	294

DINING: The 1,195-seat, non-smoking dining room is spread over two decks, with both levels connected by a grand, sweeping staircase. There are two seatings.

The cuisine in the main dining room is typical of mass banquet catering that offers standard fare comparable to that found in American family-style restaurants ashore. While menu descriptions are tempting, the actual food may be somewhat disappointing and unmemorable. The menu descriptions make the food sound better than it is (which is consistently below average), mostly disappointing and without much taste. However, a decent selection of light meals is provided, and a vegetarian menu is available. The selection of breads, rolls, fruit and cheese is quite poor, however, and could do more improvement. Caviar (once a standard menu item) incurs a hefty extra charge. There is no good caviar; special orders, tableside carving and flambeau items are not offered. Menus typically include a Welcome Aboard Dinner, French Dinner, Italian Dinner, International Dinner, and Captain's Gala Dinner.

The wine list is not very extensive, but the prices are moderate. The waiters, many of whom are from Caribbean countries, are perhaps overly friendly for some tastes – particularly on the last night of the cruise, when tips are expected.

Casual, self-serve breakfasts and luncheons can be taken in the 790-seat informal Windjammer Café. It features a great expanse of ocean-view glass windows, and the décor is bright and cheerful.

An intimate Champagne/Caviar Bar terrace can be found forward of the lower level of the two-deck-high dining room and just off the atrium for those who might like to taste something a little bit out of the ordinary, in a setting that is both bright and contemporary.

OTHER COMMENTS: *Enchantment of the Seas* is one of two of a recent breed of ships for this popular cruise line (its sister ship is *Grandeur of the Seas*), introduced in December 1996. The ship has a long profile, with a single funnel located well aft, has a nicely rounded stern (rather like the *Sovereign of the Seas*-class ships), and a Viking Crown Lounge is set amidships. This, together with the forward mast, provides three distinct focal points in its exterior profile. There is a wrap-around promenade deck outdoors (there are no cushioned pads for the deck lounge chairs, however).

A large Viking Crown Lounge (a trademark of all Royal Caribbean International ships) sits between funnel and mast, and overlooks the forward section of the swimming pool deck, as aboard *Legend of the*

Seas/Splendour of the Seas, with access provided from stairway off the central atrium.

Inside is a seven-deck-high Centrum (atrium), which provides a central focal and meeting point (the Purser's Desk and Shore Excursion Desk are located on one level). Many public entertainment rooms and facilities can be located off the atrium.

There are two show lounges; one (the principal show lounge, with 875 seats), for big production shows; the other (the secondary show lounge, with 575 seats), for smaller shows and adult cabarets. The children and teens' facilities are good, much expanded from previous ships in the fleet.

This ship is quite pretty, and will provide a good cruise vacation, particularly for first-time passengers seeking comfortable surroundings typical of what would be found in a Hyatt Hotel style setting, with fabrics and soft furnishings that blend together to provide a contemporary resort environment. The food is typical of what one would find in a big-city brasserie – adequate in quantity and nicely presented, but made from pre-mixed ingredients. This company provides a well organized, but rather homogenous cruise experience, with the same old passenger participation activities and events that have been provided for more than 25 years. The onboard currency is the US dollar.

WEAK POINTS: Standing in line for embarkation, disembarkation, shore tenders and for self-serve buffet meals is an inevitable aspect of cruising aboard all large ships. There are too many announcements, and constant contemporary pop music played around the swimming pool throughout the day and night (difficult to get away from).

MAY THE FORCE BE WITH YOU

You might be confused by the numbering system for wind velocity. There are 12 velocities, known as "force" on the Beaufort scale. They are as follows:

Force	Speed (mph)	Description/Ocean Surface	Force	Speed (mph)	Description/Ocean Surface
0	0–1	Calm; glassy (like a mirror)	7	32–38	Moderate gale; streaky white foam
1	1–3	Light wind; rippled surface	8	39–46	Fresh gale; moderately high waves
2	4–7	Light breeze; small wavelets	9	47–54	Strong gale; high waves
3	8–12	Gentle breeze; large wavelets, scattered whitecaps	10	55–63	Whole gale; very high waves, curling crests
4	13–18	Moderate breeze; small waves, frequent whitecaps	11	64–73	Violent storm; extremely high waves, froth and foam, poor visibility
5	19–24	Fresh breeze; moderate waves, numerous whitecaps	12	73+	Hurricane; huge waves, thundering white spray, visibility nil
6	25–31	Strong breeze; large waves, white foam crests			

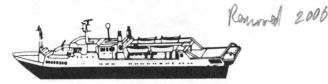

Removed 2006

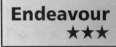

Endeavour
★★★

Small Ship: . . . . .3,132 tons	Total Crew: 64	Cabin Current: . . . . .110 and 220 volts
Lifestyle: . . . . .Standard	Passengers	Elevators: 0
Cruise Line: . . . . . . .Lindblad Expeditions	(lower beds/all berths): 113/124	Casino (gaming tables): . . . . .No
Former Names: . . . .*Caledonian Star,*	Passenger Space Ratio	Slot Machines: .No
North Star, Lindmar, Marburg	(lower beds/all berths): 27.7/25.2	Swimming Pools (outdoors): 1
Builder: . . . . . .A.G. Weser Seebeckwerft	Crew/Passenger Ratio	Whirlpools: 0
(Germany)	(lower beds/all berths): 1.7/1.9	Fitness Center: . . . . .Yes
Original Cost: .n/a	Navigation Officers: . . . . . .Scandinavian	Sauna/Steam Room: . . . . .Yes/No
Entered Service: 1966/1984	Cabins (total): .62	Massage: . . . . .No
Registry: . . . . .The Bahamas	Size Range (sq ft/m): 191.6–269.1/	Self-Service Launderette: . . . . .No
Length (Ft/m): 292.6/89.20	17.8–25.0	Lecture/Film Room: . . . . .Yes
Beam (ft/m): 45.9/14.00	Cabins (outside view): 62	Library: . . . . .Yes
Draft (f//m): 20.3/6.20	Cabins (interior/no view): 0	Zodiacs: 10
Propulsion/Propellers: . . . . .diesel	Cabins (for one person): 11	Helicopter Pad: . . . . .No
(3,236kW)/1	Cabins (with private balcony): 0	Classification Society: . . . . . .Det Norske
Passenger Decks: 6	Cabins (wheelchair accessible): 0	Veritas

---

OVERALL SCORE: 1,242 (OUT OF A POSSIBLE 2,000 POINTS)

ACCOMMODATION: The all-outside-view cabins are very compact, but reasonably comfortable, and they are decorated in warm, muted tones. All cabins feature a mini-bar/refrigerator, VCR, a decent amount of closet and drawer space (but tight for long voyages), and a clock. The cabin ceilings are rather plain, however, and bathrooms are tight, with little space for the storage of personal toiletry items, except under the sink. The "suites" are basically double the size of a standard cabin, and have a wood partition separating the bedroom and lounge area. The bathroom is still small, however.

BERLITZ'S RATINGS

	Possible	Achieved
Ship	500	267
Accommodation	200	116
Food	400	257
Service	400	282
Entertainment	N/A	N/A
Cruise	500	320

DINING: The dining room is small and charming, but the low-back chairs are small. Open seating is operated (so you can sit where you wish). The cuisine is European in style with high quality, very fresh ingredients, but not a lot of menu choice. Service is attentive and friendly.

OTHER COMMENTS: This vessel was constructed as a stern factory trawler for North Sea service, before being converted into a passenger ship – a rare occurrence for a ship that worked as a fishing vessel for 16 years. It is, today a reasonably handsome and trim ship that is extremely tidy and has been well cared for. As an expedition cruise vessel operating soft expedition cruises, there is an open bridge policy for all passengers. The vessel carries Zodiac landing craft for in-depth excursions, and there is an enclosed shore tender. An aft stairway (it is steep) leads down to the landing craft platform.

This ship (formerly known as *Cal-Star* by its many regular passengers, although its name was changed to *Endeavour* in 2001) is quite comfortable and totally unpretentious, with a warm, intimate ambience, and a casual dress code that helps make passengers feel quite at home.

For such a small ship, there is a good range of public rooms and facilities (all were nicely refurbished in mid-1998) that includes a decent lecture lounge/bar/library, where a selection of videos is stocked for in-cabin use. An excellent set of lecturers that are placed aboard for each cruise make this a real life-enrichment and learning experience for an intellectual (mainly North American and British) clientele wanting to travel and learn, while enveloped in comfortable, unpretentious surroundings (you won't need a tuxedo or any dressy clothes).

This very likeable, homey little ship provides a well-tuned destination-intensive, soft expedition-style cruise experience, at a very reasonable price. It attracts a lot of loyal repeat passengers who don't want to sail aboard ships that look like apartment blocks. The itineraries include Antarctica, where this ship started operating in December 1998. The onboard currency is the US dollar.

WEAK POINTS: The interior stairways are a little steep. The exterior stairway to the zodiac embarkation points is also steep. There is noise from the diesel engines (generators) that can be irksome, particularly on the lower decks. Communication with staff can also prove frustrating.

Europa
★★★★★ +

Small Ship:	.28,437 tons
Lifestyle:	.Luxury
Cruise Line:	.Hapag-Lloyd Cruises
Former Names:	.none
Builder:	.Kvaerner Masa-Yards (Finland)
Original Cost:	.DM260 million
Entered Service:	.Sept 1999
Registry:	.The Bahamas
Length (ft/m):	.651.5/198.6
Beam (ft/m):	.78.7/24.0
Draft (ft/m):	.20.0/6.1
Propulsion/Propellers:	.diesel-electric
	(21,600 kW)/2 azimuthing pods
	(13.3 MW each)
Passenger Decks:	.7
Total Crew:	.264

Passengers	
(lower beds/all berths):	.408/450
Passenger Space Ratio	
(lower beds/all berths):	.69.6/63.1
Crew/Passenger Ratio	
(lower beds/all berths):	.1.5/1.7
Navigation Officers:	.German
Cabins (total):	.204
Size Range (sq ft/m):	.355.2–914.9/
	33.0–85.0
Cabins (outside view):	.204
Cabins (interior/no view):	.0
Cabins (for one person):	.0
Cabins (with private balcony):	.168
Cabins (wheelchair accessible):	.2
Cabin Current:	.110 and 220 volts

Elevators:	.4
Casino (gaming tables):	.No
Slot Machines:	.No
Swimming Pools (outdoors):	.1
Swimming Pools (indoors):	.1
(indoor/outdoor with magrodome)	
Whirlpools:	.1
Fitness Center:	.Yes
Sauna/Steam Room:	.Yes/Yes
Massage:	.Yes
Self-Service Launderette:	.Yes (2)
Dedicated Cinema/Seats:	.Yes/60
Library:	.Yes
Classification Society:	.Germanischer Lloyd

OVERALL SCORE: 1,857 (OUT OF A POSSIBLE 2,000 POINTS)

ACCOMMODATION: This is provided in four configurations and 12 price categories. It consists of all-outside-view suites: 2 Penthouse Grand Suites (Hapag, and Lloyd) and 10 Penthouse Deluxe Suites (Bach, Beethoven, Brahms, Handel, Lehar, Haydn, Mozart, Schubert, Strauss, Wagner), plus 156 suites with private balcony, and 36 standard suites. There are two suites (with private balcony) for the handicapped and 8 suites with interconnecting doors (good for families). Almost all suites have a private balcony (with wide teakwood deck, and lighting), and come complete with see-through glass topped by a teakwood rail. However, 12 suites are among the most sought-after accommodation (six on each of two decks); these overlook the stern (they each have private balconies with canvas "ceilings" for shade and privacy.

GENERAL INFORMATION: ALL SUITES: Each suite features a sleeping area with twin beds that can convert to a queen-sized bed, and two bedside tables with lamps and two drawers. There is a separate lounge area (with curtain divider) and bird's-eye maple wood cabinetry and accenting (with rounded edges). Facilities include a refrigerator/mini-bar (beer and soft drinks are supplied at no extra charge), a writing/vanity desk and sofa with large table in a separate lounge area. An illuminated walk-in closet provides ample hanging rail space, six drawers, personal safe (this can be opened with a credit card), umbrella, shoehorn, and clothes brush. European duvets are provided, and, in another cruise industry first,

BERLITZ'S RATINGS

	Possible	Achieved
Ship	500	479
Accommodation	200	189
Food	400	370
Service	400	359
Entertainment	100	90
Cruise	400	370

so is a full-color daily newspaper: *Die Welt* (*Welt am Sonntag* on Sundays), or, in fact, any one of a choice of any one of about 10 different newspapers from a passenger's home region. Almost all suites have totally unobstructed views and excellent soundproofing between the suites, as well as above and below.

In what is a cruise industry first, a superb integrated color TV/computer monitor and "CIN" (Cruise Infotainment System) – 24 hours per day video and audio on-demand – is provided (at no charge), so *you* choose when *you* want to watch any one of more than 100 movies, or when you want to listen to a specific compact audio disc (there are more than 600). The infotainment system is provided by a full-sized computer located in a cabinet that also houses a refrigerator and the TV set, with a full keyboard that is located in a drawer in the adjacent vanity unit).

Restaurant seating plans, menus, ship's position and chart, deck plan, shore excursion video clips, plus other informational video clips and items are featured. The keyboard also allows you to access e-mail sent to you aboard ship and to write your own e-mails. Your own private e-mail address is provided with your tickets and other documentation (there is no charge for incoming or outgoing e-mails, only for attachments, and for internet access). A modem (data) socket is also provided should you decide to bring your own laptop computer (the ship can also provide a laptop for your use). Online connectivity is 24 hours a day, anywhere in the world.

All suites have 24-hour room service. Illuminated

walk-in closets provide a generous amount of hanging and storage space even for long voyages. Each features a 100 percent air-circulation system. Western European butlers and cabin stewardesses are featured (butlers for the 12 premium suites on Deck 10, cabin stewardesses for all other suites).

The white/gray/sea green marble-tiled bathrooms are very well designed, have light décor, and include two good size cabinets for personal toiletry items. All bathrooms feature a full bathtub (plus an integral shower and a retractable clothesline) as well as a large, separate glass-fronted shower enclosure. Thick, 100 percent cotton bathrobes are provided, as are slippers and an array of personal toiletry amenities.

PENTHOUSES (DECK 10): For those desiring even more exclusivity and a larger living space, Deck 10 features two Penthouse Grand suites, and 10 Penthouse Deluxe suites. These feature a teakwood entrance hall, spacious living room with full-size dining table and four chairs, fully stocked drinks cabinet with refrigerator butler service, complimentary bar set-up (replenished with whatever you need), laundry and ironing service included, priority spa reservations, caviar (always available on request), hand-made chocolates, canapés, petit-fours and other niceties at no extra charge. In addition, the two Penthouse Grand suites also feature larger bathrooms, with a private sauna, extensive forward views from their prime, supremely quiet location one deck above the navigation bridge, a very large wrap-around private balcony, and large flat-screen televisions.

SUITES FOR THE DISABLED (DECK 7): The suites for the handicapped are spacious, and feature electronically operated beds with hydraulic lift, while a non-walk-in closet with drawers replaces the walk-in closet in all other suites. The bathroom has a roll-in shower area. All fittings are at the correct height, and there are several grab handles, as well as an emergency call-for-help button. Wheelchair-accessible public toilets are also provided on the main restaurant/entertainment deck.

DINING: The Europa Restaurant is a beautiful dining room that is two decks high, and can accommodate all passengers in one seating, with tables assigned for dinner only (breakfast and lunch are open seating). Passengers thus keep their favorite waiter throughout each cruise (for dinner). There are two sections, forward and aft, with the aft section being slightly higher than the forward section (gently sloping carpeted wheelchair ramping is provided). In common with most German-speaking ships, both smoking and non-smoking sections are provided. There are tables for two (quite a few), four, six or eight. For superb service, a waiter and *chef de rang* (assistant waiter) are provided, so that the waiter is *always* at the station, with the *chef de rang* acting as runner. Plated presentation of food is provided for entrées with silver service for additional vegetables, as

well as tableside flambeaus. The size of portions is sensible, and never overwhelming. Just two words can be used to describe the cuisine: simply superb.

Table settings include Dibbern china, 150-gram weight Robbe & Berking silverware and Riedel wine glasses. The cuisine is very international, with many German favorites featured, as well as regional dishes from around the world. The quality of food items is extremely high. Although top-grade caviar is found on dinner menus at least once each week, caviar is always available on request (at extra cost). An extensive wine list is provided, and this includes a good selection of fine French wines, as well as an extremely fine and well-balanced selection of Austrian, German and Swiss wines.

Dining options include two intimate alternative dining spots: the Oriental Restaurant, for Euro-Asian cuisine that is both extremely creative and beautifully presented, and Venezia, for Italian cuisine (and an excellent choice of olive oils and grappa). Both are adjacent to and forward of the main restaurant, and provide the setting for a more intimate dining experience, in nicely appointed surroundings. These are available by reservation, and there is no extra charge. The Oriental Restaurant features custom-made Bauscher china, while in Venezia Rosenthal china is featured.

For more casual dining, there is a Lido Café for serve-yourself breakfasts, luncheons and dinners, with both indoor and outdoor seating and a long indoor/outdoor bar. Rosenthal china and themed evening dining are featured, when tableside service is provided (at breakfast and lunch, waiters will take your plates to a table for you). Constant variety is provided, and many special lunch buffets feature a number of popular themes and regional specialties.

In addition, *Europa* is also famous for its German sausages, available late each night in the Clipper Bar, and at a special Bavarian *Fruschoppen*.

OTHER COMMENTS: This new ship's sleek appearance should please even the most critical of passengers, with her sweeping lines, graceful profile, and the well-known Hapag-Lloyd orange/blue funnel. Stand at the aft Lido Deck fantail and you will see (if your look down) the vast sweeping curving lines of a graceful stern – unlike the box-like rears of so many of contemporary ships.

Europa is the first Hapag-Lloyd ship to feature the "pod" propulsion system, designed to improve efficiency and handling, by *pulling*, rather than *pushing*, the ship through the water, while virtually eliminating vibration. Briefly, pods, which resemble huge outboard motors, replace internal electric propulsion motors, shaft lines, rudders and their machinery, and are compact, self-contained units. When going ahead, pod units face with the propeller forward (the ship can go astern either by rotating the pods 180 degrees or by reversing the thrust).

This is a very stable ship in open-sea conditions, and there is absolutely no vibration or noise. The ship also carries seven Zodiac landing craft for use during close-up shore excursions. Port and starboard boot-washing/changing rooms are also provided. There is a jogging track for the sporting, as well as an FKK (FreiKoerper-Kultur) deck for those who enjoy nude sunbathing (complete with showers), and a wrap-around teakwood promenade deck outdoors. The deck lounge chairs are aluminum with teak armrests, and have thick cushioned pads (the name of the ship is embroidered on them).

The swimming pool is long and rectangular in shape (it was modified from its original "bottle"-shaped design in December 2000), and, while not the widest, it is certainly longer than the pools aboard most other cruise ships today; it measures 56.7 by 16.8 ft (17.3 by 5.15 meters).

Europa is simply *the* most spacious purpose-built cruise ship in the world, and the company's replacement for the previous (larger) *Europa*, which, during its 17-year history, amassed a fine clutch of loyal devotees.

With this new ship, Hapag-Lloyd has been able to reach and maintain the high standards which the ship's passengers expect and demand. The ship's principal measurements (length and beam) are very close to that of the former *Europa*, and yet the ship carries about 200 fewer passengers. So, the space per passenger is incredibly high, there is never a hint of a line anywhere, and both restaurant and show lounge seat a full complement of passengers.

Europa is also beautifully appointed, in the contemporary style so popularly described as "minimalism" in the hotel industry. Only the finest quality soft furnishings have been chosen for her interiors, and these blend traditional with modern designs and materials in a subtle manner. *Europa* has several public rooms and hallways with extremely high ceilings, and these provide an incredible sense of space and grandeur. The colors used in the ship's interior décor are light and provide a more contemporary "designer-speak" look than one would expect of a ship for German-speaking passengers.

As in the former *Europa*, public rooms include the Club Belvedere (where afternoon tea and intimate classical recitals are regular features), the Europa Lounge (the ship's main showlounge), which has a U-shaped seating configuration and a proper stage, although there are several pillars. Much of the artwork was taken from the former *Europa*, so regular passengers may be familiar with much of it.

In addition, there is a Clipper Lounge/Bar (with high ceilings), an Atrium Piano Bar (set opposite the reception and shore excursion desks), with Steinway baby grand piano. When the ship first debuted there was a casino, although this proved to be so little used that Hapag-Lloyd Cruises turned it into a multi-functional space for small cocktail parties, and meetings.

There is also a superb sidewalk Havana Bar cigar lounge set off to one side of a winding indoor promenade. This is equipped with three large glass-fronted, fully temperature-controlled and conditioned humidor cabinets, and carries an extensive range of cigars from Cuba and other countries. Cigars carried include a range of sizes (from 102mm to 232mm) of the following well-known makes: Avo Uvezian, Cohiba, Cohiba Linea 1492, Davidoff, Griffin's, Montechristo, Partagas, Romeo y Julia, and Sancho Pansa. Cigar types include Giant, Double Corona, Panetela (short, regular and long), Churchill, Lonsdale, Torpedo, Toro, Corona, Robusto, Petit Corona and Chico. The bar also serves a fine range of armagnacs, calvados and cognacs, all poured tableside, as well as Cuban beer.

Other features include a business center, an electronic golf simulator room (there are also golf driving ranges and a deck tennis court on the open deck, as well as shuffleboard), and special rooms for hobbies (arts and crafts), and for children (complete with video games). A fully stocked library (open 24 hours) has internet access via two computers with flat-screen monitors, and per minute billing to your onboard account. There's also a small cinema/meeting/function room, a hobby room (for arts and crafts), children's playroom, an electronic golf simulator room, and two shuffleboard courts.

For personal service, an experienced concierge is available to all passengers, for any special or private arrangements both aboard and ashore.

A seven-deck-high central atrium is featured, together with two glass-walled elevators (typically operated by "piccolos" on embarkation day), and a lobby on the lower level that has a Steinway grand piano and lobby bar, reception desk, concierge desk, shore excursion desk and a future cruise sales desk.

Europa excels in its fine, intellectual entertainment program, which includes a constant supply of high quality classical and contemporary music artistes, as well as a program of expert lecturers, poetry readings, and so on, together with an occasional colorful production show, and local shows from destinations throughout the world.

The Lancaster Health Spa features a wide range of beauty services and treatments, including hot stone massage, and an array of other rejuvenating treatments (including full-day spa packages). Lancaster, the well-known German cosmetics firm, operates the spa and provides the staff. The facilities include a steam room and sauna (co-ed), two shower enclosures and two foot-washing stations, relaxation room, and two changing/dressing rooms. There is also a separate gymnasium (enlarged and relocated during a modification in 2000) and a beauty salon. A special Japanese Spa is featured (this includes a cream body massage, gentle steam room and a two-tatami mat relaxation area), which is booked individually for a special 90-minute treatment that will have you floating on air when you leave.

Wheelchair passengers should note that a special ramp is provided from the swimming pool/outdoors deck down to where the lifeboats are located. When the ship was delivered there were several small lips at door thresholds (particularly at fire zone doors) throughout the ship. Some of these have now been ramped or replaced with airtight-sealing rubber strips, so that wheelchair access is now good throughout. When this latest evaluation and rating were completed, only one toilet in the public areas (outdoors on Lido Deck 8) was wheelchair-accessible, although others may be modified in the future.

This ship will appeal to all those who desire to be aboard what is arguably the most luxurious and finest of all the new (small) cruise ships today. For the German-speaking market, little else comes close. Combined with a mostly young, enthusiastic and well-trained crew, whose aim is to serve and please passengers in the most sumptuous manner and in fine surroundings, the tradition of luxury cruising, in a contemporary setting, is carried to the highest expression. Although a children's playroom is provided, *Europa* really is a ship for adults to cruise in a quiet, refined setting that mixes formality and informality well.

You may ask why the rating for this ship is so high. Well, it's all in the little details and the extra attention to personal comfort and service that this line excels. For example, if you relax at the swimming pool in a hot climate, the deck steward will not only set your deck lounge chair and cover the mattress pad with a towel, he will also serve you drinks, give you a cold towel, and spray you with Evian water to keep you cool while you take the sun. Naturally, only real glasses are used at the swimming pool and on the open decks – no plastic glasses would ever be considered, thank goodness. Flowers, pot pourri and cloth towels (paper towels are not permissible at this rating level) are provided in all public restrooms. Fresh flowers are everywhere. Each passenger has his or her own email address (all emails are free). The in-suite infotainment system is simply the best. Details, details, details – that's what *Europa* is all about, and what the ship's many repeat passengers expect. The prices for drinks and wines are also very reasonable.

In addition, excellent port information is provided (both in written form and via the television infotainment system), as are lots of extra touches not found aboard most other cruise ships today. All port taxes and gratuities are also included, although further tipping is not prohibited. The currency on board is the euro. A souvenir logbook of every cruise is provided for each passenger at the end of each cruise. When taking all things into account – the unhurried lifestyle of single seating dining, plenty of suites with private balconies, a fine

array of classical music artists and lecturers, absolutely no vibration anywhere, and the outstanding cuisine and attentive, friendly, very attentive personal service from a staff dedicated to working aboard the world's finest cruise ship – it all adds up to the very best luxurious cruise ship and cruise experience available today (unless you have your own private motor yacht).

Having said that, there *are* ships with larger penthouse suites, balconies, show lounges, health spas and other appointments, but aboard *Europa*, everything is in scale, and in relation to the requirements of its passengers. It's not just the ship itself and its facilities and appointments that contribute to the ship's high rating, though – it's also in the extensive array of details and personal attention from its fine, dedicated crew. Believe me when I say that, at present, while there are plenty of imitators, there are no equals.

German-speaking passengers might be inclined to compare *Europa* (Hapag-Lloyd Cruises) with *Deutschland* (Peter Deilmann Cruises). However, some comparisons may be in order: *Europa* has 168 balcony suites, *Deutschland* has only two. *Europa*'s suites measure 355–915 sq. ft (33–85 sq. meters); those aboard *Deutschland*'s measure approximately 161–366 sq. ft (15–34 sq. meters). *Europa*'s décor is light and contemporary, and the ship has an open feeling, with high ceilings; *Deutschland*'s décor is dark and heavy (but in a beautiful, well-stated 1920s style).

Food, creativity, variety and presentation, and service aboard *Europa* are far superior to *Deutschland*. Vibration is non-existent aboard *Europa*, while it is still quite evident aboard *Deutschland*, according to passengers. Note that there is no entry for *Deutschland* in this book, at the owner's request.

In 2003, *Europa* will operate an around-the-world cruise of 239 days, featuring an astonishing 125 port calls – the most extensive world cruise in the cruise industry. The onboard currency is the euro.

WEAK POINTS: There are really very few weak points, although perhaps an indoor swimming pool (which was located adjacent to the health spa) may be missed by the many regular passengers who cruised aboard the former *Europa*. The balcony partitions are part-partitions, but would be more private if they were of the full (floor-to-ceiling) type – although this rarely presents a problem for the ship's passengers.

√

Removed 2006

European Stars
★★★★

Large Ship: ....58,600 tons	Total Crew: 710	Cabins (wheelchair accessible): 2
Lifestyle: ....Standard	Passengers	Cabin Current: ....110 and 220 volts
Cruise Line: ....Festival Cruises	(lower beds/all berths): 1,566/2,223	Elevators: 6
Former Names: ....none	Passenger Space Ratio	Casino (gaming tables): ....Yes
Builder: ....Chantiers de l'Atlantique	(lower beds/all berths): ...37.4/27.6	Slot Machines: ....Yes
(France)	Crew/Passenger Ratio	Swimming Pools (outdoors): 1
Original Cost: ....$245 million	(lower beds/all berths): 2.2/3.1	Swimming Pools (indoors): 0
Entered Service: ....Apr 2002	Navigation Officers: ....European	Whirlpools: ....1 (thalassotherapy)
Registry: ....Italy	Cabins (total): 783	Fitness Center: ....Yes
Length (ft/m): 823.4/251.0	Size Range (sq ft/m): 139.9–236.8/	Sauna/Steam Room: ....Yes/Yes
Beam (ft/m): 94.4/28.8	13.0–22.0	Massage: ....Yes
Draft (ft/m): 22.4/6.85	Cabins (outside view): 302	Self-Service Launderette: ....No
Propulsion/Propellers: ....diesel	Cabins (interior/no view): 223	Dedicated Cinema/Seats: ....No
(31,680kW)/2 pods	Cabins (for one person): 0	Library: ....Yes
Passenger Decks: 10	Cabins (with private balcony): 132	Classification Society: ....Bureau Veritas

OVERALL SCORE: 1,496 (OUT OF A POSSIBLE 2,000 POINTS)

ACCOMMODATION: There are 11 price categories to choose from. These include 132 suites with private balcony (note that the partitions are only of the partial and not the full type), outside-view cabins and interior (no view) cabins.

Suite grade accommodation (they are not true suites, as there is no separate bedroom and lounge – in other words, it is not a "suite" of rooms) also has more room, a larger lounge area, walk-in closet, wall-to-wall vanity counter, a bathroom with combination bathtub and shower, toilet, and private balcony (with light). Bathrobes are provided.

In general, the "suites" are well laid out and nicely furnished. However, except for the very highest category, the suite bathrooms are very plain, with white plastic washbasins and white walls, and mirrors that steam up. According to the rules of *feng shui*, however, it is bad luck to place *any* mirror in such a position that it can be seen by anyone lying in bed.

No matter which accommodation grade you choose (even the smallest interior cabins are sensibly spacious, with plenty of space between lower beds), all grades of accommodation feature sheets and blankets as bed linen (no duvets), and are equipped with a television, hairdryer, mini-bar/refrigerator, personal safe (cleverly positioned behind a vanity desk mirror), bathroom with shower and toilet, and 100 percent cotton towels (except for hand towels, which, when I last sailed, were 86 percent cotton and 14 percent polyester. However, the standard grade cabins really are quite small when compared to many other new ships, at a modest 140 sq. ft (13 sq. meters).

RATINGS

	Possible	Achieved
Ship	500	408
Accommodation	200	157
Food	400	276
Service	400	307
Entertainment	100	54
Cruise	400	294

DINING: There are four dining spots, all designated as non-smoking areas). The principal dining room is the 610-seat Marco Polo Restaurant, and two seatings for meals. The cuisine featured by Festival Cruises is, in general, quite sound, and, with varied menus and good presentation, should prove a highlight for most passengers. The wine list features a wide variety of wines at fairly reasonable prices, although almost all wines are very young.

La Pergola is the second, and most formal, restaurant, and features stylish Italian cuisine. This is the restaurant assigned to all passengers occupying accommodation designated as suites, and other passengers can dine in it too, although reservations must be made.

Chez Claude, located on the starboard side aft, adjacent to the ship's funnel, is a grill area for fast food.

La Brasserie is the casual, self-serve buffet eatery, open 24 hours a day. The selections are very standardized, however, and could be better.

Additionally, Caffe Grecco, located on the upper, second level of the main lobby, is the place coffees and pastry items – as well for people-watching throughout the day. The décor is a replica of Rome's legendary Caffe Grecco.

OTHER COMMENTS: Although this ship is slightly larger, it is a close "cousin" to *Mistral* (the first new ship to be built for Festival Cruises), and sister to *European Vision*, although there is an added deck around the forward mast (this allowed for the addition of more suites with private balconies in a premium area of real estate) which also happens to provide a better balance to the ship's overall profile). A 114.8 ft-long (35-meter) mid-section was added to increase the ship's length, thus providing more space per passenger than *Mistral*. From the technical viewpoint, the ship is quite different to *Mistral*, and is fitted with an azimuthing pod propulsion system, instead of conventional rudders and propellers, in the latest configuration of high-tech propulsion systems

The lido deck surrounding the outdoor swimming pool also features whirlpool tubs and a large bandstand is set in raised canvas-covered pods. All the deck lounge chairs have cushioned pads.

Inside, the layout and passenger flow is good, as are the "you are here" deck signs. The décor is decidedly "European Moderne" – whatever that means – and it includes clean lines, minimalism in furniture designs (including some chairs that look interesting but are totally impractical unless you are prepared to face reconstructive surgery).

Facilities include: Amadeus, the ship's show lounge, and La Gondola Theatre, for plays and other theatrical presentations. There's a cigar smoking room (called Ambassador), which has all the hallmarks of a gentleman's club of former times; as well as a piano bar. The Goethe Library/Card Room has real writing desks (something many ships seem to omit today), and this ship has an Internet Café, as well an English pub called the White Lion. Gamblers will find solace in The Lido Casino, with blackjack, poker and roulette games, plus the slot machines for one-arm persons.

For the sports-minded, there is a simulated climbing wall outdoors, while other sports and fitness facilities include volleyball/basketball court, and mini-golf. The Atlantica Spa features some body-pampering treatments, as well as a gymnasium with the usual high-tech, muscle-pump machinery and gadgets.

The onboard currency is the euro. *European Stars* was built for a European company, and designed and constructed by Europeans, with European décor and colors, for European passengers, with European food, service and entertainment. In other words, as the company so strongly states, this is a ship *for Europeans* (however, the ship is also marketed in the USA, but under the company name of First European Cruises). Note that the names of the public rooms were not known at press time, so those of sister ship *European Vision* (which debuted in June 2001) have been used provisionally.

WEAK POINTS: Standing in line for embarkation, disembarkation, shore tenders and for self-serve buffet meals is an inevitable aspect of cruising aboard all large ships. The heavy smokers are virtually impossible to avoid (in typical European fashion, ashtrays are simply moved – if used at all – to wherever smokers happen to be sitting). All announcements are conducted in several languages (although these are thankfully fewer than in the past). The entertainment is of a low standard of professionalism, with intrusive animateurs that mean well, but who perform as one would expect to find in a holiday camp – with enthusiasm but little else. Entertainment is a very weak area for Festival Cruises, although this should improve somewhat as more ships are brought into service and more money is assigned to this important aspect of the company's cruise product.

The cruise line keeps prices low by providing air transportation that may be at inconvenient times, or transportation involving long journeys by bus. In other words, be prepared for a little discomfort in getting to and from your cruise in exchange for low cruise rates. The constant push for onboard revenue is also very irritating – you have to pay extra even for a visit to the ship's navigation bridge.

Removed 2006

European Vision
★★★★

Large Ship: . . . . .58,600 tons	Total Crew: 710	Cabins (wheelchair accessible): 2
Lifestyle: . . . . .Standard	Passengers	Cabin Current: . . . . .110 and 220 volts
Cruise Line: . . . . .Festival Cruises	(lower beds/all berths): 1,566/2,223	Elevators: 6
Former Names: . . . . .none	Passenger Space Ratio	Casino (gaming tables): . . . . .Yes
Builder: . . . . .Chantiers de l'Atlantique	(lower beds/all berths): 37.4/27.6	Slot Machines: . . . . .Yes
(France)	Crew/Passenger Ratio	Swimming Pools (outdoors): 2
Original Cost: . . . .$245 million	(lower beds/all berths): 2.2/3.1	Swimming Pools (indoors): 0
Entered Service: . . . . .June 2001	Navigation Officers: . . . . .European	Whirlpools: . . . . .1 (thalassotherapy)
Registry: . . . . .Italy	Cabins (total): 783	Fitness Center: . . . . .Yes
Length (ft/m): 823.4/251.0	Size Range (sq ft/m): 139.9–236.8/	Sauna/Steam Room: . . . . .Yes/Yes
Beam (ft/m): 94.4/28.8	13.0–22.0	Massage: . . . . .Yes
Draft (ft/m): 22.4/6.85	Cabins (outside view): 302	Self-Service Launderette: . . . . .No
Propulsion/Propellers: . . . . .diesel-electric	Cabins (interior/no view): 223	Dedicated Cinema/Seats: . . . . .No
(31,680kW)/2 pods	Cabins (for one person): 0	Library: . . . . .Yes
Passenger Decks: 10	Cabins (with private balcony): 132	Classification Society: . . . . .RINA

OVERALL SCORE: 1,496 (OUT OF A POSSIBLE 2,000 POINTS)

ACCOMMODATION: There are 11 price categories. These include 132 suites with private balcony (note that the partitions are only of the partial and not the full type), outside-view cabins and interior (no view) cabins.

Suite grade accommodation (they are not true suites, as there is no separate bedroom and lounge – in other words, it is not a "suite" of rooms) also has more room, a larger lounge area, walk-in closet, wall-to-wall vanity counter, a bathroom with combination bathtub and shower, toilet, and private balcony (with light). Bathrobes are provided. In general, the "suites" are well laid out and nicely furnished. However, except for the very highest category, the suite bathrooms are very plain, with white plastic washbasins and white walls, and mirrors that steam up. According to the rules of *feng shui*, however, it is bad luck to place *any* mirror in such a position that it can be seen by anyone lying in bed.

No matter which accommodation grade you choose (even the smallest interior cabins are sensibly spacious, with plenty of space between lower beds), all grades of accommodation have sheets and blankets as bed linen (no duvets), and are equipped with a TV set, hairdryer, mini-bar/refrigerator, personal safe (cleverly positioned behind a vanity desk mirror), bathroom with shower and toilet, and 100 percent cotton towels (except for hand towels, which, when I last sailed, were 86 percent cotton and 14 percent polyester).

However, the standard grade cabins really are quite small when compared to many other new ships, at a modest 140 sq. ft (13 sq. meters).

BERLITZ'S RATINGS

	Possible	Achieved
Ship	500	408
Accommodation	200	157
Food	400	276
Service	400	307
Entertainment	100	54
Cruise	400	294

DINING: There are four dining spots, all designated as non-smoking. The principal dining room is the 610-seat Marco Polo Restaurant. Typically, there are two seatings for dinner, and open seating for breakfast and lunch. However, for breakfast and lunch, you may well be seated with others with whom you may not be able to communicate very satisfactorily – such is the life aboard a ship with European passengers of different languages.

In general, the cuisine is quite acceptable, although not memorable in any way, despite the line's hype about its "excellent European gastronomy." The menus are varied and the presentation is generally sound, and should prove a highlight for most passengers. The wine list features a wide variety of wines at fairly reasonable prices, although most of the wines are very young.

La Pergola is the second (and most formal) restaurant aboard this ship, and features stylish Italian cuisine. This restaurant is assigned to all passengers occupying accommodation designated as suites, although other passengers can dine in it too, on a reservations only basis. As you might expect, the food here is superior to that in the main dining room.

Chez Claude, on the starboard side aft, adjacent to the ship's funnel, is a grill area for fast-food items.

La Brasserie is a casual, self-serve buffet eatery, open 24 hours a day. The selections are very standardized (minimal), however, and could be better.

Additionally, Café San Marco, located on the upper, second level of the main lobby, is available for coffee and pastry items – as well for people-watching.

OTHER COMMENTS: Although this ship is slightly larger, it is a close "cousin" to *Mistral,* the first new ship built for the European company Festival Cruises (known as First European Cruises in the USA), although there is an added deck around the forward mast (this allowed for the addition of more suites with private balconies in a premium area of real estate) which also happens to provide a better balance to the ship's overall profile). A 115-ft (35-meter) mid-section was added to increase the ship's length, providing more space per passenger than *Mistral.* From the technical viewpoint, the ship is quite different to *Mistral,* and is fitted with an azimuthing "pod" propulsion system (there are two pods), instead of conventional rudders and propellers, in the latest configuration of high-tech propulsion systems.

European Vision began its working life auspiciously, having been selected to be a floating hotel to accommodate the leaders and staff of the G8 summit in 2001.

The lido deck surrounding the outdoor swimming pool also features whirlpool tubs and a large bandstand is set in raised canvas-covered pods. All the deck lounge chairs have cushioned pads.

Inside, the layout and passenger flow is good, as are the "you are here" deck signs. The decks are named after European cities such as: Oxford Deck (with British public room names), Venice Deck (with Italian public room names), and Biarritz Deck (with French public room names); others are Barcelona Deck, Biarritz Deck, Copenhagen Deck, Kiel Deck, and Olympia Deck. The décor is decidedly "European Moderne" – whatever that means – and it includes clean lines, minimalism in furniture designs (including some chairs that look interesting but are totally impractical). However, the interior colors chosen are extremely good; nothing jars the senses, but rather calms them, unlike many ships today.

Facilities include Amadeus, the ship's nightclub, and La Gondola Theatre, for production shows and cabaret, plays and other theatrical presentations. There's also a cigar smoking room (called Ambassador), which has all the hallmarks of a gentleman's club; as well as Vivaldi, a piano lounge. The Goethe Library/Card Room has real writing desks (something many ships seem to omit today), and there is an extensive Internet Canter, as well an English pub called the White Lion. Gamblers will find solace in The Lido Casino, with blackjack, poker and roulette games, plus an array of slot machines.

For the sports-minded, there's a simulated climbing wall outdoors, while other sports and fitness facilities include volleyball/basketball court, and mini-golf. The Atlantica Spa has body-pampering treatments, as well as a gymnasium with great forward facing views and the usual high-tech, muscle-pump machinery and gadgets.

Anyone who is wheelchair-bound should note that there is no access to the uppermost forward and aft decks, although access throughout most of the interior of the ship is very good. The passenger hallways are a little narrow on some decks for you to pass when housekeeping carts are in place, however.

The onboard currency is the euro. *European Vision,* whose sister ship is *European Stars,* was built for a European company, and designed and constructed by Europeans, with European décor and colors, for European passengers, with European food, service and entertainment. In other words, as the company so strongly states, this is a ship *for Europeans* (although the ship is also marketed in the USA, under the company name of First European Cruises). Gratuities are recommended at €8.50 ($7.50) per person, per day. Additionally, 15 percent is added to all bar bills and heath spa treatments.

WEAK POINTS: Standing in line for embarkation, disembarkation, shore tenders and for self-serve buffet meals is an inevitable aspect of cruising aboard all large ships. Heavy smokers are everywhere, and are virtually impossible to avoid (in typical European fashion, ashtrays are simply moved – if used at all – to wherever smokers happen to be sitting). All announcements are conducted in several languages (although these are thankfully fewer than in the past). The entertainment is of a low standard of professionalism, with intrusive animateurs that mean well, but who perform as one would expect to find in a holiday camp – with enthusiasm but little else. Entertainment is a very weak area for Festival Cruises, although this should improve somewhat as more ships are brought into service and more money is assigned to this important aspect of the company's cruise product.

The company keeps prices low by providing air transportation that may be at inconvenient times, or transportation involving long journeys by bus. In other words, be prepared for a little discomfort in getting to and from your cruise in exchange for low cruise rates. The constant push for onboard revenue is also very irritating – you have to pay extra even for a visit to the ship's navigation bridge.

Explorer
★★ +

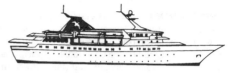

Small Ship: ....2,398 tons	
Lifestyle: ....Standard	
Cruise Line: ....Abercrombie & Kent	
Former Names: ....*Society Explorer,*	
Lindblad Explorer, World Explorer	
Builder: ...Nystad Varv Shipyard (Finland)	
Original Cost: ....$2.5 million	
Entered Service: 1969/Mar 1993	
Registry: ....Liberia	
Length (ft/m): 239.1/72.88	
Beam (ft/m): 46.0/14.03	
Draft (ft/m): 13.7/4.20	
Propulsion/Propellers: diesel (2,795kW)/1	
Passenger Decks: 6	
Total Crew: 71	

Passengers	
(lower beds/all berths): 100/114	
Passenger Space Ratio	
(lower beds/all berths): 23.9/21.0	
Crew/Passenger Ratio	
(lower beds/all berths): 1.4/1.6	
Navigation Officers: ....European	
Cabins (total): 50	
Size Range (sq ft/m): 81.8–161.4/	
7.6–15.0	
Cabins (outside view): 50	
Cabins (interior/no view): 0	
Cabins (for one person): 8	
Cabins (with private balcony): 0	
Cabins (wheelchair accessible): 0	

Cabin Current: ....220 volts	
Elevators: 0	
Casino (gaming tables): ....No	
Slot Machines: ....No	
Swimming Pools (outdoors): 1	
Whirlpools: 0	
Exercise Room: ....Yes	
Sauna/Steam Room: ....Yes/No	
Massage: ....Yes	
Self-Service Launderette: ....No	
Lecture/Film Room: ....Yes	
Library: ....Yes	
Zodiacs: ....Yes	
Helicopter Pad: ....No	
Classification Society: Det Norske Veritas	

OVERALL SCORE: 1,062 (OUT OF A POSSIBLE 2,000 POINTS)

ACCOMMODATION: There are six price categories. Whichever accommodation grade you choose, all have individual climate control.

The standard cabins are extremely small and utilitarian, although all have an outside view, and two lower beds (which cannot be pushed together to form a double bed). There is very little closet, drawer, and storage space for two persons. Even so, they are just about adequate for this type of cruising (call them cozy), where you need only casual clothing. The bathrooms (and the towels) are really tiny, however, and there is little room for your personal toiletry items. National Geographic maps are provided in all cabins.

Accommodation designated as suites feature a queen-sized bed, sofa, refrigerator, and television with VCR player. The bathrooms are marginally larger than those in the standard cabins, with a separate shower enclosure.

DINING: The dining room is cheerful and intimate, although somewhat noisy, but it does seat all passengers in one seating, with assigned tables. Features creatively presented food, although the choice is quite limited, as is the wine list. The service is smiling, attentive, and genuinely friendly, but it is quite casual.

OTHER COMMENTS: *Explorer* is the *original* expedition cruise vessel, and started expedition cruising with passengers (participants) in 1969 under the guidance of the father of expedition cruising, Lars-Eric Lindblad. It is a surprisingly strong ship, having experienced a couple of groundings (one in 1972 off the South Shetland Archipel-

BERLITZ'S RATINGS

	Possible	Achieved
Ship	500	214
Accommodation	200	94
Food	400	226
Service	400	247
Entertainment	N/A	N/A
Cruise	500	281

ago, and another in 1979). Abercrombie & Kent acquired it in 1992 and carries on the excellent tradition of providing adventure/discovery cruises to lesser-traveled regions such as the Amazon and Antarctic. As the brochure states, *"Explorer* has the comforts of a traveling base-camp."

Although a small vessel, it is fitted with all the necessary equipment for successful in-depth exploration cruising, including a fleet of Zodiac landing craft and several two-person sea kayaks. Now showing signs of wear and tear, the ship cannot compete effectively with the newer expedition-style ships, despite recent refurbishment. It does, however, have an ice-hardened hull and a well-balanced profile, and is extremely maneuverable.

There are few public rooms, but the interior decor is tasteful and cheerful, and the ambience is intimate. There is a large reference library of books associated with nature and wildlife. Good lecturers and nature specialists are on board for each cruise, provided by Abercrombie & Kent.

When cruising in the Antarctic, the ship often carries fresh fruits and other produce, and medication to research stations.

This is cruising for the serious "in-your-face" adventurer who wants to explore specialized areas of the world yet have some of the most basic creature comforts of home within reach. All shore excursions and gratuities are included. The onboard currency is the US dollar.

WEAK POINTS: The original modern-day expedition cruise vessel is now old and quirky, so you simply must not try to compare it with other small ships.

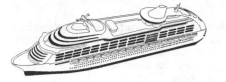

Explorer of the Seas
★★★★

Large Ship: . . . . , ...137,308 tons	Passengers		Cabin Current: . . . . .110 volts
Lifestyle: . . . . .Standard	(lower beds/all berths): 3,114/3,840		Elevators: . . . . .14 (6 glass-enclosed)
Cruise Line: Royal Caribbean International	Passenger Space Ratio		Casino (gaming tables): . . . . .Yes
Former Names: . . . . .none	(lower beds/all berths): 44.0/35.7		Slot Machines: . . . . .Yes
Builder: . . .Kvaerner Masa-Yards (Finland)	Crew/Passenger Ratio		Swimming Pools (outdoors): 3
Original Cost: . . . .$500 million	(lower beds/all berths): 2.6/3.2		Swimming Pools (indoors): 0
Entered Service: . . . . .Oct 2000	Navigation Officers: . . . . . . .Scandinavian		Whirlpools: 6
Registry: . . . . .The Bahamas	Cabins (total): 1,557		Fitness Center: . . . . .Yes
Length (ft/m): 1,020.6/311.1	Size Range (sq ft/m): 151.0–1,358.0/		Sauna/Steam Room: . . . . .Yes/Yes
Beam (ft/m): 155.5/47.4	14.0–126.1		Massage: . . . . .Yes
Draft (ft/m): 28.8/8.8	Cabins (outside view): 939		Self-Service Launderette: . . . . .No
Propulsion/Propellers: . . . . .diesel-electric	Cabins (interior/no view): 618		Dedicated Cinema/Seats: . . . . .No
(75,600kW)/3 azimuthing pods	Cabins (for one person): 0		Library: . . . . .Yes
Passenger Decks: 14	Cabins (with private balcony): 757		Classification Society: . . . . . . .Det Norske
Total Crew: 1,181	Cabins (wheelchair accessible): 26		Veritas

---

OVERALL SCORE: 1,537 (OUT OF A POSSIBLE 2,000 POINTS)

ACCOMMODATION: There is an extensive range of 22 cabin categories, in four major groupings: Premium ocean-view suites and cabins, Promenade-view (interior-view) cabins, Ocean-view cabins, and Interior (no view) cabins. Many cabins are of a similar size – good for incentives and large groups, and 300 have interconnecting doors – good for families.

A total of 138 interior (no view) cabins have bay windows that look *into* a horizontal atrium – first used to good effect aboard the Baltic passenger ferries *Silja Serenade* (1990) and *Silja Symphony* (1991) with interior (no view) cabins that look into a central shopping plaza. Regardless of what cabin grade you choose, however, all except for the Royal Suite and Owner's Suite have twin beds that convert to a queen-sized unit, television, radio and telephone, personal safe, vanity unit, mini-bar (called an Automatic Refreshment Center) hairdryer and private bathroom.

The largest accommodation includes luxuriously appointed penthouse suites (whose occupants, sadly, must share the rest of the ship with everyone else, except for their own exclusive, and private, concierge club). The grandest is the Royal Suite, positioned on the port side of the ship, and measures 1,146 sq. ft (106.5 sq. meters). It has a king-sized bed in a separate, large bedroom, a living room with an additional queen-sized sofa bed, baby grand piano (no pianist is included, however), refrigerator/wet bar, dining table, entertainment center, and large bathroom.

The slightly smaller, but still highly desirable Owner's Suites (there are 10, all located in the center

BERLITZ'S RATINGS

	Possible	Achieved
Ship	500	431
Accommodation	200	160
Food	400	252
Service	400	294
Entertainment	100	83
Cruise	400	317

of the ship, on both port and starboard sides, each measuring 468 sq. ft (43 sq. meters)) and four Royal Family suites (each measures 574 sq. ft (53 sq. meters), all of which feature similar items. However, the four Royal Family suites, which have two bedrooms (including one with third/fourth upper Pullman berths) are located at the stern of the ship and have magnificent views over the ship's wake (and seagulls).

All cabins feature a private bathroom with shower enclosure (towels are 100 percent cotton), as well as interactive television and pay-per-view movies. Cabins with "private balconies" should note that they are not so private, as the partitions are only partial, leaving you exposed to your neighbor's smoke or conversation. The balcony decking is made of Bolidt – a sort of rubberized sand – and not wood, while the balcony rail is of wood.

DINING: The main dining room is large and is set on three levels, all of which are named after explorers (Christopher Columbus, Da Gama and Magellan). A dramatic staircase connects all three levels. However, all three feature exactly the same menus and food. The dining room is totally non-smoking, there are two seatings, and tables are for four, six, eight 10 or 12.

The cuisine in the main dining room is typical of mass banquet catering that offers standard fare comparable to that found in American family-style restaurants ashore. While menu descriptions are tempting, the actual food may be somewhat disappointing and unmemorable. The menu descriptions make the food sound better than it is (which is consistently below average), mostly disappointing and without much taste. However, a decent selection of light meals is provided, and a vegetarian menu is available. The selection of breads, rolls, fruit and cheese is quite poor, however, and could do more improvement. Caviar (once a standard menu item) incurs a hefty extra charge. There is no good caviar; special orders, tableside carving and flambeau items are not offered. Menus typically include a Welcome Aboard Dinner, French Dinner, Italian Dinner, International Dinner, and Captain's Gala Dinner.

ALTERNATIVE DINING OPTIONS: Alternative dining options for casual and informal meals at all hours (according to company releases) include:

● *Cafe Promenade*, for continental breakfast, all-day pizzas and specialty coffees (provided in paper cups).
● *Windjammer Café*, for casual buffet-style breakfast, lunch and light dinner (except on the cruise's last night.
● *Island Grill* (actually a section inside the Windjammer Café), for casual dinner (no reservations necessary) featuring a grill and open kitchen.
● *Portofino*, an "upscale" (non-smoking) Euro-Italian restaurant, for dinner (reservations required).
● *Johnny Rockets*, a retro 1950s all-day, all-night eatery that has hamburgers, malt shakes (at extra cost), and jukebox hits, with both indoor and outdoor seating.
● *Sprinkles*, for round-the-clock ice cream and yogurt.

OTHER COMMENTS: *Explorer of the Seas* is a stunning, large, floating leisure resort, and sister to *Voyager of the Seas* and *Adventure of the Seas*, which debuted in 1999 and 2001 respectively, and two others still to come. The exterior design is not unlike an enlarged version of the company's *Vision*-class ships. The ships are, at present, the largest cruise vessels in the world in terms of tonnage measurement (although, to keep things in perspective, the ships are not quite as long as Norwegian Cruise Line's *Norway*, and will be eclipsed in 2004 by Cunard Line's *Queen Mary 2*).

The ship's propulsion is derived from three pod units, powered by electric motors (two azimuthing, and one fixed at the centerline) instead of conventional rudders and propellers, in the latest configuration of high-tech propulsion systems.

With its large proportions, the ship provides more facilities and options, and caters to more passengers than any other Royal Caribbean International ship has in the past, and yet the ship manages to have a healthy passenger space ratio (the amount of space per passenger). Being a "non-Panamax" ship, it is simply too large to go through the Panama Canal, thus limiting itineraries almost exclusively to the Caribbean (where few islands can accept it), or for use as a floating island resort. Spend the first few hours exploring all the many facilities and public spaces aboard this vessel and it will be time well spent.

Although this is a large ship, even the accommodation hallways are quite attractive, with artwork cabinets and wavy lines to interject and break up the monotony. In fact, there are plenty of decorative touches to help you avoid what would otherwise be a very clinical environment.

Embarkation and disembarkation take place through two stations/access points, designed to minimize the inevitable lines at the start and end of the cruise (that's over 1,500 people for each access point). Once inside the ship, you'll need good walking shoes, particularly when you need to go from one end to the other – it really is quite a long way.

The four-decks-high Royal Promenade, which is 394 ft (120 meters) long, is the main interior focal point (it's a good place to hang out, to meet someone, or to arrange to meet someone). The length of two football fields, it has two internal lobbies (atria) that rise to as many as 11 decks high. Restaurants, shops and entertainment locations front this winding street and interior "with-view" cabins look into it from above. It is designed loosely in the image of London's fashionable Burlington Arcade – although there's not a real brick in sight, and I wonder if the designers have ever visited the real thing.

The atrium houses a "traditional" English pub, with, naturally, draft beer and plenty of "street-front" seating (it's funny, but North American passengers sit down, while British passengers stand at the bar). There is also a Champagne Bar, a Sidewalk Café (for continental breakfast, all-day pizzas, specialty coffees and desserts), Sprinkles (for round-the-clock ice cream and yoghurt), and Weekend Warrior (a sports bar). There are also several shops – jewelry shop, gift shop, liquor shop and the logo souvenir shop. Altogether, the Royal promenade is a nice place to see and be seen.

The Guest Reception and Shore Excursion counters are located at the aft end of the promenade, as is an ATM machine. Things to watch for: look up to see the large moving, asteroid-like sculpture (constantly growing and contracting), parades and street entertainers.

Arched across the promenade is a captain's balcony. Meanwhile, in the center of the promenade is a stairway that connects you to the deck below, where you'll find Schooner Bar (a piano lounge) and the colorful Casino Royale. This is naturally large and full of flashing lights and noises. Casino gaming includes blackjack, Caribbean stud poker, roulette, and craps.

Aft to the casino is the Aquarium Bar, while close by are some neat displays of oceanographic interest. Royal Caribbean International has teamed up with the University of Miami's Rosenstiel School of Marine and Atmospheric Science to study the ocean and the atmosphere. To this end, a small onboard laboratory is part of project.

Action man and action woman can enjoy more sporting pursuits, such as a rock-climbing wall that's 32.8 ft high (10 meters). It is located outdoors at the aft end of the funnel. You'll get a great "buzz" being 200 ft (60 meters) above the ocean while the ship is moving – particularly when it rolls.

There's also a roller-blading track, a dive-and-snorkel shop, a full-size basketball court and 9-hole golf driving range. A ShipShape health spa measures 15,000 sq. ft (1,390 sq. meters), includes a large aerobics room, fitness center (with the usual stairmasters, treadmills, stationary bikes, weight machines and free weights), treatment rooms, men's and women's sauna/steam rooms, while another 10,000 sq ft (930 sq. meters) are devoted to a Solarium (with magrodome sliding glass roof) for relaxation after you've exercised too much.

There is also a regulation-size ice-skating rink (Studio B), featuring *real*, not fake, ice, with stadium-style seating for up to 900, and the latest in broadcast facilities. Ice Follies shows are also presented here. Slim pillars obstruct clear-view arena stage sight lines, however.

If ice-skating in the Caribbean doesn't appeal, perhaps you'd like the stunning two-deck library (open 24 hours a day). A grand $12 million has been spent on permanent artwork.

Drinking places include a neat Aquarium Bar, which comes complete with 50 tons of glass and water in four large aquariums (whose combined value is more than $1 million). Other drinking places include the small and intimate Champagne Bar, Crown & Anchor Pub, and a Connoisseur Club – for cigars and cognacs. Lovers of jazz might appreciate High Notes, an intimate room for cool music, or the Schooner Bar piano lounge. Golfers might enjoy the 19th Hole, a golf bar.

Show lovers will find that the Palace Showlounge seats 1,350-seat and spans the height of five decks. It has a hydraulic orchestra pit and stage areas, and is decorated in the style of the grand European theatres from the fin-de-siècle period.

There is a television studio, located adjacent to rooms that can be used for trade show exhibit space. Lovers can tie the knot in a wedding chapel in the sky, the Skylight Chapel (it's located on the upper level of the Observation Lounge, and even has wheelchair access via an electric stairway lift). Meanwhile, outdoors, the pool and open deck areas provide a resort-like environment.

Children's facilities are extensive. "Aquanauts" is for 3–5 year olds; "Explorers" is for 6–8 year olds; "Voyagers" is for 9–12 year olds. Optix is a dedicated area for teenagers, including a daytime club (with several computers), soda bar, disc jockey and dance floor. "Challenger's Arcade" has an array of the latest video games. Paint and Clay is an arts and crafts center for younger children. Adjacent to these indoor areas is Adventure Beach, an area for all the family. It includes swimming pools, a water slide and game areas outdoors.

In terms of sheer size, this ship presently dwarfs all other ships in the cruise industry, but in terms of personal service, the reverse is the case, unless you happen to reside in one of the top suites. Royal Caribbean International does, however, try hard to provide a good standard of programmed service from its hotel staff.

This is impersonal city life at sea, millennium-style, and a superb, well-designed alternative to a land-based resort, which is what the company wanted to build. Welcome to the real, escapist world of highly programmed resort living aboard ship. Perhaps if you dare to go outside, you might even be able to see the sea – now there's a novelty. Remember to take lots of extra pennies – you'll need them to pay for all the additional-cost items.

The ship is large, so remember that if you meet someone somewhere, and want to meet them again you'll need to make an appointment – for this really is a massive, Las Vegas-style American floating resort-city for the lively of heart and fleet of foot. The best place to arrange to meet someone is in the Royal Promenade. The onboard currency is the US dollar.

WEAK POINTS: Check-in, embarkation and disembarkation (it's better if you are a non-US resident and stay at an RCI-booked hotel, as you will complete all formalities there and then simply walk on board to your cabin). Suites and cabins with private balcony have Bolidt floors (a substance that looks like rubberized sand) instead of wood.

If you have a cabin with a door that interconnecting door to another cabin, be aware that you'll be able to hear *everything* your next-door neighbors say and do. Bathroom toilets are explosively noisy.

You'll need to plan wisely what you want to participate in; almost everything requires you to sign-up in advance (many activities take place only on sea days).

The cabin bath towels are small and skimpy. There are very few quiet places to sit and read – almost everywhere there is intrusive background music. Although the menus and food variety offered have been upgraded since the introduction, remember that you get what you pay for. Food costs are well below that for Celebrity Cruises, for example, and so you should not expect the same food quality.

Fantasy
★★★ +

Large Ship: ....70,367 tons	Passengers		Cabin Current: ....110 volts
Lifestyle: ....Standard	(lower beds/all berths): 2,056/2,634		Elevators: 14
Cruise Line: ....Carnival Cruise Lines	Passenger Space Ratio		Casino (gaming tables): ....Yes
Former Names: ....none	(lower beds/all berths): 34.4/26.7		Slot Machines: ....Yes
Builder: ...Kvaerner Masa-Yards (Finland)	Crew/Passenger Ratio		Swimming Pools (outdoors): 3
Original Cost: ....$225 million	(lower beds/all berths): 2.2/2.8		Swimming Pools (indoors): 0
Entered Service: ....Mar 1990	Navigation Officers: ....Italian		Whirlpools: 6
Registry: ....Panama	Cabins (total): 1,028		Fitness Center: ....Yes
Length (ft/m): 855.8/263.6	Size Range (sq ft/m): 173.2–409.7/		Sauna/Steam Room: ....Yes/Yes
Beam (ft/m): 103.0/31.4	16.0–38.0		Massage: ....Yes
Draft (ft/m): 25.9/7.9	Cabins (outside view): 620		Self-Service Launderette: ....Yes
Propulsion/Propellers: .....diesel-electric	Cabins (interior/no view): 408		Dedicated Cinema/Seats: ....No
(42,240kW)/2	Cabins (for one person): 0		Library: ....Yes
Passenger Decks: 10	Cabins (with private balcony): 54		Classification Society: ...Lloyd's Register
Total Crew: 920	Cabins (wheelchair accessible): 22		

OVERALL SCORE: 1,385 (OUT OF A POSSIBLE 2,000 POINTS)

ACCOMMODATION: As in sister ships *Ecstasy, Elation, Fascination, Imagination, Inspiration, Paradise* and *Sensation*), the standard outside-view and interior (no view) cabins have plain décor. They are marginally comfortable, yet spacious enough and practical (most are of the same size and appointments), with good storage space and well-designed bathrooms.

Those booking one of the outside suites will find more space, whirlpool bathtubs, and some fascinating, rather eclectic décor and furniture. These are mildly attractive, but nothing special, and they are much smaller than those aboard the ships of a similar size of several competing companies.

A gift basket is provided in all grades of accommodation; it includes aloe soap, shampoo, conditioner, deodorant, breath mints, candy, and pain relief tablets (albeit all in sample sizes).

Note that if you book accommodation in one of the suites (Category 11 or 12 in the Carnival Cruise Lines brochure) you automatically qualify for "Skipper's Club" priority check-in at any US homeland port – useful for getting ahead of the crowd.

DINING: The two large dining rooms, both with ocean-view windows (both non-smoking), are noisy, but the decor is attractive, although it is rather vivid. Dining in each restaurant is now in four seatings, for greater flexibility: 6pm, 6.45pm, 8pm and 8.45pm (these times are approximate).

Carnival meals stress quantity, not quality, although the company constantly works hard to improve the cui-

BERLITZ'S RATINGS		
	Possible	Achieved
Ship	500	395
Accommodation	200	151
Food	400	221
Service	400	270
Entertainment	100	81
Cruise	400	267

sine. While passengers seem to accept it, few find it worth remembering. However, food and its taste are still not the company's strongest points (you get what you pay for).

While the menu items sound good, their presentation and taste leave much to be desired. While meats are of a high quality, fish and seafood is not. Presentation is simple, and few garnishes are used. Many meat and fowl dishes are disguised with gravies and sauces. The selection of fresh green vegetables, breads, rolls, cheeses and fruits is limited, and there is too much use of canned fruit and jellied desserts. However, do remember that this is banquet catering, with all its attendant standardization and production cooking (it is, therefore, difficult to ask for anything remotely unusual or off-menu). The selection of breads, rolls, cheeses and fruits is limited (there is too much use of canned fruit).

Although there is a decent wine list, there are no wine waiters (the waiters are expected to serve both food and wine, which does not work well). The service is highly programmed, although the waiters are willing and reasonably friendly. However, the waiters do sing and dance (be prepared for *Simply the Best, Hot, Hot, Hot, Hot*, and other popular hits), and there are constant waiter parades; the dining room is show business – all done in the name of gratuities at the end of your cruise.

At night, the "Seaview Bistro," as the Windows on the Sea is known provides a casual (dress down) alternative to eating in the main dining rooms, serving pasta, steaks, salads and desserts (it typically is in operation between 6pm and 9pm).

In addition, there is a pâtisserie (Piazza Café) that offers specialty coffees and sweets (at an extra charge).

OTHER COMMENTS: Although externally angular and not handsome, *Fantasy* was the first in a series of eight almost identical, very successful ships built for Carnival Cruise Lines (and the company's fifth new ship). The ship, whose bows are extremely short, has the distinctive, large, swept-back wing-tipped funnel that is the trademark of Carnival Cruise Lines, in the company colors of red, white and blue. Almost vibration-free service is provided by the diesel electric propulsion system.

Decorative features include vibrant colors and an extensive use of neon lighting for total sensory stimulation. Has a six-deck-high atrium, topped by a large glass dome, features spectacular artistic centerpiece. The ship has expansive open deck areas, but they quickly become inadequate when it is full and everyone wants to be out on deck.

Inside, this ship has public entertainment lounges, bars and clubs galore, with something for everyone (except quiet space). There is a fine library and reading room, but few books. The handsome public rooms, connected by a wide indoor boulevard called "Via Marina" – with décor inspired by the ancient Roman city of Pompeii, beat a colorful mix of classic and contemporary design elements that beg your indulgence.

There is a multi-tiered showlounge is quite lavish, although 20 pillars obstruct the views from several seats. Dramatic three-deck-high glass enclosed health spa. The jogging track is "banked" for better running. The large casino has almost non-stop action, as one would expect aboard any Carnival Cruise Lines ship.

What should be of great interest to families, however, is a special partnership with Universal Studios' travel company, which packages a cruise together with a land stay and choice of three different theme parks: Universal Studios, Wet 'n Wild and Sea World. The pricing is competitive with that of the Disney land-cruise product.

Aboard the ship, kids will, I am sure, enjoy "Children's World," is a 2,500 sq. ft (230 sq. meter) play-area with games and fun stuff for kids of all ages, including Apple computers loaded with educational software, and an arts and crafts area with spin and sand art machines.

The cuisine is just so-so, but the real fun begins at sundown when Carnival really excels in sound, lights, razzle-dazzle shows and late-night sounds. From the futuristic Electricity Disco to the ancient Cleopatra's Bar, this ship will entertain you well.

Forget fashion – having fun is the *sine qua non* of a Carnival cruise. *Fantasy* features 3- and 4-day Bahamas cruises year-round, and is based on Port Canaveral. Gratuities are automatically added to your onboard account at $9.75 per person, per day (the amount charged when this book was completed); you can have this amount adjusted, although you'll have to visit the information desk to do so. The onboard currency is the US dollar.

WEAK POINTS: Standing in line for embarkation, disembarkation, shore tenders and for self-serve buffet meals is an inevitable aspect of cruising aboard all large ships. There is absolutely no escape from unnecessary and repetitious announcements (particularly for activities that bring revenue, such as art auctions, bingo, horse racing) that intrude constantly into your cruise, and a great deal of hustling for drinks, although it is sometimes done with a knowing smile.

Fascination
★★★ +

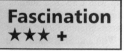

Large Ship:	.70,367 tons	Passengers		Cabin Current:	.110 volts

Large Ship: . . . . .70,367 tons
Lifestyle: . . . . .Standard
Cruise Line: . . . . . . .Carnival Cruise Lines
Former Names: . . . . .none
Builder: . . .Kvaerner Masa-Yards (Finland)
Original Cost: . . . .$315 million
Entered Service: . . . . .July 1994
Registry: . . . . .The Bahamas
Length (ft/m): 855.0/260.60
Beam (ft/m): 103.0/31.40
Draft (ft/m): 25.7/7.86
Propulsion/Propellers: . . . . .diesel-electric
(42,240kW)/2
Passenger Decks: 10
Total Crew: 920

Passengers
(lower beds/all berths): 2,056/2,634
Passenger Space Ratio
(lower beds/all berths): 34.4/26.7
Crew/Passenger Ratio
(lower beds/all berths): 2.2/2.8
Navigation Officers: . . . . .Italian
Cabins (total): 1,028
Size Range (sq ft/m): 173.2–409.7/
16.0–38.0
Cabins (outside view): 620
Cabins (interior/no view): 408
Cabins (for one person): 0
Cabins (with private balcony): 54
Cabins (wheelchair accessible): 22

Cabin Current: . . . . .110 volts
Elevators: 14
Casino (gaming tables): . . . . .Yes
Slot Machines: . . . . .Yes
Swimming Pools (outdoors): 3
Swimming Pools (indoors): 0
Whirlpools: 6
Fitness Center: . . . . .Yes
Sauna/Steam Room: . . . . .Yes/Yes
Massage: . . . . .Yes
Self-Service Launderette: . . . . .Yes
Dedicated Cinema/Seats: . . . . .No
Library: . . . . .Yes
Classification Society: . . .Lloyd's Register

OVERALL SCORE: 1,385 (OUT OF A POSSIBLE 2,000 POINTS)

ACCOMMODATION: As in sister ships *Ecstasy, Elation, Fantasy, Imagination, Inspiration, Paradise* and *Sensation*), the standard outside-view and interior (no view) cabins have plain décor. They are marginally comfortable, yet spacious enough and practical (most are of the same size and appointments), with good storage space and well-designed bathrooms.

Those booking one of the outside suites will find more space, whirlpool bathtubs, and some fascinating, rather eclectic décor and furniture. These are mildly attractive, but nothing special, and they are much smaller than those aboard the ships of a similar size of several competing companies.

A gift basket is provided in all grades of accommodation; it includes aloe soap, shampoo, conditioner, deodorant, breath mints, candy, and pain relief tablets (albeit all in sample sizes).

Note that if you book accommodation in one of the suites (Category 11 or 12 in the Carnival Cruise Lines brochure) you automatically qualify for "Skipper's Club" priority check-in at any US homeland port – useful for getting ahead of the crowd.

DINING: There are two large, noisy dining rooms (both are non-smoking) come with Carnival's typically usual efficient, fast but assertive service. The buffets are rather run-of-the-mill, with little creativity. Dining in each restaurant is now in four seatings, for greater flexibility: 6pm, 6.45pm, 8pm and 8.45pm (times are approximate).

Carnival meals stress quantity, not quality, although the company constantly works hard to improve the cui-

BERLITZ'S RATINGS

	Possible	Achieved
Ship	500	395
Accommodation	200	151
Food	400	221
Service	400	270
Entertainment	100	81
Cruise	400	267

sine. While passengers seem to accept it, few find it worth remembering. However, food and its taste are still not the company's strongest points (you get what you pay for).

While the menu items sound good, their presentation and taste leave much to be desired. While meats are of a high quality, fish and seafood is not. Presentation is simple, and few garnishes are used. Many meat and fowl dishes are disguised with gravies and sauces. The selection of fresh green vegetables, breads, rolls, cheeses and fruits is limited, and there is too much use of canned fruit and jellied desserts. However, do remember that this is banquet catering, with all its attendant standardization and production cooking (it is, therefore, difficult to ask for anything remotely unusual or off-menu). The selection of breads, rolls, cheeses and fruits is limited (there is too much use of canned fruit).

Although there is a decent wine list, there are no wine waiters (the waiters are expected to serve both food and wine, which does not work well). The service is highly programmed, although the waiters are willing and reasonably friendly. However, the waiters do sing and dance (be prepared for *Simply the Best, Hot, Hot, Hot, Hot,* and other popular hits), and there are constant waiter parades; the dining room is show business – all done in the name of gratuities at the end of your cruise.

At night, the "Seaview Bistro," as the Lido Café becomes known, provides a casual (dress down) alternative to eating in the main dining rooms, serving pasta, steaks, salads and desserts (it typically is in operation between 6pm and 9pm).

OTHER COMMENTS: Although externally angular and not handsome, *Fascination* is the fourth in a series of eight almost identical, very successful ships built for Carnival Cruise Lines (and the company's eighth new ship). The ship, whose bows are extremely short, has the distinctive, large, swept-back wing-tipped funnel that is the trademark of Carnival Cruise Lines, in the company colors of red, white and blue. Almost vibration-free service is provided by the diesel electric propulsion system.

The open deck areas are quite expansive, although they quickly become inadequate when the ship is full and everyone wants to be out on deck (the aft decks tend to be less noisy, whereas all the activities are focused around the main swimming pool and whirlpools). A well-defined "topless" sunbathing area can be found around the funnel base on Verandah Deck.

This is another ship that reflects the fine creative interior design work of Joe Farcus. It has a somewhat ungainly external profile, but the interior spaces have been well utilized. A dramatic atrium lobby spans six decks, and features cool marble and hot neon topped by a large glass dome and a spectacular artistic centerpiece called "Nucleus" which illustrates the kleig lights of a Hollywood premiere, according to Farcus.

The ship offers public entertainment lounges, bars and clubs galore, with something for everyone. The interior decor aboard all Carnival ships is themed; this one sports a sophisticated Hollywood theme that begs your indulgence. The principal public rooms are connected by a double-width indoor promenade. Excellent photo opportunities exist with some 24 superb life-like figures from the movies. Look for Marilyn Monroe and James Dean outside the casino at Stars Bar, while Humphrey Bogart and Ingrid Bergman are seated at the piano at Bogart's Café; Sophia Loren and Paul Newman are close by, and Vivien Leigh and Clark Gable can be found in Tara's Library. Meanwhile, John Wayne is for some reason at the entrance to the Passage to India Lounge, while Edward G. Robinson is inside. Outside the Diamonds Are Forever discotheque are Elizabeth Taylor and Elvis Presley. Lena Horne and Sydney Poitier can be found outside the Beverly Hills Bar, while inside are Katherine Hepburn and Spencer Tracy.

Just in case you want to gamble, you'll find Lucille Ball outside the casino. Incidentally, all the slot machines aboard all Carnival ships are linked into a big prize, called, naturally, Megacash.

The multi-tiered showlounge is lavish, and has good, though raucous, razzle-dazzle shows (sight lines are obscured from seats behind or adjacent to 20 pillars). There's a dramatic, well-segmented three-deck-high glass-enclosed health spa and gymnasium with the latest muscle-pump equipment. There's also a large shop, but it's stuffed to the gills with low-quality merchandise.

However, the real fun begins at sundown, when Carnival excels in decibels. There's no doubt that Carnival does "fun" better than anyone else, and if you want to party and live it up, then this ship should do it. Forget fashion – having fun is what Carnival's all about.

Fascination operates 3- and 4-day Caribbean cruises from Miami. Gratuities are automatically added to your onboard account at $9.75 per person, per day (the amount charged when this book was completed); you can have this amount adjusted, although you'll have to visit the information desk to do so. The onboard currency is the US dollar.

Passengers aged 16–19 now have their own hangout, called "Backstreet Club," with a CD jukebox stocked with up-to-date rock, R&B, rap and hip-hop hits, and a large dance floor. The facility has Apple iMac computers, Sony PlayStation 2 video game units, and a "mocktail lounge" – good for (non-alcoholic) drinks.

WEAK POINTS: Standing in line for embarkation, disembarkation, shore tenders and for self-serve buffet meals is an inevitable aspect of cruising aboard all large ships. There are fewer announcements in a military training camp. There is absolutely no escape from unnecessary and repetitive announcements (particularly for activities that bring revenue, such as art auctions, bingo, horse racing) that intrude constantly into your cruise, and a great deal of hustling for drinks, although it is sometimes done with a knowing smile.

✓   *Removed 2006*

Flamenco
★★ +

Mid-Size Ship: . . . . 17,042 tons
Lifestyle: . . . . Standard
Cruise Line: . . . . Festival Cruises
Former Names: *Southern Cross, Star/Ship*
Majestic, Sun Princess, Spirit of London
Builder: . . . . . .Cantieri Navale Del Tirreno
& Riuniti (Italy)
Original Cost: . . . . n/a
Entered Service: . . . . .Nov 1972/Dec 1997
Registry: . . . . .The Bahamas
Length (ft/m): 535.7/163.30
Beam (ft/m): 73.4/22.40
Draft (ft/m): 22.4/6.85
Propulsion/Propellers: . . . . .diesel
(13,450kW)/2
Passenger Decks: 7

Total Crew: 350
Passengers
(lower beds/all berths): 798/987
Passenger Space Ratio
(lower beds/all berths): 21.3/17.2
Crew/Passenger Ratio
(lower beds/all berths): 2.2/2.8
Navigation Officers: . . . . .Greek
Cabins (total): 401
Size Range (sq ft/m): 996.8–236.8/
9.0–22.0
Cabins (outside view): 272
Cabins (interior/no view): 129
Cabins (for one person): 4
Cabins (with private balcony): 0
Cabins (wheelchair accessible): 2

Cabin Current: . . . . .110 and 220 volts
Elevators: 4
Casino (gaming tables): . . . . .Yes
Slot Machines: . . . . .Yes
Swimming Pools (outdoors): 1
(+children's wading pool)
Swimming Pools (indoors): 0
Whirlpools: 0
Fitness Center: . . . . .Yes
Sauna/Steam Room: . . . . .No/No
Massage: . . . . .Yes
Self-Service Launderette: . . . . .No
Dedicated Cinema/Seats: Yes/186
Library: . . . . .Yes
Classification Society: . . .Lloyd's Register

OVERALL SCORE: 1,026 (OUT OF A POSSIBLE 2,000 POINTS)

ACCOMMODATION: There are 12 cabin price grades. Those described in the brochure as deluxe suites are reasonably spacious, with separate sleeping and living areas. All other interior and outside-view cabins are on the (very) small side, but quite well equipped, and with colorful soft furnishings. However, the cabin walls are really thin, which means you will be able to hear your next-door neighbors brushing their teeth. There is little drawer space. The cabin telephone system is rather antiquated. The bathrooms are compact but adequate, and have 100 percent cotton towels. The toilets are of the "gentle flush" and not the "barking dog suction" variety..

DINING: The Galaxy Restaurant (non-smoking), has two seatings and is quite airy, with a high ceiling and ocean-view porthole-shaped windows. However, it can be extremely noisy as the tables are very close together, as well as close to the waiter stations. The service standards are good, and being fine-tuned constantly. The quality of food and its presentation are reasonably good. There is a limited choice of breads, rolls, cheeses and fruits, which all tend to be quite standard. Informal self-service buffets for breakfast and lunch are quite decent, however, and well presented in the Satellite Cafe.

OTHER COMMENTS: This ship has a fairly handsome 1970s profile, with a rakish superstructure, an all-white hull, and a single large blue funnel. It underwent a $9 million refurbishment in 1997, after being acquired by

BERLITZ'S RATINGS

	Possible	Achieved
Ship	500	210
Accommodation	200	108
Food	400	227
Service	400	228
Entertainment	100	46
Cruise	400	207

Festival Cruises from its former owners, the now-defunct CTC Cruise Lines. There is a reasonable open deck and sunbathing space for a ship of this size, although it is tight when full, and there are no cushioned pads for the deck lounge chairs.

Inside the ship, the layout is practical. The public rooms are quite comfortable, with attractive décor and soft furnishings, while tasteful colors mixed with the extensive use of reflective surfaces provide an upbeat, contemporary feel, yet comfortable feel. Particularly nice is the Piano Bar/Casino lounge area, with its warm wood room dividers and long bar. But this is not a new ship, and cannot compare with the latest vessels. Where it does score highly is in the friendliness of the crew, which is very international.

This ship provides good very value for money, and a comfortable cruise experience in relaxed surroundings. Festival Cruises (called First European Cruises in the USA) specializes in "cruising for Europeans". The itineraries are well designed and include several sea days on longer voyages. The onboard currency is the euro.

WEAK POINTS: This is a high-density vessel, and so there will be some crowding during embarkation and disembarkation, as well as for tenders and buffets. There is no wrap-around promenade deck outdoors, although you *can* walk around the front sections of one of the open decks. There are too many loud announcements, in several languages. Non-smokers should be aware that many passengers, officers and staff are heavy smokers.

Removed 2006

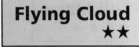

Flying Cloud
★★

Small Ship: . . . . .400 tons
Lifestyle: . . . . .Standard
Cruise Line: Windjammer Barefoot Cruises
Former Names: . . . .*Oisseau des Isles*
Builder: . . . .Ancione Chantiers Dibignon
(France)
Entered Service: 1935/1968
Registry: . . . . .Equatorial Guinea
Length (ft/m): 208.0/63.3
Beam (ft/m): 32.0/9.7
Draft (ft/m): 16.0/4.8
Type of Vessel: . . . . .barkentine
No. of Masts: 3
Sail Area (sq ft/m2): 10,500.5/975.5
Main Propulsion: . . . . .sail power

Propulsion/Propellers: diesel/1
Passenger Decks: 3
Total Crew: 28
Passengers
(lower beds/all berths): 66/66
Passenger Space Ratio
(lower beds/all berths): 5.8/5.8
Crew/Passenger Ratio
(lower beds/all berths): 2.3/2.3
Navigation Officers: . . . . . . .International
Cabins (total): 33
Size Range (sq ft/m): 60.2–148.0/
5.6–13.7
Cabins (outside view): 18
Cabins (interior/no view): 15

Cabins (for one person): 0
Cabins (with private balcony): 0
Cabins (wheelchair accessible): 0
Cabin Current: . . . . .110 volts
Elevators: 0
Casino (gaming tables): . . . . .No
Slot Machines: . . . . .No
Swimming Pools (outdoors): 0
Whirlpools: 0
Fitness Center: . . . . .No
Sauna/Steam Room: . . . . .No/No
Massage: . . . . .No
Self-Service Launderette: . . . . .No
Library: . . . . .Yes
Classification Society: . . . . .none

OVERALL SCORE: 902 (OUT OF A POSSIBLE 2,000 POINTS)

ACCOMMODATION: There are four grades. All are dimensionally challenged, particularly when compared to standard cruise ships, but this is a casual cruise experience and you will need so few clothes anyway. All are equipped with upper and lower berths, and most are quite narrow.

DINING: There is one dining room, and meals are all casual in style and service. Breakfast is served on board, as is dinner, while lunch could be either on board or at a beach, picnic-style.

OTHER COMMENTS: This ship was built in 1935 for the French Navy and originally was operated as a cadet sail-training vessel. Its interior décor includes such things as stained-glass windows, a spiral staircase, and lots of lovely wood, having been refurbished when Windjammer Barefoot Cruises bought her in 1968.

Aboard one of the Windjammer Barefoot Cruises' fleet you can let the crew do all the work, or you can lend a hand at the helm yourself, if you feel so inclined. One neat thing to do is just to sit or lie in the nets at the bows of the vessel, without a care in the world.

The mood is free and easy, the ships are equipped very simply, and only the most casual clothes are required (T-shirts and shorts), and shoes are optional, although you may need them if you go off in one of the ports. Quite possibly the most used item will be your bathing suit – better take more than one. Smoking is allowed only on the open decks.

BERLITZ'S RATINGS		
	Possible	Achieved
Ship	500	219
Accommodation	200	79
Food	400	166
Service	400	188
Entertainment	N/A	N/A
Cruise	500	250

Entertainment in the evenings consists of – you and the crew. You can put on a toga, take or create a pirate outfit and join in the fun. This is cruising free 'n' easy style – none of that programmed big-ship production show stuff here.

Jammin' aboard a Windjammer (first-time passengers are called "crewmates" while repeat passengers are called "jammers") is no-frills cruising. Indeed, it could be called an "anti-cruise." There's a no-nonsense, friendly environment, for the young at heart and those who don't feel the need for lots of programmed activities. It's all about going to sea and the romance of being at sea under sail. Those who enjoy beaches, scuba diving and snorkeling around the Caribbean will be best suited to a Windjammer Barefoot Cruises cruise.

Although itineraries (well, islands) are provided in the brochure, the captain actually decides which islands to go to in any given area, depending on sea and weather conditions. *Flying Cloud* features year-round cruises in the British and US Virgin Islands. Brochure rates might seem inexpensive, but you'll need to add on the airfare in order to get the true cost. Tips to the crew are suggested, at $50 per week.

This tall ship complies with all international safety regulations, with the exception of the 1966 fire safety standards. It sails from Tortola (British Virgin Islands). The onboard currency is the US dollar.

Other ships of the fleet which feature in this book are *Legacy, Mandalay, Polynesia,* and *Yankee Clipper.*

Fuji Maru
★★★ +

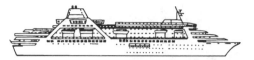

Small Ship: . . . . .23,340 tons	Passengers	Cabin Current: . . . . .100 volts
Lifestyle: . . . . .Standard	(lower beds/all berths): 328/603	Elevators: 5
Cruise Line: . . .Mitsui OSK Passenger Line	Passenger Space Ratio	Casino (gaming tables): . . . . .Yes
Former Names: . . . . .none	(lower beds/all berths): 71.1/38.7	(no cash can be won, only gifts)
Builder: . . . . .Mitsubishi (Japan)	Crew/Passenger Ratio	Slot Machines: . . . . .No
Original Cost: . . . .$63.5 million	(lower beds/all berths): 1.7/3.1	Swimming Pools (outdoors): 1
Entered Service: . . . . .Apr 1989	Navigation Officers: . . . . .Japanese	Swimming Pools (indoors): 0
Registry: .Japan	Cabins (total): 164	Whirlpools: . . . . .0 (4 Japanese Baths)
Length (ft/m): 547.9/167.00	Size Range (sq ft/m): 182.9–376.7/	Fitness Center: . . . . .Yes
Beam (ft/m): 78.7/24.00	17.0–35.0	Sauna/Steam Room: . . . . .Yes/No
Draft (ft/m): 21.4/6.55	Cabins (outside view): 164	Massage: . . . . .Yes
Propulsion/Propellers: . . . . .diesel	Cabins (interior/no view): 0	Self-Service Launderette: . . . . .Yes
(15,740kW)/2	Cabins (for one person): 0	Dedicated Cinema/Seats: Yes/142
Passenger Decks: 8	Cabins (with private balcony): 0	Library: . . . . .Yes
Total Crew: .190	Cabins (wheelchair accessible): 2	Classification Society: Nippon Kaiji Kyokai

---

OVERALL SCORE: 1,358 (OUT OF A POSSIBLE 2,000 POINTS)

ACCOMMODATION: There are two suites that are quite lovely, with separate bedroom and living room. The deluxe cabins are also of a good standard, and come with a vanity/writing desk, mini-bar/refrigerator, and full-sized, deep bathtub. Almost all of the other (standard) cabins are furnished very simply, but they are good for seminar and school cruises (they are much too small for any long voyages), with many accommodating three or four persons. The cabin insulation is reasonable, but could be better. The bathrooms are small and utilitarian, with old-style fixtures and some exposed plumbing. The folded blankets, a MOPAS (Mitsui OSK Passenger Line) tradition, are lovely.

DINING: The single, large dining room is quite attractive and has a high ceiling, but rather bright lighting, which makes it look more like a cafeteria or school dining hall. Both Japanese and Western cuisines are featured for all meals, in a single seating. The food itself is good, with simple, but colorful, presentation, and a good variety. There are several beverage machines around the ship, which are much appreciated by those attending seminars and training session cruises.

OTHER COMMENTS: *Fuji Maru* has a well thought-out, and flexible, design for multifunctional uses, but its principal use is for incentives, conventions, as a seminar and training ship, and only occasionally for individual passengers. The utilitarian outdoor decks are little used.

The interiors are plain and a little clinical, although there is some good artwork throughout to brighten things

BERLITZ'S RATINGS		
	Possible	Achieved
Ship	500	321
Accommodation	200	135
Food	400	287
Service	400	284
Entertainment	100	65
Cruise	400	266

up. There are extensive lecture and conference facilities. The largest and most flexible lecture hall is two decks high, seats 600, and converts into a sports stadium or exhibition hall for industrial product introductions. The lobby is quite elegant and open and is part of a two-level atrium.

The ship has a classic, wood-paneled library. Other features include two Japanese-style grand baths and a traditional Washitsu tatami mat room. A Hanaguruma owner's room is reasonably elegant for small formal functions. The Sakura Salon is soothing, with a blend of Western and traditional Japanese design. The media and TV systems include much high-tech equipment.

This is a fascinating exhibition, training, and educational charter cruise ship that has reasonably up-to-date facilities, although it is not ideally designed for individual passengers. As in any ship for Japanese passengers, tipping is not allowed. There are many more modern ships in the international marketplace (also serving Japanese passengers), with better facilities, more dining choices, and a less utilitarian feel and ambience, and so the score for this ship has been adjusted slightly downwards.

A specialist courier company will collect your luggage from your home before the cruise, and deliver it back after the cruise (this service available only in Japan). The onboard currency is the Japanese yen.

WEAK POINTS: The waste of open deck space, and poor maintenance of it. The deck furniture is plastic and utilitarian. The lighting is too bright, which also increases the noise level, and so there is little ambience.

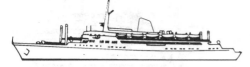

Funchal
★★ +

Small Ship . . . . .9,563 tons	Passengers	Cabin Current: . . . . .220 volts
Lifestyle: . . . . .Standard	(lower beds/all berths): 430/524	Elevators: 3
Cruise Line: Classic International Cruises	Passenger Space Ratio	Casino (gaming tables): . . . . .Yes
Former Names: . . . . .none	(lower beds/all berths): 22.218.2	Slot Machines: .Yes
Builder: . . .Helsingor Skibsvog (Denmark)	Crew/Passenger Ratio	Swimming Pools (outdoors): 1
Original Cost: .n/a	(lower beds/all berths): 2.7/3.3	Swimming Pools (indoors): 0
Entered Service: . . . . .Oct 1961/May 1986	Navigation Officers: . . .Greek/Portuguese	Whirlpools: 0
Registry: . . . . .Panama	Cabins (total): 222	Fitness Center: . . . . .Yes
Length (ft/m): 503.6/153.51	Size Range (sq ft/m): 102.2–252.9/	Sauna/Steam Room: . . . . .Yes/No
Beam (ft/m): 62.5/19.08	9.5–23.5	Massage: . . . . .No
Draft (ft/m): 20.3/6.20	Cabins (outside view): 151	Self-Service Launderette: . . . . .No
Propulsion/Propellers: . . . . .diesel	Cabins (interior/no view): 71	Dedicated Cinema/Seats: . . . . .No
(7,356kW)/2	Cabins (for one person): 14	Library: . . . . .Yes
Passenger Decks: 6	Cabins (with private balcony): 0	Classification Society: . . . . .Rinave
Total Crew: .155	Cabins (wheelchair accessible): 0	Portuguesa

OVERALL SCORE: 1,089 (OUT OF A POSSIBLE 2,000 POINTS)

ACCOMMODATION: The cabins are extremely compact yet tastefully appointed, and come in both twin and double-bedded configurations. Each now has a private bathroom, and there is just enough closet and drawer space providing you don't pack too many clothes. The cabins are decorated in very plain colors, accented with colorful soft furnishings. All cabin bathrooms have soap, shampoo, shower cap, shoeshine and sewing kits, and bathrobe.

DINING: There are two tastefully decorated dining rooms, Coimbra (which doubles as a video screening room after dinner) and Lisboa. Both have large ocean-view picture windows on port and starboard sides. There is just one seating. The food is European in style (and includes plenty of fresh fish) and is surprisingly good, as is the service from friendly Portuguese waiters. There is a decent selection of breads, cheeses and fruits, and the wine list includes Portuguese wines at modest prices.

OTHER COMMENTS: *Funchal* has a classic 1960s small ship profile with well balanced, rounded lines, and pleasing real wooden decks (no synthetic turf anywhere), including one outdoor deck with two sheltered promenades, although they do not completely encircle the ship. Its interiors have an abundance of fine woodwork and heavy-duty fittings. One deck houses all the main public rooms, the most appealing of which is the Porto Bar, reminiscent of a classy 19th century drinking club. A highly polished wooden spiral stairway is a beautiful, classic piece of decoration not found today's

BERLITZ'S RATINGS

	Possible	Achieved
Ship	500	225
Accommodation	200	101
Food	400	242
Service	400	250
Entertainment	100	58
Cruise	400	213

ships, and is reminiscent of the days of the transatlantic steamers of the early 20th century.

The mostly Portuguese staff is friendly and quite attentive, although a little reserved at first. This ship is popular with Europeans and Scandinavians during the summer and Brazilians during the winter. It provides destination-intensive cruises in a comfortable, old-world atmosphere, ideally suited to couples and solo passengers seeking good value for money and a good balance of sea days and port days, and who dislike large "warehouse" ships.There are many loyal repeat passengers.

Funchal is like an old, well-worn shoe – comfortable, but in need of a little spit and polish, and so it hovers just a tad under the three-star level (a two-and-a-half star vessel with a three-star heart). The ship and overall product is actually quite good if you enjoy small, vintage vessels with all their accompanying eccentricities. While the ship cannot be compared to the latest brand new, larger ships, *Funchal* has delightful old-world character and charm. The feeling of camaraderie and friendliness from the loyal crew (many of whom have been aboard the ship for many years) offsets some of the hardware negatives. The ship often operates under charter to various tour packagers and operators. The onboard currency is the euro.

WEAK POINTS: The open deck space for sunbathing is very small for the number of passengers carried, as is the number of deck lounge chairs available. The show lounge is poor.

Galapagos Explorer II
★★★ +

Small Ship: ....3,990 tons		Passengers		Cabin Current: ....110 volts	
Lifestyle: ....Premium		(lower beds/all berths): 100/111		Elevators: 1	
Cruise Line: ....Kleintours		Passenger Space Ratio		Casino (gaming tables): ....Yes	
Former Names: ......*Renaissance Three*		(lower beds/all berths): 39.9/35.9		Slot Machines: ....Yes	
Builder: .....Cantieri Navale Ferrari (Italy)		Crew/Passenger Ratio		Swimming Pools (outdoors): 1	
Original Cost: ....$20 million		(lower beds/all berths): 1.3/1.5		Swimming Pools (indoors): 0	
Entered Service: .....Aug 1990/Jan 1998		Navigation Officers: ....International		Whirlpools: 1	
Registry: ....Liberia		Cabins (total): 50		Fitness Center: ....No	
Length (ft/m): 289.6/88.30		Size Range (sq ft/m): 231.4–282.0/		Sauna/Steam Room: ....Yes/No	
Beam (ft/m): 50.1/15.30		21.5–26.2		Massage: ....No	
Draft (ft/m): 11.9/3.65		Cabins (outside view): 50		Self-Service Launderette: ....No	
Propulsion/Propellers: ....diesel		Cabins (interior/no view): 0		Dedicated Cinema/Seats: ....No	
(3,514kW)/2		Cabins (for one person): 0		Library: ....No	
Passenger Decks: 5		Cabins (with private balcony): 4		Classification Society: ...Registro Navale	
Total Crew: 72		Cabins (wheelchair accessible): 0		Italiano (RINA)	

OVERALL SCORE: 1,365 (OUT OF A POSSIBLE 2,000 POINTS)

ACCOMMODATION: This is located forward, with public rooms aft. Pleasant, all-outside cabins have a large picture window and combine gorgeous, highly polished imitation rosewood paneling with lots of mirrors, hand-crafted Italian furniture, and wet bar. All cabins feature a queen-sized bed, a sitting area, a mini-bar/refrigerator, TV set, VCR and hairdryer. The cabins have small closets, however; space for luggage is quite tight. The small bathrooms have showers (none have bathtubs) with a fold-down seat, real teakwood floors and marble vanities.

BERLITZ'S RATINGS

	Possible	Achieved
Ship	500	361
Accommodation	200	156
Food	400	244
Service	400	287
Entertainment	N/A	N/A
Cruise	500	317

DINING: The dining room has open seating, so you can sit where you like. It is small and elegant, and is in three sections. There are tables for two, four, six, and even eight. The meals are self-service buffet-style cold foods for breakfast and lunch (sometimes lunch will be on deck), with local delicacies. Food quality, choice and presentation are decent, but not that memorable. There is limited choice, particularly with regard to the entrées.

OTHER COMMENTS: *Galápagos Explorer II* is comfortable and inviting, but has not been particularly well maintained. Water sports facilities include an aft platform, sailfish, snorkel equipment, and several zodiacs.

It has contemporary mega-yacht looks and handsome styling. There is a wooden promenade deck outdoors. The limited number of public rooms have smart and restful décor. The main lounge doubles as a lecture room, but the piano bar is the best place to relax in the evening.

This ship provides a destination-intensive, refined, quiet and relaxed cruise for those who don't like crowds or dressing up. Naturalist guides trained at the Darwin Station lead the guided shore excursions (included in the fare).

If you *are* going on a Galápagos cruise, it is important to take along passport, short and long-sleeve cotton shirts, good walking shoes, windbreaker, mosquito repellent, sunglasses with retaining strap, and personal medication. You will need to fly from Quito to San Cristobal (via Guayaquil) to join your cruise.

Galápagos Explorer II operates three-, four-, and seven night Galápagos cruises year-round from San Cristobal. Liquor, beer, cocktails, bottled water and soft drinks are included in the fare, but wine and champagne are not. Also included are guided visits to the islands. The brochure rates may or may not include the Galapagos Islands visitor tax (about $100 depending where you book). If the cruise rates do not include the visitor tax, note that under present rules it must be paid *in cash* at Guayaquil or Quito airports or in the islands. Shore visits take place in "pangas" (local lingo for "dinghies"). Gratuities for shipboard staff are excessive, at a recommended $80 per person, per seven-night cruise. The onboard currency is the US dollar or Ecuadorian sucre.

WEAK POINTS: The tiny "dip" pool is not a swimming pool. The open deck and sunbathing space is cramped. Plastic wood is used everywhere (but it looks good). While the service is without finesse, the crew is willing. The small library is attractive, but book selection is poor. The ship does not sail well in inclement weather.

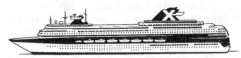

Galaxy
★★★★ +

Large Ship: ....77,713 tons	Passengers		Cabin Current: ....110 and 220 volts	
Lifestyle: ....Premium	(lower beds/all berths): 1,870/2,681		Elevators: 10	
Cruise Line: ....Celebrity Cruises	Passenger Space Ratio		Casino (gaming tables): ....Yes	
Former Names: ....none	(lower beds/all berths): 41.5/28.9		Slot Machines: ....Yes	
Builder: ....Meyer Werft (Germany)	Crew/Passenger Ratio		Swimming Pools (outdoors): 2	
Original Cost: ....$320 million	(lower beds/all berths): 2.0/2.9		Swimming Pools (indoors): 1	
Entered Service: ....Dec 1996	Navigation Officers: ....Greek		indoor/outdoor (magrodome)	
Registry: ....The Bahamas	Cabins (total): 935		Whirlpools: 4	
Length (ft/m): 865.8/263.9	Size Range (sq ft/m): 168.9–1,514.5/		Fitness Center: ....Yes	
Beam (ft/m): 105.6/32.20	15.7–140.7		Sauna/Steam Room: ....Yes/Yes	
Draft (ft/m): 25.2/7.70	Cabins (outside view): 639		Massage:........................Yes	
Propulsion/Propellers: ....diesel	Cabins (interior/no view): 296		Self-Service Launderette: ....No	
(31,500kW)/2	Cabins (for one person): 0		Dedicated Cinema/Seats: Yes/200	
Passenger Decks:..................10	Cabins (with private balcony): 220		Library: ....Yes	
Total Crew: 909	Cabins (wheelchair accessible): 8		Classification Society: ...Lloyd's Register	

OVERALL SCORE: 1,663 (OUT OF A POSSIBLE 2,000 POINTS)

ACCOMMODATION: There are 15 different grades, depending on your preference for the size and location of your living space, but the accommodation is extremely comfortable throughout this ship. Suites have more space, butler service (whether you want it or not), more and better amenities and more personal service than any of the standard cabin grades.

Occupants of all accommodation designated as suites get gold cards to open their doors (and priority service throughout the ship, free cappuccino/espresso coffees when served by a butler, welcome champagne, flowers, VCR, and use of the AquaSpa thalassotherapy pool). All occupants of standard (interior no view and outside-view) cabins have white cards. Suites that have private balconies also have floor-to-ceiling windows and sliding doors to balconies (a few suites have outward opening doors).

No matter what grade you choose, all suites and cabins haveinteractive television for booking shore excursions, ordering room service, playing electronic casino games and buying goods from the ship's boutiques (available in English, French, German, Italian and Spanish). So you don't have to leave your quarters if you don't wish to, especially if you dislike the ports of call.

Most of the suites with private balconies have floor-to-ceiling windows and sliding doors to balconies (a few have outward opening doors). All accommodation designated as suites have duvets on the beds instead of sheets/blankets. In-suite massage service is available (with the right balcony, such as those in the Sky Suites, this is an excellent service).

BERLITZ'S RATINGS

	Possible	Achieved
Ship	500	444
Accommodation	200	177
Food	400	315
Service	400	319
Entertainment	100	78
Cruise	400	330

PENTHOUSE SUITES: These two suites, located amidships, are the largest suites. Each measures 1,173 sq. ft (108.9 sq. meters), and comes with its own butler's pantry. There is an inter-connecting door so that it can link to the suite next door to become an impressive 1,515-sq. ft (141-sq. meter) apartment.

Most of the Deck 10 suites and cabins are of generous proportions, are beautifully equipped, and have balconies with full floor-to-ceiling partitions, as well as VCRs. The Sky Deck suites are also excellent, and have huge balconies (sadly, the partitions are not quite of the floor-to-ceiling type – so you can hear your neighbors or you may be subjected to their cigar or cigarette smoke). Also included are wall clock, large floor-to-ceiling mirrors, marble-topped vanity/writing desk, excellent closet and drawer space, and even dimmer-controlled ceiling lights.

STANDARD OUTSIDE-VIEW/INTERIOR (NO VIEW)-CABINS: All of the standard interior and outside cabins are of a good size and come nicely furnished with twin beds that convert to a queen-sized unit. The bathrooms, in particular, are spacious and come well equipped (with generous-size showers, hairdryers, and space for personal toiletry items). Baby-monitoring telephones are also in all cabins. But there are no cabins for singles.

DINING: The Orion Restaurant is a huge two-level dining hall. It is reminiscent of the dining halls aboard the ocean liners of the 1930s, with a grand staircase that flows between both levels and perimeter alcoves that provide more intimate dining spaces. Each level of the dining room has its own separate galley, and the noise level in the two sections is quite acceptable (more noise is noticeable on the larger, lower level, however). There are two seatings for dinner (open seating for breakfast and lunch), at tables for two, four, six, eight or 10, and the dining room is a totally no-smoking area.

The cuisine is based on menus created by Michel Roux, and executed by the chefs and cooks on board. The food has lots of taste (in particular, the sauces that accompany many of the main dishes); it also has fine color balance, and is nicely presented.

Just outside the lower-level entrance to the dining room, a champagne and caviar bar features ossetra and sevruga caviar – well presented with all the trimmings, and, of course, champagne and vodka to go with it.

For informal breakfasts and lunches, there is a two-level Oasis (lido) Cafe with several serving lines (it has a warm wood-accented décor), and eight bay windows provide some really prime seating spots. There are also two poolside grills – one located adjacent to the midships pools, the other wedged into the aft pool.

In addition, Tastings is a coffee lounge and bar for specialty coffees and pastries. For passengers in the two Presidential and 48 other suites, in-cabin dining is an option. However, the food served as room-service items is decidedly below the standard of food featured in the dining room. For those who can't live without them, freshly baked pizzas (in a box) can be delivered, in an insulated pouch, to your cabin.

Celebrity Cruises is known for its excellent cuisine and presentation, and, although it is more difficult to deliver aboard the new, larger ships, Celebrity Cruises seems to have got it just right.

OTHER COMMENTS: Slightly longer than sister ship *Century* (by 45.9 ft/14 meters), *Galaxy*'s extra length provides room for a third swimming pool, which is covered by a large glass magrodome. Although there are more than 4.5 acres (1.8 hectares) of space on the open decks, it does seem a little small and crowded when the ship is full.

Inside, there are two foyers (atriums); one is a four-deck-high main foyer, and the second is a three-deck-high atrium. There is a 1,000-seat showlounge with large side balconies and good sight lines from just about every seat. There is also a small, dedicated cinema, which doubles as a conference and meeting center with all the latest audio-visual technology that includes simultaneous translation in three languages and headsets for the hearing-impaired.

The AquaSpa, which has proved extremely popular aboard *Century*, contains 9,040 sq. ft (840 sq. meters) of space dedicated to well-being and body treatments, and includes a large fitness/exercise area, complete with all the latest high-tech muscle machines and video cycles.

The ship has a superb, somewhat whimsical collection of artwork, which casts an eclectic look at life in some of its many forms. The collection is the result of the personal work of Christina Chandris. The company's "zero announcement" policy is much appreciated by its passengers.

Apart from the "front of house" aspects of this ship, it is the "back of house" facilities, the design and flow of the main galley (23,700 sq. ft/2,200 sq. meters), where the ship really shines. The consideration for safety is second to none. This ship also has excellent tender loading platforms.

"Stratosphere," the large combination observation lounge (with forward-facing as well as wrap-around views) and discotheque, provides what is probably the best viewing room when the ship operates Alaska cruises.

For a big-ship cruise experience, this one has just about all you need to have an enjoyable and rewarding cruise experience. *Galaxy* delivers a fine product that is worth much more than the cruise fare charged when compared to several other large-ship cruise lines. Note that a 15 percent gratuity is automatically added to all bar and wine accounts. The onboard currency is the US dollar.

During the past two years (after Celebrity Cruises was bought by Royal Caribbean International), the standard of product delivery aboard all the ships in the Celebrity Cruises fleet went down as cuts were made by the new owner. However, as this book was being completed, new management was brought in to bring Celebrity Cruises back to the premium product that was envisioned when the company first started. I (and many passengers) look forward to the improvements.

WEAK POINTS: Although this is a beautiful ship, the shore excursion operation, embarkation and disembarkation remain weak links in the Celebrity Cruises operation, and the cruise staff is unpolished and has little finesse. Standing in line for embarkation, disembarkation, shore tenders and for self-serve buffet meals is an inevitable aspect of cruising aboard all large ships. The room service menu is quite poor, and room service food items are below the standard of food served in the dining room. The interactive television system can prove frustrating to use, and the larger suites have several remotes for television/audio equipment (one would be better). The one area of congestion is the Photo Gallery, when passenger flow at peak evening times is impeded. The officers have become more aloof lately, with far less contact with passengers than in the company's early days.

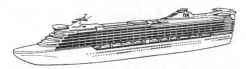

Golden Princess
★★★★

Large Ship: ....108,865 tons	Passengers	Cabin Current: ....110 and 220 volts
Lifestyle: ....Standard	(lower beds/all berths): 2,600/3,100	Elevators: 14
Cruise Line: ....Princess Cruises	Passenger Space Ratio	Casino (gaming tables): ....Yes
Former Names: ....none	(lower beds/all berths): 41.8/35.1	Slot Machines: ....Yes
Builder: ....Fincantieri (Italy)	Crew/Passenger Ratio	Swimming Pools (outdoors): 4
Original Cost: ....$450 million	(lower beds/all berths): 2.3/2.8	Swimming Pools (indoors): 0
Entered Service: ....May 2001	Navigation Officers: ......British/Italian	Whirlpools: 9
Registry: ....Bermuda	Cabins (total): 1,300	Fitness Center: ....Yes
Length (ft/m): 951.4/290.0	Size Range (sq ft/m): 161.4–764.2/	Sauna/Steam Room: ....Yes/Yes
Beam (ft/m): 118.1/36.0	15.0–71.0	Massage: ....Yes
Draft (ft/m): 26.2/8.0	Cabins (outside view): 928	Self-Service Launderette: ....Yes
Propulsion/Propellers: .....diesel-electric	Cabins (interior/no view): 372	Dedicated Cinema/Seats: ....No
(42,000kW)/2	Cabins (for one person): 0	Library: ....Yes
Passenger Decks:..................13	Cabins (with private balcony): 710	Classification Society: ...Registro Navale
Total Crew: 1,100	Cabins (wheelchair accessible): 28	Italiano (RINA)
	(18 outside/10 interior)	

OVERALL SCORE: 1,549 (OUT OF A POSSIBLE 2,000 POINTS)

ACCOMMODATION: There are six principal types of cabins and configurations: (a) grand suite, (b) suite, (c) mini-suite, (d) outside double with balcony, (e) outside double, and (f) interior (no view) double. There are, however, 35 different brochure price categories; the choice is bewildering for both travel agents and passengers. Pricing depends on two things, size and location.

(a) The largest, most lavish suite is the Grand Suite (B748, which is located at the ship's stern – a different position to the *two* Grand Suites aboard sister ship *Grand Princess*). It features a large bedroom with a queen-sized bed, huge walk-in (illuminated) closets, two bathrooms, a lounge (with fireplace and sofa bed) with wet bar and refrigerator, and a large private balcony (with hot tub that can be accessed from both balcony and bedroom).

(b/c) Suites (with a semi-private balcony) have a separate living room (with sofa bed) and bedroom (with a TV set in each). The bathroom is quite large and has both a bathtub and shower stall. The mini-suites also have a semi-private balcony, and a separate living and sleeping area (with a television in each). The bathroom is also quite spacious, with both a bathtub and shower stall. The differences between the suites and mini-suites are basically in the size and appointments, the suite being more of a square shape while mini-suites are more rectangular, and have few drawers. Plush bathrobes and fully tiled bathrooms with ample open shelf storage space are provided.

BERLITZ'S RATINGS

	Possible	Achieved
Ship	500	436
Accommodation	200	168
Food	400	256
Service	400	293
Entertainment	100	82
Cruise	400	314

Passengers occupying the best suites receive greater attention, including priority embarkation and disembarkation privileges. What is not good is that some of the most expensive accommodation has only semi-private balconies that can be seen from above, so there is no privacy whatsoever (Suites C401, 402, 409, 410, 414, 415, 420, 421, 422, 423, 424 and 425 on Caribe Deck in particular). Also, the suites D105 and D106 (Dolphin Deck), which are extremely large, have balconies that can be seen from above.

(d/e/f) The standard interior and outside-view (the outsides come either with or without private balcony) cabins are of a functional, practical, design, although almost no drawers are provided. They are very attractive, with warm, pleasing décor and fine soft furnishing fabrics.

Additionally, two family suites consist of two suites with an interconnecting door, plus a large balcony. These can sleep up to 10 (if at least four are children, or up to eight people if all are adults).

All passengers receive turndown service and chocolates on pillows each night, as well as bathrobes (on request) and toiletry amenity kits (larger, naturally, for suite/mini-suite occupants) that typically include soap, shampoo, conditioner, and hand/body lotion. A hairdryer is provided in all cabins, sensibly located at the vanity desk unit in the living area. All bathrooms are tiled and have a decent amount of open shelf storage space for personal toiletries. Princess Cruises features BBC World, CNN, CNBC, ESPN and TNT on the in-cabin color television system (when available, depending on cruise area).

Most outside cabins on Emerald Deck have views obstructed by the lifeboats. Your name is placed outside your suite or cabin – making it simple for delivery service personnel but also making it intrusive with regard to your privacy. Some cabins can accommodate a third and fourth person in upper berths. However, in such cabins, the lower beds cannot then be pushed together to make queen-sized bed. There are no cabins for singles.

Almost all balcony suites and cabins can be overlooked both from the navigation bridge wing, as well as from the port and starboard sections of the ship's discotheque – located high above the ship at the stern. Cabins with balconies on Dolphin, Caribe and Baja decks are also overlooked by passengers on balconies on the deck above; they are, therefore, not at all private. However, perhaps the least desirable balcony cabins are the eight located forward on Emerald Deck, as the balconies do not extend to the side of the ship and can be passed by walkers and gawkers on the adjacent Upper Promenade walkway (so occupants need to keep their curtains closed most of the time). Also, passengers occupying some the most expensive suites with balconies at the stern of the vessel may experience considerable vibration during certain ship maneuvers.

DINING: There are a number of "Personal Choice" dining options. For formal meals there are three principal dining rooms (Bernini, Canaletto, and Donatello). There are two seatings in one restaurant, while "anytime dining" (where you choose when and with whom you want to eat) is typically featured in the other two. All three are non-smoking and split into multi-tier sections in a non-symmetrical design that breaks what are quite large spaces into many smaller sections, for better ambience. Each dining room has its own galley.

Specially designed dinnerware and good quality linens and silverware are featured; by Dudson of England (dinnerware), Frette Egyptian cotton table linens, and silverware by Hepp of Germany. Note that 15 percent is added to all beverage bills, including wines.

Although portions are generous, the food and its presentation are disappointing and bland. The quality of fish is poor (often disguised by crumb or batter coatings), the selection of fresh green vegetables is limited, and few garnishes are used. However, do remember that this *is* big-ship banquet catering, with all its attendant standardization and production cooking. Meats are of a decent quality, although often disguised by gravy-based sauces, and pasta dishes are acceptable (though voluminous), and are typically served by section headwaiters who, in search of gratuities, may also make "something special just for you." If you like desserts, order a sundae at dinner, as most other desserts are just so-so. Ice cream ordered in the dining room is included, but if you order one anywhere else, you'll have to pay for it.

On any given cruise, the menu cycle will typically include such themes as Sailaway Dinner, Captain's Welcome Dinner, Chef's Dinner, Italian Dinner, French Dinner, Captain's Gala Dinner, and a Landfall Dinner.

There are two alternative informal dining areas: *Sabatini's Trattoria* and *Desert Rose*. Both are open for lunch and dinner. *Sabatini's* is an Italian eatery, with colorful tiled Mediterranean-style decor; it is named after *Trattoria Sabatini*, the 200-year old institution in Florence (where there is no cover charge). It has Italian-style pizzas and pastas, with a variety of sauces, as well as Italian-style entrées (including tiger prawns and lobster tail). *Sabatini's* is by reservation only, and there is a cover charge of $15 per person, for lunch or dinner (on sea days only).

Desert Rose features "southwestern American food"; by reservation only, with a cover charge of $8 per person, for lunch or dinner on sea days only. However, do note that *Desert Rose* is spread over the whole beam (width) of the ship, and two walkways intersect it, which means that it's a very open area, with people walking through it as you eat. The cuisine in both of these spots is decidedly better than in the three main dining rooms.

A poolside hamburger grill and pizza bar (no additional charge) are additional dining spots for casual bites, while extra charges will apply if you order items to eat at either the coffee bar/pâtisserie, or the caviar/champagne bar.

Other casual meals can be taken in the Horizon Court – open 24 hours a day, with large ocean-view on port and starboard sides and direct access to the two principal swimming pools and lido deck (there is no real finesse in presentation, however, as plastic plates are provided).

OTHER COMMENTS: *Golden Princess* presents a bold, forthright profile, with a racy "spoiler" effect at the stern that I personally do not consider handsome (this acts as an observation lounge with aft-facing views by day, and a noise-polluting discotheque by night). The ship has a flared snub-nosed bow and a galleon-like transom stern. At 118 ft/36 meters (but more than 43 ft/13 meters wider than the canal, including the navigation bridge wings) *Golden Princess* is too wide to transit the Panama Canal, with many balcony cabins overhanging the ship's hull.

There is a good sheltered teakwood promenade deck, which almost wraps around (three times round is equal to one mile) and a walkway which goes right to the (enclosed, protected) bow of the ship. The outdoor pools have various beach-like surroundings. One lap pool has a pumped "current" to swim against.

Unlike the outside decks, there is plenty of space inside the ship (but there are also plenty of passengers), and a wide array of public rooms to choose from, with many "intimate" (this being a relative word) spaces and places to play. The passenger flow has been well thought-out, and works with little congestion. The décor is very attractive, with lots of earth tones (well suited to both American and European tastes). In fact, this ship is the culmination of the best of all that Princess Cruises has to offer from its many years of operating what is now a well-tuned, good quality product.

Four areas center on swimming pools, one of which is two decks high and is covered by a magrodome, itself an extension of the funnel housing. A large health spa complex surrounds one of the swimming pools (you can have a massage or other spa treatment in an ocean-view treatment room). High atop the stern of the ship is a ship-wide glass-walled disco pod (I have nicknamed it the ETR – energy transfer room). It looks like an aerodynamic "spoiler" and is positioned high above the water, with spectacular views from the extreme port and starboard side windows.

An extensive collection of art works has been chosen, and this complements the elegant, non-glitzy interior design and colors well. If you see something you like, you will be able to purchase it on board – it's probably for sale.

This ship also features a Wedding Chapel (a live webcam can relay ceremonies via the internet). The ship's captain can legally marry (American) couples, due to the ship's Bermuda registry and a special dispensation (this should, however, be verified when in the planning stage, and may vary according to where you reside). Princess Cruises offers three wedding packages: Pearl, Emerald, Diamond – the fee includes registration and official marriage certificate. However, to get married *and* take your close family members and entourage with you on your honeymoon is going to cost a lot. The "Hearts & Minds" chapel can also be used for "renewal of vows" ceremonies.

Teenagers (and others) might like the array of video games ($0.50 to $3 per game), while photo enthusiasts should find "FX" (the digital photo shop) of interest – you can have your photo morphed into almost any setting. For children there is a two-deck-high playroom and teen room located in the forward section of the ship (although the video games room is located at the opposite end of the ship), and a host of trained counselors.

For entertainment, Princess Cruises prides itself on its glamorous all-American production shows, and the shows aboard this ship will not disappoint. Neither will the comfortable showlounges (the largest of which features $3 million in sound and light equipment as well as a scenery loading bay that connects directly from stage to a hull door for direct transfer to the dockside). Two other entertainment lounges help spread things around. Casino lovers should enjoy the large casino, with more than 260 slot machines. There are blackjack, craps and roulette tables, plus newer games such as Let It Ride Bonus, Spanish 21 and Caribbean Draw Progressive.

Ship lovers should enjoy the wood-paneled Wheelhouse Bar, finely decorated with memorabilia and ship models tracing part of parent company P&O's history. There is an Internet Café, with a couple of dozen AOL-linked computer terminals ($7.50 per 15 minutes when this book was completed); but it should be called an Internet Center, as there is no café – not even any coffee.

Princess Cays – Princess Cruises' own "private island" in the Caribbean – is "yours" (along with a couple of thousand other passengers) for a day on Caribbean itineraries; however, you will need to take a shore tender to get to and from it, and this can take some time. A high-tech hospital is provided, with live SeaMed telemedicine link-up to specialists at the Cedars-Sinai Medical Center in Los Angeles available for emergency help (hardly useful for international passengers who don't reside in the USA).

The dress code has been simplified – reduced to formal or smart casual (whatever that means). Note that gratuities to staff are *automatically* added to your account, at $10 per person, per day (gratuities for children are charged at the same rate). If you want to pay less, you'll need to go to the reception desk to have these charges adjusted (that could mean lining up with many other passengers wanting to do the same).

Whether this really can be considered a relaxing vacation is a moot point, but with *many choices* and "small" rooms to enjoy, the ship has been extremely well designed, and the odds are that you'll have a fine cruise vacation, in a controlled, well packaged way. The onboard currency is the US dollar.

WEAK POINTS: The cabin bath towels are too small, and drawer space is limited. There are no butlers – even for the top-grade suites. Cabin attendants have too many cabins to look after (typically 20), which cannot possibly translate to fine personal service.

The automated telephone system is truly frustrating to use, and luggage delivery is inefficient. Lines form for many things, but particularly for the purser's desk, and for open-seating breakfast and lunch in the three main dining rooms. Long lines for embarkation (an "express check-in" option is available by completing certain documentation 40 days in advance of your cruise), disembarkation, shore excursions and shore tenders are also a fact of life aboard large ships such as this one, as is waiting for elevators at peak times.

You'll have to live with the many extra charge items (such as for ice cream, and fresh squeezed orange juice) and activities (such as yoga, group exercise bicycling and kick boxing classes at $10 per session, not to mention $4 per hour for *group* babysitting services). Some of the spa (massage) treatment rooms are located directly underneath the basketball court, which makes it utterly frustrating trying to relax while the ceiling above your head is being pounded by bouncing balls. There's also a charge for using the washers ($1) and dryers ($0.50) in the self-service launderettes.

Passengers are also forced to endure countless pieces of (highly questionable) art found in almost every foyer and public room – an annoying reminder that today, cruising aboard such large ships is really like living in a bazaar of paintings surrounded by a ship. Now, what am I bid for this piece of art that is really worth only $10 – let's hear it – $1,200, do I hear $1,400, or will someone actually think it's worth more?

Grand Princess
★★★★

Large Ship: ....108,806 tons	Passengers	Cabin Current: ....110 and 220 volts
Lifestyle: ....Standard	(lower beds/all berths): 2,600/3,100	Elevators: 14
Cruise Line: ....Princess Cruises	Passenger Space Ratio	Casino (gaming tables): ....Yes
Former Names: ....none	(lower beds/all berths): 41.8/35.0	Slot Machines: ....Yes
Builder: ....Fincantieri (Italy)	Crew/Passenger Ratio	Swimming Pools (outdoors): 4
Original Cost: ....$450 million	(lower beds/all berths): 2.3/2.8	Swimming Pools (indoors): 0
Entered Service: ....May 1998	Navigation Officers: ......British/Italian	Whirlpools: 9
Registry: ....Bermuda	Cabins (total): 1,300	Fitness Center: ....Yes
Length (ft/m): 951.4/290.0	Size Range (sq ft/m): 161.4–764.2/	Sauna/Steam Room: ....Yes/Yes
Beam (ft/m): 118.1/36.0	15.0–71.0	Massage:........................Yes
Draft (ft/m): 26.2/8.0	Cabins (outside view): 928	Self-Service Launderette:..........Yes
Propulsion/Propellers: .....diesel-electric	Cabins (interior/no view): 372	Dedicated Cinema/Seats: ....No
(42,000kW)/2	Cabins (for one person): 0	Library: ....Yes
Passenger Decks: 13	Cabins (with private balcony): 710	Classification Society: ...Registro Navale
Total Crew: 1,100	Cabins (wheelchair accessible): 28	Italiano (RINA)
	(18 outside/10 interior)	

OVERALL SCORE: 1,549 (OUT OF A POSSIBLE 2,000 POINTS)

ACCOMMODATION: There are six types of cabins and configurations: (a) grand suite, (b) suite, (c) mini-suite, (d) outside double with balcony, (e) outside double, and (f) interior (no view) double. There are, however, 35 different brochure price categories; the choice is bewildering for both travel agents and passengers. Pricing depends on two things, size and location.

(a) The plushest suite is the Grand Suite, which has a hot tub accessible from both the private balcony and from the bedroom, two bedrooms, lounge, two bathrooms, a huge walk-in closet, and plenty of drawer and storage space.

(b/c) Suites (with a semi-private balcony) have a separate living room (with sofa bed) and bedroom (with a TV set in each). The bathroom is quite large and features both a bathtub and shower stall. The mini-suites also have a private balcony, and feature a separate living and sleeping area (with a television in each). The bathroom is also quite spacious and features both a bathtub and shower stall. The differences between the suites and mini-suites are basically in the size and appointments, the suite being more of a square shape while mini-suites are more rectangular, and have few drawers. Both suites and mini-suites feature really plush bathrobes, fully tiled bathrooms with ample open shelf storage space. Suite and mini-suite passengers receive priority attention, including speedy embarkation and disembarkation privileges. What is really unacceptable is that the most expensive accommodation aboard this ship has only semi-private balconies that can be seen from above and so there is absolutely no privacy whatsoever (Suites

BERLITZ'S RATINGS

	Possible	Achieved
Ship	500	436
Accommodation	200	168
Food	400	256
Service	400	293
Entertainment	100	82
Cruise	400	314

C401, 402, 409, 410, 414, 415, 420, 421/422, 423, 424 and 425 on Caribe Deck). Also, the suites D105 and D106 (Dolphin Deck) are extremely large, but their balconies can be seen from above.

(d/e/f) Both interior and outside-view (the outsides come either with or without private balcony) cabins are functional and practical, although almost no drawers are provided. They are very attractive, with warm, pleasing décor and fine soft furnishing fabrics; 80 percent of the outside cabins have a private balcony. The tiled bathrooms have a good amount of open shelf storage space for personal toiletries.

There are also two family suites. These consist of two suites with an interconnecting door, plus a large balcony, and can sleep up to 10 (if at least four are children, or up to eight people if all are adults).

All passengers receive turndown service and chocolates on pillows each night, as well as bathrobes (on request) and toiletry amenity kits (larger, naturally, for suite/mini-suite occupants) that typically include soap, shampoo, conditioner, and hand/body lotion. A hairdryer is provided in all cabins, sensibly located at the vanity desk unit in the living area. All bathrooms are tiled and have a decent amount of open shelf storage space for personal toiletries. Princess Cruises features BBC World, CNN, CNBC, ESPN and TNT on the in-cabin color TV system (when available, depending on cruise area).

Most outside cabins on Emerald Deck have views obstructed by the lifeboats. Sadly, there are no cabins for singles. Your name is placed outside your suite or cabin – making it simple for delivery service personnel but intrusive with regard to your privacy. Some cabins can accommodate a third and fourth person in upper berths. However, in such cabins, the lower beds cannot then be pushed together to make queen-sized bed.

Almost all balcony suites and cabins can be over-looked both from the navigation bridge wing, as well as from the port and starboard sections of the ship's dis-cotheque – located high above the ship at the stern. Cab-ins with balconies on Dolphin, Caribe and Baja decks are also overlooked by passengers on balconies on the deck above; they are, therefore, not at all private. How-ever, perhaps the least desirable balcony cabins are the eight located forward on Emerald Deck, as the balconies do not extend to the side of the ship and can be passed by walkers and gawkers on the adjacent Upper Prome-nade walkway (so occupants need to keep their curtains closed most of the time). Also, passengers occupying some of the most expensive suites with balconies at the stern of the vessel may experience considerable vibra-tion during certain ship maneuvers.

DINING: There are a variety of "Personal Choice" dining options. For formal meals, there are three principal dining rooms, *Botticelli*, with 504 seats, *Da Vinci*, with 486 seats, and *Michelangelo*, with 486 seats. There are two seatings in one restaurant, while the other two have "anytime din-ing" (where you choose when and with whom you want to eat) is typically available in the other two. All three are non-smoking and split into multi-tier sections in a non-symmetrical design that breaks what are quite large spaces into many smaller sections, for better ambience. Each dining room has its own galley.

Although portions are generous, the food and its pre-sentation are disappointing, and bland of taste. The qual-ity of fish is poor (often disguised by crumb or batter coatings), the selection of fresh green vegetables is lim-ited, and few garnishes are used. However, do remember that this *is* big-ship banquet catering, with all its atten-dant standardization and production cooking. Meats are of a decent quality, although often disguised by gravy-based sauces, and pasta dishes are acceptable (though volumi-nous), and are typically served by section headwaiters, in search of gratuities, who may also make "something special just for you." If you like desserts, order a sundae at dinner, as most other desserts are just so-so. Ice cream ordered in the dining room is included, but if you order one anywhere else, you'll have to pay for it.

On any given seven-day cruise, a typical menu cycle will typically include a Sailaway Dinner, Captain's Wel-come Dinner, Chef's Dinner, Italian Dinner, French Din-ner, Captain's Gala Dinner, and Landfall Dinner.

Specially designed dinnerware and high-quality linens and silverware are used; by Dudson of England (din-nerware), Frette Egyptian cotton table linens, and sil-verware by Hepp of Germany. Note that 15 percent is added to all beverage bills, including wines.

There are two alternative informal dining areas: *Saba-tini's Trattoria* and *Painted Desert*. Both are open for lunch and dinner. *Sabatini's* is an Italian eatery, with colorful tiled Mediterranean-style décor; it is named after *Trattoria Sabatini*, the 200-year old institution in Florence (where there is no cover charge). It has Ital-ian-style pizzas and pastas, with a variety of sauces, as well as Italian-style entrées (including tiger prawns and lobster tail – all provided with flair and entertainment from by the waiters). *Sabatini's* is by reservation only, and there is a cover charge of $15 per person, for lunch or dinner (on sea days only). *Painted Desert* has "south-western American food"; by reservation only, with a cover charge of $8 per person, for lunch or dinner on sea days only. However, do note that *Painted Desert* is spread over the whole beam (width) of the ship, and two walkways intersect it, which means that it's a very open area, with people walking through it as you eat. The cuisine in both of these spots is decidedly better than in the three main dining rooms.

A poolside hamburger grill and pizza bar (no additional charge) are additional dining spots for casual bites, while extra charges will apply if you order items to eat at either the coffee bar/patisserie, or the caviar/champagne bar.

Other casual meals can be taken in the Horizon Court – open 24 hours a day, with large ocean-view on port and starboard sides and direct access to the two principal swim-ming pools and lido deck (there is no real finesse in pre-sentation, however, as plastic plates are provided).

OTHER COMMENTS: *Grand Princess* presents a bold, forthright profile, with a racy "spoiler" effect at the stern that many do not consider handsome (this acts as an observation lounge with aft-facing views by day, and a stunning discotheque by night). The ship has a flared snub-nosed bow and a galleon-like transom stern. At 118 ft/36 meters (but more than 43 ft/13 meters wider than the canal, including the navigation bridge wings) *Grand Princess* is too wide to transit the Panama Canal, with many balcony cabins overhanging the ship's hull.

There is a good sheltered teakwood promenade deck, which almost wraps around (three times round is equal to one mile) and a walkway which goes right to the (enclosed, protected) bow of the ship. The outdoor pools have various beach-like surroundings. One lap pool has a pumped "current" to swim against.

Unlike the outside decks, there is plenty of space inside the ship (but there are also plenty of passengers), and a wide array of public rooms to choose from, with many "intimate" (this being a relative word) spaces and places to play. The passenger flow has been well thought out, and works with little congestion. The décor is very attractive, with lots of earth tones (well suited to both American and European tastes). In fact, this ship has the best of all that Princess Cruises has to offer from its many years of operating a fine-quality product.

Four areas center on swimming pools, one of which is two decks high and is covered by a magrodome, itself an extension of the funnel housing. A large health spa complex surrounds one of the swimming pools (you can have a massage or other spa treatment in an ocean-view treatment room). High atop the stern of the ship is a ship-wide glass-walled disco pod (I have nicknamed it the ETR – energy transfer room). It looks like an aerodynamic 'spoiler' and is positioned some 150 ft (45 meters) above the waterline, with spectacular views from the extreme port and starboard side windows (you can look along the ship's side and onto lots of "private" balconies).

An extensive collection of art works has been chosen, and this complements the interior design and colors well. If you see something you like, you will be able to purchase it on board – it's almost all for sale.

This ship also features a Wedding Chapel (a live webcam can relay ceremonies via the internet). The ship's captain can legally marry (American) couples, due to the ship's Bermuda registry and a special dispensation (this should, however, be verified when in the planning stage, and may vary according to where you reside). Princess Cruises offers three wedding packages: Pearl, Emerald, Diamond – the fee includes registration and official marriage certificate. However, to get married *and* take your close family members and entourage with you on your honeymoon is going to cost a lot. The "Hearts & Minds" chapel can also be used for "renewal of vows" ceremonies.

Another neat feature is the motion-based "virtual reality" room with its enclosed motion-based rides, and a "blue screen" studio, where passengers can star in their own videos. There is an excellent library/CD-Rom computer room, and a separate card room. For children there is a two-deck-high playroom, teen's room, and a host of specially trained counselors.

For entertainment, Princess Cruises prides itself on its glamorous all-American production shows, and the largest of the show lounges has $3 million in sound and light equipment, plus a 9-piece orchestra, and a scenery loading bay that connects directly from stage to a hull door for direct transfer to the dockside). Two other entertainment lounges help spread things around. Casino lovers should enjoy what is one of the largest casinos at sea, with more than 260 slot machines (all with dolphin-shaped handles); there are blackjack, craps and roulette tables, plus newer games such as Let It Ride Bonus, Spanish 21 and Caribbean Draw Progressive. The highlight could well be Neptune's Lair, a multimedia gaming extravaganza. Ship lovers should enjoy the wood-paneled Wheelhouse Bar, finely decorated with memorabilia and ship models tracing part of parent company P&O's history.

Princess Cays – Princess Cruises' own "private island" in the Caribbean – is "yours" (along with a couple of thousand other passengers) for a day; however, you will need to take a shore tender to get to and from it, and this can take some time. A high-tech hospital is provided with live SeaMed tele-medicine link-ups with specialists at the Cedars-Sinai Medical Center in Los Angeles available for emergency help (hardly useful for international passengers that do not reside in the USA).

This ship will appeal to those that really enjoy a big city to play in, with all the trimmings and lots of fellow passengers. But it is full of revenue centers, designed to help you part with more money. The dress code has been simplified – reduced to formal or smart casual. Gratuities are *automatically* added to your account, at $10 per person, per day (gratuities for children are charged at the same rate). If you want to pay less, you'll have to line up at the reception desk to have these charges adjusted. The onboard currency is the US dollar.

Whether this really can be considered a relaxing vacation is a moot point, but with *so many choices* and "small" rooms to enjoy, the ship has been extremely well designed; the odds are that you'll have a fine cruise vacation, in a controlled, well-packaged way.

WEAK POINTS: Standing in line for embarkation (an "express check-in" option is available by completing certain documentation 40 days in advance of your cruise), disembarkation, shore tenders and for self-serve buffet meals is an inevitable aspect of cruising aboard all large ships. If you are not used to large ships, it will probably take you some time to find your way around (take good walking shoes), despite the company's claim that this vessel offers passengers a "small ship feel, big ship choice." The cabin bath towels are small, and drawer space is very limited. There are no butlers – even for the top grade suites. Cabin attendants have too many cabins to look after (typically 20), which cannot possibly translate to fine personal service.

The automated telephone system is very frustrating for many passengers, and luggage delivery needs to be more efficient. Lines form for many things, but particularly for the purser's office, and for open-seating breakfast and lunch in the three main dining rooms. Long lines for embarkation (an "express check-in" option is available by completing certain documentation 40 days in advance of your cruise), disembarkation, shore excursions and shore tenders are also a fact of life aboard large ships, as is waiting for elevators at peak times.

You'll have to live with the many extra charge items (such as for ice cream, and fresh squeezed orange juice) and activities (such as yoga, group exercise bicycling and kick boxing classes at $10 per session, not to mention $4 per hour for *group* babysitting services). Some of the spa (massage) treatment rooms are located directly underneath the basketball court, which makes it utterly frustrating trying to relax while the ceiling above your head is being pounded by bouncing balls. There's also a charge for using the washers ($1) and dryers ($0.50) in the self-service launderettes.

Passengers also have to endure countless pieces of (highly questionable) art found in almost every foyer and public room – an annoying reminder that today, cruising aboard large ships such as *Diamond Princess, Golden Princess, Grand Princess* and *Star Princess* is really like living in a bazaar of paintings surrounded by a ship.

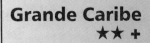

Grande Caribe
★★ +

Small Ship:	.99 tons	Passengers	
Lifestyle:	.Standard	(lower beds/all berths):	.100/100
Cruise Line:	.American Canadian	Passenger Space Ratio	
	Caribbean Line	(lower beds/all berths):	.0.99/0.99
Former Names:	.none	Crew/Passenger Ratio	
Builder:	.Blount industries (USA)	(lower beds/all berths):	.5.8/5.8
Original Cost:	.$8 million	Navigation Officers:	.American
Entered Service:	.June 1997	Cabins (total):	.50
Registry:	.USA	Size Range (sq ft/m):	.72.0–96.0/
Length (ft/m):	.183.0/55.7		6.6–8.9
Beam (ft/m):	.40.0/12.1	Cabins (outside view):	.41
Draft (ft/m):	.6.5/1.9	Cabins (interior/no view):	.9
Propulsion/Propellers:	diesel (1,044kW)/2	Cabins (for one person):	.0
Passenger Decks:	.3	Cabins (with private balcony):	.0
Total Crew:	.17	Cabins (wheelchair accessible):	.0

Cabin Current:	.110 volts
Elevators:	.0
Casino (gaming tables):	.No
Slot Machines:	.No
Swimming Pools (outdoors):	.0
Swimming Pools (indoors):	.0
Whirlpools:	.0
Fitness Center:	.0
Sauna/Steam Room:	.0/0
Massage:	.0
Self-Service Launderette:	.No
Dedicated Cinema/Seats:	.No
Library:	.Yes
Classification Society:	.American Bureau of Shipping

OVERALL SCORE: 1,089 (OUT OF A POSSIBLE 2,000 POINTS)

ACCOMMODATION: The cabins are all extremely small, relatively utilitarian units, with very little closet space (but just enough drawers) and small (very small) bathrooms. The twin beds convert to queen-sized beds (there is good storage space under the beds). There is no room service menu, and only soap is supplied (bring your own shampoo and other toiletries). Each cabin has its own air conditioner, so passengers do not have to share air with the rest of the ship (and other passengers). Refreshingly, there are no cabin keys.

DINING: The dining room seats all passengers in one open seating, so you dine with whomever you wish, so you can make new friends and enjoy different conversation each day (it is also good for small groups). The tables convert to card tables for use between meals. Passengers are welcome to bring their own alcohol, as the company does not sell it aboard ship. Effervescent, young American waitresses provide the service, although there is no finesse.

OTHER COMMENTS: *Grande Caribe* is the largest and the most contemporary of the Blount-built vessels. During passenger emergency drill, passengers are taught how to use fire extinguishers – a useful piece of training.

BERLITZ'S RATINGS

	Possible	Achieved
Ship	500	247
Accommodation	200	108
Food	400	237
Service	400	233
Entertainment	N/A	N/A
Cruise	500	264

This vessel's shallow draft enables it to cruise into off-the-beaten-path destinations well out of reach of larger ships, and also has a retractable navigation bridge – practical for those low bridges along inland waterways. *Grande Caribe*, together with sister vessel *Grande Mariner* (but not *Niagara Prince*) has stabilizers. An underwater video camera allows passengers, while seated in (dry) comfort in the lounge, to view on large-screen TV monitors what a scuba diver might see underneath the ship. Underwater lights, which attract fish and other marine life, are also fitted.

The style is unpretentious and casual (no jackets or ties) by day and night. There are two 24-passenger launches (one of which is a glass-bottomed boat), and some snorkeling equipment.

There is one lounge/bar, located on a different deck to the dining room. Water sports facilities include a glass-bottom boat, and sunfish sailboat.

This vessel will be good for anyone who does not want crowds, or entertainment of any kind, or a high standard of service. All gratuities given by passengers are pooled and shared by all the staff (although you should note that the suggested daily rate is very high). The onboard currency is the US dollar.

Grande Mariner
★★ +

Small Ship: . . . . .99 tons	Total Crew: 17	Cabin Current: . . . . .110 volts
Lifestyle: . . . . .Standard	Passengers	Elevators: 0
Cruise Line: . . . . American Canadian	(lower beds/all berths): 100/100	Casino (gaming tables): . . . . .No
Caribbean Line	Passenger Space Ratio	Slot Machines: .No
Former Names: . . . . .none	(lower beds/all berths): 0.99/0.99	Swimming Pools (outdoors): 0
Builder: . . . . .Blount industries (USA)	Crew/Passenger Ratio	Swimming Pools (indoors): 0
Original Cost: . . . .$8 million	(lower beds/all berths): 5.8/5.8	Whirlpools: 0
Entered Service: . . . . .June 1998	Navigation Officers: . . . . .American	Fitness Center: .0
Registry: . . . . .USA	Cabins (total): .50	Sauna/Steam Room: 0/0
Length (ft/m): 183.0/55.7	Size Range (sq ft/m): . .72.0–96.0/6.6–8.9	Massage: 0
Beam (ft/m): 40.0/12.1	Cabins (outside view): 41	Self-Service Launderette: . . . . .No
Draft (ft/m): 6.5/1.9	Cabins (interior/no view): 9	Dedicated Cinema/Seats: . . . . .No
Propulsion/Propellers: . . . . .diesel	Cabins (for one person): 0	Library: . . . . .Yes
(1,044kW)/2	Cabins (with private balcony): 0	Classification Society: . .American Bureau
Passenger Decks: 3	Cabins (wheelchair accessible): 0	of Shipping

OVERALL SCORE: 1,089 (OUT OF A POSSIBLE 2,000 POINTS)

ACCOMMODATION: The cabins are all extremely small, relatively utilitarian units, with very little closet space (but just enough drawers) and small (very small) bathrooms. There are 50 cabins, each with twin beds convertible to queen-sized beds (there is good storage space under the beds). There is no room service menu, and only soap is supplied (bring your own shampoo and other toiletries). Each cabin has its own air conditioner, so passengers do not have to share air with the rest of the ship (and other passengers). Refreshingly, there are no cabin keys.

BERLITZ'S RATINGS		
	Possible	Achieved
Ship	500	247
Accommodation	200	108
Food	400	237
Service	400	233
Entertainment	N/A	N/A
Cruise	500	264

DINING: The dining room seats all passengers in a single, open seating, so you dine with whomever you wish. The advantage of this is that you can make new friends and enjoy different conversation each day (it is also good for small groups). The dining tables convert to card tables for use between meals. Passengers are welcome to bring their own alcohol, as the company does not sell it aboard ship. Effervescent, young American waitresses provide the service, although there is no finesse.

OTHER COMMENTS: This is another example of a contemporary Blount-built vessel. During passenger emergency drill, passengers are taught how to use fire extinguishers – a very useful piece of training.

This vessel has a shallow draft, which enables it to cruise into off-the-beaten-path destinations well out of reach of larger ships, and also features a retractable navigation bridge – practical for those low bridges along the inland waterways. *Grande Mariner*, together with sister vessel *Grande Caribe* (but not *Niagara Prince*) has stabilizers. An underwater video camera allows passengers, while seated in (dry) comfort in the lounge, to view on large-screen TV monitors what a scuba diver might see underneath the ship. Underwater lights, which attract fish and other marine life, are also fitted.

The style is unpretentious and extremely casual (definitely no jackets or ties) both day and night. There are two 24-passenger launches (one of which is a glass bottom boat), and some snorkeling equipment.

There is one lounge/bar, located on a different deck to the dining room – a departure for ACCL from the company's former vessels. Water sports facilities include a glass-bottom boat, and sunfish sailboat.

This vessel will be good for anyone who does not want crowds, or entertainment of any kind, or a high standard of service. All gratuities given by passengers are pooled and shared by all the staff (although note that the suggested daily rate is very high for the product delivered). The onboard currency is the US dollar.

Grandeur of the Seas
★★★★

Large Ship: . . . . .74,137 tons	Passengers	Cabin Current: . . . . .110 and 220 volts
Lifestyle: . . . . .Standard	(lower beds/all berths): 1,950/2,446	Elevators: 9
Cruise Line: Royal Caribbean International	Passenger Space Ratio	Casino (gaming tables): . . . . .Yes
Former Names: . . . . .none	(lower beds/all berths): 38.0/30.3	Slot Machines: .Yes
Builder: . . .Kvaerner Masa-Yards (Finland)	Crew/Passenger Ratio	Swimming Pools (outdoors): 1
Original Cost: . . . .$300 million	(lower beds/all berths): 2.5/3.2	Swimming Pools (indoors): 1
Entered Service: . . . . .Dec 1996	Navigation Officers: . . . . .International	(indoor/outdoor w/sliding glass roof)
Registry: . . . . .The Bahamas	Cabins (total): 975	Whirlpools: 6
Length (ft/m): 916.0/279.6	Size Range (sq ft/m): 158.2–1,267.0/	Fitness Center: . . . . .Yes
Beam (ft/m): 105.6/32.2	14.7–117.7	Sauna/Steam Room: . . . . .Yes/Yes
Draft (ft/m): 25.5/7.6	Cabins (outside view): 576	Massage: . . . . .Yes
Propulsion/Propellers: . . . . .diesel-electric	Cabins (interior/no view): 399	Self-Service Launderette: . . . . .No
(50,400kW)/2	Cabins (for one person): 0	Dedicated Cinema/Seats: . . . . .No
Passenger Decks: 11	Cabins (with private balcony): 212	Library: . . . . .Yes
Total Crew: 760	Cabins (wheelchair accessible): 14	Classification Society: Det Norske Veritas

OVERALL SCORE: 1,521 (OUT OF A POSSIBLE 2,000 POINTS)

ACCOMMODATION: The suites are very well appointed and have very pleasing decor, with good wood and color accenting (the largest suite even has a baby grand piano). Category A and B cabins also have VCRs. All standard cabins have twin beds that convert to a queen-size bed, ample closet space for a one-week cruise, and a good amount of drawer space, although under-bed storage space is not good for large suitcases. The bathrooms have nine mirrors. The plastic buckets for champagne/wine are really shoddy.

DINING: The 1,195-seat, non-smoking dining room is spread over two decks, with both levels connected by a grand, sweeping staircase. There are two seatings.

The cuisine in the main dining room is typical of mass banquet catering that offers standard fare comparable to that found in American family-style restaurants ashore. While menu descriptions are tempting, the actual food may be somewhat disappointing and unmemorable. The menu descriptions make the food sound better than it is (which is consistently below average), mostly disappointing and without much taste. However, a decent selection of light meals is provided, and a vegetarian menu is available. The selection of breads, rolls, fruit and cheese is quite poor, however, and could do more improvement. Caviar (once a standard menu item) incurs a hefty extra charge. There is no good caviar; special orders, tableside carving and flambeau items are not offered. Menus typically include a Welcome Aboard Dinner, French Dinner, Italian Dinner, International Dinner, and Captain's Gala Dinner.

BERLITZ'S RATINGS

	Possible	Achieved
Ship	500	430
Accommodation	200	166
Food	400	248
Service	400	302
Entertainment	100	81
Cruise	400	294

The wine list is not very extensive, but the prices are moderate. The waiters, many of whom are from Caribbean countries, are perhaps overly friendly for some tastes – particularly on the last night of the cruise, when tips are expected.

A cavernous, 790-seat informal Windjammer Café, which features a great expanse of ocean-view glass windows, is where breakfast and lunch buffets are available as an alternative to the dining room.

An intimate terrace Champagne Bar is located forward of the lower level of the two-deck-high dining room and just off the atrium for those who might like to taste something a little out of the ordinary, in a setting that is bright and contemporary.

OTHER COMMENTS: Always evolving, the ships in the Royal Caribbean International fleet, *Grandeur of the Seas* is no exception, and presents a nice long profile, with a funnel placed well aft (almost a throwback to some ship designs used in the 1950s). It has a well-rounded stern (as have the three *Sovereign of the Seas*-class ships) and a Viking Crown Lounge in the center, just forward of the funnel. This lounge, together with the forward mast and aft funnel, provides three distinct focal points in the exterior profile. The Viking Crown Lounge sits between funnel and mast and overlooks the forward section of the swimming pool deck, as aboard *Legend of the Seas/Splendour of the Seas*, with access provided by a multi-deck atrium. No cushioned pads are provided for the plastic-webbed deck lounge chairs.

There is a wrap-around promenade deck outdoors, with a seven-deck-high atrium inside. A delightful champagne terrace bar sits forward of the lower level of the two-deck-high dining room. There is a good use of tropical plants throughout the public rooms, which helps to counteract the clinical pastel wall colors, while huge murals of opera scenes adorn several stairways.

There are two show lounges. The principal one, used for big production shows, has excellent sight lines from 98 percent of the 875 seats; the other is the secondary lounge, for smaller shows and adult cabaret, with 575 seats. There are good children's and teens' facilities, which are larger than those of previous ships in the fleet.

This is another new ship design for Royal Caribbean International (its sister ship is *Enchantment of the Seas*), with what, inside, has proven to be a good passenger flow. The vessel has a good, varied collection of artworks (including several sculptures), principally by British artists, with classical music, ballet and theater themes. The casino has a fascinating, somewhat theatrical glass-covered, but under-floor exhibit.

This ship will be good for first-time cruise passengers who want fine, very comfortable surroundings, and all the very latest in facilities, entertainment lounges and high-tech sophistication in one neat, well-packaged and a fine-tuned cruise vacation, with plenty of music and entertainment. The onboard currency is the US dollar.

WEAK POINTS: Standing in line for embarkation, disembarkation, shore tenders and for self-serve buffet meals is an inevitable aspect of cruising aboard all large ships.

Hanseatic
★★★★★

Small Ship: ....8,378 tons	Passengers	Cabin Current: ....220 volts
Lifestyle: ....Luxury	(lower beds/all berths): 184/194	Elevators: 2
Cruise Line: ....Hapag-Lloyd Cruises	Passenger Space Ratio	Swimming Pools (outdoors): 1
Former Names: ......*Society Adventurer*	(lower beds/all berths): 45.5/43.1	Whirlpools: 1
Builder: ....Rauma Yards (Finland)	Crew/Passenger Ratio	Exercise Room: ....Yes
Original Cost: ....$68 million	(lower beds/all berths): 1.5/1.5	Sauna/Steam Room: ....Yes/No
Entered Service: ....Mar 1993	Navigation Officers: ....German	Massage: ....Yes
Registry: ....The Bahamas	Cabins (total): 92	Self-Service Launderette: ....No
Length (ft/m): 402.9/122.80	Size Range (sq ft/m): 231.4–470.3/	Lecture/Film Room: ......Yes (seats 160)
Beam (ft/m): 59.1/18.00	21.5–43.7	Library: ....Yes
Draft (ft/m): 15.5/4.71	Cabins (outside view): 92	Zodiacs: 14
Propulsion/Propellers: ....diesel	Cabins (interior/no view): 0	Helicopter Pad: ....Yes
(5,880kW)/2	Cabins (for one person): 0	Classification Society: .....Germanischer
Passenger Decks: 7	Cabins (with private balcony): 0	Lloyd
Total Crew: 122	Cabins (wheelchair accessible): 2	

OVERALL SCORE: 1,740 (OUT OF A POSSIBLE 2,000 POINTS)

ACCOMMODATION: The all-outside cabins, located in the forward section of the ship, are large and very well equipped, and include a separate lounge area next to a large picture window (which has a pull-down blackout blind as well as curtains) and refrigerator. All furniture is in warm woods such as beech, and everything has rounded edges. Wood trim accents the ceiling perimeter, and acts as a divider between bed and lounge areas. Each cabin has a mini-bar, television, VCR, two locking drawers, and plenty of closet and drawer space, as well as two separate cupboards and hooks for all-weather outerwear.

All cabin bathrooms have a large bathtub, two toiletries cabinets, wall-mounted hairdryer, and bathrobe. There are only two types of cabins; 34 have double beds, others have twin beds. Towels, bed linens and pillowcases are of 100 percent cotton, and individual cotton-filled duvet covers are provided.

The suites and cabins on Bridge Deck have impeccable butler service and full in-cabin dining privileges, as well as personalized stationery. Soft drinks are supplied in the cabin refrigerator, and replenished daily, at no charge (all liquor is at extra cost, however). A very relaxed ambience prevails on board.

DINING: The dining room is elegant, warm and welcoming, and features large picture windows on two sides as well as aft, and table settings are graced with fine Rosenthal china and silverware. There is one seating for dinner, and open seating for breakfast and lunch. The cuisine and service are absolutely first-rate, but are more

BERLITZ'S RATINGS

	Possible	Achieved
Ship	500	434
Accommodation	200	172
Food	400	345
Service	400	343
Entertainment	N/A	N/A
Cruise	500	446

informal than, for example, aboard the larger *Europa* (which is at or close to the same price level). Top-quality ingredients are always used, and most items are purchased fresh when available.

The meals are very creative and nicely presented, and each is appealing to the eye as well as to the palate. There is always an excellent selection of breads, cheeses, desserts and pastry items. Note that when operating in the Arctic or Antarctic, table set-ups are often minimal, due to the possible movement of the ship (stabilizers cannot be used in much of the Antarctic region), so cutlery is provided and changed for each course.

In 1996, the ship added an alternative dining room. The Columbus Lounge, which is an informal, open seating, self-serve (or waiter service) buffet-style eatery by day, changes into an Oriental dining room at night. Reservations are required (you make them in the morning of the day you want to dine there), but there is no extra charge, and there is no tipping at any time. Also, on each cruise a full Viennese teatime is featured, as well as a regular daily teatime.

OTHER COMMENTS: Originally ordered for Society Cruises as *Society Adventurer* (although it never actually sailed under that name, due to the fact that the company declared itself bankrupt and never took possession of the ship), *Hanseatic* was designed and constructed specifically to provide world-wide expedition-style cruises in luxurious, contemporary surroundings. The ship is extremely environmentally friendly and has the latest "zero-discharge," non-polluting waste disposal system including a pollution-filtered incinerator, full biological sewage treatment plant, and a large storage capacity. This is one of only a few ships that will allow you to sign up for a tour of the engine room.

This is an outstanding ship for the best in destination-intensive exploration voyages, and is under long-term charter to Hapag-Lloyd Cruises. It has a fully enclosed bridge (with an open bridge policy, so that passengers can visit the bridge at almost any time) and an ice-hardened hull with the highest passenger vessel classification of 1A1 Super. The ship also has the very latest in high-tech navigation equipment.

A fleet of 14 Zodiac inflatable craft, each one named after a famous explorer, is used for in-depth shore landings. These craft provide the ship with tremendous flexibility in itineraries, and provide excellent possibilities for up-close wildlife viewing in natural habitats, with small numbers of passengers. Rubber boots, parkas, a boot-washing and storage room is provided for passengers, particularly useful for Arctic and Antarctic cruises.

Inside, the ship is equipped with fine quality luxury fittings and soft furnishings. There is a choice of several public rooms, all of them well furnished and decorated, and all of them have high ceilings, which help to provide an impression of space; the result is that the ship feels much larger than its actual size. The library/observation lounge provides a good selection of hardback books and videos in both the English and German languages.

Hanseatic provides destination-intensive, nature and life-enrichment cruises and expeditions in elegant, but unstuffy surroundings, to some of the world's most fascinating destinations, at a suitably handsome price. The passenger maximum is generally kept to about 150,

which means plenty of comfort and lots of space for everyone – and no lines, no hassle.

The ship is at its best when operating in Arctic and Antarctic regions (infirm passengers are advised not to consider these areas). Safety is paramount, particularly in the Antarctic and, in this regard, the ship excels with professionalism, pride and skilled seamanship. It always operates in two languages, English and German (many staff speak several languages) and caters well to both sets of passengers. All port taxes, insurance, gratuities, Zodiac trips and most shore excursions (except when the ship operates in Europe) are included. The onboard currency is the euro.

Hapag-Lloyd Cruises specializes in providing outstanding, well-planned itineraries. Where this ship really scores, however, is in its Antarctic sailings, where the experience of the captain, the cruise director and the crew really shine. The lectures, briefings, and the amount of information provided about the itinerary and ports of call are outstanding. Well qualified lecturers and naturalists accompany each cruise. Insurance, port taxes and all staff gratuities are typically included in the fare, and an expedition cruise logbook is provided at the end of each cruise for all passengers – a superb reminder of what's been seen and done during the course of your expedition adventure cruise.

WEAK POINTS: There are few negative things about this ship. It is principally marketed to German-speaking and English-speaking passengers, so other nationalities may find it hard to integrate. There are no marine quality telescopes mounted outdoors (there should be). There is, at present, no privacy curtain between cabin door and the sleeping area (there should be).

Hebridean Princess
★★★★★

Small Ship:	.2,112 tons	Passengers	
Lifestyle:	Luxury	(lower beds/all berths):	.49/49
Cruise Line:	Hebridean Island Cruises	Passenger Space Ratio	
Former Names:	Columba	(lower beds/all berths):	.43.1/43.1
Builder:	Hall Russell (Scotland)	Crew/Passenger Ratio	
Original Cost:	n/a	(lower beds/all berths):	.1.3/1.3
Entered Service:	1964/Apr 1989	Navigation Officers:	British
Registry:	Great Britain	Cabins (total):	.30
Length (ft/m):	235.0/71.6	Size Range (sq ft/m):	144.0–340.0/
Beam (ft/m):	46.0/14.0		13.4–31.6
Draft (ft/m):	10.0/3.0	Cabins (outside view):	.24
Propulsion/Propellers:	diesel	Cabins (interior/no view):	.6
	(1,790kW)/2	Cabins (for one person):	.11
Passenger Decks:	.5	Cabins (with private balcony):	.4
Total Crew:	.37	Cabins (wheelchair accessible):	.0

Cabin Current:	.240 volts
Elevators:	.0
Casino (gaming tables):	No
Slot Machines:	No
Swimming Pools (outdoors):	.0
Swimming Pools (indoors):	.0
Whirlpools:	.0
Fitness Center:	Yes
Sauna/Steam Room:	No/No
Massage:	No
Self-Service Launderette:	No
Dedicated Cinema/Seats:	No
Library:	Yes
Classification Society:	Lloyd's Register

OVERALL SCORE: 1,701 (OUT OF A POSSIBLE 2,000 POINTS)

ACCOMMODATION: All cabins have different color schemes and names (there are no numbers, and, refreshingly, no door locks, so don't ask for the door key). All are individually designed (no two cabins are identical) and created, with delightfully eclectic chintz curtains and sweeping drapes over the beds. They really are quite delightful and come in a wide range of configurations (some with single, some with double, some with twin beds), including four that have a private balcony (lovely). All except two cabins have a private bathroom with bath or shower; all feature a refrigerator, ironing board with iron, trouser press, and tea/coffee making set. All towels and bathrobe are of 100 percent cotton, as is the bed linen. Molton Brown personal toiletry items are provided.

All cabins come with real Victorian-style bathroom fittings (some are even gold-plated), and some have brass cabin portholes that actually open. Three of the newest cabins added are outfitted in Scottish Baronial style. Some cabins also have a VCR. No cabins have keys, although they can be locked from the inside.

DINING: Features include a totally non-smoking dining room with ocean-view windows, and tables that are laid with crisp white linen, and sometimes with lace overlays. Villeroy & Boch china is used. There is a single seating, at assigned tables. Some chairs have armrests while some do not. The cuisine is extremely creative, and at times outstanding – and about the same quality and presentation as *Seabourn Goddess I* and *Seabourn Goddess II*. Fresh ingredients are purchased locally – a

BERLITZ'S RATINGS		
	Possible	Achieved
Ship	500	425
Accommodation	200	177
Food	400	350
Service	400	341
Entertainment	N/A	N/A
Cruise	500	408

welcome change from the mass catering of most ships. Although there are no flambeau items (the galley has electric, not gas, cookers), what is created is beautifully presented and of the highest standard. The desserts are definitely worth saving space for.

The breakfast menu is standard each day, although you can always ask for any favorites you may have, and each day a specialty item is featured. Try the "porridge and a wee dram" – it's lovely when it is cold outside, and it sets you up for the whole day. Although there is waiter service for most things, there is also a good buffet table display for breakfast and luncheon. This little ship features a very decent wine list and extremely moderate prices (an additional connoisseur's list is also available for those seeking fine vintage wines). Many wonderful whiskeys and vintage cognacs are also available). Highly personal and attentive service from an attentive British/Scottish crew completes the picture.

OTHER COMMENTS: Small can be beautiful. The ship, originally one of three Scottish ferries built for for David MacBayne Ltd – although actually owned by the British government – was skillfully converted into a gem of a cruise ship in order to operate island-hopping itineraries in Scotland, together with the occasional jaunt to Ireland and Norway. It was re-named in 1989 by the Duchess of York. There is an outdoors deck for occasional sunbathing and al fresco meals, as well as a bar (occasionally, formal cocktail parties are held here when the weather conditions are right). There is no wrap-around deck, although inside the ship there is a mini-gym for those seeking to pedal or row themselves to the next destination. The ship carries a Zodiac inflatable runabout, as well as a rowing boat (for passenger use).

Use of the ship's small boats, speedboat, bicycles, and fishing gear are included in the price, as are entrance fees to gardens, castles, other attractions, and the occasional coach tour (depending on itinerary). The destination-intensive cruises have very creative itineraries and there really is plenty to do, despite the lack of big-ship features. Specialist guides, who give nightly talks about the destinations to be visited and some fascinating history and the local folklore, accompany all cruises.

The principal inside room is the Tiree Lounge, which features a real brick-walled fireplace, as well as a very cozy bar with a wide variety of whiskeys (the selection of single malts is excellent) and cognacs for connoisseurs.

This utterly charming little ship has stately home service and a warm, totally cosseted, traditional country house ambience that is unobtrusive but always at hand when you need it. Inspector Hercule Poirot would be very much at home here. Who needs megaships when you can take a retro-cruise aboard this absolute gem of a ship? Direct bookings are accepted.

What is so appreciated by passengers is the fact that the ship does not have photographers or some of the trappings found aboard larger ships. Passengers also love the fact that there is no bingo, horse racing, art auctions, or mindless parlor games.

Hebridean Princess has an all-UK crew, and remains one of the world's most well-kept travel secrets. A polished gem, it is especially popular with single passengers, and typically more than 50 percent of her passengers are repeaters (note that children under the age of nine are not accepted). If you cruise from Oban, you will be met at Glasgow station (or airport) and taken to/from the ship by private motor coach. All gratuities and soft drinks are included in the fare (the company earnestly requests that no additional gratuities be given).

Hebridean Island Cruises also has a slightly larger sister ship, acquired in 2001, called *Hebridean Spirit*, which offers the same style and comfort, but features more international itineraries. The onboard currency is the British pound.

WEAK POINTS: Although this vessel is strong, it does have structural limitations and noisy engines that cause some vibration (however, the engines do not run at night and the ship anchors before bedtime, providing soul-renewing peace and tranquility). Drinks (apart from soft drinks) are not included – though, at this price, they should be. It is often cold and very wet in the Scottish islands, so take plenty of warm clothing for layering.

Hebridean Spirit
★★★★★

Small Ship: ....4,200 tons	Passengers	Cabin Current: ....110/220 volts
Lifestyle: ....Luxury	(lower beds/all berths): 81/97	Dining Rooms: 1
Cruise Line: ....Hebridean Island Cruises	Passenger Space Ratio	Elevators: 1
Former Names: ....Sun Viva II,	(lower beds/all berths): 51.8/43.2	Casino (gaming tables): ....No
MegaStar Capricorn, Renaissance Six	Crew/Passenger Ratio	Slot Machines: ....No
Builder: ....Nuovi Cantieri Apuania (Italy)	(lower beds/all berths): 1.1/1.3	Swimming Pools (outdoors): 1
Entered Service: ....Mar 1991/July 2001	Navigation Officers: ....British	Swimming Pools (indoors): 0
Registry: ....Great Britain	Cabins (total): 49	Whirlpools: 0
Length (ft/m): 297.2/90.60	Size Range (sq ft/m): 215.0–365.9/	Fitness Center: ....Yes
Beam (ft/m): 50.1/15.30	20.0–34.0	Sauna/Steam Room: ....No/Yes
Draft (ft/m): 13.7/4.20	Cabins (outside view): 49	Massage:........................Yes
Propulsion/Propellers: ....diesel	Cabins (interior/no view): 0	Self-Service Launderette: ....No
(5,000kW)/2	Cabins (for one person): 18	Dedicated Cinema/Seats: ....No
Passenger Decks:...................5	Cabins (with private balcony): 8	Library: ....Yes
Total Crew: 72	Cabins (wheelchair accessible): 0	Classification Society: ....Lloyds Register

OVERALL SCORE: 1,707 (OUT OF A POSSIBLE 2,000 POINTS)

ACCOMMODATION: The cabins (with names like glens, isles, castles, and clans) are quite spacious units, measuring between 215 and 365 sq. ft (20–34 sq. meters), including bathrooms and balconies). This is quite generous for a small ship such as this one. All are decorated in a similar fashion to those aboard *Hebridean Princess*. All have outside views, and most feature wallpapered walls, lighted walk-in closets (one of the two large suites and 24 other cabins only), full-length mirror, dressing table with three-sided vanity mirrors, personalized stationery, tea/coffee-making equipment, combination large-screen color television and DVD player, refrigerator/mini-bar (always stocked with fresh milk and mineral water), direct-dial satellite telephone, personal safe, ironing board, and electric trouser press. The two suites and 14 other cabins have an additional sofa bed.

Naturally, all towels and thick, plush bathrobe are of 100 percent cotton, as is the bed linen, which features traditional sheets and blankets (not duvets), and thick, patterned bedspread. Note that there are no music channels, and there is no switch to turn announcements off in your cabin.

The bathrooms are of a reasonably decent size, and all are marble clad; they feature tiled floors, marble vanities, and shower enclosures (except for "Suite," "Glen" and "Isle" grade cabins, which have a bathtub/shower combination). An abundance of popular Molton Brown personal toiletry items is provided. Note that there is a small step between bedroom and bathroom.

The two largest suites (Saint Columba and Saint

BERLITZ'S RATINGS

	Possible	Achieved
Ship	500	432
Accommodation	200	177
Food	400	350
Service	400	341
Entertainment	N/A	N/A
Cruise	500	407

Oran) and all balcony cabins feature a combination color television and *integral* DVD player.

DINING: The Argyll Restaurant is a non-smoking dining room with ocean-view portholes, and operates with table assignments for dinner, in a single seating, and an open seating arrangement for breakfast and lunch. It is a very elegant and pleasant room, with wood paneling, fine furnishings, subtle lighting, and plenty of space around each table. A mix of chairs with and without armrests is provided. There are many tables for two, although there are also tables for four, six, and eight. Tables are always laid with crisp white linen, and ship's officers eat with passengers each night. Villeroy & Boch patterned china is used. Dinner is typically at 7.30 pm.

The cuisine is extremely creative – at times outstanding – and about the same quality and presentation (although not quite the variety) as can be found aboard *SeaDream I* and *SeaDream II*. Fresh ingredients are often purchased locally when possible – a welcome change from the mass catering of most ships. The desserts are worth saving space for. Note that Hebridean Island Cruises operates within European Community regulations concerning genetically modified foods, which are not used aboard *Hebridean Spirit*.

Breakfasts and lunches can also be taken outdoors at the alfresco Mizzen Deck Brasserie, particularly when the ship is operating in warm weather areas. Morning coffee and afternoon tea can be taken in the lounge areas or (weather permitting) on the open decks.

OTHER COMMENTS: The ship has a contemporary look, although there is also a traditional single funnel. The navigation bridge is a well-rounded half-moon design. It was one of four identical vessels originally built for Renaissance Cruises, and acquired by Hebridean Island Cruises in November 2000. After being chartered to Star Cruises until March 2001, the ship underwent an extensive redesign and refurbishment program. Its exterior design has been altered somewhat with the addition of an enclosed lounge deck forward of the single funnel, which has been made to look similar to that of sister ship *Hebridean Princess*. An open bridge policy means that passengers can go to the bridge at any time (except during maneuvers or in inclement weather conditions), and may also visit the engine room.

There is one wrap-around teakwood promenade deck outdoors, and a very reasonable amount of open deck and sunbathing space. All of the deck furniture – the tables and chairs – are made of teak and the deck lounge chairs have thick cushioned pads. All exterior handrails are of beautifully polished wood. There is also a teakwood water sports platform at the stern of the ship, where two fine, water-jet driven shore tenders (Ardbeg and Talisker) are located (these have high central rails inside for passengers to hold when standing up). The ship also carries a number of lightweight bicycles (helmets are also provided, and required), for those who like to be independent explorers in ports of call.

Inside the ship, you will find elegant interior design and the touches reminiscent of a small, lavish country house hotel (most of its original furnishings and fittings were removed in a multi-million pound refurbishment program when the ship was delivered to Hebridean Island Cruises in 2001). The Skye Lounge is the ship's main lounge, and it has the unmistakable feel of a traditional drawing room; it includes a large, white, Bath stone fireplace with an imitation log fire (safety regulations prohibit a real one). This is the focal point for all social activities and cocktail parties, although it does look a little large considering the size of the room.

Smokers can enjoy their very own (small) Lookout Room, adjacent to the Panorama Lounge (where you'll find internet-connect computer stations), located forward of the funnel, atop the ship. A humidor is provided. There is also a good travel library/reading room.

About a half-dozen bicycles are kept on board for passengers who want to go off on their own discovery pedal, otherwise, shore excursions are typically included, and always well arranged. Destination lecturers are provided during the cruise.

The ship's itineraries take participants mostly to quiet, off-the-beaten-track ports not often visited by larger cruise ships. So, what is so good about a cruise aboard this ship? It's the faultless, friendly but unobtrusive service, and the attention to detail so lacking in most large ships today. This utterly charming little ship has a warm, totally cosseted, traditional country house ambience that is unobtrusive but always at hand when you need it. Inspector Hercule Poirot would be very much at home here, as it is rather like a small, exclusive club. The fact that the ship does not have photographers and some of the trappings found aboard larger ships does not matter one bit.

Passengers really like the fact that there is no formal entertainment, game shows, bingo, horse racing, art auctions, or mindless parlor games – just good company and easy conversation, and very soft, gentle music in the lounges at certain times. Although the dress code is casual and comfortable, most passengers dress well for dinner; there are typically two formal evenings each cruise when passengers do enjoy dressing in evening dress.

Mid-morning bouillon, afternoon tea with homemade cakes and biscuits (cookies) are a lovely fact of lifestyle aboard this floating country house hotel.

All in all, a cruise aboard *Hebridean Spirit* should prove to be ideal for those who don't like large cruise ships. The service is friendly but unobtrusive; the atmosphere is quiet and sophisticated, and the ship is well run by a crew who are proud to provide the kind of personal service expected by passengers who are intellectual and well traveled.

Hebridean Island Cruises also operates a much smaller, even more intimate sister ship, mainly in the western islands off the coast of Scotland, *Hebridean Princess*. The company's brochure uses only real passengers in its photographs. Note that children under the age of nine are not accepted on board (the ship is too small to provide children's facilities, and many of the ship's repeat passengers are allergic to children running around their ship anyway).

The onboard currency is the British pound. All gratuities and all soft drinks are included in the fare (the company requests that no additional gratuities be given).

WEAK POINTS: There is no switch to turn off in-cabin announcements. There are several pillars in seemingly silly places in public rooms and hallways (although these are needed for structural reasons) and detract from the overall spaciousness of the ship. The décor consists of plastic woods instead of real woods (it looks almost too perfect in places), although it does work.

Large Ship:	.46,052 tons	Passengers	
Lifestyle:	Standard	(lower beds/all berths):	.1,452/1,800
Cruise Line:	Carnival Cruise Lines	Passenger Space Ratio	
Former Names:	none	(lower beds/all berths):	.31.7/25.5
Builder:	Aalborg Vaerft (Denmark)	Crew/Passenger Ratio	
Original Cost:	$170 million	(lower beds/all berths):	.2.2/2.7
Entered Service:	July 1985	Navigation Officers:	Italian
Registry:	The Bahamas	Cabins (total):	.726
Length (ft/m):	726.9/221.57	Size Range (sq ft/m):	.182.9–189.4/
Beam (ft/m):	.92.4/28.17		17.0–17.6
Draft (ft/m):	.25.5/7.77	Cabins (outside view):	.447
Propulsion/Propellers:	diesel	Cabins (interior/no view):	.279
	(22,360kW)/2	Cabins (for one person):	.0
Passenger Decks:	.9	Cabins (with private balcony):	.10
Total Crew:	.660	Cabins (wheelchair accessible):	.15

Cabin Current:	.110 volts
Elevators:	.8
Casino (gaming tables):	Yes
Slot Machines:	Yes
Swimming Pools (outdoors):	.3
Swimming Pools (indoors):	.0
Whirlpools:	.2
Fitness Center:	Yes
Sauna/Steam Room:	Yes/No
Massage:	Yes
Self-Service Launderette:	Yes
Dedicated Cinema/Seats:	No
Library:	Yes
Classification Society:	Lloyd's Register

OVERALL SCORE: 1,318 (OUT OF A POSSIBLE 2,000 POINTS)

ACCOMMODATION: Carnival Cruise Lines has always tried to provide an adequate amount of space in passenger cabins, and the cabins aboard *Holiday* are no exception. They are quite functional and provide all the basics; bathrooms are practical units, with decent-sized shower stalls.

A gift basket is provided in all grades of accommodation; it includes aloe soap, shampoo, conditioner, deodorant, breath mints, candy, and pain relief tablets (albeit all in sample sizes).

Note that if you book accommodation in one of the suites (Category 11 or 12 in the Carnival Cruise Lines brochure) you automatically qualify for "Skipper's Club" priority check-in at any US homeland port – useful for getting ahead of the crowd.

DINING: There are two dining rooms (Four Winds, and Seven Seas); both are large and have low ceilings, making the raised center sections seem crowded (intimate?), and noisy because they are always full. Dining in each restaurant is now in four seatings, for greater flexibility: 6pm, 6.45pm, 8pm and 8.45pm (times are approximate).

Carnival meals stress quantity, not quality, although the company constantly works hard to improve the cuisine. While passengers seem to accept it, few find it worth remembering. However, food and its taste are still not the company's strongest points (you get what you pay for, remember).

While the menu items sound good, their presentation and taste leave much to be desired. While meats are of a high quality, fish and seafood is not. Presentation is

BERLITZ'S RATINGS

	Possible	Achieved
Ship	500	355
Accommodation	200	143
Food	400	221
Service	400	275
Entertainment	100	74
Cruise	400	250

simple, and few garnishes are used. Many meat and fowl dishes are disguised with gravies and sauces. The selection of fresh green vegetables, breads, rolls, cheeses and fruits is limited, and there is too much use of canned fruit and jellied desserts. However, do remember that this is banquet catering, with all its attendant standardization and production cooking (it is, therefore, difficult to ask for anything remotely unusual or off-menu). The selection of breads, rolls, cheeses and fruits is limited (there is too much use of canned fruit).

Although there is a decent wine list, there are no wine waiters. The service is highly programmed, although the waiters are willing and reasonably friendly. However, the waiters do sing and dance, and there are constant waiter parades; the dining room is show business – all done in the name of eventual gratuities.

The Lido Café self-serve buffets are very basic, as is the selection of breads, rolls, fruit and cheeses. At night, the "Seaview Bistro," as the Lido Café becomes known, provides a casual (dress down) alternative to eating in the main dining rooms, serving pasta, steaks, salads and desserts (it typically is in operation between 6pm and 9pm).

OTHER COMMENTS: The second new ship ordered by Carnival Cruise Lines, *Holiday* is a bold, high-sided, all-white contemporary ship with short, rakish bow and stubby stern typical of so many recently built ships. The ship, whose bows are extremely short, has the distinctive, large, swept-back wing-tipped funnel that is the trademark of Carnival Cruise Lines, in the company colors of red, white and blue.

Inside, the passenger flow is quite good. There are numerous public rooms on two entertainment decks to choose from and play in, and these flow from a double-width indoor promenade. A real red-and-cream bus is located right in the middle of one of the two promenades, and this is used as a snack café.

There is a stunning, multi-tiered show lounge, although the sight lines are restricted from some seats that are located behind the several pillars.

The bright (very bright) interior décor has a distinct Broadway theme. The Carnegie Library (which has very few books) is the only public room that is not bright. The casino is good, and there is around-the-clock action. There is plenty of dazzle and sizzle entertainment, while "Camp Carnival" takes care of the junior cruisers (facilities include virtual-reality machines).

This ship, now over 10 years old, is ideal for a first cruise experience in glitzy, very lively surroundings, and for the active set who enjoy constant stimulation, loud music, and a fun-filled atmosphere, at an attractive price. The line does not provide finesse, nor does it claim to. But, forget fashion – having fun is the *sine qua non* of a Carnival cruise. There is no doubt that Carnival does a great job of providing a fun venue, but many passengers say that once is enough, and after you will want to move to a more upscale experience.

Holiday operates 7-day Southern Caribbean cruises, from San Juan. Gratuities are automatically added to your onboard account at $9.75 per person, per day; you can have this amount adjusted, although you'll have to visit the information desk to do so. The onboard currency is the US dollar.

WEAK POINTS: Standing in line for embarkation, disembarkation, shore tenders and for self-serve buffet meals is an inevitable aspect of cruising aboard all large ships. A cruise aboard this ship can be noisy and not relaxing at all (although it is good if you enjoy big-city nightlife). There is absolutely no escape from unnecessary and repetitive announcements (particularly for activities that bring revenue, such as art auctions, bingo, horse racing) that intrude constantly into your cruise, and a great deal of hustling for drinks, although it is sometimes done with a knowing smile.

Removed 2006

Large Ship: . . . . .46,811 tons	Passengers	Cabin Current: . . . . .110 volts
Lifestyle: . . . . .Premium	(lower beds/all berths): 1,354/1,660	Elevators: 7
Cruise Line: . . . . .Celebrity Cruises	Passenger Space Ratio	Casino (gaming tables): . . . . .Yes
Former Names: . . . . .none	(lower beds/all berths): 34.5/28.1	Slot Machines: . . . . .Yes
Builder: . . . . .Meyer Werft (Germany)	Crew/Passenger Ratio	Swimming Pools (outdoors): 2
Original Cost: . . . .$185 million	(lower beds/all berths): 2.1/2.5	Swimming Pools (indoors): 0
Entered Service: . . . . .May 1990	Navigation Officers: . . . . .Greek	Whirlpools: 0
Registry: . . . . .The Bahamas	Cabins (total): 677	Fitness Center: . . . . .Yes
Length (ft/m): 681.1/207.6	Size Range (sq ft/m): 172.0–340.0/	Sauna/Steam Room: . . . . .Yes/No
Beam (ft/m): 95.1/29.0	17.0–31.0	Massage: . . . . .Yes
Draft (ft/m): 23.6/7.2	Cabins (outside view): 529	Self-Service Launderette: . . . . .No
Propulsion/Propellers: . . . . .diesel	Cabins (interior/no view): 148	Dedicated Cinema/Seats: . . . . .No
(19,960kW)/2	Cabins (for one person): 0	Library: . . . . .Yes
Passenger Decks: 9	Cabins (with private balcony): 0	Classification Society: . . .Lloyd's Register
Total Crew: 642	Cabins (wheelchair accessible): 4	

OVERALL SCORE: 1,544 (OUT OF A POSSIBLE 2,000 POINTS)

ACCOMMODATION: There are 12 grades of accommodation, including outside-view suites and cabins, and interior (no view) cabins, but even the smallest cabin is considerably larger than most of the standard outside and interior (no view) cabins aboard the ships of sister company Royal Caribbean International. Note that no cabins have private balconies (they were not yet in vogue when this ship was constructed). Note that most outside cabins on Bermuda Deck have lifeboat-obstructed views.

STANDARD CABINS: All standard outside-view and interior (no view) cabins have good quality fittings with lots of wood accenting, are tastefully decorated and of an above-average size, with an excellent amount of closet and drawer space, and reasonable insulation between cabins. All have twin beds that convert to a queen-sized bed, and a good amount of closet and drawer space. The cabin soundproofing is fair to very good, depending on the location. All accommodation has interactive Celebrity Television, including pay-per-view movies.

The bathrooms have a generous shower area, and a small range of toiletries is provided (typically soap, shampoo/conditioner, body lotion, and shower cap), although bathroom towels are a little small, as is storage space for personal toiletry items. The lowest-grade outside-view cabins have a porthole, but all others have picture windows.

PRESIDENTIAL SUITES: The largest accommodation can be found in two Presidential Suites on Atlantic Deck

BERLITZ'S RATINGS		
	Possible	Achieved
Ship	500	398
Accommodation	200	158
Food	400	304
Service	400	317
Entertainment	100	68
Cruise	400	299

(Deck 10). These have butler service, and have a separate bedroom (with European duvets instead of sheets and blankets) and lounge with dining table, CD player and VCR player in addition to the large TV set. The bathroom is larger and comes with a whirlpool bathtub with integral shower.

Another 18 suites (also on Atlantic Deck) are very tastefully furnished, although they are really just larger cabins and should not be called suites. They are not as large as the suites aboard the company's seven largest vessels, *Century, Constellation Galaxy, Infinity, Mercury, Millennium,* and *Summit.* They do have a generous amount of drawer and other storage space, however, and a sleeping area (with European duvets on the beds instead of sheets and blankets) plus a lounge area. They also have good bathrooms. Butler service is standard.

DINING: Celebrity Cruises has achieved an enviable reputation for providing outstanding quality food, fine presentation and service. The Starlight Restaurant, which also has two "wings" (good for small groups) is set on a single level with a raised central section, is large, yet it feels almost intimate. There are two seatings for dinner (open seating for breakfast and lunch), at tables for two, four, six, eight or 10, and the dining room is a no-smoking area. The chairs do not have armrests, however, due to space limitations. There are separate menus for vegetarians and children. The wine list is quite extensive, and the prices quite reasonable.

A casual Coral Seas Cafe has decent self-serve buffets for breakfast (including an omelet station) and lunch (including a pasta station and vegetarian salad bar); waiters take your trays of food and escort you to tables. At night, the casual café changes into an alternative dining venue for those who want good food, but in a more casual setting than the main restaurant, with items such as grilled salmon, steaks, and rotisserie chicken, as well as specialties that change frequently (ideal for families with children).

Additionally, an outdoor grill serves fast-food items such as hamburgers and hot dogs. Caviar, at extra cost, is available in the America's Cup Club. For those who can't live without them, freshly baked pizzas (in a box) can be delivered, in an insulated pouch, to your cabin.

OTHER COMMENTS: *Horizon* is a handsome, contemporary ship (the first new ship for Celebrity Cruises), with any sharp angles softened by clever exterior styling (blue striping along the ship's hull break up the monotonous all-white exterior of so many of today's ships). There is a good amount of open deck space, and cushioned pads are provided for poolside deck lounge chairs.

Inside, the public rooms are spacious, have high ceilings, and provide very good passenger flow throughout. Elegant furnishings and appointments are the norm, with fine quality fabrics used throughout. Soothing pastel colors are relaxing, but not boring. The wood-paneled casino has a stately look (outside is a satellite-linked BankAtlantic ATM machine, with a $5 access charge).

The two-level show lounge has excellent sight lines from most seats, including the balcony level. There is nothing brash or glitzy about this ship anywhere, although the décor is a little plain and clinical in places. The two-deck-high lobby is has a peachy Miami Beach art-deco hotel look. A self-service launderette would have proven useful for longer cruises. Much appreciated by many passengers is the "zero announcement" policy.

An extensive refurbishment in 1998 saw the addition (on Deck 8) of a grand "Michael's Club" cigar-smoking lounge in what was formerly the underused discotheque (it includes a bar, fireplace, extremely comfortable chairs and leather sofas). A new library was added, complete with audio CD listening seats, card room and small business area with two computers/printers for passenger use. Also added, on Deck 7, was a small, delightful art deco-style martini bar (with 26 martinis to choose from). A room dedicated to the display of artwork (for art auctions) was added. The health spa has also been expanded. This now includes a seraglio (rasul) treatment room, relocated beauty salon, enlarged fitness/exercise areas and five massage and other treatment rooms. A Cova Café has replaced what was formerly the Plaza Bar (Cova is the name of the Milan-based coffee house that also makes exclusive chocolates and liqueurs – the original Cova Café, located near the La Scala Opera House, opened in 1756). Celebrity Cruises has an exclusive agreement with Pasticceria Confetteria Cova.).

Horizon delivers a well-defined North American cruise experience at a very modest price. Note that a 15 percent gratuity is automatically added to all bar and wine accounts. The onboard currency is the US dollar.

WEAK POINTS: Unlike the company's larger ships *Century, Galaxy, Mercury* and *Millennium*, no suites or cabins have private balconies. Trying to reach Cabin Service or the Guest Relations Desk to answer the phone (to order breakfast, for example, if you don't want to do so via the interactive television) is a matter of luck, timing and patience (a sad reminder of the automated age, and lack of personal contact). The room service menu, food items and presentation are well below the standard of food featured in the dining room.

The doors to the public restrooms and the outdoor decks are heavy. The public restrooms are clinical and need warmer décor. There are cushioned pads for poolside deck lounge chairs only, but not for chairs on other outside decks. There is a charge for using the AquaSpa/sauna/steam room complex unless you are purchasing a spa treatment. Passenger participation activities are amateurish and should be upgraded. The officers have become more aloof lately, with far less contact with passengers than when the company first started.

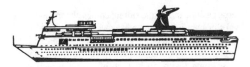

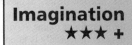

Imagination
★★★ +

Large Ship:	..............70,367 tons	Passengers
Lifestyle:	..................Standard	(lower beds/all berths):
Cruise Line:	......Carnival Cruise Lines	Passenger Space Ratio
Former Names:	.................none	(lower beds/all berths):

Large Ship: ....70,367 tons
Lifestyle: ....Standard
Cruise Line: ......Carnival Cruise Lines
Former Names: ....none
Builder: ...Kvaerner Masa-Yards (Finland)
Original Cost: ....$330 million
Entered Service: ....July 1995
Registry: ....The Bahamas
Length (ft/m): 855.0/260.6
Beam (ft/m): 103.0/31.4
Draft (ft/m): 25.9/7.9
Propulsion/Propellers: .....diesel-electric
(42,240 kW)/2
Passenger Decks: 10
Total Crew: 920

Passengers
(lower beds/all berths): 2,056/2,634
Passenger Space Ratio
(lower beds/all berths): 34.4/26.7
Crew/Passenger Ratio
(lower beds/all berths): 2.2/2.8
Navigation Officers: ....Italian
Cabins (total): 1,028
Size Range (sq ft/m): 173.2–409.7/
16.0–38.0
Cabins (outside view): 620
Cabins (interior/no view): 408
Cabins (for one person): 0
Cabins (with private balcony): 54
Cabins (wheelchair accessible): 22

Cabin Current: ....110 volts
Elevators: 14
Casino (gaming tables): ....Yes
Slot Machines: ....Yes
Swimming Pools (outdoors): 3
Swimming Pools (indoors): 0
Whirlpools: 6
Fitness Center: ....Yes
Sauna/Steam Room: ....Yes/Yes
Massage:.........................Yes
Self-Service Launderette: ....Yes
Dedicated Cinema/Seats: ....No
Library: ....Yes
Classification Society: ...Lloyd's Register

OVERALL SCORE: 1,385 (OUT OF A POSSIBLE 2,000 POINTS)

ACCOMMODATION: As in sister ships *Ecstasy, Elation, Fantasy, Fascination, Inspiration, Paradise* and *Sensation*), the standard outside-view and interior (no view) cabins have plain décor. They are marginally comfortable, yet spacious enough and practical (most are of the same size and appointments), with good storage space and well-designed bathrooms.

Those booking one of the outside suites will find more space, whirlpool bathtubs, and some fascinating, rather eclectic décor and furniture. These are mildly attractive, but nothing special, and they are much smaller than those aboard the ships of a similar size of several competing companies.

A gift basket is provided in all grades of accommodation; it includes aloe soap, shampoo, conditioner, deodorant, breath mints, candy, and pain relief tablets (albeit all in sample sizes).

Note that if you book accommodation in one of the suites (Category 11 or 12 in the Carnival Cruise Lines brochure) you automatically qualify for "Skipper's Club" priority check-in at any US homeland port – useful for getting ahead of the crowd.

DINING: There are two large, colorful, noisy dining rooms (Pride and Spirit), and both are non-smoking. Shorts are permitted in the dining room for one dinner each cruise. Dining in each restaurant is now in four seatings, for greater flexibility: 6pm, 6.45pm, 8pm and 8.45pm (times are approximate) – this should give you some idea what to expect from your dining experience. Carnival meals stress quantity, not quality, although

BERLITZ'S RATINGS

	Possible	Achieved
Ship	500	395
Accommodation	200	151
Food	400	221
Service	400	270
Entertainment	100	81
Cruise	400	267

the company constantly works hard to improve the cuisine. While passengers seem to accept it, few find it worth remembering. However, food and its taste are still not the company's strongest points (you get what you pay for, remember).

While the menu items sound good, their presentation and taste leave much to be desired. While meats are of a high quality, fish and seafood is not. Presentation is simple, and few garnishes are used. Many meat and fowl dishes are disguised with gravies and sauces. The selection of fresh green vegetables, breads, rolls, cheeses and fruits is limited, and there is too much use of canned fruit and jellied desserts. However, do remember that this is banquet catering, with all its attendant standardization and production cooking (it is, therefore, difficult to ask for anything remotely unusual or off-menu). The selection of breads, rolls, cheeses and fruits is limited (there is too much use of canned fruit).

Although there is a decent wine list, there are no wine waiters (the waiters are expected to serve both food and wine, which does not work well) – and no decent-sized wine glasses. The service is highly programmed, although the waiters are willing and reasonably friendly. However, the waiters do sing and dance (be prepared for *Simply the Best, Hot, Hot, Hot, Hot,* and other popular hits), and there are constant waiter parades; the dining room is show business – all done in the name of gratuities at the end of your cruise.

The Lido Café self-serve buffets are very basic, as is the selection of breads, rolls, fruit and cheeses. At night, the "Seaview Bistro," as the Lido Café becomes known, provides a casual (dress down) alternative to eating in the main dining rooms, serving pasta, steaks, salads and desserts (it typically is in operation between 6pm and 9pm). There's also a Pizzeria (this one is open 24 hours a day and typically serves over 500 *every* single day)!

OTHER COMMENTS: The ship has a forthright, angular appearance typical of today's space-creative designs. This is the fifth in a series of eight identically sized Carnival ships (but actually the ninth new ship for the company). The ship, whose bows are extremely short, has the distinctive, large, swept-back wing-tipped funnel that is the trademark of Carnival Cruise Lines, in the company colors of red, white and blue. At its base is a "topless" area for sunbathing.

Inside, the ship reflects the talents of interior designer Joe Farcus, whose philosophy is that the cruise ship environment should provide fantasy and an escape from routine with "entertainment architecture." Like all Carnival ships, this one has themed décor for its interiors; for this ship classical mythology and ethereal décor can be found throughout the public rooms, which are connected by a double-width indoor boulevard. The ship has expansive open deck areas and a good, well-segmented health spa, and there is also a $1 million art collection, with many items in public areas featuring some timeless mosaics.

Ship buffs will enjoy six Stephen Card paintings of clipper ships, positioned in the Grand Bar. The Victorian-style library is a curious room, with intentionally mismatched furnishings (it reminds one of Alice in Wonderland), fine oriental rugs, and even a few books. The multi-tiered show lounge is quite lavish, and almost elegant. Unfortunately, it has 20 pillars obstructing sight. The production shows are of the colorful, frenetic, razzle-dazzle type. An ATM machine is located outside the large casino, and all the slot machines aboard all Carnival ships are linked into a Megacash give-away.

This ship is one of the great floating playgrounds for young, active adults who enjoy constant stimulation, close contact with lots and lots of others, as well as the three Gs – glitz, glamour and gambling. It is a live board game with every move executed in typically grand, colorful, fun-filled Carnival Cruise Lines style. This ship will provide a great introduction to cruising for the novice passenger seeking an action-packed short cruise experience in contemporary surroundings, with a real swinging party atmosphere, and minimum fuss and finesse. You will have a fine time if you like nightlife and lots of silly participation games. Like life in the fast lane, this is cruising in theme-park fantasyland, and the dress code is extremely casual. The staff will help you have organized fun, and that is what Carnival does best. Want to party? Then this should prove to be a great ship for you. Forget fashion – having fun is the *sine qua non* of a Carnival cruise.

Imagination operates 4- and 5-day Western Caribbean cruises from Miami. Gratuities are automatically added to your onboard account at $9.75 per person, per day; you can have this amount adjusted, although you'll have to visit the information desk to do so. The onboard currency is the US dollar.

WEAK POINTS: Standing in line for embarkation, disembarkation, shore tenders and for self-serve buffet meals is an inevitable aspect of cruising aboard all large ships. This ship is not for those who want a quiet, relaxing cruise experience. There is absolutely no escape from unnecessary and repetitive announcements (particularly for activities that bring revenue, such as art auctions, bingo, horse racing) that intrude constantly into your cruise, and a great deal of hustling for drinks, although it is sometimes done with a knowing smile.

Infinity
★★★★★

Large Ship: ....90,228 tons	Passengers	Cabin Current: ....110 and 220 volts
Lifestyle: ....Premium	(lower beds/all berths): 1,950/2,450	Elevators: 10
Cruise Line: ....Celebrity Cruises	Passenger Space Ratio	Casino (gaming tables): ....Yes
Former Names: ....none	(lower beds/all berths): 46.6/37.1	Slot Machines: ....Yes
Builder: ....Chantiers de l'Atlantique	Crew/Passenger Ratio	Swimming Pools (outdoors): 2
(France)	(lower beds/all berths): 1.9/2.4	Swimming Pools (indoors): 1
Original Cost: ....$350 million	Navigation Officers: ....Greek	(with magrodome)
Entered Service: ....Mar 2001	Cabins (total): 975	Whirlpools: 4
Registry: ....The Bahamas	Size Range (sq ft/m): 165.1–2,350.0/	Fitness Center: ....Yes
Length (ft/m): 964.5/294.0	15.34–218.3	Sauna/Steam Room: ....Yes/Yes
Beam (ft/m): 105.6/32.2	Cabins (outside view): 780	Massage:.........................Yes
Draft (ft/m): 26.2/8.0	Cabins (interior/no view): 195	Self-Service Launderette: ....No
Propulsion/Propellers: .....gas turbine/2	Cabins (for one person): 0	Dedicated Cinema/Seats: Yes/368
azimuthing pods (39,000 kW)	Cabins (with private balcony): 590	Library: ....Yes
Passenger Decks: 11	Cabins (wheelchair accessible): 26	Classification Society: ...Lloyd's Register
Total Crew: 999	(17 with private balcony)	

OVERALL SCORE: 1,701 (OUT OF A POSSIBLE 2,000 POINTS)

ACCOMMODATION: There are 20 different grades of accommodation from which to choose, depending on your preference for the size and location of your living space. Almost half of the ship's accommodation features a "private" balcony; approximately 80 percent are outside-view suites and cabins, and 20 percent are interior (no view) cabins. The accommodation is extremely comfortable throughout this ship, regardless of which cabin grade you choose. Suites, naturally, have more space, butler service (whether you want it or not), more and better amenities and more personal service than if you choose any of the standard cabin grades. There are several categories of suites, but those at the stern of the ship are in a prime location and have huge balconies that are really private and not overlooked from above.

Regardless of which grade of accommodation you choose, all suites and cabins have wood cabinetry and accenting, interactive television and entertainment systems (you can go shopping, book shore excursions, play casino games, interactively, and even watch soft porn movies). Bathrooms have hairdryers, and 100 percent cotton towels.

PENTHOUSE SUITES: Two Penthouse Suites (on Penthouse Deck) are the largest accommodation aboard. Each occupies one half of the beam (width) of the ship, overlooking the ship's stern. Each measures a huge 2,530 sq. ft (235 sq. meters): 1,431.6 sq. ft (133 sq. meters) of living space, plus a huge wrap-around balcony measuring

BERLITZ'S RATINGS

	Possible	Achieved
Ship	500	454
Accommodation	200	181
Food	400	328
Service	400	330
Entertainment	100	78
Cruise	400	330

1,098 sq. ft (102 sq, meters) with 180-degree views, which occupies one half of the beam (width) of the ship, overlooking the ship's stern (it includes a wet bar, hot tub and whirlpool tub); however, note that much of this terrace can be overlooked by passengers on other decks above.

Features include a marble foyer, a separate living room (complete with ebony baby grand piano – bring your own pianist if you don't play yourself) and a formal dining room. The master bedroom has a large walk-in closet; personal exercise equipment; dressing room with vanity desk, exercise equipment; marble-clad master bathroom with twin washbasins; deep whirlpool bathtub; separate shower; toilet and bidet areas; flat-screen televisions (one in the bedroom and one in the lounge) and electronically controlled drapes. Butler service is standard, and a butler's pantry, with separate entry door, features a full-size refrigerator, temperature-controlled wine cabinet, microwave oven and good-sized food preparation and storage areas. For even more space, an interconnecting door can be opened into the adjacent suite (ideal for multi-generation families).

ROYAL SUITES: Eight Royal Suites, each measuring 733 sq. ft (68 sq. meters), are located towards the aft of the ship (four each on the port and starboard sides). Each features a separate living room with dining and lounge areas (with refrigerator, mini-bar and a Bang & Olufsen CD sound system), and a separate bedroom. There are two entertainment centers with DVD players, and two flat-screen televisions (one in the living area, one in the bedroom), and a large walk-in closet with vanity desk. The marble-clad bathroom has a whirlpool bathtub with integral shower, and there is also a separate shower enclosure, two washbasins and toilet. The teakwood decked balcony is extensive (large enough for on-deck massage) and also features a whirlpool hot tub.

CELEBRITY SUITES: Eight Celebrity Suites, each measuring 467 sq. ft (44 sq. meters), have floor-to-ceiling windows, a separate living room with dining and lounge areas, two entertainment centers with flat-screen televisions (one in the living room, one in the bedroom), and a walk-in closet with vanity desk. The marble-clad bathroom has a whirlpool bathtub with integral shower (a window with movable blind lets you look out of the bathroom through the lounge to the large ocean-view windows). Interconnecting doors allow two suites to be used as a family unit (as there is no balcony, these suites are ideal for families with small children). These suites overhang the starboard side of the ship (they are located opposite a group of glass-walled elevators), and provide stunning ocean views from the glass-walled sitting/dining area, which extends out from the ship's side. A personal computer with wood-surround screen allows direct internet connectivity. Butler service is standard.

SKY SUITES: There are 30 Sky Suites, each measuring 308 sq. ft (28.6 sq. meters), including the private balcony (some balconies may be larger than others, depending on the location). Although these are designated as suites, they are really just larger cabins that feature a marble-clad bathroom with bathtub/shower combination. The suites also have a VCR player in addition to a television, and have a larger lounge area (than standard cabins) and sleeping area. Butler service is standard.

BUTLER SERVICE: Butler service (in all accommodation designated as suites) includes full breakfast, in-suite lunch and dinner service (as required), afternoon tea service, evening hors d'oeuvres, complimentary espresso and cappuccino, daily news delivery, shoeshine service, and other personal touches.

Suite occupants in Penthouse, Royal, Celebrity and Sky suites also get welcome champagne; a full personal computer in each suite, including a printer and internet access (on request in the Sky Suites); choice of films from a video library; personalized stationery; tote bag; priority dining room seating preferences; private portrait sitting, and bathrobe; and in-suite massage service.

STANDARD OUTSIDE-VIEW/INTERIOR (NO VIEW) CABINS: All other outside-view and interior (no view) cabins feature a lounge area with sofa or convertible sofa bed, sleeping area with twin beds that can convert to a double bed, a good amount of closet and drawer space, personal safe, mini-bar/refrigerator (extra cost), interactive television, and private bathroom. The cab-

ins are nicely decorated with warm wood-finish furniture, and there is none of the boxy feel of cabins in so many ships, due to the angled placement of vanity and audio-video consoles. Even the smallest cabin has a good-sized bathroom and shower enclosure.

WHEELCHAIR-ACCESSIBLE ACCOMMODATION: Wheelchair-accessible accommodation is available in six Sky Suites, three premium outside-view, eight deluxe ocean-view, four standard ocean-view and five interior (no view) cabins measure 347 sq. ft to 362 sq. ft (32.2–33.6 sq. meters) and are located in the most practical parts of the ship and close to elevators for good accessibility (all have doorways and bathroom doorways and showers are wheelchair-accessible. Some cabins have extra berths for third or third and fourth occupants (note, however, that there is only one safe for personal belongings, which must be shared).

DINING: The Thellis Restaurant is the ship's 1,170-seat formal dining room. It is two decks high, has a grand staircase connecting the two levels, a huge glass wall overlooking the sea at the stern of the ship (electrically operated blinds provide several different backdrops), and a musician's gallery on the upper level (typically for a string quartet/quintet). There are two seatings for dinner (open seating for breakfast and lunch), at tables for two, four, six, eight or 10. The dining room is a totally no-smoking area, and, you should note, that, like all large dining halls, it can prove to be extremely noisy.

Besides this principal restaurant, there are several other dining options, particularly for those seeking more casual dining, or for an extra-special (extra cost) meal in a more intimate (and quiet) setting. Full service in-cabin dining is also available for all meals (including dinner).

For casual eating, the Las Olas Café and Grill is a self-serve buffet area, with six principal serving lines, and seating for 754; there is also a grill and pizza bar.

For champagne and caviar lovers, not to mention martinis, Carlisle's is the place to see and be seen.

ALTERNATIVE (RESERVATIONS-ONLY, EXTRA COST) DINING: The United States Restaurant is the ship's alternative *dining salon*, located adjacent to the main lobby. Actual glass paneling from the former United States Lines liner *United States* is featured (in 1952, the *United States* gained renown for the fastest transatlantic crossing by a passenger ship, and took the famed "Blue Riband" from the Cunard liner *Queen Mary*). The United States Restaurant is not nearly as luxurious as the alternative dining salons aboard sister ships *Constellation, Millennium* or *Summit*.

Fine tableside preparation is the attraction of this alternative dining room, whose classic French cuisine (but including some menu items from the famous liner *United States*) and service is outstanding (masterminded by Michel Roux, owner of a three-star Michelin restaurant near Windsor in England). This is haute cuisine at the height of professionalism, for this is, indeed, a room for a full dégustation, and not merely a dinner. However, with just 134 seats, not all passengers will be able to experience it even once during a one-week cruise (reservations are necessary, and a cover charge of $25 per person applies). A dine-in wine cellar is also a feature, as is a demonstration galley.

COVA CAFÉ DI MILANO: Additionally, a Cova Café di Milano (with 92 seats) is a signature item aboard all the ships of Celebrity Cruises, and a seagoing version of the real Café di Milano that was originally located next to La Scala Opera House in Milan (it opened in 1817). It is located in a prominent position, on the second level of the atrium lobby, and several display cases show off the extensive range of Cova coffee, chocolates and alcoholic digestives; this is *the* place to see and be seen. The Cova Cafe is for anyone who appreciates fine Italian coffees (for espresso, espresso macchiato, cappuccino, and latte), pastries and superb cakes in an elegant, refined setting.

OTHER COMMENTS: *Infinity* is a sister ship to *Constellation, Millennium* and *Summit.* Jon Bannenberg (famous for his mega-yacht designs) designed the exterior that features a royal blue and white hull, and racy lines in red, blue and gold, although it has actually turned out to look extremely ungainly (some say downright ugly). This is the second Celebrity Cruises ship to be fitted with a "pod" propulsion system (and controllable pitch propellers) coupled with a quiet, smokeless, energy-efficient *gas* turbine powerplant (two GE gas turbines provide engine power while a single GE steam turbine drives the electricity generators).

Inside, the ship features the same high-class décor and materials, and public rooms that have made the existing ships in the fleet so popular and user-friendly. But in a first for Celebrity Cruises, the atrium spans 11 decks. It is capped with a glass dome, and four glass elevators travel through the port side of the atrium. Michael's Club (a cigar and cognac specialty lounge that offers almost 20 varieties of cigars) is located on Promenade Deck.

Facilities include a combination Cinema/Conference Center, an expansive shopping arcade with a 14,447 sq.-ft (1,300 sq.-meter) retail store space (including H. Stern, Donna Karan, Fossil, and the exclusive Michel Roux culinary store), a lavish four-decks-high show lounge with the latest in staging and lighting equipment, two-level library (one level for English-language books; a second level for books in other languages); card room; compact disc listening room; art auction center (with seating that look rather more like a small chapel); Cosmos, a combination observation lounge/discotheque; an Internet Center with 18 computer stations.

One unique feature is a conservatory that includes seating, set in a botanical environment of flowers, plants, tress, mini-gardens and fountains, designed by the award-winning floral designer Emilio Robba of Paris. It is located directly in front of the main funnel and has glass walls that overlook the ship's side.

Outdoor facilities include two outdoor pools, one indoor/outdoor pool, and six whirlpools. There is a large AquaSpa (with large thalassotherapy pool under a huge solarium dome), complete with health bar for light breakfast and lunch items, and fresh squeezed fruit and vegetable juices. Spa facilities include 16 treatment rooms, plus eight treatment rooms with showers and one treatment room specifically designed for wheelchair passengers, aerobics room, gymnasium (complete with over 40 exercise machines), large male and female saunas (with large ocean-view porthole window), a co-ed thermal suite (containing several steam and shower mist rooms with different fragrances such as chamomile, eucalyptus and mint, and a glacial ice fountain), and beauty salon.

Sports facilities include a full-size basketball court, compact football, paddle tennis and volleyball, golf simulator, shuffleboard (on two different decks) and a jogging track. A 70-person capacity sports bar called Extreme (a first for a Celebrity Cruises' ship, although it just doesn't, somehow, belong) is located directly in front of the main funnel and has glass walls that overlook the ship's side. Gaming sports include Fortunes Casino, with blackjack, roulette, and numerous slot machines.

Families with children will appreciate the Fun Factory (for children) and The Tower (for teenagers).

Infinity delivers a well-defined North American cruise experience at a very modest price. The "zero announcement policy" fortunately means little intrusion. My advice is to book a suite-category cabin for all the extra benefits it brings – it really is worth it. Note that a 15 percent gratuity is automatically added to all bar and wine accounts. The onboard currency is the US dollar.

During the past two years, standards aboard the Celebrity Cruises fleet went down as cuts were made by parent company Royal Caribbean International. However, new management has been brought in to put things right. The strong points of a Celebrity cruise include the use of many European staff and service, a fine spa with a good range of facilities, treatments, taste-filled food attractively presented and served in the European fine dining tradition, and the provision of many intimate spaces and a superb collection of artwork.

WEAK POINTS: Standing in line for embarkation, disembarkation, shore tenders and for self-serve buffet meals is an inevitable aspect of cruising aboard all large ships. There is, sadly, no wrap-around wooden promenade deck outdoors. There are cushioned pads for poolside deck lounge chairs only, but not for chairs on other outside decks. Trying to reach Cabin Service or the Guest Relations Desk to answer the phone (to order breakfast, for example, if you don't want to do so via the interactive television) is a matter of luck, timing and patience. Passenger participation activities are amateurish and should be upgraded.

Inspiration
★★★ +

Large Ship:	.70,367 tons	Cabin Current:	.110 volts
Lifestyle:	Standard	Elevators:	.14
Cruise Line:	Carnival Cruise Lines	Casino (gaming tables):	Yes
Former Names:	none	Slot Machines:	Yes
Builder:	Kvaerner Masa-Yards (Finland)	Swimming Pools (outdoors):	.3
Original Cost:	$270 million	Swimming Pools (indoors):	.0
Entered Service:	Apr 1996	Whirlpools:	.6
Registry:	The Bahamas	Fitness Center:	Yes
Length (ft/m):	.855.0/260.6	Sauna/Steam Room:	Yes/Yes
Beam (ft/m):	.103.0/31.4	Massage:	Yes
Draft (ft/m):	.25.9/7.9	Self-Service Launderette:	Yes
Propulsion/Propellers:	diesel-electric	Dedicated Cinema/Seats:	No
	(42,240 kW)/2	Library:	Yes
Passenger Decks:	.10	Classification Society:	Lloyd's Register
Total Crew:	.920		

Passengers	
(lower beds/all berths):	.2,056/2,634
Passenger Space Ratio	
(lower beds/all berths):	.34.4/26.7
Crew/Passenger Ratio	
(lower beds/all berths):	.2.2/2.8
Navigation Officers:	Italian
Cabins (total):	.1,028
Size Range (sq ft/m):	.173.2–409.7/
	16.0–38.0
Cabins (outside view):	.620
Cabins (interior/no view):	.408
Cabins (for one person):	.0
Cabins (with private balcony):	.54
Cabins (wheelchair accessible):	.22

OVERALL SCORE: 1,385 (OUT OF A POSSIBLE 2,000 POINTS)

ACCOMMODATION: As in sister ships *Ecstasy, Elation, Fantasy, Fascination, Imagination, Paradise* and *Sensation*), the standard outside-view and interior (no view) cabins have plain décor. They are marginally comfortable, yet spacious enough and practical (most are of the same size and appointments), with good storage space and well-designed bathrooms.

Those booking one of the outside suites will find more space, whirlpool bathtubs, and some fascinating, rather eclectic décor and furniture. These are mildly attractive, but nothing special, and they are much smaller than those aboard the ships of a similar size of several competing companies.

A gift basket is provided in all grades of accommodation; it includes aloe soap, shampoo, conditioner, deodorant, breath mints, candy, and pain relief tablets (albeit all in sample sizes).

Note that if you book accommodation in one of the suites (Category 11 or 12 in the Carnival Cruise Lines brochure) you automatically qualify for "Skipper's Club" priority check-in at any US homeland port – useful for getting ahead of the crowd.

DINING: There are two large, rather noisy – or perhaps one should say "lively" – dining rooms, Carnivale and Mardi Gras, both of which are non-smoking. The service is attentive, but far too fast and assertive, and lacks any kind of finesse. Dining in each restaurant is now in four seatings, for greater flexibility: 6pm, 6.45pm, 8pm and 8.45pm (these times are approximate).

Carnival meals stress quantity, not quality, although

BERLITZ'S RATINGS		
	Possible	Achieved
Ship	500	395
Accommodation	200	151
Food	400	221
Service	400	270
Entertainment	100	81
Cruise	400	267

the company constantly works hard to improve the cuisine. While passengers seem to accept it, few find it worth remembering. However, food and its taste are still not the company's strongest points (you get what you pay for, remember).

While the menu items sound good, their presentation and taste leave much to be desired. While meats are of a high quality, fish and seafood is not. Presentation is simple, and few garnishes are used. Many meat and fowl dishes are disguised with gravies and sauces. The selection of fresh green vegetables, breads, rolls, cheeses and fruits is limited, and there is too much use of canned fruit and jellied desserts. However, do remember that this is banquet catering, with all its attendant standardization and production cooking (it is, therefore, difficult to ask for anything remotely unusual or off-menu). The selection of breads, rolls, cheeses and fruits is limited (there is too much use of canned fruit).

Although there is a decent wine list, there are no wine waiters (the waiters are expected to serve both food and wine, which does not work well). The service is highly programmed, although the waiters are willing and reasonably friendly. However, the waiters do sing and dance (be prepared for *Simply the Best, Hot, Hot, Hot,* and other popular hits), and there are constant waiter parades; the dining room is show business – all done in the name of gratuities at the end of your cruise.

What has improved, however, is the quality of food available at the informal food outlets such as the Brasserie Bar and Grill, which also includes a Pizzeria (open 24 hours a day – it typically serves over 500 *every single day*). At night, the "Seaview Bistro," as the Lido Café becomes known, provides a casual (dress down) alternative to eating in the main dining rooms, serving pasta, steaks, salads and desserts (it typically is in operation between 6pm and 9pm).

OTHER COMMENTS: *Inspiration* is the 10th new ship for this very successful cruise line. The ship, whose bows are extremely short, has the distinctive, large, swept-back wing-tipped funnel that is the trademark of Carnival Cruise Lines, in the company colors of red, white and blue. At its base is a "topless" area for sunbathing.

Like its seven sister ships of the same size, this vessel has a seven-deck-high atrium topped by a glass dome. The atrium features scrolled shapes resembling the necks and heads of violins, and a marble staircase. There are expansive open-deck areas and an excellent, three-deck-high glass-enclosed health spa. There are public entertainment lounges, bars and clubs galore, with something for just about everyone. The public rooms connect to wide indoor boulevards.

Various colors and design themes have been used throughout, although the ship does feature somewhat softer decor than on some of Carnival's ships. There is a $1 million art collection. Particularly fascinating is the avant-garde rendition of the famed *Mona Lisa*, in Pablo's Lounge. The decor itself is themed after the arts (in an art nouveau style) and literature.

The Shakespeare Library is a stunning, stately room (25 of his quotations adorn the oak veneer. Another dazzling room is the Rock and Roll Discotheque, with its guitar-shaped dance floor and video dance club and dozens of video monitors around the room. The ship also has a lavish, multi-tiered show lounge (although some 20 pillars cause some seats to have obstructed sight lines) and high-energy razzle-dazzle shows. The casino is large, but always humming with hopeful action.

This ship is one of the great floating playgrounds for young, active adults who enjoy constant stimulation, close contact with lots and lots of others, as well as the three Gs – glitz, glamour and gambling. It is a live board game with every move executed in typically grand, colorful, fun-filled Carnival Cruise Lines style.

Finally, the company's brochure tells it exactly like it is, by providing a good look at the unpretentious lifestyle of its passengers. This ship provides a fine adult playground for those that like to party. It will entertain you well, but do not go for the food, go for the fun, the almost non-stop, all-too-predictable action and participation activities, and for a way to visit the Caribbean in a well packaged manner that would best be described as a compact Las Vegas afloat. Forget fashion – having fun is the *sine qua non* of a Carnival cruise.

Inspiration operates 7-day Western Caribbean cruises, from New Orleans. Gratuities are automatically added to your onboard account at $9.75 per person, per day (the amount charged when this book was completed); you can have this amount adjusted, although you'll have to visit the information desk to do so. The onboard currency is the US dollar.

WEAK POINTS: Standing in line for embarkation, disembarkation, shore tenders and for self-serve buffet meals is an inevitable aspect of cruising aboard all large ships. There are no cushioned pads for the deck lounge chairs, which are plastic, and hard to sit on with just a towel for any length of time.

There is absolutely no escape from unnecessary and repetitive announcements (particularly for activities that bring revenue, such as art auctions, bingo, horse racing) that intrude constantly into your cruise, and a great deal of hustling for drinks, although it is sometimes done with a knowing smile. There is too much use of plastic on board, particularly in the informal food service areas.

Island Escape
★★★

Large Ship:	40,132 tons		
Lifestyle:	Standard		
Cruise Line:	Island		
Former Names:	*Viking Serenade,*		
	Stardancer, Scandinavia		
Builder:	Dubigeon-Normandie (France)		
Original Cost:	$100 million		
Entered Service:	Oct 1982/Mar 2002		
Registry:	Bahamas		
Length (ft/m):	623.0/189.89		
Beam (ft/m):	88.6/27.01		
Draft (ft/m):	23.6/7.20		
Propulsion/Propellers:	diesel (19,800 kW)/2		
Passenger Decks:	10		
Total Crew:	500		

Passengers
(lower beds/all berths): 1,512/1,863
Passenger Space Ratio
(lower beds/all berths): 26.5/21.5
Crew/Passenger Ratio
(lower beds/all berths): 2.4/3.0
Navigation Officers: International
Cabins (total): 756
Size Range (sq ft/m): 143.1–398.2/
13.3–37.0
Cabins (outside view): 478
Cabins (interior/no view): 278
Cabins (for one person): 0
Cabins (with private balcony): 5
Cabins (wheelchair accessible): 3

Cabin Current: 110 volts
Elevators: 5
Casino (gaming tables): Yes
Slot Machines: Yes
Swimming Pools (outdoors): 1
(magrodome)
Swimming Pools (indoors): 0
Whirlpools: 0
Fitness Center: Yes
Sauna/Steam Room: Yes/No
Massage: Yes
Self-Service Launderette: No
Dedicated Cinema/Seats: No
Library: No
Classification Society: Det Norske Veritas

OVERALL SCORE: 1,245 (OUT OF A POSSIBLE 2,000 POINTS)

ACCOMMODATION: There are just six categories of accommodation, so choosing the right one for you shouldn't be difficult. The cabins, however, are quite dimensionally challenged (in other words, because they are tight on space you should plan to take only the most minimum of clothing you can get away with). They are moderately appointed with soft furnishings that are very cheerful, with upbeat colors. However, do note that there is only a small amount of closet space, as the ship was only really designed for short cruises.

Almost all cabins have twin beds that can be pushed together to form a queen-sized bed (some cabins have an L-shaped arrangement, with immovable beds). No matter what grade of accommodation you choose, all feature a television, telephone, and three-channel radio, dressing table and mirror. There are many interior (no view) cabins, and drawers and other storage space is extremely limited. If you'd like to have more space, it's best to go for one of the suite categories.

The cabin bathrooms are *extremely* small, so you can expect to dance with the shower curtain, particularly if you have a larger than average sized body (only accommodation designated as suites have a bathtub).

Note that all outside-view cabins have even numbers, and all interior (no view) cabins have odd numbers. Also, if you are cruising with young children, there's almost no space for baby strollers. If, after looking at the deck plans, you want to book a specific cabin number, an extra charge (presently £20 per cabin) will be added to your account. Some cabins have extra Pullman

BERLITZ'S RATINGS	Possible	Achieved
Ship	500	307
Accommodation	200	112
Food	400	231
Service	400	269
Entertainment	100	61
Cruise	400	265

upper berths (good for families with young children).

ISLAND SUITE: The largest accommodation is in the "Island Suite" – towards the aft of the ship on the port side. Although it doesn't have a balcony, it's quite spacious (particularly when compared to most of the other cabins aboard the ship). A bathtub and shower are provided in the bathroom, and there's a walk-in closet, and mini-bar/refrigerator.

OTHER SUITES: Five other cabins (with balconies) are designated as suites. These are located at the stern of the vessel and have great views over the wash created by the ship's propellers, although they may be subject to a little vibration now and then (particularly when the ship is maneuvering in and out of ports). A bathtub and shower are provided in the marble-clad bathroom, and there's a walk-in closet in the sleeping area, and mini-bar/refrigerator and entertainment center in the living room. Additionally, another two suites (with balcony) are located in the forward third of the ship one deck lower than the aft-facing suites, but with the same facilities.

DINING: The Island Restaurant is the ship's main dining room, with ocean-view windows on two sides, and upbeat decor. It is open for breakfast, lunch and dinner, and you can either serve yourself form the buffets, or be served by a waiter.

A second, smaller (more intimate and exclusive) restaurant is called Oasis, and is located one deck lower than the Island Restaurant. This is an à la carte dining spot that is open only for dinner, with waiter service for all courses. Reservations are required; the ship's officers eat here, and you are welcome to join them, or invite them to your table. Oddbins, one of Britain's top high street wine merchants, provides the wine list.

Note that there are no tables for two (romantic types, please take note). The ceilings are low in both restaurants, which results in a feeling of being crowded.

The menu descriptions make the food sound better than it actually is, which is consistently average, mostly disappointing and with little taste.

OTHER COMMENTS: This ship, which has been extensively reconstructed from her original guise as a passenger-car ferry, has a fairly decent amount of open deck and sunbathing space, and there is a pool (this is really a *tiny* pool – more a "dip" pool than anything), which has a sliding glass dome (called a magrodome) that can be used in case of inclement weather.

The ship does suffer somewhat from having an extremely boxy, angular shape with a 'sponson' skirt that goes around the stern at the waterline (this is required for stability reasons). The ship underwent a $75 million reconstruction in 1991, when Royal Caribbean International (then Royal Caribbean Cruise Line) took over the ship, which remained the ugly duckling of the fleet ever since – not at all handsome, and with a very short, stubby bow. As *Viking Serenade*, the ship operated short cruises from Los Angeles to Mexico for several years, and was known as being something of a party ship (particularly during the weekend cruises), which led to a reputation for being untidy and unclean.

In November 2001 the ship was renamed *Island Escape* and transferred to Island Cruises, a new cruise line that was the result of a joint venture between the UK's First Choice Holidays and Royal Caribbean International. Onboard concessionaires include UK brands Costa Coffee, Holmes Place (health & beauty spa) and Oddbins (wine merchants). The ship began cruising in March 2002 under the new name *Island Escape*.

Inside the ship, there is a decent enough array of public rooms and facilities including a conference center and a lounge that is cantilevered around the funnel (the ocean views from it are excellent). The public rooms have contemporary, upbeat décor, with tasteful colors and furnishings that are of decent quality but some have

seen better days. The health spa facilities are quite good, and include a large gymnasium with some of the latest high-tech muscle-pumping equipment, operated as part of the spa by British specialist fitness/spa specialist Holmes Place. Other facilities include a cyber center (for internet connection and e-mail – or should that be "island mail?"), and a coffee shop (featuring Costa coffee).

Island Escape, which got off to a dubious start when the ship first debuted on cruises in the Mediterranean in spring 2002, should now provide a decent enough one-week cruise experience. The ship is marketed particularly to young British families with children. In other words, this is cruising in utterly casual, comfortable, but unpretentious surroundings that are quite upbeat, with a "let's have a party" ambience that should appeal to the young at heart. Children should have a good time, and there are plenty of planned, well supervised activities.

You can also extend your vacation with a "cruise-and-stay" package, with special pricing to make your extended vacation more affordable. Note that if you book two cruises back-to-back, the entertainment will be repeated for the second week. The dining room menus are also repeated every seven days.

Island Cruises provides scheduled or charter air service (through its wholly owned Air 2000 fleet – watch out for those of so cramped "knees-up" seats) to get you to and from the ship (from the UK). The onboard currency is the British pound.

WEAK POINTS: The ship's swimming pool is, in a word, tiny – no, a better description would be *extremely* tiny. Standing in line for embarkation, disembarkation, shore tenders and for self-serve buffet meals can be an inevitable aspect of cruising aboard all ships carrying more than 1,000 passengers. The ceilings in many public areas and hallways are quite low (the ship was originally constructed as a cruise-ferry).

There are many loud, irritating announcements and background music is played almost everywhere. Passenger participation events tend to be quite amateurish (although this depends on what you are prepared to compare them to). The cabins are *tiny* boxes, and the ship *always* feels crowded. Plastic cups are used for drinks on deck (have you ever tried drinking champagne out of a plastic glass?).

Jubilee
★★★ +

Removed 2006

Large Ship: . . . . .47,262 tons	Passengers	Cabin Current: . . . . .110 volts
Lifestyle: . . . . .Standard	(lower beds/all berths): 1,486/1,896	Elevators: 8
Cruise Line: . . . . . .Carnival Cruise Lines	Passenger Space Ratio	Casino (gaming tables): . . . . .Yes
Former Names: . . . . .none	(lower beds/all berths): 31.8/24.9	Slot Machines: . . . . .Yes
Builder: . . . . .Kockums (Sweden)	Crew/Passenger Ratio	Swimming Pools (outdoors): 3
Original Cost: . . . .$134 million	(lower beds/all berths): 2.2/2.8	Swimming Pools (indoors): 0
Entered Service: . . . . .July 1986	Navigation Officers: . . . . .Italian	Whirlpools: 2
Registry: . . . . .The Bahamas	Cabins (total): 743	Fitness Center: . . . . .Yes
Length (ft/m): 733.0/223.4	Size Range (sq ft/m): 182.9–419.8/	Sauna/Steam Room: . . . . .Yes/No
Beam (ft/m): 92.5/28.2	17.0–39.0	Massage: . . . . .Yes
Draft (ft/m): 24.7/7.5	Cabins (outside view): 453	Self-Service Launderette: . . . . .Yes
Propulsion/Propellers: . . . . .diesel	Cabins (interior/no view): 290	Dedicated Cinema/Seats: . . . . .No
(23,520 kW)/2	Cabins (for one person): 0	Library: . . . . .Yes
Passenger Decks: 9	Cabins (with private balcony): 10	Classification Society: . . .Lloyd's Register
Total Crew: .670	Cabins (wheelchair accessible): 14	

OVERALL SCORE: 1,318 (OUT OF A POSSIBLE 2,000 POINTS)

ACCOMMODATION: There are 11 different accommodation price categories (the higher the deck, the more you pay), although most cabins are of the same size.

There are 10 suites, although there are obstructed views from four of them; each has a private balcony. Almost all other cabins are relatively spacious units that are neatly appointed, and have attractive, though rather spartan, décor. Especially nice are the 10 large suites on Veranda Deck. The outside cabins have large picture windows. A gift basket is provided in all grades of accommodation; it includes aloe soap, shampoo, conditioner, deodorant, breath mints, candy, and pain relief tablets (albeit all in sample sizes).

Note that if you book accommodation in one of the suites (Category 11 or 12 in the Carnival Cruise Lines brochure) you automatically qualify for "Skipper's Club" priority check-in at any US homeland port – useful for getting ahead of the crowd.

DINING: There are two dining rooms (Bordeaux and Burgundy). They are quite cramped when full, and extremely noisy (both are non-smoking, however), and they have low ceilings in the raised sections of their centers. There are tables for four, six or eight (there are no tables for two). The décor is bright and extremely colorful, to say the least. Dining in each restaurant is now in four seatings, for greater flexibility: 6pm, 6.45pm,. 8pm and 8.45 pm (these times are approximate).

Carnival meals stress quantity, not quality, although the company constantly works hard to improve the cui-

BERLITZ'S RATINGS		
	Possible	Achieved
Ship	500	355
Accommodation	200	143
Food	400	221
Service	400	275
Entertainment	100	74
Cruise	400	250

sine. While passengers seem to accept it, few find it worth remembering. However, food and its taste are still not the company's strongest points (but you get what you pay for).

While the menu items sound good, their presentation and taste leave much to be desired. While meats are of a high quality, fish and seafood is not. Presentation is simple, and few garnishes are used. Many meat and fowl dishes are disguised with gravies and sauces. The selection of fresh green vegetables, breads, rolls, cheeses and fruits is limited, and there is too much use of canned fruit and jellied desserts. However, do remember that this is banquet catering, with all its attendant standardization and production cooking (it is, therefore, difficult to ask for anything remotely unusual or off-menu). The selection of breads, rolls, cheeses and fruits is limited (there is too much use of canned fruit).

Although there is a decent wine list, there are no wine waiters (the waiters are expected to serve both food and wine, which does not work well). The service is highly programmed, although the waiters are willing and reasonably friendly. However, the waiters do sing and dance (be prepared for *Simply the Best, Hot, Hot, Hot,* and other popular hits), and there are constant waiter parades; the dining room is show business – all done in the name of gratuities at the end of your cruise.

For casual meals, these can be taken as self-serve buffets in the Wheelhouse Bar & grill, although the foods provided are very basic, and quite disappointing, with much repetition (particularly for breakfast) and little variety. At night, the "Seaview Bistro," as the Lido Café becomes known, provides a casual (dress down) alternative to eating in the main dining rooms, serving pasta, steaks, salads and desserts (it typically is in operation between 6pm and 9pm).

OTHER COMMENTS: *Jubilee*, which was the third new-build ordered for Carnival Cruise Lines, has a bold, forthright, rather angular, all-white profile. The ship, whose bows are extremely short, has the distinctive, large, swept-back wing-tipped funnel that is the trademark of Carnival Cruise Lines, in the company colors of red, white and blue.

Inside, there are flamboyant, vivid colors in all the public rooms except for the elegant Churchill's Library, which, sadly, is almost devoid of books. A large casino has almost round-the-clock action. The numerous public rooms are spread throughout two whole decks full of entertainment rooms, bars and lounges. A fine, double width promenade deck features a white gazebo. The multi-tiered Atlantis Lounge show lounge has a large theater stage, and bold, stimulating colors. This ship provides constant entertainment and activities designed for passenger participation in a party-like setting.

This ship is a floating playground for young, active adults who enjoy constant stimulation, close contact with lots and lots of others, as well as the three Gs – glitz, glamour and gambling. It is a live board game with every move executed in typically grand, colorful, fun-filled Carnival Cruise Lines style. The ship, now

more than 10 years old, provides novice cruisers with a good first cruise experience in comfortable, but visually busy surroundings. The fun-filled, noisy, almost non-stop action equates to a stimulating vacation, targeted particularly to those who like to party and have fun. Good for families with children, and especially good for singles who want constant action (sleep *before* you cruise). Carnival provides very good value, with plenty of dazzle and sizzle entertainment and constant activities, which Carnival does so well particularly for first-time cruise passengers. Forget fashion – having fun is the *sine qua non* of a Carnival cruise.

Jubilee operates 4- and 5-day Western Caribbean cruises from Tampa. Gratuities are automatically added to your onboard account at $9.75 per person, per day; you can have this amount adjusted, although you'll have to visit the information desk to do so. The onboard currency is the US dollar.

WEAK POINTS: Standing in line for embarkation, disembarkation, shore tenders and for self-serve buffet meals is an inevitable aspect of cruising aboard all large ships. There is absolutely no escape from unnecessary and repetitive announcements (particularly for activities that bring revenue, such as art auctions, bingo, horse racing) that intrude constantly into your cruise, and a great deal of hustling for drinks. There are no cushioned pads for the deck lounge chairs. There are virtually no quiet spaces aboard to get away from crowds or noise.

Kapitan Dranitsyn
★★★

Small Ship: ....12,288 tons	Passengers	Elevators: 0
Lifestyle: ....Standard	(lower beds/all berths): 106/113	Casino (gaming tables): ....No
Cruise Line: ....Murmansk Shipping/	Passenger Space Ratio	Slot Machines: ....No
Quark Expeditions	(lower beds/all berths): 115.9/108.7	Swimming Pools (outdoors): 0
Former Names: ....none	Crew/Passenger Ratio	Swimming Pools (indoors): 1
Builder: ....Wartsila (Finland)	(lower beds/all berths): 1.1/1.2	Whirlpools: 0
Original Cost: ....n/a	Navigation Officers: ....Russian	Fitness Center: ....Yes
Entered Service: ....Dec 1980	Cabins (total): 53	Sauna/Steam Room: Yes-2/No
Registry: ....Russia	Size Range (sq ft/m): 150.6–269.0/	Massage: ....No
Length (ft/m): 434.6/132.49	14.0–25.0	Lecture/Film Room: ....No
Beam (ft/m): 86.9/26.50	Cabins (outside view): 53	Library: ....Yes
Draft (ft/m): 27.8/8.50	Cabins (interior/no view): 0	Zodiacs: 4
Propulsion/Propellers: .....diesel-electric	Cabins (for one person): 0	Helicopter Pad: ....Yes (1 helicopter)
(18,270 kW)/3	Cabins (with private balcony): 0	Classification Society: ....RS
Passenger Decks: 4	Cabins (wheelchair accessible) 0	
Total Crew: 90	Cabin Current: ....220 volts	

OVERALL SCORE: 1,164 (OUT OF A POSSIBLE 2,000 POINTS)

ACCOMMODATION: The cabins, in four price categories, are spread over four decks, and all have private facilities and plenty of storage space. Although nothing special, they are quite comfortable, with two lower berths, large closets, a small desk, and portholes that actually open. The bathrooms are practical units.

DINING: The dining room is really plain and unpretentious – like the rest of this vessel. It is totally non-smoking; there is a single seating, with assigned tables. The food is best described as really hearty fare, with generous portions (and an emphasis on fish and potatoes), served by waitresses in a dining room that is comfortable and practical. Quark Expeditions has its own catering team and so European chefs oversee the cuisine and its presentation. The wine list is pretty basic.

OTHER COMMENTS: *Kapitan Dranitsyn* is a real, working icebreaker, one of a fleet of 10 built in Finland to exacting Russian specifications for the challenging seas and conditions experienced for Arctic and polar work, and now available for charter to various tour companies. The ship, which was converted to passenger use in 1994, has an incredibly thick hull, forthright profile, and a bow like an inverted whale head. The funnel is placed just about amidships, and the accommodation block is located forward of it. An open bridge policy allows passengers to visit the bridge at almost any time. Strong diesel-electric engines (delivering 24,000 horsepower) allow it to plow through ice several feet thick.

BERLITZ'S RATINGS

	Possible	Achieved
Ship	500	267
Accommodation	200	113
Food	400	237
Service	400	224
Entertainment	N/A	N/A
Cruise	500	311

There is plenty of open deck and observation space, and a heated (but very small) indoor swimming pool. There is always a team of excellent naturalists and lecturers aboard. A helicopter is usually (but not always) carried and can be used by all passengers for sightseeing forays, as is a fleet of Zodiac rubber landing craft for in-your-face shore landings and wildlife spotting. There's also a (small) heated indoor swimming pool.

You can count on the team of naturalists and lecturers aboard being excellent. Light but warm parkas are provided for passengers, who really become participants in this kind of hands-on expedition cruising. A helicopter is usually carried and can be used by all passengers for sightseeing forays.

If you are someone who feels the call of the wild, this vessel is particularly good for tough expedition cruising, and will provide thoroughly practical surroundings, a friendly, experienced and dedicated group of crew members, and excellent value for the money in true expeditionary style. An expedition cruise logbook is typically provided at the end of each cruise for all passengers – a superb keepsake that acts as a reminder of what's been seen and done during the course of your expedition adventure cruise.

WEAK POINTS: The ship offers only basic cruise amenities and very spartan, no-frills décor. Also, you should be prepared for some tremendous roaring noise when the ship breaks through pack ice.

Kapitan Khlebnikov
★★★

Small Ship:	12,288 tons	Passengers		Elevators:	1
Lifestyle:	Standard	(lower beds/all berths):	108/114	Casino (gaming tables):	No
Cruise Line:	Murmansk Shipping/	Passenger Space Ratio		Slot Machines:	No
	Quark Expeditions	(lower beds/all berths):	113.7/107.7	Swimming Pools (outdoors):	0
Former Names:	none	Crew/Passenger Ratio		Swimming Pools (indoors):	1
Builder:	Wartsila (Finland)	(lower beds/all berths):	1.8/1.9	Whirlpools:	0
Original Cost:	n/a	Navigation Officers:	Russian	Fitness Center:	Yes
Entered Service:	1981	Cabins (total):	54	Sauna/Steam Room:	Yes-2/No
Registry:	Russia	Size Range (sq ft/m):	150.6–269/	Massage:	No
Length (ft/m):	434.6/132.49		14.0–25.0	Lecture/Film Room:	No
Beam (ft/m):	87.7/26.75	Cabins (outside view):	54	Library:	Yes
Draft (ft/m):	27.8/8.50	Cabins (interior/no view):	0	Zodiacs:	4
Propulsion/Propellers:	diesel-electric	Cabins (for one person):	0	Helicopter Pad:	Yes (1 helicopter)
	(18,270 kW)/3	Cabins (with private balcony):	0	Classification Society:	Russian Shipping
Passenger Decks:	4	Cabins (wheelchair accessible):	0		Register
Total Crew:	60	Cabin Current:	220 volts		

OVERALL SCORE: 1,164 (OUT OF A POSSIBLE 2,000 POINTS)

ACCOMMODATION: The cabins, in four categories, are spread over four decks, and all have private facilities and plenty of storage space. Although nothing special, they are quite comfortable, with two lower berths, large closets, and portholes that actually open. The bathrooms are practical units.

DINING: The dining room is really plain and unpretentious – like the rest of this vessel. It is non-smoking; there is a single seating, with assigned tables. The food is best described as really hearty fare, with generous portions (and an emphasis on fish and potatoes), served by waitresses in a dining room that is comfortable and practical. Quark Expeditions has its own catering team and so European chefs oversee the cuisine and its presentation. The wine list is pretty basic.

OTHER COMMENTS: *Kapitan Khlebnikov* is a real, working icebreaker, one of a fleet of 10 built in Finland to exacting Russian specifications for Arctic and polar work, and now available for various charters. The ship has an incredibly 45-mm (1.8-inch) thick hull, a forthright profile, and a bow that looks like an inverted whale head. The funnel is placed amidships, and the accommodation block is placed forward. An open bridge policy allows passengers to visit the bridge at almost any time. Strong diesel-electric engines (delivering 24,000 horse-

BERLITZ'S RATINGS

	Possible	Achieved
Ship	500	267
Accommodation	200	113
Food	400	237
Service	400	224
Entertainment	N/A	N/A
Cruise	500	311

power) allow it to plow through ice several feet thick. There is plenty of open deck and observation space. It has a heated (but very small) indoor swimming pool. There is always a team of excellent naturalists and lecturers aboard.

A helicopter is usually (but not always) carried and can be used by all passengers for sightseeing forays, as is a fleet of Zodiac rubber landing craft for in-your-face shore landings and wildlife spotting. Light but warm parkas are provided for passengers, who really become participants in this kind of hands-on expedition cruising.

If you are someone who feels the call of the wild, this vessel is particularly good for tough expedition cruising, and will provide thoroughly practical surroundings, a friendly, experienced and dedicated group of crew members, and excellent value for the money in true expeditionary style. An expedition cruise logbook is typically provided at the end of each cruise for all passengers – a superb keepsake that acts as a reminder of what's been seen and done during the course of your expedition adventure cruise.

WEAK POINTS: The ship offers only basic cruise amenities and a very spartan, no-frills décor. Also, you should be prepared for the tremendous roaring noise when the ship breaks through pack ice.

Kristina Regina
★★ +

Small Ship: ....4,295 tons	Passengers	Cabin Current: ....220 volts
Lifestyle: ....Standard	(lower beds/all berths): 186/245	Elevators: 0
Cruise Line: ....Kristina Cruises	Passenger Space Ratio	Casino (gaming tables): ....No
Former Names: ....Borea, Bore	(lower beds/all berths): 14.8/11.6	Slot Machines: ....No
Builder: ..Oskarshamn Shipyard (Sweden)	Crew/Passenger Ratio	Swimming Pools (outdoors): 0
Original Cost: ....n/a	(lower beds/all berths): 5.2/6.7	Swimming Pools (indoors): 0
Entered Service: 1960/1987	Navigation Officers: ....Finnish	Whirlpools: 0
Registry: ....Finland	Cabins (total): 119	Fitness Center: ....No
Length (ft/m): 327.5/99.83	Size Range (sq ft/m): 64.5–150.6/	Sauna/Steam Room: ....Yes/No
Beam (ft/m): 50.0/15.25		6.0–14.0	Massage: ....No
Draft (ft/m): 18.0/5.50	Cabins (outside view): 98	Self-Service Launderette: ....No
Propulsion/Propellers: ....diesel	Cabins (interior/no view): 21	Dedicated Cinema/Seats: ....No
	(3,233 kW)/2	Cabins (for one person): 30	Library: ....Yes
Passenger Decks: 6	Cabins (with private balcony): 0	Classification Society: ...Lloyd's Register
Total Crew: 55	Cabins (wheelchair accessible): 0	

OVERALL SCORE: 1,052 (OUT OF A POSSIBLE 2,000 POINTS)

ACCOMMODATION: There is a wide assortment of cabin sizes and configurations, from "suites" to cabins that are small, dimensionally challenged, and better described as compartments. Some cabins have a queen-sized bed; others have two lower beds, or a single bed. All grades feature a shower and toilet, radio, telephone (for internal calls only), but not much else, and they are really tiny, as are the bathrooms. As the cabins have very little closet and drawer space, do take only what's really necessary. There are also five allergy-free cabins, as well as several interconnecting cabins.

DINING: The principal dining room, Restaurant Regina, is quite charming and features Continental (European) cuisine, with a distinct accent on fish, seafood, and fresh berries. The breads and cheeses are also good. There is single seating at assigned tables, and fine, hearty, and friendly service comes with a smile.

A second dining spot, the Kotka Restaurant, features an à la carte menu (everything is cooked to order), with all items at extra cost. Additionally, continental breakfast and light snack foods can be found in the café.

OTHER COMMENTS: This is a lovely family-owned old-world ship, originally a coastal ferry, was converted specifically for close-in northern European coastal and archipelago cruises, and was extensively refurbished last in 2000. The ship originally had steam turbines powerplant, but this was converted to diesel in 1987. This is one of the few ships left today that has two funnels, and is owned by a single family, many of whose members work aboard the ship. Passengers can visit the navigation bridge at any time (conditions permitting).

Exterior features include a wrap-around wooden promenade deck outdoors. There are few public rooms (there are, however, two small conference rooms), but the ship does have some beautiful hardwoods throughout its interiors, plus lots of brass accents. The Scandinavian artwork is also quite fascinating. The ship has a good sized auditorium that doubles as a cinema and lecture hall, built into what was formerly a car deck.

In the 2000 refit and refurbishment, a small gymnasium was installed, adjacent to the sauna and tiled floor shower/changing area.

Contrary to most other ships in the cruise industry, the cruise fare includes only breakfast. However, meal packages (for lunch and dinner) can be purchased for the principal restaurant. The onboard currency is both the US dollar and the euro. Non-alcoholic drinks are complimentary. The ship's itineraries take it to the Baltic States and Russia, into White Sea ports, and to many ports in Europe and the Mediterranean.

BERLITZ'S RATINGS		
	Possible	Achieved
Ship	500	233
Accommodation	200	110
Food	400	238
Service	400	233
Entertainment	100	42
Cruise	400	196

Le Levant
★★★★ +

Small Ship: . . . . .3,504 tons	Total Crew: 50	Cabin Current: . . . . .110 and 220 volts
Lifestyle: . . . . .Premium	Passengers	Elevators: 1
Cruise Line: . . . . .Ponant Cruises/	(lower beds/all berths): 90/90	Casino (gaming tables): . . . . .No
Classical Cruises	Passenger Space Ratio	Slot Machines: .No
Former Names: . . . . .none	(lower beds/all berths): 38.9/38.9	Swimming Pools (outdoors): 1
Builder: . . . . .Leroux & Lotz (France)	Crew/Passenger Ratio	Swimming Pools (indoors): 0
Original Cost: . . . .$35 million	(lower beds/all berths): 1.8/1.8	Whirlpools: 0
Entered Service: . . . . .Jan 1999	Navigation Officers: . . . . .French	Fitness Center: . . . . .Yes
Registry: . . . . .Wallis and Fortuna	Cabins (total): 45	Sauna/Steam Room: . . . . .No/Yes
Length (ft/m): 328.0/100.00	Size Range (sq ft/m): 199.1/18.5	Massage: . . . . .No
Beam (ft/m): 45.9/14.00	Cabins (outside view): 45	Self-Service Launderette: . . . . .No
Draft (ft/m): 11.4/3.50	Cabins (interior/no view): 0	Dedicated Cinema/Seats: . . . . .No
Propulsion/Propellers: . . . . .diesel	Cabins (for one person): 0	Library: . . . . .Yes
(3,000 kW)/2	Cabins (with private balcony): 0	Classification Society: . . . .Bureau Veritas
Passenger Decks: 5	Cabins (wheelchair accessible): 0	

OVERALL SCORE: 1,609 (OUT OF A POSSIBLE 2,000 POINTS)

ACCOMMODATION: There are 45 ocean-view cabins (the brochure says "suites") and all are midships and forward, in five different price categories. Each cabin has a large ocean-view window, inlaid wood furniture and accenting, designer fabrics, two beds that will convert to a queen-size bed, a television, VCR, refrigerator, personal safe, and personal amenity kits in the marble-appointed bathrooms, all of which feature a shower (there are no cabins with bathtubs).

DINING: There are two dining rooms; the first is a wood paneled (main) Dining Room (one seating only), which has round and oval tables; the second is the more informal Veranda Restaurant, with a panoramic view overlooking the stern. Dining is in open seating, with unassigned seats, so you can dine with whomever you wish. Complimentary wines are included for lunch and dinner, and the cuisine is, naturally, classic French.

OTHER COMMENTS: *Le Levant* is a new high-class vessel looks like a streamlined private mega-yacht, and has a stunning low profile appearance with its royal blue (ice-hardened) hull and blue/white superstructure. It has two slim funnels that extend over port and starboard sides to carry any soot away from the vessel (somewhat like the design of the first four former Renaissance Cruises vessels). It was built in a specialist yacht-building yard in St. Malo, France. There is an "open bridge" policy, so passengers may visit the bridge whenever they wish (except when the ship is maneuvering in difficult conditions).

BERLITZ'S RATINGS

	Possible	Achieved
Ship	500	424
Accommodation	200	173
Food	400	312
Service	400	319
Entertainment	N/A	N/A
Cruise	500	381

A stern "marina" platform is used for shore visits, hidden in the stern, as well as six inflatable Zodiacs runabouts for landings in "soft" expedition areas such as the Amazon.

Inside, the vessel features contemporary, clean and uncluttered décor, and all the facilities of a private yacht. The public rooms are elegant and refined, with much use of wood trim and accenting. Particularly pleasing is the wood-paneled library, a feature so often lacking aboard many ships today. There is also one grand salon, which accommodates all passengers, and is used by day as a lecture room, and by night as the main lounge/bar. A resident scuba dive master is aboard for all Caribbean sailings. Each cruise has life-enrichment lecturers aboard, as well as tour leaders.

This ship is presently under charter to the New York-based Classical Cruises, who operate her in some offbeat destinations and cruise regions. In summer it may be in the Great Lakes, sailing between Toronto and Chicago, (its pencil-slim beam allows it to navigate the locks). During the fall the ship heads to Canada/New England, and in the winter to the Caribbean and South America.

This is all-inclusive cruising, with all port charges, gratuities, shore excursions and port charges are included in the cruise fare. The crew is almost entirely French. The onboard currency is the euro.

WEAK POINTS: You can walk around the uppermost accommodation deck, but there is no wrap-around promenade deck. None of the cabins has a private balcony.

Le Ponant
★★★★

Small Ship: ....1,489 tons	Propulsion/Propellers: ....diesel/
Lifestyle: ....Premium	sail power/1
Cruise Line: ....Ponant Cruises	Passenger Decks: 3
Former Names: ....none	Total Crew: 30
Builder: ....SFCN (France)	Passengers
Original Cost: ....n/a	(lower beds/all berths): 64/67
Entered Service: 1991	Passenger Space Ratio
Registry: ....France	(lower beds/all berths): 23.2/22.2
Length (ft/m): 288.7/88.00	Crew/Passenger Ratio
Beam (ft/m): 39.3/12.00	(lower beds/all berths): 2.1/2.2
Draft (ft/m): 13.1/4.00	Navigation Officers: ....French
Type of Vessel: .....high tech sail-cruiser	Cabins (total): 32
No. of Masts: 3	Size Range (sq ft/m): 139.9/13.0
Sail Area (sq ft/m2): 16,150/1,500	Cabins (outside view): 32
Main Propulsion: ......a) engine/b) sails	Cabins (interior/no view): 0

Cabins (for one person): 0
Cabins (with private balcony): 0
Cabins (wheelchair accessible): 0
Cabin Current: ....220 volts
Elevators: ....No
Casino (gaming tables): ....No
Slot Machines: ....No
Swimming Pools (outdoors): 0
Whirlpools: 0
Fitness Center: ....Yes
Sauna/Steam Room: ....No/No
Massage: ....No
Self-Service Launderette: ....No
Library: ....Yes
Classification Society: ...Lloyd's Register

OVERALL SCORE: 1,540 (OUT OF A POSSIBLE 2,000 POINTS)

ACCOMMODATION: Crisp, clean blond woods and pristine white cabins feature double or twin beds, mini-bar, personal safe, and a private bathroom. All cabins have portholes, crisp artwork, and a refrigerator. There is a limited amount of storage space, however, and few drawers. The cabin bathrooms are quite small, but efficiently designed.

DINING: The lovely Karukera dining room (open seating) have complimentary wines with lunch and dinner, and good quality food. There is fresh fish every day, and meals are true *affaires gastonomiques*. There is also a charming outdoor café under canvas sailcloth awning.

OTHER COMMENTS: Ultra sleek, very efficient, this mod-

BERLITZ'S RATINGS

	Possible	Achieved
Ship	500	399
Accommodation	200	166
Food	400	310
Service	400	319
Entertainment	N/A	N/A
Cruise	500	346

ern sail-cruise ship has three masts that rise 54.7 ft (16.7 meters) above the water line. This captivating ship has plenty of room on its open decks for sunbathing. Water sports facilities include an aft marina platform, windsurfers, water-ski boat, scuba and snorkel equipment.

The very elegant, no-glitz interior design is clean, stylish, functional and ultra-high-tech. Three public lounges have pastel décor, soft colors and great European flair.

One price fits all. The ship is marketed mainly to young, sophisticated French-speaking passengers who love yachting and the sea. This is *très* French, and *très* chic. The company also has a stunning mega-yacht cruise vessel, *Le Levant*. Gratuities are not "required," but they are expected. The onboard currency is the euro.

Legacy
★★ +

Small Ship: ....1,740 tons	Main Propulsion: ....sail power	Cabins (for one person): 0
Lifestyle: ....Standard	Propulsion/Propellers: diesel/1	Cabins (with private balcony): 0
Cruise Line: ....Windjammer Barefoot	Passenger Decks: 4	Cabins (wheelchair accessible): 0
Cruises	Total Crew: 43	Cabin Current: ....110 volts
Former Names: ....France II	Passengers	Elevators: 0
Builder: ...Forges et al Mediterranee du	(lower beds/all berths): 122/122	Casino (gaming tables): ....No
Havre (France)	Passenger Space Ratio	Slot Machines: ....No
Original Cost: ....n/a	(lower beds/all berths): 14.2/14.2	Swimming Pools (outdoors): 0
Entered Service: 1959/1997	Crew/Passenger Ratio	Whirlpools: 0
Registry: ....Equatorial Guinea	(lower beds/all berths): 2.8/2.8	Fitness Center: 0
Length (ft/m): 294.0/89.6	Navigation Officers: ....International	Sauna/Steam Room: ....No/No
Beam (ft/m): 40.0/12.1	Cabins (total): 61	Massage: ....No
Draft (ft/m): 23.0/7.0	Size Range (sq ft/m): 75.0–159.0/	Self-Service Launderette: ....No
Type of Vessel: ....barkentine	6.9–14.7	Library: ....Yes
No. of Masts: 4	Cabins (outside view): 46	Classification Society: . .American Bureau
Sail Area (sq ft/m2): 19,900/1,848.7	Cabins (interior/no view): 15	of Shipping

OVERALL SCORE: 1,029 (OUT OF A POSSIBLE 2,000 POINTS)

ACCOMMODATION: There are eight grades of accommodation (Burke's Berth, Admiral DeLuxe, Admiral Suite, Commodore Double, Commodore Triple, Ensign Cabin, Standard Cabin and Standard Single). Except for the top three grades, all other cabins are dimensionally challenged, however, particularly when compared to regular cruise ships. Remember, however, that this is a very casual cruise experience and you will need so few clothes anyway. All are equipped with upper and lower berths, mostly quite narrow.

DINING: There is one dining room, and the meals are all very simple in style and service, with little choice and only the most basic presentation. Breakfast is served on board, as is dinner, while lunch could be either on board or at a beach, picnic-style. Wine is included for dinner.

OTHER COMMENTS: When built, this barkentine with four masts served as a meteorological research and exploration vessel for the French Government before being converted into a traditional tall ship by Windjammer Barefoot Cruises in 1998–9.

Aboard one of the Windjammer Barefoot Cruises' fleet you can let the crew do all the work, or you can lend a hand at the helm yourself, if you feel so inclined. One neat thing to do is just to sit or lie in the nets at the bows of the vessel, without a care in the world.

Only the most casual clothes are required (T-shirts and shorts), and shoes are optional, although you may

BERLITZ'S RATINGS

	Possible	Achieved
Ship	500	264
Accommodation	200	100
Food	400	191
Service	400	180
Entertainment	N/A	N/A
Cruise	500	294

need them if you go off in one of the ports. Quite possibly the most used item will be your bathing suit – better take more than one. Smoking is allowed only on the open decks.

Entertainment in the evenings consists of – you and the crew. You can put on a toga, take or create a pirate outfit and join in the fun. This is cruising free 'n' easy style – none of that programmed big-ship production show stuff here.

Jammin' aboard a Windjammer (first-time passengers are called "crewmates" while repeat passengers are called "jammers") is no-frills cruising (it could be called an "anti-cruise") in a no-nonsense, friendly environment, for those who don't need programmed activities. It's best suited to young couples and (many) singles that seek sun, sea, sand and rum swizzles, and lovers of old sailing ships.

It's all about going to sea and the romance of being at sea under sail. This ship can anchor in neat little Caribbean hideaways that larger cruise ships can't get near. *Legacy* features year-round cruises in the British and U.S. Virgin Islands. Brochure rates might seem inexpensive, but you'll need to add on the airfare.

Legacy operates Caribbean cruises (from Fajardo, Puerto Rico). Other tall ships in the fleet include *Flying Cloud, Mandalay, Polynesia,* and *Yankee Clipper.* The onboard currency is the US dollar.

WEAK POINTS: It's extremely casual. There's very little room per passenger. Everything is basic, basic, basic. Tips to the crew are suggested – at $50 per week!

✓ off Gibraltar   06/09/05

Legend of the Seas
★★★★

Large Ship: ....69,130 tons
Lifestyle: ....Standard
Cruise Line: Royal Caribbean International
Former Names: ....none
Builder: Chantiers de l'Atlantique (France)
Original Cost: ....$325 million
Entered Service: ....May 1995
Registry: ....The Bahamas
Length (ft/m): 867.0/264.2
Beam (ft/m): 105.0/32.0
Draft (ft/m): 23.9/7.3
Propulsion/Propellers: ....diesel
(40,200 kW)/2
Passenger Decks: 11
Total Crew: 720

Passengers
(lower beds/all berths): 1,800/2,076
Passenger Space Ratio
(lower beds/all berths): 38.3/33.2
Crew/Passenger Ratio
(lower beds/all berths): 2.5/2.8
Navigation Officers: ....Norwegian
Cabins (total): 900
Size Range (sq ft/m): 137.7–1,147.4/
12.8–106.6
Cabins (outside view): 575
Cabins (interior/no view): 325
Cabins (for one person): 0
Cabins (with private balcony): 231
Cabins (wheelchair accessible): 17

Cabin Current: ....110 and 220 volts
Elevators: 11
Casino (gaming tables): ....Yes
Slot Machines: ....Yes
Swimming Pools (outdoors): 2
(1 with sliding roof)
Swimming Pools (indoors): 0
Whirlpools: 4
Fitness Center: ....Yes
Sauna/Steam Room: ....Yes/Yes
Massage: ....Yes
Self-Service Launderette: ....No
Dedicated Cinema/Seats: ....No
Library: ....Yes
Classification Society: Det Norske Veritas

OVERALL SCORE: 1,511 (OUT OF A POSSIBLE 2,000 POINTS)

ACCOMMODATION: Royal Caribbean International has realized that small cabins do not impress passengers. The company therefore set about designing a ship with much larger standard cabins than in any of the company's previous vessels (except sister ship *Splendour of the Seas*). Some cabins on Deck 8 also have a larger door for wheelchair access in addition to the 17 cabins for the physically handicapped, and the ship is very accessible, with ample ramped areas and sloping decks. All cabins have a sitting area and beds that convert to double configuration, and there is ample closet and drawer space. There's not much space around the bed, though, and the showers could have been better.

Cabins with balconies have glass railings rather than steel/wood to provide less intrusive sight lines. The largest accommodation, the Royal Suite, is a superb living space for those that can afford the best. It is beautifully designed, finely decorated, and features a baby grand piano, whirlpool bathtub, and other fine amenities. Several quite sitting areas are located adjacent to the best cabins amidships. Seventeen cabin categories is really too many. There are no cabins for singles.

DINING: The dining room has dramatic two-deck-high glass side walls, so many passengers both upstairs and downstairs can see both the ocean and each other in reflection (it would, perhaps, have been even better located at the stern), but it is quite noisy when full (call it atmosphere). There are two seatings, both of which are non-smoking.

BERLITZ'S RATINGS

	Possible	Achieved
Ship	500	426
Accommodation	200	163
Food	400	248
Service	400	302
Entertainment	100	78
Cruise	400	294

The cuisine is typical of mass banquet catering that offers standard fare comparable to that found in American family-style restaurants ashore. While menu descriptions are tempting, the actual food may be somewhat disappointing and unmemorable. The menu descriptions make the food sound better than it is (which is consistently below average), mostly disappointing and without much taste - the result of controlled food costs as well as the use of many mixes and pre-prepared items. However, a decent selection of light meals is provided, and a vegetarian menu is available. The selection of breads, rolls, fruit and cheese is quite poor, however, and could do more improvement. Caviar (once a standard men item) now incurs a heft extra charge. Menus typically include a Welcome Aboard Dinner, French Dinner, Italian Dinner, International Dinner, and Captain's Gala Dinner.

The wine list is not extensive, but the prices are moderate. The waiters, many from Caribbean countries, are perhaps overly friendly for some tastes – particularly on the last night of the cruise, when tips are expected.

There is also a cavernous indoor-outdoor cafe, located towards the bow and above the bridge, as well as a good-sized snack area, which provide more informal dining choices.

OTHER COMMENTS: This ship's contemporary profile looks somewhat unbalanced (but it soon grows on you), and does feature a nicely tiered stern. The pool deck amidships overhangs the hull to provide an extremely wide deck, while still allowing the ship to navigate the

Panama Canal. With engines placed midships, there is little noise and no noticeable vibration, and the ship has an operating speed of up to 24 knots.

The interior décor is quite colorful, but too glitzy for European tastes. The outside light is brought inside in many places, with an extensive amount of glass area that provides contact with sea and air – there is, in fact, over 2 acres (8,000 sq. meters) of glass. There's an innovative single-level sliding glass roof (not a magrodome) over the more formal setting of one of two swimming pools, thus providing a multi-activity, all-weather indoor-outdoor area, called the Solarium. The glass roof provides shelter for the Roman-style pool and adjacent health and fitness facilities (which are superb) and slides aft to cover the miniature golf course when required (both cannot be covered at the same time, however).

Golfers might enjoy the 18-hole, 6,000-sq. ft (560 sq.-meter) miniature golf course. It has the topography of a real course, complete with trees, foliage, grass, bridges, water hazards, and lighting for play at night. The holes themselves are 155-230 sq. ft (14.3–21.3 sq. meters).

Inside, two full entertainment decks are sandwiched between five decks full of cabins. The tiered and balconied show lounge, which covers two decks, is expansive and has excellent sight lines, and very comfortable seats. Several large-scale production shows are provided here, and the orchestra pit can be raised or lowered as required. A multi-tiered seven-deck-high atrium lobby, complete with a huge stainless steel sculpture, connects with the impressive Viking Crown Lounge via glass-walled elevators. The casino is really expansive, overly glitzy and absolutely packed. The library, outside of which is a bust of Shakespeare, is a fine facility, and has more than 2,000 books.

There is, sadly, no separate cinema. The casino could be somewhat disorienting, with its mirrored walls and lights flashing everywhere, although it is no different to those found in Las Vegas fantasy gaming halls.

As with any large ship, you can expect to find yourself standing in lines for embarkation, disembarkation, buffets and shore excursions, although the company does its best to minimize such lines.

Representing natural evolution, this ship is an outstanding new cruise vessel for the many repeat passengers who enjoy Royal Caribbean International's consistent delivery of a well-integrated, fine-tuned, very comfortable and well-liked product. With larger cabins, excellent décor and contemporary style, *Legend of the Seas* has taken Royal Caribbean International passengers, most of whom are typically from middle-America, into a much upgraded cruise experience from that of the company's other ships. The ship provides a very cost-effective cruise for all ages. The onboard currency is the US dollar.

WEAK POINTS: Standing in line for embarkation, disembarkation, shore tenders and for self-serve buffet meals is inevitable aboard all large ships.

Lirica
NYR

Removed 2006

Large Ship: ....58,600 tons	Passenger Decks: 10	Cabins (wheelchair accessible): 6
Lifestyle: ....Standard	Total Crew: 760	Cabin Current: ....110/220 volts
Cruise Line: .....Mediterranean Shipping	Passengers	Elevators: 9
Cruises	(lower beds/all berths): 1,586/2,200	Casino (gaming tables): ....Yes
Former Names: ....none	Passenger Space Ratio	Slot Machines: ....Yes
Builder: ....Chantiers de l'Atlantique	(lower beds/all berths): 36.9/26.6	Swimming Pools (outdoors): 2
(France)	Crew/Passenger Ratio	Swimming Pools (indoors): 0
Original Cost: ....$266 million	(lower beds/all berths): 2.0/2.8	Whirlpools: 2
Entered Service: ....Mar 2003	Navigation Officers: ....Italian	Fitness Center: ....Yes
Registry: ....Italy	Cabins (total): 763	Sauna/Steam Room: ....Yes/Yes
Length (ft/m): 824.3/251.25	Size Range (sq ft/m): ....n/a	Massage: ....Yes
Beam (ft/m): 94.4/28.8	Cabins (outside view): 353	Self-Service Launderette: ....No
Draft (ft/m): 22.4/6.85	Cabins (interior/no view): 272	Dedicated Cinema/Seats: ....No
Propulsion/Propellers: ....diesel	Cabins (for one person): 0	Library: ....Yes
(31,680kW)/2 pods	Cabins (with private balcony): 132	Classification Society: ....RINA

OVERALL SCORE: NYR (OUT OF A POSSIBLE 2,000 POINTS)

ACCOMMODATION: There are several different price levels for accommodation, depending on the grade and its location. Included are 132 "suites" with private balcony (note that the partitions between each balcony are of the partial and not the full wall type), outside-view cabins and interior (no view) cabins. No matter what grade of cabin you choose, all cabins feature a mini-bar and personal safe, satellite-linked television, and 24-hour room service.

DINING: There are two main dining rooms, both with large ocean view picture windows. There are two seatings for meals, in keeping with all other ships in the MSC fleet. For more casual fare, there is a grill, and a pizzeria, as well as an extensive self-serve buffet area.

OTHER COMMENTS: Very similar in size and structure to the Festival Cruises' sister ships *European Dream* and *European Vision*, but arguably with a slightly more attractive exterior profile, this is the first new build for Mediterranean Shipping Cruises (MSC), Italy's largest privately owned cruise line (formerly Star Lauro Cruises). The white funnel is sleek, with a swept-back design that closely resembles that of the Princess Cruises ships, and carries the MSC logo in gold lettering. From a technical viewpoint, the ship is quite different to *Mistral*, and is fitted with an azimuthing pod propulsion system, instead of conventional rudders and propellers, in

BERLITZ'S RATINGS		
	Possible	Achieved
Ship	500	NYR
Accommodation	200	NYR
Food	400	NYR
Service	400	NYR
Entertainment	100	NYR
Cruise	400	NYR

the latest configuration of high-tech propulsion systems.

Inside, the layout and passenger flow is good, as are the "you are here" deck signs. The décor is decidedly Italian, and includes clean lines, minimalism in furniture design, and an eclectic collection of colors and soft furnishings. Real wood and marble have been used extensively in the interiors, and the high quality reflects the commitment that MSC has in the vessel's future.

Facilities include the ship's main show lounge, a nightclub/discotheque, several lounges and bars, an internet center (with 16 terminals), virtual reality center, shopping gallery (the shops have an integrated bar and entertainment area so that shopping becomes a city-like environment where you can shop, drink, and be entertained all in one convenient area), and a children's club. Gamblers will find solace in the casino, with blackjack, poker and roulette games, together with an array of slot machines. For personal pampering, the Health Spa features some body-pampering treatments, as well as a gymnasium with the usual high-tech, muscle-pump machinery and gadgets.

The ship is designed to accommodate families with children, who have their own play center, youth counselors, and programming.

This new ship is expected to feature cruises the Mediterranean during the summer and the Caribbean during the winter. The onboard currency is the euro.

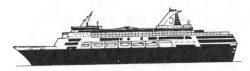

Maasdam
★★★★

Large Ship: ....55,451 tons	
Lifestyle: ....Premium	
Cruise Line: ....Holland America Line	
Former Names: ....none	
Builder: ....Fincantieri (Italy)	
Original Cost: ....$215 million	
Entered Service: ....Dec 1993	
Registry:..............The Netherlands	
Length (ft/m): 719.3/219.30	
Beam (ft/m): 101.0/30.80	
Draft (ft/m): 24.6/7.50	
Propulsion/Propellers: .....diesel-electric	
(34,560 kW)/2	
Passenger Decks:...................10	
Total Crew: 557	

Passengers
(lower beds/all berths): 1,266/1,627
Passenger Space Ratio
(lower beds/all berths): 43.8/34.0
Crew/Passenger Ratio
(lower beds/all berths): 2.2/2.9
Navigation Officers: ....Dutch
Cabins (total): 632
Size Range (sq ft/m): 186.2–1,124.8/
17.3–104.5
Cabins (outside view): 502
Cabins (interior/no view): 131
Cabins (for one person): 0
Cabins (with private balcony): 150
Cabins (wheelchair accessible): 6

Cabin Current: ....110 and 220 volts
Elevators: 12
Casino (gaming tables): ....Yes
Slot Machines: ....Yes
Swimming Pools (outdoors): 1
Swimming Pools (indoors): 1
(magrodome)
Whirlpools: 2
Fitness Center: ....Yes
Sauna/Steam Room: ....Yes/No
Massage:.........................Yes
Self-Service Launderette: ....Yes
Dedicated Cinema/Seats: Yes/249
Library: ....Yes
Classification Society: ...Lloyd's Register

OVERALL SCORE: 1,533 (OUT OF A POSSIBLE 2,000 POINTS)

ACCOMMODATION: The accommodation ranges from small interior (no view) cabins to a large penthouse suite, in 17 categories. All cabin televisions feature CNN and TNT.

The 148 interior (no view) and 336 outside (with a view) standard cabins feature twin beds that convert to a queen-size bed, and there is a separate living space with sofa and coffee table. However, although the drawer space is generally good, the closet space is actually very tight, particularly for long cruises (although more than adequate for a 7-night cruise). The bathrooms, which are tiled and compact but practical – have a good range of personal toiletries. Bathrobes and hairdryers are provided. The bathrooms are quite well laid out, but the bathtubs are small units, more like shower tubs. No cabins have inter-connecting doors (unlike *Ryndam, Veendam*).

On Navigation Deck 28, suites have accommodation for up to four. These suites also have in-suite dining as an alternative to the dining room, for private, reclusive meals. These are very spacious, tastefully decorated and well laid-out, and feature a separate living room, bedroom with two lower beds (convertible to a king-size bed), a good size living area, dressing room, plenty of closet and drawer space, marble bathroom with Jacuzzi tub.

The largest accommodation of all is a penthouse suite; there is only one, located on the starboard side of Navigation Deck. It features a king-size bed, walk-in closet with superb drawer space, oversize whirlpool bath and separate shower enclosure, living room, dressing room, large private balcony, pantry, mini-bar/refrigerator, a guest toilet and floor to ceiling windows.

BERLITZ'S RATINGS

	Possible	Achieved
Ship	500	418
Accommodation	200	162
Food	400	267
Service	400	299
Entertainment	100	77
Cruise	400	310

DINING: The two-level dining room, located at the stern is quite dramatic, and has a grand staircase (although few seem to use it), panoramic views on three sides, and a music balcony. Fine Rosenthal china and cutlery are featured (although there are no fish knives). There is open seating for breakfast and lunch, and two seatings for dinner. The waiter stations in the dining room are very noisy for anyone seated adjacent to them.

Unfortunately, Holland America Line food isn't as nice as the china it's placed on. It may be adequate for most passengers who are not used to better food, but it does not match the standard found aboard other ships in the premium segment of the industry. While USDA beef is of a good quality, fowl tends to be battery-tough, and most fish is overcooked and has the consistency of a cricket bat.

What are also definitely *not* luxurious are the endless packets of sugar, and packets (instead of glass jars) of breakfast jam, marmalade and honey, and poor quality teas. While these may be suitable for a family diner, they do not belong aboard a ship that claims to have "award-winning cuisine." Dessert and pastry items are of good quality (specifically for American tastes), although there is much use of canned fruits and jellies. Forget the selection of "international" cheeses, however, as most of it didn't come from anywhere other than the USA – which is known for its processed, highly colored cheese slices rather than fine cheese-making.

Holland America Line can provide Kosher meals, but these are prepared ashore, frozen, and brought to your table sealed in their original containers (there is no Kosher kitchen on board).

Instead of the more formal dining room, the Lido Buffet is open for casual dinners on all except the last night of each cruise (typically three nights on a 7-night cruise), in an open-seating arrangement. Tables are set with crisp linens, flatware and stemware. A set menu is featured, and this includes a choice of four entrées.

There is also an extensive, dual-line, self-serve Lido Buffet (one side is for smokers, the other side for non-smokers) for casual breakfasts and lunches (and dinners on most nights). There is much use of canned fruits (good for older passengers with few teeth) and packeted items, although there are several commercial low-calorie salad dressings. The choice of cheeses (and accompanying crackers) is very poor. The beverage station also lets it down, for it is no better than those found in family outlets ashore in the United States. In addition, a poolside grill provides basic American hamburgers and hot dogs.

OTHER COMMENTS: This is one of a series of four almost identical ships in the same series – the others being *Statendam, Ryndam* and *Veendam*. The exterior styling is rather angular (some would say boxy – the funnel certainly is), although it is softened and balanced somewhat by the fact that the hull is painted black. There is a full wrap-around teak promenade deck outdoors – excellent for strolling, and, thankfully, no sign of synthetic turf anywhere. The deck lounge chairs are wood, and come with comfortable cushioned pads.

Inside, an asymmetrical layout breaks up the interiors and helps to reduce bottlenecks and congestion. The décor is softer, more sophisticated, and far less eclectic than in sister ship *Statendam* (the first in this series of what the company terms *Statendam*-class ships), while the interiors of the latest in the series seem to improve further on the theme. In general, however, a restrained approach to interior styling is taken using a mixture of contemporary materials combined with traditional woods and ceramics. There is, fortunately, little "glitz" anywhere.

What is outstanding is the array of artworks throughout the ship (costing about $2 million), assembled and nicely displayed to represent the fine Dutch heritage of Holland America Line and to present a balance between standard itineraries and onboard creature comforts. Also noticeable are the fine flower arrangements throughout the public areas and foyers – used good effect to brighten up what to some is dull décor.

Atop the ship, with forward facing views that wrap around the sides is the Crow's Nest Lounge. By day it makes a fine observation lounge (particularly in Alaska), while by night it turns into a nightclub with extremely variable lighting.

A three-deck high atrium foyer that is quite stunning, although its sculpted centerpiece makes it look a little crowded, and leaves little room in front of the purser's office. A hydraulic magrodome (glass) roof covers the reasonably sized swimming pool/whirlpools and central Lido area (whose focal point is a large dolphin sculpture) so that this can be used in either fine or inclement weather.

The two-deck-high show lounge is basically well designed, but the ceiling is low and the sight lines from the balcony level are poor. Has a large and quite lovely, and relaxing reference library. The company keeps its ships very clean and tidy, and there is good passenger flow throughout.

Maasdam is a well-built ship, and has fairly decent interior fit and finish. Holland America Line is constantly fine-tuning its performance as a cruise operator and its regular passengers (almost all of whom are North American – there are few international passengers) find the company's ships comfortable and well run. The company continues its strong maritime traditions, although the present food and service components still let the rest of the cruise experience down.

Gratuities are extra, and they are added to your shipboard account at $10–$13 per day, according to the accommodation grade chosen. Refreshingly, the company does not add an automatic 15 percent gratuity for beverage purchases. Perhaps the ship's best asset is her friendly and personable Filipino and Indonesian crew, although communication can prove frustrating at times.

Holland America Line's many repeat passengers always seem to enjoy the fact that social dancing is always on the menu. The company also offers complimentary cappuccino and espresso coffees and free ice cream during certain hours of the day aboard its ships, as well as hot hors d'oeuvres in all bars – something other major lines seem to have dropped, or charge extra for. In the final analysis, however, the score for this ship (and its sisters *Ryndam, Statendam* and *Veendam*) ends up just a disappointing tad under what it could be if the food and food service staff were better (more professional training might help). The onboard currency is the US dollar.

WEAK POINTS: Standing in line for embarkation, disembarkation, shore tenders and for self-serve buffet meals is an inevitable aspect of cruising aboard all large ships. The service staff is Indonesian, and, although they are quite charming (for the most part), communication with them often proves frustrating for many passengers and the service is spotty and inconsistent. Passengers are forced to eat at the Lido Café on days when the dining room is closed for lunch (this is typically once or twice per cruise, depending on ship and itinerary).

The single escalator is virtually useless. There is no bell push outside the suites. The room service is poor. The charge to use the washing machines and dryers in the self-service launderette is really petty and irritating, particularly for the occupants of suites, as they pay high prices for their cruises.

Majesty of the Seas
★★★ +

Large Ship: ....73,941 tons	Total Crew: 827	Cabins (wheelchair accessible): 4
Lifestyle: ....Standard	Passengers	Cabin Current: ....110 volts
Cruise Line: ....Royal Caribbean	(lower beds/all berths): 2,350/2,744	Elevators: 11
International	Passenger Space Ratio	Casino (gaming tables): ....Yes
Former Names: ....none	(lower beds/all berths): 31.4/26.9	Slot Machines: ....Yes
Builder: ....Chantiers de l'Atlantique	Crew/Passenger Ratio	Swimming Pools (outdoors): 2
Original Cost: ....$300 million	(lower beds/all berths): 2.8/3.3	Swimming Pools (indoors): 0
Entered Service: ....Apr 1992	Navigation Officers: ....Norwegian	Whirlpools: 2
Registry: ....The Bahamas	Cabins (total): 1,175	Fitness Center: ....Yes
Length (ft/m): 879.9/268.2	Size Range (sq ft/m): 118.4–670.0/	Sauna/Steam Room: ....Yes/No
Beam (ft/m): 105.9/32.3	11.0–62.2	Massage: ....Yes
Draft (ft/m): 24.9/7.6	Cabins (outside view): 732	Self-Service Launderette: ....No
Propulsion/Propellers: ....diesel	Cabins (interior/no view): 443	Dedicated Cinema/Seats: Yes/200
(21,844 kW)/2	Cabins (for one person): 0	Library: ....Yes
Passenger Decks: 14	Cabins (with private balcony): 62	Classification Society: Det Norske Veritas

OVERALL SCORE: 1,394 (OUT OF A POSSIBLE 2,000 POINTS)

ACCOMMODATION: There are 17 price categories aboard this ship, depending on size and location.

SUITES: Thirteen suites on Bridge Deck are reasonably large and nicely furnished (the largest is the Royal Suite), with separate living and sleeping spaces, and they provide more space, with better service, and more perks than the standard-grade accommodation.

STANDARD CABINS: The standard outside-view and interior (no view) cabins are very small, however, although an arched window treatment and colorful soft furnishings do give the illusion of more space. Almost all cabins have twin beds that can be converted to a queen-sized or double bed configuration, together with moveable bedside tables. All of the standard cabins have very little closet and drawer space (you will need some luggage engineering to stow your cases). You should, therefore, think of packing only minimal clothing, which is all you really need for a short cruise. All cabins have a private bathroom, with shower enclosure, toilet and washbasin.

DINING: The two large dining rooms (both non-smoking) have Hollywood musical themes. There are tables for four, six or eight, but no tables for two, and there are two seatings. The dining operation is well orchestrated, with emphasis on highly programmed (insensitive), extremely hurried service that many find intrusive.

The cuisine is typical of mass banquet catering that

BERLITZ'S RATINGS

	Possible	Achieved
Ship	500	381
Accommodation	200	141
Food	400	245
Service	400	286
Entertainment	100	75
Cruise	400	266

offers standard fare comparable to that found in American family-style restaurants ashore. The menu descriptions make the food sound better than it is (which is consistently below average), mostly disappointing and without much taste – the result of controlled food costs as well as the use of many mixes and pre-prepared items. However, a decent selection of light meals is provided, and a vegetarian menu is available. The selection of breads, rolls, fruit and cheese is quite poor, however, and could do more improvement. Caviar (once a standard menu item) now incurs a heft extra charge. Menus typically include a Welcome Aboard Dinner, French Dinner, Italian Dinner, International Dinner, and Captain's Gala Dinner.

The wine list is not extensive, but the prices are moderate. The waiters, many from Caribbean countries, are perhaps overly friendly for some tastes – particularly on the last night of the cruise, when tips are expected.

For casual breakfasts and lunches, the Windjammer Café is the place to go, although there are often long lines at peak times, and the selection is very average.

OTHER COMMENTS: When first introduced, this ship (together with its two sister ships, *Majesty of the Seas* and *Sovereign of the Seas*) was an innovative vessel. Royal Caribbean International's trademark Viking Crown lounge and bar surrounds the funnel and provides a stunning view. The open deck space is very cramped when full, as aboard any large ship, although there seems to be plenty of it. There is a basketball court for sports lovers.

While the interior layout is a little awkward (being designed in a vertical stack, with most public rooms located aft, and accommodation located forward), the ship has an impressive array of spacious and elegant public rooms, although the décor comes from the IKEA school of interior design. A stunning five-deck-high Centrum lobby has cascading stairways and two glass-walled elevators. There is a good two-level show lounge and a decent array of shops, albeit with lots of tacky merchandise. Casino gamers will find blackjack, craps, Caribbean stud poker and roulette tables, plus an array of slot machines. Among the public rooms, the library is a nice feature for quite relaxation, and a decent selection of books. The entertainment program is quite sound, and there is a decent range of children's/teens' programs and cheerful youth counselors.

This floating resort provides a well tuned, yet impersonal short cruise experience, for a lot of passengers. The dress code is very casual. In the final analysis, you will probably be overwhelmed by the public spaces, and under whelmed by the size of the cabins. However, this is basically a well-run, fine-tuned, highly programmed cruise product geared particularly to those seeking an action-packed cruise vacation at a moderately good price, with lots of fellow passengers. The onboard currency is the US dollar.

WEAK POINTS: Standing in line for embarkation, disembarkation, shore tenders and for self-serve buffet meals is an inevitable aspect of cruising aboard all large ships. There are too many intrusive and irritating announcements. Unfortunately, the officers, junior officers and staff often forget that hospitality is the key to keeping passengers happy.

LATITUDE AND LONGITUDE

Latitude signifies the distance north or south of the equator, while **longitude** signifies distance east or west of the 0 degree at Greenwich Observatory in London ("where time begins"). Both are recorded in degrees, minutes, and seconds. At the equator, one minute of longitude is equal to one nautical mile, but as the meridians converge after leaving the equator and meeting at the poles, the size of a degree becomes smaller.

Mandalay
★★

Small Ship: ....420 tons	Main Propulsion: ....sail power	Cabins (for one person): 0
Lifestyle: ....Standard	Propulsion/Propellers: diesel/1	Cabins (with private balcony): 2
Cruise Line: ......Windjammer Barefoot	Passenger Decks: 3	Cabins (wheelchair accessible): 0
Cruises	Total Crew: 28	Cabin Current: ....110 volts
Former Names: ....Vema, Hussar	Passengers	Elevators: 0
Builder: ....Cox & Stevens (UK)	(lower beds/all berths): 72/72	Casino (gaming tables): ....No
Original Cost: ....n/a	Passenger Space Ratio	Slot Machines: ....No
Entered Service: 1923/1982	(lower beds/all berths): 5.8/5.8	Swimming Pools (outdoors): 0
Registry: ....Equitorial Guinea	Crew/Passenger Ratio	Whirlpools: 0
Length (ft/m): 236.0/71.9	(lower beds/all berths): 2.5/2.5	Fitness Center: ....No
Beam (ft/m): 33.0/10.0	Navigation Officers: ....International	Sauna/Steam Room: ....No/No
Draft (ft/m): 15.0/4.5	Cabins (total): 36	Massage: ....No
Type of Vessel: ....barkentine	Size Range (sq ft/m): 65.0–100.1/6.0–9.3	Self-Service Launderette: ....No
No. of Masts: 3	Cabins (outside view): 30	Library: ....Yes
Sail Area (sq ft/m2): 12,002.1/1,115.0	Cabins (interior/no view): 6	Classification Society: ....none

OVERALL SCORE: 902 (OUT OF A POSSIBLE 2,000 POINTS)

ACCOMMODATION: There are four grades of accommodation (Admiral's Suite, Deck Cabin, Captain's Cabin and Standard Cabin). The cabins are small (designed more for packages than people), however, particularly when compared to regular cruise ships. But this is a very casual cruise experience and you will need few clothes anyway. All cabins have upper and lower berths, and most of them are quite narrow.

DINING: There is one dining room, and meals are all very simple in style and service, with little choice and only the most basic presentation. Breakfast is served on board, as is dinner, while lunch could be either on board or at a beach, picnic-style. Wine is included for dinner.

OTHER COMMENTS: *Mandalay* was originally built for the American financier E.F. Hutton; the ship was then sold to shipping magnate George Vettelman. Windjammer Barefoot Cruises acquired the ship in 1982.

Aboard one of the Windjammer Barefoot Cruises' fleet you can let the crew do all the work, or you can lend a hand at the helm yourself, if you feel so inclined. One neat thing to do is just to sit or lie in the nets at the bows of the vessel, without a care in the world.

The mood is free and easy, the ships are equipped very simply, and only the most casual clothes are required (T-shirts and shorts), and shoes are optional, although you may need them if you go off in one of the ports. Quite possibly the most used item will be your bathing suit – so you should take more than one. Smoking is allowed only on the open decks.

BERLITZ'S RATINGS

	Possible	Achieved
Ship	500	219
Accommodation	200	79
Food	400	166
Service	400	188
Entertainment	N/A	N/A
Cruise	500	250

Entertainment in the evenings consists of – you and the crew. You can put on a toga, take or create a pirate outfit and join in the fun. This is cruising free 'n' easy style – no programmed big-ship production shows here. Everything is basic, basic, basic.

Jammin' aboard a Windjammer (first-time passengers are called "crewmates" while repeat passengers are called "jammers") is no-frills cruising in a no-nonsense, friendly environment, for the young at heart and those who don't need programmed activities. It's all about going to sea and enjoying the romance and experience of being at sea under sail.

Anyone who enjoys beaches, scuba diving and snorkeling around the Caribbean, and anyone seeking sun, sea, and sand will be best suited to a Windjammer Barefoot Cruises cruise, as well as lovers of old sailing ships.

This ship can anchor in neat little Caribbean hideaways that larger (regular) cruise ships can't get near. Although itineraries (well, islands) are provided in the brochure, the captain actually decides which islands to go to in any given area, depending on the sea and weather conditions. *Mandalay* features year-round cruises in the Caribbean, and sails from Antigua and Grenada. Although at first glance the brochure rates might seem inexpensive, but you'll need to add on the airfare in order to get the true cost. Other ships in the fleet include *Flying Cloud, Legacy, Polynesia,* and *Yankee Clipper.* The onboard currency is the US dollar.

WEAK POINTS: There's very little space per passenger. Tips to the crew are suggested – at $50 per week.

Marco Polo
★★★ +

Mid-Size Ship: . . . . .22,080 tons	Total Crew: .356	Cabins (wheelchair accessible): 2
Lifestyle: . . . . .Premium	Passengers	Cabin Current: . . . . .110 and 220 volts
Cruise Line: . . . . .Orient Lines	(lower beds/all berths): 848/915	Elevators: 4
Former Names: . . . . . .Aleksandr Pushkin	Passenger Space Ratio	Casino (gaming tables): . . . . .Yes
Builder: . . . . . .VEB Mathias Thesen Werft	(lower beds/all berths): 26.0/24.1	Slot Machines: . . . . .Yes
(Germany)	Crew/Passenger Ratio	Swimming Pools (outdoors): 1
Original Cost: . . . . .n/a	(lower beds/all berths): 2.3/2.5	Swimming Pools (indoors): 0
Entered Service: . . . . .Apr 1966/Nov 1993	Navigation Officers: . . . . . .Scandinavian	Whirlpools: 3
Registry: . . . . .The Bahamas	Cabins (total): 425	Fitness Center: . . . . .Yes
Length (ft/m): 578.4/176.28	Size Range (sq ft/m): 93.0–484.0/8.6–44.9	Sauna/Steam Room: . . . . .Yes/No
Beam (ft/m): 77.4/23.60	Cabins (outside view): 292	Massage: . . . . .Yes
Draft (ft/m): 26.8/8.17	Cabins (interior/no view): 133	Self-Service Launderette: . . . . .No
Propulsion/Propellers: . . . . .diesel	Cabins (for one person): . . .(many doubles	Dedicated Cinema/Seats: . . . . .No
(14,444 kW)/2	sold for single occupancy)	Library: . . . . .Yes
Passenger Decks: 8	Cabins (with private balcony): 0	Classification Society: . . . .Bureau Veritas

---

OVERALL SCORE: 1,386 (OUT OF A POSSIBLE 2,000 POINTS)

ACCOMMODATION: The cabins, which come in 13 different grades, are a profusion of different sizes and configurations. All are pleasingly decorated, and feature rich wood cabinetry, wood and mirror-fronted closets, adequate drawer and storage space, television, thin cotton bathrobe, and hairdryer (in the bathroom) and non-vacuum (non-noisy) toilets. Carpets curtains and bedspreads are all nicely color coordinated. Weak points include extremely poor sound insulation between cabins (you can hear you neighbors brushing their hair), and the fact that the bathrooms are small, with little storage space for toiletries (particularly during long cruises).

The largest accommodation is found in two deluxe suites and two junior suites. The deluxe suites (Dynasty and Mandarin), feature a queen-sized bed, separate living room, and marble bathroom with bathtub/shower, walk-in closet, refrigerator, television and VCR The Junior Suites feature two lower beds, lounge area, and marble bathroom with bathtub/shower, walk-in closet, and refrigerator.

Also very comfortable are the Superior Deluxe ocean-view cabins that have two lower beds (some can be converted to a queen-sized bed), marble bathroom with bathtub/shower, and refrigerator.

Note that some cabins on Upper Deck and Sky Deck have lifeboat-obstructed views. Since many passengers are of senior years, there should be 24-hour room service – but there isn't.

DINING: The Seven Seas Restaurant is nicely decorated

BERLITZ'S RATINGS

	Possible	Achieved
Ship	500	365
Accommodation	200	129
Food	400	271
Service	400	292
Entertainment	100	61
Cruise	400	268

in soft pastel colors, practical in design, and functions well, but it has a low ceiling, is noisy, and the tables are very close together. There are two seatings. There are tables for two to ten, and fine place settings and china. The food itself is of a good standard, with good presentation. The wine list is quite extensive, and the prices are very reasonable, although most wines are quite young.

Raffles is the place for informal self-serve breakfasts and lunches (there is seating inside as well as outdoors around the ship's swimming pool). On assorted evenings each cruise it also becomes an alternative dining spot, for about 75 people. Reservations are required, but there is no extra charge. A 15 percent gratuity is added to all bar and wine accounts.

OTHER COMMENTS: This ship was built as one of five almost identical sister ships for the Russian/Ukrainian fleet (it was originally constructed to re-open the Leningrad to Montreal transatlantic route in 1966, after a long absence since 1949). The ship has a fine, traditional "real-ship" profile, an extremely strong ice-strengthened hull and huge storage spaces for long voyages. After being completely refitted (from the hull and engines up) and refurbished, the ship now features well-designed destination-intensive cruises, at realistic prices.

Orient Lines, and its single ship Marco Polo was bought by Norwegian Cruise Line in 1998 (and then by Star Cruises in 2000), but continues to operate under the growing Orient Lines brand name. A second ship (Crown Odyssey) was added to the fleet in 2000.

Marco Polo is fitted with the latest navigational aids and biological waste treatment center, and carries 10 Zodiac landing craft for in-depth shore trips in eco-sensitive areas.

This is a comfortable vessel throughout and, because it has a deep draft, rides well in unkind sea conditions. There are two large, forward-facing open-deck viewing areas. There is also a helicopter-landing pad atop the ship. The wood decked aft swimming pool/lido deck area is kept in good condition. Joggers and walkers can circle around the ship – not on the promenade deck – but one deck above, although this goes past vast air intakes that are noisy, and the walkway is very narrow.

As soon as you walk aboard, you feel a warm, welcoming, homely ambiance that is instantly comforting. There is a wide range of public rooms, most of which are arranged on one horizontal deck. A sense of spaciousness pervades, as most have high ceilings. Features very tasteful interior decor, with careful use of mirrored surfaces, as well as colors that do not clash but are relaxing but not boring; the subdued lighting helps maintain an air of calmness and relaxation.

Although this ship is more than 35 years old, it is in remarkably fine shape – a tribute to the management and crew. Indeed, it's in better shape than many ships only 10 years old, and its interiors are constantly being refurbished and refreshed.

All in all, *Marco Polo* features well-planned destination-intensive cruises, and offers really good value for money in very comfortable, elegant but unpretentious surroundings, while a friendly and accommodating Filipino crew helps to make a cruise a pleasant, no-hassle experience. Despite the fact that the ship is beautifully maintained, the slightly lower score than last year reflects changing times (there's a lot of new tonnage around), less crew training in service areas, and other items.

WEAK POINTS: Avoid Cabins 310/312 as these are located close to the engine room doorway and the noise level is considerable. There is no observation lounge with forward-facing views over the ship's bows. There is a little too much use of plastic and Styrofoam cups when glass would be much better for presentation. There are many "lips" or raised thresholds, so you need to be on your guard when walking through the ship, and particularly when walking up or down the exterior stairways. This could prove difficult for wheelchair-bound passengers.

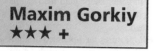

Maxim Gorkiy
★★★ +

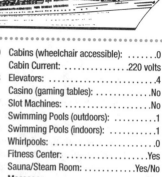

Mid-Size Ship: . . . . .24,981 tons	Total Crew: 340	Cabins (wheelchair accessible): 0
Lifestyle: . . . . .Standard	Passengers	Cabin Current: . . . . .220 volts
Cruise Line: . . . . .Phoenix Seereisen	(lower beds/all berths): 650/88	Elevators: 4
Former Names: . . . . .Hanseatic, Hamburg	Passenger Space Ratio	Casino (gaming tables): . . . . .No
Builder: . .Howaldtswerke Deutsche Werft	(lower beds/all berths): 38.4/31.7	Slot Machines: . . . . .No
(Germany)	Crew/Passenger Ratio	Swimming Pools (outdoors): 1
Original Cost: . . . .£5.6 million	(lower beds/all berths): . . . : 1.9/2.3	Swimming Pools (indoors): 1
Entered Service: . . . . .Mar 1969/Jan 1974	Navigation Officers: . . .Russian/Ukrainian	Whirlpools: 0
Registry: . . . . .The Bahamas	Cabins (total): .326	Fitness Center: . . . . .Yes
Length (ft/m): 638.8/194.72	Size Range (sq ft/m): 145.3–296.0/	Sauna/Steam Room: . . . . .Yes/No
Beam (ft/m): 87.3/26.62	13.5–27.0	Massage: . . . . .Yes
Draft (ft/m): 27.0/8.25	Cabins (outside view): 210	Self-Service Launderette: . . . . .Yes
Propulsion/Propellers: . . . . .steam turbine	Cabins (interior/no view): 116	Dedicated Cinema/Seats: Yes/290
(16,900 kW)/2	Cabins (for one person): 2	Library: . . . . .Yes
Passenger Decks: 10	Cabins (with private balcony): 0	Classification Society: Det Norske Veritas

OVERALL SCORE: 1,385 (OUT OF A POSSIBLE 2,000 POINTS)

ACCOMMODATION: The brochure shows outside-view and interior (no view) cabins in 18 grades. Most cabins are actually quite spacious, and many of them have wood paneling, accenting and trim, while the décor is comfortable and quite restful. The bathrooms are quite large and feature full-sized bathtubs in all except 20 cabins. There is a decent amount of space for the storage of one's personal toiletry items.

Cabins designated as deluxe are of a good size, come fully equipped with almost everything one would need, and have huge picture windows (most others have portholes). The in-cabin television system features both German and Russian satellite TV programming.

Anyone booking a suite or one of the top five grades receives Phoenix VIP service, which includes flowers for the cabin, a separate check-in desk and priority disembarkation.

DINING: There are three restaurants (all have one seating, with assigned tables, so you have the same waiter throughout your cruise). All three restaurants are located low down in the ship, but they are cheerfully decorated. Draught lager is always available, and the wine list has many wines from different regions of Germany, Switzerland and Austria, as well as a modest selection from France and other countries. Moderately decent food is served, and wine at lunch and dinner is included in the cruise fare, but more choice, and better presentation would be welcome.

The service is quite attentive and courteous from the

BERLITZ'S RATINGS

	Possible	Achieved
Ship	500	334
Accommodation	200	137
Food	400	288
Service	400	299
Entertainment	100	62
Cruise	400	265

well-meaning staff, although it is somewhat hurried even though there is only one seating for all meals. Cushions would be a welcome addition to some of the banquette seating.

OTHER COMMENTS: This all-white ship was originally built as *Hamburg* for the transatlantic service of the now defunct Deutsche Atlantik Linie. The ship has long, pleasing lines and outer styling, and is easily identified by its platform-topped funnel, which was designed to disperse smoke away from the aft, tiered, open decks.

In 1974 the ship was sold to the Black Sea Shipping Company and renamed *Maxim Gorkiy*. It was modernized in 1988, but on June 20, 1989 the ship gained notoriety when it rammed the cruise ship *Vasco da Gama* (presently named *Seawind Crown*) in the ice near Spitzbergen. Later in 1989, *Maxim Gorkiy* hit the headlines when it played host to an international summit in Malta between America's then president, George Bush Sr., and Russia's leader, Mikhail Gorbachev.

Since December 1992 it has been placed under long-term charter (until 2008) to Phoenix Seereisen from its present owners, Russia's Sovcomflot.

The ship has been generally well maintained, and more facilities were added during the last refurbishment. There is a generous amount of open deck and sunbathing space, and the deck lounge chairs have cushioned pads. Open-deck sports include a large basketball court aft of the funnel.

Inside, there are some handsome, well-designed, though now slightly dated, public rooms; the passenger flow is good, with few congested areas. A generous amount of wood paneling was used in the construction – most of it still looks good, although some refinishing is needed in some areas. The décor is dark and somewhat dull, although it is quite relaxing and soporific. The show lounge, an important room, is decent enough, although it simply doesn't have enough seating; the stage and lighting facilities could also be improved. The gymnasium is small, and much of the equipment needs updating. There are two relaxing winter gardens with large ocean-view windows.

An added bonus is an indoor swimming pool – always good for those times when the outdoor pool can't be used because of inclement weather.

Maxim Gorkiy will provide a very good general cruise experience in comfortable, quite elegant, but very traditional surroundings, at a modest price, although you should remember that this is an older ship that does not have the latest in facilities. This ship is particularly targeted to German-speaking passengers who appreciate good value and well-planned, destination-intensive itineraries. The mostly Russian and Ukrainian service staff provides friendly, attentive service. Port taxes, insurance and gratuities are included.

Phoenix Seereisen has, over the years, attained almost a cult status among its passengers, in that the company provides a consistently fine, very popular product for those wanting a casual cruise experience and lifestyle among friendly passengers who appreciate value for money. Where passengers are required to fly to join their cruises, the airline most used by Phoenix Seereisen is LTU. The currency on board is the euro.

Removed 2006

Melody
★★★ +

Large Ship:	.36,500 tons	Total Crew:	.535

Large Ship: . . . . .36,500 tons
Lifestyle: . . . . .Standard
Cruise Line: . . . . .Mediterranean Shipping
Cruises
Former Names: . . . .*Star/Ship Atlantic,*
Atlantic
Builder: . . . . .C.N.I.M. (France)
Original Cost: . . . .$100 million
Entered Service: . . .Apr 1982/June 1997
Registry: . . . . .Panama
Length (ft/m): 671.9/204.81
Beam (ft/m): 89.7/27.36
Draft (ft/m): 25.5/7.80
Propulsion/Propellers: . . . . .diesel
(22,070 kW)/2
Passenger Decks: 9

Total Crew: 535
Passengers
(lower beds/all berths): 1,098/1,600
Passenger Space Ratio
(lower beds/all berths): 33.2/22.8
Crew/Passenger Ratio
(lower beds/all berths): 2.0/2.9
Navigation Officers: . . . . .Italian
Cabins (total): 549
Size Range (sq ft/m): 137.0–427.0/
12.7–39.5
Cabins (outside view): 392
Cabins (interior/no view): 157
Cabins (for one person): 0
Cabins (with private balcony): 0
Cabins (wheelchair accessible): . . . . . .Yes

Cabin Current: . . . . .110 volts
Elevators: 4
Casino (gaming tables): . . . . .Yes
Slot Machines: . . . . .Yes
Swimming Pools (outdoors): 1
Swimming Pools (indoors): 1
Whirlpools: 3
Fitness Center: . . . . .Yes
Sauna/Steam Room: . . . . .Yes/No
Massage: . . . . .Yes
Self-Service Launderette: . . . . .No
Dedicated Cinema/Seats: Yes/227
Library: . . . . .Yes (2 book racks)
Classification Society: . .American Bureau
of Shipping

OVERALL SCORE: 1,259 (OUT OF A POSSIBLE 2,000 POINTS)

ACCOMMODATION: Six suites have plenty of space for families of four, and have a decent walk-in closet. The bathroom is large and has a full-size bathtub, oversize sink (large enough to bathe twins in), and an uncomfortable square toilet.

Other outside-view and interior (no view) cabins are of a decent size, and have ample closet and drawer space. Many cabins have upper berths – good for families, although with four persons there is very little space for anything else, such as luggage. The cabin insulation is extremely poor, however (you can hear your neighbors brushing their hair), and the room service menu is quite basic. Bathrooms are of a decent size, and quite practical in their facilities.

DINING: The dining room, on a lower deck, is large and quite attractive, but the tables are much too close together, and it is difficult for waiters to serve properly. Also, the chairs do not have armrests, and the noise level is extremely high. There are two seatings, and the cuisine is Italian-continental. The food quality generally is adequate for the price paid, but dishes, when presented, are not as good as the menu description would have you believe. There is a limited wine list. An attentive, multinational staff provides the service, although it needs polishing. The buffets are quite poor when compared to many other ships in this standard category.

OTHER COMMENTS: This ship (originally built for the now defunct Home Lines, then operated for many years

BERLITZ'S RATINGS

	Possible	Achieved
Ship	500	354
Accommodation	200	150
Food	400	215
Service	400	241
Entertainment	100	58
Cruise	400	241

by the now defunct Premier Cruise Lines) has a short, stubby bow and squat funnel. Her hull is all in white.

There is a good amount of outdoor deck space, but noise levels can be high when the ship is full, and there are many families with children (particularly during the summer season).

The interior is quite spacious, with plenty of public rooms, most of which have high ceilings. The décor is somewhat somber in places, and lighting is very subdued. There is a generous amount of stainless steel and teakwood trim. A large observation lounge is wasted as an informal eating area. There is a good indoor-outdoor pool area (covered by a magrodome in inclement weather). There is a fairly good children's program during peak periods, and several children's (and teens) counselors.

This ship (the largest in the MSC fleet so far) will provide a good basic cruise experience for families, at a fair price, in comfortable, modern surroundings. Typically about 60 percent of passengers will be Italian, while the rest may be a mix of other Europeans. Expect lots of extra charges. The onboard currency is the euro.

WEAK POINTS: Standing in line for embarkation, disembarkation, shore tenders and for buffet meals is inevitable aboard large ships. The almost constant loud announcements are annoying and intrusive, particularly when the ship is in port. There is no wrap-around promenade deck outdoors, nor are cushioned pads provided for the deck lounge chairs. The ship has only four elevators - not enough for this number of passengers.

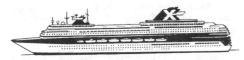

Mercury
★★★★ +

Large Ship:	...77,713 tons	Passengers	
Lifestyle:	...Premium	(lower beds/all berths):	...1,870/2,681
Cruise Line:	...Celebrity Cruises	Passenger Space Ratio	
Former Names:	...none	(lower beds/all berths):	...41.5/28.9
Builder:	...Meyer Werft (Germany)	Crew/Passenger Ratio	
Original Cost:	...$320 million	(lower beds/all berths):	...2.0/2.9
Entered Service:	...Nov 1997	Navigation Officers:	...Greek
Registry:	...The Bahamas	Cabins (total):	...935
Length (ft/m):	...865.8/263.90	Size Range (sq ft/m):	...171.0–1,514.5/
Beam (ft/m):	...105.6/32.20		15.8–140.7
Draft (ft/m):	...25.2/7.70	Cabins (outside view):	...639
Propulsion/Propellers:	...diesel	Cabins (interior/no view):	...296
	(31,500 kW)/2	Cabins (for one person):	...0
Passenger Decks:	...10	Cabins (with private balcony):	...220
Total Crew:	...909	Cabins (wheelchair accessible):	...8

Cabin Current:	...110 and 220 volts
Elevators:	...10
Casino (gaming tables):	...Yes
Slot Machines:	...Yes
Swimming Pools (outdoors):	...2
Swimming Pools (indoors):	...1
	indoor/outdoor (magrodome)
Whirlpools:	...4
Fitness Center:	...Yes
Sauna/Steam Room:	...Yes
Massage:	...Yes
Self-Service Launderette:	...No
Dedicated Cinema/Seats:	...Yes/183
Library:	...Yes
Classification Society:	...Lloyd's Register

OVERALL SCORE: 1,663 (OUT OF A POSSIBLE 2,000 POINTS)

ACCOMMODATION: The accommodation is extremely comfortable, regardless of which cabin grade you choose. Naturally, if you select a suite, you will find more space, butler service (whether you want it or not), more and better amenities and more personal service than if you choose any of the standard cabin grades.

Occupants of all accommodation designated as suites get gold cards to open their doors (and priority service throughout the ship, free cappuccino/espresso coffees when served by a butler, welcome champagne, flowers, VCR, and use of the AquaSpa thalassotherapy pool). All occupants of standard (interior no view and outside-view) cabins have white cards. Suites that have private balconies also have floor-to-ceiling windows and sliding doors to balconies (a few suites have outward opening doors).

Two Presidential Suites are located amidships. These provide spectacular living spaces, perhaps even better than those in *Century* and *Galaxy*, depending on your personal taste. There is a separate bedroom (with high-tech Sony multimedia entertainment center), large lounge (complete with dining table), huge walk-in closet with mountains of drawers, and king-sized marble-tiled bathroom with every appointment necessary.

There is in-suite dining for the two Presidential and 12 Century Suites, as well as for the 24 Sky Suites (1202, 1203, 1236 and 1237 have enormous fully private balconies, while the others are only semi-private). All suites feature full butler service, personalized stationery, and business cards. If you choose one of the forward-most Sky Deck suites, however, be warned that you may well be

BERLITZ'S RATINGS

	Possible	Achieved
Ship	500	444
Accommodation	200	177
Food	400	315
Service	400	319
Entertainment	100	78
Cruise	400	330

subject to constant music and noise from the pool deck (one deck below) between 8am and 6pm (not good if you want to relax). The closet and drawer space provided in these suites is superb. In the bathrooms of the Sky Suites, the shaving mirror is positioned too high, and in the bedroom, the TV set cannot be viewed from the bed. Push-button bell and privacy curtains should be, but are not, provided. In-suite massage is available (this really is pleasant when provided on the balcony of the Sky Suites).

The standard (interior and outside) cabins are quite spacious and nicely decorated with cheerful fabrics, and marble-topped vanity unit. The bathrooms are generous with space, tiled from floor to ceiling, and the power showers are extremely practical units.

All cabins feature interactive television for booking shore excursions, ordering cabin service items and purchasing goods from the ship's boutiques, so you don't have to leave your quarters if you don't wish to, especially if you dislike the ports of call. The system works in English, French, German, Italian and Spanish. There are five channels of music – all available from the TV set (therefore you cannot have music without having a picture). All cabins are also equipped with a "baby monitoring telephone system" which allows you to telephone your cabin whilst you are elsewhere, and have a two-way intercom to "listen in." Automatic "wake-up" calls can also be dialed in. All accommodation designated as suites have duvets on the beds instead of sheets and blankets.

DINING: The two-level formal Manhattan Restaurant, located at the ship's stern, is quite grand and elegant (each level has its own full galley); a grand staircase connects the two levels. Large picture windows provide sea views on three sides; at night, large blinds (with scenes of Manhattan, the name of the dining room) roll down electronically to cover the stern-facing windows. There are two seatings for dinner (open seating for breakfast and lunch), at tables for two, four, six, eight or 10, and the dining room is a totally no-smoking area.

Three-Michelin-starred chef Michel Roux directs the same excellent cuisine that has made Celebrity Cruises the shining star of the contemporary cruise industry. The menus are creative, and the food is very attractively presented. There is also an excellent wine list, and real wine waiters (unlike so many other large cruise companies), although prices are high (particularly for good champagne), and the wine vintages are quite young.

There are also several informal dining spots as an alternative to the main dining room: a Lido Café, with four main serving lines; a poolside grill, and another indoor/outdoor grill located behind the aft swimming pool. The Lido Cafe has fine wood paneling and is much more elegant than the informal dining areas found aboard most ships today, and has some seating in bay window areas with great ocean views.

In the center of the ship is Tastings, a delightful coffee/tea lounge; in one corner is a presentation of goodies made by COVA, the Milanese chocolatier – an exclusive to Celebrity Cruises (the original Cova Café di Milano, located adjacent to the La Scala Opera House, Milan, opened in 1817). This is *the* place to see and be seen. It is a delightful setting (as well as a good meeting place) for those who appreciate fine Italian coffees (espresso, espresso macchiato, cappuccino, and latte), pastries and superb cakes.

Finally, for those who cannot live without them, freshly baked pizzas can be ordered and delivered, in a box, inside an insulated pouch, to your cabin.

OTHER COMMENTS: This is quite a stunning ship, both inside and outside. As aboard its identical sister *Galaxy*, there is a 1,000-seat show lounge, with side balconies, and no pillars to obstruct views (there are three high-tech "dazzle and sizzle" production shows per 7-night cruise, although they consist mainly of running, jumping, smoke, colored laser lighting and little story line intelligence). Other facilities include a three-deck-high main foyer with marble floored lobby and waterfall; over 4½ acres (18,000 sq. meters) of open deck space (poolside lounge chairs have cushioned pads, those on other decks do not); a magrodome-covered indoor-outdoor pool; AquaSpa thalassotherapy pool (with several "active" water jet stations), and assorted treatment rooms including a "rasul" mud treatment room.

Other facilities include "Michael's Club," a cigar/cognac room on Promenade Deck that overlooks the atrium, a small but luxurious cinema, a large casino (this is extremely glitzy, with confusing and congested layout). The children's facilities are good (open until 10pm, it is called the "Fun Factory") as well as an outdoor play area and paddling pool.

The décor includes plenty of wood (or wood-look) paneling and accenting throughout, and many refinements have been made during the three-ship "Century Series" that Celebrity Cruises has introduced in the past few years. The ship also houses a $3.5 million living art collection with true, museum-quality pieces. The health and fitness facilities are among the nicest aboard any ship, and have been well thought-out and designed for quiet, efficient operation, with everything in just the right place.

This ship will provide you with a finely packaged cruise vacation in elegant surroundings. It is efficiently run. There are more crew members per passenger than would be found aboard other ships of the same size in the premium category, and hence service in general is very good indeed. Note that a 15 percent gratuity is automatically added to all bar and wine accounts.

During the past two years (after Celebrity Cruises was purchased by Royal Caribbean International), the standard of product delivery aboard all the ships in the Celebrity Cruises fleet went down as cuts were made by the new owner. However, new management has been brought in to put things right, and I (and many passengers) look forward to experiencing the improvements. The onboard currency is the US dollar.

WEAK POINTS: Standing in line for embarkation, disembarkation, shore tenders and for self-serve buffet meals is an inevitable aspect of cruising aboard all large ships. Trying to reach Cabin Service or the Guest Relations Desk to answer the phone (to order breakfast, for example, if you don't want to do so via the interactive television) is a matter of luck, timing and patience (a sad reminder of the automated age, and lack of personal contact). The library is disappointingly small, and poorly located away from the main flow of passengers. There is a charge for using the Aquaspa/sauna/steam room complex. The room-service menu is poor, and food items are decidedly below the standards of food featured in the dining room.

While under the direction of its former owner John Chandris, Celebrity Cruises managed to create a superb quality cruise vacation product virtually unbeatable at the prices charged in the Alaska and Caribbean markets, representing outstanding value for money. However, given the subtle changes that have occurred since Celebrity Cruises was integrated into the Royal Caribbean Cruises family in 1997, it has become evident that slippage of product delivery standards and staff have occurred, and the latest score reflects these changes. Passenger participation activities are amateurish and should be upgraded. The officers have become more aloof lately, with far less contact with passengers than when the company first started.

Millennium
★★★★★

Large Ship:	.............90,228 tons	Passengers
Lifestyle:	.................Premium	(lower beds/all berths): 1,950/2,450
Cruise Line:	..........Celebrity Cruises	Passenger Space Ratio
Former Names:	.................none	(lower beds/all berths): 46.2/36.8
Builder:	.......Chantiers de l'Atlantique	Crew/Passenger Ratio
	(France)	(lower beds/all berths): 1.9/2.4
Original Cost:	.............$350 million	Navigation Officers: ....Greek
Entered Service:	...........June 2000	Cabins (total): 975
Registry:	................The Bahamas	Size Range (sq ft/m): 170.0–2,350.0/
Length (ft/m):	.............964.5/294.0	15.7–235.0
Beam (ft/m):	................105.6/32.2	Cabins (outside view): 780
Draft (ft/m):	.................26.2/8.0	Cabins (interior/no view): 195
Propulsion/Propellers:	.....gas turbine/2	Cabins (for one person): 0
	azimuthing pods (39,000 kW)	Cabins (with private balcony): 590
Passenger Decks:	11	Cabins (wheelchair accessible): 26
Total Crew:	999	(17 with private balcony)

Cabin Current:	........110 and 220 volts
Elevators:	10
Casino (gaming tables):	............Yes
Slot Machines:	...................Yes
Swimming Pools (outdoors):	2
Swimming Pools (indoors):	1
	(with magrodome)
Whirlpools:	4
Fitness Center:	....................Yes
Sauna/Steam Room:	...........Yes/Yes
Massage:	.........................Yes
Self-Service Launderette:	...........No
Dedicated Cinema/Seats:	.......Yes/368
Library:	.........................Yes
Classification Society:	...Lloyd's Register

OVERALL SCORE: 1,701 (OUT OF A POSSIBLE 2,000 POINTS)

ACCOMMODATION: There are 20 different grades from which to choose, depending on your preference for the size and location of your living space. Almost half of the ship's accommodation has a "private" balcony; approximately 80 percent are outside-view suites and cabins, and 20 percent are interior (no view) cabins. The accommodation is extremely comfortable throughout this ship, regardless of which cabin grade you choose.

Suites, naturally, have more space, butler service (whether you want it or not), more and better amenities and more personal service than if you choose any of the standard cabin grades. There are several categories of suites, but those at the stern of the ship are in a prime location and have huge balconies that are really private and not overlooked from above.

Regardless of which grade of accommodation you choose, all suites and cabins have wood cabinetry and accenting, interactive television and entertainment systems (you can go shopping, book shore excursions, play casino games, interactively, and even watch soft porn movies). Bathrooms have hairdryers, and 100 percent cotton towels.

PENTHOUSE SUITES: Two Penthouse Suites (on Penthouse Deck) are the largest accommodation aboard. Each occupies one half of the beam (width) of the ship, overlooking the ship's stern. Each measures a huge 2,530 sq. ft. (235 sq. meters): 1,432 sq. ft. (133 sq. meters) of living space, plus a huge wrap-around balcony measuring

BERLITZ'S RATINGS

	Possible	Achieved
Ship	500	454
Accommodation	200	181
Food	400	328
Service	400	330
Entertainment	100	78
Cruise	400	330

1,098 sq. ft. (102 sq. meters) with 180-degree views, which occupies one half of the beam (width) of the ship, overlooking the ship's stern (it includes a wet bar, hot tub and whirlpool tub); however, note that much of this terrace can be overlooked by passengers on other decks above.

Features include a marble foyer, a separate living room (complete with ebony baby grand piano – bring your own pianist if you don't play yourself) and a formal dining room. The master bedroom has a large walk-in closet; personal exercise equipment; dressing room with vanity desk, exercise equipment; marble-clad master bathroom with twin washbasins; deep whirlpool bathtub; separate shower; toilet and bidet areas; flat-screen televisions (one in the bedroom and one in the lounge) and electronically controlled drapes. Butler service is standard, and a butler's pantry, with separate entry door, has a full-size refrigerator, temperature-controlled wine cabinet, microwave oven and good-sized food preparation and storage areas. For even more space, an interconnecting door can be opened into the adjacent suite (ideal for multi-generation families).

ROYAL SUITES: Eight Royal Suites, each measuring 733 sq. ft (68 sq. meters), are located towards the aft of the ship (four each on the port and starboard sides). The décor in each is different, and is in the style of a country (Africa, China, Mexico, France, India, Italy, Morocco and Portugal). Each features a separate living room with dining and lounge areas (with refrigerator, mini-bar and

Bang & Olufsen CD sound system), and a separate bedroom. There are two entertainment centers with DVD players, and two flat-screen televisions (one in the living area, one in the bedroom), and a large walk-in closet with vanity desk. The marble-clad bathroom has a whirlpool bathtub with integral shower, and there is also a separate shower enclosure, two washbasins and toilet. The teakwood decked balcony is extensive (large enough for on-deck massage) and also has a whirlpool hot tub.

CELEBRITY SUITES: Eight Celebrity Suites, each measuring 467 sq ft (44 sq. meters), feature floor-to-ceiling windows, a separate living room with dining and lounge areas, two entertainment centers with flat-screen televisions (one in the living room, one in the bedroom), and a walk-in closet with vanity desk. The marble-clad bathroom features a whirlpool bathtub with integral shower (a window with movable blind lets you look out of the bathroom through the lounge to the large ocean-view windows). Interconnecting doors allow two suites to be used as a family unit (as there is no balcony, these suites are ideal for families with small children).

These suites overhang the starboard side of the ship (they are located opposite a group of glass-walled elevators), and provide stunning ocean views from the glass-walled sitting/dining area, which extends out from the ship's side. A personal computer with wood-surround screen allows direct internet connectivity. Butler service is standard.

SKY SUITES: There are 30 Sky Suites, each measuring 308 sq ft (28.6 sq. meters), including the private balcony (note that some balconies may be larger than others, depending on the location). Although these are designated as suites, they are really just larger cabins that feature a marble-clad bathroom with bathtub/shower combination. The suites also have a VCR player in addition to a television, and have a larger lounge area (than standard cabins) and sleeping area. Butler service is standard.

BUTLER SERVICE: Butler service (in all accommodation designated as suites) includes full breakfast, in-suite lunch and dinner service (as required), afternoon tea service, evening hors d'oeuvres, complimentary espresso and cappuccino, daily news delivery, shoeshine service, and other personal touches.

Suite occupants in Penthouse, Royal, Celebrity and Sky suites also get welcome champagne; a full personal computer in each suite, including a printer and internet access (on request in the Sky Suites); choice of films from a video library; personalized stationery; tote bag; priority dining room seating preferences; private portrait sitting, and bathrobe; and in-suite massage service.

STANDARD OUTSIDE-VIEW/INTERIOR (NO VIEW) CABINS: All other outside-view and interior (no view) cabins (those not designated as suites) feature a lounge

area with sofa or convertible sofa bed, sleeping area with twin beds that can convert to a double bed, a good amount of closet and drawer space, personal safe, mini-bar/refrigerator (all items are at extra cost), interactive television, and private bathroom. The cabins are nicely decorated with warm wood-finish furniture, and there is none of the boxy feel of cabins in so many ships, due to the angled placement of vanity and audio-video consoles. Even the smallest interior (no-view) cabin has a good-sized bathroom and shower enclosure.

WHEELCHAIR-ACCESSIBLE ACCOMMODATION: Wheelchair-accessible accommodation is available in six Sky Suites, three premium outside-view cabins, eight deluxe ocean-view cabins, four standard ocean-view and five interior (no view) cabins measure 347 sq. ft to 362 sq. ft (32.2 to 33.6 sq. meters) and are located in the most practical parts of the ship and close to elevators for good accessibility (all have doorways and bathroom doorways and showers are wheelchair-accessible.

DINING: The Metropolitan Dining Room, which seats 1,224 passengers, is the ship's principal dining hall. It is two decks high, has a grand staircase connecting the two levels, a huge glass wall overlooking the sea at the stern of the ship (electrically operated blinds provide several different backdrops), and a musician's gallery on the upper level (typically for a string quartet or quintet). There are two seatings for dinner (open seating for breakfast and lunch), at tables for two, four, six, eight or 10. The dining room is a totally non-smoking area, and, you should note, that, like all large dining halls, it can prove to be extremely noisy.

As with Celebrity Cruises' other ships, there are several dining options, particularly for those seeking more casual dining spots. Full service in-cabin dining is also available for all meals (including dinner).

For casual meals, the self-serve buffet-style Ocean Café is an extensive area that features six principal serving lines, and can seat 754. At the after end of the Ocean Buffet, a separate grill/rotisserie and pizza servery provides freshly created items. Note that all pizzas are made aboard from pizza dough and do not come ready made for reheating, as with many cruise lines. On selected evenings, alternative dinners can be taken here (reservations are necessary).

There is also an outdoors grill, for hamburgers and hot dogs, roast chicken and other fast food items, adjacent to the swimming pool.

For champagne and caviar lovers, the Platinum Club has a platinum and silver art deco (belle-epoch) décor that is reminiscent of a 1930s gentleman's club. It includes a diamond-pane reflective mirror wall. It includes a Champagne Bar and a Martini Bar, each of which has a cut crystal chandelier.

COVA CAFÉ DI MILANO: The Cova Café di Milano is a signature item aboard all the ships of Celebrity Cruises, and is a seagoing version of the real Café di Milano that was originally located next to La Scala Opera House in Milan (it opened in 1817). It is located in a prominent position, on the second level of the atrium lobby, and several display cases show off the extensive range of Cova coffee, chocolates and alcoholic digestives; this is *the* place to see and be seen. It is a delightful setting (and meeting place) for anyone who appreciates fine Italian coffees (espresso, espresso macchiato, cappuccino, and latte), pastries and superb cakes.

ALTERNATIVE (RESERVATIONS-ONLY, EXTRA COST) DINING:

Celebrity Cruises created its first true alternative restaurant (actually a more accurate description would be *dining salon*) aboard this ship. The Olympic Restaurant is named after White Star Line's transatlantic ocean liner of the same name, *Olympic* (sister ship to the ill-fated *Titanic*). It is located adjacent to the atrium lobby, and has a dining lounge that is rather like an anteroom that contains figured French walnut wood paneling from the à la carte dining room of the 1911 ship, which was decorated in Louis XVI splendor, complete with ornate gold accenting. Ship buffs should be delighted with this rare find. The paneling was found in a house in the north of England, and bought at auction in 1999 (actually the entire house had to be purchased in order to get at the paneling).

Superb tableside preparation is the feature of this alternative dining room, whose classic French cuisine and service are absolutely outstanding and at the height of professionalism, for this is, indeed, a room for a full dégustation, and not merely a dinner. Throughout each dinner, a piano and violin duo plays music appropriate to the period, in costumes that have been reproduced from the designs used by the musicians aboard the trio of sister ships *Britannic, Olympic* and *Titanic*.

A wine cellar, in which it is possible to dine, is also a feature, as is a demonstration galley. The wine list is extremely extensive (with more than 200 labels represented). But the real treat for rare wine lovers is the additional list of rare vintage wines, including (when I was last aboard) a magnum of 1949 Château Petrus (at $12,400), a 1907 Heidsieck Monopole Champagne (it costs a mere $7,000, and was brought to the surface from a sunken German ship), and a Château Lafite-Rothschild Pouillac from 1890 (a real snip at $2,160).

To undertake dinner in this exquisite setting – it's rather like dining in a living museum – takes a minimum of three hours of culinary excellence and faultless service, and is, without any shadow of doubt, the very finest dining experience at sea today. Superb tableside preparation is the feature of this alternative dining room, whose classic French cuisine and service are absolutely outstanding (masterminded by Michel Roux, owner of a three-star Michelin restaurant near Windsor in England). This is haute cuisine at the height of professionalism. However, with just 134 seats, not all passengers will be able to experience it even once during a one-week cruise

(reservations are necessary, and a cover charge of $25 per person applies). A dine-in wine cellar is also provided, as is a demonstration galley, and tableside preparation is a feature of this alternative dining spot.

OTHER COMMENTS: *Millennium*, whose sister ships are *Constellation*, *Infinity* and *Summit*, is a slightly enlarged and elongated version of the company's successful trio, *Century, Galaxy* and *Mercury*, and was constructed in the same building dock where the famous former ocean liner *France* (now *Norway*) was built. Jon Bannenberg (famous as a mega-yacht designer) designed the exterior that has a royal blue and white hull, and racy lines in red, blue and gold, although it has actually turned out to look extremely ungainly (some say downright ugly).

This is the first Celebrity Cruises ship to be fitted with a "pod" propulsion system (and controllable pitch propellers) coupled with a *gas* turbine powerplant. Indeed, this is the first cruise ship in the world to be powered by quiet, smokeless, energy-efficient gas turbines (two GE gas turbines provide engine power while a single GE steam turbine drives the electricity generators). The ship was dogged by technical problems in its early days.

Inside, the ship has the same high-class décor and materials (including lots of wood, glass and marble), and public rooms that have made the existing ships in the fleet so popular and user-friendly. The atrium (with separately enclosed room for shore excursions) is a friendly four decks high and houses the reception desk, tour operator's desk, and bank. Four dramatic glass-walled elevators travel through the ship's exterior (port) side, connecting the atrium with another seven decks, thus traveling through 11 passenger decks, including the tender stations – a nice ride.

Cigar smokers will appreciate Michael's Club – a superb cigar and cognac specialty lounge that has almost 20 varieties of cigars, as well as travel humidor packs and cigar cutters – all for sale. It is approximately twice the size of the one aboard *Century*, and is decorated in an 18th-century Georgian style, with sofas, high-back chairs and writing tables.

Facilities include a combination Cinema/Conference Center, an expansive shopping arcade, with more than 14,450 sq ft (1,300 sq. meters) of retail store space (including some well known brand names: H. Stern, Donna Karan, Fossil), a lavish four-decks-high show lounge with the latest in staging and lighting equipment, two-level library (one level for English-language books; a second level for books in other languages); card room; compact disc listening room; art auction center (with seating that look rather more like a small chapel); Cosmos, a combination observation lounge/discotheque; an Internet Center featuring 19 computer stations (with wood-surround IBM flat screens).

In addition, a flower shop is enclosed in a two decks high glass circular tower. It has fresh flowers for any occasion, and a selection of Emilio Robba glass and flower creations, as well as pot pourri and other flora and fauna items.

Outdoor facilities include two outdoor pools, one indoor/outdoor pool, and six whirlpools. There is also a large AquaSpa (with large thalassotherapy pool under a huge solarium dome), complete with health bar for light breakfast and lunch items, and fresh squeezed fruit and vegetable juices. Spa facilities measuring 25,000 sq. ft (2,320 sq. meters) include 16 treatment rooms, plus eight treatment rooms with showers and one treatment room specifically designed for wheelchair passengers, aerobics room, gymnasium (complete with over 40 machines to help provide you with high-tech muscle training), large male and female saunas (with large ocean-view porthole window), a co-ed thermal suite (containing several steam and shower mist rooms with different fragrances such as chamomile, eucalyptus and mint, and a glacial ice fountain), and beauty salon. Among the different types of massage available is a superb hot and cold stone massage therapy that lasts almost 1½ hours.

Sports facilities include a full-size basketball court, compact football, paddle tennis and volleyball, golf simulator, shuffleboard (on two different decks) and a jogging track. A 70-person capacity sports bar called Extreme (a first for a Celebrity Cruises' ship, although it just doesn't, somehow, belong) is located directly in front of the main funnel and has glass walls that overlook the ship's side. Gaming sports include Fortunes Casino, with blackjack, roulette, and numerous slot machines.

Families with children will appreciate the Fun Factory (for children) and The Tower (for teenagers).

Millennium delivers a well-defined North American cruise experience at a very modest price. The "zero announcement policy" fortunately means little intrusion. Note that a 15 percent gratuity is automatically added to all bar and wine accounts.

During the past two years, the standard of product delivery aboard all the ships in the Celebrity Cruises fleet went down as cuts were made by parent company Royal Caribbean International. However, new management has been brought in to bring Celebrity Cruises back to the premium product that was envisioned when the company first started and I hope the improvements will restore the art of hospitality and a *taste of luxury*. The strong points of a Celebrity cruise include the use of many European staff and service, a fine spa with a good range of facilities, treatments, taste-filled food that is attractively presented and served in the European fine dining tradition, and the provision of many intimate spaces and a superb collection of artwork.

A cruise aboard a large ship such as this provides a wide range of choices and possibilities. If you travel in one of the suites, the benefits provide you with the highest level of personal service, while cruising in non-suite accommodation is almost like in any large ship – you'll be one of a number, with little access to the niceties and benefits of "upper class" cruising. It all depends how much you are willing to pay. One thing really is certain: cruising in a hassle-free, crime-free environment such as this is hard to beat no matter how much or how little you pay. The onboard currency is the US dollar.

WEAK POINTS: There is, sadly, no wrap-around wooden promenade deck outdoors. Standing in line for embarkation, disembarkation, shore tenders and for self-serve buffet meals is an inevitable aspect of cruising aboard all large ships. There are cushioned pads for poolside deck lounge chairs only, but not for chairs on other outside decks. Passenger participation activities are amateurish and should be upgraded. The officers have become more aloof lately, with far less contact with passengers than when the company first started.

Removed 2006

Saga Pearl
Explorer II — √
MU

Minerva
★★★★

Small Ship:	...............12,500 tons	Passengers
Lifestyle:	.................Premium	(lower beds/all berths): 352/474
Cruise Line:	.....Swan Hellenic Cruises	Passenger Space Ratio
Former Names:	..............Okean	(lower beds/all berths): 35.5/26.3
Builder:	...............Mariotti (Italy)	Crew/Passenger Ratio
Original Cost:	....................n/a	(lower beds/all berths): 2.1/3.0
Entered Service:	...........Apr 1996	Navigation Officers: ....European
Registry:	...............The Bahamas	Cabins (total): 178
Length (ft/m):	............436.3/133.0	Size Range (sq ft/m): 139.9–360.6/
Beam (ft/m):	................65.6/20.0	13.0–33.5
Draft (ft/m):	.................19.6/6.0	Cabins (outside view): 126
Propulsion/Propellers:	......2 x diesels	Cabins (interior/no view): 52
	(3,480 kW)/2	Cabins (for one person): 4
Passenger Decks:	6	Cabins (with private balcony): 12
Total Crew:	.....,............157	Cabins (wheelchair accessible): 4

Cabin Current:	...............220 volts
Elevators:	2
Casino (gaming tables):	.............No
Slot Machines:	.....................No
Swimming Pools (outdoors):	1
Swimming Pools (indoors):	0
Whirlpools:	0
Fitness Center:	...................Yes
Sauna/Steam Room:	............Yes/No
Massage:	..........................Yes
Self-Service Launderette:	..........Yes
Dedicated Cinema/Seats:	........Yes/96
Library:	..........................Yes
Classification Society:	...Registro Navale
	Italiano (RINA)

OVERALL SCORE: 1,411 (OUT OF A POSSIBLE 2,000 POINTS)

ACCOMMODATION: There are five different grades of cabins: Owner's Suite, Suite, Deluxe, Superior, and Standard, in 17 price categories, based mainly on location rather than any great difference in the size of the accommodation (note that most of the standard cabins really are quite small, particularly when compared to the "standard" cabin size on the latest ships today).

BERLITZ'S RATINGS

	Possible	Achieved
Ship	500	367
Accommodation	200	131
Food	400	283
Service	400	285
Entertainment	100	58
Cruise	400	287

OWNER'S SUITE: There are two owner's suites, 360 sq. ft (33.5 sq. meters) in size, on Bridge Deck. Facilities include a queen-sized bed, an extra-large double closet and ample drawer space; separate lounge area with sofa, table and chair, and vanity table/writing desk, television and VCR, refrigerator, hairdryer and binoculars; floor to ceiling patio doors leading to private balcony; bathroom with bath/shower combination and toilet.

SUITES: There are 10 suites, (290 sq. ft 27 sq. meters) located on Bridge Deck. Facilities include twin beds or queen-sized bed, two double closets and ample drawer space; separate lounge area with sofa, table and chair, and vanity table/writing desk, television and VCR, refrigerator, hairdryer and binoculars; floor to ceiling patio doors leading to private balcony; bathroom with bath/shower and toilet.

DELUXE: These are 226 sq. ft (21 sq. meters) in size. Facilities include twin beds or queen-sized bed, two double closets and ample drawer space; separate lounge area with sofa, table and chair, and vanity table/writing desk,

television and VCR, refrigerator, hairdryer and binoculars; large picture window; bathroom with bath/shower and toilet.

SUPERIOR: These are 162 sq. ft (15 sq. meters) in size. Facilities include twin beds or queen-sized bed, two double closets and ample drawer space; separate lounge area with sofa, table and chair, and vanity table/writing desk, television and VCR, refrigerator, hairdryer and binoculars; large picture window; bathroom with bath/shower and toilet.

STANDARD OUTSIDE-VIEW OR INTERIOR (NO VIEW) CABIN: These standard cabins are dimensionally challenged (140 sq. ft/13 sq. meters) when compared to the size of standard cabins aboard today's newest ships, which is approximately 182 sq. ft (17 sq. meters). The facilities include twin beds or queen-sized bed, two double closets and ample drawer space; separate lounge area with sofa, table and chair, and vanity table/writing desk, television and VCR, refrigerator, hairdryer and binoculars; large picture window (outside-view cabins only; or porthole, depending on deck and price category chosen); bathroom with shower enclosure (small) and toilet.

The cabin bathrooms are totally white, and have very small showers (except for the suites, which have bathtubs and green/black marble floors), although plumbing fixtures were poorly installed. Note that all cabin electrical sockets are of the standard (British) square, three-pin type. No matter what grade of accommodation you book, all grades have a pair of binoculars, hairdryer, 100 percent cotton bathrobe, TV with music channels, and direct-dial satellite-linked telephone.

DINING: The Dining Room has open seating dining (this means that you can dine with whomever you wish) in both the main restaurant and an informal indoor/outdoor cafe. The menus are quite simple, but the food is attractively presented and has good taste. A staff that is a mix of East European and Filipinos provides the dining room service. Some "quiet tables" are provided for breakfast for those who like to eat without talking – a welcome touch that more ships would be wise to adopt.

Coffees and teas are available 24 hours a day from a beverage station in the self-serve Bridge Café, which also serves casual breakfasts, luncheons, and dinners in an open seating arrangement (the menu choice is much simpler and more limited than in the dining room).

OTHER COMMENTS: Originally intended to be a spy ship (called *Okean*) for the Soviet navy, the 1989-built hull was constructed at Nikolajev on the River Ingul in Ukraine. The hull originally had a stern ramp for launching submersibles for submarine tracking. The ship was then purchased by V-Ships (the present owners), who towed it to Italy, where it was converted into a ship tailored to the requirements of Swan Hellenic Cruises as the ship's charterer and operator (originally until 2011, although *Minerva* will be handed back to the owners, the Monaco-based V-Ships group, in 2003).

It has a squat, squarely balanced profile, with a single, central funnel, and a stern that is slightly rounded. The navigation bridge, however, always looks as if it should have been located one deck higher than it is. There is ample open and shaded deck space for this size of ship (particularly in the aft section), and there is also a teak wrap-around promenade deck.

Inside, there is an excellent selection of public rooms that includes a vast, well-stocked library, with classical décor and motifs. In general, the décor throughout the ship is best described as contemporary, yet somehow restrained and not in the slightest bit glitzy (for European passengers with good taste). Cigar smokers should appreciate the special smoking room and humidor service, and high back leather chairs that provide a sense of well-being and exclusivity.

The ship has fine wool carpets throughout, with an Oriental motif running through the passageways and public rooms. Perhaps the most used public room in the ship is the library, with its fine range of reference books (many of university-standard). Passengers take delight in the multitude of puzzles and games, and jigsaw puzzles galore. The reception desk is staffed 24 hours a day.

Perhaps the most striking detail of interior decoration is the outstanding array of artwork aboard this ship. It is everywhere, in all passageways, on stairwells, in all public rooms, and cabins – most of which is provided by regular Swan Hellenic passengers (known in cruise circles as "Swanners"). The one disappointment is in the plain white ceilings in most of the public rooms.

A cruise aboard *Minerva* really is cruising for intelligent passengers (most of whom are – or were – professional people ashore) who yearn to learn more about life and times in civilizations past and present, albeit in a refined, comfortable setting. Intelligent conversation is a major part of any Swan Hellenic cruise. The company features well planned, in-depth itineraries and shore excursions (most which are included in the cruise fare) accompanied by some fine lecturers, and all gratuities and shore excursions are included (these are carried out with almost military precision). Note that this ship is not recommended for children. The onboard currency is the British pound.

This ship will be taken out of service, to be replaced by *Minerva II* (which some may know as former Renaissance Cruises' *R8*) in April 2003. Meanwhile, this *Minerva* will be chartered to Saga Cruises for approximately six months each year for three years (from May to November, starting May 2003), and the ship's name will be changed to *Saga Pearl*. Saga will probably add more cabin categories, in order to make the accommodation grades similar to those of the larger *Saga Rose*. Being a smaller ship will allow *Saga Pearl* to include ports that cannot accommodate *Saga Rose*, and so you can expect Saga to provide some fascinating itineraries for the ship. Entertainment will probably include more classical music and concerts, and light cabaret rather than the larger-scale production shows seen aboard *Saga Rose*, as well as an abundance of life-enrichment lecturers so popular with Saga passengers.

WEAK POINTS: The standard cabins are very small. There are very few cabins with private balcony.

Minerva II
NOT YET RATED

Mid-Size Ship: . . . . .30,277 tons	Passengers	Cabin Current: . . . . .110 and 220 volts
Lifestyle: . . . . .Premium	(lower beds/all berths): 698/838	Elevators: 4
Cruise Line: . . . . . .Swan Hellenic Cruises	Passenger Space Ratio	Casino (gaming tables): . . . . .Yes
Former Names: . . . . .R Eight	(lower beds/all berths): 43.3/36.1	Slot Machines: . . . . .Yes
Builder: Chantiers de l'Atlantique (France)	Crew/Passenger Ratio	Swimming Pools (outdoors): 1
Original Cost: . . . .$150 million	(lower beds/all berths): 1.8/2.2	Swimming Pools (indoors): 0
Entered Service: . . . . .Feb 2001/Apr 2003	Navigation Officers: . . . . .European	Whirlpools: 2
Registry: . . . . .Liberia	Cabins (total): 349	(+ 1 thalassaotherapy)
Length (ft/m): 593.7/181.0	Size Range (sq ft/m): 145.3–968.7/	Fitness Center: . . . . .Yes
Beam (ft/m): 83.5/25.5	13.5–90.0	Sauna/Steam Room: . . . . .No/Yes
Draft (ft/m): 19.5/6.0	Cabins (outside view): 326	Massage: . . . . .Yes
Propulsion/Propellers: . . . . .diesel	Cabins (interior/no view): 23	Self-Service Launderette: . . . . .Yes
(18,600 kW)/2	Cabins (for one person): 0	Dedicated Cinema/Seats: . . . . .No
Passenger Decks: 9	Cabins (with private balcony): 248	Library: . . . . .Yes
Total Crew: .376	Cabins (wheelchair accessible): 0	Classification Society: . . . .Bureau Veritas

OVERALL SCORE: NYR (OUT OF A POSSIBLE 2,000 POINTS)

ACCOMMODATION: There are six categories: Owner's Suites (6), Master Suite (4), Deluxe with balcony, Superior Plus with balcony, Superior with balcony, and Standard Outside View/ Standard Interior (No View) Cabins.

STANDARD OUTSIDE-VIEW AND INTERIOR (NO VIEW) CABINS: All of the standard interior (no view) and outside-view cabins (the lowest four grades) are extremely compact units, and very tight for two persons (particularly for cruises longer than five days). They have twin beds (or queen-size bed), with good under-bed storage areas, personal safe, vanity desk with large mirror, good closet and drawer space (in rich, dark woods), and bathrobe. Color TV sets carry a major news channel (where obtainable), plus a sports channel and several round-the-clock movie channels.

CABINS WITH PRIVATE BALCONY: Cabins with private balconies (66 percent of all cabins) have partial, and not full, balcony partitions, sliding glass doors, and, due to good design and layout, only 14 cabins on Deck 6 have lifeboat-obstructed views. The bathrooms, which have tiled floors and plain walls, are compact, standard units, and include a shower stall with a strong, removable hand-held shower unit, hairdryer, 100 percent cotton towels, toiletries storage shelves and retractable clothesline. Personal toiletry items include soap, shampoo, body lotion, shower cap, and shoeshine mitt.

OWNER'S SUITES/MASTER SUITES: The six Owner's Suites and four Master Suites provide the most spacious

BERLITZ'S RATINGS		
	Possible	Achieved
Ship	500	NYR
Accommodation	200	NYR
Food	400	NYR
Service	400	NYR
Entertainment	100	NYR
Cruise	400	NYR

accommodation. These are fine, large living spaces located in the forward-most and aft-most sections of the accommodation decks (particularly nice are those that overlook the stern, on Deck 6, 7 and 8). They have more extensive private balconies that really are private and cannot be overlooked by anyone from the decks above. There is an entrance foyer, living room, bedroom (the bed faces the sea, which can be seen through the floor-to-ceiling windows and sliding glass door), CD player (with selection of audio discs), bathroom with Jacuzzi bathtub, and a small guest bathroom.

DINING: Flexibility and choice are provided in four different restaurants:

The *Dining Room* has 338 seats and a raised central section. There are large ocean-view windows on three sides, several prime tables overlooking the stern, and a small bandstand for occasional live dinner music. The menu changes daily for lunch and dinner.

The *Italian Restaurant* has 96 seats, windows along two sides, and a set menu (together with added daily chef's specials).

The *Grill*, a steak house, has 98 seats, windows along two sides and a set menu (together with added daily chef's specials).

The *Bridge Café* has 154 seats indoors and 186 outdoors. It is open for breakfast, lunch and casual dinners. It is the ship's self-serve buffet restaurant, and incorporates a small pizzeria and grill.

All restaurants have open-seating dining, so you dine

when you want, with whom you wish, although reservations are typically necessary in the Swan Restaurant and The Grill, where there are mostly tables for four or six – there are few tables for two). In addition, there is a Poolside Grill and Bar for casual fast food.

OTHER COMMENTS: This ship was previously the final in a series of eight almost identical ships in the Renaissance Cruises fleet (at the time, the cruise industry's only totally non-smoking cruise line). Swan Hellenic Cruises now has this ship (larger than *Minerva*) under charter for a period of seven years. *Minerva II* can also cruise at faster speeds than *Minerva,* thus allowing the company to offer even better itineraries that cover more ground (well, water, actually). The exterior design manages to balance the ship's high sides by combining a deep blue hull with the white superstructure and large, square blue funnel.

An outside lido deck features a swimming pool, and good sunbathing space, while one of the aft decks features a thalassotherapy pool. A jogging track circles the swimming pool deck (but one deck above). The exterior decks are covered with Bolidt – a rubber and grit-like surface. The uppermost outdoors deck includes a golf driving net and shuffleboard court.

The interior décor is quite elegant, and is a throwback to ship décor of the ocean liners of the 1920s and '30s. This includes detailed ceiling cornices, both real and faux wrought iron staircase railings, leather paneled walls, *trompe l'oeil* ceilings, rich carpeting in hallways with an Oriental rug-look center section, and many other interesting (and expensive-looking) decorative touches. The overall feel is of an old-world country club. The staircase in the main, two-deck-high foyer will remind you of something similar in a blockbuster hit about a certain ship on which movie stars Kate Winslet and Leonardo di Caprio met. Regular Swan Hellenic Cruises passengers will probably be pleased with the fine taste with which its interiors have been designed and executed.

The public rooms are basically spread over three decks. The reception hall (lobby) features a staircase with intricate wrought-iron railings. A large observation lounge, the Orpheus Room, is located high atop ship. This has a long bar with forward views (for the barmen, that is), and a stack of distracting large-screen televisions; there's also an array of slot machines and various bar counter-top electronic gaming machines.

The ship has several other bars – including one in each of the restaurant entrances. An internet café with six computer terminals is located in part of the card room.

The Library is a beautiful, grand, restful room (perhaps the nicest public room), and is designed in the Regency style. It features a fireplace, a high, indented, *trompe l'oeil* ceiling, and an excellent selection of books, plus some very comfortable wingback chairs with footstools, and sofas you could sleep on.

Swan Hellenic Cruises provides a seamless cruise and tour package, geared specifically to British and North American passengers, at a price that's very hard to beat considering the destination-rich itineraries, together with pre- and post-cruise land stays at high-quality hotels, all transfers, and the fine lecturers that accompany every cruise. You should experience a fine, hassle-free cruise vacation package aboard this ship. There may not be marble bathroom fittings, or caviar and other (more expensive) niceties, but the value for money is really excellent.

A cruise aboard *Minerva II* really is a cruise for intelligent (typically retired or semi-retired) passengers (most of whom are – or were – professional people ashore) who yearn to learn more about life and times in civilizations past and present, albeit in a refined, comfortable setting. Intelligent conversation is a major part of any Swan Hellenic cruise. The company features well planned, in-depth itineraries and shore excursions (most which are included in the cruise fare) accompanied by some fine lecturers, and all gratuities and shore excursions are included (these are usually carried out with almost military precision). Note that this ship is not recommended for children.

Minerva II debuts for Swan Hellenic Cruises in April 2003, when the previous, much liked *Minerva* will be handed back to the ship's owners, V-Ships of Monte Carlo. The onboard currency is the British pound.

WEAK POINTS: There is no wrap-around promenade deck outdoors (there is, however, a small jogging track around the perimeter of the swimming pool, and port and starboard side decks), and no wooden decks outdoors (instead, they are covered by Bollidt, a sand-colored rubberized material). There is no sauna. The stairways, although carpeted, sound quite tinny.

Removed 2006

Mistral
★★★★

Large Ship: ....47,276 tons	Total Crew: 480	Cabins (wheelchair accessible): 2
Lifestyle: ....Standard	Passengers	Cabin Current: ....110 and 220 volts
Cruise Line: ....Festival Cruises	(lower beds/all berths): 1,196/1,715	Elevators: 6
Former Names: ....none	Passenger Space Ratio	Casino (gaming tables): ....Yes
Builder: ....Chantiers de l'Atlantique	(lower beds/all berths): 39.5/27.5	Slot Machines: ....Yes
(France)	Crew/Passenger Ratio	Swimming Pools (outdoors): 1
Original Cost: ....$245 million	(lower beds/all berths): 2.4/3.5	Swimming Pools (indoors): 0
Entered Service: ....July 1999	Navigation Officers: ....European	Whirlpools: ....1 (thalassotherapy)
Registry: .....Wallis & Fortuna (France)	Cabins (total): 598	Fitness Center: ....Yes
Length (ft/m): 708.6/216.00	Size Range (sq ft/m): 139.9–236.8/	Sauna/Steam Room: ....No/Yes
Beam (ft/m): 94.6/28.84	13.0–22.0	Massage:........................Yes
Draft (ft/m): 22.4/6.85	Cabins (outside view): 275	Self-Service Launderette: ....No
Propulsion/Propellers: .....diesel-electric	Cabins (interior/no view): 223	Dedicated Cinema/Seats: ....No
(31,680 kW)/2	Cabins (for one person): 0	Library: ....Yes
Passenger Decks:...................8	Cabins (with private balcony): 80	Classification Society: ....Bureau Veritas

---

OVERALL SCORE: 1,472 (OUT OF A POSSIBLE 2,000 POINTS)

ACCOMMODATION: There are three basic cabin types, in 11 different grades: suites (each of which has a private balcony, although the partitions are only of the partial, and not the full type); ocean-view standard cabins and interior (no view) standard cabins. In addition, there are two interior (no view) wheelchair accessible cabins for the handicapped. Good planning and layout means that no outside-view cabins have obstructed views of lifeboats, as aboard many ships today. The cabin numbering system goes against maritime tradition, where even-numbered cabins are located on the port side and odd-numbered cabins on the starboard side; in *Mistral*, the opposite is in effect.

All cabins have twin beds that convert to a queen-sized unit, bold, colorful bedspreads, a personal safe, a combination color TV/VCR, telephone, a personal safe, and a good amount of closet and drawer space for a one-week cruise. The bathrooms, although not large, do have a good-sized shower enclosure, and there is a decent amount of stowage space for personal toiletry items.

Accommodation designated as suites (these are really only larger cabins and not suites, as there is no separation of lounge and sleeping space), quite naturally, have more space, larger (walk-in) closets, more drawers and better storage space, plus a two-person sofa, coffee table and additional armchair, vanity desk, floor-to-ceiling mirrors and hairdryer, while the bathrooms have a bathtub/shower combination.

DINING: There are two dining rooms (and two seatings for meals), which can be configured in any of several

BERLITZ'S RATINGS

	Possible	Achieved
Ship	500	397
Accommodation	200	156
Food	400	267
Service	400	301
Entertainment	100	58
Cruise	400	293

different ways. Both have ocean-view windows. The principal dining room (L'Etoile, which seats 600) has round tables for two, four, six or eight, and a small podium complete with baby grand piano. A second dining room (Rialto, which seats 380 and is on a different deck), is used for suite passengers and anyone wishing to "upgrade" to a smaller, more intimate restaurant or for use as an alternative restaurant, and also has tables for two, four or six. Both dining rooms are non-smoking.

The food featured by Festival Cruises is quite sound, and, with varied menus and good presentation, should prove a highlight for most passengers. The wine list has a wide variety of wines at fairly reasonable prices, although almost all wines are very young.

In addition, there is a casual cafeteria for informal buffet-style breakfasts and lunches, with ocean-view windows, as well as a pleasant little coffee bar, also with ocean-view windows.

OTHER COMMENTS: *Mistral* is an all-white ship, with a single blue funnel, and blue and yellow bands to separate hull from superstructure. This was the first brand new ship for this growing European cruise line, which caters almost exclusively to European passengers, and two more ships of the same type (but marginally enlarged) soon followed (*European Vision* in 2001 and *European Stars* in 2002). Mistral is the name of a famous desert wind; it's also the name of a violin concerto. The company's older, and smaller *Azur* and *Flamenco* will, more than likely, be positioned for full charters in the future, in order to differentiate the old from the new tonnage.

Mistral is owned by a consortium of French investors, and is being operated under long-term charter to Festival Cruises, a vibrant young company that is growing rapidly. This is presently the largest ship sailing under the French flag (it is actually Wallis & Fortuna, a French possession). The ship's profile is similar to that of most new cruise ships, although the built-up stern makes the ship look a trifle bulky and less than handsome.

The ship is comparable in size to Celebrity Cruises' *Horizon* and *Zenith*, has slightly fewer cabins and therefore a better space ratio, which means the ship absorbs passengers quite well.

The lido deck surrounding the outdoor swimming pool also features whirlpool tubs and a large bandstand is set in raised canvas-covered pods. All the deck lounge chairs have cushioned pads.

Inside, the layout and passenger flow is very good, as are the "you are here" deck signs. The deck names are those of European capitals, the two decks of public rooms being Paris Deck and Rome Deck. The interior décor is light and cheerful without being glitzy in any way (with not even a hint of colored neon) and there is much use of blond wood panelling and rich, textured soft furnishings.

The names of public rooms, bars and lounges are inspired by European places or establishments (San Remo casino, Mayfair Lounge, Caffé Navona and Richlieu Library, for example).

There is a smoking room, which has all the hallmarks of a gentleman's club of former times, as well as a piano bar. The library has real writing desks (something many ships seem to omit today).

The main show lounge is tiered, and has good sight lines from most seats (banquette-style seating is featured), and there is a small balcony level at the rear. There's also a bar/lounge on the lower (main) level at the entrance to the show lounge. High atop the ship is an observation lounge with a twist – it faces *aft*, instead of forward – a pleasant change. The room also doubles as a discotheque for the late-night set. A conference center adds facilities that are good for meetings.

There is also a good-sized spa/beauty complex, set forward of the mast. This includes a fitness center with lots of muscle-toning equipment and lifecycles and life-rowing machines and a view over the bow of the ship through large floor-to-ceiling windows. There are six rooms for massage and other body treatments, as well as a sauna each for men and women, plus an aerobics exercise room. Adjacent is a video game room for teens, and a children's center. Dialysis equipment is available in the hospital, together with trained technicians.

The ship operates 7-night Mediterranean cruises from Italy during the summer and fall, and 7-night Caribbean cruises during the winter. As the ship operates in several languages (remember that this means all announcements will be in several languages too), a good number of multilingual cruise staff and reception desk staff are present at all key points. All prices aboard ship are quoted only in euros. Gratuities are not included, and 15 percent is added to all bar and spa bills.

Mistral was built for a European company, and designed and constructed by Europeans, with European décor and colors, for European passengers, with European food, service and entertainment.

WEAK POINTS: Standing in line for embarkation, disembarkation, shore tenders and for self-serve buffet meals is an inevitable aspect of cruising aboard all large ships. There is no full wrap-around promenade deck outdoors, although there is a partial walking deck on both port and starboard sides (under the lifeboats), as well as an oval jogging track atop ship. Smokers are everywhere, and are difficult to avoid (in typical European fashion, ashtrays are simply moved – if used at all – to wherever smokers happen to be sitting. The towels are small. The square chairs in the Caffe Greco are both uncomfortable and impractical. The cabins on Deck 10 are subject to noise from the Lido Deck above. The Lido Deck is virtually unusable in windy conditions.

Mona Lisa
NOT YET RATED

Mid-Size Ship: . . . . .28,891 tons	Total Crew: 417	Cabins (wheelchair accessible): 10
Lifestyle: . . . . .Standard	Passengers	Cabin Current: . . . . .220 volts
Cruise Line: . . . . .Holiday Cruises	(lower beds/all berths): 744/778	Elevators: 4
Former Names: . . .*Victoria, Sea Princess,*	Passenger Space Ratio	Casino (gaming tables): . . . . .Yes
Kungsholm	(lower beds/all berths): 38.8/37.0	Slot Machines: .Yes
Builder: . . . . .John Brown & Co. (UK)	Crew/Passenger Ratio	Swimming Pools (outdoors): 2
Original Cost: . . . .$22 million	(lower beds/all berths): 1.7/1.8	Swimming Pools (indoors): 1
Entered Service: . . . . .Apr 1966/Dec 2002	Navigation Officers: . . . . .European	Whirlpools: 1
Registry: . . . . .Great Britain	Cabins (total): .379	Fitness Center: .Yes
Length (ft/m): 660.2/201.23	Size Range (sq ft/m): 137.7–466.0/	Sauna/Steam Room: . . . . .Yes/No
Beam (ft/m): 87.1/26.57	12.8–43.3	Massage: . . . . .Yes
Draft (ft/m): 28.0/8.56	Cabins (outside view): 291	Self-Service Launderette: . . . . .Yes
Propulsion/Propellers: . . . . .diesel	Cabins (interior/no view): 88	Dedicated Cinema/Seats: Yes/289
(18,800 kW)/2	Cabins (for one person): 14	Library: . . . . .Yes
Passenger Decks: 8	Cabins (with private balcony): 0	Classification Society: . . .Lloyd's Register

OVERALL SCORE: NYR (OUT OF A POSSIBLE 2,000 POINTS)

ACCOMMODATION: There is a wide range of cabins to choose from, including six suites. Most cabins have a decent amount of space, and many of them feature fine wood paneled walls. Many cabins have been nicely refurbished over the years, and retain the look of classic ocean liner cabins. Most have excellent closet and drawer space, and fine wood-paneled walls. The bathrooms are of a generous size; the fixtures solid, and most cabins have ample storage space for personal toiletries. Some have upper and lower berths. The bathroom towels are small, however.

DINING: The tiered European-style dining room is fairly elegant, with a display of 18th-century Chinese porcelain (it has some nice etched glass panels with nautical themes – although whether these will be replaced by the new owners was uncertain when this book went to press). There are tables for two, four, six and eight, and the dining room is operated in two seatings.

The cuisine will now be tailored for German tastes, with breakfast and lunch buffets featuring a good selection of cold cuts of meat, and a good array of breads (including dark breads) and cheeses. In general, the self-serve buffets could be better in terms of both display and food quality. The wine list provides a good selection of German wines. The casual outdoor Lido Buffet has more temperature-controlled display space and better serving lines. Plastic chairs prevail.

OTHER COMMENTS: *Mona Lisa* is a solidly built ex-ocean liner and has flowing, rounded lines and a well-

BERLITZ'S RATINGS		
	Possible	Achieved
Ship	500	NYR
Accommodation	200	NYR
Food	400	NYR
Service	400	NYR
Entertainment	100	NYR
Cruise	400	NYR

balanced profile, with the mid-ship sag (called a "sheer") that makes it look like a "real" traditional ship. It has been was nicely refurbished over the years, quite well maintained, and arguably improved since it was operated by P&O Cruises (1979–2002).

The ship will be under charter to Holiday Kreutzfahrten, of Germany, until 2007. It is being promoted as a classic cruise liner, replacing the company's charter of Royal Olympic Cruises' *Triton*, which it has operated for several years. *Mona Lisa*'s open deck and sunbathing space is good, particularly for German-speaking passengers who enjoy being outdoors.

The spacious public rooms are trimmed with fine woods and have good furnishings and fabrics. A nice feature is an indoor (sea water) swimming pool, together with the usual associated saunas and gymnasium. There is a decent variety of entertainment spaces, bars and lounges, most of an intimate size.

Mona Lisa should provide an enjoyable, very traditional and conservative German cruise experience for those on a limited budget, in surroundings that are old-world, but very comfortable. Port taxes and insurance are included for all passengers, as are gratuities. The onboard currency is the euro.

WEAK POINTS: *Mona Lisa* is now an old lady – still charming in places, but well worn and decidedly out-of-date, particularly when there is so much choice of other ships in the German-speaking marketplace. The plastic deck lounge chairs are hard to keep clean, and should be replaced by teak "steamer" style chairs.

Monarch of the Seas
★★★ +

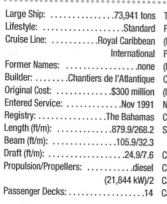

Large Ship: . . . . .73,941 tons
Lifestyle: . . . . .Standard
Cruise Line: . . . . .Royal Caribbean
International
Former Names: . . . . .none
Builder: . . . . .Chantiers de l'Atlantique
Original Cost: . . . .$300 million
Entered Service: . . . . .Nov 1991
Registry: . . . . .The Bahamas
Length (ft/m): 879.9/268.2
Beam (ft/m): 105.9/32.3
Draft (ft/m): 24.9/7.6
Propulsion/Propellers: . . . . .diesel
(21,844 kW)/2
Passenger Decks: 14

Total Crew: 858
Passengers
(lower beds/all berths): 2,354/2,744
Passenger Space Ratio
(lower beds/all berths): 31.0/26.9
Crew/Passenger Ratio
(lower beds/all berths): 2.8/3.3
Navigation Officers: . . . . .Norwegian
Cabins (total): 1,177
Size Range (sq ft/m): 118.4–670.0/
11.0–62.2
Cabins (outside view): 732
Cabins (interior/no view): 445
Cabins (for one person): 0
Cabins (with private balcony): 62

Cabins (wheelchair accessible): 4
Cabin Current: . . . . .110 volts
Elevators: 11
Casino (gaming tables): . . . . .Yes
Slot Machines: . . . . .Yes
Swimming Pools (outdoors): 2
Swimming Pools (indoors): 0
Whirlpools: 2
Fitness Center: . . . . .Yes
Sauna/Steam Room: . . . . .Yes/No
Massage: . . . . .Yes
Self-Service Launderette: . . . . .No
Dedicated Cinema/Seats: Yes-2/146 each
Library: . . . . .Yes
Classification Society: Det Norske Veritas

OVERALL SCORE: 1,394 (OUT OF A POSSIBLE 2,000 POINTS)

ACCOMMODATION: There are 17 price categories, depending on size and location.

SUITES: Thirteen suites on Bridge Deck are reasonably large and nicely furnished (the largest is the Royal Suite), with separate living and sleeping spaces. They provide more space, with better service and more perks than standard-grade accommodation.

STANDARD CABINS: The standard outside-view and interior (no view) cabins are very small, although an arched window treatment and colorful soft furnishings do give the illusion of more space. Almost all cabins have twin beds that can be converted to a queen-sized or double bed configuration, together with moveable bedside tables. All of the standard cabins have very little closet and drawer space (you will need some luggage engineering to stow your cases). You should, therefore, think of packing only minimal clothing, which is all you really need for a short cruise. All cabins feature a private bathroom, with shower enclosure, toilet and washbasin.

DINING: The two large dining rooms (both are non-smoking) have Hollywood musical themes (*Brigadoon* and *Flower Drum Song*). There are tables for four, six or eight, but no tables for two, and there are two seatings. The dining operation is well orchestrated, with emphasis on highly programmed (insensitive), extremely hurried service that many passengers find intrusive.

The cuisine is typical of mass banquet catering that offers standard fare comparable to that found in Amer-

BERLITZ'S RATINGS

	Possible	Achieved
Ship	500	381
Accommodation	200	141
Food	400	245
Service	400	286
Entertainment	100	75
Cruise	400	266

ican family-style restaurants ashore. While menu descriptions are tempting, the actual food may be somewhat disappointing and unmemorable. The menu descriptions make the food sound better than it is (which is consistently below average), mostly disappointing and without much taste – the result of controlled food costs as well as the use of many mixes and pre-prepared items. However, a decent selection of light meals is provided, and a vegetarian menu is available. The selection of breads, rolls, fruit and cheese is quite poor, however, and could do more improvement. Caviar (once a standard menu item) now incurs a heft extra charge. Menus typically include a Welcome Aboard Dinner, French Dinner, Italian Dinner, International Dinner, and Captain's Gala Dinner.

The wine list is not very extensive, but the prices are moderate. The waiters, many of whom are from Caribbean countries, are perhaps overly friendly for some tastes – particularly on the last night of the cruise, when tips are expected.

For casual breakfasts and lunches, the Windjammer Café is the place to go, although there are often long lines at peak times, and the selection is very average.

OTHER COMMENTS: The ship is almost identical in size and appearance to sister ship *Sovereign of the Seas* (the first of a trio, the third being *Monarch of the Seas*). But it has improved internal layout, public room features, passenger flow and signs. Royal Caribbean International's trademark Viking Crown lounge and bar surrounds the funnel and provides a stunning view. The open deck space is very cramped when full, as aboard any large ship, although there seems to be plenty of it. There is a basketball court for sports lovers.

Following a grounding just before Christmas 1998, the ship underwent the replacement of 460 tons of bottom shell plating. At the same time, a new facility for toddlers was created. The children's and teens' programs are good, overseen by enthusiastic youth counselors, and a busy but sound entertainment program.

While the interior layout is a little awkward (being designed in a vertical stack, with most public rooms located aft, and accommodation located forward), the ship has an impressive array of spacious and elegant public rooms, although the décor comes from the IKEA-school of interior design.

A stunning five-deck-high Centrum lobby has cascading stairways and two glass-walled elevators. There is a good two-level show lounge and decent shops, albeit with lots of tacky merchandise. Casino gamers will find blackjack, craps, Caribbean stud poker and roulette tables, plus an array of slot machines.

This floating resort provides a well tuned, yet very impersonal, short cruise experience for a lot of passengers. The dress code is very casual. There are many public rooms and spaces to play in, including a five-deck-high atrium, which really is the interior focal point of the ship, and has glass elevators. Among the public rooms, the library offers space for relaxation, and has a decent selection of books.

Monarch of the Seas provides a wide range of facilities with consistently sound, but highly programmed service from a reasonably attentive, though rather insensitive, young staff. In the final analysis, you will probably be overwhelmed by the public spaces, and underwhelmed by the size of the cabins. However, this is basically a well run, fine-tuned, highly programmed cruise product geared particularly to those seeking an action-packed cruise vacation at a moderately good price. The onboard currency is the US dollar.

WEAK POINTS: Standing in line for embarkation, disembarkation, shore tenders and for self-serve buffet meals is an inevitable aspect of cruising aboard all large ships. There are too many intrusive and irritating announcements. Because the public rooms are mostly located aft, there is often a long wait for elevators, particularly at peak times (after dinner, shows, and talks). The ship, like Cleveland, Ohio, looks tired.

Monterey
★★ +

Mid-Size Ship: ....20,040 tons	Total Crew: 280	Cabin Current: ....110 volts
Lifestyle: ....Standard	Passengers	Elevators: 2
Cruise Line: .....Mediterranean Shipping Cruises	(lower beds/all berths): 588/638	Casino (gaming tables): ....Yes
	Passenger Space Ratio	Slot Machines: ....Yes
Former Names: ......*Free State Mariner*	(lower beds/all berths): 34.0/31.4	Swimming Pools (outdoors): 1
Builder: .....Bethlehem Steel Corp. (USA)	Crew/Passenger Ratio	Swimming Pools (indoors): 0
Original Cost: ....n/a	(lower beds/all berths): 2.0/2.2	Whirlpools: 2
Entered Service: .....Dec 1952/Aug 1988	Navigation Officers: ....Italian	Fitness Center: ....Yes
Registry: ....Panama	Cabins (total): 294	Sauna/Steam Room: ....Yes/No
Length (ft/m): 563.6/171.81	Size Range (sq ft/m): 64.5–344.4/6.5–32.0	Massage: ....Yes
Beam (ft/m): 80.3/24.50	Cabins (outside view): 167	Self-Service Launderette: ....No
Draft (ft/m): 29.3/8.95	Cabins (interior/no view): 127	Dedicated Cinema/Seats: Yes/107
Propulsion/Propellers: .....steam turbine (14,400 kW)/1	Cabins (for one person): 0	Library: ....Yes
Passenger Decks: 4	Cabins (with private balcony): 0	Classification Society: . .American Bureau
	Cabins (wheelchair accessible): 0	of Shipping

OVERALL SCORE: 1,087 (OUT OF A POSSIBLE 2,000 POINTS)

ACCOMMODATION: There is a wide choice of cabin sizes and configurations – but only the top three categories have full bathtubs, while all other cabins have shower enclosures. The suites are very extremely spacious; other outside-view and interior (no view) cabins are very quite roomy and well-appointed, but most have tinny metal drawers (a carry-over from the ship's former years with the long defunct Matson Line).

The cabins located forward on Boat Deck have lifeboat-obstructed views, but other cabins on this deck are quite large; all have a window, plenty of closet and drawer space, together with a vanity desk, coffee table, sofa and chair. Bathrobes are provided for all passengers.

DINING: The two-level dining room (simply called The Restaurant) is set low down, and is charmingly decorated in soft earth tones, so the ambience is quite cozy, although it is noisy when full. There are two seatings. The ship has continental cuisine, with some decent pasta dishes and sauces. There is only the most basic selection of breads, cheeses and fruits. The service is friendly and attentive, in typical Italian style, but rather hurried.

For casual self-serve breakfasts and luncheons, there is also a casual café (Café de Paris), which has good views overlooking the aft pool deck and stern of the ship.

OTHER COMMENTS: This ship, built for the United States Maritime Commission as a C-4 cargo vessel, has a traditional, but dated 1950s ocean liner profile. It is very stable at sea, with an almost vertical bow and an

BERLITZ'S RATINGS		
	Possible	Achieved
Ship	500	262
Accommodation	200	114
Food	400	214
Service	400	234
Entertainment	100	53
Cruise	400	210

overhanging aircraft-carrier-like stern that is not at all handsome when viewed from ashore but provides a good amount of open deck space around the white-tiled swimming pool and Jacuzzis. There are partly enclosed port and starboard walking promenades, although, sadly, they do not wrap around the vessel.

The ship was refurbished in a moderate art deco style, and a new sports deck was added several years ago. There is a reasonable amount of sheltered and open deck space, and some forward open observation deck space atop some suites that were added in the late 1980s.

Inside, there are a reasonable number of public rooms to play in. All have high ceilings, although there is little elegance. There is too much cold steel and not enough warmth in the interior decoration, although this has been addressed somewhat when décor changes have been made. Rising through three decks is a large, slim totem pole, a carry-over from the ship's brief period with the now defunct Aloha Pacific Cruises.

This ship will cruise you in reasonable style and surroundings, with mainly European, and particularly Italian speaking passengers (about 60 percent). Port taxes are included. The onboard currency is the euro.

WEAK POINTS: There is no observation lounge with forward-facing views over the ship's bows. There are far too many loud, repetitive and unnecessary announcements – often in up to five languages. There is a charge for the sauna, which is located inside the beauty salon and operated by the concession.

Nantucket Clipper
★★★

Small Ship:	.1,471 tons	Passengers		Cabin Current:	.110 volts
Lifestyle:	.Standard	(lower beds/all berths):	.102/102	Elevators:	.0
Cruise Line:	.Clipper Cruise Line	Passenger Space Ratio		Casino (gaming tables):	.No
Former Names:	.none	(lower beds/all berths):	.14.4/14.4	Slot Machines:	.No
Builder:	.Jeffboat (USA)	Crew/Passenger Ratio		Swimming Pools (outdoors):	.0
Original Cost:	.$9 million	(lower beds/all berths):	.3.1/3.1	Swimming Pools (indoors):	.0
Entered Service:	.Dec 1984	Navigation Officers:	.American	Whirlpools:	.0
Registry:	.USA	Cabins (total):	.51	Fitness Center:	.No
Length (ft/m):	.207.0/63.00	Size Range (sq ft/m):	.120.5–137.7/	Sauna/Steam Room:	.No/No
Beam (ft/m):	.37.0/11.20		11.2–12.8	Massage:	.No
Draft (ft/m):	.8.0/2.40	Cabins (outside view):	.51	Self-Service Launderette:	.No
Propulsion/Propellers:	.diesel	Cabins (interior/no view):	.0	Dedicated Cinema/Seats:	.No
	(700 kW)/2	Cabins (for one person):	.0	Library:	.Yes
Passenger Decks:	.4	Cabins (with private balcony):	.0	Classification Society:	. .American Bureau
Total Crew:	.32	Cabins (wheelchair accessible):	.0		of Shipping

OVERALL SCORE: 1,213 (OUT OF A POSSIBLE 2,000 POINTS)

ACCOMMODATION: There are four grades of all-outside cabins. All are extremely small and basic. They are fairly tastefully furnished, with wood-accented trim and good sound insulation. Honeymooners and lovers should note that beds are of the twin variety, and are bolted to the deck and wall. Bathrooms are tight, but, thoughtfully, a night-light is provided, although there's little space for toiletries.

BERLITZ'S RATINGS

	Possible	Achieved
Ship	500	273
Accommodation	200	121
Food	400	265
Service	400	257
Entertainment	N/A	N/A
Cruise	500	297

DINING: The dining room is warm and inviting, and has large picture windows. There is one seating, and you can sit with whomever you wish. There are no tables for two. The ship has simple and plain American cuisine that is quite tasty, although the menu choice is limited, and the portions are small. The chefs are from the Culinary Institute of America, and all ingredients are fresh. The chocolate chip cookies are popular and are served at various times, typically in the lounge.

OTHER COMMENTS: This small, shallow draft vessel is specially built for coastal and inland cruises and is very maneuverable. It has been quite well maintained, although it is now showing signs of aging. There is a wrap-around teakwood walking deck outdoors.

This extremely high-density ship has only two public rooms – the dining room, and an observation lounge, where most passengers congregate in the evening. Passengers can visit the bridge at any time. Not recommended for night owls. Passengers are typically over 60.

The service is by young, friendly all-American college-age types. This is most definitely an "Americana" experience for those seeking particularly to learn more about the coastal ports around the USA.

The ship has a casual, unstructured lifestyle, rather like a small (but certainly not luxurious) country club afloat, with some attention to detail. This should not be compared with big-ship ocean cruising. Thankfully, there are no mindless activities or corny parlor games.

Specialist lecturers are part of every cruise. These highlight the learning experience that is an essential part of cruising with Clipper Cruise Lines. As the ship is often in coastal destinations, a few bicycles would be a welcome addition for many passengers. There is a no-smoking policy for all interior areas. The onboard currency is the US dollar.

WEAK POINTS: This really is a high-density ship, with only two public rooms: a dining room and a lounge. The engine noise level is high when the ship is underway (OK for the hard of hearing). The *per diem* price is high for what you get, and the air fare is extra.

Navigator of the Seas
NOT YET RATED

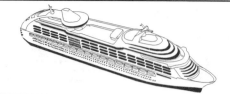

Large Ship: . . . . .137,276 tons	Total Crew: .1,185	Cabins (wheelchair accessible): 26
Lifestyle: . . . . .Standard	Passengers	Cabin Current: . . . . .110 volts
Cruise Line: . . . . .Royal Caribbean	(lower beds/all berths): 3,114/3,840	Elevators: . . . . .14 (6 glass-enclosed)
International	Passenger Space Ratio	Casino (gaming tables): . . . . .Yes
Former Names: . . . . .none	(lower beds/all berths): 44.0/35.7	Slot Machines: . . . . .Yes
Builder: . . .Kvaerner Masa-Yards (Finland)	Crew/Passenger Ratio	Swimming Pools (outdoors): 3
Original Cost: . . . .$500 million	(lower beds/all berths): 2.6/3.2	Swimming Pools (indoors): 0
Entered Service: . . . . .Spring 2003	Navigation Officers: . . . . . .Scandinavian	Whirlpools: 6
Registry: . . . . .The Bahamas	Cabins (total): 1,557	Fitness Center: . . . . .Yes
Length (ft/m): 1,020.6/311.1	Size Range (sq ft/m): 151.0–1,358.0/	Sauna/Steam Room: . . . . .Yes/Yes
Beam (ft/m): 155.5/47.4	14.0–126.1	Massage: . . . . .Yes
Draft (ft/m): 28.8/8.8	Cabins (outside view): 939	Self-Service Launderette: . . . . .No
Propulsion/Propellers: . . . . .diesel-electric	Cabins (interior/no view): 618	Dedicated Cinema/Seats: . . . . .No
(75,600 kW)/3 azimuthing pods	Cabins (for one person): 0	Library: . . . . .Yes
Passenger Decks: 14	Cabins (with private balcony): 765	Classification Society: Det Norske Veritas

---

OVERALL SCORE: NYR (OUT OF A POSSIBLE 2,000 POINTS)

ACCOMMODATION: There is an extensive range of 22 cabin categories from which to choose, in four major groupings: Premium ocean-view suites and cabins, Promenade-view (interior-view) cabins, Ocean-view cabins, and Interior (no view) cabins. Note that many cabins are of a similar size (good for incentives and large groups), and 300 have interconnecting doors (good for families).

BERLITZ'S RATINGS		
	Possible	Achieved
Ship	500	NYR
Accommodation	200	NYR
Food	400	NYR
Service	400	NYR
Entertainment	100	NYR
Cruise	400	NYR

A total of 138 interior (no view) cabins have bay windows that look *into* a horizontal atrium – first used to good effect aboard the Baltic passenger ferries *Silja Serenade* (1990) and *Silja Symphony* (1991) with interior (no view) cabins that look into a central shopping plaza. These cabins measure 157 sq. ft (15 sq. meters). Regardless of what cabin grade you choose, all except for the Royal Suite and Owner's Suite have twin beds that convert to a queen-sized unit,TV, radio and telephone, personal safe, vanity unit, mini-bar (called an Automatic Refreshment Center) hairdryer and private bathroom.

The largest accommodation includes luxuriously appointed penthouse suites (whose occupants, sadly, must share the rest of the ship with everyone else, except for their own exclusive, and private, concierge club). The grandest is the Royal Suite, which is positioned on the port side of the ship, and measures 1,146 sq. ft/106.5 sq. meters). It has a king-sized bed in a separate, large bedroom, a living room with an additional queen-sized sofa bed, baby grand piano (no pianist is included, however), refrigerator/wet bar, dining table, entertainment center, and large bathroom.

The slightly smaller, but still highly desirable,

Owner's Suites (there are 10 of these, all located in the center of the ship, on both port and starboard sides, each measuring 468 sq. ft/43 sq. meters) and four Royal Family suites (each 574 sq. ft/53 sq. meters), all featuring similar items. However, the four Royal Family suites, which have two bedrooms (including one with third/fourth upper Pullman berths) are at the stern of the ship and have magnificent views over the ship's wake (and seagulls).

All cabins have twin beds that convert to a queen-sized bed, a private bathroom with shower enclosure (towels are 100 percent cotton), as well as interactive, closed circuit and satellite television, and pay-per-view movies. Cabins with "private balconies" should note that they are not so private (the partitions are only partial, leaving you exposed to your neighbor's smoke or conversation). The balcony decking is made of Bolidt – a sort of rubberized sand – and not real wood, while the balcony rail is wood.

DINING: The main dining room, with a capacity of almost 2,000, is large and noisy. It is set on three levels, with a dramatic staircase connecting all three levels. All three have exactly the same menus and food. There are also two small private wings for private groups, each seating about 58 persons. The dining room is totally non-smoking, there are two seatings, and tables are for four, six, eight 10 or 12. The place settings, china and cutlery are of good quality.

The cuisine is typical of mass banquet catering that offers standard fare comparable to that found in American family-style restaurants ashore. While menu descriptions are tempting, the actual food may be somewhat disappointing and unmemorable. The menu descriptions make the food sound better than it is (which is consistently below average), mostly disappointing and without much taste – the result of controlled food costs as well as the use of many mixes and pre-prepared items. However, a decent selection of light meals is provided, and a vegetarian menu is available. The selection of breads, rolls, fruit and cheese is quite poor, however, and could do more improvement. Caviar (once a standard menu item) now incurs a heft extra charge. Menus typically include a Welcome Aboard Dinner, French Dinner, Italian Dinner, International Dinner, and Captain's Gala Dinner.

While the USDA prime beef is very good, other meats may not be (they are often disguised with gravies or heavy sauces). Most of the fish (apart from salmon) and seafood is overcooked and lacking in taste. Green vegetables are scarce, although salad items are plentiful. Rice is often used to replace potatoes and other sources of carbohydrates. Breads and pastry items are generally good (although some items, such as croissants, for example, may not be made on board). Dessert items are very standardized, and the selection of cheeses is poor (almost all come from the USA, known mostly for its processed, sliced, colored cheeses), as is the choice of crackers to go with the cheese.

ALTERNATIVE DINING OPTIONS: Alternative dining options for casual and informal meals at all hours (according to company releases) include:
● *Cafe Promenade*: for continental breakfast, all-day pizzas and specialty coffees (provided in paper cups).
● *Windjammer Café*: for casual buffet-style breakfast, lunch and light dinner (except for the cruise's last night).
● *Chops Grill* (this is actually a little section inside the Windjammer Café): for casual dinner (no reservations necessary) featuring a grill and open kitchen.
● *Portofino*: an "upscale" (non-smoking) Euro-Italian restaurant, with 98 seats, for dinner (reservations required).
● *Johnny Rockets*: a retro 1950s all-day, all-night eatery that features hamburgers, malt shakes (at extra cost), and jukebox hits, with both indoor and outdoor seating.
● *Sprinkles*: for round-the-clock ice cream and yoghurt (in the Royal Promenade).

OTHER COMMENTS: *Navigator of the Seas* is a stunning, large, floating leisure resort, and sister (in terms of size, looks, layout and facilities) to *Adventure of the Seas, Explorer of the Seas* and *Voyager of the Seas*, which debuted in 2001, 2000 and 1999, respectively, and one more (*Mariner of the Seas*) to make its appearance before 2005. The ships are, at present, the largest cruise vessels in the world in terms of tonnage (although, to keep things in perspective, they are not quite as long as Norwegian Cruise Line's *Norway*, and will be eclipsed in 2004 by *Queen Mary 2*).

The ship's propulsion is derived from three pod units, powered by electric motors (two azimuthing, and one fixed at the centerline) instead of conventional rudders and propellers, in the latest configuration of high-tech propulsion systems.

With its large proportions, the ship provides more facilities and options, and caters to more passengers than any other Royal Caribbean International ship has in the past, and yet the ship manages to have a healthy passenger space ratio (the amount of space per passenger). Being a "non-Panamax" ship, it is simply too large to go through the Panama Canal, thus limiting its itineraries almost exclusively to the Caribbean (where few islands can accept it), or for use as a floating island resort. Spend the first few hours exploring all the many facilities and public spaces aboard this vessel and it will be time well spent.

Although *Navigator of the Seas* is a large ship, even the accommodation hallways are warm and attractive, with artwork cabinets and wavy lines to interject and break up the monotony. In fact, there are plenty of decorative touches to help you avoid what would otherwise be a very clinical environment.

Embarkation and disembarkation take place through two stations/access points, designed to minimize the inevitable lines at the start and end of the cruise (that's more than 1,500 people for each access point). Once inside the ship, you'll need good walking shoes, particularly when you need to go from one end to the other – it really is quite a long way.

The four-decks-high Royal Promenade, which is 394 ft (120 meters) long, is the main interior focal point (it's a good place to hang out, to meet someone, or to arrange to meet someone). The length of two football fields, it has two internal lobbies (atria) that rise to as many as 11 decks high. Restaurants, shops and entertainment locations front this winding street and interior "with-view" cabins look into it from above. It is designed loosely in the image of London's fashionable Burlington Arcade – although there's not a real brick in sight, and I wonder if the designers have ever visited the real thing. It is, however, an imaginative piece of design work, and most passengers (particularly those who enjoy shopping malls) enjoy it immensely.

The super-atrium houses a "traditional" English-style pub, with draft beer and plenty of "street-front" seating (it's funny, but North American passengers sit down, while British passengers prefer to stand at the bar). There is also a Champagne Bar, a Sidewalk Café (for continental breakfast, all-day pizzas, specialty coffees and desserts), Sprinkles (for round-the-clock ice cream and yoghurt), and a sports bar. There are also several shops – for jewelry, gifts, liquor and logo souvenirs. Altogether, the Royal promenade is a nice place to see and be seen, and there is action throughout the day and night. The Guest Reception and Shore Excursion counters are located at the aft end of the promenade, as is an ATM, while opposite is the cozy Champagne Bar. Watch for the parades and street entertainers.

Arched across the promenade is a captain's balcony.

Meanwhile, in the center of the promenade is a stairway that connects you to the deck below, where you'll find the Schooner Bar (a piano lounge) and the colorful Casino Royale. This is naturally large and full of flashing lights and noises. Gaming includes blackjack, Caribbean stud poker, roulette, and craps. Aft of the casino is the Schooner Bar.

Action man and woman can enjoy more sporting pursuits, such as a rock-climbing wall that's 33 ft (10 meters) high. It is located outdoors at the aft end of the funnel. You'll get a great "buzz" being 200 ft (60 meters) above the ocean while the ship is moving – particularly when it rolls.

There's also a roller-blading track, a dive-and-snorkel shop, a full-size basketball court and 9-hole golf driving range. A ShipShape health spa measures 15,000 sq. ft (1,400 sq. meters), includes a large aerobics room, fitness center (with the usual stairmasters, treadmills, stationary bikes, weight machines and free weights), treatment rooms, men's and women's sauna/steam rooms, while another 10,000 sq. ft (930 sq. meters) is devoted to a Solarium (with magrodome sliding glass roof) for relaxation after you've exercised too much.

There is also a regulation-size ice-skating rink (Studio B), featuring *real*, not fake, ice, with "bleacher" seating for up to 900, and the latest in broadcast facilities. Ice Follies shows are also presented here. A number of slim pillars obstruct clear-view arena stage sight lines, however.

If ice-skating in the Caribbean doesn't appeal, perhaps you'd like the stunning two-deck library (it's the first aboard any ship, and it is open 24 hours a day). A grand amount of money has been spent on permanent artwork. Drinking places include a neat Aquarium Bar, which comes complete with 50 tons of glass and water in four large aquariums (whose combined value is over $1 million). Other drinking places include the small and intimate Champagne Bar, Crown & Anchor Pub, and a Connoisseur Club – for cigars and cognacs.

Lovers of jazz might appreciate the Cosmopolitan Club, an intimate room for cool music within the Viking Crown Lounge, or the Schooner Bar piano lounge. Golfers might enjoy the 19th Hole, a golf bar, as they play the Navigator Links.

Fans of production shows and adult entertainment will enjoy the 1,350-seat Metropolis Showlounge, which spans the height of five decks. It features a hydraulic orchestra pit and stage areas, and is decorated in the style of the grand European theatres from the *fin-de-siècle* period.

There is a television studio, located adjacent to rooms that can be used for trade show exhibit space. Lovers can tie the knot in a wedding chapel in the sky, called the Skylight Chapel (it's located on the upper level of the Observation Lounge, and even has wheelchair access via an electric stairway lift). Meanwhile, outdoors, the pool and open deck areas provide a resort-like environment.

Families with children have not been forgotten, and the children's facilities are extensive. "Aquanauts" is for 3–5 year olds; "Explorers" is for 6–8 year olds; "Voyagers" is for 9–12 year olds. "Fuel" is a dedicated area for teenagers, including a daytime club (with several computers), soda bar, and dance floor; there's also an array of the latest video games. Paint and Clay is an arts and crafts center for younger children. Adjacent to these indoor areas is Adventure Beach, an area for all the family; this includes swimming pools, a water slide and game areas outdoors.

In terms of sheer size, this ship dwarfs all others in the cruise industry, but in terms of personal service, the reverse is the case, unless you happen to reside in one of the top suites. Royal Caribbean International does, however, try hard to provide a good standard of programmed service from its hotel staff. This is impersonal city life at sea, millennium-style, and a superb, well-designed alternative to a land-based resort, which is what the company wanted to build. Welcome to the real, escapist world of highly programmed resort living aboard ship. Remember to take lots of extra pennies – you'll need them to pay for all the additional-cost items.

Be aware that, if you meet someone you'd like to see again, you'll need to make an appointment (arrange to meet along the Royal Promenade) – because this really is a large, Las Vegas-style floating resort-city for the lively of heart and fleet of foot. Note that this ship will probably achieve a rating score similar to that for sister ships *Adventurer of the Seas, Explorer of the Seas* and *Voyager of the Seas*. The onboard currency is the US dollar.

WEAK POINTS: Standing in line for embarkation, disembarkation, shore tenders and for self-serve buffet meals is an inevitable aspect of cruising aboard all large ships. Lines for check-in, embarkation and disembarkation (it's better if you are a non-US resident and stay at an RCI-booked hotel, as all formalities can be completed there and then you'll simply walk on board to your cabin). Suites and cabins with private balcony have Bolidt floors (a substance that looks like rubberized sand) instead of wood. If you have a cabin with a door that interconnecting door to another cabin, you should be aware that you'll probably be able to hear *everything* your next-door neighbors say and do. Bathroom toilets are explosively noisy.

You'll need to plan what you want to take part in wisely as almost everything requires you to sign-up in advance (many activities take place only on sea days). The cabin bath towels are small and skimpy. There are few quiet places to sit and read – almost everywhere you'll be bombarded with background music.

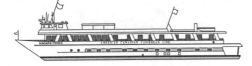

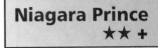

Niagara Prince
★★ +

Small Ship: ....99 tons	Total Crew: 17	Cabin Current: ....110 volts
Lifestyle: ....Standard	Passengers	Elevators: 0
Cruise Line: ....American Canadian	(lower beds/all berths): 84/94	Casino (gaming tables): ....No
Caribbean Line	Passenger Space Ratio	Slot Machines: ....No
Former Names: ....none	(lower beds/all berths): 1.1/1.0	Swimming Pools (outdoors): 0
Builder: ....Blount Industries (USA)	Crew/Passenger Ratio	Swimming Pools (indoors): 0
Original Cost: ....$7.5 million	(lower beds/all berths): 4.9/5.5	Whirlpools: 0
Entered Service: ....Nov 1994	Navigation Officers: ....American	Fitness Center: 0
Registry: ....USA	Cabins (total): 48	Sauna/Steam Room: 0/0
Length (ft/m): 177.0/53.9	Size Range (sq ft/m): ..72.0–96.0/6.6–8.9	Massage: 0
Beam (ft/m): 40.0/12.1	Cabins (outside view): 40	Self-Service Launderette: ....No
Draft (ft/m): 6.7/2.0	Cabins (interior/no view): 2	Dedicated Cinema/Seats: ....No
Propulsion/Propellers: ....diesel	Cabins (for one person): 6	Library: ....Yes
(1044 kW)/2	Cabins (with private balcony): 0	Classification Society: . .American Bureau
Passenger Decks: 3	Cabins (wheelchair accessible): 0	of Shipping

---

OVERALL SCORE: 1,087 (OUT OF A POSSIBLE 2,000 POINTS)

ACCOMMODATION: The cabins are small (designed for packages rather than people), basic, and plain. Only a metal cabinet is provided for hanging your clothes, and there are a few small metal drawers. No smoking is allowed in any cabin. The air conditioning consists of re-circulated air. Beds in 75 percent of the cabins can be made up as two singles or a queen-size bed (10 cabins have a third berth). The bathrooms are the size of a telephone kiosk (tiny), and very frustrating.

DINING: The dining room is operated in one open seating (no assigned tables), with tables for four, six, eight, or ten. Meals are served 'family-style.' The cuisine features good, wholesome American fare, with fresh-baked breads, muffins, and regional dishes. There are, perhaps, too many high-cholesterol, fatty foods for the older passengers carried. A "bring your own bottle" policy exists for those who want wine with dinner, or any alcoholic beverages (mixers are, however, available).

OTHER COMMENTS: The vessel is equipped with a unique, retractable wheelhouse for passage under low bridges on island waterway itineraries, and there is also

BERLITZ'S RATINGS

	Possible	Achieved
Ship	500	232
Accommodation	200	95
Food	400	235
Service	400	241
Entertainment	N/A	N/A
Cruise	500	284

a small platform for those who want to swim off the stern. There is also a glass-bottom boat, and a sunfish sail-boat. For other comments, see review of the company's *Grande Prince*.

An underwater video camera allows passengers to see what a scuba diver might see underneath the ship, while seated in (dry) comfort in the lounge, on large-screen TV monitors. Underwater lights, which attract fish and other marine life, are also fitted.

Cruising aboard this ship is for those who do not want or need pampering, much service, entertainment, or the facilities provided aboard regular cruise ships. This vessel is enjoyed by high percentages of repeat passengers, however, who seek a simple, unpretentious lifestyle. Take only casual clothing and the odd sweater or jacket.

Although there is no elevator, there is a stair lift for those who need a little help. All gratuities are pooled by the entire complement of staff. The onboard currency is the US dollar.

WEAK POINTS: Small, utilitarian cabins. No alcoholic beverages are available. There's no laundry aboard, so bed linen, towels and other items are all taken ashore for cleaning.

Nippon Maru
★★★ +

Small Ship:	.............21,903 tons	Passengers	
Lifestyle:	...................Standard	(lower beds/all berths):	........408/607
Cruise Line:	...Mitsui OSK Passenger Line	Passenger Space Ratio	
Former Names:	..................none	(lower beds/all berths):	.......53.6/36.0
Builder:	.....Mitsubishi Heavy Industries	Crew/Passenger Ratio	
	(Japan)	(lower beds/all berths):	..........2.5/3.7
Original Cost:	............$59.4 million	Navigation Officers:	.........Japanese
Entered Service:	...........Sept 1990	Cabins (total):	204
Registry:	.....................Japan	Size Range (sq ft/m):	......150.6–430.5/
Length (ft/m):	............546.7/166.65		14.0–40.0
Beam (ft/m):	..............78.7/24.00	Cabins (outside view):	189
Draft (ft/m):	.................21.4/6.55	Cabins (interior/no view):	15
Propulsion/Propellers:	...........diesel	Cabins (for one person):	0
	(15,740 kW)/2	Cabins (with private balcony):	0
Passenger Decks:	7	Cabins (wheelchair accessible):	2
Total Crew:	160	Cabin Current:	.............100 volts

Elevators:	5
Casino (gaming tables):	............Yes
(no cash can be won, only gifts)	
Slot Machines:	.....................No
Swimming Pools (outdoors):	1
Swimming Pools (indoors):	0
Whirlpools:	.........4 (Japanese baths)
Fitness Center:	...................Yes
Sauna/Steam Room:	............Yes/No
Massage:	.........................Yes
Self-Service Launderette:	..........Yes
Dedicated Cinema/Seats:	......Yes/135
Library:	..........................Yes
Classification Society:	.......Nippon Kaiji
	Kyokai

OVERALL SCORE: 1,391 (OUT OF A POSSIBLE 2,000 POINTS)

ACCOMMODATION: Most cabins are located forward, with public rooms positioned aft. The suites are quite large (larger than aboard sister ship *Fuji Maru*), and have a separate bedroom and living room with a solid wall divider except for the doorway, (where there is a curtain but no door). A large sofa, four chairs, and coffee table occupy one section of the lounge; there is also a vanity/writing desk. The bedroom has a good amount of closet and drawer space and two beds. The bathroom is very small, however, although there is a small vanity desk with make-up mirror. Slippers and bathrobes are provided.

The deluxe cabins are quite nicely decorated, and the living area has a table and two chairs, and two beds (they cannot be pushed together). The standard cabins are utilitarian and clinical (adequate for convention and seminar cruise passengers and those who don't mind just the basics). Many of these have a third (or third and fourth) pull-down upper Pullman berth. The lighting is minimal and quite utilitarian.

DINING: The dining room is basic and has both traditional Japanese cuisine and some Western dishes. There is one seating dining for leisure cruises, and two seatings for when the ship is under charter. The food presentation is quite decent, but rather plain, and menu choice is limited, although quite welcome by most passengers.

OTHER COMMENTS: Has a single, large, orange, swept-back funnel aft of amidships, with an exterior styling that

BERLITZ'S RATINGS

	Possible	Achieved
Ship	500	349
Accommodation	200	135
Food	400	287
Service	400	289
Entertainment	100	62
Cruise	400	269

is very traditional – not at all contemporary. There is a decent amount of open outdoors space, and the teakwood decking outdoors is good. The ship was specifically built and outfitted for Japanese passengers and the Japanese seminar/lecture marketplace.

The public rooms have very high ceilings, giving a sense of spaciousness. The well-designed public rooms have high-quality furnishings and soothing color combinations. The interior décor, including the ceilings in public areas, is plain and unexciting.

There is an elegant, quite dramatic six-deck-high atrium. Features true Japanese baths, and a washitsu tatami room. Children's activities personnel are placed onboard only for leisure cruises.

This ship is principally for older Japanese passengers (those of "silver" years) who want to cruise at moderate rates in pleasant, but not luxurious, surroundings, with Japanese food that is varied, colorful and plentiful. Tipping is not allowed.

A specialist courier company provides an excellent luggage service and will collect your luggage from your home before the cruise, and deliver it back to your home after the cruise (this service available only in Japan). The onboard currency is the Japanese yen.

WEAK POINTS: The cheap plastic deck furniture is difficult to keep clean and looks really poor and unkempt. The seats in the theater are very plain and utilitarian, and not particularly comfortable. Hospitality towards passengers could be improved (particularly by the officers).

Noordam
★★★ +

Large Ship: . . . . .33,930 tons	Total Crew: 530	Cabins (wheelchair accessible): 4
Lifestyle: . . . . .Standard	Passengers	Cabin Current: . . . . .110 and 220 volts
Cruise Line: . . . . .Holland America Line	(lower beds/all berths): 1,214/1,350	Elevators: 7
Former Names: . . . . .none	Passenger Space Ratio	Casino (gaming tables): . . . . .Yes
Builder: . . . . . . .Chantiers de l'Atlantique	(lower beds/all berths): 28.0/25.1	Slot Machines: . . . . .Yes
(France)	Crew/Passenger Ratio	Swimming Pools (outdoors): 2
Original Cost: . . . .$160 million	(lower beds/all berths): 2.2/2.5	Swimming Pools (indoors): 0
Entered Service: . . . . .Apr 1984	Navigation Officers: . . . . .Dutch	Whirlpools: 1
Registry: . . . . .The Netherlands	Cabins (total): 607	Fitness Center: . . . . .Yes
Length (ft/m): 704.2/214.66	Size Range (sq ft/m): 150.6–296.0/	Sauna/Steam Room: . . . . .Yes/No
Beam (ft/m): 89.4/27.26	14.0–27.5	Massage: . . . . .Yes
Draft (ft/m): 24.2/7.40	Cabins (outside view): 413	Self-Service Launderette: . . . . .Yes
Propulsion/Propellers: . . . . .diesel	Cabins (interior/no view): 194	Dedicated Cinema/Seats: Yes/230
(21,600 kW)/2	Cabins (for one person): 0	Library: . . . . .Yes
Passenger Decks: 10	Cabins (with private balcony): 0	Classification Society: . . .Lloyd's Register

OVERALL SCORE: 1,350 (OUT OF A POSSIBLE 2,000 POINTS)

ACCOMMODATION: There are 15 categories (9 with outside-view, 6 interior with no view). In general, most cabins have a reasonable amount of space, although they are small when compared with those of many other ships. In general, they are adequately appointed and practically laid out, with some wood furniture and fittings, wood paneling, good counter and storage space (although there is very little drawer space), a large mirror, and a private bathroom that is very modest in size.

The top three categories of cabins (which are only marginally larger and should not really be called suites or mini-suites) have bathtubs while all others have shower enclosures only. Several cabins have king- or queen-sized beds, although most have twin beds (some, but not all, can be pushed together). Note that many cabins, particularly those that are interior (no view), the bed configuration is L-shaped, and the beds cannot be pushed together.

A number of cabins also have additional upper berths for a third/fourth person. Room service is provided 24 hours a day. All cabin televisions receive CNN and TNT. The cabin insulation, however, is extremely poor, and bathroom towels are small. In addition, some cabins on Boat and Navigation Decks have obstructed views.

DINING: The dining room is reasonably large and quite attractive, with warm décor, and ample space. Breakfast and lunch are served in an open seating (so you may get a different table and different waiters for each meal), and in two seatings for dinner (where you do have the

BERLITZ'S RATINGS

	Possible	Achieved
Ship	500	323
Accommodation	200	136
Food	400	251
Service	400	284
Entertainment	100	66
Cruise	400	290

same table, and table waiters, each evening). Tables are for two (there are very few of them), four, six or eight. The service is robotic and quite basic. The Indonesian waiters appear to try hard, but communication with them is often extremely frustrating. The wine waiters are quite useless (with a very poor understanding of good wines), as are the wine glasses. Fine Rosenthal china and cutlery are featured (although there are no fish knives).

Unfortunately, Holland America Line food isn't as nice as the china it's placed on. It may be adequate for most passengers who are not used to better food, but it doesn't match the standard found aboard other ships in the premium segment of the industry. While USDA beef is of a good quality, fowl tends to be battery-tough, and most fish is overcooked and has the consistency of a cricket bat. What are also definitely *not* luxurious are the endless packets of sugar, and packets (instead of glass jars) of breakfast jam, marmalade and honey, and poor quality teas. While these may be suitable for a family diner, they do not belong aboard a ship that claims to have "award-winning cuisine." Dessert and pastry items are of good quality (specifically for American tastes), although there is much use of canned fruits and jellies. Forget the selection of "international" cheeses, however, as most come from the USA, which is known for its processed, highly colored cheese slices rather than for fine cheese making. Holland America Line can provide Kosher meals, but these are prepared ashore, frozen, and brought to your table sealed in their original containers (there is no Kosher kitchen on board).

Instead of the more formal dining room, the Lido Buffet is open for casual dinners on all except the last night of each cruise, in an open-seating arrangement. Tables are set with crisp linens, flatware and stemware. The set menu usually includes a choice of four entrées.

OTHER COMMENTS: There is a nicely raked bow, although the angular exterior design makes the ship look squat and somewhat boxy. There is a good amount of open deck space, and the traditional teakwood decks outdoors include a wrap-around promenade deck. The ship, however, has a poor build quality and suffers from excessive vibration.

The ship has quite a spacious interior design and layout, and the soothing color combinations do not jar the senses, although they are rather dark and somber. There is much polished teakwood and rosewood paneling throughout, and the ship has a fine, well-displayed collection of 17th and 18th-century artwork and Dutch artifacts. The Crow's Nest observation lounge, atop the ship, is a good retreat for many. The Explorers' Lounge is relaxing for after-meal coffee and live chamber music. The main lounge, which has a small balcony level, is reminiscent of those found on former ocean liners, and is really good only for cabaret entertainment, and not full production shows. The flower bouquets throughout the ship add warmth to the ambience.

This ship is good for older passengers wanting pleasant surroundings and food that is not highly seasoned. The company provides complimentary cappuccino and espresso coffees, and free ice cream during certain hours of the day aboard its ships, as well as hot hors d'oeuvres in all bars – something other major lines seem to have dropped, or charge extra for.

However, the latest batch of ships have more space, better facilities and more options, which leaves this one losing a few points in relation to the increased competition in the international marketplace. *Noordam*'s sister ship is now Louis Cruise Lines' *Thomson Spirit* (chartered to Thomson Cruises), following a disastrous period of liaison with United States Lines as *Patriot*.

Gratuities are extra, and they are added to your shipboard account at $10–$13 per day, according to the accommodation grade chosen. Refreshingly, the company does not add an automatic 15 percent gratuity for beverage purchases. Perhaps the ship's best asset is her friendly and personable Filipino and Indonesian crew, although communication can prove frustrating at times.

The company provides complimentary cappuccino and espresso coffees, and free ice cream during certain hours of the day aboard its ships, as well as hot hors d'oeuvres in all bars – something other major lines seem to have dropped, or charge extra for. The onboard currency is the US dollar.

WEAK POINTS: Standing in line for embarkation, disembarkation, shore tenders and for self-serve buffet meals is an inevitable aspect of cruising aboard all large ships. This ship tries to be a Holland America Line ship, but really doesn't fit in with the other (more standardized) ships in the fleet. There are simply too many interior (no view) cabins. There is a considerable amount of vibration throughout the ship, but particularly at the stern, and it's at its worst during slow maneuvering.

The charge to use the washing machines and dryers in the self-service launderette is really petty and irritating, particularly for the occupants of suites, as they pay high prices for their cruises. The room service is poor. There are many pillars that obstruct the sight lines in the show lounge.

Removed 2006

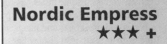

Nordic Empress
★★★ +

Large Ship: ....48,563 tons	Passengers		Cabin Current: ....110 volts
Lifestyle: ....Standard	(lower beds/all berths): 1,600/2,020		Elevators: 7
Cruise Line: Royal Caribbean International	Passenger Space Ratio		Casino (gaming tables): ....Yes
Former Names: ....none	(lower beds/all berths): 30.2/24.0		Slot Machines: Yes-220
Builder: Chantiers de l'Atlantique (France)	Crew/Passenger Ratio		Swimming Pools (outdoors): 1
Original Cost: ....$170 million	(lower beds/all berths): 2.3/2.9		(+1 wading pool)
Entered Service: ....June 1990	Navigation Officers: ......Scandinavian		Swimming Pools (indoors): 0
Registry: ....Liberia	Cabins (total): 800		Whirlpools: 4
Length (ft/m): 692.2/211.00	Size Range (sq ft/m): 117.0–818.0/		Fitness Center: ....Yes
Beam (ft/m): 100.7/30.70	10.8–76.0		Sauna/Steam Room: ....Yes/No
Draft (ft/m): 24.9/7.60	Cabins (outside view): 471		Massage: ....Yes
Propulsion/Propellers: ....diesel	Cabins (interior/no view): 329		Self-Service Launderette: ....No
(16,200 kW)/2	Cabins (for one person): 0		Dedicated Cinema/Seats: ....No
Passenger Decks: 9	Cabins (with private balcony): 69		Library: ....No
Total Crew: 685	Cabins (wheelchair accessible): 4		Classification Society: Det Norske Veritas

OVERALL SCORE: 1,306 (OUT OF A POSSIBLE 2,000 POINTS)

ACCOMMODATION: There are 15 different price categories. The largest accommodation can be found in the Royal Suite, just under the navigation bridge on the port side. This has a queen-size bed, walk-in closet, separate living area with bar, refrigerator and entertainment center; the bathroom has a whirlpool tub, and vanity dressing area. There is a private balcony.

Nine cabins have private balconies that overlook the ship's stern (these consist of two owner's suites and seven "superior" ocean-view cabins). The other cabins with private balconies also have a decent amount of living space, and a small sofa, coffee table and chair, and vanity desk.

Almost all of the other cabins are dimensionally challenged, although reasonably comfortable. No matter what grade of accommodation you choose, they all have twin beds that can convert to a queen-size configuration. The bathrooms are nicely laid-out, and have a decent amount of space for personal toiletry items. Hair dryers are not provided.

DINING: The Hollywood musical-themed Carmen Dining Room is non-smoking area. It is two decks high, and features a balcony level, as well as large windows that overlook the stern of the ship, but it is really a noisy dining room. There are two seatings. The dining operation is well orchestrated, with emphasis on highly programmed (insensitive), extremely hurried service that many find intrusive.

The cuisine is typical of mass banquet catering that offers standard fare comparable to that found in Amer-

BERLITZ'S RATINGS

	Possible	Achieved
Ship	500	343
Accommodation	200	126
Food	400	236
Service	400	270
Entertainment	100	71
Cruise	400	260

ican family-style restaurants ashore. While menu descriptions are tempting, the actual food may be somewhat disappointing and non-memorable. The menu descriptions make the food sound better than it is (which is consistently below average), mostly disappointing and without much taste – the result of controlled food costs as well as the use of many mixes and pre-prepared items. However, a decent selection of light meals is provided, and a vegetarian menu is available. The selection of breads, rolls, fruit and cheese is quite poor, and could do with improvement. Caviar (once a standard menu item) now incurs a heft extra charge. The menus typically include a Welcome Aboard Dinner, French Dinner, Italian Dinner, International Dinner, and Captain's Gala Dinner.

While the USDA prime beef is very good, other meats may not be (they are often disguised with gravies or heavy sauces). Most of the fish (apart from salmon) and seafood is overcooked and lacking in taste. Green vegetables are scarce, although salad items are plentiful. Rice is often used to replace potatoes and other sources of carbohydrates. Breads and pastry items are generally good (although some items, such as croissants, for example, may not be made on board). Dessert items are very standardized, and the selection of cheeses is poor (almost all come from the USA – a country known mostly for its processed, sliced, colored cheeses – as is the choice of crackers to go with the cheese.

The wine list is not extensive, but the prices are moderate (although there are few wines under $20). The waiters, many from Caribbean countries, are perhaps overly friendly for some tastes – particularly on the last night of the cruise, when tips are expected.

For casual breakfasts and lunches, the Windjammer Café, with its two buffet display lines, provides an alternative to the dining room, although there are often lines at peak times, and the selection is at best very average. There are no "active stations" – where items such as omelets could be made to order.

OTHER COMMENTS: This is a fine contemporary ship with a short bow and squared-off stern that looks quite stunning. *Nordic Empress* was designed specifically for the short-cruise market, for which the ship is well suited. The ship was actually designed for Admiral Cruises, which Royal Caribbean Cruise Line (as it was then called) later purchased; the original name of the ship was to have been *Future Seas*, although this name was not finally adopted. There is a polished wrap-around wood promenade deck outdoors, and there is a dramatic use of glass-enclosed viewing spaces that provide good contact from the upper, open decks to the sea.

Inside, a stunning nine-deck-high atrium is the focal point of the ship's interior design. Lots of crystal and brass are used to good effect to reflect light. An ingenious use of lighting effects provides illuminating interiors that make you feel warm. Passenger flow is generally good, although, because two seatings and two show times are operated, some congestion is inevitable adjacent to the entrance foyer at show time. The show lounge has a main floor level as well as a balcony level. However, the sightlines from the balcony are almost useless as they are ruined by railings.

A three-level casino has a sailcloth ceiling, but it is noisy. There is a superb outdoor pool deck designed for evenings under the stars, although the two swimming pools are very small. The Viking Crown Lounge, aft of the funnel, is a two-level nightclub-disco for the late-night set.

Nordic Empress is a fairly smart contemporary ship with a high passenger density, but it has an adequate array of activities for all ages. In the final analysis, you will probably be overwhelmed by the public spaces, and under whelmed by the size of the cabins. However, this is basically a well run, fine-tuned, highly programmed cruise product geared particularly to those seeking an action-packed cruise vacation at a moderately good price, with lots of fellow passengers. The onboard currency is the US dollar.

WEAK POINTS: Standing in line for embarkation, disembarkation, shore tenders and for self-serve buffet meals is an inevitable aspect of cruising aboard all large ships. Overpriced drinks are aggressively pushed as soon as passengers board the ship. The two-level show lounge has poor sight lines in the upper lateral balconies. The constant, loud announcements are irritating. The two swimming pools are very small considering the number of passengers carried.

Removed 2000

Norway
★★★ +

Large Ship: ....76,049 tons	Passengers	Cabin Current: ....110 volts
Lifestyle: ....Standard	(lower beds/all berths): 2,026/2,370	Elevators: 11
Cruise Line: ....Star Cruises	Passenger Space Ratio	Casino (gaming tables): ....Yes
Former Names: ....*France*	(lower beds/all berths): 37.5/32.8	Slot Machines: ....Yes
Builder: Chantiers de l'Atlantique (France)	Crew/Passenger Ratio	Swimming Pools (outdoors): 2
Original Cost: ....$80 million	(lower beds/all berths): 2.2/2.5	Swimming Pools (indoors): 1
Entered Service: .....Feb 1962/Oct 2001	Navigation Officers: ....Scandinavian	(plus Aquacize Pool)
Registry: ....The Bahamas	Cabins (total): 1,013	Whirlpools: 2
Length (ft/m): 1035.1/315.50	Size Range (sq ft/m): 99.0–958.0/	Fitness Center: ....Yes
Beam (ft/m): 109.9/33.50	9.2–89.0	Sauna/Steam Room: ....Yes/No
Draft (ft/m): 35.4/10.80	Cabins (outside view): 642	Massage: ....Yes
Propulsion/Propellers: ....steam turbine	Cabins (interior/no view): 371	Self-Service Launderette: ....No
(29,850 kW)/4	Cabins (for one person): 20	Dedicated Cinema/Seats: Yes/813
Passenger Decks: 12	Cabins (with private balcony): 56	Library: ....Yes
Total Crew: 920	Cabins (wheelchair accessible): 11	Classification Society: ....Bureau Veritas

OVERALL SCORE: 1,378 (OUT OF A POSSIBLE 2,000 POINTS)

ACCOMMODATION: There is an extremely wide range of suites and cabins in many different grades and configurations – from luxurious and very spacious outside suites that can accommodate up to six to tiny interior (no view) cabins. All of the cabins have nice, high ceilings, long beds, good closet and drawer space and a decent range of amenities. Many cabin bathrooms feature full-sized bathtubs, while others have only shower enclosures. Bottled water is placed in each cabin (but a charge will be made to your account if you open the bottle).

The owner's suites are extremely lavish, and the newest suites added to two decks atop the ship are very comfortable (however, all suite occupants should have had a private dining room). There are many cabins suitable for families of four or five, even six.

DINING: There are two large dining rooms (both are non-smoking) and two seatings in each. The nicest is the Windward, with its fine domed ceiling, and wall murals retained from its former days as the first-class dining room, while the Leeward (the former tourist-class restaurant) has a fine balcony level. There are few tables for two, however, and the tables are extremely close together (the result of additional suites and cabins added over the past few years).

Le Bistro is an informal alternative dining spot that provides for a change from the two restaurants (and the noise). It offers a taste of Italy in a contemporary setting.

The casual, outdoor buffet area is useful for those out on deck, but it is always crowded, with long lines to get

BERLITZ'S RATINGS		
	Possible	Achieved
Ship	500	359
Accommodation	200	146
Food	400	239
Service	400	282
Entertainment	100	78
Cruise	400	274

to what can best be described as "food as it shouldn't be presented." It never looks good, despite staff efforts to restock the displays.

Overall, the food provided is rather unmemorable fare that lacks taste and presentation quality; the menus, too, are uninspiring. There is a reasonably decent selection of breads, rolls, cheeses and fruits, however. The wine list is quite decent, and well put together, with moderate prices, although you won't find any good vintage wines. The cutlery is very ordinary (there are no fish knives). There is no formal afternoon tea, although you can make your own from various beverage stations. The service is, on the whole, adequate, nothing more, and proves that good staffs that can communicate well are quite difficult to find.

OTHER COMMENTS: Originally built as the ocean liner *France* for the Compagnie Générale de Transatlantique, the ship was once known for its food and service when operating transatlantic crossings from France to New York in the 1960s. It is still quite majestic-looking, with two large funnels, a long foredeck and a real, distinguishable "sheer" (this is the sagging centerline of the ship, which was built by laying a keel – unlike the newest ships of today, which are built in locks).

The ship's interiors, food and service, however, have almost no resemblance to its former days as an ocean liner. It was converted to become a Caribbean cruise vessel in 1979, at a cost of $130 million, and sailed for many years for Norwegian Cruise Line (owned by Star Cruises). Several years ago, some major structural alterations added two complete new glass-enclosed decks atop the ship; the new decks provide an additional 135 outside suites and junior suites, and lower the profile of the two wing-tip funnels considerably, but the balconies are not very private. Two large landing craft provide fast, efficient transportation ashore.

More recent refurbishments have also kept the interiors refreshed. Some public rooms feature art deco touches reminiscent of the former ocean liner it once was. There are two different color schemes in the forward and aft sections, which help first-time passengers to find their way around.

The public rooms are, for the most part, quite pleasing, and many have high ceilings. Soft furnishings and much marble have kept the interiors fresh. The outdoor decks are well varnished, but the synthetic turf on the ship's top deck is just not right. It has an indoor Roman Spa, set low down in the ship, with a good range of spa programs and 16 treatment rooms.

There is an extensive jogging track, although it cannot be used before 8am (it is located above some of the most expensive cabins). The Club Internationale is an elegant carry-over from its former days (when it was the first-class lounge), and is still the perfect meeting place for cocktails and sophisticated evenings.

There is an excellent proscenium Saga Theatre, complete with large balcony level, for the dazzle-and-sizzle style of production shows. Large active casino invites you to spend your money, and is very noisy.

Children and teens will have a fine time aboard this ship, with lots of activities and children's staff. It is large enough for there to be plenty of places to play.

As *France*, this was for many years the world's largest cruise ship; it is still the longest (at least until *Queen Mary 2* arrives in early 2004). *Norway* is now a floating contemporary resort with some connections to the past in its make-up, offering what NCL calls Classic Cruise Holidays.

A 15 percent gratuity is added to all bar and spa treatment accounts. The onboard currency is the US dollar.

WEAK POINTS: Standing in line for embarkation, disembarkation, shore tenders and for self-serve buffet meals is an inevitable aspect of cruising aboard all large ships. The open deck and sunbathing space is quite poor, particularly when the ship is full.

Norway does not dock anywhere because of its size and deep draft (a problem for the non-ambulatory) and passengers must go ashore by tender boats (this can take a considerable amount of time). There are just too many loud announcements, making for too much of a holiday camp atmosphere.

Norwegian Dawn
NOT YET RATED

Large Ship: . . . . .91,000 tons	Total Crew: 1,100	Cabins (wheelchair accessible): 20
Lifestyle: . . . . .Standard	Passengers	Cabin Current: . . . . .110 AC
Cruise Line: . . . . .Norwegian Cruise Lines	(lower beds/all berths): 2,244/4,080	Elevators: 12
Former Names: . . . . .none	Passenger Space Ratio	Casino (gaming tables): . . . . .Yes
Gross Tonnage: 91,000	(lower beds/all berths): 40.5/23.0	Slot Machines: . . . . .Yes
Builder: . . . . .Meyer Werft (Germany)	Crew/Passenger Ratio	Swimming Pools (outdoors): 2
Original Cost: . . . .$400 million	(lower beds/all berths): 2.0/3.7	Swimming Pools (indoors): 1
Entered Service: . . . . .Oct 2002	Navigation Officers: . . . . . . .Scandinavian	Whirlpools: . . .4 (+ 1 children's whirlpool)
Registry: . . . . .Bahamas	Cabins (total): 1,122	Fitness Center: . . . . .Yes
Length (ft/m): 964.9/294.13	Size Range (sq ft/m): 142.0–3,030.0/	Sauna/Steam Room: . . . . .Yes/Yes
Beam (ft/m): 105.6/32.2	13.2–281.5	Massage: . . . . .Yes
Draft (ft/m): 26.9/8.2	Cabins (outside view): 787	Self-Service Launderette: . . . . .No
Propulsion/Propellers: . . .diesel-electric/2	Cabins (interior/no view): 363	Dedicated Cinema/Seats: . . . . .No
pods (19.5MW each)	Cabins (for one person): 0	Library: . . . . .Yes
Passenger Decks: 12	Cabins (with private balcony): 511	Classification Society: Det Norske Veritas

OVERALL SCORE: NYR (OUT OF A POSSIBLE 2,000 POINTS)

ACCOMMODATION: This is a mix of the following grades: 36 suites, 372 standard cabins with balconies, and 107 mini-suites with balconies. Regardless of accommodation chosen, all will have tea and coffee making sets, rich cherry wood cabinetry, and bathroom with sliding door and separate toilet, shower enclosure and washbasin compartments.

The largest accommodation can be found in two huge Garden Villas, located high atop the ship in a pod that is located forward of the ship's funnel, overlooking the main swimming pool. These villas feature huge glass walls and landscaped private roof gardens (one features a Japanese-style garden, the other features a Thai-style garden) for outdoor dining (with whirlpool tubs, naturally), and huge private sunbathing areas that are completely shielded from anyone. Each has three bedrooms and bathrooms, and a large living room overlooking the lido/pool deck. These units have their own private elevator and private stairway, can be combined to create a large, 3,030 sq.-ft (281-sq.-meter) "house."

There are many suites (the smallest of which measures 290 sq. ft/27 sq. meters) in several different configurations; two are housed in a pod atop the ship, and some overlook the stern, while others are in the forward part of the ship. All are lavishly furnished, although closet space in some of the smaller units is tight.

Although they are nicely furnished and quite well equipped, the standard outside-view and interior (no view) cabins are quite small, particularly when occupied by three or four persons. Some cabins have inter-connecting doors (good for families with children), and many cabins have third and fourth person pull-down berths or trundle beds.

A small room service menu is available (all items are at extra cost, and a 15 percent service charge and a gratuity are added to your account). Bottled water is placed in each cabin (but a charge will be made to your account if you open the bottle).

BERLITZ'S RATINGS

	Possible	Achieved
Ship	500	NYR
Accommodation	200	NYR
Food	400	NYR
Service	400	NYR
Entertainment	100	NYR
Cruise	400	NYR

DINING: With what NCL calls "Freestyle Dining," you can choose which restaurant you would like to eat in, at what time, and with whom (there are no assigned dining rooms, tables or seats). All restaurants and eateries are non-smoking. NCL's dress code states that: "jeans, T-shirts, tank tops and bare feet are not permitted in restaurants."

Although there are three principal dining rooms, there are also a number of other themed eating establishments, giving a wide range of choice – though some cost extra. It would be wise to plan in advance, particularly for dinner. There are two entire decks of restaurants to choose from, involving 10 different restaurants and eateries.

● A first main dining room, Venetian, offering traditional six-course dining (open 5.30pm–midnight).

● A second main dining room, Aqua, offering traditional six-course dining (open 5.30pm–midnight).

● A third main dining room, Impressions, offering lighter cuisine (open 5.30pm–midnight).

● Bamboo, a Japanese/Thai/Chinese restaurant, with 193 seats, with sit-up sushi bar, tempura bar, show galley, and separate room with a teppanyaki grill.

● Le Bistro, a French restaurant with 66 seats, featuring Le Bistro nouvelle cuisine

● Blue Lagoon, a food court-style eatery with 88 seats, serving hamburgers, fish & chips, pot pies and wok fast dishes.

● Garden Café, an indoor/outdoor self-serve buffet eatery including "action stations" featuring made-to-order omelets, waffles, fruit, soups, ethnic specialties and pasta dishes.

● Salsas, a Spanish Tapas eatery and bar with a selection of hot and cold Tapas dishes and authentic entertainment.

● La Trattoria (located inside the indoor/outdoor buffet), featuring pasta, pizza and other popular Italian fare.

● Cagney's Steak House, arranged around the second level of the central atrium and incorporating a performance stage and a large movie screen, and serving US prime steaks and seafood.

Other eating/drinking spots include the Red Lion (an English pub for draft beer and perhaps a game of darts); Havanas, a cigar and cognac lounge; Cascades, an atrium lobby café and bar (for hot and frozen coffees, teas and pastries); a Beer Garden (for grilled foods); a Gelato Bar (for ice cream); and a Gym and Spa Bar (for health food snacks and drinks).

OTHER COMMENTS: *Norwegian Dawn* (sister to *Norwegian Star*, which debuted in 2001) was constructed in 64 blocks. It is the latest state-of-the-art vessel for Norwegian Cruise Line, and features a "pod" propulsion system. The two-pod propulsion system is powered by electric motors instead of conventional rudders and propellers in the latest configuration of high-tech propulsion systems; this gives the ship greater maneuverability, while reducing required machinery space and vibration at the stern. A large structure, which is located forward of the funnel houses a children's center, and, one deck above, the six "villa" suites.

Sports facilities include a jogging track, golf driving range, basketball and volleyball courts, as well as four levels of sunbathing decks.

Other facilities include a large Dawn Club Casino gaming area (with separate VIP/Club rooms), a Cyber Café (with 18 computer stations and internet connection), a 1,150-seat show lounge with main floor and two balcony levels, a 3,000-book library, card room, writing and study room, business center, karaoke lounge, internet café, conference and meeting rooms, and a retail shopping complex measuring 20,000 sq. ft (1,800 sq. meters).

Health devotees should enjoy the two-deck-high El Dorado health spa complex (operated by the Hawaii-based Mandara Spa), located at the stern of the ship (with large ocean-view windows on three sides). There are many facilities and services to pamper you (almost all at extra charge), including Thai massage (in the spa, outdoors on deck, in your cabin or on your private balcony). In addition, there is an indoor lap pool (measur-

ing 45 ft/14 meters), hydrotherapy pool, aromatherapy and wellness centers, and mud treatment room.

A good deal of space is devoted to children's facilities (the T-Rex Kids' Center and Teen Club) – all tucked well away from adult recreation areas. Children of all ages will get to play in a superb wet 'n' wild space-themed water park (complete with large pool, water slide, and paddle pool). They also get their own dedicated cinema (DVD movies are featured all day long), a jungle gym, painting area, and computer center. Even the toilets are at a special low height. Teens, too, are well catered for, and get their own cinema (with DVD movies), discotheque with dance floor, and their own whirlpool (hot) tub. Plus there's all the fun and facilities of a large childcare center (open 24 hours a day). There's even a room full of cots for toddlers to use for sleepovers, and even the toilets are at a special low height.

With so many dining choices (some of which cost extra) to accommodate the tastes of an eclectic mix of nationalities, it really depends on how much you are prepared to spend as to what your final cruise and dining experience will be like. To make the most of your cruise vacation, you *will* need to plan where you want to eat well in advance, and make the necessary reservations, or you may be disappointed.

More choices, including more dining options, add up to a very attractive vacation package, particularly suitable for families with children, in a very contemporary floating leisure center that really does provide ample facilities for you to have an enjoyable time. The dress code is casual – very casual (no jacket and tie needed, although you are welcome to dress formally if you so wish).

You should note that while the initial cruise fare seems very reasonable, the extra costs and charges soon mount up if you want to indulge in more than the basics. Although service levels and finesse are sometimes inconsistent, the level of hospitality is very good – made so much better and brighter by the addition of a great number of Asian female staff rather than the surly and inconsistent (Caribbean Basin) staff still found aboard some of the smaller NCL ships.

Despite the company's name (Norwegian Cruise Line), there's almost nothing Norwegian about this product, except for some of the ship's senior officers. The staff, incidentally, includes many Southeast Asians who already have service experience aboard parent company Star Cruises' big ships.

The ship is full of revenue centers, however, which are designed to help you part with even more money than what is paid for in the price of your cruise ticket. Cruising aboard large ships such as this has become increasingly an onboard revenue-based product. You can expect to be subjected to a stream of flyers advertising daily art auctions, "designer" watches, "inch of gold/silver" and other promotions, while "artworks" for auction are strewn throughout the ship.

Gratuities for staff (cabin attendants, dining room waiters, etc.) are automatically added to your onboard account at $10 per person, per day (you can, however, reduce or otherwise amend these if necessary before you disembark). In addition, a 15 percent gratuity is added to all bar and spa treatment accounts. The score and rating for this ship are expected to be similar (but not identical) to that of close sister *Norwegian Star*. The onboard currency is the US dollar.

WEAK POINTS: Standing in line for embarkation, disembarkation, shore tenders and for self-serve buffet meals is an inevitable aspect of cruising aboard all large ships – even those designated as "Freestyle." Although the suites and junior suites are quite spacious, the standard interior (no view) and outside-view cabins are very small when compared to those of other major cruise lines such as Carnival or Celebrity, particularly when occupied by three or four persons (the bathrooms, however, *are of* quite a decent size, and boast large shower enclosures). The hustling for passengers to attend art auctions is both aggressive and annoying.

Reaching room service can be an exercise in frustration. Communication (particularly between the many new Asian staff and passengers) is weak. Mindless "art auctions" are a real turn-off to a Hawaiian cruise.

HOW SYSTEMS WORK

Radar
Radar is one of the most important discoveries ever made for the development of navigational aids, providing a picture of all solid objects in a range selected by the navigator, which is from a half-mile (800 meters) to a 72-mile (116-km) radius. Its greatest asset is as an aid to collision avoidance with other ships, although it is of value in finding a position at a distance when navigational marks or charted coastlines are within its range.

Engine Telegraph
These automatic signaling devices are used to communicate orders between the bridge and the engine room. There may be three, one on the bridge and one on each bridgewing.

Bow Thruster
This small two-way handle is used to control the bow thrusters, powerful engines in the bow that push the ship away from the dockside without tugs. Some new ships may also have thrusters positioned at the stern.

Rudder Angle Indicator
This device is normally positioned in front of, and above, the quartermaster. It provides both the commanding officer and the quartermaster with a constant readout of the degrees of rudder angle, either to port (left) or starboard (right).

VHF Radio
This is a radio receiver and transmitter, operating on VHF (Very High Frequency) with a "line-of-sight" range. It is used for communicating with other ships, pilots, port authorities, and so on.

Radio Direction Finder
This operates on radio waves, enabling its operator to take bearings of shore radio stations. By crossing two or more bearings, you find the ship's position.

Depth Indicator
This equipment (which is an echo-sounder) provides a ship with a constant digital monitor readout, together with a printed chart.

Course Recorder
This records and prints all courses followed by the ship at all times.

Clearview Screen
This device makes simple but effective use of centrifugal force, where instead of an automobile-type windshield wiper, a ship has circular screens that rotate at high speed to clear rain or sea spray away, providing those on the bridge with the best possible view in even the worst weather.

Engine Speed Indicators
These provide a reading of the number of revolutions per minute being generated by the engines. Each engine has a separate indicator, giving the speed in forward or reverse.

Facsimile Recorder
This special radio device is designed to receive meteorological and oceanographic maps, satellite pictures, and other pertinent weather information transmitted by maritime broadcast stations throughout the world.

Norwegian Dream
★★★ +

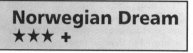

Large Ship:	.50,760 tons	Cabin Current:	.110 volts
Lifestyle:	.Standard	Elevators:	.11
Cruise Line:	.Norwegian Cruise Line	Casino (gaming tables):	.Yes
Former Names:	.*Dreamward*	Slot Machines:	.Yes
Builder:	.Chantiers de l'Atlantique (France)	Swimming Pools (outdoors):	.2
Original Cost:	.$240 million	Swimming Pools (indoors):	.0
Entered Service:	.Dec 1992	Whirlpools:	.4
Registry:	.The Bahamas	Fitness Center:	.Yes
Length (ft/m):	.754.0/229.80	Sauna/Steam Room:	.Yes/No
Beam (ft/m):	.93.5/28.50	Massage:	.Yes
Draft (ft/m):	.22.3/6.80	Self-Service Launderette:	.No
Propulsion/Propellers:	.diesel (18,480 kW)/2	Dedicated Cinema/Seats:	.No
Passenger Decks:	.10	Library:	.Yes
Total Crew:	.700	Classification Society:	.Det Norske Veritas

Passengers
(lower beds/all berths): 1,732/2,156
Passenger Space Ratio
(lower beds/all berths): 29.3/23.5
Crew/Passenger Ratio
(lower beds/all berths): 2.5/3.1
Navigation Officers: ....Norwegian
Cabins (total): 865
Size Range (sq ft/m): 139.9–349.8/ 13.0–32.5
Cabins (outside view): 695
Cabins (interior/no view): 170
Cabins (for one person): 0
Cabins (with private balcony): 48
Cabins (wheelchair accessible): 6
(+ 30 for hearing-impaired)

OVERALL SCORE: 1,381 (OUT OF A POSSIBLE 2,000 POINTS)

ACCOMMODATION: There are 15 grades of cabins. Most cabins have outside views, wood-trimmed cabinetry and warm décor, with multi-colored soft furnishings, but there is almost no drawer space (the closets have open shelves, however), so take minimal clothing. All cabins have a sitting area, but this takes away any free space, making movement pretty tight. The bathrooms are small but practical, although there is little space for storage of personal toiletry items. Bottled water is placed in each cabin (but you pay for it once you open the bottle).

There are 18 suites (12 with a private entrance and a small, private balcony), each with separate living room and bedroom, fine quality cabinetry, and lots of closet and drawer space. Occupants of suites get "concierge" service, which provides extra personal attention. In addition, 16 suites and 70 cabins have inter-connecting doors – good for families cruising together, or perhaps for those that want separate "his and hers" living spaces. There are several cabins specially equipped for the hearing-impaired. Note that all cabins on the port side of the ship are designated non-smoking.

DINING: The two main full-service dining rooms are: The Terraces (arguably the nicest, with windows that look out over the ship's tiered aft decks), and the Four Seasons (with approximately 450 seats), located amidships. All are non-smoking and feature the same menu and food, in an open seating, come when you want (and with whom) arrangement (NCL calls it "Freestyle Din-

BERLITZ'S RATINGS		
	Possible	Achieved
Ship	500	377
Accommodation	200	145
Food	400	237
Service	400	282
Entertainment	100	73
Cruise	400	267

ing"). The Four Seasons is the largest, and has some prime tables at ocean-view window seats in a section that extend from the ship's port and starboard sides in half-moon shapes (nice for lunch, but it's either dark or the curtains are drawn for dinner). However, this ship was not built with this kind of "free for all" dining arrangements in mind. Consequently, the flow, timing, and successfulness of this concept aboard this ship simply doesn't work well, if at all. The dress code states that: "jeans, T-shirts, tank tops and bare feet are not permitted in restaurants."

In addition to the two principal dining rooms, there are also a number of other themed eating establishments, giving a wide range of choice – although it would be wise to plan in advance – particularly for dinner. Italian fare is served in the Trattoria (formerly the Sun Terraces), which overlooks the aft swimming pool. There is also The Bistro, which features informal evening dining at no extra charge in more intimate surroundings. A 200-seat Sports Bar (typically open between 6am and 1am) features breakfast, luncheon, dinner, and snacks throughout the day. There's also a poolside pizzeria, and a small coffee lounge.

While "Freestyle" dining works best aboard the newer, larger ships in the fleet, aboard *Norwegian Dream* and sister ship *Norwegian Wind* it simply creates food outlets instead of restaurants, and causes untold confusion. Although the various menus make meals sound appetizing, overall, the food provided is rather non-memorable fare that lacks taste and presentation quality, and is often overcooked. There is a reasonably decent selection of breads, rolls, and fruits, although the selection of cheeses is poor. The wine list is quite decent and well put together, with moderate prices, although you won't find any good vintage wines. There are many types of beer (including some on draught in the popular Sports Bar & Grill). The cutlery is very ordinary (there are no fish knives). There is no formal afternoon tea, although you can make your own from various beverage stations. The service is, on the whole, adequate, nothing more, and proves that good staffs that can communicate well are hard to find.

You can eat breakfast or lunch in any dining room when it's "open seating." A lavish "chocoholics" buffet is featured once each cruise – this is a firm favorite among Norwegian Cruise Line's repeat passengers.

OTHER COMMENTS: Built first (its sister ship is *Norwegian Wind*), this vessel has a fairly handsome profile (despite a large, square funnel) that was better balanced before it underwent a "chop and stretch" operation in spring 1998. A completely new mid-section was added, and the funnel was adapted so that it could be "folded" over to allow the ship topass under the low bridges on Germany's Kiel Canal. Included in the 131-ft (40-meter) mid-section were 251 new passengers cabins and 50 crew cabins, together with several new or enlarged public rooms (although there simply are not enough) including a 60-seat conference center. Some innovative features were incorporated in the original design, and these have been kept and enhanced. The passenger flow is generally good – indeed, the ship seems to absorb passengers quite well for much of the time, except at peak traffic times around meal times.

However, following the "stretch" its exterior shape is now not as handsome. The lifeboats are inboard. There is a blue rubber-covered wrap-around promenade deck outdoors. The tiered pool deck is neat, as are the multi-deck aft sun terraces and all the fore and aft connecting exterior stairways.

The overall exterior design emphasizes a clever and extensive use of large windows that create a sense of open spaces, although the interior design provides many smaller public rooms rather than the large hangers found aboard so many other ships. However, there is no big atrium lobby, as one might expect. The pastel interior colors used are quite soothing, and it is considered by many to be a pretty ship inside. The entrance lobby is not at all attractive, and feels rather confined for a ship of this size.

This ship has proven highly successful for Norwegian Cruise Line's younger, active sports-minded passengers (when the ship operates Caribbean itineraries), and provides a good alternative to the larger ships and their larger passenger numbers, although there are plenty of other passengers to keep you company.

The ship is full of revenue centers, however, designed to part you from your money. You can expect to be subjected to a stream of flyers advertising daily art auctions, "designer" watches, "inch of gold/silver" and other promotions, while "artworks" for auction are strewn throughout the ship.

Gratuities for staff (cabin attendants, dining room waiters, etc) are automatically added to your onboard account at $10 per person, per day (you can, however, reduce or otherwise amend these if necessary before you disembark). In addition, a 15 percent gratuity is added to all bar and spa treatment accounts. The onboard currency is the US dollar.

WEAK POINTS: Standing in line for embarkation, disembarkation, shore tenders and for self-serve buffet meals is an inevitable aspect of cruising aboard all large ships. The hustling for passengers to attend art auctions is very aggressive and annoying, as is the constant bombardment for revenue activities and the daily junk mail that arrives at one's cabin door. The room service menu is still poor and could be improved. The outdoor stairways are numerous and confusing. Getting from the ship's fore to aft areas on some of the decks is confusing and the layout is thus rather disjointed. The carpeted steel interior stairwell steps are quite tinny. When the ship was "stretched" it reduced the amount of outdoor space per passenger, and this is reflected in increased density around the pools. There simply are not enough public rooms to absorb the increase in passengers well.

Norwegian Majesty
★★★ +

Large Ship:	.40,876 tons	Total Crew: 620

Large Ship: ....40,876 tons
Lifestyle: ....Standard
Cruise Line: ......Norwegian Cruise Line
Former Names: ....*Royal Majesty*
Builder: ....Kvaerner Masa-Yards
X(Finland)
Original Cost: ....$229 million
Entered Service: ....Sept 1992/Nov 1997
Registry: ....The Bahamas
Length (ft/m): 680.0/207.20
Beam (ft/m): 90.5/27.60
Draft (ft/m): 20.3/6.20
Propulsion/Propellers: ....diesel
(21,120 kW)/2
Passenger Decks: 9

Total Crew: 620
Passengers
(lower beds/all berths): 1,460/1,790
Passenger Space Ratio
(lower beds/all berths): 27.9/22.8
Crew/Passenger Ratio
(lower beds/all berths): 2.0/2.5
Navigation Officers: ....Norwegian
Cabins (total): 730
Size Range (sq ft/m): 118.4–374.5/
11.0–34.8
Cabins (outside view): 481
Cabins (interior/no view): 249
Cabins (for one person): 0
Cabins (with private balcony): 0

Cabins (wheelchair accessible): 7
Cabin Current: ....110 and 220 volts
Elevators: 6
Casino (gaming tables): ....Yes
Slot Machines: ....Yes
Swimming Pools (outdoors): 2
Swimming Pools (indoors): 0
Whirlpools: 3
Fitness Center: ....Yes
Sauna/Steam Room: ....Yes/No
Massage: ....Yes
Self-Service Launderette: ....No
Dedicated Cinema/Seats: Yes/100
Library: ....Yes
Classification Society: ...Lloyd's Register

OVERALL SCORE: 1,386 (OUT OF A POSSIBLE 2,000 POINTS)

ACCOMMODATION: There are 22 different price grades – a bewildering choice, and too many for a ship of this size. The suites have concierge service and extra goodies such as late afternoon snacks and hors d'oeuvre items. Although they cannot be considered large, they are quite well equipped, and come with VCRs as well as televisions. Bottled water is placed in each cabin (but a charge will be made if you open the bottle).

Almost all other outside-view and interior (no view) cabins are on the small side, but quite comfortable. The closets are really small, so suitcases have to be stored under the bed to keep them out of the way (this is also the best place for shoes). The bathrooms are a little tight, although there is a generous amount of room in the shower enclosures. A number of cabins are designated for non-smokers. Many cabins on Norway and Viking Decks have obstructed views; so check the deck plans carefully.

DINING: With what NCL's "Freestyle Dining," you choose which restaurant you wish to eat in, at what time, and with whom (there are no assigned dining rooms, tables or seats). All restaurants and eateries are non-smoking. NCL's dress code states that: "jeans, T-shirts, tank tops and bare feet are not permitted in restaurants."

Although there are two principal dining rooms, there are also a number of other themed eating establishments, giving a wide range of choice – although it would be wise to plan in advance, particularly for dinner.

The main dining rooms: Seven Seas, with 636 seats,

BERLITZ'S RATINGS

	Possible	Achieved
Ship	500	395
Accommodation	200	156
Food	400	246
Service	400	255
Entertainment	100	69
Cruise	400	265

and the more intimate Four Seasons (added when the ship was "stretched" in 1999) with 266 seats. However, they are quite noisy and the tables are close together, which means that correct service is difficult. The food, menu, creativity and service are basically quite sound, with a good selection of breads and bread rolls, but the choice of cheeses and fruits is limited (almost all cheeses are American). Some dinners are "themed" in the evening, a feature that has been popular with NCL passengers for years.

There is also a 56-seat Le Bistro Restaurant, which serves Italian- and Continental-style cuisine for alternative dinners in an intimate environment (no reservations are needed).

For casual, self-serve meals, the Café Royale is a small buffet dining spot with 112 seats (not nearly enough for the number of passengers now carried). It is open for breakfast, lunch and snacks. An outdoor grill (oddly named the Piazza San Marco) serves fast food items, including pizza (this can also be delivered to your cabin). A small coffee bar/lounge in an open passageway (street café) serves a variety of coffees, coffee-flavored drinks, "flaming" specialty drinks, and teas.

Overall, the food provided is rather unmemorable fare that lacks taste and presentation quality. The menus, too, are uninspiring. There's a reasonably good selection of breads, rolls, cheeses and fruits, however. The wine list is quite decent, and is well arranged, with moderate prices, although you won't find good vintage wines. The cutlery is very ordinary (there are no fish knives). There is no formal afternoon tea, although you can make your own from various beverage stations. The service is, on the whole, adequate, nothing more, and proves that good staffs that can communicate well are difficult to find.

OTHER COMMENTS: This smart, stylish, contemporary cruise ship, originally built for the now-defunct Majesty Cruise Line, now has an improved profile and is generally a well-designed vessel (its original lines were those of a Baltic ferry, albeit with a rounded bow, and not at all handsome). The ship underwent a $53.3 million, 110-ft (34-meter) "chop and stretch" and refurbishment operation in 1999, which added more cabins, new public rooms, much more open deck space and two new elevators, while all other existing public spaces were refreshed. For a real "wind-in-the-hair" experience, passengers can actually stand at the very bow of this ship (weather permitting) as all the mooring ropes and winches are on the deck below.

The open deck and sunbathing space has been improved (there are now two swimming pools, plus a splash pool for children). The ship's exterior profile is sleeker and more aerodynamic. Cutting the ship in half, however, required some ingenuity, for, unlike *Norwegian Dream* and *Norwegian Wind*, it was never designed for such a splicing operation.

Inside, it is quite a pretty ship, and is tastefully appointed, with lots of wood paneling and chrome/copper accents, reasonably discreet lighting, soothing colors, no glitz and almost no neon lighting. Wide passageways provide a feeling of inner spaciousness. The ship has a nice touch of elegance and open walking areas provide a fine feel to it. The circular lobby is bright and classical in appearance.

There are several public rooms, bars and lounges. The Royal Observatory observation lounge has fine views, but is sometimes used as a karaoke lounge. The show lounge, while comfortable, is poorly designed, with 14 pillars obstructing the sight lines. Families with children will find "Kid's Korner" a useful place to deposit young ones for a full program of activities.

This ship will provide you with a comfortable cruise experience in warm, fairly elegant surroundings, with generally good food (and plenty of it), and a modicum of hospitality from a reasonably friendly crew, although there is little service finesse. The ship is full of revenue centers, however, which are designed to help part you from your money. You can expect to be subjected to a stream of flyers advertising daily art auctions, "designer" watches and other promotions, while "artworks" for auction are strewn throughout the ship.

Gratuities for staff (cabin attendants, dining room waiters, etc.) are automatically added to your onboard account at $10 per person, per day (you can, however, reduce or otherwise amend these if necessary before you disembark). In addition, a 15 percent gratuity is added to all bar and spa treatment accounts. The onboard currency is the US dollar.

WEAK POINTS: There are several repetitive announcements for revenue-producing activities, and the increased amount of squeezing for onboard revenue makes a cruise less enjoyable than it should be. The hustling for passengers to attend art auctions is aggressive and annoying, as is the constant bombardment for revenue activities and the daily junk mail that arrives at one's cabin door. The spa facilities are poor and basic. There are no cushioned pads for the plastic deck chairs. The buffet area is simply too small for the extra number of passengers carried (while the ship was expanded, the buffet and seating areas were not). While adequate for 3- and 4-day cruises, the ship is only moderately comfortable for 7-day cruises. Standing in line for embarkation, disembarkation, shore tenders and for self-serve buffet meals is inevitable aboard all large ships.

Norwegian Sea
★★★ +

Removed 2006

Large Ship:	42,276 tons	Passengers		Cabin Current:	110 volts
Lifestyle:	Standard	(lower beds/all berths):	1,510/1,798	Elevators:	6
Cruise Line:	Norwegian Cruise Line	Passenger Space Ratio		Casino (gaming tables):	Yes
Former Names:	Seaward	(lower beds/all berths):	28.0/23.5	Slot Machines:	Yes
Builder:	Wartsila (Finland)	Crew/Passenger Ratio		Swimming Pools (outdoors):	2
Original Cost:	$120 million	(lower beds/all berths):	2.3/2.8	Swimming Pools (indoors):	0
Entered Service:	June 1988	Navigation Officers:	Norwegian	Whirlpools:	2
Registry:	The Bahamas	Cabins (total):	755	Fitness Center:	Yes
Length (ft/m):	708.6/216.0	Size Range (sq ft/m):	109.7–269.1/	Sauna/Steam Room:	Yes/No
Beam (ft/m):	95.1/29.0		10.2–25.0	Massage:	Yes
Draft (ft/m):	22.9/7.0	Cabins (outside view):	512	Self-Service Launderette:	No
Propulsion/Propellers:	diesel	Cabins (interior/no view):	243	Dedicated Cinema/Seats:	No
	(21,120 kW)/2	Cabins (for one person):	0	Library:	No
Passenger Decks:	9	Cabins (with private balcony):	0	Classification Society:	Det Norske
Total Crew:	680	Cabins (wheelchair accessible):	4		Veritas

OVERALL SCORE: 1,382 (OUT OF A POSSIBLE 2,000 POINTS)

ACCOMMODATION: There are 16 cabin categories. This ship was built before balcony cabins came into vogue – so there are none. The cabins are of average size for a standard cruise ship (which translates to " a bit cramped for two") although they are quite tastefully appointed and comfortable, with warm, pastel colors, bright soft furnishings and a touch of art deco styling; however, the walls and ceilings are plain and simple. Audio channels are available via the TV set, although the picture cannot be turned off. The bathrooms are efficient units that are quite well designed, although they are basic; hairdryers (they are weak) are included in all bathrooms. Bottled water is placed in each cabin (but a charge will be made to your account if you open the bottle).

If you book a suite or one of two upper-grade cabins, you'll get a little more space, a lounge area with table and sofa that converts into another bed (good for families), European duvets, and a refrigerator (top three categories only). The bathrooms also have a bathtub, shower and retractable clothesline.

DINING: With NCL's "Freestyle Dining," you can choose which restaurant you would like to eat in, at what time, and with whom (there are no assigned dining rooms, tables or seats). All restaurants and eateries are non-smoking. NCL's dress code states that: "jeans, T-shirts, tank tops and bare feet are not permitted in restaurants."

Although there are two principal dining rooms, there are also a number of other themed eating establishments, giving a wide range of choice – although it would be

BERLITZ'S RATINGS		
	Possible	Achieved
Ship	500	365
Accommodation	200	148
Food	400	237
Service	400	284
Entertainment	100	74
Cruise	400	274

wise to plan in advance, particularly for dinner.

There are two main dining rooms: Four Seasons, with 372 seats, and Seven Seas, with 476 seats. They are both comfortable, and have pastel décor. The cuisine, for a mass-market ship, ranges from adequate to reasonably good. Vegetables (few green ones are used) tend to be overcooked. Fish and poultry items are good. Meat is disappointing. The emphasis is on Tex-Mex cuisine, with a wide choice of hot and spicy courses.

There are alternative dining spots. For casual breakfast and lunch, there's the Big Apple Café (436 seats), which has indoor and outdoor seating. There's also the intimate 82-seat Le Bistro, open for informal dinners; and Gatsby's is a popular wine bar that has a good wine and champagne list. Le Bistro and Gatsby's are both located high in the ship and have large ocean-view picture windows. The selection of wines is good, but the glasses are small. The breakfast and luncheon buffets are poor and need more variety and better ingredients.

Overall, the food provided is rather unmemorable fare that lacks taste and presentation quality. The menus, too, are uninspiring. There's a reasonably decent selection of breads, rolls, cheeses and fruits, however. The wine list is quite decent and well arranged, together with moderate prices, although you won't find any good vintage wines. The cutlery is very ordinary (there are no fish knives). There is no formal afternoon tea, although you can make your own from various beverage stations. The service is adequate, nothing more, and proves that good staffs that can communicate well are difficult to find.

OTHER COMMENTS: This angular yet reasonably attractive vessel has a contemporary European cruise-ferry profile with a sharply raked bow and sleek mast and funnel added. There is a full wrap-around promenade deck outdoors (although it is a plain steel deck, painted nautical blue).

This ship is quite well designed, with generally sound passenger flow and no major areas of congestion, and an abundance of public rooms and open interior spaces, many with high ceilings. The interior décor is designed to remind you of sea and sky by stressing the colors of coral, blue and mauve. Although the hallways and stairways are plain, two glass-walled stairways provide good connection with sea and sky. There's a good gymnasium/fitness center for those that want to work their muscles; it is located around the mast and is accessible only from the outside deck (not good when it rains).

The Crystal Court lobby is two decks high and is pleasing without being overwhelming, although at times it appears quite cluttered. It has a tube-shaped crystal and water sculpture and seatback-less seating around its perimeter.

The 770-seat theater-show lounge (called "Cabaret") provides large-scale dazzle and sizzle shows with lots of energy and volume (including a shortened version of the musical *Grease*), although 12 thick pillars obstruct the sight lines from many seats. There is a large nightclub (again there are several pillars obstructing sight lines), and a disco (correctly called "Boomers"). For those seeking a more intimate lounge, the mahogany-paneled Oscar's Lounge is the place to go.

This ship will provide a cruise in good taste for first-time cruise passengers who want to have fun in comfortable surroundings, at a sensible, competitive price. If you like sports bars, country and western music, hoedowns and amateurish participation games, this ship will prove a lot of fun.

It is full of revenue centers, however, designed to part you from your money. You can expect to be subjected to a stream of flyers advertising daily art auctions, "designer" watches and other promotions, while "artworks" for auction are strewn throughout the ship.

Gratuities for staff (cabin attendants, dining room waiters, etc) are added to your onboard account at $10 per person, per day (you can reduce or otherwise amend these if necessary before you disembark). In addition, a 15 percent gratuity is added to all bar and spa treatment accounts. The onboard currency is the US dollar.

WEAK SPOTS: Standing in line for embarkation, disembarkation, shore tenders and for self-serve buffet meals is an inevitable aspect of cruising aboard all large ships. The open decks are cluttered and largely unclean. Food buffets (very poor presentation, quality of ingredients). Food service and supervision needs work. The hustling for passengers to attend art auctions is very aggressive and annoying, as is the constant bombardment for revenue activities and the daily junk mail that arrives at one's cabin door. Badly dented and scuffed panels in the accommodation hallways are unattractive. The steps on the stairways are tinny. There is no library. The constant background music in the hallways is irritating. There is too much use of synthetic turf on the upper outdoors decks (this gets very soggy when wet). There are no cushioned pads for the deck lounge chairs. The cruise staff is very young and rather amateurish.

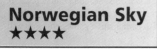

Removed 2006

Norwegian Sky
★★★★

Large Ship:	....	.77,104 tons
Lifestyle:	....	.Standard
Cruise Line:	......	Norwegian Cruise Line
Former Names:	....	.none
Builder:	....	.Lloyd Werft (Germany)
Original Cost:	....	.$332 million
Entered Service:	....	.Aug 1999
Registry:	....	.The Bahamas
Length (ft/m):	....	.853.0/260.00
Beam (ft/m):	....	.105.8/32.25
Draft (ft/m):	....	.26.2/8.00
Propulsion/Propellers:	.....	diesel-electric (50,000 kW)/2
Passenger Decks:	....	.12
Total Crew:	....	.800
Passengers		
(lower beds/all berths):	.....	.2,002/2,450
Passenger Space Ratio		
(lower beds/all berths):	....	.38.5/31.4
Crew/Passenger Ratio		
(lower beds/all berths):	....	.2.6/3.2
Navigation Officers:	....	.Norwegian
Cabins (total):	....	.1,001
Size Range (sq ft/m):	.....	.120.5–488.6/ 11.2–45.4
Cabins (outside view):	....	.574
Cabins (interior/no view):	....	.427
Cabins (for one person):	....	.0
Cabins (with private balcony):	....	.252
Cabins (wheelchair accessible):	....	.6
Cabin Current:	....	.110 volts
Elevators:	....	.12
Casino (gaming tables):	....	.Yes
Slot Machines:	....	.Yes
Swimming Pools (outdoors):	....	.2
Swimming Pools (indoors):	....	.0
Whirlpools:	....	.5
Fitness Center:	....	.Yes
Sauna/Steam Room:	....	.Yes/Yes
Massage:	....	.Yes
Self-Service Launderette:	....	.No
Dedicated Cinema/Seats:	....	.No
Library:	....	.Yes
Classification Society:	.....	.Germanischer Lloyd

OVERALL SCORE: 1,507 (OUT OF A POSSIBLE 2,000 POINTS)

ACCOMMODATION: There are 26 categories: 17 for outside-view suites and cabins, and nine for interior (no view) cabins. All of the standard outside-view and interior (no view) cabins have two lower beds that can convert to a queen-sized bed, a small lounge area with sofa and table, and a decent amount of closet space, but very little drawer space, and the cabins themselves are disappointingly small. Over 200 outside-view cabins each have their own private balcony. Each cabin has a small vanity/writing desk, color television (typically CNN, ESPN, and TNT), personal safe, climate control, and a laptop computer connection socket. Audio can be obtained only through the TV set. Bottled water is placed in each cabin (but a charge will be made to your account if you open the bottle).

The largest accommodation is found in four owner's suites, each of which has a hot tub, large teak table, two chairs and two deck lounge chairs outside on a huge, very private, forward-facing teakwood floor balcony just under the ship's navigation bridge, with large floor-to-ceiling windows. Each suite has a separate lounge and bedroom. The lounge has a large dining table and four chairs, two two-person sofas, large television, DVD/CD player, coffee table, queen-sized pull-down Murphy's bed, guest closet, writing desk, wet bar with two bar stools, refrigerator and sink, several cupboards for glasses, and several drawers and other cupboards for storage. The bedroom, which has sliding wood half-doors that look into the lounge, has a queen-sized bed (with European duvet) under a leaf-glass chandelier, vanity desk, television, walk-in closet with plenty of

BERLITZ'S RATINGS

	Possible	Achieved
Ship	500	402
Accommodation	200	152
Food	400	287
Service	400	284
Entertainment	100	78
Cruise	400	304

hanging rail space, five open shelves and large personal safe. The white-tiled bathroom, although not large, has a full-size bathtub with retractable clothesline above, separate shower enclosure with glass doors, deep washbasin, and toiletries cabinets.

There are also 10 Junior Suites – each of which has a private teak decked balcony; these suites face aft in a secluded position and overlook the ship's wash. They have almost the same facilities as found in the owner's suites, with the exception of the outdoor hot tub, and the fact that there is less space.

DINING: With NCL's "Freestyle Dining," you can choose which restaurant you would like to eat in, at what time, and with whom (there are no assigned dining rooms, tables or seats). All restaurants and eateries are non-smoking. NCL's dress code states that "jeans, T-shirts, tank tops and bare feet are not permitted in restaurants."

Although there are two principal dining rooms, there are also a number of other themed eating establishments, giving a wide range of choice – although it would be wise to plan in advance, particularly for dinner.

The main dining rooms are Four Seasons, with 564 seats, and Seven Seas, with 604 seats. Both are non-smoking. Tables for four, six or eight have an open seating "come when you want" arrangement.

A third, smaller dining room, Horizons Restaurant, has Italian cuisine and 84 seats. It is available as an à la carte dining option (it has pleasant half-moon alcoves and several tables for two), for which there is an extra charge of $10 per person (including gratuity).

Other dining options include an 84-seat "Le Bistro" alternative dining spot for some very fine meals (including such desserts as flaming cherries jubilee and chocolate fondue), and "Ciao Chow," a casual Italian/Southeast Asian eatery. Both are by reservation, and each incurs a $10 per person cover charge (including gratuity).

There is also a sports bar and grill (complete with a wall of television screens and live satellite-televised sports action), a pizzeria, Gatsby's wine bar (with complimentary tapas), a champagne and caviar bar and an ice-cream bar.

Overall, the food provided is rather unmemorable fare that lacks taste and presentation quality; the menus, too, are uninspiring. There is a reasonably good selection of breads, rolls, cheeses and fruits. The wine list is quite decent and well arranged, with moderate prices, although you won't find many good vintage wines. The cutlery is very ordinary (there are no fish knives). There is no formal afternoon tea, although you can make your own from various beverage stations. The service is, on the whole, adequate, nothing more, and proves that good staffs that can communicate well are difficult to find.

OTHER COMMENTS: This ship was created from the hull of what was to be *Costa Olympia* (a sister to *Costa Victoria*), which was purchased for $40 million but not completed when the shipyard went into bankruptcy. Norwegian Cruise Line was thus able to build this ship in about 20 months, or about two-thirds of the time it would normally have taken. Some parts of the ship differ from the original; for example, the navigation bridge is located one deck lower than aboard *Costa Victoria*.

The amount of outdoor space is very good, and the extra wide pool deck (the extra width created from port and starboard "overhangs" that resulted from balconies being added to cabins on two decks below), with its two swimming pools and four Jacuzzi tubs. On the "catwalk" deck above the pools, there is an electric "skymobile" beverage cart.

There is a two-level, 1,001-seat show lounge, with large proscenium stage for the high-energy dazzle and sizzle shows that NCL passengers enjoy. It has staged the first sea-going production of one of Cameron Mackintosh's musicals. However, the sight lines are obstructed from many seats by several slim pillars, and the sight lines in the balcony are blocked almost completely due to the fact that the safety rail is so poorly positioned.

A separate cabaret lounge, the black and white themed Checkers Lounge is equipped with what NCL states is the longest bar at sea, at 98 ft (30 meters) long. At present, however, this honor goes to *Aida*. Other features include a large casino, shopping arcade, children's playroom (there is also a splash pool in a prime open deck area forward atop ship), a video arcade, large

health/fitness spa – including an aerobics room and separate gymnasium (open 24 hours a day), and several treatment rooms.

Other facilities include a small conference room with an "Out of Africa" décor theme, library and beauty salon, Churchill's cigar smoking lounge (adjoining the Windjammer Bar) for cigars and cognac, and an Internet Café, with 14 computer terminals and coffee available from an adjacent bar. Those with a black belt in shopping might appreciate the fact that all the shops on board are run by Colombian Emeralds, and showcase a wide range of goods, from inexpensive to very expensive.

Sports fans will appreciate the large basketball/volleyball court, baseball-batting cage, golf-driving range, platform tennis, shuffleboard and table tennis facilities, and sports bar with 24-hour *live* satellite television coverage of sports events and major games. Joggers will find a wrap-around indoor/outdoor-jogging track.

With this ship, Norwegian Cruise Line has made an effort to provide more and better public room and entertainment facilities and options than previously, so you get a lot of ship for your money. *Norwegian Sky* tries to be all things to all people, and is a resort at sea. The ship certainly has more choices and options for eating than the smaller NCL vessels. The ship is full of revenue centers, however, designed to part you from your money. You can expect to be subjected to a stream of flyers advertising daily art auctions, "designer" watches and other promotions.

Gratuities for staff (cabin attendants, dining room waiters, etc) are automatically added to your onboard account at $10 per person, per day (you can, however, reduce or otherwise amend these if necessary before you disembark). In addition, a 15 percent gratuity is added to all bar and spa treatment accounts. The onboard currency is the US dollar.

WEAK POINTS: Standing in line for embarkation, disembarkation, shore tenders and for self-serve buffet meals is an inevitable aspect of cruising aboard all large ships. The hustling for passengers to attend art auctions is very aggressive and annoying, as is the constant bombardment for revenue activities and the daily junk mail that arrives at one's cabin door. There are too many announcements – particularly annoying are those that state what is already written in the daily program. Anyone in the Four Seasons dining room wanting to use the restroom must exit the dining room and go across the atrium to locate the nearest one. There is little connection to the sea from many public rooms. The ceilings in the cabins are very plain and uninteresting. The passenger hallways are extremely plain, boring, and void of artwork – in other words, they are very institutional, as are some of the stairwells. "Freestyle" disembarkation isn't.

Norwegian Star
★★★★

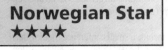

Large Ship: . . . . .91,740 tons	Passengers	Cabin Current: . . . . .110 AC
Lifestyle: . . . . .Standard	(lower beds/all berths): 2,244/4,080	Elevators: 12
Cruise Line: . . . . . .Norwegian Cruise Line	Passenger Space Ratio	Casino (gaming tables): . . . . .No
Former Names: . . . . .none	(lower beds/all berths): 40.8/22.4	Slot Machines: . . . . .No
Builder: . . . . .Meyer Werft (Germany)	Crew/Passenger Ratio	Swimming Pools (outdoors): 2
Original Cost: . . . .$400 million	(lower beds/all berths): 2.0/3.7	Swimming Pools (indoors): 1
Entered Service: . . . . .Dec 2001	Navigation Officers: . . . . . . .Scandinavian	Whirlpools: . . .4 (+ 1 children's whirlpool)
Registry: . . . . .Panama	Cabins (total): 1,122	Fitness Center: . . . . .Yes
Length (ft/m): 964.9/294.13	Size Range (sq ft/m): 142.0–3,030.0/	Sauna/Steam Room: . . . . .Yes/Yes
Beam (ft/m): 105.6/32.2	13.2–281.5	Massage: . . . . .Yes
Draft (ft/m): 26.9/8.2	Cabins (outside view): 787	Self-Service Launderette: . . . . .No
Propulsion/Propellers: . . .diesel-electric/2	Cabins (interior/no view): 363	Dedicated Cinema/Seats: Yes/151
azimuthing pods (19.5 MW each)	Cabins (for one person): 0	Library: . . . . .Yes
Passenger Decks: 12	Cabins (with private balcony): 509	Classification Society: Det Norske Veritas
Total Crew: 1,100	Cabins (wheelchair accessible): 20	

OVERALL SCORE: 1,522 (OUT OF A POSSIBLE 2,000 POINTS)

ACCOMMODATION: With 29 different price grades, this is a mix that includes something for everyone. There are 36 suites (including two of the very largest aboard any cruise ship); 372 "balcony-class" standard cabins with private balconies; 415 outside-view cabins (no balcony); 363 interior (no view) cabins; 36 suites with balconies, and 20 wheelchair-accessible cabins for the physically challenged. Suites and cabins with private balconies have easy-to-use sliding glass doors.

Regardless of the accommodation (and thus the price you pay for your cruise), all feature a powerful hairdryer (located in the cabin itself, and not, thankfully, in the bathroom), and a tea and coffee making sets, rich cherry wood cabinetry, and a bathroom with a sliding door and a separate toilet, shower enclosure and washbasin compartments. There is plenty of wood accenting throughout all accommodation, including wood frames surrounding balcony doors – a nice touch that will be subliminally appreciated by passengers.

The largest accommodation is in two huge Garden Villas (named Vista, and Horizon), located high atop the ship in a pod that is located forward of the ship's funnel, and overlooks the main swimming pool. These villas feature huge glass walls and landscaped private roof gardens (one has a Japanese-style garden, the other a Thai-style garden) for outdoor dining (with whirlpool tubs, naturally), and huge private sunbathing areas that are completely shielded from anyone; the garden itself extends to 1,720 sq. ft (160 sq. meters). Each suite has three bedrooms (one with a sliding glass door that leads

BERLITZ'S RATINGS

	Possible	Achieved
Ship	500	421
Accommodation	200	156
Food	400	293
Service	400	284
Entertainment	100	66
Cruise	400	302

to the garden) and bathrooms (one bathroom has a large corner bathtub, and two washbasins set in front of large glass walls that overlook the side of the ship as well as the swimming pool, although most of the view is of the overlarge waterslide), and a large living room (with Yamaha baby grand piano) with glass dining table and eight chairs, overlooking the lido/ pool deck. These units have their own private elevator and private stairway, and can be combined to create a large, 3,000 sq.-ft (280 sq.-meter) "house."

There are many suites (the smallest measures 290 sq. ft/27 sq. meters) in several different configurations. Two are housed in a pod atop the ship, and some overlook the stern, while others are in the forward part of the ship. All are lavishly furnished, although closet space in some of the smaller units is tight.

Although they are nicely furnished and quite well equipped, the standard outside-view and interior (no view) cabins are quite small, particularly when occupied by three or four persons. Some cabins have interconnecting doors (good for families with children), and many cabins have third and fourth person pull-down berths or trundle beds.

A small room service menu is available (all items are at extra cost, and a 15 percent service charge and a gratuity are automatically added to your account). Bottled water is placed in each cabin (but a charge will be made to your account if you open the bottle).

DINING: With Norwegian Cruise Line's "Freestyle Dining," you can choose which restaurant or dining spot you would like to eat in, at what time, and with whom. With many choices, you can eat in a different restaurant every night – just like going out on the town ashore. There are no assigned dining rooms, tables or seats, although you could, for example, eat in the same restaurant every day if you so wish – even to the point of having the same waiter, as in traditional cruising). Freestyle Dining also appears to work far better for individuals rather than large groups. All restaurants and eateries are non-smoking. NCL's dress code states that: "jeans, T-shirts, tank tops and bare feet are not permitted in restaurants," although I have observed that this is not followed in practice, particularly when families with young children are aboard at peak holiday times. On Formal Nights, many passengers want to eat in the two large main dining rooms, and this can create a logjam.

Although there are two main dining rooms: Versailles Restaurant, and Aqua Restaurant (both open from 5:30pm until midnight daily), there are several other themed eating establishments, giving a wide range of choice. It would be wise to plan in advance, particularly for dinner. In fact, there are two entire decks of dining establishments to choose from, involving 10 different restaurants and eateries, and 11 different menus nightly.

● *Versailles,* the ornate 375-seat first main dining room, is decorated in brilliant red and gold. This offers the traditional six-course dining experience (open 5.30pm-midnight).

● *Aqua*: a contemporary-styled 374-seat second main dining room, offering lighter cuisine (open 5.30pm-midnight), and an open galley where you can view the preparation of pastries and dessert items.

● *Soho*: Pacific Rim cuisine is where East meets West (California and Asian cuisine) in culinary terms. Has a live lobster tank (the first aboard a ship outside Southeast Asia). A main dining area that can seat 132, plus private dining rooms (each seats 10). A collection of pop art (including Andy Warhol) adorns the walls.

● *Ginza*: a Japanese restaurant, with 193 seats, a sit-up sushi bar, tempura bar, show galley, and separate "teppanyaki grill" room.

● *Le Bistro*: a French restaurant, with 66 seats, serving nouvelle cuisine and six courses.

● *Blue Lagoon*: a funky food court-style eatery with 88 seats (both indoors and outdoors on the Promenade Deck), featuring hamburgers, fish and chips, potpies and fast (wok stir-fried) dishes.

● *Market Café*: a large indoor/outdoor self-serve buffet eatery, with almost 400 ft (120 meters) of buffet counter space. "Action Stations" has made-to-order omelets, waffles, fruit, soups, ethnic specialties and pasta dishes.

● *La Trattoria*, an Italian (evening only) dining spot located within the indoor/outdoor buffet area, has pasta, pizza and other popular Italian fare.

● *Las Ramblas*: a Spanish tapas eatery and bar with a selection of hot and cold Tapas dishes and authentic entertainment.

● *Endless Summer*: a Hawaiian themed restaurant –

arranged around the second level of the central atrium and incorporating a performance stage and a large movie screen.

Other eating/drinking spots include the *Red Lion* (an English pub for draft beer and perhaps a game of darts); *Havana Club*, a cigar and cognac lounge; *Java Cafe*, an atrium lobby café and bar (for hot and frozen coffees, teas and pastries); a *Beer Garden* (for grilled foods); a *Spinkles* (an ice cream bar); a *Gym and Spa Bar* (for health food snacks and drinks); and *Gatsby's* wine bar (located at the entrance to *Soho*).

OTHER COMMENTS: *Norwegian Star* is the latest state-of-the-art vessel for Norwegian Cruise Line, and has a "pod" propulsion system – the first of a pair of sister ships (the second being *Norwegian Dawn*, which debuted in 2002). The pod propulsion system gives the ship more maneuverability, while reducing required machinery space and vibration at the stern. A large structure located forward of the funnel houses a children's center, and, one deck above, the two outstanding "villa" suites described in the accommodation section above.

Sports facilities include a jogging track, golf driving range, basketball and volleyball courts, as well as four levels of sunbathing decks. There are plenty of deck lounge chairs (the number is greater than the number of passengers carried), which is good news for the several days spent at sea on the Hawaii cruise itinerary. Water slides are included for the adult swimming pools (children have their own pools at the ship's stern – out of sight of the adult areas).

Inside the ship, you'll be met by a truly eclectic mix of bright colors and décor that you probably wouldn't have in your home (unless you were color-blind), and yet, somehow, it works extremely well in this large ship setting that is meant to attract young, active types.

Facilities include an Internet Café (with 17 computer stations and internet connection), a 1,150-seat show lounge with main floor and two balcony levels, 3,000-book library, card room, writing and study room, business center, karaoke lounge, conference and meeting rooms and associated facilities, and a retail shopping complex measuring 20,000 sq. ft (1,800 sq. meters).

Health devotees should enjoy the two decks high health spa complex (operated by the Hawaii-based Mandara Spa), located at the stern of the ship (with large ocean-view windows on three sides). There are many facilities and services to pamper you (almost all at extra charge), including Thai massage (in the spa, outdoors on deck, in your cabin or on your private balcony). In addition, there is an indoor lap pool (measuring 45 ft/14 meters), hydrotherapy pool, aromatherapy and wellness centers, and mud treatment room.

Children of all ages will get to play in a superb wet 'n' wild space-themed water park (complete with large pool, water slide, and paddle pool). They also get their own dedicated cinema (DVD movies are featured all day long), a jungle gym, painting area, and computer center.

Even the toilets are at a special low height. Teens, too, are well catered for, and get their own cinema (with DVD movies), discotheque with dance floor, and their own whirlpool (hot) tub.

With so many dining choices (some costing extra) to accommodate the tastes of an eclectic mix of nationalities, what your final cruise and dining experience will be like really depends on how much you are prepared to spend. To make the most of your vacation, you *will* need to plan where you want to eat well in advance, and make the necessary reservations, or you may be disappointed. More choices, including more dining options, add up to a very attractive vacation package, particularly suitable for families with children, in a very contemporary floating leisure center that really does provide ample facilities for you to have an enjoyable time, as well as provide you with the opportunity to immerse yourself in all things Hawaiian. The dress code is casual – very casual (no jacket and tie needed, although you are welcome to dress formally if you so wish).

While the initial cruise fare seems very reasonable, the extra costs and charges soon mount up if you want more than the basics. Although service levels and finesse are sometimes inconsistent (this was especially true when the ship was first went into service), the level of hospitality is very good – made so much better and brighter by the addition of a great number of Asian female staff rather than the surly and inconsistent (Caribbean Basin) staff still found on some of the smaller NCL ships.

Despite the company's name (Norwegian Cruise Line), there's almost nothing Norwegian about this product, except for some of the ship's senior officers. The staff, incidentally, includes many Southeast Asians who already have service experience aboard parent company Star Cruises' big ships.

The ship is full of revenue centers, however, designed to help you part with your money. You can expect to be subjected to a stream of flyers advertising daily art auctions, "designer" watches and other promotions, while "artworks" for auction are strewn throughout the ship.

Gratuities for staff (cabin attendants, dining room waiters, etc) are added to your onboard account at $10 per person, per day (you can reduce or otherwise amend these if necessary before you disembark). In addition, a 15 percent gratuity is added to all bar and spa treatment accounts. The onboard currency is the US dollar.

WEAK POINTS: Standing in line for embarkation, disembarkation, shore tenders and for self-serve buffet meals is an inevitable aspect of cruising aboard all large ships – even those designated as "Freestyle." There is not really that much time spent in ports in the Hawaiian islands – the only full day is on the island of Oahu. Although the suites and junior suites are quite spacious, the standard interior (no view) and outside-view cabins are very small when compared to those of other major cruise lines such as Carnival or Celebrity, particularly when occupied by three or four persons (the bathrooms, however, *are of* quite a decent size, and have large shower enclosures). The hustling for passengers to attend art auctions is both aggressive and annoying.

Reaching room service tends to be an exercise in frustration. Communication (particularly between the many new Asian staff and passengers) remains weak. Mindless "art auctions" are a real turn-off on a Hawaiian cruise.

Norwegian Sun
★★★★

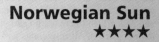

Large Ship:	.............77,104 tons	Passengers	
Lifestyle:	.................Standard	(lower beds/all berths):	.....2,002/2,400
Cruise Line:	......Norwegian Cruise Line	Passenger Space Ratio	
Former Names:	................none	(lower beds/all berths):	........38.5/32.1
Builder:	.........Lloyd Werft (Germany)	Crew/Passenger Ratio	
Original Cost:	............$332 million	(lower beds/all berths):	.........2.0/2.4
Entered Service:	............Nov 2001	Navigation Officers:	.........Norwegian
Registry:	................The Bahamas	Cabins (total):	1,001
Length (ft/m):	..........853.0/260.00	Size Range (sq ft/m):	......120.5–488.6/
Beam (ft/m):	.............105.8/32.25		11.2–45.4
Draft (ft/m):	.................26.2/8.00	Cabins (outside view):	675
Propulsion/Propellers:	.....diesel-electric	Cabins (interior/no view):	326
	(50,000 kW)/2	Cabins (for one person):	0
Passenger Decks:	12	Cabins (with private balcony):	252
Total Crew:	980	Cabins (wheelchair accessible):	6

Cabin Current:	..............110 volts
Elevators:	12
Casino (gaming tables):	............Yes
Slot Machines:	....................Yes
Swimming Pools (outdoors):	2
Swimming Pools (indoors):	0
Whirlpools:	4
Fitness Center:	.....................Yes
Sauna/Steam Room:	...........Yes/Yes
Massage:	.......................Yes
Self-Service Launderette:	...........No
Dedicated Cinema/Seats:	...........No
Library:	........................Yes
Classification Society:	.....Germanischer Lloyd

OVERALL SCORE: 1,517 (OUT OF A POSSIBLE 2,000 POINTS)

ACCOMMODATION: There are 30 different price categories, including 6 grades of suites, 15 grades of outside-view cabins and nine grades of interior (no view) cabins, so choosing the right accommodation for your needs requires some thought.

All of the standard outside-view and interior (no view) cabins feature common facilities, such as: two lower beds that can convert to a queen-sized bed, a small lounge area with sofa and table, and a decent amount of closet and drawer space, although the cabins themselves are disappointingly small. Over 200 outside-view cabins each have their own private balcony (balcony doors open outwards, but the doors are difficult to close because the door handles are not very user-friendly). Each cabin has a small vanity/writing desk, color television, personal safe, refrigerator, climate control, and laptop computer connection socket. Bottled water is placed in each cabin (but a charge will be made to your account if you open the bottle).

There are two Honeymoon/Anniversary Suites, located at the front of the ship, with forward facing and side views. Each suite has a separate lounge and bedroom. The lounge features a large dining table and chairs, two sofas, large television, DVD/CD player, coffee table, queen-sized pull-down Murphy's bed, guest closet, writing desk, wet bar with two bar stools, refrigerator and sink, several cupboards for glasses, and several drawers and other cupboards for storage. The sleeping area has twin beds that convert to a queen-sized bed, and walk-in closet with a good amount of hanging space. The tiled bathroom, although not large, has a full-

BERLITZ'S RATINGS

	Possible	Achieved
Ship	500	410
Accommodation	200	152
Food	400	289
Service	400	284
Entertainment	100	78
Cruise	400	304

size whirlpool bathtub and shower, retractable clothesline, deep wash-basin, and personal toiletries cabinets.

The largest accommodation can be found in two Owner's Suites – each with a hot tub, large teak table, two chairs and two deck lounge chairs outside on a huge, private, forward-facing teak floor balcony just under the ship's navigation bridge, with large floor-to-ceiling windows. Each suite has a separate lounge and bedroom. The lounge has a large dining table and chairs, two sofas, large TV set, DVD/CD player, coffee table, queen-sized pull-down Murphy's bed, guest closet, writing desk, wet bar with two bar stools, refrigerator and sink, several cupboards for glasses, and several drawers and other cupboards for storage. The bedroom, with sliding wood half-doors that look into the lounge, has a queen-sized (with European duvet) bed under a leaf-glass chandelier, vanity desk, TV set, walk-in closet with plenty of hanging rail space, several open shelves and large personal safe. The tiled bathroom, although not large, has a full-size bathtub with retractable clothesline above, separate shower enclosure with glass doors, deep washbasin, and personal toiletries cabinets.

There are also a number of other suites – each with a private teakwood balcony; these suites face aft in a secluded position and overlook the ship's wash. They have some of the same facilities as found in the owner's suites, with the exception of the outdoor hot tub, and the fact that there is less space.

All cabins have tea/coffee making sets, personal safe, satellite-linked telephone, and private bathroom with bath or shower.

DINING: With NCL's "Freestyle Dining," you can choose which restaurant you would like to eat in, at what time, and with whom (there are no assigned dining rooms, tables or seats). All restaurants and eateries are non-smoking. Although there are two principal (large) dining rooms, there are also a number of other themed eating establishments, giving a wide range of choice – although it would be wise to plan in advance, particularly for dinner. All restaurants and eateries are non-smoking, and some incur an extra charge. NCL's dress code states that: "jeans, T-shirts, tank tops and bare feet are not permitted in restaurants."

The two main dining rooms – the 564-seat Four Seasons Dining Room, and the 604-seat Seven Seas Dining Room, have tables for four, six or eight (there are no tables for two).

Sandwiched between the two (rather like a train carriage) is a third, 84-seat Italian Restaurant, Il Adagio, available as an à la carte dining option (for which there is an extra charge), with window-side tables for two or four persons. Reservations are necessary.

There are also several other dining options, most of located on one of the upper-most decks of the ship, with great views from large picture windows. These include:
● *Le Bistro*: a 90-seat alternative dining spot for some fine French-style meals, including tableside cooking. Reservations are necessary for dinner.
● *Las Ramblas*: a Spanish/Mexican style eatery featuring tapas light snack items.
● *Ginza*: a Japanese Restaurant, with a sushi bar and a teppanyaki grill (show cooking in a "U"-shaped setting where you sit around the chef). Reservations are necessary for dinner.
● *East Meets West*: a Pacific Rim Fusion Restaurant, featuring à la carte California/Hawaii/Asian cuisine. Reservations are necessary for dinner.
● *Pacific Heights*: a Healthy Living Restaurant (with 80 seats), featuring spa cuisine and Cooking Light menus. Reservations are necessary for dinner.
● *Garden Café*: a 24-Hour restaurant indoor/outdoor self-serve buffet-style eatery with fast foods and salads.

Although the various menus make meals sound appetizing, overall, the food provided is rather unmemorable fare that lacks taste and is mostly overcooked. However, the presentation is generally quite good. There is a reasonably decent selection of breads, rolls, and pastry items, but the selection of cheeses is very poor.

The wine list is well balanced, with a wide selection of wines to suit various tastes and pocket books. A connoisseur list is available for those seeking premium wines, although the vintages tend to be young. There are many types of beer (including some on draught in the popular Sports Bar & Grill).

The cutlery is very ordinary (European should note that there are no fish knives). There is no formal afternoon tea, although you can make your own from various beverage stations (but only the most basic ingredients are supplied – it's difficult to get fresh milk, for exam-

ple, as non-dairy "creamers" are typically supplied). The service is, on the whole, adequate, nothing more, and proves that good staffs that can communicate well are quite hard to find.

OTHER COMMENTS: This is a close sister ship to *Norwegian Sky* (but with improved outfitting and finishing detail), with one additional deck of balcony cabins, and crew cabins have been added to accommodate an additional 200 (mainly smiling Asian) crew.

The amount of outdoor space is quite good, and the extra wide pool deck (the extra width created from port and starboard "overhangs" that resulted from balconies being added to cabins on two decks below), with its two swimming pools and four Jacuzzi tubs, and plenty of deck lounge chairs, albeit arranged in rows, camp-style.

There is a two-level show lounge with more than 1,000 seats, and this incorporates a large proscenium stage for the high-energy dazzle and sizzle shows that Norwegian Cruise Line's North American passengers seem to enjoy. However, the sight lines are obstructed in a number of seats by several slim pillars, although there is not as much obstruction as aboard the sister ship *Norwegian Sky*.

A separate cabaret lounge, Dazzles Lounge, is equipped with an extremely long bar. Other features include a large casino (this will operate 24 hours a day, with special facilities and rooms for high-rollers and "club" members), a shopping arcade, children's playroom (there is also a splash pool in a prime open deck area forward atop ship), and a video arcade.

There is also a large health/fitness spa (including an aerobics room and separate gymnasium), and several treatment rooms, all operated by the Hawaii-based Mandara Spa (now part of the Steiner Group).

Other facilities include a small conference room, library and beauty salon, a lounge for smoking cigars and drinking cognac, and an Internet Café, located on the Promenade Deck within the ship's atrium lobby, with 20 computer stations.

Those with a black belt in shopping might appreciate the fact that there are numerous shops, showcasing a wide range of goods, from inexpensive to very expensive. Columbian Emeralds is the joint venture operator.

Sports fans will appreciate the large basketball/volleyball court, baseball-batting cage, golf-driving range, platform tennis, shuffleboard and table tennis facilities, and sports bar with 24-hour *live* satellite television coverage of sports events and major games. Joggers will also find a wrap-around indoor-outdoor jogging track.

Young passengers will find an array of facilities for a range of ages, which include a children's playroom called Kid's Korner (for "junior sailors" ages 3–5; (First Mates (ages 6–9); Navigators (ages 10–12); and Teens (ages 13–17).

With this ship, Norwegian Cruise Line has made an effort to provide more and better public rooms and more entertainment facilities than aboard its smaller ships – so you get a lot of ship for your money. *Norwegian Sun* tries hard to be all things to all people. The ship certainly has plenty of options for eating.

The ship is full of revenue centers, however, which are designed to help you part you from your money. You can expect to be subjected to a stream of flyers advertising daily art auctions, "designer" watches, and other promotions, while "artworks" for auction are strewn throughout the ship.

Gratuities for staff (cabin attendants, dining room waiters, etc) are added to your onboard account at $10 per person, per day (you can, however, reduce or otherwise amend these before you disembark). In addition, a 15 percent gratuity is added to all bar and spa treatment accounts. The onboard currency is the US dollar.

WEAK POINTS: Standing in line for embarkation, disembarkation, shore tenders and for self-serve buffet meals is an inevitable aspect of cruising aboard all large ships. The standard interior (no view) and outside-view cabins are very small when compared to those of other major cruise lines such as Carnival or Celebrity. The food in the large dining rooms is a weak point. There are too many plastic plates, Styrofoam and plastic cups and plastic stirrers in use in the casual eateries. . The hustling for passengers to attend art auctions is very aggressive and annoying.

QUOTABLE QUOTES

These are some of the questions I have been asked by passengers cruising for the first time:

"Does the crew sleep on board?"

"How far above sea level are we?"

"Is the island surrounded by water?"

"Are all Caribbean islands the same size?"

"How does the captain know which port to go to?"

"Can we get off in the Panama Canal?"

"Does the ship generate its own electricity?"

"Does this elevator go up as well as down?"

"Will this elevator take me to my cabin?"

"Why is the sauna so hot?"

"What time's the midnight buffet?"

"Are there two seatings at the midnight buffet?"

"Can I please have some hot iced tea?"

"Do we have to stay up until midnight to change our clocks?"

"Does the chef cook himself?"

"What do they do with the ice sculptures after they melt?"

"How many fjords to the dollar?"

"What time's the 2 o'clock tour?"

"Where's the bus for the walking tour?"

Norwegian Wind
★★★ +

Large Ship:	50,760 tons	Cabin Current:	110 volts
Lifestyle:	Standard	Elevators:	10
Cruise Line:	Norwegian Cruise Line	Casino (gaming tables):	Yes
Former Names:	Windward	Slot Machines:	Yes
Builder:	Chantiers de l'Atlantique (France)	Swimming Pools (outdoors):	2
Original Cost:	$240 million	Swimming Pools (indoors):	0
Entered Service:	June 1993	Whirlpools:	2
Registry:	The Bahamas	Fitness Center:	Yes
Length (ft/m):	754.0/229.8	Sauna/Steam Room:	Yes/No
Beam (ft/m):	93.5/28.5	Massage:	Yes
Draft (ft/m):	22.3/6.8	Self-Service Launderette:	No
Propulsion/Propellers:	diesel (18,480 kW)/2	Dedicated Cinema/Seats:	No
Passenger Decks:	10	Library:	Yes
Total Crew:	700	Classification Society:	Det Norske Veritas

Passengers
(lower beds/all berths): 1,732/2,156
Passenger Space Ratio
(lower beds/all berths): 29.3/23.5
Crew/Passenger Ratio
(lower beds/all berths): 2.5/3.1
Navigation Officers: Norwegian
Cabins (total): 866
Size Range (sq ft/m): 139.9–349.8/ 13.0–32.5
Cabins (outside view): 696
Cabins (interior/no view): 170
Cabins (for one person): 0
Cabins (with private balcony): 48
Cabins (wheelchair accessible): 6
(+ 30 for hearing impaired)

OVERALL SCORE: 1,381 (OUT OF A POSSIBLE 2,000 POINTS)

ACCOMMODATION: There are 15 grades of cabins. The majority of cabins have outside views and feature wood-trimmed cabinetry and warm decor, with multicolored soft furnishings, but there is almost no drawer space (the closets have open shelves, however), so take minimal clothing. All cabins have a sitting area, but this takes away any free space, making movement pretty tight. The bathrooms are small but practical, although there is little space for storage of personal toiletry items.

BERLITZ'S RATINGS	Possible	Achieved
Ship	500	377
Accommodation	200	145
Food	400	237
Service	400	282
Entertainment	100	73
Cruise	400	267

There are 18 suites (12 of which have a private entrance and a small, private balcony), each with separate living room and bedroom, fine quality cabinetry, and lots of closet and drawer space. Occupants of suites receive "concierge" service, which provides extra personal attention. In addition, 16 suites and 70 cabins have inter-connecting doors – good for families cruising together, or perhaps for those that want separate "his and hers" living spaces. Several cabins are specially equipped for the hearing-impaired. All cabins on the port side of the ship are designated non-smoking. Bottled water is placed in each cabin (but a charge will be made to your account if you open the bottle).

DINING: The two main full-service dining rooms are: The Terraces (arguably the nicest, with windows that look out over the ship's tiered aft decks), and the Four Seasons (with approximately 450 seats), located amidships. All are non-smoking and feature the same menu and food, in an open seating, come when you want (and with whom) arrangement (NCL calls it "Freestyle Dining"). The Four Seasons is the largest, and has some prime tables at ocean-view window seats in a section that extend from the ship's port and starboard sides in half-moon shapes (nice for lunch, but it's either dark or the curtains are drawn for dinner). However, this ship was not built with this kind of "free for all" dining arrangements in mind. Consequently, the flow, timing, and concept aboard this ship are simply not successful. The dress code states that: "jeans, T-shirts, tank tops and bare feet are not permitted in restaurants."

In addition to the two principal dining rooms, there are also a number of other themed eating establishments, giving a wide range of choice – although it would be wise to plan in advance, particularly for dinner. Italian fare is served in the Trattoria (formerly the Sun Terraces), which overlooks the aft swimming pool. There is also The Bistro, which features informal evening dining at no extra charge in more intimate surroundings. A 200-seat Sports Bar (typically open between 6am and 1am) has breakfast, luncheon, dinner, and snacks throughout the day. There's also a poolside pizzeria, and a small coffee lounge.

While "Freestyle" dining works best aboard the newer, larger ships in the fleet, aboard *Norwegian Wind* and its sister ship *Norwegian Dream* it simply creates food outlets instead of restaurants, and causes untold confusion. Although the various menus make meals sound appetizing, overall, the food provided is rather unmemorable fare that lacks taste and presentation quality, and is often overcooked. There is a reasonably decent selection of breads, rolls, and fruits, although the selection of cheeses is poor. The wine list is quite decent and well put together, with moderate prices, although you won't find any good vintage wines. There are many types of beer (including some on draught in the popular Sports Bar & Grill).

The cutlery is very ordinary (there are no fish knives). There is no formal afternoon tea, although you can make your own from various beverage stations. The service is adequate, nothing more, and proves that good staffs that can communicate well are quite difficult to find.

You can eat breakfast or lunch in any of the dining rooms when it's "open seating." A lavish "chocoholics" buffet is featured once each cruise – established as a firm favorite among Norwegian Cruise Line's repeat passengers.

OTHER COMMENTS: *Norwegian Wind* is the sister ship to *Norwegian Dream*, and, as such, has a moderately handsome profile (despite a large, square blue funnel), that was actually rather better balanced before the ship underwent a "chop and stretch" operation in 1998. A completely new mid-section was added, and the funnel was adapted so that it could be "folded" over to allow the ship to transit the Kiel Canal in Germany. Included in the 130-ft (40-meter) section were 251 new passengers cabins and 50 crew cabins, together with several new or enlarged public rooms (although there simply are not enough) including a 60-seat conference center. Some innovative features were incorporated in the original design, and these have been enhanced. The passenger flow is generally good – indeed, the ship seems to absorb passengers quite well for much of the time, except at peak traffic times between dinner seatings.

There is a blue rubber-covered wrap-around promenade deck outdoors. The tiered pool deck is neat, as are the multi-deck aft sun terraces and all her fore and aft connecting exterior stairways.

The overall exterior design emphasizes a clever and extensive use of large windows that create a sense of open spaces, although the interior design provides many smaller public rooms rather than the large hangers found aboard so many other ships. However, there is no big atrium lobby, as one might expect. The pastel interior colors used are quite soothing, and is considered by many to be a pretty ship inside. The entrance lobby is not at all attractive, and feels rather confined for a ship of this size.

This ship has proven highly successful for Norwegian Cruise Line's younger, active sports-minded passengers, and provides a good alternative to the larger ships and their larger passenger numbers, although there will be plenty of other passengers to keep you company. The dress code is casual, and there are no formal nights when you have to dress up.

The ship is full of revenue centers, however, designed to part you from your money. You can expect to be subjected to a stream of flyers advertising daily art auctions, "designer" watches and other promotions, while "artworks" for auction are strewn throughout the ship.

Gratuities for staff (cabin attendants, dining room waiters, etc) are automatically added to your onboard account at $10 per person, per day (you can, however, reduce or otherwise amend these if necessary before you disembark). In addition, a 15 percent gratuity is added to all bar and spa treatment accounts. The onboard currency is the US dollar.

WEAK POINTS: Standing in line for embarkation, disembarkation, shore tenders and for self-serve buffet meals is an inevitable aspect of cruising aboard all large ships. The hustling for passengers to attend art auctions is very aggressive and annoying, as is the constant bombardment for revenue activities and the daily junk mail that arrives at one's cabin door. The room service menu is still poor and could be improved. The outdoor stairways are numerous and confusing. The carpeted steel interior stairwell steps are quite tinny. When the ship was "stretched" it reduced the amount of outdoor space per passenger, and this is reflected in increased density around the pools. There simply are not enough public rooms to absorb the increase in passengers well.

Removed 2006

OceanBreeze
★★ +

Mid-Size Ship: . . . . .21,486 tons	Total Crew: 370	Cabins (wheelchair accessible): 0
Lifestyle: . . . . .Standard	Passengers	Cabin Current: . . . . .110 volts
Cruise Line: Imperial Majesty Cruise Line	(lower beds/all berths): 780/1,012	Elevators: 1
Former Names: . . . . .*Azure Seas, Calypso,*	Passenger Space Ratio	Casino (gaming tables): . . . . .Yes
Monarch Star, Southern Cross	(lower beds/all berths): 27.5/21.2	Slot Machines: .Yes
Builder: . . . . .Harland & Wolff (UK)	Crew/Passenger Ratio	Swimming Pools (outdoors): 1
Original Cost: .n/a	(lower beds/all berths): 2.1/2.7	Swimming Pools (indoors): 0
Entered Service: . . . .Mar 1955/May 1992	Navigation Officers: . . . . . . .International	Whirlpools: 1
Registry: . . . . .The Bahamas	Cabins (total): .390	Fitness Center: .Yes
Length (ft/m): 603.8/184.06	Size Range (sq ft/m): 96.8–398.2/	Sauna/Steam Room: . . . . .No/No
Beam (ft/m): 80.0/24.41	9.0–37.0	Massage: . . . . .Yes
Draft (ft/m): 26.1/7.97	Cabins (outside view): 236	Self-Service Launderette: . . . . .No
Propulsion/Propellers: . . . . .steam turbine	Cabins (interior/no view): 154	Dedicated Cinema/Seats: Yes/55
(14,900 kW)/2	Cabins (for one person): 0	Library: . . . . .Yes
Passenger Decks: 9	Cabins (with private balcony): 0	Classification Society: . . . .Lloyds Register

---

OVERALL SCORE: 1,095 (OUT OF A POSSIBLE 2,000 POINTS)

ACCOMMODATION: There are a wide variety of cabin shapes, sizes and configurations to choose from, in 11 price categories. Most are moderately comfortable and nicely decorated in earth tones and pastel colors. Although they are not large and have only basic appointments, all have one or two lower beds, and heavy-duty fittings. Many interior (no view) cabins are actually larger than some of the outside-view cabins. Most cabins have very plain walls. The lighting is minimal; there is little drawer space, although the closet space is sufficient for two (particularly for two night cruises). The bathrooms are very basic; most have a shower enclosure, and soap and shampoo are provided.

On Boat Deck there are 12 larger suites, three of which have forward views over the ship's long foredeck; these come with a separate bedroom and living area (with television), are very comfortable, and could sleep five or six – good for families with children. All suites come with a mini-bar/refrigerator.

Room service is available 24 hours daily, although the menu is limited.

DINING: The 500-seat Caravelle Restaurant, located on a lower deck, has a warm, cheerful ambience. There are two seatings, at tables for two, four, six or 10; the chairs, however, do not have armrests. The cuisine is generally basic but sound, and there is plenty of it, but it certainly is not gourmet food, despite what the brochure claims, and the presentation is minimal. However, having said that, there is enough of a variety to please just about

BERLITZ'S RATINGS

	Possible	Achieved
Ship	500	263
Accommodation	200	110
Food	400	215
Service	400	244
Entertainment	100	54
Cruise	400	209

everyone. Lunch and dinner menus include a vegetarian appetizer and entrée. The service is reasonable and attentive, but extremely hurried (particularly for first seating). There is only the most basic choice of cheeses and fresh fruits.

For the short cruise product that this ship provides, the wine list is actually quite extensive (it focuses on wines from the USA and the New World) and the prices reflect extremely good value for money in a short cruise.

Casual, self-serve, food is available buffet-style for breakfast, lunch and midnight snacks in the self-serve Café Miramar (the room also acts as a show lounge and nightclub). You can, however, also sit outside, under a canvas-style awning.

OTHER COMMENTS: *OceanBreeze* is a real vintage ship, originally built to operate line voyages from England to Australia in the 1950s for the long-defunct Shaw Savill line. The ship, which was christened in a naming ceremony by England's Queen Elizabeth II, has a long, low profile, and is easily identified by its single funnel almost at the very stern in what was, when built, a radical departure from all other passenger vessels of the period. The new owners have thoughtfully provided a display of the ship's history (including a letter from Queen Elizabeth II) can be found in three wooden showcases close to the ship's main lounge.

The ship, which has a dark blue hull and white superstructure, has been maintained quite well, although now showing its age in several areas – it is, after all, well over 40 years old. The large areas of wooden open decks (complete with wooden deck lounge chairs and thick blue cushioned pads) are still in a very reasonable condition. One bonus feature is the fact that the ship has steam turbine propulsion; this translates to little or no vibration, unlike many of today's newer ships that are powered by diesel or diesel-electric engines.

A refurbishment of the ship in 2000 revitalized its interiors, although some of the interesting art deco features and wood and etched glass doors (a carry-over from its former days as an ocean liner) have been kept. The Monte Carlo casino is on two levels (in what used to be the cinema, with a bar on the upper level), and is nicely decorated in an art deco style. Other features include a health and fitness/spa area, gift shop, and video arcade. There is a cardroom/library, although there are no books (there really is *no* time to relax and read on a two-night cruise – with one day in port).

There is a main lounge (for evening shows, shore excursion lectures), although, with its single deck height, it quickly becomes crowded, and the sight lines are poor.

All in all, *OceanBreeze* is an old, but very reasonable ship for those wanting a pleasant short cruise getaway for a modest price, in casual, no-frills surroundings. You should note that the program is a busy one and, because the cruise is only two days long, there will be little time to relax. The ship will provide you with a taste of the pleasures of cruising, all in a package that relieves you of some of the decision-making normally necessary for a typical land-based two-night vacation break.

OceanBreeze was bought by Imperial Majesty Cruise Line in May 2000 and operates short cruises from Ft. Lauderdale to the Bahamas. Note that (when this book was completed) $19.50 per person per two-night cruise is added to your onboard account – for gratuities (you can, however, decline or change this amount by visiting the Purser's Desk). Note also that a 15 percent gratuity is added to all bar accounts. The onboard currency is the US dollar.

WEAK POINTS: Do expect lines for embarkation, disembarkation, shore excursions and the self-serve buffets. There are many smokers among the passengers, and the entertainment is of the low budget variety.

Ocean Majesty
★★★ +

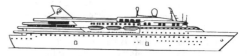

Mid-Size Ship: . . . . .10,417 tons	Passenger Decks: 8	Cabins (wheelchair accessible): 2
Lifestyle: . . . . .Standard	Total Crew: 235	Cabin Current: . . . . .110 and 220 volts
Cruise Line: . . . . . . .Majestic International	Passengers	Elevators: 3
Cruises	(lower beds/all berths): 535/621	Casino (gaming tables): . . . . .Yes
Former Names: . . . . . . .Homeric, Olympic,	Passenger Space Ratio	Slot Machines: . . . . .Yes
Ocean Majesty, Kypros Star, Sol	(lower beds/all berths): 19.4/16.7	Swimming Pools (outdoors): 1
Christina, Juan March	Crew/Passenger Ratio	Swimming Pools (indoors): 0
Builder: . .Union Navale de Levante (Spain)	(lower beds/all berths): 2.2/2.6	Whirlpools: 1
Original Cost: . . . .$65 million	Navigation Officers: . . . . .Greek	Fitness Center: . . . . .Yes
Entered Service: 1966/Apr 1994	Cabins (total): 273	Sauna/Steam Room: . . . . .Yes/No
Registry: .Greece	Size Range (sq ft/m): 96.8–182.9/	Massage: . . . . .Yes
Length (ft/m): 443.8/135.30	9.0–17.0	Self-Service Launderette: . . . . .No
Beam (ft/m): 62.9/19.20	Cabins (outside view): 186	Dedicated Cinema/Seats: . . . . .No
Draft (ft/m): 19.5/5.95	Cabins (interior/no view): 87	Library: . . . . .Yes
Propulsion/Propellers: . . . . .diesel	Cabins (for one person): 11	Classification Society: . .American Bureau
(12,200 kW)/2	Cabins (with private balcony): 8	of Shipping

---

OVERALL SCORE: 1,274 (OUT OF A POSSIBLE 2,000 POINTS)

ACCOMMODATION: There are too many cabin categories for a ship of this size. Most of the cabins are small but quite functional, with a decent amount of closet and drawer space. The ceilings are very plain, and the soundproofing could be better, but the overall impression is that they are neat and tidy. All cabins have twin lower beds or double beds. Some also have one or two additional upper (Pullman) berths.

The tiled bathrooms (all have a shower; none have a bathtub) are bright and functional, with good lighting, but do lack space for the storage of personal toiletry items.

Although there are two wheelchair accessible cabins, wheelchair access throughout much of the ship will prove difficult, and is not recommended.

DINING: The dining room features two seatings, and is set low down in the ship. Although it is reasonably attractive, it is also extremely noisy, particularly at tables adjacent to the waiter stations, which seem to be everywhere. There are few tables for two, and most passengers dine at large tables that seat eight. The cuisine is continental in style, with a decent enough selection of menu items, highlighted by Greek specialties and signature dishes. There is a small selection of breads, fruits and cheeses, and the buffets are generally simple, unimaginative and repetitive affairs.

OTHER COMMENTS: This ship has a pleasing, balanced, somewhat handsome profile, with an aft funnel. The ship's name, *Ocean Majesty*, however, seems a little ill

BERLITZ'S RATINGS

	Possible	Achieved
Ship	500	324
Accommodation	200	141
Food	400	248
Service	400	259
Entertainment	100	63
Cruise	400	239

suited to a small ship such as this. It underwent an extensive transformation into a smart cruise vessel (1994), with the exception of hull, shaft and propellers, and was placed under charter to the British company Page & Moy in 1995.

The conversion was accomplished quite well, and, although the built-up stern is not particularly handsome, there is a unique "walk-through" funnel. There is a good amount of open deck space for the size of the vessel, but the plastic deck furniture is tacky.

There are several good public rooms, bars and lounges, furnished with good quality materials and soft furnishing fabrics. The décor includes an abundance of highly polished mirrored surfaces.

Cruising aboard this ship will provide a busy, destination-oriented experience in very casual but comfortable surroundings. The ship is of an ideal size for cruising in the Aegean and Mediterranean areas, and can get into many ports that larger ships cannot.

This ship is often chartered to various tour operators and packagers. This means the standards of product delivery can vary. During each summer, the ship is under charter to Page & Moy for cruises to Northern Europe and the Baltic (when the food and its presentation is improved). The onboard currency is the British pound.

WEAK POINTS: This is a high-density vessel, so expect lines for shore excursions and buffets. No cabins have bathtubs. Has a somewhat awkward interior layout and steep interior stairways with short steps.

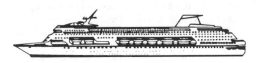

Ocean Village
NOT YET RATED

Large Ship: . . . . .63,524 tons	Total Crew: 514
Lifestyle: . . . . .Standard	Passengers
Cruise Line: . . . . .Ocean Village	(lower beds/all berths): 1,624/1,692
Former Names: . . .*Arcadia, Star Princess,*	Passenger Space Ratio
FairMajesty	(lower beds/all berths): 39.1/37.5
Builder: Chantiers de L'Atlantique (France)	Crew/Passenger Ratio
Original Cost: . . . .$200 million	(lower beds/all berths): 3.1/3.2
Entered Service: . . . . Mar 1987/May 2003	Navigation Officers: . . . . .British
Registry: . . . . .Great Britain	Cabins (total): .812
Length (ft/m): 810.3/247.00	Size Range (sq ft/m): 148.0–538.2/
Beam (ft/m): 105.6/32.20	13.7–50.0
Draft (ft/m): 26.9/8.20	Cabins (outside view): 622
Propulsion/Propellers: . . . . .diesel-electric	Cabins (interior/no view): 190
(39,000kW)/2	Cabins (for one person): 0
Passenger Decks: 12	Cabins (with private balcony): 64

Cabins (wheelchair accessible): 8
Cabin Current: . . . . .220 volts
Elevators: 9
Casino (gaming tables): . . . . .Yes
Slot Machines: . . . . .Yes
Swimming Pools (outdoors): 3
Swimming Pools (indoors): 0
Whirlpools: 4
Fitness Center: . . . . .Yes
Sauna/Steam Room: . . . . .Yes/No
Massage: . . . . .Yes
Self-Service Launderette: . . . . .Yes
Dedicated Cinema/Seats: Yes/205
Library: . . . . .No
Classification Society: . . .Lloyd's Register

BERLITZ'S OVERALL SCORE: NYR (OUT OF A POSSIBLE 2,000 POINTS)

ACCOMMODATION: There are four basic types, in 14 different price grades. These include two grades of suites: 36 suites with private balcony and bathtub, plus separate shower enclosure, 2 suites with shower, but no balcony. There are also 28 suites with private balcony, and shower. All other accommodation consists of standard outside-view and interior (no view) grade cabins. Many passengers like to fall asleep with soft music playing however, because music is only available through the TV set, you can't obtain any of the music channels without having a TV picture on.

STANDARD OUTSIDE-VIEW/INTERIOR (NO VIEW) CABINS: All are equipped with twin beds that can (in most cases) be placed together to form a queen-sized bed. All have a good amount of storage space, including wooden drawer units, plus some under-bed space for luggage, and a walk-in (open) closet. A direct dial telephone is provided. However, the sound insulation between cabins is actually quite poor (televisions late at night can be particularly irritating, as can loud children). A number of cabins also have third and fourth person berths (in which case the drawer and storage space becomes tight, and there is only one personal safe), good for families with children.

The bathrooms are of a modular design, and are of quite a decent size, with good shower enclosures, and a retractable clothes line. None have bathtubs, except in one of the grades designated as suites, as the ship was

BERLITZ'S RATINGS		
	Possible	Achieved
Ship	500	NYR
Accommodation	200	NYR
Food	400	NYR
Service	400	NYR
Entertainment	100	NYR
Cruise	400	NYR

originally built for American passengers (who prefer showers). Soap is provided, and a soap/shampoo dispenser is fitted into the shower enclosure (although there is no conditioner).

SUITES: For more living space, choose one of the suite grades. Some have a small private balcony (although the partitions are not of the full floor-to-ceiling type, so you may hear your neighbors – or smell their smoke). Suite occupants also get a 100 percent cotton bathrobe.

DINING: The idea of Ocean Village (the company) is that the whole cruise experience should be casual, with none of the stuffiness normally associated with traditional dining. So, the dining concept is simple: meals are taken in a self-serve buffet style setting, so you can dress as casually as you like. There are several dining spots, including two large self-serve buffet restaurants (Waterfront, and Plantation), a bistro, La Luna pizzeria on deck for lunch or dinner (there is a cover charge at night, and reservations are necessary). All dining spots are non-smoking.

Plantation and The Waterfront both have large ocean-view windows, self-serve buffet display counters, and there are plenty of tables, most of which are for four, six or eight persons. Plantation is open 24 hours a day, while The Waterfront has set opening hours, detailed in the daily program. At night, Plantation has Asian and Oriental themed buffets.

For a little more attention, better food, and more flair in presentation, try The Bistro (located in one corner of the Waterfront Restaurant). It has Mediterranean cuisine created by celebrity chef James Martin (à la carte items cost extra and reservations are needed), and there is a decent wine list.

In general, the food is expected to be typical of what you would find in a couples-only or family-style vacation village (modern British with a Mediterranean touch), with plenty of choices for families with children. It is likely to be quite straightforward, unfussy and unpretentious, with little use of garnishes. Vegetarian dishes are incorporated into the menu each day. The service is warm and lighthearted. You'll be able to have the "Great British Breakfast" as well as light, healthy fare.

OTHER COMMENTS: The ship was originally designed and built for Sitmar Cruises, a company absorbed into Princess Cruises in 1988 before the ship was completed. It was extensively refurbished in 1997 at the Harland & Wolff shipyard in Belfast, and reconfigured specifically for British cruise passengers. Until March 2003 the ship's name is *Arcadia* and it is operated by P&O Cruises (the parent company of Ocean Village).

After a refurbishment intended to brighten the interior passageways, public rooms and dining spots, *Arcadia* will morph into *Ocean Village,* a trendy, upbeat ship designed for younger couples and families who want to take a cruise, but don't want the sedentary "eat when we tell you to and relax" image typical of traditional cruise ships.

In the 2003 refit, several new cabins have been added, although the overall number of crew has been reduced; the casino was relocated, displacing the library, and the former casino has been turned into a new internet center/bar called Connexions.

Ocean Village is well proportioned, with a good amount of open deck space. On the open deck are two swimming pools (one has sloping steps, while the other has vertical steps; one has a sit-in bar), while the aft pool will probably be used by families with children. Four hot tubs sit on a raised platform, and two shower cubicles stand adjacent to a poolside bar.

The ship's interiors are upbeat and trendy in a high-street sort of fashion, but also include a few items that have a link with the past, such as the art deco touches of stainless steel balustrades. There aren't a lot of public rooms to play in, although one nice feature is the fact that the public rooms do have ceilings that are higher than average for contemporary cruise ships.

The focal point of the interior is a three-deck-high foyer, highlighted by a stainless-steel kinetic sculpture (it resembles a Swiss Army knife) that brings one's attention to the multi-deck horseshoe-shaped staircase. There is a domed observation lounge atop the ship (it sits atop the ship, forward of the mast, like a lump of camembert cheese). Although it is a little out of the traffic flow, it is a restful spot for cocktails; at night it turns into a night-spot/discotheque.

The largest public room is the two-deck-high show lounge (The Marquee); it is horseshoe-shaped, with main and balcony levels, and there are adequate sight lines from most of the banquette-style seating. There are several shops (one always carries chocolates) set around the second and third levels of the three-deck high atrium lobby, plus a dedicated cinema. Other facilities include a casino (aft of the upper level of the two-deck high show lounge). There is a beauty salon, gymnasium, and wellness center (called the Karma Spa), including a sauna/steam room complex, located on the lowest passenger deck.

Families should enjoy extensive children's facilities. The children's indoor play area (Base Camp) is located aft, while the exterior aft decks have an outdoor paddling pool and games areas. There's also a Night Nursery for sleepovers (operates 6pm–2am, and there may be an additional charge). Teenagers are catered to with their own area, The Hideout. Babies under 6 months old are not accepted as passengers.

Ocean Village begins fly-cruise operations in May 2003, with the ship based on Palma de Majorca. Special fly-cruise packages have been created (for British passengers) from five UK airports (Birmingham, Edinburgh, London Gatwick, London Stanstead, and Manchester). You can take a 7-day or 14-day cruise, (there are two different itineraries, alternating each week), and add on a one-week or two-week stay at a choice of Majorcan family resort hotels, one of which is exclusive to Ocean Village.

As part of the "fusion cruise-stay" vacation, a variety of active sports is available. These include mountain biking, abseiling, jet skiing, jeep safaris, quad biking, parasailing, helicopter flight-seeing, and snorkeling (all are at extra cost). The ship carries a "fleet" of mountain bikes. Both active and passive cruising are therefore on offer.

In marketing terms, this ship and casual dress-down product is designed to compete head to head with Island Cruises' *Island Escape,* with the same kind of itineraries and cost structure, to appeal specifically to the British vacation market.

Given all the facts and projections available when this book was completed, the overall score for this ship and product would probably end up somewhere just over 1,500 points, which equals three-and-a-half stars. However, in practice, who knows? The next edition of this book will tell. Gratuities to staff are included in the cruise/vacation price.

WEAK POINTS: Standing in line for embarkation, disembarkation, shore tenders and for self-serve buffet meals tends to happen with ships of this size. Sadly, there is no full wrap-around promenade deck outdoors (open port and starboard walking areas stretch only partly along the sides). There is no library.

Oceana
NOT YET RATED

Large Ship: ....77,499 tons	Passengers	Cabin Current: ....110 and 220 volts
Lifestyle: ....Standard	(lower beds/all berths): 2,016/2,272	Elevators: 11
Cruise Line: ....P&O Cruises	Passenger Space Ratio	Casino (gaming tables): ....Yes
Former Names: ....*Ocean Princess*	(lower beds/all berths): 38.4/34.1	Slot Machines: ....Yes
Builder: ....Fincantieri (Italy)	Crew/Passenger Ratio	Swimming Pools (outdoors): 4
Original Cost: ....$300 million	(lower beds/all berths): 2.3/2.5	Swimming Pools (indoors): 0
Entered Service: .....Feb 2000/Nov 2002	Navigation Officers: ....British	Whirlpools: 5
Registry: ....Great Britain	Cabins (total): 975	Fitness Center: ....Yes
Length (ft/m): 857.2/261.30	Size Range (sq ft/m): 158.2–610.3/	Sauna/Steam Room: ....Yes/Yes
Beam (ft/m): 105.6/32.20	14.7–56.7	Massage: ....Yes
Draft (ft/m): 24.6/7.95	Cabins (outside view): 603	Self-Service Launderette: ....Yes
Propulsion/Propellers: .....diesel-electric	Cabins (interior/no view): 372	Dedicated Cinema/Seats: ....No
(28,000 kW)/2	Cabins (for one person): 0	Library: ....Yes
Passenger Decks: 10	Cabins (with private balcony): 410	Classification Society: ....Lloyds Register
Total Crew: 850	Cabins (wheelchair accessible): 19	

OVERALL SCORE: NYR (OUT OF A POSSIBLE 2,000 POINTS)

ACCOMMODATION: There are 19 different cabin grades, designated as: suites (with private balcony), mini-suites (with private balcony), outside-view twin-bedded cabin with balcony, outside-view twin bedded cabin, and interior (no view) twin-bedded cabins. Although the standard outside-view and interior (no view) cabins are a little small, they are well designed and functional in layout, and have earth tone colors accentuated by splashes of color from the bedspreads. Proportionately, there are quite a lot of interior (no view) cabins. Many of the outside-view cabins have private balconies, and all seem to be quite well soundproofed, although the balcony partition is not of the floor to ceiling type, so you can hear your neighbors clearly (or smell their smoke). The balconies are very narrow, and only just large enough for two small chairs, and there is no dedicated outdoor balcony lighting. Many cabins have third- and fourth-person upper bunk beds – these are good for families with children.

SUITES: The largest accommodation is in six suites, two on each of three decks at the aft of the ship (with a private balcony giving great views over the stern). Each of these suites, named *Oronsay, Orcades, Orion, Orissa, Orsova, Orontes* (all P&O ships of yesteryear), has a large private balcony. They are well laid out, and have large, marble-clad bathrooms with two washbasins, a Jacuzzi bathtub, and a separate shower enclosure. The bedroom has generous amounts of wood accenting and detailing, indented ceilings, and TV sets in both bedroom and lounge areas, which also have a dining room table and four chairs.

BERLITZ'S RATINGS

	Possible	Achieved
Ship	500	NYR
Accommodation	200	NYR
Food	400	NYR
Service	400	NYR
Entertainment	100	NYR
Cruise	400	NYR

MINI-SUITES: Mini-suites typically have two lower beds that convert to a queen-sized bed. There is a separate bedroom/sleeping area with vanity desk, and a lounge with sofa and coffee table, indented ceilings with generous amounts of wood accenting and detailing, walk-in closet, and a larger, marble-clad bathroom with Jacuzzi bathtub and separate shower enclosure. There is a private balcony.

STANDARD OUTSIDE-VIEW/INTERIOR (NO VIEW) CABINS: A reasonable amount of closet and abundant drawer and other storage space is provided in all cabins (adequate for 7 nights but a little tight for longer cruises), as are a TV set and refrigerator. Each night a chocolate will appear on your pillow. The cabin bathrooms are practical, and come with all the details one needs, although they really are tight spaces, best as one-person at-a-time units. They do, however, have a decent shower enclosure, a small amount of shelving for personal toiletries, real glasses, hairdryer and bathrobe.

You can receive BBC World channel on the in-cabin color television system (when available, depending on cruise area), as well as movies (there is no dedicated theater aboard this ship).

DINING: There are two principal dining rooms, *Adriatic* and *Ligurian*. Both dining rooms are non-smoking, as are the dining rooms aboard all ships of P & O Cruises, and which one you are assigned to will depend on the location of your accommodation. Each has its own galley and each is split into multi-tier sections, which help create a feeling of intimacy, although there is a lot of noise from the waiter stations, adjacent to many tables. Breakfast and lunch are provided in an open seating arrangement, while dinner is in two seatings.

The cuisine is decidedly British – a little adventurous at times, but always, always with plenty of curry dishes and other standard British items. The presentation is good, though – better than other ships in the P&O Cruises fleet. Don't expect exquisite dining – this is British hotel catering that doesn't pretend to offer caviar and other gourmet foods. But what it does present is attractive and tasty, with some excellent gravies and sauces to accompany meals. In keeping with the Britishness of P&O Cruises, the desserts are always good. A statement in the onboard cruise folder states that P&O Cruises does not knowingly purchase genetically modified foods. The service is provided by a team of friendly stewards – most from the island of Goa, with which P&O has had a long relationship.

On most cruises, a typical menu cycle will include a Sailaway Dinner, Captain's Welcome Dinner, Chef's Dinner, Italian Dinner, French Dinner, Captain's Gala Dinner, and Landfall Dinner. The wine list is reasonable, but the company has, sadly, seen fit to eliminate all wine waiters. A 15 percent is added to all beverage bills, including wines (whether you order a £10 bottle or a £100 bottle of wine, even though it takes the same amount of service to open and pour the wine).

The Plaza self-serve buffet is open 24 hours a day, and is located above the navigation bridge, with some commanding views. At night, this large room (there are two food lines – one each on both port and starboard sides) is transformed into an informal dinner setting with sit-down waiter service.

Outdoors on deck, with a sheltered view over the Riviera Pool, the Riviera Grill has fast-food items for those who don't want to change from their sunbathing attire.

For informal eats, there is also *Café Jardin*, for pizzas and light snacks; it is located on the uppermost level of the four deck high atrium lobby.

In addition, there is also a pâtisserie (for cappuccino/espresso coffees and pastries), a wine/caviar bar (Magnums). The cabin service menu is very limited, and presentation of the food items featured is poor.

OTHER COMMENTS: Although large, this all-white ship has a good profile, and is well balanced by its large funnel, which contains a deck tennis/basketball/volleyball court in its sheltered aft base. There is a wide, teakwood wrap-around promenade deck outdoors, real teak steamer-style deck chairs (complete with royal blue cushioned pads), and 93,000 sq. ft (8,600 sq. meters) of space outdoors. A great amount of glass area on the upper decks provides plenty of light and connection with the outside world.

The ship, while large, absorbs passengers well, and has an almost intimate feel, which is what the interior designers intended. Its interiors are very pretty and warm,

with attractive colors and welcoming décor that includes some very attractive wall murals and other artwork.

There is a wide range of public rooms, with several intimate rooms and spaces, so that you don't feel overwhelmed by large spaces. The décor is tasteful, with attractive color combinations that are warm and do not clash (nothing is brash). The interior focal point is a large four-deck-high atrium lobby with winding, double stairways and two panoramic glass-walled elevators.

The main public entertainment rooms are located under three decks of passenger cabins. There is plenty of space throughout the public areas, and the traffic flow is quite good. There are two show lounges (Footlights, and Starlights), one at each end of the ship. One is a fine 550-seat, theater-style show lounge (movies may also be shown here occasionally) and the other is a 480-seat cabaret-style lounge, complete with bar.

A glass-walled health spa complex is located high atop ship and includes a gymnasium with high-tech machines. One swimming pool is "suspended" aft between two decks (there are two other pools, although they are not large for the size of the ship).

The library is a warm room and has six large buttery leather chairs for listening to compact audio discs, with ocean-view windows. There is a conference center for up to 300, as well as a business center, with computers, copy and fax machines.

The collection of artwork is quite good, particularly on the stairways, and helps make the ship feel smaller than it is, and is more coordinated than before (when the ship was operated by Princess Cruises). The Monte Carlo Club Casino, while large, is not really in the main passenger flow and so it does not generate the "walk-through" factor found aboard so many ships.

The most traditional room aboard is the Yacht and Compass Bar, decorated in the style of a turn-of-the-century gentleman's club, with wood paneling and comfortable seating.

Ballroom dance fans will be pleased to note that there are several good-sized wooden dance floors. The ship always carries a professional dance couple as hosts and teachers, and there is plenty of dancing time included in the entertainment programming.

Children have their own Treasure Chest (for ages 2–5), The Hideout (for 6–9 years olds), and for older children (aged 10–13) there is The Buzz Zone.

At the end of the day, as is the case aboard most large ships, if you live in the best accommodation (suites), you will be well attended; if you do not, you will merely be one of a very large number of passengers. One nice feature is the captain's cocktail party – it is held in the four-deck-high main atrium so you can come and go as you please, with no standing in line (to have your photograph taken with the captain) if you don't want to.

However, note that in the quest for increased onboard revenue (and shareholder value), even birthday cakes are an extra cost item, as are espressos and cappuccinos (fake ones, made from instant coffee, are available in the dining rooms). Also at extra cost are ice cream, and bottled water (these can add up to a considerable amount on an around-the-world cruise, for example). You can expect to be subjected to a stream of flyers advertising daily art auctions, "designer" watches and other promotions. For gratuities (which are optional), you should typically allow £3.50 (about $5.50) per person, per day. The onboard currency is the British pound.

A fine British brass band send-off accompanies all sailings from Southampton. Other touches include church bells that sound throughout the ship for the inter-denominational Sunday church service. A coach service for any passengers embarking or disembarking in Southampton covers much of the UK. Car parking is also available (there is one rate for undercover parking, one rate for parking in an open compound).

This book was published before *Ocean Princess* had left the Princess Cruises fleet to P&O Cruises to become *Oceana.* Although not yet rated as *Oceana,* the evaluations and ratings in effect when the ship was operated as *Ocean Princess* (1,539 points, 4 Stars) are expected to be reasonably similar when the ship is re-evaluated.

WEAK POINTS: There are a number of dead ends in the interior layout, so it's not as user-friendly as it should be. Standing in line for disembarkation, shore tenders and for self-serve buffet meals is an inevitable aspect of cruising aboard all large ships. You may be subjected to announcements for revenue-producing activities such as art auctions, bingo, horse racing that intrude constantly into your cruise.

The digital voice announcing elevator deck stops is irritating to passengers (many of whom have threatened to rip out the speaker system). The cabin numbering system is illogical, with numbers going through several hundred series on the same deck. The walls of the passenger accommodation decks are very plain (some artwork would be an improvement).

The swimming pools are actually rather small and will be crowded when the ship is full; also the pool deck is cluttered with white, plastic deck lounge chairs, which don't have cushioned pads. Waiting for tenders in anchor ports can prove irritating, but typical of large ship operations. Shuttle buses, which used to be provided free in some ports, are no longer complimentary.

Oceanic
★★ +

Large Ship: ....38,772 tons	Total Crew: 565	Cabins (wheelchair accessible): 1
Lifestyle: ....Standard	Passengers	Cabin Current: ....110 volts
Cruise Line: ....Pullmantur Cruises	(lower beds/all berths): 1,124/1,800	Elevators: 5
Former Names: ...*Big Red Boat I, Oceanic*	Passenger Space Ratio	Casino (gaming tables): ....Yes
Builder: ....Cantieri Riuniti dell' Adriatico	(basis 2): 34.7/21.54	Slot Machines: ....Yes
(Italy)	Passenger Space Ratio	Swimming Pools (outdoors): 2
Original Cost: ....$40 million	(all berths): 21.5/3.1	Swimming Pools (inside): 0
Entered Service: .....Apr 1965/May 2001	Navigation Officers: ....Spanish	Whirlpools: 3
Registry: ....Spain	Cabins (total): 562	Fitness Center: ....Yes
Length (ft/m): 782.1/238.40	Size Range (sq ft/m): 139.9–454.2/	Sauna/Steam Room: ....No/No
Beam (ft/m): 96.5/29.44	13.0–42.2	Massage:.........................Yes
Draft (ft/m): 28.2/8.60	Cabins (outside view): 252	Self-Service Launderette: ....No
Propulsion/Propellers: .....steam turbine	Cabins (interior/no view): 310	Cinema/Seats: ....No
(45,100 kW)/2	Cabins (for one person): 0	Library: ....Yes
Passenger Decks: 10	Cabins (with private balcony): 21	Classification Society: ....Bureau Veritas

OVERALL SCORE: 1,093 (OUT OF A POSSIBLE 2,000 POINTS)

ACCOMMODATION: *Oceanic* has a wide range of suites and standard outside-view and interior (no view) cabins, in different 12 price categories (seven for outside-view suites, junior suites and cabins, and five for interior cabins without a view). There are far more interior (no view) cabins than outside-view cabins. There are eight deluxe suites, each with a private balcony; 65 suites (13 with a private balcony), the rest being a mixture of inside (no view) and outside (sea-view) cabins. Many of the suites have their views obstructed by lifeboats.

The ceiling height is good, which helps give an impression of space. All cabins have heavy-duty furniture and are quite well equipped, although many are now in need of refurbishment. Many cabins have double beds. All cabins have a television, telephone, and climate control.

DINING: The Seven Continents Restaurant, which operates in two seatings, is large and cheerful, but it is extremely noisy when full (some might call it ambience). The tables (for between two and eight persons) are very close together, and chairs do not have armrests (there is simply not enough room for them). All meals are included in the price. The cuisine is adequate, no more, and dining room service is of only a very basic standard – there is absolutely no finesse in service. Although food is plentiful, there is a limited selection of breads, cheeses and fruits. The wine list is reasonably decent (with many Spanish wines featured), and the prices are reasonable.

BERLITZ'S RATINGS

	Possible	Achieved
Ship	500	263
Accommodation	200	124
Food	400	222
Service	400	220
Entertainment	100	56
Cruise	400	208

OTHER COMMENTS: Built with a strong, riveted hull, originally as an ocean liner for Home Lines, *Oceanic* (the ship's first name), it underwent a successful conversion to provide cheap and cheerful family cruises following its purchase by Premier Cruise Lines in 1985. When Premier went into bankruptcy in 2000, the ship was purchased at auction, and is now owned and operated by Spain-based tour operator Pullmantur Cruises.

There is a reasonable amount of open teakwood-covered deck space for sunbathing, but it becomes cramped and noisy when the ship is full, and there are no cushioned pads for the white plastic deck lounge chairs (except on the deck lounge chairs located along the inside promenade deck). The twin swimming pools atop the ship have a sliding magrodome roof that can be used in inclement weather.

The ship's interiors and public rooms have changed little since the ship was operated by Premier Cruise Lines, and some artwork (particularly on the stairways) exist from its original operator, Home Lines.

The interiors have upbeat décor, and cheerful soft furnishing fabrics. One neat feature is the enclosed promenades (popular on the old ocean liners crossing the North Atlantic in all weather conditions) for strolling around the ship, or for just sitting; however, table tennis tables do restrict the flow around this promenade deck. During a refurbishment in May 2000, a new kid's room and teen room were built, and an Internet Café was installed. Framed photographs and paintings, which are for sale, are placed on the walls of the main lounge deck.

One interesting feature of the former ocean liner can be found on the aft of Lounge Deck, which has a bar outdoors (with San Miguel beer on draft), and a small enclosure with original brass emergency steering equipment, made by Hastie of Greenock, Scotland, together with the ship's wheel.

Although the ship got off to a rather chaotic start under the new operators, Pullmantur Cruises, it has now settled down and will provide a family with children with a busy, fun-filled cruise aboard a classic ship setting. But it certainly does remind me of a summer camp at sea, particularly when school vacations mean lots (and I mean *lots*) of children have the run of the ship, the complaints of many passengers who have cruised aboard other cruise ships. The onboard currency is the euro.

WEAK POINTS: There are many, many interior (no view) cabins. There are lines everywhere. There is much congestion at the self-service buffets for breakfast and lunch. The noise pollution is high throughout the ship, with constant repetitive announcements, and music throughout all hallways and on open decks. The interiors need more attention to detail, and cleanliness could be better. Many public rooms have numerous support pillars to obstruct sight lines. Smokers are everywhere – there is no escape.

SAFETY MEASURES

Fire Control

If anyone sounds the fire alarm, an alarm is automatically set off on the bridge. A red panel light will be illuminated on a large plan, indicating the section of the ship that has to be checked so that the crew can take immediate action.

Ships are sectioned into several zones, each of which can be tightly closed off. In addition, almost all ships have a water-fed sprinkler system that can be activated at the touch of a button, or automatically activated when sprinkler vials are broken by fire-generated heat. New electronic fire detection systems are being installed aboard ships in order to increase safety further.

Emergency Ventilation Control

This automatic fire damper system also has a manual switch that is activated to stop or control the flow of air to all areas of the ship, in this way reducing the fanning effect on flame and smoke via air-conditioning and fan systems.

Watertight Doors Control

Watertight doors throughout the ship can be closed off, in order to contain the movement of water flooding the ship. A master switch activates all the doors in a matter of seconds. All watertight doors can be operated electrically and manually, which means that nobody can be trapped in a watertight compartment.

Stabilizers Control

The ship's two stabilizing fins can be extended, housed, or controlled. They normally operate automatically under the command of a gyroscope located in the engine control room.

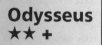

Ramoved 2006

Odysseus
★★ +

Small Ship: ....9,821 tons	Total Crew: 194	Cabins (wheelchair accessible): 0
Lifestyle: ....Standard	Passengers	Cabin Current: ....110 volts
Cruise Line: ......Royal Olympic Cruises	(lower beds/all berths): 452/484	Elevators: 1
Former Names: ......*Aquamarine, Marco*	Passenger Space Ratio	Casino (gaming tables): ....Yes
Polo, Princesa Isabel	(lower beds/all berths): 21.7/20.2	Slot Machines: ....Yes
Builder: .....Astilleros Espanoles (Spain)	Crew/Passenger Ratio	Swimming Pools (outdoors): 1
Original Cost: ....n/a	(lower beds/all berths): 2.3/2.4	Swimming Pools (indoors): 0
Entered Service: 1962/2000	Navigation Officers: ....Greek	Whirlpools: 4
Registry: ....Greece	Cabins (total): 226	Fitness Center: ....Yes
Length (ft/m): 483.1/147.30	Size Range (sq ft/m): 102.2–279.8/	Sauna/Steam Room: ....Yes/No
Beam (ft/m): 61.2/18.67	9.5–26.0	Massage:........................Yes
Draft (ft/m): 24.1/7.35	Cabins (outside view): 183	Self-Service Launderette: ....No
Propulsion/Propellers: ....diesel	Cabins (interior/no view): 43	Dedicated Cinema/Seats: ....No
(6,766 kW)/2	Cabins (for one person): 0	Library: ....Yes
Passenger Decks: 7	Cabins (with private balcony): 0	Classification Society: ...Lloyd's Register

OVERALL SCORE: 1,071 (OUT OF A POSSIBLE 2,000 POINTS)

ACCOMMODATION: The attractive, fairly roomy, mostly outside-view cabins have either sofa beds which convert from a sofa during the day into and a bed by night or twin beds (few cabins have genuine double beds). There is a reasonable amount of closet and drawer space, and tasteful gray wood cabinetry that, in most cabins, includes a writing/vanity desk. Some cabins have third/fourth upper Pullman berths. The cabin bathrooms, however, are really quite small, (particularly the shower enclosures) and very basic, with little storage space, and harsh fluorescent lighting. Personal amenities provided include soap, shampoo/bath foam, perfumed hand lotion, shower cap, and sewing kit. The towels are of 100 percent cotton. Note that some cabins in the center of the ship on Poseidon Deck and Venus Deck are subject to throbbing diesel generator noise.

There is a 24-hour room service menu, but any in-cabin food/beverage service tends to be very basic, without the finesse found aboard more expensive vessels.

The largest accommodation comprises four suites; each has a separate lounge and sleeping area (with double bed), plenty of closet, drawer and other storage space, and a reasonably large bathroom.

DINING: The dining room is quite basic in furnishings and setting, and because it is small, it does tend to be extremely noisy, due to the low ceiling height and the location of waiter stations. Because it is small, there are two seatings (both non-smoking). The chairs do not have armrests and are quite small, and low. The food is Con-

BERLITZ'S RATINGS

	Possible	Achieved
Ship	500	268
Accommodation	200	116
Food	400	213
Service	400	223
Entertainment	100	48
Cruise	400	203

tinental, and includes many well-known Greek dishes. Reasonably warm, attentive service is provided in typical Greek fashion, but the menu choice is rather limited, and presentation is inconsistent. The quality and selection of breads, cheeses, and fruits could be better. You should note that dining room seating and table assignments are typically provided by the restaurant manager (maitre d') upon embarkation (this may or may not be so when the ship is under charter and an open seating is operated).

An informal eatery is available poolside for casual buffet-style breakfasts and lunches, although the selection is quite limited. Seating is at plastic deck chairs, which, without cushions, are uncomfortable. A very basic beverage station is provided, with plastic cups.

OTHER COMMENTS: This moderately attractive traditional vessel has a balanced, somewhat low profile, with a royal blue, riveted hull and white superstructure. It was acquired and completely reconstructed by Epirotiki Cruise Line (now part of Royal Olympic Cruises) in 1987. There is ample open deck and sunbathing space. There are twin teakwood-decked sheltered promenade walking areas.

There is a reasonable range of public rooms for the size of the vessel. Almost all have dated Mediterranean décor, very plain colors, and very little artwork. Almost all of the public rooms are located on one principal deck, so finding them is easy. The show lounge, located forward, is quite poor, as four large pillars obstruct sight lines from many seats. A small nightclub/disco is popular with the late-night set.

This ship is really best suited to those who want to cruise at a modest cost, in adequate, but dated surroundings, aboard a comfortable smaller vessel which features interesting and popular destination-intensive itineraries mainly in the Aegean and Mediterranean.

The ship is often placed under charter to various tour operators, and packages are sold by a number of cruise-tour companies in various countries. This means that passengers are likely to consist of a wide mix of nationalities, and daily programs and announcements, therefore, could well be in several languages.

Under Greek Seaman's Union rules, all gratuities (suggested at $9 per person per day) are pooled among the crew (you give them to the chief steward). The exception to this is when the ship is operating under charter and the charterer/operator includes gratuities in the fare. The onboard currency is the euro.

WEAK POINTS: The dining room is small and extremely noisy. There is no wrap-around outdoor promenade deck. Some of the interior stairways are very steep and have very short steps. There are only two bars. The company provides little port information for passengers wishing to go ashore individually, but heavily sells its own shore excursion programs. The staff hospitality factor is adequate; more training is needed. In fact, there is little consistency across the company's range of ships with regard to standards of food, service and hospitality.

QUOTABLE QUOTES

Overheard in Alaska:
"Are the glaciers always here?"

Overheard in the cigar smoking room: "I'm looking for a no-smoking seat"

Overheard in the dining room in the Caribbean:
"Is all the salmon smoked? I am a non-smoker"
"Waiter, this vichyssoise is cold."
"Was the fish caught this morning by the crew?"

Overheard on an Antarctic cruise:
"Where is the good shopping in Antarctica?"

Overheard on a cruise taking in the British Isles:
"Windsor Castle is terrific. But why did they build it so close to the airport?"

Overheard on a Greek islands cruise: "Why did the Greeks build so many ruins?"

Overheard in the dining room:
Passenger: "Waiter: What is caviar?"
Waiter: "Fish eggs, sir."
Passenger: "In that case, I'll have two, over-easy!"

Overheard on a QE2 round-Japan cruise, in Kagoshima, with Mount Suribaya in the background: "Can you tell me what time the volcano will erupt? I want to be sure to take a photograph."

Removed 2006

Olympia Countess
★★★

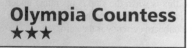

Mid-Size Ship: . . . . .17,593 tons	Total Crew: 350	Cabins (wheelchair accessible): 0
Lifestyle: . . . . .Standard	Passengers	Cabin Current: . . . . .110 and 220 volts
Cruise Line: . . . . . .Royal Olympic Cruises	(lower beds/all berths): 846/959	Elevators: 2
Former Names: . . . . . .*Olympic Countess,*	Passenger Space Ratio	Casino (gaming tables): . . . . .Yes
Awani Dream I, Cunard Countess	(lower beds/all berths): 20.7/18.3	Slot Machines: .Yes
Builder: . . . .Burmeister & Wein (Denmark)	Crew/Passenger Ratio	Swimming Pools (outdoors): 1
Original Cost: . . . .£12 million	(lower beds/all berths): 2.4/2.7	Swimming Pools (indoors): 0
Entered Service: . . . . .Aug 1976/1998	Navigation Officers: . . . . .Greek	Whirlpools: 2
Registry: . . . . .Panama	Cabins (total): .423	Fitness Center: . . . . .Yes
Length (ft/m): 536.6/163.56	Size Range (sq ft/m): 87.1–264.8/	Sauna/Steam Room: . . . . .Yes/No
Beam (ft/m): 74.9/22.84	8.1–24.6	Massage: . . . . .No
Draft (ft/m): 19.0/5.82	Cabins (outside view): 281	Self-Service Launderette: . . . . .No
Propulsion/Propellers: . . . . .diesel	Cabins (interior/no view): 142	Dedicated Cinema/Seats: Yes/126
(15,670 kW)/2	Cabins (for one person): 0	Library: . . . . .Yes
Passenger Decks: 8	Cabins (with private balcony): 0	Classification Society: . . .Lloyd's Register

---

OVERALL SCORE: 1,240 (OUT OF A POSSIBLE 2,000 POINTS)

ACCOMMODATION: The cabins are mostly of a standard (very compact) size, and come in light colors and plain, but pleasant décor that is adequate for short cruises. They are best described as space-efficient units with metal fixtures and poor insulation – you can talk to your neighbors without having to use the telephone! Cabins on the lowest deck (Poseidon Deck) suffer from vibration and the odor of diesel fuel. The cabin bathrooms are small modular units, good for one, but just about impossible for two.

DINING: The single dining room has large ocean-view picture windows on two sides, and seating is mostly at tables for four, six or eight. There are two seatings. Reasonable banquet food is standard, tailored for American and European passengers. Out-of-the-ordinary requests are difficult. There is a limited selection of fresh fruits and cheeses, but good, cheerful service from an attentive Greek staff.

Additionally, a casual self-serve open-air area is available at the stern of the ship for breakfast, lunches and (sometimes, depending on the itinerary) buffet dinners.

OTHER COMMENTS: Originally built for Cunard Line as an informal Caribbean cruise vessel, the ship was bought in 1997 by Royal Olympic Cruises from its for-

BERLITZ'S RATINGS

	Possible	Achieved
Ship	500	326
Accommodation	200	121
Food	400	247
Service	400	251
Entertainment	100	52
Cruise	400	243

mer operators, the now defunct Awani Dream Cruises, of Indonesia, who purchased the vessel from Cunard.

Olympia Countess still displays a contemporary profile, with crisp, clean lines and a distinctive swept-back funnel (its almost identical twin presently operates as *Rhapsody* for Mediterranean Shipping Cruises).

Inside, there is a good selection of public rooms, most with attractive, light colors and cheerful décor. The show lounge is a single-level room with raised seating on its port and starboard sides (eight pillars obstruct the sight lines, however, and the ceiling is low). Aft of the show lounge is a good indoor-outdoor entertainment lounge/nightclub that incorporates a large aft open deck area – a good facility for warm-weather cruises.

Passengers seeking a casual, destination-intensive cruise will probably like this comfortable vessel, which is a change from the newer, larger ships of today, and is well suited to cruising in the Aegean/Mediterranean region. Gratuities (suggested at $9 per person per day) are pooled among the crew. The onboard currency is the US dollar.

WEAK POINTS: This is a very high-density ship. The outside decks need attention. Too many loud, unnecessary announcements do not make for a relaxing cruise.

Removed 2006

Olympia Explorer
★★★★

Mid-Size Ship: ....24,500 tons	Passengers	Cabin Current: ....110 and 230 volts
Lifestyle: ....Standard	(lower beds/all berths): 840/920	Elevators: 4
Cruise Line: ......Royal Olympic Cruises	Passenger Space Ratio	Casino (gaming tables): ....Yes
Former Names: ....none	(lower beds/all berths): 29.1/26.6	Slot Machines: ....Yes
Builder: ....Blohm & Voss (Germany)	Crew/Passenger Ratio	Swimming Pools (outdoors): 1
Original Cost: ....$175 million	(lower beds/all berths): 2.3/2.5	Swimming Pools (indoors): 0
Entered Service: ....May 2001	Navigation Officers: ....Greek	Whirlpools: 0
Registry: ....Gibraltar	Cabins (total): 420	Fitness Center: ....Yes
Length (ft/m): 590.5/180.0	Size Range (sq ft/m): 140.0–258.0/	Sauna/Steam Room: ....Yes/No
Beam (ft/m): 83.6/25.5	13.0–23.9	Massage: ....Yes
Draft (ft/m): 23.2/7.1	Cabins (outside view): 296	Self-Service Launderette: ....No
Propulsion/Propellers: ....diesel	Cabins (interior/no view): 124	Dedicated Cinema/Seats: ....No
(37,800 kW)/2	Cabins (for one person): 0	Library: ....Yes
Passenger Decks: 8	Cabins (with private balcony): 24	Classification Society: .....Germanischer
Total Crew: 360	Cabins (wheelchair accessible): 4	Lloyd

OVERALL SCORE: 1,432 (OUT OF A POSSIBLE 2,000 POINTS)

ACCOMMODATION: The accommodation, in 11 price grades, consists of 12 Sky Suites (with balcony), 12 Balcony Cabins (with a covered, and not an open ceiling, and with full partitions – so you can't hear your neighbor or smell their smoke), 20 Junior Suites, 292 cabins (double occupancy), 72 cabins (two lower beds and a third, upper berth), 4 cabins (two lower beds, two upper berths) and 4 wheelchair accessible cabins (with spacious bathrooms and roll-in showers).

BERLITZ'S RATINGS		
	Possible	Achieved
Ship	500	411
Accommodation	200	158
Food	400	273
Service	400	284
Entertainment	100	60
Cruise	400	246

STANDARD CABINS: The standard interior (no view) and outside-view cabins are quite compact (some interior cabins are larger than others), but practically laid-out, and the décor includes warm blond wood cabinetry, accents and facings, and pleasing soft furnishings. The bathrooms are small, but have a decent-sized shower enclosure, and storage facilities for personal toiletry items. All cabins include television (with pay-per-view movies), hairdryer, mini-bar/refrigerator and personal safe. The Junior Suites simply have a little more room than the standard cabins.

SKY SUITES: The largest accommodation can be found in 12 Sky Suites, all of which have names) located high atop the ship and in the forward-most section. They have large private balconies (some are more like large terraces), floor-to-ceiling windows, limited butler service, and 24-hour dining service (although the glass-topped table is far too low for use as a dining table for anything other than snacks). Some of the suites have walk-in closets, while others have closets facing the entrance-way; all, however, have an abundance of drawer and hanging space, and chrome pullout shoe rack and tie rack. The bathroom has a combination bathtub/shower (although the bathtub is extremely small and is really only for sitting in) and a retractable clothesline; a thick 100 percent cotton bathrobe is also provided. All suites feature wood paneled walls with vanity desk, stocked mini-bar/refrigerator, sofa, coffee table (this is fixed and cannot be raised for dining), and sleeping area partly separated from the lounge area by a wood/glass divider. Note that four of the suites have huge structures above their balconies that constitute port side and starboard side gangway lowering mechanisms; they are noisy in ports of call and anchor ports, and thus the balconies cannot be considered very private. Also, you should note that when the ship is traveling at speed, considerable wind sweeps across the balcony, rendering it all but useless.

DELUXE (BALCONY) SUITES: The 12 cabins with private balconies have superb electric sliding doors to the balconies (they operate by compressed air filling a "skirt" around the door frame to keep them absolutely airtight and soundproof). Facilities include wood-paneled walls with vanity desk, stocked mini-bar/refrigerator, sofa, and drinks table (this is fixed and cannot be raised for dining). There is a separate sleeping area (with twin or queen-sized bed), vanity/make-up desk with a good amount of drawer space. There is a decent amount of closet space and an abundance of drawer and hanging space, chrome pullout shoe rack baskets, and tie rack.

The bathroom has a combination bathtub/shower (although the bathtub is extremely small and is really only for sitting in) and a retractable clothesline; a thick 100 percent cotton bathrobe is also provided.

DINING: The 470-seat Dining Room, located aft, has picture windows on three sides. There are two seatings, and there are tables for two, four, six or eight. It has a semi-circular walkway, with minimalist décor, as its entrance. The décor in the dining room itself is warm and welcoming, and quite tasteful, carried out as it is in what is best described as a "Greek Moderne" style.

For casual breakfast and lunch self-service buffets, the Garden Restaurant is a pleasant, but very basic room, with large picture windows and an open feel to the room. There is seating for 210 indoors and 199 outdoors, where there is also a bar with sailcloth-style cover. The layout of the buffet line is atrocious; it is too small, and causes congestion – a testament to poor, inflexible shipbuilding in the 21st century.

Additional munching outlets include a pizza serving area/salad bar, and an ice cream bar.

OTHER COMMENTS: This is the second new ship (sister ship *Olympia Voyager* was the first) ordered by Royal Olympic Cruises (a combination of two old-established former cruise companies: Epirotiki Lines and Sun Line Cruises), and takes the company into the contemporary cruise market with new ships. The ship has a compact outer design, complete with a royal blue hull, for this medium-size, but high-density ship. There is a streamlined funnel, and the fast speed (up to 27 knots) enables it to operate busy (destination-intensive) itineraries.

The exterior hull design is similar to that found in naval frigates, with a slender fore-body, and two engine rooms (forward and amidships) capable of providing a 27-knot speed (and even some additional power in reserve). The ship is thus designed for destination-intensive (port-hopping) itineraries that can be covered in a shorter time, which allows passengers more time in each port.

There is a reasonable amount of open deck space (provided the ship isn't full), although there are not many deck lounge chairs; all exterior railings are made – unusually so – of stainless steel. The seawater swimming pool is located aft, and is quite small (most passengers will be enjoying the destinations featured by this cruise line); adjacent are two shower enclosures.

The interior design combines contemporary conveniences with quiet, restrained décor intended to remind one of the Mediterranean region the ship is specifically designed for, with warm colors and an abundance of blond woods and opaque glass paneling.

Perhaps the most striking, yet subtle, features in terms of design and decoration can be found in the artwork. Of particular note are the two flowing poems that are etched in illuminated opaque glass panels that are backlit on the stairways (these are, ironically, by poets from Greece and Cyprus – the two countries where the owning companies of Royal Olympic Cruises are located).

Most of the public rooms are located on one principal deck in a horizontal-flow layout that makes it easy to quickly find your way around, with a slightly winding open passageway that links several leisure lounges in one neat "street scene" (the artwork consists of valuable rocks and gems from Greece and the islands). A cigar smoking room, just aft of the main show lounge, attracts cigar and cognac devotees and comes complete with fireplace. There's also a library and a separate card room, and a piano lounge with bar.

A casino (with its own bar) features blackjack, roulette and aces poker tables, while another section houses 44 slot machines (tokens only).

One of the nicest and most useful facilities aboard this ship can be found in the Spa. This is well run by a Greek concession, and provides Ayervedic massage as well as Swedish Remedial/Aromatherapy massage, a hydrotherapy bath, mosaic tiled steam room and sauna (both are co-ed – so you will need to wear a bathing suit), and several treatment rooms, all in an area that is secluded from the main passenger flow.

Other facilities include a show lounge (with 420 seats, and many pillars that obstruct the sight lines from too many seats), a nightclub, piano bar, library and card room.

The program of special interest guest lecturers that accompanies each cruise is very good; these may be destination, cultural, lifestyle, or ex-government lecturers.

The crew typically consists of a Greek and international mix, with Greek officers. There is a good degree of warmth and friendliness throughout the ship – a factor that so many cruise lines seem to have neglected. While service is not perfect, it comes with a smile. Gratuities are given directly to dining room stewards and cabin stewardesses, and are not pooled as they are aboard most Greek-flag ships. The onboard currency is the euro.

WEAK POINTS: There is no full wrap-around promenade deck outdoors, although you can walk around parts of the vessel outdoors. There are no dedicated facilities or rooms for the large numbers of children or teens that are typically carried during the July/August summer holidays. There is no public toilet that is accessible by wheelchair. There simply are not enough deck lounge chairs considering the number of passengers carried, and not enough open deck space. Overall, the cabins are very small for anything longer than 7-day cruises. The sight lines in the show lounge are appalling – from about 40 percent of the seats.

Removed 2006

Olympia Voyager
★★★★

Mid-Size Ship: . . . . .24,391 tons	Passengers	Cabin Current: . . . . .110 and 230 volts
Lifestyle: . . . . .Standard	(lower beds/all berths): 840/920	Elevators: 4
Cruise Line: . . . . . .Royal Olympic Cruises	Passenger Space Ratio	Casino (gaming tables): . . . . .Yes
Former Names: . . . . .none	(lower beds/all berths): 29.0/26.5	Slot Machines: . . . . .Yes
Builder: . . . . .Blohm & Voss (Germany)	Crew/Passenger Ratio	Swimming Pools (outdoors): 1
Original Cost: . . . .$150.8 million	(lower beds/all berths): 2.3/2.5	Swimming Pools (indoors): 0
Entered Service: . . . . .July 2000	Navigation Officers: . . . . .Greek	Whirlpools: 0
Registry: . . . . .Greece	Cabins (total): 420	Fitness Center: . . . . .Yes
Length (ft/m): 590.5/180.0	Size Range (sq ft/m): 140.0–258.0/	Sauna/Steam Room: . . . . .Yes/No
Beam (ft/m): 83.6/25.5	13.0–23.9	Massage: . . . . .Yes
Draft (ft/m): 23.2/7.1	Cabins (outside view): 294	Self-Service Launderette: . . . . .No
Propulsion/Propellers: . . . . .diesel	Cabins (interior/no view): 126	Dedicated Cinema/Seats: . . . . .No
(37,800 kW)/2	Cabins (for one person): 0	Library: . . . . .Yes
Passenger Decks: 8	Cabins (with private balcony): 12	Classification Society: . . . . .Germanischer
Total Crew: .360	Cabins (wheelchair accessible): 4	Lloyd

OVERALL SCORE: 1,409 (OUT OF A POSSIBLE 2,000 POINTS)

ACCOMMODATION: The accommodation, in 11 price grades, consists of 12 Sky Suites, 16 Bay Window Suites, 20 Junior Suites, 292 cabins (double occupancy), 72 cabins (two lower beds, one upper berth), 4 four-person cabins (two lower beds, two upper berths) and 4 wheelchair accessible cabins (with spacious bathrooms and roll-in showers).

STANDARD CABINS: The standard interior (no view) and outside-view cabins are quite compact, but practically laid-out, and the décor includes warm blond wood cabinetry, accents and facings, and pleasing soft furnishings. The bathrooms are small, but have a decent-sized shower enclosure, and good storage facilities for personal toiletry items. All cabins include television (with pay-per-view movies), hairdryer, mini-bar/refrigerator and a personal safe. You should note that only one personal safe is provided in each cabin, although there could be as many as four persons sharing the same cabin.

JUNIOR SUITES: The accommodation designated as Junior Suites simply have a little more room than the standard interior (no view) and outside-view cabins. The bathrooms are small, but have a decent-sized shower enclosure, and good storage facilities for personal toiletry items.

BAY WINDOW SUITES: There are 16 bay window cabins (Acropolis, Aphea, Athos, Corinthia, Delos, Delphi, Dodoni, Knossos, Lindos, Meteore, Mistra, Olympia, Sounion, Sparta, Thiva, Velos) in the forward section of the ship; each features a large window that extends over the side of the ship, and a lounge area and sleeping area.

BERLITZ'S RATINGS

	Possible	Achieved
Ship	500	399
Accommodation	200	157
Food	400	263
Service	400	284
Entertainment	100	60
Cruise	400	246

SKY SUITES: The largest accommodation can be found in 12 Sky Suites (Andromeda, Arcas, Ariadne, Bolina, Cadmos, Cassiope, Harmonia, Hersilia, Myrtilos, Parthenos, Perseas, Theseas) located high atop the ship and in the forward-most section. They have large private balconies (some are more like large terraces), floor-to-ceiling windows, limited butler service, and 24-hour dining service (although the glass-topped table is far too low for use as a dining table for anything other than snacks). Some of the suites have walk-in closets, while others have closets facing the entranceway; all, however, have an abundance of drawer and hanging space, and chrome pullout shoe rack and tie rack. The bathroom has a combination bathtub/shower (although the bathtub is extremely small and is really only for sitting in) and a retractable clothesline; a thick 100 percent cotton bathrobe is also provided.

All suites have wood paneled walls with vanity desk, stocked mini-bar/refrigerator, sofa, coffee table (this is fixed and cannot be raised for dining), and sleeping area partly separated from the lounge area by a wood/glass divider. Arcas, Ariadne, Myrtilos and Parthenos have huge structures above their balconies that constitute port side and starboard side gangway lowering mechanisms; they are noisy in ports of call and anchor ports, and thus the balconies cannot be considered very private. Also, you should note that when the ship is traveling at speed, considerable wind sweeps across the balcony rendering it all but useless.

Outside-view and interior (no-view) cabins located

aft on Deck 3 (Neptune Deck: Numbers 3120–3138 and 3121–3151) are subject to a substantial amount of throbbing noise from the diesel engines, and should be avoided if at all possible (unless you like throbbing engine noise, that is).

DINING: The 470-seat Selenes Dining Room is located aft and has picture windows on three sides. There are two seatings, and there are tables for two, four, six or eight. It has a semi-circular walkway, with minimalist décor, as its entrance. The décor in the dining room itself is warm and welcoming, and quite tasteful, carried out as it is in what is best described as a "Greek Moderne" style.

For casual breakfast and lunch self-service buffets, the Horizon Garden Restaurant is a pleasant, but very basic room, with large picture windows and an open feel to the room. There is seating for 210 indoors and 199 outdoors, where there is also a bar. The layout of the buffet line is atrocious; it is too small, and causes congestion – a testament to poor, inflexible shipbuilding in the 21st century.

Additional munching outlets include a pizza serving area/salad bar, and an ice cream bar.

OTHER COMMENTS: This is the first new ship ever ordered by this company (a combination of two former companies, Epirotiki Lines and Sun Line Cruises), and is intended to take the company into the contemporary cruise market with new ships, like many other companies today. The ship has a compact outer design, complete with a royal blue hull, for this medium-size, but high-density ship. There is a streamlined funnel, and its fast speed (up to 27 knots) enables it to operate busy (destination-intensive) itineraries.

The exterior hull design (called a Fast Monohull) is very close to that found in naval frigates, with a slender fore-body, and two engine rooms (forward and midships) capable of providing a 27-knot speed (and even some additional power in reserve). The ship is thus designed for destination-intensive (port-hopping) itineraries that can be covered in a shorter time, which allows passengers more time in each port.

There is a reasonable amount of open deck space (provided the ship isn't full), although there are not many deck lounge chairs; all exterior railings are made – unusually so – of stainless steel. The seawater swimming pool is located aft, and is quite small (most passengers will be enjoying the destinations served by this cruise line); adjacent are two shower enclosures.

The interior design combines contemporary conveniences with quiet, restrained décor intended to remind one of the Mediterranean region the ship is specifically designed for, with warm colors and an abundance of wood and opaque glass paneling.

Perhaps the most striking, yet subtle, features in terms of design and decoration can be found in the artwork. Of particular note are the two flowing poems etched in illuminated opaque glass panels on the stairways (these are,

ironically, by poets from Greece and Cyprus – the two countries where the owning companies of Royal Olympic Cruises are located). One poem, from 1911 (called *Ithaca*) by the Alexander the Greek poet Constantinos Petrou Kavafis, complements the poem, *Let's Say*, by the Cypriot poet Yannis Papadopoulos. Also, two entertaining large canvasses (that, in turn are composed of four smaller ones) cleverly separate the dining room.

Most public rooms are located on one principal deck in a horizontal-flow layout that makes it easy to quickly find your way around, with a slightly winding open passageway that links several leisure lounges in one neat "street scene." There's a smoking room, adjacent to the main show lounge, for cigar and cognac devotees (with a black fireplace from the 1890s). In the popular Silenes Piano Bar, three ship models are cleverly displayed behind large glass wall panels.

A casino (with its own bar) features blackjack, roulette and aces poker tables, while another section houses 44 slot machines (tokens only).

Other facilities include a show lounge with 420 seats (and many pillars to obstruct the sight lines from many seats), a nightclub, piano bar, library and card room.

One of the nicest and most useful facilities can be found in the Jade Spa. This is well run by a Greek concession, and provides Ayervedic massage as well as Swedish Remedial/Aromatherapy massage, a hydrotherapy bath, mosaic tiled steam room and sauna (both are co-ed, so you will need to wear a bathing suit), and several treatment rooms, all in an area secluded from the main passenger flow.

The program of special interest guest lecturers that accompanies each cruise is very good; these may be destination, cultural, lifestyle, or ex-government lecturers.

The crew typically consists of a Greek and international mix, with Greek officers. There is a good degree of warmth and friendliness throughout the ship – a factor that so many cruise lines seem to have neglected. While service is not perfect, it comes with a smile. Gratuities are given directly to dining room stewards and cabin stewardesses, and are not pooled as they are aboard most ships belonging to Greek companies. The onboard currency is the euro.

WEAK POINTS: There is no full wrap-around promenade deck outdoors, although you can walk around parts of the vessel outdoors. There is considerable vibration when the ship is under way at high speed, and during maneuvering at slow speeds. There are no dedicated facilities or rooms for the large numbers of children or teens that are typically carried during the July/August summer holidays. There is no public toilet accessible by wheelchair. The self-service buffet line is awful. There simply are not enough deck lounge chairs considering the number of passengers carried, and not enough open deck space. Overall, the cabins are very small for anything longer than 7-day cruises. The sight lines in the showlounge are appalling – from about 40 percent of the seats.

Oosterdam
NOT YET RATED

Large Ship: ....85,920 tons	Passengers	Elevators: 14
Lifestyle: ....Premium	(lower beds/all berths): 1,848/2,272	Casino (gaming tables): ....Yes
Cruise Line: ....Holland America Line	Passenger Space Ratio	Slot Machines: ....Yes
Former Names: ....none	(lower beds/all berths): 46.4/37.8	Swimming Pools (outdoors): 2
Builder: ....Fincantieri (Italy)	Crew/Passenger Ratio	+1 children's pool
Original Cost: ....$400 million	(lower beds/all berths): 2.1/2.6	Swimming Pools (indoors): 1
Entered Service: ....June 2003	Navigation Officers: ....European	(indoor/outdoor)
Registry: ....The Netherlands	Cabins (total): 924	Whirlpools: 5
Length (ft/m): 959.6/292.50	Size Range (sq ft/m): 185.0–1,318.6/	Fitness Center: ....Yes
Beam (ft/m): 105.6/32.25	17.1–122.5	Sauna/Steam Room: ....Yes/Yes
Draft (ft/m): 25.5/7.80	Cabins (outside view): 788	Massage: ....Yes
Propulsion/Propellers: .....diesel-electric	Cabins (interior/no view): 136	Self-Service Launderette: ....Yes
(34,000 kW)/2 pods	Cabins (for one person): 0	Dedicated Cinema/Seats: Yes/170
(17.6 MW each)	Cabins (with private balcony): 810	Library: ....Yes
Passenger Decks: 10	Cabins (wheelchair accessible): 28	Classification Society: ...Lloyd's Register
Total Crew: 842	Cabin Current: ....110 volts	

OVERALL SCORE: NYR (OUT OF A POSSIBLE 2,000 POINTS)

ACCOMMODATION: In keeping with cruise industry trends, there are more cabins with private balconies than aboard any other Holland America Line ships at present (with the exception of sister *Zuiderdam*).

Note that some cabins on the lowest accommodation deck (Main Deck) have views obstructed by lifeboats. Some cabins that can accommodate a third and fourth person have very little closet space, and only one personal safe.

BERLITZ'S RATINGS

	Possible	Achieved
Ship	500	NYR
Accommodation	200	NYR
Food	400	NYR
Service	400	NYR
Entertainment	100	NYR
Cruise	400	NYR

PENTHOUSE VERANDAH SUITES: These two suites have the largest accommodation (1,126 sq. ft/104.6 sq. meters). These have a separate bedroom with a king-size bed; there's also a walk-in closet, dressing room, living room, dining room, butler's pantry, mini-bar and refrigerator, and private balcony (verandah). The main bathroom has a large whirlpool bathtub, two washbasins, toilet, and plenty of storage space for personal toiletry items. Personalized stationery and complimentary dry cleaning are included, as are hot hors d'oeuvres daily and other goodies.

DELUXE VERANDAH SUITES: DeLuxe Verandah Suites Next in size are 60 of these suites (563 sq. ft/52.3 sq. meters). These have twin beds that convert to a king-size bed, vanity desk, lounge area, walk-in closet, mini-bar and refrigerator, and bathroom with full-size bathtub, washbasin and toilet. Personalized stationery and complimentary dry cleaning are in-

cluded, as are hot hors d'oeuvres and other goodies.

VERANDAH SUITES: There are 100 of these Verandah Suites (actually they are cabins, not suites, and measure (284 sq. ft/26.3 sq. meters). Twin beds can convert to a queen-size bed; there is also a lounge area, mini-bar and refrigerator, while the bathroom features a bathtub, wash-basin and toilet. Floor to ceiling windows open onto a private balcony (verandah).

OUTSIDE-VIEW CABINS: Standard outside cabins (197 sq. ft/18.3 sq. meters) have twin beds that can be converted to make a queen-size bed. There's also a small sitting area, while the bathroom features a bathtub/shower combination. The interior (no view) cabins are slightly smaller (182.9 sq. ft/17 sq. meters).

DINING: With this ship, there are more dining options, from full-service meals in the main dining room (two decks high, with balcony level), to more informal eateries located high in the ship, to casual, self-serve buffet-style meals and fast-food outlets.

The main dining room is two decks high, (the galley is located underneath the restaurant, accessed by port and starboard escalators), and is located at the stern of the ship. It provides a traditional Holland America Line dining experience, with friendly service from smiling Indonesian stewards.

Note that Holland America Line can provide Kosher

meals, although these are prepared ashore, frozen, and brought to your table sealed in their original containers (there is no Kosher kitchen on board).

There is also an alternative, slightly more upscale dining spot atop the ship. It seats approximately 150; the dining spot also has a show kitchen where chefs can be seen at work, and is on two of the uppermost decks of the ship, located at the top of the atrium lobby. Fine table settings, china and silverware are featured, as well as leather bound menus. There is also a stage and dance floor. Reservations are required and there is a cover charge of $15 per person (for service and gratuity).

For casual meals, while there is an extensive self-serve buffet area. The large eatery that wraps around the funnel housing and extends aft, with fine views over the multi-deck atrium. It includes a separate pizzeria, salad bar and dessert buffet.

There's also an outdoor self-serve buffet (adjacent to the fantail pool), which serves fast food items such as hamburgers and hot dogs, chicken and fries, as well as two smaller buffets adjacent to the midships pool area.

OTHER COMMENTS: This is another in the latest generation of new, large ships for Holland America Line (sister to *Zuiderdam*), designed to appeal to a younger, more vibrant holidaymakers. The basic hull design is shared with Carnival's *Carnival Legend, Carnival Pride* and *Carnival Spirit*, and Costa Cruises' *Costa Atlantica* and *Costa Mediterranea*. Podded propulsion is provided, powered by a diesel-electric system, with small gas turbine located in the funnel for the reduction of emissions. This will provide the ship with more maneuverability, while reducing required machinery space and vibration at the stern. Each pod has a forward-facing propeller that can be turned through 360 degrees, and houses an electric motor and propeller, replacing the traditional long shaft, propeller and rudder system of the past.

A complete wrap-around exterior teak promenade deck is a feature enjoyed by many Holland America Line regular passengers, and teak "steamer" style deck lounge chairs are also provided. Exterior glass elevators, mounted midships on both port and starboard sides, provide fine ocean views from any one of the 10 decks that the elevators travel to.

In keeping with the traditions of Holland America Line, a large collection of artwork and Dutch maritime memorabilia has become standard on all its new ships.

There are two centrally located swimming pools outdoors, and one can be used in inclement weather due to its retractable sliding glass roof (called a magrodome) cover. Two whirlpool tubs, adjacent to the swimming pools, are abridged by a bar. Another smaller pool is available for children; it incorporates a winding water slide that spans two decks in height. There is also an additional whirlpool tub outdoors.

When you first walk into the ship, you'll be greeted by the immense size of the dramatic lobby space that spans eight decks. The atrium lobby, with its two grand stairways, presents a stunning wall decoration that is best seen from any of the multiple viewing balconies on each deck above the main lobby floor level.

There are two whole entertainment/public room decks, the upper of which also features an exterior promenade deck – something new for this fun cruise line. Although it doesn't go around the whole ship, it's long enough to do some serious walking on. Additionally, there is also a jogging track outdoors, located around the ship's mast and the forward third of the ship.

Without doubt, the most dramatic room aboard this ship is the show lounge. It spans four decks in the forward section of the ship. The main floor level has a bar in its starboard aft section. Spiral stairways at the back of the lounge connect all levels. Stage shows are best seen from the upper three levels, from where the sight lines are reasonably good.

Other facilities include a winding shopping street with several boutique stores and logo shops.

The casino is large (one has to walk through it to get from the restaurant to the show lounge on one of the entertainments decks), and is equipped with all the gaming paraphernalia and slot machines you can think of.

A large, two-decks-high health spa – called the Ocean Spa – is located directly above the navigation bridge. Facilities include a solarium, eight treatment rooms, sauna and steam rooms for men and women, a beauty parlor, and a large gymnasium with floor-to-ceiling windows on three sides and forward-facing ocean views, and the latest high-tech muscle-pumping machines.

Gratuities are extra, and they are added to your shipboard account at $10–$13 per day, according to the accommodation grade chosen. Refreshingly, the company does not add an automatic 15 percent gratuity for beverage purchases. Perhaps the ship's best asset is its friendly and personable Filipino and Indonesian crew, although communication can be problematical.

The company provides complimentary cappuccino and espresso coffees, and free ice cream during certain hours of the day, as well as hot hors d'oeuvres in all bars.

The onboard currency is the US dollar.

WEAK POINTS: The information desk in the lobby is small in comparison to the size of the lobby. Many of the private balconies are not so private, and can be overlooked from various public locations. Many pillars obstruct the passenger flow and lines of sight throughout the ship. Standing in line for embarkation, disembarkation, shore tenders and for self-serve buffet meals can be an inevitable aspect of cruising aboard all large ships. The charge to use the washing machines and dryers in the self-service launderette is petty, particularly for the occupants of suites, as they pay high prices for their cruises. Communication (in English) with many of the staff, particularly in the dining room and buffet areas, can prove very frustrating. It may be difficult to escape from smokers, and people walking around in unsuitable clothing, clutching plastic sport drinks bottles.

✓ Guernsey 15/09/05

Oriana
★★★★

Large Ship:	.............69,153 tons	Passengers
Lifestyle:	...................Premium	(lower beds/all berths): 1,828/1,975
Cruise Line:	.............P&O Cruises	Passenger Space Ratio
Former Names:	..................none	(lower beds/all berths): 37.8/35.0
Builder:	........Meyer Werft (Germany)	Crew/Passenger Ratio
Original Cost:	............£200 million	(lower beds/all berths): 2.4/2.5
Entered Service:	............Apr 1995	Navigation Officers: ....British
Registry:	................Great Britain	Cabins (total): 914
Length (ft/m):	...........853.0/260.0	Size Range (sq ft/m): 150.6–500.5/
Beam (ft/m):	..............105.6/32.2	14.0–46.5
Draft (ft/m):	.................25.9/7.9	Cabins (outside view): 594
Propulsion/Propellers:	..........diesel	Cabins (interior/no view): 320
	(47,750 kW)/2	Cabins (for one person): 112
Passenger Decks:	10	Cabins (with private balcony): 118
Total Crew:	760	Cabins (wheelchair accessible): 8

Cabin Current: ....110 and 220 volts
Elevators: 10
Casino (gaming tables): ....Yes
Slot Machines: ....Yes
Swimming Pools (outdoors): 3
Swimming Pools (indoors): 0
Whirlpools: 5
Fitness Center: ....Yes
Sauna/Steam Room: ....Yes/Yes
Massage: ....Yes
Self-Service Launderette: ....Yes
Dedicated Cinema/Seats: Yes/189
Library: ....Yes
Classification Society: ...Lloyd's Register

OVERALL SCORE: 1,530 (OUT OF A POSSIBLE 2,000 POINTS)

ACCOMMODATION: There is a wide range of cabin configurations and categories (in 18 grades), including family cabins with extra beds (110 cabins can accommodate up to four persons). The standard interior (no view) cabins and outside-view cabins are well equipped, although disappointingly small. There is much use of rich, warm limed oak or cherry wood in all cabins, which makes even the least expensive four-berth cabin seem inviting. All cabins feature a decent amount of closet and drawer space, small refrigerator, television, full-length mirror, and blackout curtains (essential for North Cape cruises). Satellite television provided typically would include BBC World, although reception may not be good in all areas.

A good number of cabins have been provided for passengers traveling singly. Anyone traveling singly who is sharing a cabin should note that only one personal safe is provided in most twin-bedded cabins. Although the cabins for four persons (family cabins) do have four small personal safes, there are no privacy curtains.

The standard cabin bathrooms are very compact units, and have mirror-fronted cabinets, although the lighting is quite soft (not strong enough for the application of make-up). All bathrooms feature a wall-mounted hairdryer (it would be better placed at the vanity desk in the living area). A Molton Brown "hair and body sport wash" dispenser is mounted in all bathrooms. Note that it is difficult to use the dispenser while in the bathtub (in those cabins with bathtubs), and neither shampoo nor conditioner is provided.

There are eight suites, each measuring 500 sq. ft (46

BERLITZ'S RATINGS

	Possible	Achieved
Ship	500	427
Accommodation	200	157
Food	400	260
Service	400	309
Entertainment	100	82
Cruise	400	295

sq. meters). All have butler service (there are two butlers). Features include a separate bedroom with two lower beds convertible to a queen-sized bed, walk-in dressing area, two double closets, plenty of drawer space. The lounge area has a sofa, armchairs and table, writing desk binoculars, umbrella, trouser press, iron and ironing board, two televisions, VCR, personal safe, hairdryer and refrigerator. The bathroom features a whirlpool bath, shower and toilet, and there is also a guest bathroom. The whirlpool bathtubs are reasonable, although they have high sides to step over, and most are of the dimensionally challenged type where you sit in them rather than lie in them. All in all, the suites, and particularly the bathrooms, are very disappointing when compared with similar sized suites in other ships. The private balcony is suitably large enough, and has two deck lounge chairs, tables and chairs.

Other balcony cabins (called outside deluxe) measure 210 sq. ft (19 sq. meters) and, although the balconies are small, they do have good partitions, rubber matting on the deck and a thick wooden railing. Inside, there is a curtain to separate the sleeping and living areas. There is plenty of closet and drawer space. The bathrooms are somewhat disappointing, however, and have a very small, very plain sink (one would expect marble or granite units in these grades).

Some suites and cabins with balconies have an interconnecting door, and include a trouser press, ironing board and iron – neatly tucked into a cupboard, binoculars, umbrella, a large atlas, and a second TV set as well as a sliding glazed panel between bedroom and sitting room.

DINING: There are two restaurants, allocated according to the cabin grade and location you choose. The Peninsular Restaurant is located amidships, while the Oriental Restaurant is located aft. Both are moderately handsome (each has tables for two, four, six or eight). Both have interesting ceilings, chandeliers and décor; the chinaware is Wedgwood, the silverware Elkington. The Oriental Restaurant has windows on three sides, including those overlooking the wash at the stern. Two seatings are featured in each restaurant, both of which are non-smoking (in fact, all dining spots are non-smoking). For those who are interested, a statement in the cruise folder in your cabin states that P&O Cruises does not knowingly purchase genetically modified foods.

The meals are mostly of the unmemorable "Middle-England" (unpretentious) variety, and the presentation lacks creativity (the cuisine does improve on the around-the-world cruise, however). Curries are heavily featured, however, particularly on the luncheon menus. Afternoon tea is disappointing, with a poor selection of teas and sandwiches.

The Conservatory offers self-serve breakfast and luncheon buffets, and 24-hour self-serve beverage stands (although the selection of teas is poor and it's often hard to find teaspoons – only plastic stirrers are provided). On selected evenings, it becomes a reservation-only alternative restaurant, Le Bistro, with sit-down service, typically featuring French Bistro, Indian or Southeast Asian cuisine – popular with the ship's mainly British clientele.

A former aerobics room (which was not used very much) has been turned into the popular (particularly with children and teenage passengers) Al Fresco Pizzeria (however, the pizza slices are bread-based and not made from pizza dough).

OTHER COMMENTS: The ship is quite conventional: evolutionary rather than revolutionary, but the first new ship for P&O Cruises for more than 25 years. This is a ship that takes *Canberra*'s traditional appointments and public rooms and adds more up-to-date touches, together with better facilities and passenger flow, and a feeling of timeless elegance.

For a little diversion, early references to the name *Oriana* are contained in 16th-century English romances. Various musical anthologies were composed to celebrate Elizabeth I as *Oriana*, culminating in a collection of 26 madrigals published by Thomas Morley in 1601 under the title "The Triumphs of Oriana." Although attributed to 23 different composers, each madrigal ends with the words "Long Live Fair Oriana."

Back to the ship: the interiors are gentle, welcoming and restrained. There is a splendid amount of open deck and sunbathing space, an important plus for her outdoors-loving British passengers. Has an extra-wide wrap-around promenade deck outdoors. The stern superstructure is nicely rounded and has several tiers that overlook the aft decks, pool and children's outdoor facilities.

Inside, the well laid-out design provides good horizontal passenger flow, and wide passageways. Very noticeable are the fine, detailed ceiling treatments. As it is a ship for all types of people, specific areas have been designed to attract different age groups and lifestyles.

There is a four-deck-high atrium with a soft waterfall. It is elegant but not glitzy, and is topped by a dome of Tiffany glass. The large number of public entertainment rooms provides plenty of choice, with lots of nooks and crannies in which to sit and read.

The Theatre Royal, designed by John Wyckham, is the ship's main show lounge. Decorated in rich reds, it was created specifically for drama and light theatrical presentations. It has individually air-conditioned seats, an orchestra pit, revolving stage and excellent acoustics. The theater seats would provide better stage sight lines if they were staggered, however.

The Pacific Lounge is a nightclub that doubles as a second show lounge for cabaret acts and comedy acts, although its many pillars obstruct the stage view.

The L-shaped Anderson's Lounge (named after the founder of the Peninsular Steam Navigation Company in the 1830s) features a series of 19th-century marine paintings, and is decorated in the manner of a fine British gentleman's club. Although there is no fireplace (there is one aboard the equivalent room aboard *Aurora*), it is a popular lounge.

Atop the ship and forward is the Crow's Nest, a U-shaped room with two small wings that can be closed off for small groups. There is a long bar, giving the barmen have a great view of the bow, while passengers sitting at the bar have a view of a ship model (a former P&O ship *Ranpura*) in a glass case. Two small stages are set into the forward port and starboard sections, and there is a wooden dance floor. The lounge has both smoking and non-smoking sections, although smoke lingers everywhere.

The library is a fine room, with a good range of hardback books (and a librarian), inlaid wood tables skillfully crafted by Lord Linley's company, and some comfortable chairs. On the second day of almost any cruise, however, the library will have been almost stripped of books by word-hungry passengers. Adjacent is Thackeray's, the writing room (known as the sleeping room in the afternoons); it is named after the novelist William Makepeace Thackeray, a P&O passenger in 1844. Without a doubt, the most restful room is the Curzon Room, used occasionally for piano recitals.

Meanwhile, Lord's Tavern is the most sporting place to pitch a beverage or two, or take part in a sing-along (rather like group karaoke). It is decorated with cricket memorabilia.

The carpeting throughout the ship is of an excellent quality, much of it custom designed and made from 100 percent wool. There are some fine pieces of sculpture that add the feeling of a floating museum, and original artworks by all-British artists that include several tapestries and sculptures.

The Oasis Spa is located forward and almost atop the ship. It is quite large, and provides all the latest alternative treatment therapies, and there is a gymnasium with the latest high-tech muscle toning equipment. The co-ed sauna is a large facility (most ships have separate saunas for men and women), and there is also a steam room.

Children and teens have "Club Oriana" programs with their own rooms (Peter Pan and Decibels), and their own outdoor pool. Children can be entertained until 10pm, which gives parents time to have dinner and go dancing. The cabins also have a baby-listening device. A special night nursery for small children (ages 2 to 5) is available at no extra charge (6pm–2am).

There is a wide variety of mainly British entertainment aboard the ships of P&O Cruises. There is also a program of theme cruises (antiques, The Archers, art appreciation, classical music, comedy, cricket, gardening, jazz, motoring, popular fiction, Scottish dance, sequence dancing). Check with your travel agent to see what is available when you intend to take your cruise.

Oriana provides a decent, standardized cruise experience for its mainly British passengers (of all dialects) who do not want to fly to join a cruise ship. However, in the quest for increased onboard revenue, even birthday cakes are an extra cost, as are real espressos and cappuccinos (fake ones, made from instant coffee, are available in the dining rooms). Ice cream and bottled water also cost extra (and can add up to a considerable amount on an around-the-world cruise, for example).

A fine British brass band send-off accompanies all sailings. Other touches include church bells sounded throughout the ship for the interdenominational Sunday church service. The onboard currency is the British pound. For gratuities (optional), you should allow £3 (US$4.50) per person, per day.

WEAK POINTS: Standing in line for embarkation, disembarkation, shore tenders and for self-serve buffet meals is inevitable aboard all large ships. Smokers seem to be everywhere, as is the smell of stale smoke. Cabin soundproofing is quite poor. Shuttle buses, which used to be provided free in some ports, are no longer complimentary (except on the around-the-world cruise). During school holidays, you should be aware that there will be many children aboard; this can be a cause of irritation and frustration to many older passengers.

Orient Venus
★★★ +

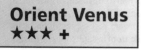

Small Ship: . . . . .21,884 tons	Total Crew: 120	Cabins (wheelchair accessible): 0
Lifestyle: . . . . .Standard	Passengers	Cabin Current: . . . . .110 volts
Cruise Line: . . . . .Venus Cruise	(lower beds/all berths): 390/606	Elevators: 3
Former Names: . . . . .none	Passenger Space Ratio	Casino (gaming tables): . . . . .No
Builder: . . . . .Ishikawajima Heavy	(lower beds/all berths): 56.1/36.1	Slot Machines: .No
Industries (Japan)	Crew/Passenger Ratio	Swimming Pools (outdoors): 1
Original Cost: . . . .$150 million	(lower beds/all berths): 3.2/5.0	Swimming Pools (indoors): 0
Entered Service: . . . . .July 1990	Navigation Officers: . . . . .Japanese	Whirlpools: 0
Registry: . . . . .Japan	Cabins (total): 195	Fitness Center: . . . . .Yes
Length (ft/m): 570.8/174.00	Size Range (sq ft/m): 182.9–592.0/	Sauna/Steam Room: . . . . .No/No
Beam (ft/m): 78.7/24.00	17.0–55.0	Massage: . . . . .No
Draft (ft/m): 21.3/6.52	Cabins (outside view): 195	Self-Service Launderette: . . . . .Yes
Propulsion/Propellers: . . . . .diesel	Cabins (interior/no view): 0	Dedicated Cinema/Seats: Yes/606
(13,830 kW)/2	Cabins (for one person): 0	Library: . . . . .Yes
Passenger Decks: 6	Cabins (with private balcony): 2	Classification Society: Nippon Kaiji Kyokai

---

OVERALL SCORE: 1,382 (OUT OF A POSSIBLE 2,000 POINTS)

ACCOMMODATION: There are just four cabin grades (royal, deluxe, state and standard). The all-outside standard cabins, many of which have upper berths for third/fourth passengers, have décor that is best described as plain, with a reasonable amount of closet space and little drawer space.

The largest suites (of which there are two) have an expansive lounge area with large, plush armchairs, coffee table, and window-side chairs and drinks table, floor-to-ceiling windows, and a large private balcony. There is a separate sleeping room (curtained off from the living room) with twin- or queen-sized bed, vanity/office desk, and large bathroom.

All grades of accommodation have a tea drinking set (with electric hot water kettle), color television, telephone, and stocked refrigerator.

DINING: The main dining room, which operates a single seating with assigned tables, is quite attractive, and there is plenty of space around the dining tables. In addition, an alternative Romanesque Grill is unusual, with its classic period Roman décor and a high, elegant ceiling. The ship offers reasonably good, but quite commercial Japanese cuisine (washoku) exclusively.

OTHER COMMENTS: *Orient Venus* was the first cruise ship built for its owners, Venus Cruise, which is part of Japan Cruise Line, which is, itself, part of SHK Line Group, a joint venture between Shin Nohonkai, Hankyu and Kanpu ferry companies (operating more than 20

BERLITZ'S RATINGS		
	Possible	Achieved
Ship	500	338
Accommodation	200	120
Food	400	291
Service	400	283
Entertainment	100	62
Cruise	400	288

ferries). This is a conventional-shaped ship with a reasonably graceful profile. There is a decent amount of open deck and sunbathing space, which is not often used. There is also an expansive amount of open deck space for sunbathing, aft of funnel.

Inside the ship, the Night and Day Lounge set at funnel base looks forward over the swimming pool. Windows of the Orient is a small attractive, peaceful forward observation lounge. The conference facilities are excellent, and consist of both main and small conference rooms with 620 movable seats. There is a fine array of public rooms with tasteful and very inviting décor. The horseshoe-shaped main lounge has very good sight lines to the platform stage.

This cruise ship, with its western-style décor, will provide its mostly Japanese corporate passengers with extremely comfortable surroundings, and offers a superb cruise and seminar/learning environment and experience. *Orient Venus* was joined by a new, slightly larger sister ship, *Pacific Venus,* in 1998.

A specialist courier company provides an excellent luggage service and will collect your luggage from your home before the cruise, and deliver it back to your home after the cruise (this service available only in Japan). The onboard currency is the Japanese yen.

WEAK POINTS: The ship does not really cater well to individual passengers. The décor is rather plain in many public rooms. The crew-to-passenger ratio is quite poor, but typical of seminar-intensive ships.

Pacific Princess
NOT YET RATED

Mid-Size Ship: . . . . .30,277 tons	Total Crew: 373	Cabins (wheelchair accessible): 3
Lifestyle: . . . . .Premium	Passengers	Cabin Current: . . . . .110 and 220 volts
Cruise Line: . . . . . .P&O Cruises Australia/	(lower beds/all berths): 686/826	Elevators: 4
Princess Cruises	Passenger Space Ratio	Casino (gaming tables): . . . . .Yes
Former Names: . . . . .R Three	(lower beds/all berths): 44.1/36.6	Slot Machines: .Yes
Builder: Chantiers de l'Atlantique (France)	Crew/Passenger Ratio	Swimming Pools (outdoors): 1
Original Cost: . . . .$150 million	(lower beds/all berths): 1.8/2.2	Swimming Pools (indoors): 0
Entered Service: . . . . .Aug 1999/Nov 2002	Navigation Officers: . . . . .European	Whirlpools: . . . . . .2 (+ 1 thalassotherapy)
Registry: . . . . .Gibraltar	Cabins (total): .344	Fitness Center: .Yes
Length (ft/m): 593.7/181.0	Size Range (sq ft/m): . . . . .145.3 – 968.7/	Sauna/Steam Room: . . . . .No/Yes
Beam (ft/m): 83.5/25.5	13.5 – 90.0	Massage: . . . . .Yes
Draft (ft/m): 19.5/6.0	Cabins (outside view): 317	Self-Service Launderette: . . . . .Yes
Propulsion/Propellers: . . . . .diesel-electric	Cabins (interior/no view): 27	Dedicated Cinema/Seats: . . . . .No
(18,600kW)/2	Cabins (for one person): 0	Library: . . . . .Yes
Passenger Decks: 9	Cabins (with private balcony): 232	Classification Society: . . . .Bureau Veritas

BERLITZ'S OVERALL SCORE: NYR (OUT OF A POSSIBLE 2,000 POINTS)

ACCOMMODATION: There is a variety of about eight different cabin types to choose from (however, when this book was completed, specific cabin category details were not available). All of the standard interior (no view) and outside-view cabins are extremely compact units, and extremely tight for two persons (particularly for cruises longer than seven days). Cabins have twin beds (or queen-size bed), with good under-bed storage areas, personal safe, vanity desk with large mirror, good closet and drawer space (in rich, dark woods), and bathrobe. Color televisions carry a major news channel (where it is obtainable), plus a sports channel and several round-the-clock movie channels.

The cabins that have private balconies (66 percent of all cabins, or 73 percent of all outside view cabins) have partial, and not full, balcony partitions, sliding glass doors, and, due to good design and layout, only 14 cabins on Deck 6 have lifeboat-obstructed views. The bathrooms, which have tiled floors and plain walls, are compact, standard units, and include a shower enclosure with a removable, strong hand-held shower unit, hairdryer, 100 percent cotton towels, toiletries storage shelves and a retractable clothesline.

MINI-SUITES: The 52 accommodation units designated as mini-suites, are in reality simply larger cabins than the standard varieties, as the sleeping and lounge areas are not divided. While not overly large, the bathrooms have a good-sized bathtub and ample space for storing personal toiletry items. The living area has a refrigerated

BERLITZ'S RATINGS

	Possible	Achieved
Ship	500	NYR
Accommodation	200	NYR
Food	400	NYR
Service	400	NYR
Entertainment	100	NYR
Cruise	400	NYR

mini-bar, lounge area with breakfast table, and a balcony with two plastic chairs and a table.

OWNER'S SUITES: The 10 Owner's Suites are the most spacious accommodation, and are fine, large living spaces located in the forward-most and aft-most sections of the accommodation decks (particularly nice are those that overlook the stern, on Deck 6, 7 and 8). They have more extensive balconies that really are private and cannot be overlooked by anyone from the decks above. There is an entrance foyer, living room, bedroom (the bed faces the sea, which can be seen through the floor-to-ceiling windows and sliding glass door), CD player, bathroom with Jacuzzi bathtub, as well as a small guest bathroom.

DINING: Flexibility and choice are what this mid-sized ship's dining facilities are all about. There are four different dining spots:

● The *Main Dining Room* has 338 seats, and includes a large raised central section. There are large ocean-view windows on three sides, several prime tables overlooking the stern, and a small bandstand for occasional live dinner music.

● The *Sabatini's Trattoria* is an Italian restaurant, with 96 seats, windows along two sides, and a set menu (typically with added daily chef's specials).

● The *Sterling Steakhouse*, an "American steak house," has 98 seats, windows along two sides, and a set menu (together with added daily chef's specials).

● The *Lido Cafe* has seating for 154 indoors and 186

outdoors. It is open for breakfast, lunch and casual dinners. It is the ship's self-serve buffet restaurant (open 24 hours a day), and has a small pizzeria and grill.

All restaurants have open-seating dining, so you dine when you want, with whom you wish, although reservations may be necessary in *Sabatini's Trattoria* and *Sterling Steakhouse*, where there are mostly tables for four or six (there are few tables for two). In addition, there is a Poolside Grill and Bar for those fast-food items provided for on-deck munching.

OTHER COMMENTS: This ship was one of eight almost identical ships ordered and operated by the now defunct Renaissance Cruises, the industry's first totally non-smoking cruise line. As one of the "R-class" ships, this one operated in Tahiti, and was delivered by the shipyard through French government funding. After the collapse of Renaissance Cruises (following the September 11, 2001, attacks on the United States), P&O Princess Cruises announced the lease/purchase of this ship, together with sister ship *R Three* (now named *Pacific Princess*). Both ships debuted in 1999, and are of an ideal size for operating in warm water regions.

A lido deck has a swimming pool, and good sunbathing space, while one of the aft decks has a thalassaotherapy pool (it's part of a spa package and incurs an extra charge). A jogging track circles the swimming pool deck (but one deck above). The uppermost outdoors deck includes a golf driving net and shuffleboard court.

The interior décor is quite stunning and elegant, a throwback to ship décor of the ocean liners of the 1920s and '30s, executed in fine taste. This includes detailed ceiling cornices, both real and faux wrought-iron staircase railings, leather-paneled walls, *trompe l'oeil* ceilings, rich carpeting in hallways with an Oriental rug-look center section, and many other interesting (and expensive-looking) decorative touches. The overall feel is of an old-world country club. The staircase in the main, two-deck-high foyer will remind you of something similar in a blockbuster hit movie about a certain ship (*Titanic*), where the stars, Kate Winslet and Leonardo di Caprio, met.

The public rooms are basically spread over three decks. This is totally a non-smoking ship (there is no smoking anywhere, including cabins, dining room, public rooms, *or* on the open decks – although the crew have their own smoking room).

The reception hall (lobby) has a staircase with intricate wrought-iron railings. A large observation lounge, the Horizon Lounge, is located high atop ship. This has a long bar with forward views (for the barmen, that is), and a stack of distracting large-screen televisions; there's also an array of slot machines and bar counter-top electronic gaming machines.

There are plenty of bars – including one in the entrance to each of the restaurants. Perhaps the nicest of all bars and lounges are in the casino bar/lounge that is a beautiful room reminiscent of London's grand hotels. It has an inviting marble fireplace (in fact there are *three* such fireplaces aboard) and comfortable sofas and individual chairs.

The Library is a beautiful, grand room, designed in the Regency style, and has a fireplace, a high, indented, *trompe l'oeil* ceiling, and an excellent selection of books, as well as some very comfortable wingback chairs with footstools, and sofas you could sleep on.

Pacific Princess cruises for part of the year under the Princess Cruises banner in French Polynesia, and six months under the P&O Cruises (Australia) brand name in Australia (cruises from Sydney). Although there may not be marble bathroom fittings, or caviar and other (more expensive) niceties, the value for money is extremely good, and you have the opportunity to cruise in comfort aboard a mid-sized ship with plenty of dining choices. There's very little entertainment, but it is certainly not needed in these cruise areas.

With the introduction of *Pacific Princess* (and sister ship *Tahitian Princess*), Princess Cruises has provided rather smart replacements for a previous pair of similarly-sized ships (*Island Princess* and *Pacific Princess*) that were operated for many years to the delight of passengers not wanting to cruise aboard the larger ships in the fleet.

In common with all ships in the Princess Cruises fleet, 15 percent will typically be added to all bar accounts (drink prices are moderate, while beer prices are high), and a standard gratuity (about $10 per person, per day) will be automatically added to your onboard account (if you think this is too much and want to reduce the amount, you'll need to go to the reception desk to do so).

Although not yet rated, it is expected that, given that the ship, its food, style and staffing and service levels will be similar to those of other Princess Cruises ships, the overall score is expected to be in the region of 1,500 points, which would equate to four stars.

WEAK POINTS: There is no wrap-around promenade deck outdoors (there is, however, a small jogging track around the perimeter of the swimming pool, and port and starboard side decks), and no wooden decks outdoors (instead, they are covered by Bolidt, a sand-colored rubberized material). There is no sauna. The room service menu is extremely limited. Suggested gratuities are high (there is even a gratuities slot at the reception desk). Stairways, although carpeted, are tinny. In order to keep the prices low, often the air routing to get to/from your ship is not the most direct.

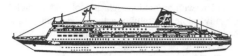

Pacific Sky
★★★ +

Large Ship: ....46,392 tons	Passengers	Cabin Current: ....110 and 220 volts
Lifestyle: ....Standard	(lower beds/all berths): 1,200/1,550	Elevators: 6
Cruise Line: ......P&O Cruises (Australia)	Passenger Space Ratio	Casino (gaming tables): ....Yes
Former Names: ....*Sky Princess, Fairsky*	(lower beds/all berths): 38.6/34.3	Slot Machines: ....Yes
Builder: ..............C.N.I.M. (France)	Crew/Passenger Ratio	Swimming Pools (outdoors): 3
Original Cost: ....$156 million	(lower beds/all berths): 2.1/2.8	Swimming Pools (indoors): 0
Entered Service: .....Mar 1984/Nov 2000	Navigation Officers: ....British	Whirlpools: 1
Registry: ....Great Britain	Cabins (total): 600	Fitness Center: ....Yes
Length (ft/m): 788.6/240.39	Size Range (sq ft/m): 168.9–519.9/	Sauna/Steam Room: ....Yes/No
Beam (ft/m): 91.3/27.84	15.7–48.3	Massage: ....Yes
Draft (ft/m): 26.7/8.15	Cabins (outside view): 385	Self-Service Launderette: ....Yes
Propulsion/Propellers: .....steam turbine	Cabins (interior/no view): 215	Dedicated Cinema/Seats: Yes/283
(21,700 kW)/2	Cabins (for one person): 0	Library: ....Yes
Passenger Decks: 11	Cabins (with private balcony): 10	Classification Society: ...Lloyd's Register
Total Crew: 550	Cabins (wheelchair accessible): 10	

OVERALL SCORE: 1,253 (OUT OF A POSSIBLE 2,000 POINTS)

ACCOMMODATION: There are 19 grades of accommodation: two suite categories, eight outside-view cabin grades and nine interior (no view) cabin grades. The cabins are, for the most part, fairly spacious, comfortable, and well-appointed, with all the essentials and good-sized rectangular showers. There are, however, too many interior (no view) cabins. The cabin walls and ceilings are plain and unappealing, and could do with some splashes of color to brighten them.

BERLITZ'S RATINGS		
	Possible	Achieved
Ship	500	338
Accommodation	200	139
Food	400	237
Service	400	230
Entertainment	100	63
Cruise	400	254

The largest accommodation can be found in the 10 Lido Deck suites, all of which are named after famous places (Capri, Portofino, Estoril, Monaco, Malaga on the port side, and Antibes, Minorca, St. Tropez, San Remo, Amalfi on the starboard side). These are really very fine living spaces, and provide extra comforts such as a mini-bar/refrigerator, walk-in closet, and a larger bathroom (with bathtub and shower), and a private balcony. All have a queen-sized bed, with the exception of Amalfi and Malaga, which have fixed twin beds.

There are 28 mini-suites, which each has separate sleeping and living areas, with dressing table, sofa, coffee table and chairs, and mini-bar/refrigerator.

Many cabins have one or two additional upper berths, making them extremely cramped when occupied (storage of luggage can be a problem), but they are useful for families with children. All cabins suffer from inadequate soundproofing, but all have a color television, and two lower beds. A room service menu is available 24 hours a day. Cabins at the aft end of Aloha Deck may be subject to noise from the adjacent Children's Playroom.

DINING: There are two dining rooms (Regency and Savoy), assigned according to the accommodation you choose. Both are non-smoking, are brightly lit and have pleasant décor. There are two seatings, and tables are for four, six or eight there are no tables for two). The food is largely standard fare and a little repetitive; quality, flair and presentation could be better. Mainly friendly male Filipino waiters provide the dining room service, although it lacks any finesse and I receive many complaints from passengers about careless service and tables not being served separately, issues which need addressing.

For casual daytime snacking, there is the Al Fresco self-serve buffet on deck, with New Zealand ice cream, milkshakes and pastries (all at extra cost).

Other casual dining alternatives include the Pizzeria, open 24 hours a day. There's also Harry's Café de Waves (based on the Sydney icon, and famous for its world renowned "Pie and Peas"), for snacks, including hot dogs. Both the Pizzeria and Harry's Café de Waves are extra charge outlets, and not included in the cruise price.

OTHER COMMENTS: This well-designed vessel has a short, sharply raked bow and a large, swept-back funnel. This was the first cruise ship to have steam turbine machinery since Cunard Line's *Queen Elizabeth 2* debuted in 1969, so there is almost no vibration (it was originally ordered by Sitmar Cruises, which was itself acquired by Princess Cruises in 1988). *Pacific Sky* is a much more contemporary, and spacious ship, with many more facilities than the ship it replaces, *Fair Princess*.

Inside the ship, the layout is quite comfortable and it is easy to find one's way around – good signing also helps. The clean, bland, clinical, yet oddly tasteful minimalist interior decor lacks warmth – some flowers and greenery are needed. There is a decent enough array of public rooms, including some expansive shopping space on Rodeo Drive. There are nine bars/lounges to choose from, including a new Sports Bar.

Of the major public entertainment rooms, the Pacific Sky Showlounge has decent visibility from most seats following improvements that were made by the ship's previous owners, (Princess Cruises), although it is only a single-level room (most new cruise ships have at least two levels for their showlounges).

The Horizon Lounge, set atop the ship, is restful at night. The casino has a split configuration. Although the health spa/fitness facilities are decent, there are simply not enough treatment rooms.

Another lounge, the newly added Verandah Lounge (formerly a café) includes a dance floor and live music, while the Starlight Lounge is also for dancing and lively late-night cabaret. The ship has its own dedicated cinema (something that few new ships seem to provide), complete with balcony level.

Children have their own area, too, aft on Aloha Deck, complete with an outdoor splash pool, and a whole, brightly colored roomful of activities and fun things. Note that no children under 18 months old are accepted as passengers by P&O Holidays.

This ship provides a reasonably well-balanced, pleasing cruise experience for the mature passenger, with plenty of space and little crowding, although service does suffer from carelessness and lack of training and supervision. British officers and Filipino dining staff help to create a fairly friendly ambience aboard this ship, which commenced operations in November 2000 when it was renamed *Pacific Sky*, with a home base in Sydney, Australia.

The onboard currency is the Australian dollar.

WEAK POINTS: Standing in line for embarkation, disembarkation, shore tenders and for self-serve buffet meals is an inevitable aspect of cruising aboard all large ships, and this one is no exception. Sadly, there is no wrap-around promenade deck outdoors, although there is a decent *enclosed* promenade deck. There are simply too many interior (no view) cabins. Public restrooms are often out of order, and cleanliness leaves much to be desired; some of this due to problems with the ship's plumbing.

Pacific Venus
★★★★ +

Mid-Size Ship: ....26,518 tons	Total Crew: 180	Cabin Current: ....110 volts
Lifestyle: ....Standard	Passengers	Elevators: 4
Cruise Line: ....Venus Cruise	(lower beds/all berths): 532/720	Casino (gaming tables): ....Yes
Former Names: ....none	Passenger Space Ratio	Slot Machines: ....No
Builder: ....Ishikawajima Heavy	(lower beds/all berths): 49.8/36.8	Swimming Pools (outdoors): 1
Industries (Japan)	Crew/Passenger Ratio	(+ 1 for children)
Original Cost: ....$114 million	(lower beds/all berths): 2.9/4.0	Swimming Pools (indoors): 0
(Yen13 billion)	Navigation Officers: ....Japanese	Whirlpools: 1
Entered Service: ....Apr 1998	Cabins (total): 266	Fitness Center: ....Yes
Registry: ....Japan	Size Range (sq ft/m): 164.6–699.6/	Sauna/Steam Room: ....No/Yes
Length (ft/m): 601.7/183.4	15.3–65.0	Massage: ....Yes
Beam (ft/m): 82.0/25.0	Cabins (outside view): 250	Self-Service Launderette: ....Yes (2)
Draft (ft/m): 21.3/6.5	Cabins (interior/no view): 16	Dedicated Cinema/Seats: Yes/94
Propulsion/Propellers: ....diesel	Cabins (for one person): 0	Library: ....Yes
(13,636 kW)/2	Cabins (with private balcony): 20	Classification Society: ....Nippon Kaiji
Passenger Decks: 7	Cabins (wheelchair accessible): 1	Kyokai

OVERALL SCORE: 1,647 (OUT OF A POSSIBLE 2,000 POINTS)

ACCOMMODATION: There are six different types of accommodation: royal suites, suites, deluxe cabins, state cabins (in four different price grades), and standard cabins, all located from the uppermost to lowermost decks, respectively.

The four Royal Suites are decorated in two different styles – one contemporary, one more traditional Japanese style. Each has a private balcony, with sliding door (teak table and two chairs), an expansive lounge area with large sofa and plush armchairs, coffee table, window-side chairs and drinks table, floor-to-ceiling windows, and a VCR. There is a separate bedroom, with twin- or queen-sized bed, vanity/writing desk, large walk-in closet with personal safe, and a large bathroom with a tiny Jacuzzi bathtub. The bathroom has ocean-view windows, separate shower and his/hers sinks.

Sixteen suites also have private balconies (with teak table and two chairs), a good-sized living area with vanity/writing desk, dining table, chair and curved sofa, separate sleeping area, and bathroom with deep bathtub slightly larger than the Royal suites, and single large sink. There is ample lighted closet and drawer space (two locking drawers instead of a personal safe), and a VCR.

The 20 Deluxe cabins have large picture windows fronted by a large, curtained arch, sleeping area with twin (or queen) beds, plus a daytime sofa that converts into a third bed.

The 210 state cabins, (172 of which have upper berths for third passengers), have décor that is best described as

BERLITZ'S RATINGS		
	Possible	Achieved
Ship	500	430
Accommodation	200	156
Food	400	326
Service	400	329
Entertainment	100	80
Cruise	400	326

basic, with a reasonable closet, but little drawer space.

The 16 standard cabins are really plain, but accommodate three persons, although drawer and storage space is tight.

All cabin grades have a tea drinking set (with electric hot water kettle), color TV, telephone, stocked mini-bar/refrigerator (all items included in the cruise price). Bathrooms have a hairdryer, and lots of Shiseido personal toiletry items (particularly in the suites, which include after-shave, hair liquid, hair tonic, skin lotion, body lotion, milky lotion, shampoo, rinse, razor, toothbrush, toothpaste, sewing kit, shower cap, hairbrush, clothes brush and shoe horn). All room service menu items cost extra. All passengers receive a yukata (Japanese-style light cotton robe); suite occupants also get a plush bathrobe.

DINING: The main dining room (Primavera) is located aft, with ocean views on three sides. Passengers dine in one seating, and tables are for six, 10 or 12. The food consists of both Japanese and Western items; the menu is varied and the food is attractively presented.

A second, intimate, yet moderately stately 42-seat alternative restaurant, called Grand Siècle, has an à la carte menu, which incurs an extra charge for everything; it is decorated in Regency-style, with much fine wood paneling and a detailed, indented ceiling.

OTHER COMMENTS: Venus Cruise is part of Japan Cruise Line, which is itself part of SHK Line Group, a joint venture between Shin Nohonkai, Hankyu and Kanpu ferry companies (operating more than 20 ferries). The company also owns and operates the slightly smaller and more basic *Orient Venus,* used principally for the charter and incentive group market. *Pacific Venus*, which is being operated for individual cruises (no charters) is one deck higher than its sister ship, and is slightly longer and beamier.

There is a good amount of open deck space aft of the funnel, good for deck sports, while protected sunbathing space is provided around the small swimming pool (all deck lounge chairs have cushioned pads).

The base of the funnel itself is the site of a day/night lounge, which overlooks the swimming pool (it is slightly reminiscent of Royal Caribbean International's lounges). There is a wrap-around (rubber-coated) promenade deck outdoors.

Inside the ship, the high passenger space ratio means that there is plenty of space per passenger. The décor is clean and fresh, with much use of pastel colors and blond woods.

One deck (Deck 7) has a double-width indoor promenade off which the dining rooms are located. The three-deck-high atrium has a crystal chandelier as its focal point.

Facilities include male and female Grand Baths, which include bathing pool and health/cleansing facilities. There are special rooms for meetings and conference organizers, for times when the ship is chartered. There is a piano salon with colorful low-back chairs, a large main hall (with a finely sculptured high ceiling and 720 moveable seats – production shows are performed here), a 350-seat main lounge for cabaret shows, a small theater, a library and card room, a casino, two private karaoke rooms, a Japanese chashitsu room for tea ceremonies (a tatami-matted room), and a beauty salon. There is a 24-hour vending machine corner (juice, beer, camera film and other items), self-service launderette (no charge), and several (credit card/coin) public telephone booths.

Overall, this company provides a well-packaged cruise in a ship that presents a very comfortable, serene environment. The dress code is relaxed and no tipping is allowed. The onboard currency is the Japanese yen.

WEAK POINTS: There are few cabins with private balcony. The open walking promenade decks are rubber-coated steel – teak would be more desirable.

Paloma I
★★ +

Small Ship: ....12,586 tons	Total Crew: 170	Cabins (wheelchair accessible): 0
Lifestyle: ....Standard	Passengers	Cabin Current: ....220 volts
Cruise Line: D&P Cruises/Hansa Touristik	(lower beds/all berths): 354/400	Elevators: 2
Former Names: ....Paloma, Dimitri	Passenger Space Ratio	Casino (gaming tables): ....No
Shostakovich	(basis 2/all berths): 35.5/31.4	Slot Machines: ....Yes
Builder: ......Szczesin Stocznia (Poland)	Crew/Passenger Ratio	Swimming Pools (outdoors): 1
Original Cost: ....n/a	(lower beds/all berths): 2.0/2.3	Swimming Pools (indoors): 0
Entered Service: 1980	Navigation Officers: ....Ukrainian	Whirlpools: 0
Registry: ....The Bahamas	Cabins (total): 177	Fitness Center: ....Yes
Length (ft/m): 449.9/137.15	Size Range (sq ft/sq m): 100–320/	Sauna/Steam Room: ....Yes/No
Beam (ft/m): 68.8/21.00	9.2–29.7	Massage: ....Yes
Draft (ft/m): 19.0/5.8	Cabins (outside view): 93	Self-Service Launderette: ....No
Propulsion/Propellers: ....diesel	Cabins (interior/no view): 84	Dedicated Cinema/Seats: ....No
(12,806 kW)/2	Cabins (for one person): 0	Library: ....Yes
Passenger Decks: 6	Cabins (with private balcony): 0	Classification Society: ....KM

OVERALL SCORE: 1,032 (OUT OF A POSSIBLE 2,000 POINTS)

ACCOMMODATION: There are 10 cabin price grades, although there is little difference in the size of most of these price categories, the difference in price being for deck and location. Of these, there are 3 suites, 6 junior suites, the rest of the accommodation being standard exterior view and interior (no view) cabins.

SUITES/JUNIOR SUITES: The three suites have a completely separate bedroom with plenty of closet space (although there are no drawers, there are a few shelves), and a large bathroom with shower enclosure. The six junior suites have only a larger bathroom, with shower enclosure. The suites and junior suites each have a television and video player.

STANDARD EXTERIOR VIEW/INTERIOR (NO VIEW) CABINS: The standard cabins are very small and somewhat utilitarian in their fittings and furnishings; there is almost no drawer space, and the under-bed storage space for luggage is tight (however, you may need to use your suitcase as storage space, particularly for small items of clothing). Many cabins are fitted with upper Pullman berths, although these are seldom used, except by families with children.

All cabins come with a private bathroom, with shower enclosure, and a small cabinet for personal toiletry items (note that only soap is supplied, so do take your own shampoo, conditioner, hand cream and any other personal toiletries that you might need).

Note that there is no room service menu, nor is it possible to obtain tea/coffee in your cabin.

BERLITZ'S RATINGS		
	Possible	Achieved
Ship	500	224
Accommodation	200	97
Food	400	228
Service	400	235
Entertainment	100	38
Cruise	400	210

DINING: The dining room is totally non-smoking, and seats approximately 370 passengers in one seating (a real bonus for leisurely dining). It is quite attractive, and has large picture windows on three sides, although the ceiling is quite low. There is also a small, additional section that could be used as a private dining room, useful for small groups. Meals are provided by an Italian maritime catering company, which does a fine job (taking into account the low price of a cruise aboard this ship).

High-quality meats and plenty of fresh vegetables is the mainstay of the cuisine. Although fish dishes are disappointing, vegetarian meals are creative. Service is provided by Ukrainian waiters and waitresses. Although they have little finesse and not much knowledge regarding the food, they are attractive, smile, and try hard. The wine list is also quite basic, with young wines being the mainstay of the list.

OTHER COMMENTS: *Paloma I* has a square, rather angular profile with a boxy stern (complete with fold-down aft ramp), stubby bow and a fat funnel – otherwise it's moderately handsome! The navigation bridge is of the (almost) fully enclosed type for all-weather operation. There is a small helicopter landing deck.

The ship was originally built in Poland as one of a series of five sister ships (the original names of the five were: *Dimitriy Shostakovich, Konstantin Simonov, Lev Tolstoi, Mikhail Sholokhov,* and *Petr Pervyy*). They were designed for carrying both cars and passengers on line voyages (principally within Europe and Russia) with a large aft ramp for loading cars and stores. The loading ramp is still in use for loading stores, and, when *Paloma I* operates during the summer on European/Mediterranean itineraries, passengers can drive to the port of embarkation and park their cars on board (the ship can carry up to 50 cars).

Inside the ship, the interior décor is reasonably smart, and consists principally of soft pastel colors, with no glitz in evidence anywhere. Public rooms include a main lounge (low budget, basic evening shows are performed here, although 13 pillars obstruct the sight lines); beer bar, which doubles as a video showing room (but the wooden seats are hard); three bars (one indoors, one by the swimming pool, and one "beer garden").

The ship is comfortable, and there is no glitz anywhere. The lifestyle is very casual, although you may want to take a jacket and tie/cocktail dress for the one Captain's Dinner evening typical of each cruise. The main thing is that the ship is clean and tidy, and the staff is warm and friendly. Holsten beer (from Hamburg) appears to sponsor the provision of beer mats, glasses and ashtrays.

Paloma I is owned by an Italian company (Di Maio Cruises), and is presently under charter to Hansa Touristik of Germany, a company well known for providing cruise holidays at very low prices. A cruise aboard *Paloma I* will give you a basic but comfortable cruise experience at very modest rates, but you should not expect too much. Book this ship because you want to go to the destinations and itineraries, which are attractive, and not because of the ship.

While most of the service crew is Ukrainian, there is also a sprinkling of Germans and Austrians in key hotel management positions. Tickets come in a nice pouch that includes pocket guides to the ports of call. The onboard currency is the euro.

WEAK POINTS: Both interior and exterior staircases are quite steep, the ship having been originally constructed as a roll-on, roll-off passenger ferry. There is no observation lounge with forward-facing views over the ship's bows. The amount of open deck and sunning space is limited (particularly if the ship is full) and the small swimming pool is really merely a "dip" pool. The port and starboard open promenade decks are steel, painted blue.

Paradise
★★★ +

Large Ship:	..............70,367 tons	Passengers	Cabin Current:	...............110 volts
Lifestyle:	...................Standard	(lower beds/all berths): 2,052/2,594	Elevators:	14
Cruise Line:	.......Carnival Cruise Lines	Passenger Space Ratio	Casino (gaming tables):	............Yes
Former Names:	.................none	(lower beds/all berths): 34.2/26.7	Slot Machines:	.....................Yes
Builder:	...Kvaerner Masa-Yards (Finland)	Crew/Passenger Ratio	Swimming Pools (outdoors):	3
Original Cost:	............$300 million	(lower beds/all berths): 2.2/2.8	Swimming Pools (indoors):	0
Entered Service:	.............Nov 1998	Navigation Officers:	Whirlpools:	6
Registry:	....................Panama	Cabins (total):	1,026	Fitness Center:	....................Yes
Length (ft/m):	.............855.0/260.6	Size Range (sq ft/m): 173.2–409.7/	Sauna/Steam Room:	..........Yes/Yes
Beam (ft/m):	...............103.3/31.5	16.0–38.0	Massage:	........................Yes
Draft (ft/m):	.............25.9/7.9	Cabins (outside view):	618	Self-Service Launderette:	..........Yes
Propulsion/Propellers:	.....diesel-electric	Cabins (interior/no view):	408	Dedicated Cinema/Seats:	..........No
	(42,842 kW)/2 azimuthing pods	Cabins (for one person):	0	Library:	..........................Yes
Passenger Decks:	10	Cabins (with private balcony):	26	Classification Society:	...Lloyd's Register
Total Crew:	920	Cabins (wheelchair accessible):	22		

OVERALL SCORE: 1,390 (OUT OF A POSSIBLE 2,000 POINTS)

ACCOMMODATION: As in sister ships *Ecstasy, Elation, Fantasy, Fascination, Imagination, Inspiration,* and *Sensation*), the standard outside-view and interior (no view) cabins have plain décor. They are marginally comfortable, yet spacious enough and practical (most are of the same size and appointments), with good storage space and well-designed bathrooms.

Those booking one of the outside suites will find more space, whirlpool bathtubs, and some fascinating, rather eclectic décor and furniture. These are mildly attractive, but nothing special, and they are much smaller than those aboard the ships of a similar size of several competing companies.

A gift basket is provided in all grades of accommodation; it includes aloe soap, shampoo, conditioner, deodorant, breath mints, candy, and pain relief tablets (albeit all in sample sizes).

Note that if you book accommodation in one of the suites (Category 11 or 12 in the Carnival Cruise Lines brochure) you automatically qualify for "Skipper's Club" priority check-in at any US homeland port – useful for getting ahead of the crowd.

DINING: There are two dining rooms (Destiny and Paradise); both are non-smoking. They have splashy, colorful décor, and are large, very crowded and very noisy. While the menu descriptions sound inviting, the food, when it arrives, is not. It is adequate, but no more, although the company (which provides its own catering) has made improvements. You get what you pay for when it comes to food costs, and this company pays

BERLITZ'S RATINGS

	Possible	Achieved
Ship	500	395
Accommodation	200	151
Food	400	221
Service	400	270
Entertainment	100	81
Cruise	400	272

very little. Dining in each restaurant is now in four seatings, for greater flexibility: 6pm, 6.45pm, 8pm and 8.45pm (times are approximate).

Carnival meals stress quantity, not quality, although the company constantly works hard to improve the cuisine. While passengers seem to accept it, few find it worth remembering. Food and its taste are still not the company's strongest points.

While the menu items sound good, their presentation and taste leave much to be desired. While meats are of a high quality, fish and seafood is not. Presentation is simple, and few garnishes are used. Many meat and fowl dishes are disguised with gravies and sauces. The selection of fresh green vegetables, breads, rolls, cheeses and fruits is limited, and there is too much use of canned fruit and jellied desserts. However, do remember that this is banquet catering, with all its attendant standardization and production cooking (it is, therefore, difficult to ask for anything remotely unusual or off-menu). The selection of breads, rolls, cheeses and fruits is limited (there is too much use of canned fruit).

Although there is a decent wine list, there are no wine waiters (the waiters are expected to serve both food and wine, which does not work well) and no decent-sized wine glasses. The service is highly programmed, although the waiters are willing and reasonably friendly. However, the waiters do sing and dance (be prepared for *Simply the Best, Hot, Hot, Hot, Hot,* and other popular hits), and there are constant waiter parades; the dining room is show business – all done to attract gratuities.

For casual meals, there's the Lido Cafe, which,

aboard this ship, has some improvements and additions worthy of note, such as: an orange juice machine, where you put in oranges and out comes fresh juice (better than the concentrate stuff supplied in the dining room). The Pizzeria is open 24 hours a day – and typically serves more than 500 *every* single day. There's also a sushi bar – things are looking up. At night, the "Seaview Bistro," as the Lido Café becomes known, provides a casual (dress down) alternative to eating in the main dining rooms, serving pasta, steaks, salads and desserts (it typically is in operation between 6pm and 9pm).

OTHER COMMENTS: *Paradise* is the eighth in a series of eight mega-ships of the same series and identical internal configuration, and the 13th new ship for this cruise line. It is a very successful design for this successful company that targets the mass market, and particularly the first-time passenger. The ship's appearance is bold, forthright, and angular, and is typical of today's space-creative designs. What is new, however, is the pod propulsion system, which gives the ship more maneuverability, while reducing required machinery space and vibration at the stern. The ship, whose bows are extremely short, has the distinctive, large, swept-back wing-tipped funnel that is the trademark of Carnival Cruise Lines, in the company colors of red, white and blue. At its base is a "topless" area for sunbathing.

Like a breath of fresh air, this is a totally *non-smoking* ship (and that includes the crew), including all open decks. There is a fine of $250 for *anyone* caught smoking, and you will be put off at the next port. Passengers must sign a document agreeing to this policy prior to embarkation.

All of the principal public rooms are set off to one side of a double-width boulevard. There's a three-deck-high glass-enclosed health spa and gymnasium with the latest muscle-pump equipment, and a banked outdoor jogging track. A large shop is stuffed to the gills with low-quality merchandise. The large casino has gaming tables for blackjack, craps, roulette, Caribbean stud poker, as well as slot machines (all slot machines aboard all Carnival ships are linked into a big prize, called, naturally, Megacash).

The décor includes splashy, showy, public rooms and interior colors – pure Las Vegas, ideal for some tastes.

There are public entertainment lounges, bars and clubs galore, with something for everyone, including a children's playroom, larger than aboard the other ships in this series. Some busy colors and design themes abound in the handsome public rooms – these are connected by wide indoor boulevards and beg your attention and indulgence. There is also a good art collection, much of it bright and vocal. The Blue Riband library is a fine room, as aboard most Carnival ships; although there are few books, there are models of ocean liners. One neat feature (not found aboard previous ships in this series) is an atrium bar, complete with live classical music.

It's a real "life on the ocean rave for the young at heart, if you enjoy people and noise. Children are provided with good facilities, including their own two-level Children's Club (including an outdoor pool), and are well cared for with "Camp Carnival," the line's extensive children's program. The general passenger flow is good, and the interior design is clever, functional, wacky, and outrageously colorful. The ship is arguably better than the ports of call.

The company has grown dramatically over the past few years and has improved its product substantially. In 1996, the company introduced a "Vacation Guarantee" program (the first of its kind in the industry) to great success – particularly for first-time passengers who do not know whether they will enjoy cruising (few passengers ever consider leaving the cruise).

Carnival *does not* try to sell itself as a luxury cruise line and consistently delivers *exactly* what it says in its brochures (nothing more, nothing less), for which there is a huge, growing first-time cruise audience. It delivers a well-packaged cruise vacation, with smart new ships that have the latest high-tech entertainment facilities and features.

This ship is one of the great floating playgrounds for young, active adults who enjoy constant stimulation, close contact with lots and lots of others, as well as the three Gs – glitz, glamour and gambling. It is a live board game with every move executed in typically grand, colorful, fun-filled Carnival Cruise Lines style. This ship is ideally suited to those who like big city life ashore and want it on their vacation, and for those who like lively action, constant entertainment, and nightlife at any hour. Forget fashion – having fun is the *sine qua non* of a Carnival cruise.

Paradise operates alternating 7-day Eastern and Western Caribbean cruises from Miami. Gratuities are automatically added to your onboard account at $9.75 per person, per day (the amount charged when this book was completed); you can have this amount adjusted, although you'll have to visit the information desk to do so. The onboard currency is the US dollar.

WEAK POINTS: This ship is not for those who want a quiet, relaxing cruise experience. There are simply too many annoying announcements, and a great deal of hustling for drinks. The balconied showlounge is large, but 20 pillars obstruct the views from several seats. Shore excursions are booked via the in-cabin ("Fun Vision") television system (there is no longer a shore excursion desk, and thus no one to answer questions). In fact, getting anyone to answer your questions can prove utterly frustrating. Standing in line for embarkation, disembarkation, shore tenders and for self-serve buffet meals is an inevitable aspect of cruising aboard all large ships. The service is very, very basic, and completely without a hint of finesse.

Paul Gauguin
★★★★ +

Small Ship: ....18,800 tons	Total Crew: 206	Cabins (wheelchair accessible): 1
Lifestyle: ....Luxury	Passengers	Cabin Current: ....110 volts
Cruise Line: ......Radisson Seven Seas	(lower beds/all berths): 320/320	Elevators: 4
Cruises	Passenger Space Ratio	Casino (gaming tables): ....Yes
Former Names: ....none	(lower beds/all berths): 58.7/58.7	Slot Machines: ....Yes
Builder: Chantiers de l'Atlantique (France)	Crew/Passenger Ratio	Swimming Pools (outdoors): 1
Original Cost: ....$150 million	(lower beds/all berths): 1.5/1.5	Swimming Pools (indoors): 0
Entered Service: ....Jan 1998	Navigation Officers: ....European	Whirlpools: 0
Registry: ....Wallis & Fortuna	Cabins (total): 160	Fitness Center: ....Yes
Length (ft/m): 513.4/156.50	Size Range (sq ft/m): 200.0–534.0/	Sauna/Steam Room: ....No/Yes
Beam (ft/m): 72.1/22.00	18.5–49.6	Massage: ....Yes
Draft (ft/m): 16.8/5.15	Cabins (outside view): 160	Self-Service Launderette: ....No
Propulsion/Propellers: .....diesel-electric	Cabins (interior/no view): 0	Dedicated Cinema/Seats: ....No
(9,000 kW/2	Cabins (for one person): 0	Library: ....Yes
Passenger Decks: 7	Cabins (with private balcony): 80	Classification Society: ....Bureau Veritas

OVERALL SCORE: 1,645 (OUT OF A POSSIBLE 2,000 POINTS)

ACCOMMODATION: The outside-view cabins, half of which have private balconies, are nicely equipped, although they are strictly rectangular (and none have more interesting shapes). Most have large windows, except those on the lowest accommodation deck, which have portholes. Each has queen- or twin-sized beds (convertible to queen), and wood-accented cabinetry with rounded edges. A minibar/refrigerator (stocked with complimentary soft drinks) VCR, personal safe, hairdryer and umbrellas are standard. The marble-look appointed bathrooms are nice and large and have a bathtub as well as a separate shower enclosure. Bathrobes are provided for all passengers, and soft drinks and mineral water are free.

The two largest suites have a private balcony at the front and side of the vessel. Although there is a decent amount of in-cabin space, with a beautiful long vanity unit (and plenty of drawer space), the bathrooms are disappointingly small and plain, and too similar to all other standard cabin bathrooms. Butler service is provided in all accommodation designated as Owners Suite, Grand Suites, Oceanview "A" and "B" category suites (this was inaugurated in 2002).

DINING: The main dining room ("L'Etoile") features lunch and dinner, while La Veranda, an alternative dining spot, is open for breakfast, lunch and dinner. Both dining rooms provide "open seating" which means that passengers can choose when they want to dine and with whom. This provides a good opportunity to meet new people for dinner each evening. La Veranda provides

BERLITZ'S RATINGS

	Possible	Achieved
Ship	500	425
Accommodation	200	169
Food	400	326
Service	400	320
Entertainment	100	77
Cruise	400	328

dinner by reservation, with alternating French and Italian menus; the French menus are provided by Jean-Pierre Vigato, a two-star Michelin chef with his own restaurant ("Apicius") in Paris.

The dining operation is well orchestrated, with cuisine and service of a high standard. Complimentary standard table wines are served with dinner (although a connoisseur selection is available, at extra cost, for real wine lovers), and mineral water, fruit juices and soft drinks are complimentary throughout the ship – a nice touch.

An outdoor bistro provides informal cafe fare on deck aft of the pool, while the Connoisseur Club offers a luxurious retreat for cigars, cognacs, and wine tasting.

OTHER COMMENTS: Built by a French company, managed and operated by the US-based Radisson Seven Seas Cruises, this ship is extremely spacious. While it could carry more passengers, under French law operating in the Polynesian islands, it is not permitted to do so. The ship has a look that is quite well balanced, and all in gleaming white, and is topped by a single funnel.

This smart ship also has a retractable aft marina platform, and carries two water skiing boats and two inflatable craft for water sports. Windsurfers, kayaks, plus scuba and snorkeling gear are available for your use (all except scuba gear are included in the cruise fare).

Inside, there is a pleasant array of public rooms, and both the artwork and the decor have a real French Polynesia look and feel. The interior colors are quite restful, although a trifle bland.

Expert lecturers on Tahiti and Gauguin accompany each cruise, and a Fare (pronounced *foray*) Tahiti Gallery offers books, videos, and other materials on the unique art, history, and culture of the islands. Three original Gauguin sketches are displayed under glass. There is a good health spa program with treatment services provided by Carita of Paris, although the changing facilities are very limited. There is no sauna, and use of the steam room incurs an extra charge (it should be free).

The library is pleasant enough, although it really could be larger. This ship (a more deluxe version of the company's popular *Song of Flower*) presents Radisson Seven Seas Cruises with the opportunity to score very high marks with its passengers, as the company is known for its attention to detail and passenger care.

A no-tie policy means that the dress code is very relaxed – every day. The standard itinerary means that the ship docks only in Papeete and shore tenders are used in all other ports. There is little entertainment, as the ship stays overnight in several ports (so little is needed). The ship's high crew-to-passenger ratio translates to highly personalized service, and, overall, this is a pleasing product. Where the ship really shines is in the provision of a lot of water sports equipment, and its shallow draft allows it to navigate and anchor in lovely little places that larger ships couldn't possibly get to. All in all, it's a delightful cruise and product, and all gratuities to staff are included. The euro is now the currency in Tahiti and its islands, as Tahiti is part of France.

WEAK POINTS: Although it sounds exotic, the itinerary is only marginally interesting to the well traveled, the best island experience being in Bora Bora. The ship's shallow draft means there could be some movement, as it is rather high-sided for its size. A minimum purchase rule in the ship's boutique is irritating (however, this is due to local Government rules); the same is true of the casino (you must pay $10 to play – again, local government rules). The spa is very small, and the fitness room is windowless.

Polaris
★★ +

Small Ship:	2,214 tons	Passengers		Cabin Current:	220 volts

Small Ship: . . . . .2,214 tons
Lifestyle: . . . . .Standard
Cruise Line: . . . . . . .Lindblad Expeditions
Former Names: *Lindblad Polaris, Oresund*
Builder: . . . . . . .Aalborg Vaerft (Denmark)
Original Cost: .n/a
Entered Service: 1960/May 1987
Registry: . . . . .Ecuador
Length (ft/m): 236.6/72.12
Beam (ft/m): 42.7/13.03
Draft (ft/m): 13.7/4.30
Propulsion/Propellers: . . . . .diesel
. . . .(2,354 kW)/2
Passenger Decks: 4
Total Crew: 44

Passengers
(lower beds/all berths): 82/84
Passenger Space Ratio
(lower beds/all berths): 27.0/26.3
Crew/Passenger Ratio
(lower beds/all berths): 1.8/1.8
Navigation Officers: . . . . .Ecuadorian
Cabins (total): 41
Size Range (sq ft/m): 99.0–229.2/
. . . . .9.2–21.3
Cabins (outside view): 41
Cabins (interior/no view): 0
Cabins (for one person): 0
Cabins (with private balcony): 0
Cabins (wheelchair accessible): 0

Cabin Current: . . . . .220 volts
Elevators: 0
Casino (gaming tables): . . . . .No
Slot Machines: . . . . .No
Swimming Pools (outdoors): 0
Whirlpools: 0
Exercise Room: . . . . .No
Sauna/Steam Room: . . . . .Yes/No
Massage: . . . . .No
Self-Service Launderette: . . . . .No
Lecture/Film Room: . . . . .No
Library: . . . . .Yes
Zodiacs: 8
Helicopter Pad: 0
Classification Society: . . . .Bureau Veritas

OVERALL SCORE: 1,097 (OUT OF A POSSIBLE 2,000 POINTS)

ACCOMMODATION: The cabins, all of which are above the waterline, are fairly roomy and nicely appointed, but there is little drawer space. Some have been refurbished, and have large (lower) beds. Each has a hairdryer; refreshingly, cabin keys are not used. The cabin bathrooms are really tiny, however, so take only what you need. There is no cabin service menu.

BERLITZ'S RATINGS

	Possible	Achieved
Ship	500	244
Accommodation	200	105
Food	400	229
Service	400	233
Entertainment	N/A	N/A
Cruise	500	286

DINING: The dining room has big picture windows and a wrap-around view. Seating is now at individual tables (formerly family style) in a leisurely single seating. Has good food, with a major emphasis on local fish and seafood dishes. There is also a fine wine list. Breakfast and lunch are buffet-style. There is friendly service from an attentive staff.

OTHER COMMENTS: This "soft" expedition cruise vessel, of modest proportions, has a dark blue hull and white superstructure. It has been well maintained and operated, having been skillfully converted from a former Scandinavian ferry. It sports a fantail and improved aft outdoor lounge area, and carries several Zodiac inflatable rubber landing craft, as well as a glass-bottom boat.

Inside, although there are few public rooms, the Scandinavian-style interior furnishings and décor are very tidy and welcoming, accented by lots of wood trim. Has a friendly, very intimate atmosphere on board,

with Filipino service staff. There is a good team of lecturers and nature observers, whose daily recaps are a vital part of the experience. A restful, well-stocked library helps passengers learn more about the region and the natural world.

If you *are* going on a Galápagos cruise, it is important that you remember to take with you: passport, short and long-sleeve cotton shirts, good walking shoes, windbreaker, mosquito repellent (mosquitos are at their worst between December and July, particularly in Bartolome), sunglasses with retaining strap, and any personal medication. You will need to take a flight from Quito to San Cristobal (via Guayaquil) to join your cruise.

Polaris is a good small vessel, which now operates year-round nature-intensive "soft" expedition cruises around the Galápagos Islands. This is an area to which the ship is well suited (only 90 passengers from any one ship are allowed at any one time in the Galápagos Islands, where tourism is managed well by the local Equadorians). In fact, this ship is among the best suited to this region.

Bottled water is provided at no extra charge. All of the port charges are included in this product, which is marketed by Lindblad Expeditions and Noble Caledonia, together with other specialist packagers. The onboard currency is the US dollar or Ecuadorian sucre.

Polynesia
★★

Small Ship: ....430 tons	Main Propulsion: ....sail power	Cabins (for one person): 0
Lifestyle: ....Standard	Propulsion/Propellers: diesel/1	Cabins (with private balcony): 0
Cruise Line: ....Windjammer Barefoot	Passenger Decks: 4	Cabins (wheelchair accessible): 0
Cruises	Total Crew: 45	Cabin Current: ....110 volts
Former Names: ....*Argus*	Passengers	Elevators: 0
Builder: .....Haan & Oerlemans (Holland)	(lower beds/all berths): 110/122	Casino (gaming tables): ....No
Original Cost: ....n/a	Passenger Space Ratio	Slot Machines: ....No
Entered Service: 1938/1975	(lower beds/all berths): 3.9/3.5	Swimming Pools (outdoors): 0
Registry: ....Equatorial Guinea	Crew/Passenger Ratio	Whirlpools: 0
Length (ft/m): 248.0/75.5	(lower beds/all berths): 2.4/2.7	Fitness Center: ....No
Beam (ft/m): 36.0/10.9	Navigation Officers: ....International	Sauna/Steam Room: ....No/No
Draft (ft/m): 18.0/5.4	Cabins (total): 55	Massage: ....No
Type of Vessel: ....topsail schooner	Size Range (sq ft/m): 68.0–104.0/6.3–9.6	Self-Service Launderette: ....No
No. of Masts: 4	Cabins (outside view): 14	Library: ....Yes
Sail Area (sq ft/m2): 18,000/1,672.2	Cabins (interior/no view): 41	Classification Society: ....none

OVERALL SCORE: 902 (OUT OF A POSSIBLE 2,000 POINTS)

ACCOMMODATION: There are four grades (designated as Admiral Suite, Deck Cabin, Standard Cabin, and Bachelor/ette Cabin). The cabins are very small, however, particularly when compared to regular cruise ships. But remember that this is a very casual cruise experience and you will need so few clothes anyway. All are equipped with upper and lower berths, and most are quite narrow.

DINING: There is one dining room, with views to the outside through real portholes, and meals are all very simple in style and service, with little choice and only the most basic presentation. Breakfast is served on board, as is dinner, while lunch could be either on board or at a beach, picnic-style. Wine is included for dinner.

OTHER COMMENTS: *Polynesia* was built to be part of the great Portuguese Grand Banks fleet. It was featured in the May 1952 edition of *National Geographic* magazine and in *The Quest of the Schooner Argus* by the late maritime writer, Allen Villers. Windjammer Barefoot Cruises acquired *Polynesia* in 1975.

Aboard one of this company's fleet you can let the crew do all the work, or you can lend a hand at the helm yourself. One neat thing to do is just to sit or lie in the nets at the bows of the vessel, without a care in the world.

The mood is free and easy, the ships are equipped very simply, and only the most casual clothes are required (T-shirts and shorts), and shoes are optional, although you may need them if you go off in one of the ports. Quite possibly the most used item will be your

BERLITZ'S RATINGS		
	Possible	Achieved
Ship	500	219
Accommodation	200	79
Food	400	166
Service	400	188
Entertainment	N/A	N/A
Cruise	500	250

bathing suit – better take more than one! Smoking is allowed only on the open decks.

Entertainment in the evenings consists of – you and the crew. You can put on a toga, take or create a pirate outfit and join in the fun. This is cruising free 'n' easy style – none of that programmed big-ship production show stuff here.

Jammin' aboard a Windjammer (first-timers are "crewmates" while repeat passengers are "jammers") is no-frills cruising in a no-nonsense, friendly environment, for the young at heart and those who don't need programmed activities. It's all about the romance of being at sea under sail. Those who enjoy beaches, scuba diving and snorkeling around the Caribbean will be best suited to a Windjammer Barefoot Cruises cruise. This ship can anchor in neat little sheltered Caribbean hideaways that larger (regular) cruise ships can't get near.

Although itineraries (well, islands) are provided in the brochure, the captain actually decides which islands to go to in any given area, depending on sea and weather conditions. *Polynesia* features year-round cruises in the Caribbean. The brochure rates might seem inexpensive, but remember that you will need to add on the air fare.

Other tall ships in the fleet include *Flying Cloud, Legacy, Mandalay,* and *Yankee Clipper.* The onboard currency is the US dollar.

WEAK POINTS: There's very little room per passenger. Everything is basic, basic, basic. Tips to the crew are strongly suggested – at $50 per week.

Removed 2006

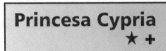

Princesa Cypria
★ +

Mid-Size Ship: . . . . .9,984 tons	Total Crew: 180	Cabin Current: . . . . .110 volts
Lifestyle: . . . . .Standard	Passengers	Dining Rooms: 2
Cruise Line: . . . . .Louis Cruise Lines	(lower beds/all berths): 548/633	Elevators: 2
Former Names: . . . .*Asia Angel/*	Passenger Space Ratio	Casino (gaming tables): . . . . .Yes
Lu Jiang/Princesse Margrethe	(lower beds/all berths): 18.2/15.7	Slot Machines: .Yes
Builder: . . . . . . .Cantieri del Terreno (Italy)	Crew/Passenger Ratio	Swimming Pools (outdoors): 0
Original Cost: . . . . .n/a	(lower beds/all berths): 3.0/3.5	Swimming Pools (indoors): 0
Entered Service: 1968/July 1989	Navigation Officers: . . . . . .Cypriot/Greek	Whirlpools: 0
Registry: . . . . .Cyprus (P3CQ3)	Cabins (total): 274	Fitness Center: .No
Length (ft/m): 409.9/124.95	Size Range (sq ft/m): . . . . .n/a	Sauna/Steam Room: . . . . .No/No
Beam (ft/m): 63.1/19.25	Cabins (outside view): 144	Massage: . . . . .No
Draft (ft/m): 20.9/5.40	Cabins (interior/no view): 129	Self-Service Launderette: . . . . .No
Propulsion/Propellers: . . . . .diesel	Cabins (for one person): 0	Movie Theater/Seats: . . . . .No
(12,000bhp)/2	Cabins (with private balcony): 0	Library: . . . . .No
Passenger Decks: 6	Cabins (wheelchair accessible): 0	Classification Society: Det Norske Veritas

---

OVERALL SCORE: 691 (OUT OF A POSSIBLE 2,000 POINTS)

ACCOMMODATION: This ship has very small, spartan cabins with virtually no closet and drawer space, and some 171 are without private facilities. The bathrooms are tiny.

DINING: The Curium Restaurant, with 338 seats, is located forward and high up in the ship and has large picture windows, while a second dining room, the Tamassos Restaurant, with 160 seats, is set amidships. Typically, an open seating prevails. The food is adequate, and basic, but no more, and service comes without finesse. The wine list is poor.

OTHER COMMENTS: The low foredeck and short, stubby bows are typical of this former ferry, whose profile is stunted and poorly balanced, particularly at the stern, where some new cabins were added during a reconstruction of the ship in 1989–90. The open deck and sunning space is very limited. The exterior maintenance and open deck areas need more work. It is an extremely

BERLITZ'S RATINGS

	Possible	Achieved
Ship	500	130
Accommodation	200	73
Food	400	169
Service	400	170
Entertainment	N/A	N/A
Cruise	500	149

high-density ship, so public rooms are always crowded.

The ship carries cars and passengers on short voyages (typically lasting two or three days). It suits passengers looking for really low fares and completely unpretentious surroundings, in a cruise that goes to the Holy Land. It is ideal for backpackers wishing to visit several ports.

The public rooms are basically attractive. *Cypria* has a fairly friendly atmosphere, and lovers of old ships will find it pleasant, although it cannot compare with more modern and contemporary tonnage. The onboard currency is the Cyprus pound.

WEAK POINTS: The space per passenger ratio is very low, which translates to a very densely populated ship, and that means that it is hard to find any quiet spaces at all. Low ceilings and too many support pillars add to the rather confined feeling. There is little separation of smokers and non-smokers.

Princesa Marissa
★★

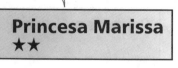

Small Ship: ....10,487 tons	Passengers	Cabin Current: ....220 volts
Lifestyle: ....Standard	(lower beds/all berths): 628/839	Dining Rooms: 2
Cruise Line: ....Louis Cruise Lines	Passenger Space Ratio	Elevators: 1
Former Names: ...*Princessan, Finnhansa*	(lower beds/all berths): 16.6/12.4	Casino (gaming tables): ....Yes
Builder: ....Wartsila (Finland)	Crew/Passenger Ratio	Slot Machines: ....Yes
Original Cost: ....n/a	(lower beds/all berths): 3.3/4.5	Swimming Pools (outdoors): 0
Entered Service: 1966/June 1987	Navigation Officers: ....Cypriot/Greek	Swimming Pools (indoors): 0
Registry: ....Cyprus	Cabins (total): 314	Whirlpools: 0
Length (ft/m): 440.6/134.30	Size Range (sq ft/m): 75.3–226.0/	Fitness Center: ....No
Beam (ft/m): 65.2/19.90	7.0–21.0	Sauna/Steam Room: ....Yes/No
Draft (ft/m): 18.7/5.70	Cabins (outside view): 148	Massage: ....No
Propulsion/Propellers: ....diesel	Cabins (interior/no view): 166	Self-Service Launderette: ....No
(10,300 kW)/2 (CP)	Cabins (for one person): 0	Movie Theater/Seats: ....No
Passenger Decks: 9	Cabins (with private balcony): 0	Library: ....No
Total Crew: 185	Cabins (wheelchair accessible): 0	Classification Society: Det Norske Veritas

OVERALL SCORE: 901 (OUT OF A POSSIBLE 2,000 POINTS)

ACCOMMODATION: The standard cabins are fairly smart and functional, although the bathrooms are very small. A whole section of new cabins, added in 1995, are of a good size, and have large picture windows; the décor is bright and cheerful, and they also have good, practical bathrooms.

DINING: There are two dining rooms. Both are quite attractive (the forward one is a little more intimate), and have comfortable chairs. There are two seatings. There are both à la carte and buffet style meals, and the menu choice includes three entrées. There is also a full vegetarian menu. The selections of breads and ice cream sundaes are good. In fact, the food is perhaps the best part of a cruise aboard this vessel.

OTHER COMMENTS: This former ferry has a square stern, twin funnels and a short, stubby bow. There is very little open deck and sunbathing space, however.

BERLITZ'S RATINGS

	Possible	Achieved
Ship	500	203
Accommodation	200	91
Food	400	205
Service	400	204
Entertainment	100	37
Cruise	400	161

The interiors are quite smart and tidy, and the ship has been well maintained. The public room décor is attractive, with warm, fairly bright contemporary colors, well-designed fabrics and soft furnishings. There are some limited facilities for meetings and small conferences.

The ship provides low fare transportation in unstuffy surroundings and typically operates year-round short cruises to Egypt and Israel (principally for residents of Cyprus and for British passengers on holiday there) that include shore excursions. The onboard currency is the Cyprus pound.

WEAK POINTS: The passenger density is high. Also, the ceilings are low, and typical of ferry construction. There are few crew members for so many passengers. Passengers must board through the aft car deck, but that is no real hardship. There is little separation of smokers and non-smokers.

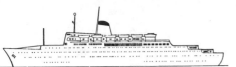

Removed 2006

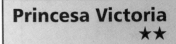

Princesa Victoria
★★

Mid-Size Ship: . . . . .14,583 tons	Total Crew: 230	Cabins (wheelchair accessible): 0
Lifestyle: . . . . .Standard	Passengers	Cabin Current: . . . . .115 volts
Cruise Line: . . . . .Louis Cruise Lines	(lower beds/all berths): 568/750	Elevators: 3
Former Names: . . . .The Victoria, Victoria,	Passenger Space Ratio	Casino (gaming tables): . . . . .Yes
Dunottar Castle	(lower beds/all berths): 25.6/19.4	Slot Machines: . . . . .Yes
Builder: . . . . .Harland & Wolff (UK)	Crew/Passenger Ratio	Swimming Pools (outdoors): 2
Original Cost: .n/a	(lower beds/all berths): 2.4/3.2	Swimming Pools (indoors): 0
Entered Service: . . . . .July 1936/Jan 1993	Navigation Officers: . . . . . . .Cypriot/Greek	Whirlpools: 0
Registry: .Cyprus	Cabins (total): 287	Fitness Center: . . . . .Yes
Length (ft/m): 572.8/174.60	Size Range (sq ft/m): 156.0–258.3/	Sauna/Steam Room: . . . . .Yes/No
Beam (ft/m): 71.9/21.92	14.5–24.0	Massage: . . . . .No
Draft (ft/m): 27.8/8.50	Cabins (outside view): 216	Self-Service Launderette: . . . . .No
Propulsion/Propellers: . . . . .diesel	Cabins (interior/no view): 71	Dedicated Cinema/Seats: Yes/250
(10,450 kW)/2	Cabins (for one person): 8	Library: . . . . .Yes
Passenger Decks: 7	Cabins (with private balcony): 0	Classification Society: . . .Lloyd's Register

OVERALL SCORE: 895 (OUT OF A POSSIBLE 2,000 POINTS)

ACCOMMODATION: The standard cabins are fairly spacious, and have heavy-duty furniture and fittings. The suite rooms are cavernous, and the large bathrooms come with deep, full bathtubs, something not seen on today's cruise vessels.

DINING: The dining room is set low down, but is comfortable and has a fine two-deck high center section with barrel-shaped ceiling, music balcony and lots of wood paneling. There are two seatings. The standard of cuisine is good, particularly bearing in mind the price. There are three entrées, as well as a complete vegetarian menu. Salads, bakery items and fruits are reasonable.

OTHER COMMENTS: This ship has a long history. Originally built for the Union Castle Line (for voyages from England to South Africa), it was then operated for many years by Chandris Cruises before being bought by Louis

BERLITZ'S RATINGS

	Possible	Achieved
Ship	500	198
Accommodation	200	88
Food	400	204
Service	400	205
Entertainment	100	37
Cruise	400	163

Cruise Lines. It has been extremely well maintained, despite its age. There is a generous amount of open deck space and twin outdoor swimming pools (although there are no showers on deck). Inside, the center stairway is built in true art deco style. There is a friendly, old-world ambience on board. The Riviera Club is a contemporary room that is totally out of keeping with the rest of ship.

Princesa Victoria provides a good cruise experience for first-time cruisers and particularly for anyone seeking to optimize their hotel vacation in Cyprus. This really is an old ship, however, and does not have the ultra-contemporary facilities of most modern ships. The onboard currency is the Cyprus pound.

WEAK POINTS: The repetitive announcements are annoying. There is little separation of smokers and non-smokers, and the ship is old and worn in many places.

Yalim 8/6/05   *Remared 2006*

Princess Danae
★★★

Mid-Size Ship: . . . . .17,074 tons	Passenger Decks: 7	Cabins (wheelchair accessible): 0
Lifestyle: . . . . .Standard	Total Crew: 240	Cabin Current: . . . . .220 volts
Cruise Line: . . . . .Classic International	Passengers	Elevators: 2
Cruises	(lower beds/all berths): 560/670	Casino (gaming tables): . . . . .Yes
Former Names: . . . . .Baltica,	Passenger Space Ratio	Slot Machines: . . . . .Yes
Starlight Express, Danae,	(lower beds/all berths): 30.4/25.4	Swimming Pools (outdoors): 1
Therisos Express, Port Melbourne	Crew/Passenger Ratio	Swimming Pools (indoors): 0
Builder: . . . . .Swan, Hunter (UK)	(lower beds/all berths): 2.3/2.7	Whirlpools: 2
Original Cost: .n/a	Navigation Officers: . . . . .European	Fitness Center: . . . . .Yes
Entered Service: . . . . . . .July 1955/1997	Cabins (total): 280	Sauna/Steam Room: . . . . .Yes/No
Registry: .Panama	Size Range (sq ft/m): 200.0–270.0/	Massage: . . . . .Yes
Length (ft/m): 532.7/162.39	18.5–25.0	Self-Service Launderette: . . . . .No
Beam (ft/m): 70.0/21.34	Cabins (outside view): 215	Dedicated Cinema/Seats: Yes/275
Draft (ft/m): 41.9/12.80	Cabins (interior/no view): 65	Library: . . . . .Yes
Propulsion/Propellers: . . . . .diesel	Cabins (for one person): 0	Classification Society: . .American Bureau
(9,850 kW)/2	Cabins (with private balcony): 6	of Shipping

---

OVERALL SCORE: 1,101 (OUT OF A POSSIBLE 2,000 POINTS)

ACCOMMODATION: Most cabins are of good size (in eight categories) and have heavy-duty furniture and fittings with ample closet and drawer space. Note that the cabins located under the disco can suffer from thumping noise late at night. The lower-grade cabins are really plain. While 210 cabin bathrooms have a bathtub and shower, 70 have a shower only. Cabin insulation is poor.

BERLITZ'S RATINGS		
	Possible	Achieved
Ship	500	288
Accommodation	200	116
Food	400	234
Service	400	223
Entertainment	100	42
Cruise	400	198

DINING: The dining room is decorated quite nicely and has a high ceiling. It has open seating dining (dine with whoever you wish) and Continental/European cuisine. The service is fairly attentive, although the noise level is high from the open waiter stations.

OTHER COMMENTS: *Princess Danae* is a solidly built ship, with good lines and a reasonably balanced profile, originally built for a now-defunct Greek operator, Carras Cruises. Costa Cruises then operated the ship for many years before it was bought by its present owners, Classic International Cruises. There is a decent amount of open deck space for sunbathing.

There is a pleasing traditional shipboard ambience, combined with a mixture of both traditional and con-temporary features, including many original interior appointments of decent quality. There are a number of spacious public rooms, although the décor is conservative. A new bar amidships was recently added. There is a roomy, traditional cinema.

This ship underwent a refurbishment early in 1996, but the fit and finish of the areas that were changed is extremely poor. It provides a moderately comfortable, cruise experience.

The ship features Caribbean cruises from Santo Domingo in winter, from Brazil during the summer, and Mediterranean cruises during some summer months. It is often placed under charter to various tour operators (of various nationalities), and so the character of the ship changes, as does the level of food and service provided (the principal constituent parts of the cruise experience). In other words, use the rating only as a guide, as the actual product can be inconsistent. The onboard currency is the US dollar.

WEAK POINTS: There is no observation lounge with forward-facing views over the ship's bows. There is little finesse in the hospitality department, and service is, at best, perfunctory.

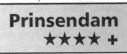

Prinsendam
★★★★ +

Mid-Size Ship: ....37,845 tons	Total Crew: 460	Cabins (wheelchair accessible): 4
Lifestyle: ....Premium	Passengers	Cabin Current: ....110 volts
Cruise Line: ......Holland America Line	(lower beds/all berths): 794/840	Elevators: 4
Former Names: ....*Seabourn Sun,*	Passenger Space Ratio	Casino (gaming tables): ....Yes
Royal Viking Sun	(lower beds/all berths): 47.6/46.4	Slot Machines: ....Yes
Builder: ....Wartsila (Finland)	Crew/Passenger Ratio	Swimming Pools (outdoors): 2
Original Cost: ....$125 million	(lower beds/all berths): 1.7/1.8	Swimming Pools (indoors): 0
Entered Service: ....Dec 1988/May 2002	Navigation Officers: ....European	Whirlpools: 2
Registry:..............The Netherlands	Cabins (total): 396	Fitness Center: ....Yes
Length (ft/m): 674.2/205.5	Size Range (sq ft/m): 137.7–723.3/	Sauna/Steam Room: ....Yes/Yes
Beam (ft/m): 91.8/28.0	12.8–67.2	Massage: ....Yes
Draft (ft/m): 23.6/7.2	Cabins (outside view): 368	Self-Service Launderette: ....Yes
Propulsion/Propellers: ....diesel	Cabins (interior/no view): 25	Dedicated Cinema/Seats: Yes/101
(21,120 kW)/2	Cabins (for one person): 2	Library: ....Yes
Passenger Decks: 8	Cabins (with private balcony): 145	Classification Society: Det Norske Veritas

OVERALL SCORE: 1,670 (OUT OF A POSSIBLE 2,000 POINTS)

ACCOMMODATION: There are 15 grades – up from the 10 grades when the ship was operated by its previous owner, Seabourn Cruise Line. These range from Penthouse Verandah Suites to standard interior (no view) cabins added when Holland America Line took over the ship in 2002.

PENTHOUSE VERANDAH SUITE : The Penthouse Verandah Suite (723 sq. ft/67 sq. meters), is a most desirable living space, although not as large as other penthouse suites aboard some other ships. It is light and airy, and has two bathrooms, one of which has a large whirlpool bathtub with ocean views, and anodized gold bathroom fittings. The living room contains a large dining table and chairs, large sofas, and plenty of space to spread out. There is also a substantial private balcony, and butler service.

DELUXE VERANDAH SUITES: There are 18 of these (8 on Sports Deck/10 on Lido Deck). Located in the forward section of the ship, they have large balconies, two sofas, large bar/entertainment center, (mini-bar/refrigerator, color television, VCR and CD player); bathrooms have separate toilet, sink and toiletries cabinets, connecting sliding door into the bedroom, large mirror, two toiletries cabinets, plenty of storage space, full bathtub, and anodized gold fittings. Each evening the butler brings different goodies – hot and cold hors d'oeuvres and other niceties. Liquor and wines are included in the cruise fare. If you do choose one of these suites, it might be best on the starboard side where they are located in a private hallway, while those on the port side (including

BERLITZ'S RATINGS	Possible	Achieved
Ship	500	430
Accommodation	200	174
Food	400	322
Service	400	323
Entertainment	100	81
Cruise	400	340

the Penthouse Verandah Suite) are positioned along a public hallway. The 10 suites on Lido Deck are positioned along private port and starboard side hallways.

Passengers in Penthouse and Deluxe Verandah Suites are provided with a private concierge lounge, high tea served in the suite each afternoon, hors d'oeuvres before dinner each evening (on request), complimentary laundry pressing and dry cleaning, private cocktail parties with captain, priority disembarkation, and more.

OTHER CABIN GRADES: Most of the other cabins (spread over six other decks) are of generous proportions and are well appointed with just about everything you would need (including a VCR). Many of them (about 38 percent) have a small, private balcony. All cabins have walk-in closets, lockable drawers (the line calls them "safe drawers"), full-length mirrors, hairdryers, and ample cotton towels. A few cabins have third berths, while some have interconnecting doors (good for couples who want two bathrooms and more space, or for families with children).

In all grades of accommodation, passengers receive a basket of fresh fruit, fluffy cotton bathrobes, evening turndown service, and a Holland America Line signature tote bag. Filipino and Indonesian cabins stewards and stewardesses provide unobtrusive personal service.

Four well-equipped, L-shaped cabins for the handicapped are quite well designed, fairly large, and are equipped with special wheel-in bathrooms with shower facilities and closets.

DINING: The La Fontaine Dining Room wraps around the aft end of Lower Promenade Deck and has extensive ocean-view windows that provide plenty of light; a second, smaller (quieter) section is located along the starboard side. There is plenty of space around tables for waiters to serve properly. A good number of window-side tables are for two persons, although there are also tables for four, six or eight. Crystal glasses, and Rosenthal china and fine cutlery are provided. There are two seatings for dinner, at assigned tables, and an open seating arrangement for breakfast and lunch (you'll be seated by restaurant staff when you enter).

A smaller, quieter room is the Odyssey Dining Room, with 48 seats, and wood paneled décor that increases the feeling of intimacy and privacy. The cuisine is Italian, and seating preference is given to occupants of accommodation designated as suites. Reservations are required, although there is no extra charge. The Odyssey is open for both lunch and dinner.

The food is creative and well presented, with good use of color combinations and garnishes. Note that Holland America Line can provide Kosher meals, but these are prepared ashore, frozen, and brought to your table sealed in their original containers (there is no Kosher kitchen on board). There is a well-chosen wine list, although there is much emphasis on California wines, the prices of which are quite high.

There is also the decent Lido Restaurant, for casual dining and self-serve buffet-style meals. This restaurant, which has both indoor and outdoor seating, was enlarged during the latest dry-docking of the ship, and has incorporated space originally used as an alternative dining spot, thus providing more seating indoors.

OTHER COMMENTS: *Prinsendam* is a contemporary, well-designed ship that has sleek, flowing lines, a sharply raked bow, and a well-rounded profile, with lots of floor-to-ceiling glass. Originally ordered and in service as a Royal Viking Line ship, it was bought by Seabourn Cruise Line in 1998. Following an extensive refit and refurbishment program (which sadly didn't go far enough), the ship was renamed *Seabourn Sun* in 1999 (when it was then the largest ship in the Seabourn Cruise Line fleet). In 2002, it was transferred to Holland America Line as *Prinsendam*, and the ship's hull was changed from all-white to a dark blue hull with white superstructure. The shore tenders are thoughtfully air-conditioned and even have radar and a toilet.

Wide teak wood decks provide excellent walking areas including a decent wrap-around promenade deck outdoors. The swimming pool (outdoors on Lido Deck) is not large, but it is quite adequate, while the deck above has a croquet court and golf driving range.

Inside, the name changes of the ship's public rooms reflect the traditions of Holland America Line. There are two glass-walled elevators at the aft elevator bank. Separate baggage elevators mean passengers do not have to wait long for luggage on embarkation day. The interior layout is very spacious (it is even more ideal when a maximum of 600 passengers are aboard). Impressive public rooms and tasteful décor now reign. Two handrails – one of wood, one of chrome – are provided on all stairways, a thoughtful touch.

The Crow's Nest, the ship's forward observation lounge, is simply one of the most elegant, but contemporary (at least in décor), lounges at sea. Pebble Beach is the name of the electronic golf simulator room, complete with wet bar, with play possible on 11 virtual courses. The Erasmus Library (formerly the Ibsen Library) is well organized, although it is simply not large enough for long-distance cruising. The former Compass Rose room is now the Explorer's Lounge.

The Oak Room is the ship's cigar/pipe smoker's lounge; it has a marble fireplace, which sadly cannot be used due to United States Coast Guard regulations. I have always thought it would make a fine library, although it is also excellent as a cigar smoking room. Adjacent to the Java Café and Bar, a firm favorite with Holland America Line regulars.

The Health Spa is extensive and stretches across the beam at the aft part of the ship. It includes six treatment rooms (with integral showers), a rasul chamber (for mud treatments, combined with gentle steam), a gymnasium with views over the stern (it is located where an aft swimming pool used to be – for those who remember it when it was a Royal Viking ship), and separate sauna, steam room, and changing rooms for ladies and gents.

There is a computer-learning center, with 10 workstations (although there is little privacy when receiving one's emails). A lecture is provided to present subjects of cultural interest, while gentlemen "dance hosts" provide partners for ladies traveling alone.

Whether by intention or not, the ship has a definite two-class feeling, with passengers in "upstairs" penthouse suites and "A" grade staterooms gravitating to the somewhat quieter Stella Polaris lounge (particularly at night), while other passengers (the participants) go to the main entertainment deck.

This ship has a wide range of facilities, including a concierge, self-service launderettes (useful when on long voyages), an excellent guest lecture program, 24-hour information office, and true 24-hour cabin service, for the discriminating passenger who demands spacious personal surroundings, and good food and service, regardless of price. This ship operates mainly long-distance cruises in great comfort, and free shuttle buses are provided in almost all ports of call.

While *Prinsendam* isn't perfect (the perfect ship has not yet been delivered), the few design flaws (for example: poorly designed bar service counters) are minor points. Even though the hardware is not perfect, the software (personnel and service) is generally sound.

A cruise aboard *Prinsendam* should prove to be a civilized travel experience (although, as with any ship, the larger the cabin the better the experience for many of the regulars), with plenty of space per passenger, uncluttered surroundings, and no lines anywhere. Holland America Line also provides cappuccino and espresso coffees and free ice cream during certain hours of the day aboard its ships, as well as hot hors d'oeuvres in all bars – something other major lines seem to have dropped, or charge extra for.

Note that gratuities are extra, and they are added to your shipboard account at $10–$13 per day, according to the accommodation grade chosen. Refreshingly, the company does not add an automatic 15 percent gratuity for beverage purchases. Perhaps the ship's best asset is its friendly and personable Filipino and Indonesian crew, although communication can prove frustrating at times.

Prinsendam is an extremely comfortable ship in which to cruise – smaller (except for *Noordam*) than other Holland America Line ships, and more refined, although dining is now in two seatings. The ship has some fine, elegant decorative features (Dutch artwork and memorabilia). Added benefits include a fine health spa facility, spacious, wide teakwood decks and teak deck lounge chairs. However, the good points are marred by the bland quality of the dining room food (all geared to American tastes) and service, and the lack of understanding of what it takes to make a "luxury" cruise experience, despite what is stated in the company's brochures. The onboard currency is the US dollar.

WEAK POINTS: There are only four elevators, so anyone with walking disabilities may have to wait for some time during periods of peak usage (e.g. before meals). The cabin ceilings are plain. This spacious ship shows signs of wear and tear in some areas (particularly in the accommodation passageways), despite recent refurbishments. The library is far too small (particularly for some of the long cruises operated by this ship) and difficult to enter for anyone confined to a wheelchair.

Professor Molchanov
★★

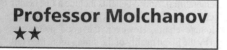

Small Ship: ....1,753 tons	
Lifestyle: ....Standard	
Cruise Line: ......Oceanwide Expeditions	
Former Names: ....none	
Builder: ....Wartsila (Finland)	
Original Cost: ....n/a	
Entered Service: 1983	
Registry: ....Russia	
Length (ft/m): 234.9/71.6	
Beam (ft/m): 42/12.8	
Draft (ft/m): 15.0/4.6	
Propulsion/Propellers: ....diesel	
(2,327 kW)/2	
Passenger Decks: 3	
Total Crew: 20	

Passengers
(lower beds/all berths): 52/52
Passenger Space Ratio
(lower beds/all berths): 33.7/33.7
Crew/Passenger Ratio
(lower beds/all berths): 2.6/2.6
Navigation Officers: ....Russian
Cabins (total): 26
Size Range (sq ft/m): ....n/a
Cabins (outside view): 29
Cabins (interior/no view): 0
Cabins (for one person): 6
Cabins (with private balcony): 0
Cabins (wheelchair accessible): 0
Cabin Current: ....220 volts

Elevators: 0
Casino (gaming tables): ....No
Slot Machines: ....No
Swimming Pools (outdoors): 0
Swimming Pools (indoors): 0
Whirlpools: 0
Fitness Center: ....No
Sauna/Steam Room: ....Yes/No
Massage: ....No
Self-Service Launderette: ....No
Dedicated Cinema/Seats: ....No
Library: ....Yes
Classification Society: .Russian Shipping
Register

OVERALL SCORE: 947 (OUT OF A POSSIBLE 2,000 POINTS)

ACCOMMODATION: With the exception of a single "suite," almost all other cabins are very small, spartan, and rather clinical. There are two-berth cabins with shower and toilet, or there are two-bed cabins on the lowest deck, whose occupants must share a bathroom.

DINING: There are two dining rooms (the galley is located between them), each with a single seating. The meals are hearty international fare, with no frills. When the ship is under charter to Quark Expeditions, western rather than Russian chefs oversee the food operation, and the quality of meals and variety of foods is much better.

OTHER COMMENTS: This all-white vessel was originally specially constructed in Finland for the former Soviet Union's polar and oceanographic research program and should not be taken as a cruise ship, although it was converted in the early 1990s to carry passengers, and then fitted out specifically for expedition cruising when refurbished in 1996. Other ships in the same series are *Akademik Boris Petrov, Akademik Golitsyn,*

BERLITZ'S RATINGS

	Possible	Achieved
Ship	500	227
Accommodation	200	87
Food	400	203
Service	400	188
Entertainment	N/A	N/A
Cruise	500	242

Akademik M.A. Laurentiev, Akademik Nikolaj Strakhov, Livonia, Akademik Shokalskiy, Professor Khromov and *Professor Multanovskiy.* It has an ice-hardened, steel hull, which is good for cruising in both the Arctic and Antarctic regions. All passengers have access to the navigation bridge. There are several Zodiac landing craft for close-in shore excursions and nature observation trips.

Inside, the limited public rooms consist of a library and lounge/bar. The dining rooms also serve as a lecture room. The medical facilities are good.

This is expedition style cruising, in a very small ship with limited facilities. However, it provides a somewhat primitive, but genuine adventure experience, taking you "up-close and personal" to places others only dream about. The bigger ships cannot get this close to Antarctica or the Arctic, but this little vessel will sail you close to the face of the ice continent.

Quark Expeditions charters this ship for the Antarctic (winter) season, and has its own staff and lecturers on board, as well as oversees the food, to make sure that everything is up to the company's usual high standard.

Professor Multanovskiy
★★

Small Ship: ....1,753 tons	Passengers	Elevators: 0
Lifestyle: ....Standard	(lower beds/all berths): 49/49	Casino (gaming tables): ....No
Cruise Line: ......Oceanwide Expeditions	Passenger Space Ratio	Slot Machines: ....No
Former Names: ....none	(lower beds/all berths): 35.7/35.7	Swimming Pools (outdoors): 0
Builder: ....Wartsila (Finland)	Crew/Passenger Ratio	Swimming Pools (indoors): 0
Original Cost: ....n/a	(lower beds/all berths): 1.9/1.9	Whirlpools: 0
Entered Service: 1983	Navigation Officers: ....Russian	Fitness Center: ....No
Registry: ....Russia	Cabins (total): 29	Sauna/Steam Room: ....Yes/No
Length (ft/m): 234.9/71.6	Size Range (sq ft/m): ....n/a	Massage: ....No
Beam (ft/m): 42/12.8	Cabins (outside view): 29	Self-Service Launderette: ....No
Draft (ft/m): 15.0/4.6	Cabins (interior/no view): 0	Dedicated Cinema/Seats: ....No
Propulsion/Propellers: ....diesel	Cabins (for one person): 9	Library: ....Yes
(2,327 kW)/2	Cabins (with private balcony): 0	Classification Society: ..Russian Shipping
Passenger Decks: 3	Cabins (wheelchair accessible): 0	Register
Total Crew: 25	Cabin Current: ....220 volts	

OVERALL SCORE: 947 (OUT OF A POSSIBLE 2,000 POINTS)

ACCOMMODATION: With the exception of a single "suite," almost all other cabins are very small, spartan, and rather clinical. There are two-berth cabins with shower and toilet, or there are two-bed cabins on the lowest deck, whose occupants must share a bathroom.

DINING: There are two dining rooms (the ship's galley is actually located between them), and all passengers are accommodated in a single seating. The meals are hearty international fare, with no frills. When the ship is under charter to Quark Expeditions, western rather than Russian chefs oversee the food operation, and the quality of meals and variety of foods is much better.

OTHER COMMENTS: This vessel, which has a dark hull and white superstructure, was originally specially built in Finland for the former Soviet Union's polar and oceanographic research program and should not be taken as a cruise ship, although it was converted in the early 1990s to carry passengers, and then fitted out specifically for expedition cruising when refurbished in 1996.

Other ships in the same series are *Akademik Boris Petrov, Akademik Golitsyn, Akademik M.A. Laurentiev,*

BERLITZ'S RATINGS		
	Possible	Achieved
Ship	500	227
Accommodation	200	87
Food	400	203
Service	400	188
Entertainment	N/A	N/A
Cruise	500	242

Akademik Nikolaj Strakhov, Akademik Shokalskiy, Livonia, Professor Khromov and *Professor Molchanov.*

This ship is typically operated under charter to various "expedition" cruise companies. It has an ice-hardened, steel hull, which is good for cruising in both the Arctic and Antarctic regions. All passengers have access to the navigation bridge. There are several Zodiac landing craft for close-in shore excursions and nature observation trips.

Inside, the limited public rooms consist of a library and lounge/bar. The dining rooms also serve as a lecture room. The medical facilities are good.

This is expedition style cruising, in a very small ship with limited facilities. However, it provides a somewhat primitive, but genuine adventure experience, taking you "up-close and personal" to places others only dream about. The bigger ships cannot get this close to Antarctica or the Arctic, but this little vessel will sail you close to the face of the ice continent.

Quark Expeditions charters this ship for the Antarctic (winter) season, and has its own staff and lecturers on board. It also oversees the food, to make sure that everything is up to its usual high (Quark) standard.

Mahé Seychelles

Queen Elizabeth 2
★★★★★ to ★★★ +

Large Ship:	...............70,327 tons	
Lifestyle:	............Luxury/Premium	
Cruise Line:	..............Cunard Line	
Former Names:	.................none	
Builder:	...Upper Clyde Shipbuilders (UK)	
Original Cost:	.............£29 million	
Entered Service:	............May 1969	
Registry:	.................Great Britain	
Length (ft/m):	.........962.93/293.50	
Beam (ft/m):	.............105.1/32.03	
Draft (ft/m):	.................32.4/9.87	
Propulsion/Propellers:	.....diesel-electric	
	(99,900 kW)/2	
Passenger Decks:	13	
Total Crew:	1,015	

Passengers
(lower beds/all berths): 1,782/1,906
Passenger Space Ratio
(lower beds/all berths): 39.4/36.8
Crew/Passenger Ratio
(lower beds/all berths): 1.7/1.8
Navigation Officers: ....British
Cabins (total): 950
Size Range (sq ft/m): 107.0–1,184.0/
10.0–110.0
Cabins (outside view): 657
Cabins (interior/no view): 293
Cabins (for one person): 151
Cabins (with private balcony): 32
Cabins (wheelchair accessible): 4

Cabin Current: ....110 and 220 volts
Elevators: 13
Casino (gaming tables): ....Yes
Slot Machines: ....Yes
Swimming Pools (outdoors): 1
Swimming Pools (indoors): 1
(+ AquaSpa pool)
Whirlpools: 4
Fitness Center: ....Yes
Sauna/Steam Room: ....Yes/Yes
Massage: ....Yes
Self-Service Launderette: ....Yes
Dedicated Cinema/Seats: Yes/530
Library: ....Yes
Classification Society: ...Lloyd's Register

OVERALL SCORE (OUT OF A POSSIBLE 2,000 POINTS)
GRILL CLASS: 1,754   CARONIA CLASS: 1,622   MAURETANIA CLASS: 1,383

BERLITZ'S RATINGS		
Grill Class	Possible	Achieved
Ship	500	441
Accommodation	200	177
Food	400	351
Service	400	350
Entertainment	100	84
Cruise	400	351

BERLITZ'S RATINGS		
Caronia Class	Possible	Achieved
Ship	500	416
Accommodation	200	152
Food	400	320
Service	400	318
Entertainment	100	84
Cruise	400	332

BERLITZ'S RATINGS		
Mauretania Class	Possible	Achieved
Ship	500	350
Accommodation	200	99
Food	400	279
Service	400	273
Entertainment	100	84
Cruise	400	298

ACCOMMODATION: There is a vast range of accommodation grades and cabin configurations from which to choose. The most exclusive (and therefore expensive) accommodation can be found in the Queen Elizabeth and Queen Mary split-level penthouses on Signal Deck. Next are another 30 suites and suites on Signal Deck and Sun Deck (several on Sun Deck have private balconies, although some have lifeboat-obstructed views) and 10 suites on Boat Deck. Then come the large cabins on Decks 1, 2 and 3, while the smallest outside-view cabins are to be found lower down on Decks 4 and 5 (these have portholes, which tend to make the cabins seem smaller than they are, with little natural light available), and interior (no-view) cabins. When unkind weather conditions are encountered on crossings of the North Atlantic, the portholes of Deck 5 cabins may have to be closed.

Note that whichever grade you choose, bathroom cabinets have a lot of storage space – important for anyone choosing this ship for long voyages. Almost all bathrooms were replaced in a 1997 refit, although some that were not replaced are quite tacky in places.

SUITES: Many of the suites and cabins on Deck 3, 2, 1, Boat Deck, Sports Deck and Signal Deck have fine wood-paneled walls, generous closet and drawer space, thick, real wood furniture and large, marble bathrooms. From sumptuous, understated two-level suites with private balconies, walk-in closets, stocked refrigerators and mini-bars and bathrooms large enough for four, to modest interior (no-view) cabins that are compact but quite well equipped, you pay for the amount of space and grade you want, and, more important, the location.

Additionally, the accommodation you choose will determine in which of the ship's five restaurants you will dine. Note that some suites on Sun Deck and Boat Deck have lifeboat-obstructed views (not shown in the brochure), which are the same price as for those without obstructed views – very odd.

PENTHOUSE SUITES: The Penthouse Suites (on Signal Deck and Sun Deck) are among the most refined and quiet living spaces at sea. During the ship's 1999 refit, three new suites were added to the list of exclusive living spaces: the Aquitania and Carinthia suites on 2 Deck, and the wheelchair-accessible Caledonia suite on Boat Deck. Occupants of these most exclusive suites have room service food items supplied by chefs from the Queens Grill (during dining hours).

WHEELCHAIR-ACCESSIBLE CABINS: Physically challenged passengers will appreciate four cabins that are specially equipped for wheelchair-bound passengers, created using the guidelines of the American Disabled Association (ADA). The cabin door is wide enough for a wheelchair (no "lip"); the bathroom door slides open electronically at the touch of a button (located at wheelchair height), and the floor is flat. The full-length bathtub has special assist handles, and the toilet has grab bars. Closets have hanging rails with hydraulically balanced lever to lower them towards the outside of the closet, to the right height. There is an intercom, alarm, and remote controls for lighting, curtains and doors.

These cabins are also good for the hearing-impaired, with three brightly colored lighted signs on the cabin bulkhead, as well as a telephone system for the deaf. While these cabins are specially designed for the physically challenged, their ingenious design would not upset a regular passenger.

DINING: There are five principal full-service restaurants (all of which include many tables for two, unlike so many ships being introduced today) and two informal dining spots: The Lido (breakfast lunch and dinner) and The Pavilion Grill (for lunchtime fast-food items only). In order of excellence they are: Queens Grill, Britannia Grill and Princess Grill, Caronia Restaurant (very nicely refurbished in 1999, with rich wood paneling, pleasing chandeliers and a quieter, and more elegant décor), and Mauretania Restaurant.

One-seating dining is featured in all except the Mauretania Restaurant, which operates two seatings (note that this is where the student waiters cut their teeth, and food and service are adequate at best). There are both smoking and non-smoking sections in all restaurants. The menus are varied, creative and well balanced, and include spa/light/healthy-eating items.

The Queens Grill has its own separate galley, the best waiters and service, a fine, formal atmosphere for dinner, and food that can be best described as memorable (you can also order from the à la carte menu, as well as "off-menu"). The Britannia Grill, Princess Grill and Mauretania Restaurant share the same galley, but the service and setting in the intimate Britannia Grill and Princess Grill is far superior. The Caronia and Mauretania Restaurants have good, creative and varied menus, with service provided by the least experienced waiters.

QUEENS GRILL: Fine dining (with many items cooked to order à la minute) is exemplified in the Queens Grill, the ship's most formal restaurant. This is comparable to a very good shore-side gourmet restaurant, and features

tableside carvings, flambeaus and outstanding presentation by dedicated *British* traditional restaurant managers and headwaiters who really do excel in the art of hospitality. The room, whose décor is classic black and white, features individual chairs (there are, fortunately, no tables with banquette seats) and there are many tables for two. The cuisine includes many traditional British favorites, together with extensive French dishes as well as regional specialties from around the world. Regular travelers know that special orders are always possible.

BRITANNIA GRILL/PRINCESS GRILL: Some frequent travelers might, however, prefer the smaller and more intimate Britannia Grill or Princess Grill (this dining spot remains much as it was when the ship debuted more than 30 years ago), which offer almost the same kind of tableside service and fine cuisine. During 2000, the food budget for the ship was cut severely, so you can expect to find some decrease in the quality and variety of foods available. Also, note that the tables in all the Grill Rooms are very close together, more tables having been squeezed in over the years to accommodate the increase in Grill-class capacity. Regular travelers know that special orders are always possible.

CARONIA RESTAURANT: This wood-paneled restaurant (formerly the first-class dining room) is large, but extremely comfortable. At the entrance, three steps lead down into the well of the restaurant were designed so that ladies in gowns could make an elegant entrance that could be seen by most diners. The food, while similar to the grill rooms, is presented with polished service and good attention from the international mix of waiters and waitresses.

MAURETANIA RESTAURANT: This restaurant, the entrance of which leads off from the lovely Crystal Bar, operates two seatings. Its focal point is a "white horse" sculpture that is bathed in blue light; there is also a mural of Cunard cruising scenes on one wall, as well as a model of the former Cunard world-wide cruising ship *Caronia*. The restaurant has tables for 2, 4, 6, 8 or 10, and many dining alcoves, which help to make it appear smaller than it really is.

The food is quite good, well presented, and comes with service that is reasonably correct, the waiters and waitresses in this restaurant being the new breed (those with the least training). Note that the Mauretania Restaurant may operate as a one-seating dining room when the ship is not full.

CASUAL DINING: THE LIDO CAFE: Casual dinners can be taken in The Lido, an intensive casual dining spot that invites a tremendous throughput during the entire day (casual dress code), which has its own galley, bar and beverage station. The luncheon and midnight buffets provide a good range of foods, although at peak times there are lines at this popular eatery.

CASUAL DINING: THE PAVILION: For casual fast food, this place is located aft, just under The Lido Café. Here you can find hamburgers, hot dogs, veggie burgers, and other grilled fast-food items.

OTHER COMMENTS: *Queen Elizabeth 2* is a true *ocean liner*, designed and built for the differing weather and sea conditions of the North Atlantic. The ship sports a dark blue hull and single, large funnel, and performs a regular schedule of transatlantic crossings as well as several cruises each year, plus an annual around-the-world cruise (typically from January to April). It is still the fastest, as well as the most integrated ocean liner in the world (I stress that it is important to think of this ship as an *ocean liner* rather than as a cruise ship in the more contemporary sense of the word). A good range of joint travel programs and tour configurations is integrated into the marketing of this ship. In contrast to so many ships where formal dress has all but disappeared, the dress code is *mostly formal* – though it is becoming less so as the company's new American owners market to a more casual population who insist on dressing down. Gentleman social hosts are provided as dancing partners for ladies traveling alone – a popular program that was started in the 1970s.

Originally constructed with steam turbine propulsion, the ship underwent a $160 million refit in Bremen, Germany, in 1986. The original steam turbines were extracted and exchanged for a diesel-electric propulsion system, resulting in greater speed, better economy and more reliability. A new, fatter funnel was constructed, designed to better keep any soot off the expansive open decks. The ship has a long foredeck (rather like the long snout of a 4.5-liter vintage Bentley), unsurpassed by any other cruise ship today. That foredeck makes it look powerful, yet at the same time sleek and so graceful.

Over the years, the ship has undergone a number of extensive multi-million dollar interior refurbishments that have included numerous structural changes designed to facilitate better passenger flow and provide greater dining space. Fine wood paneling and more traditional furnishings have replaced many of the original laminates that were all the tacky rage in the 1960s. The décor is now more reminiscent of the ocean liners of yesteryear – which is what passengers expect.

At the end of 1999, the ship had a further $33.1 million refurbishment (including $19 million on technical items). Bathrooms in all accommodation grades have been entirely replaced; all now feature marble fixtures and jazzy art deco-style toiletry cabinets. Several new suites were added. Other facilities include a large library with more than 7,000 books, and an integrated Cunard memorabilia shop. There is also a dedicated florist. The latest enhancements have provided grace, pace and space in what is a ship for all reasons.

OTHER COMMENTS – TRANSATLANTIC CROSSINGS: This is still the fastest passenger ship in service, and even at a speed of close to 30 knots there is almost no vibration at the stern. Interestingly, this ship can go backwards faster than most cruise ships can go forwards, if ever it were necessary to do so (19 knots backwards has been recoded). There is a wide range of facilities and public rooms with high ceilings, including garage space for up to 12 cars.

QE2 is a veritable city at sea, and, like any city, there are several parts of town. There are *three* distinct classes: Grill Class, Caronia Class and Mauretania Class. Grill Class accommodation consists of outstanding penthouse suites (with butler service only in the Sun Deck and Sports Deck suites and room service food items provided by Queens Grill chefs, a stocked mini-bar refrigerator, daily fresh fruit and personalized stationery), and large outside-view cabins (with standard cabin service in One Deck and Two Deck cabins that is nothing special).

Dining is in one of three grill rooms: Queens Grill (named after former Cunard transatlantic liners *Queen Elizabeth* and *Queen Mary*), Britannia Grill or Princess Grill, according to the accommodation grade chosen.

Caronia Class accommodation consists of outside-view double cabins, and interior (no-view) and outside-view single cabins, with dining in the beautifully paneled Caronia Restaurant (decorated in an Italian style).

Mauretania Class accommodation features the lowest-priced cabin grades, but dining is in two seatings in the Mauretania Restaurant.

All passengers enjoy the use of all public rooms, except for the Queens Grill Lounge, which is reserved exclusively for passengers in Grill Class accommodation. *QE2* has real wood "steamer" deckchairs (as well it should). Those on Sun Deck (also known as the "helicopter deck" can be reserved (for a small fee) when crossing the Atlantic. Grill Class is the most desirable and sophisticated way to cross the Atlantic; Caronia Class (formerly known as first class) is good but definitely not what it used to be, while Mauretania Class (formerly known as transatlantic class) provides comfortable travel in a price-sensitive setting.

In the final analysis, *Queen Elizabeth 2* is a fine transatlantic liner that provides a very civilized experience, particularly for those who don't like to fly as well as for those who enjoy the essence of British life and the grace and pace of days at sea without ports of call. The large amount of personal luggage allowed is also especially useful for anyone relocating between continents, or for extended vacations. When you arrive in either New York or Southampton, after six days of not having to lift a finger, it often proves to be a bittersweet anti-climax. It also provides a disquieting reminder that life ashore has to be faced after the calming effects of *QE2* on one's inner being. Indeed, there is probably nothing more pleasing to the soul or more civilized than a transatlantic crossing, being cosseted in the finery of dining in either of the three grill restaurants with their fine cuisine, presentation and overall dining experience. Gratuities are automatically charged to your onboard account (you will need to visit the information desk to make any changes necessary). In addition, 15 percent is added to all bar and wine, and health spa/salon bills.

OTHER COMMENTS – CRUISES: The extensive refit in December 1999 resulted in the most cohesive interior décor the ship has been given in years. The public rooms and passenger hallways were refreshed and color-coordinated for the better. The Penthouse Suites are truly superb and quiet – and are among the most refined living spaces at sea (all bathrooms were replaced in 1996).

Ship buffs can enjoy the Heritage Trail, a ship-wide display consisting of more than two dozen exhibits of Cunard ocean liner history and ship models, as well as some superb paintings of former Cunard liners, spread around the ship. It includes a stunning 16-ft (5-meter) illuminated model of the company's 1907 *Mauretania* (strangely located outside the Caronia Restaurant, while a model of the former *Caronia* is located in the Mauretania Restaurant). There is a great abundance of memorabilia items (some further items are available for sale in the memorabilia bookshop/library).

There is a substantial amount of fine artwork, sculptures and paintings. Two huge, beautiful paintings can be found hanging in the "D" Deck foyer between Boat Deck and Upper Deck. They are the 1948 painting of Queen Elizabeth, the Queen Mother, by Sir Oswald Birley (this used to be aboard RMS *Queen Elizabeth*); and the 1949 painting of Princess Elizabeth and Prince Philip, which used to be aboard RMS *Caronia*.

The ship's wide range of facilities include a Grand Lounge (a dedicated show lounge with thrust stage, three seating tiers and good sound system); Tour and Travel Center (for shore excursions, theater tickets and concierge services); Business Center, Shopping Concourse which has a limited amount of brand name merchandise at high European prices. The Yacht Club is a nautical, practical and popular aft-facing room that becomes a nightclub (afternoon recorded classical concerts here are a bonus). An extensive indoor spa includes a 10-station AquaSpa, and several comfortable treatment rooms (treatments are at extra cost); fitness center, and beauty salons for men and women; a safety deposit center and passenger accounts office; and an automated telephone system. Sports facilities include a paddle tennis court, golf driving ranges, basketball, shuffleboard, ring toss and other deck games.

The Queens Room is a real ballroom, with a large dance floor, for society dancing to a big band (during the day it is a quiet, stately room with very comfortable lounge chairs), and delightful stand-up cocktail parties. The Midships Lobby, the ship's embarkation point, has a distinctive, ocean liner image, with fine bird's-eye maple woodwork and wrap-around murals of the former and present Cunard Queens. A large computer center (with daily lectures and 22 computer workstations) is a real bonus. There is also a dedicated florist and flower shop, and a large self-service launderette (no charge).

The Lido, a large, informal bistro dining spot with 24-hour hot beverage stations, is also a bonus on cruises and all espresso and cappuccino coffees are free. The elegant Chart Room Bar (formerly the Midships Bar) is a charming, quiet drinking spot (it contains a piano from the liner *Queen Mary*).

There is a large cinema/concert hall (with 530 seats), complete with balcony level and 9-ft-long (2.7-meter) Bosendorfer piano. The Golden Lion Pub has Victorian décor and a selection of over 20 beers (both bottled and draught). There is also a superb library, much loved by passengers (without doubt one of the best at sea, with over 7,000 books, in about a dozen languages). This, combined with a memorabilia bookshop, has real professional librarians. The Player's Club Casino has fitting art deco and blond wood décor.

QE2 has British officers, with an international hotel staff that is fairly attentive and service-oriented, although many do not speak English well, as is the case aboard so many ships today. There is a decent enough entertainment mix (although it could perhaps be more British in style and more in keeping with the character of the ship), and there is an extensive range of lecture programs. The laundry and dry-cleaning facilities are very good; there are also self-service (no charge) launderettes. There are, as well, English nannies and some facilities for children. This ship offers refined living at sea for those in upper-grade accommodation – otherwise it is just a large ship, albeit with fine facilities.

Tender ports should be avoided whenever possible, however, although the double-deck shore tenders used are very practical units.

MORE ABOUT QE2: The Orient Express Boat Train is chartered by Cunard Line, and runs between London's Waterloo Station and Southampton Docks; the train pulls up right alongside the Ocean Terminal to connect with all transatlantic voyages of the ship. This special train consists exclusively of Pullman carriages, richly paneled and fitted with individual deep-upholstery seats. Complimentary hot canapés and champagne are served. Passengers traveling from London to Southampton can complete all formalities and ship check-in procedures on the train, and simply walk directly on board *QE2* on arrival. Baggage loaded onto the train's baggage carriage in Waterloo is delivered directly to your cabin.

The Cunard Line/British Airways *Concorde* program is also worth experiencing. Combining a *QE2* transatlantic crossing with a one-way British Airways *Concorde* flight is, without doubt, the ultimate way to go on a round-trip transatlantic journey. Six days one-way, and 3 hours, 15 minutes the other way remain one of the great modern travel experiences. And, with special, Cunard-subsidized fares, there is every reason to indulge at least once in this short lifetime.

In 1997 *QE2* became the first cruise ship to have an email address. The ship has traveled more than *5 million nautical miles* (including about 700 visits to New York and about 600 to Southampton), blends high-tech engineering with traditional ocean liner facilities, and has hosted more famous faces than any other ship afloat. *QE2* is much like a well-worn shoe – comfortable, but a little tired and frayed around the edges in places, which makes it a difficult ship to evaluate. Sadly, there are fewer British crewmembers serving than passengers expect, and fewer of the crew speak English when in passenger areas. However, it has a wonderful, loyal following, and provides the only civilized way to cross the North Atlantic with the space, pace and grace of a real Cunard liner. As a cruise ship (particularly on short cruises of less than seven days) the ship is a real mismatch, and waiting for tenders (when the ship is at anchor and shore tenders must be used) is a pain.

If you occupy one of the top-level (Grill Class) suites, with butler service and all the trimmings of finery, your experience should be nothing short of superb, highly civilized quiet living at sea. However, the many who occupy lower-grade accommodations (Caronia Class and Mauretania Class), may find that the ship does not quite come up to their high expectations. However, if you have to consider economic budgeting, taking a longer cruise in lower-grade accommodation may well be preferable to taking a shorter cruise in higher-priced accommodation. There may well be some inconsistencies and frustrations when sailing aboard *QE2*, but they will seem insignificant when compared to the splendid experience you will have when sailing the world's most legendary ship. There is no question that the staff are more stressed when the ship is operating crossings (particularly in a westbound direction, when five hours are lost during the six-day crossing of the time zones), as all passengers are aboard all day long, every day – as opposed to cruises, when passengers go off in ports of call, giving staff have more breathing time.

Will *QE2* survive the onslaught of the mega-ships? I believe it will, simply because it isn't one of them, and it does have a lifestyle that somehow will still be in vogue when its rivals have become floating night clubs.

When its new consort *Queen Mary 2* is introduced in 2004, *Queen Elizabeth 2* will no longer operate regular transatlantic crossings. Instead, it will become strictly a cruise ship, initially operating its annual around-the-world cruise from January to April and devoting the rest of the year to a variety of cruises. The final transatlantic crossing is scheduled for April 2004. The onboard currencies are the British pound and the US dollar.

WEAK POINTS: *QE2*, perhaps the most famous of all passenger ships, is now almost 35 years old, and it is difficult to compare it with the latest contemporary ships that have more light, multiple balconies (these are not really considered practical on crossings of the North Atlantic) and more flexible, high-tech facilities. Although the interior passageways are wide, there is a feeling of being enclosed, and cabins with portholes simply seem dated (however, you should bear in mind the fact that this is an *ocean liner* and *not* a cruise ship).

Sadly, there is no forward observation lounge (there was when the ship was first constructed). Missing are a few grand, flowing staircases, the air of romance, and the high standard of food service personnel of the ocean liners of former years. The show lounge is poor when compared with those aboard newer ships; the sight lines and seating could be better, and much of the entertainment is unremarkable and quite forgettable.

The shops are, for the most part, tacky, and not at all representative of the elegance of ocean liner travel. They are run by a concession more used to high street and mass market trading than Bond Street and are a constant source of complaint from passengers.

The cabins on Five Deck (the lowest of the accommodation decks) are adequate, no more. Following recent refurbishments, there are fewer small, intimate hideaway bars. You cannot have just a sauna, or use of the steam room without paying a charge for a "Spa Experience" package. As a "classless" cruise ship, the layout is rather disjointed, but as a transatlantic liner, the layout is beautifully designed to keep you in your place.

Queen Mary 2
NOT YET RATED

Large Ship: ....150,000 tons	
Lifestyle: ....Luxury/Premium	
Cruise Line: ....Cunard Line	
Former Names: ....none	
Builder: Chantiers de l'Atlantique (France)	
Original Cost: ....$780 million	
Entered Service: ....Jan 2004	
Registry: ....Great Britain	
Length (ft/m): 1,131.9/345.03	
Beam (ft/m): 134.5/41.00	
Draft (ft/m): 32.6/9.95	
Propulsion/Propellers: ......gas turbine	
(103,000kW) and diesel-electric/4 pods	
(2 azimuthing, 2 fixed/21.5 MW each)	
Passenger Decks: 17	

Total Crew: 1,254	
Passengers	
(lower beds/all berths): 2,620/3,090	
Passenger Space Ratio	
(lower beds/all berths): 57.2/48.5	
Crew/Passenger Ratio	
(lower beds/all berths): 2.0/2.4	
Navigation Officers: ....British	
Cabins (total): 1,310	
Size Range (sq ft/m): 194.0–1,650.0/	
18.0–153	
Cabins (outside view): 1,017	
Cabins (interior/no view): 293	
Cabins (for one person): 0	
Cabins (with private balcony): 944	

Cabins (wheelchair accessible): 30	
Cabin Current: ....110 and 220 volts	
Elevators: 22	
Casino (gaming tables): ....Yes	
Slot Machines: ....Yes	
Swimming Pools (outdoors): 3	
Swimming Pools (indoors): 2	
Whirlpools: 8	
Fitness Center: ....Yes	
Sauna/Steam Room: ....Yes/Yes	
Massage:.........................Yes	
Self-Service Launderette: ....Yes	
Dedicated Cinema/Seats: ....No	
Library: ....Yes	
Classification Society: ...Lloyd's Register	

OVERALL SCORE: NYR (OUT OF A POSSIBLE 2,000 POINTS)

INTRODUCTION: In January 2004, the cruising world will witness the birth of a new Queen. *Queen Mary 2* will be the largest passenger ocean liner ever built, and the most expensive. Due to be handed over to Cunard Line in December 2003 and scheduled to start operations the following month, the ship is designed to introduce passengers to the pleasures of crossing the North Atlantic on a regular schedule, with all the very latest high-tech facilities and conveniences, in a user-friendly setting that promises to be the world's most luxurious ship. *Queen Mary 2* will be an ideal method of crossing the North Atlantic in style, particularly for the many people who dislike flying. It is destined to become the successor to all other ocean liners that have ever sailed.

I thought it would be good to provide an early view of what the ship will offer, so you can make your bookings early – the waiting list is already long.

ACCOMMODATION: There are 10 categories, in 25 price grades. From standard outside-view cabins to the most opulent suites afloat, there will be something for every taste and pocketbook – a choice unrivalled aboard any other cruise vessel. Perhaps the most noticeable difference between this ship and *QE2* is the addition of a large number of cabins with private balconies (75 percent of all cabins have them). Some cabins look inwards to the atrium lobby, which spans six decks. All suites and cabins have internet connectivity.

All grades of accommodation will have a minimum of a 20-inch color television with concealed interactive

BERLITZ'S RATINGS

	Possible	Achieved
Ship	500	NYR
Accommodation	200	NYR
Food	400	NYR
Service	400	NYR
Entertainment	100	NYR
Cruise	400	NYR

keyboard. Other features will include digital video on demand, music on demand (with 3,000 titles), audio books on demand, and email and digital photographs preview and purchase (the system can be blocked so that children cannot access it).

For the largest accommodation in the cruise industry, two combinations offer the equivalent of a large house at sea. At the front of the ship, you can combine the Queen Elizabeth and Queen Mary suites with the Queen Anne and Queen Victoria suites to produce one huge suite measuring 5,016 sq. ft (466 sq. meters). Even this can be eclipsed at the other end of the ship, by joining Grand Duplex apartments at the lower level to the adjacent penthouses to produce an unprecedented 8,288 sq. ft (770 sq. meters).

BALMORAL/SANDRINGHAM DUPLEXES – GRADE Q1): The largest stand-alone accommodation can be found in the Balmoral and Sandringham Duplexes (2,249 sq. ft/209 sq. meters). These are located aft in prime real estate territory, with superb views along the entire length of the ship. Upstairs is a bedroom with wood-framed king-size bed, and large private balcony; downstairs is a living room with sofa, coffee table, dining table, and writing desk. There are two marble-clad bathrooms with whirlpool bath and separate shower enclosure, toilet and bidet, and two washbasins.

QUEEN ELIZABETH/QUEEN MARY SUITES – GRADE Q2): The Queen Elizabeth Suite and Queen Mary Suite (1,194 sq. ft/111 sq. meters) are both located just under the navigation bridge, with good views over the ship's long bows. There are living and dining areas, with a large private balcony (but not as large as the Balmoral/Sandringham duplex balconies). The master, marble-clad bathroom has a whirlpool bathtub and shower enclosure, and a second bathroom with a shower enclosure (no bathtub). Each suite has the convenience of private elevator access.

QUEEN ANNE/QUEEN VICTORIA SUITES – GRADE Q3): These two suites (796.5 sq. ft/74 sq. meters) have the most commanding views over the ship's long bows. They consist of a bedroom with master, marble-clad bathroom with whirlpool bathtub and separate shower enclosure; separate living/dining area, and a second bathroom with a shower enclosure (no bathtub).

DUPLEX APARTMENTS: There are three duplex apartments: Buckingham and Windsor (each 1,291 sq. ft/120 sq. meters), and Hollywood (1,566 sq. ft/145 sq. meters). Each has a gymnasium, balcony, butler and concierge service, and superb views over the ship's stern.

PENTHOUSE SUITES (GRADE Q4): There are six penthouse suites (758 sq. ft/70 sq. meters). These have a living and dining area, large private balcony, bedroom and dressing room with master, marble-clad bathroom with whirlpool bathtub and separate shower enclosure.

SUITES (506 SQ FT – GRADE Q5/Q6): These 82 suites (506 sq. ft/47 sq. meters) have a large private balcony, living area, dressing room, marble-clad bathroom with whirlpool bathtub and separate shower enclosure. Beds can be arranged in a king-size or twin-bed configuration.

JUNIOR SUITES (GRADE P1/P2): There are 76 Junior Suites (381 sq. ft/35 sq. meters). Each has a lounge area, large private balcony, and marble-clad bathroom with whirlpool bathtub and separate shower enclosure. Beds can be arranged in a king-size or twin-bed configuration.

DELUXE/PREMIUM BALCONY CABINS: These 782 cabins (248 sq. ft/23 sq. meters) include a sitting area with sofa, and bathroom with shower enclosure. Beds can be arranged in a king-size or twin-bed configuration.

STANDARD OUTSIDE-VIEW/INTERIOR (NO VIEW) CABINS: There are 62 outside-view cabins and 281 interior (no view) cabins measuring 194 sq. ft/18 sq. meters). Beds can be arranged in a king-size or twin-bed configuration.

ATRIUM VIEW CABINS: These are 12 of these interior cabins (194 sq. ft/18 sq. meters), but each has an unusual view – into the six-deck high atrium lobby. Beds can be arranged in a king-size or twin-bed configuration. An ensuite bathroom has a shower enclosure, washbasin, toilet, and cabinet for personal toiletries.

WHEELCHAIR ACCESSIBLE CABINS: There are 30 suites and cabins (in various categories) specially designed for wheelchair and other handicapped passengers. Facilities for blind passengers will include Braille signs and tactile room signs. Eight special wheelchair-accessible elevators are provided to service the dining areas.

Additionally, some 36 cabins have been designated to accommodate deaf or hearing-impaired passengers. There are headsets in the Royal Theatre and Planetarium, and close captioned television.

DINING: Naturally, you should expect lavish dining, and accept nothing less. In all there are 14 bars, and 7 galleys serving 10 dining rooms and eateries. All dining rooms and eateries have ocean-view windows. One of the most famous chefs in the world, Daniel Boulud, is Cunard Line's culinary consultant.

BRITANNIA RESTAURANT: The main dining room, the Britannia Restaurant, seats 1,347, and spans the full beam of the ship. It is a lavish room two decks high and has a superb grand staircasewhich enables you to make your entry in style. Above the staircase is a light well and large, classic columns add to the sense of grandeur, while the centerpiece backdrop to the staircase is a huge tapestry of a Cunard ocean liner. I know it's a cliché but Cunard is hoping that Britannia rules the waves. Breakfast will be in an open-seating arrangement, while dinner is in two seatings.

QUEEN GRILL/PRINCESS GRILL: There are two Grill Rooms (Queens Grill and Princess Grill), which I would rather call *dining salons*. As in smaller "sister" ship *Queen Elizabeth 2*, which restaurant you dine in will depend on your accommodation grade (and the price paid). The Queens Grill and Princess Grill are located aft, and have fine ocean view widows; they are quite large and less intimate than those aboard *QE2*. Passengers in the most spacious and luxurious suites, therefore, may feel less special, being mixed, as they will be, among all others in Grill Class accommodation. The Queens Grill is decorated in gold, and passengers who dine in this exclusive establishment have their own Queens Grill Bar and Terrace. This was a chance for Cunard to dispense with waiter stations, but alas, they are still in place.

TODD ENGLISH RESTAURANT: This alternative 216-seat restaurant (reservations are necessary, although there will be no cover charge or charge for gratuities) is named after Todd English, the famous chef whose restaurant in Boston (Olives) has become one of the best-known in high gastronomic circles. This represents the American television chef's first venture at sea. The restaurant will feature his noted Mediterranean cuisine. The room has been designed with intimate detailing and architecture and overlooks the Pool Terrace, allowing for al fresco dining.

KING'S COURT: This informal eatery will feature self-serve breakfast and lunch. At night, decorated screens will transform the area into four different indoor/outdoor restaurants. Themes will range from Italian, Asian, a British carvery (for roast meats), and a Chef's Galley. The Chef's Galley will feature a live demonstration of the meal preparation that will be broadcast via close circuit TV onto a large screen. "Street entertainment" will be performed throughout the area in the evenings.

DINE IN YOUR SUITE/CABIN: If you are shy and retiring and want complete privacy, or if you are recuperating from a busy working life, you can also order from the restaurant menus and have breakfast, lunch and dinner served in your own suite or cabin.

OTHER COMMENTS: A ship of superlatives, *Queen Mary 2* is the largest passenger ship ever built (in terms of gross tonnage, length, and beam) and is five times the length of Cunard Line's first ship, *Britannia*. *Queen Mary 2* (22 ft/6.7 meters longer than the original *Queen Mary*) is the first new ship to be built for *Cunard* since 1969, when running mate *Queen Elizabeth 2* sailed on its maiden crossing from Southampton to New York. Like *QE2*, *Queen Mary 2* will be used for transatlantic crossings for much of the year, but no world cruises (these will, at present, be operated only by *QE2*).

Queen Mary's exterior design bears an uncanny resemblance to that of *QE2*, and for good reason, because it was designed by naval architect Stephen Payne, an ocean liner enthusiast. This is a superbly designed ship, able to weather any unkind conditions on the North Atlantic, or anywhere else.

Its power and propulsion system comprises an environmentally friendly Rolls-Royce marine gas turbine and diesel-electric power plant developing 157,000 horsepower (117.2 MW) – enough to provide power to the 200,000 inhabitants of its home port, Southampton. The ship is propelled by the world's first four-pod propulsion system (made by Rolls-Royce-owned Kamewa and Alstom Power Motors), which will be able to power through the waters of the North Atlantic at up to 30 knots. Each pod weighs 250 tons, has a forward-facing highly polished stainless-steel propeller that can be turned through 360 degrees, and houses an electric motor and propeller, replacing the traditional long shaft, propeller and rudder system of the past. The pods are powered by a diesel-electric system.

Queen Mary 2 is being built at the Chantiers de l'Atlantique shipyard in France, in a dry dock measuring 1,360 by 207 ft (415 by 63 meters), with an overhead gantry crane that stands 203 ft (62 meters) high. The first steel was cut on January 16, 2002, while the keel laying took place on July 4, 2002 – 162 years to the day that the first Cunard steamship, *Britannia*, made its first crossing. Since 1840, Cunard Line has operated transatlantic crossings every year, both in peacetime and in wartime – a remarkable achievement. The huge ship,

which is being constructed in 94 blocks, each weighing up to 600 tons, will be completed an incredibly short 24 months later (964 days, to be exact).

Externally, the ship looks like a larger sister to the ever-popular *Queen Elizabeth 2*, although the stern is slightly boxier and more angular, and doesn't have the roundness of *Queen Elizabeth 2*. Of course, *Queen Mary 2* has more decks and a lot of balcony cabins, which add to the powerful, but bulky look. It sports a gloriously long foredeck, and a large, contemporary funnel and beautifully tiered stern. *QM2* is too wide of beam to transit the Panama Canal.

One delightful feature (there are many) concerns the whistle of the original *Queen Mary*; one of two aboard the original ship, the whistle was carried to Europe by *Queen Elizabeth 2* prior to fitting *Queen Mary 2* in the shipyard. Manufactured by Kockums in Sweden, it has been inspected, cleaned and converted from steam power to air power for its new role. It is 7 ft long and 3 ft high (2.1 by 0.9 meters), and weighs 1,400 pounds (635 kg). It was tuned so that it would not disturb passengers on deck, but could be heard 10 miles away.

There is a wide wrap-around promenade deck outdoors, and once around is 2,034 ft (620 meters), or well over one-third of a mile (inside the ship are several other walking promenades – good if the weather is inclement when crossing the North Atlantic). A full line of teak "steamer" chairs will be placed on the open promenade deck, and still leave plenty of room for walkers to pass.

The ship's interiors are designed by Robert Tillberg, a Norwegian company. Its interior designs provide style and elegance throughout, with towering public spaces, sweeping staircases and grand public rooms – a salute to the former Cunard liners of yesteryear and the traditions of transatlantic crossings. High ceilings (typically two decks of *Queen Mary 2* are the equivalent of three decks in height of a regular cruise vessel) provide a greater sense of space and grandeur.

Once inside the ship, you'll need good walking shoes, particularly when you need to go from one end to the other – it really is quite a long way. When first entering the ship, passengers will see a spacious atrium lobby that spans six decks, and has a dramatic staircase and exclusive works of art.

Let's take a deck by deck preview at the facilities and public rooms featured aboard what promises to be the most superlative ocean liner ever (starting at the lowest deck and working our way upward, forward to aft):

● **Deck 2** has Illuminations, and the Royal Court Theatre, the lower level of the six-deck high atrium lobby, the Purser's Desk, Video Arcade, Empire Casino, Golden Lion Pub, and the lower level of the two-deck high Britannia Restaurant.

● **Deck 3** has the upper level of Illuminations and the Royal Court Theatre, the second level of the six-deck high atrium lobby, Mayfair Shops, Sir Samuel's, The Chart Room, Champagne Bar, the upper level of the Britannia Restaurant, the Queens Room, and the G32 Nightclub.

● **Decks 4/Deck 5/Deck 6** have accommodation and the third, fourth and fifth levels of the six-deck high atrium lobby; at the aft end of Deck 6 are the facilities for children, including an outdoor pool (Minnows Pool).

● **Deck 7** features the Canyon Ranch Spa, the Winter Garden, the sixth and uppermost level of the six-deck high atrium lobby, expansive King's Court Buffet, Queens Grill Lounge, Queens Grill and Princess Grill dining salons.

● **Deck 8** (forward) has the upper level of the Canyon Ranch Spa, and the Library and Bookshop. The center section has accommodation. In the aft section are the alternative restaurant Todd English, Terrace Bar, and swimming pool outdoors.

● **Deck 9** (forward) has the Commodore Club, Boardroom and the Cigar Club. The rest of the deck has accommodation and a Concierge Club for suite occupants.

● **Deck 10** has accommodation only.

● **Deck 11** (forward) has an outdoors observation area. The rest of the deck has accommodation. The aft section outdoors has a whirlpool tub and sunbathing deck.

● **Deck 12** (forward) has accommodation. The mid-section has an indoor/outdoor pool (with sliding glass roof), and golf areas (Fairways). The aft section has the Boardwalk Café, dog kennels, and shuffleboard courts.

● **Deck 13** has the Sports Centre, Regatta Bar, a splash pool, and extensive outdoor sunbathing space.

In all there are 14 lounges, clubs and bars. There is an observation lounge with commanding views forward over the ship's bows, called the Commodore Club; light jazz will be featured in this bar, which is connected to the Boardroom, and Cigar Lounge. Included is a Golden Lion Pub, a wine bar (Sir Samuel's), a nautically-themed cocktail bar (The Chart Room), and Champagne Bar. Bars outdoors include the Regatta Bar and Terrace Bar. The ship's G32 nightclub, which has a main and mezzanine level, is located at the aft end of the ship, away from passenger cabins; it is named after the number designated to the ship by its French builder. The Empire Casino will have a bar, and the latest high-tech slot machines, and traditional gaming tables.

The Royal Court Theatre has tiered seating for 1,094, and is the main location for evening entertainment, with "full-scale" West End-style productions as well as featured headline entertainers.

The Queens Room is a grand ballroom, with the largest dance floor at sea. The room will have a dramatic high ceiling, crystal chandeliers, highly comfortable armchairs, and will be used for dancing, cocktail parties, and afternoon teas.

Queen Mary 2 will contain the first full-scale planetarium at sea. Called Illuminations, it is a multi-function space that also functions as a grand cinema, a 500-seat lecture hall and even a broadcasting studio. As a planetarium, it will also feature high-tech programs and virtual reality films. A Maritime Quest Exhibit will feature a history of shipbuilding on Scotland's River Clyde, including John Brown's Shipyard, the yard that

built *Queen Elizabeth* and *Queen Mary* in the 1930s.

Health Spa and Beauty Services are provided in a 20,000 sq. ft (1,850 sq. meter) Canyon Ranch Spa, set on two levels. A rasul chamber (for couples) will be included in the range of treatments, including many variations on the theme of massage and bodyworks, as will Ayurvedic massage, aromatherapy and seaweed treatments, facials and masks, conditioning body scrubs and therapeutic body cocoons. A thalassotherapy pool and whirlpool are part of the facilities of the extensive spa. In all, there are 24 treatment rooms. The gymnasium will have the latest high-tech muscle-pumping equipment, as well as free weights.

Adjacent to the spa is a colonial-style Winter Garden, where flowers will bloom year-round. This peaceful garden setting is for relaxation; a string quartet could well be playing for afternoon tea.

There will be five swimming pools, including one that can be enclosed under a retractable sliding glass roof (known as a magrodome); this will be useful in inclement weather conditions (particularly useful for crossings of the North Atlantic). A large sunning area (21,100 sq. ft/1,960 sq. meters) of open sunning space) includes a sports bar at one end. Sports facilities include electronic golf simulator, putting green, giant chess board and a paddle tennis court.

The ship's Library and Bookshop is located forward; it will have 8,000 books, and coffees will be available. Full-time librarians will be in attendance, and the area will include leather sofas and armchairs.

ConneXions, a unique education center, will include seven sophisticated classrooms for Cunard Line's College at Sea program. Classes in such things as computer training, seamanship and navigation, art and wine appreciation, languages and photography will be taught. Internet access can be found in the Internet Center.

Children have their own space, with a dedicated play area. the Play Zone. Real English nannies will supervise toddlers, while older children get to use The Zone. Dogs can also have a life of their own aboard this ship, with 12 kennels and a private "dogs-only" exercise run.

SOME FUN STATISTICS: The ship is as long as 36 London double-decker buses (or four football fields).

Propulsion power is equivalent to 1,600 family cars.

The ship towers 236 ft (72 meters) from the top of the funnel to the base of the keel – taller than the Statue of Liberty, the equivalent of a 23-storey building.

There will be 30,000 sq. yards (25,000 sq meters) of carpet and 1,550 miles (2,500 km) of electric cabling.

WEAK POINTS: There are no single cabins. Unlike *QE2*, it has no dedicated cinema – a shame since the ship is specifically built for the North Atlantic crossings, when a cinema is much appreciated by frequent passengers during the day and evening. The grill rooms are too large to be intimate, and are more akin to the kind of grill/steakhouses one finds in large North American cities.

Removed 2006

R-5 Blue Dream
★★★★

Mid-Size Ship: ....30,277 tons	Passengers		Cabin Current: ....110 and 220 volts
Lifestyle: ....Premium	(lower beds/all berths): 698/824		Elevators: 4
Cruise Line: ....Pullmantur Cruises	Passenger Space Ratio		Casino (gaming tables): ....Yes
Former Names: ....R Five	(lower beds/all berths): 43.3/36.7		Slot Machines: ....Yes
Builder: Chantiers de l'Atlantique (France)	Crew/Passenger Ratio		Swimming Pools (outdoors): 1
Original Cost: ....$150 million	(lower beds/all berths): 1.8/2.2		Swimming Pools (indoors): 0
Entered Service: ....Feb 2000/May 2002	Navigation Officers: ....European		Whirlpools: 2
Registry: ....Liberia	Cabins (total): 349		(+ 1 thalassotherapy hot tub)
Length (ft/m): 593.7/181.0	Size Range (sq ft/m): 145.3–968.7/		Fitness Center: ....Yes
Beam (ft/m): 83.5/25.5	13.5–90.0		Sauna/Steam Room: ....No/Yes
Draft (ft/m): 19.5/6.0	Cabins (outside view): 328		Massage: ....Yes
Propulsion/Propellers: ....diesel	Cabins (interior/no view): 21		Self-Service Launderette: ....Yes
(18,600kW)/2	Cabins (for one person): 0		Dedicated Cinema/Seats: ....No
Passenger Decks: 9	Cabins (with private balcony): 249		Library: ....Yes
Total Crew: 376	Cabins (wheelchair accessible): 0		Classification Society: ...Bureau Veritas

---

OVERALL SCORE: 1,481 (OUT OF A POSSIBLE 2,000 POINTS)

ACCOMMODATION: There are eight cabin price categories. All of the standard interior (no view) and outside-view cabins (the lowest four grades) are extremely compact and, and extremely tight for two persons (particularly for cruises longer than five days). If you can afford it, choose a suite or cabin with its own balcony.

STANDARD INTERIOR (NO VIEW)/ STANDARD OUTSIDE-VIEW CABINS: These have twin beds (convertible to a queen-size bed), with good under-bed storage areas, personal safe, vanity desk with large mirror, good closet and drawer space in rich, dark woods, and bathroom.

SUPERIOR EXTERIOR VIEW CABINS WITH BALCONY: The cabins with private balconies (66 percent of all cabins) have partial, and not full, balcony partitions, sliding glass doors, and, due to good design and layout, only 14 cabins on Deck 6 have lifeboat-obstructed views. The bathrooms, which have tiled floors and plain walls, are compact, standard units, and include a shower stall with a strong, removable hand-held shower unit, hairdryer, 100 percent cotton towels, toiletries storage shelves and retractable clothesline. Personal toiletry items include soap, shampoo, body lotion, shower cap, and shoeshine mitt.

JUNIOR SUITES: There are 52 mini-suites, which in reality are large cabins, as the sleeping and lounge areas are not divided. While not overly large, the bathrooms have a good-sized bathtub and ample space for storing personal

BERLITZ'S RATINGS

	Possible	Achieved
Ship	500	423
Accommodation	200	157
Food	400	273
Service	400	283
Entertainment	100	63
Cruise	400	282

toiletry items. The living area has a refrigerated mini-bar, lounge area with breakfast table, and a balcony with two plastic chairs and a table.

DE-LUXE SUITES: The 10 De-Luxe Suites provide the most spacious accommodation, and are fine, large living spaces located in the forward-most and aft-most sections of the accommodation decks (particularly nice are those that overlook the stern, on Deck 6, Deck 7 and Deck 8). They have more extensive private balconies that really are private and cannot be overlooked by anyone from the decks above.

There is an entrance foyer, living room, bedroom (the bed faces the sea, which can be seen through the floor-to-ceiling windows and sliding glass door), CD player (with selection of audio discs), bathroom with Jacuzzi bathtub, and a small guest bathroom.

No matter what grade of accommodation you choose, all have color televisions that carry European news and sports channel (where obtainable), and several movie channels.

DINING: Flexibility and choice are provided in this ship, with four different restaurants:
● The *Club Restaurant*, the equivalent of a main dining room, has 338 seats, and a raised central section. There are large ocean-view windows on three sides, several prime tables overlooking the stern, and a small bandstand for occasional live dinner music. The menu changes daily for lunch and dinner.
● The *Italian Restaurant* is located at the back of the

ship; it has 96 seats, windows along two sides, and a set menu (together with added daily chef's specials).

● The *Grill Room*, also located at the aft of the ship, provides grill food. It has 98 seats, and windows along two sides and a set menu (together with added daily chef's specials).

● The *Panorama Buffet* has indoor seating for 154 (not enough during cruises to cold areas or in the winter months), and 186 seats outdoors. Many tables have window views. It is open for breakfast, lunch and very casual dinners. It is the ship's self-serve casual buffet restaurant, and incorporates a small pizzeria and grill. Basic salads, meat carving station, and a selection of hams and cheeses are available every day.

All restaurants have open-seating dining, so you dine when you want, with whom you wish, although reservations are necessary in the Italian Restaurant and The Grill, where there are mostly tables for four or six (there are few tables for two). Service in all the restaurants is generally very good, and attentive. In addition, there is a Poolside Grill and Bar. Note that all cappuccino and espresso coffees are an extra cost, even when ordered in the restaurants.

OTHER COMMENTS: Originally built for the now defunct Renaissance Cruises, this was one of a series of eight almost identical ships (with almost identical interior décor) in what was the cruise industry's first totally non-smoking cruise line. Pullmantur Cruises has chartered this ship – its first contemporary ship, and has used the original name of the ship, adding the words *Blue Dream*.

The exterior design manages to balance the ship's high sides by combining a deep blue hull with the white superstructure and large, square blue funnel. A lido deck features a tiny – and I mean tiny – swimming pool, and good sunbathing space, while one of the aft decks has a (seawater) thalassaotherapy pool. A jogging track circles the swimming pool deck (but one deck above). The uppermost outdoors deck includes a golf driving net and shuffleboard court.

The interior décor is quite stunning and elegant, a throwback to ship décor of the ocean liners of the 1920s and '30s. This includes detailed ceiling cornices, both real and faux wrought-iron staircase railings, leather-paneled walls, *trompe l'oeil* ceilings, rich carpeting in hallways with an Oriental rug-look center section, and many other interesting (and expensive-looking) decorative touches. The overall feel is of an old-world country club.

The staircase in the main, two-deck-high foyer will remind you of something similar in a blockbuster hit about a certain ship, where movie stars Kate Winslet and Leonardo di Caprio met. Passengers will probably be pleased with the fine taste with which the interiors have been designed and executed.

The public rooms are basically spread over three decks. The reception hall (lobby) has a staircase with intricate wrought-iron railings. A large observation lounge, the Sports Bar, is located high atop ship. This has a long bar with forward views (for the barmen, that is, as passengers sitting at the bar face aft), and a stack of distracting large-screen TV screens; there's also an array of slot machines and bar counter-top electronic gaming machines. There are plenty of other bars – including one in each of the restaurant entrances.

The Library is a beautiful, grand, restful room (perhaps the nicest public room aboard this ship), and is designed in the Regency style. It has a fireplace, a high, indented, *trompe l'oeil* ceiling, and a good selection of books, as well as some very comfortable wingback chairs with footstools, and sofas you could sleep on. Internet-connect computers are provided (their use incurs an extra cost).

Pullmantur Cruises provides a decent cruise, geared specifically to Spanish-speaking passengers (the language on board is Spanish), at a price that is very hard to beat, considering the destination-rich itineraries. Pre- and post-cruise land stays are also available at decent quality, large hotels. So, while the bathroom fittings may not be marble, and caviar and other (more expensive) niceties may not be provided, the value for money is very good. There is some evening entertainment if you want it. The onboard currency is the euro.

WEAK POINTS: There is no wrap-around promenade deck outdoors (there is, however, a small jogging track above and around the perimeter of the swimming pool on Deck 10, and walking sections on port and starboard side decks on Deck 5). There are no wooden decks outdoors (instead, they are covered by Bollidt, a sand-colored rubberized material). There is no sauna. The room service menu is extremely limited. Suggested gratuities are high (there is even a gratuities slot at the reception desk). The stairways, although carpeted, are quite tinny.

Radiance of the Seas
★★★★

Large Ship: ....90,090 tons	Passengers	Cabin Current: ....110 volts
Lifestyle: ....Standard	(lower beds/all berths): 2,100/2,500	Elevators: 9
Cruise Line: ....Royal Caribbean	Passenger Space Ratio	Casino (gaming tables): ....Yes
International	(lower beds/all berths): 42.9/36.0	Slot Machines: ....Yes
Former Names: ....none	Crew/Passenger Ratio	Swimming Pools (outdoors): 2
Builder: ....Meyer Werft (Germany)	(lower beds/all berths): 2.4/2.9	Swimming Pools (indoors): 0
Original Cost: ....$350 million	Navigation Officers: ....Norwegian	Whirlpools: 3
Entered Service: ....Apr 2001	Cabins (total): 1,050	Fitness Center: ....Yes
Registry: ....The Bahamas	Size Range (sq ft/m): 165.8–1,216.3/	Sauna/Steam Room: ....Yes/Yes
Length (ft/m): 961.9/293.2	15.4–113.0	Massage:.........................Yes
Beam (ft/m): 105.6/32.2	Cabins (outside view): 813	Self-Service Launderette: ....No
Draft (ft/m): 27.8/8.5	Cabins (interior/no view): 237	Dedicated Cinema/Seats: Yes/40
Propulsion/Propellers: .....Gas turbine/2	Cabins (for one person): 0	Library: ....Yes
azimuthing pods (20 MW each)	Cabins (with private balcony): 577	Classification Society: ....Det Norske
Passenger Decks:.................13	Cabins (wheelchair accessible): 14	Veritas
Total Crew: 858	(8 with private balcony)	

OVERALL SCORE: 1,546 (OUT OF A POSSIBLE 2,000 POINTS)

ACCOMMODATION: There is a wide range of suites and standard outside-view and interior (no view) cabins to suit different tastes, requirements, and depth of wallet, in 10 different categories and 19 different price groups.

Apart from the largest suites (six owner's suites), which have king-sized beds, almost all other cabins have twin beds that convert to a queen-sized bed (all sheets are of 100 percent Egyptian cotton, although the blankets are of nylon). All cabins have rich (but faux) wood cabinetry, including a vanity desk (with hairdryer), faux wood drawers that close silently (hooray), television, personal safe, and three-sided mirrors. Some cabins have ceiling recessed, pull-down berths for third and fourth persons, although closet and drawer space would be extremely tight for four persons (even if two of them are children), and some have interconnecting doors (so families with children can cruise together, in separate, but adjacent cabins. Note that audio channels are available through the television; however, if you want to go to sleep with soft music playing in the background you'll need to put a towel over the television screen, as it is impossible to turn the picture off.

Most bathrooms feature tiled accenting and a terrazzo-style tiled floor, and a shower enclosure in a half-moon shape (it *is* rather small, however, considering the size of many North American passengers), 100 percent Egyptian cotton towels, a small cabinet for personal toiletries and a small shelf. In reality, there is little space to stow personal toiletries for two (or more).

BERLITZ'S RATINGS

	Possible	Achieved
Ship	500	433
Accommodation	200	163
Food	400	259
Service	400	298
Entertainment	100	81
Cruise	400	312

The largest accommodation consists of a family suite with two bedrooms. One bedroom has twin beds (convertible to queen-sized bed), while a second has two lower beds and two upper Pullman berths, a combination that can sleep up to eight persons (this would be suitable for large families).

Occupants of accommodation designated as suites also get the use of a private Concierge Lounge (where priority dining room reservations, shore excursion bookings and beauty salon/spa appointments can be made).

DINING: "Cascades" is the name of the main dining room; it spans two decks (the upper deck level has floor-to-ceiling windows, while the lower deck level has picture windows), and is a lovely, but noisy, dining hall – reminiscent of those aboard the transatlantic liners in their heyday. It seats 1,104, and has cascading water themed décor. There are tables for two, four, six, eight or 10 in two seatings. Two small private dining rooms (Breakers, with 94 seats and Tides, with 30 seats) are located off the main dining room. No smoking is permitted in the dining venues.

The cuisine is typical of mass banquet catering that offers standard fare comparable to that found in American family-style restaurants ashore. The menu descriptions make the food sound better than it is (which is consistently below average), mostly disappointing and without much taste – the result of controlled food costs as well as the use of many mixes and pre-prepared items.

However, a decent selection of light meals is provided, and a vegetarian menu is available. The selection of breads, rolls, fruit and cheese is quite poor, however, and could do more improvement. Caviar (once a standard men item) now incurs a hefty extra charge. Menus typically include a Welcome Aboard Dinner, French Dinner, Italian Dinner, International Dinner, Captain's Gala Dinner. One thing this company does once each cruise is to feature a "Galley Buffet" whereby passengers go through a section of the galley picking up food for a midnight buffet. There is an adequate wine list, with moderate prices.

For a change from the main dining room, there are two alternative dining spots: Portofino, with 112 seats (and a magnificent "cloud" ceiling), featuring Italian cuisine, and Chops Grille Steakhouse, with 95 seats and an open (show) kitchen, serving premium meats in the form of chops and steaks. Both alternative dining spots have food that is of a much higher quality than in the main dining room, with extremely good presentation. There is an additional charge of $20 per person (this includes gratuities to staff), and reservations *are* required for both dining spots, which are typically open between 6pm and 11pm. Do be prepared to eat a *lot* of food (perhaps this justifies the cover charge). The dress code is smart casual.

Also, casual meals can be taken (for breakfast, lunch and dinner) in the self-serve, buffet-style Windjammer Café, which can be accessed directly from the pool deck. It has islands dedicated to specific foods, and indoors and outdoors seating.

Additionally, there is the Seaview Café, open for lunch and dinner. Choose from the self-serve buffet, or from the menu for casual, fast-food seafood items including fish sandwiches, popcorn shrimp, fish 'n' chips, as well as non-seafood items such as hamburgers and hot dogs. The décor, naturally, is marine- and ocean related.

OTHER COMMENTS: This is the first Royal Caribbean International ship to use gas and steam turbine power instead of the more conventional diesel or diesel-electric combination (two gas turbines, one steam turbine). Podded propulsion power is also provided, instead of the previous conventional rudder and propeller shafts. As is common aboard all RCI vessels, the navigation bridge is of the fully enclosed type (good for cruising in cold-weather areas such as Alaska).

Radiance of the Seas is a streamlined contemporary ship, and has a two-deck-high wrap-around structure in the forward section of the funnel. Along the ship's starboard side, a central glass wall protrudes, giving great views (cabins with balconies occupy the space directly opposite on the port side). The gently rounded stern has nicely tiered decks, which gives the ship an extremely well balanced look.

Inside the ship, the décor is contemporary, yet elegant, bright and cheerful, designed for active, young hip and trendy types. A nine-deck high atrium lobby has glass-walled elevators (on the port side of the ship) that travel through 12 decks, face the sea and provide a link with nature and the ocean. The Centrum (as the atrium is called), has several public rooms connected to it: the guest relations (the contemporary term for purser's office) and shore excursions desks, a Lobby Bar, Champagne Bar, the Library, Royal Caribbean Online, the Concierge Club, and a Crown & Anchor Lounge. A great view can be had of the atrium by looking down through the flat glass dome high above it.

Other facilities include a three-level show lounge (Aurora Theatre) with 874 seats (including 24 stations for wheelchairs) and good sight lines from most seats; a second entertainment lounge for more casual cabaret shows (the Colony Club); and a delightful, but very small library. A shop called "Books, Books and Coffee" sells books, chocolates, various coffees, pastries and cakes – it's rather like a small Seattle coffee house. There's also a Champagne Bar, and a large Schooner Bar (a popular favorite aboard RCI ships) that houses maritime art in an integral art gallery. The entrance to the Schooner Bar, which has a finely detailed ceiling, has cannons, cannon balls, and a distinct, strong aroma of smoked wood.

Gambling devotees should enjoy Casino Royale, which has a French Art Nouveau decorative theme, and includes 11 crystal chandeliers (although it's difficult to see them for all the slot machines and gaming tables). There's also a small dedicated screening room for movies (with space for two wheelchairs), as well as a 194-seat conference center, and a business center.

The Viking Crown Lounge (a Royal Caribbean International trademark) is a large structure set around the base of the ship's funnel. It functions as an observation lounge during the daytime (with views forward over the swimming pool). In the evening, the space features Starquest – a futuristic, high-energy dance club, and Hollywood Odyssey – a more intimate and relaxed entertainment venue for softer mood music and "black box" theater.

For those who wish to go online, Royal Caribbean Online is a dedicated computer center that has 12 IBM computers with high-speed Internet access for sending and receiving email, located in a semi-private setting (in addition, data ports are provided in all cabins). Four more internet-access computer terminals are located in Books 'n' Coffee, a bookshop with coffee and pastries, located in an extensive area of shops.

As aboard *Adventure of the Seas, Explorer of the* Seas and *Voyager of the* Seas (the largest ships in the RCI fleet), there is a 30-ft high (9-meter) rock-climbing wall with five separate climbing tracks. There's no charge – but, once you've done it, the typical passenger reaction is: "been there, done that, what's next?"

Other sports facilities include a 9-hole miniature golf course (with novel 17th-century decorative ornaments), and an indoor/outdoor country club with golf simulator, a jogging track, and basketball court. Want to play pool? Well, you can, thanks to two special tables (called STables), whose technology was engineered for keeping North Sea oil platforms stable during rough seas.

A climate-controlled 10,176 sq. ft (945 sq. meter) indoor/outdoor Solarium (with magrodome sliding glass roof that can be closed in cool or inclement weather conditions) provides facilities for relaxation. It has a fascinating African themed décor, and includes a whirlpool and counter current swimming under a retractable magrodome roof. There's even a bronze statue of a lion-cub lounging on a bench dipping its left front paw and hind leg into the pool, as well as three huge 16-ft (4.8-meter) high carved stone elephants, with cascading waterfalls. Fitness/spa facilities, which are located on two decks, include a gymnasium (with 44 cardiovascular machines), 50-person aerobics room, ladies and gent's sauna and steam rooms, and therapy treatment rooms (no, the masseurs are not from the Zulu tribe!). There is also an exterior jogging track.

Youth facilities include Adventure Ocean, an "edutainment" area with four separate age-appropriate sections for junior passengers: Aquanaut Center (for ages 3–5); Explorer Center (for ages 6–8); Voyager Center (for ages 9–12); and the Optix Teen Center (for ages 13–17). There is also Adventure Beach, which includes a splash pool complete with waterslide; Surfside, with computer lab stations with entertaining software; and Ocean Arcade, a video games hangout.

The artwork aboard this ship is really eclectic (so there should be something for all tastes), and provides a spectrum and a half of color works. It ranges from Jenny M. Hansen's *A Vulnerable Moment* glass sculpture to David Buckland's *Industrial and Russian Construc-* *tionism 1920s* in photographic images on glass and painted canvas, to a huge multi-deck high contemporary bicycle-cum-paddlewheel sculpture design suspended in the atrium.

With this new ship, Royal Caribbean International has introduced a new, more upgraded ship (somewhat approaching Celebrity Cruises' *Millennium*), while the product delivery is much more casual and unstructured than RCI has previously been delivering. *Radiance of the Seas* offers more space and more comfortable public areas (and several more intimate spaces), slightly larger cabins and more dining options – for the younger, active, hip and trendy set – than most other RCI ships.

There is also a grand amount of glass that provides more contact with the ocean around you; of course, more glass means more cleaning of glass. However, at the end of the day, the overall product is similar to that delivered aboard other ships in the fleet. In the overall analysis, while the ship is quite delightful in many ways, the onboard operation is less spectacular, and suffers from a lack of service staff. The onboard currency is the US dollar.

WEAK POINTS: Many of the "private" balcony cabins are not very private, as they can be overlooked by anyone standing in the port and starboard wings of the Solarium, and from other locations. Standing in lines for embarkation, the reception desk, disembarkation, for port visits, shore tenders and for the self-serve buffet stations in the Windjammer Café is an inevitable aspect of cruising aboard this large ship. There are no cushioned pads for the deck lounge chairs. Spa treatments are extravagantly expensive.

Radisson Diamond
★★★★ +

Removed 2006

Small Ship: ....20,295 tons	Passengers	Cabins (wheelchair accessible): 2
Lifestyle: ....Premium	(lower beds/all berths): 354/354	Cabin Current: ....110 and 220 volts
Cruise Line: Radisson Seven Seas Cruises	Passenger Space Ratio	Elevators: 3
Former Names: ....none	(lower beds/all berths): 57.3/57.3	Casino (gaming tables): ....Yes
Builder: ....Rauma Yards (Finland)	Crew/Passenger Ratio	Slot Machines: ....Yes
Original Cost: ....$125 million	(lower beds/all berths): 1.7/1.7	Swimming Pools (outdoors): 1
Entered Service: ....May 1992	Navigation Officers: ......Scandinavian/	Swimming Pools (indoors): 0
Registry: ....The Bahamas	European	Whirlpools: 1
Length (ft/m): 430.4/131.2	Cabins (total): 177	Fitness Center: ....Yes
Beam (ft/m): 104.9/32.0	Size Range (sq ft/m): 220.6–552.0/	Sauna/Steam Room: ....Yes/Yes
Draft (ft/m): 26.2/8.0	20.5–48.5	Massage: ....Yes
Propulsion/Propellers: ....diesel	Cabins (outside view): 177	Self-Service Launderette: ....No
(11,340kW)/2 nozzles	Cabins (interior/no view): 0	Dedicated Cinema/Seats: ....No
Passenger Decks: 6	Cabins (for one person): 0	Library: ....Yes
Total Crew: 200	Cabins (with private balcony): 123	Classification Society: Det Norske Veritas

OVERALL SCORE: 1,591 (OUT OF A POSSIBLE 2,000 POINTS)

ACCOMMODATION: This ship has nicely designed, spacious, and well-equipped all outside-view cabins, most of which have private balconies with outdoor lights (those without balconies have large windows instead). All are furnished in blond woods, with marble bathroom vanities and a tiny bathtub. There are bay windows in 47 units designated as suites.

All cabins are of the same dimensions, with the exception of two "VIP" master suites with private balconies (and Rousseau-inspired wall murals). Each cabin has an oversized window or floor-to-ceiling balcony windows/door. Each has a spacious sitting area with sofa and chairs, dressing table with hair dryer, mini-bar and refrigerator, telephone, color remote-control television with integral VCR, twin beds that convert to a queen-sized unit, two good, adjustable reading lamps that are bright, a personal safe (somewhat hidden and awkward for older passengers to reach and operate), full-length mirror, and excellent drawer space.

The closet space, however, is really minimal, adequate for short cruises, but tight for two on a 7-night cruise, worse for longer cruises. Each cabin has a mini-bar that is stocked with beer and soft drinks; half-liter bottles of four liquors are provided. Bottled mineral water is provided. The cabin bathrooms have really small tubs (they are really shower tubs).

Butler service is featured in all accommodation designated as Master Suites (this was inaugurated in 2002).

Two wheelchair-accessible cabins, formerly located about as far from the elevators as one could get, have sensibly been relocated so that they are adjacent to the

BERLITZ'S RATINGS

	Possible	Achieved
Ship	500	392
Accommodation	200	168
Food	400	328
Service	400	328
Entertainment	100	78
Cruise	400	297

elevators. These have wheel-in bathrooms and shower areas, and all fittings are sensibly provided at an accessible height.

DINING: The two-deck-high dining room is spacious and quite elegant, has a 270-degree view over the stern, and open seating is featured, so you can dine with whomever you wish, when you wish (within dining room hours, of course). The cuisine quality and food presentation is European in style, and outstanding in quality, choice, and presentation. Health foods and dietary specials are always available. The waitresses (there are no waiters) are really charming, and superbly supervised by experienced headwaiters. As far as wines go, although fairly decent whites and reds are included for lunch and dinner, a separate wine list is available for those who appreciate better wines (at extra cost).

"Don Vito" is the name of a 50-seat alternative Italian casual indoor/outdoor dining spot (there is no extra charge). Run like a real restaurant ashore (make your reservations early each day you want to eat there), this informal dining spot features fine homemade pasta dishes daily, has a fine menu, including cream sauces and exotic garnishes. Each day has a different menu, and the food is presented, in small portions, course by course. It is lovingly prepared and exquisite to taste, although somewhat rich. Seating is at sturdy, practical glass-topped wooden tables for two, four, or six. Tableside dessert flambeaus are often featured – oh, and the waiters serenade you.

"The Grill" is the place for casual breakfasts and

lunches, with seating in various nooks and crannies. The self-serve buffets are of high quality, with good choice and variety.

You can also be very private if you wish and dine, course by course, in your cabin – or on the balcony (in the right setting, and if weather conditions permit). Dining is definitely the vessel's strong point.

OTHER COMMENTS: This ship features a very innovative design, based on the SWATH (Small Waterplane Area Twin Hull) technology. It is thus very stable when at sea (except, of course, in rough seas), with four stabilizing fins (two on the inner side of each pontoon), so that motion is really minimized when compared with conventional (monohull) vessels. The wide beam of this design also provides outstanding passenger space, although the public rooms are stacked vertically and are contained mostly on the inside of the ship's structure, which is like a sea-going version of a Radisson hotel ashore. The design was novel when first introduced, but, sensibly, has not been repeated in any ship order since (its propulsion system translates to a very slow service speed, making long voyages in open water – such as transatlantic crossings – quite time-consuming).

At the stern of the vessel, there is a retractable, free-floating water sports marina platform, but it is really only useful in dead calm sea conditions. There are jet-skis, and a water-ski boat. There is also a little-used underwater viewing area (it actually consists of just two portholes). There is a good outdoor jogging track, although fitness fanatics will find the gymnasium quite small.

Inside, the central focal point is a five-deck-high atrium, which has glass-enclosed elevators (together with the staircase, however, they take up most of the space). There is a well-stocked library and video center, and a sophisticated business center with facilities that are ideal for small groups and conventions. For groups and meetings, the high-tech audio and video conferencing facilities, and a high-tech security system that uses approximately 50 cameras to monitor just about everywhere, provide a good feeling of security and exclusivity. The one problem with groups is that public rooms may be taken over (reserved for private functions and parties, for example) to the annoyance of regular (non-group) passengers (ask your travel agent to check your sailing).

Other facilities include a casino, with gaming tables on one side of a passageway that connects to the show lounge; it has slot machines on the opposite side to the gaming tables – a sensible arrangement for serious game players who don't want the sound of slot machines to intrude.

This semi-submersible, twin-hulled cruise vessel, which some say looks like a white-caped "Batman" from the stern, certainly has the most unusual and distinctive looks of any cruise ship, although its design has not been as successful as hoped. It should appeal to those seeking a high standard of personalized service in fairly sophisticated and personable, somewhat "hotel-style" surroundings, with mainly unstructured daytime activities, and a dress code that is casual by day and a little more dressy at night. The food and standard of onboard service are very good, which helps to make up for the design and structural shortcomings of the vessel. Flowers and greenery also help. One nice plus is the fact that all gratuities are included. The onboard currency is the US dollar.

WEAK POINTS: The design means that many public rooms are inside, with little or no connection with the sea. The ship has a maximum speed of 12.5 knots, which makes it fine for leisurely island cruising, but slow going on longer itineraries. The spaciousness of the ship, while providing flexibility of the several individual public rooms, actually detracts from the overall flow, and the awkward one-way (contra-flow) interior staircase around the atrium can prove to be quite frustrating.

Also awkward is the multilevel entertainment room (show lounge). While the health spa facilities are good, the elevator does not reach the facilities. The meet-and-greet service is inconsistent and remains the subject of passenger complaints.

Regal Empress
★★

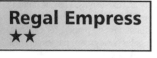

Mid-Size Ship: . . . . .21,909 tons	Passengers		Cabin Current: . . . . . . .110 and 220 volts	
Lifestyle: . . . . .Standard	(lower beds/all berths): 905/1,068		Elevators: 3	
Cruise Line: . . . . .Regal Cruises	Passenger Space Ratio		Casino (gaming tables): . . . . .Yes	
Former Names: . . . . . . .Caribe I, Olympia	(lower beds/all berths): 24.2/20.5		Slot Machines: . . . . .Yes	
Builder: . . . . .Alex Stephen & Son (UK)	Crew/Passenger Ratio		Swimming Pools (outdoors): 1	
Original Cost: . . . . .n/a	(lower beds/all berths): 2.2/2.6		Swimming Pools (indoors): 0	
Entered Service: . . . . .Oct 1953/May 1993	Navigation Officers: . . . . .European		Whirlpools: 2	
Registry: . . . . .The Bahamas	Cabins (total): .457		Fitness Center: . . . . .Yes	
Length (ft/m): 611.8/186.5	Size Range (sq ft/m): 104.4–296.0/		Sauna/Steam Room: . . . . .No/No	
Beam (ft/m): 79.0/24.1	9.7–27.5		Massage: . . . . .Yes	
Draft (ft/m): 28.2/8.6	Cabins (outside view): 230		Self-Service Launderette: . . . . .No	
Propulsion/Propellers: . . . . .diesel	Cabins (interior/no view): 227		Dedicated Cinema/Seats: Yes/90	
(10,742kW)/2	Cabins (for one person): 9		Library: . . . . .Yes	
Passenger Decks: 8	Cabins (with private balcony): 8		Classification Society: . . .Lloyd's Register	
Total Crew: .396	Cabins (wheelchair accessible): 1			

OVERALL SCORE: 917 (OUT OF A POSSIBLE 2,000 POINTS)

ACCOMMODATION: There is a wide range of cabin sizes and configurations, in 12 suite/cabin price grades. Most are small, yet spacious enough, with a reasonable amount of closet and drawer space, and heavy-duty fittings. However, the décor is generally quite dark and dull.

The largest accommodation can be found in four "Admiral Suites," which have views over the ship's bows (when you stand up, that is), and in eight suites with private (covered and enclosed) verandahs that were added in 1999, as were TV sets in all cabins (although some are positioned at odd angles, and often do not work).

Many cabins have additional upper berths, while some cabins can accommodate five persons. Otis Spunkmeyer cookies can be found on your pillow each night (this makes a change from those mint chocolates most cruise lines use).

DINING: The old-world Caribbean Dining Room is a step back in time to a more gracious era, with its original oil paintings on burnished wood paneling, ornate lighting fixtures and etched glass panels, and original murals depicting New York and Rio. There are two seatings, and the whole dining room is non-smoking. Don't expect a table for two, as most tables are for groups of six or more, with a few tables for four.

The food is plentiful and of a reasonably decent standard considering the price (although there is much use of rice instead of potatoes and other starch-rich alternatives), with the exception of the self-serve buffets, which are really very basic, under-creative, and totally forget-

BERLITZ'S RATINGS

	Possible	Achieved
Ship	500	218
Accommodation	200	95
Food	400	193
Service	400	206
Entertainment	100	38
Cruise	400	167

table. Lunches are quite repetitive. While the freshly baked breads (and different flavored butters daily) are good (passengers like the garlic bread, and the donut machine), the selection of real cheeses and fresh fruits is not.

La Trattoria is the place for casual self-serve buffet breakfasts, lunches and dinners. This eatery features Italian and other European-style cuisines.

OTHER COMMENTS: This ship – now almost 50 years old – has a traditional, balanced ocean liner profile, and, for many years, sailed as a transatlantic liner between Greece and the United States. There is a good amount of open deck space for sun worshippers, although this can become very crowded when the ship is full. Traditional liner features include polished teakwood decking and handrails. Although the ship is old, Regal Cruises is spending a lot of time and effort to maintain it.

There is an enclosed (air-conditioned) promenade deck is popular with strollers, and for those that like to sit and read.

Inside the ship you'll find plenty of real woods heavy brass and art deco detailing throughout many of the public rooms, with fine satin woods and brass featured on the ship's interior staircases. Considering that the ship carries approximately 1,000 passengers, there really are very few public rooms other than a casino, a single-level show lounge (with slightly raised port and starboard sections, but poor sight lines from many seats except for the first few rows), a nightclub/disco, and a piano lounge.

There is, however, a fine, old-fashioned library with

untouched, original wood paneling and wood beam ceiling; the book selection, however, is poor and out of date, and the dog-eared paperbacks just do not look right (hardback books are better); and no magazines are provided. There is also an Internet Café (it's actually a bar), for those who simply must connect while at sea.

Junior passengers are divided in to two groups: Juniors (ages 6–11) and Teens (12–18 years), although facilities are minimal, as the vessel simply wasn't built to cater to many youngsters.

This ship provides a basic, no-frills cruise experience at low cost, in reasonably adequate surroundings. Do note that, although it underwent some much-needed refurbishment in 1997, it is a very old ship, with a disjointed layout. The service is perfunctory at best (communication with many crew members can prove frustrating if you don't speak their language), and there is much hustling for gratuities. The onboard currency is the US dollar.

WEAK POINTS: This is a high-density ship that feels very crowded and makes it difficult to find any quiet places to relax. There are no cushioned pads for the deck lounge chairs outside on the open decks. Expect to be in a line for embarkation, the self-serve buffet meals, and, particularly when disembarking. The ship is extremely cramped, with little space to move around when full, particularly on the short "party" cruises. It has an awkward layout, and many passageways do not extend for the length of the ship. Many ceilings in public rooms are low. Passengers (on longer cruises) often complain that the washing machines and dryers are out of order. Finally, tipping glasses stationed around the ship (on many cruises) are grossly insulting.

QUOTABLE QUOTES

These are some of the questions I have been asked over the years by passengers taking a cruise for the first time:

"Will we have time to take the shore excursion?"

"If I don't buy a shore excursion, am I allowed off in port?"

"Are the entertainers paid?"

"Why don't we have a Late Night Comedy Spot in the afternoon?"

"Is the mail brought in by plane?"

"Why aren't the dancers fully dressed?"

"How do we know which photos are ours?"

"Will the ship wait for the tour buses to get back?"

"Will I get wet if I go snorkeling?"

"Do the Chinese do the laundry by hand?"

"Does the ship dock in the middle of town?"

"Is the doctor qualified?"

"Who's driving the ship if the captain is at the cocktail party?"

"Does the sun always rise on the left side of the ship?"

"Is trapshooting held outside?"

"I'm married, but can I come to the Singles Party?"

"Should I put my luggage outside the cabin before or after I go to sleep?"

"Does an outside cabin mean it's outside the ship?"

Regal Princess
★★★★

Large Ship: ....69,845 tons	Passengers	Cabin Current: ....110 and 220 volts
Lifestyle: ....Standard	(lower beds/all berths): 1,590/1,910	Elevators: 9
Cruise Line: ....Princess Cruises	Passenger Space Ratio	Casino (gaming tables): ....Yes
Former Names: ....none	(lower beds/all berths): 43.9/36.5	Slot Machines: ....Yes
Builder: ....Fincantieri Navali (Italy)	Crew/Passenger Ratio	Swimming Pools (outdoors): 2
Original Cost: ....$276.8 million	(lower beds/all berths): 2.2/2.7	Swimming Pools (indoors): 0
Entered Service: ....Aug 1991	Navigation Officers: ....Italian	Whirlpools: 4
Registry: ....Great Britain	Cabins (total): 795	Fitness Center: ....Yes
Length (ft/m): 811.0/247.2	Size Range (sq ft/m): 189.4–586.6/	Sauna/Steam Room: ....Yes/Yes
Beam (ft/m): 105.6/32.2	17.6–54.5	Massage:..........................Yes
Draft (ft/m): 25.5/7.8	Cabins (outside view): 624	Self-Service Launderette:..........Yes
Propulsion/Propellers: ....diesel	Cabins (interior/no view): 171	Dedicated Cinema/Seats: Yes/169
(24,000kW)/2	Cabins (for one person): 0	Library: ....Yes
Passenger Decks: 12	Cabins (with private balcony): 184	Classification Society: ...Registro Navale
Total Crew: 696	Cabins (wheelchair accessible): 10	Italiano (RINA)

OVERALL SCORE: 1,448 (OUT OF A POSSIBLE 2,000 POINTS)

ACCOMMODATION: There are 26 different price grades. In general, the cabins are well designed and have large bathrooms as well as good soundproofing. Walk-in closets, refrigerator, personal safe, color television and an interactive video system are provided in all cabins, as are chocolates on your pillow each night. Princess Cruises carries BBC World, CNN, CNBC, ESPN and TNT on the in-cabin color television system (when available, depending on cruise area). Twin beds convert to queen-size beds in standard cabins. Bathrobes and personal toiletry amenities are provided. The outside-view handicapped cabins have their views obstructed by lifeboats.

The 14 most expensive suites (each of which has a large private balcony) are very well equipped, with a practical design that positions most things in just the right place. They have the following names (in alphabetical order): Amalfi, Antibes, Cannes, Capri, Corfu, La Palma, Madeira, Majorca, Malaga, Marbella, Monaco, Portofino, St. Tropez, and Sorrento. The bedroom is separated from the living room by a heavy wooden door, and there are televisions in both rooms. The closet and drawer space is very generous, and there is enough of it even for long cruises.

DINING: The Palm Court dining room is a non smoking room (all dining rooms aboard Princess Cruises ships are non-smoking), and is large, although the galley divides it into a U-shape. However, there are no tables for two, although the line's marketing tag line states that this is "The Love Boat" line. Some of the most desirable

BERLITZ'S RATINGS

	Possible	Achieved
Ship	500	365
Accommodation	200	148
Food	400	264
Service	400	290
Entertainment	100	78
Cruise	400	303

tables overlook the stern. There are two seatings.

Despite the fact that the portions are generous, the food and its presentation are somewhat disappointing, and bland of taste. The quality of fish is poor (often disguised by crumb or batter coatings), the selection of fresh green vegetables is limited, and few garnishes are used. However, do remember that this *is* big-ship banquet catering, with all its attendant standardization and production cooking. Meats are of a decent quality, although often disguised by gravy-based sauces, and pasta dishes are acceptable (though voluminous), and are typically served by section headwaiters who, in search of gratuities, may also make "something special just for you." If you like desserts, order a sundae at dinner, as most other desserts are just so-so. Remember that ice cream ordered in the dining room is included, but if you order one anywhere else, you'll have to pay for it.

On any given seven-day cruise, a typical menu cycle will include a Sailaway Dinner, Captain's Welcome Dinner, Chef's Dinner, Italian Dinner, French Dinner, Captain's Gala Dinner, and Landfall Dinner. The general service level is quite reasonable, but it always seems hurried, particularly for those who are at the first dinner seating. The wine list is average, with a heavy emphasis on Californian wines. Note that 15 percent is added to all beverage bills, including wines (whether you order a $15 bottle or a $120 bottle).

There is an excellent pizzeria, however, for informal meals; this is particularly popular at lunchtime and in the afternoons. Themed late-night buffets are provided, but afternoon teas are poor. For sweet snacks during the day, a Pâtisserie (items are at extra charge) is located in the spacious lobby.

OTHER COMMENTS: This was the second ship in the 70,000-ton range for Princess Cruises, and as such foreshadowed the even larger ships this successful company went on to build. The ship has an interesting, jumbo-airplane look to it when viewed from the front, with a dolphin-like upper structure (made of lightweight aluminum alloy), and a large upright "dustbin-like" funnel (also made from aluminum alloy) placed aft.

Inside, innovative and elegant styling of the period is mixed with traditional features and a spacious interior layout. The interior spaces are well designed, although the layout itself is somewhat disjointed. An understated décor of soft pastel shades is highlighted by some very colorful artwork.

An observation dome, set high atop the ship like the head of a dolphin, has a large casino, numerous rubber trees, a dance floor and live music. The ship has decent health and fitness facilities. A striking, elegant three-deck-high atrium has a grand staircase with fountain sculpture (real, stand-up cocktail parties are held here). Characters Bar, located adjacent to the pizzeria on the open deck forward, has wonderful drink concoctions and some unusual glasses.

This ship provides a very pleasant cruise in elegant and very comfortable surroundings, and fine-tuned staff will make you feel welcome. Princess Cruises provides white-gloved stewards to take you to your cabin when you embark, another nice touch. *Regal Princess* has undergone an extensive refit (remodeled atrium and dining room, new 24-hour Lido restaurant and evening bistro, and new children's center).

The ship is full of revenue centers, however, designed to help part you from your money as efficiently as possible. You can expect to be subjected to a stream of flyers advertising daily art auctions, "designer" watches, and other promotions, while "artworks" for auction are strewn throughout the ship.

Note that gratuities to staff are *automatically* added to your account, at $10 per person, per day (gratuities for children are charged at the same rate). If you want to pay less, you'll need to go to the reception desk to have these charges adjusted (that could mean lining up with many other passengers wanting to do the same). The onboard currency is the US dollar.

WEAK POINTS: The open deck space is very limited for the size of the ship and the number of passengers carried, and, sadly, there is no forward observation viewpoint outdoors. There is no wrap-around promenade deck outdoors (the only walking space being along the sides of the ship). In fact, there is little contact with the outdoors at all. The sunbathing space is really limited when the ship is full, although with passenger age range often of 50 years old and above, perhaps this is not quite so crucial. There are too many support pillars in the public rooms that obstruct the sight lines and flow. Inside, the layout is disjointed, and takes getting used to. Galley fumes seem to waft constantly over the aft open decks.

The automated telephone system is frustrating for many passengers, and luggage delivery needs to be more efficient. Lines form for many things, but particularly for the purser's office, and for open-seating breakfast and lunch in the dining room. Long lines for embarkation (an "express check-in" option is available by completing certain documentation 40 days in advance of your cruise), disembarkation, shore excursions and shore tenders are also a fact of life aboard large ships such as this one, as is waiting for elevators at peak times.

Rhapsody
★★★

Removal 2006

Mid-Size Ship: . . . . .17,495 tons
Lifestyle: . . . . .Standard
Cruise Line: . . . . .Mediterranean Shipping Cruises
Former Names: . . . .*Cunard Princess, Cunard Conquest*
Builder: . . . .Burmeister & Wein (Denmark)
Original Cost: . . . .£12 million
Entered Service: . . . .Mar 1977/May 1995
Registry: . . . . .Panama
Length (ft/m): 541.0/164.9
Beam (ft/m): 76.1/23.2
Draft (ft/m): 19.0/5.82
Propulsion/Propellers: . . . . .diesel
(15,670kW)/2

Passenger Decks: 8
Total Crew: .350
Passengers
(lower beds/all berths): 788/959
Passenger Space Ratio
(lower beds/all berths): 22.2/18.1
Crew/Passenger Ratio
(lower beds/all berths): 2.2/2.7
Navigation Officers: . . . . .Italian
Cabins (total): 394
Size Range (sq ft/m): 87.1–264.8/8.1–24.6
Cabins (outside view): 267
Cabins (interior/no view): 127
Cabins (for one person): 0
Cabins (with private balcony): 0

Cabins (wheelchair accessible): 0
Cabin Current: . . . . .220 volts
Elevators: 2
Casino (gaming tables): . . . . .Yes
Slot Machines: . . . . .Yes
Swimming Pools (outdoors): 1
Swimming Pools (indoors): 0
Whirlpools: 2
Fitness Center: . . . . .Yes
Sauna/Steam Room: . . . . .Yes/No
Massage: . . . . .No
Self-Service Launderette: . . . . .No
Dedicated Cinema/Seats: Yes/135
Library: . . . . .Yes
Classification Society: . . .Lloyd's Register

OVERALL SCORE: 1,194 (OUT OF A POSSIBLE 2,000 POINTS)

ACCOMMODATION: Although the cabins are small and compact, with somewhat tinny (noisy) metal fixtures and thin walls that provide extremely poor cabin insulation, they are adequate for short cruises. The soft furnishings are pleasing, and the closet and drawer space reasonable. The bathrooms are adequate, if tight, with little storage space for toiletries.

BERLITZ'S RATINGS		
	Possible	Achieved
Ship	500	323
Accommodation	200	121
Food	400	216
Service	400	238
Entertainment	100	62
Cruise	400	234

turn was renamed Mediterranean Shipping Cruises, as a replacement for its *Achille Lauro*, which caught fire and sank in 1995. There is a good amount of open deck space for sun-worshippers. There is a good selection of public rooms with attractive décor, in light, bright colors, including an observation lounge above the bridge, overlooking the bow.

The ship has an excellent indoor-outdoor entertainment nightclub and bar, which incorporates the occasional use of an aft open deck area. The show lounge, a one deck high room with raised seating on its port and starboard sides, has eight pillars that obstruct sight lines (the ceiling height is also very low).

This ship will provide a very comfortable first cruise experience, featuring destination-intensive itineraries, in a pleasing, casual, but very high-density environment.

This vessel is now marketed mostly to Europeans and to Italian passengers in particular (who form about 60 percent of the passengers). While it still looks sharp following an extensive refit and refurbishment in 1997, the standard of food and service offered are disappointingly commonplace. The onboard currency is the euro.

DINING: A pleasant, bubbly dining room has sea views from large picture windows, but is fairly noisy due to its open design. There are two seatings. The standard "banquet" food is reasonable and tailored mainly to Italian passengers, with typical Italian dishes including plenty of pasta (but sadly no tableside cooking). The service is bubbly, cheerful, attentive, and comes with a smile, but it lacks finesse. There is a limited selection of breads and fruits. The cabin service menu is very limited.

Additionally, a casual self-serve open-air area is available for breakfast, lunches and (sometimes, depending on the itinerary) buffet dinners.

OTHER COMMENTS: This ship is almost identical to her sister, *Olympic Countess* (the former *Cunard Countess*), with the same contemporary profile and good looks. It was acquired in 1995 by StarLauro Cruises, which in

WEAK POINTS: There is no outdoor wrap-around promenade deck outdoors. The cabins really are very small.

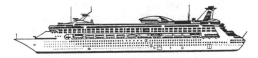

Rhapsody of the Seas
★★★★

Large Ship: . . . . .78,491 tons	Passengers	Cabin Current: . . . . .110 and 220 volts
Lifestyle: . . . . .Standard	(lower beds/all berths): 2,000/2,435	Elevators: 9
Cruise Line: Royal Caribbean International	Passenger Space Ratio	Casino (gaming tables): . . . . .Yes
Former Names: . . . . .none	(lower beds/all berths): 39.2/32.2	Slot Machines: . . . . .Yes
Builder: Chantiers de l'Atlantique (France)	Crew/Passenger Ratio	Swimming Pools (outdoors): 1
Original Cost: . . . .$275 million	(lower beds/all berths): 2.6/3.1	Swimming Pools (indoors): 1
Entered Service: . . . . .May 1997	Navigation Officers: . . . . .International	(inside/outside)
Registry: . . . . .The Bahamas	Cabins (total): 1,000	Whirlpools: 6
Length (ft/m): 915.3/279.0	Size Range (sq ft/m): 135.0–1,270.1/	Fitness Center: . . . . .Yes
Beam (ft/m): 105.6/32.2	12.5–118.0	Sauna/Steam Room: . . . . .Yes/Yes
Draft (ft/m): 24.9/7.6	Cabins (outside view): 593	Massage: . . . . .Yes
Propulsion/Propellers: . . . . .diesel-electric	Cabins (interior/no view): 407	Self-Service Launderette: . . . . .No
(50,400kW)/2	Cabins (for one person): 0	Dedicated Cinema/Seats: . . . . .No
Passenger Decks: 11	Cabins (with private balcony): 229	Library: . . . . .Yes
Total Crew: .765	Cabins (wheelchair accessible): 14	Classification Society: Det Norske Veritas

OVERALL SCORE: 1,519 (OUT OF A POSSIBLE 2,000 POINTS)

ACCOMMODATION: The standard interior (no view) and exterior view cabins are of an adequate size, and have just enough functional facilities to make them comfortable for a one-week cruise, but longer might prove confining. The décor is bright and cheerful, although the ceilings are plain; colorful soft furnishings make one's home away from home look like the inside of a modern Scandinavian hotel – minimalist, yet colorful. Twin lower beds convert to queen-sized beds, and there is a reasonable amount of closet and drawer space (there is little room to maneuver between the bed and desk/television unit).

The bathrooms are small but functional, although the shower units themselves are small, and there is no cabinet for one's personal toiletry items. The towels could be larger and thicker. In the passageways, upbeat artwork depicts musical themes, from classical to jazz and popular.

Choose a "C" grade suite if you want spacious accommodation that includes a separate (curtained-off) sleeping area, a good-sized outside balcony (with part, not full, partition), lounge with sofa, two chairs and coffee table, three closets, plenty of drawer and storage space, television and VCR. The bathroom is large and has a full-size bathtub, integral shower, and two washbasins/two toiletries cabinets.

For the ultimate accommodation aboard this ship, choose the Royal Suite, which resembles a Palm Beach apartment, and comes complete with a white baby grand (player) piano. It has a separate bedroom with king-size bed, living room with queen-size sofa bed, refrigera-

BERLITZ'S RATINGS

	Possible	Achieved
Ship	500	428
Accommodation	200	166
Food	400	248
Service	400	302
Entertainment	100	81
Cruise	400	294

tor/mini-bar, dining table, entertainment center, and vanity dressing area. The décor is simple and elegant, with pastel colors, and wood accented ceiling treatments. Located just under the starboard side navigation bridge wing, it has its own private balcony.

DINING: The two-level main dining room (Edelweiss) is attractive and works well, although the noise level can be high. There are two seatings. The quality and serving of meals aboard Royal Caribbean International ships has become quite robotic over the past few years.

The cuisine is typical of mass banquet catering that offers standard fare comparable to that found in American family-style restaurants ashore. The menu descriptions make the food sound better than it is (which is consistently below average), mostly disappointing and without much taste – the result of controlled food costs as well as the use of many mixes and pre-prepared items. However, a decent selection of light meals is provided, and a vegetarian menu is available. The selection of breads, rolls, fruit and cheese is quite poor, however, and could do more improvement. Caviar (once a standard men item) now incurs a hefty extra charge.

Menus typically include a Welcome Aboard Dinner, French Dinner, Italian Dinner, International Dinner, Captain's Gala Dinner. One thing this company does once each cruise is to feature "Galley Buffet" whereby passengers go through a section of the galley picking up food for a midnight buffet. There is an adequate wine list, with moderate prices.

The informal dining spots are well designed, with

contemporary décor and colors, but the food is really basic fare and disappointing, the four-sided self-service buffet area is small for the number of passengers that use it. More money needs to be spent for better-quality ingredients. Each evening, buffets have a different theme, something this company has been doing for more than 25 years – perhaps the time has come for more creativity.

OTHER COMMENTS: This striking ship shares design features that make many (but not all) of the Royal Caribbean International ships identifiable, including a Viking Crown Lounge, a terrific multi-level night spot (the music can be loud and overbearing, however, as can the cigarette smoke around the bar). The Viking Crown Lounge (which is also the ship's disco) aboard this and sister ship *Vision of the Seas* is positioned just forward of the center of the ship. The funnel located well aft – a departure from all other RCI ships to date - which feature the lounge positioned around or at the base of, the funnel. The ship's stern is beautifully rounded. There is a reasonable amount of open-air walking space, although this can become cluttered with deck lounge chairs.

There is a wide range of interesting public rooms, lounges and bars to play in, and the interiors have been cleverly designed to avoid congestion and aid passenger flow into revenue areas. Speaking of which, for those who enjoy gambling, the astrologically-themed casino is large and glitzy (although not as bold as aboard some of the company's other ships), again typical of most of the new large ships; a couple of pieces of "electrostatic" art in globe form provide fascinating relief.

There is, as one might expect, a large shopping area, although the merchandise is consistently tacky, and identical to that found in most American malls. The artwork throughout the ship is really upbeat and colorful, and has a musical theme: classical, jazz, popular and rock 'n' roll. Much improved over previous new ships in the fleet is the theater, with more entrances and fewer bottlenecks; there are still pillars obstructing sight lines from many seats, however. Also improved are the facilities for children and teens.

There are good health spa facilities, set in a spacious environment on one of the uppermost decks. The décor has Egypt as its theme, with pharaohs lining the pool.

Ship lovers will enjoy the chair fabric in the Shall We Dance lounge, with its large aft-facing windows, and the glass case-enclosed mechanical sculptures.

Royal Caribbean International provides a consistently good, highly programmed cruise vacation for those seeking to travel in a large ship with a large number of other lively passengers. What, in particular, makes this ship feel warm and cozy are the use of fine, light wood surfaces throughout her public rooms, as well as the large array of potted plants everywhere. The onboard currency is the US dollar.

WEAK POINTS: Standing in line for embarkation, disembarkation, shore tenders and for self-serve buffet meals is an inevitable aspect of cruising aboard all large ships. The daily program is so full of the day's events, in small type size, is that it is *extremely* difficult to read. The light colored carpeting used on the stairwells is impractical.

Rotterdam
★★★★

Large Ship:	.............59,652 tons	
Lifestyle:	..................Premium	
Cruise Line:	......Holland America Line	
Former Names:	.................none	
Builder:	.............Fincantieri (Italy)	
Original Cost:	.............$250 million	
Entered Service:	.............Dec 1997	
Registry:	............The Netherlands	
Length (ft/m):	..........777.5/237.00	
Beam (ft/m):	.............105.8/32.25	
Draft (ft/m):	.................25.5/7.80	
Propulsion/Propellers:	.....diesel-electric	
	(37,500kW)/2	
Passenger Decks:	12	
Total Crew:	593	

Passengers
(lower beds/all berths): 1,320/1,668
Passenger Space Ratio
(lower beds/all berths): 45.1/35.7
Crew/Passenger Ratio
(lower beds/all berths): 2.2/2.8
Navigation Officers: ....Dutch
Cabins (total): 660
Size Range (sq ft/m): 184.0–1,124.8/
                                   17.1–104.5
Cabins (outside view): 542
Cabins (interior/no view): 118
Cabins (for one person): 0
Cabins (with private balcony): 160
Cabins (wheelchair accessible): 20

Cabin Current: ....110 and 220 volts
Elevators: 12
Casino (gaming tables): ....Yes
Slot Machines: ....Yes
Swimming Pools (outdoors): 1
Swimming Pools (indoors): 1
                            (magrodome cover)
Whirlpools: 2
Fitness Center: ....Yes
Sauna/Steam Room: ....Yes/Yes
Massage:.........................Yes
Self-Service Launderette:...........Yes
Dedicated Cinema/Seats: Yes/235
Library: ....Yes
Classification Society: . . .Lloyd's Register

OVERALL SCORE: 1,541 (OUT OF A POSSIBLE 2,000 POINTS)

ACCOMMODATION: This is spread over five decks (a number of cabins have full or partially obstructed views). Interestingly, no cabin is more than 144 ft (44 metres) from a stairway, which makes it easier to get from cabins to public rooms. All cabin doors have a bird's-eye maple look, and hallways have framed fabric panels to make them warmer and less clinical. Cabin televisions carry CNN and TNT.

BERLITZ'S RATINGS

	Possible	Achieved
Ship	500	430
Accommodation	200	165
Food	400	281
Service	400	276
Entertainment	100	77
Cruise	400	312

All standard inside and outside cabins are tastefully furnished, and have twin beds that convert to a queen-sized bed (space is tight for walking between beds and vanity unit). There is a decent amount of closet and drawer space, although this will prove tight for the longer voyages featured. The bathrooms, which are fully tiled, are disappointingly small (particularly for long cruises) and have small shower tubs, utilitarian personal toiletries cupboards, and exposed under-sink plumbing. There is no detailing to distinguish them from bathrooms aboard the *Statendam*-class ships, given that this ship is claimed by Holland America Line to be the "flagship" of the fleet.

There are 36 full verandah suites (Navigation Deck), including four penthouse suites, which share a private Concierge Lounge with a concierge to handle such things as special dining arrangements, shore excursions and special requests – although strangely there are no butlers for these suites, as aboard ships with similar facilities. Each suite has a separate steward's entrance and separate bedroom, dressing and living areas. Suite passengers get personal stationery, complimentary laundry and ironing, cocktail-hour hors d'oeuvres and other goodies, as well as priority embarkation and disembarkation. The concierge lounge, with its latticework teak detailing and private library is accessible only by private key-card.

Handicapped passengers have 20 cabins to choose from, including two of the large "penthouse" suites (which include concierge services). However, there are different cabin configurations, and it is wise to check with your booking agent.

DINING: There is one principal, large two-level dining room (La Fontaine), with tables for four, six or eight, similar to the *Statendam*-class ships (there are just nine tables for two). Open seating is featured for breakfast and lunch, with two seatings for dinner (with both smoking and no-smoking sections on both upper and lower levels). Fine Rosenthal china and good cutlery are used (although there are no fish knives).

Unfortunately, Holland America Line food isn't as nice as the china it's placed on. It may be adequate for most passengers who are not used to better food, but it doesn't match the standard found aboard other ships in the premium segment of the industry. While USDA beef is of a good quality, fowl tends to be battery-tough, and most fish is overcooked and has the consistency of a baseball bat. What are also definitely *not* luxurious are the endless packets of sugar, and packets (instead of glass jars) of breakfast jam, marmalade and honey, and poor quality teas. While these may be suitable for a family diner, they do not belong aboard a ship that claims to have "award-winning cuisine." Dessert and pastry items are of good quality (specifically for American tastes), although there is much use of canned fruits and jellies. Forget the selection of "international" cheeses, however, as most of it didn't come from anywhere other than the USA – a country that is known for processed, highly colored cheese slices rather than fine cheese making. Note that Holland America Line can provide Kosher meals, but these are prepared ashore, frozen, and brought to your table sealed in their original containers (there is no Kosher kitchen on board).

Instead of the more formal dining room, the Lido Buffet is open for casual dinners on all except the last night of each cruise, in an open-seating arrangement. Tables are set with crisp linens, flatware and stemware. A set menu is featured, and this includes a choice of four entrées.

The food is marginally better than that presently served aboard other Holland America Line ships, with better buffets and more attention to detail, although it does not come up to the standard of other ships in the premium segment of the industry.

There is also an 88-seat Odyssey Italian alternative restaurant, decorated in the manner of an opulent baroque Italian villa, and available to all passengers on a reservation basis. This alternative restaurant is a first on any Holland America Line ship (there's no extra charge). The room, whose basic color is black with gold accenting, is divided into three sections. The cuisines from the Perugia, Tuscany and Umbria regions of Italy are featured, although the portions are very small.

OTHER COMMENTS: The current *Rotterdam* has been constructed to look like a slightly larger (longer and beamier), but certainly a much sleeker version of the *Statendam*-class ships, while retaining the graceful lines of the former *Rotterdam*, including a nicely raked bow, as well as the familiar interior flow and design style. Also retained is the twin-funnel feature well recognized by former Holland America Line passengers, though it has been somewhat more streamlined. The new *Rotterdam* (the sixth Holland America Line ship to bear the name) is capable of 25 knots, which is useful for longer itineraries.

The focal interior point is a three-deck high atrium, in an oval, instead of circular, shape. The atrium's focal point is a huge "one-of-a-kind" clock, which includes an astrolabe, an astrological clock and 14 other clocks in a structure that takes up three decks. Instead of just two staircases aboard the *Statendam*-class ships, *Rotterdam* has three (better from the viewpoint of safety and passenger accessibility). There is a magrodome-covered pool on the Lido Deck between the mast and the ship's twin funnels, as aboard the company's *Statendam*-class ships, which have only one large, very square funnel.

The interior public spaces also carry on the same layout and flow as found aboard the *Statendam*-class ships. The interior décor is best described as restrained, with much use of wood accenting. One room has a glass ceiling similar to that found aboard a former *Statendam*. As a whole, the decor of this ship is extremely refined, with much of the traditional ocean liner detailing so loved by frequent Holland America Line passengers. Additions are children's and teens' play areas, although these really are token gestures by a company that traditionally does not cater well to children. Popcorn is available at the Wajang Theatre for moviegoers, while adjacent is the popular Java Cafe. The casino, which is located in the middle of a major passenger flow, has blackjack, roulette, poker and dice tables alongside the requisite rows of slot machines.

The artwork consists of a collection of 17th-century Dutch and Japanese artifacts together with contemporary works specially created for the ship, although there seems little linkage between some of the items.

Holland America Line's new flagship replaced the former ship of the same name when it was retired in 1997 – just in time for the start of the company's 125th anniversary in 1998. It is a most contemporary ship for Holland America Line, with lighter, brighter décor. It is an extremely comfortable vessel in which to cruise, with some fine, elegant and luxurious decorative features. However, these are marred by the poor quality of dining room food and service and the lack of understanding of what it takes to make a "luxury" cruise experience, despite what is touted in the company's brochures.

Gratuities are extra, and they are added to your shipboard account at $10–$13 per day, according to the accommodation grade chosen. Refreshingly, the company does not add an automatic 15 percent gratuity for beverage purchases. Perhaps the ship's best asset is its friendly and personable Filipino and Indonesian crew, although communication can prove frustrating at times.

The company provides complimentary cappuccino and espresso coffees, and free ice cream during certain hours of the day aboard its ships, as well as hot hors d'oeuvres in all bars – something other major lines seem to have dropped, or charge extra for. The onboard currency is the US dollar.

WEAK POINTS: Standing in line for embarkation, disembarkation, shore tenders and for self-serve buffet meals is an inevitable aspect of cruising aboard all large ships. With one whole deck of suites (and a dedicated, private concierge lounge, and preferential passenger treatment), the company has in effect created a two-class ship. The charge to use the washing machines and dryers in the self-service launderette is really petty and irritating, particularly for the occupants of suites, as they pay high prices for their cruises. Communication (in English) with many of the staff, particularly in the dining room and buffet areas, can prove very frustrating. Room service is poor. Non-smokers should avoid this ship, as smokers are everywhere.

Royal Clipper
★★★★

Small Ship: ....5,061 tons	Propulsion/Propellers: diesel (3,700kW)/1	Cabins (for one person): 0
Lifestyle: ....Premium	Passenger Decks: 5	Cabins (with private balcony): 14
Cruise Line: ....Star Clippers	Total Crew: 100	Cabins (wheelchair accessible): 0
Former Names: ....none	Passengers	Cabin Current: ....110 and 220 volts
Builder: ....De Merwede (Holland)	(lower beds/all berths): 228/255	Elevators: 0
Original Cost: ....$75 million	Passenger Space Ratio	Casino (gaming tables): ....No
Entered Service: ....Oct 2000	(lower beds/all berths): 22.1/19.8	Slot Machines: ....No
Registry: ....Luxembourg	Crew/Passenger Ratio	Swimming Pools (outdoors): 3
Length (ft/m): 439.6/134.0	(lower beds/all berths): 2.2/2.5	Whirlpools: 0
Beam (ft/m): 54.1/16.5	Navigation Officers: ....International	Fitness Center: ....Yes
Draft (ft/m): 18.5/5.6	Cabins (total): 114	Sauna/Steam Room: ....No/Yes
Type of Vessel: sail-cruise (square rigger)	Size Range (sq ft/m): 100.0–320.0/	Massage: ....Yes
No. of Masts: 5	9.3–29.7	Self-Service Launderette: ....No
Sail Area (sq ft/m2): 56,000/5,204.5	Cabins (outside view): 108	Library: ....Yes
Main Propulsion: ....42 sails	Cabins (interior/no view): 6	Classification Society: ...Lloyd's Register

OVERALL SCORE: 1,540 (OUT OF A POSSIBLE 2,000 POINTS)

ACCOMMODATION: There are eight grades: Owner's Suite (2), Deluxe Suite (14), and Categories 1–6. No matter what grade you choose, all have polished wood-trimmed cabinetry and wall-to-wall carpeting, personal safe, full-length mirror, small television with audio channels and 24-hour text-based news, and private bathroom. All feature twin beds (86 of which convert into a queen-size bed, while 28 are fixed queen-size beds that cannot be separated), hairdryer and satellite-linked telephone. The six interior (no view) cabins, and a handful of other cabins have a permanently fixed double bed.

Most cabins feature a privacy curtain, so that you cannot be seen from the hallway when the cabin attendant opens the door (useful if you are not wearing any clothes). In addition, 27 cabins sleep three.

The two owner's suites, located at the very aft of the ship, provide the most lavish accommodation, and have one queen-size bed and one double bed, a separate living area with semi-circular sofa, large vanity desk, wet bar/refrigerator, marble-clad bathroom with whirlpool bathtub, plus one guest bathroom, and butler service. The two suites have an interconnecting door, so that the combined super-suite can sleep eight persons. However, there is no private balcony.

The 14 "Deck Suites" have interesting names: Ariel, Cutty Sark, Doriana, Eagle Wing, Flying Cloud, France, Golden Gate, Gloria, Great Republic, Passat, Pommern, Preussen, and Thermopylae. However, they are not actually suites, as the sleeping area cannot be separated from the lounge – they are simply larger cabins with a more

BERLITZ'S RATINGS		
	Possible	Achieved
Ship	500	406
Accommodation	200	157
Food	400	288
Service	400	296
Entertainment	N/A	N/A
Cruise	500	393

luxurious interior, more storage space and a larger bathroom. Each has two lower beds convertible to a queen-size, small lounge area, mini-bar/refrigerator, writing desk, small private balcony, and marble-clad bathroom with combination whirlpool bathtub/shower, washbasin and toilet, and butler service. The door to the balcony can be opened so that fresh air floods the room (note that there is a 12-inch (30-cm) threshold to step over.

There are no curtains, only roll-down blinds for the windows and balcony door. The balcony itself typically has two white plastic chairs and drinks table; however, teak chairs and table would be more in keeping with the nature of the ship. The 14 balconies are not particularly private, and most have ship's tenders or zodiacs overhanging them, or some rigging obscuring the views.

Two other "name cabins (Lord Nelson and Marco Polo – designated as Category 1 cabins) are located aft, but do not have private balconies, although the facilities are similar.

The interior (no view) cabins and the lowest grades of outside-view cabins are extremely small and tight, with very little room to move around the beds. Therefore, take only the minimum amount of clothing and luggage, as there will simply not be enough room for it. When in cabins where beds are linked together to form a double bed, you will have to clamber up over the front of the bed, as both sides have built-in storm barriers (this applies in inclement weather conditions only).

There is a small room service menu (all items are at extra cost).

DINING: The dining room is constructed on several connecting levels (getting used to the steps is not easy), and seats all passengers at one seating under a three-deck-high atrium dome. You can sit with whom you wish at tables for four, six, eight or 10. However, it is a noisy dining room, due to the positioning of the many waiter stations, and poor training, and mealtimes are therefore not as enjoyable as one would wish them to be. Some tables are poorly positioned such that correct waiter service is impossible, and much reaching over has to be done in order to serve everyone.

One corner can be closed off for private parties. Breakfasts and lunches are self-serve buffets, while dinner is a sit-down affair with table service, although the ambience is always friendly and lighthearted. The wine list consists of very young wines, and prices are quite high.

The cuisine is certainly nothing to write home about. Although perfectly acceptable, it certainly cannot be considered in the same class as that found aboard ships such as *Sea Cloud* or *Sea Cloud II*.

OTHER COMMENTS: The culmination of an owner's childhood dream, *Royal Clipper* is truly a stunning sight under sail. Being marketed as the largest true fully rigged sailing ship in the world, this is a logical extension of the company's two other, smaller, the 4-masted tall ships (*Star Clipper* and *Star Flyer*). *Royal Clipper*'s 5-masted design is based on the only other 5-masted sailing ship to be built, the 1902-built *Preussen*, and has approximately the same dimensions, albeit 46 ft (14 meters) shorter (it is much larger than the famous *Cutty Sark*, for example). It is almost 40 ft (12.1 meters) longer than the largest sailing ship presently in commission – the four-mast Russian barkentine *Sedov*. However, to keep things in perspective, *Royal Clipper* is the same length overall as *Wind Song*, *Wind Spirit* and *Wind Star* – the computer-controlled cruise-sail vessels of Windstar Cruises.

The construction time for this ship was remarkably short, due to the fact that its hull had been almost completed (at Gdansk shipyard, Poland) for another owner (the ship was to be named *Gwarek*) but became available to Star Clippers for completion and fitting out. The ship is instantly recognizable due to its geometric blue and white hull markings. Power winches, as well as hand winches, are employed in deck fittings, as well as a mix of horizontal furling for the square sails and hydraulic power assist to roll the square sails along the yardarm. The sail handling system, which was designed by the ship's owner, Mikael Krafft, is such that it can be converted from a full rigger to a schooner in an incredibly short amount of time.

Her masts reach as high as 197 ft (60 meters) above the waterline, and the top 19 ft (5.8 meters) can be hinged over 90 degrees to clear bridges, cable lines and other port-based obstacles. Up to 42 sails can be used: 26 square sails (fore upper topgallant, fore lower topgallant, fore upper topsail, fore lower topsail, foresail, main royal, main upper topgallant, main lower top-

gallant, main upper topsail, main lower topsail, mainsail, middle royal, middle upper topgallant, middle lower topgallant, middle upper topsail, middle lower topsail, middle course, mizzen upper topgallant, mizzen lower topgallant, mizzen upper topsail, mizzen lower topsail, mizzen course, jigger topgallant, jigger upper topsail, jigger lower topsail, crossjack), 11 staysails (main royal staysail, main topgallant staysail, main topmast staysail, middle royal staysail, middle topgallant staysail, middle topmast staysail, mizzen royal staysail, mizzen topgallant staysail, mizzen topmast staysail, jigger topgallant staysail, jigger topmast staysail); 4 jibs (flying jib, outer jib, inner jib, fore topmast staysail) and 1 gaff-rigged spanker, it looks quite magnificent when under full sail – an area of some 54,360 sq. ft (5,050 sq. meters). Also, watching the sailors manipulate ropes, rigging and sails is like watching a ballet – the precision and cohesion of a group of men who make it all look so simple.

As a passenger, you are allowed to climb to special lookout points aloft – maybe even for a glass of champagne! Passengers are also allowed on the bridge at any time (but not in the galley or engine room).

There is a large amount of open deck space and sunning space aboard this ship – something most tall ships lack, although, naturally, this is laid with ropes for the rigging. A marina platform can be lowered at the stern of the vessel, from where you can use the surfboards, sailing dinghies, take a ride on the ship's own banana boat, or go water-skiing or swimming. Snorkeling gear is available at no cost, while scuba diving is available at an extra charge. You will be asked to sign a waiver if you wish to use the water sports equipment.

Inside, a midships atrium that is three decks high sits under one of the ship's three swimming pools, and sunlight streams down through a piano lounge on the uppermost level inside the ship and down into the dining room, which is on the lower level. A forward observation lounge is a real plus, and this is connected to the piano lounge via a central corridor. An Edwardian library/card room is decorated with a belle époque fireplace.

A lounge, the Captain Nemo Club, is where passengers can observe fish and sea life when the ship is at anchor, through thick glass portholes (floodlit from underneath at night – to attract the fish). It is also adjacent to the ship's health spa, which incorporates a beauty salon, Moroccan steam room (for which there is a charge) and gymnasium. Thai massage as well as traditional massage, and other beauty treatments, are available.

This delightful, quite spectacular tall ship for tourists operates 7-night and 14-day cruises in the Grenadines and Lower Windward Islands of the Caribbean during the winter and 7-night and 14-night cruise in the Mediterranean during the summer. It is good to note that the officers navigate using both traditional (sextant) and contemporary methods (advanced electronic positioning system).

Being a tall ship with true sailing traditions, there is, naturally, a parrot (sometimes kept in a large, gilded cage, but often seen around the ship on someone's shoulder), which is part of the crew (as aboard all Star Clippers' ships). The general ambience on board is extremely relaxed, friendly and casual – completely unpretentious. The passenger mix is international (often consisting of a good cross-section of yachting types) and the dress code is casual at all times (shorts and casual tops are the order of the day – yachting wear), with no ties needed at any time.

There is no doubt that *Royal Clipper* is a superb vessel for the actual experience of sailing – a tall ship probably without equal, as much more time is spent actually under sail than aboard almost any other tall ship (including the smaller *Sea Cloud* and *Sea Cloud II*). However, apart from the sailing experience, it is in the cuisine and service that the lack of professionalism and poor standards of delivery shows. Much of this is the result of insufficient training and supervision, which the company is slowly addressing. The result is a score that could be higher if the cuisine and service were better.

The suites and cabins are larger than those aboard the tall ships of the Windjammer Barefoot Cruises fleet, while, in general, smaller than aboard *Sea Cloud* and *Sea Cloud II*. While the food and service are far superior to the Windjammers, both are well below the standard found aboard *Sea Cloud* and *Sea Cloud II*. I do not include the Windstar Cruises ships (*Wind Song, Wind Spirit, Wind Star, Wind Surf*), because they cannot, in any sense of the word, be considered tall ships. *Royal Clipper*, however, is exactly that – a real, working, wind-and-sails-in-your-face tall ship with a highly personable captain and crew that welcome you as if you were part of the team. What also gives the ship a little extra in the scoring department is the fact that many water sports are included in the price of your cruise. The onboard currency is the US dollar.

WEAK POINTS: The food, its quality, variety, presentation and service are still the weakest points of a cruise aboard this tall ship – although it is better than that provided aboard the company's smaller vessels, *Star Clipper* and *Star Flyer*. This ship is not for the physically impaired, or for children. The steps of the internal stairs are steep, as in most sailing vessels. The tipping system, where all tips are pooled (the suggested amount is $8 per passenger, per day), causes concern for many passengers.

Royal Princess
★★★★

Removed 2005

Large Ship: . . . . .44,348 tons	Passengers	Cabin Current: . . . . .110 and 220 volts
Lifestyle: . . . . .Standard	(lower beds/all berths): 1,200/1,275	Elevators: 6
Cruise Line: . . . . .Princess Cruises	Passenger Space Ratio	Casino (gaming tables): . . . . .Yes
Former Names: . . . . .none	(lower beds/all berths): 36.9/34.7	Slot Machines: . . . . .Yes
Builder: . . . . .Wartsila (Finland)	Crew/Passenger Ratio	Swimming Pools (outdoors): 2
Original Cost: . . . .$165 million	(lower beds/all berths): 2.3/2.4	(+2 splash pools)
Entered Service: . . . . .Nov 1984	Navigation Officers: . . . . .British	Swimming Pools (indoors): 0
Registry: . . . . .Great Britain	Cabins (total): 600	Whirlpools: 2
Length (ft/m): 754.5/230.0	Size Range (sq ft/m): 186.0–1,126.0/	Fitness Center: . . . . .Yes
Beam (ft/m): 95.8/29.2	17.2–104.5	Sauna/Steam Room: . . . . .Yes/No
Draft (ft/m): 25.5/7.8	Cabins (outside view): 600	Massage: . . . . .Yes
Propulsion/Propellers: . . . . .diesel	Cabins (interior/no view): 0	Self-Service Launderette: . . . . .Yes
(29,160kW)/2	Cabins (for one person): 0	Dedicated Cinema/Seats: Yes/150
Passenger Decks: 9	Cabins (with private balcony): 152	Library: . . . . .Yes
Total Crew: 520	Cabins (wheelchair accessible): 4	Classification Society: . . .Lloyd's Register

OVERALL SCORE: 1,528 (OUT OF A POSSIBLE 2,000 POINTS)

ACCOMMODATION: The all-outside cabins (152 of which have private balconies) represent just four accommodation types (including suites), although there are 20 price categories. All are quite well thought out, very comfortable and well appointed. The suites are extremely attractive, and have good personal toiletry kits.

All cabins have a full bathtub and shower, three-sided mirrors, and color television. Note that Princess Cruises features BBC World, CNN, CNBC, ESPN and TNT on the in-cabin color television system (when available, depending on cruise area). Bathrobes are provided for all passengers, as are chocolates on your pillow each night. Prompt, attentive room service is available 24 hours a day. Note that some cabins on both Baja Deck and Caribe Deck do have views that are obstructed by the lifeboats. The cabin numbering system is extremely illogical, with numbers going through several hundred series on the same deck.

DINING: The elegant Continental Dining Room (all dining rooms aboard Princess Cruises' ships are non-smoking) is set low down, adjacent to the lobby. There are two seatings for dinner. The service is reasonably friendly, and sound.

Despite the fact that the portions are generous, the food and its presentation are somewhat disappointing, and bland of taste. The quality of fish is poor (often disguised by crumb or batter coatings), the selection of fresh green vegetables is limited, and few garnishes are used. However, do remember that this *is* big-ship banquet catering, with all its attendant standardization and pro-

BERLITZ'S RATINGS

	Possible	Achieved
Ship	500	406
Accommodation	200	170
Food	400	265
Service	400	296
Entertainment	100	78
Cruise	400	313

duction cooking. Meats are of a decent quality, although often disguised by gravy-based sauces, and pasta dishes are acceptable (though voluminous), and are typically served by section headwaiters that may also make "something special just for you" – in search of gratuities and good comments. If you like desserts, order a sundae at dinner, as most other desserts are just so-so. Remember that ice cream ordered in the dining room is included, but if you order one anywhere else, you'll have to pay for it.

On any given seven-day cruise, a typical menu cycle will include a Sailaway Dinner, Captain's Welcome Dinner, Chef's Dinner, Italian Dinner, French Dinner, Captain's Gala Dinner, and Landfall Dinner. The wine list is average, with a heavy emphasis on California wines. Note that 15 percent is added to all beverage bills, including wines (whether you order a $15 bottle or a $120 bottle, although it's the same amount of service to open and pour the wine).

The in-cabin service menu is really basic and could include more items. The indoor-outdoor Lido Café was expanded dramatically in a refit not long ago and now features 24-hour food availability for casual dining (plastic plates are provided, however), and better beverage stations that translates to less standing in lines.

OTHER COMMENTS: This ship has handsome, contemporary outer styling, with a short, well-raked bow. Quality materials were used throughout. There is an excellent amount of outdoor deck and sunbathing space, and traditional wrap-around teakwood deck.

Well-designed, though slightly unconventional interior layout and passenger flow provides passenger cabins that are located above the public room decks. Features include large, beautifully appointed and spacious public rooms rather than the smaller, more intimate public rooms and lounges found aboard many ships today. There are spacious passageways and delightful, imposing staircases. Contemporary without being the least bit garish, the decor reflects the feeling of space, openness and light.

The Horizon Lounge, set around the funnel base, has fine views, and makes for a peaceful environment during the day. This ship will provide a fine cruise experience in spacious, elegant surroundings, at the appropriate price, although attention to the small details of service finesse is often missing.

When this ship debuted, it was a state-of-the-art vessel. It is amazing to see that now it lags behind the latest ships in several ways. Although still a fine ship (particularly well liked by American and British passengers), there is increasing competition in the marketplace.

The ship is full of revenue centers, however, designed to help part you from your money. You can expect to be subjected to a stream of flyers advertising daily art auctions, "designer" watches and other promotions, while "artworks" for auction are strewn throughout the ship.

Note that gratuities to staff are *automatically* added to your account, at $10 per person, per day (gratuities for children are charged at the same rate). If you want to pay less, you'll need to go to the reception desk to have these charges adjusted (that could mean lining up with many other passengers wanting to do the same). The onboard currency is the US dollar.

WEAK POINTS: The automated telephone system is frustrating for many passengers, and luggage delivery is not efficient. Standing in line for embarkation (an "express check-in" option is available by completing certain documentation 40 days in advance of your cruise), disembarkation, shore tenders and for self-serve buffet meals is an inevitable aspect of cruising aboard all large ships, as is waiting for elevators at peak times. The signs throughout the ship are adequate at best, and some of them are difficult to read.

Royal Star
★★ +

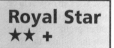

Small Ship: ....5,360 tons	Passenger Decks: 5	Cabins (wheelchair accessible): 0
Lifestyle: ....Standard	Total Crew: 130	Cabin Current: ....110 and 220 volts
Cruise Line: ......African Safari Cruises/	Passengers	Elevators: 1
Star Line Cruises	(lower beds/all berths): 222/255	Casino (gaming tables): ....Yes
Former Names: ....Ocean Islander,	Passenger Space Ratio	Slot Machines: ....Yes
San Giorgio, City of Andros	(lower beds/all berths): 24.1/21.0	Swimming Pools (outdoors): 1
Builder: ....Cantieri Riuniti dell' Adriatico	Crew/Passenger Ratio	Swimming Pools (indoors): 0
(Italy)	(lower beds/all berths): 1.7/1.9	Whirlpools: 0
Original Cost: ....n/a	Navigation Officers: ....Greek	Fitness Center: ....Yes
Entered Service: 1956/Dec 1990	Cabins (total): 111	Sauna/Steam Room: ....Yes/No
Registry: ....The Bahamas	Size Range (sq ft/m): 107.0–398.0/	Massage: ....Yes
Length (ft/m): 367.4/112.00	10.0–37.0	Self-Service Launderette: ....No
Beam (ft/m): 51.0/15.55	Cabins (outside view): 97	Dedicated Cinema/Seats: ....No
Draft (ft/m): 18.2/5.56	Cabins (interior/no view): 14	Library: ....Yes
Propulsion/Propellers: ....diesel	Cabins (for one person): 0	Classification Society: . .American Bureau
(4,817kW)/2	Cabins (with private balcony): 1	of Shipping

OVERALL SCORE: 1,069 (OUT OF A POSSIBLE 2,000 POINTS)

ACCOMMODATION: There are eight grades. Except for one President Suite, which has its own private balcony terrace, the cabins are not large, although they are quite pleasingly decorated with good-quality furnishings and ample closet and drawer space. The cabin bathrooms, however, are really tiny, although the suites have two bathrooms, with hairdryer. There is a limited cabin service menu.

BERLITZ'S RATINGS		
	Possible	Achieved
Ship	500	264
Accommodation	200	108
Food	400	213
Service	400	237
Entertainment	100	46
Cruise	400	201

DINING: The Belvedere Restaurant is a charming dining room, with reasonably good service and an international cuisine, although standards are variable. There are two seatings. There is a limited selection of breads, cheeses, and fruits, and the choice of teas is poor. The dining room service is provided by Filipino and Indonesian waiters.

OTHER COMMENTS: The African Safari Club, a Swiss hotel and tour operator, has been specializing in land-based safaris and East African resort stays for over 30 years. The company, started by Swiss businessman Karl Ruedin, which manages 13 hotels in Kenya, has been operating this ship for several years (as African Safari Cruises and Star Line Cruises) in conjunction with these land-based safaris.

Royal Star is a charming little vessel (formerly operated by the now defunct Ocean Cruise Lines), with a well-balanced profile. There is an open-bridge policy for all passengers while the ship is at sea (weather permitting). The ship has reasonable open deck space for sunbathing (but do remember this operates for much of the year close to the equator, so the sun is *incredibly* strong).

Royal Star, now well over 40 years old, is quite suited to cruising in sheltered areas. Moderately clean and tidy, it has a reasonably warm, friendly, relaxed and personable ambience, although service finesse is lacking. Although it is now quite old, the interior décor is reasonably attractive, accented by brass railings and solid wood doors. Has a newly improved (but small) fitness center. There is little entertainment; it is very low-key (and low budget), and the crew provides much of it.

But the ship is only one part of the cruise/safari equation. The main reason for taking this ship is to get to the safari portion of your vacation, in the lands of the Masai Tribe. The scenery is spectacular, and this cruise/safari combination is a great way to experience the big animals of Kenya's best game parks. So the fact that the ship *is* old, small, and lacks the facilities, or the food, service or entertainment levels you might expect of better ships, should be kept in perspective. The official currency on board is the US dollar.

The African Safari Club has its own DC10 aircraft to transport you from Frankfurt (or Basle) to Mombasa (check with your travel agent in case a visa is needed). It also has an internal airline (Skytrail) to transport tourists to the high plains, as well as a fleet of four-wheel-drive vehicles.

WEAK POINTS: The vessel's cleanliness leaves much to be desired, particularly in the "back of house" areas.

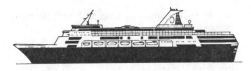

Ryndam
★★★★

Large Ship:	...............55,451 tons	Passengers		
Lifestyle:	...................Premium	(lower beds/all berths):	.....1,266/1,627	
Cruise Line:	.......Holland America Line	Passenger Space Ratio		
Former Names:	..................none	(lower beds/all berths):	........43.8/34.0	
Builder:	.............Fincantieri (Italy)	Crew/Passenger Ratio		
Original Cost:	............$215 million	(lower beds/all berths):	.........2.2/2.9	
Entered Service:	............Nov 1994	Navigation Officers:	.......British/Dutch	
Registry:	..............The Netherlands	Cabins (total):	633	
Length (ft/m):	.............719.3/219.3	Size Range (sq ft/m):	.....186.2–1,124.8/	
Beam (ft/m):	................101.0/30.8		17.3–104.5	
Draft (ft/m):	.................24.6/7.5	Cabins (outside view):	502	
Propulsion/Propellers:	.....diesel-electric	Cabins (interior/no view):	131	
	(34,560kW)/2	Cabins (for one person):	0	
Passenger Decks:	10	Cabins (with private balcony):	150	
Total Crew:	557	Cabins (wheelchair accessible):	6	

Cabin Current: ....110 and 220 volts
Elevators: 12
Casino (gaming tables): ....Yes
Slot Machines: ....Yes
Swimming Pools (outdoors): 1
Swimming Pools (indoors): 1
(magrodome)
Whirlpools: 2
Fitness Center: ....Yes
Sauna/Steam Room: ....Yes/No
Massage: ....Yes
Self-Service Launderette: ....Yes
Dedicated Cinema/Seats: Yes/249
Library: ....Yes
Classification Society: ...Lloyd's Register

OVERALL SCORE: 1,533 (OUT OF A POSSIBLE 2,000 POINTS)

ACCOMMODATION: This ranges from small interior (no view) cabins to a large penthouse suite, in 17 categories. All cabin televisions carry CNN and TNT.

The 148 interior (no view) and 336 outside (with a view) standard cabins have twin beds that convert to a queen-size bed, and there is a separate living space with sofa and coffee table. However, although the drawer space is generally good, the closet space is actually very tight, particularly for long cruises (although more than adequate for a 7-night cruise). The bathrooms are tiled, and compact but practical – they come with a good range of personal toiletry amenities. Bathrobes are also provided, as are hairdryers. The bathrooms are quite well laid out, but the bathtubs are small units better described as shower tubs. Some cabins have interconnecting doors – good for families with children – or older couples with their own butler/maid or nurse (*Ryndam, Veendam* only).

On Navigation Deck 28 suites have accommodation for up to four. These suites also have in-suite dining as an alternative to the dining room, for private, reclusive meals. These are very spacious, tastefully decorated and well laid-out, and have a separate living room, bedroom with two lower beds (convertible to a king-size bed), a good size living area, dressing room, plenty of closet and drawer space, marble bathroom with Jacuzzi tub.

The largest accommodation of all is a penthouse suite; there is only one, located on the starboard side of Navigation Deck. It has a king-size bed, walk-in closet with superb drawer space, oversize whirlpool bath and separate shower enclosure, living room, dressing room, large

BERLITZ'S RATINGS

	Possible	Achieved
Ship	500	418
Accommodation	200	162
Food	400	267
Service	400	299
Entertainment	100	77
Cruise	400	310

private balcony, pantry, mini-bar/refrigerator, a guest toilet and floor to ceiling windows.

DINING: The two-level Rotterdam Dining Room, located at the stern is quite dramatic, and has a grand staircase (although few seem to use it), panoramic views on three sides, and a music balcony. It has open seating for breakfast and lunch, and two seatings for dinner. The waiter stations in the dining room are very noisy for anyone seated adjacent to them. Fine Rosenthal china and cutlery are used (although there are no fish knives).

Unfortunately, Holland America Line food isn't as nice as the china it's placed on. It may be adequate for most passengers who are not used to better food, but it does not match the standard found aboard other ships in the premium segment of the industry. While USDA beef is of a good quality, fowl tends to be battery-tough, and most fish is overcooked and has the consistency of a baseball bat. What are also definitely *not* luxurious are the endless packets of sugar, and packets (instead of glass jars) of breakfast jam, marmalade and honey, and poor quality teas. While these may be suitable for a family diner, they do not belong aboard a ship that claims to have "award-winning cuisine." Dessert and pastry items are of good quality (specifically for American tastes), although there is much use of canned fruits and jellies. Forget the selection of "international" cheeses, however, as most of it didn't come from anywhere other than the USA – a country better known for processed, highly colored cheese slices than for fine cheese making. Note that Holland America Line can provide Kosher meals, but these are prepared ashore, frozen, and brought to your table sealed in their original containers (there is no Kosher kitchen on board).

A small alternative restaurant was introduced in 2002. The 66-seat Pinnacle Grill has Pacific Northwest cuisine (Dungeness crab, Alaska salmon, halibut and other regional specialties). The new venue (reservations are necessary, and a cover/service charge of $15 applies) was created out of a section of the Explorers Lounge and the private dining wing of the main dining room. A Bvlgari show plate, Rosenthal china, Reidel wine glasses, and Frette table linen are used. The Pinnacle Grill promises to be a much better dining experience than the main dining room.

There is also an extensive, dual-line (self-serve) Lido Buffet (one side is for smokers, the other side for non-smokers) for casual breakfasts and lunches. For the buffets, there is much use of canned fruits (good for dentally challenged older passengers) and packeted items, although there are several commercial low-calorie salad dressings. The choice of cheeses (and accompanying crackers) is very poor. The beverage station also lets it down, for it is no better than those found in family outlets ashore in the United States. In addition, a poolside grill provides basic American hamburgers and hot dogs.

OTHER COMMENTS: This is one of a series of four almost identical ships in the same series – the others being *Maasdam, Statendam,* and *Veendam*. The exterior styling is rather angular (some would say boxy – the funnel certainly is), although it is softened and balanced somewhat by the fact that the hull is painted black. There is a full wrap-around teakwood promenade deck outdoors – excellent for strolling, and, thankfully, no sign of synthetic turf anywhere. The deck lounge chairs are wood, and come with comfortable cushioned pads.

Inside, an asymmetrical layout breaks up the interiors and helps to reduce bottlenecks and congestion. The décor is softer, more sophisticated, and far less eclectic than in sister ship *Statendam*, while the interiors of *Ryndam* seem to improve further on the theme. In general, however, a restrained approach to interior styling is taken, using a mixture of contemporary materials combined with traditional woods and ceramics. There is, fortunately, little "glitz" anywhere.

What is outstanding is the array of artworks throughout the ship (costing about $2 million), assembled and nicely displayed to represent the fine Dutch heritage of Holland America Line. Also noticeable are the fine flower arrangements throughout the public areas and foyers – used to good effect to brighten up what some consider dull décor.

Atop the ship, with forward facing views that wrap around the sides is the Crow's Nest Lounge. By day it makes a fine observation lounge (particularly in Alaska),

while by night it turns into a nightclub with extremely variable lighting.

The three-deck high atrium foyer is quite stunning, although its sculptured centerpiece makes it look a little crowded, and leaves little room in front of the purser's office. A hydraulic magrodome (glass) roof covers the reasonably sized swimming pool/whirlpools and central Lido area (whose focal point is a large dolphin sculpture) so that this can be used in either fine or inclement weather.

The two-deck-high show lounge is basically well designed, but the ceiling is low and the sight lines from the balcony level are poor. There is a large and quite lovely and relaxing reference library. The company keeps its ships very clean and tidy throughout, and there is good passenger flow throughout.

Ryndam is a well-built ship, and has fairly decent interior fit and finish. Holland America Line is constantly fine-tuning its performance as a cruise operator and its regular passengers (almost all of whom are North American – there are few international passengers) find the company's ships very comfortable and well run. The company continues its strong maritime traditions, although the present food and service components still let the rest of the cruise experience down.

Holland America Line's many repeat passengers always seem to enjoy the fact that social dancing is on the menu. The company provides complimentary cappuccino and espresso coffees, and free ice cream during certain hours of the day aboard its ships, as well as hot hors d'oeuvres in all bars – something other major lines seem to have dropped, or charge extra for. In the final analysis, however, the score for this ship (and its sisters *Maasdam, Statendam* and *Veendam*) ends up just a disappointing tad under what it could be if the food and food service staff were better (more professional training might help). This ship is now deployed year-round in the Caribbean, where its rather dark interior décor contrasts with the strong sunlight of the sub-tropical region. The onboard currency is the US dollar.

WEAK POINTS: Standing in line for embarkation, disembarkation, shore tenders and for self-serve buffet meals is an inevitable aspect of cruising aboard all large ships. Although the Indonesian service staff is quite charming (for the most part), communication with them often proves frustrating for many passengers, and service is spotty and inconsistent. Passengers are forced to eat at the Lido Café on days when the dining room is closed for lunch (this is typically once or twice per cruise, depending on ship and itinerary). The single escalator is virtually useless. There is no bell push outside the suites. The charge to use the washing machines and dryers in the self-service launderette is really petty and irritating, particularly for the occupants of suites, as they pay high prices for their cruises. Room service is poor.

Saga Ruby – see Caronia
Saga Pearl – see Minerva
✓ Geirangerfjord
7/03

Saga Rose
★★★★

Mid-Size Ship: ....24,474 tons	Total Crew: 350	Cabins (wheelchair accessible): 8
Lifestyle: ....Premium	Passengers	Cabin Current: ....110 volts
Cruise Line: ....Saga Shipping	(lower beds/all berths): 584/620	Elevators: 4
Former Names: ......*Gripsholm, Sagafjord*	Passenger Space Ratio	Casino (gaming tables): ....No
Builder: ......Forges et Chantiers de la	(lower beds/all berths): 40.8/39.4	Slot Machines: ....No
Mediteranee (France)	Crew/Passenger Ratio	Swimming Pools (outdoors): 1
Original Cost: ....$30 million	(lower beds/all berths): 1.6/1.7	Swimming Pools (indoors): 1
Entered Service: .....Oct 1965/May 1997	Navigation Officers: ....British	Whirlpools: 0
Registry: ....The Bahamas	Cabins (total): 322	Fitness Center: ....Yes
Length (Ft/m): 619.6/188.88	Size Range (sq ft/m): 96.8–387.5/	Sauna/Steam Room: ....Yes/No
Beam (ft/m): 80.3/24.49	9.0–36.0	Massage: ....Yes
Draft (ft/m): 27.0/8.25	Cabins (outside view): 290	Self-Service Launderette: ....Yes
Propulsion/Propellers: ....diesel	Cabins (interior/no view): 32	Dedicated Cinema/Seats: Yes/181
(20,150kW)/2	Cabins (for one person): 60	Library: ....Yes
Passenger Decks: 7	Cabins (with private balcony): 26	Classification Society: Det Norske Veritas

OVERALL SCORE: 1,423 (OUT OF A POSSIBLE 2,000 POINTS)

ACCOMMODATION: There are 22 different grades: 3 designated as suites, 10 outside-view grades and 2 interior (no view) cabins (7 grades are designated for single occupancy, including one with a private balcony). Several cabins have interconnecting doors (useful for couples who, for whatever reason, like to have more space, and a bathroom each), and some have views obstructed by lifeboats.

No matter what grade you choose, all have fine quality fittings and appointments. All cabins have excellent insulation, and have been refurbished. There are also many single cabins (useful for passengers who enjoy the privacy of their own space without having to share with someone else). There is a generous amount of drawer, under-bed storage and illuminated closet space, and all cabins have European duvets, and a small personal lockbox. All bathrooms have a combination bathtub/shower.

The service provided by the cabin stewards and stewardesses is good. Soft, 100 percent cotton bathrobes and towels are provided, as well as several personal toiletry items: shampoo/conditioner, body lotion, bath gel, shower cap and soap.

Those who choose a cabin with a private balcony will find a teak decked balcony, with see-through railings, enough space for two deck lounge chairs and table, and an outside light. The cabin voltage is 110 volts, so do take an adapter if you have a 220-volt electrical appliance (such as a hairdryer).

DINING: The dining room is superb in the classic sense, and has a central ceiling two decks high, with large

BERLITZ'S RATINGS		
	Possible	Achieved
Ship	500	362
Accommodation	200	152
Food	400	280
Service	400	274
Entertainment	100	81
Cruise	400	274

ocean-view picture windows on the port and starboard sides and a horse-shoe-shaped grand staircase at the forward end. One-seating dining is featured at assigned tables, with tables for two (there are lots of these), four, six, eight or 10. The chinaware is Royal Doulton, while the flatware is also of a good quality.

The cuisine is quite creative, with a good variety of menu choices, and good-quality ingredients are used. The entrées are generally well presented, pastries and dessert items are of a good standard, and there is a reasonable choice of cheeses and fruits. There is a fairly comprehensive wine list, and the prices are very modest. Generally, the service is good, in the style of a grand hotel, from thoughtful and attentive waiters.

For casual meals, the Lido Café is available as a serve-yourself venue for breakfast and luncheon, and the outdoors aft of the café is expansive and very useful for al fresco dining. Several special theme buffets are provided for each cruise.

OTHER COMMENTS: This is still a finely proportioned, traditional cruise ships afloat today, and presents a sweeping profile and line of sheer, with clean, delightfully rounded lines, royal blue hull and well placed buff-colored funnel amidships. This ship has classic liner styling and profile, and really does *look* like a ship. Like an aging Bentley, this ship will hopefully not go out of style. In fine maritime tradition, the ship's bell and whistle are sounded at noon each day. There is a wrap-around teakwood promenade deck outdoors, and thick pads for all deck lounge chairs. The ship has expansive open deck and sunbathing areas, and lots of nooks and crannies for privacy.

This classic ship, built in the mid-1960s for long-distance cruising, provides a traditional ship experience for discriminating passengers over the age of 50 (note that those under 50 are not accepted as passengers). Constructed to a high standard (the French shipyard that built it actually went bankrupt as a result of the losses incurred), this ship has been quite well maintained and is operated with pride by the present owners, who have spent considerable sums of money in restoring it to fine condition.

The interiors are spacious, with high-ceilinged public rooms and tasteful décor (although there are, perhaps, too many low-back chairs). There are fine quality furnishings and fittings, including hardwoods, brass and stainless steel. In fact, it is quite difficult to find any plastic in the interior fittings, except for the laminates used to line the walls of the accommodation areas.

Public room facilities include a real ballroom/main lounge – among the nicest afloat for proper cocktail parties (where you stand and mingle, rather than sit), with furniture that can be moved for almost any configuration, and a large wood dance floor.

Other facilities include an indoor swimming pool (and adjacent fitness center) as well as an outdoor pool, lots of recreational space and delightful little nooks and crannies outdoors. The Britannia Lounge (observation lounge) is a fine room for social activities (or a spot of quiet reading), while the adjacent North Cape Bar provides a good bar and hangout for the cocktail crowd. The ship also has a delightful piano bar/lounge (Shakespeare's), a real, large traditional cinema (good for lectures as well as films), a nightclub, computer-learning center (in what used to be the upper level of the nightclub), and a good library.

Saga Rose fits like an old shoe – most passengers find it so comfortable that they don't want to discard it. It was made from the best materials and fits well as soon as you "put it on." The ship attracts passengers that appreciate quality surroundings, decent service, and low drink prices. Designed and created for long-distance cruising, it excels in quiet, refined living, and has numerous nights at sea and extended itineraries in surroundings of good comfort. Its high repeat passenger base confirms that there is a place for a ship such as this.

A voyage aboard her should prove to be a most pleasurable travel experience. Entertainment has now improved, and the program of string quartet and other classical concerts is much appreciated by passengers (especially delicious are the themes afternoon tea concerts: Chocolate, English, and Viennese).

This is classic cruising for its mainly British passengers (the ship is based at Dover and Southampton), under the banner of Saga Cruises. *Saga Rose* is a gracious old lady, now in her mid-thirties. Although the ship looks quite tired in places, it continues to offer passengers the chance to cruise in comfortable surroundings of high quality, with roaming worldwide itineraries, and service that is friendly and unobtrusive. Port taxes, insurance and gratuities are included, and if you pay for your onboard expenses with a Saga Visa Card you get a 5 percent discount. The onboard currency is the US dollar.

Note that in May 2003 another vessel will join the Saga Cruises fleet: *Saga Pearl* (ex-*Minerva*), which will be operated for six months a year for three years.

WEAK POINTS: The interiors of *Saga Rose* are quite dark (restful) and somber in places (particularly the accommodation hallways). There are few balcony cabins. Access to some of the upper grade cabins is a little disjointed. The elevator does not go down as far as the indoor pool deck ("C" Deck).

Removed 2006

St. Helena
★★★

Small Ship: ....6,767 tons	Passengers	Cabin Current: ....220 volts
Lifestyle: ....Standard	(lower beds/all berths): 98/128	Elevators: 1
Cruise Line: ....St. Helena Shipping	Passenger Space Ratio	Casino (gaming tables): ....No
Former Names: ....none	(lower beds/all berths): 69.0/52.8	Slot Machines: ....Yes (3)
Builder: ......A&P Appledore (Scotland)	Crew/Passenger Ratio	Swimming Pools (outdoors): 1
Original Cost: ....£32 million	(lower beds/all berths): 1.8/2.4	Swimming Pools (indoors): 0
Entered Service: ....Oct 1990	Navigation Officers: ..British/St. Helenian	Whirlpools: 0
Registry: ....England	Cabins (total): 49	Fitness Center: ....No
Length (ft/m): 344.4/105.0	Size Range (sq ft/m): 51.0–202.0/	Sauna/Steam Room: ....No/No
Beam (ft/m): 62.9/19.2	4.8–18.7	Massage: ....No
Draft (ft/m): 19.6/6.0	Cabins (outside view): 37	Self-Service Launderette: ....Yes
Propulsion/Propellers: ....diesel	Cabins (interior/no view): 12	Dedicated Cinema/Seats: ....No
(6,534kW)/2	Cabins (for one person): 0	Library: ....Yes
Passenger Decks:..................4	Cabins (with private balcony): 0	Classification Society: ...Lloyd's Register
Total Crew: 53	Cabins (wheelchair accessible): 1	

OVERALL SCORE: 1,155 (OUT OF A POSSIBLE 2,000 POINTS)

ACCOMMODATION: This is in two-, three-, or four-berth cabins (there are 11 grades, a lot for such a small vessel). These are quite simply furnished, yet comfortable. The bathrooms are quite small, and of the "me first, you next" variety. There are nine cabins that do not have private facilities.

DINING: The non-smoking dining room has two seatings, which, on such a small ship, is rather disruptive. The food is very British, with hearty breakfasts and a relatively simple menu, attractively presented on fine china. Afternoon tea, complete with freshly baked cakes, is a must. If you want tea or coffee at any time, you can make it yourself in the steward's pantry – even in the middle of the night.

OTHER COMMENTS: This is a fine little combination of contemporary working cargo-passenger ship that has all modern conveniences, including stabilizers and air-conditioning, although, unlike almost all cruise vessels, no bulbous bow exists. Passengers can even take their pets. It operates just like a full-size cruise vessel, and has an "open bridge" policy. The tiny swimming pool, however, is really only a "dip" pool.

Inside, the décor is tasteful and reasonably homey, though extremely plain, with little imagination when it comes to color and warmth. A connection with British royalty can be seen in a photograph of Prince Andrew and the Duchess of York prominently displayed on board (Prince Andrew named the ship when launched in 1989, and had visited both St. Helena and Ascension when he served in the Falklands War). There is a pleasant

BERLITZ'S RATINGS		
	Possible	Achieved
Ship	500	250
Accommodation	200	123
Food	400	261
Service	400	268
Entertainment	N/A	N/A
Cruise	500	253

library/reading lounge (audio recordings and videos are also available). A complimentary self-service launderette is available.

The brochure states that landing at Ascension is at times "a hazardous process" because of slippery and steep wharf steps – now that's telling it like it is. The atmosphere is decidedly British. The staff is warm, welcoming, eager to see you enjoying the journey, and delightful to sail with.

The ship operates a regular Cardiff–Tenerife–St. Helena–Ascension Island–Tristan Da Cunha–Capetown line service, which is like a mini-cruise, or long voyage, with lots of days at sea. There are, at present, about six round-trip sailings a year. The island of St. Helena, the final place of exile for Napoleon Bonaparte, was once owned by the East India Company, and that company's logo can be seen in the badge on the funnel.

Occasionally, a special theme sailing is organized, such as one for ornithologists. And for those who have yet to meet Father Neptune when crossing the Equator, rest assured that you will get to meet him.

Don't go for the ship, but go for the route, and to get to St. Helena and Ascension. Although the ship is comfortable, it really is little more than basic. The onboard currency is the US dollar.

WEAK POINTS: The plastic deck furniture spoils the outdoors (teak tables and chairs would not only look much better, but they would also withstand the inclement weather sometimes encountered while crossing this vast expanse of open ocean). The diesel engines are noisy.

Sapphire
★★★

Small Ship: . . . . .12,183 tons	Total Crew: 250	Cabin Current: . . . . .110 volts
Lifestyle: . . . . .Standard	Passengers	Elevators: 5
Cruise Line: . . . . .Louis Cruise Lines	(lower beds/all berths): 576/650	Casino (gaming tables): . . . . .Yes
Former Names: . . . . . .*Princesa Oceanica,*	Passenger Space Ratio	Slot Machines: .Yes
Sea Prince V, Sea Prince, Ocean	(lower beds/all berths): 21.1/18.7	Swimming Pools (outdoors): 1
Princess, Princess Italia, Italia	Crew/Passenger Ratio	Swimming Pools (indoors): 0
Builder: . . .Cantieri Navale Felszegi (Italy)	(lower beds/all berths): 2.3/2.6	Whirlpools: 0
Original Cost: .n/a	Navigation Officers: . . . . .Greek	Fitness Center: .No
Entered Service: . . . . .Aug 1967/Apr 1996	Cabins (total): 288	Sauna/Steam Room: . . . . .No/No
Registry: .Cyprus	Size Range (sq ft/m): 75.3–226.0/	Massage: . . . . .Yes
Length (ft/m): 491.7/149.8	7.0–21.0	Self-Service Launderette: . . . . .No
Beam (ft/m): 70.9/21.5	Cabins (outside view): 149	Dedicated Cinema/Seats: Yes/170
Draft (ft/m): 21.6/6.6	Cabins (interior/no view): 139	Library: . . . . .Yes
Propulsion/Propellers: . . . . .diesel	Cabins (for one person): 0	Classification Society: . . .Registro Navale
(11,050kW)/2	Cabins (with private balcony): 0	Italiano (RINA)
Passenger Decks: 8	Cabins (wheelchair accessible): 0	

OVERALL SCORE: 1,210 (OUT OF A POSSIBLE 2,000 POINTS)

ACCOMMODATION: The outside-view and interior (no view) cabins are available in several grades, the price depending on the location of the cabin and deck of location. The reasonable-sized cabins have pleasing, though plain, décor, furnishings, and fittings. In almost all cases, the cabin closet and drawer space is very limited. All have tiled bathrooms, but they are small. There is a 24-hour cabin service menu, although there is only a limited choice of items.

DINING: The dining room is charming and has an art deco feel, a raised center ceiling, and lovely etched glass dividers, but the noise level is high from the waiter stations. There are two seatings. Service is reasonably attentive from a willing, friendly staff. The cuisine is international, but do remember that this is a low-cost cruise, and so you shouldn't expect high-class cuisine.

For casual breakfast and luncheon, the Café de Paris (located indoors but looking out onto the pool deck) is the place (it also has a bar).

OTHER COMMENTS: *Sapphire* has had many previous names and owners, and an interesting life, including a time, when, in 1993, the ship sank in the Amazon River before being bought by its present owners and refitted. It has long, low-slung, handsome lines and a swept-back aft-placed funnel – all of which combine to provide a very attractive profile for this small ship. Louis Cruise

BERLITZ'S RATINGS

	Possible	Achieved
Ship	500	296
Accommodation	200	137
Food	400	239
Service	400	257
Entertainment	100	61
Cruise	400	220

Lines purchased the ship in 1995 and, following an extensive refurbishment, placed it into service in 1996. Since it took over the ship, the company has lavished much care and attention in keeping it in excellent condition.

There is a good amount of open deck and sunbathing space, but the heated swimming pool is very small, and is really only a "dip" pool.

Inside, the contemporary interior décor is fairly smart. There is a mix of attractive colors, together with much use of mirrored surfaces, which help to give the public rooms a feeling of spaciousness and warmth. Most public rooms do have a low ceiling height, however. Harry's Bar is perhaps the most popular gathering place, although there are few seats (the gaming tables are adjacent). There is also a cinema with comfortable seating.

This ship will take you to some decent destinations in good, contemporary surroundings, and in a relaxed, casual, yet comfortable style. The realistic, inexpensive price of this product is a bonus for first-time passengers seeking a cruise aboard a mid-sized ship that is still considered very much a "traditional" cruise ship rather than one of the floating mega-resorts operated by the major cruise lines.

WEAK POINTS: The ceilings are quite low throughout the ship, with the exception of a couple of the public rooms. Some cabins are subject to noise from the engines and generators.

Seabourn Legend
★★★★★

Small Ship:	9,975 tons	Total Crew:	150	Cabins (wheelchair accessible):	4
Lifestyle:	Luxury	Passengers		Cabin Current:	110 and 220 volts
Cruise Line:	Seabourn Cruise Line	(lower beds/all berths):	200/200	Elevators:	3
Former Names:	*Queen Odyssey,*	Passenger Space Ratio		Casino (gaming tables):	Yes
	Royal Viking Queen	(lower beds/all berths):	49.8/49.8	Slot Machines:	Yes
Builder:	Schichau Seebeckwerft	Crew/Passenger Ratio		Swimming Pools (outdoors):	1
	(Germany)	(lower beds/all berths):	1.3/1.3	Swimming Pools (indoors):	0
Original Cost:	$87 million	Navigation Officers:	Norwegian	Whirlpools:	3
Entered Service:	Mar 1992/July 1996	Cabins (total):	100	Fitness Center:	Yes
Registry:	Bahamas	Size Range (sq ft/m):	277.0–590.0/	Sauna/Steam Room:	Yes/Yes
Length (ft/m):	439.9/134.10		25.7–54.8	Massage:	Yes
Beam (ft/m):	62.9/19.20	Cabins (outside view):	100	Self-Service Launderette:	Yes
Draft (ft/m):	16.7/5.10	Cabins (interior/no view):	0	Dedicated Cinema/Seats:	No
Propulsion/Propellers:	diesel (7,280kW)/2	Cabins (for one person):	0	Library:	Yes
Passenger Decks:	6	Cabins (with private balcony):	6	Classification Society:	Det Norske Veritas

OVERALL SCORE: 1,786 (OUT OF A POSSIBLE 2,000 POINTS)

ACCOMMODATION: This is spread over three decks, and there are nine price categories, the price depending on size and location. All suites are comfortably large and very nicely equipped with everything one might need (they are, for example, larger than those aboard the smaller *Sea-Dream I* and *SeaDream II*, but then the ship is also larger, and carries almost twice as many passengers).

All suites have a sleeping area (European duvets are standard) and separate lounge area with VCR and television, vanity desk, mini-bar and refrigerator (stocked with soft drinks, and two bottles of your favorite liquor when you embark), a large walk-in closet (illuminated automatically when you open the door), electronic personal safe, and wall-mounted clock and barometer. However, many suites have a vanity desk with mirror opposite the bed, which definitely does not conform to the principles of *feng shui*. A full passenger list is also provided (Seabourn Cruise Line is one of only a handful of cruise lines to do so).

Marble-clad bathrooms have one or two washbasins (depending on the accommodation grade), a decent (but not full-sized) bathtub (four suites have a shower enclosure only – no bathtub), plenty of storage areas, 100 percent thick cotton towels, plush terrycloth bathrobe, designer soaps and Molton Brown personal amenity items. A selection of five special bath preparations by Molton Brown (Intoxicating Sensual Bath, Invigorating Ginseng Bath, Warming Eucalyptus Bath, Yuan Zhi Peacemaker Bath, and Oceanic De-Tox Bath) can be ordered from your stewardess, who will prepare your bath for you.

BERLITZ'S RATINGS		
	Possible	Achieved
Ship	500	461
Accommodation	200	186
Food	400	347
Service	400	353
Entertainment	100	86
Cruise	400	353

Course-by-course in-cabin dining is available during dinner hours (the cocktail table can be raised to form a dining table); there is 24-hour room service. Also provided are: personalized stationery, and fancy ticket wallet (suitably boxed and nicely packaged before your cruise). Non-smoking cabins are available. Menus for each dinner are delivered to your suite during the day.

In 2001, Seabourn Cruise Line added 36 French balconies to suites on two out of three accommodation decks. These are not balconies in the true sense of the word, but do have two doors that open wide onto a tiny teakwood balcony that is just 27 cm (about 10½ inches) wide. The balconies do allow you to have fresh sea air, however, together with some salt spray, as well as ascertain the outside temperature so that you know how to dress accordingly.

Four Owner's suites (Ibsen/Grieg, each measuring 530 sq. ft/49 sq. meters and Eriksson/Heyerdahl, each 575 sq. ft/53 sq. meters), and two Classic Suites (Queen Maud/Queen Sonja, each 400 sq. ft/37 sq. meters) offer superb, private living spaces. Each has a walk-in closet, second closet, full bathroom plus a guest toilet with washbasin. There is a fully secluded forward- or side-facing balcony, with sun lounge chairs and wooden drinks table (Ibsen/Grieg do not have a balconies). The living area has ample bookshelf space (including a complete edition of *Encyclopaedia Britannica*), large refrigerator/drinks cabinet, television and VCR (plus a second TV set in the bedroom). All windows, as well as the door to the balcony, have manually operated blackout blinds, and a complete blackout is possible in both bed-room and living room.

DINING: The part-marble, part-carpeted dining room (The Restaurant) has portholes and elegant décor but it is not as warm and intimate as that found aboard the smaller Sea-Dream ships, with their wood paneling. The silverware (150 gram weight – the best available) is by Robbe & Berking. Open-seating dining means that you can dine when you want, with whom you wish. Course-by-course meals can also be served in your cabin.

Dining is a memorable affair, and rightly so. The menus are nicely balanced, with a wide selection of foods and regional cuisine, although the Charlie Palmer-based cuisine includes some internationally unacceptable spelling (examples: filet of beef and fillet of fish both incorrectly spelled). Seabourn Cruise Line's fine, creative cuisine is artfully presented, with many items cooked to order. Special orders are available, and caviar is always available on request. Tableside flambeaus are presented, as are flaming desserts cooked at your table. There is always a good selection of exotic fruits and cheeses.

Each day, basic table wine is included for lunch and dinner, but all others (the decent ones) cost extra. The wine list is quite extensive, with prices ranging from moderate to high; many of the wines come from the smaller, more exclusive vineyards. The European dining room staff is hand picked and provides excellent, unhurried service.

In addition, relaxed breakfasts (available until at least 10am – civilized enough for late-risers) and lunch buffets and informal alternative, casual candlelight dinners (except on formal nights) can be taken in the popular Veranda Cafe, adjacent to the swimming pool, instead of in the dining room. In-suite, course-by-course dining is available at any time.

OTHER COMMENTS: This is a strikingly sleek ship with a handsome profile, almost identical in looks to *Seabourn Pride* and *Seabourn Spirit*, but built to a higher standard, with streamline "decorator" bars (made by Mercedes Benz) located along the side of the upper superstructure (could that make it Carbourne Cruise Line?), and a slightly different swept-over funnel design. Seabourn Cruise Line was originally called Signet Cruise Line, but changed its name due to the fact that it was already a registered name in North America. The ship has two fine mahogany water taxis for use as shore tenders. There is also an aft water sports platform and marina, which can be used in suitably calm warm-water areas. Water sports facilities include a small, enclosed "dip" pool, sea kayaks, snorkel equip-ment, windsurfers, water ski boat, and Zodiac inflatable boats. An open-bridge policy exists, so you can visit the ship's navigation bridge at almost any time (except during bad weather or especially tricky maneuvers).

Inside, there is a wide central passageway throughout the accommodation areas. The finest quality interior fix-tures, fittings, and fabrics have been combined in its sumptuous public areas to present an outstanding, ele-gant décor, with warm color combinations (there is no glitz anywhere) and some fine artwork. A 360-degree mural in the reception lobby has the ship's interior designer painted into the mural. The dress code, relaxed by day, is more formal at night.

A small but well equipped health spa/fitness center (The Spa at Seabourn) has sauna and steam rooms (with separate facilities for men and women), and a separate exercise room, with video tapes for private, individual aerobics workouts, and a beauty salon. Spa treatment prices are equal to those in an expensive land-based spa (examples: Hot Stone Therapy $178 for 75 minutes).

During the past two years, there have been many com-plaints about how the standards aboard the Seabourn ships have gone down, particularly with regards to main-tenance (the Seabourn ships are over 10 years old), and that food, presentation and service wasn't what it used to be. However, the company has now turned this around, and attention has been given to the ships. Today, I am happy to report that the product delivered is extremely good, and is more consistent (particularly in areas of food and service) than, say, the Silversea Cruises ships, which are larger and carry more passengers. However, the Seabourn ships are smaller than the Silversea ships, and larger than, and not quite as intimate as the Sea-Dreams, although the food, presentation and service have returned to their former fine levels.

Seabourn Legend provides discerning passengers with an outstanding level of personal service and an utterly civ-ilized cruise experience. For a grand, small ship cruise experience in fine surroundings, with only just over 100 other couples as neighbors, this ship is difficult to beat. All drinks (with the exception of premium brands and con-noisseur wines) are included, as are gratuities, fine aroma-therapy bath selections from Molton Brown and large soaps by Bronnley, Chanel and Hermès, short massages on deck, open-seating dining, use of watersports equipment, one complimentary *Exclusively Seabourn* shore excursion per cruise, and movies under the stars. *Seabourn Legend* is able to cruise to places where large cruise ships can't, thanks to its ocean-yacht size.

Note that port charges and insurance are not included. The onboard currency is the US dollar.

In the final analysis, both the Seabourns and Sea-Dreams provide an excellent product, and both are supe-rior to other upscale ships such as *Seven Seas Navigator* and *Seven Seas Mariner*, but still not quite up to the stan-dard of *Europa*.

WEAK POINTS: The plastic chairs on the open decks really are unacceptable for this type of ship and should be changed to stainless steel or teak. There is no wrap-around promenade deck outdoors. The range of cigars offered is very limited in comparison to ships such as *Europa*. The Club suffers from over-amplified music. Non-American passengers should note that almost all entertainment and activities are geared towards American tastes, despite the increasingly international passenger mix.

Seabourn Pride
★★★★★

Small Ship: ....9,975 tons	Passengers	Cabin Current: ....110 and 220 volts
Lifestyle: ....Luxury	(lower beds/all berths): 200/200	Elevators: 3
Cruise Line: ......Seabourn Cruise Line	Passenger Space Ratio	Casino (gaming tables): ....Yes
Former Names: ....none	(lower beds/all berths): 49.8/49.8	Slot Machines: ....Yes
Builder: ....Seebeckwerft (Germany)	Crew/Passenger Ratio	Swimming Pools (outdoors): 1
Original Cost: ....$50 million	(lower beds/all berths): 1.3/1.3	(plus 1 aft marina-pool)
Entered Service: ....Dec 1988	Navigation Officers: ....Norwegian	Swimming Pools (indoors): 0
Registry: ....Bahamas	Cabins (total): 100	Whirlpools: 3
Length (ft/m): 439.9/134.10	Size Range (sq ft/m): 277.0–575.0/	Fitness Center: ....Yes
Beam (ft/m): 62.9/19.20	25.7–53.4	Sauna/Steam Room: ....Yes/Yes
Draft (ft/m): 16.8/5.15	Cabins (outside view): 100	Massage: ....Yes
Propulsion/Propellers: ....diesel	Cabins (interior/no view): 0	Self-Service Launderette: ....Yes
(5,355kW)/2	Cabins (for one person): 0	Dedicated Cinema/Seats: ....No
Passenger Decks: 6	Cabins (with private balcony): 6	Library: ....Yes
Total Crew: 150	Cabins (wheelchair accessible): 4	Classification Society: Det Norske Veritas

OVERALL SCORE: 1,785 (OUT OF A POSSIBLE 2,000 POINTS)

ACCOMMODATION: The all-outside cabins (called suites in brochure-speak) are comfortably large and beautifully equipped with everything, including refrigerator, personal safe, television and VCR, personalized stationery, and large walk-in illuminated closet with wooden hangers. Electric blackout blinds are provided for the large windows in addition to curtains. All cabinetry is made of blond woods, with softly rounded edges, and cabin doors are neatly angled away from passageway (each pair of cabins also has a further door fronting on the passageway outside). The cabin ceilings are, however, quite plain.

All the suites are comfortably large and beautifully equipped with everything one could need (they are, for example, larger than those aboard the smaller *SeaDream I* and *SeaDream II*, but then the ship is also larger, and carries almost twice as many passengers).

All suites have a sleeping area (European duvets are standard) and separate lounge area with VCR and television, vanity desk, mini-bar and refrigerator (stocked with soft drinks, and two bottles of your favorite liquor when you embark), a large walk-in closet (illuminated automatically when you open the door), electronic personal safe, and wall-mounted clock and barometer. However, many suites have a vanity desk with mirror opposite the bed, which does not conform with the principles of *feng shui*. A full passenger list is also provided (Seabourn Cruise Line is one of only a handful of cruise lines to do so).

Marble-clad bathrooms feature one or two washbasins (depending on the accommodation grade), a decent (but

BERLITZ'S RATINGS

	Possible	Achieved
Ship	500	460
Accommodation	200	186
Food	400	347
Service	400	353
Entertainment	100	86
Cruise	400	353

not full-sized) bathtub (four suites have a shower enclosure only – no bathtub), plenty of storage areas, 100 percent thick cotton towels, plush terrycloth bathrobe, designer soaps and Molton Brown personal amenity items.

A selection of five special bath preparations by Molton Brown can be ordered from your stewardess, who will prepare your bath for you: Intoxicating Sensual Bath, Invigorating Ginseng Bath, Warming Eucalyptus Bath, Yuan Zhi Peacemaker Bath, and Oceanic De-Tox Bath.

In 2001, Seabourn Cruise Line added 36 French balconies to suites on two out of three accommodation decks. These are not balconies in the true sense of the word, but they do have two doors that open wide, onto a tiny teakwood balcony that is just 27 cm (about 10½ inches) wide. The balconies allow you to have fresh sea air, however, together with some salt spray, as well as ascertain the outside temperature so that you know how to dress accordingly.

Course-by-course in-cabin dining is available during dinner hours (the cocktail table can be raised to form a dining table); there is 24-hour room service. Also provided are: personalized stationery, and fancy ticket wallet (suitably boxed and nicely packaged before your cruise). Non-smoking cabins are available. Menus for each dinner are delivered to your suite during the day.

Four Owner's suites (King Haakon/King Magnus, each measuring 530 sq. ft/49 sq. meters, and Amundsen/Nansen, each 575 sq. ft/53 sq. meters), and two Classic Suites (King Harald/King Olav, each 400 sq. ft/ 37 sq. meters) offer superb, private living spaces. Each has a walk-in closet, second closet, full bathroom plus a guest toilet with washbasin. There is a fully secluded forward- or side-facing balcony, with sun lounge chairs and wooden drinks table. The living area has ample bookshelf space (including a complete edition of *Encyclopedia Britannica*), large refrigerator/drinks cabinet, television and VCR (plus a second TV set in the bedroom). All windows, as well as the door to the balcony, have manually operated blackout blinds, and a complete blackout is possible in both bedroom and living room.

DINING: The part marble, part carpeted dining room (The Restaurant) has portholes and elegant décor but it is not as warm and intimate as that found aboard the smaller Sea-Dream ships, with their wood paneling. The silverware (150 gram weight – the best available) is by Robbe & Berking. Open-seating dining means that you can dine when you want, with whom you wish. Course-by-course meals can also be served in your cabin.

The menus are nicely balanced, with a wide selection of foods and regional cuisine, although the Charlie Palmer-based cuisine includes some internationally unacceptable spelling (examples: filet of beef and fillet of fish both incorrectly spelled). Seabourn Cruise Line's fine, creative cuisine is artfully presented, with many items cooked to order. Special orders are available, and caviar is always available on request. Tableside flambeaus are presented, as are flaming desserts cooked at your table. There is always a good selection of exotic fruits and cheeses.

Each day, basic table wine is included for lunch and dinner, but all others (the decent ones) cost extra. The wine list is quite extensive, with prices ranging from moderate to high; many of the wines come from the smaller, more exclusive vineyards. The hand-picked European dining room staff provides excellent, unhurried service.

In addition, relaxed breakfasts (available until at least 11am – civilized enough for late-risers) and lunch buffets and informal alternative, casual candlelight dinners (except on formal nights) can be taken in the popular Veranda Café adjacent to the swimming pool, instead of in the dining room. In-suite, course-by-course dining is available at any time.

OTHER COMMENTS: This luxuriously appointed cruise vessel has sleek exterior styling handsome profile with swept-back, rounded lines, and is an identical sister vessel to *Seabourn Spirit*. It has two fine mahogany water taxis for use as shore tenders. There is also an aft water sports platform and marina, which can be used in suitably calm warm-water areas. Water sports facilities include a small, enclosed "dip" pool, sea kayaks, snorkel equipment, windsurfers, water ski boat, and Zodiac inflatable boats. An open-bridge policy exists, so you can visit the ship's navigation bridge at almost any time (except during bad weather or especially tricky maneuvers).

There is an aft water sports platform and marina, used in suitably calm, warm-water areas. Water sports facilities include an aft platform, enclosed marina pool, banana boat, pedalos, scuba, sea kayaks, snorkel, windsurfers, and water-ski boat.

There is a wide central passageway throughout the accommodation areas. Inviting, sumptuous public areas have warm colors. Fine quality interior fixtures, fittings, and fabric combine to present an outstanding, elegant décor, color combinations, and artwork. For a small ship, there is wide range of public rooms. These include a main lounge (staging small cabaret shows), nightclub (this was expanded in 1999), an observation lounge with bar, large, deep armchairs, and a cigar smoking area complete with cabinet, cigar humidor and small selection of good cigars (this was added in 1999). There is a small business center, small meeting room, and a small casino with roulette and blackjack tables, with a few slot machines tucked away.

A small, but well-equipped health spa/fitness center has sauna and steam rooms (separate facilities for men and women), and a separate exercise room, with video tapes for private, individual aerobics workouts, and a beauty salon.

Not for the budget-minded, this ship is for those desiring the utmost in supremely elegant, stylish, small-ship surroundings, but is perhaps too small for long voyages in open waters.

During the past two years, there have been many complaints about falling standards aboard the Seabourn ships had gone down, particularly with regards to maintenance (they are now over 10 years old), and that food, presentation and service wasn't what it used to be. However, the company has now turned this around, and the product delivered is extremely good.

Seabourn Pride provides discerning passengers with an outstanding level of personal service and an utterly civilized cruise experience. For a grand, small ship cruise experience in fine surroundings, with only just over 100 other couples as neighbors, this ship is difficult to beat. All drinks (with the exception of premium brands and connoisseur wines) are included, as are gratuities, fine aromatherapy bath selections from Molton Brown and large soaps by Bronnley, Chanel and Hermès, short massages on deck, open-seating dining, use of watersports equipment, one complimentary *Exclusively Seabourn* shore excursion per cruise, and movies under the stars. *Seabourn Pride* is able to cruise to places where large cruise ships can't, due to its ocean-yacht size. Note that port charges and insurance are not included. The onboard currency is the US dollar.

WEAK POINTS: The deck lounge chairs are plastic (although light and easy to store, they are second-class, and should be made of wood or stainless steel). There is no wrap-around promenade deck outdoors. There are no seat cushions on the wooden chairs at the indoor/outdoor cafe. There is only one dryer in the self-service launderette. Non-American passengers should note that almost all entertainment and activities are geared towards American tastes, despite the increasingly international passenger mix.

Seabourn Spirit
★★★★★

Small Ship: . . . . .9,975 tons	Passengers	Cabin Current: . . . . .110 and 220 volts
Lifestyle: .Luxury	(lower beds/all berths): 200/200	Elevators: 3
Cruise Line: . . . . . . .Seabourn Cruise Line	Passenger Space Ratio	Casino (gaming tables): . . . . .Yes
Former Names: . . . . .none	(lower beds/all berths): 49.8/49.8	Slot Machines: . . . . .Yes
Builder: . . . . .Seebeckwerft (Germany)	Crew/Passenger Ratio	Swimming Pools (outdoors): 1
Original Cost: . . . .$50 million	(lower beds/all berths): 1.3/1.3	(plus aft marina-pool)
Entered Service: . . . . .Nov 1989	Navigation Officers: . . . . .Norwegian	Swimming Pools (indoors): 0
Registry: . . . . .Bahamas	Cabins (total): 100	Whirlpools: 3
Length (ft/m): 439.9/134.10	Size Range (sq ft/m): 277.0–575.0/	Fitness Center: . . . . .Yes
Beam (ft/m): 62.9/19.20	25.7–53.4	Sauna/Steam Room: . . . . .Yes/Yes
Draft (ft/m): 16.8/5.15	Cabins (outside view): 100	Massage: . . . . .Yes
Propulsion/Propellers: . . . . .diesel	Cabins (interior/no view): 0	Self-Service Launderette: . . . . .Yes
(5,355kW)/2	Cabins (for one person): 0	Dedicated Cinema/Seats: . . . . .No
Passenger Decks: 6	Cabins (with private balcony): 6	Library: . . . . .Yes
Total Crew: .150	Cabins (wheelchair accessible): 4	Classification Society: Det Norske Veritas

---

OVERALL SCORE: 1,785 (OUT OF A POSSIBLE 2,000 POINTS)

ACCOMMODATION: The all-outside cabins (called suites in brochure-speak) are comfortably large and beautifully equipped with everything, including refrigerator, personal safe, VCR, personalized stationery, and large walk-in illuminated closet with wooden hangers. Electric blackout blinds are provided for the large windows in addition to curtains. All cabinetry is made of blond woods, with softly rounded edges, and cabin doors are neatly angled away from passageway (each pair of cabins also has a further door fronting on the passageway outside). The cabin ceilings are, however, quite plain.

All the suites are comfortably large and beautifully equipped with everything one could need (they are, for example, larger than those aboard the smaller *SeaDream I* and *SeaDream II*, but then the ship is also larger, and carries almost twice as many passengers).

All suites feature a sleeping area (European duvets are standard) and separate lounge area with VCR and television, vanity desk, mini-bar and refrigerator (stocked with soft drinks, and two bottles of your favorite liquor when you embark), a large walk-in closet (illuminated automatically when you open the door), electronic personal safe, and wall-mounted clock and barometer. However, many suites have a vanity desk with mirror opposite the bed, which definitely does not conform to the principles of *feng shui*. A full passenger list is also provided (Seabourn Cruise Line is one of only a handful of cruise lines to do so).

Marble-clad bathrooms feature one or two wash-basins (depending on the accommodation grade), a

BERLITZ'S RATINGS

	Possible	Achieved
Ship	500	460
Accommodation	200	186
Food	400	347
Service	400	353
Entertainment	100	86
Cruise	400	353

decent (but not full-sized) bathtub (four suites have a shower enclosure only – no bathtub), plenty of storage areas, 100 percent thick cotton towels, plush terrycloth bathrobe, designer soaps and Molton Brown personal amenity items. A selection of five special bath preparations by Molton Brown can be ordered from your stewardess, who will prepare your bath for you: Intoxicating Sensual Bath, Invigorating Ginseng Bath, Warming Eucalyptus Bath, Yuan Zhi Peacemaker Bath, and Oceanic De-Tox Bath.

Course-by-course in-cabin dining is available during dinner hours (the cocktail table can be raised to form a dining table); there is 24-hour room service. Also provided are: personalized stationery, and fancy ticket wallet (suitably boxed and nicely packaged before your cruise). Non-smoking cabins are available. Menus for each dinner are delivered to your suite during the day.

In 2001, Seabourn Cruise Line added 36 French balconies to suites on two out of three accommodation decks. These are not balconies in the true sense of the word, but they do feature two doors that open wide, onto a tiny teakwood balcony that is just 27 cm (about 10½ inches) wide. The balconies do allow you to have fresh sea air, however, together with some salt spray, as well as ascertain the outside temperature so that you know how to dress accordingly.

Four Owner's suites (Bergen/Oslo, each measuring 530 sq. ft/49 sq. meters and Copenhagen/Stockholm, each 575 sq. ft/53 sq. meters), and two Classic Suites (Helsinki/Reykjavik, each 400 sq. ft/37 sq. meters) offer superb, private living spaces. Each has a walk-in closet, second closet, full bathroom plus a guest toilet with washbasin. There is a fully secluded forward- or side-facing balcony, with sun lounge chairs and wooden drinks table. The living area has ample bookshelf space (including a complete edition of *Encyclopedia Britannica*), large refrigerator/drinks cabinet, television and VCR (plus a second TV set in the bedroom). All windows, as well as the door to the balcony, have manually operated blackout blinds, and a complete blackout is possible in both bedroom and living room.

DINING: The part-marble, part-carpeted dining room (The Restaurant) has portholes and elegant décor but it is not as warm and intimate as that found aboard the smaller SeaDream ships, with their wood paneling. The silverware (150 gram weight – the best available) is by Robbe & Berking. Open-seating dining means that you can dine when you want, with whom you wish. Course-by-course meals can also be served in your cabin.

The menus are nicely balanced, with a wide selection of foods and regional cuisine, although the Charlie Palmer-based cuisine includes some internationally unacceptable spelling (examples: filet of beef and fillet of fish both incorrectly spelled). Seabourn Cruise Line's fine, creative cuisine is artfully presented, with many items cooked to order. Special orders are available, and caviar is always available on request. Tableside flambeaus are presented, as are flaming desserts cooked at your table. There is always a good selection of exotic fruits and cheeses.

Basic table wine is included for lunch and dinner, but all others (the decent ones) cost extra. The wine list is quite extensive, with prices ranging from moderate to high; many of the wines come from the smaller, more exclusive vineyards. The hand-picked European dining room staff provides excellent, unhurried service.

In addition, relaxed breakfasts (available until at least 11am – civilized enough for late-risers) and lunch buffets and informal alternative, casual candlelight dinners (except on formal nights) can be taken in the popular Veranda Café adjacent to the swimming pool, instead of in the dining room. In-suite, course-by-course dining is available at any time.

OTHER COMMENTS: This luxuriously appointed cruise vessel has sleek exterior styling handsome profile with swept-back, rounded lines, and is an identical sister vessel to *Seabourn Spirit*. It has two fine mahogany water taxis for use as shore tenders. There is also an aft water sports platform and marina, which can be used in suitably calm warm-water areas. Water sports facilities include a small, enclosed "dip" pool, sea kayaks, snorkel equipment, windsurfers, water ski boat, and Zodiac inflatable boats. An open-bridge policy exists, so you can visit the ship's navigation bridge at almost any time (except during bad weather or especially tricky maneuvers).

There is an aft water sports platform and marina,

used in suitably calm, warm-water areas. Water sports facilities include an aft platform, enclosed marina pool, banana boat, pedalos, scuba, sea kayaks, snorkel, windsurfers, and water-ski boat.

There is a wide central passageway throughout the accommodation areas. Inviting, sumptuous public areas have warm colors. Fine quality interior fixtures, fittings, and fabric combine to present an outstanding, elegant décor, color combinations, and artwork. For a small ship, there is wide range of public rooms. These include a main lounge (staging small cabaret shows), nightclub (expanded in 1999), an observation lounge with bar, large, deep armchairs, and a cigar smoking area complete with cabinet, cigar humidor and small selection of good cigars (this was added in 1999). There is also a small business center, small meeting room, even a small casino with roulette and blackjack tables, with a few slot machines tucked away.

A small but well equipped health spa/fitness center has sauna and steam rooms (separate facilities for men and women), and a separate exercise room, with video tapes for private, individual aerobics workouts, and a beauty salon.

During the past two years, there have been many complaints about falling standards aboard the Seabourn ships had gone down, particularly with regards to maintenance (they are now over 10 years old), and that food, presentation and service wasn't what it used to be. However, the company has now turned this around, and the product delivered is extremely good.

Seabourn Pride provides discerning passengers with an outstanding level of personal service and an utterly civilized cruise experience. For a grand, small ship cruise experience in fine surroundings, with only just over 100 other couples as neighbors, this ship is difficult to beat. All drinks (with the exception of premium brands and connoisseur wines) are included, as are gratuities, fine aromatherapy bath selections from Molton Brown and large soaps by Bronnley, Chanel and Hermès, short massages on deck, open-seating dining, use of watersports equipment, one complimentary *Exclusively Seabourn* shore excursion per cruise, and movies under the stars. *Seabourn Pride* is able to cruise to places where large cruise ships can't, due to its ocean-yacht size. Note that port charges and insurance are not included. The onboard currency is the US dollar.

WEAK POINTS: The deck lounge chairs are plastic (although light and easy to store, they are second-class, and should be made of wood or stainless steel). There is no wrap-around promenade deck outdoors. There are no seat cushions on the wooden chairs at the indoor/outdoor café. There is only one dryer in the self-service launderette. Non-American passengers should note that almost all entertainment and activities are geared towards American tastes, despite the increasingly international passenger mix.

SeaDream I
★★★★★

Small Ship:	...............4,260 tons	Passengers		Cabins (wheelchair accessible):	0

Small Ship: ....4,260 tons
Lifestyle: ....Luxury
Cruise Line: ......Seadream Yacht Club
Former Names: .....Seabourn Goddess I,
Sea Goddess I
Builder: ....Wartsila (Finland)
Entered Service: .....Apr 1984/May 2002
Registry: ....The Bahamas
Length (ft/m): 343.8/104.81
Beam (ft/m): 47.9/14.60
Draft (ft/m): 13.6/4.17
Propulsion/Propellers: ....diesel
(3,540kW)/2
Passenger Decks: 5
Total Crew: 89

Passengers
(lower beds/all berths): 108/108
Passenger Space Ratio
(lower beds/all berths): 39.4/39.4
Crew/Passenger Ratio
(lower beds/all berths): 1.2/1.2
Navigation Officers: ....Norwegian/
Scandinavian
Cabins (total): 54
Size Range (sq ft/m): 195.0–490.0/
18.1–45.5
Cabins (outside view): 58
Cabins (interior/no view): 0
Cabins (for one person): 0
Cabins (with private balcony): 0

Cabins (wheelchair accessible): 0
Cabin Current: ....110 and 220 volts
Elevators: 1
Casino (gaming tables): ....Yes
Slot Machines: ....Yes
Swimming Pools (outdoors): 1
Swimming Pools (indoors): 0
Whirlpools: 1
Fitness Center: ....Yes
Sauna/Steam Room: ....Yes/No
Massage:.........................Yes
Self-Service Launderette: ....No
Dedicated Cinema/Seats: ....No
Library: ....Yes
Classification Society: ...Lloyd's Register

OVERALL SCORE: 1,790 (OUT OF A POSSIBLE 2,000 POINTS)

ACCOMMODATION: There are three types, and five price categories: Yacht Club (standard) Cabin, Commodore Club Suite, and Owner's Suite.

YACHT CLUB CABINS: Incorrectly called "suites" in the brochure, the standard cabins are, more correctly, fully equipped "mini-suites" with an outside view through windows or portholes (depending on the deck and price category you choose). Each measures 195 sq. ft (18.1 sq. meters), which is not large by today's cruise ship standards – however, it *is* large compared to cabins aboard many private motor yachts, and *extremely* large when compared to ocean-going racing yachts. The sleeping area has twin beds (these can be put together to form a queen-size configuration); beds are positioned next to the window (or porthole) so that you can entertain in the living area without going past the sleeping area (as you must aboard the slightly larger Seabourn or Silversea ships, for example); a curtain separates the sleeping and lounge areas. All cabinetry and furniture is of thick blond wood, with nicely rounded edges.

A long vanity desk in the sleeping area has a large mirror above it (however, there is no three-sided mirror for women to see the back of their hair) and two small drawers for cosmetic items; there is also a brass clock located on one wall. Note that *feng shui* advises against placing a mirror opposite your bed. In the lounge area, a long desk has six drawers, plus a vertical cupboard unit that houses a sensible safe, refrigerator and drinks cabinet (stocked your choice of drinks). There is also a 20-inch (51.5-mm) flat-screen television, CD and DVD

BERLITZ'S RATINGS

	Possible	Achieved
Ship	500	441
Accommodation	200	173
Food	400	371
Service	400	370
Entertainment	N/A	N/A
Cruise	500	435

player, and an MP3 audio player (with a choice of over 100 selections). The beds have the finest linens, including thick cotton duvets, and non-allergenic pillows (and duvets) are also available. There's little room under the beds for luggage, although this can be taken away and stored for you.

One drawback is the fact that the insulation between cabins is not as good as it could be, although rarely does this present a problem, as most passengers aboard the two SeaDreams are generally extremely quiet, considerate types who are allergic to noise. Incidentally, a sleep suit (pyjama) is supplied in case you want to sleep out on deck under the stars in one of the on-deck two-person beds, but more of those later.

Since the ship became *SeaDream I,* all bathrooms have been totally refurbished. The old tiling has been discarded and replaced by a new décor that is more hip and trendy, with softer colors and larger (beige) marble tiles. The former (tiny) sit-in bathtubs have been taken out (these will be missed by many regular European passengers) and replaced by a multi-jet power glassed-in shower enclosure. A new washbasin set in a marble-look surround and two glass shelves make up the facilities, while an under-sink cupboard provides further space for larger personal toiletry items. Bulgari personal toiletry amenities are provided. Gorgeously thick, plush, 100 percent cotton SeaDream-logo bathrobes and towels are also supplied. However, the bathrooms *are* small (particularly for those who are of larger than average build), despite their having been completely rebuilt (although the doors still open inward), so space inside really is at a premium. The toilet is located in a rather awkward position, and, unless you close the door, you can see yourself in the mirror facing of the closets, opposite the bathroom door.

COMMODORE CLUB SUITES: For larger accommodation, choose one of 16 Commodore Club Suites. These consist of two standard cabins with an interconnecting door, thus providing you with a healthy 380 sq. ft (36 sq. meters) of living space. One cabin is made into a lounge and dining room (with table and up to four chairs), while the other becomes your sleeping area. The advantage is that you get two bathrooms (his and hers).

OWNER'S SUITE: For the largest living space aboard this ship, go for the Owner's Suite. This measures a grand 490 sq. ft (45.5 sq. meters). It's the only accommodation with a bathroom that incorporates a real full-sized bathtub, and a separate show enclosure.

All passengers receive personalized stationery, a personal email address, a sleep suit, Bulgari personal toiletry amenities, 24-hour room service, and "sweet dreams" chocolates.

DINING: The dining salon is extremely elegant and inviting, and has bird's-eye maple wood paneled walls and wood-accented décor. It is cozy, yet with plenty of space around each table for fine service, and the ship provides a floating culinary celebration in an open-seating arrangement, so you can dine whenever, and with whomever you want. A grand piano is located at one end, for quiet dinner music. Course-by-course meals can also be served in your cabin, or out on deck.

Tables can be configured for two, four, six, or eight. They are immaculately laid with settings of real glass base (show) plates, pristine white monogrammed table linen, and fresh flowers, while wall sconces house some superb glass ornaments). Candlelit dinners are part of the inviting setting. There is even a box of spare spectacles for menu reading in case you forget your own. You get leather-bound menus, and supremely attentive, close to impeccable personalized European service.

The SeaDream Yacht Club experience really is all about dining. This ship will not disappoint, and culinary excellence prevails. Only the very freshest and finest quality ingredients are used in the best culinary artistry. Fine, unhurried European service is provided.

The ship features exquisite, creative cuisine, and everything is prepared individually to order. Special orders are welcomed, and flaming desserts are showcased at your tableside. You can also dine, course by course in your suite for any meal, at any time (you can also eat à la carte 24 hours a day if you wish). There is plenty of fine quality caviar, at any time of the day or night. Thankfully, there's never a hint of baked Alaska!

Good-quality table wines are included in the cruise fare for lunch and dinner. Real wine connoisseurs, however, will appreciate the availability of an extra wine

list, of special vintages and premier crus (at extra cost). If you want to do something different with a loved one, you can also arrange to dine one evening on the open (but covered) deck, overlooking the swimming pool and stern – it can be a magical and very romantic setting.

A new, informal Topside Restaurant has been created from what used to be the outdoor café. Now it has glass sides and a glass roof. Informal dining is the theme here, whether for breakfast, lunch or dinner. Teak tables and chairs add an additional (but essential and expected) touch of finery. And if you are hungry, no matter at what time of the day or night, you can "raid the pantry" and find something tasty to eat. Additionally, caviar (sevruga malossol) and champagne (Pommery) are always available whenever you want them.

OTHER COMMENTS: This small ship was originally built with money from about 800 investors, and operated under the Norske Cruise banner. It has an ultra-sleek profile, with deep blue hull and white superstructure, and the ambience of a private club. After the ship was acquired by SeaDream Yacht Club in 2001, it was completely refurbished, with many changes to both public rooms and outdoor areas, and several new features were added to create what is now an extremely contemporary, chic, and desirable vessel.

At the stern is a small, retractable, water sports platform. Equipment carried for sporting types include a water-ski boat, sailboat, two wave runners (jet skis), seven kayaks, wake boards, snorkeling equipment and two Zodiacs.

The use of all this equipment is *included* in the price of your cruise. Note, however, the sea conditions have to be just right (minimal swell) for these items to be used, which, on average is once or twice in a 7-night cruise. You may also be allowed to swim off the stern platform if conditions permit. Ten mountain bikes are also carried, so you can pedal away when ashore.

A new "top of the yacht" bar, crafted in warm wood, has been added, as have eight special alcoves equipped with two-person sun loungers with very thick pads. At the front part of the deck there are more sun loungers and a couple of hammocks, as well as a golf simulator (with a choice of 30 courses). You can sleep under the stars if you wish and sleep suits (pyjama) are provided.

Inside, there is a delightful feeling of unabashed but discreet sophistication. Elegant, chic public rooms have flowers and pot pourri everywhere. The main social gathering places are the lounge, a delightful library/ living room with a selection of about 800 books, a piano bar, and a casino (two blackjack tables and five slot machines). The library has been enlarged and moved to what formerly a lounge area, and now provides a very comfortable, warm and cozy setting.

A new (Asian-style) spa has been created, housed together with a small gymnasium, and beauty salon. There are three massage rooms, a sauna, and steam shower enclosure. Meanwhile, golfers should enjoy the electronic golf simulator, with a choice of several golf courses to play.

The two SeaDream ships really are the ultimate boutique vessels – like having your own private yacht in which hospitality and anticipation are art forms practiced to a high level. The staff is delightful and accommodating ("no" is not in their vocabulary); if there is anything special you want, you have only to ask, and they will be only too happy to oblige – in the style of the best European hotels. The dress code is resort casual by day (one could almost live in one's bathrobe), informal by night. Oriental rugs are a feature of the lobby. Fine-quality furnishings and fabrics are used throughout, with marble and blond wood accents add warmth.

So what type of persons will enjoy the SeaDream Yacht Club experience? Answer: those who enjoy life without dressing up, bingo, discos, or entertainment, and those seeking a totally unstructured lifestyle, with the attraction of watersports at no extra charge. It is for experienced, independent travelers who don't like regular cruise ships, large ships, glitzy lounges, a platoon of people and kids running around, or dressing up (no tuxedos or gowns allowed). The SeaDreams provide the setting for personal indulgence and refined, unstructured and languorous private living at sea, in a casual setting.

One delightful feature of each cruise in warm weather areas is a "caviar in the surf" beach barbeque.

All drinks (with the exception of premium brands and connoisseur wines) and gratuities are included, while port charges and insurance are not included. Goodies include a useful canvas tote/beach bag, and scrumptious chocolates are, of course, provided in your cabin/suite. Life could hardly be better at sea – so, as many regular SeaDream Yacht Club passengers say, why bother with ports of call at all? Embarkation never starts before 3pm, in case you are eager to get aboard. These pocket-sized ships would be ideal for charters.

The price of a cruise is just that: the price of a cruise. Air and/or other travel arrangements can be made on your own, or through your own travel agent, or you can use the excellent services of Total Travel Marine (with offices in London and Miami and 24-hour, 365-day service), the agency that specializes in first, business or coach air arrangements as partner to SeaDream Yacht Club. The onboard currency is the US dollar.

WEAK POINTS: Although these were the first of the mega-yacht-style ships when they were built, none of the cabins has a private balcony (ships with private balconies made their debut just a couple of years later).

SeaDream II
★★★★★

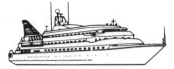

Small Ship:	.4,260 tons	Passengers	
Lifestyle:	.Luxury	(lower beds/all berths):	108/108
Cruise Line:	.SeaDream Yacht Club	Passenger Space Ratio	
Former Names:	.Seabourn Goddess II,	(lower beds/all berths):	39.4/39.4
	Sea Goddess II	Crew/Passenger Ratio	
Builder:	.Wartsila (Finland)	(lower beds/all berths):	1.2/1.2
Original Cost:	.$34 million	Navigation Officers:	.Norwegian/
Entered Service:	.May 1985/Jan 2002		Scandinavian
Registry:	.The Bahamas	Cabins (total):	.58
Length (ft/m):	.343.8/104.81	Size Range (sq ft/m):	.195.0–490.0/
Beam (ft/m):	.47.9/14.60		18.1–45.5
Draft (ft/m):	.13.6/4.17	Cabins (outside view):	.58
Propulsion/Propellers: diesel (3,540kW)/2		Cabins (interior/no view):	.0
Passenger Decks:	.5	Cabins (for one person):	.0
Total Crew:	.89	Cabins (with private balcony):	.0

Cabins (wheelchair accessible): .0
Cabin Current: .110 and 220 volts
Elevators: .1
Casino (gaming tables): .Yes
Slot Machines: .Yes
Swimming Pools (outdoors): .1
Swimming Pools (indoors): .0
Whirlpools: .1
Fitness Center: .Yes
Sauna/Steam Room: .Yes/No
Massage: .Yes
Self-Service Launderette: .No
Dedicated Cinema/Seats: .No
Library: .Yes
Classification Society: .Lloyd's Register

OVERALL SCORE: 1,790 (OUT OF A POSSIBLE 2,000 POINTS)

ACCOMMODATION: There are three types, and five price categories: Yacht Club (standard) Cabin, Commodore Club Suite, and Owner's Suite.

YACHT CLUB CABINS: Incorrectly called "suites" in the brochure, the standard cabins are, more correctly, fully equipped "mini-suites" with an outside view through windows or portholes (depending on the deck and price category). Each measures 195 sq. ft (18.1 sq. meters), which is not large by today's cruise ship standards – however, it *is* large compared to cabins aboard many private motor yachts, and *extremely* large when compared to ocean-going racing yachts. The sleeping area has twin beds (these can be put together to form a queen-size configuration); beds are positioned next to the window (or porthole) so that you can entertain in the living area without going past the sleeping area (as you must aboard the slightly larger Seabourn or Silversea ships, for example); a curtain separates the sleeping and lounge areas. All cabinetry and furniture is of thick blond wood, with nicely rounded edges.

A long vanity desk in the sleeping area has a large mirror above it (however, there is no three-sided mirror for women to see the back of their hair) and two small drawers for cosmetic items; there is also a brass clock located on one wall. Note that in the world of *feng shui* placing a mirror opposite your bed is frowned upon. In the lounge area, a long desk has six drawers, plus a vertical cupboard unit that houses a sensible safe, refrigerator and drinks cabinet (stocked your choice of drinks). There is also a 20-inch (51.5-mm) flat-screen television,

BERLITZ'S RATINGS		
	Possible	Achieved
Ship	500	441
Accommodation	200	173
Food	400	371
Service	400	370
Entertainment	N/A	N/A
Cruise	500	435

CD and DVD player, and an MP3 audio player (with a choice of over 100 selections). The beds have the finest linens, including thick cotton duvets, and non-allergenic pillows (and duvets) are also available. There's little room under the beds for luggage, although this can be taken away and stored for you.

One drawback is the fact that the insulation between cabins is not as good as it could be, although rarely does this present a problem, as most passengers aboard the two SeaDreams are generally extremely quiet, considerate types who are allergic to noise. Incidentally, a sleep suit (pyjamas) is supplied in case you want to sleep out on deck under the stars in one of the on-deck two-person beds, but more of those later.

Since the ship became *SeaDream II*, all bathrooms have been totally refurbished. The old tiling has been discarded and replaced by a new décor that is more hip and trendy, with softer colors and larger (beige) marble tiles. The former (tiny) sit-in bathtubs have been taken out (these will be missed by many regular European passengers) and replaced by a multi-jet power glassed-in shower enclosure. A new washbasin set in a marble-look surround and two glass shelves make up the facilities, while an under-sink cupboard provides further space for larger personal toiletry items. Bulgari personal toiletry amenities are provided. Gorgeously thick, plush, 100 percent cotton SeaDream-logo bathrobes and towels are also supplied. However, the bathrooms *are* small (particularly for those who are of larger than average build), despite their having been completely rebuilt (although the doors still open inward), so space inside really is at a premium. The toilet is located in a rather awkward position, and, unless you close the door, you can see yourself in the mirror facing of the closets, opposite the bathroom door.

COMMODORE CLUB SUITES: For larger accommodation, choose one of 16 Commodore Club Suites. These consist of two standard cabins with an interconnecting door, thus providing you with a healthy 380 sq. ft (36 sq. meters) of living space. One cabin is made into a lounge and dining room (with table and up to four chairs), while the other becomes your sleeping area. The advantage is that you get two bathrooms (his and hers).

OWNER'S SUITE: For the largest living space aboard this ship, go for the Owner's Suite. This measures a grand 490 sq. ft (45.5 sq. meters). It's the only accommodation with a bathroom that incorporates a real full-sized bathtub, and a separate show enclosure.

All passengers receive personalized stationery, personal email address, sleep suit, Bulgari personal toiletry amenities, 24-hour room service, and "sweet dreams" chocolates.

DINING: The dining salon is extremely elegant and inviting, and has bird's-eye maple wood-paneled walls and wood-accented décor. It is cozy, yet with plenty of space around each table for fine service, and the ship provides a floating culinary celebration in an open-seating arrangement, so you can dine whenever, and with whomever you want. A grand piano is located at one end, for quiet dinner music. Course-by-course meals can also be served in your cabin, or out on deck.

Tables can be configured for two, four, six, or eight. They are immaculately laid with settings of real glass base (show) plates, pristine white monogrammed table linen, and fresh flowers, while wall sconces house some superb glass ornaments). Candlelit dinners are part of the inviting setting. There is even a box of spare spectacles for menu reading in case you forget your own. You get leather-bound menus, and supremely attentive, close to impeccable personalized European service.

The SeaDream Yacht Club experience really is all about dining. This ship will not disappoint, and culinary excellence prevails. Only the very freshest and finest quality ingredients are used in the best culinary artistry. Fine, unhurried European service is provided.

The ship has exquisite, creative cuisine, and everything is prepared individually to order. Special orders are welcomed, and flaming desserts are showcased at your tableside. You can also dine, course by course in your suite for any meal, at any time (you can also eat à la carte 24 hours a day if you wish). There is plenty of fine-quality caviar, at any time of the day or night. And, thankfully, there's never a hint of baked Alaska!

Good-quality table wines are included in the cruise fare for lunch and dinner. Real wine connoisseurs, however, will appreciate the availability of an extra wine list, of special vintages and premier crus (at extra cost). If you want to do something different with a loved one, you can also arrange to dine one evening on the open (but covered) deck, overlooking the swimming pool and stern – it can be a magical and very romantic setting.

A new, informal Topside Restaurant has been created from what used to be the outdoor café. Now it has glass sides and a glass roof. Informal dining is the theme here, whether for breakfast, lunch or dinner. Teak tables and chairs add an additional (but essential and expected) touch of finery. And if you are hungry, no matter at what time of the day or night, you can "raid the pantry" and find something tasty to eat. Additionally, caviar (sevruga malossol) and champagne (Pommery) are always available whenever you want them.

OTHER COMMENTS: This small ship was originally built with money from about 800 investors, and operated under the Norske Cruise banner. It has an ultra-sleek profile, with deep blue hull and white superstructure, and the ambience of a private club. When it was acquired by SeaDream Yacht Club in 2001, the ship was completely refurbished, with many changes to both public rooms and outdoor areas, and several new features were added to create what is now an extremely contemporary, chic, and desirable ship.

At the stern is a small, retractable, water sports platform. Equipment carried for sporting types include a water-ski boat, sailboat, two wave runners (jet skis), seven kayaks, wake boards, snorkeling equipment and two Zodiacs.

The use of all this equipment is *included* in the price of your cruise. Note, however, the sea conditions have to be just right (minimal swell) for these items to be used, which, on average is once or twice in a 7-night cruise. You may also be allowed to swim off the stern platform if conditions permit. Ten mountain bikes are also carried, so you can pedal away when ashore.

A new "top of the yacht" bar, crafted in warm wood, has been added, as have eight special alcoves equipped with two-person sun loungers with very thick pads. At the front part of the deck there are more sun loungers and a couple of hammocks, as well as a golf simulator (with a choice of 30 courses). You can sleep under the stars and sleep suits (pyjamas) will be provided.

Inside, there is a delightful feeling of unabashed but discreet sophistication. Elegant, chic public rooms have flowers and pot pourri everywhere. The main social gathering places are the lounge, a delightful library/ living room with a selection of about 800 books, a piano bar, and a casino (two blackjack tables and five slot machines). The library has been enlarged and moved to what was formerly a lounge area, and now provides a very comfortable, warm and cozy setting.

A new (Asian-style) spa has been created, housed together with a small gymnasium, and beauty salon. There are three massage rooms, a sauna, and steam shower enclosure. Meanwhile, golfers should enjoy the new electronic golf simulator, with a choice of several golf courses to play.

The two SeaDream ships really are the ultimate boutique vessels – like having your own private yacht in which hospitality and anticipation are art forms practiced to a high level. The staff is delightful and accommodating ("no" is not in their vocabulary); if there is anything special you want, you have only to ask, and they will be only too happy to oblige – in the style of the best European hotels. The dress code is resort casual by day (one could almost live in one's bathrobe), informal by night. Oriental rugs are a feature of the lobby. Fine-quality furnishings and fabrics are used throughout, with marble and blond wood accents add warmth.

So what type of persons will enjoy the SeaDream Yacht Club experience? Answer: those who enjoy life without dressing up, bingo, discos, or entertainment, and those seeking a totally unstructured lifestyle, with the attraction of watersports at no extra charge. It is for experienced, independent travelers who do not like regular cruise ships, large ships, glitzy lounges, a platoon of people and kids running around, or dressing up (no tuxedos or gowns allowed. The SeaDreams provide the setting for personal indulgence and refined, unstructured and languorous private living at sea, in a casual setting.

One delightful feature of each cruise in warm weather areas is a "caviar in the surf" beach barbeque.

All drinks (with the exception of premium brands and connoisseur wines) and gratuities are included, while port charges and insurance are not included. Goodies include a useful canvas tote/beach bag, and scrumptious chocolates are, of course, provided in your cabin/suite. Life could hardly be better at sea – so, as many regular SeaDream Yacht Club passengers say, why bother with ports of call at all? Embarkation never starts before 3pm, in case you are eager to get aboard. These pocket-sized ships would be ideal for charters.

The price of a cruise is just that: the price of a cruise. Air and/or other travel arrangements can be made on your own, or through your own travel agent, or you can use the excellent services of Total Travel Marine (with offices in London and Miami and 24-hour, 365-day service), the agency that specializes in first, business or coach air arrangements as partner to SeaDream Yacht Club. The onboard currency is the US dollar.

WEAK POINTS: Although these SeaDream ships were the first of the mega-yacht-style ships when they were built, none of the cabins has a private balcony (ships with private balconies made their debut just a couple of years later).

Sea Bird
★★

Small Ship: ....99.7 tons	Passengers	Cabin Current: ....110 volts
Lifestyle: ....Standard	(lower beds/all berths): 70/70	Elevators: 0
Cruise Line: ....Lindblad Expeditions	Passenger Space Ratio	Casino (gaming tables): ....No
Former Names: ......*Majestic Explorer*	(lower beds/all berths): 1.4/1.4	Slot Machines: ....No
Builder: ....Whidbey Island	Crew/Passenger Ratio	Swimming Pools (outdoors): 0
(USA)	(lower beds/all berths): 3.1/3.1	Swimming Pools (indoors): 0
Original Cost: ....n/a	Navigation Officers: ......Scandinavian	Whirlpools: 0
Entered Service: 1981	Cabins (total): 36	Fitness Center: ....No
Registry: ....The Bahamas	Size Range (sq ft/m): 73.0–202.0/	Sauna/Steam Room: ....No/No
Length (ft/m): 151.9/46.3	6.7–18.7	Massage: ....No
Beam (ft/m): 30.8/9.4	Cabins (outside view): 36	Self-Service Launderette: ....No
Draft (ft/m): 8.0/2.4	Cabins (interior/no view): 0	Dedicated Cinema/Seats: ....No
Propulsion/Propellers: diesel/2	Cabins (for one person): 2	Library: ....No
Passenger Decks: 4	Cabins (with private balcony): 0	Classification Society: ..American Bureau
Total Crew: 22	Cabins (wheelchair accessible): 0	of Shipping

BERLITZ'S OVERALL SCORE: 943 (OUT OF A POSSIBLE 2,000 POINTS)

ACCOMMODATION: All the cabins aboard this little ship have an outside view through picture windows, except for those on the lowest deck, which have portholes. Some cabins have double beds, some have twin beds (they can be pushed together to form a queen-sized bed), and some are for singles (at a surcharge of 150 percent). There is plenty of room to stow your luggage. All cabins have a private bathroom, although it really is tiny. There is no room service for food or beverages.

DINING: The dining room (non-smoking), which has ocean-view picture windows, is large enough to accommodate all passengers in a single seating. The tables are not assigned, and so you can sit with whom you like. The food is unpretentious, good and wholesome, although its presentation is very plain, with no frills, and features regional specialties. The wine list is very limited, and is comprised mostly of wines from California.

OTHER COMMENTS: The vessel carries a fleet of motor-

BERLITZ'S RATINGS

	Possible	Achieved
Ship	500	185
Accommodation	200	83
Food	400	204
Service	400	214
Entertainment	N/A	N/A
Cruise	500	257

ized Zodiac landing craft for use as shore tenders and for up-close shore exploration. A number of sea kayaks are also carried. An open-bridge policy means you can go to the navigation bridge at any time.

The vessel is small enough to operate in ports and narrow inlets inaccessible to larger ships. Lecturers and recap sessions are held daily.

This small craft (and sister ship *Sea Lion*) is adequate for looking at nature and wildlife close-up, in modest but comfortable surroundings that provide an alternative to big-ship cruising. It best suits older couples and single travelers who enjoy learning about nature, geography, history and other life sciences in casual, non-dressy surroundings without a hint of pretension. Operates cruises in Alaska, Baja California and the Sea of Cortes. Tipping is suggested at about $7 per person per day. The onboard currency is the US dollar.

WEAK POINTS: In the cabins, the mattresses are enclosed in a wood frame with sharp corners, which you can bang into constantly.

Sea Cloud
★★★★★

Small Ship:	2,532 tons	Main Propulsion:	sail power
Lifestyle:	Luxury	Propulsion/Propellers:	diesel (4,476kW)/2
Cruise Line:	Sea Cloud Cruises	Passenger Decks:	3
Former Names:	Sea Cloud of Grand	Total Crew:	60
	Cayman, IX-99, Antama, Patria,	Passengers	
	Angelita, Sea Cloud, Hussar	(lower beds/all berths):	68/69
Builder:	Krupp Werft (Germany)	Passenger Space Ratio	
Entered Service:	Aug 1931/1979	(lower beds/all berths):	37.2/36.6
	(restored)	Crew/Passenger Ratio	
Registry:	Malta	(lower beds/all berths):	1.1/1.1
Length (ft/m):	359.2/109.5	Navigation Officers:	European
Beam (ft/m):	48.28/14.9	Cabins (total):	34
Draft (ft/m):	16.8/5.13	Size Range (sq ft/m):	102.2–409.0/
Type of Vessel:	barkentine		9.5–38.0
No. of Masts:	4 (17.7 meters)/30 sails	Cabins (outside view):	34
Sail Area (sq ft/m2):	32,292/3,000	Cabins (interior/no view):	0

Cabins (for one person):	0
Cabins (with private balcony):	0
Cabins (wheelchair accessible):	0
Cabin Current:	220 volts
Elevators:	0
Casino (gaming tables):	No
Slot Machines:	No
Swimming Pools (outdoors):	0
Whirlpools:	0
Fitness Center:	No
Sauna/Steam Room:	No/No
Massage:	No
Self-Service Launderette:	No
Library:	Yes
Classification Society:	Germanischer Lloyd

OVERALL SCORE: 1,704 (OUT OF A POSSIBLE 2,000 POINTS)

ACCOMMODATION: Because *Sea Cloud* was built as a private yacht, there is a wide variation in cabin sizes and configurations. Some cabins have double beds, while some have twin beds (side by side or in an "L"-shaped configuration) that are fixed and cannot be placed together. Many of the original cabins have a fireplace (now with an electric fire).

All of the accommodation is very comfortable, but those on Main Deck (Cabins 1–8) were part of the original accommodation aboard this ship. Of these, the two owner's suites (Cabins 1 and 2) are really opulent, and feature real, original Chippendale furniture, fine gilt detailing, a real fireplace, French canopy bed, and large Italian Carrara marble bathrooms with gold fittings. The Owner's Cabin Number 1 is decorated in white throughout, and has a fireplace and Louis Phillippe chairs. Owner's Cabin Number 2 is completely paneled in rich woods, and retains the mahogany secretary used 60 years ago by Edward F. Hutton (Marjorie Post's husband) himself.

Other cabins (both the original ones, and some newer additions) are all beautifully furnished (all were refurbished in 1993) and are surprisingly large for the size of the ship. There is a good amount of closet and drawer space and all cabins feature a personal safe and telephone. The cabin bathrooms, too, are quite luxurious, and equipped with really everything you will need, including bathrobes and hairdryer, and an assortment of personal toiletry items (there is also a 110 volt AC shaver socket in each bathroom). The "new" cabins are

BERLITZ'S RATINGS

	Possible	Achieved
Ship	500	423
Accommodation	200	173
Food	400	348
Service	400	335
Entertainment	N/A	N/A
Cruise	500	425

rather small for two persons, so it's best to take minimal luggage.

There is no cabin food or beverage service. Also, note that if you occupy one of the original cabins on Main Deck you will probably be subjected to some noise when the motorized capstans are used to raise and lower or trim the sails. On one day each cruise, an "open-house" cocktail party is held on the Main Deck, with all cabins available for any passengers to see.

DINING: The dining room, created from the original owner's living room/saloon, is located in the center of the vessel. It is exquisite and elegant in every detail (it also houses the ship's library) has beautiful wood paneled walls and a wood beam ceiling. There is ample space at each table, so there is never a crowded feeling, and meals are taken in an open-seating arrangement, so you can sit and dine with whom you wish, where you wish. German chefs are in charge, and the cuisine is very international, with a good balance of *nouvelle cuisine* and regional dishes featured (depending on which region the ship is sailing in). Outstanding quality food and cuisine are featured throughout. Place settings for dinner (often by candlelight) are navy blue, white and gold Bauscher china.

European wines are typically provided for lunch and dinner (soft drinks and bottled water are included in the price, while alcoholic drinks cost extra). There is always excellent seafood and fish (this is always purchased fresh, locally, when available, as are most other ingredients). For breakfast and lunch, there are self-serve buffets. These are really good, and beautifully presented (typically indoors for breakfast and outdoors on the Promenade Deck for lunch). Meal times are announced by the ship's bell. On the last day of each cruise, homemade ice cream is produced.

OTHER COMMENTS: *Sea Cloud* is the oldest and most beautiful sailing ship in the world, and the largest private yacht ever built (at three times the size of Captain Cook's *Endeavour*). It is a beautiful, completely authentic 1930s barkentine whose three masts are almost as high as a 20-story building (the main mast is 178 ft/ 54 meters above the main deck). This was the largest private yacht ever built when completed in 1931 by E.F. Hutton for his wife, Marjorie Merriweather Post, the American cereal heiress. Originally constructed for $1 million as *Hussar* in the Krupp shipyard in Kiel, Germany, this steel-hulled yacht is immensely impressive when in port, but exhilarating when under full sail.

During World War II, the vessel saw action as a weather observation ship, under the code name *IX-99*. You can still see five chevrons on the bridge, one for each half-year of duty, serving as a reminder of those important years.

There is plenty of deck space, even under the vast expanse of white sail, and the promenade deck outdoors still has wonderful varnished sea chests. The decks themselves are made of mahogany and teak, and wooden "steamer"-style deck lounge chairs are provided. One of the most beautiful aspects of sailing aboard this ship is its "Blue Lagoon," located at the very stern of the vessel. Weather permitting, you can lie down on the thick blue padding and gaze up at the stars and night sky – it's one of the great pleasures – particularly when the ship is under sail, with engines turned off.

The original engine room (with diesel engines) is still in operation for the rare occasions when sail power can't be used. An open-bridge policy is the norm (except during times of poor weather or navigational maneuvers).

In addition to its retained and refurbished original suites and cabins, with their gorgeous wood paneling and antiques and dressers, some newer, smaller cabins were added in 1979 when a consortium of German yachtsmen and businessmen purchased the ship. The owners spent $7.5 million refurbishing it. Many original oil paintings adorn the interior walls.

The interiors exude warmth, and are finely hand crafted. There is much antique mahogany furniture, fine original oil paintings, gorgeous carved oak paneling, parquet flooring and burnished brass everywhere, as well as some finely detailed ceilings. There is absolutely no doubt that Marjorie Merryweather Post was accustomed only to the very finest things in life. The ship was designed by Gibbs & Cox and Cox & Stevens, then the foremost ship design firm in North America.

Sea Cloud is, without doubt, the ultimate, most romantic sailing ship afloat today. Although there are many imitations, there still is none better than this beautiful vintage vessel. The ship is still kept close to its original state when built. It operates under charter for much of the year, and sails in both the Caribbean and European/Mediterranean waters.

A cruise aboard *Sea Cloud* is, in summary, a truly exhilarating experience, and the ship exudes as much warmth and ambience today as it did when first launched. This is really a ship like no other, for the discerning few to relish the uncompromising comfort and elegance of a bygone era. A kind of stately home afloat, *Sea Cloud* remains one of the finest and nicest travel experiences in the world, and a wonderful escape from the stress and strain of contemporary life ashore. The activities are few, and so relaxation is the key, in a setting that provides fine service and style, but in an unpretentious way.

The only "dress-up" night is the Captain's Welcome Aboard Dinner, but otherwise, smart casual clothing is all that is needed (no tuxedo). The dress code is casual (note that mini-skirts would be impractical due to the steep staircases in some places – trousers are more practical). Also note that a big sailing vessel such as this can heel to one side occasionally (so take flat shoes rather than high heels).

The crew is made up from a number of nationalities, and the sailors who climb the rigging and set the sails include females as well as males. On the last night of the cruise, the sailors' choir sings seafaring songs for all. Gratuities are suggested at $15 per person, per day, although these can be charged to your onboard account. The US dollar is used as the onboard currency.

The German owning company, Sea Cloud Cruises, also operates the new river vessel *River Cloud*, introduced in 1996, for cruises on the Danube, Main, Mosel and Rhine areas, and, in 2001 introduced a brand new companion sailing ship, *Sea Cloud II*.

Sea Cloud is, for part of each year, under charter to Hapag-Lloyd Cruises. On those occasions, white and red wines and beer are included for lunch and dinner; soft drinks, espresso and cappuccino coffees are also included at any time; shore excursions are an optional extra, as are gratuities. Details may be different for other charter operators (such as Abercrombie & Kent).

Note that passengers are not permitted to climb the rigging, as may be possible aboard some other tall ships. This is because the mast rigging on this vintage sailing ship is of a very different type to the more modern sailing vessels. However, passengers may be able participate occasionally in the furling and unfurling of the sails.

Although now just over 70 years old, *Sea Cloud* is so lovingly maintained and operated that anyone who sails aboard it cannot fail to be impressed. If you seek entertainment, casinos, bingo, horse racing and flashy resort cruising, this is not the ship for you. However, if you want to be part of one of the most exclusive communities at sea aboard a ship that is nothing other than utterly graceful, serene and calming, you will love *Sea Cloud*. The food and service are extremely good, as is the interaction between passengers and crew, many of whom have worked aboard it for many, many years. One really important bonus is the fact that the doctor on board is available *at no charge* for medical emergencies or seasickness medication.

In 2001, the ship suffered a fire while in Rijeka, which put it out of commission for many months. However, all necessary repairs have been painstakingly made and it is now in its beautiful original condition again.

RIGGING: For the sailors among you, the sails are (in order, from fore to aft mast, top to bottom):
Fore Mast: flying jib, outer jib, inner jib, fore topmast staysail, fore royal, fore topgallant, fore upper-top sail, fore lower-top sail, foresail.
Main Mast: main royal staysail, main topgallant staysail, main topmast staysail, skysail, main royal, main topgallant, main upper topsail, main lower topsail, main sail.
Mizzen Mast: mizzen royal staysail, mizzen topgallant staysail, mizzen topmast staysail, mizzen royal topsail, mizzen topgallant, mizzen upper topsail, mizzen lower topsail, mizzen course.
Spanker Mast: spanker top mast staysail, spanker staysail, spanker-gaff topsail, spanker.

WEAK POINTS: Some staircases are steep, as they are aboard almost all sailing vessels.

17/07/05 Dundee √

Sea Cloud II
★★★★★

Small Ship: ....3,849 tons	Main Propulsion: ....sail power	Cabins (interior/no view): 0
Lifestyle: ....Luxury	Propulsion/Propellers: diesel (2,500kW)/2	Cabins (for one person): 0
Cruise Line: ....Sea Cloud Cruises	Passenger Decks: 4	Cabins (with private balcony): 0
Former Names: ....none	Total Crew: 60	Cabins (wheelchair accessible): 0
Builder: ......Astilleros Gondan, Figueras	Passengers	Cabin Current: ....110 and 220 volts
(Spain)	(lower beds/all berths): 96/96	Elevators: 0
Original Cost: ....DM 50 million	Passenger Space Ratio	Swimming Pools (outdoors): 0
Entered Service: ....Feb 2001	(lower beds/all berths): 40.0/40.0	Whirlpools: 0
Registry: ....Malta	Crew/Passenger Ratio	Exercise Room: ....Yes
Length (ft/m): 383.8/117.0	(lower beds/all berths): 1.6/1.6	Sauna/Steam Room: ....Yes/No
Beam (ft/m): 52.9/16.15	Navigation Officers: . .American/European	Massage: ....No
Draft (ft/m): 17.7/5.4	Cabins (total): 48	Self-Service Launderette: ....No
Type of Vessel: ....barkentine	Size Range (sq ft/m): 215.2–322.9/	Library: ....Yes
No. of Masts: ....3 (24 sails)	20.0–30.0	Classification Society: .....Germanischer
Sail Area (sq ft/m2): 32,292/3,000	Cabins (outside view): 48	Lloyd

---

BERLITZ'S OVERALL SCORE: 1,709 (OUT OF A POSSIBLE 2,000 POINTS)

ACCOMMODATION: The décor in the cabins is very tasteful 1920s retro, with lots of bird's-eye maple wood paneling, brass accenting, and beautiful molded white ceilings. All cabins have a vanity desk, hairdryer, refrigerator (typically stocked with soft drinks and bottles water), and a combination television/video player. All cabins have a private bathroom with shower enclosure (or bathtub/shower combination), and plenty of storage space for your personal toiletries. Note that the cabin electrical current is 220 volts, although all bathrooms also include a 110-volt socket (but only for shavers).

There are two suites. Naturally, these have more space (but not as much space as the two owner's suites aboard sister vessel *Sea Cloud*), and comprise a completely separate bedroom (with four-poster bed) and living room, while the marble-clad bathroom has a full-sized bathtub.

There are 16 junior suites. These provide a living area and sleeping area with twin beds that convert to a queen-sized bed. The marble-clad bathroom is quite opulent, and has a small bathtub/shower combination, with lots of little cubbyholes to store personal toiletry items.

DINING: The one-seating dining room operates an open-seating policy, so you can dine with whom you wish, when you wish (within operating hours). It is decorated in a light, modern maritime style, with wood and carpeted flooring, comfortable chairs with armrests, and circular light fixtures. The gold-rimmed plateware used for the captain's dinner (which is typically a candlelit affair) has the ship's crest embedded in the white porce-

BERLITZ'S RATINGS

	Possible	Achieved
Ship	500	435
Accommodation	200	173
Food	400	344
Service	400	333
Entertainment	N/A	N/A
Cruise	500	424

lain; it is extremely elegant (and highly collectible). The cuisine is very good, with small portions that are well presented, and accompanying sauces that are light and complementary, and not at all heavy. House wines are typically included for lunch and dinner.

OTHER COMMENTS: This new, three-mast tall ship is slightly longer than the original *Sea Cloud*, and has the look, ambience and feel of a 1930s sailing vessel, but with all the latest high-tech navigational aids. The ship complements the company's beautiful, original, 1931-built *Sea Cloud* in almost every way, including its external appearance – except for a very rounded stern in place of the counter stern of sister ship *Sea Cloud*).

Despite some appallingly low standards in the original fitting out of its interiors and carpeting by a shipyard that needs to learn the meaning of the word "quality," Sea Cloud Cruises quickly acted to correct the irritating items, and can now satisfy those seeking the very best of luxurious comfort and surroundings inside a wonderful sailing vessel.

A small water sports platform is built into the aft quarter of the starboard side (with adjacent shower), and the ship carries four inflatable craft for close-in shore landings, as well as snorkeling equipment.

Completely elegant in décor, but using modern materials to reproduce the period intended, the interior designers have managed to continue the same beautiful traditional look and design as that of its sister ship, *Sea Cloud*. These design details and special decorative touches will make you feel instantly at home. Whether the modern materials used will stand up to 70 years of use like those of the original *Sea Cloud* remains to be seen, although they are of a high quality. In any event, passengers who have sailed aboard the original *Sea Cloud* will no doubt compare the original with the new.

The main lounge is elegance personified, with sofa and large individual tub chair seating around oval drinks tables. The ceiling is ornate, with an abundance of wood detailing, and an oval centerpiece is set around skylights to the open deck above. A bar is set into the aft port side of the room, which also has audio-visual aids built in – for lectures and presentations.

One of the most treasured aspects of sailing aboard this ship is the "Blue Lagoon," located at the very stern of the vessel – part of the outdoor bar and casual dining area. Weather permitting, you can lie down on thick blue padding and gaze up at the stars and warm night sky – it's one of the great pleasures – particularly when the ship is under sail, with the engines turned off.

Overall, *Sea Cloud II* is one of the most luxurious true sailing ships in the world, although it is not the largest (that distinction goes to competitor Star Clippers' *Royal Clipper*). However, in terms of interior deign, degree of luxury in appointments, the passenger flow, fabrics, food and service, the ceiling height of pub-lic rooms, larger cabins, great open deck space, better passenger space ratio and crew to passenger ratio, there is none better than *Sea Cloud II*. If you sail both vessels (as I have), I am absolutely certain you would agree with me, and that your overall sail-cruise experience will be a truly memorable one.

Note that your personal experience will depend on which company is operating the ship under charter at the time of your sailing, and exactly what is to be included in the package. This is, however, as exclusive as it gets – sailing in the lap of luxury.

RIGGING: This consists of up to 24 sails: flying jib, outer jib, inner jib; fore royal, fore topgallant, fore upper topsail, fore lower topsail, fore course; main royal staysail, main topgallant staysail, main topmast stay-sail; sky sail, main royal, main topgallant, main upper topsail, main lower topsail, main sail; mizzen topgallant staysail, mizzen topmast staysail; mizzen gaff topsail, mizzen upper gaff sail, mizzen lower gaff sail, middle gaff, upper gaff.

WEAK POINTS: If you have sailed in the original cabins aboard the original *Sea Cloud* before, you will probably be disappointed with the more limited space and deco-ration of the equivalent cabins aboard this ship.

Sea Lion
★★

Small Ship:	.99.7 tons	Passengers		Cabin Current:	.110 volts
Lifestyle:	.Standard	(lower beds/all berths):	.72/76	Elevators:	.0
Cruise Line:	.Lindblad Expeditions	Passenger Space Ratio		Casino (gaming tables):	.No
Former Names:	.*Great Rivers Explorer*	(lower beds/all berths):	.1.3/1.3	Slot Machines:	.No
Builder:	.Whidbey Island	Crew/Passenger Ratio		Swimming Pools (outdoors):	.0
	(USA)	(lower beds/all berths):	.3.2/3.4	Swimming Pools (indoors):	.0
Original Cost:	.n/a	Navigation Officers:	.Scandinavian	Whirlpools:	.0
Entered Service:	.1982	Cabins (total):	.37	Fitness Center:	.No
Registry:	.The Bahamas	Size Range (sq ft/m):	.73.0–202.0/	Sauna/Steam Room:	.No/No
Length (ft/m):	.151.9/46.3		6.7–18.7	Massage:	.No
Beam (ft/m):	.30.8/9.4	Cabins (outside view):	.37	Self-Service Launderette:	.No
Draft (ft/m):	.8.0/2.4	Cabins (interior/no view):	.0	Dedicated Cinema/Seats:	.No
Propulsion/Propellers:	.diesel/2	Cabins (for one person):	.2	Library:	.No
Passenger Decks:	.4	Cabins (with private balcony):	.0	Classification Society:	.American Bureau
Total Crew:	.22	Cabins (wheelchair accessible):	.0		of Shipping

OVERALL SCORE: 943 (OUT OF A POSSIBLE 2,000 POINTS)

ACCOMMODATION: All the cabins aboard this little ship have an outside view through picture windows, except for those on the lowest deck, which have portholes. Some cabins have double beds, some have twin beds (they can be pushed together to form a queen-sized bed), and some are for singles (at a surcharge of 150 percent). There is plenty of room to stow your luggage. All cabins have a private bathroom, although it really is tiny. There is no room service for food or beverages.

DINING: The dining room (non-smoking), which has ocean-view picture windows, is large enough to accommodate all passengers in a single seating. The tables are not assigned, and so you can sit with whom you like. The food is unpretentious, good and wholesome, although its presentation is very plain, with no frills, and features regional specialties. The wine list is very limited, and is comprised mostly of wines from California.

OTHER COMMENTS: The vessel carries a fleet of motor-

BERLITZ'S RATINGS		
	Possible	Achieved
Ship	500	185
Accommodation	200	83
Food	400	204
Service	400	214
Entertainment	N/A	N/A
Cruise	500	257

ized Zodiac landing craft for use as shore tenders and for up-close shore exploration. A number of sea kayaks are also carried. An open-bridge policy means that you are allowed to go to the navigation bridge at any time.

The vessel is small enough to operate in ports and narrow inlets inaccessible to larger ships. Lectures and recap sessions are held each day.

This small craft (together with sister ship *Sea Bird*) is adequate for looking at nature and wildlife close-up, in modest but comfortable surroundings that provide an alternative to big-ship cruising. It would best suit older couples and single travelers who enjoy learning about nature, geography, history and other life sciences, in casual, non-dressy surroundings without a hint of pretension.

Cruises visit Alaska, Baja California and the Sea of Cortes. Tipping is suggested at about $7 per person per day. The onboard currency is the US dollar.

WEAK POINTS: In the cabins, the mattresses are enclosed in a wood frame with sharp corners, which you can bang into constantly.

Sea Princess

★★★★

Large Ship: ....77,499 tons	Passengers	Cabin Current: ....110 and 220 volts
Lifestyle: ....Standard	(lower beds/all berths): 2,100/2,250	Elevators: 11
Cruise Line: ....Princess Cruises	Passenger Space Ratio	Casino (gaming tables): ....Yes
Former Names: ....none	(lower beds/all berths): 36.9/34.4	Slot Machines: ....Yes
Builder: ....Fincantieri (Italy)	Crew/Passenger Ratio	Swimming Pools (outdoors): 3
Original Cost: ....$300 million	(lower beds/all berths): 2.1/2.5	Swimming Pools (indoors): 0
Entered Service: ....Dec 1998	Navigation Officers: ....Italian	Whirlpools: 5
Registry: ....Great Britain	Cabins (total): 1,050	Fitness Center: ....Yes
Length (ft/m): 857.2/261.3	Size Range (sq ft/m): 158.2–610.3/	Sauna/Steam Room: ....Yes/Yes
Beam (ft/m): 105.6/32.2	14.7–56.7	Massage: ....Yes
Draft (ft/m): 26.5/8.1	Cabins (outside view): 652	Self-Service Launderette: ....Yes
Propulsion/Propellers: .....diesel-electric	Cabins (interior/no view): 398	Dedicated Cinema/Seats: ....No
(46,080kW)/2	Cabins (for one person): 0	Library: ....Yes
Passenger Decks: 10	Cabins (with private balcony): 446	Classification Society: ...Registro Navale
Total Crew: 900	Cabins (wheelchair accessible): 20	Italiano (RINA)

OVERALL SCORE: 1,539 (OUT OF A POSSIBLE 2,000 POINTS)

ACCOMMODATION: There are 28 different cabin grades: 20 outside-view and 8 interior (no view) cabins. Although the standard outside (view) and interior (no view) cabins are a little small, they are well designed and functional in layout, and have earth tone colors accentuated by splashes of color from the bedspreads. Proportionately, there are quite a lot of interior (no view) cabins. Many of the outside-view cabins have private balconies, and all seem to be quite well soundproofed, although the balcony partition is not floor to ceiling type, so you can hear your neighbors clearly (or smell their smoke). Note that the balconies are very narrow and only just large enough for two small chairs, and there is no dedicated lighting.

A reasonable amount of closet and abundant drawer and other storage space is provided in all cabins – adequate for a 7-night cruise. There's also a color television, and refrigerator. Each night a chocolate will appear on your pillow. The cabin bathrooms are practical, and come complete with all the details one needs, although they really are tight spaces, best described as one person at-a-time units. They do, however, have a decent shower enclosure, a small amount of shelving for your personal toiletries, real glasses, a hairdryer and a bathrobe.

The largest accommodation can be found in six suites, two on each of three decks located at the stern of the ship, with large private balcony. These are well laid out, and have large bathrooms with two sinks, a Jacuzzi bathtub, and a separate shower enclosure. The bedroom has generous amounts of wood accenting and detailing, indented ceilings, and television sets in both bedroom

BERLITZ'S RATINGS		
	Possible	Achieved
Ship	500	428
Accommodation	200	162
Food	400	266
Service	400	291
Entertainment	100	86
Cruise	400	306

and lounge areas. The suites also have a dining room table and four chairs.

Mini-suites typically have two lower beds that convert into a queen-sized bed. There is a separate bedroom/sleeping area with vanity desk, and a lounge with sofa and coffee table, indented ceilings with generous amounts of wood accenting and detailing, walk-in closet, and larger bathroom with Jacuzzi bathtub and separate shower enclosure.

Princess Cruises carry BBC World, CNN, CNBC, ESPN and TNT on the in-cabin color television system (when available, depending on cruise area).

DINING: There are two main dining rooms, Neapolitan, and Sicilian (both are non-smoking, as are the dining rooms aboard all ships of Princess Cruises) and which one you are assigned to depends on the location of your accommodation. Each dining room has its own galley and is split into multi-tier sections, which help create a feeling of intimacy, although there is a lot of noise from the waiter stations, which are adjacent to many tables. Breakfast and lunch are provided in an open-seating arrangement, while dinner is in two seatings.

Despite the fact that the portions are generous, the food and its presentation are somewhat disappointing, and bland of taste. The quality of fish is poor (often disguised by crumb or batter coatings), the selection of fresh green vegetables is limited, and few garnishes are used. However, do remember that this *is* big-ship banquet catering, with all its attendant standardization and production cooking. Meats are of a decent quality,

although often disguised by gravy-based sauces, and pasta dishes are acceptable (though voluminous), and are typically served by section headwaiters who, in search of gratuities, may also make "something special just for you." If you like desserts, order a sundae at dinner, as most other desserts are just so-so. Remember that ice cream ordered in the dining room is included, but if you order one anywhere else, you'll have to pay for it.

On any given seven-day cruise, a typical menu cycle will include a Sailaway Dinner, Captain's Welcome Dinner, Chef's Dinner, Italian Dinner, French Dinner, Captain's Gala Dinner, and Landfall Dinner. The wine list is reasonable, but not good, and the company has, sadly, seen fit to eliminate all wine waiters. Note that 15 percent is added to all beverage bills, including wines (whether you order a $15 bottle or a $120 bottle, even though it takes the same amount of service to open and pour the wine).

For some really good meat, however, consider the *Sterling Steakhouse*; it's for those that want to taste four different cuts of Angus beef from the popular "Sterling Silver" brand of USDA prime meats – Filet Mignon, New York Strip, Porterhouse, and Rib-Eye – all presented on a silver tray. There is also a barbecue chicken option, plus the usual baked potato or French fries as accompaniments. This is available as an alternative to the dining rooms, between 6.30pm and 9.30pm only, at an additional charge of $8 per person. However, it is not, as you might expect, a separate, intimate dining room, but is located in a section of the Horizon Buffet, with its own portable bar and some decorative touches to set it apart (from the regular Horizon Buffet).

The Horizon Buffet is open 24 hours a day and, at night, has an informal dinner setting with sit-down waiter service; a small bistro menu is also available. The buffet displays are, for the most part, quite repetitious, but better than they have been in the past few years (there is no real finesse in presentation, however, as plastic plates are provided, instead of trays). The cabin service menu is very limited, and presentation of the food items featured is poor.

There is also a pâtisserie (for cappuccino/espresso coffees and pastries), a wine/caviar bar, and a pizzeria (complete with cobblestone floors and wrought iron decorative features), and excellent pizzas (there are six to choose from).

OTHER COMMENTS: Although large, this all-white ship has a profile that is well balanced by a large, stylish, swept-back funnel, which contains a deck tennis/basketball/volleyball court in its sheltered aft base. There is a wide, teakwood wrap-around promenade deck outdoors, some real teak steamer-style deck chairs (with royal blue cushioned pads), and 93,000 sq. ft (8,600 sq. meters) of outdoors space. A great amount of glass area on the upper decks provides plenty of light and connection with the outside world.

The ship actually absorbs passengers quite well, and some areas have an almost intimate feel to them, which is what the interior designers intended. The interiors are very attractive, with warm colors and welcoming décor that includes countless wall murals and other artwork. The signs around the ship could be better, however.

There is a wide range of public rooms, with several intimate rooms and spaces so that you don't get the feel of being overwhelmed by large spaces. The décor is tasteful, with attractive color combinations that are warm and don't clash (nothing is brash). The interior focal point is a huge four-deck-high atrium lobby with winding, double stairways, complete with two panoramic glass-walled elevators.

The main public entertainment rooms are located under three cabin decks. There is plenty of space, the traffic flow is good, and the ship absorbs people well. There are two show lounges, one at each end of the ship; one is a superb 550-seat, theater-style lounge (movies are also shown here) and the other is a 480-seat cabaret-style lounge with bar.

A glass-walled health spa complex is located high atop ship with gymnasium and high-tech machines. One swimming pool is "suspended" aft between two decks (there are two other pools, although they are not large for the size of the ship).

The library is a very warm room and has six large buttery leather chairs for listening to compact audio discs, with ocean-view windows. There is a conference center for up to 300, as well as a business center, with computers, copy and fax machines. The collection of artwork is good, particularly on the stairways, and helps make the ship feel smaller than it is, although in places it doesn't always seem coordinated. The casino, while large, is not really in the main passenger flow and so it does not generate the "walk-through" factor found aboard so many ships.

The most traditional room aboard is the Wheelhouse Lounge/Bar, which is decorated in the style of a late 19th-century gentleman's club, complete with wood paneling and comfortable seating. The focal point is a large ship model from the P&O collection archives: *Arandora Star*.

At the end of the day, as is the case aboard most large ships today, if you live in the top suites, you will be well attended; if you do not, you will merely be one of a very large number of passengers. One nice feature is the captain's cocktail party – it is held in the four-deck-high main atrium, so you can come and go as you please, and there's no standing in line to have your photograph taken with the captain if you don't want to.

The ship is full of revenue centers, however, designed to help you part you from your money. You can expect to be subjected to a stream of flyers advertising daily art auctions, "designer" watches and other promotions, while "artworks" for auction are strewn throughout the ship.

Gratuities to staff are *automatically* added to your account, at $10 per person, per day (gratuities for children are charged at the same rate). If you want to pay less, you'll need to go to the reception desk to have these charges adjusted (that could mean lining up with many other passengers wanting to do the same). The onboard currency is the US dollar.

In May 2003, *Sea Princess* will be moved from the Princess Cruises fleet to the UK-based parent company P&O Cruises. The ship will be renamed *Adonia*, and will replace *Arcadia*, which will be placed into a new cruise line, named Ocean Village, and targeted to a younger audience. *Adonia* will cater to an adults-only clientele. Many of the public rooms will undergo name changes to better reflect the tastes of P&O's mainly British passengers.

WEAK POINTS: Standing in line for embarkation (an "express check-in" option is available by completing certain documentation 40 days in advance of your cruise), disembarkation, shore tenders and for self-serve buffet meals is an inevitable aspect of cruising aboard all large ships. There is no escape from repetitious announcements (for activities that bring revenue, such as art auctions, bingo, horse racing) that intrude on your cruise vacation (depending on itinerary). In-your-face art auctions are overbearing, and the paintings, lithographs and faux framed pictures are strewn throughout the ship (and clash irritatingly with its interior décor). These are an annoying intrusion into what should be a vacation, not a cruise in a floating "art" store.

The digital voice announcing elevator deck stops is irritating to passengers (many of whom tell me they would like to rip out the speaker system). There are a number of dead ends in the interior layout, so it's not as user-friendly as it should be.

The cabin numbering system is extremely illogical, with numbers going through several hundred series on the same deck. The walls of the passenger accommodation decks are very plain (perhaps some artwork would come in useful here?).

The swimming pools are quite small, considering the number of passengers carried, and the pool deck is cluttered with white, plastic deck lounge chairs, without cushioned pads. Waiting for tenders in anchor ports can prove irritating, but again, it's typical of large ship operations. Charging for the machines in the self-service launderette is annoying (even though it's minimal).

Removed 2006

Seawing
★★ +

Mid-Size Ship: ....16,710 tons	Passenger Decks: 7	Cabins (wheelchair accessible): 0
Lifestyle: ....Standard	Total Crew: 334	Cabin Current: ....110 volts
Cruise Line: ......Sun Cruises/My Travel/	Passengers	Elevators: 4
Louis Cruise Lines	(lower beds/all berths): 784/926	Casino (gaming tables): ....Yes
Former Names: ....*Southward*	Passenger Space Ratio	Slot Machines: ....Yes
Builder: ......Cantieri Navale del Tirreno	(lower beds/all berths): 21.3/18.0	Swimming Pools (outdoors): 1
et Riuniti (Italy)	Crew/Passenger Ratio	Swimming Pools (indoors): 0
Original Cost: ....n/a	(lower beds/all berths): 2.5/2.9	Whirlpools: 0
Entered Service: .....Nov 1971/Mar 1995	Navigation Officers: ....International	Fitness Center: ....Yes
Registry: ....The Bahamas	Cabins (total): 392	Sauna/Steam Room: ....Yes/No
Length (ft/m): 535.7/163.30	Size Range (sq ft/m): 89.3–255.1/8.3–23.7	Massage: ....Yes
Beam (ft/m): 74.7/22.79	Cabins (outside view): 260	Self-Service Launderette: ....No
Draft (ft/m): 21.3/6.50	Cabins (interior/no view): 132	Dedicated Cinema/Seats: Yes/198
Propulsion/Propellers: ....diesel	Cabins (for one person): 0	Library: ....Yes
(13,400kW)/2	Cabins (with private balcony): 0	Classification Society: Det Norske Veritas

OVERALL SCORE: 1,072 (OUT OF A POSSIBLE 2,000 POINTS)

ACCOMMODATION: According to the Sun Cruises/My Travel brochure, there are three cabin grades (Standard, Superior and Deluxe) and five price categories. Note that, in the past, cabins were not assigned until you arrived at the ship; however, now you *can* book the cabin you want.

The 10 Boat Deck deluxe cabins are reasonably spacious for the size of the vessel, although the two forward-facing units overlook the mooring deck; these can prove noisy, and are much smaller than the other eight suites. All the suites and deluxe cabins are quite comfortable, and have full bathtubs.

All other outside-view and interior (no view) cabins are very compact (dimensionally challenged, in fact), yet they are basically clean and tidy, with adequate closet space for a one-week cruise. Room service food items incur an extra charge.

DINING: The dining room is reasonably charming, with warm colors. There are tables for four, six, eight or 10, in two seatings. The cuisine is basic, no-frills British motorway café fare – adequate for those who don't expect much in the way of presentation or quality, but definitely not memorable. Indeed, it is quantity, not quality, that prevails, but it's all provided at a low cost – as is a cruise aboard this ship. Presentation is a weak point. Remember that, like anything, you get what you pay for. If you enjoy going out to eat, and like being adventurous, then you will be disappointed. There is an adequate, but limited, wine list, and the wines are almost all very young – typical of those found in supermarkets.

BERLITZ'S RATINGS

	Possible	Achieved
Ship	500	237
Accommodation	200	101
Food	400	221
Service	400	231
Entertainment	100	52
Cruise	400	230

Wine prices are modest, as are the prices for most alcoholic beverages.

There is a self-serve buffet for casual breakfasts and luncheons, although the selection is quite limited, and the presentation is repetitive.

OTHER COMMENTS: This ship, which was formerly operated for many years by Norwegian Cruise Line, was the first vessel with which Airtours entered the cruise marketplace. However, in 2000 the ship was transferred to Louis Cruise Lines' sister company Royal Olympic Cruises as part of a deal under which Direct Cruises (a company owned by Airtours) was released from a four-year full charter of *Apollon*. Instead, *Seawing* was provided to Louis Cruise Lines as compensation. Airtours Sun Cruises (My Travel) operates the ship under charter during the summer months, while Royal Olympic Cruises typically operates the ship during the winter.

Seawing has a clean, though somewhat dated profile, with rakish superstructure, dual funnels and inboard lifeboats. The open deck and sunbathing space is rather limited, however, and the swimming pool is small.

Inside, there is a good selection of comfortable public rooms with bright, fairly contemporary and upbeat decor. Perhaps the favorite is the nightclub, set high atop adjacent to the ship's forward mast. There is also a cinema with a balcony. The show lounge is adequate for cabaret-style shows, although there are too many pillars causing obstruction to the sight lines. Families with children will find lots to do, and Airtours has special staff to provide activities and entertainment for youngsters.

Airtours Sun Cruises/My Travel provides good value for money with these cruises, designed for the young at heart. This ship provides all the right ingredients for an active, fun-filled short cruise vacation for sun loving couples and families at the right price, but the ship shows its age in places. This is basic, but reasonably sound, cruising for those wanting a no-frills vacation in pleasant surroundings, at a really modest price level. Onboard drinks prices are very reasonable. The product is tailored specifically to the UK family cruise market, and the on-board currency is the pound sterling.

Airtours/My Travel is known for packaging its products really well, and this ship represents an excellent buy for families who want to cruise, but on a limited budget. Also, if you want a little more than the basics, Sun Cruises/My Travel offers special packages – good for celebrating something special. These come in four packages – bronze, silver, gold and platinum, with each adding a little extra cost. Want to buy the captain? Go for gold or platinum and you get breakfast in bed with champagne, flowers, fruit basket, and dinner at the captain's table.

Airtours/My Travel also has its own fleet of aircraft, and this is one reason that the company is able to offer complete cruise-air-stay packages at such low rates. Sun Cruises/ My Travel typically does a fine job in getting you and your luggage from airplane to ship without having to go through immigration (although this will depend on the itinerary and operating area) in foreign countries whenever possible – so your cruise vacation is as seamless as possible.

The Sun Cruises/My Travel brochures do tell it like it is – so you know before you go exactly what you will get for your money, with the exception of its claim to "first class food," which is an exaggeration. If you want just the basics, you pay the least amount. If you want all the goodies, choose a wider "premium" seat with extra leg room on your Airtours aircraft, choose your own cabin, choose your dinner seating, breakfast in bed and dinner with the captain (no, not in bed) – then you'll pay for all those "privileges." Note, however, that, however you choose to cruise, all gratuities are included. Insurance is also included (but you will be charged for it) unless you decline it on the booking form. The onboard currency is the US dollar.

WEAK POINTS: Like the other ships in the fleet, the space per passenger is quite tight when the ship is full (which is most of the time). The cabin televisions are extremely small (except for those in the suites). Note that couples who travel without children will be surrounded by large number of children during the summer months – and, thus, increased noise levels. There is little choice of tea and coffee. There are no cushioned pads for the deck lounge chairs.

Sensation
★★★ +

Large Ship: ....70,367 tons	Total Crew: 920	Cabins (wheelchair accessible): 20
Lifestyle: ....Standard	Passengers	Cabin Current: ....110 volts
Cruise Line: ......Carnival Cruise Lines	(lower beds/all berths): 2,040/2,594	Elevators: 14
Former Names: ....none	Passenger Space Ratio	Casino (gaming tables): ....Yes
Builder: ....Kvaerner Masa-Yards	(lower beds/all berths): 34.4/26.7	Slot Machines: ....Yes
(Finland)	Crew/Passenger Ratio	Swimming Pools (outdoors): 3
Original Cost: ....$300 million	(lower beds/all berths): 2.2/2.8	Swimming Pools (indoors): 0
Entered Service: ....Nov 1993	Navigation Officers: ....Italian	Whirlpools: 6
Registry: ....The Bahamas	Cabins (total): 1,020	Fitness Center: ....Yes
Length (ft/m): 855.0/260.6	Size Range (sq ft/m): 173.2–409.7/	Sauna/Steam Room: ....Yes/Yes
Beam (ft/m): 104.0/31.4	16.0–38.0	Massage: ....Yes
Draft (ft/m): 25.9/7.9	Cabins (outside view): 618	Self-Service Launderette: ....Yes
Propulsion/Propellers: .....diesel-electric	Cabins (interior/no view): 402	Dedicated Cinema/Seats: ....No
(42,240kW)/2	Cabins (for one person): 0	Library: ....Yes
Passenger Decks: 10	Cabins (with private balcony): 54	Classification Society: ...Lloyd's Register

OVERALL SCORE: 1,385 (OUT OF A POSSIBLE 2,000 POINTS)

ACCOMMODATION: As in sister ships *Ecstasy, Elation, Fantasy, Fascination, Imagination, Inspiration,* and *Paradise*), the standard outside-view and interior (no view) cabins have plain décor. They are marginally comfortable, yet spacious enough and practical (most are of the same size and appointments), with good storage space and well-designed bathrooms.

Those booking one of the outside suites will find more space, whirlpool bathtubs, and some fascinating, rather eclectic décor and furniture. These are mildly attractive, but nothing special, and they are much smaller than those aboard the ships of a similar size of several competing companies.

A gift basket is provided in all grades of accommodation; it includes aloe soap, shampoo, conditioner, deodorant, breath mints, candy, and pain relief tablets (albeit all in sample sizes).

Note that if you book accommodation in one of the suites (Category 11 or 12 in the Carnival Cruise Lines brochure) you automatically qualify for "Skipper's Club" priority check-in at any US homeland port – useful for getting ahead of the crowd.

DINING: There are two huge, noisy dining rooms (Ecstasy and Fantasy, both non-smoking) with the usual efficient, assertive service. Dining in each restaurant is now in four seatings, for greater flexibility: 6pm, 6.45pm, 8pm and 8.45pm (these times are approximate).

Carnival meals stress quantity, not quality, although the company constantly works hard to improve the cuisine. While passengers seem to accept it, few find it

BERLITZ'S RATINGS

	Possible	Achieved
Ship	500	395
Accommodation	200	151
Food	400	221
Service	400	270
Entertainment	100	81
Cruise	400	267

worth remembering. However, food and its taste are still not the company's strongest points (you get what you pay for, remember).

While the menu items sound good, their presentation and taste leave much to be desired. Meats are of a high quality, but fish and seafood is not. Presentation is simple, and few garnishes are used. Many meat and fowl dishes are disguised with gravies and sauces. The selection of fresh green vegetables, breads, rolls, cheeses and fruits is limited, and there is too much use of canned fruit and jellied desserts. However, do remember that this is banquet catering, with all its attendant standardization and production cooking (it is, therefore, difficult to ask for anything remotely unusual or off-menu). The selection of breads, rolls, cheeses and fruits is limited (there is too much use of canned fruit).

Although there is a decent wine list, there are no wine waiters (the waiters are expected to serve both food and wine, which does not work well). The service is highly programmed, although the waiters are willing and reasonably friendly. However, the waiters do sing and dance (be prepared for *Simply the Best, Hot, Hot, Hot, Hot,* and other popular hits), and there are constant waiter parades; the dining room is show business – all done in the name of gratuities at the end of your cruise.

The Lido Café self-serve buffets are very basic, as is the selection of breads, rolls, fruit and cheeses. At night, the "Seaview Bistro," as the Lido Café becomes known, provides a casual (dress down) alternative to eating in the main dining rooms, serving pasta, steaks, salads and desserts (it typically is in operation between 6pm and 9pm). The Pizzeria is open 24 hours a day – and typically serves over 500 *every* single day.

OTHER COMMENTS: *Sensation* is the seventh in a string of newbuilds for Carnival Cruise Lines (and third in a series of eight *Fantasy*-class ships), and features almost vibration-free operational service from its diesel-electric propulsion system. The ship, whose bows are extremely short, has the distinctive, large, swept-back wing-tipped funnel that is the trademark of Carnival Cruise Lines, in the company colors of red, white and blue. At its base is a "topless" area for sunbathing.

Inside, the general passenger flow is good, and the interior design is clever, functional, and extremely colorful. A dramatic six-deck-high atrium, with cool marble and hot neon, is topped by a large colored glass dome, and features a spectacular artistic centerpiece. There are expansive open-deck areas and a good health spa/fitness center, with a large gymnasium and the latest high-tech muscle machines. There are public entertainment lounges, bars and clubs galore, with something for everyone. Dazzling colors and design themes in handsome public rooms connected by wide boulevards indoors.

There is also a $1 million art collection, much of it bright and vocal. The library is a lovely room, but there are few books (Carnival perhaps feels that its passengers do not read). The Michelangelo Lounge is a creative thinker's delight, while Fingers Lounge is sheer sensory stimulation. Lavish, but elegant multi-tiered showlounge (there are 20 pillars to obstruct some sight lines) and high energy razzle-dazzle shows. Dramatic three-deck-high glass enclosed health spa. There is a banked jogging track. The large casino has non-stop action and features plenty of gaming tables and the latest high-tech slot machines.

This ship is a fine floating playground for young, active adults who enjoy constant stimulation, close contact with lots and lots of others, as well as the three Gs – glitz, glamour and gambling. It is a live board game with every move executed in typically grand, colorful, fun-filled Carnival Cruise Lines style. This ship will entertain you well. Forget fashion – having fun is the *sine qua non* of a Carnival cruise.

Sensation operates 7-night cruises year-round from the Port of Tampa, Florida. Gratuities are automatically added to your onboard account at $9.75 per person, per day (the amount charged when this book was completed); you can have this amount adjusted, although you'll have to visit the information desk to do so. The onboard currency is the US dollar.

WEAK POINTS: Standing in line for embarkation, disembarkation, shore tenders and for self-serve buffet meals is an inevitable aspect of cruising aboard all large ships. This vessel is not for those who want a quiet, relaxing cruise experience. As in most Carnival ships, there is a sense of overwhelming sensory indulgence, as if you are in the midst of a video game parlor. There are too many loud, repetitive announcements. The constant and aggressive hustling for drinks by bar waiters is irritating, as are drinks in plastic glasses.

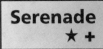

Mid-Size Ship: . . . . .14,173 tons	Total Crew: 320	Cabin Current: . . . . .110 and 220 volts
Lifestyle: . . . . .Standard	Passengers	Elevators: 2
Cruise Line: . . . . .Louis Cruise Lines	(lower beds/all berths): 600/739	Casino (gaming tables): . . . . .Yes
Former Names: . . .*Mermoz, Jean Mermoz*	Passenger Space Ratio	Slot Machines: .Yes
Builder: . . . . .Chantiers de l'Atlantique	(lower beds/all berths): 23.6/19.1	Swimming Pools (outdoors): 2
(France)	Crew/Passenger Ratio	Swimming Pools (indoors): 0
Original Cost: . . . . .n/a	(lower beds/all berths): 1.8/2.3	Whirlpools: . . . . .Yes
Entered Service: . . . .May 1957/Sept 1999	Navigation Officers: . . . . . .Cypriot/Greek	Fitness Center: . . . . .No
Registry: . . . . .The Bahamas	Cabins (total): .300	Sauna/Steam Room: . . . . .Yes/No
Length (ft/m): 531.5/162.01	Size Range (sq ft/m): . . . . .n/a	Massage: . . . . .Yes
Beam (ft/m): 65.0/19.82	Cabins (outside view): 230	Self-Service Launderette: . . . . .No
Draft (ft/m): 20.9/6.40	Cabins (interior/no view): 70	Dedicated Cinema/Seats: Yes/240
Propulsion/Propellers: . . . . .diesel	Cabins (for one person): 0	Library: . . . . .Yes
(8,000kW)/2	Cabins (with private balcony): 0	Classification Society: . . . .Bureau Veritas
Passenger Decks: 9	Cabins (wheelchair accessible): 0	

OVERALL SCORE: 790 (OUT OF A POSSIBLE 2,000 POINTS)

ACCOMMODATION: All cabins are equipped with lower beds. The cabins are quite small and equipped with only basic facilities, but they are tastefully furnished, cozy and quite comfortable, with solid fixtures and lots of wood everywhere. There is a fair amount of closet and drawer space, but the cabin bathrooms are very small (and there is little room for storage of toiletry items). Although bathrobes were provided for all passengers, they may not be under the new operators.

DINING: The main dining room has assigned tables for two, four, six, or eight. There is a smaller Grill Room, with wicker furniture. In general, the food is creatively presented. The service is provided by waiters of many nationalities, most quite friendly and attentive.

OTHER COMMENTS: *Serenade* has traditional 1950s lines and now looks very dated. It was operated for many years by the now-defunct Paquet Cruises. Louis

BERLITZ'S RATINGS

	Possible	Achieved
Ship	500	204
Accommodation	200	99
Food	400	170
Service	400	168
Entertainment	N/A	N/A
Cruise	500	149

Cruise Lines bought it in 1999, and now operates it in the Mediterranean. There is a reasonable amount of open deck and sunbathing space, although much of the teakwood decking is not in good condition.

Inside, the ship has what can be best described as a reasonably chic art deco-style décor that is rather eclectic, with a pastel color scheme and a "colonial" ambience. The spa and solarium are good spaces, with a main emphasis on hydrotherapy treatments. However, apart from the main lounge, there are few public rooms.

This ship has a fine, perhaps somewhat eclectic character, and is for those who enjoy being aboard an older ship, with all its quirks and idiosyncrasies, albeit for a moderate price. The dress code is casual throughout. The onboard currency is the Cyprus pound.

WEAK POINTS: There is no observation lounge with forward-facing views over the ship's bows. The ship is tired and worn out, and should be replaced.

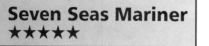

Seven Seas Mariner
★★★★★

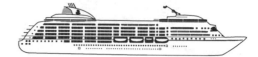

Mid-Size ship: . . . . .48,015 tons	Total Crew: 445	Cabins (wheelchair accessible): 6
Lifestyle: . . . . .Luxury/Premium	Passengers	Cabin Current: . . . . .110 volts
Cruise Line: . . . . . . .Radisson Seven Seas	(lower beds/all berths): 708/752	Elevators: 5
Cruises	Passenger Space Ratio	Casino (gaming tables): . . . . .Yes
Former Names: . . . . .none	(lower beds/all berths): 67.8/63.8	Slot Machines: . . . . .Yes
Builder: Chantiers de l'Atlantique (France)	Crew/Passenger Ratio	Swimming Pools (outdoors): 1
Original Cost: . . . .$240 million	(lower beds/all berths): 1.6/1.7	Swimming Pools (indoors): 0
Entered Service: . . . . .Mar 2001	Navigation Officers: . . . . .French	Whirlpools: 3
Registry: .France	Cabins (total): 354	Fitness Center: . . . . .Yes
Length (ft/m): 713/217.3	Size Range (sq ft/m): 301.3–1,528.4/	Sauna/Steam Room: . . . . .Yes/Yes
Beam (ft/m): 95.1/29.0	28.0–142.0	Massage: . . . . .Yes
Draft (ft/m): 21.4/6.5	Cabins (outside view): 354	Self-Service Launderette: . . . . .Yes (3)
Propulsion/Propellers: . . .diesel-electric/2	Cabins (interior/no view): 0	Dedicated Cinema/Seats: . . . . .No
azimuthing pods (8.5 MW each)	Cabins (for one person): 0	Library: . . . . .Yes
Passenger Decks: 9	Cabins (with private balcony): 354	Classification Society: . . . .Bureau Veritas

OVERALL SCORE: 1,703 (OUT OF A POSSIBLE 2,000 POINTS)

ACCOMMODATION: This is the cruise industry's first "all-suite, all-balcony" ship (terminology that marketing departments enjoy, although it is not actually correct, as not all accommodation has sleeping areas completely separated from living areas). However, all grades of accommodation have private, marble-clad bathrooms with bathtub, and all suite entrances are neatly recessed away from the passenger hallways, to provide an extra modicum of quietness. In comparison with *Seven Seas Navigator*, the bathrooms aboard this ship are not as large in the lower grade of accommodation.

MASTER SUITE: The largest accommodation (1,580 sq. ft/147 sq. meters), in two Master Suites, has two separate bedrooms, living room with TV/VCR and CD player, walk-in closet, dining area, large, two marble-clad bathrooms with bathtub and separate shower enclosure, and two private teakwood-decked balconies. These suites are located on the deck under the ship's navigation bridge, one balcony providing delightful forward-facing views, while a second balcony provides port or starboard views. Butler service is provided. To keep things in perspective, these two Master Suites are nowhere near as large as the two Penthouse Suites aboard the much larger Celebrity Cruises ships *Infinity, Millennium* and *Summit* (which measure 2,350 sq. ft/218 sq. meters).

MARINER SUITE: Six Mariner Suites (739 sq. ft/69 sq. meters), located on port and starboard sides of the atrium on three separate decks, have a separate bedroom, living

BERLITZ'S RATINGS

	Possible	Achieved
Ship	500	449
Accommodation	200	177
Food	400	334
Service	400	324
Entertainment	100	83
Cruise	400	336

room with TV/VCR and CD player, walk-in closet, dining area, large, marble-clad bathroom with bathtub and separate shower enclosure, and a good sized private balcony with either port or starboard views. Butler service is provided.

GRAND SUITE): Two Grand Suites (707 sq. ft/66 sq. meters) are located one deck above the ship's navigation bridge, and have a separate bedroom, living room with TV/VCR and CD player, walk-in closet, dining area, two marble-clad bathrooms (one with bathtub and separate shower enclosure, the second with a bathtub and a separate shower enclosure), and a good sized private balcony with port or starboard views. Butler service is provided.

SEVEN SEAS SUITES: Six spacious suites (697 sq. ft/65 sq. meters) overlook the ship's stern (two suites are located on each of four decks) and have very generous private balcony space and good wrap-around views over the ship's stern and to port or starboard. However, the balconies are only semi-private and can be partly overlooked by neighbors in Horizon Suites as well as from above. Another two Seven Seas Suites are located just aft of the ship's navigation bridge and measure a slightly smaller 600 sq ft (56 sq. meters) and have balconies with either port or starboard views. These suites have a separate bedroom, living room with TV/VCR and CD player, walk-in closet, dining area, large, and marble-clad bathroom with a combination bathtub/shower.

HORIZON SUITES: There are 12 Horizon Suites (522 sq.

ft/48 sq. meters) overlooking the ship's stern (three suites are located on each of four decks, sandwiched between the Seven Seas Suites) and have a good-sized balcony (though not as large as the Seven Seas Suites) and good views. These suites have a separate bedroom, living room with TV/VCR, walk-in closet, dining area, large, marble-clad bathroom with a combination bathtub/shower.

ALL OTHER CABINS: All other cabins (Categories A–H in the brochure, listed as Deluxe Suites and Penthouse Suites) are 300 sq. ft (28 sq. meters) and have twin beds that can convert to a queen-sized bed (European duvets are standard), small walk-in closet, marble-lined bathroom with combination bathtub/shower, 100 percent cotton bathrobe 100 percent cotton towels, vanity desk, hairdryer, TV/VCR, refrigerator (stocked with soft drinks and bar set-up on embarkation), personal safe. In these suites, the sleeping area is separated from the living area only by partial room dividers, and therefore is a cabin (albeit a good-sized one), and not a suite.

Six wheelchair-accessible suites are located as close to an elevator as one could possibly get, and provide ample living space, together with a large roll-in shower and all bathroom fittings located at the correct height.

DINING: There are four different dining venues, all operated on an open seating basis, so that you can sit with whom you want, when you wish. In reality, this means that dining aboard ship is like dining on land – you can go to a different dining spot each night. The downside of this is that waiters don't get to know and remember your preferences. Reservations are required in two of the four dining spots. In general, the cuisine is very good, with creative presentation and a wide variety of food choices.

The main dining room is the 570-seat Compass Rose Restaurant, located in the center of the ship. It has a light, fresh décor, and seating at tables for two, four, six or eight. A large pre-dinner drinks bar is conveniently located adjacent on the starboard side. Fine Dudson china is used.

Off to the port side of the Compass Rose Restaurant is Latitudes – with 80 seats, the smallest of the specialty restaurants for alternative dining, with tableside preparation of dishes from all parts of the world (the décor, too, is an interesting, rather eclectic mix from several parts of the world). There is seating for two, four or six, and reservations are required.

A 120-seat "supper club," called Signatures – which has its own dedicated galley – is located one deck above the main galley (for convenient vertical supply and staff access), and has ocean views along the room's port side. It is directed and staffed by chefs wearing the white toque and blue riband of Le Cordon Bleu in Paris, the world's most prestigious culinary authority, and so the cuisine is classic French. Doors open onto a covered area outdoors, complete with stage and dance floor. Porsgrund china is used, as are silver show plates and

the very finest silverware. Seating is at tables of two, four, or six, and reservations are required.

For more casual meals, La Veranda is a large self-serve indoor/outdoor café with seats for 450 (the teakwood-decked outdoor seating is particularly pleasant), and the décor is fresh and light. This eatery has several food islands and substantial counter display space. There is also an outdoor grill, adjacent to the swimming pool.

As another variation on the dining theme, you can also choose to dine in your cabin. There is a 24-hour room service menu, and, during regular dinner hours, the full dining room menu is available.

OTHER COMMENTS: This is the largest ship in the Radisson Seven Seas Cruises fleet, and the first to receive a "pod" propulsion system, replacing the traditional shaft and rudder system (the pods have forward-facing propellers that can be turned through 360 degrees). The ship was (for the technically minded) built in 32 blocks, using the same hull design as for Festival Cruises' *Mistral*, although the interior design is totally different. In the fitting out stage, for example, many changes were made to accommodate Radisson Seven Seas Cruises' need for all-outside-view suites. Consequently, its passenger space ratio is now the highest in the cruise industry, at just a fraction above those for *Europa*. *Seven Seas Mariner* is operated by Radisson Seven Seas Cruises, although the ship is actually owned by a joint-venture company established with ship managers V-Ships.

There is a wide range of public rooms to play in, almost all located below the accommodation decks. Three sets of stairways (forward, center, aft) mean it is easy to find your way around the vessel. An atrium lobby spans nine decks, with the lowest level opening directly onto the tender landing stage.

Facilities include a delightful observation lounge, a casino, a shopping concourse (conveniently located opposite the casino) – complete with open market area, a garden lounge/promenade arcade, a large library with internet-connect computers, business center, card room and a conference room.

The main show lounge spans two decks and is quite stunning, and the sight lines are very good from almost all seats. There is also a nightclub (Stars) with an oval-shaped dance floor, a cigar-smoking lounge (called the Connoisseur Club, for cigars, cognacs and other assorted niceties), and the usual photo gallery.

Health and fitness facilities include an extensive health spa with gymnasium and aerobics room, beauty parlor, and separate changing, sauna and steam rooms for men and women. Specialist Judith Jackson operates the spa and beauty services, located not at the top of the ship, as is common with many other ships today, but just off the atrium. Sports devotees can play in the paddle tennis court, golf driving and practice cages.

With the introduction of *Seven Seas Mariner*, Radisson Seven Seas Cruises has clearly moved into a new breed of larger ships that are more economical to operate, and provide more choices for passengers. However, the downside of a larger ship such as this is that there is a loss of the sense of intimacy that the company's smaller ships have previously been able to maintain. Thus, some of the former personal service of the smaller ships has been absorbed into a larger structure. Another downside is the fact that this ship is simply too large to enter the small harbors and berths that the company's smaller ships can, and so loses some of the benefits of small upscale ship cruising.

So, it's swings and roundabouts when it comes to scoring the ship. At present, it scores very highly in terms of hardware and software, but operationally may lose a few points if it is deemed that it can enter only mid-size ship ports. By comparison, this ship is a more upscale version of the eight ships in the Renaissance Cruises fleet – with better food, more choices, and a staff that is more hospitality-conscious and generally better trained. *Seven Seas Mariner*, therefore, has ended

up just a tad over the score base needed for it to join the "Berlitz Five Star" Club.

Gratuities are included, as are complimentary bar set-ups on embarkation and complimentary table wines for dinner (although premium and connoisseur selections are available at extra cost). The onboard currency is the US dollar.

WEAK POINTS: Service and hospitality are sometimes spotty and inconsistent – the result more of a multi-nationality crew mix provided by a maritime personnel supply agency that appears not to understand quality. The same carpeting is used throughout the public areas – with no relief or change of color or pattern on the stairwells. The décor is a little glitzy in places. The ship is too large to get into some of the smaller ports of call that the smaller ships in the fleet can get into. Also, much of the intimacy and close-knit ambience of the smaller vessels is missing.

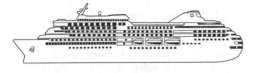

Seven Seas Navigator
★★★★ +

Small Ship: . . . . .28,550 tons	Passengers	Cabin Current: . . . . .110 and 220 volts
Lifestyle: . . . . .Luxury/Premium	(lower beds/all berths): 490/530	Elevators: 5
Cruise Line: . . . . . . .Radisson Seven Seas	Passenger Space Ratio	Casino (gaming tables): . . . . .Yes
Cruises	(lower beds/all berths): 58.2/53.8	Slot Machines: .Yes
Former Names: . . . . .none	Crew/Passenger Ratio	Swimming Pools (outdoors): 1
Builder: . . . . .T. Mariotti (Italy)	(lower beds/all berths): 1.5/1.6	Swimming Pools (indoors): 0
Original Cost: . . . .$200 million	Navigation Officers: . . . . .European/	Whirlpools: 2
Entered Service: . . . . .Aug 1999	International	Fitness Center: . . . . .Yes
Registry: . . . . .The Bahamas	Cabins (total): .245	Sauna/Steam Room: . . . . .Yes/Yes
Length (ft/m): 559.7/170.6	Size Range (sq ft/m): 301.3–1,173.3/	Massage: . . . . .Yes
Beam (ft/m): 71.5/21.8	28.0–109.0	Self-Service Launderette: . . . . .Yes
Draft (ft/m): 21.3.0/6.5	Cabins (outside view): 245	Dedicated Cinema/Seats: . . . . .No
Propulsion/Propellers: . . . . .diesel	Cabins (interior/no view): 0	Library: . . . . .Yes
(13,000kW/2	Cabins (for one person): 0	Classification Society: . . .Registro Navale
Passenger Decks: 8	Cabins (with private balcony): 196	Italiano (RINA)
Total Crew: 325	Cabins (wheelchair accessible): 4	

OVERALL SCORE: 1,653 (OUT OF A POSSIBLE 2,000 POINTS)

ACCOMMODATION: There are 11 grades. The company markets this as an "all-suite" ship. Even the smallest suite is quite large, and all have outside views. Almost 90 percent of all suites feature a private balcony, with floor-to-ceiling sliding glass doors, while 10 suites are interconnecting, and 38 suites have an extra bed for a third occupant. By comparison, even the smallest suite aboard this ship is more than twice the size of the smallest cabin aboard the world's largest cruise ship, Royal Caribbean International's *Explorer of the Seas.*

All grades of accommodation have a walk-in closet, European king-sized bed or twin beds, wooden cabinetry with nicely rounded edges, plenty of drawer space, mini-bar/refrigerator (stocked with complimentary soft drinks and bar set-up on embarkation), television/VCR, personal safe and other accoutrements of fine living at sea in the latest design format. The marble-appointed bathroom has a full-size bathtub, as well as a separate shower enclosure, 100 percent cotton bathrobe and towels, and hairdryer.

The largest living spaces can be found in four master suites, with forward-facing views (all have double-length side balconies). Each suite has a completely separate bedroom with dressing table; the living room has a full dining room table and chairs for up to six persons, wet bar, counter and bar stools, large 3-person sofa and six armchairs, and an audio-visual console/entertainment center. Each suite has a large main, marble-clad, fully tiled bathroom with full-sized bathtub and separate

BERLITZ'S RATINGS

	Possible	Achieved
Ship	500	416
Accommodation	200	180
Food	400	332
Service	400	318
Entertainment	100	83
Cruise	400	324

shower enclosure, a separate room with bidet, toilet and washbasin, with plenty of shelf and other storage space for personal toiletry items. There is a separate guest bathroom.

Next in size are the superb Navigator Suites, which have a completely separate bedroom, walk-in closet, large lounge with mini-bar/refrigerator (stocked with complimentary soft drinks and bar set-up on embarkation), personal safe, compact disc player, large television/VCR player, and dining area with large table and four chairs. The marble-clad, fully tiled bathroom has a full-sized bathtub with hand-held shower, plus a separate shower enclosure (the door to which is only 18 inches/45 cm, however), large washbasin, toilet and bidet, and ample shelf space for personal toiletry items. It is unfortunate that the Navigator Suites are located in the center of the ship, as they are directly underneath the swimming pool deck. They are, thus, subject to noise attacks at 6am daily, when deck cleaning is carried out, and chairs are dragged across the deck directly over the suites. They are further subjected to noise attacks whenever pool deck stewards drag and drop deck lounge chairs into place. Despite these comments, the Navigator Suites are delightful living spaces.

Four suites for the physically challenged have private balconies, and are ideally located adjacent to the elevators (correcting a mistake made when the company's *Radisson Diamond* was constructed, when they were located as far from any elevators as they possibly could be). However, while the suites are very practical, it is almost impossible to access the balcony, because of the "lip" or "threshold" at the bottom of the sliding glass door.

DINING: The Compass Rose Dining Room has large ocean-view picture windows and open seating dining, which means that you may be seated when and with whom you wish. Complimentary wines are served during dinner, although a connoisseur wine list is available for those who prefer to choose a vintage wine (at extra cost). The company also features "heart healthy" cuisine. Although most of the dining room is non-smoking, a small section is available for smokers.

An alternative dining spot, Portofino Grill, has informal Italian dining for dinner (reservations are required). The Grill is part of a larger restaurant with indoor/outdoor seating. For fast-food items, there is also a small indoor/outdoor Grill, adjacent to the swimming pool.

You can also choose to dine in your cabin. There is a 24-hour room service menu; also, during regular dinner hours, you can choose from the full dining room menu.

OTHER COMMENTS: This new ship was built using a hull already constructed in St. Petersburg, Russia, as the research vessel *Akademik Nikolay Pilyugin*. After launching the hull, the name *Blue Sea* was used for a short time. The superstructure was incorporated into the hull in an Italian shipyard – the result being that what was (for all intents and purposes) a new ship was delivered in record time. However, the result is less than handsome – particularly at the ship's stern. It is, however, large enough to be stable over long stretches of water, and there is an excellent amount of space per passenger.

The interiors have a mix of classical and contemporary Italian styling and décor throughout, with warm, soft colors and fine quality soft furnishings and fabrics.

The Vista Lounge is forward-view observation lounge. At the opposite end of the ship is Galileo's, a large piano lounge with good views over the stern.

A Navigator's Lounge has warm mahogany and cherry wood paneling and large, comfortable, mid-back tub chairs. Meanwhile, next door, cigars and cognac (and other niceties) can be taken in the delightful Connoisseur's Club – the first aboard a Radisson Seven Seas Cruises vessel.

There is a two-deck-high show lounge, with reasonable sight lines from most seats (although several pillars obstruct the views from some of the side balcony seats). The extensive library also has several computers with direct email/internet access (for a fee).

The ship is designed for worldwide cruise itineraries, and is one of the most in the Radisson Seven Seas Cruises fleet. As with all ships in the Radisson Seven Seas Cruises fleet, all gratuities are included. The onboard currency is the US dollar.

WEAK POINTS: There is no wrap-around promenade deck outdoors, although there is a jogging track high atop the aft section of the ship around the funnel housing. Two of the upper, outer decks are laid with green Astroturf, which cheapens the look of the ship – these decks would be better in teak. The ceilings in several public rooms (including the main restaurant) are quite low, which makes the ship feel smaller and more closed in than it is. The ship suffers from a considerable amount of vibration, which detracts from the comfort level when compared with other vessels of the same size. Service and hospitality are spotty and inconsistent.

Nice 2004 ✓

Silver Cloud
★ ★ ★ ★ ★

Small Ship: . . . . .16,927 tons	Passengers	Cabin Current: . . . . . . .110 and 220 volts
Lifestyle: . . . . .Luxury	(lower beds/all berths): 296/315	Elevators: 4
Cruise Line: . . . . .Silversea Cruises	Passenger Space Ratio	Casino (gaming tables): . . . . .Yes
Former Names: . . . . .none	(lower beds/all berths): 57.1/53.7	Slot Machines: . . . . .Yes
Builder: . . . . .Visentini/Mariotti (Italy)	Crew/Passenger Ratio	Swimming Pools (outdoors): 1
Original Cost: . . . .$125 million	(lower beds/all berths): 1.4/1.5	Swimming Pools (indoors): 0
Entered Service: . . . . .Apr 1994	Navigation Officers: . . . . .Italian	Whirlpools: 2
Registry: . . . . .The Bahamas	Cabins (total): 148	Fitness Center: . . . . .Yes
Length (ft/m): 514.4/155.8	Size Range (sq ft/m): 240.0–1,314.0/	Sauna/Steam Room: . . . . .Yes/Yes
Beam (ft/m): 70.62/21.4	22.2–122.0	Massage: . . . . .Yes
Draft (ft/m): 17.3/5.3	Cabins (outside view): 148	Self-Service Launderette: . . . . .Yes
Propulsion/Propellers: . . . . .diesel	Cabins (interior/no view): 0	Dedicated Cinema/Seats: Yes/306
(11,700kW)/2	Cabins (for one person): 0	Library: . . . . .Yes
Passenger Decks: 6	Cabins (with private balcony): 110	Classification Society: . . .Registro Navale
Total Crew: 210	Cabins (wheelchair accessible): 2	Italiano (RINA)

OVERALL SCORE: 1,717 (OUT OF A POSSIBLE 2,000 POINTS)

ACCOMMODATION: The all-outside suites (75 percent of which have fine private teakwood balconies) have convertible queen-to-twin beds and are beautifully fitted out with just about everything one needs, including huge floor-to-ceiling windows, large walk-in closets, dressing table, writing desk, stocked mini-bar/refrigerator (no charge), and fresh flowers. The marble floor bathrooms have

BERLITZ'S RATINGS

	Possible	Achieved
Ship	500	435
Accommodation	200	181
Food	400	339
Service	400	340
Entertainment	100	77
Cruise	400	345

bathtub, single vanity and plenty of towels. Personalized stationery, bathrobes, and a decent amenities kit is provided in all cabins. The top grades of suites also have CD-players.

All cabins have televisions and VCR. However, the walk-in closets do not actually provide much hanging space (particularly for such items as full-length dresses), and it would be better for the door to open outward instead of inward (the drawers themselves are poorly positioned). Although the cabin insulation above and below each cabin is good, the insulation between cabins is not (a privacy curtain installed between entry door and sleeping area would be most useful), and light from the passageway leaks into the cabin, making it hard to achieve a dark room.

Note that the cabins with balconies on the lowest deck can suffer from sticky salt spray when the ship is moving, so the balconies require lots of cleaning. Each evening, the stewardesses bring plates of canapés to your suite – just right for a light bite with cocktails.

DINING: The contemporary dining room has an attractive arched gazebo center and a wavy ceiling design as

its focal point, and is set with fine Limoges china and well-balanced Christofle flatware. Meals are served in an open seating, which means you can eat when you like (within the given dining room opening times), and with whom you like. Meals can also be served, course-by-course, in your suite, although the balcony tables are rather low for dining outdoors. The dining is good throughout the ship, with a choice of formal and informal areas, but the cuisine and presentation don't quite match up to products such as the smaller Seabourn Cruise Line ships. Standard table wines are included for lunch and dinner, but there is also a "connoisseur list" of premium wines at extra charge. The house champagne is Moet & Chandon.

An alternative Italian restaurant, Cucina Italiana, is very popular for evening alternative dining. By day it acts as the informal Terrace Cafe, but by night turns into a delightful, intimate dining spot, complete with candlelight and print tablecloths.

The ship also provides 24-hour in-cabin dining service (full course by course dinners are available).

OTHER COMMENTS: *Silver Cloud* has quite a handsome profile, with a sloping stern reminiscent of an "Airstream" trailer. The size is just about ideal for highly personalized cruising in an elegant environment. The vertical cake-layer stacking of public rooms aft and the location of accommodation units forward ensures quiet cabins. There is a synthetic turf-covered wrap-around promenade deck outdoors, and a spacious swimming pool deck.

The spacious interior is well planned, with elegant

décor and fine quality soft furnishings. This is accented by the gentle use of brass and fine woods and very creative ceilings throughout. The spa areas need improvement, and the tiled decor is bland and uninviting.

There is a useful business center as well as a CD-ROM and hardback book library, open 24 hours a day. There is an excellent two-level show lounge with tiered seating, but the entertainment is disappointing and not as good as when the ship first debuted.

In 2000, a new concession took over the health spa and improved upon the services and range of personal treatments available. The Mandara Spa (originating in Bali) includes what are known as Ayervedic treatments. Massages, however, are extremely expensive, at approximately $2 per minute.

There is an excellent amount of space per passenger and there is no hint of a line anywhere in this unhurried environment. Excellent documentation is provided before your cruise, all of which comes in a high-quality document wallet.

An elegant onboard ambience prevails, and there is no pressure, no hype, and an enthusiastic staff to pamper you, with a high ratio of Europeans. Insurance is extra (it *was* included when Silversea Cruises first started). Refreshingly, all drinks, gratuities and port taxes *are* included, and, refreshingly, no further tipping anywhere

on board is allowed. This ship is perhaps ideal for those who enjoy spacious surroundings, excellent food, and some entertainment. It would be difficult not to have good cruise vacation aboard this ship, albeit at a fairly high price.

Silversea Cruises has come a long way since its inception, and continues to refine its product. The company's many international passengers react well to the ambience, food, service and the staff, most of who go out of their way to please.

Few ships make it to a five-star rating today, but Silversea Cruises has earned an enviable reputation for high quality in a short space of time. The onboard currency is the US dollar.

WEAK POINTS: Some vibration is evident when bow thrusters or the anchors are used, particularly in the forward-most cabins. Plastic deck lounge chairs and patio tables for the alternative dining spot do not signal a luxury product; these should be changed to teak or other sustainable hardwood variety. The self-service launderette is poor and not large enough for longer cruises, when passengers like to be able to do their own small items. Sadly, crew facilities are minimal, and so keeping consistency is difficult, as high crew turnover is a fact of life. The artwork is quite poor.

Silver Shadow
★★★★★

Small Ship: . . . . .28,258 tons	Passengers	Cabin Current: . . . . .110 and 220 volts
Lifestyle: . . . . .Luxury	(lower beds/all berths): 388/400	Elevators: 5
Cruise Line: . . . . .Silversea Cruises	Passenger Space Ratio	Casino (gaming tables): . . . . .Yes
Former Names: . . . . .none	(lower beds/all berths): 72.8/70.6	Slot Machines: . . . . .Yes
Builder: . . . . .Visentini/Mariotti	Crew/Passenger Ratio	Swimming Pools (outdoors): 1
(Italy)	(lower beds/all berths): 1.3/1.3	Swimming Pools (indoors): 0
Original Cost: . . . .$150 million	Navigation Officers: . . . . .Italian	Whirlpools: 2
Entered Service: . . . . .Sept 2000	Cabins (total): 194	Fitness Center: . . . . .Yes
Registry: . . . . .The Bahamas	Size Range (sq ft/m): 287.0–1,435.0/	Sauna/Steam Room: . . . . .Yes/Yes
Length (ft/m): 610.2/186.0	26.6–133.3	Massage: . . . . .Yes
Beam (ft/m): 81.8/24.8	Cabins (outside view): 194	Self-Service Launderette: . . . . .Yes
Draft (ft/m): 19.6/6.0	Cabins (interior/no view): 0	Dedicated Cinema/Seats: . . . . .No
Propulsion/Propellers: diesel/2	Cabins (for one person): 0	Library: . . . . .Yes
Passenger Decks: 7	Cabins (with private balcony): 157	Classification Society: . . .Registro Navale
Total Crew: .295	Cabins (wheelchair accessible): 2	Italiano (RINA)

OVERALL SCORE: 1,757 (OUT OF A POSSIBLE 2,000 POINTS)

ACCOMMODATION: There are seven grades. Regardless of the size or grade of accommodation you choose, all have double vanities in the marble-floored bathrooms, which also have a bathtub and separate shower enclosure. Silversea-monogrammed Frette bed linen is provided in all grades, as are soft down pillows, 100 percent cotton bathrobes and a range of personal toiletry amenities by Bulgari, and personalized stationery.

VISTA SUITES: These suites (287 sq. ft/27 sq. meters) do not have a private balcony. Instead there is a large window, twin beds that convert to a queen-sized bed, sitting area, television and VCR, refrigerator, writing desk, personal safe, cocktail cabinet, dressing table with hairdryer, and walk-in closet. The bathroom is marble-clad in gentle colors, and has two (his 'n' hers) washbasins, full-sized bathtub, separate shower enclosure, and toilet.

VERANDA SUITES: Each of the Veranda Suites (really a Vista Suite plus a veranda) measures 345 sq. ft (33 sq. meters) and have convertible twin-to-queen beds. They are well fitted out with just about everything you would need, including large floor-to-ceiling windows, large walk-in closet, dressing table, writing desk, stocked mini-bar/refrigerator (all drinks are included in the price of your cruise), and fresh flowers. The marble-clad bathrooms have two (his 'n' hers) washbasins, full-sized bathtub, separate shower enclosure, and toilet.

SILVER SUITES: The Silver Suites measure 701 sq. ft

BERLITZ'S RATINGS		
	Possible	Achieved
Ship	500	454
Accommodation	200	180
Food	400	339
Service	400	349
Entertainment	100	86
Cruise	400	349

(65 sq. meters). These are much wider than the Vista Suites or Veranda Suites and have a separate bedroom, an entertainment center with CD player, TV/VCR unit (in both bedroom and living room) and much more living space that includes a large dining area with table and four chairs. The marble-clad bathrooms have two (his 'n' hers) washbasins, full sized bathtub, separate shower enclosure, and toilet.

OWNER'S SUITES: The two Owner's Suites, each of which measures 1,208 sq. ft (112 sq. meters), are much larger units and includes an extra bathroom for guests, as well as more living space. There is a 200 sq.-ft (18 sq.-meter) veranda, two bedrooms (with queen-sized beds), two walk-in closets, two living rooms, two sitting areas, separate dining area, an entertainment center with flat-screen plasma television in the living room and TV/VCR player in each bedroom, telephones, refrigerators, cocktail cabinet, writing desk, dressing tables with hairdryers. There are two marble-clad bathrooms, one with a full sized whirlpool bathtub and two washbasins, separate toilet, and separate shower, as well as a powder room for guests. Owner's Suites can be either a one- or two-bedroom configuration.

ROYAL SUITES: Stately accommodation can be found in two Royal Suites, which measure either 1,312 sq. ft (122 sq. meters) or 1,352 sq. ft (126 sq. meters). These are two-bedroom suites, with two teakwood verandas, two living rooms, sitting areas, dining area, queen-size beds, an entertainment center with flat-screen plasma television in the living room and TV/VCR player in each bedroom, telephones, refrigerators, cocktail cabinet, writing desk, two closets, dressing tables with hair-dryers. There are two marble-clad bathrooms, one with a full sized whirlpool bathtub and two washbasins, sep-arate toilet, and separate shower, as well as a powder room for guests. Royal Suites can be either a one- or two-bedroom configuration.

GRAND SUITES: There are two Grand Suites, one of which measures 1,286 sq. ft (119 sq. meters), while the other (including an adjoining suite with interconnect-ing door) measures 1,435 sq. ft (133 sq. meters). These have two bedrooms, two large walk-in closets, two liv-ing rooms, Bang & Olufsen entertainment centers, and large, forward-facing, private verandas that face for-wards. These really are sumptuous apartments that fea-ture all the comforts of home, and then some.

HANDICAP SUITES: There are two suites for the physi-cally disabled (535 and 537), both of which are adja-cent to an elevator, as well as being next to each other. They measure a generous 398 sq. ft (37 sq. meters). The suites are well equipped with an accessible hanging rail, and roll-in bathroom with roll-in shower unit.

DINING: The main dining room (called, simply, "The Restaurant") provides open-seating dining in elegant surroundings. Three grand chandeliers provide an up-ward focal point, while you can dine when you want, and with whom you wish (within the given dining room opening times), in these refined surroundings. Meals can also be served, course-by-course, in your suite, although the balcony tables are rather low for dining outdoors. The dining is good throughout the ship, with a choice of formal and informal areas, although the cui-sine and presentation doesn't quite match up to that of products such as the smaller Seabourn Cruise Line ships. Cristofle silverware is provided. Standard table wines are included for lunch and dinner, but there is also a "connoisseur list" of premium wines at extra charge. The house champagne is Moet & Chandon.

A poolside Grill provides a casual alternative day-time dining spot, for grill and fast food items. Dinner can also be served course by course in your own suite.

For even more informal dining, there is an informal Terrace Café – this has been popular aboard the com-pany's two (smaller) ships, *Silver Cloud* and *Silver Wind*). In the evening this has regional Italian cuisine.

Adjacent to the café is a wine bar as well as a cigar smoking room (more of this later). Once each cruise, there's a "Galley Brunch" in the ship's galley, trans-formed for the occasion into a large "chef's kitchen."

OTHER COMMENTS: *Silver Shadow* is the second gen-eration of vessels in the Silversea Cruises fleet, and is slightly larger than the company's first two ships, *Silver Cloud* and *Silver Wind*, with a more streamlined for-ward profile and large, sleek single funnel. However, the stern section is not particularly handsome. The design of this new ship (its sister ship is *Silver Whis-per*) has evolved from the experience and success gained from the first pair. There is a generous amount of open deck and sunning space.

"The Humidor, by Davidoff" is the ship's cigar smok-ing lounge; it has 25 seats and has been created in the style of an English smoking club, with candlelit evenings. All the cigars for sale are provided by Davidoff, the well-known purveyor of fine cigars. It was Zino Davidoff, son of founder Henri Davidoff, who created the revolutionary "cigar cellar" (now called a humidor). In case you're won-dering, the air is changed 62 times each hour, so there is little of the stale smell you might expect from such rooms.

Other new additions include a champagne bar and a computer-learning center, with four computer terminals.

The Mandara Spa (originating in Bali) operates the health spa facilities, much expanded when compared to smaller sisters *Silver Cloud* and *Silver Wind*, and spe-cializes in what are known as Ayervedic treatments. Massages, however, are extremely expensive, at approx-imately $2 per minute.

Silversea Cruises has "all-inclusive" fares, including gratuities (they do not, however, include vintage wines, or massage, or other personal services), but they do include many things that are at extra cost compared aboard the ships of many other cruise lines. The pas-senger mix includes many nationalities, which actually makes for a more interesting experience, although the majority of passengers are typically North American. The onboard currency is the US dollar.

WEAK POINTS: The swimming pool is surprisingly small, as is the fitness room. Plastic deck lounge chairs and patio tables for the alternative dining spot do not signal a luxury product; these should be changed to teak or other sustainable hardwood variety.

Removed 2006

Small Ship: ....5,092 tons	Total Crew: 130	Cabin Current: ....220 volts
Lifestyle: ....Standard	Passengers	Elevators: 0
Cruise Line: ....Mano Maritime	(lower beds/all berths): 314/425	Casino (gaming tables): ....Yes
Former Names: ....*Royal Dream,*	Passenger Space Ratio	Slot Machines: ....Yes
Odessa Song, Bashkiriya	(lower beds/all berths): 16.2/11.9	Swimming Pools (outdoors): 1
Builder: ....VEB Mathias Thesen	Crew/Passenger Ratio	Swimming Pools (indoors): 0
(Germany)	(lower beds/all berths): 2.4/3.2	Whirlpools: 0
Original Cost: ....n/a	Navigation Officers: ....Ukrainian	Fitness Center: ....No
Entered Service: 1964/1998	Cabins (total): 157	Sauna/Steam Room: ....Yes/No
Registry: ....Malta	Size Range (sq ft/m): ....n/a	Massage: ....No
Length (ft/m): 400.5/122.1	Cabins (outside view): 134	Self-Service Launderette: ....No
Beam (ft/m): 52.4/16.0	Cabins (interior/no view): 23	Dedicated Cinema/Seats: ....No
Draft (ft/m): 18.3/5.59	Cabins (for one person): 0	Library: ....Yes
Propulsion/Propellers: diesel/2	Cabins (with private balcony): 0	Classification Society: ..Hellenic Register
Passenger Decks: 6	Cabins (wheelchair accessible): 0	

OVERALL SCORE: 811 (OUT OF A POSSIBLE 2,000 POINTS)

ACCOMMODATION: The Silver Iris and Silver Jasmine suites are the largest of the seven cabin grades, which is really too many for such a small ship. These have a separate living room and bedroom, plus a bathroom with full-sized bathtub.

Other cabins are small and basic, yet reasonably comfortable, and the few interior (no view) cabins are fairly large. Most cabins have beds in an "L"-shaped configuration; some cabins have third and fourth upper berths, although the closet and drawer space is extremely limited when all are occupied; all have a private bathroom with shower (soap and shampoo are provided). The cabin insulation is poor, and drawer space is very modest.

DINING: The dining room, which is set low down in the ship (it also has a low ceiling) and has portholes, has Middle Eastern décor. There are two seatings. The food is surprisingly good, with lots of fresh salads and vegetables, plus good meats and local fish. There is certainly plenty of variety. Kosher food can also be supplied – for a surcharge of about $19 per passenger, per day.

OTHER COMMENTS: This former Russian vessel has a large square funnel, and is now operated under a 15-year charter to Mano Maritime of Haifa, Israel. There is very little outdoor walking space, although there is a

BERLITZ'S RATINGS

	Possible	Achieved
Ship	500	191
Accommodation	200	93
Food	400	250
Service	400	22
Entertainment	100	48
Cruise	400	207

decent amount of open deck and sunbathing space. The swimming pool is really just a "dip" pool, and the painted steel decks forward of the pool really should be covered with wood or other heat-absorbing materials.

There are just two principal public rooms. One is the main lounge/show lounge, which has a bar on the port side adjacent to the entrance. The lounge seating is arranged around a circular wooden dance floor. The second room acts as the ship's disco at night. There is also a small room for children.

Silver Star (no connection with Silversea Cruises) is an older vessel that has received extensive refit and refurbishment work, and typically operates 7-night Mediterranean cruises almost exclusively for the local Israeli market. The ship itself is very basic, but the food provides a highlight.

Some cruises are designated as special holiday cruises (Passover, Yom Haatzmaut, Shavuot, Rosh Hashana, Sukkot, and Hannukah) and attract higher cruise rates. All passengers are provided with a photo ID/charge card (Mano Card). Port charges are extra, as are handling fees and administrative expenses.

WEAK POINTS: This is a very high-density ship that has little space per person. There is a charge for use of the sauna.

Silver Whisper
★★★★★

Small Ship:	.28,258 tons	Passengers	
Lifestyle:	.Luxury	(lower beds/all berths):	.388/400
Cruise Line:	.Silversea Cruises	Passenger Space Ratio	
Former Names:	.none	(lower beds/all berths):	.72.8/70.6
Builder:	.Visentini/Mariotti	Crew/Passenger Ratio	
	(Italy)	(lower beds/all berths):	.1.3/1.3
Original Cost:	.$150 million	Navigation Officers:	.Italian
Entered Service:	.July 2001	Cabins (total):	.194
Registry:	.The Bahamas	Size Range (sq ft/m):	.287.0–1,435.0/
Length (ft/m):	.610.2/186.0		26.6–133.3
Beam (ft/m):	.81.8/24.8	Cabins (outside view):	.194
Draft (ft/m):	.19.6/6.0	Cabins (interior/no view):	.0
Propulsion/Propellers:	.diesel/2	Cabins (for one person):	.0
Passenger Decks:	.7	Cabins (with private balcony):	.157
Total Crew:	.295	Cabins (wheelchair accessible):	.2

Cabin Current:	.110 and 220 volts
Elevators:	.5
Casino (gaming tables):	.Yes
Slot Machines:	.Yes
Swimming Pools (outdoors):	.1
Swimming Pools (indoors):	.0
Whirlpools:	.2
Fitness Center:	.Yes
Sauna/Steam Room:	.Yes/Yes
Massage:	.Yes
Self-Service Launderette:	.Yes
Dedicated Cinema/Seats:	.No
Library:	.Yes
Classification Society:	.Registro Navale Italiano (RINA)

OVERALL SCORE: 1,757 (OUT OF A POSSIBLE 2,000 POINTS)

ACCOMMODATION: There are seven grades. All have double vanities in the marble-floored bathrooms, which also have a bathtub and separate shower enclosure. Silversea-monogrammed Frette bed linen is provided in all grades, as are soft down pillows, 100 percent cotton bathrobes and a range of personal toiletry amenities by Bulgari, and personalized stationery.

BERLITZ'S RATINGS		
	Possible	Achieved
Ship	500	454
Accommodation	200	180
Food	400	339
Service	400	349
Entertainment	100	86
Cruise	400	349

VISTA SUITES: These suites measure 287 sq. ft (27 sq. metes), and do not have a private balcony. Instead there is a large window, twin beds that convert to a queen-sized bed, sitting area, TV and VCR player, refrigerator, writing desk, personal safe, cocktail cabinet, dressing table with hairdryer, and walk-in closet. The bathroom is marble-clad in gentle colors, and has two (his 'n' hers) washbasins, full sized bathtub, separate shower enclosure, and toilet.

VERANDA SUITES: Each of the Veranda Suites (really a Vista Suite plus a veranda) measures 345 sq. ft (32 sq. meters) and has convertible twin-to-queen beds. They are well fitted-out with just about everything you would need, including large floor-to-ceiling windows, large walk-in closet, dressing table, writing desk, stocked mini-bar/refrigerator (all drinks are included in the price of your cruise), and fresh flowers. The marble-clad bathrooms have two (his 'n' hers) washbasins, full sized bathtub, separate shower enclosure, and toilet.

SILVER SUITES: The Silver Suites measure 701 sq. ft (65 sq. meters). These are much wider than the Vista

Suites or Veranda Suites and have a separate bedroom, an entertainment center with CD player, TV/VCR unit (in both bedroom and living room) and much more living space that includes a large dining area with table and four chairs. The marble-clad bathrooms have two (his 'n' hers) washbasins, full sized bathtub, separate shower enclosure, and toilet.

OWNER'S SUITES: The two Owner's Suites, each 1,208 sq. ft (112 sq. meters), are much larger units and includes an extra bathroom for guests, as well as more living space. There is a 200 sq. ft (18 sq. meter) veranda, two bedrooms (with queen-sized beds), two walk-in closets, two living rooms, two sitting areas, separate dining area, an entertainment center with flat-screen plasma television in the living room and TV/VCR player in each bedroom, telephones, refrigerators, cocktail cabinet, writing desk, dressing tables with hairdryers. There are two marble-clad bathrooms, one with a full sized whirlpool bathtub and two washbasins, separate toilet, and separate shower, plus a powder room for guests. Owner's Suites can be either a one- or two-bedroom configuration.

ROYAL SUITES: Stately accommodation can be found in two Royal Suites, which measure either 1,312 sq. ft (122 sq. meters) or 1,352 sq. ft (126 sq. meters). These are two-bedroom suites, with two teakwood verandas, two living rooms, sitting areas, dining area, queen-size beds, an entertainment center with flat-screen plasma television in the living room and TV/VCR player in each bedroom, telephones, refrigerators, cocktail cabinet, writing desk, two closets, dressing tables with hair-dryers. There are two marble-clad bathrooms, one with a full sized whirlpool bathtub and two washbasins, sep-arate toilet, and separate shower, as well as a powder room for guests. Royal Suites can be either a one- or two-bedroom configuration.

GRAND SUITES: There are two Grand Suites, one which 1,286 sq. ft (119 sq. meters), while the other (including an adjoining suite with interconnecting door) measures 1,435 sq. ft (133 sq. meters). These have two bedrooms, two large walk-in closets, two living rooms, Bang & Olufsen entertainment centers, and large, forward-fac-ing, private verandas that face forwards. These really are sumptuous apartments that have all the comforts of home, and then some.

HANDICAP SUITES: There are two suites for the physi-cally disabled (535 and 537), both of which are adja-cent to an elevator, as well as being next to each other. They measure a generous 398 sq. ft (37 sq. meters). The suites are well equipped with an accessible hanging rail, and roll-in bathroom with roll-in shower unit.

DINING: The main dining room (called, simply, "The Restaurant") provides open-seating dining in elegant surroundings. Three grand chandeliers provide an up-ward focal point, while you can dine when you want, and with whom you wish (within the given dining room opening times), in these refined surroundings. Meals can also be served, course-by-course, in your suite, although the balcony tables are rather low for dining outdoors. The dining is good throughout the ship, with a choice of formal and informal areas, although the cui-sine and presentation doesn't quite match up to that of products such as the smaller Seabourn Cruise Line ships. Cristofle silverware is provided. Standard table wines are included for lunch and dinner, but there is also a "connoisseur list" of premium wines at extra charge. The house champagne is Moet & Chandon.

A poolside Grill provides a casual alternative day-time dining spot. Dinner can also be served course by course in your own suite.

For even more informal dining, there's an informal Terrace Café (this has proved popular aboard the com-pany's two (smaller) ships, *Silver Cloud* and *Silver Wind*). In the evening this room has themed dinners.

Adjacent to the café is a wine bar as well as a cigar smoking room (more of this later). Once each cruise, there's a "Galley Brunch" in the ship's galley, trans-formed for the occasion into a large "chef's kitchen."

OTHER COMMENTS: *Silver Whisper* is the second gen-eration of vessels in the Silversea Cruises fleet (its sis-ter ship is *Silver Shadow*), and is slightly larger than the company's first two ships, *Silver Cloud* and *Silver Wind*, with a more streamlined profile and large, sleek single funnel. The design of this new ship has evolved from the experience and success gained from the first pair.

"The Humidor, by Davidoff" is the ship's cigar smok-ing lounge; it has 25 seats and has been created in the style of an English smoking club, with candlelit evenings. All the cigars for sale are provided by David-off, the well-known purveyor of fine cigars. It was Zino Davidoff, son of founder Henri Davidoff, who created the revolutionary "cigar cellar" (now called a humidor). In case you're wondering, the air is changed 62 times each hour, so there is little of the stale smell you might expect from such rooms.

Other facilities include a wine bar, computer learning center, and cigar-smoking lounge. The Mandara Spa (originating in Bali) operates the health spa, much expanded when compared to smaller sisters *Silver* Cloud and *Silver* Wind, and specializes in what are known as Ayervedic treatments. Massages, however, are extremely expensive, at approximately $2 per minute.

Silversea Cruises have "all-inclusive" fares (they do not, however, include vintage wines, or massage, or other personal services), but they do include many things that are at extra cost compared aboard the ships of many other cruise lines in the industry. The passenger mix includes many nationalities, which actually makes for a more interesting experience, although the majority of passengers are typically American. The onboard cur-rency is the US dollar.

WEAK POINTS: Plastic deck lounge chairs and patio tables for the alternative dining spot do not signal a lux-ury product; these should be changed to teak or other sustainable hardwood variety.

Silver Wind

★★★★★

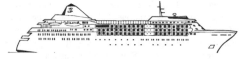

Small Ship:	...............16,927 tons	Passengers		Cabin Current:	........110 and 220 volts
Lifestyle:	.....................Luxury	(lower beds/all berths):	.........296/315	Elevators:	4
Cruise Line:	..........Silversea Cruises	Passenger Space Ratio		Casino (gaming tables):	............Yes
Former Names:	.................none	(lower beds/all berths):	.......57.1/53.7	Slot Machines:	....................Yes
Builder:	........Visentini/Mariotti (Italy)	Crew/Passenger Ratio		Swimming Pools (outdoors):	1
Original Cost:	.............$125 million	(lower beds/all berths):	..........1.5/1.5	Swimming Pools (indoors):	0
Entered Service:	.............Jan 1995	Navigation Officers:	............Italian	Whirlpools:	2
Registry:	...........................Italy	Cabins (total):	148	Fitness Center:	....................Yes
Length (ft/m):	............514.4/155.8	Size Range (sq ft/m):	.....240.0–1,314.0/	Sauna/Steam Room:	..........Yes/Yes
Beam (ft/m):	..............70.62/21.4		22.2–122.0	Massage:	.........................Yes
Draft (ft/m):	..................17.3/5.3	Cabins (outside view):	148	Self-Service Launderette:	..........Yes
Propulsion/Propellers:	..........diesel	Cabins (interior/no view):	0	Dedicated Cinema/Seats:	.......Yes/306
	(11,700kW)/2	Cabins (for one person):	0	Library:	.........................Yes
Passenger Decks:	6	Cabins (with private balcony):	110	Classification Society:	...Registro Navale
Total Crew:	197	Cabins (wheelchair accessible):	2		Italiano (RINA)

OVERALL SCORE: 1,717 (OUT OF A POSSIBLE 2,000 POINTS)

ACCOMMODATION: The all-outside suites (75 percent of which have fine private teakwood balconies) have convertible queen-to-twin beds and are beautifully fitted out with just about everything one needs, including huge floor-to-ceiling windows, large walk-in closets, dressing table, writing desk, stocked mini-bar/refrigerator (no charge), and fresh flowers. The marble floor bathrooms have bathtub, single vanity and plenty of towels. Personalized stationery, bathrobes, and a decent amenities kit is provided in all cabins. The top grades of suites also have CD-players.

All cabins have TV and VCR. However, the walk-in closets don't actually provide much hanging space (particularly for such items as full-length dresses), and it would be better for the door to open outward instead of inward (the drawers themselves are poorly positioned). Although the cabin insulation above and below each cabin is good, the insulation between cabins is not (a privacy curtain installed between entry door and sleeping area would be most useful), and light from the passageway leaks into the cabin, making it hard to achieve a dark room.

Note that the cabins with balconies on the lowest deck can suffer from sticky salt spray when the ship is moving, so the balconies require lots of cleaning. Each evening, the stewardesses bring plates of canapés to your suite – just right for a light bite with cocktails.

DINING: The contemporary dining room has an attractive arched gazebo center and a wavy ceiling design

BERLITZ'S RATINGS		
	Possible	Achieved
Ship	500	435
Accommodation	200	181
Food	400	339
Service	400	340
Entertainment	100	77
Cruise	400	345

as its focal point, and is set with fine Limoges china and well-balanced Christofle flatware. Meals are served in an open seating, which means you can eat when you like (within the given dining room opening times), and with whom you like. Meals can also be served, course-by-course, in your suite, although the balcony tables are rather low for dining outdoors. The dining is good throughout the ship, with a choice of formal and informal areas, although the cuisine and presentation doesn't quite match up to that of products such as the smaller Seabourn ships. Standard table wines are included for lunch and dinner, but there is also a "connoisseur list" of premium wines at extra charge. The house champagne is Moet & Chandon.

An alternative Italian restaurant, Cucina Italiana, is very popular for evening alternative dining. By day it acts as the informal Terrace Café, but by night turns into a delightful, intimate dining spot, complete with candlelight and print tablecloths.

The ship also provides 24-hour in-cabin dining service (full course by course dinners are available).

OTHER COMMENTS: *Silver Wind* has a quite handsome profile, with a sloping stern reminiscent of an "Airstream" trailer. The size is just about ideal for highly personalized cruising in an elegant environment. The vertical cake-layer stacking of public rooms aft and the location of accommodation units forward ensures quiet cabins. There is a synthetic turf-covered wraparound promenade deck outdoors, and a fairly spa-

spacious swimming pool and sunbathing deck. The spacious interior is well planned, with elegant décor and fine quality soft furnishings. It is accented by the gentle use of brass and fine woods and very creative ceilings throughout. The spa areas need improvement, and the tiled decor is bland and uninviting.

There is a useful business center as well as a CD-ROM and hardback book library, open 24 hours a day. There is an excellent two-level show lounge with tiered seating, but the entertainment is disappointing and not as good as when the ship first debuted.

In 2000, a new concession took over the health spa and improved upon the services and range of personal treatments available. The Mandara Spa (originating in Bali) includes what are known as Ayervedic treatments. Massages, however, are extremely expensive, at approximately $2 per minute.

There is an excellent amount of space per passenger and there is no hint of a line anywhere in this unhurried environment. Excellent documentation is provided before your cruise, all of which comes in a high-quality document wallet.

An elegant onboard ambience prevails, and there is no pressure, no hype, and an enthusiastic staff to pamper you, with a high ratio of Europeans. Insurance is extra (it *was* included when Silversea Cruises first started). Refreshingly, all drinks, gratuities and port taxes *are* included, and, refreshingly, no further tipping anywhere on board is allowed. This ship is perhaps ideal for those who enjoy spacious surroundings, excellent food, and some entertainment. It would be difficult not to have good cruise vacation aboard this ship, albeit at a fairly high price. Silversea Cruises has come a long way since its inception, and continues to refine its product. The company's many international passengers react well to the ambience, food, service and the staff, most of who go out of their way to please.

Few ships make it to a five-star rating today, but Silversea Cruises has earned an enviable reputation for high quality in a short space of time. The onboard currency is the US dollar.

WEAK POINTS: The artwork is of very poor quality. Some vibration is evident when bow thrusters or the anchors are used, particularly in the forward-most cabins. Plastic deck lounge chairs and patio tables for the alternative dining spot do not enhance a luxury product; these should be changed to teak or other sustainable hardwood variety. The self-service launderette is poor and not large enough for longer cruises, when passengers like to be able to do their own small items. Sadly, crew facilities are minimal, and so keeping consistency is difficult, as high crew turnover is a fact of life. The quality of artwork is poor.

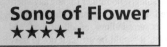

Song of Flower
★★★★ +

Removed 2006

Small Ship: ....8,282 tons	Total Crew: 144	Cabins (wheelchair accessible): 0
Lifestyle: ....Luxury	Passengers	Cabin Current: ....220 volts
Cruise Line: ......Radisson Seven Seas	(lower beds/all berths): 198/198	Elevators: 2
Cruises	Passenger Space Ratio	Casino (gaming tables): ....Yes
Former Names: ......*Explorer Starship*	(lower beds/all berths): 41.8/41.8	Slot Machines: ....Yes
Builder: ....KMV (Norway)/Lloyd Werft	Crew/Passenger Ratio	Swimming Pools (outdoors): 1
(Germany)	(lower beds/all berths): 1.3/1.3	Swimming Pools (indoors): 0
Original Cost: ....n/a	Navigation Officers: ....Norwegian	Whirlpools: 1
Entered Service: 1986/Feb 1990	Cabins (total): 99	Fitness Center: ....Yes
Registry: ....The Bahamas	Size Range (sq ft/m): 183.0–398.0/	Sauna/Steam Room: ....Yes/No
Length (ft/m): 407.4/124.2	17.0–37.0	Massage: ....Yes
Beam (ft/m): 52.4/16.0	Cabins (outside view): 99	Self-Service Launderette: ....No
Draft (ft/m): 16.0/4.9	Cabins (interior/no view): 0	Dedicated Cinema/Seats: ....No
Propulsion/Propellers: diesel (5,500kW)/2	Cabins (for one person): 0	Library: ....Yes
Passenger Decks: 6	Cabins (with private balcony): 10	Classification Society: Det Norske Veritas

---

OVERALL SCORE: 1,626 (OUT OF A POSSIBLE 2,000 POINTS)

ACCOMMODATION: There are six different price categories. There are 10 elegant suites; 10 cabins are strictly for non-smokers. All other cabins are well equipped, complete with bathrobes and slippers, refrigerator, and VCR. All suites have excellent closet and drawer space. Many have bathtubs, but they are tiny (shower tubs would be a better description). Disabled passengers should choose a cabin with a shower instead of a bath. Sadly, there are no in-cabin dining facilities for dinner.

DINING: The Galaxy Dining Room is charming (better when the ship is stationary and there's no vibration) and has warm colors, a welcoming ambience, and one seating, with no assigned tables. There are several tables for two, as well as tables for four six or eight persons. Very creative food and presentation is featured, with small portions, attractively presented. All alcoholic and non-alcoholic beverages are included, with the exception of some premium wines. The personal service is excellent.

A recent addition is an alternative dining spot called A Taste of Italy, created in what was formerly the casino (until it was moved to a new location).

OTHER COMMENTS: This is an excellent small cruise ship (it was originally built as the roll-on, roll-off vessel *Begonia* in 1974 and fully converted in 1986). Operated for a while as *Explorer Starship* by the Seattle-based Exploration Cruise Lines until the line's bankruptcy, the ship was then bought by Japan's Meijo Corporation.

The ship has tall, twin funnels that give a somewhat

BERLITZ'S RATINGS

	Possible	Achieved
Ship	500	395
Accommodation	200	162
Food	400	337
Service	400	344
Entertainment	100	73
Cruise	400	315

squat profile. If only the foredeck and bow could be a little longer, it would provide a sleeker appearance, rather than its unfortunate ferry shape.

Song of Flower has been well maintained and cared for and is very clean throughout, although its interiors are now looking tired. There is a good amount of sheltered open deck and sunbathing space. Water sports facilities include snorkel equipment.

Inside, the interior décor is warm, with many pastel colors used in the public rooms, passageways, and on the stairways. High-quality soft furnishings and fabrics have been used throughout, to good effect, making the ship very comfortable, though not luxurious, by any means. The health spa facility is very compact and short on space, but is reasonably adequate.

The well-tiered show lounge is good, comfortable, and has good sight lines from almost all seats. The warm, caring staff really does try to anticipate your needs. Totally understated elegance and a warm, informal lifestyle are the hallmarks of a cruise aboard this nice ship. *Song of Flower* should provide a fine, destination-intensive, yet relaxing, friendly and unpretentious cruise experience, delivered with a sprinkling of style and panache. Gratuities are included, and no further tipping is allowed, although port charges are extra. The onboard currency is the US dollar.

WEAK POINTS: Announcements for the day's activities are unnecessary when everything is listed in the daily program. Vibration, particularly at the stern, and at some tables in the dining room, is still a problem.

Sovereign of the Seas
★★★ +

Large Ship: ....73,192 tons	Total Crew: 825	Cabins (wheelchair accessible): 6
Lifestyle: ....Standard	Passengers	Cabin Current: ....110 volts
Cruise Line: ....Royal Caribbean	(lower beds/all berths): 2,276/2,852	Elevators: 13
International	Passenger Space Ratio	Casino (gaming tables): ....Yes
Former Names: ....none	(lower beds/all berths): 32.1/25.6	Slot Machines: ....Yes
Builder: Chantiers de l'Atlantique (France)	Crew/Passenger Ratio	Swimming Pools (outdoors): 2
Original Cost: ....$183.5 million	(lower beds/all berths): 2.7/3.4	Swimming Pools (indoors): 0
Entered Service: ....Jan 1988	Navigation Officers: ....Norwegian	Whirlpools: 2
Registry: ....The Bahamas	Cabins (total): 1,138	Fitness Center: ....Yes
Length (ft/m): 879.9/268.2	Size Range (sq ft/m): 118.4–670.0/	Sauna/Steam Room: ....Yes/No
Beam (ft/m): 105.9/32.3	11.0–62.2	Massage: ....Yes
Draft (ft/m): 24.9/7.6	Cabins (outside view): 722	Self-Service Launderette: ....No
Propulsion/Propellers: ....diesel	Cabins (interior/no view): 416	Dedicated Cinema/Seats: Yes-2/144 each
(21,844kW)/2	Cabins (for one person): 0	Library: ....Yes
Passenger Decks: 12	Cabins (with private balcony): 0	Classification Society: Det Norske Veritas

OVERALL SCORE: 1,386 (OUT OF A POSSIBLE 2,000 POINTS)

ACCOMMODATION: There are 17 price categories, depending on the size and location of the accommodation chosen. Some cabins have interconnecting doors (particularly useful for families with children).

SUITES: Thirteen suites on Bridge Deck (the largest is the Royal Suite) are reasonably large and nicely furnished, with separate living and sleeping spaces. They provide more space, with better service, and more perks than the standard-grade accommodation.

STANDARD CABINS: The standard outside-view and interior (no view) cabins are very small, although an arched window treatment and colorful soft furnishings do give the illusion of more space. Almost all cabins have twin beds that can be converted to a queen-sized or double bed configuration, together with moveable bedside tables. All of the standard cabins have very little closet and drawer space (you will need some luggage engineering to stow your cases). You should, therefore, think of packing only minimal clothing, which is all you really need for a short cruise. All cabins have a private bathroom, with shower enclosure, toilet and washbasin.

DINING: The two dining rooms, Gigi and Kismet (located on two different decks, one above the other), provide seating at tables for four, six, or eight (there are no tables for two). Both dining rooms are non-smoking area, and there are two seatings. The food is pretty average, and doesn't seem to have much taste. The dining operation is well orchestrated, with emphasis on highly

BERLITZ'S RATINGS

	Possible	Achieved
Ship	500	381
Accommodation	200	141
Food	400	244
Service	400	286
Entertainment	100	73
Cruise	400	261

programmed (some passengers find it quite insensitive), extremely hurried service that many find intrusive. The waiters, many from the Caribbean, are perhaps overly friendly for some tastes – particularly on the last night of the cruise, when tips are expected.

The cuisine is typical of mass banquet catering that offers standard fare comparable to that found in American family-style restaurants ashore. The menu descriptions make the food sound better than it is, which is consistently below average – the result of controlled food costs as well as the use of many mixes and pre-prepared items. However, a decent selection of light meals is provided, and a vegetarian menu is available. The selection of breads, rolls, fruit and cheese is quite poor, and could do more improvement. Caviar (once a standard menu item) now incurs a hefty extra charge. Menus typically include a Welcome Aboard Dinner, French Dinner, Italian Dinner, International Dinner, Captain's Gala Dinner. One thing this company does once each cruise is to feature "Galley Buffet" whereby passengers go through a section of the galley picking up food for a midnight buffet. There is an adequate wine list, with moderate prices.

For casual breakfasts and lunches, the Windjammer Café is the place to go, although there are often long lines at peak times, and the selection is extremely average.

OTHER COMMENTS: This is a handsome mega-ship with well-balanced profile, nicely rounded lines and high superstructure, but the open deck space is adequate, no more. A Viking Crown Lounge is built around the funnel and has superb views. The ship has a wide wrap-around outdoors polished wood deck, and there is a basketball court for sports fans.

While the interior layout is a little awkward (being designed in a vertical stack, with most public rooms located aft, and accommodation located forward), the ship has an impressive array of spacious and elegant public rooms, although the décor comes from the IKEA-school of interior design. A stunning five-deck-high Centrum lobby has cascading stairways and two glass-walled elevators. There is a good two-level show lounge and a decent array of shops, albeit with lots of tacky merchandise. Casino gamers will find blackjack, craps, Caribbean stud poker and roulette tables, plus an array of slot machines. Among the public rooms, the library is a nice place for relaxation, and has a decent selection of books. The entertainment program is quite sound, and there is a good range of children's and teens' programs and cheerful youth counselors.

This floating resort provides a well tuned, yet very impersonal short cruise experience, for a lot of passen-gers. The dress code is very casual. The ship was exten-sively refurbished in 1997, when 220 new third and fourth berths were added to increase capacity to more than 2,800, and the shopping area was increased. More seats in the dining rooms were also added.

In the final analysis, you will probably be over-whelmed by the public spaces, and underwhelmed by the size of the cabins. However, this is basically a well run, fine-tuned, highly programmed cruise product geared to those seeking an action-packed cruise vacation at a moderately good price, with lots of fellow passen-gers. The onboard currency is the US dollar.

WEAK POINTS: There are no cabins with private bal-conies. Standing in line for embarkation, disembarka-tion, shore tenders and for self-serve buffet meals is an inevitable aspect of cruising aboard all large ships. There is congested passenger flow in some areas. There are too many intrusive and irritating announcements. The ship is well used during these short cruises, and always looks tired and worn in some spots.

Spirit of '98
★★ +

Small Ship: ....99 tons	Passengers	Cabin Current: ....110 volts
Lifestyle: ....Standard	(lower beds/all berths): 96/96	Elevators: 1
Cruise Line: ....Cruise West	Passenger Space Ratio	Casino (gaming tables): ....No
Former Names: ....*Pilgrim Belle,*	(lower beds/all berths): 1.0/1.0	Slot Machines: ....No
Victorian Empress	Crew/Passenger Ratio	Swimming Pools (outdoors): 0
Builder: ......Bender Shipbuilding (USA)	(lower beds/all berths): 3.2/3.2	Swimming Pools (indoors): 0
Original Cost: ....n/a	Navigation Officers: ....American	Whirlpools: 0
Entered Service: 1984/1993	Cabins (total): 49	Fitness Center: 0
Registry: ....USA	Size Range (sq ft/m): 80.0–510.0/	Sauna/Steam Room: ....No/No
Length (ft/m): 192.0/58.2	7.4–47.3	Massage: ....No
Beam (ft/m): 40.0/12.1	Cabins (outside view): 49	Self-Service Launderette: ....No
Draft (ft/m): 9.3/2.8	Cabins (interior/no view): 0	Dedicated Cinema/Seats: ....No
Propulsion/Propellers: diesel/1	Cabins (for one person): 0	Library: ....Some bookshelves
Passenger Decks: 4	Cabins (with private balcony): 0	Classification Society: . .American Bureau
Total Crew: 30	Cabins (wheelchair accessible): 1	of Shipping

OVERALL SCORE: 1,018 (OUT OF A POSSIBLE 2,000 POINTS)

ACCOMMODATION: There are six grades of cabin. The Owner's Suite is the largest accommodation in the Cruise West fleet, and has large picture windows on three sides. It consists of two rooms; a lounge/living room with game table, TV/VCR, refrigerator and fully stocked complimentary bar. There is a separate bedroom with a king-sized bed, and large bathroom with Jacuzzi bathtub.

There are also four irregular-shaped deluxe cabins at the front of the vessel, with decent closet space, a queen-sized bed (or twin beds that convert to a double bed), and a bathroom with a separate shower enclosure. Two of the cabins also have an extra sofa bed.

The other cabins are quite small, but are reasonably comfortable, and have a large picture window. While a few cabins have queen-sized or double beds, most have single beds that cannot be moved together. Each cabin has its own private bathroom, although these really are tiny, and have a wall-mounted shower. There is no room service for food or snack items.

DINING: The Klondyke Dining Room, decorated in the style of 100 years ago, is an elegant room. The cuisine is decidedly plain and simple though tasty Americana fare (expect lots of seafood), as is the cutlery (no fish knifes are used, for example). The ingredients are mostly fresh, and local. Wine and full bar services are provided.

OTHER COMMENTS: This distinctive-looking vessel was built to resemble a late 1800s coastal cruising vessel. It is particularly suited to in-depth, in-your-face glacier

BERLITZ'S RATINGS

	Possible	Achieved
Ship	500	205
Accommodation	200	126
Food	400	202
Service	400	214
Entertainment	N/A	N/A
Cruise	500	271

spotting, and for close-in cruising along the coastline of Alaska. There is only one public room – the Grand Salon, although it is a large room.

You are much closer to nature aboard a small cruise vessel such as this. There are no lines, no loud rap and rock music, no shows, no casino. There is a viewing area outdoors right at the ship's bow. There is an "open bridge" policy, and the company is concerned about protecting the natural environment.

This ship and cruise are best suited to adult couples and single travelers (typically aged 60-plus) who enjoy learning about nature, geography, history and other life sciences, in a casual, totally unpretentious setting, and who don't mind sharing confined spaces.

The dress code is absolutely casual (not even a jacket for men is needed, and no ties, please). However, do take comfortable walking shoes, as well as photographic materials for wildlife spotting. Smoking is permitted only on the outside decks. All tips are pooled by all staff, using the amounts recommended in the cruise line's brochure of $10 per passenger, per day (this is high for the services offered). The cruising areas are Alaska, the Pacific Northwest, and California's wine country. The onboard currency is the US dollar.

WEAK POINTS: The ship is very small. There is an almost constant throbbing from the diesel engines/generator. There is no doctor on board (except for cruises in the Sea of Cortes), and so anyone with medical problems should really not consider this vessel. There are no cushioned pads for the deck lounge chairs.

Spirit of Alaska
★★

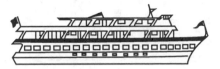

Small Ship: ....97 tons	Passengers	Elevators: 0
Lifestyle: ....Standard	(lower beds/all berths): 78/78	Casino (gaming tables): ....No
Cruise Line: ....Cruise West	Passenger Space Ratio	Slot Machines: ....No
Former Names: ....Pacific Northwest	(lower beds/all berths): 1.2/1.2	Swimming Pools (outdoors): 0
Explorer	Crew/Passenger Ratio	Swimming Pools (indoors): 0
Builder: ....Blount Marine (USA)	(lower beds/all berths): 3.9	Whirlpools: 0
Original Cost: ....n/a	Navigation Officers: ....American	Fitness Center: 0
Entered Service: 1980/1991	Cabins (total): 39	Sauna/Steam Room: ....No/No
Registry:.........................USA	Size Range (sq ft/m): ...80–128/7.4–11.6	Massage: 0
Length (ft/m): 143.0/43.5	Cabins (outside view): 27	Self-Service Launderette: 0
Beam (ft/m): 28.5/8.6	Cabins (interior/no view): 12	Dedicated Cinema/Seats: ....No
Draft (ft/m): 7.5/2.2	Cabins (for one person): 0	Library: ....Some bookshelves
Propulsion/Propellers: diesel/1	Cabins (with private balcony): 0	Classification Society: . .American Bureau
Passenger Decks: 4	Cabins (wheelchair accessible): 0	of Shipping
Total Crew: 20	Cabin Current: ....110 volts	

OVERALL SCORE: 936 (OUT OF A POSSIBLE 2,000 POINTS)

ACCOMMODATION: There are five grades of cabin. All are small when compared to most cruise ships, but they are reasonably comfortable. A few have double beds, but most have single beds that cannot be moved together. Each cabin has its own private bathroom, although these really are tiny, and have a wall-mounted shower. Each cabin has a small sink. There is no room service for food or snacks.

BERLITZ'S RATINGS

	Possible	Achieved
Ship	500	175
Accommodation	200	83
Food	400	202
Service	400	214
Entertainment	N/A	N/A
Cruise	500	262

DINING: The dining room has very plain décor, but the open-seating policy means that you can dine with whomever you wish, in one seating. The cuisine is decidedly plain though tasty Americana fare (expect lots of seafood). The ingredients are mostly fresh, and local. Wine and full bar services are provided.

OTHER COMMENTS: This vessel, which was originally built for the American Canadian Caribbean Line, is particularly suited to in-depth, in-your-face glacier spotting and for close in cruising along the coastline of Alaska. There is only one public room inside the ship – the Glacier View Lounge. Smoking is permitted only on the outside decks.

You are much closer to nature aboard a small cruise vessel such as this. There are no lines, no loud rap and rock music blaring, no shows, no cabaret, and no casino. There is a viewing area outdoors right at the ship's bow. One bonus is the fact that at the bow of the vessel, a "bow gangway" comes into its own for landing passengers. There is an "open bridge" policy, so you can visit the wheelhouse whenever you wish (except possibly during difficult maneuvers). The company has a genuinely caring attitude towards protecting the natural environment.

This ship and cruise are best suited to adult couples and single travelers (typically aged 60-plus) who enjoy learning about nature, geography, history and other life sciences, in a casual, totally unpretentious setting, and who don't mind sharing confined spaces. This ship could be good for those who really do not large cruise ships and endless lines.

There is only one public room inside the ship – the Riverview Lounge. The dress code is absolutely casual (not even a jacket for men is needed, and no ties, please). However, do take comfortable walking shoes, as well as photographic materials for wildlife spotting. Smoking is permitted only on the outside decks.

All tips are pooled by all staff, using the amounts recommended in the cruise line's brochure of $10 per passenger, per day (this is high for the services offered). This ship features cruises in Alaska and the Pacific Northwest. The ship was laid-up in 2002 due to the after-effects of the terrorist attacks on the United States, but was expected to be in operation again in 2003. The onboard currency is the US dollar.

WEAK POINTS: The ship is very small, and there are no nooks and crannies to hide away in (except for your cabin). There is an almost constant throbbing from the diesel engines/generator. There is no doctor on board, and so anyone with medical problems should really not consider this vessel. There are no cushioned pads for the deck lounge chairs.

Spirit of Columbia
★★

Small Ship: ....98 tons	Passengers	Cabin Current: ....110 volts
Lifestyle: ....Standard	(lower beds/all berths): 78/82	Elevators: 0
Cruise Line: ....Cruise West	Passenger Space Ratio	Casino (gaming tables): ....No
Former Names: ....*New Shoreham II*	(lower beds/all berths): 1.2/1.1	Slot Machines: ....No
Builder: ....Blount Marine	Crew/Passenger Ratio	Swimming Pools (outdoors): 0
(USA)	(lower beds/all berths): 3.9/4.1	Swimming Pools (indoors): 0
Original Cost: ....n/a	Navigation Officers: ....American	Whirlpools: 0
Entered Service: 1979/1995	Cabins (total): 39	Fitness Center: 0
Registry: ....USA	Size Range (sq ft/m): 80–121.0/	Sauna/Steam Room: 0/0
Length (ft/m): 143.0/43.5	7.4–11.2	Massage: 0
Beam (ft/m): 28.0/8.5	Cabins (outside view): 27	Self-Service Launderette: 0
Draft (ft/m): 6.5/1.9	Cabins (interior/no view): 12	Dedicated Cinema/Seats: ....No
Propulsion/Propellers: diesel/1	Cabins (for one person): 0	Library: ....Some bookshelves
Passenger Decks: 4	Cabins (with private balcony): 0	Classification Society: . .American Bureau
Total Crew: 20	Cabins (wheelchair accessible): 0	of Shipping

OVERALL SCORE: 936 (OUT OF A POSSIBLE 2,000 POINTS)

ACCOMMODATION: There are five grades of cabin. All are small when compared to most cruise ships, but they are reasonably comfortable. A few have double beds, but most have single beds that cannot be moved together (romantics please note). Each cabin has its own private bathroom, although these really are tiny, and feature a wall-mounted shower. Each cabin also has a small sink. There is no room service for food or snack items.

DINING: The dining room has minimal décor, but the open-seating policy means that you can dine with whomever you wish, in one seating. The cuisine is decidedly plain and simple Americana fare (expect good seafood), as is the cutlery (no fish knifes are used, for example), although it is quite tasty. This is due to the fact that the ingredients are mostly fresh, and local. Wine and full bar services are provided.

OTHER COMMENTS: This vessel, originally built for the American Canadian Caribbean Line, is particularly suited to in-depth, in-your-face glacier spotting and for close in cruising along the coastline of Alaska.

You are much closer to nature aboard a small cruise vessel such as this. There are no lines, no loud rap and rock music blaring, no shows, no cabaret, and no casino. There is a viewing area outdoors right at the ship's bow. One bonus is the fact that a direct access loading ramp can be opened up from the lounge, for landing passengers. There is an "open bridge" policy, so you can visit

BERLITZ'S RATINGS

	Possible	Achieved
Ship	500	175
Accommodation	200	83
Food	400	202
Service	400	214
Entertainment	N/A	N/A
Cruise	500	262

the wheelhouse whenever you wish (except possibly during difficult maneuvers). The company has a genuinely caring attitude towards protecting the natural environment.

This ship and cruise are best suited to adult couples and single travelers (typically aged 60-plus) who enjoy learning about nature, geography, history and other life sciences, in a casual, totally unpretentious setting, and who don't mind sharing confined spaces. This ship could be good for those who really don't like large cruise ships and endless lines.

There is only one public room inside the ship – the Riverview Lounge. The dress code is absolutely casual (not even a jacket for men is needed, and no ties, please). However, do take comfortable walking shoes, as well as photographic materials for wildlife spotting. Smoking is permitted only on the outside decks.

All tips are pooled by all staff, using the amounts recommended in the cruise line's brochure of $10 per passenger, per day (this is high for the services offered). This ship features cruises in Alaska and the Pacific Northwest The onboard currency is the US dollar.

WEAK POINTS: The ship is very small, and there are no nooks and crannies to hide away in (except for your cabin). There is an almost constant throbbing from the diesel engines/generator. Remember that there is no doctor on board, and so anyone with medical problems should really not consider this vessel. There are no cushioned pads for the deck lounge chairs.

Spirit of Discovery
★★

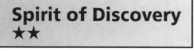

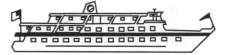

Small Ship:	.94 tons	Passengers	
Lifestyle:	Standard	(lower beds/all berths):	.84/84
Cruise Line:	Cruise West	Passenger Space Ratio	
Former Names:	*Independence,*	(lower beds/all berths):	1.1/1.1
	Columbia	Crew/Passenger Ratio	
Builder:	Blount Marine (USA)	(lower beds/all berths):	4.2/4.2
Original Cost:	n/a	Navigation Officers:	American
Entered Service:	1982/1992	Cabins (total):	43
Registry:	USA	Size Range (sq ft/m):	64–126.0/
Length (ft/m):	166.0/50.5		5.9–11.7
Beam (ft/m):	37.0/11.2	Cabins (outside view):	43
Draft (ft/m):	7.5/2.2	Cabins (interior/no view):	0
Propulsion/Propellers:	diesel/1	Cabins (for one person):	2
Passenger Decks:	3	Cabins (with private balcony):	0
Total Crew:	20	Cabins (wheelchair accessible):	0

Cabin Current:	110 volts
Elevators:	0
Casino (gaming tables):	No
Slot Machines:	No
Swimming Pools (outdoors):	0
Swimming Pools (indoors):	0
Whirlpools:	0
Fitness Center:	0
Sauna/Steam Room:	0/0
Massage:	0
Self-Service Launderette:	No
Dedicated Cinema/Seats:	No
Library:	Some bookshelves
Classification Society:	American Bureau of Shipping

OVERALL SCORE: 936 (OUT OF A POSSIBLE 2,000 POINTS)

ACCOMMODATION: There are six grades of cabin to choose from. All are small when compared to most cruise ships, but they are reasonably comfortable, and have a large picture window and small clothes closet. A few cabins have double beds, but most have single beds that cannot be moved together. Each cabin has its own private bathroom, although these really are tiny, and have a wall-mounted shower. Each cabin also has a small sink. There is no room service for food or snack items.

DINING: The dining room has very plain décor, but the open-seating policy means that you can dine with whomever you wish, in one seating. The cuisine is decidedly plain and simple Americana fare (expect lots of seafood), as is the cutlery (no fish knifes are used, for example), although it is quite tasty. This is due to the fact that the ingredients are mostly fresh, and local. Wine and full bar services are provided.

OTHER COMMENTS: This vessel, originally built for the American Canadian Caribbean Line, is particularly suited to in-depth, in-your-face glacier spotting and for close in cruising along the coastline of Alaska.

There is only one public room inside the ship – the Glacier View Lounge. Smoking is permitted only on the outside decks.

You are much closer to nature aboard a small cruise vessel such as this. There is a viewing area outdoors right at the ship's bow. There are no lines, no loud rap

BERLITZ'S RATINGS

	Possible	Achieved
Ship	500	175
Accommodation	200	83
Food	400	202
Service	400	214
Entertainment	N/A	N/A
Cruise	500	262

and rock music blaring, no shows, no cabaret, and no casino. There is an "open bridge" policy, so you can visit the wheelhouse whenever you wish (except possibly during difficult maneuvers). The company has a genuinely caring attitude towards protecting the natural environment.

This ship and cruise are best suited to adult couples and single travelers (typically aged 60-plus) who enjoy learning about nature, geography, history and other life sciences, in a casual, totally unpretentious setting, and who don't mind sharing confined spaces. This ship could be good for those who really do not large cruise ships and endless lines.

The dress code is absolutely casual (not even a jacket for men is needed, and no ties, please). However, do take comfortable walking shoes, as well as photographic materials for wildlife spotting. All tips are pooled by all staff, using the amounts recommended in the cruise line's brochure of $10 per passenger, per day (this is high for the services offered).

This ship cruises in Alaska and the Pacific Northwest The onboard currency is the US dollar.

WEAK POINTS: The ship is very small, and there are no nooks and crannies to hide away in (except for your cabin). There is an almost constant throbbing from the diesel engines/generator. Remember that there is no doctor on board, and so anyone with medical problems should really not consider this vessel. There are no cushioned pads for the deck lounge chairs.

Spirit of Endeavour
★ ★

Small Ship: . . . . .95 tons	Passengers	Cabin Current: . . . . .110 volts
Lifestyle: . . . . .Standard	(lower beds/all berths): 102/107	Elevators: 0
Cruise Line: . . . . .Cruise West	Passenger Space Ratio	Casino (gaming tables): . . . . .No
Former Names: . . . .*Nantucket Clipper,*	(lower beds/all berths): 0.9/0.8	Slot Machines: .No
SeaSpirit	Crew/Passenger Ratio	Swimming Pools (outdoors): 0
Builder: . . . . .Jeffboat (USA)	(lower beds/all berths): 3.6/3.8	Swimming Pools (indoors): 0
Original Cost: .n/a	Navigation Officers: . . . . .American	Whirlpools: 0
Entered Service: 1983/1996	Cabins (total): .51	Fitness Center: .0
Registry: . . . . .USA	Size Range (sq ft/m): 110.0–153.0/	Sauna/Steam Room: 0/0
Length (ft/m): 217.0/66.1	10.2–14.2	Massage: 0
Beam (ft/m): 37.0/11.3	Cabins (outside view): 51	Self-Service Launderette: 0
Draft (ft/m): 8.5/2.5	Cabins (interior/no view): 0	Dedicated Cinema/Seats: . . . . .No
Propulsion/Propellers: diesel/1	Cabins (for one person): 0	Library: . . . . .Yes
Passenger Decks: 4	Cabins (with private balcony): 0	Classification Society: . .American Bureau
Total Crew: 28	Cabins (wheelchair accessible): 0	of Shipping

OVERALL SCORE: 946 (OUT OF A POSSIBLE 2,000 POINTS)

ACCOMMODATION: There are four grades of cabin. All are small when compared to most cruise ships, but they are reasonably comfortable for this small size of vessel, and have a large picture window (just four cabins on Main deck have a porthole), a clothes closet, television and VCR. A few cabins have twin beds that can convert into a queen-sized bed, but most have single beds that cannot be moved together. Each cabin has its own private bathroom, although these really are tiny, and have a wall-mounted shower. Several cabins have a Pullman-berth for a third occupant. Each cabin also has a small sink. There is no room service for food or snack items.

DINING: The Resolution Dining Room has plain décor, but an open-seating policy ch means that you can dine with whomever you wish. The cuisine is decidedly plain and simple Americana fare (expect lots of seafood), as is the cutlery (no fish knifes are used), although it is quite tasty. This is because the ingredients are mostly fresh, and local. Wine and full bar services are provided.

OTHER COMMENTS: This vessel, originally built for Clipper Cruise Line, is the flagship of the Cruise West fleet, and is particularly suited to in-depth, in-your-face glacier spotting and for "up-close" cruising along the coastline of Alaska. There is only one public room inside the ship – the Explorer Lounge. Smoking is permitted only on the outside decks.

You are much closer to nature aboard a small cruise vessel such as this. There is a viewing area outdoors

BERLITZ'S RATINGS

	Possible	Achieved
Ship	500	185
Accommodation	200	83
Food	400	202
Service	400	214
Entertainment	N/A	N/A
Cruise	500	262

right at the ship's bow. There are no lines, no loud rap and rock music blaring, no shows, no cabaret, and no casino. An "open bridge" policy means that you can visit the wheelhouse whenever you wish (except possibly during difficult manoeuvres). The company has a genuinely caring attitude towards protecting the natural environment.

This ship and cruise are best suited to adult couples and single travellers (typically aged 60-plus) who enjoy learning about nature, geography, history and other life sciences, in a casual, totally unpretentious setting, and who don't mind sharing confined spaces. This ship might be good for those who really do not large cruise ships and endless lines.

The dress code is absolutely casual (not even a jacket for men is needed, and no ties, please). However, do take comfortable walking shoes, as well as photographic materials for wildlife spotting. All tips are pooled by all the staff, using the amounts recommended in the cruise line's brochure of $10 per passenger, per day (this is high for the services offered). The cruising areas are Alaska, the Sea of Cortes, and California's wine country. The onboard currency is the US dollar.

WEAK POINTS: The ship is very small, and there are no nooks and crannies to hide away in (except for your cabin). There is an almost constant throbbing from the diesel engines/generator. There is no doctor on board (except for the Sea of Cortes cruises), and so anyone with medical problems should not consider this vessel. There are no cushioned pads for the deck lounge chairs.

Spirit of Glacier Bay
★★

Small Ship: . . . . .97 tons	Passengers	Cabin Current: . . . . .110 volts
Lifestyle: . . . . .Standard	(lower beds/all berths): 52/54	Elevators: 0
Cruise Line: . . . . .Cruise West	Passenger Space Ratio	Casino (gaming tables): . . . . .No
Former Names: . . . . .*Glacier Bay Explorer,*	(lower beds/all berths): 1.8/1.7	Slot Machines: . . . . .No
New Shoreham I	Crew/Passenger Ratio	Swimming Pools (outdoors): 0
Builder: . . . . .Blount Marine (USA)	(lower beds/all berths): 3.4/3.6	Swimming Pools (indoors): 0
Original Cost: . . . . .n/a	Navigation Officers: . . . . .American	Whirlpools: 0
Entered Service: 1971/1990	Cabins (total): .27	Fitness Center: 0
Registry: . . . . .USA	Size Range (sq ft/m): 55.0–72.0/	Sauna/Steam Room: 0/0
Length (ft/m): 125.0/38.1	5.1–6.6	Massage: 0
Beam (ft/m): 28.0/8.5	Cabins (outside view): 14	Self-Service Launderette: 0
Draft (ft/m): 6.5/1.9	Cabins (interior/no view): 13	Dedicated Cinema/Seats: . . . . .No
Propulsion/Propellers: diesel/1	Cabins (for one person): 2	Library: . . . . .Some bookshelves
Passenger Decks: 3	Cabins (with private balcony): 0	Classification Society: . .American Bureau
Total Crew: 15	Cabins (wheelchair accessible): 0	of Shipping

OVERALL SCORE: 913 (OUT OF A POSSIBLE 2,000 POINTS)

ACCOMMODATION: There are three grades of cabin. All are small when compared to most cruise ships, but they are reasonably comfortable, and most have a large picture window and small clothes closet. A few cabins have double beds, but most have single beds that cannot be moved together. Two cabins on the lowest deck, in the front of the ship have upper and lower berths. Each cabin has its own private bathroom, although these really are tiny, and feature a wall-mounted shower. Each cabin also has a small sink. There is no room service for food or snack items.

DINING: The dining room has really plain décor, but the open-seating policy means that you can dine with whomever you wish, in one seating. The cuisine is decidedly plain and simple Americana fare (expect lots of seafood), as is the cutlery (no fish knifes are used, for example), although it is quite tasty. This is because the ingredients are mostly fresh, and local. Wine and full bar services are provided.

OTHER COMMENTS: This vessel, originally built for the American Canadian Caribbean Line, is particularly suited to in-depth, in-your-face glacier spotting and for close in cruising along the coastline of Alaska. There is only one public room inside the ship – the Glacier View Lounge. Smoking is permitted only on the outside decks.

You are much closer to nature aboard a small cruise vessel such as this. There is a viewing area outdoors right at the ship's bow. There are no lines, no loud rap and rock music blaring, no shows, no cabaret, and no

BERLITZ'S RATINGS		
	Possible	Achieved
Ship	500	166
Accommodation	200	75
Food	400	202
Service	400	214
Entertainment	N/A	N/A
Cruise	500	256

casino. One bonus is the fact that at the bow of the vessel, a "bow gangway" comes into its own for landing passengers. There is an "open bridge" policy, so you can visit the wheelhouse whenever you wish (except possibly during difficult manoeuvres). The company has a genuinely caring attitude towards protecting the natural environment.

This ship is best suited to adult couples and single travellers (typically aged 60-plus) who enjoy learning about nature, geography, history and other life sciences, in a casual, totally unpretentious setting, and who don't mind sharing confined spaces. This could be a good choice for those who really do not large cruise ships and endless lines.

The dress code is absolutely casual (not even a jacket for men is needed, and no ties, please). However, do take comfortable walking shoes, as well as photographic materials for wildlife spotting. All tips are pooled by all staff, using the amounts recommended in the cruise line's brochure of $10 per passenger, per day (this is high for the cruise offered).

The ship's cruising areas are Alaska and the Pacific Northwest The onboard currency is the US dollar.

WEAK POINTS: The ship is very small, and there are no nooks and crannies to hide away in (except for your cabin). There is an almost constant throbbing from the diesel engines/generator. Remember that there is no doctor on board, and so anyone with medical problems should really not consider this vessel. There are no cushioned pads for the deck lounge chairs.

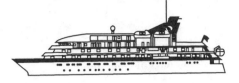

Spirit of Oceanus
★★★

Small Ship:	4,200 tons	Passengers	
Lifestyle:	Standard	(lower beds/all berths):	114/127
Cruise Line:	Cruise West	Passenger Space Ratio	
Former Names:	...MegaStar Sagittarius,	(lower beds/all berths):	37.5/33.0
	Sun Viva, Renaissance Five	Crew/Passenger Ratio	
Builder:	Nuovi Cantieri Apuania	(lower beds/all berths):	2.0/4.7
	(Italy)	Navigation Officers:	American
Entered Service:	1991/2001	Cabins (total):	57
Registry:	The Bahamas	Size Range (sq ft/m):	215.0–353.0/
Length (ft/m):	294.5/89.7		20.0–32.7
Beam (ft/m):	50.1/15.30	Cabins (outside view):	57
Draft (ft/m):	13.2/4.05	Cabins (interior/no view):	0
Propulsion/Propellers:	diesel	Cabins (for one person):	0
	(5,000kW)/2	Cabins (with private balcony):	12
Passenger Decks:	5	Cabins (wheelchair accessible):	0
Total Crew:	55	Cabin Current:	110 volts

Dining Rooms:	1
Elevators:	1
Casino (gaming tables):	No
Slot Machines:	No
Swimming Pools (outdoors):	1
Swimming Pools (indoors):	0
Whirlpools:	1
Fitness Center:	Yes
Sauna/Steam Room:	No/No
Massage:	Yes
Self-Service Launderette:	No
Dedicated Cinema/Seats:	No
Library:	Yes
Classification Society:	American Bureau of Shipping

OVERALL SCORE: 1,218 (OUT OF A POSSIBLE 2,000 POINTS)

ACCOMMODATION: There are six categories. Fine all-outside-view cabins (called "suites" in the brochure) combine highly polished imitation rosewood paneling with lots of mirrors, and fine, hand crafted Italian furniture. All suites have twin beds that can convert to a queen-sized bed, a sitting area with three-person sofa, one individual chair, coffee table, mini-bar/refrigerator (stocked with juices and bottled water), TV/VCR, direct-dial satellite telephone, and a bowl of fresh fruit on embarkation day. While closet space is good, space for stowing luggage is tight, and there is little drawer space (each cabin has three drawers, two of which are lockable, plus several open shelves in a separate closet). There are no music channels in the cabins, and there is no switch to turn off announcements in your cabin.

The marble bathrooms are compact units that have showers (no bathrooms have a bathtub) with fold-down (plastic) seat, real teakwood floor, marble vanity, large mirror, recessed towel rail (good for storing personal toiletries), and built-in hairdryer. Note that there is a high "lip" into the bathroom.

DINING: The Restaurant, which has an open-seating policy, is bright, elegant, welcoming, and non-smoking. It is on the lowest deck and has portholes rather than windows, due to international maritime construction and insurance regulations. There are tables for two, four, six, or eight. Dinners are normally sit-down affairs, although, depending on the itinerary and length of cruise, there

BERLITZ'S RATINGS

	Possible	Achieved
Ship	500	339
Accommodation	200	150
Food	400	211
Service	400	237
Entertainment	N/A	N/A
Cruise	500	281

could be an occasional buffet. Breakfast and lunch are typically self-serve buffets and can be taken at the poolside (weather permitting), in your cabin, or in the restaurant.

OTHER COMMENTS: This ship has contemporary exterior styling, a private yacht-like look and handsome styling with twin, flared funnels. The navigation bridge is a well-rounded half-moon design. This was one of four identical vessels (out of a series of eight) originally built for Renaissance Cruises, but now the ship is now being operated by its fourth owner since new.

There is a teakwood promenade deck outdoors, and a reasonable amount of open deck and sunbathing space. The deck furniture is teak and the deck lounge chairs have thick cushioned pads. There is a teakwood water sports platform at the stern of the ship (not used in Alaska), plus a number of zodiac inflatable rubber landing craft. Snorkeling gear is provided (not used in Alaska).

The main lounge, the focal point for social activities, has six pillars that destroy sight lines to the small stage area. There is also a very small book and video library.

The ship was acquired by Cruise West in 2001 and is the only ocean-going vessel in the fleet. It cruises Alaska and British Columbia during the summer, while in the winter it sails to Tahiti, the Fijian Islands and other Pacific Ocean itineraries. What's really nice is that there are no lines, no loud rap and rock music blaring, no shows, no cabaret, and no casino – just you, the ship and nature. The onboard currency is the US dollar.

Splendour of the Seas
★★★★

Large Ship:	.69,130 tons
Lifestyle:	Standard
Cruise Line:	Royal Caribbean International
Former Names:	none
Builder:	Chantiers de l'Atlantique (France)
Original Cost:	$325 million
Entered Service:	Mar 1996
Registry:	The Bahamas
Length (ft/m):	867.0/264.2
Beam (ft/m):	105.0/32.0
Draft (ft/m):	24.5/7.3
Propulsion/Propellers:	diesel (40,200kW)/2
Passenger Decks:	11
Total Crew:	720
Passengers	
(lower beds/all berths):	1,804/2,064
Passenger Space Ratio	
(lower beds/all berths):	38.3/33.4
Crew/Passenger Ratio	
(lower beds/all berths):	2.5/2.8
Navigation Officers:	Norwegian
Cabins (total):	902
Size Range (sq ft/m):	137.7–1,147.4/ 12.8–106.6
Cabins (outside view):	575
Cabins (interior/no view):	327
Cabins (for one person):	0
Cabins (with private balcony):	231
Cabins (wheelchair accessible):	17
Cabin Current:	110 and 220 volts
Elevators:	11
Casino (gaming tables):	Yes
Slot Machines:	Yes
Swimming Pools (outdoors):	2 (1 with sliding roof)
Swimming Pools (indoors):	0
Whirlpools:	4
Fitness Center:	Yes
Sauna/Steam Room:	Yes/Yes
Massage:	Yes
Self-Service Launderette:	No
Dedicated Cinema/Seats:	No
Library:	Yes
Classification Society:	Det Norske Veritas

OVERALL SCORE: 1,511 (OUT OF A POSSIBLE 2,000 POINTS)

ACCOMMODATION: Royal Caribbean International has realized that small cabins do not please passengers. The company therefore set about designing a ship with much larger standard cabins than in any of the company's previous vessels (except sister ship *Legend of the Seas*). Some cabins on Deck 8 also have a larger door for wheelchair access in addition to the 17 cabins for the physically handicapped, and the ship is very accessible, with ample ramped areas and sloping decks. All cabins have a sitting area and beds that convert to double configuration, and there is ample closet and drawer space, although there is not much space around the bed (and the showers could have been better designed).

Cabins with balconies have glass railings rather than steel/wood to provide less intrusive sight lines. The largest accommodation, the Royal Suite, is a superb living space for those that can afford the best. It is beautifully designed, finely decorated, and has a baby grand piano, whirlpool bathtub, and other fine amenities. Several quite sitting areas are located adjacent to the best cabins amidships. Seventeen cabin categories is really too many. There are no cabins for singles.

DINING: The two-deck-high dining room has dramatic two-deck-high glass side walls, so many passengers both upstairs and downstairs can see both the ocean and each other in reflection (it would, perhaps, have been even better located at the stern), but it is quite noisy when full (call it atmosphere). There are two seatings.

BERLITZ'S RATINGS	Possible	Achieved
Ship	500	426
Accommodation	200	163
Food	400	248
Service	400	302
Entertainment	100	78
Cruise	400	294

The well orchestrated dining operation emphasizes highly programmed (insensitive), extremely hurried service that many find intrusive.

The cuisine is typical of mass banquet catering that offers standard fare comparable to that found in American family-style restaurants ashore. The menu descriptions make the food sound better than it is (which is consistently below average), mostly disappointing and without much taste – the result of controlled food costs as well as the use of many mixes and pre-prepared items. However, a decent selection of light meals is provided, and a vegetarian menu is available. The selection of breads, rolls, fruit and cheese is quite poor, however, and could do more improvement. Caviar (once a standard menu item) now incurs a hefty extra charge. Menus typically include a Welcome Aboard Dinner, French Dinner, Italian Dinner, International Dinner, Captain's Gala Dinner. One thing this company does once each cruise is to feature "Galley Buffet" whereby passengers go through a section of the galley picking up food for a midnight buffet. There is an adequate wine list, with moderate prices.

For casual meals, there is also a cavernous indoor-outdoor café, located towards the bow and above the bridge, as well as a good-sized snack area, which provide more informal dining choices.

OTHER COMMENTS: This ship's contemporary profile looks somewhat unbalanced (but it soon grows on you), and does sport a nicely tiered stern. The pool deck amidships overhangs the hull to provide an extremely wide deck, while still allowing the ship to navigate the Panama Canal. With engines placed amidships, there is little noise and no noticeable vibration, and the ship has an operating speed of up to 24 knots.

The interior décor is quite colorful, but too glitzy for European tastes. The outside light is brought inside in many places, with an extensive amount of glass area that provides contact with sea and air (there's more than 2 acres/8,000 sq. meters of glass). There's an innovative single-level sliding glass roof (not a magrodome) over the more formal setting of one of two swimming pools, providing a large, multi-activity, all-weather indoor-outdoor area, called the Solarium. The glass roof provides shelter for the Roman-style pool and adjacent health and fitness facilities (which are superb) and slides aft to cover the miniature golf course when required (both cannot be covered at the same time, however).

Golfers might enjoy the 18-hole, 6,000 sq.-ft (557 sq.-meter) miniature golf course, with the topography of a real golf course, complete with trees, foliage, grass, bridges, water hazards, and lighting for play at night. The holes are 155–230 sq. ft. (14–21 sq. meters).

Inside, two full entertainment decks are sandwiched between five decks full of cabins. The tiered and balconied show lounge, which covers two decks, is expansive and has excellent sight lines, and very comfortable seats. Several large-scale production shows are provided here, and the orchestra pit can be raised or lowered as required. A multi-tiered seven-deck-high atrium lobby, complete with a huge stainless steel sculpture, connects with the impressive Viking Crown Lounge via glass-walled elevators. The casino is really expansive, overly glitzy and absolutely packed. The library, outside of which is a bust of Shakespeare, is a fine facility, and carries more than 2,000 books.

The casino could be somewhat disorienting, with its mirrored walls and lights flashing everywhere, although it is no different to those found in Las Vegas fantasy gaming halls. As with any large ship, you can expect to find yourself standing in lines for embarkation, disembarkation, buffets and shore excursions, although the company does its best to minimize such lines.

Representing natural evolution, this ship is an outstanding new cruise vessel for the many repeat passengers who enjoy Royal Caribbean International's consistent delivery of a well-integrated, fine-tuned, very comfortable and well-liked product. The onboard currency is the US dollar.

WEAK POINTS: There is, sadly, no separate cinema. Standing in line for embarkation, disembarkation, shore tenders and for self-serve buffet meals is inevitable when cruising aboard all large ships.

Star Clipper
★★★★

Small Ship:	...............3,025 tons	Main Propulsion: ....sail power
Lifestyle:	..................Standard	Propulsion/Propellers: ....diesel
Cruise Line:	.............Star Clippers	(1,030kW)/1
Former Names:	.................none	Passenger Decks: 4
Builder:	..........Scheepswerven van	Total Crew: 72
	Langerbrugge (Belgium)	Passengers
Original Cost:	.............$30 million	(lower beds/all berths): 170/180
Entered Service:	............May 1992	Passenger Space Ratio
Registry:	.................Luxembourg	(lower beds/all berths): 17.7/16.8
Length (ft/m):	.............366.1/111.6	Crew/Passenger Ratio
Beam (ft/m):	................49.2/15.0	(lower beds/all berths): 2.3/2.5
Draft (ft/m):	..................17.7/5.6	Navigation Officers: ....European
Type of Vessel:	.....barentine schooner	Cabins (total): 85
No. of Masts:	...............4 (208 ft)	Size Range (sq ft/m): 95.0–150.0/
Sail Area (sq ft/m2):	....36,221/3,365/16	8.8–14.0
	manually furled sails	Cabins (outside view): 78

Cabins (interior/no view): 6
Cabins (for one person): 0
Cabins (with private balcony): 0
Cabins (wheelchair accessible): 0
Cabin Current: ....110 volts
Elevators: 0
Casino (gaming tables): ....No
Slot Machines: ....No
Swimming Pools (outdoors): 2
Whirlpools: 0
Fitness Center: ....No
Sauna/Steam Room: ....No/No
Massage: ....No
Self-Service Launderette: ....No
Library: ....Yes
Classification Society: ...Lloyd's Register

OVERALL SCORE: 1,402 (OUT OF A POSSIBLE 2,000 POINTS)

ACCOMMODATION: There are six price grades; generally the higher the deck, the more expensive your cabin will be. The cabins are quite well equipped and comfortable; they have wood-trimmed cabinetry and wall-to-wall carpeting, two-channel audio, color television, lockable personal safe and full-length mirrors. The bathrooms are very compact but practical units, and feature gray marble tiling, a toiletries cabinet, some under-shelf storage space, washbasin, small shower stall and toilet. There is no "lip" to prevent water from the shower from moving over the bathroom floor. The bed linen is of a mix of 50 percent cotton and 50 percent polyester.

The deluxe cabins are larger, and additional features include a full-sized bathtub and mini-bar/refrigerator. There is no cabin food or beverage service.

The cabins in the lowest price grade are interior cabins with upper and lower berths, and not two lower beds – so someone will need to be agile to climb up to the upper berth (a ladder is provided, of course). A handful of cabins have a third, upper Pullman-style berth (note that closet and drawer space will be at a premium with three persons in a cabin, so do take only the minimal amount of clothing you can).

DINING: The dining room is quite attractive, and has lots of wood accenting and nautical décor. There are buffet breakfasts and lunches, together with a mix of buffet and à la carte dinners (generally a choice of two entrées). There is one (open) seating. The seating arrangement

BERLITZ'S RATINGS

	Possible	Achieved
Ship	500	382
Accommodation	200	134
Food	400	249
Service	400	271
Entertainment	N/A	N/A
Cruise	500	366

(mostly with tables of six) makes it difficult for waiters to serve properly. However, you can dine with whomever you wish, and this *is* supposed to be a casual experience. While cuisine aboard the Star Clippers ships is perhaps less than the advertised "gourmet" excellence (as far as presentation and choice are concerned), it is fairly creative, and one has to take into account the tiny galley provided.

Perhaps fewer passenger cabins and more room in the galley would have enabled the chefs to provide a better dining experience than the present arrangement. There is a limited choice of bread rolls, pastry items, and fruits.

Tea and coffee should be, but is not, available 24 hours a day, particularly in view of the fact that there is no cabin food service at all. When it is available, paper cups are provided (real china would be better).

OTHER COMMENTS: This is one of a pair of almost identical tall ships (its sister ship is *Star Flyer*). It is a sailing vessel with cruise accommodation that evokes memories of the 19th-century clipper sailing ships. This is an accurate four-mast, barentine-rigged vessel with graceful lines, a finely shaped hull and masts that are 63 ft (19.3 meters) tall. Breathtaking when under full sail, the ship displays excellent sea manners. This working clipper ship relies on the wind about 80 percent of the time. A diesel engine is used as backup in emergencies, for generating electrical power and for desalinating the approximately 40 tons of seawater each day for shipboard needs. The crew performs almost every task, including hoisting, trimming, winching and repairing the sails.

Water sports facilities include a water ski boat, sunfish, scuba and snorkel equipment, and eight Zodiac inflatable craft. Sports directors provide basic dive instruction (for a fee).

The whole cruise experience evokes the feeling of sailing aboard some famous private yacht. *Star Flyer* (sister to *Star Clipper*), the first clipper sailing ship to be built for 140 years, became the first commercial sailing vessel to cross the North Atlantic in 90 years.

Some of the amenities of large modern cruise vessels are provided, such as air-conditioning, cashless cruising, occasional live music, a small shop, and a pool to "swim" in (actually "dip" would be a better description). Inside the vessel, classic Edwardian nautical décor throughout is clean, warm, intimate, and inviting. The paneled library has a fireplace, and chairs that are supremely comfortable. A cruise aboard this ship means no lines, no hassle, and "Sailing a Square Rigger" classes are a part of every cruise.

Each morning, passengers gather for "captain's story-time" – normally held on an open deck area adjacent to the bar – which, incidentally, has a fine collection of single malt whiskies. The captain also explains sailing maneuvers when changing the rigging or directing the ship as it sails into port, and notes the important events of the day. Passengers are encouraged to lend a hand, pulling on thick ropes to haul up the main sail. And they love it.

The vessel promotes total informality and provides a carefree sailing cruise experience in a totally unstructured setting at a modest price. Take minimal clothing: short-sleeved shirts and shorts for the men, shorts and tops for the ladies are the order of the day (and night). No jackets, ties, high-heeled shoes, cocktail dresses, or the slightest hint of formal wear is needed.

The deck crew consists of real sailors, brought up with yachts and tall ships—and most would not set foot aboard a cruise ship.

It is no exaggeration to say that to be sailing aboard either *Star Clipper* or *Star Flyer* is to seem to have died and gone to yachtsman's heaven, as there is plenty of sailing during the course of a typical one-week cruise. Even the most jaded passenger should enjoy the feel of the wind and sea close at hand. Just don't expect good food to go with what is decidedly a fine sailing experience – which is what *Star Clipper* is all about. Note that 12.5 percent is added to all beverage purchases. The onboard currency is the US dollar.

WEAK POINTS: The food, its quality, variety, presentation and service are still the weakest points of a cruise aboard this tall ship – and is not as good as what is provided aboard the company's larger flagship, *Royal Clipper*. This ship is not for the physically impaired, or for children. The steps of the internal stairs are steep, as in most sailing vessels. The tipping system, where all tips are pooled (the suggested amount is $8 per passenger, per day), causes concern for many passengers.

Star Flyer
★★★★

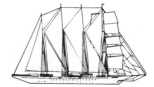

Small Ship: ....3,025 tons	Main Propulsion: ....sail power	Cabins (interior/no view): 6
Lifestyle: ....Standard	Propulsion/Propellers: ....diesel	Cabins (for one person): 0
Cruise Line: ....Star Clippers	(1,030kW)/1	Cabins (with private balcony): 0
Former Names: ....none	Passenger Decks: 4	Cabins (wheelchair accessible): 0
Builder: ....Sheepswerven van	Total Crew: 72	Cabin Current: ....110 volts
Langerbrugge (Belgium)	Passengers	Elevators: 0
Original Cost: ....$25 million	(lower beds/all berths): 170/180	Casino (gaming tables): ....No
Entered Service: ....July 1991	Passenger Space Ratio	Slot Machines: ....No
Registry: ....Luxembourg	(lower beds/all berths): 17.7/16.8	Swimming Pools (outdoors): 2
Length (ft/m): 366.1/111.6	Crew/Passenger Ratio	Whirlpools: 0
Beam (ft/m): 49.2/15.0	(lower beds/all berths): 2.3/2.5	Fitness Center: ....No
Draft (ft/m): 17.7/5.6	Navigation Officers: ....European	Sauna/Steam Room: ....No/No
Type of Vessel: .....barkentine schooner	Cabins (total): 84	Massage: ....No
No. of Masts: ....4 (208 ft)	Size Range (sq ft/m): 95.0–150.0/	Self-Service Launderette: ....No
Sail Area (sq ft/m2): 36,221/3,365/16	8.8–14.0	Library: ....Yes
manually furled sails	Cabins (outside view): 78	Classification Society: ...Lloyd's Register

OVERALL SCORE: 1,402 (OUT OF A POSSIBLE 2,000 POINTS)

ACCOMMODATION: There are six price grades; generally, the higher the deck, the more expensive your cabin will be. The cabins are quite well equipped and comfortable; they have wood-trimmed cabinetry and wall-to-wall carpeting, two-channel audio, color television, lockable personal safe and full-length mirrors. The bathrooms are very compact but practical units, and have gray marble tiling, a toiletries cabinet, some under-shelf storage space, washbasin, small shower stall and toilet. There is no "lip" to prevent water from the shower from moving over the bathroom floor. The bed linen is of a mix of 50 percent cotton and 50 percent polyester. A handful of cabins have a third, upper Pullman-style berth (note that closet and drawer space will be at a premium with three persons in a cabin, so do take only the minimal amount of clothing you can).

The deluxe cabins are larger, and additional features include a full-sized bathtub and mini-bar/refrigerator. Note that there is no cabin food or beverage service.

The cabins in the lowest price grade are interior cabins with upper and lower berths, and not two lower beds – so someone will need to be agile to climb up to the upper berth (a ladder is provided, of course). A handful of cabins have a third, upper Pullman-style berth (note that closet and drawer space will be at a premium with three persons in a cabin, so do take only the minimum amount of clothing you can).

DINING: The dining room is quite attractive, and has lots of wood accenting and nautical décor. There are buffet

BERLITZ'S RATINGS

	Possible	Achieved
Ship	500	382
Accommodation	200	134
Food	400	249
Service	400	271
Entertainment	N/A	N/A
Cruise	500	366

breakfasts and lunches, together with a mix of buffet and à la carte dinners (generally a choice of two entrées). There is one (open) seating. The seating arrangement (mostly with tables of six) makes it difficult for waiters to serve properly. However, it is in an open-seating arrangement, so you can dine with whomever you wish, and this *is* supposed to be a casual experience. While cuisine aboard the Star Clippers ships is perhaps less than the advertised "gourmet" excellence (as far as presentation and choice are concerned), it is nevertheless fairly creative, and one has to take into account the tiny galley provided.

Perhaps fewer passenger cabins and more room in the galley would have enabled the chefs to produce better results than the present arrangement. There is a limited choice of bread rolls, pastry items, and fruits.

Tea and coffee should be, but is not, available 24 hours a day, particularly in view of the fact that there is no cabin food service at all. When it is available, paper cups are provided (real china would be better).

OTHER COMMENTS: *Star Flyer* is one of a pair of almost identical tall ships (the sister ship is *Star Clipper*). It is a sailing vessel with cruise accommodation that evokes memories of the 19th-century clipper sailing ships. Accurate four-mast, barkentine-rigged vessel with graceful lines, a finely shaped hull and masts that are 63 ft (19.3 meters) tall. Breathtaking when under full sail, the ship displays excellent sea manners. This working clipper ship relies on the wind about 80 percent of the time.

A diesel engine is used as backup in emergencies, for generating electrical power and for desalinating the approximately 40 tons of seawater each day for shipboard needs. The crew performs almost every task, including hoisting, trimming, winching and repairing the sails.

Water sports facilities include a water ski boat, sunfish, scuba and snorkel equipment, and eight Zodiac inflatable craft. Sports directors provide basic dive instruction (for a fee).

The whole cruise experience evokes the feeling of sailing aboard some famous private yacht a century ago. *Star Flyer,* the first clipper sailing ship to be built for 140 years, became the first commercial sailing vessel to cross the North Atlantic in 90 years.

Some of the amenities of large modern cruise vessels are provided, such as air-conditioning, cashless cruising, occasional live music, a small shop, and a pool to "swim" in (actually "dip" would be a better description). Inside the vessel, classic Edwardian nautical decor throughout is clean, warm, intimate, and inviting. The paneled library has a fireplace, and chairs that are supremely comfortable. A cruise aboard it means no lines, no hassle, and "Sailing a Square Rigger" classes are a part of every cruise.

Each morning, passengers gather for "captain's story-time" – normally held on an open deck area adjacent to the bar – which, incidentally, has a fine collection of single malt whiskies. The captain also explains sailing maneuvers when changing the rigging or directing the ship as it sails into port, and notes the important events of the day. Passengers are encouraged to lend a hand, pulling on thick ropes to haul up the main sail. And they love it.

The vessel promotes informality and provides a carefree sailing cruise experience in a totally unstructured setting at a modest price. Take minimal clothing: short-sleeved shirts and shorts for the men, shorts and tops for the ladies are the order of the day (and night). No jackets, ties, high-heeled shoes, cocktail dresses, or the slightest hint of formal wear is needed. The deck crew consists of real sailors, brought up with yachts and tall ships—and most would not set foot aboard a cruise ship.

It is no exaggeration to say that to be sailing aboard either *Star Clipper* or *Star Flyer* is to seem to have died and gone to yachtsman's heaven, as there is plenty of sailing during the course of a typical one-week cruise. Even the most jaded passenger should enjoy the feel of the wind and sea close at hand – just don't expect good food to go with what is decidedly a fine sailing experience – which is what *Star Clipper* is all about. Note that 12.5 percent is added to all beverage purchases. The onboard currency is the US dollar.

WEAK POINTS: The food, its quality, variety, presentation and service are still the weakest points of a cruise aboard this tall ship – and is not as good as what is provided aboard the company's larger flagship, *Royal Clipper*. This ship is not for the physically impaired, or for children. The steps of the internal stairs are steep, as in most sailing vessels. The tipping system, where all tips are pooled (the suggested amount is $8 per passenger, per day), causes concern for many passengers.

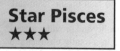

Star Pisces
★★★

Large Ship:	.............40,012 tons	
Lifestyle:	..................Standard	
Cruise Line:	..............Star Cruises	
Former Names:	...............*Kalypso*	
Entered Service:	1990	
Builder:	.............Wartsila (Finland)	
Original Cost:	.........SEK650 million	
Registry:	....................Panama	
Length (ft/m):	............579.3/176.6	
Beam (ft/m):	.................97.1/29.6	
Draft (ft/m):	...................20.3/6.2	
Propulsion/Propellers:	..........diesel (23,760kW)/2	
Passenger Decks:	12	
Total Crew:	750	

Passengers (lower beds/all berths):	.....1,394/1,900
Passenger Space Ratio (lower beds/all berths):	.......28.7/21.0
Crew/Passenger Ratio (lower beds/all berths):	.........1.8/2.5
Navigation Officers:	.......Scandinavian
Cabins (total):	718
Size Range (sq ft/m):	......67.8–145.3/ 6.3–13.5
Cabins (outside view):	303
Cabins (interior/no view):	415
Cabins (for one person):	42
Cabins (with private balcony):	0
Cabins (wheelchair accessible):	6

Cabin Current:	...............220 volts
Elevators:	5
Casino (gaming tables):	............Yes
Slot Machines:	.....................Yes
Swimming Pools (outdoors):	1
Swimming Pools (indoors):	1
Whirlpools:	3
Fitness Center:	....................Yes
Sauna/Steam Room:	...........Yes/Yes
Massage:	........................Yes
Self-Service Launderette:	..........No
Dedicated Cinema/Seats:	..........No
Library:	.........................Yes
Classification Society:	.......Det Norske Veritas

OVERALL SCORE: 1,247 (OUT OF A POSSIBLE 2,000 POINTS)

ACCOMMODATION: There are six grades of accommodation. Except for some large "imperial" suites, almost all cabins are *extremely* small, and come with just the basic facilities, and very little closet and drawer space. Many cabins have third- and fourth-person upper berths - which are good for families who don't mind tight quarters. The cabin insulation is quite poor, and the bathrooms are really tiny.

The largest suites are very spacious, and are decorated in luxurious, richly lacquered materials, feature two bathrooms, butler service, a private club meeting room, private sun deck and spa.

DINING: There are seven restaurants that together provide a wide choice of cuisine and dining styles. A Chinese restaurant has live fish tanks from which to select your fish and seafood. A Japanese restaurant includes a sushi bar, waitresses in kimonos, and private tatami rooms. An Italian restaurant has candlelight dining. A Spice Island buffet restaurant has items such as laksa, satay and hawker delights. In addition, there are three other snack cafés. The cruise fare includes only the basic buffets restaurants – all other restaurants are à la carte, and expensive.

OTHER COMMENTS: This ship is wide and squat looking in the water, has Scandinavian design combined with a touch of the Orient. The large blue funnel has a single, large yellow (gold) star as the company's logo. Although the outdoor deck and sunbathing space is limited, it is little used by its Asian passengers.

BERLITZ'S RATINGS

	Possible	Achieved
Ship	500	277
Accommodation	200	123
Food	400	275
Service	400	265
Entertainment	100	56
Cruise	400	251

There is a helipad, a huge duty-free shopping center and a supermarket. The Regal Casino (essentially for VIPs) is large and has a high, detailed ceiling. There is also a second casino for general use. Has a fine health club for men (with many "extra" services). There are many meeting rooms, conference auditoriums and a business center. The extensive facilities for children include computers and educational rooms, play areas and a huge video machine section. There is free ice cream for kids, excellent Asian hospitality, and lots of activities for the whole family.

Skillfully converted into a cruise vessel for the Asian family market, this ship was based on Hong Kong for several years before being moved into her new cruise area. The ship offers short cruises, with lots of Asian hospitality, choice of dining venues and styles, an abundance of karaoke and gambling opportunities, all in a modern ship with colorful surroundings. The initial ticket price is extremely low, but almost everything on board costs extra. The ship operates short cruises from Osaka, Japan to Korea. All gratuities are included.

WEAK POINTS: Standing in line for embarkation, disembarkation, shore tenders and for self-serve buffet meals is an inevitable aspect of cruising aboard all large ships. This is a very high-density ship, and that means that many of the public rooms will always be crowded. The open deck space is poor, although this is mostly unused by Asian passengers. The cabins (and bathrooms) really are *very* small – particularly when occupied by three or four persons.

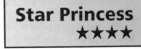

Star Princess
★★★★

Large Ship: ....108,977 tons	Passengers		Cabin Current: ....110 volts
Lifestyle: ....Standard	(lower beds/all berths): 2,602/3,102		Elevators: 14
Cruise Line: ....Princess Cruises	Passenger Space Ratio		Casino (gaming tables): ....Yes
Former Names: ....none	(lower beds/all berths): 41.8/35.1		Slot Machines: ....Yes
Builder: ....Fincantieri	Crew/Passenger Ratio		Swimming Pools (outdoors): 4
(Italy)	(lower beds/all berths): 2.3/2.8		Swimming Pools (indoors): 0
Original Cost: ....$460 million	Navigation Officers: ......British/Italian		Whirlpools: 9
Entered Service: ....Feb 2002	Cabins (total): 1,301		Fitness Center: ....Yes
Registry: ....Bermuda	Size Range (sq ft/m): 161.4–764.2/		Sauna/Steam Room: ....Yes/Yes
Length (ft/m): 951.4/290.0	15.0–71.0		Massage:.........................Yes
Beam (ft/m): 118.1/36.0	Cabins (outside view): 935		Self-Service Launderette: ....Yes
Draft (ft/m): 26.2/8.0	Cabins (interior/no view): 366		Dedicated Cinema/Seats: ....No
Propulsion/Propellers: .....diesel-electric	Cabins (for one person): 0		Library: ....Yes
(42,000kW)/2	Cabins (with private balcony): 711		Classification Society: ...Registro Navale
Passenger Decks:.................13	Cabins (wheelchair accessible): 28		Italiano (RINA)
Total Crew: 1,200	(18 outside/10 interior)		

OVERALL SCORE: 1,549 (OUT OF A POSSIBLE 2,000 POINTS)

ACCOMMODATION: There are six principal types of cabins and configurations: (a) grand suite, (b) suite, (c) mini-suite, (d) outside-view double cabins with balcony, (e) outside-view double cabins, and (f) interior (no view) double cabins. These come in 35 different brochure price categories; the choice is quite bewildering for both travel agents and passengers; pricing depends on two things, size and location.

(a) The largest, most lavish suite is the Grand Suite (B748, which is located at the ship's stern – a different position to the *two* Grand Suites aboard *Grand Princess*). It has a large bedroom with queen-sized bed, huge walk-in (illuminated) closets, two bathrooms, a lounge (with fireplace and sofa bed) with wet bar and refrigerator, and a large private balcony on the port side (with hot tub that can be accessed from both balcony and bedroom).

(b/c) Suites (with a semi-private balcony) have a separate living room (with sofa bed) and bedroom (with a television in each). The bathroom is quite large and has both a bathtub and shower stall. The mini-suites also have a private balcony, and a separate living and sleeping area (with a television in each). The bathroom is also quite spacious and has both a bathtub and shower enclosure. The differences between the suites and mini-suites are basically in the size and appointments, the suite being more of a square shape while mini-suites are more rectangular, and have few drawers. Both suites and mini-suites have plush bathrobes, and fully tiled bathrooms

BERLITZ'S RATINGS		
	Possible	Achieved
Ship	500	436
Accommodation	200	168
Food	400	256
Service	400	293
Entertainment	100	82
Cruise	400	314

with ample open shelf storage space. Suite and mini-suite passengers receive greater attention, including priority embarkation and disembarkation privileges. What is not good is that the most expensive accommodation has only semi-private balconies that can be seen from above and so there is little privacy (Suites C401, 402, 409, 410, 414, 415, 420, 421, 422, 423, 424 and 425 on Caribe Deck in particular). Also, the suites D105 and D106 (Dolphin Deck), which are extremely large, have balconies that are overlooked from above.

(d/e/f). Both interior (no view) and outside-view (the outsides come either with or without private balcony) cabins are of a functional, practical, design, although almost no drawers are provided. They are quite attractive, with warm, pleasing décor and fine soft furnishing fabrics; 80 percent of the outside-view cabins have a private balcony. Bathrooms have tild floors, and a good amount of open shelf storage space for personal toiletries, although the modular bathrooms are all in a plain beige color. Interior (no view) cabins measure 160 sq. ft (14.4 sq. meters), while the standard outside-view cabins measure 228 sq. ft (21 sq. meters).

The 28 wheelchair-accessible cabins measure 250–385 sq. ft (23.2–35.7 sq. meters). Surprisingly, there is no mirror for dressing, and no full-length hanging space for long dresses (yes, some passengers in wheelchairs *do* also use mirrors and full-length clothing). Additionally, two family suites consist of two suites with an interconnecting door, plus a large balcony. These can sleep up to 10 (if at least four are children, or up to eight people if all are adults).

All passengers receive turndown service and chocolates on pillows each night, as well as bathrobes (on request) and toiletry amenity kits (larger, naturally, for suite/mini-suite occupants) that typically include soap, shampoo, conditioner, and hand/body lotion. A hairdryer is provided in all cabins, sensibly located at the vanity desk unit in the living area. All bathrooms have tiled floors, and there is a decent amount of open shelf storage space for personal toiletries, although the plain beige décor is very basic and unappealing. Note that Princess Cruises typically carries CNN, CNBC, ESPN and TNT on the in-cabin color television system (when available, depending on cruise area).

Most outside cabins on Emerald Deck have views obstructed by the lifeboats. There are no cabins for singles. Your name is placed outside your suite or cabin in a documents holder – making it simple for delivery service personnel but also making it intrusive as far as privacy is concerned. There is 24-hour room service (but some items on the room service menu are not available during early morning hours).

Some cabins can accommodate a third and fourth person in upper berths. However, in such cabins, the lower beds cannot then be pushed together to make queen-sized bed.

Note that almost all balcony suites and cabins can be overlooked both from the navigation bridge wing, as well as from the port and starboard sections of the ship's discotheque – located high above the ship at the stern. Cabins with balconies on Dolphin, Caribe and Baja decks are also overlooked by passengers on balconies on the deck above. They are, therefore, not at all private. However, perhaps the least desirable balcony cabins are eight balcony cabins located forward on Emerald Deck, as the balconies do not extend to the side of the ship and can be passed by walkers and gawkers on the adjacent Upper Promenade walkway (so occupants need to keep their curtains closed most of the time). Also, passengers occupying some the most expensive suites with balconies at the stern of the vessel may experience considerable vibration during certain ship maneuvers.

DINING: As befits the size of the ship, there are a variety of dining options. For formal meals there are three principal dining rooms (Amalfi, with 504 seats; Capri, with 486 seats; and Portofino, with 486 seats), and seating is assigned according to the location of your cabin. There are two seatings in one restaurant (Amalfi), while "anytime dining" (where you choose when and with whom you want to eat) is typically offered by the other two. All three are non-smoking and split into multi-tier sections in a non-symmetrical design that breaks what are quite large spaces into many smaller sections, for better ambience. Each dining room has its own galley.

Specially designed dinnerware and high-quality linens and silverware are used in the main dining rooms;

by Dudson of England (dinnerware), Frette Egyptian cotton table linens, and silverware by Hepp of Germany. Note that 15 percent is added to all beverage bills, including wines (whether you order a $15 bottle or a $120 bottle, although it's the same amount of service to open and pour the wine).

Despite the fact that the portions are generous, the food and its presentation are somewhat disappointing, and bland of taste. The quality of fish is poor (often disguised by crumb or batter coatings), the selection of fresh green vegetables is limited, and few garnishes are used. However, do remember that this *is* big-ship banquet catering, with all its attendant standardization and production cooking. Meats are of a decent quality, although often disguised by gravy-based sauces, and pasta dishes are acceptable (though voluminous), and are typically served by section headwaiters that may also make "something special just for you" – in search of gratuities and good comments. If you like desserts, order a sundae at dinner, as most other desserts are just so-so. Remember that ice cream ordered in the dining room is included, but if you order one anywhere else, you'll have to pay for it.

ALTERNATIVE (EXTRA CHARGE) EATERIES: Two alternative informal dining areas are provided: *Sabatini's Trattoria* and *Tequila's*. Both are open for lunch and dinner on days at sea. *Sabatini's* is an Italian eatery, with colorful tiled Mediterranean-style décor; it is named after *Trattoria Sabatini*, the 200-year old institution in Florence (where there is no cover charge). It features Italian-style pizzas and pastas, with a variety of sauces, as well as Italian-style entrées (including tiger prawns and lobster tail – all provided with flair and entertainment from by the staff of waiters (by reservation only, with a cover charge of $15 per person, for lunch or dinner on sea days only).

Tequila's has "southwestern American" food; by reservation only, with a cover charge of $8 per person, for lunch or dinner on sea days only. However, do note that *Tequila's* is spread over the whole beam (width) of the ship, and two walkways intersect it, which means that it's a very open area, with people walking through it as you eat – not a very comfortable arrangement. The cuisine in both of these spots is decidedly better than in the three main dining rooms, with better quality ingredients and more attention to presentation and taste.

A poolside hamburger grill and pizza bar (no additional charge) are additional dining spots for casual bites, while extra charges will apply if you order items to eat at either the coffee bar/pâtisserie, or the caviar/champagne bar.

Other casual meals can be taken in the Horizon Court, which is open 24 hours a day. It has large ocean-view on port and starboard sides and direct access to the two principal swimming pools and lido deck. There is no real finesse in presentation, however, as plastic plates are provided.

OTHER COMMENTS: The design for this large cruise ship, whose sister ships are *Golden Princess* and *Grand Princess*, presents a bold, forthright profile, with a racy "spoiler" effect at its galleon-like transom stern that I (and others) do not consider handsome (the "spoiler" acts as a stern observation lounge by day, and a stunning discotheque by night). *Star Princess* is quite a ship. At 118 ft/36 meters, including the navigation bridge wings and with many balcony cabins overhanging the ship's hull, it is too wide – by more than 43 ft/13 meters – to transit the Panama Canal. When the ship was delivered by the shipyard in Italy, *Star Princess* went through the Suez Canal (the largest passenger ship ever to do so), then sailed to Singapore for its maiden voyage, before going to Los Angeles; thus the ship did almost an around-the-world sailing before commencing service on the US west coast.

A few changes (compared with *Golden Princess* and *Grand Princess*) have been incorporated, including a substantially enlarged and much improved children's area (the Fun Zone) at the stern of the vessel. Also different (and improved) is the layout of the Lotus Spa (particularly the placement of the saunas/changing rooms).

There is a good sheltered teakwood promenade deck, which almost wraps around (three times round is equal to one mile) and a walkway which goes right to the (enclosed, protected) bow of the ship. The outdoor pools have various beach-like surroundings. One lap pool has a pumped "current" to swim against.

Unlike the outside decks, there is plenty of space inside the ship (but there are also plenty of passengers), and a wide array of public rooms to choose from, with many "intimate" (this being a relative word) spaces and places to play. The passenger flow has been well thought out, and works with little congestion. The décor is attractive, with lots of earth tones (well suited to both American and European tastes). In fact, this is a culmination of the best of all that Princess Cruises has to offer from its many years of operating what is now a well-tuned, good quality product.

Four areas center on swimming pools, one of which is two decks high and is covered by a magrodome, itself an extension of the funnel housing. High atop the stern of the ship is a ship-wide glass-walled disco pod (I have nicknamed it the ETR – energy transfer room). It looks like an aerodynamic "spoiler" and is positioned high above the water, with spectacular views from the extreme port and starboard side windows.

A large health spa complex, with Japanese-style décor, surrounds all of the swimming pools (you can have a massage or other spa treatment in an ocean-view treatment room). Lotus Spa treatments include Chakra hot stone massage, Asian Lotus ritual (offering massage with reflexology, reiki and shiatsu massage), deep-tissue sports therapy massage, lime and ginger salt glow, wild strawberry back cleanse, and seaweed mud wraps, among others devised to make you feel good (and part with your money). It is unfortunate, however (perhaps a lack of knowledge or respect on the part of the interior designer), that the Japanese symbol on the door of on of the steam inhalation rooms means *insect* – not a nice thing to call passengers!

An extensive collection of art works has been chosen, and this complements the interior design and colors well. If you see something you like, you will be able to purchase it on board – it's almost all for sale.

Like its sister ships *Golden Princess* and *Grand Princess,* it has a Wedding Chapel (a live web-cam can relay ceremonies via the internet). The ship's captain can legally marry (American) couples, thanks to the ship's Bermuda registry and a special dispensation (which should be verified when in the planning stage, according to where you reside). Princess Cruises offers three wedding packages – Pearl, Emerald, Diamond. The fee includes registration and official marriage certificate. However, to get married *and* take your close family members and entourage with you on your honeymoon is going to cost a lot of money. The "Hearts & Minds" chapel is also useful for "renewal of vows" ceremonies.

For children, there is a two-deck-high playroom, teen room, and a host of specially trained counselors. Children have their own pools, hot tubs, and open deck area at the stern of the ship, thankfully away from adult areas. There are more netted-in areas; one section has a dip pool, while another has a mini-basketball court.

For entertainment, Princess Cruises prides itself on its glamorous all-American production shows, and the shows aboard this ship (typically two per 7-day cruise) will not disappoint. Neither will the comfortable show lounges (the largest of which has $3 million in sound and light equipment, as well as a 9-piece orchestra, and a scenery loading bay that connects directly from stage to a hull door for direct transfer to the dockside). Two other entertainment lounges help spread things around.

Gaming lovers should enjoy what is presently one of the largest casinos at sea (Grand Casino), with more than 260 slot machines; there are blackjack, craps and roulette tables, plus newer games such as Let It Ride Bonus, Spanish 21 and Caribbean Draw Progressive. But the highlight could well be the specially linked slot machines that provide a combined payout.

Other features include a decent library/CD-Rom computer room, and a separate card room. Ship lovers should enjoy the wood-paneled Wheelhouse Bar, finely decorated with memorabilia and ship models tracing part of parent company P&O's history (this ship highlights the 1950-built cargo ship *Ganges*. A sports bar, Shooters, has two billiard tables, as well as eight television screens.

A high-tech hospital is provided, with live SeaMed tele-medicine link-ups with specialists at the Cedars-Sinai Medical Center in Los Angeles available for emergency help.

The ship provides with a stunning, grand resort playground in which to roam when you are not ashore. Princess Cruises delivers a consistently fine, well-packaged vacation product, with a good sense of style, at an attractive, highly competitive price, and this ship will appeal to those that really enjoy a big city to play in, with all the trimmings and lots of fellow passengers. The ship is full of revenue centers, however, designed to help part you from your money. As cruising aboard large ships such as this has become increasingly an onboard revenue-based product, you can expect to be subjected to a stream of flyers advertising daily art auctions, "designer" watches and other promotions, while "art-works" for auction are strewn throughout the ship.

The dress code has been simplified – reduced to formal or smart casual (which seems to be translated by many as jeans and trainers). Note that gratuities to staff are *automatically* added to your account, at $10 per person, per day (gratuities for children are charged at the same rate). If you want to pay less, you'll need to go to the reception desk to have these charges adjusted (that could mean lining up with many other passengers wanting to do the same). The onboard currency is the US dollar.

Whether this really can be considered a relaxing vacation is a moot point, but with *so many choices* and "small" rooms to enjoy, the ship has been extremely well designed, and the odds are that you'll have a fine cruise vacation.

WEAK POINTS: If you are not used to large ships, it will take you some time to find your way around this one, despite the company's claim that this vessel offers passengers a "small ship feel, big ship choice." The cabin bath towels are small, and drawer space is very limited. There are no butlers – even for the top-grade suites (which are not really large in comparison similar suites aboard some other ships). Cabin attendants have too many cabins to look after (typically 20), which does not translate to fine personal service.

The automated telephone system is frustrating, and luggage delivery is inefficient. Lines form for many things, but particularly for the purser's office, and for open-seating breakfast and lunch in the three main dining rooms. Long lines for shore excursions and shore tenders are also a fact of life aboard large ships such as this, as is waiting for elevators at peak times, embarkation (an "express check-in" option is available by completing certain documentation 40 days in advance of your cruise) and disembarkation, and booking spa appointments on the day of embarkation.

You'll have to live with the many extra charge items (such as for ice cream, and fresh squeezed orange juice) and activities (such as yoga, group exercise bicycling and kick boxing classes at $10 per session, not to mention $4 per hour for *group* babysitting services – at the time this book was completed).

Some of the spa (massage) treatment rooms are located directly underneath the jogging track. There's also a charge for using the washers ($1) and dryers ($0.50) in the self-service launderettes.

Passengers are also forced to endure countless pieces of (highly questionable) art found in almost every foyer and public room – an annoying reminder that today, cruising aboard large ships such as *Golden Princess*, *Grand Princess* and *Star Princess* is really like living in a bazaar of paintings surrounded by a ship. Now, what am I bid for this piece of art that is really worth only $10? Let's hear it. $1,200? Do I hear $1,400? Or will someone actually imagine it's worth even more?

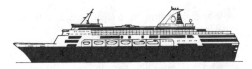

Large Ship: ....55,451 tons	Passengers	Cabin Current: ....110 and 220 volts
Lifestyle: ....Premium	(lower beds/all berths): 1,266/1,627	Elevators: 12
Cruise Line: ....Holland America Line	Passenger Space Ratio	Casino (gaming tables): ....Yes
Former Names: ....none	(lower beds/all berths): 43.8/34.0	Slot Machines: ....Yes
Builder: ....Fincantieri (Italy)	Crew/Passenger Ratio	Swimming Pools (outdoors): 1
Original Cost: ....$215 million	(lower beds/all berths): 2.2/2.9	Swimming Pools (indoors): 1
Entered Service: ....Jan 1993	Navigation Officers: ....Dutch	(magrodome)
Registry: ....The Netherlands	Cabins (total): 633	Whirlpools: 2
Length (ft/m): 719.4/219.3	Size Range (sq ft/m): 186.2–1,124.8/	Fitness Center: ....Yes
Beam (ft/m): 101.0/30.8	17.3–104.5	Sauna/Steam Room: ....Yes/No
Draft (ft/m): 24.6/7.5	Cabins (outside view): 502	Massage:.........................Yes
Propulsion/Propellers: .....diesel-electric	Cabins (interior/no view): 131	Self-Service Launderette: ....Yes
(34,560kW)/2	Cabins (for one person): 0	Dedicated Cinema/Seats: Yes/249
Passenger Decks:..................10	Cabins (with private balcony): 150	Library: ....Yes
Total Crew: 557	Cabins (wheelchair accessible): 6	Classification Society: ...Lloyd's Register

OVERALL SCORE: 1,533 (OUT OF A POSSIBLE 2,000 POINTS)

ACCOMMODATION: This ranges from small interior (no view) cabins to a large penthouse suite (with ocean views), in 17 categories. All cabin televisions carry CNN and TNT.

The interior (no view) and outside-view standard cabins have twin beds that convert to a queen-size bed, and there is a separate living space with sofa and coffee table. However, although the drawer space is generally good, the closet space is very tight, particularly for long cruises (although more than adequate for a 7-night cruise). The bathrooms are tiled, and compact but practical – they come with a good range of personal toiletry amenities. Bathrobes are also provided, as are hairdryers. The bathrooms are quite well laid out, but the bathtubs are small units better described as shower tubs. Some cabins have interconnecting doors (*Ryndam, Veendam* only).

On Navigation Deck 28 suites have accommodation for up to four persons. These also have in-suite dining as an alternative to the dining room, for private, reclusive meals. These are very spacious, tastefully decorated and well laid-out, and have a separate living room, bedroom with two lower beds (convertible to a king-size bed), a good size living area, dressing room, plenty of closet and drawer space, marble bathroom with Jacuzzi tub.

The largest accommodation of all can be found in one Penthouse Suite, located on the starboard side of Navigation Deck. It has a king-size bed, walk-in closet with superb drawer space, oversize whirlpool bath and separate shower enclosure, living room, dressing room, large private balcony, pantry, mini-bar/refrigerator, a guest toilet and floor to ceiling windows.

BERLITZ'S RATINGS

	Possible	Achieved
Ship	500	418
Accommodation	200	162
Food	400	267
Service	400	299
Entertainment	100	77
Cruise	400	310

DINING: The two-level Rotterdam Dining Room, located at the stern is quite dramatic, and has a grand staircase (although few seem to use it), panoramic views on three sides, and a music balcony. There is open seating for breakfast and lunch, and two seatings for dinner. The waiter stations in the dining room are very noisy for anyone seated adjacent to them. Fine Rosenthal china and cutlery are featured (although there are no fish knives).

Unfortunately, Holland America Line food isn't as nice as the china it's placed on. It may be adequate for most passengers who are not used to better food, but it does not match the standard found aboard other ships in the premium segment of the industry. While USDA beef is of a good quality, fowl tends to be battery-tough, and most fish is overcooked and has the consistency of a cricket bat. What are also definitely *not* luxurious are the endless packets of sugar, and packets (instead of glass jars) of breakfast jam, marmalade and honey, and poor quality teas. While these may be suitable for a family diner, they do not belong aboard a ship that claims to have "award-winning cuisine."

Dessert and pastry items are of good quality (specifically geared to American tastes) although there is much use of canned fruits and jellies. Forget the selection of "international" cheeses, however, as most of it didn't come from anywhere other than the USA – a country that is better known for its processed, highly colored slices than for fine cheese-making. Note that Holland America Line can provide Kosher meals, but these are prepared ashore, frozen, and brought to your table sealed in their original containers (there is no Kosher kitchen on board).

A small alternative restaurant was introduced in 2002. The 66-seat Pinnacle Grill has Pacific Northwest cuisine (Dungeness crab, Alaska salmon, halibut and other regional specialties). The new venue (reservations are necessary, and a cover/service charge of $15 applies) was created out of a section of the Explorers Lounge and the private dining wing of the main dining room. A Bvlgari show plate, Rosenthal china, Reidel wine glasses, and Frette table linen are used. The Pinnacle Grill promises to be a much better dining experience than the main dining room.

There is also an extensive, dual-line (self-serve) Lido Buffet (one side is for smokers, the other side for non-smokers) for casual breakfasts and lunches. For the buffets, there is much use of canned fruits (good for dentally challenged older passengers) and packeted items, although there are several commercial low-calorie salad dressings. The choice of cheeses (and accompanying crackers) is very poor. The beverage station also lets it down, for it is no better than those found in family outlets ashore in the United States. In addition, a poolside grill provides basic American hamburgers and hot dogs.

OTHER COMMENTS: *Statendam* is the first of a series of four almost identical ships in the same series – the others being *Maasdam, Ryndam* and *Veendam*. The exterior styling is rather angular (some would say boxy – the funnel certainly is), although it is softened and balanced somewhat by the fact that the hull is painted black. There is a full wrap-around teakwood promenade deck outdoors – excellent for strolling, and, thankfully, there's no sign of synthetic turf. The deck lounge chairs are wood, and come with comfortable cushioned pads.

Inside, an asymmetrical layout breaks up the interiors and helps to reduce bottlenecks and congestion. The décor is a little harsh and eclectic. In general, however, a mixture of contemporary materials is combined with traditional woods and ceramics. There is, fortunately, not too much "glitz" anywhere.

What is outstanding is the array of artworks throughout the ship (costing about $2 million), assembled and nicely displayed to represent the fine Dutch heritage of Holland America Line and to present a balance between standard itineraries and onboard creature comforts. Also noticeable are the fine flower arrangements throughout the public areas and foyers – used good effect to brighten up what to some is dull décor.

Atop the ship, with forward facing views that wrap around the sides is the Crow's Nest Lounge. By day it makes a fine observation lounge (particularly in Alaska),

while by night it turns into a nightclub with extremely variable lighting.

A three-deck high atrium foyer that is quite stunning, although its sculptured centerpiece makes it look a little crowded, and leaves little room in front of the purser's office. A hydraulic magrodome (glass) roof covers the reasonably sized swimming pool/whirlpools and central Lido area (whose focal point is a large dolphin sculpture) so that this can be used in either fine or inclement weather.

The two-deck-high show lounge is basically well designed, but the ceiling is low and the sight lines from the balcony level are poor. It has a large, lovely and relaxing reference library. The company keeps its ships very clean and tidy, and there is good passenger flow.

Statendam is basically a well-built ship, and has fairly decent interior fit and finish. Holland America Line is constantly fine-tuning its performance as a cruise operator and its regular passengers (almost all of whom are North American – there are few international passengers) find the company's ships very comfortable and well-run. The company continues its strong maritime traditions, although the present food and service components let down the rest of the cruise experience.

Holland America Line's many repeat passengers seem to enjoy the fact that social dancing is always on the menu. The company provides complimentary cappuccino and espresso coffees, and free ice cream during certain hours of the day aboard its ships, as well as hot hors d'oeuvres in all bars – something other major lines seem to have dropped, or charge extra for. In the final analysis, however, the score for this ship (and its sisters *Maasdam, Ryndam, Veendam*) ends up just a disappointing tad under what it could be if the food and food service staff were better (more professional training might help). The onboard currency is the US dollar.

WEAK POINTS: Standing in line for embarkation, disembarkation, shore tenders and for self-serve buffet meals is an inevitable aspect of cruising aboard all large ships. The service staff is Indonesian, and, although they are quite charming (for the most part), communication often proves frustrating for many passengers and service is spotty and inconsistent.

Note that passengers are forced to eat at the Lido Café on days when the dining room is closed for lunch (this is typically once or twice per cruise, depending on ship and itinerary). The single escalator is virtually useless. There is no bell push outside the suites. The charge to use the washing machines and dryers in the self-service launderette is really petty and irritating, particularly for the occupants of suites, as they pay high prices for their cruises. Room service is poor.

Removed 2006

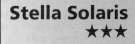

Stella Solaris
★★★

Mid-Size Ship:	17,832 tons	Total Crew:	320

Mid-Size Ship: . . . . .17,832 tons
Lifestyle: . . . . .Standard
Cruise Line: . . . . . .Royal Olympic Cruises
Former Names: . . . .*Stella V, Camboge*
Builder: . . .Ateliers et Chantiers de France
(France)
Original Cost: .n/a
Entered Service: . . . .July 1953/June 1973
Registry: .Greece
Length (ft/m): 545.1/166.15
Beam (ft/m): 72.4/22.08
Draft (ft/m): 25.8/7.88
Propulsion/Propellers: . . . . .diesel
(17,900kW)/2
Passenger Decks: 8

Total Crew: 320
Passengers
(lower beds/all berths): 658/700
Passenger Space Ratio
(lower beds/all berths): 27.1/25.4
Crew/Passenger Ratio
(lower beds/all berths): 1.9/2.1
Navigation Officers: . . . . .Greek
Cabins (total): 329
Size Range (sq ft/m): 96.8–226.0/
9.0–21.0
Cabins (outside view): 250
Cabins (interior/no view): 79
Cabins (for one person): 0
Cabins (with private balcony): 0

Cabins (wheelchair accessible): 0
Cabin Current: . . . . . . .110 and 220 volts
Elevators: 3
Casino (gaming tables): . . . . .Yes
Slot Machines: . . . .Yes (in separate room)
Swimming Pools (outdoors): 1
Swimming Pools (indoors): 0
Whirlpools: 0
Fitness Center: . . . . .Yes
Sauna/Steam Room: . . . . .No/Yes
Massage: . . . . .Yes
Self-Service Launderette: . . . . .No
Dedicated Cinema/Seats: Yes/275
Library: . . . . .Yes
Classification Society: . . .Lloyd's Register

OVERALL SCORE: 1,193 (OUT OF A POSSIBLE 2,000 POINTS)

ACCOMMODATION: There are 11 grades: 166 suites and deluxe cabins with ocean views; 163 standard interior (no view) and outside-view cabins. The outside-view cabins can best be described as adequate (particularly those on Sapphire, Ruby and Emerald decks), although many of them have what amounts to almost a full bathtub; the interior (no-view) cabins have very small bathrooms, however. All bathrooms have lovely mosaic-tiled floors, but the plumbing is exposed.

The cabin décor has been only slightly changed over the years, but presently has slightly brighter fabrics and colors than previously, although the old pegboard ceilings remain as a reminder that the ship was built in the 1950s, when such things were in vogue. The insulation between cabins, and between decks, is *extremely* poor. The accommodation passageways are reasonably wide, however. The telephone system is archaic, but at least there is real human operator to connect you, and not some automated system with voice mail.

The suites on Boat Deck all have names of Greek islands such as Milos, Samos – and look out onto the promenade deck outdoors, a feature not found aboard many ships today. Some cabins even have windows that can be opened. However, those located in the aft third of the ship are subject to the irritating noise of deck lounge chairs being moved on the pool deck above, at most inconvenient times.

The floor-to-ceiling height of 6.75 ft (2 meters) is typical of older ships, but rarely found aboard today's new builds, and provides an even better sense of spa-

BERLITZ'S RATINGS

	Possible	Achieved
Ship	500	329
Accommodation	200	136
Food	400	213
Service	400	248
Entertainment	100	57
Cruise	400	210

ciousness. There is an abundance of closet and drawer space, a vanity unit, television (cannot be seen from the bed, only in the lounge area, which is separated from the bedroom by a lattice-work panel), and telephone. The bathrooms come with a decent-sized bathtub, small toiletries cabinet, and hairdryer. Bathrobes may be obtained upon request (suite passengers only).

Many cabins located on aft on Sapphire Deck and amidships on Emerald Deck are subject to throbbing engine noise. The towels are thin, although they are of 100 percent cotton. Personal amenities provided are soap, shampoo (doubles as bath foam) and body lotion.

A room service menu with limited items such as sandwiches and cookies and beverages is available 24 hours a day (better selection available 7am–11pm).

DINING: The large, high-ceilinged dining room (totally non-smoking) has tables for four or six (although when the ship is not full, tables for two can be arranged). The room's focal point is a huge mural in shades of bronze, copper and gold that depicts scenes from Greek mythology. There are two seatings. The cuisine includes a wide variety of food, with spa and vegetarian dishes on lunch and dinner menus. However, the food has very little taste. Open seating for breakfast and lunch (a breakfast buffet is also set up in the dining room, but a regular à la carte breakfast men is also available). The dining room seating and table assignments are handled by the maître d' when you embark.

The old-world service from the Greek dining room

stewards adds to the experience, although it is not nearly as good as it was in former years, and is far too hurried.

The wine list is a mixture of a couple of good wines (but poor vintages) and a selection of reasonably priced wines, including many from Greece.

Informal breakfast and lunch buffets are available in the Lido Cafe (inside) adjacent to the pool, although the room is very small. The selection really is very limited, as is the food display. Breakfast includes too many tinned fruits and packaged items.

The ship makes fresh potato chips on board, revered by repeat passengers, and available in all bars, on most days – a nice touch.

OTHER COMMENTS: This ship has a traditional ship profile, with a royal blue hull and a large, attractive funnel amidships. It was originally built to carry cargo and passengers to Indonesia during the war the French waged in that area in the 1950s. The ship was successfully converted into a cruise vessel in the early 1970s, when it was operated by Sun Line (Sun Line merged with Epirotiki Lines into Royal Olympic Cruises in 1995). Because the ship has a deep draft, it is very stable at sea.

Although this is now one of the oldest cruise ships still in active service, it is reasonably clean and tidy, although maintenance is fighting a losing battle. There is an expansive amount of open deck space, and this includes a wrap-around promenade deck (part-enclosed, part-outdoors). Much of the teakwood decking and caulking are now well worn, but the well-polished railings are in excellent condition. There is an attractive figure-of-eight pool and sunbathing area, although open deck space is tight. The mostly Greek staff is selectively friendly (more so towards females than males), and some of them have been with the company for many years. But communication with many of the non-Greek staff (from eastern Europe and Asian countries) is limited, and can prove somewhat frustrating.

Inside, the public rooms have good quality, solid furniture and fixtures, although everything has that well-worn look (sagging seats, broken springs). Sadly, there is no forward observation lounge, although there is a feeling of space and old-world grace. The elevators are large, and can even accommodate wheelchairs (although wheelchair access to most of the ship is awful).

There are also plenty of public restrooms – although, for some reason, many seem to be permanently locked. The fresh flowers that were formerly everywhere are now mostly missing. The show lounge, which is combined with a bar (which itself is home to three blackjack tables and one roulette table) is large, with old-style chairs and banquette seating; all the shows feature cabaret-style entertainers, but sight lines are obstructed from many seats by eight pillars. A health spa added a few years ago, provides some much-needed facilities, although the $10 per person charge to use the steam room (incorrectly called a "Turkish Bath") is irritating.

This ship is for the much older passenger who seeks a relaxed, unhurried and old world cruise experience in decent, though very tired, surroundings, at reasonable cost, with reasonably friendly service, but without the hype of the more contemporary ships. One nice feature is that the toilets are quiet (not like the "barking dog" vacuum toilets aboard more modern ships).

The itineraries are well planned and interesting. There are always a number of lecturers aboard, as well as one or two gentlemen dance "hosts" (at least on the longer winter cruises). Gratuities ("suggested" at $9 per person, per day) are given to the Chief Steward, then pooled and shared among the crew. *Stella Solaris* was laid-up in 2002 because of fleet operational changes within the company. However, when this book was completed, it was expected that it would be brought back into service in 2003. The onboard currency is the euro.

WEAK POINTS: There is no observation lounge with forward-facing views over the ship's bows. This ship and onboard product really is tired and worn, as is many of the crew, who seem to have lost the art of hospitality (unless they know you well). Considerable financial investment is needed to improve the interiors, which are dark and somber. Completely gone is the grace of yesteryear. The seats in the cinema are not staggered, so sight lines are poor. Likewise, there are obstructed views from many seats in the show lounge.

Port information literature is very limited for those who want to go ashore independently. The in-cabin audio channels are not available at night. There is absolutely no enforcement of smoking and no-smoking areas. The vibration at the stern is irritating.

Large Ship: ....91,000 tons	Passengers	Cabin Current: ....110 and 220 volts
Lifestyle: ....Premium	(lower beds/all berths): 1,950/2,450	Elevators: 10
Cruise Line: ....Celebrity Cruises	Passenger Space Ratio	Casino (gaming tables): ....Yes
Former Names: ....none	(lower beds/all berths): 46.6/37.1	Slot Machines: ....Yes
Builder: ....Chantiers de l'Atlantique	Crew/Passenger Ratio	Swimming Pools (outdoors): 2
(France)	(lower beds/all berths): 1.9/2.4	Swimming Pools (indoors): 1
Original Cost: ....$350 million	Navigation Officers: ....Greek	(with magrodome)
Entered Service: ....Nov 2001	Cabins (total): 975	Whirlpools: 4
Registry: ....The Bahamas	Size Range (sq ft/m): 165.1–2,530.0/	Fitness Center: ....Yes
Length (ft/m): 964.5/294.0	15.34–235.0	Sauna/Steam Room: ....Yes/Yes
Beam (ft/m): 105.6/32.2	Cabins (outside view): 780	Massage: ....Yes
Draft (ft/m): 26.2/8.0	Cabins (interior/no view): 195	Self-Service Launderette: ....No
Propulsion/Propellers: .....gas turbine/2	Cabins (for one person): 0	Dedicated Cinema/Seats: Yes/368
azimuthing pods (39,000kW)	Cabins (with private balcony): 590	Library: ....Yes
Passenger Decks:.................11	Cabins (wheelchair accessible): 26	Classification Society: ...Lloyd's Register
Total Crew: 999	(17 with private balcony)	

OVERALL SCORE: 1,701 (OUT OF A POSSIBLE 2,000 POINTS)

ACCOMMODATION: There are 20 different grades, giving you a wide choice of size and location. Almost half the accommodation has a "private" balcony; approximately 80 percent are outside-view suites and cabins, and 20 percent are interior (no view) cabins. The accommodation is extremely comfortable throughout this ship, regardless of which grade you choose. Suites, naturally, have more space, butler service (whether you want it or not), more and better amenities and more personal service than if you choose any of the standard cabin grades. There are several categories of suites, but those at the stern of the ship are in a prime location and have huge balconies that are really private and not overlooked from above.

All suites and cabins have wood cabinetry and accenting, interactive television and entertainment systems (you can go shopping, book shore excursions, play casino games, interactively, and even watch soft porn movies). Bathrooms have hairdryers, and 100 percent cotton towels.

PENTHOUSE SUITES: Two Penthouse Suites (on Penthouse Deck) are the largest accommodation aboard. Each occupies one half of the beam (width) of the ship, overlooking the ship's stern. Each measures a huge 2,530 sq. ft (235 sq. meters) – 1,432 sq. ft (133 sq. meters) of living space, plus a huge wrap-around balcony measuring 1,098 sq. ft (102 sq. meters) with 180-degree views, which occupies one-half of the beam (width) of the ship,

BERLITZ'S RATINGS

	Possible	Achieved
Ship	500	454
Accommodation	200	181
Food	400	328
Service	400	330
Entertainment	100	78
Cruise	400	330

overlooking the ship's stern (it includes a wet bar, hot tub and whirlpool tub); however, note that much of this terrace can be overlooked by passengers on other decks above.

Features include a marble foyer, a separate living room (complete with ebony baby grand piano – bring your own pianist if you don't play yourself) and a formal dining room. The master bedroom has a large walk-in closet; personal exercise equipment; dressing room with vanity desk, exercise equipment; marble-clad master bathroom with twin washbasins; deep whirlpool bathtub; separate shower; toilet and bidet areas; flat-screen televisions (one in the bedroom and one in the lounge) and electronically controlled drapes. Butler service is standard, and a butler's pantry, with separate entry door, has a full-size refrigerator, temperature-controlled wine cabinet, microwave oven and good-sized food preparation and storage areas. For even more space, an interconnecting door can be opened into the adjacent suite (ideal for multi-generation families).

ROYAL SUITES: Eight Royal Suites, each measuring 733 sq. ft 68 sq. meters), are located towards the aft of the ship (four each on the port and starboard sides). Each features a separate living room with dining and lounge areas (with refrigerator, mini-bar and Bang & Olufsen CD sound system), and a separate bedroom. There are two entertainment centers with DVD players, and two flat-screen televisions (one in the living area, one in the bedroom), and a large walk-in closet with vanity desk.

The marble-clad bathroom has a whirlpool bathtub with integral shower, and there is also a separate shower enclosure, two washbasins and toilet. The teakwood decked balcony is extensive (large enough for on-deck massage) and also has a whirlpool hot tub.

CELEBRITY SUITES: Eight Celebrity Suites, each measuring 467 sq. ft (44 sq. meters), have floor-to-ceiling windows, a separate living room with dining and lounge areas, two entertainment centers with flat-screen televisions (one in the living room, one in the bedroom), and a walk-in closet with vanity desk. The marble-clad bathroom has a whirlpool bathtub with integral shower (a window with movable blind lets you look out of the bathroom through the lounge to the large ocean-view windows). Interconnecting doors allow two suites to be used as a family unit (as there is no balcony, these suites are ideal for families with small children). These suites overhang the starboard side of the ship (they are located opposite a group of glass-walled elevators), and provide stunning ocean views from the glass-walled sitting/dining area, which extends out from the ship's side. A personal computer with wood-surround screen allows direct internet connectivity. Butler service is standard.

SKY SUITES: There are 30 Sky Suites, each measuring 308 sq. ft (28.6 sq. meters), including the private balcony (some balconies may be larger than others, depending on the location). Although these are designated as suites, they are really just larger cabins that feature a marble-clad bathroom with bathtub/shower combination. The suites also have a VCR player in addition to a TV set, and have a larger lounge area (than standard cabins) and sleeping area. Butler service is standard.

BUTLER SERVICE: Butler service (in all accommodation designated as suites) includes full breakfast, in-suite lunch and dinner service (as required), afternoon tea service, evening hors d'oeuvres, complimentary espresso and cappuccino, daily news delivery, shoeshine service, and other personal touches.

Suite occupants in Penthouse, Royal, Celebrity and Sky suites also get welcome champagne; a full personal computer in each suite, including a printer and internet access (on request in the Sky Suites); choice of films from a video library; personalized stationery; tote bag; priority dining room seating preferences; private portrait sitting, and bathrobe; and in-suite massage service.

STANDARD OUTSIDE-VIEW/INTERIOR (NO VIEW) CABINS: All other outside-view and interior (no view) cabins feature a lounge area with sofa or convertible sofa bed, sleeping area with twin beds that can convert to a double bed, a good amount of closet and drawer space, personal safe, mini-bar/refrigerator (extra cost), interactive television, and private bathroom. The cabins are nicely decorated with warm wood-finish furniture, and there is none of the boxy feel of cabins in so many ships, due to the angled placement of vanity and audio-video consoles. Even the smallest cabin has a good-sized bathroom and shower enclosure.

WHEELCHAIR-ACCESSIBLE ACCOMMODATION: Wheelchair-accessible accommodation is available in six Sky Suites, three premium outside-view, eight deluxe ocean-view, four standard ocean-view and five interior (no view) cabins measuring from 347 to 362 sq. ft (32.2 to 33.6 sq. meters) and are located in the most practical parts of the ship and close to elevators for good accessibility (all have doorways and bathroom doorways and showers are wheelchair-accessible). Some cabins have extra berths for third or third and fourth occupants (note, however, that there is only one safe for personal belongings, which must be shared).

DINING: The 1,170-seat Cosmopolitan Restaurant, the ship's formal dining room. It is two decks high, has a grand staircase connecting the two levels, a huge glass wall overlooking the sea at the stern of the ship (electrically operated blinds provide several different backdrops), and a musician's gallery on the upper level (typically for a string quartet/quintet). There are two seatings for dinner (open seating for breakfast and lunch), at tables for two, four, six, eight or 10. The dining room is a totally no-smoking area, and, you should note, that, like all large dining halls, it can prove to be extremely noisy.

As a tribute to the French Line ship *Normandie,* a statue created by Leon-Georges Baudry, called "La Normandie," that once overlooked the ship's grand staircase and for the past 47 years graced the Fontaineblue Hotel in Miami, can now be seen in this dining room.

There are other dining options, including one for those seeking more casual dining spots – or for that extra-special (extra cost) meal in more intimate and exclusive settings. Full service in-cabin dining is also available for all meals (including dinner).

For casual eating, the Waterfall Café is a self-serve buffet area, with six principal serving lines, and 754 seats; there is also a grill and pizza bar.

For champagne and caviar lovers, the Platinum Club has a platinum and silver art deco décor that is reminiscent of a 1930s gentleman's club. It includes a diamond-pane reflective mirror wall. There's also a Martini Bar.

ALTERNATIVE (RESERVATIONS-ONLY, EXTRA COST) DINING: The Normandie Restaurant is an alternative dining room, adjacent to the conference center. It has gold lacquered paneling form the smoking room of the original French Line ship. Fine tableside preparation is the feature of this alternative dining room, whose classic French cuisine and service is outstanding (masterminded by Michel Roux, owner of a three-star Michelin restaurant near Windsor, England). This is haute cuisine at the height of professionalism. However, with just 134 seats, not all passengers can experience it even once during a one-week cruise (reservations are necessary, and a cover charge of $25 per person applies). There is a dine-in wine cellar (with more than 200 labels from around the world), and a demonstration galley. Tableside preparation is a feature of this alternative dining spot.

COVA CAFÉ DI MILANO: The Cova Café di Milano is a signature item aboard all Celebrity Cruises ships, and a seagoing version of the real Café di Milano originally located next to La Scala Opera House in Milan (it opened in 1817). It is in a prominent position, on the second level of the atrium lobby, and several display cases show off the extensive range of Cova coffee, chocolates and alcoholic digestives; this is *the* place to see and be seen. It is a delightful setting (and meeting place) for those who appreciate fine Italian coffees (for espresso, espresso macchiato, cappuccino, latte), pastries and superb cakes in an elegant, refined setting.

OTHER COMMENTS: *Summit* is a sister ship to *Infinity* and *Millennium*. Jon Bannenberg (famous as a mega-yacht designer) designed the exterior that features a royal blue and white hull, and racy lines in red, blue and gold, although it has actually turned out to look extremely ungainly (some say downright ugly). This is the third Celebrity Cruises ship to be fitted with a "pod" propulsion system (and controllable pitch propellers) coupled with a quiet, smokeless *gas* turbine powerplant (two GE gas turbines provide engine power while a single GE steam turbine drives the electricity generators).

Inside, the ship has the high-class décor and materials and public rooms that have made the existing ships in the fleet so popular and user-friendly. But in a first for Celebrity Cruises, the atrium spans 11 decks. It is capped with a glass dome, and four glass elevators travel through the port side of the atrium. Michael's Club (a cigar and cognac specialty lounge that has almost 20 varieties of cigars) is located on Promenade Deck.

Facilities include a combination Cinema/Conference Center, an expansive shopping arcade, with 14,500 sq. ft (1,300 sq. meters) of retail store space, a lavish four-decks-high show lounge with the latest in staging and lighting equipment, two-level library (one level for English-language books; a second level for books in other languages), card room, music room, and a combination observation lounge/discotheque.

One unique feature is a conservatory which includes many seats set in a botanical environment of flowers, plants, tress, mini-gardens and fountains, designed by the award-winning floral designer Emilio Robba of Paris. It is located directly in front of the main funnel and has glass walls that overlook the ship's side.

Outdoor facilities include two outdoor pools, one indoor/outdoor pool (with magrodome cover), and several whirlpools. Spa facilities include an AquaSpa (a multi-station thalassotherapy pool), 16 treatment rooms, plus eight treatment rooms with showers and one treatment room specifically designed for wheelchair passengers, aerobics room, gymnasium (complete with over 40 machines), large male and female saunas (with large ocean-view porthole window), a co-ed thermal suite (containing several steam and shower mist rooms with different fragrances such as chamomile, eucalyptus and mint, and a glacial ice fountain), and beauty salon. Among the different types of massage available is a delightful hot and cold stone massage therapy that lasts almost 1½ hours (the cost is about $175).

Sports facilities include a full-size basketball court, compact football, paddle tennis and volleyball, golf simulator, shuffleboard (on two different decks) and a jogging track. Gaming sports include a large casino, with blackjack, roulette, and numerous slot machines.

Families with children will appreciate the Fun Factory (for children) and The Tower (for teenagers).

Summit delivers a well-defined North American cruise experience at a very modest price. The "zero announcement policy" fortunately means little intrusion. A 15 percent gratuity is added to bar and wine accounts.

During the past two years, the standard of product delivery aboard all Celebrity Cruises ships went down as cuts were made by parent company Royal Caribbean International. However, new management has improved the situation. The strong points of a Celebrity cruise include the use of many European staff and service, a fine spa with a good range of facilities, treatments, taste-filled food attractively presented and served in the European fine dining tradition, and the provision of many intimate spaces and a superb collection of artwork.

If you travel in one of the suites, the benefits provide you with the highest level of personal service, while cruising in non-suite accommodation is almost like in any large ship – you'll be one of a number, with little access to the niceties and benefits of the "upper class" cruising. The onboard currency is the US dollar.

WEAK POINTS: There is no wrap-around wooden promenade deck outdoors. Standing in line for embarkation, disembarkation, shore tenders and for self-serve buffet meals is inevitable aboard all large ships. There are cushioned pads for poolside deck lounge chairs only, but not for chairs on other outside decks. Trying to reach Cabin Service or the Guest Relations Desk to answer the phone (to order breakfast, for example, if you don't want to do so via the interactive television) is a matter of luck, timing and patience. Passenger participation activities are amateurish and should be upgraded. The officers have become more aloof lately, with far less contact with passengers than when the company first started.

Sun Bay I
★★★★

Removed 2006

Small Ship:	2,842 tons	Passengers		Cabin Current:	220 volts
Lifestyle:	Premium	(lower beds/all berths):	92/92	Elevators:	0
Cruise Line:	Sun Bay Cruises	Passenger Space Ratio		Casino (gaming tables):	No
Former Names:	none	(lower beds/all berths):	30.8/30.8	Slot Machines:	No
Builder:	Cassens-Werft (Holland)	Crew/Passenger Ratio		Swimming Pools (outdoors):	No
Original Cost:	DM 35 million	(lower beds/all berths):	1.9/1.9	Swimming Pools (indoors):	No
Entered Service:	June 2001	Navigation Officers:	German	Whirlpools:	1
Registry:	The Bahamas	Cabins (total):	46	Fitness Center:	Yes
Length (ft/m):	290.3/88.5	Size Range (sq ft/m):	156.0–247.5/	Sauna/Steam Room:	Yes/No
Beam (ft/m):	45.9/14.0		14.5–23	Massage:	Yes
Draft (ft/m):	11.4/3.5	Cabins (outside view):	46	Self-Service Launderette:	No
Propulsion/Propellers:	diesel	Cabins (interior/no view):	0	Dedicated Cinema/Seats:	No
	(3,000kW)/2	Cabins (for one person):	0	Library:	Yes
Passenger Decks:	4	Cabins (with private balcony):	9	Classification Society:	Germanischer
Total Crew:	50	Cabins (wheelchair accessible):	0		Lloyd

OVERALL SCORE: 1,425 (OUT OF A POSSIBLE 2,000 POINTS)

ACCOMMODATION: There are four price categories in two cabin types: 9 Suites, measuring 247 sq. ft (23 sq. meters); 34 Comfort Cabins, 172 sq. ft (16 sq.meters); and 3 Comfort cabins, 156 sq. ft (14.5 sq. meters).

All suites and cabins have twin beds (four comfort cabins have a double bed), television, sofa, drinks table, vanity desk with hairdryer, mini-bar/ refrigerator, and personal safe, while bathrooms all have a good-sized shower enclosure (no suites/cabins have bathtubs) with soap/shampoo dispenser, black granite washbasin, white marble-clad walls, and 100 percent cotton bathrobes and towels. The beds are quite novel, as they are wider at the head end, narrower at the foot end, with specially designed mattresses (the interior designer has obviously noticed that couples typically put their feet together when sleeping).

The largest accommodation is in the nine suites (Amrum, Baltrum, Borkum, Helgoland, Ilsedom, Juist, Nordernay, Rugen, Sylt), each with a private balcony. One suite is located forward, with forward-facing views, and has a characterful sloping ceiling. The balconies have partitions that are almost private, and a teakwood deck. Two of the suites can be joined together through an interconnecting wall. One bedroom has two pull-down Murphy beds, so that it can be used as a lounge in the daytime.

DINING: The Dining Room accommodates all passengers in one seating and operates on an open-seating basis. It is nicely decorated in warm, contemporary colors, and has ocean-view windows along one side. A self-serve buffet offers salads, cold cuts and cheeses. The service is

BERLITZ'S RATINGS		
	Possible	Achieved
Ship	500	372
Accommodation	200	157
Food	400	308
Service	400	255
Entertainment	100	61
Cruise	400	272

provided by Ukrainian staff. Sea Chefs of Hamburg provides the food, which is extremely good. The wine list is quite sound for a small ship carrying fewer than 100 people.

A casual self-serve buffet (the Seagull Buffet) is on one of the open decks aft, with teak tables and chairs.

OTHER COMMENTS: Watersports enthusiasts will find an array of windsurfers, kayaks, water-ski boat, banana boat, and scuba and snorkeling gear. At the stern, there is a wide platform at the stern of the ship, for accessing the equipment, or for swimming directly from. There is a surprisingly good amount of open deck space – far better, in proportion, than many ships far larger, and much of it with teakwood decking. Although there is no swimming pool, there is a whirlpool tub on the open deck.

Facilities include a main lounge, with bar and small dance floor, a boutique, fitness room, and the ship's information desk doubles as a business center.

This is the first really small yacht-like ship for German-speaking passengers. It's like a small private club. The ambience is unpretentious, unhurried, but subtly elegant at the same time. Except for the dining room (which can double as a conference room), there is only one public room: the main lounge, complete with bar, dance floor and bandstand. Columbus Seereisen is the charterer/operator. The onboard currency is the euro.

WEAK POINTS: *Sun Bay I* is not fitted with stabilizers, which could mean an unpleasant ride in bad weather. The dining room chairs do not have armrests.

Removed 2006

Small Ship: . . . . .2,842 tons	Passengers	Cabin Current: . . . . .220 volts
Lifestyle: . . . . .Premium	(lower beds/all berths): 92/92	Elevators: 0
Cruise Line: . . . . .Sun Bay Cruises	Passenger Space Ratio	Casino (gaming tables): . . . . .No
Former Names: . . . . .none	(lower beds/all berths): 30.8/30.8	Slot Machines: . . . . .No
Builder: . . . . .Cassens-Werft (Holland)	Crew/Passenger Ratio	Swimming Pools (outdoors): . . . . .No
Original Cost: . . . . .DM 35 million	(lower beds/all berths): 1.9/1.9	Swimming Pools (indoors): . . . . .No
Entered Service: . . . . .June 2002	Navigation Officers: . . . . .German	Whirlpools: 1
Registry: . . . . .The Bahamas	Cabins (total): .46	Fitness Center: . . . . .Yes
Length (ft/m): 290.3/88.5	Size Range (sq ft/m): 156.0–247.5/	Sauna/Steam Room: . . . . .Yes/No
Beam (ft/m): 45.9/14.0	14.5–23	Massage: . . . . .Yes
Draft (ft/m): 11.4/3.5	Cabins (outside view): 46	Self-Service Launderette: . . . . .No
Propulsion/Propellers: . . . . .diesel	Cabins (interior/no view): 0	Dedicated Cinema/Seats: . . . . .No
(3,000kW)/2	Cabins (for one person): 0	Library: . . . . .Yes
Passenger Decks: 4	Cabins (with private balcony): 9	Classification Society: . . . . .Germanischer
Total Crew: 50	Cabins (wheelchair accessible): 0	Lloyd

OVERALL SCORE: 1,425 (OUT OF A POSSIBLE 2,000 POINTS)

ACCOMMODATION: There are four price categories in two cabin types: 9 Suites, measuring 247 sq. ft (23 sq. meters); 34 Comfort Cabins, 172 sq. ft (16 sq.meters); and 3 Comfort cabins, 156 sq. ft (14.5 sq. meters).

All suites and cabins have twin beds (four comfort cabins have a double bed), television, sofa, drinks table, vanity desk with hairdryer, mini-bar/refrigerator, and personal safe, while bathrooms all have a good-sized shower enclosure (no suites/cabins have bathtubs) with soap/shampoo dispenser, black granite washbasin, white marble-clad walls, and 100 percent cotton bathrobes and towels. The beds are quite novel, as they are wider at the head end, narrower at the foot end, with specially designed mattresses (the interior designer has obviously noticed that couples typically put their feet together when sleeping).

The largest accommodation is in the nine suites (Amrum, Baltrum, Borkum, Helgoland, Ilsedom, Juist, Nordernay, Rugen, Sylt), each with a private balcony. One suite is located forward, with forward-facing views, and has a characterful sloping ceiling. The balconies have partitions that are almost private, and a teakwood deck. Two of the suites can be joined together through an interconnecting wall. One bedroom has two pull-down Murphy beds, so that it can be used as a lounge in the daytime.

DINING: The Dining Room accommodates all passengers in one seating and operates on an open-seating basis. It is nicely decorated in warm, contemporary colors, and has ocean-view windows along one side. A self-serve buffet offers salads, cold cuts and cheeses. The service is

BERLITZ'S RATINGS

	Possible	Achieved
Ship	500	372
Accommodation	200	157
Food	400	308
Service	400	255
Entertainment	100	61
Cruise	400	272

provided by Ukrainian staff. Sea Chefs of Hamburg provides the food, which is extremely good. The wine list is quite sound for a small ship carrying fewer than 100 people.

A casual self-serve buffet (the Seagull Buffet) is on one of the open decks aft, with teak tables and chairs.

OTHER COMMENTS: Watersports enthusiasts will find an array of windsurfers, kayaks, water-ski boat, banana boat, and scuba and snorkeling gear. At the stern, there is a wide platform at the stern of the ship, for accessing the equipment, or for swimming directly from. There is a surprisingly good amount of open deck space – far better, in proportion, than many ships far larger, and much of it with teakwood decking. Although there is no swimming pool, there is a whirlpool tub on the open deck.

Facilities include a main lounge, with bar and small dance floor, a boutique, fitness room, and the ship's information desk doubles as a business center.

Together with sister ship *Sun Bay I,* this is a really small yacht-like ship for German-speaking passengers. It's like a small private club. The ambience is unpretentious, unhurried, but subtly elegante. Except for the dining room (which doubles as a conference room), there is only one public room: the main lounge, with bar, dance floor and bandstand. Unlike *Sun Bay I.* it has stablisiers – good news in bad weather. Columbus Seereisen is the charterer/operator. The onboard currency is the euro.

WEAK POINTS: The dining room chairs do not have armrests.

Sunbird
★★★ +

Now Thomson Destiny *Majored 08/09/05* (handwritten)

Large Ship: ....37,584 tons	Passengers	Cabin Current: ....110 volts
Lifestyle: ....Standard	(lower beds/all berths): 1,450/1,611	Elevators: 7
Cruise Line: ......Sun Cruises (My Travel)	Passenger Space Ratio	Casino (gaming tables): ....Yes
Former Names: ....*Song of America*	(lower beds/all berths): 25.9/23.3	Slot Machines: ....Yes
Builder: ....Wartsila (Finland)	Crew/Passenger Ratio	Swimming Pools (outdoors): 2
Original Cost: ....$140 million	(lower beds/all berths): 2.6/2.9	Swimming Pools (indoors): 0
Entered Service: ....Dec 1982/May 1999	Navigation Officers: ....International	Whirlpools: 0
Registry: ....The Bahamas	Cabins (total): 725	Fitness Center: ....Yes
Length (ft/m): 705.0/214.88	Size Range (sq ft/m): 118.4–425.1/	Sauna/Steam Room: ....Yes/No
Beam (ft/m): 93.1/28.40	11.0–39.5	Massage: ....Yes
Draft (ft/m): 22.3/6.80	Cabins (outside view): 425	Self-Service Launderette: ....No
Propulsion/Propellers: ....diesel	Cabins (interior/no view): 300	Dedicated Cinema/Seats: ....No
(16,480kW)/2	Cabins (for one person): 0	Library: ....Yes
Passenger Decks: 11	Cabins (with private balcony): 9	Classification Society: ....Det Norske
Total Crew: 540	Cabins (wheelchair accessible): 0	Veritas

OVERALL SCORE: 1,275 (OUT OF A POSSIBLE 2,000 POINTS)

ACCOMMODATION: This is provided in five grades (L-Shaped Twin, Parallel Twin, Deluxe, Penthouse Suite and Grand Penthouse Suite), making it an easy matter to select your cabin. You can now also book the exact cabin and location you want if you pay an extra charge of £50 per cabin (roughly US$75), which also lets you choose whether you want to dine at the early or late evening seating.

Most cabins are of a similar size (which is actually very small when compared to today's newer ships) and the insulation between them is quite poor. The cabins also have mediocre closets and very little storage space, yet somehow everyone seems to manage (the ship was built originally for one-week Caribbean cruises). However, they are just about adequate for a one-week cruise, as you will need only a small selection of mainly casual clothes (you'll probably have to put your shoes – and luggage – under the bed).

Most bathrooms typically contain a washbasin, toilet, and shower, with very little space for your personal toiletry items. Although they are reasonably cheerful, the shower enclosure is small, and has a curtain that you will probably end up dancing with. Towels are of 100 percent cotton.

In some cabins, twin beds are fixed in a parallel mode (some are moveable and can be made into a queen-sized bed), while others may be in an "L" shape. Note that in almost all cabins there is a "lip" or threshold (of about 9 inches/23 cm) at the bathroom door to step over.

For a little more money than a standard two-bed cabin, you can get more space and a larger cabin if you

BERLITZ'S RATINGS

	Possible	Achieved
Ship	500	329
Accommodation	200	120
Food	400	241
Service	400	259
Entertainment	100	63
Cruise	400	263

book one of the 21 deluxe grade cabins on Promenade Deck. These typically have twin beds that convert to a queen-sized bed, set diagonally into a sleeping area adjacent to outside-view windows. There is more drawer space, more closet space, and the bathroom has a half-size bathtub and shower combination – bathrobes are also provided. The largest of these deluxe grade cabins is Cabin 7000.

For even more exclusivity, you can book one of the nine Penthouse Suites (*Owner's Suite, Commodore's Suite, Amerigo Verspucci, Christoforo Columbus, Henry the Navigator, James Cook, Leif Ericson, Sir Francis Drake, Vasco da Gama*). All are located in a private area, have fine wood paneling and trim, and come with additional space and better, more personalized service.

The additional space includes a lounge area with sofa (this converts to a double bed – making it ideal for families with children), coffee table and two chairs, a vanity desk, combination TV/VCR, an abundance of drawers, illuminated closets (with both hanging space and several shelves), excellent storage space, king-sized bed, and bathrobes. The bathroom is fully tiled, and has a full-sized enamel bathtub (few ships have enamel tubs today) with shower, pink granite-look washbasin, and plenty of storage space for personal toiletry items. Suite occupants also get a semi-private balcony (the door of which is extremely heavy and difficult to open) with drinks table and two teak chairs.

Private, butler service is standard. You will also be able to eat in your suite from the full dining room menu for breakfast, lunch and dinner – although there is no dining table in the suite. Book either the *Owner's Suite* or *Commodore's Suite* (called Grand Penthouse Suites in the brochure), and you'll get even more room – plus views over the ship's bows (through windows with electric blinds) and a larger balcony (these can, however, be overlooked from the open deck above), more floor space, and a walk-in closet – otherwise they have the same facilities as for the other suites mentioned above. Missing are a bedside telephone and a bathroom telephone.

Do note that, no matter what suite or cabin grade you book, the cabin voltage is 110 volts so British passengers (the majority aboard the ships of Sun Cruises/My Travel) will need to take a US-style adapter for any electrical appliances such as a hairdryer. Note that, in the past, cabins were not assigned until you arrived at the ship; however, now you *can* book the cabin you want. The accommodation deck hallways are also very narrow on some decks. There is a Room Service Menu, but all items (including breakfast) are at extra cost, unless you are in one of the suites.

DINING: The Seven Seas Restaurant is a large room, and consists of a central main section, and two long, narrow wings (called the Magellan Room and Galileo Room on port and starboard sides respectively, and have large, ocean-view windows. However, the low ceiling creates a high level of ambient noise. There are two seatings – both are non-smoking. There are tables for two (but only 14), four, six or eight (window tables are for two or six). The service is average in this efficiently run dining room operation. The food is of a generally decent quality and the portions are quite substantial, although the menus are standard and deviation is difficult. Bottled water is offered, although it costs extra; the ship's drinking water (for which there is no charge) is adequate.

So, what's the cuisine like? In a nutshell, it's basic, no-frills cuisine – acceptable for those who do not expect much in the way of presentation or quality, but certainly not memorable. There is plenty of it, however; indeed, it is quantity, not quality, that prevails, but do remember that it is all provided at a low cost – as is a cruise aboard this ship, compared to more expensive cruise products. Presentation is a weak point, and there are no fish knives. So, it's best to remember that, like anything in life, you get what you pay for. If you enjoy going out to eat, and enjoy being adventurous with your food and eating habits – then you could be disappointed.

There is an adequate, but limited, wine list, and the wines are almost all very young – typical of those you might find in your local supermarket. Wine prices are quite modest, as are the prices for most alcoholic beverages. The same glasses are used for both red and white wines, and they are small.

For casual, self-serve breakfasts and lunches, the Veranda Café, is the alternative choice, although the tables and seats outdoors are of metal and plastic, and the buffets are extremely basic – the kind one would expect to find in a school from the 1950s. However,

remember that the price is low – and then you'll understand why you get plastic cups and plastic stirrers (teaspoons are unheard of). At night you can "dine" under the steel and canvas canopy, where the café becomes a pleasant, outdoors alternative to the dining room – and includes waiter service and food that's cooked à la minute. Additionally, during lunchtime, baguettes are available at the bar forward of the forward swimming pool.

OTHER COMMENTS: This is the largest ship in the Sun Cruises/My Travel fleet. It is a smart-looking and contemporary, with nicely rounded lines, a sharply raked bow, and a single funnel with a cantilevered, wrap-around lounge. The side of the all-white ship has the company's new corporate logo (My Travel) painted on the side. When the ship first debuted (for previous owners Royal Caribbean International), it was named by famous opera singer Beverly Sills.

Smaller sister ships *Carousel* and *Sundream* were also purchased from the same company, although in the case of *Sunbird*, the lounge that wraps around the funnel housing was not removed. The lounge (called the "Chart Room") is a fine place from which to observe the world around and below you.

Sunbird was acquired by the UK-based Airtours in 1999. There is a decent amount of open deck and sunbathing space (but it certainly will be crowded when the ship is full, which is most of the time), and nicely polished wooden decks and rails. There are two swimming pools – the aft pool being designated for children, the forward pool for adults.

Inside, there is a good array of public rooms. The principal public rooms all have high ceilings, and are located one deck up from the dining room, in a convenient horizontal layout. These include the main show lounge (Can Can Lounge), casino (Casino Royale) and nightclub (Oklahoma Lounge). There is also a small conference center for meetings and group business, as well as an Internet Café (with six computer terminals – but no café).

When Sun Cruises/My Travel first started in cruising, its ships were effectively under the control of an outside management company. Now, however, all the ships and personnel are under direct Sun Cruises/My Travel ownership and management, which has resulted a more consistent product.

Of the ships in the fleet, *Sunbird* is the largest and provides more facilities and choice – particularly for the many repeat passengers that the company has acquired. This ship should prove to be a good choice if you are a *first-time* passenger seeking a well rounded, destination-intensive cruise at a *very modest* price (book between January and March and you get half-price cabin upgrades). The pre- and post-cruise land stays are also well organized. Sun Cruises/My Travel provides a consistent, well-tuned and well-packaged, fun product, in comfortable surroundings, and it should prove to be a good vacation that is particularly suited to couples and families with children. Note, however, that Sun CruisesMy Travel does not actively market or specialize in cruises for families with children because the children's and youth facilities are limited (there is also no evening babysitting service for youngsters).

Airtours is known for packaging its products really well, and this ship represents an excellent buy for families who want to cruise, but on a limited budget. Also, if you want a little more than the basics, Sun Cruises/My Travel offers special packages – good for celebrating something special. These come in four packages – bronze, silver, gold and platinum, with each adding a little extra cost. Want to buy the captain? Go for gold or platinum and you get breakfast in bed with champagne, flowers, fruit basket, and dinner at the captain's table.

Airtours also has its own fleet of aircraft, and this is one reason that the company is able to offer complete cruise-air-stay packages at such low rates. Sun Cruises/My Travel does a fine job in getting you and your luggage from airplane to ship without having to go through immigration (depending on itinerary) in foreign countries whenever possible – so your cruise vacation is as seamless as possible.

The company's brochures tell it like it is – so you know before you go exactly what you will get for your money, with the exception of its claim to "first class food," which is a gross exaggeration. However, Sun Cruises/My Travel provides cruises for "working man," at very modest prices. If you want just the basics, you pay the least amount. If you want all the goodies – choose a wider "premium" seat with extra leg room on your Airtours aircraft, choose your own cabin, choose your dinner seating, breakfast in bed and dinner with the captain, then you'll pay for all those "privileges." Note that however you choose to cruise, all gratuities are included. Insurance is also included – although you will be charged for it unless you decline it on the booking form. The onboard currency is the British pound.

WEAK POINTS: Standing in line for embarkation, disembarkation, shore tenders and for self-serve buffet meals is an inevitable aspect of cruising aboard all large ships. Like the other ships in the fleet, the space per passenger (particularly on the open decks) is very tight when the ship is full (which is most of the time). Non-smokers will find it extremely difficult to escape from smokers who walk through public rooms. The cabin televisions are very small (except for those in the suites). Note that couples that travel without children will be surrounded by large number of children during the summer months – and, thus, increased noise levels. The food is of low-budget quality, and the presentation is quite poor. There is little choice of tea and coffee. There are no cushioned pads for the deck lounge chairs.

Removed 2000

Large Ship: . . . . .22,945 tons	Passengers	Cabin Current: . . . . .110 volts
Lifestyle: . . . . .Standard	(lower beds/all berths): 1,076/1,257	Elevators: 4
Cruise Line: . . . . . Sun Cruises/My Travel	Passenger Space Ratio	Casino (gaming tables): . . . . .Yes
Former Names: . . . .*Song of Norway*	(lower beds/all berths): 21.3/18.2	Slot Machines: .Yes
Builder: . . . . .Wartsila (Finland)	Crew/Passenger Ratio	Swimming Pools (outdoors): 1
Original Cost: . . . .$13.5 million	(lower beds/all berths): 2.5/2.9	Swimming Pools (indoors): 0
Entered Service: . . . .Nov 1970/May 1997	Navigation Officers: . . . . . . .International	Whirlpools: 0
Registry: . . . . .The Bahamas	Cabins (total): 538	Fitness Center: . . . . .Yes
Length (ft/m): 637.5/194.32	Size Range (sq ft/m): 118.4–265.8/	Sauna/Steam Room: . . . . .No/No
Beam (ft/m): 78.8/24.03	11.0–24.7	Massage: . . . . .No
Draft (ft/m): 21.9/6.70	Cabins (outside view): 346	Self-Service Launderette: . . . . .No
Propulsion/Propellers: . . . . .diesel	Cabins (interior/no view): 192	Dedicated Cinema/Seats: . . . . .No
(13,400kW)/2	Cabins (for one person): 0	Library: . . . . .Yes
Passenger Decks: 8	Cabins (with private balcony): 0	Classification Society: . . . . . . .Det Norske
Total Crew: 423	Cabins (wheelchair accessible): 0	Veritas

OVERALL SCORE: 1,226 (OUT OF A POSSIBLE 2,000 POINTS)

ACCOMMODATION: The cabins are split into just four price grades (Standard, Superior, Promenade and Deluxe) and six types, making it an easy matter to select the type of accommodation you want.

Most cabins are of a similar size (dimensionally challenged comes to mind for most of them) and the insulation between them is quite poor, but do remember that this ship is now over 20 years old. The cabins also have mediocre closets and very little storage space, yet somehow everyone seems to manage (the ship was built originally for Caribbean cruising). They really are adequate for a one-week cruise, as you will need only casual clothes, and, with these destination-intensive cruises, you really will not need many clothes anyway (shoes can always go under the bed). The bathrooms are very small (they are best described as functional rather than attractive), and the showers have a curtain you will probably need to dance with (larger than average persons may well become frustrated quickly).

The best advice I can give you therefore is to take only casual clothing and only the things you really need. Do note that cabin voltage is 110 volts (American two flat pin sockets are provided), so you may need to take adapters for electrical appliances such as a hairdryer. Note that, in the past, cabins were not assigned until you arrived at the ship; however, now you *can* book the cabin you want; an extra charge of £50 (roughly US$75) *per cabin* will be applied for this privilege, which also grants you the right to choose whether you want to dine at the early or late seating for dinner.

BERLITZ'S RATINGS

	Possible	Achieved
Ship	500	310
Accommodation	200	115
Food	400	236
Service	400	253
Entertainment	100	56
Cruise	400	256

The largest cabins are named after famous explorers. Only the owner's suite has a refrigerator.

DINING: The large "King and I" Dining Room is reasonably attractive, but noisy. There are two seatings. It is a good operation, but the food, while consistent in quality and presentation, is not memorable. The service, by friendly Filipino waiters and wine waiters, is generally adequate.

So, what's the cuisine like? In a nutshell, it's basic, no-frills cuisine – acceptable for those who do not expect much in the way of presentation or quality, but certainly not memorable. There is plenty of it, however; indeed, it is quantity, not quality, that prevails, but do remember that it is all provided at a low cost – as is a cruise aboard this ship, compared to more expensive cruise products. Presentation is a weak point, and there are no fish knives. So, it's best to remember that, like anything in life, you get what you pay for. If you enjoy going out to eat, and enjoy being adventurous with your food and eating habits – then you could be disappointed.

There is an adequate, but limited, wine list, and the wines are almost all very young – typical of those you might find in your local supermarket. Wine prices are quite modest, as are the prices for most alcoholic beverages. The same glasses are used for both red and white wines, and they are small.

OTHER COMMENTS: This smart ship, built originally for many years by Royal Caribbean International (then Royal Caribbean Cruise Line), has sleek modern lines, with a sharply raked bow, and a single red funnel, aft of which is a large amount of open deck space for sports. The side of the all-white ship has the company's new corporate logo (My Travel) painted on the side.

There is a polished wrap-around wooden deck outdoors – good for strolling, but make sure you wear shoes with non-slip soles. There is a reasonable amount of open deck space, but it does get crowded when the ship is full (which is almost always), particularly around the small swimming pool.

Inside the ship, the layout is quite logical, which makes it easy to find one's way around. The décor is based on themed Broadway musicals, with fairly bright, crisp, clean colors. The passageways are not wide, but they do contain lots of artwork and wood trim. In fact, there is an abundance of artwork throughout this ship. There are several lounges and bars to choose from, most of which are located on one deck.

This is the sister ship to *Carousel*, and was "stretched" in 1978 when operated by Royal Caribbean International. *Sundream*, which commenced operations for Sun Cruises/My Travel (one of Britain's Big Three tour companies) in 1997, caters efficiently to novice passengers with well-programmed flair, and provides an activity-filled cruise product in comfortable, but fairly busy surroundings, at very modest cruise rates for its mainly British and Canadian passengers.

Airtours is known for packaging its products really well, and this ship represents an excellent buy for families who want to cruise, but on a limited budget. Also, if you want a little more than the basics, Sun Cruises/My Travel offers special packages – good for celebrating something special. These come in four packages – bronze, silver, gold and platinum, with each adding a little extra cost. Want to buy the captain? Go for gold or platinum and you get breakfast in bed with champagne, flowers, fruit basket, and dinner at the captain's table.

Note that Sun Cruises does not actively market or specialize in cruises for families with children, and the children's and youth facilities are limited (and there is no evening babysitting service for youngsters).

Airtours also has its own fleet of aircraft, and this is one reason that the company is able to offer complete cruise-air-stay packages at such low rates. Sun Cruises/My Travel does a fine job in getting you and your luggage from airplane to ship without having to go through immigration (this does depend on the itinerary and operational region) in foreign countries whenever possible – so your cruise vacation is as seamless as possible.

Sun Cruises/My Travel brochures tell it like it is – so you know before you go exactly what you will get for your money, with the exception of its claim to "first class food," which is a gross exaggeration. If you want just the basics, you pay the least amount. If you want all the goodies – choose a wider "premium" seat with extra leg room on your Airtours aircraft, choose your own cabin, choose your dinner seating, breakfast in bed and dinner with the captain – you'll pay for all those "privileges." Note, however, that, however you choose to cruise, all gratuities are included. Insurance is also included (but you will be charged for it) unless you decline it on the booking form. The onboard currency is the British pound.

WEAK POINTS: Standing in line for embarkation, disembarkation, shore tenders and for self-serve buffet meals is an inevitable aspect of cruising aboard all large ships. There are many announcements. The accommodation deck hallways are very narrow. Many seats in the "My Fair Lady" show lounge have poor sight lines, obstructed by several pillars. Like the other ships in the fleet, the space per passenger (particularly on the open decks) is very tight when the ship is full (which is most of the time). The cabin televisions are extremely small (except for those in the suites).

Note that couples who travel without children will be surrounded by large number of children during the summer months – and, thus, increased noise levels. The food is of low quality, and the presentation is quite poor. There is little choice of tea and coffee. There are no cushioned pads for the deck lounge chairs.

Sun Princess
★★★★

Large Ship: ....77,499 tons	Passengers	Cabin Current: ....110 and 220 volts
Lifestyle: ....Standard	(lower beds/all berths): 1,950/2,250	Elevators: 11
Cruise Line: ....Princess Cruises	Passenger Space Ratio	Casino (gaming tables): ....Yes
Former Names: ....none	(lower beds/all berths): 39.7/34.4	Slot Machines: ....Yes
Builder: ....Fincantieri (Italy)	Crew/Passenger Ratio	Swimming Pools (outdoors): 4
Original Cost: ....$300 million	(lower beds/all berths): 2.0/2.5	Swimming Pools (indoors): 0
Entered Service: ....Dec 1995	Navigation Officers: ....Italian	Whirlpools: 5
Registry: ....Great Britain	Cabins (total): 975	Fitness Center: ....Yes
Length (ft/m): 857.2/261.3	Size Range (sq ft/m): 134.5–753.4/	Sauna/Steam Room: ....Yes/Yes
Beam (ft/m): 105.6/32.2	12.5–70.0	Massage: ....Yes
Draft (ft/m): 26.5/8.1	Cabins (outside view): 603	Self-Service Launderette: ....Yes
Propulsion/Propellers: .....diesel-electric	Cabins (interior/no view): 372	Dedicated Cinema/Seats: ....No
(28,000kW)/2	Cabins (for one person): 0	Library: ....Yes
Passenger Decks: 10	Cabins (with private balcony): 410	Classification Society: ...Registro Navale
Total Crew: 900	Cabins (wheelchair accessible): 19	Italiano (RINA)

OVERALL SCORE: 1,539 (OUT OF A POSSIBLE 2,000 POINTS)

ACCOMMODATION: The brochure shows 28 different cabin grades: 20 outside-view and 8 interior (no view) cabins. Although the standard outside-view and interior (no view) cabins are a little small, they are well designed and functional in layout, and have earth tone colors accentuated by splashes of color from the bedspreads. Proportionately, there are quite a lot of interior (no view) cabins. Many of the outside-view cabins have private balconies, and all seem to be quite well soundproofed, although the balcony partition is not floor to ceiling type, so you can hear your neighbors clearly (or smell their smoke). Note that the balconies are very narrow, only just large enough for two small chairs, and there is no dedicated lighting.

A reasonable amount of closet and abundant drawer and other storage space is provided in all cabins – adequate for a 7-night cruise, as are a television and refrigerator. Each night a chocolate will appear on your pillow. The cabin bathrooms are practical, and come complete with all the details one needs, although they really are tight spaces, best described as one person at-a-time units. They do, however, have a decent shower enclosure, a small amount of shelving for your personal toiletries, real glasses, a hairdryer and a bathrobe.

The largest accommodation can be found in six suites, two on each of three decks located at the stern of the ship, with large private balcony. These are well laid out, and have large bathrooms with two sinks, a Jacuzzi bathtub, and a separate shower enclosure. The bedroom has generous amounts of wood accenting and detailing, indented ceilings, and television sets in both bedroom

BERLITZ'S RATINGS

	Possible	Achieved
Ship	500	428
Accommodation	200	162
Food	400	266
Service	400	291
Entertainment	100	86
Cruise	400	306

and lounge areas. The suites have a dining room table and four chairs.

The mini-suites typically have two lower beds that convert into a queen-sized bed. There is a separate bedroom/sleeping area with vanity desk, and a lounge with sofa and coffee table, indented ceilings with generous amounts of wood accenting and detailing, walk-in closet, and larger bathroom with Jacuzzi bathtub and separate shower enclosure.

Princess Cruises typically features BBC World, CNN, CNBC, ESPN and TNT on the in-cabin color television system (when available, depending on cruise area).

DINING: There are two principal dining rooms, Marquis, and Regency (both are non-smoking, as are the dining rooms aboard all the ships of Princess Cruises); which one you are assigned to depends on the location of your accommodation. Each has its own galley and each is split into multi-tier sections, which help create a feeling of intimacy, although there is a lot of noise from the waiter stations adjacent to many tables. Breakfast and lunch are provided in an open-seating arrangement, while dinner is typically in two seatings.

Despite the fact that the portions are generous, the food and its presentation are somewhat disappointing, and bland of taste. The quality of fish is poor (often disguised by crumb or batter coatings), the selection of fresh green vegetables is limited, and few garnishes are used. However, do remember that this *is* big-ship banquet catering, with all its attendant standardization and production cooking. Meats are of a decent quality,

although often disguised by gravy-based sauces, and pasta dishes are acceptable (though voluminous), and are typically served by section headwaiters who, in search of gratuities, may also make "something special just for you." If you like desserts, order a sundae at dinner, as most other desserts are just so-so. Remember that ice cream ordered in the dining room is included, but if you order one anywhere else, you'll have to pay for it.

On any given 7-day cruise, a typical menu cycle will include a Sailaway Dinner, Captain's Welcome Dinner, Chef's Dinner, Italian Dinner, French Dinner, Captain's Gala Dinner, and Landfall Dinner. The wine list is reasonable, but not good, and the company has, sadly, dispensed with wine waiters. Note that 15 percent is added to all beverage bills, including wines (whether you order a $15 bottle or a $120 bottle, even though it takes the same amount of service to open and pour the wine).

For some really good meat, however, consider the *Sterling Steakhouse*; it's for those that want to taste four different cuts of Angus beef from the popular "Sterling Silver" brand of USDA prime meats – Filet Mignon, New York Strip, Porterhouse, and Rib-Eye – all presented on a silver tray. There is also a barbecue chicken option, plus the usual baked potato or French fries as accompaniments. This is available as an alternative to the dining rooms, between 6.30pm and 9.30pm only, at an additional charge of $8 per person. However, it is not, as you might expect, a separate, intimate dining room, but is located in a section of the Horizon Buffet, with its own portable bar and some decorative touches to set it apart from the regular Horizon Buffet.

The Horizon Buffet is open 24 hours a day, and, at night, has an informal dinner setting with sit-down waiter service; a small bistro menu is also available. The buffet displays are, for the most part, quite repetitious, but better than they have been in the past few years (there is no real finesse in presentation, however, as plastic plates are provided, instead of trays). The cabin service menu is very limited, and presentation of the food items featured is poor.

There is also a pâtisserie (for cappuccino/espresso coffees and pastries), a wine/caviar bar, and a pizzeria (complete with cobblestone floors and wrought-iron decorative features), and excellent pizzas (there are six to choose from).

OTHER COMMENTS: Although large, this all-white ship has a good profile, and is well balanced by its large funnel, which contains a deck tennis/basketball/volleyball court in its sheltered aft base. There is a wide, teakwood wrap-around promenade deck outdoors, some real teak steamer-style deck chairs (complete with royal blue cushioned pads), and 93,000 sq. ft (8,600 sq. meters) of space outdoors. A great amount of glass area on the upper decks provides plenty of light and connection with the outside world.

The ship, while large, absorbs passengers well, and has an almost intimate feel to it, which is what the interior designers intended. The interiors are very pretty and warm, with attractive colors and welcoming décor that includes some very attractive wall murals and other artwork. The signs around the ship could be improved, however.

There is a wide range of public rooms, with several intimate rooms and spaces so that you do get the feel of being overwhelmed by large spaces. The décor is quite tasteful, with attractive color combinations that are warm and do not clash (nothing is brash). The interior focal point is a huge four-deck-high atrium lobby with winding, double stairways, complete with two panoramic glass-walled elevators.

The main public entertainment rooms are located under three cabin decks. There is plenty of space, the traffic flow is good, and the ship absorbs people well. There are two show lounges, one at each end of the ship; one is a superb 550-seat, theater-style show lounge (movies are also shown here) and the other is a 480-seat cabaret-style lounge, complete with bar.

A glass-walled health spa complex is located high atop ship and includes a gymnasium with high-tech machines. One swimming pool is "suspended" aft between two decks (there are two other pools, although they are not large for the size of the ship).

The library is a very warm room and has six large buttery leather chairs for listening to compact audio discs, with ocean-view windows. There is a conference center for up to 300, as well as a business center, with computers, copy and fax machines. The collection of artwork is good, particularly on the stairways, and helps make the ship feel smaller than it is, although in places it doesn't always seem co-coordinated. The casino, while large, is not really in the main passenger flow and so it does not generate the "walk-through" factor found aboard so many ships.

The most traditional room aboard is the Wheelhouse Lounge/Bar, which is decorated in the style of a late 19th-century gentleman's club, complete with wood paneling and comfortable seating. The focal point is a large ship model from the P&O archives.

At the end of the day, as is the case aboard most large ships today, if you live in the top suites, you will be well attended; if you do not, you will merely be one of a very large number of passengers. One nice feature is the captain's cocktail party – it is held in the four-deck-high main atrium so you can come and go as you please – and there's no standing in line to have your photograph taken with the captain if you don't want to.

The ship is full of revenue centers, however, designed to help part you from your money. As cruising aboard large ships such as this has become increasingly an onboard revenue-based product, you can expect to be subjected to a stream of flyers advertising daily art auctions, "designer" watches and other promotions, while "artworks" for auction are strewn throughout the ship.

Note that gratuities to staff are *automatically* added to your account, at $10 per person, per day (gratuities for children are charged at the same rate). If you want to pay less, you'll need to go to the reception desk to have these charges adjusted (that could mean lining up with many other passengers wanting to do the same). The onboard currency is the US dollar.

WEAK POINTS: Standing in line for embarkation (an "express check-in" option is available by completing certain documentation 40 days in advance of your cruise), disembarkation, shore tenders and for self-serve buffet meals is an inevitable aspect of cruising aboard all large ships. There is absolutely no escape from unnecessary and repetitious announcements (particularly for activities that bring revenue, such as art auctions, bingo, horse racing) that intrude constantly into your cruise. In-your-face art auctions are simply overbearing, and the paintings, lithographs and faux framed pictures that are strewn throughout the ship (and clash irritatingly with the interior décor) are an annoying intrusion into what should be a vacation, not a cruise inside a floating "art" emporium.

The digital voice announcing elevator deck stops is irritating to passengers (many of whom tell me they would like to rip out the speaker system). There are a number of dead ends in the interior layout, so it's not as user-friendly as a ship this size should be. The cabin numbering system is extremely illogical, with numbers going through several hundred series on the same deck. The walls of the passenger accommodation decks are very plain (some artwork would be an improvement).

The swimming pools are quite small for so many passengers, and the pool deck is cluttered with white, plastic deck lounge chairs, which do not have cushioned pads. Waiting for tenders in anchor ports can prove irritating, but typical of large ship operations. Charging for the machines in the self-service launderette is trifling (even though it's only $1 per wash, $0.50 per dryer cycle, and $0.50 for washing powder).

WHERE THE CAT CAME FROM

Cruise passengers sometimes ask about the origin of the saying "He let the cat out of the bag"

On board a square-rigger 150 years ago, this would have sent shudders through one's spine – for it meant that a sailor had committed an offense serious enough to have the "cat o' nine tails" extracted from its bag.

The "cat" was a whip made of nine lengths of cord, each being about 18 inches (45 cm) long with three knots at the end, all fixed to a rope handle. It could seriously injure, or even kill, the victim. It is no longer carried on today's tall ships, having been outlawed by the US Congress in 1850, and then by Britain's Royal Navy in 1879.

SuperStar Aries
★★★ +

Removed 2006

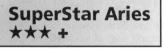

Mid-Size Ship: . . . . .37,301 tons	Passengers	Cabin Current: . . . . . . .110 and 220 volts
Lifestyle: . . . . .Premium	(lower beds/all berths): 678/1,006	Elevators: 4
Cruise Line: . . . . .Star Cruises	Passenger Space Ratio	Casino (gaming tables): . . . . .Yes
Former Names: *SuperStar Europe, Europa*	(lower beds/all berths): 55.0/37.0	Slot Machines: . . . . .Yes
Builder: . . . . . .Bremer Vulkan (Germany)	Crew/Passenger Ratio	Swimming Pools (outdoors): 2
Original Cost: . . . .$120 million	(lower beds/all berths): 1.2/1.7	(1 magrodome)
Entered Service: . . . . .Jan 1982/1999	Navigation Officers: . . . . .European	Swimming Pools (indoors): 1 (fresh water)
Registry: . . . . .Bahamas	Cabins (total): .339	Whirlpools: 0
Length (ft/m): 654.9/199.63	Size Range (sq ft/m): 135.6–683.5/	Fitness Center: . . . . .Yes
Beam (ft/m): 93.8/28.60	12.6–63.5	Sauna/Steam Room: . . . . .Yes/No
Draft (ft/m): 27.6/8.42	Cabins (outside view): 283	Massage: . . . . .Yes
Propulsion/Propellers: . . . . .diesel	Cabins (interior/no view): 56	Self-Service Launderette: . . . . .Yes
(21,270 kW)/2	Cabins (for one person): 0	Dedicated Cinema/Seats: Yes/238
Passenger Decks: 10	Cabins (with private balcony): 6	Library: . . . . .Yes
Total Crew: 560	Cabins (wheelchair accessible): 1	Classification Society: Det Norske Veritas

---

OVERALL SCORE: 1,396 (OUT OF A POSSIBLE 2,000 POINTS)

ACCOMMODATION: There is a wide range of suites and cabins from which to choose, reflecting Star Cruises' pricing and grading system according to the deck and location chosen.

All of the original cabins are quite spacious, and all were refurbished in 1995 and refreshed again in 1999 when Star Cruises acquired the ship. All have illuminated closets, dark wood cabinetry with rounded edges, several full-length mirrors, color television and VCR, mini-bar/refrigerator, and personal safe, hairdryer, excellent cabin insulation. There is a small room service menu (for such things as omelets, fried noodles, chicken wings, etc.), and all items are at extra cost.

Most cabins can now accommodate one or two additional persons, which mean the ship's original spacious feel has been greatly eroded in order to cater more to families with children. However, the cabins are, in general, much larger than those found in almost all other ships in the Star Cruises fleet.

The bathrooms have deep bathtubs (cabins without bathtub have a large shower enclosure), a three-head shower unit, two deep sinks (not all cabins), large toiletries cabinet and handsome personal toiletry amenities. The bath towels, although made of 100 percent cotton, are a little small.

The largest accommodation can be found in suites added during the 1999 refit. However, because of their location (they were created from what were formerly officers' cabins) they have lifeboat-obstructed views. Six other suites had private balconies added (Beethoven, Handel, Haydn, Mozart, Schubert, Wagner). These are

BERLITZ'S RATINGS		
	Possible	Achieved
Ship	500	380
Accommodation	200	143
Food	400	263
Service	400	288
Entertainment	100	58
Cruise	400	264

all quite generous living spaces. There is a separate bedroom (with either queen-sized or twin beds), illuminated closets, and vanity desk. The lounge includes a wet bar with refrigerator and glass cabinets and large audio-visual center complete with large-screen TV/VCR and compact disc player. The marble-clad bathroom has a large shower enclosure, with retractable clothesline. Burberry personal toiletry amenities are provided, as are a bathrobe, weight scale, and good-sized towels.

Occupants of suites are in Admiral Class, and can order from the "breakfast in bed" menu, as well as have free access to the indoor spa, and priority embarkation and disembarkation and other extras.

DINING: The Grand Restaurant is large, with ocean-view windows on two sides, and a good amount of space around each table. There are two seatings for meals, and classic white Schonwald chinaware (from Germany) is used. There is also a large, extremely varied self-serve cold table for all meals, with colorful displays of a wide variety of foods, located in the center of the restaurant. One side of the room has been converted into Taipan, an à la carte, extra-charge Chinese dining spot, with its own Chinese galley for authentic Chinese cuisine.

For casual meals, self-serve Asian and Western breakfasts, luncheons and supper buffets are provided at the Clipper Terrace, an outdoor area near one of the swimming pools (and the recently added Star Club Casino).

OTHER COMMENTS: Originally constructed for Hapag-

Lloyd, this was the flagship of the German cruise industry for many years before the company ordered a replacement that came into service in 1999. Star Cruises bought the ship in April 1998 and leased it back to Hapag Lloyd until July 1999, when it went into drydock for a $15 million refit and renovation.

Exterior changes include a new sponson stern – added in order to comply with the latest stability regulations, although *SuperStar Aries* still retains a moderately handsome, well-balanced profile. There is an excellent amount of outdoor deck and sunbathing space, although the former FKK (nude sunbathing) deck is now a crew recreation deck (no, it's not nude sunbathing any longer).

The ship was originally constructed with a wide range of good-sized public rooms, most of them with high ceilings that promoted an even greater sense of spaciousness. Dark, restful colors were applied in many public rooms and cabins, and subtle, hidden lighting was used throughout, particularly on the stairways. Two casinos were added during the 1999 refit; one for general use, as well as a private club for VIP members only.

The indoor swimming pool aboard this ship is *larger* than most *outdoor* pools aboard new, much larger ships; adjacent facilities include a sauna, fitness/exercise center, coin-operated solarium, hydrotherapy bath, spa bar, and beauty salon.

Star Cruises has made some changes to some public rooms and open areas, while leaving others alone. Sadly, a large casino has been added – located in what was formerly the cinema, with a spiral stairway that connects to a slot machine room on the deck below. Additionally, two private gambling clubs were installed, and, for the Asian market, a karaoke room. A children's playroom has replaced the former flower shop.

When operated by its former owners (Hapag-Loyd Cruises), it was the food, service and quiet, refined ambience that the many repeat passengers enjoyed, together with the excellent space ratio. Under Star Cruises, however, while the hospitality, and the range and variety of food were altered to cater to different nationalities and religions, the whole feeling of the ship also changed – and not for the better. Star Cruises also converted some public rooms to casino gaming areas – perhaps too many, which also changed the character of the ship.

A decent level of Asian hospitality is presently provided in what is a very informal, relaxed setting, with an extremely casual dress code (in reality, there is no dress code, particularly for Asean nation passengers).

There is no question that the ship's personality has changed as Star Cruises has provided for its specialized local markets. However, this has also taken away many of the niceties and facilities which were in place previously. In 2000 and 2001 *SuperStar Aries* operated in two different markets – Japan and Thailand, and thus the ship's character changed accordingly, as did all the directional signs; in 2002 *SuperStar Aries* was moved back into the local market for cruises to Thailand and China. At present, the ship is disjointed, and the push for additional onboard revenue has made a negative impact on what was formerly a very nice ship and product.

Further, the poor training and supervision of staff has led to a much lower level of service and product delivery than required to keep the ship's previous high rating.

WEAK POINTS: There is no wrap-around promenade deck outdoors (there are, however, half-length port and starboard promenades). The sight lines in the show lounge are quite poor from many of the seats (the room was originally built more for use as a single level concert salon than a room for shows). At present, the ship's décor is too dark, and several public rooms have been completely spoiled.

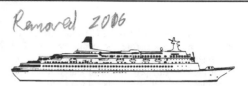

SuperStar Capricorn
★★★ +

Mid-Size Ship: . . . . .28,078 tons	Passenger Decks: 8	Cabin Current: . . . . .110 and 220 volts
Lifestyle: . . . . .Standard	Total Crew: 600	Cabin TV: . . . . .Yes
Cruise Line: . . .Hyundai Merchant Marine	Passengers	Elevators: 5
Former Names: . . . . .Hyundai Keumgang,	(lower beds/all berths): 804/1,366	Casino (gaming tables): . . . . .Yes
SuperStar Capricorn, Golden Princess,	Passenger Space Ratio (basis 2): 34.9	Slot Machines: . . . . .Yes
Sunward, Birka Queen, Royal Viking Sky	Passenger Space Ratio (all berths): . .20.5	Swimming Pools (outdoors): 2
Builder: . . . . .Wartsila (Finland)	Navigation Officers: . . . . .International	Swimming Pools (indoors): 1
Original Cost: . . . .$22.5 million	Cabins (total): .429	Whirlpools: 1
Entered Service: . . . .June 1973/Dec 2001	Size Range (sq ft/m): 135.6–579.1/	Fitness Center: .Yes
Registry: .Panama	12.6–53.8	Sauna/Steam Room: . . . . .Yes/Yes
Length (ft/m): 674.1/205.47	Cabins (outside view): 358	Massage: . . . . .Yes
Beam (ft/m): 82.6/25.20	Cabins (interior/no view): 71	Self-Service Launderette: . . . . .Yes
Draft (ft/m): 24.7/7.55	Cabins (single occupancy): 2	Movie Theater/Seats: . . . . .No
Propulsion/Propellers: . . . . .diesel	Cabins (with private balcony): 10	Library: . . . . .Yes
(13,400kW)/2 (CP)	Cabins (wheelchair accessible): 0	Classification Society: Det Norske Veritas

---

OVERALL SCORE: 1,364 (OUT OF A POSSIBLE 2,000 POINTS)

ACCOMMODATION: There is something for every taste and wallet, from spacious suites with separate bedrooms, to small interior (no view) cabins. While most cabins are for two persons, some can accommodate a third, fourth, or even a fifth person.

SUITES: Anyone wanting the largest space should consider a suite. These have a separate bedroom with ample closet and other storage space, lounge with large windows (with large TV/VCR, refrigerator and mini-bar), and bathroom with full-size bathtub and shower, and separate toilet. There is also a private outdoor balcony.

STANDARD OUTSIDE-VIEW/INTERIOR (NO VIEW) CABINS: The cabins are quite well equipped, and there is plenty of good (illuminated) closet, drawer and storage space (the drawers are metal and tinny, however, and in some closets they consist of wire baskets – like you might find in inexpensive hotels)., and the insulation between some of the lower grade cabins could be better. The bathrooms are of a decent size, but access is awkward in some of them. Some cabins have a small bathtub, although many have only a shower enclosure.

DINING: The main dining room is quite spacious and has a high ceiling; it is generally quiet, and provides a reasonably elegant setting for cuisine that is very standard Southeast Asian cuisine. There are two seatings.

OTHER COMMENTS: This ship has outer styling that is quite handsome, a benefit from its former life as a Royal

BERLITZ'S RATINGS

	Possible	Achieved
Ship	500	356
Accommodation	200	152
Food	400	271
Service	400	264
Entertainment	100	55
Cruise	400	266

Viking Line ship. After approximately three years spent carrying South Korean passengers to North Korea to visit the famous Mount Kumgang near the demilitarized zone in Kangwon Province, Hyndai Merchant Marine handed the ship back to owners Star Cruises, who now operate the ship on cruises within Southeast Asia.

There is a good amount of open deck and sunbathing space; in fact, there is plenty of space everywhere, and littlee sense of crowding. There is a good wrap-around promenade deck outdoors, as well as decent fitness and sports facilities.

Inside, the décor is quite tasteful, with splashes of bright colors and high ceilings. There are lots of public rooms, including a karaoke lounge and private karaoke rooms. The casino action is, to say the least, very lively.

This ship, which was "stretched" in 1982 (a mid-section was built and inserted to make the ship longer), should provide a decent cruise experience in spacious, nicely furnished surroundings. It was purchased by Star Cruises in 1996 and went through an extensive $5 million refit that added an indoor swimming pool and a video arcade. Note that all gratuities are included.

WEAK POINTS: However, anyone sailing aboard this ship should note that the food is extremely basic and simple fare, and will not in any way compare with international cuisine. Note that a number of cabins located in the aft section of the three lowest passenger accommodation decks can prove to be uncomfortable, with noise from throbbing engines and generator units a major source (particularly from cabins adjacent to the engine casing).

SuperStar Gemini
★★★ +

Mid-Size Ship: . . . . .19,046 tons	Total Crew: 470	Cabins (wheelchair accessible): 4
Lifestyle: . . . . .Standard	Passengers	Cabin Current: . . . . .110 and 220 volts
Cruise Line: . . . . .Star Cruises	(lower beds/all berths): 808/900	Elevators: 4
Former Names: . . . . .Crown Jewel	Passenger Space Ratio	Casino (gaming tables): . . . . .Yes
Builder: . . . . . . .Union Navale de Levante	(lower beds/all berths): 23.5/21.1	Slot Machines: . . . . .Yes
(Spain)	Crew/Passenger Ratio	Swimming Pools (outdoors): 1
Original Cost: . . . .$100 million	(lower beds/all berths): 1.7/1.9	Swimming Pools (indoors): 0
Entered Service: . . . Aug 1992/July 1995	Navigation Officers: . . . . . .Scandinavian	Whirlpools: . . . . .3 (2 outside/1 inside)
Registry: . . . . .Panama	Cabins (total): 404	Fitness Center: . . . . .Yes
Length (ft/m): 537.4/163.81	Size Range (sq ft/m): 139.9–349.8/	Sauna/Steam Room: . . . . .Yes/Yes
Beam (ft/m): 73.8/22.50	13.0–32.5	Massage: . . . . .Yes
Draft (ft/m): 17.7/5.40	Cabins (outside view): 281	Self-Service Launderette: . . . . .No
Propulsion/Propellers: . . . . .diesel	Cabins (interior/no view): 123	Dedicated Cinema/Seats: . . . . .No
(13,200kW)/2	Cabins (for one person): 0	Library: . . . . .Yes
Passenger Decks: 9	Cabins (with private balcony): 10	Classification Society: Det Norske Veritas

OVERALL SCORE: 1,322 (OUT OF A POSSIBLE 2,000 POINTS)

ACCOMMODATION: There are six price categories for the accommodation, which consists of executive suites (220.7–377.8 sq. ft/20.5–35.1 sq. meters), junior suites (225–258.3 sq. ft/20.9–24 sq. meters), ocean-view cabins with double bed (134.5–212 sq. ft/12.5–19.7 sq. meters), ocean-view cabins with twin beds (137.8 sq. ft/12.8 sq. meters), smaller ocean-view cabins with window (114.1–148.5 sq. ft/10.6–13.8 sq. meters), and interior (no view) cabins (127–150.7 sq. ft/11.8–14 sq. meters). There are four cabins for the handicapped, and several cabins have interconnecting doors (good for families with children).

Eight of the Executive Suites have a private balcony, although the partitions are not of the floor-to-ceiling type – so you can hear your neighbors clearly, or smell their smoke). Junior Suites are really little larger than standard and larger standard cabins, but with more closet space). Both types of suite are nicely furnished. The sleeping area can be curtained off from the living area. A tea/coffee making set, and laser disc player are provided (Executive Suites only).

The standard outside-view and interior (no view) cabins, almost all of which are the same size, are really quite small (they somehow remind me of caravan accommodation), although they are nicely furnished, and trimmed with blond wood cabinetry. Most of them feature broad picture windows (some deluxe cabins on Deck 6 and Deck 7 have lifeboat-obstructed views). They are practical and comfortable, with wood-trimmed accents and multi-colored soft furnishings, but there is almost no drawer space, and the closet space is extremely small.

BERLITZ'S RATINGS

	Possible	Achieved
Ship	500	348
Accommodation	200	132
Food	400	253
Service	400	265
Entertainment	100	58
Cruise	400	266

The bathrooms are reasonably decent considering the size of the ship, and each has two small toiletries cabinets, although the shower cubicle is small. The cabin soundproofing is quite poor; the 100 percent cotton towels are thin; there is little room for luggage, so take only what is really necessary (casual clothing only, no formal attire needed – even the captain's gala dinner night asks for "smart casual" attire). Bathrobes, slippers and toiletry amenities are provided in all cabins, as well as a small color television, telephone, and bottled water.

None of the cabins has a bathtub. Hairdryers are not supplied for any cabin category, so take your own if you need to use one. Also, there is no room service for such items as coffee or tea, nor is there a menu for snacks. The cabin numbering system and signage is confusing.

DINING: The attractive Ocean Palace dining room is located aft and has large picture windows on three sides (although the accenting in the center of the ceiling makes the room appear round). There are two seatings. It is not open for dinner each night, but is dependent on the itinerary.

The ambience is good, but there are few tables for two (most tables are for four, six or eight). Meals feature international cuisine with an Oriental touch, and there is open seating for all meals, except for dinner on the one "formal" night of the cruise. On the six-day cruise, one night includes a barbecue outside on the pool deck (the main dining room is closed on this night). The wine list itself is reasonable, but the wines are all young and prices are high (the cost of wines and spirits in Southeast Asia is high due to high import duties) and champagne is incredibly expensive.

There is also an informal cafe, called Mariner's Buffet (a pork-free eatery). Breakfast here always includes some Southeast Asian dishes such as Nasi Lemak, and Fried Noodles, as well as western favorites. Lunch and dinner are also provided in this eatery. Australian passengers will appreciate the ample supply of Vegemite.

There is a good selection of beer, including some regional varieties, and some draft lager.

OTHER COMMENTS: *SuperStar Gemini* is a handsome mid-sized cruise ship with smart exterior styling (the largest cruise vessel ever built in Spain). There is a wrap-around promenade deck outdoors.

Although the fit and finish was originally poor, Star Cruises has made the ship's interiors much warmer and more colorful. Inside, the ship has a traditional layout that provides reasonable horizontal passenger flow, although the passageways are narrow. There are picture windows in almost all of the public rooms that connect passengers with the sea and the outside light.

There is a fair amount of open deck and sunbathing space, including a neat area high atop the ship in front of a glass windbreak area – lovely for those balmy evenings outdoors, away from the crowds inside. Cushioned pads are provided for the deck lounge chairs.

Other features include a five-deck-high glass-walled atrium, and a karaoke/disco lounge. The décor is attractive, with upbeat art deco color combinations and splashy, colorful soft furnishings. The artwork is fairly plain and simple and could be improved. The fitness center/spa area is decent but quite cramped.

This very informal ship caters to a mix of Australian, European (mainly British and German) as well as Southeast Asian passengers, and announcements may be in several languages. The ship presently operates Andaman Sea cruises. The dress code is totally casual.

All in all, the company provides really good value for money, cruising in a homely ship that is bright, contemporary, and very informal. The staff is young, though, and needs more training, experience and supervision in the arts of hospitality, service and flexibility. Gratuities are included and no further tipping is allowed. All in all, you should have an enjoyable, fun voyage for a destination-intensive week, with acceptable, but not memorable food and service.

WEAK POINTS: The staff could be better trained, and there is a high turnover. There are simply too many loud announcements. Music plays constantly in public spaces, hallways, and on open decks, making a relaxing cruise experience totally impossible.

Removed 2006

SuperStar Leo
★★★★

Large Ship:	.75,338 tons	Passengers	
Lifestyle:	.Standard	(lower beds/all berths):	.1,974/2,800
Cruise Line:	.Star Cruises	Passenger Space Ratio	
Former Names:	.none	(lower beds/all berths):	.38.1/26.9
Builder:	.Meyer Werft (Germany)	Crew/Passenger Ratio	
Original Cost:	.$350 million	(lower beds/all berths):	.1.5/2.1
Entered Service:	.Oct 1998	Navigation Officers:	.Scandinavian
Registry:	.Panama	Cabins (total):	.987
Length (ft/m):	.879.2/268.0	Size Range (sq ft/m):	.150.6–638.3/
Beam (ft/m):	.105.6/32.2		14.0–59.3
Draft (ft/m):	.25.9/7.9	Cabins (outside view):	.608
Propulsion/Propellers:	.2 diesels	Cabins (interior/no view):	.379
	(50,400kW)/2	Cabins (for one person):	.0
Passenger Decks:	.10	Cabins (with private balcony):	.391
Total Crew:	.1,300	Cabins (wheelchair accessible):	.4

Cabin Current:	.240 volts
Elevators:	.9
Casino (gaming tables):	.Yes
Slot Machines:	.Yes
Swimming Pools (outdoors):	.2
Swimming Pools (indoors):	.0
Whirlpools:	.4
Fitness Center:	.Yes
Sauna/Steam Room:	.Yes/Yes
Massage:	.Yes
Self-Service Launderette:	.No
Dedicated Cinema/Seats:	.No
Library:	.Yes
Classification Society:	.Det Norske Veritas

OVERALL SCORE: 1,497 (OUT OF A POSSIBLE 2,000 POINTS)

ACCOMMODATION: There are 7 different types, in 15 price categories.

Three whole decks of cabins have private balconies, while two-thirds of all cabins have an outside view. Both the standard outside-view and interior (no view) cabins really are very small (particularly in light of the fact that all cabins have extra berths for a third/fourth person), although the bathrooms have a good-sized shower enclosure. In other words, take only the very smallest amount of clothing you can (there's almost no storage space for luggage).

All cabins have a personal safe, 100 percent cotton towels and 100 percent cotton duvets or sheets.

Choose one of the six largest Executive Suites (named Hong Kong, Malaysia, Shanghai, Singapore, Thailand and Tokyo) and you'll have an excellent amount of private living space, with separate lounge, and bedroom. Each has a large, en-suite bathroom that is part of the bedroom and open to it – as is the trend in high-cost, interior architect-designed bathrooms ashore. It has a gorgeous mosaic tiled floor, kidney bean-shaped whirlpool bathtub, two sinks, separate shower enclosure (with floor-to-ceiling ocean-view window) and separate toilet (with glass door). There are televisions in the lounge, bedroom and bathroom.

The Singapore and Hong Kong suites and the Malaysia and Thai suites can be combined to form a double suite (good for families with children and maid).

Choose one of the 12 Zodiac suites (each is named after a sign of the Zodiac) and you will get the second largest accommodation aboard the ship. Each suite has a

BERLITZ'S RATINGS		
	Possible	Achieved
Ship	500	421
Accommodation	200	154
Food	400	286
Service	400	278
Entertainment	100	61
Cruise	400	297

separate lounge, bedroom, and bathroom, and an interconnecting door to an ocean-view cabin with private balcony (good for families). All cabinetry features richly lacquered woods, large (stocked) wet bar with refrigerator, dining table (with a top that flips over to reveal a card table) and four chairs, sofa and drinks table, and trouser press. The bedrooms are small, but have a queen-sized bed; there is a decent amount of drawer space, although the closet space is rather tight (it contains two personal safes). The large en-suite bathrooms are similarly designed to those in the Executive Suites.

A small room service menu is available (all items are at extra cost, and both a 15 percent service charge as well as a gratuity are added to your account).

DINING: There is certainly plenty of choice when it comes to fine dining and informal trans-ethnic eating spots. There are, in all, eight places to eat (all are non-smoking). You will, therefore, need to plan where you want to eat well in advance, or you may be disappointed. These are included in the price of the cruise:

● *Windows on the World*: this is the ship's equivalent of a main dining room. It seats 632 in two seatings, is two decks high at the aft-most section, and has huge cathedral-style windows set in three sections overlooking the ship's stern and wake. There are no waiter stations adjacent to the tables – they are tucked neatly away in side wings, thus avoiding the high noise levels normally found in large dining rooms.

● *Raffles Café*: a large self-serve buffet restaurant with

indoor/outdoor seating for 400, and, as you might expect, pseudo-Raffles Hotel-like décor, with rattan chairs, overhead fans, and wood paneling.

● *Garden Room Restaurant*: with 268 seats, featuring Chinese cuisine

The following are à la carte (extra-cost) restaurants:

● *Taipan*: a Chinese Restaurant, with traditional Hong Kong-themed décor and items such as dim sum made from fresh, not frozen, ingredients (there are also two small private dining rooms).

● *Shogun*: a Japanese restaurant and sushi bar, for sashimi, sushi, and tempura. A section can be closed off to make the Samurai Room, with 22 seats, while a traditional Tatami Room has seats for eight. There's also a teppanyaki grill, with 10 seats, where the chef cooks in front of you.

● *Maxim's*: this is a small à la carte restaurant with ocean-view windows, and has fine cuisine and dining in the classic French style.

● *Blue Lagoon*: a small, casual street café with about 24 seats, featuring noodle dishes, fried rice and other Southeast Asian cuisine (adjacent is a karaoke street bar called The Bund).

In the atrium lobby there is also a casual pâtisserie serving several types of coffees, teas, cakes and pastries (at extra cost).

OTHER COMMENTS: *SuperStar Leo* was the first brand new ship ordered by Star Cruises specifically for the Southeast Asian market. There is a wrap-around promenade deck outdoors, good for strolling.

Inside, there are two indoor boulevards, and a stunning, six-deck-high central atrium lobby, with three glass-walled elevators and ample space to peruse the shops and cafés that line its inner sanctum. The lobby itself is modeled after the lobby of the Hyatt Hotel in Hong Kong, with little clutter from the usual run of desks found aboard other cruise ships; instead, there is only the reception desk – no desk for shore excursions or for banking.

The casino complex is at the forward end of the atrium boulevard on Deck 7. This includes a large general purpose, brightly lit casino, called Maharajah's, with gaming tables and slot machines. There's also a smaller, "members only" gaming club, as well as VIP gaming rooms, one of which has its own access to the upper level of the showlounge.

The interior design theme revolves around art, architecture, history and literature. The ship has a mix of both eastern and western design and décor details, and public room names have been chosen to appeal to a mixture of Australian, European and Asian passengers. Three stairways are each carpeted in a different color, which helps new cruise passengers find their way around easily.

The main show lounge (Moulin Rouge, with 973 seats) is two decks high (a separate balcony level is reserved for "club" members only), with almost no support columns to obstruct the sight lines, and a revolving stage for Broadway-style reviews and other production shows (typically to recorded music – there is no live showband). The show lounge can also be used as a large-screen cinema, with superb surround sound.

A 450-seat room atop the ship functions as an observation lounge during the day and a nightclub at night, with live music. From it, a spiral stairway takes you down to a navigation bridge viewing area, where you can see the captain and bridge officers at work.

There is a business center (complete with conference center - good for small groups) and writing room, as well as private mahjong and karaoke rooms, and a smoking room, for those who enjoy cigars and cognac. A shopping concourse is set around the second level of the lobby.

Sports facilities include a jogging track, golf driving range, basketball and tennis courts, as well as four levels of sunbathing decks. Health devotees should enjoy Caesar's (Cleopatra's for women) and the Nero Fitness Center, with facilities and services to pamper you (all at extra charge – even for use of the sauna and steam rooms), including Thai massage outdoors on deck.

Families with children should note that teens have their own huge video arcade, while children get to play in a wet 'n' wild aft pool (complete with pirate ship and caves) and two whirlpool tubs. Plus there's all the fun and facilities of Charlie's childcare center (open 24 hours a day), which includes a painting room, computer learning center, and small cinema. There's even a room full of cots for toddlers to use for sleepovers, and even the toilets are at a special low height. Over 15,000 sq. ft (1,400 sq. meters) is devoted to children's facilities – all tucked well away from adult recreation areas.

Ideally suited to families with children, the dress code is extremely casual (no jacket and tie needed). Watch out for the extra costs and charges to mount up if you order more than the basics. With many dining choices (some of which cost extra) to accommodate different tastes and styles, your cruise and dining experience will largely depend on how much you are prepared to spend. For priority check-in, disembarkation, generally better service, book "Balcony Class" rather than "Non-Balcony-Class" accommodation. *SuperStar Leo* is based in Hong Kong. All gratuities are included.

WEAK POINTS: Standing in line for embarkation, disembarkation, shore tenders and for self-serve buffet meals is an inevitable aspect of cruising aboard all large ships. The cabins with balconies cabins have extremely narrow balconies, and the cabins themselves are very small (the ship was originally constructed for 3- and 4-day cruises). While the ship is quite stunning and offers a wide choice of dining venues, keeping consistency of product delivery depends on the quality of the service and supervisory staff. There are many extra-cost items (in addition to the à la carte dining spots), such as for morning tea, afternoon tea, and childcare. There are many loud and intrusive inevitable entertainment and activity announcements.

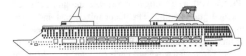

SuperStar Virgo
★★★★

Large Ship:	.75,338 tons	Passengers		Cabin Current:	.240 volts

Large Ship: ....75,338 tons
Lifestyle: ....Standard
Cruise Line: ....Star Cruises
Former Names: ....none
Builder: ....Meyer Werft (Germany)
Original Cost: ....$350 million
Entered Service: ....Aug 1999
Registry: ....Panama
Length (ft/m): 879.2/268.0
Beam (ft/m): 105.6/32.2
Draft (ft/m): 25.9/7.9
Propulsion/Propellers: ....diesel
(50,400kW)/2
Passenger Decks: 10
Total Crew: 1,300

Passengers
(lower beds/all berths): 1,974/2,800
Passenger Space Ratio
(lower beds/all berths): 38.1/26.9
Crew/Passenger Ratio
(lower beds/all berths): 1.5/2.1
Navigation Officers: ......Scandinavian
Cabins (total): 987
Size Range (sq ft/m): 150.6–638.3/
14.0–59.3
Cabins (outside view): 608
Cabins (interior/no view): 379
Cabins (for one person): 0
Cabins (with private balcony): 391
Cabins (wheelchair accessible): 4

Cabin Current: ....240 volts
Elevators: 9
Casino (gaming tables): ....Yes
Slot Machines: ....Yes
Swimming Pools (outdoors): 2
Swimming Pools (indoors): 0
Whirlpools: 4
Fitness Center: ....Yes
Sauna/Steam Room: ....Yes/Yes
Massage: ....Yes
Self-Service Launderette: ....No
Dedicated Cinema/Seats: ....No
Library: ....Yes
Classification Society: ....Det Norske
Veritas

OVERALL SCORE: 1,522 (OUT OF A POSSIBLE 2,000 POINTS)

ACCOMMODATION: There are seven types of accommodation, in 15 price categories. Three entire decks of cabins feature private balconies, while two-thirds of all cabins have an outside view. Both the standard outside-view and interior (no view) cabins really are very small (particularly in light of the fact that all cabins have extra berths for a third/fourth person), so take only the very smallest amount of clothing you can (there's almost no storage space for luggage).

All cabins have a personal safe, 100 percent cotton towels and 100 percent cotton duvets or sheets. Bathrooms have a good-sized shower enclosure, and include personal toiletry items such as Burberry soap, conditioning shampoo and body lotion.

For more space, choose one of 13 suites. Each suite has a separate lounge/dining room, bedroom, and bathroom, and an interconnecting door to an ocean-view cabin with private balcony (with light). All cabinetry features richly lacquered woods, large (stocked) wet bar with refrigerator, dining table (with a top that flips over to reveal a card table) and four chairs, sofa and drinks table, and trouser press.

The bedroom is small, completely filled by its queen-sized bed; there is a reasonable amount of drawer space (but the drawers are very small), and the closet space is rather tight (it contains two personal safes). A large en-suite bathroom is part of the bedroom and open to it – as is the trend in high-cost, interior architect-designed bathrooms ashore, and features a gorgeous mosaic tiled floor, kidney bean-shaped whirlpool bathtub, two sinks, sep-

BERLITZ'S RATINGS

	Possible	Achieved
Ship	500	421
Accommodation	200	156
Food	400	293
Service	400	284
Entertainment	100	66
Cruise	400	302

arate shower enclosure (with floor-to-ceiling ocean-view window) and separate toilet (with glass door). There are televisions in the lounge, bedroom and bathroom.

For even more space, choose one of the six largest suites (Boracay, Nicobar, Langkawi, Majorca, Phuket, and Sentosa) and you'll have a generous amount of private living space, with a separate lounge, dining area, bedroom, large bathroom, and private balcony (with light). All cabinetry features richly lacquered woods, large (stocked) wet bar with refrigerator, dining table (with a top that flips over to reveal a card table) and four chairs, sofa and drinks table, and trouser press. The bedrooms are small, completely filled by its queen-sized bed; there is a reasonable amount of drawer space (but the drawers are very small), and the closet space is rather tight (it contains two personal safes). The large en-suite bathrooms are similar to those in the suites already described. The Boracay and Sentosa suites and the Phuket and Langkawi suites can be combined to form a double suite (good for families with children, and maid). There are televisions in the lounge, bedroom and bathroom.

A small room service menu is available (all items are at extra cost, and both a 15 percent service charge as well as a gratuity are added to your account).

DINING: There is certainly plenty of choice when it comes to fine dining and informal trans-ethnic eating spots with a total of eight places to eat (all are non-smoking). You will need to plan where you want to eat well in advance, or you may be disappointed. The following eateries are ncluded in the price of the cruise:

● *Bella Vista*: the equivalent of a main dining room. It seats over 600 in an open seating arrangement, although, in effect the restaurant operates two seatings. The aft section is two decks high, and huge cathedral-style windows are set in three sections overlooking the ship's stern. There are no waiter stations adjacent to the tables – instead they are tucked neatly away in side wings, thus avoiding the high noise levels normally found in large dining rooms.

● *Mediterranean Buffet*: this is a large self-serve buffet restaurant with indoor/outdoor seating for 400.

● *The Pavilion Room*: features traditional Cantonese Chinese cuisine, including dim sum at lunchtime.

The following are à la carte (extra-cost) dining spots:

● *Noble* House: a Chinese Restaurant, with traditional Hong Kong-themed décor and items such as dim sum (there are also two small private dining rooms).

● *Palazzo*: a beautiful, if slightly ostentatious Italian restaurant. It has fine food, and something very unusual – a genuine Renoir painting displayed in a strategic focal point (well protected by cameras and alarms).

● *Samura*: a Japanese restaurant and sushi bar (for sashimi and sushi). There are two teppanyaki grills, each with 10 seats, where the chef cooks in front of you. The menu is extensive.

● *The Taj*: an Indian/Vegetarian dining spot that offers a range of food in a self-serve buffet setup.

● *Blue Lagoon*: a casual 24-hour street café with noodle dishes, fried rice and other Southeast Asian dishes.

● *Out of Africa*: a casual karaoke café and bar, where coffees, teas and pastries are available.

OTHER COMMENTS: *SuperStar Virgo* is the second new ship ordered specifically for the Asian market. The all-white ship has a distinctive red/blue funnel with gold star logo. There is a wrap-around promenade deck outdoors, good for strolling.

Inside, there are two indoor boulevards, and a stunning, six-deck-high central atrium lobby, with three glass-walled elevators and ample space to peruse the shops and cafés that line its inner sanctum. There is no clutter from the usual run of desks found aboard other cruise ships; instead, there is only a reception desk, tour booking desk, and concierge.

The casino complex can be found at the forward end of the atrium boulevard on Deck 7. This includes a large general purpose, brightly lit casino, called Oasis, with gaming tables and slot machines. There's also a smaller, "members only" gaming club, as well as VIP gaming rooms, one of which has its own access to the upper level of the showlounge.

The décor aboard *SuperStar Virgo* is much more European in design, taste and color combinations than sister ship *SuperStar Leo*, and the layout has been modified and improved slightly (for a slightly different market). The lobby, for example, has become an Italian

Piazza, with a stunning *trompe l'oeil* and multi-colored stained-glass ceiling. The décor mixes east and west, and public room names have been chosen to appeal to a mixture of Australian, European and Asian passengers. Three stairways are each carpeted in a different color, which helps new cruise passengers find their way around easily.

The main show lounge (The Lido, with 973 seats) is two decks high (a separate balcony level is reserved for "club" members only), with almost no support columns to obstruct the sight lines, and a revolving stage for Broadway-style reviews. Shows that have included live tigers have given way to lavish production shows (one of which is an extra-cost topless dancer "girlie" show). The show lounge also turns into a large-screen cinema, with excellent surround sound.

The 450-seat Galaxy of the Stars Lounge is set atop the ship. It is an observation lounge by day and a nightclub at night, with live music. From it, a spiral stairway takes you down to a navigation bridge viewing area, where you can see the captain and bridge officers at work.

There is a business center (complete with six meeting rooms) a large library and writing room, as well as private mahjong and karaoke rooms, and a smoking room, for those who enjoy cigars and cognac. A shopping concourse is set around the second level of the lobby, and includes a wine shop.

Sports facilities include a jogging track, golf driving range, basketball and tennis courts, as well as four levels of sunbathing decks. Health devotees should enjoy the Apollo Health Spa, with facilities and services to pamper you (all at extra charge – even for use of the sauna and steam rooms), including Thai massage outdoors on deck.

Families with children should note that teens have their own huge video arcade, while children get to play in a wet 'n' wild aft pool (complete with pirate ship and caves) and two whirlpool tubs. Plus there's all the fun and facilities of Charlie's childcare center (open 24 hours a day), which includes a painting room, computer learning center, and small cinema. There's even a room full of cots for toddlers to use for sleepovers, and even the toilets are at a special low height. About 15,000 sq. ft (1,400 sq. meters) is devoted to children's facilities – all tucked well away from adult recreation areas.

Star Cruises has established a Southeast Asian regional cruise audience for its diverse fleet of ships. *SuperStar Virgo* is a fine ship for the active local market, and is certainly the most stunning and luxurious of any of the ships sailing year-round from this busy popular Southeast Asian port.

SuperStar Virgo is based in Singapore. The passenger mix is international, although the local (regional) market has now been developed, so you can expect to find lots of families with children (who are allowed to roam around the ship uncontrolled), particularly on the weekend (Friday–Sunday) cruise. There are lots of activities and entertainment (some are extra-cost items), and a lot of young passengers.

More choices, more dining options, and Asian hospitality all add up to a very attractive vacation package that is particularly suitable for families with children, in a very contemporary floating leisure center that operates from Singapore. The dress code is casual – very casual (no jacket and tie needed), and the ship operates under a "no-tipping" policy. While the initial cruise fare seems very reasonable, the extra costs and charges soon mount up if you want to indulge in more than the basics. Although service levels and finesse remain inconsistent, hospitality is very good.

With so many dining choices (some of which cost extra) to accommodate the tastes of an eclectic mix of nationalities, your enjoyment of the cruise may depend largely on how much you are prepared to spend. For priority check-in, disembarkation, generally better service, and priority booking of the à la carte dining spots,

choose "Balcony Class" accommodation. All gratuities are included.

WEAK POINTS: Standing in line for embarkation, disembarkation, shore tenders and for self-serve buffet meals is an inevitable aspect of cruising aboard all large ships. The "balcony class" cabins have extremely narrow balconies. While the ship is quite stunning and offers a wide choice of dining venues, keeping consistency of product delivery depends on the quality of the service and supervisory staff, and more training is needed. There are many extra cost items (in addition to the à la carte dining spots), such as for morning tea, afternoon tea, most cabaret shows (except a crew show), and childcare. There are some inevitable entertainment and activity announcements (in English and Mandarin). Finding your way around the many areas blocked by portable "crowd containment" ribbon barriers can prove frustrating at times.

Tahitian Princess
NOT YET RATED

Mid-Size Ship: . . . . .30,277 tons	
Lifestyle: . . . . .Premium	
Cruise Line: . . . . .Princess Cruises	
Former Names: . . . . .R Four	
Builder: Chantiers de l'Atlantique (France)	
Original Cost: . . . .$150 million	
Entered Service: . . . . .Nov 1999/Dec 2002	
Registry: . . . . .Gibraltar	
Length (ft/m): 593.7/181.0	
Beam (ft/m): 83.5/25.5	
Draft (ft/m): 19.5/6.0	
Propulsion/Propellers: . . . . .diesel-electric	
(18,600kW)/2	
Passenger Decks: 9	
Total Crew: .373	

Passengers
(lower beds/all berths): 686/826
Passenger Space Ratio
(lower beds/all berths): 44.1/36.6
Crew/Passenger Ratio
(lower beds/all berths): 1.8/2.2
Navigation Officers: . . . . .European
Cabins (total): 344
Size Range (sq ft/m): . . . . .145.3 – 968.7/
13.5 – 90.0
Cabins (outside view): 317
Cabins (interior/no view): 27
Cabins (for one person): 0
Cabins (with private balcony): 232
Cabins (wheelchair accessible): 3

Cabin Current: . . . . . . .110 and 220 volts
Elevators: 4
Casino (gaming tables): . . . . .Yes
Slot Machines: . . . . .Yes
Swimming Pools (outdoors): 1
Swimming Pools (indoors): 0
Whirlpools: 2
(+ 1 thalassotherapy)
Fitness Center: . . . . .Yes
Sauna/Steam Room: . . . . .No/Yes
Massage: . . . . .Yes
Self-Service Launderette: . . . . .Yes
Dedicated Cinema/Seats: . . . . .No
Library: . . . . .Yes
Classification Society: . . . .Bureau Veritas

OVERALL SCORE: NYR (OUT OF A POSSIBLE 2,000 POINTS)

ACCOMMODATION: There is a variety of about eight different cabin types to choose from (however, when this book was completed, specific cabin category details were not available). All of the standard interior (no view) and outside-view cabins (the lowest four grades) are extremely compact units, and extremely tight for two persons (particularly for cruises longer than seven days). Cabins feature twin beds (or queen-size bed), with good under-bed storage areas, personal safe, vanity desk with large mirror, good closet and drawer space (in rich, dark woods), and bathrobe. Color televisions carry a major news channel (where obtainable), plus a sports channel and several round-the-clock movie channels.

The cabins that have private balconies (66 percent of all cabins, or 73 percent of all outside view cabins) have partial, and not full, balcony partitions, sliding glass doors, and, due to good design and layout, only 14 cabins on Deck 6 have lifeboat-obstructed views. The bathrooms, which have tiled floors and plain walls, are compact, standard units, and include a shower enclosure with a removable, strong hand-held shower unit, hairdryer, 100 percent cotton towels, toiletries storage shelves and a retractable clothesline.

MINI-SUITES: The 52 accommodation units designated as mini-suites, are in reality simply larger cabins than the standard varieties, as the sleeping and lounge areas are not divided. While not overly large, the bathrooms have a good-sized bathtub and ample space for storing personal toiletry items. The living area features a refriger-

BERLITZ'S RATINGS		
	Possible	Achieved
Ship	500	NYR
Accommodation	200	NYR
Food	400	NYR
Service	400	NYR
Entertainment	100	NYR
Cruise	400	NYR

ated mini-bar, lounge area with breakfast table, and a balcony with two plastic chairs and a table.

OWNER'S SUITES: The 10 Owner's Suites are the most spacious accommodation, and are fine, large living spaces located in the forward-most and aft-most sections of the accommodation decks (particularly nice are those that overlook the stern, on Deck 6, 7 and 8). They have more extensive balconies that really are private and cannot be overlooked by anyone from the decks above. There is an entrance foyer, living room, bedroom (the bed faces the sea, which can be seen through the floor-to-ceiling windows and sliding glass door), CD player, bathroom with Jacuzzi bathtub, as well as a small guest bathroom.

DINING: Flexibility and choice are what this mid-sized ship's dining facilities are all about. There are four different dining spots:
● The *Main Dining Room* has 338 seats, and includes a large raised central section. There are large ocean-view windows on three sides, several prime tables overlooking the stern, and a small bandstand for occasional live dinner music.
● The *Sabatini's Trattoria* is an Italian restaurant, with 96 seats, windows along two sides, and a set menu (typically with added daily chef's specials).
● The *Sterling Steakhouse* is an "American steak house," has 98 seats, and windows along two sides and a set menu (together with added daily chef's specials).
● The *Lido Cafe* has seating for 154 indoors and 186

outdoors. It is open for breakfast, lunch and casual dinners. It is the ship's self-serve buffet restaurant (open 24 hours a day), and incorporates a small pizzeria and grill. Basic salads, a meat carving station, and a reasonable selection of cheeses are featured daily.

All restaurants feature open seating dining, so you dine when you want, with whom you wish, although reservations may be necessary in *Sabatini's Trattoria* and *Sterling Steakhouse*, where there are mostly tables for four or six (note that there are few tables for two). In addition, there is a Poolside Grill and Bar for those fast food items for on-deck munching.

OTHER COMMENTS: This ship was one of eight almost identical ships ordered and operated by the now defunct Renaissance Cruises, which was the cruise industry's first totally non-smoking cruise line. As one of the "R-class" ships, this one operated in Tahiti, and was delivered by the shipyard through French government funding. After the collapse of Renaissance Cruises (following the September 11, 2001 terrorist attacks on the USA) P&O Princess Cruises announced the lease/purchase of this ship, together with sister ship *R Four* (now named *Tahitian Princess*). Both ships debuted in 1999, and are of an ideal size for operating in the warm water regions of Tahiti.

The exterior design manages to balance the ship's high sides by combining a deep blue hull with the white superstructure and large, square blue funnel. A lido deck features a swimming pool, and good sunbathing space, while one of the aft decks has a thalassaotherapy pool. A jogging track circles the swimming pool deck (but one deck above). The uppermost outdoors deck includes a golf driving net and shuffleboard court.

The interior décor is quite stunning and elegant, a throwback to ship décor of the ocean liners of the twenties and thirties, executed in fine taste. This includes detailed ceiling cornices, both real and faux wrought-iron staircase railings, leather paneled walls, *trompe l'oeil* ceilings, rich carpeting in hallways with an Oriental rug-look center section, and many other interesting (and expensive-looking) decorative touches. The overall feel is of an old-world country club. The staircase in the main, two-deck-high foyer will remind you of something similar in a blockbuster hit movie about a certain ship (*Titanic*), where the stars, Kate Winslet and Leonardo di Caprio met.

The public rooms are basically spread over three decks. This is totally a non-smoking ship (there is no smoking anywhere, including cabins, dining room, public rooms, *or* on the open decks – although the crew have their own smoking room).

The reception hall (lobby) has a staircase with intricate wrought-iron railings. A large observation lounge, the Horizon Lounge, is located high atop ship. This has a long bar with forward views (for the barmen, that is), and a stack of distracting large-screen televisions; there's also an array of slot machines and bar counter-top electronic gaming machines.

There are plenty of bars – including one in the entrance to each of the restaurants. Perhaps the nicest of all bars and lounges can be found in the casino bar/lounge that is a beautiful room reminiscent of London's grand hotels. It features an inviting marble fireplace (in fact there are *three* such fireplaces aboard) and comfortable sofas and individual chairs.

The Library is a grand room, designed in the Regency style (it was designed by Scottish ships interior designer John McNeece), and has a fireplace, a high, indented, *trompe l'oeil* ceiling, and an excellent selection of books, plus some comfortable wingback chairs with footstools, and sofas you can easily fall asleep on.

Tahitian Princess cruises year-round on three different 10-day itineraries in the warm water regions of Tahiti and the South Pacific. Although there may not be marble bathroom fittings, or caviar and other (more expensive) niceties, the value for money is extremely good, and will provide you with a chance to cruise in comfort aboard a mid-sized ship with some interesting dining choices. There's very little entertainment, but it is certainly not needed in these cruise areas. With the introduction of *Tahitian Princess* (and sister ship *Pacific Princess*), Princess Cruises has provided rather smart replacements for a previous pair of similarly-sized ships (named *Island Princess* and *Pacific Princess*) that were operated for many years to the delight of passengers not wanting to cruise aboard the larger ships in the fleet.

Note that, in common with all ships in the Princess Cruises fleet, 15 percent will typically be added to all bar accounts (drink prices are moderate, while beer prices are high), and a standard gratuity (about $10 per person, per day) will be automatically added to your onboard account. If you think this is too much and want to reduce the amount, you'll need to go to the reception desk to do so.

Although not yet rated, it is expected that, given the ship, its food, style and staffing and service levels will be similar to those of other Princess Cruises ships. The overall score is expected to be in the region of 1,500 points, which would equate to four stars.

WEAK POINTS: There is no wrap-around promenade deck outdoors (there is, however, a small jogging track around the perimeter of the swimming pool, and port and starboard side decks), and no wooden decks outdoors (instead, they are covered by Bollidt, a sand-colored rubberized material). There is no sauna. Stairways, although carpeted, are tinny. In order to keep the prices low, often the air routing to get to and from your ship is often not the most direct.

The Emerald
★★★

Mid-Size Ship: . . . . .26,431 tons	Total Crew: 412	Cabin Current: . . . . .110 and 220 volts
Lifestyle: . . . . .Standard	Passengers	Elevators: 3
Cruise Line: . . . . .Louis Cruise Lines	(lower beds/all berths): 990/1,198	Casino (gaming tables): . . . . .Yes
Former Names: . . . .*Regent Rainbow,*	Passenger Space Ratio	Slot Machines: . . . . .Yes
Diamond Island, Santa Rosa	(lower beds/all berths): 26.6/22.0	Swimming Pools (outdoors): 1
Builder: . . . . .Newport News Shipbuilding	Crew/Passenger Ratio	Swimming Pools (indoors): 0
(USA)	(lower beds/all berths): 2.4/2.9	Whirlpools: 2
Original Cost: . . . .$25 million	Navigation Officers: . . . . .Greek/European	Fitness Center: . . . . .Yes
Entered Service: . . . .June 1958/Apr 1997	Cabins (total): 500	Sauna/Steam Room: . . . . .Yes/No
Registry: . . . . .Cyprus	Size Range (sq ft/m): 124.8–304.6/	Massage: . . . . .Yes
Length (ft/m): 599.0/182.57	11.6–28.3	Self-Service Launderette: . . . . .No
Beam (ft/m): 84.0/25.60	Cabins (outside view): 338	Dedicated Cinema/Seats: . . . . .No
Draft (ft/m): 27.5/8.38	Cabins (interior/no view): 162	Library: . . . . .Yes
Propulsion/Propellers: . . . . .steam turbine	Cabins (for one person): 10	Classification Society: . . .American Bureau
(16,400kW)/2	Cabins (with private balcony): 0	of Shipping
Passenger Decks: 10	Cabins (wheelchair accessible): 2	

OVERALL SCORE: 1,143 (OUT OF A POSSIBLE 2,000 POINTS)

ACCOMMODATION: This ship has a varied mix of cabins both old and new that offer a wide range of configurations, presented in just three main categories: premier, superior and standard (although there are, in effect, seven price levels).

Note that cabins are not assigned until you are at the embarkation port for check-in unless you pay a supplement in order to pre-book. Even then, you will only be informed of your cabin on the day of embarkation. This ad-hoc method of assigning cabins means that those who book first (and those who arrive first at the embarkation port) probably will get the best cabins, in the best locations.

Many of the original cabins are quite spacious, with good closet and drawer space, while newer ones are a little more compact, and have poor insulation. Continental breakfast in your cabin will cost about $7.50 (£4.50) per person extra (each time). There is also a 24-hour cabin service menu for snacks, all at extra cost.

DINING: The dining room has large ocean-view windows and an interesting, neat orchestra balcony. There are two seatings. While it won't win any awards, the food quality and its presentation are actually quite decent considering the cost of a cruise, although the variety is limited. The service is friendly and quite attentive, although you should not expect grand hotel-style service.

OTHER COMMENTS: After being laid up for more than 10 years, this solid, American-built, former ocean liner

BERLITZ'S RATINGS

	Possible	Achieved
Ship	500	268
Accommodation	200	120
Food	400	220
Service	400	249
Entertainment	100	58
Cruise	400	228

underwent a great amount of reconstruction (costing a whopping $72 million) in Greece in 1992. Louis Cruise Lines spent more on another refit in 1997. With new upper decks added, its profile is not exactly handsome (it does have a decent "sheer" along its waistline, however). The open deck and sunbathing space is limited when the ship is full, although there are a good number of deck lounge chairs. There is, however, a good wrap-around promenade deck outdoors, with plenty of chairs.

The ship's interiors are quite pleasant and surprisingly comfortable, and have a warm décor that is contemporary without being at all brash. Many of the public rooms have high ceilings, and these a spacious ocean liner feel to the ship, and there are some fine wrought-iron railings on the stairways. The artwork, unfortunately, does look like the low budget stuff it is and could do with being upgraded.

For short cruises, this ship provides a range of public spaces that, in turn, promote a good party ambience and a number of bars for drinking in. The casino is quite large, and has a high ceiling.

During the summer, the ship is based on Palma Majorca, under charter to Thomson Cruises. *The Emerald* operates Mediterranean cruises, and is quite well suited for this task. During the winter, the ship is based on Barbados, and operates two alternating Caribbean itineraries. Thomson's wholly owned airline (Britannia Airways) will probably fly you to your port of embarkation. Despite the minor criticisms, Thomson will provide you with quite a decent cruise experience, and this ship and the cruise product therefore achieves a very respectable rating. Hotel add-ons can extend your cruise vacation, and Thomson has a fine collection from which to choose, depending on your needs, budget, and whether you are traveling with children (or grandchildren) or not.

Thomson does a good job of providing a range of entertainment to suit its clientele, and the shows, although not of the top professional variety, are, nonetheless fun and entertaining for the whole family. Note that all gratuities are included in the cruise fare, so you don't have to bother about who to tip and when – it's all done for you.

The onboard currency is the British pound.

WEAK POINTS: The high density of this vessel means that there is little room to move about when full, although cruise lines often translate this to "ambience." The sight lines in the show lounge really are very poor (particularly from the port and starboard side seating areas, where there is obstruction from 12 thick pillars, and the entertainment is typical of the low-budget type.

WATERTIGHT CONTRACTS

Cruise lines are masters of small print when it comes to contracts. A clause in the ticket typically reads: "The Carrier's legal responsibility for death, injury, illness, damage, delay, or other loss or detriment of person or property of whatever kind suffered by the Passenger will, in the first instance, be governed by the Athens Convention relating to the Carriage of Passengers and their Luggage by Sea, 1974, with protocols and amendments, together with the further provisions of the International Convention on Limitation of Liability for Maritime Claims, 1976, with revisions and amendments (hereinafter collectively referred to as the "Convention"). The Carrier shall not be liable for any such death, injury, illness, damage, delay, loss, or detriment caused by Act of God, war or warlike operations, civil commotions, labor trouble, interference by Authorities, perils of the sea, or any other cause beyond the control of the Carrier, fire, thefts or any other crime, errors in the navigation or management of the Vessel, or defect in, or unseaworthiness of hull, machinery, appurtenances, equipment, furnishings, or supplies of the Vessel, fault or neglect of pilot, tugs, agents, independent contractors, such as ship's Physician, Passengers or other persons on board not in the Carrier's employ or for any other cause of whatsoever nature except and unless it is proven that such death, injury, illness, damage, delay, loss resulting from Carrier's act or omission was committed with the intent to cause such loss or with knowledge that such loss would probably result therefrom and in that event the Carrier's liability therefore shall not exceed the specified limitations per Passenger in Special Drawing Rights (S.D.R.) as defined in the applicable conventions or in any further revision and/or amendment thereto as shall become applicable."

✓ *Barelona* 09/09/05

The Iris
NOT YET RATED

Small Ship: ....12,688 tons	Total Crew: 170	Cabin Current: ....220 volts
Lifestyle: ....Standard	Passengers	Elevators: 2
Cruise Line: ....Mano Maritime	(lower beds/all berths): 487/750	Casino (gaming tables): ....Yes
Former Names: ....Francesca,	Passenger Space Ratio	Slot Machines: ....Yes
Konstantin Simonov	(lower beds/all berths): 26.0/16.9	Swimming Pools (outdoors): 1
Builder: ......Szczesin Stocznia (Poland)	Crew/Passenger Ratio	Swimming Pools (indoors): 0
Original Cost: ....n/a	(lower beds/all berths): 2.8/4.4	Whirlpools: 1
Entered Service: .....Apr 1982/Mar 2001	Navigation Officers: ....European	Fitness Center: ....Yes
Registry: ....Malta	Cabins (total): 245	Sauna/Steam Room: ....Yes/No
Length (ft/m): 422.2/128.7	Size Range (sq ft/m): ....n/a	Massage: ....Yes
Beam (ft/m): 68.8/21.0	Cabins (outside view): 159	Self-Service Launderette: ....Yes
Draft (ft/m): 19.0/5.8	Cabins (interior/no view): 86	Dedicated Cinema/Seats: ....No
Propulsion/Propellers: ....diesel	Cabins (for one person): 3	Library: ....No
(12,800kW)/2	Cabins (with private balcony): 0	Classification Society: ..Russian Shipping
Passenger Decks: 7	Cabins (wheelchair accessible): 1	Register

OVERALL SCORE: NYR (OUT OF A POSSIBLE 2,000 POINTS)

ACCOMMODATION: There are 13 large suites and 30 large outside-view cabins, the other accommodation being a variety of outside-view and interior (no view) cabins.

Except for the 13 large cabins classed as "suites," all are small and somewhat utilitarian in their fittings and furnishings. There is very little drawer space, and the under-bed storage space for luggage is tight. Many cabins are fitted with upper Pullman berths. All have a private bathroom, with shower, and a small cabinet for personal toiletry items (only soap is supplied).

The suites have a much larger bathroom, with bathtub and shower combination, and each has a television and video player. The two largest of the "luxe" cabins have a separate bedroom with plenty of closet and drawer space, and a large bathroom with bathtub and shower combination.

DINING: The dining room, which has a low ceiling, has two seatings. The food is surprisingly good, with lots of fresh salads and vegetables, as well as good meats and local fish. There is certainly plenty of variety. Kosher food can also be supplied for a surcharge of around $19 per passenger, per day.

OTHER COMMENTS: *The Iris* has a square, angular profile with a boxy stern (complete with fold-down car ramps), stubby bow and a fat funnel placed amidships –

BERLITZ'S RATINGS

	Possible	Achieved
Ship	500	NYR
Accommodation	200	NYR
Food	400	NYR
Service	400	NYR
Entertainment	100	NYR
Cruise	400	NYR

otherwise it's a moderately handsome vessel. Has a fully enclosed bridge for all-weather operation. There is also a small helicopter landing deck, and the ship can also accommodate about 20 private cars.

This vessel was originally built in Poland as one of a series of five sister ships (the original names of the five being: *Dimitriy Shostakovich, Konstantin Simanov, Lev Tolstoi, Mikhail Sholokhov,* and *Petr Pervyy*). It was designed for carrying both cars and passengers on line voyages, although it is now used solely as a cruise ship, having been extensively reconstructed for pleasure cruising activities, and placed under charter to Israel's Mano Maritime in 2001.

Some cruises are designated as special holiday cruises (Passover, Yom Haatzmaut, Shavuot, Rosh Hashana, Sukkot, and Hannukah) and cost more. All passengers are provided with a photo ID/charge card (Mano Card). To the cost of your cruise, you need to add port charges, handling fees and administrative expenses.

WEAK POINTS: Both interior and exterior staircases are quite steep, the ship having been originally constructed as a ro-ro/passenger ferry. There is no observation lounge with forward-facing views over the ship's bows. Has a limited amount of open deck and sunning space (particularly if the ship is full) and a tiny swimming pool that is really merely a "dip" pool. The port and starboard open promenade decks are of painted steel.

The Jasmine
NOT YET RATED

Small Ship:	.............12,811 tons	Total Crew:	150
Lifestyle:	..................Standard	Passengers	
Cruise Line:	............Mano Maritime	(lower beds/all berths):	........450/750
Former Names:	.......*Palmira, Natasha,*	Passenger Space Ratio	
	Lev Tolstoi	(lower beds/all berths):	.......28.4/17.0
Builder:	......Szczesin Stocznia (Poland)	Crew/Passenger Ratio	
Original Cost:	.....................n/a	(lower beds/all berths):	.........3.0/5.0
Entered Service:	........1981/Mar 2002	Navigation Officers:	.........European
Registry:	........St. Vincent/Grenadines	Cabins (total):	225
Length (ft/m):	..........449.9/137.15	Size Range (sq ft/m): 118.4–322.9/11–30	
Beam (ft/m):	..............68.8/21.00	Cabins (outside view):	159
Draft (ft/m):	...................19.0/5.8	Cabins (interior/no view):	86
Propulsion/Propellers:	..........diesel	Cabins (for one person):	3
	(12,800kW)/2	Cabins (with private balcony):	0
Passenger Decks:	7	Cabins (wheelchair accessible):	1

Cabin Current:	...............220 volts
Elevators:	2
Casino (gaming tables):	............Yes
Slot Machines:	.......................Yes
Swimming Pools (outdoors):	1
Swimming Pools (indoors):	0
Whirlpools:	1
Fitness Center:	....................Yes
Sauna/Steam Room:	...........Yes/No
Massage:	.........................Yes
Self-Service Launderette:	...........Yes
Dedicated Cinema/Seats:	...........No
Library:	...........................No
Classification Society: ..Russian Shipping Register	

OVERALL SCORE: NYR (OUT OF A POSSIBLE 2,000 POINTS)

ACCOMMODATION: There are eight grades, spread over five decks. There are two large Royal Suites, 13 Presidential Suites, the other accommodation being a variety of outside-view and interior (no view) cabins.

STANDARD OUTSIDE-VIEW/INTERIOR (NO VIEW) CABINS: All regular cabins are very small and somewhat utilitarian in their fittings and furnishings. There is little drawer space, and the under-bed storage space for luggage is tight. Most cabins are fitted with one or two beds and one or two upper Pullman berths. All suites/cabins have a private bathroom, with shower, and a small cabinet for toiletries (only soap is supplied).

ROYAL SUITES/PRESIDENTIAL SUITES: The two Royal Suites have a separate bedroom with plenty of closet and drawer space, and a large bathroom with bathtub and shower combination. The Presidential suites have a much larger bathroom, with bathtub and shower combination, and each has a TV/VCR. The Presidential Suites with the best location are situated directly under the ship's navigation bridge (although if the ship is pitching in poor weather conditions, the movement will be felt here).

DINING: The restaurant, which seats about 420, and is operated in two seatings. It has large picture windows on three sides, although the ceiling is quite low. The food is surprisingly good, with lots of fresh salads and vegetables, as well as good meats and local fish. There is certainly plenty of variety. Kosher food can also be supplied for a surcharge of about $19 per passenger, per day.

BERLITZ'S RATINGS		
	Possible	Achieved
Ship	500	NYR
Accommodation	200	NYR
Food	400	NYR
Service	400	NYR
Entertainment	100	NYR
Cruise	400	NYR

OTHER COMMENTS: *The Jasmine* has a square, angular profile with a boxy stern (complete with fold-down car ramps), stubby bow and a fat funnel placed amidships. There's a fully enclosed bridge for all-weather operation, and a small helicopter landing deck. The ship can carry up to 80 private cars. Outdoors facilities include a small swimming pool, regulation volleyball court, and sun deck.

Inside, there is a range of public rooms, although the ceilings are quite low. These include a main lounge (The Palace), duty-free store, casino with tables and slot machines, (very) small children's playroom, and beauty salon. In 2004, a new, enlarged health spa will open.

This Polish-built vessel was designed for carrying both cars and passengers on line voyages, although it is now used solely as a cruise ship, having been extensively reconstructed for pleasure cruising activities, and placed under charter to Israel's Mano Maritime in 2002.

Some cruises are designated as special holiday cruises (Passover, Yom Haatzmaut, Shavuot, Rosh Hashana, Sukkot, and Hannukah) and cost more. All passengers are provided with a photo ID/charge card (Mano Card). To the cost of your cruise, you need to add port charges, handling fees and administrative expenses.

WEAK POINTS: Both interior and exterior staircases are quite steep. There is no observation lounge with forward-facing views over the ship's bows. Has a limited amount of open deck and sunning space, and a tiny swimming pool that is really merely a "dip" pool. The port and starboard open promenade decks are of painted steel.

Removed 2006

The Topaz
★★

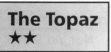

Large Ship: . . . . .31,500 tons	Total Crew: 550	Cabin Current: . . . . .110 volts
Lifestyle: . . . . .Standard	Passengers	Elevators: 4
Cruise Line: . .Topaz International Cruises	(lower beds/all berths): 1,056/1,386	Casino (gaming tables): . . . . .Yes
Former Names: . . .Olympic, FiestaMarina,	Passenger Space Ratio	Slot Machines: . . . . .Yes
Carnivale, Empress of Britain,	(lower beds/all berths): 30.0/22.7	Swimming Pools (outdoors): 2
Queen Anna Maria	Crew/Passenger Ratio	Swimming Pools (indoors): 0
Builder: . . . . . . .Fairfield Shipbuilding (UK)	(lower beds/all berths): 1.9/2.5	Whirlpools: 1
Original Cost: . . . .£7.5 million	Navigation Officers: . . . . .Greek	Fitness Center: . . . . .Yes
Entered Service: . . . . .Apr 1956/1994	Cabins (total): 528	Sauna/Steam Room: . . . . .No/No
Registry: . . . . .Panama	Size Range (sq ft/m): 100.7–301.3/	Massage: . . . . .Yes
Length (ft/m): 640.0/195.08	9.36–28.0	Self-Service Launderette: . . . . .No
Beam (ft/m): 87.0/26.51	Cabins (outside view): 228	(has ironing room)
Draft (ft/m): 29.0/8.84	Cabins (interior/no view): 300	Dedicated Cinema/Seats: . . . . .No
Propulsion/Propellers: . . . . .steam turbine	Cabins (for one person): 6	Library: . . . . .No
(22,400kW)/2	Cabins (with private balcony): 0	Classification Society: . . .Lloyd's Register
Passenger Decks: 9	Cabins (wheelchair accessible): 0	

OVERALL SCORE: 1,023 (OUT OF A POSSIBLE 2,000 POINTS)

ACCOMMODATION: There is a wide range of cabins and many different configurations (a carry-over from the ship's days as a transatlantic liner). But they are assigned in only four categories: suites and superior outside-view cabins, standard outside-view cabins, standard interior (no view) cabins, and single interior (no view) cabins. Many come with rich wood furniture, and all have been redecorated at some stage. Many cabins have third and fourth berths – good for families with children.

The Topaz is now an old ship, however, and most of the cabin bathrooms are small, even in the five "suites." The smallest cabins are very small (particularly the bathrooms). The cabins are not assigned until the day of embarkation, so you cannot choose when you book, except for the *grade* of cabin you pay for, unless you pay a supplement in order to pre-book a specific cabin number (an extra £25, or $40 per cabin applies).

DINING: There are two dining rooms, although they do become crowded and noisy. The décor is pleasing. Dining is in an open-seating arrangement, so you can dine when you want, and with whom you want. The food is certainly not for gourmets – it rather consists of quantity instead of quality. While fish dishes are quite poor, the meat dishes are reasonable, although there is little use of garnishes, and presentation could be better.

The 24-hour informal eatery, called the Yacht Club, while a good piece of design; in practice, however, it is a very poor operation.

BERLITZ'S RATINGS

	Possible	Achieved
Ship	500	220
Accommodation	200	103
Food	400	210
Service	400	233
Entertainment	100	52
Cruise	400	205

OTHER COMMENTS: This solidly built former ocean liner has a large funnel amidships, and the "sheer" that was typically found in classic ocean liners of yesteryear. This 1950s ship has had many lives, and many changes of name. It has also been through a number of refurbishments over the years (it is now well over 40 years old, but has been quite well maintained). Before it was bought by Topaz International (and chartered to Thomson Cruises), the ship had spent a great deal time being operated by Carnival Cruise Lines. All of the lifeboats are of the open-air type and should be updated (if it rains, you get wet). Teakwood outdoor and glass-enclosed indoor promenade decks encircle the ship.

Inside the ship, the colors are bright and stimulating, and the public rooms have jazzy décor, but it's so nice to see several public rooms with high ceilings. The casino is large for a ship that is catering principally to Europeans. Some delightful original woods and polished brass can be found throughout her public spaces, a large whirlpool has been added, and there is a colorful tiled outdoor deck.

When this book was completed, the ship was still under charter to Thomson Cruises, a British tour operator that provides a good, basic cruise vacation at very attractive prices, in a very casual setting. This could be the right ship for a first cruise, at a very modest price, to some fascinating destinations. Do remember, however, that this *is* an old ship, and does not have the latest high-tech facilities and features. It will continue cruising for

Thomson Cruises until spring 2003, but will be replaced by the much newer *Thomson Spirit* (ex-*Patriot*), which should provide a more contemporary setting for future Thomson Cruises passengers.

Thomson does a good job of providing a range of entertainment to suit its clientele, and the shows, although not of the top professional variety, are, nonetheless fun and entertaining for the whole family. While the entertainment facilities are limited at best (the single level show lounge is poor), the entertainment is quite acceptable. Variety shows provide a good amount of fun for the family clientele that the ship attracts (particularly during the peak school holiday periods).

The Topaz reflects Thomson's first foray into "all-inclusive" pricing, whereby all drinks, including beer and basic wines, as well as all gratuities, are included in the cruise fare (this is particularly good for families with children, who need constant soft drinks). However, you will be asked to pay extra for any drinks from the "premium brands" list, as well as for champagne. Note that shore excursions, laundry/cleaning, purchases from the ship's shops are *not* included in the "all inclusive" price (neither are alcoholic drinks after 2am).

During the summer, the ship is based on Palma Majorca, under charter to Thomson Cruises. *The Emerald* operates Mediterranean cruises, and is quite well suited for this task. Thomson's wholly owned airline (Britannia Airways) will probably fly you to your port of embarkation. Despite the minor criticisms about the ship, Thomson will provide you with quite a decent cruise experience, and provides a worry-free way to take a vacation. Hotel add-ons can extend your cruise vacation, and Thomson has a fine collection from which to choose, depending on your needs, budget, and whether you are traveling with children (or grandchildren). The onboard currency is the British pound.

WEAK POINTS: The announcements and constant background music are irritating. Expect some lines (queues in British English) for embarkation, disembarkation, buffets and shore excursions. The ship is old and tired, and probably past its "sell by" date.

Removed 2006

The World
NOT YET RATED

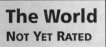

Small Ship:	43,524 tons	Passenger Space Ratio		Current: ....110/220 volts
Lifestyle:	Luxury	(lower beds/all berths):	109.9/44.5	Elevators: 4
Cruise Line:	ResidenSea	Crew/Passenger Ratio		Casino (gaming tables): ....Yes
Former Names:	none	(lower beds/all berths):	1.1/3.1	Slot Machines: ....Yes
Builder: ...Fosen MEK Versteder (Norway)		Navigation Officers: ....Scandinavian		Swimming Pools (outdoors): 1
Original Cost:	$266 million	Private Apartments (total):	110	Swimming Pools (indoors): 1
Entered Service:	Feb 2002	Size Range (sq ft/m): ...1,300.3–3,243.1/		Whirlpools: 1
Registry:	The Bahamas		102.8–301.2	Fitness Center: ....Yes
Length (ft/m):	644.1/196.35	Guest Suites:	88	Sauna/Steam Room: ....Yes/Yes
Beam (ft/m):	97.7/29.8	Size Range (sq ft/m): 259–648/24.0–60.1		Massage: ....Yes
Draft (ft/m):	21.9/6.7	Suites (outside view):	198	Self-Service Launderette: ....Yes
Propulsion/Propellers:	diesel/2	Suites (interior/no view):	0	Dedicated Cinema/Seats: ....No
Passenger Decks:	9	Suites (for one person):	0	Library: ....Yes
Total Crew:	320	Suites (with private balcony):	198	Classification Society: ....Det Norske
Passengers		Suites (wheelchair accessible):	2	Veritas
(lower beds/all berths):	396/976	(+2 for hearing impaired)		

OVERALL SCORE: NYR (OUT OF A POSSIBLE 2,000 POINTS)

APARTMENTS FOR RESIDENTS: There are 110 elegant residences in five different sizes and price ranges, costing between $2.3 million and $12 million per apartment for a 50-year lease, plus maintenance charges of approximately 5 per cent annually (this fee goes towards shipboard operations, and the servicing of the residences). A few owned apartments are also available for rent.

BERLITZ'S RATINGS		
	Possible	Achieved
Ship	500	NYR
Accommodation	200	NYR
Food	400	NYR
Service	400	NYR
Entertainment	100	NYR
Cruise	400	NYR

The residences range in size from 1,106 to 3,242 sq. ft (102.7 to 301.1 sq. meters). Owners choose between four different design styles (the designers are Nina Campbell, Juan Pablo Molyneux, Luciano Di Pilla, and Yran & Storbraaten). All have a fully equipped kitchen (with top-of-the-line refrigerator, oven, microwave, and dishwasher), 2–3 bedrooms (each with its own bathroom, naturally), living and dining room area, and private terrace. All have built-in modem access. Chefs are available for private meals in the apartments. Apartment owners also have a say in the creation of the ship's itineraries and other matters through the Resident's Committee.

GUEST ACCOMMODATION: An additional 88 guest suites, in five size and configuration categories (all with musical names: Adagio, Libretto, Sonata and Rhapsody) are available for family and friends of apartment owners, and for general cruise passenger use.

ADAGIO SUITES: There are eight Adagio Suites (six of which have lifeboat-obstructed views, the other two, which are for the handicapped, do not). They measure 259–325 sq. ft (24–30.1 sq. meters), and have a large picture window (no private balcony), two beds that can convert to a queen-sized bed, sitting area, cocktail cabinet with refrigerator, dressing table with built-in hairdryer, writing desk, personal safe, television and VCR. The marble-clad bathroom has a bathtub (except for two handicapped suites) and separate shower enclosure.

LIBRETTO SUITES: There are Six Libretto Suites. They are square in shape and measure 271–309 sq. ft (25.1–28.7 sq. meters), and have two beds that can convert to a queen-sized bed, sitting area, cocktail cabinet with refrigerator, dressing table with built-in hairdryer, writing desk, personal safe, television and VCR. The marble-clad bathroom has a bathtub (except for two handicapped suites) and separate shower enclosure.

CONCERTO SUITES: There are 18 Concerto Suites, each with a private balcony. They measure 294–319 sq. ft (27.3–29.6 sq. meters), and have two beds that can convert to a queen-sized bed, sitting area, cocktail cabinet with refrigerator, dressing table with built-in hairdryer, writing desk, personal safe, television and VCR. The marble-clad bathroom has a bathtub (except for two handicapped suites) and separate shower enclosure.

SONATA SUITES: There are 52 Sonata Suites, each with a private balcony. They measure 328–348 sq. ft (30.4–32.3 sq. meters), and have two beds that can convert to a queen-sized bed, sitting area, cocktail cabinet with refrigerator, dressing table with built-in hairdryer, writing desk, personal safe, television and VCR. The marble-clad bathroom has a bathtub (except for two handicapped suites) and separate shower enclosure. Three of the suites have an interconnecting door to another Sonata Suite, providing ideal his 'n' hers facilities for couples, or lavish accommodation for families with children.

RHAPSODY SUITES: There are four large Rhapsody Suites (two at the stern facing aft) created by the Signature Designers of the apartments; each with a large private balcony. They measure 598–648 sq. ft (55.5–60.1 sq. meters), and have a large living room that includes a dining table, cocktail cabinet with refrigerator, dressing table with built-in hairdryer, writing desk, television and VCR. There is a completely separate bedroom with its own dressing table with built-in hairdryer, two beds that convert to a queen-sized bed, and a large walk-in closet.

OTHER INFORMATION: If you want to be assured of space for future cruises, you can also book "tailored time" in blocks of 100, 200 or 300 days in Adagio, Libretto, Concerto or Sonata suites, and use the time purchased over a 24-month period. This is like owning an apartment without actually having to buy one or pay the annual maintenance charges. It's ideal for those who would like an apartment, but want to keep their main residence ashore, where they can keep their cars and pets and do things they could not do aboard ship. All apartments have kitchens that are enclosed in steel, and are thus self-contained fire zones that automatically seal themselves shut (just in case you burn the toast or something more serious). It's interesting that several apartment owners purchased their apartment over the internet (a new meaning to the phrase "on-liner"). There are also two suites for the hearing-impaired and two suites that are designed to be totally wheelchair accessible.

You can also rent one of the actual residences (when available); rates start at about $2,100 per apartment, per day, depending on the season (food not included, and the rental is limited to two persons per bedroom).

DINING: There are several restaurants, cafés and bars, including a gourmet market/delicatessen. Some (*Portraits, Marine Restaurant & Bar, Fredy's Deli*) are located off the equivalent of Main Street on Deck 5 (called The Village), while others (*Regatta, Tides, East Restaurant & Sushi Bar*, and *The Pool Grill*) are located up on Deck 11.

Several dining plans are available. Some examples:
Breakfast only: $18.50 per person, per day.
Lunch only: $52.50 per person, per day.
Dinner only: $75.00 per person, per day.
Complete Full Day plan: $125 per person, per day.

Deck 5 Eateries
● *Portraits*: the name of the most upscale restaurant aboard the ship, for contemporary French cuisine, with tableside cooking its specialty. It is located on a low deck, on the starboard side of the ship. Smoking is not permitted.
● *The Marina Restaurant and Bar*: for seafood, steak and rotisserie items. It is located on a lower deck at the ship's stern, and has an open "show" kitchen. Smoking is permitted, and there is seating for 88 indoors, 94 outdoors, and 10 at the bar.
● *Fredy's Deli* is a gourmet market/delicatessen (fresh produce, meat, fish and seafood, bakery items, pasta, tea and coffee) that also doubles as a street café (with a 24-hour delivery service to all suites). Naturally, kosher, vegetarian and diabetic meals are available.

Deck 11 Eateries
● *Tides Restaurant*: for casual self-serve buffet meals in a Mediterranean style (with more than a touch of Northern Italian cuisine). It is wrapped around the stern of the ship, with tables overlooking the ship's wash, and extends along the port and starboard sides; there are also some tables indoors (there are 76 indoor seats and 122 seats outdoors). Smoking is permitted only at the outdoors tables.
● *East Restaurant & Sushi Bar*: this is an Asian restaurant and sushi bar. It is located on a high deck, on the starboard side of the ship, with seating for 62 persons. The restaurant aims to serve *authentic* sashimi, sushi and tempura items. Tables are fitted with removable turntables for Asian-style (not including Japanese) dining. Smoking is not permitted.
● The *Pool Grill* is for casual meals by the pool (weather permitting). Smoking is permitted in this area, which has 128 seats at tables, and another 14 at the counter.
● *Regatta* backs onto the *Pool Grill* but on the inside. There are 72 seats, and sports are the main focus here.

OTHER COMMENTS: Is it a ship, or a floating apartment house? Well, to be truthful, it's both. It's a ship because it moves in the water, like other ships. And it has apartments can be purchased (like a home ashore), and suites that can be occupied by anyone paying the appropriate cruise fare.

So, it *is* possible to travel the world without leaving home – the ultimate virtual travel reality in what is the first residential *des res* (desirable residence) community at sea (not including naval submarines, of course). High-wealth owners like to make their own decisions, so democracy afloat could prove to be difficult, as the apartment owners get to (sort of) choose the ship's itineraries. Each apartment buyer owns a piece of the captain! In any event, the ship's occupants create their own set of social settings, and the chance of romantic adventures afloat within a semi-permanent community could make for a fascinating study in human behavior. The mix of apartment owners is approximately 40 percent North American and 60 percent other nationals.

Hopefully, apartment owners will like, and get on

with, their neighbors. But what if they don't? You couldn't pretend you're not in, could you? So how about the dress, or undress, code? Well, once you have purchased your apartment, it really is all up to you. But it could prove to be a fashion model's nightmare – imagine being seen in the same clothes twice in any given year. The questions surrounding the occupants and operation of *ResidenSea* remain countless, but I am sure that, like wealthy people on land, most will get on famously. Given that the apartments have sold extremely well, it appears that owners will be happy at sea.

The ship was blessed in a ceremony in Oslo, Norway, on February 19, 2002, by three Norwegian priests, who poured a mixture of holy water and champagne (some say it's one and the same) in the main lobby. The hull of the ship was built in Sweden; it was then towed 757 nautical miles to Rissa, Norway, for outfitting. At the ship's official naming ceremony in Venice on May 17, 2002, Ann Weedon, the first person to purchase an apartment aboard the ship, named the ship in a traditional champagne ceremony.

The exterior design is not overly handsome, and definitely suggests apartments at sea, with rows and rows of private balconies extending throughout the ship's superstructure (surprisingly, some of the balconies are not overly large). A marina folds out to provide a platform for watersports equipment and swimming; the marina is adjacent to an indoor pool.

Inside the ship, the entrance lobby is a restrained two decks high, but has an elegant domed atrium. Pleasure facilities include a cigar smoking lounge, show lounge/theatre for lectures, musical and theatrical performances (called the Colosseo Theater, although there are only 192 seats), a large library, an Internet Café, a Hobby Room, and a chapel. Business facilities include computers and fax machines, and a conference center, meeting rooms, and secretarial services. The 24-hour services include a concierge staff, housekeeping service, security and medical services, catering, hair and beauty salon, travel agency, and laundry and dry cleaning.

The health, beauty and fitness facilities occupy 6,545 sq. ft (608 sq. meters) and are provided by Clinique La Prairie, the renowned Swiss private clinic. Forget vegetable juices, here you can try the injections of "CLP extract" a concentrated solution of biologically active substances that was refined at the institute (created from selected sheep raised at the clinic's own farm).

One deck is almost completely given over to sports facilities. These include a full-size tennis court; paddle tennis court; paddle tennis court; volleyball court; jogging track; golf pro shop, and driving and putting ranges; two indoor artificial grass greens; target greens, sand bunker; 40-course golf simulator. The World Golf and Country Club has the first onboard 700 sq.-ft (65 sq.-meter) real grass greens in the world (the eco-friendly golf balls dissolve into fish food after 96 hours in the water).

Children's facilities include a play center (called the Junior Lounge), located on the Sports Deck.

ResidenSea Members have reciprocal privileges in private clubs around the world (these are quite useful for the times they are based on land). The ResidenSea Club itself occupies 51,345 sq. ft (4,770 sq. meters) of fine dining, entertainment, activities, recreation and shopping space.

The ship's operational plans call for the vessel to be in port for around 250 days in each year, and will maintain a continuous circumnavigation of the world, ostensibly in pursuit of fair weather and special international events. Itineraries in 2002 varied from 5 to 19 days, including many overnight calls and more than 60 multiple-day calls.

Doctors and medical staff are on call 24 hours a day, and there is a helipad in case medical evacuations become necessary.

So, what's it really like? Well, it is, without doubt the ultimate private address – and the ultimate waterborne stretch limo. Some of the ship's facilities, interior décor and accommodation provided may well set the benchmark for all other (normal) cruise ships. The ship provides the most elegant and luxurious setting in which to travel in comfort and privacy.

This is decadence upon the sea – *The World* as one's oyster. Whether an ambiance can be created year-round will depend entirely on the number of apartment occupants and cruise guests sailing at any given time, and on the class and behaviour of all aboard – including, of course, the personnel, which are expected to be impeccable as well as utterly discreet, with a mix of European waiters and an international hotel, housekeeping and social staff. The role of the cruise director has been changed to fit the clientele, to become the Enrichment Director. To make all your arrangements ashore and aboard, there's a concierge.

If you choose to cruise as a "regular" cruise passenger, note that the ship does stay in ports of call around the world for several days at a time, so you will need to be very selective with regard to itineraries if you want to visit several other destinations along the way. Choose this ship if you want to enjoy the spa and watersports facilities, and for its golfing ashore programs. But don't choose it if you're looking for lots of entertainment – there's very little. If you purchase a cruise, all gratuities are included in your cruise fare, and none are expected (although they are *not* prohibited, by any means).

Finally, if someone wanted to pay for me, would I go? Absolutely! Why? Because it is a unique experience in the annals of a serious cruise enthusiast. The onboard currency is the US dollar.

WEAK POINTS: There is no wrap-around promenade deck outdoors. Apartment occupants (or anyone else) cannot take their pets with them, or their cars (although they probably *could* take their lovers for private jollies). When few of the owners are in residence, unless there are regular passengers, there is little atmosphere in the public rooms and dining spots.

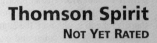

Thomson Spirit
NOT YET RATED

Large Ship:	.33,930 tons	Passenger Decks:	.10
Lifestyle:	Standard	Total Crew:	.510
Cruise Line:	.Louis Cruise Lines/	Passengers	
	Thomson Cruises	(lower beds/all berths):	.1,214/1,350
Former Names:	.Nieuw Amsterdam,	Passenger Space Ratio	
	Patriot, Nieuw Amsterdam	(lower beds/all berths):	.28.0/25.1
Builder:	.Chantiers de l'Atlantique	Crew/Passenger Ratio	
	(France)	(lower beds/all berths):	.2.3/2.6
Original Cost:	.$150 million	Navigation Officers:	.European
Entered Service:	.July 1983/May 2002	Cabins (total):	.607
Registry:	.The Bahamas	Size Range (sq ft/m):	.150.6–296.0/
Length (ft/m):	.704.2/214.66		14.0–27.5
Beam (ft/m):	.89.4/27.26	Cabins (outside view):	.413
Draft (ft/m):	.24.6/7.52	Cabins (interior/no view):	.194
Propulsion/Propellers:	.diesel	Cabins (for one person):	.0
	(21,600 kW)/2	Cabins (with private balcony):	.0

Cabins (wheelchair accessible):	.4
Cabin Current:	.110 and 220 volts
Elevators:	.7
Casino (gaming tables):	.Yes
Slot Machines:	.Yes
Swimming Pools (outdoors):	.2
Swimming Pools (indoors):	.0
Whirlpools:	.1
Fitness Center:	.Yes
Sauna/Steam Room:	.Yes/No
Massage:	.Yes
Self-Service Launderette:	.Yes (3)
Dedicated Cinema/Seats:	.Yes/230
Library:	.Yes
Classification Society:	.American Bureau of Shipping

OVERALL SCORE: NYR (OUT OF A POSSIBLE 2,000 POINTS)

ACCOMMODATION: As the ship was not in service for Thomson Cruises when this book was completed, I will provide descriptions of the accommodation when the ship was operated by its previous operator, United States Lines. Although the accommodation will probably change little, the names probably will be altered to reflect British tastes.

With the exception of one "Presidential Suite," all other accommodation comes in just four types: Parlor Suite, Superior Ocean-view stateroom, Ocean-view Stateroom, and Interior (no view) stateroom, and 15 price grades: 10 outside-view and five interior (no view) grades. In general, most of the cabins are quite small (below the industry standard of 170 sq. ft/15.7 sq. meters). They are reasonably well appointed and practically laid out. Some have wood furniture, fittings, or accenting, good counter and storage space (although there is very little drawer space), a large dressing mirror, and private bathrooms that are adequate, but no more.

The top cabin categories (which are only marginally larger and should not be called suites or mini-suites) have full-sized bathtubs while all others have showers. Several cabins have king- or queen-sized beds, although most have twin beds.

The largest accommodation can be found in the Presidential Suite (on Eagle Deck), a new suite created when United States Lines purchased the ship. Small by comparison to suites aboard many other ships, it measures 464 sq. ft (43.1 sq. meters), and is decorated in the style

BERLITZ'S RATINGS

	Possible	Achieved
Ship	500	NYR
Accommodation	200	NYR
Food	400	NYR
Service	400	NYR
Entertainment	100	NYR
Cruise	400	NYR

of a "Pacific White House" with American Federal décor, cherry wood cabinetry, and Murano (Italian) glass light fixtures. There is a king-sized bed, walk-in closet, wet bar, study and dining areas, television, VCR, and stereo system. The bathroom includes a whirlpool tub, double sink unit, and a separate powder room.

A number of cabins also have additional berths for a third/fourth person. Room service is provided 24 hours a day. All cabin televisions carry BBC World. The cabin insulation, however, is extremely poor, and bathroom towels are small. In addition, some cabins on Bridge Deck and Mariner Deck have obstructed views.

DINING: The dining room is reasonably large and quite attractive, with warm décor and ample space. Breakfast and lunch are served in an open-seating arrangement (so you may get a different table and different waiters for each meal), and in two seatings for dinner (where you do have the same table, and table waiters, each evening). Although there are a few tables for two, most are for four, six or eight persons.

Dessert and pastry items will typically be of good quality, and made specifically for British tastes, although there is much use of canned fruits and jellies.

Instead of the more formal dining room, the Lido Buffet is open for casual dinners on all except the last night of each cruise, in an open-seating arrangement. Tables are set with crisp linens, flatware and stemware. The set menu includes a choice of four entrées.

OTHER COMMENTS: The ship, originally built for and operated by Holland America Line, has a bow with a shapely rake to it, although the angular exterior design makes the ship look squat and extremely boxy. The ship's exterior has a deep blue hull, with a white superstructure. There is a decent amount of open teakwood deck space (particularly at the aft section of the ship), and the traditional outdoors teakwood decks include a wrap-around promenade deck. Unfortunately, the ship has always suffered from its poor build quality and excessive vibration since new.

The ship had a disastrous liaison with United States Lines, as *Patriot*, following its sale by Holland America Line to United States Lines in 2000. However, that venture was short-lived, and United States Lines collapsed in a sea of debt owed to US taxpayers in October 2001. Carnival Corporation (owners of Holland America Line) repurchased the ship for the amount outstanding ($79.8 million), and then chartered it to Louis Cruise Lines, who in turn has sub-chartered it to Thomson Cruises for a three-and-a-half year period, to replace one of the older ships the company had previous chartered. *Thomson Spirit* has a sister ship in the slightly newer, 1984-built *Noordam*, presently operated by Holland America Line.

Thomson first operated cruises in the 1970s, and then abandoned them, only to start cruises operations again in the mid-1990s (it has proven to be a highly successful venture, offering good value for money, particularly for families with children).

The ship has quite a spacious interior design and layout, and most of the public rooms are located on a single deck. The soothing color combinations do not jar the senses (most are pretty nondescript, although there are splashes of color). There is much polished teakwood and rosewood paneling throughout. For quieter moments, try the Observation Lounge, located atop the ship; it has a wooden dance floor. The Mid-Ship Lounge is relaxing for after-meal coffee with live music. The main lounge, which has a small balcony level, is reminiscent of the ocean liners of yesteryear.

For younger passengers, a teen center includes internet-access computer terminals, while younger children (those ages 5 through 12) have their own space, which includes a movie viewing room.

It's good to see a tour operator like Thomson Cruises charter and operate this newer ship, particularly in light of the fact that the competition in the cruise industry is increasing. This ship is quite acceptable for passengers wanting pleasant surroundings and an all-British ambiance. However, many newer ships have more space, better facilities and more options, and these leave this ship losing a few points in relation to the increased competition in the international marketplace.

Perhaps the best part of cruising aboard *Thomson Spirit* lies in the destinations, and not the ship. Hotel add-ons can extend a cruise vacation, and Thomson has a fine collection, depending on your needs, budget, and whether you are traveling with children (or grandchildren). The eventual score and rating for this ship is expected to be much higher than the older ship that *Thomson Spirit* is replacing (*The Topaz*). The onboard currency is the British pound.

It is expected that, in the UK market, Thomson will be going head to head with P&O's new Ocean Village cruise concept for the young at heart. However, Thomson has a major advantage in that it owns its own airline, and has much experience in operating fly-cruises to the Mediterranean (the company offers airlift from many UK airports).

WEAK POINTS: Standing in line for embarkation, disembarkation, shore tenders and for self-serve buffet meals is an inevitable aspect of cruising aboard all large ships (those carrying more than 1,000 passengers). There are too many interior (no-view) cabins in relation to the number of outside-view cabins aboard this ship. There is a considerable amount of vibration throughout the ship, particularly at the stern, and is particularly noticeable during slow maneuvering. There are no cabins with private balconies. The cabins really are quite small when compared to the newer ships in the cruise industry. The spa and gymnasium are also quite small, and the beauty salon is located in a completely different area to the health and fitness facilities.

Removed 2006 ✓

Triton
★★ +

Mid-Size Ship: . . . . .14,155 tons	Total Crew: 265	Cabins (wheelchair accessible): 0
Lifestyle: . . . . .Standard	Passengers	Cabin Current: . . . . .110 and 220 volts
Cruise Line: . . . . . .Royal Olympic Cruises	(lower beds/all berths): 756/945	Elevators: 2
Former Names: . . . . . .Cunard Adventurer,	Passenger Space Ratio	Casino (gaming tables): . . . . .Yes
Sunward II	(lower beds/all berths): 18.7/14.9	Slot Machines: .Yes
Builder: Rotterdamsche Dry Dock (Holland)	Crew/Passenger Ratio	Swimming Pools (outdoors): 1
Original Cost: .n/a	(lower beds/all berths): 2.8/3.5	Swimming Pools (indoors): 0
Entered Service: . . . . .Oct 1971/May 1992	Navigation Officers: . . . . .Greek	Whirlpools: 0
Registry: .Greece	Cabins (total): .378	Fitness Center: . . . . .Yes
Length (ft/m): 491.1/149.70	Size Range (sq ft/m): 118.4–131.3/	Sauna/Steam Room: . . . . .Yes/No
Beam (ft/m): 70.5/21.50	11.0–12.2	Massage: . . . . .Yes
Draft (ft/m): 19.22/5.86	Cabins (outside view): 236	Self-Service Launderette: . . . . .No
Propulsion/Propellers: . . . . .diesel	Cabins (interior/no view): 142	Dedicated Cinema/Seats: Yes/96
(19,860kW)/2	Cabins (for one person): 0	Library: . . . . .No
Passenger Decks: 7	Cabins (with private balcony): 0	Classification Society: . . .Lloyd's Register

OVERALL SCORE: 1,039 (OUT OF A POSSIBLE 2,000 POINTS)

ACCOMMODATION: *Triton* has cabins in eight grades, most of which are small (narrow) and basic. The closet and drawer space (the drawers are rather tinny) is minimal, and cabin soundproofing is very poor. There are 32 cabins (in the two highest grades) with a bathtub/shower, otherwise the cabin bathrooms have very small shower units, and little space for personal toiletry items (however, the ship operates short cruises, so you won't need to take much).

BERLITZ'S RATINGS

	Possible	Achieved
Ship	500	270
Accommodation	200	96
Food	400	205
Service	400	226
Entertainment	100	53
Cruise	400	189

DINING: While the dining room is reasonably attractive and has contemporary colors and ambience, it is also very noisy. There are two seatings for dinner on most nights (open seating for the first night of the cruise), and open seating for breakfast and lunch. The cuisine is continental, which means much use of oils and salt. The choice is reasonable, but the presentation is spotty and inconsistent. There is a limited (repetitious) choice of bread rolls and fruits. The Greek dining room staff provides service that can be best described as selectively friendly, but it is hurried. Dining room seating and table assignments for the cruise (except for the first night) are done by the maître d' upon embarkation.

Casual breakfast and lunch (with limited choices) can also be taken outside on deck adjacent to the swimming pool, or in the main lounge when the weather is poor.

OTHER COMMENTS: *Triton*, together with a sister ship, was originally built for Overseas National Airways but was then purchased by Cunard Line when ONA went bankrupt. It was later purchased by Royal Olympic

Cruises for informal cruises, has a reasonably handsome profile, a deep clipper bow, and twin funnels. The ship has been fairly well maintained, although it is now showing its age. There is a wrap-around painted steel outdoors promenade deck of sorts, as well as a decent amount of open deck space for sunbathing, and a small "kidney-shaped" swimming pool, although space is extremely tight when the ship is full (which is most of the time). Much of the open space outdoors is covered by canvas awnings, much appreciated by many passengers as a shelter from the intensity of the summer sun.

Inside, a good general layout and passenger flow makes it easy to find your way around in a short time. There is a good choice of public rooms, most of which are dressed in cheerful, warm colors. However, the décor and artwork is eclectic, some of it left over from the ship's former days with Norwegian Cruise Line and Cunard, while the deck names are Greek.

There's a good nightclub with forward observation views. The show lounge is a single level room, with sight lines obstructed by six pillars and the fact that there is no sloping floor, so only those passengers seated in the first few rows can see below waist level. There is no library (although there is a token gesture of two unkempt bookcases with a few old paperbacks).

On one of the upper decks, a dance floor is provided outdoors, with a bar by the name of Jailhouse Rock – it's good for lively nights under the summer stars (but it is not used early and late in the season when the weather is cooler).

These destination-intensive itineraries (typically from April to November) are excellent for those who want to see many places in a short time (there are two ports of call on most days), but, be warned, they are *extremely* busy, particularly on the first day (there are no days at sea). In other words, these three- and four-night cruises are not for relaxing, but are for sightseeing.

Triton is a decent down-home ship for short cruises around the Greek islands and Mediterranean. The dress code is very casual throughout (there are no formal nights), so leave your coats and ties and long dresses at home, as you simply do not need them. Gratuities (suggested at $8 per person per day) are pooled among the crew on the last day.

Forget about such things as chocolates on your pillow, and the other niceties associated with cruising aboard other cruise lines, this one will get you around the Greek islands in low-budget surroundings; with food that is more quantity than quality, and service that is mostly indifferent. Of course, with two sets of passengers each week, it is hard to provide friendly contact. The onboard currency is the euro.

WEAK POINTS: This really is a high-density ship with crowded public areas. Expect lines for buffets and shore excursions. There are too many announcements for tours, in many languages, when in ports of call. The nature of the Greek island cruises means that crew contracts are seasonal, and, at the end of the season (end of October/beginning of November) most crew are tired and clearly want to go home – and it shows – to the detriment of the product.

FUN FACTS

● Cruise ship design is interesting. Aesthetically, the beauty of design lies in curves, and not in straight lines. Today's large cruise ships, designed merely for cruising in warm weather regions and not for voyaging across the North Atlantic (heaven forbid, the delivery voyage was enough), are made of straight lines. They are boxy and cold in appearance, yet of course they provide much more usable space inside the ship (some call it warehouse cruising). Take a look at *Norway* (the former liner *France*) and you won't find a straight line anywhere. Then take a look at *Imagination* and compare the two.

● Beatrice Muller, in her early 80s, makes her permanent home at sea. She lives year-round aboard Cunard Line's *Queen Elizabeth 2*, paying a set amount to reside in Cabin 4068. She prefers being aboard the ship rather than sit around in a retirement home in Britain's damp climate, and proves that the world is her oyster. She loves it because she doesn't have to deal with the daily drudgery of shopping, doesn't need a car, or pay electric, gas or telephone bills. She communicates with her family by using the email from the computer center.

● Norwegian Cruise Line has a "chocoholic" buffet aboard its ships once each cruise. This midnight extravaganza should satisfy even the most dedicated addicts.

● Cruise lines and charity go hand in hand. Cunard donated 1,500 pieces of classic furniture from the 1994 refit of *Queen Elizabeth 2* to the Salvation Army for its adult rehabilitation program. Crew aboard the same ship, when on its annual around-the-world cruise, donate money to buy guide dogs for the blind, or an ambulance for the St. John's Ambulance Brigade in the UK. Princess Cruises made a "sizeable" contribution to UNICEF following the death of Audrey Hepburn in 1993 (she named the company's *Star Princess*, now operating as *Arcadia* for P&O Cruises). Passengers of Hapag-Lloyd's *Europa* have donated more than 1 million euros to children's homes in Vietnam. Both Holland America Line and Princess Cruises have contributed heavily to the Raptor Center in Juneau, Alaska.

● The sky's the limit: now you can have a private astrological report including a horoscope analysis provided for you in two special "astroflash" booths set up aboard Norwegian Cruise Lines newest ship, *Norwegian Sky*.

● Times were different then. In the mid-1960s there were 12 "bell boys" ("piccolos" in hotelspeak) aboard the Cunard Line's RMS *Queen Elizabeth* and *Queen Mary*. They manned the elevators and opened the doors to the various restaurants. Each day, before they were allowed to work, they all lined up and their fingernails were inspected.

Removed 2006

Universe Explorer
★★ +

Mid-Size Ship: . . . . .22,162 tons	Total Crew: 365	Cabins (wheelchair accessible): 0
Lifestyle: . . . . .Standard	Passengers	Cabin Current: . . . . .110 volts
Cruise Line: . . . . . .World Explorer Cruises	(lower beds/all berths): 737/846	Elevators: 3
Former Names: . . . .*Enchanted Seas,*	Passenger Space Ratio	Casino (gaming tables): . . . . .No
Queen of Bermuda, Canada Star, Liberte,	(lower beds/all berths): 30.0/24.7	Slot Machines: . . . . .No
Island Sun, Volendam, Monarch Sun, Brasil	Crew/Passenger Ratio	Swimming Pools (outdoors): 1
Builder: . . . . . . .Ingalls Shipbuilding (USA)	(lower beds/all berths): 2.0/2.3	Swimming Pools (indoors): 0
Original Cost: . . . .$26 million	Navigation Officers: . . . . .European/	Whirlpools: 0
Entered Service: . . . .Sept 1958/Nov 1990	Scandinavian	Fitness Center: . . . . .Yes
Registry: . . . . .Panama	Cabins (total): 371	Sauna/Steam Room: . . . . .No/No
Length (ft/m): 617.4/188.2	Size Range (sq ft/m): 103.3–292.7/	Massage: . . . . .Yes
Beam (ft/m): 84.3/25.7	9.6–27.2	Self-Service Launderette: . . . . .No
Draft (ft/m): 27.2/8.3	Cabins (outside view): 291	Dedicated Cinema/Seats: Yes/167
Propulsion/Propellers: . . . . .steam turbine	Cabins (interior/no view): 80	Library: . . . . .Yes
(19,000kW)/2	Cabins (for one person): 5	Classification Society: . .American Bureau
Passenger Decks: 8	Cabins (with private balcony): 0	of Shipping

---

OVERALL SCORE: 1,063 (OUT OF A POSSIBLE 2,000 POINTS)

ACCOMMODATION: The cabins, with many sizes and configurations, are priced in eight grades, depending on size, location and facilities. Most are generously proportioned for a ship of this size, with heavy-duty furniture and fittings, and good closet and drawer space. The bathrooms are, however, old-fashioned and utilitarian, as are their fittings, although they are still quite practical. Many cabins are set aside for single occupancy.

BERLITZ'S RATINGS

	Possible	Achieved
Ship	500	253
Accommodation	200	101
Food	400	206
Service	400	246
Entertainment	100	49
Cruise	400	208

DINING: The Hamilton Dining Room is located on the starboard side of the ship. It is charming and warm, and has large windows that provide plenty of light. There are two seatings. The menu choice is somewhat limited and quite basic, but service is attentive and comes with a smile, even if it is without finesse. There is only a moderate selection of bread rolls, cheeses (mostly of the standard supermarket processed kind) and fruits.

OTHER COMMENTS: This ship has a classic, compact 1960s traditional ocean liner profile that is quite low and rather squat, and has had an extensive amount of refurbishment over the years. It has nicely finished teakwood decks outdoors. Being an older ship, there are spacious promenade areas for walking outdoors, as well as plenty of sheltered and open sunbathing space.

Inside, the public rooms are moderately spacious and well appointed. Almost all have high ceilings, pleasing, but dated décor and colors that do not jar the senses. The Mid Ocean Lounge (the ship's show lounge) is ade-

quate, but it can't compare with those on larger, more modern ships, and the sight lines are poor. Although there used to be a large casino, this has been turned into a library and computer center while the ship is operated by World Explorer Cruises. The library houses about 16,000 books, and mounds of clippings, brochures, travel articles and cultural pieces.

This ship will provide a reasonably enjoyable cruise experience in comfortable surroundings reminiscent of old-world style. Cruise itineraries are relaxed and relatively unhurried.

Where the ship scores well with passengers is in the program of lecturers and educational features for passengers who want to learn more about their cruise surroundings than found aboard the more regular cruise vessels. You will get more out of your cruise if you become an avid *participant*, immersing yourself in the local cultures and traditions of the places you visit.

Other good points include the fact that there is no loud music anywhere – instead, there are classical concerts and dance music after dinner. The ship offers a mixture of 14-night Alaska cruises in the summer, with cruises to the Western Caribbean and Yucatán Peninsula in the winter, as well as an annual around-the-world cruise under the "Semester at Sea" banner for schoolchildren. The onboard currency is the US dollar.

WEAK POINTS: Being an older ship, there are no cabins with private balconies. Accommodation hallways are quite dim, with inconsistent lighting.

Van Gogh

★★ +

Mid-Size Ship: ....15,402 tons	Total Crew: 250	Refrigerator: ....No
Lifestyle: ....Standard	Passengers	Dining Rooms: 1
Cruise Line: ....Nouvelle Frontieres	(lower beds/all berths): 506/795	Elevators: 1
Former Names: ......Club I, Odessa Sky,	Passenger Space Ratio	Casino (gaming tables): ....Yes
Gruziya	(lower beds/all berths): 30.4/19.3	Slot Machines: ....Yes
Gross Tonnage: 15,402	Crew/Passenger Ratio	Swimming Pools (outdoors): 1
Builder: ....Wartsila (Finland)	(lower beds/all berths): 2.0/3.1	Swimming Pools (indoors): 0
Original Cost: ....$25 million	Navigation Officers: ....Ukrainian	Whirlpools: 0
Entered Service: ...June 1975/May 1999	Cabins (total): 253	Fitness Center: ....Yes
Registry: ....St. Vincent & the Grenadines	Size Range (sq ft/m): ...90–492/8.4–45.7	Sauna/Steam Room: ....Yes/No
Length (ft/m): 512.6/156.27	Cabins (outside view): 148	Massage: ....Yes
Beam (ft/m): 72.3/22.05	Cabins (interior/no view): 105	Self-Service Launderette: ....Yes
Draft (ft/m): 19.4/5.92	Cabins (for one person): 0	Dedicated Cinema/Seats: Yes/140
Propulsion/Propellers: ....diesel	Cabins (with private balcony): 0	Library: ....Yes
(13,430kW)/2	Cabins (wheelchair accessible): 0	Classification Society: ....Det Norske
Passenger Decks: 7	Cabin Current: ....220 volts	Veritas

---

OVERALL SCORE: 1,098 (OUT OF A POSSIBLE 2,000 POINTS)

ACCOMMODATION: Four suites on Boat Deck offer the largest accommodation, with sweeping forward views. These provide very spacious accommodation for the size of the ship, have full-sized bathtubs, good closet and drawer space and reasonably decent artwork. Another six suites are almost as large but don't have the fine forward-facing views.

All other cabins are very small and sparingly furnished, but quite adequate for short cruises. Most cabins have very little drawer space (particularly poor are those that accommodate three or four persons), and the insulation between cabins is poor.

One cabin has been "adapted" for the handicapped, although it would be difficult to get even a junior collapsible wheelchair through the cabin door.

DINING: There is a rather plain (non-smoking) dining room, but it has nicely decorated soft furnishings, and is moderately comfortable. There are tables for four, six or eight (none for two), assigned for the cruise's duration. Dinner is in two seatings, typically at 7pm and 9pm.

Casual, self-serve breakfast and lunch buffets are available on the port side of the swimming pool, although the choice is quite limited.

OTHER COMMENTS: One of a series of five sister ships (although today their interiors vary greatly), this is a fairly smart looking vessel with a squarish 1970s profile and smart, square funnel (with the Nouvelles Frontières logo emblazoned in red). Has a good outdoor promenade area.

BERLITZ'S RATINGS

	Possible	Achieved
Ship	500	273
Accommodation	200	117
Food	400	206
Service	400	238
Entertainment	100	50
Cruise	400	214

A past refit added a cinema, new nightclub, foyer, bar and more cabins, while a 1999 refit refreshed the interior décor prior to its long-term charter to French tour operator Nouvelles Frontières.

The ship was laid up at Montreal, Canada, for more than a year, after which it was then taken to Wilhelmshaven, Germany, where it was laid up for two more years. It was then purchased by the Dutch firm Eltek in August 1998 and operated by Club Cruise specifically for short cruises from Rotterdam for Dutch passengers. However, that venture proved short-lived, and the ship then provided comfortable, unpretentious cruises for French-speaking passengers, under charter to Nouvelles Frontières. At the time this book was completed, the ship was being operated for other tour operators in the European market. Thus, the currency used on board will depend on the country of origin of the tour operator.

Inside, most of the public rooms (which are few) are located on one horizontal deck, There is a Captain's Bar (neatly decorated in maritime paraphernalia, brass portholes, etc.), casino with tables and slot machines (tokens only), and boutique. Other facilities include a Sky Bar atop the ship (behind which, and outside, is a topless sunbathing area), with a circular bar. There's also a small cinema and discotheque.

WEAK POINTS: Communication with many of the staff can prove frustrating even though they are reasonably friendly. There are no cushioned pads for the deck lounge chairs. The gangway is narrow.

Veendam
★★★★

Large Ship:	.55,451 tons	Passengers		Cabin Current:	.110 and 220 volts
Lifestyle:	Premium	(lower beds/all berths):	.1,266/1,627	Elevators:	.12
Cruise Line:	Holland America Line	Passenger Space Ratio		Casino (gaming tables):	Yes
Former Names:	none	(lower beds/all berths):	.43.8/34.0	Slot Machines:	Yes
Builder:	Fincantieri (Italy)	Crew/Passenger Ratio		Swimming Pools (outdoors):	1
Original Cost:	$215 million	(lower beds/all berths):	.2.2/2.9	Swimming Pools (indoors):	1
Entered Service:	May 1996	Navigation Officers:	British/Dutch		(magrodome)
Registry:	The Bahamas	Cabins (total):	.633	Whirlpools:	2
Length (ft/m):	.719.3/219.3	Size Range (sq ft/m):	.186.2–1,124.8/	Fitness Center:	Yes
Beam (ft/m):	.101.0/30.8		17.3–104.5	Sauna/Steam Room:	Yes/No
Draft (ft/m):	.24.6/7.5	Cabins (outside view):	.502	Massage:	Yes
Propulsion/Propellers:	diesel-electric	Cabins (interior/no view):	.131	Self-Service Launderette:	Yes
	(34,560kW)/2	Cabins (for one person):	0	Dedicated Cinema/Seats:	Yes/249
Passenger Decks:	10	Cabins (with private balcony):	.150	Library:	Yes
Total Crew:	.561	Cabins (wheelchair accessible):	6	Classification Society:	Lloyd's Register

OVERALL SCORE: 1,533 (OUT OF A POSSIBLE 2,000 POINTS)

ACCOMMODATION: The accommodation ranges from small interior (no view) cabins to a large penthouse suite, in 17 categories. All cabin televisions carry CNN and TNT.

The 148 interior (no view) and 336 outside (with a view) standard cabins have twin beds that convert to a queen-size bed, and there is a separate living space with sofa and coffee table. However, although the drawer space is generally good, the closet space is actually very tight, particularly for long cruises (although more than adequate for a 7-night cruise). The bathrooms are tiled, and compact but practical – they come with a good range of personal toiletry amenities. Bathrobes are also provided, as are hairdryers. The bathrooms are quite well laid out, but the bathtubs are small units better described as shower tubs. Some cabins have interconnecting doors – good for families with children, or older couples with their own butler/maid or nurse (*Maasdam, Ryndam, Veendam* only, not *Statendam*).

On Navigation Deck 28, suites have accommodation for up to four. These also have in-suite dining as an alternative to the dining room, for private, reclusive meals. These are very spacious, tastefully decorated and well laid-out, and feature a separate living room, bedroom with two lower beds (convertible to a king-size bed), a good size living area, dressing room, plenty of closet and drawer space, marble bathroom with Jacuzzi tub.

The largest accommodation of all is a penthouse suite; there is only one, located on the starboard side of Navigation Deck. It has a king-size bed, walk-in closet with superb drawer space, oversize whirlpool bath and separate shower enclosure, living room, dressing room, large private balcony, pantry, mini-bar/refrigerator, a guest toilet and floor to ceiling windows.

BERLITZ'S RATINGS

	Possible	Achieved
Ship	500	418
Accommodation	200	162
Food	400	267
Service	400	299
Entertainment	100	77
Cruise	400	310

DINING: The two-level Rotterdam Dining Room, located at the stern, is quite dramatic, and has a grand staircase (although few seem to use it), panoramic views on three sides, and a music balcony. It has open seating for breakfast and lunch, and two seatings for dinner. The waiter stations in the dining room are very noisy for anyone seated adjacent to them. Fine Rosenthal china and cutlery are used (although there are no fish knives).

Unfortunately, Holland America Line food isn't as nice as the china it's placed on. It may be adequate for most passengers who are not used to better food, but it does not match the standard found aboard other ships in the premium segment of the industry. While USDA beef is of a good quality, fowl tends to be battery-tough, and most fish is overcooked and has the consistency of a cricket bat. What are also definitely *not* luxurious are the endless packets of sugar, and packets (instead of glass jars) of breakfast jam, marmalade and honey, and poor quality teas. While these may be suitable for a family diner, they do not belong aboard a ship that claims to have "award-winning cuisine."

Dessert and pastry items are of good quality (specifically for American tastes), although there is much use of canned fruits and jellies. Forget the selection of "international" cheeses, however, as most of it didn't come from anywhere other than the USA – a country that is better known for its processed, highly colored slices than for fine cheese-making. Holland America Line can provide Kosher meals, but these are prepared ashore, frozen, and brought to your table sealed in their original containers (there is no Kosher kitchen on board).

Instead of the more formal dining room, the Lido Buffet is open for casual dinners on all but the last night of a cruise, in an open-seating arrangement. Tables are set with crisp linens, flatware and stemware. A set menu includes a choice of four entrées.

There is also an extensive, dual-line (self-serve) Lido Buffet (one side is for smokers, the other side for non-smokers) for casual breakfasts and lunches. For the buffets, there is much use of canned fruits (good for dentally challenged older passengers) and packeted items, although there are several commercial low-calorie salad dressings. The choice of cheeses (and accompanying crackers) is very poor. The beverage station also lets it down, for it is no better than those found in family outlets ashore in the United States. In addition, a poolside grill provides basic American hamburgers and hot dogs.

OTHER COMMENTS: This is one of a series of four almost identical ships in the same series – the others being *Maasdam, Statendam, Ryndam.* The exterior styling is rather angular (some would say boxy – the funnel certainly is), although it is softened and balanced somewhat by the fact that the hull is painted black. There is a full wrap-around teakwood promenade deck outdoors – excellent for strolling, and, thankfully, no sign of synthetic turf anywhere. The deck lounge chairs are wood, and come with comfortable cushioned pads.

Inside, an asymmetrical layout breaks up the interiors and helps to reduce bottlenecks and congestion. The décor is softer, more sophisticated, and far less eclectic than in sister ship *Statendam* (the first in this series of what the company terms *Statendam*-class ships), while the interiors of the latest in the series seem to improve further on the theme. In general, however, a restrained approach to interior styling is taken using a mixture of contemporary materials combined with traditional woods and ceramics. There is, fortunately, little "glitz" anywhere.

What is outstanding is the array of artworks throughout the ship (costing about $2 million), assembled and nicely displayed to represent the fine Dutch heritage of Holland America Line and to present a balance between standard itineraries and onboard creature comforts. Also noticeable are the fine flower arrangements throughout the public areas and foyers – used good effect to brighten up what to some is dull décor.

Atop the ship, with forward facing views that wrap around the sides is the Crow's Nest Lounge. By day it makes a fine observation lounge (particularly in Alaska), while by night it turns into a nightclub with extremely variable lighting.

A three-deck high atrium foyer is quite stunning, although its sculpted centerpiece makes it look a little crowded, and leaves little room in front of the purser's office. A hydraulic magrodome (glass) roof covers the reasonably sized swimming pool/whirlpools and central Lido area (whose focal point is a large dolphin sculpture) so that this can be used in either fine or inclement weather.

The two-deck-high show lounge is basically well designed, but the ceiling is low and the sight lines from the balcony level are poor. There is a large reference library, quite lovely and relaxing. The company keeps its ships very clean and tidy, and there is good passenger flow throughout.

Veendam is a well-built ship, and has fairly decent interior fit and finish. Holland America Line is constantly fine-tuning its performance as a cruise operator and its regular passengers (almost all of whom are North American – there are few international passengers) find the company's ships very comfortable and well run. The company continues its strong maritime traditions, although the present food and service components still let the rest of the cruise experience down.

Gratuities are extra, and they are added to your shipboard account at $10–$13 per day, according to the accommodation grade chosen. Refreshingly, the company does not add an automatic 15 percent gratuity for beverage purchases. Perhaps the ship's best asset is its friendly and personable Filipino and Indonesian crew, although communication can prove frustrating at times.

Holland America Line's many repeat passengers seem to enjoy the fact that social dancing is always on the menu. The company provides complimentary cappuccino and espresso coffees, and free ice cream during certain hours of the day aboard its ships, as well as hot hors d'oeuvres in all bars – something other major lines seem to have dropped, or charge extra for.

In the final analysis, however, the score for this ship (and its sisters *Maasdam, Ryndam, Statendam*) ends up just a disappointing tad under what it could be if the food and food service staff were better (more professional training and better supervision might help). The onboard currency is the US dollar.

WEAK POINTS: Standing in line for embarkation, disembarkation, shore tenders and for self-serve buffet meals is an inevitable aspect of cruising aboard all large ships. The service staff is Indonesian, and, although quite charming (for the most part) communication with them often proves frustrating for many passengers, and service is spotty and inconsistent. Note that passengers are forced to eat at the Lido Café on days when the dining room is closed for lunch (this is typically once or twice per cruise, depending on ship and itinerary).

The single escalator is virtually useless. There is no bell push outside the suites. The charge to use the washing machines and dryers in the self-service launderette is really petty and irritating, particularly for the occupants of suites, as they pay high prices for their cruises. Room service is poor.

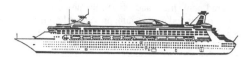

Vision of the Seas
★★★★

Large Ship: ....78,491 tons	Passengers	Cabin Current: ....110 and 220 volts
Lifestyle: ....Standard	(lower beds/all berths): 2,000/2,435	Elevators: 9
Cruise Line: Royal Caribbean International	Passenger Space Ratio	Casino (gaming tables): ....Yes
Former Names: ....none	(lower beds/all berths): 39.2/32.2	Slot Machines: ....Yes
Builder: Chantiers de l'Atlantique (France)	Crew/Passenger Ratio	Swimming Pools (outdoors): 1
Original Cost: ....$275 million	(lower beds/all berths): 3.0/3.6	Swimming Pools (indoors): 1
Entered Service: ....May 1998	Navigation Officers: ....International	(inside/outside)
Registry: ....The Bahamas	Cabins (total): 1,000	Whirlpools: 6
Length (ft/m): 915.3/279.0	Size Range (sq ft/m): 135.0–1,270.1/	Fitness Center: ....Yes
Beam (ft/m): 105.6/32.2	12.5–118.0	Sauna/Steam Room: ....Yes/Yes
Draft (ft/m): 24.9/7.6	Cabins (outside view): 593	Massage: ....Yes
Propulsion/Propellers: .....diesel-electric	Cabins (interior/no view): 407	Self-Service Launderette: ....No
(50,400kW)2	Cabins (for one person): 0	Dedicated Cinema/Seats: ....No
Passenger Decks: 11	Cabins (with private balcony): 229	Library: ....Yes
Total Crew: 765	Cabins (wheelchair accessible): 14	Classification Society: Det Norske Veritas

OVERALL SCORE: 1,519 (OUT OF A POSSIBLE 2,000 POINTS)

ACCOMMODATION: There are 18 cabin categories, in 11 pricing units.

The standard interior (no view) and exterior view cabins are of an adequate size, and have just enough functional facilities to make them comfortable for a one-week cruise, but longer might prove confining. The décor is bright and cheerful, although the ceilings are plain; colorful soft furnishings make one's home away from home look like the inside of a modern Scandinavian hotel – minimalist, yet colorful. Twin lower beds convert to queen-sized beds, and there is a reasonable amount of closet and drawer space (there is little room to maneuver between the bed and desk/television unit).

The bathrooms are small but functional, although the shower units themselves are small, and there is no cabinet for one's personal toiletry items. The towels could be larger and thicker.

Choose a "C" grade suite if you want spacious accommodation that includes a separate (curtained-off) sleeping area, a good-sized outside balcony (with part, not full, partition), lounge with sofa, two chairs and coffee table, three closets, plenty of drawer and storage space, television and VCR. The bathroom is large and has a full-size bathtub, integral shower, and two washbasins/two toiletries cabinets.

For the ultimate accommodation aboard this ship, choose the Royal Suite, which resembles a Palm Beach apartment, and comes complete with a white baby grand (player) piano. It has a separate bedroom with king-size bed, living room with queen-size sofa bed, refrigerator/mini-bar, dining table, entertainment center, and van-

BERLITZ'S RATINGS

	Possible	Achieved
Ship	500	428
Accommodation	200	166
Food	400	248
Service	400	302
Entertainment	100	81
Cruise	400	294

ity dressing area. The décor is simple and elegant, with pastel colors, and wood accented ceiling treatments. Located just under the starboard side navigation bridge wing, it has its own private balcony.

DINING: The non-smoking dining room is set on two levels with large ocean-view picture windows on two sides (rectangular windows on the upper level, large circular windows on the lower level) and a large connecting stairway. There are two seatings.

The cuisine is typical of mass banquet catering that offers standard fare comparable to that found in American family-style restaurants ashore. While menu descriptions are tempting, the actual food may be somewhat disappointing and unmemorable. The menu descriptions make the food sound better than it is (which is consistently below average), mostly disappointing and without much taste – the result of controlled food costs as well as the use of many mixes and pre-prepared items. However, a decent selection of light meals is provided, and a vegetarian menu is available.

The selection of breads, rolls, fruit and cheese is quite poor, however, and could do more improvement. Caviar (once a standard menu item) now incurs a hefty extra charge. Menus typically include a Welcome Aboard Dinner, French Dinner, Italian Dinner, International Dinner, Captain's Gala Dinner.

The Windjammer Café is the ship's informal dining spot, and offers more choice for those who enjoy casual meals, in a contemporary setting, with attractive colors and décor, and large ocean-view windows that provide plenty of light. However, only the basics are available at the beverage stations.

OTHER COMMENTS: This striking ship, sixth in the Vision-class of vessels, shares design features that make all Royal Caribbean International ships identifiable, including a Viking Crown Lounge (which is also the ship's disco). Aboard this ship (and sister ship Rhapsody of the Seas, which debuted in 1998) the Viking Crown Lounge is located just forward of the center of the ship, with the funnel located well aft – a departure from all other RCI ships to date. The ship's stern is beautifully rounded. There is a reasonable amount of open-air walking space, although this can become cluttered with deck lounge chairs (which do not have cushioned pads).

Inside, the ship provides the latest incarnation of RCI's interpretation of a floating contemporary hotel, and presents the nicest mix of colors and décor of any of the Vision-class ships, with lots of warm beige and pink tones (particularly in the expansive atrium).

The artwork (which cost $6 million) is plentiful, colorful and very creative (much seems to have been inspired by that aboard Galaxy, which belongs to sister company Celebrity Cruises), with more previously blank wall space covered with interesting artworks of differing shapes and sizes. Most noticeable is the extensive use of glass (two beautiful glass sculptures stand out – one in the atrium (at the entrance to a Champagne Bar), one on the upper level of the Viking Crown Lounge). There are plenty of public rooms, bars and lounges to play in, as well as a large, well-lit casino.

The spa, with its solarium and indoor/outdoor dome-covered pool, Inca- and Mayan-theme décor, sauna/ steam rooms and gymnasium, provides a haven for the health-conscious and fitness buff (although there is a pizza bar forward of the pool area). There is a lovely "Mayan Serpent" sculpture in the solarium.

The Viking Crown Lounge is a multi-level nightspot (the music can be loud and overbearing, however, and so can cigarette smoke around the bar – one of few places where smokers can light up). Perhaps the best atmosphere can be found in the nautical-theme Schooner Bar. The Library features an excellent array of hardback books, as well as a neat wooden sculpture of something that looks like the Tin Man from The Wizard of Oz.

The entertainment throughout is upbeat (in fact, it is difficult to get away from music and noise), but is typical of the kind of resort hotel found ashore in Las Vegas. There is even background music in all corridors and elevators, and constant music outdoors on the pool deck. If you want a quiet relaxing vacation, this is the wrong ship. If you enjoy big-city life, with a fine array of sounds and entertainment around you, this could be just right. The onboard currency is the US dollar.

WEAK POINTS: Standing in line for embarkation, disembarkation, shore tenders and for self-serve buffet meals is inevitable aboard all large ships. The staff is only mildly accommodating, and only a small percentage say hello when passing you in the corridors (this included the officers). In other words, the hospitality factor is below average. The elevators talk to you ("going up/ going down" is informative, but monotonous, although the illuminated picture displays of decks is good).

Rigu . 9/06/05

Vistamar
★★★ +

Small Ship:	.7,478 tons	Total Crew:	.110	Cabins (wheelchair accessible):	0
Lifestyle:	Standard	Passengers		Cabin Current:	.220 volts
Cruise Line:	Plantours & Partners	(lower beds/all berths):	.299/320	Elevators:	1
Former Names:	none	Passenger Space Ratio		Casino (gaming tables):	No
Builder:	Union Navale de Levante	(lower beds/all berths):	.25.3/23.3	Slot Machines:	No
	(Spain)	Crew/Passenger Ratio		Swimming Pools (outdoors):	1
Original Cost:	$45 million	(lower beds/all berths):	.2.7/2.9	Swimming Pools (indoors):	0
Entered Service:	Sept 1989	Navigation Officers:	Spanish	Whirlpools:	0
Registry:	Spain	Cabins (total):	.152	Fitness Center:	Yes
Length (ft/m):	.396.9/121.00	Size Range (sq ft/m):	.129.1–150.6/	Sauna/Steam Room:	Yes/No
Beam (ft/m):	.55.1/16.82		12.0–14.0	Massage:	Yes
Draft (ft/m):	.14.9/4.55	Cabins (outside view):	.126	Self-Service Launderette:	No
Propulsion/Propellers:	diesel	Cabins (interior/no view):	.26	Dedicated Cinema/Seats:	No
	(3,900kW)/2	Cabins (for one person):	.5	Library:	Yes
Passenger Decks:	6	Cabins (with private balcony):	.11	Classification Society:	Bureau Veritas

OVERALL SCORE: 1,262 (OUT OF A POSSIBLE 2,000 POINTS)

ACCOMMODATION: The passenger accommodation areas are located forward, while public rooms are positioned aft, which means there is a minimal amount of noise in the cabins. There are 11 cabin grades, but in just two different sizes: suites with private (covered) balcony and queen-size bed; outside-view or interior (no view) cabins for two, three or four persons, all with fixed, wide single beds. All of the cabins are reasonably comfortable, although the bathrooms are *extremely* small and tight (there is a considerable "lip" to step over to access the bathroom), and both closet and drawer space is limited. Cabins have twin beds with wooden headboard, small vanity/writing desk, color television, climate-control, telephone, and hairdryer. Most of the cabinetry is made with a wood finish.

There are 11 suites, each of which has a small, narrow, private, covered balcony outdoors. The suites are: Alboran, Algarve, Almeria, Armador, Cadiz, Cordoba, Granada, Huelva, Jaen, Malaga, Seville – all of which are regions of Andalucia. They also have a more spacious bathroom, with a large bathtub and integral shower. The living area s also larger, and comes with a sofa, coffee table, vanity/writing desk, and a larger color television. Note that Armador is the owner's suite, and comes with a circular bathtub with integral shower, set against large picture windows (wonderful for the Arctic and Antarctic cruises that this company typically operates in the appropriate season).

No matter what accommodation grade or location they choose, all passengers get personal amenities that

BERLITZ'S RATINGS

	Possible	Achieved
Ship	500	311
Accommodation	200	129
Food	400	247
Service	400	271
Entertainment	100	60
Cruise	400	244

include soap, shampoo, body lotion and bath/shower gel, and shoeshine mitt. Accommodation hallways are provided either in hospital green, powder blue, or hot pink.

DINING: The Andalucia Restaurant is quite warm and inviting, with contemporary colors and décor, and large picture windows, although the six pillars detract from the otherwise attractive room. The room's focal point is a model of a sailing vessel with an emerald green hull (about the same color as the fabrics on the dining room chairs. There is one seating for all passengers (so meals are leisurely), with assigned tables for four, six or eight (there are no tables for two). Window-side tables are for six, and all chairs have armrests.

The food is reasonably adequate, and quite sound, and dinners typically come with a choice of three entrees (plus a vegetarian selection). The selection of cooked green vegetables, breads, cheeses and fruits is limited, and the overall cuisine really is of quite a low standard (it could be said to be quite similar to that found aboard other ships operated for German-speaking passengers, such as *Berlin, Delphin* – which have two seatings for dinner). The service is adequate, no more, as is the wine list. Note that sekt (sweet sparkling wine) is provided for breakfast, while white and red table wines are provided for lunch and dinner.

OTHER COMMENTS: *Vistamar* has a moderately smart, reasonably contemporary, but rather squat small ship profile. The ship, which has an ice-hardened hull, also carries several inflatable rubber landing craft for close-up landings during certain itineraries that include the Arctic and Antarctic.

There is an "open bridge" policy, so you can join the captain and other navigation officers at almost any time. There is a good open observation deck at the forward-most part of the ship – atop the navigation bridge, although the other open deck and sunbathing space is a little limited, particularly on the aft open deck around the small outdoor pool (it is really only a "dip" pool, although it has a large splash surround).

As stated, the interior layout has all the public rooms located aft, in a "cake-layer" stacking, with a single, central staircase that takes up most of the space in an atrium lobby that spans three decks (with a glass elevator that is shaped like half a cable car). Features include wood-trimmed interior décor, which is jazzy, attractive and warm, although the mirrored metallic ceilings are somewhat irritating.

A four-deck high atrium with a "sky dome" has a glass-walled elevator and a wrap-around staircase, and is the focal point of the ship's interior. The library has comfortable high wingback chairs, but there are not very many books. There is also a Card Room, and board games are available.

The ship's main lounge, Don Fernando, is named after Senor Don Fernando Abril Martorell, the president of the Union Navale de Levante shipyard that constructed *Vistamar* in 444 days (perhaps if more time had

been taken, the ship would have been built better). Additionally, there is a rather jazzy nightclub/disco, with acres of glass, set around the base of the funnel, with a long bar, and dance floor, for the late night set.

This ship has been under charter to Plantours & Partners, specifically for German-speaking passengers, since 1991, and the product is aimed at the inexpensive standard market. The dress code is ultra-casual (no tuxedos, no ties required). While the ship is not in the best condition, and maintenance is spotty, there is a warm, friendly ambiance, which attracts many repeat passengers.

There is an abundance of greenery throughout the ship, which helps to make it feel warm, more comfortable and less clinical. The ship is quite small, and so passengers can enjoy interesting destination-intensive cruises, with many port calls that larger ships simply cannot get into. Tipping is recommended at 5–6 euros (the onboard currency) per person, per day.

WEAK POINTS: The tiny "dip" swimming pool is virtually useless. There is a distinct odor of diesel fuel at the upper level of the lobby, where there is also a complete lack of air-conditioning. The ship's hotel operation is rather sloppy and needs streamlining. There is no walking track or wrap-around promenade deck outdoors. The fit, finish and maintenance of this ship are all quite poor, and well below the standard expected. The sight lines in the single-level show lounge are very poor, and there is a lack of good stage lighting.

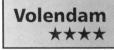

Volendam
★★★★

Large Ship:	.63,000 tons	Passengers	
Lifestyle:	.Premium	(lower beds/all berths):	.1,440/1,850
Cruise Line:	.Holland America Line	Passenger Space Ratio	
Former Names:	.none	(lower beds/all berths):	.43.7/34.0
Builder:	.Fincantieri (Italy)	Crew/Passenger Ratio	
Original Cost:	.$300 million	(lower beds/all berths):	.2.5/2.5
Entered Service:	.Nov 1999	Navigation Officers:	.Dutch
Registry:	.The Netherlands	Cabins (total):	.720
Length (ft/m):	.781.0/238.00	Size Range (sq ft/m):	.113.0–946.0/
Beam (ft/m):	.105.8/32.25		10.5–87.8
Draft (ft/m):	.25.5/7.80	Cabins (outside view):	.581
Propulsion/Propellers:	.diesel-electric	Cabins (interior/no view):	.139
	(37,500kW)/2	Cabins (for one person):	.0
Passenger Decks:	.10	Cabins (with private balcony):	.197
Total Crew:	.561	Cabins (wheelchair accessible):	.23

Cabin Current:	.110 volts
Elevators:	.12
Casino (gaming tables):	.Yes
Slot Machines:	.Yes
Swimming Pools (outdoors):	.2
Swimming Pools (indoors):	.1
	(magrodome cover)
Whirlpools:	.2
Fitness Center:	.Yes
Sauna/Steam Room:	.Yes/Yes
Massage:	.Yes
Self-Service Launderette:	.Yes (2)
Dedicated Cinema/Seats:	.Yes/205
Library:	.Yes
Classification Society:	.Lloyds Register

OVERALL SCORE: 1,541 (OUT OF A POSSIBLE 2,000 POINTS)

ACCOMMODATION: The range is similar to that found aboard the similarly sized *Rotterdam*, and comprises 17 different categories. There is one penthouse suite, and 28 suites, with the rest of the accommodation a mix of outside-view and interior (no view) cabins, and many more balcony cabins ("mini-suites") aboard this ship than aboard the slightly smaller *Statendam*-class ships (*Maasdam, Ryndam, Statendam, Veendam*).

All standard interior and outside cabins are tastefully furnished, and have twin beds that convert to a queen-sized bed (space is tight for walking between beds and vanity unit). There is a decent amount of closet and drawer space, although this will prove tight for the longer voyages featured. All cabin televisions carry CNN and TNT. The bathrooms, which are fully tiled, are disappointingly small (particularly for long cruises) and have small shower tubs, utilitarian personal toiletries cupboards, and exposed under-sink plumbing. There is no detailing to distinguish them from bathrooms aboard the *Statendam*-class ships.

There are 28 full Verandah Suites (Navigation Deck), and one Penthouse Suite. All suite occupants share a private Concierge Lounge (the concierge handles such things as special dining arrangements, shore excursions, private parties and special requests). Strangely, there are no butlers for these suites, as aboard ships with similar facilities. Each Verandah Suite has a separate bedroom, dressing and living areas. Suite passengers get personal stationery, complimentary laundry and ironing, cocktail hour hors d'ouvres and other goodies, as well as priority embarkation and disembarkation. The concierge lounge,

BERLITZ'S RATINGS

	Possible	Achieved
Ship	500	430
Accommodation	200	165
Food	400	281
Service	400	276
Entertainment	100	77
Cruise	400	312

with its latticework teak detailing and private library, is accessible only by private key-card.

For the ultimate in accommodation and living space aboard this ship, choose the Penthouse Suite. It has a separate steward's entrance, a large bedroom with king-size bed, separate living room (with baby grand piano) and a dining room, dressing room, walk-in closet, butler's pantry, and private balcony (though the balcony is no large than that of any other suite). Other facilities include an audio-visual center with television and VCR, wet bar with refrigerator, large bathroom with Jacuzzi bathtub, separate toilet with bidet, and a guest bathroom (with toilet and washbasin).

With the exception of the penthouse suite, located forward on the starboard side, the bathrooms in the other suites and "mini-suites" are a little disappointing – neither as spacious nor as opulent as one would expect. All outside-view suites and cabin bathrooms feature a bathtub/shower while interior (no view) cabins have a shower only. Also, note that the 23 cabins for the mobility-limited have a roll-in shower enclosure for wheelchair users (none have bathtubs, no matter what the category).

DINING: There is one main dining room, and one alternative dining spot (open for dinner only). The 747-seat Rotterdam Dining Room is quite a grand room, and is spread over two decks, with ocean views on three sides with a grand staircase to connect the upper and lower levels. There are two seatings for dinner, open seating for breakfast and lunch, and both smoking and non-smoking sections are provided. Fine Rosenthal china and cutlery are featured (although there are no fish knives).

Unfortunately, Holland America Line food isn't as nice as the china it's placed on. It may be adequate for most passengers who are not used to better food, but it does not match the standard found aboard other ships in the premium segment of the industry. While USDA beef is of a good quality, fowl tends to be battery-tough, and most fish is overcooked and has the consistency of a baseball bat. What are also definitely *not* luxurious are the endless packets of sugar, and packets (instead of glass jars) of breakfast jam, marmalade and honey, and poor quality teas. While these may be suitable for a family diner, they do not belong aboard a ship that claims to have "award-winning cuisine." Dessert and pastry items are of good quality (specifically for American tastes), although there is much use of canned fruits and jellies. Forget the selection of "international" cheeses, however, as most of it didn't come from anywhere other than the USA – a country better known for its processed, highly colored slices than for fine cheesemaking. Note that Holland America Line can provide Kosher meals, but these are prepared ashore, frozen, and brought to your table sealed in their original containers (there is no Kosher kitchen on board).

The alternative, casual-dress Marco Polo Restaurant seats 88, and there is no charge, although reservations *are* required. It is created in the style of a California artists' bistro and provides Italian cuisine (this has a set menu together with nightly specials). Passengers thus have more choice and an occasional change of venue (anyone booking suite-grade accommodation get priority reservations).

In addition, there is the Lido Buffet, self-serve café that has proved popular aboard all Holland America Line ships for casual breakfasts and luncheons. There is also an outdoor grill for those who enjoy hamburgers, hot dogs and other grilled fast-food items. The Lido Buffet is also open for casual dinners on each night except for the last one, in an open-seating arrangement. Tables are set with crisp linens, flatware and stemware. A set menu includes a choice of four entrées.

OTHER COMMENTS: This is the third ship of the same name for Holland America Line and the first of the evolving generation after the *Statendam*-class ships. Its sister ship is *Zaandam*. The ship's name *Volendam* is derived from the fishing village of the same name, located north of Amsterdam, Holland. The hull is dark blue, in keeping with all Holland America Line ships. Although similar in size to the line's flagship *Rotterdam*, this ship has a single funnel, not unlike that found aboard the company's much smaller *Noordam*.

Having been built to approximately the same size as the company's newest *Rotterdam*, the same layout and public rooms have been incorporated into the interiors. This carries on the same flow and comfortable feeling so passengers will immediately feel at home aboard almost any ship in the Holland America Line fleet.

Volendam features three principal passenger stairways, which is so much better than two stairways, particularly the viewpoints of safety, accessibility and passenger flow. There is a magrodome-covered pool on the Lido Deck between the mast and the ship's funnel. The health spa facilities are quite extensive, and include gymnasium, separate saunas and steam rooms for men and women, and more treatment rooms (each has a shower and toilet). Practice tennis courts can be fund outdoor, as well as the traditional shuffleboard courts, and jogging track, not to mention a full wrap-around teakwood promenade deck.

The principal interior design theme is flowers, from the 17th to the 21st centuries. The interior focal point is a huge crystal sculpture, "Caleido," in the three-deck-high atrium, by one of Italy's leading contemporary glass artists, Luciano Vistosi. The health spa facilities include more treatment rooms (each has a shower and toilet).

In the casino bar (also known as the ship's sports bar), a cinematic theme presents visions of Hollywood, and includes a collection of costumes, props, photos and posters of movies and the stars who made them.

At the Lido Deck swimming pool, leaping dolphins are the focal point, but they are of a different design to that seen aboard the *Statendam*-class ships. The pool itself is also one deck higher than the *S*-class ships, with the positive result being the fact that there is now direct access between the aft and midships pools (not so aboard the *S*-class ships).

This ship is perhaps best for older passengers who seek safe, pleasant surroundings and food that is not too adventurous. Holland America Line provides complimentary cappuccino and espresso coffees, and free ice cream during certain hours of the day aboard its ships, as well as hot hors d'oeuvres in all bars – something other major lines seem to have dropped, or charge extra for.

Gratuities are extra, and they are added to your shipboard account at $10–$13 per day, according to the accommodation grade chosen. Refreshingly, the company does not add an automatic 15 percent gratuity for beverage purchases. Perhaps the ship's best asset is its friendly and personable Filipino and Indonesian crew, although communication can prove frustrating at times.

The onboard currency is the US dollar.

WEAK POINTS: Standing in line for embarkation, disembarkation, shore tenders and for self-serve buffet meals is an inevitable aspect of cruising aboard all large ships. The entertainment is still a weak point. Communication with staff is not easy. Room service is poor. The charge to use the washing machines and dryers in the self-service launderette is really petty and irritating, particularly for the occupants of suites, as they pay high prices for their cruises.

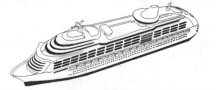

Voyager of the Seas
★★★★

Large Ship: . . . . .137,280 tons
Lifestyle: . . . . .Standard
Cruise Line: Royal Caribbean International
Former Names: . . . . .none
Builder: . . .Kvaerner Masa-Yards (Finland)
Original Cost: . . . .$500 million
Entered Service: . . . . .Nov 1999
Registry: . . . . .The Bahamas
Length (ft/m): 1,020.6/311.1
Beam (ft/m): 155.5/47.4
Draft (ft/m): 28.8/8.8
Propulsion/Propellers: . . . . .diesel-electric
(42,000 kW)/3 azimuthing pods
(14 MW each)
Passenger Decks: 14

Total Crew: 1,176
Passengers
(lower beds/all berths): 3,114/3,838
Passenger Space Ratio
(lower beds/all berths): 44.0/35.7
Crew/Passenger Ratio
(lower beds/all berths): 2.6/3.2
Navigation Officers: . . . . . .Scandinavian
Cabins (total): 1,557
Size Range (sq ft/m): 151.0–1,358.0/
14.0–126.1
Cabins (outside view): 939
Cabins (interior/no view): 618
Cabins (for one person): 0
Cabins (with private balcony): 757

Cabins (wheelchair accessible): 26
Cabin Current: . . . . .110 volts
Elevators: . . . . .14 (6 glass-enclosed)
Casino (gaming tables): . . . . .Yes
Slot Machines: . . . . .Yes
Swimming Pools (outdoors): 3
Swimming Pools (indoors): 0
Whirlpools: 6
Fitness Center: . . . . .Yes
Sauna/Steam Room: . . . . .Yes/Yes
Massage: . . . . .Yes
Self-Service Launderette: . . . . .No
Dedicated Cinema/Seats: . . . . .No
Library: . . . . .Yes
Classification Society: Det Norske Veritas

OVERALL SCORE: 1,537 (OUT OF A POSSIBLE 2,000 POINTS)

ACCOMMODATION: There is a wide range of 22 cabin categories, in four major groupings: Premium ocean-view suites and cabins, interior (atrium-view) cabins, Ocean-view cabins, and Interior (no view) cabins. Note that many cabins are of a similar size (good for incentives and large groups), and 300 have interconnecting doors (good for families.

A total of 138 interior (no view) cabins have bay windows that look *into* an interior horizontal atrium – a cruise industry first when the ship debuted. Regardless of what cabin grade you choose, however, all except for the Royal Suite and Owner's Suite have twin beds that convert to a queen-sized unit, television, radio and telephone, personal safe, vanity unit, hairdryer and private bathroom.

The largest accommodation includes luxuriously appointed penthouse suites (whose occupants, sadly, must share the rest of the ship with everyone else, except for their own exclusive, and private, concierge club). The grandest is the Royal Suite, positioned on the port side of the ship. It has a king-sized bed in a separate, large bedroom, a living room with an additional queen-sized sofa bed, baby grand piano (no pianist is included, however), refrigerator/wet bar, dining table, entertainment center, and large bathroom.

The 10 slightly smaller, but still highly desirable Owner's Suites (located in the center of the ship, on both port and starboard sides) and the four Royal Family suites have similar items. However, the four Royal Family suites, which have two bedrooms (including one with third/fourth upper Pullman berths) are located at

BERLITZ'S RATINGS

	Possible	Achieved
Ship	500	431
Accommodation	200	160
Food	400	252
Service	400	294
Entertainment	100	83
Cruise	400	317

the stern of the ship and have magnificent views over the ship's wash.

All cabins have a private bathroom, as well as interactive television and pay-per-view movies, including an X-rated channel, where you must enter a "pin" code to prevent children from watching. Some grades have a refrigerator/mini-bar, although there is no space left in the refrigerator, because it is stocked with "take-and-pay" items. Note: if you take anything from the mini-bar/refrigerator on the day of embarkation in Miami, Florida sales tax will be added to your bill. Cabins with "private balconies" should note that they are not so private, as the partitions are only partial, leaving you exposed to your neighbor's smoke or conversation. The balcony decking is made of Bolidt – a sort of rubberized sand – and not wood, while the balcony rail is of wood.

DINING: The main dining room is extremely large and is set on three levels, each with an operatic name and theme: Carmen, La Boheme and Magic Flute. All are connected by a dramatic three-deck high staircase – but all three have the same menus and food. The dining room is totally non-smoking and there are two seatings.

The cuisine is typical of mass banquet catering that offers standard fare comparable to that found in American family-style restaurants ashore. The menu descriptions make the food sound better than it is (which is consistently below average), mostly disappointing and without much taste – the result of controlled food costs as well as the use of many mixes and pre-prepared items. However, a decent selection of light meals is provided, and a vegetarian menu is available. The selection of breads, rolls, fruit and cheese is quite poor and could do more improvement. Caviar (once a standard menu item) incur a hefty extra charge. Menus typically include a Welcome Aboard Dinner, French Dinner, Italian Dinner, International Dinner, Captain's Gala Dinner.

ALTERNATIVE DINING OPTIONS: Alternative dining options for casual and informal meals at all hours (according to company releases) include:
● *Cafe Promenade*: for continental breakfast, all-day pizzas and specialty coffees (provided in paper cups).
● *Windjammer Café*: for casual buffet-style breakfast, lunch and light dinner (except for the cruise's last night).
● *Island Grill* (this is actually a section inside the Windjammer Café): for casual dinner (no reservations necessary) featuring a grill and open kitchen.
● *Portofino*: this is an "upscale" (non-smoking) Euro-Italian restaurant, for dinner only. Reservations are required, and a $6 gratuity per person is charged). The food and its presentation are better than the food in the dining room, although the restaurant is not large enough for all passengers to try even once during a cruise.
● *Johnny Rockets*, a retro 1950s all-day, all-night eatery that features hamburgers, malt shakes, and jukebox hits, with both indoor and outdoor seating, and all-singing, all-dancing waitresses that'll knock your socks off, if you can stand the noise.
● *Sprinkles*: for round-the-clock ice cream and yoghurt, pastries and coffee.

OTHER COMMENTS: *Voyager of the Seas* is a large, immensely impressive floating resort (one of five such ships, the others being *Explorer of the Seas* and *Adventure of the Seas*, which debuted in 2000 and 2001 respectively, and two more to follow). The exterior design is not unlike an enlarged version of the company's *Vision*-class ships. It is the largest cruise vessel in the world in terms of tonnage measurement (although, to keep things in perspective, it is not quite as long as the Norwegian Cruise Line's *Norway*, and will be eclipsed in 2004 by *Queen Mary 2*). After a difficult life in the shipyard, where a fire caused havoc and necessitated the replacement of some 80 cabins and the whole of the main restaurant, the ship debuted without further problems.

Its propulsion is derived from three pod units, powered by electric motors (two azimuthing, and one fixed at the centerline) instead of conventional rudders and propellers, in the latest configuration of high-tech propulsion systems.

With its large proportions, it provides more facilities and options, and caters to more passengers than any other Royal Caribbean International ship has in the past, and yet the ship manages to have a healthy passenger space ratio (the amount of space per passenger). It is simply too large to go through the Panama Canal, thus limiting itineraries almost exclusively to the Caribbean (where few islands can accept it), or for use as a floating island resort. Spend the first few hours wandering exploring all the many facilities and public spaces aboard this vessel and it will be time well spent.

Although this is a large ship, even the accommodation hallways are attractive, with artwork cabinets and wavy corridors to break the monotony. In fact, there are plenty of decorative touches to help you avoid what would otherwise be a clinical environment.

At certain times, passengers are allowed to stand right at the bow of the ship at the observation point, perhaps with arms spread in an "eagle-like" position, just like the stars in the film *Titanic*. What a photo opportunity! However, for the best ones, as in in the film, you'll need to bring a helicopter. Those seeking a view of the navigation bridge can see what's happening from a special spot above the bridge.

Embarkation and disembarkation take place through two stations/access points, designed to minimize the inevitable lines at the start and end of the cruise (that's over 1,500 people for each access point). Once inside the ship, you'll need good walking shoes, particularly when you need to go from one end to the other – it really is quite a long way.

The four-decks-high Royal Promenade, the interior focal point of the ship, is a good place to arrange to meet someone. It is 394 ft (120 meters) long – the length of two football fields, and has two internal lobbies (atria) that rise to as many as 11 decks high, one at each end. There are 16 elevators in four banks of four. The entrance to one of three levels of the main restaurant, together with shops and entertainment locations are spun off from this "boulevard," while interior "with-view" cabins (with rather useless bay windows) look into it from above.

It houses a traditional English "pub" ("Pig 'n' Whistle), a Champagne Bar, a Sidewalk Café (for continental breakfast, all-day pizzas and specialty coffees), Sprinkles (for round-the-clock ice-cream and yoghurt), Scoreboard (a sports bar), Spinners (a revolving gaming arcade) and a captain's balcony arched across the promenade. There are also several shops – jewelry shop, gift shop, liquor shop and a logo souvenir shop, as well as a bright red telephone kiosk that houses an ATM cash machine. Altogether, it's a nice place to see and be seen, and street performers complete the scene. It really is a cross between a shopping arcade and an amusement park (Florida's Aventura meets New York's Coney Island crowd). The chairman of Royal Caribbean International even donated his own beloved Morgan sports car to grace the Royal Promenade (which is supposedly designed in the image of London's fashionable Burlington Arcade). Actually, by far the best view of the whole promenade is from one of the 138 premium-price cabins that look into it, or from a "captain's bridge" that crosses above it.

The ship's Casino Royale is large. Gaming includes blackjack, Caribbean stud poker, craps, and roulette (including the world's largest interactive roulette wheel that is activated by a roulette ball tower four decks high).

For the more sporting, youthful passengers, there is

activity galore – including a rock-climbing wall that's 32.8 ft high (10 meters), with five separate climbing tracks. It is located outdoors at the aft end of the funnel. You'll get a great "buzz" being 200 ft (60 meters) above the ocean while the ship is moving. There is a 30-minute instruction period before anyone is allowed to climb, and this is done in pairs. The cost: it's free, and all safety gear is included.

Other sports facilities include a roller-blading track, a dive-and-snorkel shop, a full-size basketball court and 9-hole, par 26 golf course; there's also a roller-blading track, and a dive-and-snorkel shop. A 15,000 sq.-ft (1,400 sq.-meter) health spa includes a large aerobics room, fitness center (with the usual stairmasters, treadmills, stationary bikes, weight machines and free weights), treatment rooms, men's and women's sauna/steam rooms, while another 10,000 sq. ft (930 sq. meters) of space is devoted to a relaxing Solarium.

The 1,350-seat show lounge is five decks high. It has hydraulic pit and stage areas, and is decorated in the style of the La Scala opera house in Milan. A second show lounge (Studio B, a regulation-size ice-skating rink that features real, not fake, ice) has arena seating for up to 900, and the latest in broadcast facilities. A number of slim pillars obstruct the clear-view arena stage sight lines, however. An Ice Follies show is presented by a professional ice-skating show team each cruise.

If ice-skating in the Caribbean doesn't particularly appeal, you might like to visit the stunning two-deck library (it's the first aboard any ship, and is open 24 hours a day). A whopping $12 million has been spent on permanent artwork.

Drinking places include a neat Aquarium Bar, complete with 50 tons of glass and water in four large aquariums (whose combined value is over $1 million). Other drinking places include the small and intimate Champagne Bar, Crown & Anchor Pub, and a Connoisseur Club – for cigars and cognacs. Lovers of jazz might appreciate High Notes, an intimate room for cool music, or the Schooner Bar piano lounge. Golfers might enjoy the 19th Hole, a golf bar.

There is a large television studio, located adjacent to rooms that can be used for trade show exhibit space. Lovers could tie the knot in a wedding chapel in the sky, the Skylight Chapel (it's located on the upper level of the Viking Crown Lounge).

Families with children, and the children's facilities are extensive. "Aquanauts" is for 3–5 year olds. "Explorers" is for 6–8 year olds. "Voyagers" is for 9–12 year olds. "Optix" is a dedicated area for teenagers, including a daytime club (with computers), soda bar, disk jockey and dance floor. "Challenger's Arcade" features an array of the latest video games. "Virtual Submarine" is a virtual reality underwater center for all ages. "Computer Lab" has 14 computer stations loaded with fun and games. "Paint and Clay" is an arts and crafts center for younger children. Adjacent to these indoor areas is "Adventure Beach," an area for all the family to enjoy: it includes swimming pools, a water slide and game areas outdoors.

Royal Caribbean International has, since its inception, always been an innovator in the cruise industry, and will probably remain so with this new vessel, the first of three such ships to be placed into service by the company. *Voyager of the Seas* operates 7-night western Caribbean cruises year-round from Miami.

In terms of sheer size, this ship presently dwarfs all other ships in the cruise industry, but in terms of personal service, the reverse is the case, unless you happen to reside in one of the top suites. Royal Caribbean International does, however, try hard to provide a good standard of programmed service from its hotel staff. This is impersonal city life at sea, and a superb, well-designed alternative to a land-based resort, which is what the company wanted to build. Welcome to the real, escapist world of highly programmed resort living aboard ship. Perhaps if you dare to go outside, you might even be able to see the sea – now there's a novelty! Remember to take lots of extra pennies: you'll need them to pay for all the additional-cost items. The on-board currency is the US dollar.

The ship is large, so remember that if you meet someone somewhere, and want to meet them again you'll need to make an appointment – for this really is a large, Las Vegas-style American floating resort-city for the lively of heart and fleet of foot. Good advice is to arrange to meet somewhere along the Royal Promenade.

WEAK POINTS: Standing in line for embarkation, disembarkation, shore tenders and for self-serve buffet meals is an inevitable aspect of cruising aboard all large ships. Check-in, embarkation (better if you are a non-US resident and stay at an RCI-booked hotel, as you will complete all formalities there and simply walk on board to your cabin) and disembarkation (non-US citizens can be held up for over an hour by slow US Immigration processing in the terminal after leaving the ship). Suites and cabins with private balcony have Bolidt floors (a substance that looks like rubberized sand) instead of wood. If you have a cabin with a door that interconnecting door to another cabin, be aware that you'll be able to hear *everything* your next-door neighbors say and do. Bathroom toilets are explosively noisy.

You'll need to plan what you want to take part in wisely as almost everything requires you to sign-up in advance (many activities take place only on sea days). The cabin bath towels are small and skimpy. There are very few quiet places to sit and read (almost everywhere there is intrusive acoustic wallpaper (background music). Although the menus and food variety offered have been upgraded since the ship's introduction, remember that you get what you pay for. Food costs are well below that for Celebrity Cruises, for example, and so you should not expect the same food quality.

Wilderness Adventurer
★★

Small Ship: ....89.5 tons	Passengers	Cabin Current: ....110 volts
Lifestyle: ....Standard	(lower beds/all berths): 68/76	Elevators: 0
Cruise Line: ....Glacier Bay Cruises	Passenger Space Ratio	Casino (gaming tables): ....No
Former Names: ....*Caribbean Prince*	(lower beds/all berths): 1.1/1.0	Slot Machines: ....No
Builder: ....Blount Shipyards (USA)	Crew/Passenger Ratio	Swimming Pools (outdoors): 0
Original Cost: ....$6 million	(lower beds/all berths): 3.4/3.8	Swimming Pools (indoors): 0
Entered Service: 1983/1997	Navigation Officers: ....American	Whirlpools: 0
Registry: ....USA	Cabins (total): 34	Fitness Center: 0
Length (ft/m): 156.6/47.7	Size Range (sq ft/m): 70.0–88.0/	Sauna/Steam Room: ....No/No
Beam (ft/m): 38.0/11.0	6.5–8.1	Massage: ....No
Draft (ft/m): 6.5/1.8	Cabins (outside view): 30	Self-Service Launderette: ....No
Propulsion/Propellers: ....diesel	Cabins (interior/no view): 4	Dedicated Cinema/Seats: ....No
(1,472kW)/1	Cabins (for one person): 0	Library: ....Yes
Passenger Decks: 3	Cabins (with private balcony): 0	Classification Society: . .American Bureau
Total Crew: 20	Cabins (wheelchair accessible): 0	of Shipping

OVERALL SCORE: 939 (OUT OF A POSSIBLE 2,000 POINTS)

ACCOMMODATION: The cabins (there are only three types to choose from – one on each of three decks) really are utilitarian, *ultra-tiny*, no-frills units that are just about adequate if you are not used to, or do not want, anything better. While 14 cabins have a double bed, all others have two lower beds, and 8 also have an upper (Pullman) berth. Each cabin has a private bathroom, although these really are minuscule. There is no room service for food or snack items.

BERLITZ'S RATINGS

	Possible	Achieved
Ship	500	181
Accommodation	200	83
Food	400	204
Service	400	214
Entertainment	N/A	N/A
Cruise	500	257

DINING: The dining room has minimal décor, but the open-seating policy means you can dine with whomever you wish, in a single seating. The cuisine is decidedly plain and simple American fare, as is the cutlery (no fish knifes are used, for example), but it is rather tasty. This is because the ingredients are all fresh. A full-service bar provides wines and other alcoholic beverages.

OTHER COMMENTS: This vessel, built for the American Canadian Caribbean Line, is good for real in-depth, up-close cruising along the coastline of Alaska. One bonus is the fact that at the bow of the vessel, a "bow gangway" comes into its own for landing passengers. The ship is also equipped with a unique, retractable wheelhouse for passage under low bridges on inland waterways, and there is also a platform for those who want to swim off the stern. A fleet of two-person kayaks is carried, for up-close, in-your-face personal exploration of the Alaska shoreline. Water sports facilities include a glass-bottom boat/sunfish sailboat (not used on Alaska itineraries).

The dress code is absolutely casual (not even a jacket for men is needed, and no ties, please). There is an ample supply of snorkeling gear, so there is really no need to take your own (Mexico's Sea of Cortez itineraries only – from January through March).

Make sure that you take comfortable walking shoes, as well as photographic materials for wildlife spotting (particularly in Alaska).

Glacier Bay Crusies (formerly known as Alaska's Glacier Bay Tours and Cruises) has, since 1996, been owned by Goldbelt, an Alaska Tlingit Indian company. The cruises are *very* expensive (particularly when compared with other ships operating in the same areas), and are for those who want to up close to nature and wildlife, in a small environment (note that all shore excursions are included, however). All tips are pooled and shared among all the staff, using the amounts recommended in the cruise line's brochure of $8–12 per passenger, per day, which is high for the services offered. The onboard currency is the US dollar.

WEAK POINTS: There is an almost constant throbbing from the diesel engines/generator. Remember that there is no doctor on board, and so anyone with medical problems should really not consider this vessel.

Wilderness Discoverer
★★

Small Ship: ....99 tons	Passengers	Cabin Current: ....110 volts
Lifestyle: ....Standard	(lower beds/all berths): 84/98	Elevators: 0
Cruise Line: ....Glacier Bay Cruises	Passenger Space Ratio	Casino (gaming tables): ....No
Former Names: ....*Mayan Prince*	(lower beds/all berths): 1.1/1.0	Slot Machines: ....No
Builder: ....Blount Industries (USA)	Crew/Passenger Ratio	Swimming Pools (outdoors): 0
Original Cost: ....$7.5 million	(lower beds/all berths): 4.2/4.4	Swimming Pools (indoors): 0
Entered Service: ......June 1992/1998	Navigation Officers: ....American	Whirlpools: 0
Registry:........................USA	Cabins (total): 42	Fitness Center: ....No
Length (ft/m): 169.0/51.5	Size Range (sq ft/m): 88.0–196.0/	Sauna/Steam Room: ....No/No
Beam (ft/m): 38.0/11.5	8.1–18.2	Massage: ....No
Draft (ft/m): 6.7/2.0	Cabins (outside view): 37	Self-Service Launderette: ....No
Propulsion/Propellers: ....diesel	Cabins (interior/no view): 5	Dedicated Cinema/Seats: ....No
(1,472kW)/1	Cabins (for one person): 0	Library: ....Yes
Passenger Decks:...................3	Cabins (with private balcony): 0	Classification Society: . .American Bureau
Total Crew: 22	Cabins (wheelchair accessible): 0	of Shipping

---

OVERALL SCORE: 939 (OUT OF A POSSIBLE 2,000 POINTS)

ACCOMMODATION: There are four cabin grades spread over three decks, and all are dimensionally challenged, so take only the most minimal amount of clothing and personal effects you possible can. There are six cabins on the lowest deck that do not have a window, and they are *really tiny*. While 7 cabins have a double bed, all others have two lower beds, and several also have an upper (Pullman) berth. There is no room service for food or snack items or beverages. The air-conditioning consists of re-circulated air, much like that found aboard aircraft, and is, therefore, not very fresh. Each cabin has its own private bathroom, although these really are minuscule.

DINING: The dining room is mildly attractive and has a single, open seating policy (so you can dine with whomever you wish). The food is reasonably sound Americana fare, with good presentation and decent creativity. Wines and other alcoholic drinks are obtainable from a full-service bar.

OTHER COMMENTS: This vessel, originally built for the American Canadian Caribbean Line, based on the US east coast, is small and squat, has a shallow draft, being

BERLITZ'S RATINGS

	Possible	Achieved
Ship	500	181
Accommodation	200	83
Food	400	204
Service	400	214
Entertainment	N/A	N/A
Cruise	500	257

designed specifically for in-depth coastal cruising. It is equipped with a unique, retractable wheelhouse, although this is no longer used. In 2001 it acquired a floating dock, and a small fleet of kayaks and Zodiac landing craft.

A cruise aboard the ship is for those who really enjoy the camaraderie of others. There is very little service, and no entertainment. Indeed, unless you go to your cabin, there is no getting away from other passengers. Take only very casual clothing, as the attire is strictly non-dressy.

Glacier Bay Cruises (formerly known as Alaska's Glacier Bay Tours and Cruises) has, since 1996, been owned by Goldbelt, an Alaska Tlingit Indian company. *Wilderness Discoverer* presently operates five-night round-trip cruises from Juneau, to Haines, Skagway, Sitka, Glacier Bay and Tracy Arm, Alaska during the summer. The cruises are *very* expensive (particularly when compared with other ships operating in the same areas), and are for those who want to up close to nature and wildlife, in a small environment (note that all shore excursions are included, however).

Gratuities are expected, at about $8–$12 per person, per day. The onboard currency is the US dollar.

Wind Song
★★★★

Renamed 2006

Small Ship: . . . . .5,350 tons	Main Propulsion: . . . . . .a) engines/b) sails	Cabins (interior/no view): 0
Lifestyle: . . . . .Premium	Propulsion/Propellers: . . . . .diesel-electric	Cabins (for one person): 0
Cruise Line: . . . . .Windstar Cruises	(1,400kW)/1	Cabins (with private balcony): 0
Former Names: . . . . .none	Passenger Decks: 5	Cabins (wheelchair accessible): 0
Builder: . . . .Ateliers et Chantiers du Havre	Total Crew: 88	Cabin Current: . . . . .110 volts
(France)	Passengers	Casino (gaming tables): . . . . .Yes
Original Cost: . . . .$34.2 million	(lower beds/all berths): 148/159	Slot Machines: . . . . .Yes
Entered Service: . . . . .July 1987	Passenger Space Ratio	Swimming Pools (outdoors): . .1 (dip pool)
Registry: . . . . .The Bahamas	(lower beds/all berths): 36.1/33.6	Whirlpools: 1
Length (ft/m): 439.6/134.0	Crew/Passenger Ratio	Fitness Center: . . . . .Yes
Beam (ft/m): 51.8/15.8	(lower beds/all berths): 1.6/1.8	Sauna/Steam Room: . . . . .Yes/No
Draft (ft/m): 13.4/4.1	Navigation Officers: . . . . .European	Massage: . . . . .Yes
Type of Vessel: . . . . . .computer-controlled	Cabins (total): 74	Self-Service Launderette: . . . . .No
sail-cruiser	Size Range (sq ft/m): 182.9–220.6/	Library: . . . . .Yes
No. of Masts: . . . . . .4/6 self-furling sails	17.0–20.5	Classification Society: . . . .Bureau Veritas
Sail Area (sq ft/m2): 21,489/1,996.4	Cabins (outside view): 74	

OVERALL SCORE: 1,518 (OUT OF A POSSIBLE 2,000 POINTS)

ACCOMMODATION: Regardless of the category you choose, all cabins are very nicely equipped, have crisp, inviting décor, and a mini-bar/refrigerator (stocked when you embark, but all drinks are at extra cost), 24-hour room service, personal safe, television (with CNN, when available, for news) that rotates so that it is viewable from the bed and the bathroom, video player, compact disc player, plenty of storage space, and two portholes. The cabins all have two portholes with outside views, and dead-lights (steel covers that provide a complete blackout at night and can be closed in inclement weather conditions). The décor is a pleasant mix of rich woods, natural fabrics and colorful soft furnishings, and hi-tech yacht-style amenities. However, note that some of the cabinetry is looking a little tired, and has that "I've been varnished many times look." A basket of fruit is provided, and replenished daily.

The bathrooms are compact units, designed in a figure of eight, with a teakwood floor in the central section. There is a good amount of storage space for personal toiletry items in two cabinets, as well as under-sink cupboard space; a wall-mounted hairdryer is also provided. The shower enclosure (no cabins have bathtubs) is circular (like many of today's passengers), and has both a hand-held, as well as a fixed shower (so you can wash your hair without getting the rest of your body wet). Soap, shampoo and après-sun soothing lotion is provided, as is a vanity kit and shower cap. Note, however, that the lighting is not strong enough for women to apply

BERLITZ'S RATINGS

	Possible	Achieved
Ship	500	382
Accommodation	200	164
Food	400	295
Service	400	300
Entertainment	N/A	N/A
Cruise	500	377

make-up – this is better applied at the vanity desk in the cabin, which has stronger overhead (halogen) lighting. Bathrobes and towels are of 100 percent cotton.

DINING: There is one rather chic and elegant dining room (The Restaurant), with ocean views from large, picture windows, a lovely wood ceiling and wood paneling on the walls. California-style nouvelle cuisine is served, with dishes that are attractively presented. Additionally, "signature" dishes, created by master chefs Joachim Splichal and Jeanne Jones, are offered daily. Open seating means you dine when you want and with whomever you wish to.

When the company first started, European waiters provided service with practiced European finesse. However, those waiters have been replaced by Indonesians and Filipinos, whose communication skills at times can prove frustrating, although the service is pleasant enough. The selection of breads, cheeses, and fruits could be better. There is a big push to sell wines, although the prices are extremely high, as they are for most alcoholic drinks (even bottled water is the highest in the industry, at $7 per liter bottle).

There is often casual dinner on the open deck under the stars, with grilled seafood and steaks. At the bars, hot and cold hors d'oeuvres appear at cocktail times.

OTHER COMMENTS: *Wind Song* is one of three identical vessels (a fourth, *Wind Saga*, was never built). This is a long, sleek-looking craft that is part-yacht, part-cruise ship, with four giant masts that tower 170 ft (52 meters) above the deck (they are actually 204 ft, or 62 meters) high, and fitted with computer-controlled sails; the masts, sails and rigging alone cost $5 million. The computer keeps the ship on an even keel (via the movement of a water hydraulic ballast system of 142,653 gallons/540,000 liters), so there is no heeling (rolling) over 6 degrees.

There is little open deck space when the ship is full, due to the amount of complex sail machinery. There is a tiny dip pool. At the stern is a small water sports platform for those who enjoy all the goodies the ship offers (but only when at anchor, and only in really calm sea conditions). Water sports facilities include a banana boat kayaks, sunfish sailboats, windsurf boards, water ski boat, scuba and snorkel equipment, and four Zodiacs. You will be asked to sign a waiver if you wish to use the water sports equipment.

The interior is finely crafted, with pleasing, blond woods, together with soft, complementary colors and décor that is chic, even elegant, but a little cold. Note that the main lounge aboard *Wind Star* is of a different design than *Wind Song* and *Wind Spirit*.

No scheduled activities help to make this a real relaxing, unregimented "get away from it all" vacation. The Windstar ships will cruise you in extremely comfortable surroundings that are bordering on contemporary luxury, yet in an unstructured environment. They will provide a very relaxing, virtually unstructured cruise experience that is just right for seven idyllic nights in sheltered areas (but can be disturbing when a Windstar vessel is in small ports with several huge cruise ships). This ship is ideal for couples who do not like large ships. The dress code is casual (no jackets and ties required), even for dinner (the brochure states casual elegance). There are no formal nights or theme nights.

You will probably be under sail for less than 40 percent of the time (conditions and cruise area winds permitting). Gratuities are "not required" by the friendly, smiling staff, according to the brochure, but passengers find they are always accepted. The onboard currency is the US dollar.

WEAK POINTS: There is very little open deck space, and the swimming pool is really only a tiny "dip" pool. Be prepared for the "whine" of the vessel's generators, which are needed to run the air-conditioning and lighting systems 24 hours a day. That means you will also hear it at night in your cabin (any cabin), and takes most passengers a day or two to get used to. Beverage prices are high.

The library is small, and needs more hardback fiction. Although the staff is friendly, they are casual and a little sloppy in the finer points of service at times.

● **Note: In late 2002, after this book was completed, *Wind Song* caught fire and became a constructive total loss.**

WATER MUSIC

Tall ship lovers who are also music lovers may like to know about "The Tall Ship Suite," a work in three movements: The Race Begins (10 mins, 24 secs); The Open Sea (10 mins, 42 secs); Landfall and the Grand Parade of Sail (6 mins, 28 secs). It was jointly composed and orchestrated by Dave Roylance and Bob Gavin. The two composers met in Liverpool in 1980 and composed the suite in 1992 in commemoration of the Grand Regatta Columbus '92. The work, played by the Royal Liverpool Philharmonic Orchestra conducted by Bill Conifer, is available on compact disc.

Also on the disc are two other works by the same composing team: "Ocean Fantasia," a tone poem (18 mins,19 secs), and "Voyager," an orchestral piece (8 mins,11 secs). With strong themes and excellent scoring, this music should be in every tall ship lover's music library.

Wind Spirit
★★★★

Removed 2006

Small Ship: . . . . .5,350 tons	Main Propulsion: . . . . . .a) engines/b) sails	Cabins (interior/no view): 0
Lifestyle: . . . . .Premium	Propulsion/Propellers: . . . . .diesel-electric	Cabins (for one person): 0
Cruise Line: . . . . .Windstar Cruises	(1,400kW)/1	Cabins (with private balcony): 0
Former Names: . . . . .none	Passenger Decks: 5	Cabins (wheelchair accessible): 0
Builder: . . . . .Ateliers et Chantiers	Total Crew: 88	Cabin Current: . . . . .110 volts
du Havre (France)	Passengers	Casino (gaming tables): . . . . .Yes
Original Cost: . . . .$34.2 million	(lower beds/all berths): 148/159	Slot Machines: . . . . .Yes
Entered Service: . . . . .Apr 1988	Passenger Space Ratio	Swimming Pools (outdoors): . .1 (dip pool)
Registry: . . . . .The Bahamas	(lower beds/all berths): 36.1/33.6	Whirlpools: 1
Length (ft/m): 439.6/134.0	Crew/Passenger Ratio	Fitness Center: . . . . .Yes
Beam (ft/m): 51.8/15.8	(lower beds/all berths): 1.6/1.8	Sauna/Steam Room: . . . . .Yes/No
Draft (ft/m): 13.4/4.1	Navigation Officers: . . . . .European	Massage: . . . . .Yes
Type of Vessel: . . . . .computer-controlled	Cabins (total): 74	Self-Service Launderette: . . . . .No
sail-cruiser	Size Range (sq ft/m): 185.0–220.0/	Library: . . . . .Yes
No. of Masts: . . . . . .4/6 self-furling sails	17.0–22.5	Classification Society: . . . .Bureau Veritas
Sail Area (sq ft/m2): 21,489/1,996.4	Cabins (outside view): 74	

OVERALL SCORE: 1,518 (OUT OF A POSSIBLE 2,000 POINTS)

ACCOMMODATION: Regardless of the category you choose, all cabins are very nicely equipped, have crisp, inviting décor, and a mini-bar/refrigerator (stocked when you embark, but all drinks are at extra cost), 24-hour room service, personal safe, television (with CNN, when available, for news) that rotates so that it is viewable from the bed and the bathroom, video player, compact disc player, plenty of storage space, and two portholes. The cabins all have two portholes with outside views, and deadlights (steel covers that provide a complete blackout at night and can be closed in inclement weather conditions). The décor is a pleasant mix of rich woods, natural fabrics and colorful soft furnishings, and hi-tech yacht-style amenities. However, note that some of the cabinetry is looking a little tired, and has that "I've been varnished many times look." A basket of fruit is provided, and replenished daily.

The bathrooms are compact units, designed in a figure of eight, with a teakwood floor in the central section. There is a good amount of storage space for personal toiletry items in two cabinets, as well as under-sink cupboard space; a wall-mounted hairdryer is also provided. The shower enclosure (no cabins have bathtubs) is circular (like many of today's passengers), and features both a hand-held as well as a fixed shower (so you can wash your hair without getting the rest of your body wet). Soap, shampoo and après-sun soothing lotion is provided, as is a vanity kit and shower cap. Note, however, that the lighting is not strong enough for women to

BERLITZ'S RATINGS		
	Possible	Achieved
Ship	500	382
Accommodation	200	164
Food	400	295
Service	400	300
Entertainment	N/A	N/A
Cruise	500	377

apply make-up – this is better applied at the vanity desk in the cabin, which has stronger overhead (halogen) lighting. Bathrobes and towels are of 100 percent cotton.

DINING: There is one rather chic and elegant dining room (The Restaurant), with ocean views from large, picture windows, a lovely wood ceiling and wood paneling on the walls. California-style nouvelle cuisine is served, with dishes that are attractively presented. Additionally, "signature" dishes, created by master chefs Joachim Splichal and Jeanne Jones, are offered daily. Open seating means you dine when you want and with whomever you wish to.

When the company first started, European waiters provided service with practiced European finesse. However, those waiters have been replaced by Indonesians and Filipinos, whose communication skills at times can prove frustrating, although the service is pleasant enough. The selection of breads, cheeses, and fruits could be better. There is a big push to sell wines, although the prices are extremely high, as they are for most alcoholic drinks (even bottled water is the highest in the industry, at $7 per liter bottle).

There is often casual dinner on the open deck under the stars, with grilled seafood and steaks. At the bars, hot and cold hors d'oeuvres appear at cocktail times.

OTHER COMMENTS: *Wind Spirit* is one of three identical vessels (a fourth, *Wind Saga*, was never built). This is a long, sleek-looking craft that is part-yacht, part-cruise ship, with four giant masts that tower 170 ft (52 meters) above the deck (they are actually 204 ft, or 62 meters) high, and fitted with computer-controlled sails; the masts, sails and rigging alone cost $5 million. The computer keeps the ship on an even keel (via the movement of a water hydraulic ballast system of 142,653 gallons/540,000 liters), so there is no heeling (rolling) over 6 degrees.

There is little open deck space when the ship is full, due to the amount of complex sail machinery. There is a tiny dip pool. At the stern is a small water sports platform for those who enjoy all the goodies the ship offers (but only when at anchor and only in really calm sea conditions). Water sports facilities include a banana boat kayaks, sunfish sailboats, windsurf boards, water ski boat, scuba and snorkel equipment, and four Zodiacs. You will be asked to sign a waiver if you wish to use the water sports equipment.

The ship features a finely crafted interior with pleasing, blond woods, together with soft, complementary colors and decor that is chic, even elegant, but a little cold. Note that the main lounge aboard *Wind Star* is of a different design to that of *Wind Spirit*.

No scheduled activities help to make this a real relaxing, unregimented "get away from it all" vacation. The Windstar ships will help you to cruise in very comfortable, contemporary surroundings that are bordering on the luxurious, yet in an unstructured environment. They will provide a very relaxing, virtually unstructured cruise experience that is just right for seven idyllic nights in sheltered areas (but can be disturbing when a Windstar vessel is in small ports with several huge cruise ships). This ship is ideal for couples who do not like large ships. The dress code is casual (no jackets and ties required), even for dinner (the brochure states casual elegance). There are no formal nights or theme nights.

You will probably be under sail for less than 40 percent of the time (conditions and cruise area winds permitting). Gratuities are "not required" by the friendly, smiling staff, according to the brochure, but passengers find they are always accepted. The onboard currency is the US dollar.

WEAK POINTS: There is very little open deck space, and the swimming pool is really only a tiny "dip" pool. Be prepared for the "whine" of the vessel's generators, which are needed to run the air-conditioning and lighting systems 24 hours a day. That means you will also hear it at night in your cabin (any cabin), and takes most passengers a day or two to get used to.

Beverage prices are high. The library is small, and needs more hardback fiction. The staff, though friendly, is casual and a little sloppy at times in the finer points of service.

Wind Star
★★★★

Small Ship: ....5,350 tons	Main Propulsion: ......a) engines/b) sails	Cabins (interior/no view): 0
Lifestyle: ....Premium	Propulsion/Propellers: .....diesel-electric	Cabins (for one person): 0
Cruise Line: ....Windstar Cruises	(1,400kW)/1	Cabins (with private balcony): 0
Former Names: ....none	Passenger Decks: 5	Cabins (wheelchair accessible): 0
Builder: ....Ateliers et Chantiers	Total Crew: 88	Cabin Current: ....110 volts
du Havre (France)	Passengers	Casino (gaming tables): ....Yes
Original Cost: ....$34.2 million	(lower beds/all berths): 148/168	Slot Machines: ....Yes
Entered Service: ....Dec 1986	Passenger Space Ratio	Swimming Pools (outdoors): ..1 (dip pool)
Registry: ....The Bahamas	(lower beds/all berths): 36.1/33.6	Whirlpools: 1
Length (ft/m): 439.6/134.0	Crew/Passenger Ratio	Fitness Center: ....Yes
Beam (ft/m): 51.8/15.8	(lower beds/all berths): 1.6/1.8	Sauna/Steam Room: ....Yes/No
Draft (ft/m): 13.4/4.1	Navigation Officers: ....European	Massage:........................Yes
Type of Vessel: ......computer-controlled	Cabins (total): 74	Self-Service Launderette: ....No
sail-cruiser	Size Range (sq ft/m): 185.0–220.0/	Library: ....Yes
No. of Masts: ......4/6 self-furling sails	17.0–22.5	Classification Society: ....Bureau Veritas
Sail Area (sq ft/m2): 21,489/1,996.4	Cabins (outside view): 74	

OVERALL SCORE: 1,518 (OUT OF A POSSIBLE 2,000 POINTS)

ACCOMMODATION: Regardless of the category you choose, all cabins are very nicely equipped, have crisp, inviting décor, and a mini-bar/refrigerator (stocked when you embark, but all drinks are at extra cost), 24-hour room service, personal safe, television (with CNN, when available, for news) that rotates so that it is viewable from the bed and the bathroom, video player, compact disc player, plenty of storage space, and two portholes. The cabins all have two portholes with outside views, and deadlights (steel covers that provide a complete blackout at night and can be closed in inclement weather conditions). The décor is a pleasant mix of rich woods, natural fabrics and colorful soft furnishings, and hi-tech yacht-style amenities. However, note that some of the cabinetry is looking a little tired, and has that "I've been varnished many times look." A basket of fruit is provided, and replenished daily.

The bathrooms are compact units, designed in a figure of eight, with a teakwood floor in the central section. There is a good amount of storage space for personal toiletry items in two cabinets, as well as under-sink cupboard space; a wall-mounted hairdryer is also provided. The shower enclosure (no cabins have bathtubs) is circular (like many of today's passengers), and features both a hand-held, as well as a fixed shower (so you can wash your hair without getting the rest of your body wet). Soap, shampoo and après-sun soothing lotion is provided, as is a vanity kit and shower cap. Note, however, that the lighting is not strong enough for women to

BERLITZ'S RATINGS		
	Possible	Achieved
Ship	500	382
Accommodation	200	164
Food	400	295
Service	400	300
Entertainment	N/A	N/A
Cruise	500	377

apply make-up – this is better applied at the vanity desk in the cabin, which has stronger overhead (halogen) lighting. Bathrobes and towels are of 100 percent cotton.

DINING: There is one rather chic and elegant dining room (The Restaurant), with ocean views from large, picture windows, a lovely wood ceiling and wood paneling on the walls. California-style nouvelle cuisine is served, with dishes that are attractively presented. Additionally, "signature" dishes, created by master chefs Joachim Splichal and Jeanne Jones, are offered daily. Open seating means you dine when you want and with whomever you wish to. Both smoking and no-smoking sections are provided.

When the company debuted, European waiters provided service with practiced European finesse; however, those waiters have been replaced by Indonesians and Filipinos, whose communication skills at times can prove frustrating, although the service is pleasant enough. The selection of breads, cheeses, and fruits could be better. There is a big push to sell wines, although the prices are extremely high, as they are for most alcoholic drinks (even bottled water is the highest in the industry, at $7 per liter bottle).

Tthere is often casual dinner on the open deck under the stars, with grilled seafood and steaks. At the bars, hot and cold hors d'oeuvres appear at cocktail times.

OTHER COMMENTS: *Wind Star* is one of three identical vessels (a fourth, *Wind Saga*, was never built). This is a long, sleek-looking craft that is part-yacht, part-cruise ship, with four giant masts that tower 170 ft (52 meters) above the deck (they are actually 204 ft, or 62 meters) high, and fitted with computer-controlled sails; the masts, sails and rigging alone cost $5 million. The computer keeps the ship on an even keel (via the movement of a water hydraulic ballast system of 142,653 gallons/540,000 liters), so there is no heeling (rolling) over 6 degrees. When the masts for *Wind Star* (first of the three original Windstar vessels) were lowered into position, a US silver dollar, dated 1889, was placed under mast number two (the main mast).

There is little open deck space when the ship is full, due to the amount of complex sail machinery. There is a tiny dip pool. At the stern is a small water sports platform for those who enjoy all the goodies the ship offers (but only when at anchor, and only in really calm sea conditions). Water sports facilities include a banana boat kayaks, sunfish sailboats, windsurf boards, water ski boat, scuba and snorkel equipment, and four Zodiacs. You will be asked to sign a waiver if you wish to use the water sports equipment.

The ship has a finely crafted interior with pleasing, blond woods, together with soft, complementary colors and décor that is chic, even elegant, but a little cold. Note that the main lounge aboard *Wind Star* is of a different design to that of *Wind Spirit*.

No scheduled activities help to make this a real relaxing, unregimented "get away from it all" vacation. The Windstar ships will cruise you in extremely comfortable surroundings that are bordering on contemporary luxury, yet in an unstructured environment. They will provide a very relaxing, virtually unstructured cruise experience that is just right for seven idyllic nights in sheltered areas (but can be disturbing when a Windstar vessel is in small ports with several huge cruise ships). This ship is ideal for couples who do not like large ships. The dress code is casual (no jackets and ties required), even for dinner (the brochure states casual elegance). There are no formal nights or theme nights.

You will probably be under sail for less than 40 percent of the time (conditions and cruise area winds permitting). Gratuities are "not required" by the friendly, smiling staff, according to the brochure, but passengers find they are always accepted. The onboard currency is the US dollar.

WEAK POINTS: There is very little open deck space, and the swimming pool is really only a tiny "dip" pool. Be prepared for the "whine" of the vessel's generators, which are needed to run the air-conditioning and lighting systems 24 hours a day. That means you will also hear it at night in your cabin (any cabin), and takes most passengers a day or two to get used to.

Beverage prices are high. The library is small, and needs more hardback fiction. The staff, though friendly, is casual and can be a little sloppy at times in the finer points of service.

Wind Surf
★★★★ +

Small Ship: . . . . .14,745 tons	Main Propulsion: . . . . . .a) engines/b) sails	Cabins (for one person): 0
Lifestyle: . . . . .Premium	Propulsion/Propellers: diesel (9,120kW)/2	Cabins (with private balcony): 0
Cruise Line: . . . . .Windstar Cruises	Passenger Decks: 8	Cabins (wheelchair accessible): 0
Former Names: . . . .*Club Med I*	Total Crew: 163	Cabin Current: . . . . .220 volts
Builder: . . . . .Ateliers et Chantiers	Passengers	Elevators: 2
du Havre (France)	(lower beds/all berths): 308/308	Casino (gaming tables): . . . . .Yes
Original Cost: . . . .$140 million	Passenger Space Ratio	Slot Machines: . . . . .Yes
Entered Service: . . . .Feb 1990/May 1998	(lower beds/all berths): 47.8/47.8	Swimming Pools (outdoors): 2
Registry: . . . . .The Bahamas	Crew/Passenger Ratio	Whirlpools: 2
Length (ft/m): 613.5/187.0	(lower beds/all berths): 1.8/1.8	Fitness Center: . . . . .Yes
Beam (ft/m): 65.6/20.0	Navigation Officers: . . . . .European	Sauna/Steam Room: . . . . .Yes/No
Draft (ft/m): 16.4/5.0	Cabins (total): 154	Massage: . . . . .Yes
Type of Vessel: . . . . .high-tech sail-cruiser	Size Range (sq ft/m): 188.0–375.6/	Self-Service Launderette: . . . . .No
No. of Masts: . . . .5/7 computer-controlled	57.3–114.5	Library: . . . . .Yes
sails	Cabins (outside view): 154	Classification Society: . . . .Bureau Veritas
Sail Area (sq ft/m2): 26,910/2,500	Cabins (interior/no view): 0	

OVERALL SCORE: 1,567 (OUT OF A POSSIBLE 2,000 POINTS)

ACCOMMODATION: There are just three price categories, making your choice a simple one. Regardless of the category you choose, all cabins are very nicely equipped, have crisp, inviting décor, and a mini-bar/refrigerator (stocked when you embark, but all drinks are at extra cost), 24-hour room service, personal safe, television (with CNN, when available, for news) that rotates so that it is viewable from the bed and the bathroom, video player, compact disc player, plenty of storage space, and two portholes. Videos and compact discs are available from the ship's library. There are six 4-person cabins; 35 doubles are fitted with an extra Pullman berth, and several cabins have an interconnecting door (good for families). However, note that some of the cabinetry is looking a little tired, and has that "I've been varnished many times look." A basket of fruit is provided, and replenished daily.

The bathrooms are compact units, designed in a figure of eight, with a teakwood floor in the central section. There is a good amount of storage space for personal toiletry items in two cabinets, as well as under-sink cupboard space; a wall-mounted hairdryer is also provided. The shower enclosure (no cabins have bathtubs) is circular (like many of today's passengers), and features both a hand-held, as well as a fixed shower (so you can wash your hair without getting the rest of your body wet). Soap, shampoo and après-sun soothing lotion is provided, as is a vanity kit and shower cap. Note, however, that the lighting is not strong enough for women to apply make-up – this is better applied at the vanity desk

BERLITZ'S RATINGS

	Possible	Achieved
Ship	500	422
Accommodation	200	166
Food	400	299
Service	400	289
Entertainment	N/A	N/A
Cruise	500	391

in the cabin, which has stronger overhead (halogen) lighting. Bathrobes and towels are of 100 percent cotton, while bed linen is of a mix of 50 percent cotton/50 percent polyester (with 100 percent cotton sheets available on request).

In 1998, 31 new suites were added to Deck 3 during an extensive refit (one Owner's Suite plus 30 suites that were created by using two former standard cabins for one suite). Adding these resulted in a decrease of passenger capacity to 308 from the 386 of the ship's former owners (Club Mediterranée). All except one of the new suites have two bathrooms (so that a couple can have one bathroom each), a separate living/dining area, sleeping area (this can be curtained off from the lounge), two writing desks (there is even enough room for you to have an in-suite massage), and four portholes instead of two.

There are also two TV sets (one in the lounge, on in the sleeping area), VCR and CD player. However, note that movies cannot be watched from the bed – only from the sofa in the lounge area. Popcorn (for movie viewing) is available by calling room service.

DINING: The 272-seat Restaurant has tables for two, four or six, and open seating (with no pre-assigned tables), so you can sit with whom you wish, when you like. It is open only for dinner, which is typically between 7.30pm and 9.30pm. Both smoking and no-smoking sections are provided. California-style nouvelle cuisine is served, with dishes that are attractively presented. Additionally, "signature" dishes, created by master chefs Joachim Splichal and Jeanne Jones, are offered daily.

A 124-seat Bistro provides an alternative venue to the main restaurant (for dinner). The menus are basically the same as in the dining room, and the Bistro really provides an overflow to the dining room – particularly when the ship is full. The Bistro is thus not a bistro at all. It is located high atop the ship (on Star Deck) and has picture windows on port and starboard sides, an open kitchen, and tables for two, four or six. This is a no-smoking dining spot. Reservations are required for dinner, and passengers are restricted to two visits per 7-day cruise.

The Veranda, located amidships (on Star Deck) has its own open terrace for informal, self-serve breakfast and lunch buffets. It really is very pleasant to be outside, eating an informal meal on a balmy night. Do try the bread pudding – the ship is famous for it (available after lunch each day). Additionally, a permanent barbecue is also set up aft of the Veranda, for fresh grilled items for breakfast and lunch.

The Compass Rose, an indoor/outdoor bar, provides snack items plus some pastries and coffee for breakfast.

Windstar Cruises food product is generally very good, although highly geared toward American tastes. Europeans and other nationals should note that items such as bacon is fried to death, and the choice of cheeses and teas is poor. The service is also fast, geared towards American impatience. Consequently, leisurely dining is quite difficult.

OTHER COMMENTS: One of a pair of the world's largest sail-cruisers, *Wind Surf* is part-cruise ship, part-yacht (its sister ship operates as *Club Med II*). This is a larger, grander sister to the original three Windstar Cruises vessels. Five huge masts of 164 ft/50 meters (these actually rise 221 feet, or 67.5 meters above sea level) carry seven triangular, self-furling sails (made of Dacron) with a total surface area of 26,881 sq. ft (2,497 sq. meters). No human hands touch the sails, as everything is handled electronically by computer control from the bridge.

The computer keeps the ship on an even keel (via the movement of a water hydraulic ballast system of 266,814 gallons/1 million liters), so there is no heeling (rolling) over 6 degrees. When the ship is not using the sails, four diesel-electric motors propel the ship at up to approximately 12 knots.

There is a large, hydraulic water sports platform at the stern (swimming from it is not allowed, however), and extensive water sports facilities include 12 windsurfers, 3 sailboats, 2 water-ski boats, 20 single scuba tanks, snorkels, fins and masks, and 4 inflatable zodiac motorized boats (for water-skiing, etc), and all at no extra charge (except for the scuba tanks). Note that you will be asked to sign a waiver if you wish to use the water sports equipment.

There are two (saltwater) swimming pools (really little more than dip pools); one is located amidships on the uppermost deck of the ship, while the other is located aft, together with two hot tubs, and an adjacent bar.

In December 2000, the ship underwent further internal redesign, with enhancement of some features and the addition of new ones. A new gangway was installed, which has improved embarkation/disembarkation. A business center has been added; this incorporates a computer center (with 10 internet-access computer terminals so passengers can *Windsurf* the net), and a meeting room for between 30 and 60 persons. In the ship's casino/main lounge, which has an unusually high ceiling for the size of the ship, the dance floor has thankfully been relocated for better access and flow.

The health spa (with a staff of 10) features a co-ed sauna (bathing suits are required), beauty salon, several treatment rooms for massage, facials and body wraps; there is also a decent gymnasium (on a separate deck – with ocean views), and an aerobics workout room. Unfortunately, the spa facilities are split on three separate decks, making them rather disjointed. Special spa packages can be pre-booked through your travel agent before you arrive at the ship.

Other facilities include an integrated main lounge and enlarged casino (with 4 blackjack and one roulette table, and 21 slot machines).

Wind Surf is a good choice for couples seeking the "California Casual" dress code (no jackets or ties required) and informality found aboard this vessel, yet don't want the inconvenience of the workings of a *real* tall ship. The high quality of food and its presentation is a definite plus, as is the policy of no music in passenger hallways or elevators – in other words, it's a delightful, peaceful environment.

Wind Surf cruises from Barbados (November–March) and from Nice (May–October). However, the European itineraries are really port-intensive, which means you sail each night and are in port each day. With such itineraries, there seems little point to having the sails.

This ship has become a somewhat larger sister ship (with more space per passenger) for the other original Windstar Cruises vessels presently operating (*Wind Spirit* and *Wind Star*). All gratuities and port taxes are included in the brochure price (no additional gratuities are expected), which itself is considerably higher than those of the three smaller vessels in the fleet. The onboard currency is the US dollar.

WEAK POINTS: There are no showers at either of the two swimming pools (they really are just dip pools for cooling off) – passengers get into pool or hot tubs, while covered in oil or lotion, an unhygienic arrangement. Art auctions simply do not belong aboard this sail-cruise vessel (hopefully they will have disappeared by the time you read this). Don't even think about purchasing a cigar from the onboard shop – because the air temperature in the shop is high, cigars will be dry and absolutely worthless (they should, of course, be sold from a properly kept humidor).

Removed 2006

World Discoverer
NOT YET RATED

Small Ship: ....6,000 tons	Passengers	Cabin Current: ....220 volts
Lifestyle: ....Premium	(lower beds/all berths): 164/164	Dining Rooms: 1
Cruise Line: ....Society Expeditions	Passenger Space Ratio	Elevators: 2
Former Names: ..*Dream 21, Baltic Clipper*	(lower beds/all berths): 36.5/36.5	Casino (gaming tables): ....Yes
Sally Clipper, Delfin Clipper	Crew/Passenger Ratio:	Slot Machines: ....Yes
Builder: ....Rauma-Repola (Finland)	(lower beds/all berths): 1.8/1.8	Swimming Pools (outdoors): 1
Original Cost: ....$50 million	Navigation Officers: ......Scandinavian	Swimming Pools (indoors): 0
Entered Service: ....July 1989/2001	Cabins (total): 82	Whirlpools: 1
Registry: ....The Bahamas	Size (sq ft/m): 215.2–375.0/	Fitness Center: ....Yes
Length (ft/m): 354.9/108.20	20.0–34.8	Sauna/Steam Room: ....Yes/No
Beam (ft/m): 51.1/15.60	Cabins (outside view): 82	Massage: ....Yes
Draft (ft/m): 14.3/4.38	Cabins (interior/no view): 0	Self-Service Launderette: ....No
Propulsion/Propellers: diesel (4,500kw)/2	Cabins (for one person): 0	Movie Theater/Seats: ....No
Passenger Decks: 5	Cabins (with private balcony): 0	Library: ....No
Total Crew: 90	Cabins (wheelchair accessible): 0	Classification Society: ...Lloyd's Register

OVERALL SCORE: NYR (OUT OF A POSSIBLE 2,000 POINTS)

ACCOMMODATION: There are six types, and seven price grades. The cabins, which are extremely large for such a small ship as this, are fitted out to a fairly high standard, with ample closet and drawer space. All have outside views and feature twin beds that can convert to a queen-sized bed, television, telephone, VCR, hairdryer, refrigerator, and lockable drawer for valuables. All feature finely crafted wood cabinetry.

Although only eight suites (including the owner's suite) have a private balcony to either port or starboard side), another 20 cabins have what is termed a "French" balcony; these are simply glass doors that open onto a few inches of space outdoors, and should *not* be interpreted as private balconies (they do, however, allow you to take fresh air). The owner's suite and junior suites have whirlpool bathtubs; otherwise, there is simply more space.

The owner's suite is the largest accommodation, and features two rooms, linked by an interconnecting door, to provide a separate lounge, bedroom, and two bathrooms.

DINING: The dining room is spacious and has pastel-colored décor. The dining room accommodates all passengers in one seating.

OTHER COMMENTS: Twin swept-back outboard funnels highlight the smart exterior design of this small specialist cruise ship, which has an ice-hardened hull, and carries fleet of Zodiac inflatable landing craft for in-your-face shore excursions. This "new" *World Discoverer* (the previous one, built in 1974, was beached in

BERLITZ'S RATINGS		
	Possible	Achieved
Ship	500	NYR
Accommodation	200	NYR
Food	400	NYR
Service	400	NYR
Entertainment	N/A	N/A
Cruise	500	NYR

the Solomon Islands in 1999 and was declared a constructive total loss) is the smaller of two similar ships originally constructed new for Baltic Sea cruises for the Finnish company Delfin Cruises, which went bankrupt in 1990; the larger sister ship is used for gambling junkets, and is based in Hong Kong. The ship was originally built to a high standard of fit and finish. In the late 1990s, Samsung shipyard in South Korea bought the vessel. The shipyard actually dismantled this ship and rebuilt it again – just to learn how western shipyards build cruise vessels.

A fleet of Zodiac inflatable rubber craft is carried for in-your-face shore landings, as is a glass-bottom boat and snorkeling gear. An open-bridge policy means that you can visit the ship's navigation bridge at almost any time.

The accommodation is located forward, with all public rooms aft; this helps keep noise to a minimum in cabins. The interior has Scandinavian design elements.

World Discoverer provides a comfortable cruise experience in tasteful surroundings. All passengers (expedition cruise participants) receive a pre-cruise amenities package that includes a field guide, backpack, carry-on travel bag, and luggage tags. An expedition cruise log is provided at the end of each cruise for all participants.

Lecturers provide in-depth education about wildlife, geography and other interesting subjects that enrich the expedition cruise experience. Onboard currencies are the US dollar and the euro.

WEAK POINTS: There is no wrap-around promenade deck outdoors.

Removed 2006

World Renaissance
★★ +

Small Ship: ....11,724 tons	Passenger Decks: 8
Lifestyle: ....Standard	Total Crew: 204
Cruise Line: ......Royal Olympic Cruises	Passengers
Former Names: ....*Awani Dream,*	(lower beds/all berths): 481/599
World Renaissance, Renaissance,	Passenger Space Ratio
Homeric Renaissance	(lower beds/all berths): 24.3/19.5
Builder: Chantiers de l'Atlantique (France)	Crew/Passenger Ratio
Original Cost: ....n/a	(lower beds/all berths): 2.2/2.9
Entered Service: ....May 1966/Jan 1996	Navigation Officers: ....Greek
Registry: ....Greece	Cabins (total): 241
Length (ft/m): 492.1/150.02	Size Range (sq ft/m): 110–270/10.2–25.0
Beam (ft/m): 69.0/21.06	Cabins (outside view): 178
Draft (ft/m): 22.9/7.00	Cabins (interior/no view): 63
Propulsion/Propellers: ....diesel	Cabins (for one person): 1
(10,060kW)/2	Cabins (with private balcony): 0

Cabins (wheelchair accessible): 0
Cabin Current: ....110 volts
Elevators: 1
Casino (gaming tables): ....Yes
Slot Machines: ....Yes
Swimming Pools (outdoors): 2
Swimming Pools (indoors): 0
Whirlpools: 0
Fitness Center: ....Yes
Sauna/Steam Room: ....Yes/No
Massage: ....Yes
Self-Service Launderette: ....No
Dedicated Cinema/Seats: Yes/110
Library: ....Yes
Classification Society: ...Lloyd's Register

OVERALL SCORE: 1,096 (OUT OF A POSSIBLE 2,000 POINTS)

ACCOMMODATION: Some of the cabins have some fine wood paneling. They are homey and reasonably spacious, though certainly not luxurious. The cabin bathrooms are tiled, but are very small, and there is little space for toiletries.

DINING: The dining room is reasonably pleasant, although there are no tables for two, the tables are close together, and there are two seatings. The cuisine is predominantly Indonesian, with plenty of spicy foods. There is therefore a limited selection of breads, pastry, fruit and cheeses. The service is quite basic and there is really very little finesse.

OTHER COMMENTS: This ship has traditional 1960s styling and profile topped by a slender funnel; it was operated for many years by Epirotiki Lines (now part of Royal Olympic Cruises), and is now back with ROC after a short sojourn in Indonesia with Awani Dream Cruises, who ceased operations in late 1997. It has a

BERLITZ'S RATINGS

	Possible	Achieved
Ship	500	244
Accommodation	200	105
Food	400	238
Service	400	243
Entertainment	100	50
Cruise	400	216

pencil-slim funnel and white superstructure atop a royal blue hull.

The ship has a generous amount of open deck and sunbathing space for its size. The interior layout, however, is disjointed and awkward, and signage could be better.

Inside the ship, the décor can be said to be both "colonial" and eclectic, with some touches that still remind one of her original days as a French ship. Although the main lounge is comfortable, there are few other public rooms, and therefore the ship always feels busy (crowded).

The library, as a room is a restful place to relax. the ship has a friendly Greek staff and good basic service, although there is not much refinement. The onboard currency is the euro.

WEAK POINTS: The ship has a steep passenger gangway in most ports of call. There is no wrap-around promenade deck outdoors, and there are no cushioned pads for the deck lounge chairs.

Yamal
★★★

Small Ship: ....23,445 tons	Passengers		Elevators: 0
Lifestyle: ....Standard	(lower beds/all berths): 100/100		Casino (gaming tables): ....No
Cruise Line: ....Poseidon Arctic	Passenger Space Ratio		Slot Machines: ....No
Voyages	(lower beds/all berths): 234.0/234.0		Swimming Pools (indoors): 1
Former Names: ....none	Crew/Passenger Ratio		Whirlpools: 0
Builder: ....Baltic Shipyard &	(lower beds/all berths): 0.6/0.6		Fitness Center: ....Yes
Engineering (Russia)	Navigation Officers: ...Russian/Ukrainian		Sauna/Steam Room: Yes-2/No
Original Cost: ....$150 million	Cabins (total): 56		Massage: ....No
Entered Service: ....Nov 1992	Size Range (sq ft/m): 130.0–300.0/		Self-Service Launderette: ....Yes
Registry: ....Russia	14.3–27.8		Lecture/Film Room: ......Yes (seats 100)
Length (ft/m): 492.1/150.0	Cabins (outside view): 56		Library: ....Yes
Beam (ft/m): 98.4/30.0	Cabins (interior/no view): 0		Zodiacs: 4
Draft (ft/m): 36.0/11.0	Cabins (for one person): 3		Helicopter Pad: ....2 helicopters for
Propulsion/Propellers: ..nuclear-powered	Cabins (with private balcony): 0		passenger use
turbo-electric (55,950kW)/3	Cabins (wheelchair accessible): 0		Classification Society: ..Russian Shipping
Passenger Decks: 4	Cabin Current: ....220 volts		Registry
Total Crew: 150	Dining Rooms: 1		

OVERALL SCORE: 1,246 (OUT OF A POSSIBLE 2,000 POINTS)

ACCOMMODATION: All of the cabins are generously sized (considering the type of specialized vessel this is), and all are outside, with private facilities, television (for in-house viewing), VCR (suites only), refrigerator and desk. There is, however, a limited amount of closet and drawer space in most cabins. The bathrooms are small and utilitarian, and you will need to take your own favourite toiletry items.

DINING: The dining room is nicely appointed, and all passengers dine in one seating. The carbohydrate-rich food is surprisingly hearty, with plenty of meat and potato dishes, but little fruit and cheese. But then, these are not meant to be gourmet cruises. When the ship is under charter to western companies, western rather than Russian chefs oversee the food operation, and the selection of foods is better.

OTHER COMMENTS: The ultimate in technology accompanies this special ship, one of a fleet of four that comprise the world's most powerful icebreakers, with a 48mm-thick (about 3 inches) armored double hull. Propulsion power is provided by two nuclear-powered reactors (encased in 160 tons of steel), which provide the steam for propulsion via a pair of steam turbines. Each steam turbine operates three generators, and these in turn produce DC power to the electric propulsion motors that power the three powerful four-bladed propellers, each of which weighs about seven tons. The ship carries

BERLITZ'S RATINGS		
	Possible	Achieved
Ship	500	307
Accommodation	200	120
Food	400	244
Service	400	250
Entertainment	N/A	N/A
Cruise	500	331

enough fuel for four years without refueling. Its icebreaking capability is assisted by an air bubbling system that delivers hot water from jets located below the surface.

Yamal is one of few surface ships ever to reach the North Pole. Two helicopters are carried for reconnaissance and passenger sightseeing use; their use is included in the expedition fare, and provide you with a bird's-eye view of the polar landscape. The ship also carries a fleet of Zodiac inflatable landing craft for "up close and personal" shore landings.

Rugged, unpretentious, yet surprisingly comfortable surroundings prevail inside. There are two lounges. A tiered lecture theater with stage is the setting for a team of biologists, scientists, geologists, and other lecturers. There is a heated indoor sea-water pool. The ship is now operated by the Russian-owned Poseidon Arctic Voyages, and attentive and friendly Russian service is provided. Expedition participants (passengers) are also allowed on the bridge at almost all times. Light but warm parkas are provided for everyone.

Yamal, one of six ships built between 1959 and 1993, is occasionally placed under charter to various operators. It is quite an incredible vessel, with a strong hull and reinforced bow for negotiating extremely tough ice conditions (although the vessel really is noisy when plowing through ice). This is one of the most exciting, seat-of-your-pants expedition cruise experiences available today. The onboard currency is the US dollar.

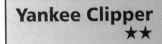

Yankee Clipper ★★

Small Ship: . . . . .327 tons	Propulsion/Propellers: diesel/1
Lifestyle: . . . . .Standard	Passenger Decks: 3
Cruise Line: . . . . . .Windjammer Barefoot	Total Crew: 24
Cruises	Passengers
Former Names: . . . . . . .Pioneer, Cressida	(lower beds/all berths): 64/64
Builder: . . . . .Krupp (Germany)	Passenger Space Ratio
Entered Service: 1927/1965	(lower beds/all berths): 5.1/5.1
Registry: . . . . .Equitorial Guinea	Crew/Passenger Ratio
Length (ft/m): 197.0/60.0	(lower beds/all berths): 2.6/2.6
Beam (ft/m): 30.0/9.1	Navigation Officers: . . . . . . .International
Draft (ft/m): 17.0/5.1	Cabins (total): 32
Type of Vessel: . . . . .schooner	Size Range (sq ft/m): . .65.0–86.0/6.0–7.9
No. of Masts: .3	Cabins (outside view): 32
Sail Area (sq ft/m2): 8,000/743.2	Cabins (interior/no view): 0
Main Propulsion: . . . . .sail power	Cabins (for one person): 0

Cabins (with private balcony): 0	
Cabins (wheelchair accessible): 0	
Cabin Current: . . . . .110 volts	
Elevators: 0	
Casino (gaming tables): . . . . .No	
Slot Machines: . . . . .No	
Swimming Pools (outdoors): 0	
Whirlpools: 0	
Fitness Center: . . . . .No	
Sauna/Steam Room: . . . . .No/No	
Massage: . . . . .No	
Self-Service Launderette: . . . . .No	
Library: . . . . .Yes	
Classification Society: . . . . .none	

OVERALL SCORE: 902 (OUT OF A POSSIBLE 2,000 POINTS)

ACCOMMODATION: There are four grades: Deck Cabin, Captain's Cabin, Captain's Double, and Standard Cabin. The cabins are dimensionally challenged (more for packages than people), however, particularly when compared to regular cruise ships. Remember, however, that this is a very casual cruise experience and you will need so few clothes anyway. All of the cabins are equipped with upper and lower berths, and most of them are quite narrow.

DINING: There is one dining room, and meals are all very simple in style and service, with little choice and only the most basic presentation. Breakfast is served on board, as is dinner, while lunch could be available either on board or at a beach, picnic-style. Wine (don't expect it to be very good) is included for dinner.

OTHER COMMENTS: The ship was built as one of the only armor-plated privated yachts in the world, for the German industrialist Alfred Krupp. Confiscated during World War II as a war prize, it was later acquired by the Vanderbilts. It joined the Windjammer Barefoot Cruises fleet in 1965. Aboard this fleet, you can let the crew do all the work, or you can lend a hand at the helm. One neat thing to do is just to sit or lie in the nets at the bows of the vessel, without a care in the world.

The mood is free and easy, the ships are equipped very simply, and only the most casual clothes are required (T-shirts and shorts). Shoes are optional, although you may need them if you go off in one of the ports. Quite possibly the most used item will be your

BERLITZ'S RATINGS

	Possible	Achieved
Ship	500	219
Accommodation	200	79
Food	400	166
Service	400	188
Entertainment	N/A	N/A
Cruise	500	250

bathing suit – better take more than one. Smoking is allowed only on the open decks.

Jammin' aboard a Windjammer is no-frills cruising in a no-nonsense, friendly environment, for the young at heart and those who don't need programmed activities. It's all about going to sea and the romance of being at sea under sail. Those who enjoy beaches, scuba diving and snorkeling around the Caribbean will be best suited to such a cruise. This ship can anchor in neat little Caribbean hideaways that larger (regular) cruise ships can't get near.

Entertainment in the evenings consists of – you and the crew. You can put on a toga, take or create a pirate outfit and join in the fun. This is cruising free 'n' easy style – none of that programmed big-ship production show stuff here.

Although itineraries (well, islands) are provided in the brochure, the captain actually decides which islands to go to in any given area, depending on sea and weather conditions. *Flying Cloud* features year-round cruises in the British and US Virgin Islands. Brochure rates might seem inexpensive, but you'll need to add on the airfare in order to get the true cost.

Yankee Clipper sails in the Caribbean, from Grenada. Other tall ships in the fleet include *Flying Cloud, Legacy, Mandalay,* and *Polynesia.* The onboard currency is the US dollar.

WEAK POINTS: It's extremely basic. There's little space per passenger. Everything is basic. Tips to the crew are suggested – at a whopping $50 per week per person.

Yorktown Clipper

★★★

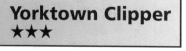

Small Ship:	2,354 tons	Passengers		Cabin Current:	110 volts
Lifestyle:	Standard	(lower beds/all berths):	138/138	Elevators:	0
Cruise Line:	Clipper Cruise Line	Passenger Space Ratio		Casino (gaming tables):	No
Former Names:	none	(lower beds/all berths):	17.0/17.0	Slot Machines:	No
Builder:	First Coast Shipbuilding (USA)	Crew/Passenger Ratio		Swimming Pools (outdoors):	0
Original Cost:	$12 million	(lower beds/all berths):	3.4/3.4	Swimming Pools (indoors):	0
Entered Service:	Apr 1988	Navigation Officers:	American	Whirlpools:	0
Registry:	USA	Cabins (total):	69	Fitness Center:	No
Length (ft/m):	257.0/78.30	Size Range (sq ft/m):	121.0–138.0/	Sauna/Steam Room:	No/No
Beam (ft/m):	43.0/13.10		11.2–12.8	Massage:	No
Draft (ft/m):	8.0/2.43	Cabins (outside view):	69	Self-Service Launderette:	No
Propulsion/Propellers:	diesel	Cabins (interior/no view):	0	Dedicated Cinema/Seats:	No
	(1,044kW)/2	Cabins (for one person):	0	Library:	Yes
Passenger Decks:	4	Cabins (with private balcony):	0	Classification Society:	American Bureau
Total Crew:	40	Cabins (wheelchair accessible):	0		of Shipping

---

OVERALL SCORE: 1,230 (OUT OF A POSSIBLE 2,000 POINTS)

ACCOMMODATION: The all-outside cabins are really quite small, but, with lots of wood-accented trim and restful colors, they are reasonably comfortable and tastefully furnished. The bathrooms, likewise, are small, with little space for toiletry items, but a night-light is provided, so you don't have to turn on bright lights in the middle of the night – a thoughtful touch. There is no room service for food and beverage items, as found aboard larger ships.

DINING: The dining room is warm and fairly inviting and has large picture windows, although there are no tables for two. There is one open-seating, so you dine with whom you wish. The service is provided by a young, all-American, mid-western team; they tend to smile a lot and are quite friendly, so you can forgive them a little for the lack of finesse. The food, however, is of a good quality, and made from locally purchased fresh ingredients. There is little menu choice, but the food provided is nicely presented. There is an adequate but very limited selection of breads and fruits.

OTHER COMMENTS: This small vessel was built specifically to operate coastal and inland waterway cruises. The draft is shallow, and the ship has good maneuverability, and has been well maintained since new. There is a teakwood outdoor sun deck. Inflatable rubber Zodiac craft are used for close-in shore excursions.

Inside, there is a glass-walled observation lounge.

BERLITZ'S RATINGS

	Possible	Achieved
Ship	500	285
Accommodation	200	121
Food	400	265
Service	400	257
Entertainment	N/A	N/A
Cruise	500	302

This ship offers a decidedly American experience for those seeking to learn more about the coastal ports around the USA during the summer months, while Caribbean cruises are featured in winter.

The lifestyle is casual and completely unregimented. This can best be compared to a small, congenial country club without any of the pretentiousness, and a good antidote to cruising aboard large ships. There are no mindless activities or corny games, and no entertainment as such, except for an occasional movie after dinner (the dining room converts to a movie screening room). There are always one or two lecturers aboard each sailing, which highlights the learning experience that is an essential part of cruising with Clipper Cruise Lines.

This really should not be compared with big ship ocean cruising. The price, however, is high for what you get when compared to many other ships, and the air fare is extra. There is a no-smoking policy throughout all interior areas.

The onboard currency is the US dollar.

WEAK POINTS: This really is a high-density ship, and there are only two public rooms: a dining room and a lounge. The engine noise level is high when the ship is underway (not so noticeable for those who may be hard of hearing). The per-diem price is high for what you get, and air fare is extra. Although there is a wrap-around teakwood walking deck outdoors, it is quite narrow.

Zaandam
★★★★

Large Ship:	.63,000 tons	Passengers	
Lifestyle:	Premium	(lower beds/all berths):	....1,440/1,850
Cruise Line:	Holland America Line	Passenger Space Ratio	
Former Names:	none	(lower beds/all berths):	...43.7/34.0
Builder:	Fincantieri (Italy)	Crew/Passenger Ratio	
Original Cost:	$300 million	(lower beds/all berths):	...2.5/2.5
Entered Service:	May 2000	Navigation Officers:	Dutch
Registry:	The Netherlands	Cabins (total):	720
Length (ft/m):	777.5/237.00	Size Range (sq ft/m):	113.0–339.2/
Beam (ft/m):	105.8/32.25		10.5–34.3
Draft (ft/m):	25.5/7.80	Cabins (outside view):	581
Propulsion/Propellers:	diesel-electric	Cabins (interior/no view):	139
	(37,500kW)/2	Cabins (for one person):	0
Passenger Decks:	12	Cabins (with private balcony):	197
Total Crew:	561	Cabins (wheelchair accessible):	23

Cabin Current: ....110 volts
Elevators: 12
Casino (gaming tables): ....Yes
Slot Machines: ....Yes
Swimming Pools (outdoors): 2
Swimming Pools (indoors): 1
(magrodome cover)
Whirlpools: 2
Fitness Center: ....Yes
Sauna/Steam Room: ....Yes/Yes
Massage:..........................Yes
Self-Service Launderette:...........Yes
Dedicated Cinema/Seats: Yes/205
Library: ....Yes
Classification Society: ... .Lloyds Register

OVERALL SCORE: 1,541 (OUT OF A POSSIBLE 2,000 POINTS)

ACCOMMODATION: The range is comparable to that found aboard the similarly sized *Rotterdam*, and comprises 17 different categories. There is one penthouse suite, 28 suites, and 168 mini-suites, with the rest of the accommodation comprised of a mix of outside-view and interior (no view) cabins. However, there are many more balcony cabins (called "mini-suites") aboard this ship than aboard the slightly smaller *Statendam*-class ships (*Maasdam, Ryndam, Statendam, Veendam*).

BERLITZ'S RATINGS		
	Possible	Achieved
Ship	500	430
Accommodation	200	165
Food	400	281
Service	400	276
Entertainment	100	77
Cruise	400	312

All standard interior and outside cabins are tastefully furnished, and have twin beds that convert to a queen-sized bed (space is tight for walking between beds and vanity unit). There is a decent amount of closet and drawer space, although this will prove tight for the longer voyages featured. All cabin televisions carry CNN and TNT. The bathrooms, which are fully tiled, are disappointingly small (particularly for long cruises) and have small shower tubs, utilitarian personal toiletries cupboards, and exposed under-sink plumbing. There is no detailing to distinguish them from bathrooms aboard the *Statendam*-class ships.

There are 28 full verandah suites (Navigation Deck), and one penthouse suites. All suite occupants share a private Concierge Lounge (the concierge handles such things as special dining arrangements, shore excursions and special requests). Strangely, there are no butlers for these suites, as aboard ships with similar facilities. Each Verandah Suite has a separate bedroom, dressing and living areas. Suite passengers get personal stationery, complimentary laundry and ironing, cocktail hour hors d'oeuvres and other goodies, as well as priority embarkation and disembarkation. The concierge lounge, with its latticework teak detailing and private library, is accessible only by private key-card.

The ultimate in accommodation and living space can be found in the Penthouse Suite. It has a separate steward's entrance, and has a large bedroom with king-size bed, separate living room (with baby grand piano) and a dining room, dressing room, walk-in closet, butler's pantry, private balcony (the balcony is no large than the balcony of any of the other suites).

Other facilities include an audio-visual center with television and VCR, wet bar with refrigerator, large bathroom with Jacuzzi bathtub, separate toilet with bidet, and a guest bathroom (with toilet and washbasin).

With the exception of the penthouse suite, located forward on the starboard side, the bathrooms in the other suites and "mini-suites" are a little disappointing – not as spacious or opulent as one might expect. All outside-view suites and cabin bathrooms have a bathtub/shower while interior (no view) cabins have a shower only. Also, note that the 23 cabins for the mobility-limited have a roll-in shower enclosure for wheelchair users (none have bathtubs, no matter what the category).

DINING: The Rotterdam Dining Room (the ship's main dining room) is quite a grand room, and is spread over two decks, with ocean views on three sides with a grand staircase to connect the upper and lower levels. There are two seatings for dinner, open seating for breakfast and lunch, and both smoking and non-smoking sections are provided. Fine Rosenthal china and cutlery are featured (although there are no fish knives).

Unfortunately, Holland America Line food isn't as nice as the china it's placed on. It may be adequate for most passengers not used to better food, but it does not match the standard found aboard other ships in the premium segment of the industry. While USDA beef is of a good quality, fowl tends to be battery-tough, and most fish is overcooked and has the consistency of a baseball bat. What are *not* luxurious are the endless packets of sugar, and packets (instead of glass jars) of breakfast jam, marmalade and honey, and poor quality teas.

Dessert and pastry items are of good quality (specifically for American tastes), although there is much use of canned fruits and jellies. Forget the selection of "international" cheeses, however, as most of it didn't come from anywhere other than the USA. Holland America Line can provide Kosher meals, but these are prepared ashore, frozen, and brought to your table sealed in their original containers (there is no Kosher kitchen on board).

An alternative, casual-dress Marco Polo Restaurant (dinner only, with reservations required) seats 88, and there is no extra charge. It serves what is best described as California-Italian cuisine (this has a set menu together with nightly specials). Passengers thus have more choice and an occasional change of venue (anyone booking suite-grade accommodation get priority reservations).

In addition, there is the Lido Buffet, a casual, self-serve café that has proved popular aboard all Holland America Line ships for casual breakfasts and luncheons, as well as an grill outdoors for the inevitable hamburgers, hot dogs and other grilled fast-food items. The Lido Buffet is also open for casual dinners on several nights each cruise (typically three nights on a 7-night cruise), in an open-seating arrangement. Tables are set with crisp linens, flatware and stemware. A set menu is featured, and this includes a choice of four entrées.

OTHER COMMENTS: The hull is dark blue, in keeping with all Holland America Line ships. Although similar in size to the line's flagship *Rotterdam*, this ship has a single funnel, and is a sister ship to *Volendam*.

Zaandam has three principal passenger stairways, which is so much better than two stairways, particularly the viewpoints of safety, accessibility and passenger flow. There is a magrodome-covered pool on the Lido Deck between the mast and the ship's funnel. The health spa facilities are quite extensive, and include gymnasium, separate saunas and steam rooms for men and women, and more treatment rooms (each has a shower and toilet). Practice tennis courts can be fund outdoor, as well as the traditional shuffleboard courts, and jogging track, not to mention a full wrap-around teakwood promenade deck.

The interior décor is best described as restrained, with much use of wood accenting, and the design theme of music incorporated throughout. Music memorabilia is scattered throughout the ship, in fabrics, posters, and – believe it or not – real instruments. The musical instruments and other memorabilia were acquired from the "Pop and Guitars" auction at Christie's in London in 1997. They include a Fender Squire Telecaster guitar signed by Mick Jagger, Keith Richards, Charlie Watts, Ronnie Wood and Bill Wyman of the Rolling Stones; a Conn Saxophone signed on the mouthpiece by former US President Bill Clinton; an Ariana acoustic guitar signed by David Bowie and Iggy Pop; a Fender Stratocaster guitar signed in silver ink by the members of the rock band Queen; a Bently "Les Paul" style guitar signed by various artists, including Carlos Santana, Eric Clapton, BB King, Robert Cray, Keith Richards and Les Paul.

As a whole, the décor is quite refined, with much traditional ocean liner detailing. Additions are children's and teens' play areas, although these really are token gestures by a company that traditionally does not cater well to children. Popcorn is even available at the Wajang Theatre for moviegoers (just like ashore), while adjacent is the popular Java Café. The casino has blackjack, roulette, stud poker and dice tables alongside the requisite rows of slot machines.

The vessel's focal point is a three-deck-high atrium, around which the ship's main offices can be found (reception desk, shore excursions desk, photo shop, and photo gallery). It also houses a fanciful pipe organ, complete with puppets that move in time with the music.

As in *Volendam*, the Lido Deck swimming pool is located one deck higher than the *S*-class ships, so that you can now have direct access between the aft and midships pools aboard this ship (not so aboard the *S*-class ships). This provided more space on the Navigation Deck below for extra cabins to be accommodated.

This ship is best for older passengers who are looking for safe, pleasant surroundings and food that isn't too adventurous. Holland America Line provides complimentary cappuccino and espresso coffees, and free ice cream during certain hours of the day aboard its ships, as well as hot hors d'oeuvres in all bars – something other major lines seem to have dropped, or charge extra for. Very pleasing is the fact that the company, unlike many others, does not add an automatic 15 percent for beverage purchases. The onboard currency is the US dollar.

WEAK POINTS: Standing in line for embarkation, disembarkation, shore tenders and for self-serve buffet meals is inevitable aboard large ships. With one whole deck of suites (and a dedicated, private concierge lounge, with preferential passenger treatment), the company has in effect created a two-class ship. The charge to use the washing machines and dryers in the self-service launderette is petty and irritating, particularly for the occupants of suites, as they pay high prices for their cruises. Communication (in English) with many of the staff, particularly in the dining room and buffet areas, can be frustrating. Room service is poor. Non-smokers should avoid this ship, as smokers are everywhere.

Zenith
★★★★

Large Ship:	47,255 tons	Passengers	
Lifestyle:	Premium	(lower beds/all berths):	1,378/1,800
Cruise Line:	Celebrity Cruises	Passenger Space Ratio	
Former Names:	none	(lower beds/all berths):	34.2 /26.2
Builder:	Meyer Werft (Germany)	Crew/Passenger Ratio	
Original Cost:	$210 million	(lower beds/all berths):	2.0/2.6
Entered Service:	Apr 1992	Navigation Officers:	Greek
Registry:	The Bahamas	Cabins (total):	689
Length (ft/m):	681.0/207.59	Size Range (sq ft/m):	172.2–500.5/
Beam (ft/m):	95.1/29.00		16.0–46.50
Draft (ft/m):	23.6/7.20	Cabins (outside view):	541
Propulsion/Propellers:	diesel	Cabins (interior/no view):	148
	(19,960kW)/2	Cabins (for one person):	0
Passenger Decks:	9	Cabins (with private balcony):	0
Total Crew:	670	Cabins (wheelchair accessible):	4

Cabin Current:	110 volts
Elevators:	7
Casino (gaming tables):	Yes
Slot Machines:	Yes
Swimming Pools (outdoors):	2
Swimming Pools (indoors):	0
Whirlpools:	3
Fitness Center:	Yes
Sauna/Steam Room:	Yes/No
Massage:	Yes
Self-Service Launderette:	No
Dedicated Cinema/Seats:	No
Library:	Yes
Classification Society:	Lloyd's Register

OVERALL SCORE: 1,545 (OUT OF A POSSIBLE 2,000 POINTS)

ACCOMMODATION: There are 12 grades, including outside-view suites and cabins, and interior (no view) cabins, but even the smallest cabin is considerably larger than most of the standard outside and interior (no view) cabins aboard the ships of sister company Royal Caribbean International. Note that no suites or cabins have private balconies (they were not yet in vogue when this ship was constructed). Also, most outside cabins on Bahamas Deck have lifeboat-obstructed views.

STANDARD CABINS: All standard outside-view and interior (no view) cabins have good-quality fittings with lots of wood accenting, are tastefully decorated and of an above-average size, with an excellent amount of closet and drawer space, and reasonable insulation between cabins. All have twin beds that convert to a queen-sized bed, and a good amount of closet and drawer space. The cabin soundproofing is fair to very good, depending on the location. All accommodation has interactive Celebrity Television, including pay-per-view movies.

The bathrooms have a generous shower area, and a small range of toiletries is provided (typically soap, shampoo/conditioner, body lotion, and shower cap), although bathroom towels are a little small, as is storage space for personal toiletry items. The lowest-grade outside-view cabins have a porthole, but all others have picture windows.

ROYAL SUITES: The largest accommodation can be found in two Royal Suites on Atlantic Deck (Deck 10).

BERLITZ'S RATINGS

	Possible	Achieved
Ship	500	399
Accommodation	200	158
Food	400	304
Service	400	317
Entertainment	100	68
Cruise	400	299

These have butler service, and have a separate bedroom and lounge, dining area with glass dining table (with CD player and VCR player in addition to the large television). The bathroom is also larger and has a whirlpool bathtub with integral shower. Butler service is standard.

Another 20 suites (also on Atlantic Deck) are very tastefully furnished, although they are really just larger cabins and shouldn't be called suites. They are not as large as the suites aboard the company's larger ships, *Century, Constellation Galaxy, Infinity, Mercury, Millennium,* and *Summit.* They do have a generous amount of drawer and other storage space, however, and a sleeping area (with European duvets on the beds instead of sheets and blankets) plus a lounge area. They also have good bathrooms. Butler service is standard.

All accommodation designated as suites do however, suffer from noise generated on the swimming pool deck directly above. No suites or cabins have private balconies (they weren't in vogue when this ship was built).

DINING: The Caravelle Dining Room, which has a raised section in its center, has several tables for two, as well as for four, six or eight (in banquettes), although the chairs do not have armrests. There are two seatings for dinner (open seating for breakfast and lunch), at tables for two, four, six, eight or 10, and the dining room is a totally no-smoking area. The cuisine, its presentation and service are really extremely good. There is a separate menu for vegetarians and children. An extensive wine cellar means that the wine list features a fine selection of vintage and non-vintage wines and champagnes from around the world. The wine sommeliers are knowledgeable, and wine suggestions are provided on all dinner menus.

For informal meals, the Windsurf Café (non-smoking) has good buffets for breakfast (including an omelet station) and luncheon (including a pasta station, rotissereie and pizza ovens). At peak times, however, the buffets is simply too small. At night, the dining area changes into an alternative dining spot for those who want good food but in a more casual setting than the main restaurant, with items such as grilled salmon, steaks, and rotisserie chicken, as well as specialties that change frequently.

The Grill, located outdoors adjacent to (but aft of) the Windsurf Café, serves typical fast-food items. And for those that cannot live without them, freshly baked pizzas (in a box) can be delivered, in an insulated pouch, to your cabin.

OTHER COMMENTS: This ship, now over 10 years old, has a smart, contemporary profile that gives the impression of power and speed owing to its blue paint striping along the sides, separating the hull from the superstructure, as in its two-years-older sister *Horizon*. The funnel is instantly recognizable in royal blue, with a white "X," the company's logo.

Inside, there is a similar interior layout (to sister ship *Horizon)* and elegant and restrained décor that most find a little warmer, and an enlarged and enhanced forward observation lounge with a larger dance floor that is a pleasant setting for cocktails and late-night dance music.

The feeling is one of uncluttered surroundings. Intelligent, well-chosen art works are provided throughout the ship, and soothing pastel colors and high-quality soft furnishings are used throughout the ship's interiors.

The principal deck that houses many of the public entertainment rooms has a double-width indoor promenade. Facilities include an excellent show lounge, with main and balcony levels, and good sight lines from almost all seats (however, the railing at the front of the balcony level does impede viewing).

There is a good-sized library, which was relocated and enlarged in a 1999 refit. There is a good (seasonal) program for children and teenagers, with specially trained youth counselors. The large, elegantly appointed

casino has its own bar, while outside is a satellite-linked BankAtlantic ATM machine (with a $5 access charge) in case you didn't bring enough cash. An art deco-style hotel-like lobby (reminiscent of hotels in Miami Beach) has a two-deck-high ceiling and a spacious feel to it.

The 1999 refurbishment added a delightful "Michael's Club" cigar smoking lounge (complete with fireplace and bookshelves containing leather-bound volumes) in what was formerly an underused discotheque, as well as the enlarged library and a small business center. Also added was a popular martini bar, a room dedicated to the display of art (for art auctions), an expanded health spa (this now includes a rasul treatment room, AquaJet and dry flotation bath), and an enlarged beauty salon with ocean-view windows; and a fine Cova Café (the original Cova Café, located near the La Scala Opera House, opened in 1756).

This ship will provide a well-packaged cruise vacation in elegant, calming surroundings, with finely presented food in a formal dining room setting, and service from a well trained service staff that include a large percentage of Europeans. Almost all passengers feel that the company exceeds their expectations. The onboard currency is the US dollar.

WEAK POINTS: Standing in line for embarkation, disembarkation, shore tenders and for self-serve buffet meals is an inevitable aspect of cruising aboard all large ships. Unlike the company's larger ships *Century, Galaxy, Mercury* and *Millennium*, no suites or cabins have private balconies. Trying to reach Cabin Services or the Guest Relations Desk to answer the phone (to order breakfast, for example, if you don't want to do so via the interactive television) is a matter of luck, timing and patience. The doors to the public restrooms and the outdoor decks are rather heavy. The public restrooms are clinical and need some softer décor. There are cushioned pads for poolside deck lounge chairs only, but not for chairs on other outside decks.

Participation activities tend to be amateurish and should be upgraded. The officers have become more aloof lately, with far less contact with passengers than when the company first started. The production shows are quite poor.

Zuiderdam
NOT YET RATED

Large Ship: . . . . .85,920 tons	Passengers	Elevators: 14
Lifestyle: . . . . .Premium	(lower beds/all berths): 1,848/2,272	Casino (gaming tables): . . . . .Yes
Cruise Line: . . . . . . .Holland America Line	Passenger Space Ratio	Slot Machines: . . . . .Yes
Former Names: . . . . .none	(lower beds/all berths): 46.4/37.8	Swimming Pools (outdoors): . . . . .2+1
Builder: . . . . .Fincantieri (Italy)	Crew/Passenger Ratio	children's pool
Original Cost: . . . .$400 million	(lower beds/all berths): 2.1/2.6	Swimming Pools (indoors): 1
Entered Service: . . . . .Dec 2002	Navigation Officers: . . . . .European	(indoor/outdoor)
Registry: . . . . .The Netherlands	Cabins (total): .924	Whirlpools: 5
Length (ft/m): 951.4/290.00	Size Range (sq ft/m): 185.0–1,318.6/	Fitness Center: . . . . .Yes
Beam (ft/m): 105.6/32.25	17.1–122.5	Sauna/Steam Room: . . . . .Yes/Yes
Draft (ft/m): 25.5/7.80	Cabins (outside view): 788	Massage: . . . . .Yes
Propulsion/Propellers: . . . . .diesel-electric	Cabins (interior/no view): 136	Self-Service Launderette: . . . . .Yes
(34,000 kW)/2 pods	Cabins (for one person): 0	Dedicated Cinema/Seats: Yes/170
(17.6 MW each)	Cabins (with private balcony): 810	Library: . . . . .Yes
Passenger Decks: 10	Cabins (wheelchair accessible): 28	Classification Society: . . .Lloyd's Register
Total Crew: .842	Cabin Current: . . . . .110 volts	

OVERALL SCORE: NYR (OUT OF A POSSIBLE 2,000 POINTS)

ACCOMMODATION: In keeping with cruise industry trends, there are more cabins with private balconies than aboard any other Holland America Line ships at present.

PENTHOUSE VERANDAH SUITES: The largest accommodation (1,126 sq. ft/104.6 sq. meters) can be found in two Penthouse Verandah Suites. These have a separate bedroom with a king-size bed; there's also a walk-in closet, dressing room, living room, dining room, butler's pantry, mini-bar and refrigerator, and private balcony (verandah). The main bathroom has a large whirlpool bathtub, two washbasins, toilet, and plenty of storage space for personal toiletry items. Personalized stationery and complimentary dry cleaning are included, as are hot hors d'oeuvres daily and other goodies.

DELUXE VERANDAH SUITES: Next in size are 60 De-Luxe Verandah Suites (563 sq. ft/52.3 sq. meters). These feature twin beds that can convert to a king-size bed, vanity desk, lounge area, walk-in closet, min-bar and refrigerator, and bathroom with full-size bathtub, washbasin and toilet. Personalized stationery and complimentary dry cleaning are included, as are hot hors d'oeuvres daily and other goodies.

VERANDAH SUITES: There are 100 of these Verandah Suites (actually they are cabins, not suites, and measure 284 sq. ft/26.3 sq. meters). Twin beds can convert to a queen-size bed; there is also a lounge area, mini-bar and

BERLITZ'S RATINGS		
	Possible	Achieved
Ship	500	NYR
Accommodation	200	NYR
Food	400	NYR
Service	400	NYR
Entertainment	100	NYR
Cruise	400	NYR

refrigerator, while the bathroom features a bathtub, washbasin and toilet. Floor to ceiling windows open onto a private balcony (verandah).

OUTSIDE-VIEW CABINS: Standard outside cabins (197 sq. ft/18.3 sq. meters) have twin beds that can be converted to make a queen-size bed. There's also a small sitting area, while the bathroom has a bathtub/shower combination. The interior (no view) cabins are slightly smaller, at 182.9 sq ft/17 sq. meters.

It is well to note that a number of cabins on the lowest accommodation deck (Main Deck) have views obstructed by lifeboats. Some cabins that can accommodate a third and fourth person have *very little* closet space, and there's only one personal safe. There is no separate radio in each cabin – instead, audio channels are provided on the in-cabin television system (however, you can't turn the picture off – not very romantic for late at night sounds with your loved one).

DINING: There are several dining options, from full-service meals in the huge main dining room, to more informal eateries located high in the ship, to casual, self-serve buffet-style meals and fast-food outlets.

The La Fontaine (main) dining room is two decks high, (the galley is underneath the restaurant, accessed by port and starboard escalators). Located at the stern of the ship, it seats 1,045. It is traditional Holland America Line in its operation, with friendly service from smiling Indonesian stewards, and has Rosenthal china.

Holland America Line can provide Kosher meals, but they are prepared ashore, frozen, and brought to your table sealed in their original containers (there is no Kosher kitchen on board).

ALTERNATIVE (RESERVATIONS REQUIRED) DINING SPOT: The Odyssey Restaurant is an alternative, slightly more upscale dining spot (with much better food and presentation than in the main dining room) atop the ship, located on two of its uppermost decks, directly above the Lido Buffet (at the top of the nine decks high atrium lobby). It seats approximately 130, and features a show kitchen where chefs can be seen preparing their master-pieces. Fine table settings, china and silverware are featured, as are leather-bound menus. There is also a stage and dance floor, so dining can be combined with dancing in this true supper club atmosphere. Reservations are required and there is a cover charge of $15 per person for service and gratuity.

INFORMAL EATERIES: For casual eating, there is an extensive Lido Café and Pizzeria, which form an eatery that wraps around the funnel housing and extends aft; there are also some fine views over the ship's central multi-deck atrium. It includes a separate pizzeria, a separate salad bar and separate dessert buffet, although movement around the buffet area is *very slow*, and requires you to stand in line for everything.

Additionally, there is an outdoor self-serve buffet (adjacent to the fantail pool), which serves fast-food items such as hamburgers and hot dogs, chicken and fries, as well as two smaller buffets adjacent to the midships swimming pool area.

OTHER COMMENTS: *Zuiderdam* is one of what is known as the "Vista" class ships (several other ships in the Carnival Cruise Lines and Costa Cruises fleets are also of the same size and general design), designed to appeal to a younger, more vibrant market. The basic hull design is shared in common with Carnival's *Carnival Legend*, *Carnival Pride* and *Carnival Spirit*, and Costa Cruises' *Costa Atlantica* and *Costa Mediterranea*.

The propulsion is provided by two azimuthing "pods" which are hung under the ship's stern (rather like giant outboard motors). These replace the conventional shaft and rudder system (the pods have forward-facing propellers that can be turned through 360 degrees). The pods are powered by a diesel-electric system. In addition, a small gas turbine is located in the funnel for the reduction of emissions.

A complete wrap-around exterior promenade deck is a feature enjoyed by many. Exterior glass elevators, mounted midships on both port and starboard sides, provide fine ocean views from any one of the 10 decks that the elevators travel to. In keeping with the traditions of Holland America Line, a large collection of artwork is a standard feature of all its ships, including this one.

There are two centrally located swimming pools out-doors, and one of the pools can be used in inclement weather due to its retractable magrodome (glass dome) cover. Two whirlpool tubs, located adjacent to the swimming pools, are abridged by a bar. Another smaller pool is available for children.

When you first walk into the ship, you'll be greeted by the immense size of the dramatic lobby space that spans eight decks. The atrium lobby, with its two grand stairways, presents a stunning wall decoration that is best seen from any of the multiple viewing balconies on each deck above the main lobby floor level. Alternatively, you could take a drink from the lobby bar and look upwards – the surroundings are quite stunning.

There are two whole entertainment/public room decks, the upper of which also features an exterior promenade deck – something new for this fun cruise line. Although it doesn't go around the whole ship, it's long enough to do some serious walking on. Additionally, there is also a jogging track outdoors, located around the ship's mast and the forward third of the ship.

Without doubt, the most dramatic public room aboard this ship is the Queens Lounge, the ship's show lounge; it spans three decks in the forward section of the ship. The main floor level has a bar in its starboard aft section, while the upper two levels. Spiral stairways at the back of the lounge connect all levels. Stage shows are best seen from the upper levels, from where the sight lines are reasonably good. Other facilities include a winding shopping street with boutique stores and logo shops.

The casino is large (one has to walk through it to get from the restaurant to the showlounge on one of the entertainments decks), and this is equipped with all the gaming paraphernalia and array of slot machines you can think of – all designed, of course, to entertain you while you are relieved of your money.

A large, two-decks-high health spa – called the Ocean Spa – is located directly above the navigation bridge. Facilities include a solarium, eight treatment rooms, sauna and steam rooms for men and women, a beauty parlor, and a large gymnasium with floor-to-ceiling windows on three sides, including forward-facing ocean views.

So, what's it like to cruise aboard a ship of this size? Holland America Line's many repeat passengers seem to enjoy the fact that social dancing is always on the menu. The company also offers complimentary cappuccino and espresso coffees and free ice cream during certain hours of the day aboard its ships, as well as hot hors d'oeuvres in all bars - something other major lines seem to have dropped, or charge extra for.

Gratuities are extra, and they are added to your ship-board account at $10–$13 per day, according to the accommodation grade chosen. Refreshingly, the company does not add an automatic 15 percent gratuity for beverage purchases. Perhaps the ship's best asset is its friendly and personable Filipino and Indonesian crew, although communication can prove frustrating at times. In the final analysis, however, the score for this ship will probably end up just a disappointing tad under what it could be if the food and food service staff were better (more professional training might help). The onboard currency is the US dollar.

WEAK POINTS: The information desk in the lobby is small in comparison to the size of the lobby. Many of the private balconies are not so private, and can be overlooked from various public locations. Many pillars obstruct the passenger flow and lines of sight throughout the ship. Indeed, the many pillars in the dining room make it extremely difficult for the waiters and the proper service of food. Standing in line for embarkation, disembarkation, shore tenders and for self-serve buffet meals can be an inevitable aspect of cruising aboard all large ships. The charge to use the washing machines and dryers in the self-service launderette is petty, particularly for the occupants of suites, as they pay high prices for their cruises. Communication (in English) with many of the staff, particularly in the dining room and buffet areas, can prove very frustrating. It may be difficult to escape from smokers, and people walking around in unsuitable clothing, clutching plastic sport drinks bottles.

A PASSENGER'S PRAYER

"Heavenly Father, look down on us, Your humble, obedient passengers who are doomed to travel the seas and waterways of this earth, taking photographs, mailing postcards, buying useless souvenirs, and walking around in ill-fitting swimwear.

"We beseech You, oh Lord, to see that our plane is not hijacked, our luggage is not lost, and that our oversized carry-ons go unnoticed.

"Protect us from surly and unscrupulous taxi drivers, avaricious porters, and unlicensed, English-speaking guides in foreign places.

"Give us this day Divine guidance in the selection of our cruise ships and our travel agents — so that we may find our bookings and dining room reservations honored, our cabins of generous proportions, that our luggage arrives before the first evening meal, and that our beds are made up.

"We humbly ask that our shower curtains do not provoke us into meaningless frustration and destructive thoughts.

"We pray that our cabin telephones work, the operator (human or electrical) speaks our tongue, and that there are no phone calls from our children forcing us to abandon our cruise early.

"Lead us, dear Lord, to good, affordable restaurants in the world ashore, where the food is superb, the waiters friendly, and the wine included in the price of a meal.

"Please grant us a cruise director who does not "cream" excessively from the spoils of bingo or horse racing, or does not stress only those jewelry stores from which he accepts an offering.

"Grant us the strength to take shore excursions — to visit the museums, cathedrals, spice stalls, and gift shops listed in Berlitz Pocket Guides.

"And if on our return journey by non-air-conditioned buses we slip into slumber, have mercy on us for our flesh is weak, hot, and tired.

"Give us the wisdom to tip correctly at the end of our voyage. Forgive us for under-tipping out of ignorance, and over-tipping out of fear. Please make the chief purser and ship's staff loves us for what we are and not for what we can contribute to their worldly goods or company comment forms.

"Dear God, keep our wives from shopping sprees and protect them from bargains they do not need or cannot afford. Lead them not into temptation in St. Thomas or Hong Kong for they know not what they do.

"Almighty Father, keep our husbands from looking at foreign women and comparing them to us. Save them from making fools of themselves in cafés and nightclubs. Above all, please do not forgive them their trespasses for they know exactly what they do.

"And when our voyage is over and we return home to our loved ones, grant us the favor of finding someone who will look at our home videos and listen to our stories, so our lives as tourists will not have been in vain. This we ask you in the name of our chosen cruise line, and in the name of American Express, Visa, MasterCard, and our banks. Amen."

Ocean-going Ships to Debut: 2003–2006

CRUISE LINE	NAME OF SHIP	TONS	COST (US$m)
2003 (13 Ships)			
Aida Cruises	*AIDAaura*	42,200	200
Carnival Cruise Lines	*Carnival Glory*	110,000	450
Costa Cruises	*Costa Mediterranea*	85,700	377
Costa Cruises	*Costa Fortuna*	105,000	418.5
Crystal Cruises	*Crystal Serenity*	68,000	350
Cunard Line	*Queen Mary 2*	150,000	700
Holland America Line	*Oosterdam*	85,700	400
Mediterranean Shipping Cruises	*Lirica*	60,000	266
Norwegian Coastal Voyages	*to be announced*	16,053	105
Princess Cruises	*Island Princess*	88,000	360
Princess Cruises	*Diamond Princess*	113,000	460
Radisson Seven Seas Cruises	*Seven Seas Voyager*	46,000	200
Royal Caribbean Internatonal	*Serenade of the Seas*	90,090	400
Royal Caribbean International	*Navigator of the Seas*	137,300	600
2004 (13 Ships)			
Carnival Cruise Lines	*Carnival Miracle*	85,900	375
Carnival Cruise Lines	*Carnival Valor*	110,000	450
Costa Cruises	*Costa Magica*	105,000	418.5
Holland America Line	*to be announced*	85,700	400
Mediterranean Shipping Cruises	*Opera*	60,000	266
Norwegian Coastal Voyages	*to be announced*	15,000	105
Princess Cruises	*Crown Princess*	108,000	460
Princess Cruises	*Sapphire Princess*	113,000	460
Royal Caribbean Internatonal	*Jewel of the Seas*	90,090	400
Royal Caribbean International	*Mariner of the Seas*	137,300	600
2005 (3 Ships)			
Carnival Cruise Lines	*to be announced*	110,000	450
Cunard Line	*to be announced*	85,000	400
Holland America Line	*to be announced*	85,700	400
2006 (1 Ship)			
Holland America Line	*to be announced*	85,700	400

Notes

- This chart shows ships under firm contract. It is given in alphabetical order according to cruise line.

Delivery/debut dates may be brought forward or put back, therefore precise months are not listed.
tba = to be announced

LENGTH (feet)	LENGTH (meters)	PASSENGERS (lower bed capacity)	BUILDER	MONTH
662.7	202.0	1,300	Aker MTW Werft (Germany)	March
951.4	290.0	2,974	Fincantieri (Italy)	Summer
959.6	292.5	2,114	Kvaerner Masa-Yards (Finland)	Spring
893.0	272.2	2,720	Sestri Cantieri Navale (Italy)	November
777.8	237.1	1,080	Chantiers de l'Atlantique (France)	June
1131.8	345.0	2,800	Chantiers de l'Atlantique (France)	December
957.0	291.7	1,848	Fincantieri (Italy)	June
824.1	251.2	1,600	Chantiers de l'Atlantique (France)	March
444.5	135.5	618	Kleven Werft (Norway)	Summer
948.1	289.0	1,950	Chantiers de l'Atlantique (France)	June
964.5	294.0	2,600	Mitsubishi Heavy Industries (Japan)	July
708.6	216.0	720	Fincantieri (Italy)	April
961.9	293.2	2,100	Meyer Werft (Germany)	Autumn
1,019.7	311.0	3,114	Kvaerner Masa-Yards (Finland)	Spring
957.0	291.7	2,124	Kvaerner Masa-Yards (Finland)	Spring
951.4	290.0	2,974	Fincantieri (Italy)	Autumn
983.0	272.2	2,700	Sestri Cantieri Navale (Italy)	November
957.0	291.7	1,848	Fincantieri (Italy)	April
824.1	251.2	1,600	Chantiers de l'Atlantique (France)	Spring
444.5	135.5	674	Kleven Werft (Norway)	Summer
951.4	290.0	2,600	Fincantieri (Italy)	April
964.5	294.0	2,600	Mitsubishi Heavy Industries (Japan)	May
961.9	293.2	2,100	Meyer Werft (Germany)	June
1,019.7	311.0	3,114	Kvaerner Masa-Yards (Finland)	Spring
951.4	290.0	2,974	Fincantieri (Italy)	Autumn
957.0	291.7	1,968	Fincantieri (Italy)	January
957.0	291.7	1,800	Fincantieri (Italy)	October
957.0	291.7	1,800	Fincantieri (Italy)	May

BOOKING AND BUDGETING

Is it better to book cruises directly or through a travel agent?

And what hidden extras should you look for when calculating costs?

The Internet

While the Internet may be a good *resource* tool, it is not the place to book your cruise, unless you know *exactly* what you want. Questions cannot be asked, and most of the information provided by the cruise companies is strictly marketing hype. Most sites providing cruise ship reviews have something to sell, and the sound-byte information provided can be misleading.

The Internet vs Travel Agents

So, you've found a discounted rate for your cruise on the net. That's fine. But, if a cruise line suddenly offers special discounts for your sailing, or cabin upgrades, or things go wrong with your booking, your internet booking service may prove very unfriendly. Your travel agent, however, can probably work magic in making those special discounts work for *you*. It's called personal service.

Travel Agents

Travel agents do not generally charge for their services, although they earn a commission from cruise lines. Consider a travel agent as your business advisor, not just a ticket agent. He/she will handle all matters relevant to your booking and should have the latest information on changes of itinerary, cruise fares, fuel surcharges, discounts, and any other related items, including insurance in case you have to cancel prior to sailing. Most travel agents are linked into cruise line computer systems and have access to most shipboard information.

There is *no* "Best Cruise Line in the World" or "Best Cruise Ship" — only the ship and cruise that's right for *you*. Your travel agent should find exactly the *right ship* for *your needs* and *lifestyle*. Some sell only a limited number of cruises and are known as "preferred suppliers," because they receive special "overrides" on top of their normal commission (they probably know their limited number of ships well, however).

If *you* have chosen a ship and cruise, be firm and book exactly what you want, or change agencies. In the UK, look for a member of the Guild of Professional Cruise Agents. PSARA (Passenger Shipping Association of Retail Agents) provides in-depth agent training in the UK, as well as a full "bonding" scheme to protect passengers from failed cruise lines. In the US, look for a member of NACOA (National Association of Cruise Oriented Agencies), or a CLIA (Cruise Lines International Association) affiliated agency.

Questions to Ask a Travel Agent

● Is air transportation included in the cabin rate quoted? If not, what will be the extra cost?
● What other extra costs will be involved? These can include port charges, insurance, gratuities, shore excursions, laundry, and drinks.
● What is the cruise line's cancellation policy?
● If I want to make changes to my flight, routing, dates, and so on, will the insurance policy cover everything in case of missed or canceled flights?
● Does your agency deal with only one, or several different insurance companies?
● Does the cruise line offer advance booking discounts or other incentives?
● Do you have preferred suppliers, or do you book any cruise on any cruise ship?
● Have you sailed aboard the ship I want to book, or that you are recommending?
● Is your agency bonded and insured? By whom?
● If you book the shore excursions offered by the cruise line, is insurance coverage provided?

Reservations

Plan ahead and book early. After choosing a ship, cruise, date, and cabin, you pay a deposit that is roughly 10 percent for long cruises, 20 percent for short cruises (most cruise lines ask for a set amount). The balance is normally payable 45 to 60 days before departure. For a late reservation, you pay in full when space is confirmed (when booking via the internet, for example). Cruise lines reserve the right to change prices in the event of tax increases, fluctuating rates of exchange, fuel surcharges, or other costs beyond their control.

When you make your reservation, also make special dining requests known: seating preference, smoking or nonsmoking sections.

After the line has received full payment, your cruise ticket will be sent. Check all documents. Make sure the ship, date, and cruise details are correctly noted. Verify any connecting flight times.

Extra Costs

Cruise brochures boldly proclaim that "almost everything's included," but in most cases you will find this is not strictly true. In fact, for some cruises "all-exclusive" would be a more appropriate term.

In the aftermath of the September 11, 2001, terrorist attacks in the USA, many cruise lines cut their fares dramatically in order to attract business. At the same time, the cost of many onboard items went up. So allow for extra onboard costs.

Your fare covers the ship as transportation, your cabin, meals, entertainment, activities, and service on board; it typically does not include alcoholic beverages, laundry, dry cleaning or valet services, shore excursions, meals ashore, gratuities, port charges, cancellation insurance, optional onboard activities such as gambling.

Expect to spend about $25 a day per person on extras, plus another $10–$12 a day per person in gratuities. Genuine exceptions can be found in some small ships (those with fewer than 500 passengers) where just about everything *is* included.

Calculate the total cost of your cruise (not including any extra-cost services you might decide you want once on board) with the help of your travel agent. Here are the approximate prices per person for a typical seven-day cruise aboard a well-rated mid-size or large cruise ship, based on an outside-view two-bed cabin:

Cruise fare	*$1,200*
Port charges	*$100 (if not included)*
Gratuities	*$50*
Total per person	*$1,350*

Typical Extra-cost Items

'Alternative' Dining (cover charge)	$15–$25 a person
Baby-sitting (per hour)	$5
Bottled Water	$2.50–$7 (per bottle)
Cappuccino/Espresso	$1.50–$2.50
Cartoon Character Bedtime "Tuck-In" Service	$20
Wash One Shirt	$1.50–$3
Dry-Clean Dress	$3–$7.50
Dry-Clean Jacket	$4–$8
Golf Simulator	$15 (30 minutes)
Group Bicycling Class	$10 per class
Hair Wash/Set	$17–$28
Haircut (men)	$20
Ice Cream	$1–$3.75
In-cabin Movies	$6.95–$12.95
Kick-Boxing Class	$10 per class
Laundry Soap	$0.50–1.50
Massage	$1.50-plus a minute (plus tip)
Satellite Phone/Fax	$6.95–$15 per minute
Send/Receive e-mails	$0.75 per minute
Sodas (soft drinks)	$1–$2
Souvenir Photo	$6–$8
Trapshooting (three or five shots)	$5, $8
Video Postcard	$4.95–$6.95
Wine/Cheese Tasting	$10–$15
Wine with Dinner	$7–$500
Yoga Class	$10 per class

This comes to less than $200 per person per day. For this price, you wouldn't even get a decent hotel room in London, New York, Tokyo, or Venice.

However, your 7-day cruise can become expensive when you start adding on a few extra touches. For example, add two flight-seeing excursions in Alaska (at about $200 each), two cappuccinos each a day ($25), a scotch and soda each a day ($35), a massage ($100), 7 mineral waters ($28), 30 minutes' access to the internet for emails ($30), three other assorted excursions $120), and gratuities $50). That's an extra $788 – without even one bottle of wine with dinner! So a couple will need to add an extra $1,576 for a 7-day cruise (plus the cruise fare, of course, and the cost of getting to and from your local airport, or ship port).

Discounts and Incentives

Book ahead to get the best discounts (discounts decrease closer to the cruise date).

You may be able to reserve a cabin grade, but not a specific cabin — "tba" (to be assigned). Some lines will accept this arrangement and may even upgrade you. It is useful to know that the first cabins to be sold out are usually those at minimum and maximum rates. Note: Premium rates apply during Christmas/New Year cruises.

Cancellations and Refunds

Take out full cancellation insurance (if it is not included), as cruises (and air transportation to/from them) must be paid in full before your tickets are issued. Without such insurance, if you cancel at the last minute (even for medical reasons) you could lose the whole fare. Insurance coverage can be obtained from your travel agent, and paying by credit card makes sense (you'll probably get your money back in case the travel agency goes out of business) or through the internet. Beware of policies sold by the cruise lines – they may well be no good if the cruise line goes out of business.

Cruise lines usually accept cancellations more than 30 days before sailing, but all charge full fare if you don't turn up on sailing day, whatever the reason. Other cancellation fees depend on the cruise and length of trip. Many lines do not return port taxes, which are not part of the cruise fare.

Medical Insurance

Whether you intend to travel overseas or cruise down a local river, and your present medical insurance does not cover you, you should look into extra coverage for your cruise. A "passenger protection program" may be offered by the cruise line, the charge for which will appear on your final invoice, unless you decline. It is worth every penny, and it typically covers such things as evacuation by air ambulance, high-limit baggage, baggage transfers, personal liability, and missed departure.

Port Taxes/Handling Charges

These are assessed by individual port authorities and are usually shown in the brochure. Port charges form part of the final payment, although they can be changed right up to the day of embarkation.

Air/Sea Packages

When your cruise fare includes "free air" (as in a one-way or round-trip air ticket), note that airline arrangements usually cannot be changed without paying a premium, as cruise lines often book group space on aircraft to obtain the lowest rates.

If you do make changes, remember that, if the airline cancels your flight, the cruise line is under no obligation to help you or return your cruise fare if you don't reach the ship on time. If flying to a foreign country, allow extra time (particularly in winter) for flight delays and cancellations.

Airlines often use a "hub-and-spoke" system, which can prove frustrating. Because of changes to air schedules, cruise and air tickets may not be sent to passengers until a few days before the cruise.

In Europe, air/sea packages generally start at a major metropolitan airport; some include first-class rail travel from outlying districts. In the United States, many cruise lines include connecting flights from suburban airports as part of the package.

Most cruise lines allow you to jet out to join a ship in one port and fly home from another. An advantage is that you only have to check your baggage once at the departure airport. The baggage transfer from plane to ship is handled for you. Note that this does not include intercontinental fly/ cruises, where you must claim your baggage at the airport on arrival to clear it though customs.

Travel Insurance

Although I have mentioned Cancellation and Medical Insurance already, it would be wise to further consider the following: cruise lines and travel agents routinely sell travel cover policies that, on close inspection, appear to wriggle out of payment due to a litany of exclusion clauses, most of which are never explained to you. Some examples:
● "Pre-existing" medical conditions.
● "Valuables" left unattended on a tour bus (even though the tour guide says it is safe and that the driver will lock the door).

How to get the best travel insurance deal:
● Allow time to shop around and don't accept the first travel insurance policy you are offered.
● Read the contract carefully and make sure you know exactly what you are covered for.
● Beware of the "box ticking" approach to travel cover, which is often done quickly at the travel agent's office in lieu of providing expert advice. However, watch out for questions relating to "pre-existing medical conditions" as this little gem alone could cost you dearly. Insurers should not, in reality, be allowed to apply exclusions that have not been clearly pointed out to the policyholder.
● Do ask for a detailed explanation of all exclusions, excesses, and limitations.
● Check out the procedure you need to follow if you are the victim of a crime (such as your wallet or camera being stolen while on a shore excursion). Incidentally, if anything does happen, *always* obtain a police report as soon as possible. Note that many insurance policies will only reimburse you for the *secondhand* value of an item that has been lost or stolen, rather than the full cost of replacement. You will also probably be required to produce the original receipt for any such items claimed.
● Watch out for exclusions for "hazardous sports." These could include things typically offered as shore excursions aboard ships. Examples: horse riding (there goes that horse riding on the beach excursion in Jamaica) or cycling (mountain biking excursions in Alaska, Antigua or Rhodes, for example), or jet skiing (most beaches).
● If you purchase travel cover over the internet, do check the credentials of the company that is underwriting the scheme. It is best to deal with well-established names, and not to take what appears to be the cheapest deal offered.

Guaranteed Single Rates

Although some singles travel with friends or family, many others like to travel alone. For this reason, cruise lines have established several programs to accommodate them. One is the "Guaranteed Single" rate, which provides a set price without having to be concerned about which cabin to choose. Some cruise lines have guaranteed singles' rates, but the line and *not* the passenger picks the cabin. If the line does not find a roommate, the single passenger may get the cabin to himself/herself at no extra charge.

Guaranteed Share Programs

A "Guaranteed Share" program allows you to pay the normal double-occupancy rate, but the cruise line will find another passenger of the same sex to share the double cabin with you. Some cruise lines do not advertise a guaranteed-share program in their brochures but will often try to accommodate such bookings, particularly when demand for space is light. You could book a guaranteed share basis cabin only to find that you end up with a cabin to yourself. As cruise lines are apt to change such things at short notice, it is best to check with your travel agent for the latest rates, and read the fine print. ❏

DON'T LEAVE HOME WITHOUT...

*Cruise ships are well stocked for most people's everyday needs,
but there are certain things you need to take with you*

Baggage

There is generally no limit to the amount of personal baggage you can take on your cruise (towels, soap, shampoo, and shower caps are provided aboard most cruise ships). Do allow extra space for purchases on the cruise.

Tag all luggage with your name, ship, cabin number, sailing date, and port of embarkation (tags are provided with your tickets). Baggage transfers from airport to ship are generally smooth and problem-free when handled by the cruise line.

Liability for loss or damage to baggage is contained in the passenger contract (part of your ticket). Do take out insurance (the policy should extend from the date of departure until two or three days after your return home).

Clothing

If you think you might not wear it, don't take it, as closet space aboard many ships is at a premium. So, unless you are on an extended cruise, keep your luggage to a minimum.

For cruises to tropical areas, where the weather is warm to hot with high humidity, casual wear should include plenty of lightweight cottons and other natural fibers. Synthetic materials do not "breathe" as well and often retain heat. Clothes should be as opaque as possible to counteract the sun's ultraviolet rays. Take a lightweight cotton sweater or windbreaker for the evenings, when the ship's air-conditioning will seem even more powerful after a day in the sun. Pack sunglasses and a hat. Rainstorms in the tropics are infrequent and don't last long, but they can give you a good soaking, so take inexpensive, lightweight rainwear for excursions you go on.

The same is true for cruises to the Mediterranean, Greek Isles, or North Africa, although there will be little or no humidity for most of the year. Certain areas may be dusty as well as dry. In these latitudes, the weather can be changeable and cool in the evenings from October to March, so take extra sweaters and a windbreaker.

For cruises to Alaska, the North Cape, or the Norwegian fjords, take some warm comfortable clothing layers, plus a raincoat or parka for the northernmost port calls. Cruises to Alaska and the Land of the Midnight Sun are operated during the peak summer months, when temperatures are pleasant and the weather less likely to be poor.

Unless you are traveling to northern ports such as St. Petersburg in winter, you will not need thermal underwear. However, you will need thermal underwear, and thick socks – and a topcoat – if you take an adventure cruise to the Antarctic Peninsula or through the Northwest Passage.

In destinations with a strong religious tradition, like Venezuela, Haiti, the Dominican Republic, Colombia, and countries in the Far East, shorts or bare shoulders may cause offense, so cover up.

Aboard ship, dress rules are relaxed by day, but in the evening what you wear should be tasteful. Men should take a blazer or sports jacket and ties for the dining room and for any "informal" occasions. Transatlantic crossings are normally more elegant and require formal attire.

For formal nights (usually two out of seven), women can wear a long evening gown, elegant cocktail dress, or a smart pants suit. Gentlemen are expected to wear either a tuxedo or dark business suit and tie. These "rules" are less rigid on short and moderately priced cruises. If you are the athletic type, pack sportswear (and gym shoes) for the gymnasium or aerobics classes.

No matter where you are going, comfortable low- or flat-heeled shoes are a must for women, except for formal nights. Light, airy walking shoes are best for walking. If you are in the Caribbean or Pan-Pacific region and you are not used to heat and humidity, your ankles may swell, so tight shoes are not recommended. Rubber soles are best for walking on the deck of a ship.

Formal: Tuxedo, dinner jacket or dark suit for men; evening gown or other appropriate formal attire for women.

Informal: Jacket and tie for men; cocktail dress, dressy pantsuit, or the like for women.

Casual (Elegant): While this is an oxymoron, it generally means long trousers (no shorts or jeans), proper collared and sleeved shirt (gentlemen); skirt or slacks and top for women.

Casual (Relaxed): Slacks over sweater or open shirt (no tie) for men (no beach wear or muscle shirts); a blouse with skirt, slacks, or similar comfortable attire for women. Shoes are required.

Documents

A passport is the most practical proof of your citizenship and identification. Visas are required for some countries (allow time to obtain these). On most cruises, you will hand in your passport to the purser on embarkation. This helps the ship to clear customs and immigration inspection on arrival in ports of call. Your passport will be returned before you reach the port of disembarkation.

Flying...and Jet Lag

Several cruise lines have "air deviation" desks that allow you to change your flights and connections, for a fee (typically $25–$50 per person).

Air travel today is fast and efficient. But even experienced travelers find that the stress of international travel can persist long after the flight is over. Eastbound flights tend to cause more pronounced jet lag than westbound flights. Jet aircraft are generally pressurized to some 8,000 ft (2,400 meters) in altitude, causing discomfort in the ears and the stomach, and swollen feet. A few precautions should reduce the less pleasant effects of flying around the world. Plan as far in advance of your cruise as possible. Take a daytime flight, so that you can arrive at, or close to, your normal bedtime. Try to be as quiet as possible before flying, and allow for another five hours of rest after any flight that crosses more than five time zones.

Note: Babies and small children are less affected by changes in time because of their shorter sleeping and waking cycles. But adults generally need more time to adjust.

Medication

Take any medicine and other medical supplies that you need, plus spare eyeglasses or contact lenses. In many countries it may be difficult to find certain medicines. Others may be sold under different names. If you are taking a long cruise, ask your doctor for names of alternatives.

The ship's pharmacy will stock certain standard remedies, but do not expect a supply of the more unusual or obscure medicines. Remember to take along a doctor's prescription for any medication.

Also, be advised that if you run out of your medication and you need to get a supply aboard ship, most ships will require that you see the doctor, even if you have a prescription. There is a charge for each visit, plus the cost of any medication.

Let spouses/companions carry a supply of your medicine and medical supplies. Do not pack medication in any luggage to be checked in when flying, but take it in your carry-on.

Money Matters

Most ships operate primarily in US dollars or euros, but a few use other currencies (check with your travel agent or supplier). Major credit cards and traveler's checks are accepted on board (few lines take personal checks). You sign for drinks and other services, as part of "cashless cruising." Some large ships have ATM cash machines (although a "transaction fee" is assessed).

Pets

Pets are not allowed aboard cruise ships (although a handful of cargo-passenger ships still carry them), with two exceptions. The first is aboard the scheduled transatlantic services of Cunard Line's QE2, which has 16 air-conditioned kennels (plus a genuine British lamppost and New York fire hydrant) and cat containers, plus several special cages for birds. The second is aboard the scheduled South Atlantic service from England to Cape Town and the Ascension Islands aboard *St. Helena*.

Photography

Use low-speed film in tropical areas such as the Caribbean or South Pacific (high-speed film is easily damaged by heat). Take plenty of film with you; standard sizes are available in the ship's shop, but the selection will be limited, particularly if you use slide film. If you buy film during a port visit, try to obtain it from an air-conditioned store, and check the expiration date.

Keep film cool, as the latent image on exposed film is fragile and easily affected by heat. There will be professional photographers on board who may develop print film for you, for a fee.

When taking photographs in ports of call, respect the wishes of local inhabitants. Ask permission to photograph someone close-up. Most will smile and tell you to go ahead. But some people are superstitious or afraid of having their picture taken and will shy away from you. Do not press the point. ❑

SIX FIRSTS

● In 1903 the British liner *Lucania* became the first ship to acquire wireless equipment, which enabled it to keep in touch with both sides of the Atlantic Ocean at the same time.

● The first ship-to-shore wireless telegraphy took place on the American passenger ship *St. Paul* in 1899.

● The first twin-screw passenger ship was the Compagnie Générale Transatlantique's 3,200-ton *Washington*, built in 1863 and converted in 1868.

● The first floating eclipse expedition was led by the US astronomer Ted Pedas in 1972, when 800 passengers sailed to a spectacular rendezvous with a total sun eclipse in the North Atlantic.

● The first passenger ship to exceed 80,000 tons was the Compagnie Générale Transatlantique's *Normandie*, which measured at 82,799 tons in 1936.

● The first gravity lifeboats were installed aboard the Compagnie Générale Transatlantique's *Ile de France* in 1928.

WHAT TO EXPECT

If you've never been on a cruise before, here is what you need

to know about a typical initial embarkation process

Make sure sure you have your passport and any visas required (in some countries – such as the People's Republic of China, or Russia – you might go ashore on organized excursions under a group visa). Pack any medication you may need, and advise family members and friends where you are going.

You already have been sent your cruise tickets and documents by the cruise line or your travel agent. A typical document package might include:

- Air ticket
- Cruise ticket
- Luggage tage
- Embarkation card (to fill out before you get to the embarkation point)
- Discount coupons for the shops on board
- Bon Voyage gift selection form
- Shore excursion brochure
- Onboard credit account form
- Guide to services on board (including e-mail)
- Ship's telephone and fax contact numbers
- Coupon for tuxedo rental

Assume that you've arrived at the airport closest to your ship's embarkation point, and retrieved your luggage. It is probable that there will be a representative from the cruise line waiting, holding aloft the company's sign. You will be asked to place your luggage in a cluster together with those of other passengers. The next time you see your luggage should be aboard your ship, where it will be delivered to your cabin.

Go to the registration (check-in) area in the terminal building. For large ships, numerous desks will be set up. Go to the desk that displays the first letter of your surname, wait in line (having filled out all embarkation, registration, and immigration documents), and then check in. If your accommodation is designated as a "suite," there should be a separate check-in facility (sometimes called gold card service).

If you are cruising from a US port and you are a non-US citizen or "Resident Alien," you will go to a separate desk to check in (*Note*: Do not buy duty-free liquor to take on board – it will not be allowed by the cruise line and will be confiscated until the last day of the cruise). You will be asked for your passport, which you deposit with the check-in personnel (be sure to ask for a receipt – it is, after all, a valuable document). If you are cruising from any other port in the world that is not a US port, be advised that each country has its own check-in requirements, setups, and procedures (passport control and inspection, for example).

Documents in hand, you will probably go through a security-screening device, for both your person and hand luggage (just like at airports). Next, you'll walk a few paces towards the gangway. This may be a covered, airport-type gangway, or an open gangway (hopefully with a net underneath it in case you drop something over the side). The gangway could be flat, or you may have to walk up (or down) an incline, depending on the location of the gangway, the tide, or other local conditions.

As you approach the gangway you will probably be greeted by the ship's photographers, a snap-happy team ready to take your photograph, bedraggled as you may appear after having traveled for hours. If you do not want your photograph taken, say "no" firmly, and proceed.

Once on the gangway, you will feel a heightened sense of anticipation. At the ship end of the gangway, you will find a decorated (hopefully) entrance and the comfortable feel of air-conditioning if the weather is hot. The ship's cruise staff will welcome you aboard. Give them your cabin number, and a steward should magically appear to take your carry-on luggage from you and take you directly to your cabin. At last you've arrived.

The door to your cabin should be unlocked and open. If it is locked, ask the steward to obtain the key to open the door. Aboard the newest ships, you will probably be handed an electronically coded key card, which you insert into the door lock. Once inside the cabin, put down your personal effects and take a good look. Is it clean? Is it tidy? Are the beds properly made? Check under them to make sure the floor is clean (on one cruise I found a pair of red ladies shoes, but, alas, no lady to go with them). Make sure there is ice in the ice container. Check the bathroom, bathtub (if there is one), or shower. Make sure there are towels and soap. If all is clean and shipshape, fine.

If there are problems, bring them to the attention of your cabin steward immediately. Or call the purser's office (or reception desk), and explain the problem, then quietly, but firmly request that someone in a supervisory position see you to resolve it. The housekeeping in cruise ships is generally very good, but sometimes when "turn-around" time is tight, when passengers disembark in the morning and new passengers embark in the afternoon, little things get overlooked. They shouldn't, but they do (just as in any hotel ashore).

One thing you also should do immediately is to remember the telephone number for the ship's hospital, doctor, or for medical emergencies, just so you know how to call for help if any medical emergency should arise.

Your luggage probably will not have arrived yet (if it is a ship carrying more than 500 passengers) so don't sit in the cabin waiting for it. Once you've oriented yourself with the cabin and its features, put your hand luggage away somewhere, and, deck plan in hand, take a walk.

Familiarize yourself with the layout of the ship. Learn which way is forward, which way is aft, and how to reach your cabin from the main stairways. This is also a good time to learn how to get from your cabin to the outside decks in an emergency. A Passenger Lifeboat Drill typically takes place *before* the ship sails. This means that the drill will not disturb your cruise (or your sleep) should it be held the next morning. Regulations dictate that a drill *must* take place within 24 hours after the ship sails from the embarkation port.

After the drill (you'll find your lifejacket in the cabin and directions to your assembly station will be posted on the back of the cabin door), you can take off the lifejacket and *relax*. By now, your luggage probably will have arrived.

Unpack, then go out on deck just before the ship sails. It's always a magical moment, and a good time to meet some new faces. You'll soon be ready for that first night's dinner. It is simply amazing how the sea air gives you an appetite. ❏

CRUISE LINES BY MARKET CLASSIFICATION

LUXURY
Crystal Cruises
Cunard Line
Hapag-Lloyd Cruises (3)
Hebridean Island Cruises
Radisson Seven Seas Cruises
(3)
Sea Cloud Cruises
Seabourn Cruise Line
SeaDream Yacht Club
Silversea Cruises

PREMIUM
Abercrombie & Kent
Celebrity Cruises
Classical Cruises
Club Mediterranee Cruises
Fred Olsen Cruise Lines
Golden Sea Cruises
Holland America Line
Lindblad Expeditions
NYK Cruises
Noble Caledonia
Orient Lines
Ponant Cruises
Quark Expeditions
Radisson Seven Seas Cruises
(3)
Saga Shipping
Society Expeditions
Sun Bay Cruises

Swan Hellenic Cruises
Venus Cruise (Japan Cruise Line)
Windstar Cruises

STANDARD
A'Rosa Cruises (4)
Aida Cruises (4)
Airtours Sun Cruises
American Canadian Caribbean Line
American Cruise Lines
Arcalia Shipping (2)
Carnival Cruise Lines
Canodros
Classic International Cruises (2)
Clipper Cruise Line
Costa Cruises
Cruise West
Delphin Seereisen
Disney Cruise Line
Festival Cruises (1)
First Choice Cruises
First European Cruises (1)
Galapagos Cruises
Glacier Bay Cruiseline
Golden Sea Cruises
Golden Star Cruises
Hansa Touristik
Hapag-Lloyd Cruises (3)
Imperial Majesty Cruise Line

Islas Galapagos y Turismos
Island Cruises
Kleintours
Kristina Cruises
Louis Cruise Lines
Mano Maritime
Mediterranean Shipping Cruises
Mitsui OSK Passenger Line
New Paradise Cruises
Noble Caledonia
Norwegian Cruise Line
P&O Cruises
P&O Cruises (Australia)
Phoenix Seereisen
Plantours & Partner
Princess Cruises
Pullmantur Cruises
Regal Cruises
Royal Caribbean International
Royal Olympic Cruises
St. Helena Shipping
Seetours (4)
Spanish Cruise Line
Star Cruises
Star Clippers
Star Line Cruises
Thomson Cruises
Transocean Tours
Windjammer Barefoot Cruises
World Explorer Cruises

Notes:
(1) This company operates under different brand names in Europe and North America.
(2) These companies are one and the same.
(3) This company has different ships for different market segments and is thus listed under more than one market classification.
(4) Seetours operates both A'Rosa Cruises and Aida Cruises

WHERE TO FIND THE MAJOR CRUISE LINES

NORTH AMERICA

Abercrombie & Kent
1520 Kensington Road
Oak Brook
IL 60523-2141. USA
www.aandktours.com

American Canadian Caribbean Line
461 Water Street
Warren
RI 02885. USA
www.accl-smallships.com

American Cruise Lines
One Marine Park
Haddam
CT 06438. USA
www.americancruiselines.com

Carnival Cruise Lines
3655 NW 87 Avenue
Miami
FL 33178-2428. USA
www.carnival.com

Celebrity Cruises
1050 Port Boulevard
Miami
FL 33124. USA
www.celebrity-cruises.com

Classical Cruises
132 East 70 Street
New York
NY 10021. USA
www.classicalcruises.com

Clipper Cruise Line
7711 Bonhomme Avenue
St. Louis
MO 63105. USA
www.clippercruise.com

Club Med Cruises
75 Valencia Ave.
Coral Gables
FL 33134. USA
www.clubmed.com

Costa Cruises
World Trade Center
80 SW 8 Street, 27th Floor
Miami

FL 33130-3097. USA
www.costacruises.com

Cruise West
2401 Fourth Avenue, Suite 700
Seattle
WA 98121-1438. USA
www.cruisewest.com

Crystal Cruises
2049 Century Park East,
Suite 1400, Los Angeles
CA 90067. USA
www.crystalcruises.com

Cunard Line
6100 Blue Lagoon Drive,
Suite 400
Miami
FL 33126. USA
www.cunard.com

Disney Cruise Line
210 Celebration Place,
Suite 400
Celebration
FL 33747-4600. USA
www.disney.com/
DisneyCruise

First European Cruises
95 Madison Avenue,
Suite 1203, New York
NY 10016. USA
www.first-european.com

Glacier Bay Cruiseline
107 West Denny Way,
Suite 303, Seattle
WA 98101. USA
www.glacierbaytours.com

Holland America Line
300 Elliott Avenue West
Seattle
WA 98119. USA
www.hollandamerica.com

Lindblad Expeditions
720 Fifth Avenue, Suite 605
New York
NY 10019. USA
www.expeditions.com

Mediterranean Shipping Cruises
420 5th Avenue
New York
NY 10018. USA
www.msccruisesusa.com

Norwegian Coastal Voyages
405 Park Avenue
New York
NY 10022. USA
www.coastalvoyage.com

Norwegian Cruise Line
7665 Corporate Center Drive
Miami
FL 33126. USA
www.ncl.com

Orient Lines
7665 Corporate Center Drive
Miami
FL 33126. USA
www.orientlines.com

Princess Cruises
24305 Town Center Drive
Santa Clarita
CA 91355-4999. USA
www.princesscruises.com

Quark Expeditions
980 Post Road
Darien
CT 06820. USA
www.quark-expeditions.com

Radisson Seven Seas Cruises
600 Corporate Drive, Suite 410
Ft. Lauderdale
FL 33180. USA
www.rssc.com

Regal Cruises
300 Regal Cruises Way
Palmetto
FL 34220. USA
www.regalcruises.com

ResidenSea
5200 Blue Lagoon Drive,
Suite 790
Miami
FL 33126. USA
www.residensea.com

Royal Caribbean International
1050 Caribbean Way
Miami
FL 33132-2096. USA
www.royalcaribbean.com

Royal Olympic Cruises
One Rockefeller Plaza
New York
NY 10020. USA
www.royalolympiccruises.com

Seabourn Cruise Line
6100 Blue Lagoon Drive
Suite 400, Miami
FL 33126. USA
www.seabourn.com

SeaDream Yacht Club
2601 South Bayshore Drive,
Penthouse 1B
Coconut Grove
FL 33133
seadreamyachtclub.com

Silversea Cruises
110 E. Broward Boulevard
Suite 300
Ft. Lauderdale
FL 33301. USA
www.silversea.com

Society Expeditions, Inc.
2001 Western Ave., Suite 300
Seattle
WA 98121. USA
www.societyexpeditions.com

Star Clippers
4101 Salzedo Avenue
Coral Gables
FL 33146. USA
www.star-clippers.com

Voyager Cruise Line
520 Pike Street, Suite 1400
Seattle
WA 98101. USA
www.voyagercruiseline.com

Windjammer Barefoot Cruises
1759 Bay Road
Miami Beach
FL 33119. USA
www.windjammer.com

Windstar Cruises
300 Elliott Avenue West
Seattle
WA 98119. USA
www.windstarcruises.com

World Explorer Cruises
555 Montgomery Avenue
San Francisco
CA 94111. USA
www.wecruise.com

REST OF THE WORLD

A'Rosa Cruises
Am Seehafen 1
Siemenstrasse 90
63203 New Isenberg
GERMANY
www.a-rosa.de

Aida Cruises
Am Seehafen 1
Siemenstrasse 90
63203 New Isenberg
GERMANY
www.aida.de

Airtours Sun Cruises
Parkway Four, Parkway Business Centre
300 Princess Road
Manchester
M14 7QU
UK
www.airtours.co.uk

Canodros
Guayaquil
Ecuador
www.canodros.com

Costa Crociere (Costa Cruises)
Via Gabriele D'Annunzio, 2/80
16121 Genoa
ITALY
www.costacruises.com

Delphin Seereisen
Blumenstrasse 20
63004 Offenbach/Main
GERMANY
www:delphin-cruises.com

Festival Cruises
99 Akti Miouli
GR 185 38, Piraeus
GREECE
www.festivalcruises.com

Fred Olsen Cruise Lines
Fred Olsen House
White House Road
Ipswich
Suffolk 1P1 5LL
ENGLAND
www.fredolsen.co.uk

Golden Sea Cruises
Filonos 64
Piraeus 185 35
GREECE

Golden Star Cruises
85 Akti Miaouli
Piraeus
GREECE 185 38
www.goldenstarcruises.com

Hansa Touristik
Contrescarpe 36
28203 Bremen
GERMANY
www.hansatourstik.com

Hapag-Lloyd Cruises
Ballindamm 25
D-20095 Hamburg
GERMANY
www.hlkf.com

Hebridean Island Cruises
Griffin House
Broughton Hall
Skipton
North Yorkshire BD23 3AN
ENGLAND

Kristina Cruises
16 Kirkkokatu
Kotka 48100
FINLAND
www.kristinacruises.com

Louis Cruise Lines
54-58 Evangoros Avenue
(P.O. Box 1306)
Nicosia
CYPRUS
www.louiscruises.com

Mitsui OSK Passenger Line
Shuwa-Kioicho Park Building
Kioicho 3-6
Chiyoda-ku
Tokyo 192-8552
JAPAN
www.mopas.co.jp.com

NYK Line (Nippon Yusen Kaisha)
Yusen Building
3-2 Marunouchi 2-choime
Chiyoda-ku
Tokyo 100-0005
JAPAN
www.asukacruise.co.jp

New Paradise Cruises
P.O. Box 50157
3601 Limassol
CYPRUS
www.paradise.com.cy

Orient Lines
1, Derry Street
Kensington
London W8 5NN
ENGLAND
www.orientlines.com

P&O Cruises
77 New Oxford Street
London WC1A 1PP
ENGLAND
www.pocruises.com

P&O Cruises (Australia)
P.O. Box 5287
Sydney 2001
New South Wales
AUSTRALIA
www.pocruises.com.au

Phoenix Seereisen
Kolnstrasse 80
53111 Bonn
GERMANY
www.phoenixreisen.com

Plantours & Partner
Obern Street 69
Bremen 28195
GERMANY

Ponant Cruises
60 Boulebard Marchal Juin
44100 Nantes
FRANCE
www.ponant.com

St. Helena Shipping
The Shipyard
Porthleven
Cornwall TR13 9JA
ENGLAND
rms-st-helena.com

Saga Cruises
Folkestone
Kent
ENGLAND
www.saga.co.uk

Sea Cloud Cruises
Ballindamm 17
D-200095 Hamburg
GERMANY
www.seacloud.com

Seetours
Frankfurterstrasse 233
63263 Neu-Isenburg
GERMANY
www.seetours.de

Star Cruises
Star Cruises Terminal
Pulau Indah
PO Box No. 288
42009 Pelabuhan Klang
Selangor Darul Ehsan
MALAYSIA
www.starcruises.com.my

Star Line Cruises
P.O. Box 81443
Mombasa
KENYA

Swan Hellenic Cruises
77 New Oxford Street
London WC1A 1PP
ENGLAND
www.swan-hellenic.co.uk

Thomson Cruises
Greater London House
Hampstead Road
London NW1 7SD
ENGLAND
www.thomson-holidays.com

Transocean Tours
Postfach 10 09 07
28009 Bremen
GERMANY
www.transocean.de

Venus Cruise
Umeda Hanshin Daiichi Building
5-25, Umeda 2-chome
Kita-ku
Osaka 530-0001
JAPAN
www.venus-cruise.co.jp

SHIPS RATED BY SCORE

Ship	Score	Rating	Ship	Score	Rating
LARGE SHIPS			Carnival Pride	1,474	4
(over 1,000 passengers)			Carnival Spirit	1,474	4
			Mistral	1,472	4
Queen Elizabeth 2 (Grill Class)	1,754	5	Carnival Destiny	1,455	4
Constellation	1,701	5	Carnival Triumph	1,455	4
Infinity	1,701	5	Carnival Victory	1,455	4
Millennium	1,701	5	Regal Princess	1,448	4
Summit	1,701	5	Crown Odyssey	1,445	4
Century	1,663	4+	Costa Atlantica	1,438	4
Galaxy	1,663	4+	Costa Victoria	1,406	4
Mercury	1,663	4+	Costa Europa	1,394	3+
Queen Elizabeth 2 (Caronia Class)	1,622	4+	Majesty of the Seas	1,394	3+
Disney Magic	1,553	4+	Monarch of the Seas	1,394	3+
Disney Wonder	1,553	4+	Paradise	1,390	3+
Golden Princess	1,549	4	Elation	1,387	3+
Grand Princess	1,549	4	Norwegian Majesty	1,386	3+
Star Princess	1,549	4	Sovereign of the Seas	1,386	3+
Aurora	1,548	4	Ecstasy	1,385	3+
Brilliance of the Seas	1,546	4	Fantasy	1,385	3+
Radiance of the Seas	1,546	4	Fascination	1,385	3+
Zenith	1,545	4	Imagination	1,385	3+
Horizon	1,544	4	Inspiration	1,385	3+
Amsterdam	1,543	4	Sensation	1,385	3+
Rotterdam	1,541	4	Queen Elizabeth 2		
Volendam	1,541	4	(Mauretania Class)	1,383	3+
Zaandam	1,541	4	Norwegian Sea	1,382	3+
Dawn Princess	1,539	4	Norwegian Dream	1,381	3+
Sea Princess	1,539	4	Norwegian Wind	1,381	3+
Sun Princess	1,539	4	Norway	1,378	3+
Adventure of the Seas	1,537	4	Arcadia	1,374	3+
Explorer of the Seas	1,537	4	Costa Romantica	1,369	3+
Voyager of the Seas	1,537	4	Costa Classica	1,368	3+
Maasdam	1,533	4	Noordam	1,350	3+
Ryndam	1,533	4	Celebration	1,318	3+
Statendam	1,533	4	Holiday	1,318	3+
Veendam	1,533	4	Jubilee	1,318	3+
Oriana	1,530	4	Nordic Empress	1,306	3+
AIDAcara	1,529	4	Sunbird	1,275	3+
Royal Princess	1,528	4	Melody	1,259	3+
Norwegian Star	1,522	4	Pacific Sky	1,253	3+
SuperStar Virgo	1,522	4	Star Pisces	1,247	3
Enchantment of the Seas	1,521	4	Island Escape	1,245	3
Grandeur of the Seas	1,521	4	Costa Tropicale	1,237	3
Rhapsody of the Seas	1,519	4	Carousel	1,226	3
Vision of the Seas	1,519	4	Sundream	1,226	3
Norwegian Sun	1,517	4	Oceanic	1,093	2+
Legend of the Seas	1,511	4	The Topaz	1,023	2
Splendour of the Seas	1,511	4	A'Rosa Blu	NYR	NYR
Norwegian Sky	1,507	4	Adonia	NYR	NYR
SuperStar Leo	1,497	4	AIDAvita	NYR	NYR
European Stars	1,496	4	Carnival Conquest	NYR	NYR
European Vision	1,496	4	Carnival Glory	NYR	NYR
Carnival Legend	1,474	4	Coral Princess	NYR	NYR

Ship	Score	Rating	Ship	Score	Rating
Costa Mediterranea	NYR	NYR	Regal Empress	917	2
Crystal Serenity	NYR	NYR	Aegean I	897	2
Diamond Princess	NYR	NYR	Princesa Victoria	895	2
Lirica	NYR	NYR	Serenade	790	1+
Navigator of the Seas	NYR	NYR	Princesa Cypria	691	1+
Norwegian Dawn	NYR	NYR	Minerva II	NYR	NYR
Ocean Village	NYR	NYR	Mona Lisa	NYR	NYR
Oceana	NYR	NYR	Pacific Princess	NYR	NYR
Oosterdam	NYR	NYR	Tahitian Princess	NYR	NYR
Queen Mary 2	NYR	NYR			
Thomson Spirit	NYR	NYR	**SMALL SHIPS**		
Zuiderdam	NYR	NYR	(up to 500 passengers)		
MID-SIZE SHIPS			Europa	1,857	5+
(500–1,000 passengers)			SeaDream I	1,790	5
			SeaDream II	1,790	5
Crystal Symphony	1,758	5	Seabourn Legend	1,786	5
Crystal Harmony	1,725	5	Seabourn Pride	1,785	5
Seven Seas Mariner	1,703	5	Seabourn Spirit	1,785	5
Prinsendam	1,670	4+	Silver Shadow	1,757	5
Asuka	1,660	4+	Silver Whisper	1,757	5
Pacific Venus	1,647	4+	Hanseatic	1,740	5
Caronia	1,494	4	Silver Cloud	1,717	5
Astor	1,486	4	Silver Wind	1,717	5
R-5 Blue Dream	1,481	4	Sea Cloud II	1,709	5
Astoria	1,476	4	Hebridean Spirit	1,707	5
Olympia Explorer	1,432	4	Sea Cloud	1,704	5
Black Watch	1,429	4	Hebridean Princess	1,701	5
Saga Rose	1,423	4	Seven Seas Navigator	1,653	4+
Olympia Voyager	1,409	4	Paul Gauguin	1,645	4+
SuperStar Aries	1,396	3+	Song of Flower	1,626	4+
Marco Polo	1,386	3+	Le Levant	1,609	4+
Maxim Gorkiy	1,385	3+	Radisson Diamond	1,591	4+
SuperStar Capricorn	1,364	3+	Wind Surf	1,567	4+
Braemar	1,325	3+	Clelia II	1,546	4
SuperStar Gemini	1,322	3+	Le Ponant	1,540	4
Ocean Majesty	1,274	3+	Royal Clipper	1,540	4
Olympia Countess	1,240	3	Club Med 2	1,532	4
Costa Marina	1,224	3	Wind Spirit	1,518	4
Costa Allegra	1,206	3	Wind Star	1,518	4
Rhapsody	1,194	3	Bremen	1,461	4
Stella Solaris	1,193	3	Clipper Odyssey	1,451	4
Albatros	1,144	3	Sun Bay I	1,425	4
The Emerald	1,143	3	Sun Bay II	1,425	4
Princess Danae	1,101	3	Minerva	1,411	4
Van Gogh	1,098	2+	Star Clipper	1,402	4
Ocean Breeze	1,095	2+	Star Flyer	1,402	4
Monterey	1,087	2+	Nippon Maru	1,391	3+
Seawing	1,072	2+	C. Columbus	1,383	3+
Universe Explorer	1,063	2+	Orient Venus	1,382	3+
Triton	1,039	2+	Galapagos Explorer	1,365	3+
Bolero	1,034	2+	Fuji Maru	1,358	3+
Flamenco	1,026	2+	Delphin	1,297	3+
Azur	1,008	2+	Vistamar	1,262	3+
Ausonia	996	2+	Yamal	1,246	3

Ship	Score	Rating	Ship	Score	Rating
Endeavour	1,242	3	Spirit of Endeavour	946	2
Yorktown Clipper	1,230	3	Sea Bird	943	2
Spirit of Oceanus	1,218	3	Sea Lion	943	2
Nantucket Clipper	1,213	3	Akademik Sergey Vavilov	942	2
Sapphire	1,210	3	Wilderness Adventurer	939	2
Clipper Adventurer	1,175	3	Wilderness Discoverer	939	2
Kapitan Dranitsyn	1,164	3	Spirit of Alaska	936	2
Kapitan Khlebnikov	1,164	3	Spirit of Columbia	936	2
St. Helena	1,155	3	Spirit of Discovery	936	2
Polaris	1,097	2+	Spirit of Glacier Bay	913	2
World Renaissance	1,096	2+	Flying Cloud	902	2
Black Prince	1,093	2+	Mandalay	902	2
Funchal	1,089	2+	Polynesia	902	2
Grande Caribe	1,089	2+	Yankee Clipper	902	2
Grande Mariner	1,089	2+	Princesa Marissa	901	2
Niagara Prince	1,087	2+	Arion	859	2
Odysseus	1,071	2+	American Glory	835	2
Royal Star	1,069	2+	American Eagle	827	2
Calypso	1,062	2+	Silver Star	811	2
Explorer	1,062	2+	Atalante	645	1
Kristina Regina	1,052	2+	Ambassador I	620	1
Paloma I	1,032	2+	The Iris	NYR	NYR
Legacy	1,029	2+	The Jasmine	NYR	NYR
Spirit of '98	1,018	2+	The World	NYR	NYR
Caribe	1,005	2+	World Discoverer	NYR	NYR
Professor Molchanov	947	2			
Professor Multanovskiy	947	2			

NYR = Not Yet Rated

Index

*Numbers in **bold** refer to pages containing ship reviews*

Credits

Photography:

Jan Butchofsky-Houser/
  Houserstock 3
Carnival Cruise Lines back cover
(top right), 52, 59, 109
Corbis 14, 15, 16, 17
Costa Crociere 121
Cunard 21
Jon Davison 25
Delta Queen Steamboat
  Company 87

Glyn Genin 1, 4/5, 7, 9, 43, 47, 95
Mary Ann Hemphill 12, 13, 63
Holland America Line 38, 40, 57,
68
Dave G. Houser 96, 115
Axel Krause/Apa 85
Bob Krist back cover (top left),
10, 11, 44, 49, 51,
Buddy Mays/Travel Stock 97
Princess Cruises 31
Seabourn Cruise Line 99
Storto Shooting front cover, 122
Topham Picturepoint 18, 19
Douglas Ward back cover (top

center), 42, 55, 61, 69, 70, 73, 74,
77, 81, 86, 88, 90, 92, 100, 103,
107, 117, 123
Windjammer Barefoot Cruises
622

Art Director: Klaus Geisler
Production: Sylvia George
Cartography Editor:
Zoë Goodwin

Map Production Tyne Mapping
© 2003 Apa Publications GmbH & Co.
Verlag KG (Singapore branch)

DEAR PASSENGER,

You are most welcome to send me your observations concerning any recent cruises taken. Please complete the following basic information when sending comments concerning your recent cruise experiences.

Although I cannot acknowledge receipt of this comment form, or any letters, because of my non-stop travel schedule, I do thank you for your input, and for purchasing this book.

Cruise Date . . . .   Ship Name . . . .

Cruise Line . . . .   Suite/Cabin Number . . . .

Dining Room Seating (tick box):   ❏ Open   ❏ First   ❏ Second

Your Comments . . . .

Your Pet Peeves

(1) . . . .

(2) . . . .

(3) . . . .

Your name . . . . Age . . . .

Address . . . .

. . . .

. . . .

Please send to the address below:

Mr Douglas Ward
The Maritime Evaluations Group
Canada House
1 Carrick Way
New Milton
Hampshire BH25 6UD
United Kingdom